TAXATION OF CHARITIES AND NONPROFIT ORGANISATIONS

JAMES KESSLER QC
ETIENNE WONG
and
JON-SELOUS BORLACE

VOLUME TWO

THIRTEENTH EDITION

Key Haven Publications Ltd
P. O. Box 669, Oxford, OX3 3AU
Tel: 01865 352121
http://www.khpplc.co.uk

CONTENTS IN BRIEF

CHAPTER TWENTY TWO

GIFTS OF WORKS OF ART TO CHARITY

22.1 Works of art: Introduction

This chapter discusses the relief for gifts of works of art to charity.

There is a separate relief for remittance basis taxpayers who lend works of art to museums: the loan is not regarded as a taxable remittance. We do not discuss that relief here, as it is fully discussed in Kessler, *Taxation of Non-Residents and Foreign Domiciliaries*.[1]

22.2 Gift to Nation: Cultural gifts scheme

Following many years of lobbying[2] and a consultation paper,[3] sch 14 FA 2012 provides a relief for gifts of pre-eminent works of art. The relief is

1 (21st ed., 2022-23), para 19.31 (Public access rule) online version *https://www.foreigndomiciliaries.co.uk*

2 Goodison Review "Securing the Best for our Museums: Private Giving and Government Support", (2004) *http://webarchive.nationalarchives.gov.uk/20130129110402/http://www.hm-treasury.gov.uk/d/ACF10B6.pdf*
MacGregor Report on the Role Endowments Could Play in DCMS Funded Museums and Galleries (2010) *https://www.gov.uk/government/uploads/system/uploads/attachment_data/file/77725/Endowments_paper_20101208.pdf*

3 "Gifts of pre-eminent objects and works of art to the nation" *https://www.gov.uk/government/uploads/system/uploads/attachment_data/file/81429/consult_gifts_of_art.pdf*

called "Gifts to the nation". The name is more catchy than apt. DCMS call it the "Cultural Gifts Scheme" ("CGS"). DCMS published the text of the CGS in 2013[4] updated in January 2015 (the "CGS document"). The CGS is administered by the Arts Council.

The CGS document provides an overview:

> *Overview of the Scheme*
>
> 11. The CGS will work as follows:
>
> - A person (an individual acting in a private capacity) or a company with a tax liability in the UK who wholly owns an object, considered to be pre-eminent, offers to donate the object for the benefit of the public or the nation;
> - Offers to donate objects which are considered pre-eminent should be made to the Arts Council. Each offer will be registered as set out in this document. Applications will be considered by the Panel on a first come, first served basis;
> - Objects which the Panel assesses as not being pre-eminent will be rejected. Applications may also be rejected by the Panel where acceptance would cause the annual limit for AIL and CGS to be exceeded, if negotiations have not been concluded within 2 years (see paragraph 57) or if the Panel otherwise considers that the offer should not be accepted. There should be no presumption that an object will be accepted automatically if it is considered pre-eminent. Where applications are rejected, the Arts Council will write to the applicant informing them of the decision and explaining the reason(s) for it;
> - Where the Panel considers that the requirements of the Scheme have been met and that an object is pre-eminent, the object's fair market value has been agreed by the Panel and the Panel considers that the gift should be accepted for the benefit of the public or the nation, the Panel will then make a recommendation to the relevant Minister (being either the Secretary of State for Culture, Media and Sport, the Welsh Ministers, the Scottish Ministers or the Northern Ireland Department for Culture, Arts and Leisure) regarding the pre-eminence, valuation and (if applicable) the proposed allocation;
> - Following the agreement to the recommendation by the relevant Minister and confirmation from the Secretary of State for Culture, Media and Sport that acceptance is within the annual limit, the applicant will receive a letter of acceptance. The letter of acceptance will include: the agreed value of the object or objects; a schedule of

4 *https://www.gov.uk/government/uploads/system/uploads/attachment_data/file/540689/Cultural_Gifts_Scheme_DCMS_guidance.pdf*

how the tax reduction or reductions will be applied; and the name of the institution to which the object will be transferred if already known. The applicant will need to accept the terms within 30 days of the date of the letter of acceptance. The terms in the letter of acceptance, once accepted by the donor, are the "agreed terms" for the purposes of the Scheme

- The gift will then be made pursuant to the agreed terms and the object will transfer from the donor to be held for the benefit of the public or the nation;
- The Arts Council will inform HMRC of the donation, and, where the donor is an individual, provide details of how the tax reduction is to be applied. HMRC will not apply the tax reduction to a person's tax liability unless and until the Panel has confirmed to HMRC that the relevant conditions for the tax reduction have been met;
- As set out in Schedule 14 to the Finance Act 2012, the maximum value of the tax reduction is 30% of the agreed value of the object that is being donated where the donor's liability is to income tax and capital gains tax, and 20% of the agreed value of the object where the donor's liability is to corporation tax. For individuals, the tax reduction can be spread across a maximum of five tax years, beginning with the tax year in which the offer is formally registered by the Arts Council (the "offer registration date" described in paragraphs 16 and 17 below). Alternatively, individual donors can choose to apply the tax reduction to a single year being either the tax year in which the application is registered or one of the subsequent four tax years. Companies will not be able to spread the tax reduction: the tax reduction can be used only to offset the company's corporation tax liability generated in the accounting period in which the offer was registered by the Arts Council;
- Subject to the rules and exceptions contained within Schedule 14 to the Finance Act 2012, the donor will not be liable for capital gains tax or inheritance tax on the donation. Schedule 14 also contains provisions relating to objects which have previously been conditionally exempted from inheritance tax or where estate duty has been deferred.

The CGS document sets out the differences between the CGS and the Acceptance in Lieu scheme[5]. The two schemes together share a £40 million annual limit:

8. Although the CGS shares many similarities with the Acceptance in

5 This scheme is beyond the scope of this book.

> Lieu Scheme (the "AIL Scheme") which allows works of art, land and buildings to be accepted into public ownership in lieu of inheritance tax, the CGS is different in a number of respects. In particular, the CGS provides an opportunity, where certain conditions are met, for owners of objects or collections of objects, who wish to see those objects placed in eligible institutions in the UK, to make a gift of the object during their lifetime and in the knowledge that objects will be transferred to an eligible institution, subject to certain conditions, including to hold and manage the object, to maintain it in good condition and to make it accessible to the public. The CGS also differs from the AIL Scheme because the CGS does not allow the eligible institution to which the object is transferred to fund the difference between the amount of tax reduction available and the amount of the object's agreed open market value (called a "hybrid offer"). The CGS is not appropriate for gifts of land and buildings which may, in suitable circumstances and subject to certain conditions, qualify for forms of tax relief.
>
> 9. The CGS, together with the AIL Scheme, will operate within a £40 million annual limit for both schemes. This means that the annual reduction in tax liabilities and amount accepted in lieu of tax under both schemes must, together, not exceed £40 million in each tax year, starting 6 April. The Acceptance in Lieu Panel ("the Panel") will take into account the value of any other gifts of cultural objects and offers in lieu of tax it has already recommended or is considering recommending before making a new recommendation in relation to an offer to a Minister, so as not to exceed the annual limit. When presenting its recommendations to Ministers on donations under the CGS, the Panel will also seek agreement from the Secretary of State for Culture, Media and Sport that acceptance of the gift will not breach the annual limit for the relevant year. The Secretary of State for Culture, Media and Sport will have overall responsibility for ensuring that the annual limit is not exceeded.

It is later specified in the CGS document that the annual limit will be a relevant consideration whenever an application for the relief is received:

> 26. The Panel will assess the information submitted with the application. In particular, it will assess whether the object is pre-eminent, whether the value stated on the application is the object's fair market value as at the date of registration and whether a preferred institution is an eligible institution. The Panel will take such expert advice as it considers necessary to assist it in its assessment. The Panel will also take account of the annual limit for the relevant year to ensure that acceptance of any object will not exceed that limit.

22.2.1 *"Qualifying gift"*

Para 1 sch 14 FA 2012 provides:

> (1) For the purposes of this Schedule, a person makes a "qualifying gift" if the person makes a gift in the circumstances described in sub-paragraph (2).
> (2) The circumstances are—
> (a) the person offers to give pre-eminent property to be held for the benefit of the public or the nation,
> (b) the person is legally and beneficially entitled to the property and the property is not owned jointly (or in common) with others,
> (c) the offer is made in accordance with a scheme set up by the Secretary of State for the purposes of this Schedule,
> (d) the offer is registered in accordance with the scheme,
> (e) the offer, or a part of the offer, is accepted in accordance with the scheme, and
> (f) the gift is made pursuant to the offer, or the part of the offer, accepted.

The CGS document is therefore more than mere guidance. In order to qualify for the relief, an offer of a relevant cultural gift must be made in accordance with the terms of the CGS document.

Para 22 sch 14 FA 2012 defines pre-eminent property:

> (1) In this Schedule, "pre-eminent property" means—
> (a) any picture, print, book, manuscript, work of art, scientific object or other thing that the relevant Minister is satisfied is pre-eminent for its national, scientific, historic or artistic interest,
> (b) any collection or group of pictures, prints, books, manuscripts, works of art, scientific objects or other things if the relevant Minister is satisfied that the collection or group, taken as a whole, is pre-eminent for its national, scientific, historic or artistic interest, or
> (c) any object that is or has been kept in a significant building if it appears to the relevant Minister desirable for the object to remain associated with the building.
> (2) A "significant building" is any building falling within section 230(3)(a) to (d) of IHTA 1984 (acceptance of property in lieu of tax)[6].

---

6 Section 230(3) IHTA 1984 provides:
(3)This section also applies to any objects which are or have been kept in any building—

> (3) "National interest" includes interest within any part of the United Kingdom.
> (4) In determining whether an object or collection or group of objects is pre-eminent, regard is to be had to any significant association of the object, collection or group with a particular place.

The CGS document provides:

> 13. ... Works by living artists can be considered by the Panel to be pre-eminent.

More specific guidance on how the status of a proffered object will be reviewed by the Panel is provided later in the CGS document:

> 28. ... The Panel will consider applications only on the basis that the object, if accepted, will be held for the benefit of the public or the nation, i.e. displayed in a space under the control and management of an eligible institution (see paragraphs 33 to 37). It will not consider offers for the donation of objects which are to be placed on extended or permanent loan to an institution which is not an eligible institution. Unlike the AIL Scheme, the CGS will not consider hybrid offers (see paragraph 8 above).
> 29. The Panel will also take into account the physical condition of the object. If an object is in poor condition the Panel is likely to reject it.
> 30. The Panel will reject an application if it does not consider the object to be pre-eminent. Similarly, the Panel may reject an application, even where the object is pre-eminent, where acceptance of the object would or could breach the annual limit, if negotiations have not been concluded within 2 years, or where other objects which are pre-eminent are preferred. The Panel may agree to review its recommendations in

---

(a) if the Board have determined to accept or have accepted that building in satisfaction or part satisfaction of tax or of estate duty, or

(b) if the building or any interest in it belongs to Her Majesty in right of the Crown or of the Duchy of Lancaster, or belongs to the Duchy of Cornwall or belongs to a Government department or is held for the purposes of a Government department, or

(c) if the building is one of which the Secretary of State is guardian under the M1Ancient Monuments and Archaeological Areas Act 1979 or of which the Department of the Environment for Northern Ireland is guardian under the Historic Monuments and Archaeological Objects (Northern Ireland) Order 1995, or

(d) if the building belongs to any body within Schedule 3 to this Act,

in any case where it appears to the Secretary of State desirable for the objects to remain associated with the building.

exceptional circumstances, for example, where new and important evidence comes to light.

22.2.2 *"Eligible institution"*

The donee must be an eligible institution. The CGS document provides:

> 33. Objects may only be transferred to eligible institutions. For the purposes of the CGS, an eligible institution is an institution or body that is willing to accept an object and which falls within categories (a) or (b) below:
>
> (a) any museum, art gallery, library, archive or other similar institution having as its purpose or one of its purposes the preservation for the public benefit of a collection of historic, artistic or scientific interest; or
>
> (b) any body having as its purpose or one of its purposes the provision, improvement or preservation of amenities enjoyed or to be enjoyed by the public.
>
> 34. Where the application does not specify a preferred institution, the availability of the object will be advertised by the Arts Council on its website. Where a gift of manuscripts or archives is made without a wish, the National Archives will advertise the availability on its website and may, if it considers it appropriate, place additional adverts in other media. In these cases, the National Archives will advise the Panel on the appropriate eligible institution. The Panel will assess the responses to the advert and consider the merits of each before making a recommendation on transfer to the relevant Minister, who will have ultimate responsibility for deciding on the transferee.
>
> 35. Applicants may express a wish on the application form that the object be transferred to an eligible institution of their choice. The Panel will consider any such preferred institution and take into account factors such as:
>
> (a) the institution's collections policy;
>
> (b) its existing holdings;
>
> (c) the level of public access that it will provide;
>
> (d) its ability to provide proper care and maintenance for the object;
>
> (e) its security and environmental controls; and
>
> (f) any connection it has to the owner, the object, or its creator.
>
> 36. Whilst an applicant may express a wish for an object to go to a particular institution, the Panel will also take overall account of the regional spread of allocations, particularly outside London, to ensure that regional museums and galleries are well supported.
>
> 37. If the Panel considers the preferred eligible institution is not appropriate for any reason, it will advise the applicant and provide an

opportunity for the applicant to name an alternative eligible institution, before any recommendation is put forward for approval by the relevant Minister. If an eligible institution cannot be agreed the Arts Council will advertise the object as described in paragraph 34.

22.2.3 *Relief for individual*

The relief for individuals is in part 2 sch 14. Para 2(1) sch 14 FA 2012 provides:

> This Part applies to an individual's liability to income tax and capital gains tax.

There is no relief for trustees; para 2(2) sch 14 FA 2012 (unnecessarily) makes the point expressly:

> It does not apply to any liability arising as a trustee or personal representative.

Para 2(3) sch 14 FA 2012 keeps IHT outside the relief:

> Subject to sub-paragraph (2)—
> (a) a reference in this Part to an individual's "tax liability" is to the individual's liability to income tax and capital gains tax, and
> (b) references to an amount of or on account of "tax" are to be read accordingly.

The CGS document summarises the requirements for donor eligibility:

> 12. ...Donors must be legally and beneficially entitled to the object and the object must not be owned jointly (or in common) with others. An object jointly owned would not therefore be eligible for consideration. Artists may donate their own work. In general, when a professional artist donates their own work, they automatically trigger a charge to tax and may also be liable for VAT. This will continue to apply to donations made under CGS...

We do not agree that in general, when a professional artist donates their own work, they automatically trigger a charge to tax; see 18.7.2 (Deemed trading receipt).

22.2.4 *Basic rule*

Para 3 sch 14 FA 2012 provides that the relief (in short) can be spread over up to 5 years:

> (1) If an individual ("N") makes a qualifying gift, a portion of N's tax

liability for each relevant tax year is to be treated as satisfied, as if N had paid that portion when it became due (or on the offer registration date, if the portion became due before that date).
(2) A "relevant tax year" is a tax year identified in the agreed terms[7] as a tax year to which this paragraph is to apply.
(3) Up to 5 tax years may be identified in the agreed terms, but each one must be either—
  (a) the tax year in which the offer registration date[8] falls, or
  (b) one of the 4 tax years following that tax year.

The CGS document provides:

> 47. ...No revision of the Agreed Tax Schedule will be permitted, even where the donor's tax liability is found to be lower or higher than anticipated for a particular tax year. If the donor's tax liability turns out to be lower than expected, then the element of tax reduction for that year which goes unused will be lost.
> 48. Should an individual who made a donation die at any time during that five year period without benefitting from the full amount of the applicable tax reduction, the amount of the unused reduction will be lost and their estate will not be able to claim any part of it to offset against any liability.
> 49. Where an offer of a gift is accepted under the Scheme, resulting in an amount of the tax liability being treated as having been satisfied (as set out in the Scheme) then no late payment interest or late payment penalties will be payable on that amount from the date of registration. However, if a qualifying gift was not made for any reason (for example, because the offer was rejected or withdrawn by the donor), then the donor would be required to pay to HMRC both the tax due and any late payment interest due up to and including the date of payment. If the tax and interest remains unpaid within 30 days the donor will be subject to late payment penalties.
> 50. Where a tax reduction has been applied but the qualifying gift is later set aside or declared void, for example it was discovered that the donor was not the legal owner or the item was not authentic, the tax reduction applied will have to be repaid together with any late payment interest and late payment penalties in respect of it.

---

7 Para 1(3) sch 14 FA 2012 provides a commonsense definition: "In this Schedule— (a) "the agreed terms" means the terms on which acceptance is agreed, as recorded in the manner prescribed by the scheme".

8 Para 1(3) sch 14 FA 2012 provides a commonsense definition: "In this Schedule— ... (b) "the offer registration date" means the date when the offer was registered in accordance with the scheme."

> 51. Individual donors will be able to specify whether they want the tax reduction to be set against income tax or capital gains tax first. This preference will apply to all years in the Agreed Tax Schedule. Any balance remaining will be set against any outstanding liability under the other head of duty. For example, if an individual has a tax reduction available of £200,000 with an income tax liability of £100,000 and a capital gains tax liability of £300,000 the donor may specify the tax reduction to be set first against income tax and then against capital gains tax. In that case the whole of the income tax liability will be extinguished, leaving a balance of £100,000 to be set against the capital gains tax liability of £300,000. Alternatively the donor may opt to set the tax reduction against the capital gains tax liability, leaving £100,000 capital gains tax and £100,000 income tax to pay.
>
> 52. The offer registration date will be treated as the date of disposal of the object for capital gains tax purposes and for corporation tax on chargeable gains if the gift is accepted.

The "offer registration date" is set out in paras 16 and 17 of the CGS document:

> 16. Subject to the annual limit not already having been exceeded, the Arts Council will normally register the application under the Scheme within 30 days of receiving all the required information (the "offer registration date"). The required information is set out in paragraph 19 below. Applicants who do not provide all the required information will be contacted by the Arts Council and requested to provide this as soon as possible. The application will not be formally registered until the Arts Council is satisfied that it has received all the required information. In addition, an application may not be registered where the value set out in the application is considered by the Panel to be wholly unsupported by the evidence submitted by the applicant or by any other information known to the Panel. Registration of the application by the Panel should not give rise to any expectation by the applicant that the value set out in the application will be agreed.
>
> 17. The offer registration date has consequences for valuation and tax purposes. Whereas the Panel may take some time to agree the value of an object, the final agreed value will be the value of the object as at the offer registration date. The Arts Council will notify the offer registration date to HMRC within 30 days after the offer registration date. The offer registration date will be recorded by HMRC for tax purposes, should the application succeed.

22.2.5 *Relief*

In short, the relief is 30% of the value of the asset. If the individual sold the asset and gave the proceeds to charity, the IT relief is worth more, even after allowing for CGT.

Para 4 sch 14 FA 2012 provides:

> 4(1) The portion of N's tax liability for a relevant tax year that is to be treated as satisfied is an amount equal to the smaller of—
> (a) the tax reduction figure allocated to that tax year, and
> (b) the amount of N's tax liability for that tax year less any portion of that amount that is treated as satisfied in consequence of any qualifying gift made by N on a previous occasion.
> (2) The amount determined under sub-paragraph (1) may be nil.
> (3) The tax reduction figure allocated to a tax year is such part of the total tax reduction figure as is expressed in the agreed terms to be allocated to that tax year.
> (4) The figures allocated to the relevant tax years must in total add up to no more than the total tax reduction figure.
> (5) "The total tax reduction figure" is 30% of the value set out in the agreed terms as the agreed value of the property forming the subject of the qualifying gift.
> (6) The Treasury may by order substitute a different percentage for the percentage specified for the time being in sub-paragraph (5).
> **Order in which benefit is applied**
> 5(1) If the tax reduction figure allocated to a relevant tax year is less than the amount determined under paragraph 4(1)(b) for that tax year, the benefit of paragraph 3(1) is to be applied to N's tax liability in the order specified in the agreed terms.
> (2) If no order is specified, the order is—
> (a) first, to N's liability to income tax for that year, and
> (b) then, to N's liability to capital gains tax for that year.

Once the terms have been agreed, the Arts Council will provide HMRC with the necessary information. The CGS document provides:

> 45. Following the formal acceptance of a donation by the relevant Minister and confirmation of receipt of the object in an acceptable condition by the agreed eligible institution, the Arts Council will confirm in writing to HMRC:
> - The name of the donor;
> - details of the object or objects (including the agreed value of the object);
> - the Agreed Tax Schedule and in the case of individuals only, details

of the order in which the individual would like the tax reduction to be offset against their relevant liabilities (income tax or capital gains tax);

- its belief that the requirements of the CGS have all been met;
- that the title of the object has been transferred pursuant to the CGS; and
- that receipt of the object in acceptable condition has been confirmed by the recipient eligible institution.

Section 809YE ITA provides a relief against the remittance charge which could apply to remittance basis taxpayers.[9]

22.2.6 *Interest and penalties*

Para 6 sch 14 FA 2012 provides:

> (1) This paragraph explains the effect of paragraph 3(1) as regards late payment interest and late payment penalties.[10]
> (2) The effect is that liability to pay amounts specified in sub-paragraph (3) ceases when the qualifying gift is made, as if the liability had never arisen.
> (3) The amounts are—
> (a) any late payment interest that accrued on the relevant portion during the negotiation period, and
> (b) any late payment penalty to which N became liable in the negotiation period for failing to pay the relevant portion (together with any interest on such a penalty).
> (4) "The relevant portion" is the portion of N's tax liability for a relevant tax year that is treated under paragraph 3 as satisfied.
> (5) In determining for the purposes of sub-paragraph (2) whether or to what extent—
> (a) late payment interest accruing on an amount of or on account of N's tax liability for the relevant tax year is attributable to the relevant portion, or
> (b) a late payment penalty incurred for failing to pay an amount of or on account of N's tax liability for the relevant tax year is

---

9 See Kessler, *Taxation of Non-Residents and Foreign Domiciliaries* (21st ed., 2022-23), para 19.39 (Exempt property clawback charge) online version *https://www.foreigndomiciliaries.co.uk*

10 Para 24 sch 14 FA 2012 provides:
"late payment interest" means interest under section 101 of FA 2009, or under or by virtue of Part 9 of TMA 1970, on amounts payable to HMRC;
"late payment penalty" means a penalty under Schedule 56 to FA 2009.

attributable to the relevant portion, any attribution or apportionment is to be done in the way that maximises the relief obtained by N by virtue of this paragraph.

(6) "The negotiation period" is the period—

(a) beginning with the offer registration date, and

(b) ending with the day on which the qualifying gift is made.

(7) Nothing in this paragraph affects any late payment interest that accrued, or any late payment penalty to which N became liable, before the offer registration date.

Paragraph 38 of the Explanatory Notes to the FA 2012, as cited in the CGS document, provides:

> Paragraph 6 ensures that where an offer of a gift is accepted under the scheme, resulting in an amount of the tax liability being treated as having been satisfied (as set out in the scheme) then no late payment interest or late payment penalties will be payable on that amount from the date of registration. It is being explored whether, and to what extent, provisions should be made to defer payments of tax, interest and late payment penalties during the negotiation period in respect of tax becoming payable on or after the registration of an offer, where the offer has been made in good faith. However, if a qualifying gift was not made for any reason (say, for example, because the offer was rejected in accordance with the scheme or because the offer was withdrawn by the donor), then the donor would be required to pay to HMRC both the tax due and any late payment interest due up to and including the date of payment. It is currently envisaged that if the tax and interest remains unpaid within 30 days the donor will be subject to late payment penalties.

22.2.7 *Change to tax liability*

Para 7 sch 14 FA 2012 provides:

> (1) If the amount of N's tax liability for a relevant tax year is revised at any time, the portion of that liability that is treated under paragraph 3(1) as satisfied is to be re-calculated.
>
> (2) But nothing in this paragraph permits any revision of the agreed terms.

22.2.8 *Gift set aside*

Para 8 sch 14 FA 2012 provides:

> If a qualifying gift is set aside or declared void after it is made—
>
> (a) the portion of N's tax liability for each relevant tax year that is treated as satisfied ceases to be treated as satisfied,

(b) the effect described in paragraph 6 is negated, and
(c) N is required to pay the portion due for each relevant tax year, together with any late payment interest and late payment penalties in respect of it, by the later of—
   (i) the end of the period of 30 days beginning with the day on which the gift was set aside or declared void, and
   (ii) the day by which N would have been required to pay those amounts but for this Schedule.

This will rarely if ever apply.

22.2.9 *Tax deferral for negotiations*

Para 9 sch 14 FA 2012 provides:

> (1) An individual who makes an offer in the circumstances described in paragraph 1 (a "potential donor") may make a request under this paragraph if—
> (a) the offer is registered in accordance with the scheme,
> (b) the offer includes a proposal ("the donor proposal") of what should be in the agreed terms,
> (c) the potential donor will be required to pay an amount of or on account of tax for a relevant tax year by a certain date, and
> (d) the negotiations are not expected to conclude before that date (referred to as "the due date").
>
> (2) For the purposes of this paragraph, the negotiations "conclude" when—
> (a) a qualifying gift is made pursuant to the offer,
> (b) the offer is withdrawn by the potential donor, or
> (c) the offer is rejected.
>
> (3) A request under this paragraph is a request that the potential donor's obligation to pay the amount by the due date be suspended until the negotiations conclude.
>
> (4) But the running total of amounts for which suspension may be requested under this paragraph in respect of the same offer and the same relevant tax year must not exceed the proposed tax reduction figure for that tax year.
>
> (5) "The proposed tax reduction figure" for a tax year is the amount shown in the donor proposal as the proposed tax reduction figure for that year.
>
> (6) A request under this paragraph—
> (a) must be made in writing to HMRC at least 45 days before the due date, and
> (b) must be accompanied by a copy of the donor proposal and such

other information as an officer of Revenue and Customs may reasonably require.

(7) In considering whether or to what extent to agree to a request, HMRC must have regard to all the circumstances of the case (including, for example, the creditworthiness of the potential donor).

(8) HMRC may impose conditions with respect to the suspension.

10(1) Suspension under paragraph 9 of a potential donor's obligation to pay an amount of or on account of tax stops the donor from becoming liable to late payment penalties for or in connection with the failure to pay that amount by the due date.

(2) But it does not stop late payment interest from accruing on that amount from the due date.

(3) HMRC may by notice in writing to the potential donor withdraw its agreement to the suspension with effect from such date, before conclusion of the negotiations, as may be specified in the notice.

(4) If it does so, the potential donor must pay the amount, together with any late payment interest that has accrued on it since the due date, by the end of the period of 30 days beginning with the date specified in the notice.

(5) The last day of that 30-day period is to be treated for the purposes of any enactment relating to late payment penalties as the date on or before which the amount must be paid.

(6) Paragraph 11 explains what happens once the negotiations conclude (depending on the outcome of the negotiations).

Para 11 sch 14 FA 2012 provides:

(1) This paragraph applies if a potential donor's obligation to pay an amount of or on account of tax remains suspended under paragraph 9 when the negotiations conclude (within the meaning of that paragraph).

(2) The potential donor must pay the amount, together with any late payment interest that has accrued on it since the due date, within the period of 30 days beginning with the day on which the negotiations concluded.

(3) The last day of that 30-day period is to be treated for the purposes of any enactment relating to late payment penalties as the date on or before which the amount must be paid.

(4) But if the negotiations conclude because a qualifying gift is made pursuant to the offer or a part of the offer—

- (a) sub-paragraph (2) is to be read subject to paragraph 3(1) (and its effect as described in paragraph 6), and
- (b) accordingly, the potential donor is only required to pay so much as is not treated as satisfied under paragraph 3(1).

(5) If the negotiations conclude in relation to a part only of the offer—
  (a) this paragraph is to be given effect as far as reasonably practicable in relation to that part, and
  (b) on receipt of a revised copy of the donor proposal, HMRC may give effect to paragraph 9 in relation to the part of the offer that remains under negotiation.

22.2.10 *Corporation tax*

Sch 14 FA 2012 provides similar rules for CT:

> 12(1) This Part applies to a company's liability to corporation tax.
> (2) A reference in this Part to a company's "tax liability" is to the company's liability to corporation tax.
> (3) References to an amount of or on account of "tax" are to be read accordingly.
> **The basic rule**
> 13(1) If a company ("C") makes a qualifying gift, a portion of C's tax liability for the relevant accounting period is to be treated as satisfied, as if C had paid that portion when it became due (or on the offer registration date, if the portion became due before that date).
> (2) "The relevant accounting period" is the accounting period of C's in which the offer registration date falls.
> **The portion treated as satisfied**
> 14(1) The portion of C's tax liability for the relevant accounting period that is to be treated as satisfied is an amount equal to the smaller of—
>   (a) the tax reduction figure, and
>   (b) the amount of C's tax liability for that period less any portion of that amount that is treated as satisfied in consequence of any qualifying gift made by C on a previous occasion.
> (2) The amount determined under sub-paragraph (1) may be nil.
> (3) The tax reduction figure is—
>   (a) 20% of the value set out in the agreed terms as the agreed value of the property forming the subject of the qualifying gift, or
>   (b) such lower figure as may be specified in the agreed terms as the tax reduction figure.
> (4) The Treasury may by order substitute a different percentage for the percentage specified for the time being in sub-paragraph (3)(a).

The following provisions relate to late payment and negotiations, and duplicate the IT provisions; this need not be set out again here.

There is no relief for non-resident companies which are (in general) subject to IT and not to CT. That is a breach of EU law but in practice perhaps this issue will not arise.

22.2.11 *Relevant minister*

Para 23 sch 14 FA 2012 navigates some delicate devolution areas:

(1) For the purposes of paragraph 22, "the relevant Minister" is—

- (a) for items with a purely Scottish interest, the Scottish Ministers,
- (b) for items with some Scottish interest but with no Northern Irish interest and no Welsh interest, the Secretary of State and the Scottish Ministers concurrently,
- (c) for items with a purely Northern Irish interest, the Northern Ireland Department of Culture, Arts and Leisure,
- (d) for items with some Northern Irish interest but with no Scottish interest and no Welsh interest, the Secretary of State and the Northern Ireland Department of Culture, Arts and Leisure concurrently,
- (e) for items with a purely Welsh interest, the Welsh Ministers,
- (f) for items with some Welsh interest but with no Scottish interest and no Northern Irish interest, the Secretary of State and the Welsh Ministers concurrently, and
- (g) for any other items, the Secretary of State.

(2) If an item within sub-paragraph (1)(g) has more than one devolved interest, the Secretary of State must consult the appropriate Minister for each such interest before making a decision under paragraph 22 affecting the item.

(3) An item has a purely Scottish interest if—

- (a) it is located in Scotland, and
- (b) the offer contains—
  - (i) no wish about where the item is to be displayed, or
  - (ii) a wish that it is to be displayed in Scotland.

(4) An item has some Scottish interest if it does not have a purely Scottish interest but—

- (a) it is located in Scotland, or
- (b) the offer contains a wish that it is to be displayed in Scotland.

(5) An item has no Scottish interest if it does not have a purely Scottish interest and it does not have some Scottish interest.

(6) References to items with a purely Northern Irish or purely Welsh interest, to items with some Northern Irish or some Welsh interest and to items with no Northern Irish interest or no Welsh interest are to be read in accordance with sub-paragraphs (3) to (5), but replacing references to Scotland with references to Northern Ireland or, as the case may be, Wales.

(7) A "devolved interest" is some Scottish interest, some Northern Irish interest or some Welsh interest.

(8) "The appropriate Minister" is—

- (a) if the item has some Scottish interest, the Scottish Ministers,
- (b) if the item has some Northern Irish interest, the Northern Ireland Department of Culture, Arts and Leisure, and

(c) if the item has some Welsh interest, the Welsh Ministers.

(9) "Item" means an object or collection or group of objects.

The CGS document sets out the role of the Relevant Minister:

Recommendation to the Relevant Minister

38. Where the Panel considers that an application meets all the requirements, and that the offer should be accepted, it will make a recommendation to the relevant Minister that the object is pre-eminent and (subject to the availability of funds) should be accepted on behalf of the nation. The identity of the relevant Minister who will agree to the recommendation that an object is pre-eminent will depend on where the object is located and whether there is a wish as to where the object is displayed. This is discussed further in paragraphs 53 to 55.

39. Where the relevant Minister accepts the Panel's recommendations the Arts Council will ensure that the Secretary of State for Culture, Media and Sport has confirmed that the acceptance of the gift is within the annual limit for the CGS and AIL Schemes. Only when it is satisfied that accepting the gift will not breach the ceiling will the Arts Council write to the applicant accepting the gift. The Secretary of State for Culture, Media and Sport is responsible for ensuring that the CGS and AIL schemes remain within the agreed annual limit. The Arts Council will then issue a letter of acceptance to the donor which will include the agreed valuation; a schedule of how the tax reduction or reductions will be applied; and the name of the institution to which the object will be transferred where this is already known. The applicant will need to accept the terms within 30 days of the date of the letter of acceptance. The terms in the letter of acceptance, once accepted by the donor, are the "agreed terms" for the purposes of the Scheme;

22.2.12 *Applications*

The CGS document sets out the procedure for making an application under the CGS:

15. The process for all applications under the CGS will be administered by the Arts Council. Applications to donate objects are to be made in writing to the Arts Council using the application form at the end of this Guidance.

16. Subject to the annual limit not already having been exceeded, the Arts Council will normally register the application under the Scheme within 30 days of receiving all the required information (the "offer registration date"). The required information is set out in paragraph 19 below. Applicants who do not provide all the required information will be contacted by the Arts Council and requested to provide this as soon as

possible. The application will not be formally registered until the Arts Council is satisfied that it has received all the required information. In addition, an application may not be registered where the value set out in the application is considered by the Panel to be wholly unsupported by the evidence submitted by the applicant or by any other information known to the Panel. Registration of the application by the Panel should not give rise to any expectation by the applicant that the value set out in the application will be agreed.

17. The offer registration date has consequences for valuation and tax purposes. Whereas the Panel may take some time to agree the value of an object, the final agreed value will be the value of the object as at the offer registration date. The Arts Council will notify the offer registration date to HMRC within 30 days after the offer registration date. The offer registration date will be recorded by HMRC for tax purposes, should the application succeed.

18. The registration of an application should not give rise to any right or expectation that the object will be accepted under the Scheme and it is not to be taken as approval that any of the conditions of the CGS have been satisfied.

19. The application must include the following information:

a) Full details of the object, for example, artist or designer, title, medium, dimensions, date, provenance, exhibition history and any associated literature or correspondence which might help illustrate any of these points. Applicants who are considering donating archival material may find it helpful to refer to notes which apply to the AIL Scheme and which are available from the Arts Council's website ...;

b) A valuation and information about who has provided the valuation, together with evidence of auctions, sales or other information which may help to justify the valuation (see paragraphs 20 and 21 for further advice on valuations);

c) Evidence of good legal title and detailed evidence of provenance, including details of the ownership of the object between 1933-1945, where applicable. The applicant must confirm, by completing the application form, that they have full and unencumbered title to the object, with unrestricted right to transfer title free from all third party rights or claims (including, where appropriate, copyright claims);

d) At least three good quality colour photographs and a high resolution jpeg of the object. Where an application relates to intangible objects, e.g. video installations or other electronic records, any printed images relating to the objects should be provided, where these are available;

e) A current condition report;

f) A statement setting out why the object is considered to be pre-eminent (see paragraphs 27 to 30);

g) Contact details of the applicant or their agents and details of where the object can be inspected;

h) An Interim Tax Reduction Schedule (the "Interim Tax Schedule") will need to be completed and signed by the donor in relation to their tax affairs. The Interim Tax Schedule will specify, on the basis of the applicant's valuation, the amount and, for individuals only, state which tax years (for up to five tax years beginning with the year in which the offer is registered) the applicant would like the tax reduction to be spread and which tax they would like to offset first (income tax or capital gains tax). Alternatively, individual donors can choose to apply the tax reduction to a single year being either the tax year in which the application is registered or one of the subsequent four tax years. This form must be submitted with the application form;

i) In the event that negotiations are prolonged, the applicant may apply to HMRC to suspend the payment of the tax. This only applies to the tax liability that the tax reduction would, if agreed by Arts Council, be expected to offset. Applicants will need to write to HMRC once the Arts Council has confirmed to HMRC that it has registered the offer. Suspension of an individual's tax liability is at HMRC's discretion and HMRC will consider each application on a case by case basis. Applicants should be aware that a request to suspend tax does not mean that it will be automatically approved. Any suspension request received prior to confirmation from ACE to HMRC of registration will be rejected. For individuals, a Suspension Request Form is included for information in the application pack. Companies will need to contact HMRC directly;

j) Details of an individual's Tax Office, their Unique Tax Reference and National Insurance Number. Donors will also be required to sign a declaration, giving their consent to the Arts Council, HMRC and DCMS to exchange information relating to their proposed donation and the tax reduction associated with it, where the exchange of this information is necessary for the consideration of their offer and the administration of the Scheme;

k) The preferred eligible institution (if any) to which the applicant would wish to see the object transferred and the reasons for their preference (see paragraphs 35 to 37); and

l) The donor will need to sign the application form as well as the

> Interim Tax Schedule.

The address for applications is provided:

> 62. Applicants should complete an application form and submit an electronic copy and a signed hard copy together with the supporting material outlined in paragraph 19 to the Arts Council at the following addresses:
>
> catherine.higgs@artscouncil.org.uk
> Cultural Gifts Scheme
> Acquisitions, Exports, Loans and Collections Unit
> Arts Council England
> 21 Bloomsbury Street
> LONDON WC1B 3HF.

22.2.13 *Valuation*

It is the responsibility of the taxpayer to provide an initial, estimated valuation. The CGS document provides:

> *How should the object be valued?*
>
> 20. Applicants are required to provide information concerning the object's estimated value. The value of each object should be its fair market value. This is taken to mean the price at which the object could reasonably be expected to change hands in an open and unrestricted market, where buyer and seller are both knowledgeable, informed and prudent, with neither being under any compulsion to buy and sell and where the value is unaffected by any consideration relating to past or future transactions between the parties.
>
> 21. The objective therefore is to agree an estimate of what the object might have fetched in the saleroom, i.e. the open market value at the time of registration. The valuation should be fully justified by the applicant in their application and should be accompanied by substantiating evidence. The value will not take into account any costs of disposal, i.e. the costs of professional fees or tax are excluded.
>
> 22. The costs to the applicant of establishing and agreeing the value of the object, and of transferring title to the object, will not be taken into account when determining the fair market value and will be the sole responsibility of the applicant.
>
> 23. Based on the applicant's valuation, an applicant will need to provide an Interim Tax Schedule. If they wish to spread the tax reduction beyond the tax year in which the offer is registered they will need to include this information in the Interim Tax Schedule. This is described in paragraphs 47 to 49.
>
> 24. Applicants should note that the value set out in the application does

> not give rise to any right or expectation that the value will be accepted by the Panel. As set out in paragraphs 31 to 32, the Panel will consider the valuation and may seek to agree a revised value.
>
> 25. The date at which the value of the object is to be agreed for the purposes of the CGS will be the offer registration date (see paragraphs 16 and 17 above).

This valuation is subject to confirmation by the Acceptance in Lieu panel. The CGS document provides:

> 31. Where the Panel finds that an object is pre-eminent, it will then confirm that it is prepared to recommend the value or, where appropriate, advise the applicant of an alternative value at which it would recommend acceptance of the object.
>
> 32. For individual applicants, once the value of the object has been agreed between the Panel and the applicant, the applicant will have the opportunity to amend the Interim Tax Schedule if the agreed value is different from the value provided at the offer registration date.. Any amendments need to be agreed by the Panel. This will then become the Agreed Tax Reduction Schedule (the "Agreed Tax Schedule") and will then form part of the agreed terms and no amendments or other revisions will be permitted. This means that if, in any of the prescribed years, the donor's actual tax liability is less than the amount of tax reduction set out in the Agreed Tax Schedule for that year, the difference cannot be carried forward into any future years and will therefore be lost to the donor. On the other hand, if the donor's tax affairs are such that, in any of the prescribed years, the donor's actual tax liability is more than the amount of tax reduction set out in the Agreed Tax Schedule for that year, the donor will only be able to claim the amount of tax reduction set out in the Agreed Tax Schedule for that year. Any remaining tax will need to be paid on time. This allows the Panel to have certainty for future year commitments when managing the annual limit.

22.2.14 *Time limit for negotiation*

There is a time limit for negotiations. In this regard, the CGS document provides:

> 57. Applicants should note that where negotiations have not been concluded within two years of the offer registration date the Panel will review the application. Negotiations are "concluded" when either a qualifying gift is made pursuant to the offer, or the offer is withdrawn or rejected (para 9 and 18 of Schedule 14). Where the Panel considers that there is no reasonable prospect of negotiations being concluded within a

reasonable time, subject to an absolute limit of three years, the application will be rejected. If negotiations have not been concluded within three years of the offer registration date the Panel will reject the application. If any tax had been suspended by HMRC the applicant will be required to pay the outstanding tax and the interest accrued.

58. If the applicant still wishes to gift the object for the benefit of the public or the nation they will need to submit a new application and the process will start again. The applicant will not be able to use the tax reduction against tax accrued in the years that the previous offer was being negotiated.

22.2.15 *Confidentiality*

The CGS document contains an undertaking that, although gifts under the CGS will usually be publicised, the taxpayer concerned is entitled to his usual confidentiality.

It is not difficult to imagine that these two principles may create a conflict between the interests of DCMS and the donor, and there is not currently any suggestion of how such a conflict will be resolved.

> 59. On completion of the gift and delivery to an eligible institution, an announcement will be made by the Arts Council, or by the relevant body in Scotland, Wales or Northern Ireland, depending on which Minister has accepted the object. The announcement will provide details of the gifted object and the amount of the tax reduction applied. Images of the object provided by the applicant to the Panel for the purposes of assessment of the gift will be used for publicity purposes.
>
> 60. Where for any reason an application is not accepted or is withdrawn no announcement will be made.
>
> 61. The rules of customer confidentiality apply throughout and accordingly the name of the donor will remain confidential unless the donor gives specific written consent for their right of confidentiality to be waived. For the avoidance of doubt, this consent will be separate to the consent given to HMRC, DCMS and the Panel to exchange taxpayer information between themselves for the purposes of an application under the Scheme.

22.2.16 *Delivery*

The CGS document provides:

> *Transfer of objects from the donor*
>
> 40. The donor will be required to sign a deed to transfer title. The legal and beneficial title in the object would usually transfer from the donor to the relevant Minister in return for the tax reduction. It is possible,

however, in cases where an eligible institution is agreed at an early stage, following recommendation by the Panel, for title to the object to transfer, at the direction of the relevant Minister, from the donor directly to the agreed eligible institution, i.e. instead of to the relevant Minister.

41. In cases where the eligible institution is not identified at an early stage, e.g. because the donor has not expressed a wish and the availability of the object is advertised, then, following recommendation by the Panel, title to the object may transfer from the donor to the relevant Minister. Until such time as an eligible institution is identified, the relevant Minister may direct that the object is transferred to a nominated person (which will also be an eligible institution) to hold and manage the object on a temporary basis. Once an institution is identified for permanent transfer, the object will transfer from the relevant Minister to that institution.

42. Objects will be transferred to the eligible institution on such conditions as the relevant Minister directs. The conditions of transfer will usually include the following, as appropriate, to ensure each object is protected and accessible to the public:

- The eligible institution shall, at its own expense, maintain the object in its existing condition and make good any repairable damage.
- The object shall be made accessible to the public. This may be on such terms as are appropriate to the nature and condition of the object, taking into account the long term preservation of the object. Where appropriate this may be reflected in a requirement that the object is available to the public for a number of days per year and in most cases this will amount to a minimum of 100 days. For other objects, particularly archive and manuscript material, this may not be appropriate and "available to the public" may require the object to be available for study by the public in, for example, a reading room;
- Title to the object may not be transferred or disposed of whether by sale or otherwise, without the prior consent of the relevant Minister. The object may not be transferred to another institution except for short periods of exhibition (appropriate to the nature and condition of the object), preservation or restoration without the prior consent of the relevant Minister; and
- If the eligible institution to which the object has been transferred is unable to fulfil any or all of the conditions, it shall notify the Panel immediately and may be required to surrender the object to the relevant Minister, who will seek advice from the Panel as to a new eligible institution to which the object can be transferred.

43. The Arts Council will liaise with the owner of the object and the eligible institution to which it is to be transferred either permanently or temporarily, pending a decision on permanent transfer, regarding the

collection and transportation of the object. The donor will be responsible for arranging any insurance and transport and bearing any costs.

44. The object will remain the responsibility of the donor until legal title has passed and the object has been received in acceptable condition by the agreed eligible institution.

22.3 IT relief for other assets: Critique

A case for allowing income tax relief (QIDR or Gift Aid) on all gifts of all assets is set out by Venables, "Gift Aid Relief for Gifts in Kind" CLPR Vol. 3, Issue 3, p.139.[11] The point was summarily dismissed in the Review of Charity Taxation Consultative Document (1997) but since income tax relief has been allowed for quoted shares (2000), for land (2002) and works of art (2012), the case for allowing relief for other assets is stronger. The administrative problems could be kept within limits by a fairly high minimum value limit, which would stop, eg gifts of jumble to charity shops from qualifying for relief.

The coalition government (2010-15) similarly rejected a proposal by the Gift Aid Forum to extend Gift Aid relief to donated goods and donated expenses:

> This would move Gift Aid away from being a relief on donations of cash and add considerable complexity to the system, particularly in relation to valuation and the need to prevent fraud.[12]

Tax avoidance schemes (ab)using QIDR show that there are indeed challenges in tax reliefs of this kind.

---

11 *http://www.khpplc.co.uk/reviews*

12 Letter from Justine Greening (Economic Secretary to the Treasury) to CIOT, December 2010 *http://webarchive.nationalarchives.gov.uk/20130129110402/http://www.hm-treasury.gov.uk/d/gift_aid_forum_letter_to_peter_fanning_from_est_031210.pdf*

CHAPTER TWENTY THREE

CGT RELIEF ON DISPOSALS TO CHARITY

Cross references

The following topics are considered elsewhere:
  7.24 (Tainted donation: CGT)
  9.18 (Liquidation)

23.1 Disposal of asset to charity

This chapter considers:

(1) CGT relief for disposals to a charity (**"donor CGT relief"**)

(2) Comparable IT reliefs on transfers to charities of:

  (a) offshore funds

  (b) deeply discounted securities

  (c) securities within the accrued income scheme

  (d) income streams

Individuals and trusts pay CGT on chargeable gains and UK companies pay corporation tax. For present purposes (more or less) the same rules apply and we refer for simplicity to CGT.

23.2 CGT on gifts generally

In money terms (one might say, in economic reality, but that is not a helpful concept in tax) a gift does not give rise to a gain: it normally gives rise to a loss to the donor. However, s.17(1) TCGA provides:

> Subject to the provisions of this Act, a person's acquisition or disposal of an asset shall for the purposes of this Act be deemed to be for a consideration equal to the market value of the asset—
> (a) where he acquires or, as the case may be, disposes of the asset otherwise than by way of a bargain made at arm's length, and in particular where he acquires or disposes of it
> [i] by way of gift or
> [ii] on a transfer into settlement by a settlor or
> [iii] by way of distribution from a company in respect of shares in the company, or
> (b) where he acquires or, as the case may be, disposes of the asset
> [i] wholly or partly for a consideration that cannot be valued,
> [ii] or in connection with his own or another's loss of office or employment or diminution of emoluments,
> [iii] or otherwise in consideration for or recognition of his or another's services or past services in any office or employment or of any other service rendered or to be rendered by him or another.

A chargeable gain may therefore accrue to the donor on making a gift.

23.3 Donor CGT relief

23.3.1 *History of relief*

At the inception of CGT in 1965 there was no relief for gifts to charity: a gift to charity gave rise to a chargeable gain on the basis of market value. That must have been a strong disincentive to charitable giving (though mitigated to some extent in the earliest years by 1965 CGT rebasing).

Relief was introduced by the Heath administration in 1972, and is now in s.257 TCGA.

23.3.2 *Application conditions*

Section 257(1) sets out the conditions for the relief:

> Subsection (2) below shall apply where a disposal of an asset is made otherwise than under a bargain at arm's length—

(a) to a charity or a registered club[1] or
(b) to any bodies mentioned in Schedule 3 to the Inheritance Tax Act 1984 (gifts for national purposes, etc) ...

We refer to this as **"donor CGT relief"**. (It must not be confused with the distinct CGT relief which applies on disposals *by* a charity, ie when a gain accrues to the charity, which we refer to as **"charity's CGT relief"**).[2]

The disposal must be "otherwise than under[3] a bargain at arm's length", so the relief applies to all disposals within s.17 TCGA. The relief applies in particular to:

(1) pure gifts; and
(2) sales at a deliberate undervalue

The standard tax definition of charity applies.[4]

The disposal must be "to" a charity. What is the position if a lease is surrendered, or a debt on a security is released? It is considered that there is a disposal "to" the charity (even though there is no acquisition by the charity) so the relief applies.[5]

The relief applies in a straightforward way on a disposal to charity by individuals and companies. For a disposal to charity by trustees see 23.15 (Private trust: Disposal to charity).

No claim is needed: the relief is compulsory. This is probably deliberate because where a loss arises, the relief would not be advantageous to the taxpayer.

23.3.3 *Position of donor*

The relief is in s.257(2) TCGA which provides:

> [A] Sections 17(1) and 258(3) shall not apply;
> [B] but if the disposal is by way of gift (including a gift in settlement)

---

1 ie a CASC: see 41.2 (Types of club and terminology).
2 See 5.1 (Taxation of charity capital gains).
3 The TCGA sometimes refers to disposals *by way of* a bargain *made* at arm's length; and other times refers to disposals *under* a bargain at arm's length. The two expressions might be taken to be identical. However, the better view is that the expression "under" a bargain at arm's length is wider than the expression "by way of" a bargain made at arm's length. It is significant that the expression "under" a bargain made at arm's length is generally used in relieving sections, eg donor CGT relief hold-over relief.
4 See 3.4 (Tax definition of charity).
5 See 15.12 (Waiver of debt).

> or for a consideration not exceeding the sums allowable as a deduction under section 38, then—
> (a) the disposal and acquisition shall be treated for the purposes of this Act as being made for such consideration as to secure that neither a gain nor a loss accrues on the disposal...

Section 257(2)[A] disapplies s.17(1); so one does not substitute market value for the actual consideration.

If this were all, an allowable loss would usually accrue on gifts to charity (and on sales to a charity at an undervalue). Section 257(2)[B](a) prevents this.

Thus the position for the donor is as follows:

(1) A disposal to a charity is treated as made for such consideration as secures that neither a gain nor a loss accrues if:
    (a) It is a gift
    (b) The transfer is for a consideration less than the base cost, ie less than the sums allowable as a deduction under s.38 TCGA.[6]
    (c) The transfer is made for a consideration which cannot be valued.
(2) If an asset is disposed of to a charity for consideration which exceeds the base cost, tax is computed on the actual consideration not market value. Benefits received which are not "consideration" are ignored.

23.3.4 *Position of charity*

A charity will only be concerned with gains accruing on its own disposals in the exceptional case where it fails to qualify for charity's CGT relief, under s.256 TCGA.

The base cost of the asset in the hands of the charity will be the consideration which it is treated as receiving under the rules set out above. In the case of the gift that will be the donor's base cost. A charity will not normally know what that base cost is, and the donor would certainly be surprised to be asked, so it is just as well that relief in practice makes the point irrelevant.

For the position where the asset given is a qualifying investment, see 21.16 (Position of charity).

For completeness we should mention s.257(2)(b) TCGA, which provides:

> if the disposal is by way of gift (including a gift in settlement) or for a

---

6 Note that a company's indexation relief does not count as "base cost".

> consideration not exceeding the sums allowable as a deduction under section 38, then ...
>
> (b) where, after the disposal, the asset is disposed of by the person who acquired it under the disposal, its acquisition by the person making the earlier disposal shall be treated for the purposes of this Act as the acquisition of the person making the later disposal.

If after a gift of an asset to a charity, the asset is later disposed of by the charity, the acquisition of the asset by the donor is to be treated as the acquisition of the asset by the charity. The practical effect would seem to be in connection with time apportionment, 1982 rebasing and (for corporate charities) indexation relief.

It is considered that s.257(2)(b) serves no useful purpose, and repeal would be a small but worthwhile simplification.

23.3.5 *Gift of venture capital trust*

Section 257 TCGA requires that:

> ... the disposal is not one in relation to which section 151A(1) has effect.

Section 151A(1) TCGA provides:

> A gain or loss accruing to an individual on a qualifying disposal of any ordinary shares in a company which—
>
> (a) was a venture capital trust at the time when he acquired the shares, and
>
> (b) is still such a trust at the time of the disposal,
>
> shall not be a chargeable gain or, as the case may be, an allowable loss.

No relief is needed in this case, so this restriction can only be helpful.

23.4 "Consideration"

"Consideration" is a fundamental term for many tax purposes, including in particular the following charity tax issues:

(1) Donor CGT relief

(2) IHT charity exemption for trusts[7]

"Consideration" is a common term in tax and other statutes. The term is

---

7 See 24.26 (Acquired for consideration). James Kessler QC discusses "consideration" in more detail in *Kessler, Taxation of Nonresidents & Foreign Domiciliaries* (21st ed., 2022-23) App 4.2 (Consideration)
online version *www.foreigndomiciliaries.co.uk*

not usually defined. Its meaning is discussed in the cases:

> The word "consideration" is a term of art in English law, and I think that, used in an English statute, it must be assumed to bear its ordinary meaning in the law, save in so far as the provisions of the statute indicate some other meaning. In its usage in English law the central feature of consideration is reciprocity ... . Something is given in return for something else. It may, for example, be a promise in return for a promise or a payment in return for a promise. It can be a detriment to the promise or a benefit to the promisor. But whatever its form, I think that reciprocity is involved. It is essentially mutual.

The emphasis on *English* law is debatable, so far as we are concerned with the word (consideration) in a statute which also applies in Scotland. But reciprocity is inherent in the general sense of the word consideration, It is not a specifically English law idea; so the point does not matter.

Another example from a non-tax case:

> In our view the meaning of the word "consideration" must be the legal meaning of it and not any common or garden meaning; that really goes without saying. ... In our judgment the word "consideration" connotes the existence of something in the shape of a contract or a bargain between the parties. ... Consideration deals with the situation where there is a contract or a bargain and something moving the other way.[8]

Context may of course show that "consideration" is used in a special sense.[9] But the above is the starting point.

23.4.1 *Contract not required*

A contract in English law requires consideration. But consideration does not require a contract:

> [The reference to consideration in what is now s.5(2)(a) VATA 1984] is not necessarily contemplating the existence of a contract. A barrister, for example, receives consideration for his services from a solicitor, but there is no contract. That, however, is a different point and does not, I think, indicate any different meaning of consideration to that which I have mentioned.[10]

In some tripartite cases the courts are prepared to regard as consideration

---

8 *R v Braithwaite* [1983] 1 WLR 385 at p.391.

9 For instance, in the VAT context of *Apple & Pear*, an EU-law concept of "consideration" was adopted in preference to the English contract law meaning.

10 *C&E Commissioners v Apple & Pear Development Council* [1985] STC 383 at p.389.

benefits received as a result of a payment, in the absence of a contractual relationship between the parties.[11]

The fact that the disponor receives some benefit as a result of a disposal does not necessarily mean that person receives consideration. In *Ball v National and Grindlays Bank* 47 TC 287, the bank entered into covenants to pay income for the benefit of children of employees. The bank received a benefit in the form of motivated staff. Nevertheless, the payments were not made for consideration, there being no bargain between the employees and the bank that the covenants should be made.[12] It may alternatively be said that the benefit received was too indirect.

The fact that the benefit would not have been received but for the disposal does not entail that the benefit is necessarily consideration for the disposal. The distinction is recognised in another context in *Pritchard v Arundale* 47 TC 680 at 687.

In complex cases the courts will not "unpick the constituent parts of the bargain and put a value on those parts".[13] Covenants given by a charity which are merely incidental to the main transaction may in some circumstances be disregarded as:

(1) not "consideration" at all; contrast *Mouatt v Betts Motors* [1959] AC 71; or
(2) consideration of no value; contrast *Fielder v Vedlynn* 65 TC 145.

23.4.2 *"In money or money's worth"*

Statute frequently refers to consideration "in money or money's worth". The only effect of the words *in money or money's worth* is that one ignores consideration of marriage.[14] However, consideration of marriage is not nowadays an important concept.

The expression also excludes consideration of "natural love and affection" but that is not consideration in the true sense at all.[15] So there

---

11 eg *Unilever v IRC* 76 TC 300 in the High Court at [46] reversing the Special Commissioners (but without any substantial discussion of the issue). The Court of Appeal did not consider the point.

12 The drafter took this point on board in drafting s.401 ITEPA: "In consideration of *or in consequence of or otherwise in connection with* ..."

13 *Wilson v Clayton* 77 TC 1 at [50].

14 Marriage was formerly regarded as a contract, and agreeing to marry was consideration for the contract. However, marriage consideration is not "money or money's worth".

15 The phrase seems rather inapt: it is a traditional conveyancer's phrase which probably antecedes the modern sense of "consideration".

is no practical difference between "consideration" and consideration "in money or money's worth". The words "in money or money's worth" do not add anything.

23.5 Qualifying corporate bond

Normally no chargeable gains arise on the disposal of a qualifying corporate bond ("**QCB**") so CGT relief is irrelevant. However a gain does accrue when the QCB is acquired in a reorganisation within s.116 TCGA.

The CG Manual provides:

> **CG66624: Gifts: of Qualifying Corporate Bonds to Charities etc**[16]
> [Jun 2016]
> This paragraph applies if a person holds qualifying corporate bonds (QCBs) issued following a takeover or share reorganisation. In brief TCGA92/S116 (10) requires the computation of the gain that would have arisen if the shares had been sold at their market value at the date of reorganisation. This gain is deferred and accrues on a later disposal of the QCBs. See CG53723.
> If the disposal is to a charity and comes within TCGA92/S257, there will no charge by reference to the deferred gain either on the donor, or on the charity on a subsequent disposal of the QCBs.

This is correct. The same point is made in RI 23.

This is useful where:

(1) A person has exchanged shares for a QCB, under a reorganisation within s.116 TCGA.
(2) The QCB has become of little value.

On a disposal of the QCB, the gain on the share-for-QCB exchange accrues under s.116(10) TCGA. The tax may exceed the value of the QCB. If the QCB is given to a charity, no CGT is due.

23.6 Offshore fund

On the disposal of a non-reporting offshore fund, an offshore income gain may arise which is subject to income tax. The gain is computed on CGT principles.[17] This incorporates donor's CGT charity relief. On the

---

16 The "etc" refers to bodies within Schedule 3 IHTA.

17 See reg. 38, 39 Offshore Funds (Tax) Regulations 2009. For a full discussion of offshore funds, see Kessler, *Taxation of Non-Residents and Foreign Domiciliaries* (21st ed., 2022-23), Chapters 66-67 (Offshore Funds) online version *https://www.foreigndomiciliaries.co.uk*

disposal of an interest in an offshore fund to charity there will in principle be no gain and no income tax charge will arise.

23.7 Deeply discounted security

On the disposal of a deeply discounted security, a profit may arise which is subject to income tax.[18] On a disposal which is not at arm's length, such as a gift to charity, the profit is computed by reference to market value at the time of disposal. There is no relief for gifts to charity. Qualifying investment donation relief will apply if the deeply discounted security is a qualifying investment. In other cases it is likely to be better to give other assets, or to sell and give the cash proceeds under Gift Aid.

23.8 Accrued income scheme

On a transfer of assets within the accrued income scheme, income may arise to the transferor which is subject to income tax.[19] There is no relief for gifts to charity. Qualifying investment donation relief will apply if the security is a qualifying investment. In other cases might sometimes be better to give other assets, or to sell and give the cash proceeds under Gift Aid, or to make the transfer ex div. But the amounts involved may not be very significant.

23.9 Transfer of income stream

On a transfer of an income stream to charity within the income stream code, income may arise to the transferor which is subject to income tax.[20] There is no relief for gifts to charity. But in practice this is not likely to arise.

23.10 Gift to foreign charity

The tax definition of "charity" applies so (in short) a gift to a foreign

---

18 See s.439, 440 ITTOIA. For a discussion of deeply discounted securities, see Kessler, *Taxation of Non-Residents and Foreign Domiciliaries* (20th ed., 2021-22), Chapter 28 (Deeply Discounted Securities) online version *https://www.foreigndomiciliaries.co.uk*

19 See s.616 ITA. For a discussion of the accrued income scheme, see Kessler, *Taxation of Non-Residents and Foreign Domiciliaries* (21st ed., 2022-23), Chapter 28 (Accrued Income Profits) online version *https://www.foreigndomiciliaries.co.uk*

20 For a discussion of the income stream code, see Kessler, *Taxation of Non-Residents and Foreign Domiciliaries* (21st ed., 2022-23), Chapter 54 (Transfer of Income Streams) online version *https://www.foreigndomiciliaries.co.uk*

(non-EU) charity will not qualify for CGT relief.[21] A person who wishes to make a gift to a foreign charity which might give rise to a chargeable gain should consider making a gift to a UK or EU charity. The UK charity may then lend or transfer the asset to the foreign charity. Care may be needed to avoid a deemed gain by the charity: see 5.5 (Deemed gain). Consider the GAAR. The use of a UK charity will usually be required in order to secure the IHT charitable exemption.

23.11 Planning: Selection of assets

If a person wishes to give assets to a charity it is obviously sensible as far as possible to select those assets which (if otherwise disposed of) would give rise to the greatest chargeable gain. It is wasteful to give (say) gilts to a charity (which would not give rise to a chargeable gain) or assets which have fallen in value, and at the same time to retain other assets pregnant with gain.

23.12 Gift/sale by charity

From a narrow CGT viewpoint it is better to give assets to a charity rather than for an individual to sell the assets and give to charity the proceeds of sale. A sale by an individual would give rise to CGT, whereas if the charity receives the assets *in specie* and later decides to sell, the gain is exempt. The authors are aware of cases where HMRC have not accepted the channelling of a sale through a charity. It may be alleged that the transfer to the charity was an "inserted step" and a fiscal nullity under the GAAR. It is considered that the HMRC argument should be firmly resisted. The disposal to the charity cannot properly be characterised as an "inserted step": see *Reynaud v IRC* [1999] STC SCD 185. It may well be that HMRC do not now take this point. Still, the best course is to transfer an asset to a charity before it is "preordained" that the sale will be completed. The issue of the GAAR should not arise.

23.13 Gift of assets *v.* sale & cash gift

Only a gift of cash or qualifying investments to a charity qualifies for income tax relief. In the case of other assets, a donor should ask himself which relief would be more valuable: relief from income tax or from capital gains tax. It may be appropriate to sell and make a cash gift.

---

21 See 3.6 (Jurisdiction condition).

Example 1

Suppose an individual wishes to give £100,000 to a charity. There are two possibilities:

(1) The individual may give assets worth £100,000 to the charity. The gift qualifies for CGT relief–on the inherent gain–but no income tax relief (unless the assets are qualifying investments).

(2) The individual may give £80,000 qualifying for Gift Aid . The donor may then sell the same assets in order to raise the necessary cash. This qualifies for Gift Aid income tax relief but not CGT relief.

In that example the donor did not mind whether the charity received assets or cash. The donor may desire to transfer a specific asset to a charity.

Example 2

An individual wishes to give a picture to a charity. The picture is worth £500,000.

Suppose the base cost of the picture for CGT purposes is nil. A disposal of the picture would give rise to a chargeable gain of £500,000. The donor could simply give the picture to the charity. The gift enjoys CGT relief.

Suppose that the base cost of the picture is £500,000 so that no capital gain would accrue on the disposal. CGT relief is of no value to the individual, but income tax relief on £500,000 would be valuable. Or suppose that the base cost of the picture is £200,000 so that the capital gain which would accrue on its disposal is £300,000. For suggestions, see 15.19 (Acquisition of property rule) and 28.3 (QIDR).

23.14 Asset with inherent loss

It may happen that a person wishes to give to a charity a specific asset with a loss; that is, the present value of the asset is less than the CGT base cost. A simple gift to the charity would not give rise to an allowable loss. That is wasteful and should be avoided. To this problem there are a number of solutions.

If the asset could be sold on the open market and the proceeds given to charity then the donor enjoys both a CGT allowable loss and income tax relief under Gift Aid.

It is more difficult where the donor wishes the charity to have the specific asset and not cash. Possibly the asset could be given to an appropriate third party which would allow the charity use of the asset.

It must be borne in mind that a loss accruing on a disposal to a connected person is only allowable against a gain accruing on a disposal to the same person.[22] An individual is connected with the trustees of a charitable settlement of which they are a settlor. Any person who makes a gift to a charitable trust would appear to become a "settlor" of that trust. However, a person is not connected to a charitable company unless they have control of that company (or if they and persons connected with him have control). In this area, therefore, a charitable company would appear to receive better treatment than a charitable trust.

23.14.1 *Critique*

The CGT legislation is unjust in its treatment of losses. The symmetry of wording masks an asymmetry of treatment. It makes good sense to provide that if a person is gifting their capital gain to charity then they should not pay tax on it, but it makes no sense to provide that if on a gift to charity they should happen to realise a loss, that loss should not be an allowable loss. For, unlike the gain, the loss remains theirs in economic reality and is not transferred to the charity. Section 257 ought to be amended so that the consideration which the donor is deemed to receive (and that which the charity is deemed to give) for the asset is the lower of its market value and the maximum amount of such consideration consistent with the donor not realising a gain on the disposal.

23.15 Private trust: Disposal to charity

On the occasion when a person (including a charity) becomes absolutely entitled to property as against a trustee, the trustee is deemed to dispose of the property and re-acquire it at market value: s.71 TCGA. Section 257(1) TCGA disapplies section 17 but does not provide relief against section 71.[23] Relief is provided instead by section 257(3) TCGA which provides:

> Where—
>
> (a) otherwise than on the termination of a life interest (within the meaning of section 72) by the death of the person entitled thereto, any assets or parts of any assets forming part of settled

---

22 Curiously this rule does not apply on gifts to certain clubs; see s.18(4) TCGA. However, such clubs will rarely be charities.

23 In the absence of s.257(3) it would be arguable that s.257(1) by implication provided relief from s.71; but the context shows that relief is available (if at all) under s.257(3); if subsection (3) does not apply one cannot obtain relief under subsection (1).

property are, under section 71, deemed to be disposed of and reacquired by the trustee, and

(b) the person becoming entitled as mentioned in section 71(1) is
    [i] a charity,
    [ii] a registered club or
    [iii] a body mentioned in Schedule 3 to the Inheritance Tax Act 1984 (gifts for national purposes, etc),

then, if no consideration is received by any person for or in connection with any transaction by virtue of which the charity, registered club or other body becomes so entitled, the disposal and reacquisition of the assets to which the charity, registered club or other body becomes so entitled shall, notwithstanding section 71, be treated for the purposes of this Act as made for such consideration as to secure that neither a gain nor a loss accrues on the disposal.

The condition at the end of s.257(3) is aimed at avoidance schemes involving the sale of an equitable interest, but it applies further than that. The point was discussed in *Abacus v NSPCC* [2001] STC 1344, in the context of a so-called "flip-flop" scheme:

(1) Trustees of a non-resident trust borrowed funds from Coutts and secured the funds on shares.
(2) The Trustees appointed the shares to the charity absolutely.

Patten J said:

> Although the appointment in question was made in favour of charity it is at the very least strongly arguable and in my view probably right to suppose that the exemption granted by s.257 of the 1992 Act does not apply so as to exclude the charge. This is because by virtue of s.257(3) the deemed disposal and re-acquisition so as to secure neither a gain nor a loss which forms the basis of exemption only applies where "no consideration is received by any person for or in connection with any transaction by virtue of which the charity or other body becomes so entitled". It must be strongly arguable that the transaction referred to in s.257(3) would encompass the so called "flip flop" scheme as a whole. If that is right then consideration was provided in at least three possible ways;
> [i] in the form of the bank loan from Coutts;
> [ii] in the form of the obligation of the trustees to repay the Coutts loan;
> [iii] by the transfer of cash borrowed from Coutts in order to fund the

> two new settlements.[24]
>
> No trustee properly advised could have executed the 3 April appointment on the basis that s.257 was likely to prevent a charge arising under s.71(1) ...

This comment was made in the context of an application to declare that the trustees' appointment was void (the trustees had failed to take the relevant tax matters into account). HMRC was not party to the hearing and the court would not have heard a full argument on the CGT position. The authors suggest that the "transaction" referred to in section 257(3) is not the "flip-flop" arrangement as a whole: it is the appointment to the charity, for that is the transaction "by virtue of which the charity becomes ... entitled". Nevertheless the consideration received at [i] and [ii] is "in connection with" that transaction and so the judge was correct to conclude that the relief in s.257(3) would not apply.

A disposal which does not qualify for this relief might qualify for hold-over relief, if the relevant conditions are satisfied.

For additional questions on a transfer from a non-resident trust to charity, see 32.1 (Payment to charity from non-resident trust).

23.15.1 *Incidental cost of disposal*

The concept of consideration being received "in connection with" a transaction is quite common in anti-avoidance provisions. It occurs in particular in para 3(1) sch 4A TCGA.[25] RI 259 discusses this:

> Our view is that "consideration" in this context does not extend to the incidental costs of the transaction, in particular reasonable fees charged by professional advisors for giving guidance as to the legal and fiscal effects of the transaction or for drafting and executing the relevant paperwork.

This is a sensible result and a purposive if non-literal interpretation, since it is not the intention of the provision to stop relief merely because there were such incidental costs.

---

24 It is hard to see that the payment in [iii] is "consideration": see 23.4 ("Consideration"). But points [i] and [ii] do involve receipt of consideration.

25 "... a disposal is 'for consideration' if consideration is given or received by any person for, or otherwise in connection with, any transaction by virtue of which the disposal is effected."

23.16 Sale to museum, etc

Section 258(2) TCGA provides:

> A gain shall not be a chargeable gain if it accrues on the disposal of an asset which is property which has been or could be designated under section 31 of the Inheritance Tax Act 1984 ("the 1984 Act") (designation and undertakings) and—
>
> (a) the disposal is by way of sale by private treaty to a body mentioned in Schedule 3 to the 1984 Act (museums, etc), or is to such a body otherwise than by sale, or
>
> (b) the disposal is to the Board in pursuance of section 230 of the 1984 Act (acceptance of property in satisfaction of tax).

That refers us to s.31(1) IHTA:

> The Treasury may designate under this section—
>
> (a) any relevant object which appears to the Board to be pre-eminent for its national, scientific, historic or artistic interest;
>
> (aa) any collection or group of relevant objects which, taken as a whole, appears to the Board to be pre-eminent for its national, scientific, historic or artistic interest;]6
>
> (b) any land which in the opinion of the Treasury is of outstanding scenic or historic or scientific interest;
>
> (c) any building for the preservation of which special steps should in the opinion of the Treasury be taken by reason of its outstanding historic or architectural interest;
>
> (d) any area of land which in the opinion of the Treasury is essential for the protection of the character and amenities of such a building as is mentioned in paragraph (c) above;
>
> (e) any object which in the opinion of the Treasury is historically associated with such a building as is mentioned in paragraph (c) above.

This applies to arms length sales (unlike the usual CGT charity exemption) but the purchase price will reflect the CGT saving. On this topic, see Tennant "A little sweetener" Taxation Magazine (29 April 2010), vol 165 no 4252 p.16.

CHAPTER TWENTY FOUR

INHERITANCE TAX RELIEFS FOR CHARITIES

Cross references

The following topics are considered elsewhere:
43.2 (IHT political party exemption)
44.2 (IHT housing association exemption)

The next three chapters consider will drafting, gifts of share of residue to charity, and variation of wills.

24.1 Introduction

A gift made by an individual is generally a transfer of value. The transfer may be exempt, potentially exempt, or chargeable. IHT is charged on a chargeable transfer.[1]

A gift to charity will not normally be a chargeable transfer, by virtue of one or more of the following reliefs:

IHTA	**Relief**	**See para**
s.12	Dispositions allowable for income tax	24.3
s.21	Normal expenditure out of income	24.4
s.23	IHT charity exemption	24.6

A gift to charity cannot be a potentially exempt transfer: if it fails to qualify for relief, it is a chargeable transfer.

24.2 IHT: Promise to transfer to charity

Section 5(5) IHTA provides:

> Except in the case of a liability imposed by law, a liability incurred by a transferor shall be taken into account only to the extent that it was incurred for a consideration in money or money's worth.

A binding promise to transfer money or assets to charity (not for consideration) is not a transfer of value for IHT purposes. Instead, the individual makes a transfer of value when they carry out the promise.

A binding promise usually requires a deed of covenant. Thus if (say) an individual covenants to pay £x on 1 December each year for four years, they make transfers of value of £x if and when they pay the money due. These transfers qualify for the IHT charity exemption.

If the individual defaults on the covenant then no transfer of value is made.

On the death of the individual, their estate is valued without allowing for a deduction for any sums due under the covenant. However s.38 IHTA

---

1 See ss 1-3 IHTA.

provides:

> (1) Such part of the value transferred shall be attributable to specific gifts[2] as corresponds to the value of the gifts...
> (6) For the purposes of this section, any liability of the transferor which is not to be taken into account under section 5(5) above ... shall be treated as a specific gift...

Suppose:
(1) an individual dies after making the deed of covenant, and
(2) the covenant binds the executors, who make the payment to charity

The payment to charity is a "specific gift" for the purposes of the allocation of exemption rules. Thus outstanding payments under the covenant qualify for the IHT charity exemption, in computing the IHT on the death of the individual.

24.3 Disposition allowable for IT

Section 12(1) IHTA provides:

> A disposition made by any person is not a transfer of value if it is allowable in computing that person's profits or gains for the purposes of income tax or corporation tax or would be so allowable if those profits or gains were sufficient and fell to be so computed.

This would apply to gifts by traders which qualify for a deduction.[3] Donations of Qualifying Investments would qualify under this exemption as they are deductible in the computation of total income, if the reference to "profits or gains" includes a reference to total income. But it may be that "profits or gains" refers only to income, and does not include the technical concept "total income".

It is doubtful whether Gift Aid payments qualify for relief under s.12 but the question is academic since such payments will qualify for exemption

---

2 Section 42(1) IHTA provides some definitions:
"In this Chapter—
"gift", in relation to any transfer of value, means the benefit of any disposition or rule of law by which, on the making of the transfer, any property becomes (or would but for any abatement become) the property of any person or applicable for any purpose;
"given" shall be construed accordingly;
"specific gift" means any gift other than a gift of residue or of a share in residue."

3 See 18.2 (Charity gift: Deductible expense).

under another head.

24.4 Normal expenditure out of income

Section 21(1) IHTA provides:

> A transfer of value is an exempt transfer if, or to the extent that, it is shown—
>
> (a) that it was made as part of the normal expenditure of the transferor, and
>
> (b) that (taking one year with another) it was made out of his income, and
>
> (c) that, after allowing for all transfers of value forming part of his normal expenditure, the transferor was left with sufficient income to maintain his usual standard of living.

A series of payments to charity will usually qualify for exemption by virtue of this exemption. A single cash gift would not qualify for relief under this heading as it would not satisfy condition (a). Substantial gifts would not satisfy condition (c) unless the donor's income comfortably exceeded the amount given. A gift of an asset (as opposed to cash) may not qualify for relief as condition (b) might not be satisfied. In such cases one may have to turn to the IHT charity exemption.

24.5 IHT charity relief: History

18th and 19th century legacy, probate and succession duties had no charity exemption.[4] Neither did estate duty when it was introduced, in 1894. However when the gifts *inter vivos* period was increased, in stages, from the original one year to seven years, the period for gifts to charity remained at one year. FA 1972 introduced an estate duty charity relief cautiously capped at £50k. The story since then (like Gift Aid, 20 years later) is one of gradual erosion of the limit. The relief was carried across to CTT in the FA 1975 (retaining a limit, now £100k, for gifts within one year of death). The limit on the relief (by then £250k) was finally abolished by the Thatcher administration in 1983.

24.6 IHT charity exemption

Section 23(1) IHTA provides:

---

4 19th century protests are outlined in Owen, *English Philanthropy 1660–1960*, p.338. The equivalent duties in Ireland had a charity relief. In assessing the significance of this history, it should be borne in mind that tax rates were low compared to today.

> Transfers of value are exempt to the extent that the values transferred by them are attributable to property which is given to charities or registered clubs.

We call this the **"IHT charity exemption"**.

24.6.1 *Value transferred exceeds asset value*

A transfer of value is fully exempt even if the value transferred exceeds the value of the property received by the charity. HMRC agree. Statement of Practice E13 provides:

> 2. Where the value transferred (ie the loss to transferor's estate as a result of the disposition) exceeds the value of the gift in the hands of a charity, etc, the Board take the view that the exemption extends to the whole value transferred.

However, s.161 IHTA (related property) prevents most tax planning opportunities which might otherwise arise, other than long-term planning. This provides:

> (1) Where the value of any property comprised in a person's estate would be less than the appropriate portion of the value of the aggregate of that and any related property, it shall be the appropriate portion of the value of that aggregate.
> (2) For the purposes of this section, property is related to the property comprised in a person's estate if—
> (a) it is comprised in the estate of his spouse or civil partner; or
> (b) it is or has within the preceding five years been—
> (i) the property of a charity, or held on trust for charitable purposes only, or
> (ii) the property of a body mentioned in section 24, 24A, or 25above,
>
> and became so on a transfer of value which was made by him or his spouse or civil partner after 15th April 1976 and was exempt to the extent that the value transferred was attributable to the property.
> (3) The appropriate portion of the value of the aggregate mentioned in subsection (1) above is such portion thereof as would be attributable to the value of the first-mentioned property if the value of that aggregate were equal to the sums of the values of that and any related property, the value of each property being determined as if it did not form part of that aggregate.

24.7 "Given to charities"/"donor"

Section 23(6) IHTA provides:

> For the purposes of this section—
> (a) property is given to charities if
> [i] it becomes the property of charities or
> [ii] is held on trust for charitable purposes only ...
> and "donor" shall be construed accordingly.

If an individual sells an asset to a charity at an undervalue then the asset becomes property of the charity. The asset is therefore "given" to charity (as that expression is defined) and so the transfer of value on the sale is exempt.

Suppose:

(1) X lends money to a charity, or sells an asset leaving the debt outstanding; and
(2) X later waives the debt

It is suggested that the relief applies, on the basis that:

(1) The debt is given to charity in the general sense of the phrase; the definition in s.23(6) is inclusive and not exclusive; or
(2) The transfer is attributable to the money or asset sold, which is "given to charity" within the defined s.23(6) meaning.[5]

The same point arises if a person wishes to surrender a lease to a charity.

Suppose:

(1) a Will was unclear, or of uncertain validity; and
(2) a charity and individual beneficiaries agreed to divide the estate in certain proportions.

Could HMRC argue that the gift to charity under the Will was invalid, so there is no charity relief, even in relation to the charity's share? In practice HMRC will normally accept the validity and construction of the Will accepted by the beneficiaries. Strictly, it might be argued that the true effect of the Will (which may differ from that accepted by the beneficiaries out of court) should govern the tax relief. If there were any doubt as to the application of the IHT charity exemption, an instrument of variation may be appropriate.

---

5 For Gift Aid, see 15.12 (Waiver of debt). A similar point arises for CGT donor relief: see 23.3 (Donor CGT relief).

Could an individual beneficiary argue that on the true construction of the Will the charity should have received a larger share of the estate, or the whole of the estate, and the IHT charity exemption should be applied accordingly? It is considered that charity relief is restricted to the amount that actually passes to the charity, as the estate is administered, so that the funds which end up with the individual beneficiary are not "given" to charity – even if, had the matter come to trial, the charity would have succeeded in its claim to the whole of the estate.

It was assumed without argument in a Scottish case, *Guild v IRC* [1991] STC 281, that the IHT charity exemption is not affected where (following a *cy-près* application) an estate given to charity by Will was transferred to a non-charitable trust. (That could probably only happen in Scotland, whose charity law differs from English law.)

24.8 "Charities/charitable purposes"

24.8.1 *"Charities"*

Section 23(6) IHTA provides:

> For the purposes of this section—
> (a) property is given to charities if
> [i] it becomes the property of charities

The standard tax definition of charity applies for para [i].[6] This brings in the jurisdiction condition, so subject to the EU-law arguments, a gift to a charity outside the EU and EEA will not qualify for the relief under s.23(6)(a)[i]. For instance, an American charitable company is not a "charity" within the tax definition, as it does not meet the jurisdiction requirement.

The IHT Manual provides:

> **IHTM11112 meaning of 'charity' and 'charitable'** [Sept 2016]
> ... Eligibility to the exemption is determined at the date of the transfer of value. HMRC Charities administer a non-statutory approvals process so that charities can obtain certainty in advance of receiving a donation. Those charities that are receiving UK tax reliefs at 1 April 2010 will automatically qualify. A list of charities that have gained approval will be available on the HMRC Charities website in due course.
> If a charity meets all the conditions it may qualify for the exemption without having formal approval from HMRC Charities. In these cases,

6 See 3.4 (Tax definition of charity).

you may need to make further checks to establish the charitable status. In general, transfers made to a charity in England and Wales that has been registered with the Charities Commission can be accepted as exempt without enquiry. Similarly, transfers to charities that have been approved by HMRC Charities can be accepted as exempt without enquiry unless there are indications that the status of the charity has changed since the approval was given.

24.8.2 *Trust for charitable purposes*

Section 23(6) IHTA provides:

> For the purposes of this section—
> (a) property is given to charities if it ...
> [ii] is held on trust for charitable purposes only ...

Under s.23(6)(a)[ii], there is no express jurisdiction requirement.

In *Routier v HMRC*[7] the Court of Appeal held that this should be implied. Although the statute did not actually say so, "trust" means a trust governed by UK law and subject to the jurisdiction of UK courts. On appeal, the Supreme Court held that this judge-made restriction should not be implied, as it was in breach of EU free movement of capital:

> 50. On its face, section 23 of the Inheritance Tax Act does not impose any restriction on the free movement of capital. In particular, it does not discriminate between gifts to charities governed by the law of the United Kingdom and gifts to charities governed by the law of other EU member states or third countries. It is, on its face, entirely compliant with article 56 EC. That is so even if section 272 of the Inheritance Tax Act and section 989 of the Income Tax Act are taken into account, since those provisions, on their face, are equally non-discriminatory.
> 51. The only relevant restriction which existed at any material time, and with which this appeal is concerned, is the restriction imposed by the judicial gloss which was placed on the words now found in section 989 of the Income Tax Act in the case of *Dreyfus*: a restriction which, when incorporated into section 23 of the Inheritance Tax Act, has the effect of confining relief under that provision to trusts governed by the law of a part of the United Kingdom and subject to the jurisdiction of United Kingdom courts.

7 [2016] EWCA Civ 938. This was said to follow from *Camille and Henry Dreyfus Foundation v IRC* 36 TC 126 which implied a jurisdiction condition into the pre-2010 definition of charity for IT purposes.

The reader may question whether the Court of Appeal was right as a simple matter of domestic law to add a gloss to the UK statute; but as far as domestic law is concerned, that ship has sailed. However it sunk in the collision with EU law:

> There can be no doubt that the *Dreyfus* gloss on the language of section 989 of the Income Tax Act, as applied to section 23, is incompatible with article 56 EC. It is plain that the restriction of relief from inheritance tax to trusts governed by the law of a part of the United Kingdom cannot be justified under EU law.
>
> 52. Article 56 EC is directly applicable as law in the United Kingdom, and must be given effect in priority to inconsistent national law, whether judicial or legislative in origin. It follows that the *Dreyfus* gloss on the language of section 989 of the Income Tax Act cannot be applied to section 23 in situations falling within the scope of article 56. The resultant position is as set out in para 49 above: applying section 23 without incorporating the *Dreyfus* gloss, there is no relevant restriction on the availability of relief beyond the conditions appearing on the face of the provision. That result is in conformity with article 56. Since it is undisputed that the Coulter Trust satisfied those conditions at the relevant time, it follows that it qualifies for the relief.
>
> 53. That is the conclusion which the Court of Appeal should have reached, once it had decided that the *Dreyfus* gloss on the language of section 989 of the Income Tax Act, if incorporated into section 23 of the Inheritance Tax Act, imposed a restriction which was incompatible with article 56. Having reached that decision, the court could not apply that entirely judge-made restriction, and therefore had to apply section 23 without the gloss placed on the language used in section 989 of the Income Tax Act in the *Dreyfus* case. It would then have arrived at a result which complied with article 56.
>
> 54. With great respect to the Court of Appeal, it should not have concerned itself with a hypothetical restriction concerned with the existence of mutual assistance agreements, even if it considered that such a restriction might have been justifiable under EU law and might have been imposed by Parliament. The fact was that there was no such restriction in existence. Neither section 23 of the Inheritance Tax Act nor section 989 of the Income Tax Act made relief for trusts in third countries conditional on there being a mutual assistance agreement in place. The fact that such a restriction, if it had existed, might have been in conformity with EU law did not mean that it could be imposed by the court, by means of a purported interpretation of the language used in section 23.

55. Having reached the conclusion that section 23 of the Inheritance Tax Act can be brought into conformity with article 56 by disapplying the *Dreyfus* gloss on the meaning of the words contained in section 989 of the Income Tax Act, and that, having done so, the gift to the Coulter Trust qualifies for relief under section 23, it is unnecessary for this court to decide the other issues in dispute between the parties: in particular, whether the Court of Appeal was correct to hold that the Dreyfus gloss applied to both limbs of section 23(6), and whether it was correct to hold that a general requirement that there be a mutual assistance agreement in place at the time of the testator's death would constitute a justifiable restriction on freedom of movement of capital under EU law. The Court of Appeal's decision cannot stand, even if it was correct in its determination of those issues.

24.8.3 *Foreign charity: planning*

If a person wishes to make a gift to a charity which does not or might not qualify for relief (in short, charities outside the EU or EU charities not on the HMRC approved list) the solution is

(1) to make a gift to a UK or EU charity whose objects allow it to support the intended charitable activities;
(2) that charity may in due course transfer its assets to a suitable foreign charity without loss of IHT relief.

If this is done by will it may be necessary to wait two years to avoid s.143 IHTA.

The absence of charity relief for non-EU charities may be overlooked by will drafters. When a testator has made a gift to a non-EU charity (or to an EU body which does not quite fit the UK definition of charity) it should be possible to vary the will after death so as to direct the gift to a tax-exempt charity.

24.9 HMRC practice

24.9.1 *Selection trusts*

The IHT Manual provides:

IHTM11129: Procedure: selection trusts [Aug 2016]
The position can be complicated where persons other than the testator (IHTM12001)(for example, the personal representatives (IHTM05012) or trustees) have the power to select charitable bodies or objects that benefit.
Situations you may encounter are:

> **A trust or bequest directing the trustees to appoint or distribute to bodies described as 'charities' or 'charitable'.**
> These can be immediately accepted as qualifying for charity exemption without identifying the recipients if the Will (IHTM12041) has effect under UK law. A Will can be accepted as having effect under UK law where the deceased died domiciled (IHTM13002) in the UK, unless the Will shows an intention that some other law is to apply. Where the Will has effect under UK law the use of words allowing others to choose the charitable objects is construed as allowing them to choose between such institutions in the UK whose objects are exclusively charitable in accordance with the law of England and Wales. In practice 'charitable' can be taken as having the same meaning under the law in Scotland and Northern Ireland.

This is correct for English law but concessionary for Scotland and Northern Ireland.[8]

> There is one exception to the above: if the trustees/executors are given the power to decide the identity of the charitable donees in cases of doubt or dispute. These are not charitable selection trusts (*Re Raven* [1915] 1 Ch 673 and *Re Wynn* [1952] Ch 271).

This is not correct. The cases cited show that a provision authorising trustees to determine the identity of beneficiaries may be void. It does not follow that the charitable gift made by the will is void.

The Manual continues:

> Refer the case to Technical if the deceased was domiciled outside the UK, if there is otherwise doubt about which law governs the interpretation of the Will or, if our view is challenged.
> **A bequest for purposes which appear to be charitable, but which does not restrict the selection to bodies described as 'charities' or 'charitable'**
> This does not qualify for relief. This is because distributions may be made to bodies working in that field which are not themselves charitable (IHTM11112)(for example, those operated for financial gain). Actual appointments or distributions to qualifying charities may be exempt if IHTA84/S144 applies (see below).

Whether or not this is correct depends on the construction of the will. It will not often be correct in practice.

---

8 See 3.15.2 (Tax position of Scots law charity).

> If there is any reference to bodies outside of the EU or other specified country in any of the above situations the requirements of IHTA84/S23 are not satisfied because distributions might be made to non-qualifying charities. You should refuse relief underIHTA84/S23.
> **Example**
> A Will contains a clause stating 'I devise and bequeath all the residue of my estate … unto my executors upon trust that the executors shall apply the same for such charitable institutions or such other charitable objects in the UK and South Africa, or either of those places as they may in their absolute discretion select'
> This bequest does not qualify for charity exemption.

Again it is a matter of construction of the will. It may be on the correct construction gifts can only be made to charities for foreign objects which are charities for tax purposes. In that case the relief applies.

> However, if appointments or distributions are made to qualifying charities within two years of a death, exemption may be due on these, provided Section 144 IHTA 1984 applies. If it is claimed that appointments or distributions (IHTM35181) come within Section 144 IHTA 1984, refer the case to Technical.
> **(This text has been withheld because of exemptions in the [Freedom of Information] Act 2000)**

It is surprising that material on this straightforward technical point should be sensitive. Perhaps the omitted material relates to arrangements to identify evasion involving fraudulent charities.

24.9.2 *HMRC scrutiny*

The former CTO Manual M.293 provided:

> You may accept that the gift is to a charity if:
> - it does not exceed £10,000 and
> - on the basis of the information [that][9] the parties have paid it to a registered UK Charity.

This passage is not found in this form in the IHT Manual, but we would not be surprised if it is one of the unpublished instructions "withheld because of exemptions in the Freedom of Information Act".

The IHT Manual provides:

9 The original erroneously read: "they have".

IHTM11135: Procedure: categories of gift accepted as exempt in limited circumstances [19 Aug 2016]
Gifts to bodies in the following categories may or may not be charitable (IHTM11112), depending on the precise terms of the gift. However it has been agreed with HMRC Charities that a gift to an organisation within the following categories may be accepted as charitable provided:
- The gift is of a reasonable amount (This content has been withheld because of exemptions in the Freedom of Information Act 2000)
- the organisation is based in the UK, EU or other specified country (IHTM11128), and
- the gift is straightforward (IHTM11124)

You should follow the procedure at IHTM11130 and contact the taxpayer or agent s if these conditions are not satisfied or there is any doubt about whether the body falls into one of the following categories. You will also need to be sure of the identity of the beneficiary of the gift.

Category 1
- Cathedrals (including those described as minsters or abbeys and the friends of cathedrals etc)
- Diocesan Boards of Finance
- Church officers (including the minister, rector, vicar, church wardens) where the gift is for the upkeep of the church.
- Parish churches which may also be minsters or abbeys
- Parochial Church Councils
- Churches of recognised denominations including chapels and mission halls
- Missionary societies
- Moral welfare associations
- Sunday Schools

Category 2
- Child welfare associations
- Children's homes
- Community centres
- Convalescent homes
- Homes for the blind
- Hospital homes
- Groups for people with learning disabilities
- Old people's welfare committees
- Orphanages
- Groups for disabled people

Category 3
(Some bodies within this category may come within the Sch 3 exemption (IHTM11221) for health service bodies (IHTM11227)
- Area health authorities
- Hospices
- Hospitals (including private hospitals)
- Hospital management committees
- Leagues of friends of hospitals
- Medical research funds
- Nursing associations
- Patient amenity funds attached to hospitals
- Samaritan funds attached to hospitals

Category 4
Any branch of any organisation which is governed by Royal Charter and which is itself acceptable as charitable. Notable examples are
- Boy Scouts
- British Red Cross
- Girl Guides
- Royal British Legion (branches not clubs)
- St John Ambulance Brigade
- Sea Cadet Corps

24.10 Date for charitable status

The IHT Manual provides:

> **IHTM11113: General outline: 'charitable status' and date for determining status** [19 Aug 2016]
> ... As a general rule the beneficiary needs to have charitable status at the date of transfer for the exemption to apply....

This is in principle correct.

24.10.1 *Charity registers after gift*

The IHT Manual continues:

> But, a beneficiary who appears to be given charitable status after the date of transfer may qualify for exemption, if:
> [1] the charity was not previously registered with the Charity Commission but applied to register as a result of the legacy[10] ...

There are two possible scenarios here. Usually the beneficiary will have been a charity before registration. Then IHT relief applies.[11] The author of the IHT Manual passage may have assumed (wrongly) that unregistered bodies did not qualify for IHT relief.

The other (perhaps rarer) possibility is that the beneficiary had to make changes in its constitution in order to qualify for registration. Then IHT relief does not strictly apply, unless s.142 or 144 IHTA provide relief. If the author of the Manual intended IHT relief to apply here, the HMRC practice is concessionary.

24.10.2 *CASC registers after gift*

The IHT Manual continues:

> *Example (Tanya)*
> T dies in December 2010.
> A local sports club which has existed for several years applies in August 2011 under [what is now s.658 CTA 2010] to become a Community Amateur Sports Club (which gives it charitable status for tax purposes).
> A legacy by T to that club is not exempt in December 2010.

This is correct if (prior to registration as a CASC) the sports club was not

---

10 The Manual continues with two other non-contentious examples:
> "[2] the deceased's will creates a charitable trust, or
> [3] the deeming provisions of s.142 IHTA or s.144 IHTA apply because of a instrument of variation (IHTM35011) or a qualifying distribution (IHTM35181) from a discretionary trust."

11 See 3.7.1 (English charity).

a charity. However (depending on its constitution) it may well have been a charity.

> But if in, say, November 2011 the residuary beneficiary under T's Will makes an instrument of variation (to which IHTA84/S142 (1) applies) that benefits the club, the charity exemption will apply.

This is a concession.

The Manual concludes:

> Generally, you do not need to check that the beneficiary had charitable status at the date of the transfer. You only need to check this if you have good reason to believe the beneficiary was not a charity at the relevant date. If this is the case you should refer the file with an explanatory note to Technical (IHTM11125).

24.11 Anti-avoidance: Introduction

Section 23 IHTA contains eight anti-avoidance provisions. Section 56 IHTA contains further anti-avoidance provisions relating to trusts. Some of the provisions are widely drafted and affect arrangements with no tax avoidance element in them. Most of these rules apply in the same way to the IHT spouse exemption, so passages in the IHT Manual on the spouse exemption are set out here where relevant.

24.12 Application for charitable purposes

Section 23(5) IHTA provides:

> In the case of any property which is given to charities, subsection (1) above shall not apply in relation to the property if it or any part of it may become applicable for purposes other than
> [a] charitable purposes or
> [b] those of a body mentioned in section 24 or 25 below or,
> [c] where it is land, of a body mentioned in section 24A below.

We call this the **"application for charitable purposes rule"**.

An example would be a transfer to charity on terms that part of the money transferred should be used for non-charitable purposes.

The references in para [b] and [c] are as follows:

Section	**Topic**	**See para**
24	Political parties	43.2
25	National purposes	24.35
24A	Housing associations	44.1

Another example may be a trust to pay income to charity, with power to appoint to A (not a charity) is a "charity" for tax purposes, albeit a temporary charity. A gift to such a trust would not qualify for IHT charity relief as it breaches the application for charitable purposes rule. However, temporary gifts to charity can qualify for IHT relief if structured in the form of long term loans of money, or leases or licences of property.[12]

IHT relief is wholly lost even if only part of the property may become applied for non-charitable purposes.

24.13 Postponed gift rule

Section 23(2) IHTA provides:

> Subsection (1) above shall not apply in relation to property if the testamentary or other disposition by which it is given—
>
> (a) takes effect on the termination after the transfer of value of any interest or period.

We call this the **"postponed gift rule"**.

"Takes effect" means "takes effect in possession". Thus a gift to a trust for an individual for life, with remainder to charity, does not qualify for the IHT charity exemption, even in part, though the charity does receive a valuable reversionary interest at the time of the gift. But there is relief on the IHT charge (if applicable) on the death of the life tenant with an estate interest in possession, when the charity becomes absolutely entitled.

24.13.1 *Postponed gift rule: Practice*

The IHT Manual has an interesting passage:

> **IHTM11092: Exceptions where the exemption does not apply: postponed gifts** [19 Aug 2016]
>
> Under IHTA84/S18 (3) (a) a transfer to a spouse or civil partner (IHTM11032) is not exempt if it 'takes effect on the termination after the transfer of value (IHTM04024) of any interest or period'. We interpret the term 'takes effect' as 'takes effect in possession' as any other interpretation would be unworkable.
>
> However, IHTA84/S18 (3) (a) does not apply - and so spouse or civil partner exemption is available
>
> - where the gift to the spouse or civil partner depends on survival for a specified period of less than twelve months. If the survival period is more than 12 months, spouse or civil partner exemption is

12 See 24.28 (Loans and use of property).

excluded (IHTM11093) under IHTA84/S18 (3) (b)

Example

A gift by Will to the deceased's spouse absolutely on condition that they survive the deceased by one month is exempt if they do survive for that period.

- where under IHTA84/S29 (2) the transfer of value is a loan by one spouse or civil partner (IHTM11042) to the other, or a disposition allowing the other spouse or civil partner use of property

The application of the postponed gifts provision in IHTA84/S18 (3) (a) can depend on fine points of construction of any Will (IHTM12041) or other instrument. You need to be particularly careful with gifts under which payment of capital and/or interest is

- deferred until a specific date that is more than a year after the death, or
- subject to discretionary powers of trustees over and above the usual demands of administration to which executors are normally subject

Example

'I give to my wife....a pecuniary legacy of £100,000 and I declare that such legacy shall not begin to carry interest until three years from my death' We would consider that this provision confers on the widow an immediate vested legacy in possession. It is not prevented from being such a legacy just because it does not carry interest for three years. The full £100,000, subject to any adjustment underIHTA84/S.39A, is exempt. You should not discount the £100,000 to reflect the provision about interest.

You should refer any doubtful case to Technical for advice.

The same must apply to gifts to charity. The reason is presumably that a three year delay is regarded as administrative and not dispositive. A 30 year delay would fall on the other side of the line.

24.14 Conditional gift rule

Section 23(2) IHTA provides:

> Subsection (1) above shall not apply in relation to property if the testamentary or other disposition by which it is given ...
>
> (b) depends on a condition which is not satisfied within twelve months after the transfer.

We call this the **"conditional gift rule"**.

This rule seems unnecessary: a conditional gift must fail the application for charitable purposes rule.

By implication, a gift which depends on a condition which is satisfied within twelve months must be taken to satisfy the application for charitable purposes rule. Thus the conditional gift rule extends rather than limits the IHT charity exemption.

Suppose a testator leaves £100,000 to charity on condition that the charity pays £80,000 to A. Suppose the condition is satisfied within 12 months. It seems at first sight that the gift is entirely exempt, as the conditional gift rule is clearly satisfied. There is a risk that a court would hold that only £20,000 is given to charity. This is the HMRC view. The IHT Manual provides:

> **IHTM11093: Exceptions where the exemption does not apply: conditional gifts** [19 Aug 2016]
> Under IHTA84/S18 (3) (b), a gift to a spouse or civil partner (IHTM11032) is not exempt if it depends on a condition which is not satisfied within twelve months after the transfer.
> ***Example***
> In his will Adam leaves his wife a legacy which
> - is dependant on his wife surviving Adam for more than twelve months, and
> - does not carry the intermediate income
>
> The legacy is not exempt
> A different situation arises where a bequest to a spouse or civil partner is made on condition that the spouse or civil partner makes a specified provision for a chargeable beneficiary within a period of 12 months or more.
> If the spouse or civil partner does, in fact, satisfy the condition within a year of the death, IHTA84/S18 (3) (b) does not prevent the spouse or civil partner exemption applying. But you should, of course, adjust the amount of exemption to reflect the reduced benefit to the spouse or civil partner.
> IHTA84/S18 (3) (b) does not apply where the transfer between spouses or civil partners is:
> - a loan (IHTM11042) by one spouse or civil partner to another or
> - a disposition allowing the other spouse or civil partner the use of property.

The same practice will apply to gifts to charity.

24.15 Conditional gift to charity

If a person makes a conditional or defeasible gift to charity, and the gift becomes unconditional or indefeasible within one year, then IHT charity relief applies. For instance suppose a charity fundraising appeal is made to purchase a particular asset: donors are told that if insufficient funds are raised, so the asset is not purchased, their contributions will be returned. So long as the condition is satisfied within twelve months, IHT charity relief is available on gifts to the fund.

Nevertheless, a person should not normally make such gifts. There are two possible risks:

(1) the condition may be satisfied after a delay of more than one year; in which case IHT charity relief is lost; or

(2) the condition may not be satisfied at all, in which case the property will revert to the donor. Nevertheless the donor has still made a chargeable transfer on making the conditional gift. The fact that it has become void does not alter that. In particular, s.150 IHTA (voidable transfers) does not provide any relief.

In this sort of case it is suggested that the individual should *covenant* to make the gift if the relevant condition is satisfied. The making of the covenant is not a transfer of value.[13] There is a transfer only when the condition is satisfied and the donor makes the transfer under the covenant. That transfer will qualify for IHT charity relief in a straightforward way as it is not conditional. This is also necessary in order to qualify for Gift Aid relief.[14]

24.16 Defeasible gift rule

Section 23(2) IHTA provides:

> Subsection (1) above shall not apply in relation to property if the testamentary or other disposition by which it is given ...
>
> (c) is defeasible;
>
> and for this purpose any disposition which has not been defeated at a time twelve months after the transfer of value and is not defeasible after that time shall be treated as not being defeasible (whether or not it was capable of being defeated before that time).

We call this the **"defeasible gift rule"**.

This rule seems unnecessary. A defeasible or conditional gift will not qualify for the IHT charity exemption because of the application for charitable purposes rule: see above.

While in strict conveyancing language "defeasible" is distinguished from

13 See 24.2 (IHT: Promise to transfer to charity).

14 See 15.16 (Repayment rule: Condition B).

"determinable" in the present context this is not significant, as (1) the statute is not using language in its strict conveyancing sense; and (2) other anti-avoidance provisions will fill any gap.

A gift which is indefeasible after twelve months is treated as indefeasible even though it could have been defeated within twelve months. It is considered that any gifts which satisfy the defeasible gift rule must by implication be treated as satisfying the application for charitable purposes rule. Thus the defeasible gift rule also extends rather than limits the charity exemption.

This is useful on occasions to put matters right. Suppose X gives property to a temporary charitable trust (ie a trust for charity subject to a power to appoint the property to other persons). The gift is chargeable, since (i) it breaches the application for charitable purposes rule and (ii) it is defeasible. If the power is released within one year the gift is exempt.

Where property is not settled property, and so passes under a person's will, the benefit of the charity exemption may be obtained by a variation under s.142 IHTA, or (in the case of discretionary will trusts) by a deed of appointment under s.144 IHTA, provided the property passes to charity within two years of the death. Those sections do not apply to settled property but the defeasible gifts rule can be used to allow a little flexibility. Suppose property is held on trusts under which L has an estate interest in possession, and the trustees are minded to appoint that the property should pass to charity after the death of L. If they are not quite sure and wish to keep some flexibility, they could appoint that the property passes to charity *defeasibly* on the death of L, allowing the appointment to be defeated within one year of the death of L. Provided that the appointment is not defeated, the charity exemption will be applicable. The result is comparable to a discretionary will trust, though the requirements to obtain relief are somewhat stricter.

In *Bailhache Labesse Trustees v HMRC* [2008] STC (SCD) 869 trustees held property on trust for A for life, with remainder on common form discretionary trusts, and subject thereto for named charities. Within 12 months of the death of A, the trustees appointed the property to the charities absolutely. The Commissioners rightly held that the IHT charity exemption did not apply on the death of A. The tax planning moral is that the trustees should have made an appointment during the lifetime of A, so that on the death of A the property passed absolutely to the charities (or at least conditionally or defeasibly, the gift becoming absolute within 12 months of the death of A). In that case relief would have applied.

24.17 Entire interest rule

Section 23(3) IHTA provides:

> Subsection (1) above shall not apply in relation to property which is an interest in other property if—
>
> (a) that interest is less than the donor's,[15] ...
>
> and for this purpose any question whether an interest is less than the donor's shall be decided as at a time twelve months after the transfer of value.

We call this the **"entire interest rule"**.

There are two conditions for this to apply:

(1) the property is an interest in other property; and
(2) the interest is less than the donor's.

An example would be the gift of an option to purchase the donor's property; or the grant of an easement.

Suppose a testator provides in their will that their house is to pass as to one-half to charity, and as to the other half to their children. The charity's interest is less than the donor's. But it is not an interest in other property. HMRC agree. The IHT Manual provides:

> **IHTM11176: Exclusions from exemption: gift less than donor's whole interest or for a limited period** [19 Aug 2016]
>
> Under IHTA84/S23 (3) a gift to a charity is not exempt if the property given is an interest in other underlying property and either
>
> - that interest is less than the donor's full interest (this must be established at a time twelve months after the transfer), or
> - the property is given for a limited period
>
> This exception does not apply simply because the gift is an undivided share of the property.
>
> *Example (Joseph)*
>
> J owned the freehold interest in the whole of Hall Farm. The effect of IHTA84/S23 (3) on possible alternative gifts by will is:
>
> - a gift of a half share of Hall Farm to a charity: IHTA84/S23 (3 does not prevent the exemption applying...

If a person grants a lease to charity, it is considered that this restriction does not apply. A lease is not an interest in other property. A lease is an estate in land, but "land" in that sense is not property. In English land law, one owns estates or interests in land, but land itself is not capable of

15 "Donor" is widely defined: see 24.7 ("Given to charities" "donor").

ownership. If that were wrong, however, s.29 IHTA would provide relief.[16] It seems that HMRC do not agree. The IHT Manual provides:

> **IHTM11176: Exclusions from exemption: gift less than donor's whole interest or for a limited period** [19 Aug 2016]
> ... ***Example** (Joseph)*
> J owned the freehold interest in the whole of Hall Farm. The effect of IHTA84/S23 (3)on possible alternative gifts by will is ...
> - a gift of a leasehold interest to a charity: IHTA84/S23 (3) prevents the exemption from applying.
>
> But if J had owned only a leasehold interest in Hall Farm and had given the whole of that leasehold interest to the charity, IHTA84/S23 (3) would not have prevented the exemption from applying.

We cannot see the purpose of the entire interest rule, and would be grateful to any reader who could explain. The rule derives from the estate duty charity relief which was disapplied where a gift was "less than the full interest of the donor in the property given".[17] It is not clear why the estate duty wording was rewritten: perhaps it was recognised that the former wording was too wide.

The entire interest rule is restricted in the case of national institutions.[18]

24.18 Limited period rule

Section 23(3) IHTA provides:

> Subsection (1) above shall not apply in relation to property which is an interest in other property if ...
> (b) the property is given for a limited period;

We call this the **"limited period rule"**.

For instance, a trust to pay income to charity for a fixed period, with remainder to another person (not a charity), is (for that period) an income tax charity. A gift to such a trust does not qualify for the IHT charity exemption because of the limited period rule as well as the application for charitable purposes rule. Such gifts can qualify for relief if they are structured in the form of leases or loans.[19]

This rule is restricted in the case of national institutions.[20]

---

16 See 24.28 (Loans and use of property).
17 Para 3 Sch 26 FA 1972.
18 See 24.35 (Gift to national institution).
19 See 24.28 (Loans and use of property).
20 See 24.35 (Gift to national institution).

24.19 Retained interest rule: Land

Section 23(4) IHTA provides:

> Subsection (1) above shall not apply in relation to any property if—
>
> (a) the property is land or a building and is given subject to an interest reserved or created by the donor[21] which entitles him, his spouse or
> civil partner or a person connected with him to possession of, or to occupy, the whole or any part of the land or building rent-free or at a rent less than might be expected to be obtained in a transaction at arm's length between persons not connected with each other ...

We call this the **"retained interest rule"**.

Thus if a person retains a lease and gifts the freehold reversion of land to charity the charity exemption does not apply (unless market rent is paid). Likewise if the donor grants a lease to their spouse, and gives the reversion to charity: there is no charity exemption on the gift to charity.

There is no objection to a gift to a charity subject to a lease at a low rent for the benefit of the donor's cohabitee or employee. Such persons are not "connected" with the donor.

It might be argued that the retained interest rule only applies to lifetime dispositions. If the donor grants a lease to their child, and gives the reversion to charity *by will* there is no difficulty because a deceased person is not "connected" with anyone. However, the tax charge on the donor's death involves a notional transfer of value immediately before death, at which time the connected person rules will apply; see s.4 IHTA.

For the purpose of the retained interest rule:

> any question whether property is given subject to an interest shall be decided as at a time twelve months after the transfer of value.

See s.23(4) IHTA.

This is useful on occasions to put matters right. Suppose a donor has given land to a charity retaining a right of occupation. They may clearly avoid a tax charge if, within one year of their gift, they surrender their interest to the charity.

It is arguable that the reference at the end of s.23(4) to *an interest* means an interest within the meaning of s.23(4)(a), that is, an interest giving

---

21 "Donor" is widely defined: see 24.7 ("Given to charities" "donor").

(broadly) a benefit to the donor or a connected person. If that is correct, the donor may also avoid the tax charge if they transfer their interest to a person not connected to them. However, the better view is that, although one determines whether the land is subject to an interest at the end of the twelve months, the question whether the interest confers entitlement on the donor (or connected person) is to be determined at the moment of gift.

On whether a contractual licence is an "interest" see 30.5.3 (Licence route).

24.20 Retained interest rule: Non-land

Section 23(4) IHTA provides:

> Subsection (1) above shall not apply in relation to any property if ...
> (b) the property is not land or a building and is given subject to an interest reserved or created by the donor other than—
> (i) an interest created by him for full consideration in money or money's worth, or
> (ii) an interest which does not substantially affect the enjoyment of the property by the person or body to whom it is given;
>
> and for this purpose any question whether property is given subject to an interest shall be decided as at a time twelve months after the transfer of value.

Interests not reserved or created by the donor are not affected.

24.21 Gift to charity, gift over to other charity

Suppose a testator makes a gift to charity A, so long as some condition is satisfied and if it is not, to charity B. Alternatively, the gift to charity A is defeasible and the gift to charity B may take effect if the first gift is defeated. On any basis the property will belong to a charity. (This is not an academic example. For instance, a testator may wish to make a gift of a picture to the Tate Gallery so long as the picture is displayed, with a gift over to Cancer Research if it ceases to be on show.) It is considered that the gift itself sets out a gift to charity which qualifies for exemption. Thus conditions or limitations of this kind do not spoil the tax relief.

24.22 Acquisition of reversionary interest/settlement power from charity

Section 55(1) IHTA provides:

> Notwithstanding section 5(1) above, where a person entitled to an

> interest (whether in possession or not) in any settled property acquires a reversionary interest expectant (whether immediately or not) on that interest, the reversionary interest is not part of his estate for the purposes of this Act.

This prevents a simple avoidance scheme. Suppose:

(1) property is held upon trusts under which A (an elderly individual) has an estate interest in possession, remainder to B.

(2) A purchases B's reversionary interest.

Since the reversionary interest is not part of A's estate, A is deemed to make a transfer of value of the purchase price. In the absence of this rule, the scope for avoidance is obvious.

It often happens that an artificial deeming provision to stop one avoidance scheme opens up potential for another. Hence s.56(1) IHTA provides:

> Sections 18 and 23 to 27 above shall not apply in relation to property which is given in consideration of the transfer of a reversionary interest if, by virtue of section 55(1) above, that interest does not form part of the estate of the person acquiring it.

The IHT Manual explains:

> **IHTM11162: Settled property: acquisition of a reversionary interest from a charity (anti-avoidance)** [19 Aug 2016]
> Most reversionary interests (IHTM16231) are excluded property. This could provide an opportunity to avoid Inheritance Tax in the following circumstances.
> ***Example*** (*Anna and Bill*)
> A wishes to make a gift of £100,000 to B. A settles the £100,000 on herself for a short term, after which it will revert to B. B immediately sells his future right to receive the assets to the charity for £99,000. A then buys the reversion back from the charity for £100,000 to allow the charity a small profit.
> Without the following provision, the payment by A would be exempt.
> But, under IHTA84/S56 (1) charity exemption does not apply to property
> - given to a charity (IHTM11112) in return for a reversionary interest (IHTM16231) in settled property (IHTM16000), if
> - by reason of IHTA84/S55 (1) that reversionary interest does not form part of the IHT estate of the person acquiring it - that is when the person acquiring it already has a prior interest in the same property
>
> This provision is designed to prevent misuse of the charity exemption. In the example above, because of IHTA84/S55 (1) and IHTA84s/S56 (2), the reversion A purchases from the charity is not part of her estate

and IHTA84/S10 (1) cannot apply to the transaction. Consequently the £100,000 A pays to the charity in consideration for the reversion is a transfer of value. But for IHTA84/S56 (1) that transfer of value would be exempt under.IHTA84/S23 (1). The result would have been a gift of £99,000 from A to B without any charge to IHT. IHTA84/S56 (1) prevents this by making the £100,000 paid by A to the charity for the reversion into a chargeable transfer. It is not a potentially exempt transfer (PET) (IHTM14024) because the donee, the charity, is not an individual.

The IHT Manual also considers this in the context of the spouse exemption:

IHTM11095: Exceptions where the exemption does not apply: acquisition of a reversion [19 Aug 2016]
There are two special rules when a person
- with an interest, whether in possession (IHTM16062) or not (IHTM42222), in any settled property (IHTM16000)
- acquires a reversionary interest (IHTM16231), whether immediately or not, expectant on that prior interest

The rules are
- the reversion is not part of the acquirer's estate (IHTM04029) for IHT purposes (so that any consideration given for the acquisition of the reversion reduces the acquirer's estate) ((IHTA84/S55 (1)), and
- spouse or civil partner (IHTM11032) exemption does not apply to any property given by the acquirer in consideration for the reversion (IHTA84/S56 (1)).

IHTA84/S56 (1) is designed to prevent misuse of spouse or civil partner exemption to avoid a charge under HTA84/S55 (1).
Example *(Andy, Ben, Cathy)*
A wishes to make a gift of £100,000 to B. The first step is for A to settle £100,000 on himself for a short time with remainder to B. A cannot make a tax-free gift to B by simply buying B's reversion even for its full value. Under IHTA84/S55 (1) and IHTA84/S55 (2), IHTA84/S10 (1) is prevented from applying and the sum A pays B for the reversion is treated as a gift from A to B.
Without any provision to the contrary it would be possible to bypass IHTA84/S55 by exploiting spouse or civil partner exemption. B would sell the reversion to A's wife, C, who in turn would sell it to A. The payment by A to C would be an exempt transfer (the reversion he purchased would not be part of his IHT estate but the payment would be an exempt transfer under IHTA84/S18). So the combined estates of husband and wife would have been diminished, and B would have received the benefit, without any IHT charge. IHTA84/S56 (1) prevents

a scheme of this nature by denying IHTA84/S18 exemption for the payment by A to C. That payment is a Potentially Exempt Transfer (PET) (IHTM04057).
IHTA84/S56 (1) does not apply to a transfer so far as it is a loan (IHTM11042) or a disposition allowing another person the use of property.

24.23 IHT exemption on termination of IIP

24.23.1 *Lifetime termination*

The termination of an estate interest in possession is a transfer of value: s.52 IHTA provides:

> (1) Where at any time during the life of a person beneficially entitled to an interest in possession in settled property his interest comes to an end, tax shall be charged, subject to section 53 below, as if at that time he had made a transfer of value and the value transferred had been equal to the value of the property in which his interest subsisted.
> ...
> (2A) Where the interest mentioned in subsection (1) ... above is one to which the person became beneficially entitled on or after 22nd March 2006, that subsection applies in relation to the coming to an end of the interest only if the interest is—
> (a) an immediate post-death interest,
> (b) a disabled person's interest, or
> (c) a transitional serial interest.

This transfer of value may qualify for the IHT charity exemption. The legislation often distinguishes between an actual transfer of value and a transfer of value deemed to be made under s.52 IHTA. However, the reference to "transfer of value" in s.23 IHTA includes a transfer of value deemed to be made under s.52. This is nowhere directly stated, but it is perhaps assumed in s.56 IHTA and in practice HMRC accept this. The IHT Manual provides:

> **IHTM11161: Settled property: background** [19 Aug 2016]
> Subject to the general exceptions (IHTM11171) and the specific exceptions for settled property mentioned on this and the following pages, exemption for transfers of value to charities or registered clubs is available on the termination of a qualifying interest in possession (IHTM16091) in settled property (IHTM16000).
> ...

Example 4 (Laura)
L has a qualifying interest in possession (IHTM16062) for life, in a trust set up under her late husband's Will. On her death it passes to a qualifying charity. L brings the settlement to an end by surrendering her life interest to that charity. The charity exemption applies.

24.23.2 *Termination on death*

Section 4(1) IHTA provides:

> On the death of any person tax shall be charged as if, immediately before his death, he had made a transfer of value and the value transferred by it had been equal to the value of his estate immediately before his death.

Since the estate of a person normally includes property in which they have an estate IP, this brings into charge property in which a person has an estate IP on their death. The IHT charity exemption is available. HMRC accept this. The IHT Manual provides:

> **IHTM11161. Background** [19 Aug 2016]
> ...
> ***Example 1*** (*Laura*)
> L has a qualifying interest in possession (IHTM16062) for life, in a trust set up under her late husband's Will. On L's death the property passes to a charity absolutely. On L's death the charity exemption is available.
> ***Example 2*** (*Laura and Robin*)
> L has a qualifying interest in possession (IHTM16062) for life, in a trust set up under her late husband's Will. On L's death the property passes to R absolutely. While L's life interest still subsists, R gives his future interest to a charity. On L's death the charity exemption is available.
> Charity exemption applies to a termination of a qualifying interest in possession in settled property, but only if the charity then takes absolutely and indefeasibly. So when the qualifying interest in possession comes to an end the settlement also comes to an end (at least to the extent to which the settled property is given to charities (IHTM11112)). If the gift to the charity does not bring the settlement to an end in relation to the settled property concerned, then IHTA84/S56 (3) (a) prevents exemption from applying.
> ***Example 3***
> L has a qualifying interest in possession (IHTM16062) for life, in a trust set up under her late husband's Will. On L's death one half passes to a charity absolutely and the other half to R for life, then to Josh. On L's death the settlement of the half given to the charity comes to an end, so that half is exempt.

24.24 Gift of IIP to charity

Section 56 IHTA imposes four additional anti-avoidance rules for trusts. Section 56(3)(a) IHTA provides:

> Sections 23 to 27 above shall not apply in relation to any property if—
> (a) the property is an interest in possession in settled property and the settlement does not come to an end in relation to that settled property on the making of the transfer of value ...

This prevents another simple avoidance scheme. Suppose:
(1) property is held upon trusts under which A (an elderly individual) has an estate interest in possession, remainder to B.
(2) A gives the interest in possession to a charity.
Under s.56(3)(a) the gift is a chargeable transfer so no IHT is saved by A.

24.25 Charity purchases equitable interest

Section 56(3)(b) IHTA provides:

> Sections 23 to 27 above shall not apply in relation to any property if ...
> (b) immediately before the time when it becomes the property of the exempt body[22] it is comprised in a settlement and, at or before that time, an interest under the settlement is or has been acquired for a consideration in money or money's worth by that or another exempt body.

This prevents another simple tax avoidance scheme. Suppose:
(1) Property is held upon trusts under which A (an elderly individual) has an estate interest in possession, remainder to B.
(2) B sells the reversionary interest to the charity for market value (broadly equal to the value of the trust fund).
The sale is not a transfer of value but the IHT charity exemption does not apply on the death of A.

Section 56(4) IHTA provides:

> for the purposes of subsection (3)(b) there shall be disregarded any acquisition from a charity, political party or body within sections 23 to 25.

---

22 Section 56(4) IHTA defines "exempt body":
"In subsection (3)(b) above 'exempt body' means a charity, political party or other body within sections 23 to 25 above or the trustees of a settlement in relation to which a direction under paragraph 1 of Schedule 4 to this Act has effect."

The IHT Manual provides:

IHTM11162: Settled property: acquisition of a reversionary interest from a charity (anti-avoidance) [19 Aug 2016]
Most reversionary interests (IHTM16231) are excluded property. This could provide an opportunity to avoid Inheritance Tax in the following circumstances.
Example (*Anna and Bill*)
A wishes to make a gift of £100,000 to B. A settles the £100,000 on herself for a short term, after which it will revert to B. B immediately sells his future right to receive the assets to the charity for £99,000. A then buys the reversion back from the charity for £100,000 to allow the charity a small profit.
Without the following provision, the payment by A would be exempt.
But, under IHTA84/S56 (1) charity exemption does not apply to property

- given to a charity (IHTM11112) in return for a reversionary interest (IHTM16231) in settled property (IHTM16000), if
- by reason of IHTA84/S55 (1) that reversionary interest does not form part of the IHT estate of the person acquiring it - that is when the person acquiring it already has a prior interest in the same property

This provision is designed to prevent misuse of the charity exemption. In the example above, because of IHTA84/S55 (1) and IHTA84s/S56 (2), the reversion A purchases from the charity is not part of her estate and IHTA84/S10 (1) cannot apply to the transaction. Consequently the £100,000 A pays to the charity in consideration for the reversion is a transfer of value. But for IHTA84/S56 (1) that transfer of value would be exempt under .IHTA84/S23 (1). The result would have been a gift of £99,000 from A to B without any charge to IHT. IHTA84/S56 (1) prevents this by making the £100,000 paid by A to the charity for the reversion into a chargeable transfer. It is not a potentially exempt transfer (PET) (IHTM14024) because the donee, the charity, is not an individual.
IHTM11163: Settled property: purchase of a reversionary interest by a charity between April 1976 and April 1978 (anti-avoidance) [19 Aug 2016]
When a reversionary interest (IHTM16231) in settled property (IHTM16000) was purchased by a charity (IHTM11112) between 16 April 1976 and 11 April 1978 (both dates inclusive), charity exemption under IHTA84/S23 does not apply in relation to the non-relevant settled property when it becomes the property of the charity on the termination of the prior interest. ((IHTA84/S56 (2) and IHTA84/S56 (7))
Example (*Leroy and Rosie*)
Property is put into trust for L for life with remainder to R absolutely. In 1977 R sells her reversionary interest to a charity. The settled property

is not exempt under IHTA84/S23 when L's life interest comes to an end. You should note that exemption is excluded by IHTA84/S56 (2) and IHTA84/S56 (7) only when the charity purchases the reversion. Exemption is available when the acquisition of the reversion (whenever acquired) is not for monetary consideration. This is the case

- whatever the date of death of the reversioner, and whether or not the reversion was chargeable to Estate Duty, Capital Transfer Tax or IHT in their estate, and
- (if it was so chargeable) whether or not the duty or tax had been paid at the time when the prior interest terminated. In particular, you should not restrict exemption on the grounds that part of the settled property was applicable in payment of duty or tax in the reversioner's estate.

IHTM11164: Settled property: purchase of a reversionary interest by a charity after 12 April 1978 (anti-avoidance) [19 Aug 2016]

With one exception (mentioned below) charity exemption and the exemptions at IHTA84/S24 to IHTA84/S27 do not apply to any property by reason of IHTA84/S56 (3)(b) if:

- immediately before becoming the property of the 'exempt body' it was comprised in a settlement, and
- on or after 12 April 1978
- an interest in the settlement is or has been acquired for a consideration in money or money's worth by the same organisation or another 'exempt body'

'Exempt body' is defined by IHTA84/S56 (4) as a charity (IHTM11112), political party (IHTM11191) or other body within IHTA84/S23 to IHTA84/S26 or the trustees of a maintenance fund for historical buildings (IHTM11250) and similar property.

The exception (referred to above) is that IHTA84/S56 (3) (b) does not apply if the purchase was from an exempt body within IHTA84/S23 to IHTA84/S25. However this exception only applies to purchases from exempt bodies within IHTA84/S23 to IHTA84/S25, not from the full range of exempt bodies as defined in IHTA84/S56 (4).

So, where the exempt body has purchased a reversionary interest (IHTM16231), exemption will only be due if the reversion was bought from a body within IHTA84/S23 to IHTA84/S25.

Note

'Exempt body' used to include certain private bodies which preserve national heritage property for public benefit. The relevant provisions were repealed in 1998. It is possible, if unlikely, that before 1998 one of these bodies purchased a reversion which would not fall in until later.

Any such case should be referred to Technical for guidance before allowing exemption.

24.25.1 *Pre-1978 acquisition*

Section 56(8) IHTA provides:

> Subsection (3)(b) above shall not apply where the acquisition of the interest was before 12th April 1978.

24.26 Acquired for consideration

24.26.1 *"Acquired"*

SP E5 provides:

> The Commissioners for HMRC consider that the general intention of IHTA 1984 s 101 is to treat the participators as beneficial owners for all the purposes of that Act. Consequently, the conditions of IHTA 1984 ss 52(2), 53(2) are regarded as satisfied where it is the company that in fact becomes entitled to the property or disposes of the interest.

The IHT Manual provides:

> **IHTM11063: Settled property: exclusion from exemption in connection with a reversionary interest** [19 Aug 2016]
> ... A person is treated as acquiring a reversion for the purposes of IHTA84/S56 (5) if it is acquired by a close company (IHTM16241) in which they are a participator or by the trustees of a settlement in which they have an interest in possession (IHTM16246). IHTA84/S56 (5) does not apply where the person concerned acquired the reversion before 12 April 1978 - IHTA84/S56 (8).

24.26.2 *Acquired "for consideration"*

Section 56(5) IHTA provides:

> For the purposes of subsections (2) and (3) above, a person shall be treated as acquiring an interest for a consideration in money or money's worth if he becomes entitled to it as a result of transactions which include a disposition for such consideration[23] (whether to him or another) of that interest or of other property.

See 23.4 ("Consideration"). The IHT Manual states:

23 The words "for such consideration" were accidentally omitted on consolidation! They were restored by para 2 Sch 7 F(No 2)A 1987 for events on or after 17 March 1987.

IHTM11063: Settled property: exclusion from exemption in connection with a reversionary interest [19 Aug 2016]
When applied to settled property, spouse or civil partner (IHTM11032) exemption is subject to certain general limitations and exceptions (IHTM11091). In addition there is one exception that only applies to settled property

- where a person acquires a reversionary interest (IHTM16231) in settled property for a monetary consideration ((IHTA/S56 (2))
- the spouse or civil partner exemption does not apply in relation to the settled property when it becomes the property of the purchaser on the termination of the prior interest

For transfers on or after 22 March 2006, spouse or civil partner exemption only applies where the reversionary interest is a qualifying interest in possession (IHTM16061)
Example (*Linda and Ryan*)
Property is put into trust for L for life. On her death it passes to R. L's civil partner buys R's reversion (after April 1976). The property is not exempt under IHTA84/S18 when L's life interest comes to an end.
This exception does not apply where the reversionary interest was bought before 16 April 1976. In addition, the exception does not apply to a transfer so far as it is a loan or a disposition (IHTM04023) allowing another person the use of property.
For the purposes of the exception, a person is treated as acquiring an interest for a monetary consideration if they acquire it 'as a result of transactions which include a disposition for such consideration (whether to themselves or another) of that interest or of other property'. So spouse or civil partner exemption is excluded whether the reversion was purchased by the person beneficially entitled to it when the prior interest comes to an end or by a predecessor in title. If the reversion has been purchased at any stage, the exemption is excluded.
Example (*Lee and Richard*)
Property is put into trust for L for life with remainder to R. L buys R's reversion and then gives it to his wife. The property is not exempt under IHTA84/S18 when L's life interest comes to an end.

24.27 Consideration: Transitional rules

24.27.1 *Acquisition 1976-1978*

Section 56(8) IHTA disapplies s.56(5) for acquisitions before 12 April 1978:

subsection (5) above shall not apply where the person concerned became entitled to the interest before that date. [12 April 1978]

Instead, for acquisitions between 16 April 1976 and 12 April 1978, s.56(7) sets out another anti-avoidance rule:

> Subsection (2) above shall not apply where the acquisition of the reversionary interest was before 16th April 1976; and where the acquisition was on or after that date but before 12th April 1978 that subsection shall have effect—
> (a) with the substitution for the words "section 18 above" of the words "sections 18 and 23 to 25 above", and
> (b) with the insertion after the word "person" in both places where it occurs of the words "or body".

In its current form, s.56(2) does not concern charities. Amended as indicated, s.56(2) provides:

> Where a person or body acquires a reversionary interest in any settled property for a consideration in money or money's worth, sections 18 above shall not apply in relation to the property when it becomes the property of that person or body on the termination of the interest on which the reversionary interest is expectant.

24.27.2 *Acquisition pre-1976*

Interests acquired before 16 April 1976 are not affected by these rules (but such cases are now likely to be rare).

24.28 Loans and use of property

A loan repayable on demand is not a transfer of value (assuming the borrower is solvent) even if it is interest free. Likewise a licence revocable without notice even if it is rent free. By contrast, a loan or licence to a charity on favourable terms for a period not terminable on demand would in principle be a transfer of value. In the discussion below we describe this as a **"fixed term"** loan or licence.

A fixed term loan would probably not qualify for the IHT charity exemption because it would breach the application for charitable purposes rule. A fixed term licence would not qualify for the IHT charity exemption it would breach the limited period rule.

However, s.29 IHTA provides (so far as relevant):

> (1) If or to the extent that a transfer of value is a disposition whereby the use of money or other property is allowed by one person to another ("the

> borrower"), the preceding provisions of this Chapter shall apply to it with the following modifications ...
> (5) For the purposes of sections 23 ...
> (a) the value transferred shall be treated as attributable to the property of which the borrower is allowed the use, and
> (b) that property shall be treated as given to, or as becoming the property of, the borrower unless the use allowed includes use for purposes other than charitable purposes ...;
> and sections 23(2) to (6) ... shall not apply.

Thus a grant of a licence of land or other property to charity would be exempt from IHT, even though the donor retains the property licensed.

The grant of a lease with vacant possession to charity on favourable terms is also arguably exempt, even though the donor retains the freehold reversion. It may be objected that a lease is a separate item of property. But this is to construe the language of s.29 as if it were in a conveyancing statute; the word "use" should be given a natural meaning; a lease is simply a device to allow the charity use of land.

24.29 Home for dependant, then charity

Suppose an individual owns a property occupied by X, a dependant, relative, or friend. They wish the property to be occupied by X for their life, and after the death of X to pass to charity. In the case of a spouse or civil partner, this is easy.[24] It is assumed here that X is not the spouse or civil partner.

If the individual provides in their Will that the property be held on trust for X for life with remainder to charity, there is no IHT charity exemption at their death because of the postponed gift rule.

If the individual provides in their Will that their executors should grant a lease for life to X, and gives the reversion to charity there is no IHT charity exemption at their death because of the entire interest rule.

If the individual grants a lease for life to X during their life, and then during their life gives the reversion to charity, the gift qualifies for exemption only if X is not connected to them. Otherwise the relief is lost because of the retained interest rule. This course would be possible if X were a cohabitee, but not if X were an aunt.

The proposed solution is to grant in the lifetime of the individual a lease to X for life, and to gift the reversion to the charity by Will. The grant of

24 See 26.2 (Residue to charity, provision for spouse).

the lease to the individual may well be exempt under s.11(3) IHTA. Even if this exemption does not apply, the transfer of value will be limited to the reduction in the estate and will be a PET. See s.170 IHTA. The gift to charity qualifies for exemption.

24.30 Fund for dependant, then charity

Suppose now that an individual wishes to make financial provision to X for life, with remainder to charity on the death of X.

If the individual provides in their Will that the property be held on trust for X for life with remainder to charity, there is no IHT charity exemption at their death because of the postponed gift rule.

One solution is that the individual should lend the funds to X, the loan repayable after the death of X. (If the individual does not wish X to have control over the money, they may lend to a trust for the benefit of X.) The loan may be exempt by s.11(3) IHTA. If not, the transfer of value is limited by the life expectancy of X. Then the individual gives the benefit of the loan to charity by Will. This gift to charity qualifies for exemption.

24.31 Reservation of benefit

Section 102(5) FA 1986 provides:

> This section does not apply if or, as the case may be, to the extent that the disposal of property by way of gift is an exempt transfer by virtue of any of the following provisions of Part II of the 1984 Act ...
> (d) section 23 (gifts to charities);
> (e) section 24 (gifts to political parties);
> (ee) section 24A (gifts to housing associations);
> (f) section 25 (gifts for national purposes, etc)...

So the GWR rules do not apply to a transfer which is exempt by virtue of the IHT charity exemption and similar exemptions.

It is suggested that the GWR rules do not apply to a gift which qualifies for both the IHT charity exemption and some other exemption, such as the annual exemption, or normal expenditure out of income.[25]

The rules would in principle apply where a gift fails to qualify for the IHT charity exemption because it falls foul of the anti-avoidance rules. In such circumstances, if the donor enjoys any benefit from the property they give

25 If that were wrong then inter-spouse gifts which qualified for these exemptions would also fall within the scope of GWR, which is absurd and has never been suggested.

to the charity, the usual GWR rules do apply.

It is arguable that the GWR rule could apply where a gift is not a transfer of value by virtue of s.12 IHTA.[26] In practice the authors have not known HMRC to take this point.

24.32 Charity makes ex gratia payment

It may happen that a charity receives property from an estate where the testator intended some other person to receive the funds. For instance, the testator may have intended to revoke the gift to charity, but which failed to do so because of some oversight or legal technicality. In such cases the charity may transfer the property to the individual who was intended to have it.[27]

Will this benevolent conduct by the charity have the effect of losing the IHT charity exemption? Section 143 IHTA provides:

> Where
> [1] a testator expresses a wish that property bequeathed by his will should be transferred by the legatee to other persons, and
> [2] the legatee transfers any of the property in accordance with that wish within the period of two years after the death of the testator,
> this Act shall have effect as if the property transferred had been bequeathed by the will to the transferee.

This will not usually apply. For instance, suppose a testator intended to revoke a gift to charity, but died before making a new will, or the later will was invalid as not properly executed. In those cases the testator has not expressed a wish that the property given to charity should be transferred *by the legatee* to other persons.

In cases where s.143 might apply, it should not be difficult to avoid that result and retain the benefit of the IHT charity exemption for the transferee: the transfer should be postponed until more than two years after the testator's death. Alternatively, the transfer may be made not to the transferee but to some trust of which they may be a beneficiary.

---

26 See 24.3 (Dispositions allowable for income tax). The argument to the contrary would be that a transaction which is not a transfer of value is outside GWR generally: see Kessler, *Taxation of Non-Residents and Foreign Domiciliaries* (21st ed., 2022-23), see 76.9 (Gift of excluded property) online version *https://www.foreigndomiciliaries.co.uk*

27 See 4.21.6 (Ex-gratia payment).

24.33 Close co IHT code: Charity relief

Section 94(1) IHTA provides:

> ... where a close[28] company makes a transfer of value, tax shall be charged as if each individual to whom an amount is apportioned under this section had made a transfer of value of such amount as after deduction of tax (if any) would be equal to the amount so apportioned, less the amount (if any) by which the value of his estate is more than it would be but for the company's transfer; ...[29]

HMRC say:

> So far as the company's transfer of value relates to property given to charity or to the national institutions or bodies mentioned above, then the exemptions for gifts to those bodies extend to the amounts apportioned to the individual participators.[30]

Taxation of Companies and Company Reconstructions, formerly [31] stated that:

> ... the transfer of value treated as made by the shareholder under section 94(1), does not have any corresponding "value transferred" attached to it, and the exemptions (in particular section 23 - charities) do not apply unless there is some "value transferred". Thus a gift of property outside Gift Aid[32] to a charity by a close company should strictly speaking result in a chargeable transfer by the shareholders, unless concessionary relief is given.

The textbook went on to note that HMRC do not take this point. It is considered that HMRC's approach is right as a matter of law. When s.94

---

28 Section 102(1) IHTA defines "close company" to include a non-resident close company.

29 These provisions are considered in more detail in Kessler, *Taxation of Non-Residents and Foreign Domiciliaries* (21st ed., 2022-23), para 79.1 (Transfer of value by close co) and following.

30 "The Arts are your Business" (1980) a booklet prepared in conjunction with the Inland Revenue and issued by the Association for Business Sponsorship of the Arts, referred to in Hansard HC Deb 09 March 1981 vol 1000 cc260-1W
http://hansard.millbanksystems.com/written_answers/1981/mar/09/arts-sponsorship-tax-benefits
The passage was printed in Yellow Tax Handbook 2015/16; it is not in current edition, but there is no reason to think that HMRC practice has changed.

31 [Looseleaf], Sweet & Maxwell, A11.4.4, but now deleted.

32 Authors' note: A Gift Aid payment qualifies for the exemption in s.94(2)(a).

deems there to be "a transfer of value of [a certain] amount" the deeming is firstly that there is a transfer of value and secondly that the value transferred is of that amount. It is impossible to have a transfer of value of an amount because a transfer of value is a disposition and is not an amount (unlike the value transferred, which is an amount). If the textbook were right, then s.94 would never apply because IHT is not charged on a transfer of value: it is charged on the *value transferred* by a chargeable transfer![33] However, since the HMRC view is known the point is not likely to arise.

24.34 Deferred shares

In the HMRC view there is a charge to IHT when deferred shares come to rank equally with another class of shares.[34] However, it would be possible to avoid the issue by a gift (or even a sale) of the undeferred shares to a charitable trust, or a charitable company which is not a close company, before the relevant date. Section 98 IHTA does not impose an IHT charge on the charity in those circumstances.

24.35 Gift to national institution

Section 25 IHTA provides:

> (1) A transfer of value is an exempt transfer to the extent that the value transferred by it is attributable to property which becomes the property of a body within Schedule 3 to this Act.
> (2) Subsections (2) to (5) of section 23 and subsection (4) of section 24 above shall apply in relation to subsection (1) above as they apply in relation to section 24(1), except that section 23(3) shall not prevent subsection (1) above from applying in relation to property consisting of the benefit of an agreement restricting the use of land.

We refer to bodies within schedule 3 as **"national institutions"**. That is not a particularly helpful label but it is difficult to think of a better one to describe the disparate list, which is considered below.

Most national institutions are charities and do not need this relief. It

---

33 We would have reached this view even without s.3(4) IHTA but that arguably makes the position clearer.

34 Statement in *Law Society's Gazette*, 11th September 1991. The law on this point is unclear but that may be the better view; see Kessler, *Taxation of Non-Residents and Foreign Domiciliaries* (21st ed., 2022-23), para 79.8 (Deferred shares) online version *https://www.foreigndomiciliaries.co.uk*

survives for historical reasons: before 1983 there was a limit on the exempt amount for gifts to charities within a year of death but there was no limit for gifts to national institutions. It is now only relevant in very special cases:

(1) for national institutions which are not charities; and
(2) restricting the s.23(3) charity IHT relief restrictions.[35]

24.35.1 *"National institutions"*

Schedule 3 IHTA provides the list:

The National Gallery
The British Museum
The National Museums of Scotland
The National Museum of Wales
The Ulster Museum
Any other similar national institution which exists wholly or mainly for the purpose of preserving for the public benefit a collection of scientific, historic or artistic interest and which is approved for the purposes of this Schedule by the Treasury
Any museum or art gallery in the United Kingdom which exists wholly or mainly for that purpose and is or has been maintained by a local authority or university in the United Kingdom
Any library the main function of which is to serve the needs of teaching and research at a university in the United Kingdom
The Historic Buildings and Monuments Commission for England

---

35 See 24.17 (Entire interest rule); 24.18 (Limited period rule). This is essentially for the benefit of the National Trust. The IHT Manual provides:

IHTM11223: Gifts for National Purposes: qualifications specific to the exemption [Jun 2016]

The exemption is subject to the same exclusions (IHTM11171) that apply to charity exemption (IHTM11101), but with certain qualifications under IHTA84/S25 (2) which allow exemption that would otherwise be excluded. The situations where IHTA84/S25 (2) applies to allow the exemption are:

- the IHTA84/S23 (3) exclusion of gifts of less than the donor's whole interest or for a limited period (IHTM11176) does not prevent the IHTA84/S25 (1) exemption from applying to property consisting of the benefit of an agreement restricting the use of land
- gifts of land to the National Trust may be accompanied by a memorandum of wishes under which the donor or other person is permitted to reside in the house and receive the rent during their lifetime. The memorandum has no legal force and the reservation, no matter for whose benefit, does not prevent exemption under IHTA84/S25 from applying.

The National Trust for Places of Historic Interest or Natural Beauty
The National Trust for Scotland for Places of Historic Interest or Natural Beauty
The National Art Collections Fund
The Trustees of the National Heritage Memorial Fund
The Friends of the National Libraries
The Historic Churches Preservation Trust
Natural England
Scottish Natural Heritage
The Natural Resources Body for Wales
The Marine Management Organisation
Any local authority[36]
Any Government department[37] (including the National Debt Commissioners)
Any university or university college in the United Kingdom
A health service body, within the meaning of section 986 of the CTA 2010

Section 986 CTA 2010 defines "health service body":

In section 985 "health service body" means a body mentioned in the following table:

Body	**Provision under which body established**
the Common Services Agency for the Scottish Health Service	s.10 of the National Health Service (Scotland) Act 1978
a Health and Social Services	Art 16 of the Health and Personal Social Board Services (Northern Ireland) Order 1972 SI 1972/1265
a Health and Social Care trust	Art 10 of the Health and Personal Social Services (Northern Ireland) Order 1991 (SI 1991/194 (NI 1))
a Health Board	s.2(1)(a) National Health Service (Scotland) Act 1978
a Local Health Board	s.11 of the National Health Service (Wales) Act 2006
a National Health Service trust	s.25 of the National Health Service Act 2006 or s.18 of the National Health Service (Wales) Act 2006
an NHS foundation trust	s.30 of the National Health Service Act 2006
the Northern Ireland Central Services Agency for the Health and Social Services	Art 26 of the Health and Personal Social Services (Northern Ireland) Order 1972 (SI 1972/1265 (NI 14))
a Primary Care Trust	s.18 of the National Health Service Act 2006

36 See 45.2 ("Local Authority").

37 Section 272 IHTA provides that "Government department includes a Northern Ireland government department." The IHT Manual provides:

HTM11226: Gifts for National Purposes: government department [Jun 2016]
The definition of 'government department' is contained in .IHTA84/S272. It includes the National Debt Commissioners, and departments in Northern Ireland. Following the devolution of powers to the Scottish Parliament with the passing of the Scotland Act 1998, S.I. 1999 No. 1820. The Scotland Act 1998 (Consequential Modifications (No.2) Order 1999 paragraph 2(2) ensured that the definition of 'government department' in IHTA84/S272 includes the Scottish Administration.

the Scottish Dental Practice Board	s.4 of the National Health Service (Scotland) Act 1978
a special health and social services agency	Art 3 of the Health and Personal Social Services (Special Agencies) (Northern Ireland) Order 1990 (SI 1990/247 (NI 3))
a Special Health Authority	s.28 of the National Health Service Act 2006 or s.22 of the National Health Service (Wales) Act 2006
a Special Health Board	s.2(1)(b) National Health Service (Scotland) Act 1978
a Strategic Health Authority	s.13 of the National Health Service Act 2006

The Inheritance Tax Manual comments on the category

> Any other similar national institution which exists wholly or mainly for the purpose of preserving for the public benefit a collection of scientific, historic or artistic interest and which is approved for the purposes of this para by the Board:

IHTM11224: Gifts for National Purposes: qualifying Bodies [Jun 2016]

... Approval has, to date, been given to

The British Library
The British Museum[38]
The Fleet Air Arm Museum
The Geological Museum
The Imperial War Museum
Lambeth Palace Library
The London Museum
The National Army Museum
The National Galleries of Scotland
The National Library of Scotland
The National Library of Wales
The National Maritime Museum
The National Museums and Galleries on Merseyside
The National Museum of Antiquities, Scotland[39]
The National Portrait Gallery
The National Postal Museum
The National History Museum
Portsmouth Royal Naval Museum
The RAF Museum
The Royal Botanic Gardens, Kew
The Royal Marines Museum
The Science Museum
Submarine Museum
The Tate Museum
The Tower Armouries
The Ulster Folk Museum
The Victoria and Albert Museum
The Wallace Collection

24.35.2 *National institutions*: *Critique*

It is suggested that the overlap between s.23 and s.25 IHTA should be abolished. All charitable bodies ought to be taken off the list in schedule 3, so that s.25 only applies to non-charitable bodies (eg local authorities) who actually need the relief. If some of the charities (eg the National Trust) need wider IHT exemptions, that ought to be dealt with expressly. The current duplication can only cause confusion.

---

38 Before 1 September 1992- the Natural History Museum

39 Before 1 October 1985.

In 2016, Schedule 3 was amended to bring back within the scope of existing legislation certain museums and galleries that previously benefited from the advantageous tax provisions currently provided by the inheritance tax legislation, but which have lost this benefit because some local authorities have placed their museum's collections into independent charitable trusts which are not within the terms of the legislation. This was done through the addition of the words "or has been". However, we ask whether there was any need for this if the collection is already in a charity: have they simply got muddled here?

24.36 Gift to charity from pension fund

There is a relief from the charge to tax on legacies paid from unused registered pension schemes when those legacies are paid to charity. The tax rate on legacies paid from unused registered pension schemes is 55% so the relief is valuable. The effect of the relief is that the drawing from the pension and the payment to the charity will incur no tax charge at all, provided the legacy is used for charitable purposes.

The legislation is found in schedule 29 FA 2004. Paragraph 18 provides:

> (1) A lump sum death benefit is a charity lump sum death benefit if—
> (b) there are no dependants of the member,
> (c) it is paid in respect of the member's drawdown pension fund in respect of an arrangement at the date of the member's death, and
> (d) it is paid to a charity nominated by the member.
>
> (1A) A lump sum death benefit is also a charity lump sum death benefit if—
> (a) the member had reached the age of 75 at the date of the member's death,
> (b) there are no dependants of the member,
> (c) it is paid in respect of relevant uncrystallised funds[40] in respect of a money purchase arrangement at the date of the member's death, and

40 Defined by reference in para 18(1B) sch 29 FA 2004: "Relevant uncrystallised funds" has the meaning given by paragraph 15(2).
Para 15(2) sch 29 FA 2004 provides:
"Relevant uncrystallised funds" means such of the sums and assets held for the purposes of the arrangement at the member's death as—
(a) had not been applied for purchasing a scheme pension, a lifetime annuity, a dependants' scheme pension or a dependants' annuity, and
(b) had not been designated under the arrangement as available for the payment of drawdown pension.

(d) it is paid to a charity nominated by the member.

(2) A lump sum death benefit is also a charity lump sum death benefit if—

(a) it is paid on the death of a dependant of the member,

(c) there are no other dependants of the member,

(d) it is paid in respect of the dependant's drawdown pension fund at the date of the dependant's death in respect of an arrangement relating to the member, and

(e) it is paid to a charity nominated by the member or, if the member made no nomination, by the dependant.

HMRC's Registered Pensions Scheme Manual RPSM10106090 [25 April 2014] summarises as follows:

> **What is a charity lump sum death benefit?**
> Broadly a charity lump sum death benefit is a lump sum paid to a charity if:
> - a member [of the pension scheme] receiving a drawdown pension, or
> - a dependant [of a member of a pension scheme] getting a dependant drawdown pension
>
> dies and there are no other dependants of the member.
>
> ...
>
> **When can a charity lump sum death benefit be paid?**
> If the member (or dependant) died on or after 6 April 2011 there is no requirement that the member (or dependant) had to be age 75 or over when they died. The lump sum can be paid whatever the age of the member (or dependant) when they died.
> A charity lump sum death benefit can also be paid if the member dies on or after 6 April 2011 and all the following apply:
> - the member was 75 or older when they died,
> - the member had uncrystallised rights (benefits that have not started to be put into payment) under any type of arrangement when they died, and
> - there are no dependants of the member.

The charity must be chosen by the member of the pension scheme or, in relevant cases, a charity chosen by the dependent of a member. Charity for these purposes bears its usual tax meaning. RPSM10106090 provides:

> If the charity does not use the payment for charitable purposes the payment will not have been a charity lump sum death benefit. It will be treated as an unauthorised member payment (see RPSM04104020, which deals with the taxation of such payments).

This relief will be more advantageous than IHT relief on death.

24.37 10-year and exit charges

24.37.1 *Charity property not relevant property*

Section 58 IHTA provides:

> (1) In this Chapter "relevant property" means settled property in which no qualifying interest in possession subsists, other than—
> (a) property held for charitable purposes only, whether for a limited time or otherwise ...

For the meaning of charitable purposes, see 24.8.2 (Trust for charitable purposes).

A permanent charity is not within the scope of IHT 10-year and exit charges.

For property leaving a temporary charitable trust, see 31.3 (Temporary charitable trust).

24.37.2 *Charity exit charge relief*

Section 76(1) IHTA provides relief from the exit charge which would otherwise apply when property in a non-charitable, relevant property trust becomes held on charitable trusts (and so ceases to be relevant property):

> Tax shall not be charged under this Chapter (apart from section 79 below) in respect of property which
> [i] ceases to be relevant property, or
> [ii] ceases to be property to which section 70, 71, 71A, 71D, 72, 73 or 74 above or paragraph 8 of Schedule 4 to this Act applies,
> on becoming—
> (a) property held for charitable purposes only without limit of time (defined by a date or otherwise);
> (b) the property of a political party qualifying for exemption under section 24 above; or
> (c) the property of a body within Schedule 3 to this Act;

Section 76(3) IHTA deals with special cases where the value passing to charity is less than the amount on which the exit charge is charged (which is the reduction in the value of the trust fund)

> If the amount on which tax would be charged apart from this section in respect of any property exceeds the value of the property immediately after it becomes property of a description specified in paragraphs (a) to

(c) of subsection (1) above (less the amount of any consideration for its transfer received by the trustees), that subsection shall not apply but the amount on which tax is charged shall be equal to the excess.

Section 76(4) IHTA is supplemental:

The reference in subsection (3) above to the amount on which tax would be charged is a reference to the amount on which it would be charged—

(a) assuming (if it is not in fact so) that the tax is not paid out of settled property, and

(b) apart from Chapters I and II of Part V of this Act;

and the reference in that subsection to the amount on which tax is charged is a reference to the amount on which it would be charged on that assumption and apart from those Chapters.

Section 76(5) (8) are common form anti-avoidance provisions:

Section	**Topic**	**See para**
76(5)	Defeasible transaction	24.16
76(6)	Charitable purposes only	24.12
76(7)(8)	Interest acquired for consideration	24.25

(5) Subsection (1) above shall not apply in relation to any property if the disposition by which it becomes property of the relevant description is defeasible; but for this purpose a disposition which has not been defeated at a time twelve months after the property concerned becomes property of the relevant description and is not defeasible after that time shall be treated as not being defeasible, whether or not it was capable of being defeated before that time.

(6) Subsection (1) above shall not apply in relation to any property if it or any part of it may become applicable for purposes other than charitable purposes or purposes of a body mentioned in subsection (1)(b), or (c) above.

(7) Subsection (1) shall not apply in relation to any property if, at or before the time when it becomes property of the relevant description, an interest under the settlement is or has been acquired for a consideration in money or money's worth by an exempt body otherwise than from a charity or a body mentioned in subsection (1)(b) or (c) above.

(8) In subsection (7) above "exempt body" means a charity or a body mentioned in subsection (1)(b), or (c) above; and for the purposes of subsection (7) above a body shall be treated as acquiring an interest for a consideration in money or money's worth if it becomes entitled to the interest as a result of transactions which include a disposition for such consideration (whether to that body or to another person) of that interest

or of other property.

24.38 Inheritance tax on charity

A permanently charitable trust is not subject to inheritance tax. In particular, the trust will be exempt from the IHT trust regime. Section 58(1) IHTA provides:

> (1) In this Chapter "relevant property" means settled property in which no qualifying interest in possession subsists, other than—
> (a) property held for charitable purposes only, whether for a limited time or otherwise;...

There is no express jurisdiction requirement. It is arguable that this relief applies to settled property even if the settlement is not governed by a UK law (though the purposes must be charitable according to English law). But for practical purposes, in the light of *Routier v HMRC* [2019] UKSC 43 it is necessary to proceed on the basis that relief only applies to trusts subject to the jurisdiction of the UK courts, and charities established in EU member states (and some EEA countries) would nevertheless qualify for the relief by virtue of retained EU law.[41] Other foreign charities would not qualify.

For taxation of a temporary charitable trust see 31.3 (Temporary charitable trust).

24.39 IHT on members of charitable companies

The rights of a member of a charitable company are not within the scope of IHT because:

(1) The rights are not property, or not property to which an individual is beneficially entitled,[42] so they do not form part of the individual's estate for IHT purposes.
(2) The rights should have nil market value.

This should be so even if:

(1) the charitable company is not a charity within the tax definition, eg a

---

41 See 3.20 (EU law).

42 See *Children's Investment Fund v AG*: [2017] EWHC 1379 (Ch at [46]."Members of a charitable company limited by guarantee without a share capital do not generally have a personal proprietary interest in their shares, since they cannot benefit personally from their membership as a result of the restrictions contained in sections 197, 198 and 201 of the Charities Act 2011."

non-EU charity, (though in such a case the nature of the rights of the member may need further investigation)

(2) the charitable company has a share capital (though this is probably academic as charitable companies in practice do not have a share capital)

The rights of a member of a temporary charitable company may constitute valuable property.

CHAPTER TWENTY FIVE

CHARITY LEGACY RELIEF

25.1 Charity legacy relief

This chapter discusses the IHT relief in sch 1A IHTA which we call **"charity legacy relief"**.

The development of the relief can be traced through consultation and response papers[1] but these are now of historical interest only.

In short, the rate of IHT on an estate that makes a charitable gift of 10% or more of the estate will be 36% rather than 40%. The consultation paper

1 HMRC Consultation Document, "A new incentive for charitable legacies" (2011) *https://www.att.org.uk/system/files_force/file_uploads/Incentive_charitable_legacies_HMRC.pdf?download=1*
"A new incentive for charitable legacies A lower rate of inheritance tax when leaving 10% of an estate to charity Summary of Responses", (December 2011).

gives a simple example:

	With legacy	**No legacy**
Estate value	850,000	850,000
less lifetime gift		
less available NR band	-325,000	-325,000
net estate for 10% test	525,000	
less charity legacy	-52,500	
taxable estate	472,500	525,000
IHT due @ 36%	170,100	
IHT due @ 40%		210,000
Residue[2]	627,400	640,000

The charitable legacy of £52.5k results in a reduction in the amount left to other beneficiaries of £12.6k = 24% of the charitable legacy.

It is melancholic to compare this example with the complexities of the (slightly) more real life examples below. Moreover the example is correct but misleading: the 24% saving will only be achieved if the testator is prepared to let the tax rules determine the amount of the legacy, to the exclusion of all other considerations.

25.2 "D" and "TP"

Para 1(1) sch 1A IHTA provides:

> This Schedule applies if—
> (a) a chargeable transfer is made (under section 4) on the death of a person ("D"), and
> (b) all or part of the value transferred by the chargeable transfer is chargeable to tax at a rate other than nil per cent.

Para 1(2) sch 1A IHTA provides:

> The part of the value transferred that is chargeable to tax at a rate other than nil per cent is referred to in this Schedule as "TP".

D stands for the **D**eceased, and TP stands for **T**axable **P**roperty.

25.3 Charitable giving condition

The relief applies if the charitable giving condition is met.[3]

Para 2(2) sch 1A IHTA provides:

2 Ie, the amount left for distribution to non-charitable beneficiaries, the estate value less the charitable legacy and IHT.

3 See 25.6 (The relief).

> For the purposes of this paragraph, the charitable giving condition is met if, for one or more components of the estate[4] (taking each component separately), the donated amount is at least 10% of the baseline amount.

The IHT Manual calls this the "10% test".

25.4 Components of estate

Para 3(1) sch 1A IHTA provides:

> For the purposes of paragraph 2, the components of the estate are—
> (a) the survivorship component,
> (b) the settled property component, and
> (c) the general component.

We consider them in the same order, though the general component is the most important. In outline:

Component	**Meaning**	**See para**
Survivorship	Joint property	25.4.1
Settled property	Estate IP property	25.4.2
General	Individual's free estate	25.4.3

25.4.1 *Survivorship component*

Para 3(2) sch 1A IHTA provides:

> The survivorship component is made up of all the property comprised in the estate that, immediately before D's death, was joint (or common) property liable to pass on D's death—
> (a) by survivorship (in England and Wales or Northern Ireland),
> (b) under a special destination (in Scotland), or
> (c) by or under anything corresponding to survivorship or a special destination under the law of a country or territory outside the United Kingdom.

In England and Northern Ireland, survivorship will generally involve land held as joint tenants and joint bank accounts.

The Manual comments on joint bank accounts:

> **IHTM45004: Components of the estate: survivorship component** [Jun 2016]
> Note that where:

4 Para 10 sch 1A IHTA provides: "In this Schedule, in relation to D ... "the estate" means D's estate immediately before death".

- property is held in joint names of the deceased and another for convenience; but
- the deceased provided all the funds so that the full value of the property is charged to tax at death,[5]

the property should still be treated as part of the survivorship component because as a matter of fact, the funds pass to the surviving owner.

In Scotland, special destination is wider than joint ownership in England. The Scottish Law Commission say:[6]

> 6.61 A special destination is a destination in a document of title to property which passes the property, or the deceased's share of the property, from the deceased to a specified person or class of persons on the deceased's death. The most common special destination is the survivorship destination. In its simplest form the title is "to A and B equally between them and wholly to the survivor". While A and B are alive they are co-owners, but when one dies his or her share passes automatically to the survivor who ends up owning the whole property. This is often inserted in the titles of dwelling houses owned by married and other couples. Special destinations are not confined to heritable property; they are also met in share or bond certificates.
> 6.62 In the 1990 Report, this Commission took the view that special destinations, other than survivorship destinations, in future documents should cease to have effect in passing property on death.[7] Other special destinations, such as "to A whom failing B" and "to A and B in conjunct fee and liferent" are seldom used and it was considered that any advantages in having them were outweighed by the dangers that the owners of property and their executors were ignorant of their legal effects and the likelihood of conflicting provisions in the owners' wills. We now think that there is no need for legislative intervention. People should be free to use whatever destination they wish and should have to accept the risk that it may fail to give effect to their intentions. Although we have not carried out a recent survey, anecdotal evidence is that special destinations other than survivorship destinations are rarely used in current practice so that the scale of the mischief does not warrant statutory abolition. Finally, it has been pointed out that the survivorship destination "to A and B equally between them and wholly to the

---

5 See Kessler, *Taxation of Non-Residents and Foreign Domiciliaries*, (21st ed., 2022-23) para 92.3 (Joint account: IHT) online version *https://www.foreigndomiciliaries.co.uk*

6 The Scottish Law Commission, Report on Succession (2009).

7 Footnote original: Paras 6.2-6.6 for property and paras 6.23-6.26 for leases.

> survivor" is in fact a half share to A whom failing B and a half share to B whom failing A, so that it makes no sense to allow survivorship destinations but ban destinations of the type "to A whom failing B". We also see no need to define a special destination and are content to leave this to the existing law and its development by the courts.

This is important not only for Scottish estates, but also for property which passes under foreign dispositions.

25.4.2 *Settled property component*

Para 3(3) sch 1A IHTA provides:

> The settled property component is made up of all the settled property comprised in the estate[8] in which there subsisted, immediately before D's death, an interest in possession to which D was beneficially entitled immediately before death.

The drafter clearly had in mind an estate interest in possession, ie one to which s.49 IHTA applies, where the trust property is treated as in the estate of the life tenant. This is not stated expressly but it is considered that must be implied.

If there is a non-estate interest in possession, no election will be made under para 7 so it does not normally matter whether or not that counts as a settled property component. The issue could arise in the rare case where D had an estate interest in possession in one trust, a non-estate interest in possession in another trust, and elected that the settled property component should be merged with the general component. But in practice that may never happen.

25.4.3 *General component*

Para 3(4) sch 1A IHTA provides:

> The general component is made up of all the property comprised in the estate[9] other than—
> (a) property in the survivorship component,
> (b) property in the settled property component, and
> (c) property that forms part of the estate by virtue of section 102(3) of the FA 1986 (gifts with reservation).

8 Para 10 sch 1A IHTA provides: "In this Schedule, in relation to D ... "the estate" means D's estate immediately before death".

9 Para 10 sch 1A IHTA provides: "In this Schedule, in relation to D ... "the estate" means D's estate immediately before death".

25.4.4 *GWR property*

The IHT Manual provides:

> **IHTM45006**: **Components of the estate: reservation of benefit property** [Jun 2016]
> [1] Property in which a reservation of benefit subsists (IHTM04071) is not included as a component of the estate as such property cannot by itself qualify for the reduced rate.
> [2] This is because the reservation of benefit rules do not apply to gifts to charity, FA86/S102(5)(d).[10]
> [3] However, such property may be eligible for the reduced rate if an election to merge it with, say, the general component is made, IHTA84/Sch1A/Para 7(5) (b).

The issue will not often arise. Gifts with reservation are never made except by accident.

25.5 "Donated"/"baseline" amounts

The terms "donated amount" and "baseline amount" matter as the charitable giving condition requires that the donated amount must be 10% of the baseline amount.

Strictly one should not refer to donated or baseline amounts in the abstract, but a donated amount and baseline amount for each of the general/survivorship/settled component of an estate. An estate may have up to 3 components and so may have 3 donated amounts and 3 baseline amounts.

25.5.1 *"Donated amount"*

Para 4 sch 1A IHTA provides:

> The donated amount, for a component of the estate,[11] is so much of the value transferred by the relevant transfer[12] as (in total) is attributable to property that—
> (a) forms part of that component, and

---

10 This is not in fact the correct reason for the rule; but it does not matter.

11 See 25.4 (Components of the estate).

12 Para 10 sch 1A IHTA provides:
"In this Schedule, in relation to D ...
"the relevant transfer" means the transfer of value that D is treated (under section 4) as having made immediately before death."

(b) is property in relation to which section 23(1) [IHT charity exemption] applies.

The donated amount for the general component depends on the terms of the will of the deceased (and any instrument of variation).

The donated amount for the settled component depends on the terms of the settlement(s).

The IHT Manual comments on the donated amount for the survivorship component:

> **IHTM45004: Components of the estate: survivorship component**
> [Jun 2016]
> [The manual outlines para 3(2) Sch 1A IHTA and continues:]
> Normally, property passing by survivorship will not qualify for charity exemption and will not be entitled to the reduced rate. However, the surviving joint owner is liable for the tax attributable to the joint property under IHTA84/S200(1)(c) (IHTM30022) and they may choose to redirect part of their entitlement to charity by an Instrument of Variation in order to benefit from the reduced rate.
> Sometimes, such a variation may simply sever a joint tenancy (IHTM15081) with the result that the joint property passes under the deceased's Will. IHTA84/Sch1A/Para 3(2) says that the survivorship component includes all the property comprised in the deceased's estate that, immediately before death was liable to pass by survivorship. For this reason this type of variation does not result in the severed property "switching" to the general component. You should continue to include the joint property in the survivorship component for the purposes of the 10% test.
> However, because this component takes into account all joint property, where there are a number of items of joint property that the deceased held with different joint owners, action by a single joint owner may not be enough to benefit from the lower rate as the charitable giving condition (IHTM45002) is unlikely to be met for this component as a whole.

25.5.2 *"Baseline amount"*

Para 5 sch 1A IHTA provides:

> The baseline amount, for a component of the estate,[13] is the amount calculated in accordance with the following steps—

13 See 25.4 (Components of the estate).

Step 1
Determine the part of the value transferred by the chargeable transfer[14] that is attributable to property in that component.
Step 2
Deduct from the amount determined under Step 1 the appropriate proportion of the available nil-rate band.
"The appropriate proportion" is a proportion equal to the proportion that the amount determined under Step 1 bears to the value transferred by the chargeable transfer as a whole.
"The available nil-rate band" is the amount (if any) by which—
(a) the nil-rate band maximum (increased, where applicable, in accordance with section 8A [transferable nil rate band]), exceeds
(b) the sum of the values transferred by previous chargeable transfers made by D in the period of 7 years ending with the date of the relevant transfer.[15]
Step 3
Add to the amount determined under Step 2 an amount equal to so much of the value transferred by the relevant transfer as (in total) is attributable to property that—
(a) forms part of that component, and
(b) is property in relation to which section 23(1) [IHT charity exemption] applies.
The result is the baseline amount for that component.

The need to amend in light of the residence NRB seems to have been overlooked.

25.6 The relief

Para 2 sch 1A IHTA provides:

(1) If the charitable giving condition is met—
(a) the tax charged on the part of TP that qualifies for the lower rate of tax is to be charged at the lower rate of tax, and
(b) the tax charged on any remaining part of TP is to be charged at the rate at which it would (but for this Schedule) have been

---

14 Para 10 sch 1A IHTA provides "In this Schedule, in relation to D—
"the chargeable transfer" means the chargeable transfer mentioned in paragraph 1(1)".

15 Para 10 sch 1A IHTA provides:
"In this Schedule, in relation to D ...
"the relevant transfer" means the transfer of value that D is treated (under section 4) as having made immediately before death."

charged on the whole of TP in accordance with section 7.

...

(5) The part of TP that "qualifies for the lower rate of tax" is the part attributable to all the property in each of the components for which the donated amount is at least 10% of the baseline amount.
(6) The lower rate of tax is 36%.

25.7 HMRC examples

25.7.1 *General component only*

The IHT Manual provides:

IHTM45010: Calculating the baseline amount: estate with a single estate component [Aug 2016]
Most estates will contain just the deceased's free estate which is part of the general component (IHTM45007).[16] In these cases, establishing the donated amount (IHTM45002) and the baseline amount (IHTM45009) will be straightforward.
Example (Robert)
R died on 17 June 2012 leaving an estate valued at £750,000 after deduction of liabilities. He leaves a legacy of £50,000 to the National Trust.
The donated amount is £50,000.

The HMRC analysis is as follows:

The baseline amount is calculated following the steps in IHTA/Sch1A/Para 5 as follows

Estate on death	£750,000	
Legacy to charity (donated amount)	-£50,000	
Chargeable transfer	£700,000	(step 1)
Less nil-rate band	-£325,000	
	£375,000	(step 2)
Add back legacy to charity	£50,000	
Baseline amount	£425,000	(step 3)

The charitable giving condition (IHTM45002) or 10% test requires that the donated amount is at least 10% of the baseline amount. Here the legacy of £50,000 is more than 10% of £425,000 (or £42,500) so the estate qualifies for the reduced rate. The reduced tax liability will be £135,000 compared to £150,000 at full rate.

The next example is the same except there was a lifetime gift (a failed PET):

---

16 Authors' footnote: We doubt is that is correct, for estates above the IHT nil rate band, but it does not matter.

IHTM45011 calculating the baseline amount with a single estate component and lifetime cumulative total [Aug 2016]
Step 2 in calculating the baseline amount (IHTM45009) provides that the available nil-rate band is deducted from the chargeable transfer to establish the baseline amount. Where there are chargeable transfers in the seven years prior to death, they will reduce the amount of the nil-rate band that can be deducted.
Example
James died on 17 July 2012 leaving an estate valued at £750,000 after deduction of liabilities. He leaves a legacy of £50,000 to the RNIB. He had given £150,000 to his daughter 4 years before he died.
The donated amount is £50,000.

The HMRC analysis is as follows:

The baseline amount is calculated following the steps in IHTA/Sch1A/Para 5 as follows

Estate on death	£750,000	
Legacy to charity (donated amount)	-£50,000	
Chargeable transfer	£700,000	(step 1)
Less nil-rate band	-£175,000	(£325,000 – £150,000)[17]
	£525,000	(step 2)
Add back legacy to charity	£50,000	
Baseline amount	£575,000	(step 3)

The charitable giving condition (IHTM45002) or 10% test requires that the donated amount is at least 10% of the baseline amount. Here the legacy of £50,000 is less than 10% of £575,000 or £57,500, so the estate does not qualify for the reduced rate.

The Manual continues with some IHT planning advice:

It would, however, be possible for the beneficiaries of the estate to increase the legacy to charity by another £7,500 by executing an Instrument of Variation (IHTM35011), so that the 10% test is met. This would reduce the liability at full rate from £210,000 to that at reduced rate of £186,300 – a tax saving of £23,700, which more than pays for the additional payment to charity.

25.7.2 *Estate with 2 or 3 components*

The IHT Manual provides:

IHTM45012: Calculating the baseline amount: estate with two or more estate components [Aug 2016]
Where there are two or more components to the estate, the donated amount (IHTM45002) and the baseline amount (IHTM45009) must be calculated separately for each component and the reduced rate applied to the component(s)

17 Authors' footnote: The IHT annual exemption has been ignored.

that meet the 10% test. It will not be uncommon in these circumstances for one component to be taxed at the full rate and another at the reduced rate.

Example

Elizabeth died on 17 May 2012 leaving assets owned personally valued at £750,000 after deduction of liabilities.

She bequeaths 10% of the residue of her estate to Cancer Research.

She held a joint bank account with her son, Andrew, which had a balance of £60,000 at death. Both contributed equally to the account so £30,000 is included in her estate as joint property passing by survivorship.

The HMRC analysis is as follows:

In this case the estate contains two components, a survivorship component and a general component. The donated amount in the general component is £75,000. The joint account passes by survivorship to Andrew, so the survivorship component cannot qualify for the reduced rate.

The baseline amount for the general component is calculated following the steps in IHTA/Sch1A/Para 5 as follows

Estate on death	£750,000	
Legacy to charity (donated amount)	-£75,000	
Chargeable transfer	£675,000	(step 1)
Less proportion of nil-rate band[18]	-£311,170	
	£363,830	(step 2)
Add back legacy to charity	£75,000	
Baseline amount	£438,830	(step 3)

The charitable giving condition (IHTM45002) or 10% test requires that the donated amount is at least 10% of the baseline amount. Here the legacy of £75,000 exceeds 10% of £438,830 or £43,883, so the general component qualifies for the reduced rate. The reduced tax liability will be £130,978.80 compared to £145,532 at full rate.

The tax on the survivorship component will be

Chargeable transfer	£30,000
Less proportion of nil-rate band[19]	-£13,830
	£16,170
Tax at 40%	£6,468

Where the amount qualifying for charity exemption in one component exceeds the 10% test (as is the case in this example) the beneficiaries of the estate may want to consider making an election to merge the components (IHTM45035) to gain the maximum benefit from the reduced rate.

25.8 Interaction with revaluation relief

The IHT Manual provides:

---

18 £675,000 ÷ (£675,000 + £30,000) × £325,000 = £311,170

19 £30,000 ÷ (£675,000 + £30,000) × £325,000 = £13,830

> **IHTM45024: Reduced rate for charities: treatment of reduced rate on COMPASS: Example where changes to values affect whether the reduced rate applies or not** [Jun 2014]
> **Example**
> Helen died on 20 July 2012 leaving an estate valued at £555,000 after deduction of liabilities, when the IHT400 is delivered. She leaves a legacy of £30,000 to the RSPCA.
> The donated amount is £30,000.

The HMRC analysis of the position before revaluation relief is as follows:

> The baseline amount is calculated as follows:

Estate on death	£655,000	
Legacy to charity (donated amount)	-£30,000	
Chargeable transfer	£625,000	(step 1)
Less nil-rate band	-£325,000	
	£300,000	(step 2)
Add back legacy to charity	£30,000	
Baseline amount	£330,000	(step 3)

> To qualify for the reduced rate the donated amount must be at least 10% of the baseline amount. As the legacy of £30,000 is less than 10% of £330,000 (or £33,000) so the estate does not qualify for the reduced rate.

The could execute a deed of variation; but revaluation relief makes that unnecessary. The HMRC analysis is as follows:

> One of the assets in the estate is a house valued at £450,000 at the date of death. In the year following Helen's death the house is sold for £410,000 and Loss on sale relief is claimed. This reduces the value of the death estate to £615,000.
> The amended calculation of the baseline amount is:

Estate on death	£615,000	
Legacy to charity (donated amount)	-£30,000	
Chargeable transfer	£585,000	(step 1)
Less nil-rate band	-£325,000	
	£265,000	(step 2)
Add back legacy to charity	£30,000	
Baseline amount	£295,000	(step 3)

> The legacy of £30,000 is now more than 10% of £295,000 (or £29,500) so the estate now qualifies for the reduced rate.

25.9 Interaction with instalment relief

The IHT Manual provides:

> **IHTM45025: Reduced rate for charities: treatment of reduced rate on COMPASS: examples of calculations for temporary workaround** [Jun 2014]
> **Example** (Elizabeth)
> E died on 17 May 2012 leaving an estate valued at £800,000 after deduction of

liabilities, consisting of personal estate of £300,000 and her house valued at £500,000.
She bequeaths 10% of the residue of her estate to Cancer Research.
Her executors elect to pay the tax on the house by instalments.

The HMRC analysis is as follows:

The baseline amount is calculated following the steps in IHTA/Sch1A/Para 5 as follows

Estate on death	£800,000	
Legacy to charity (donated amount)	- £80,000	
Chargeable transfer	£720,000	(step 1)
Less [proportion of][20] nil-rate band	- £325,000	
	£395,000	(step 2)
Add back legacy to charity	£80,000	
Baseline amount	£475,000	(step 3)

The charitable giving condition (IHTM45002) or 10% test requires that the donated amount is at least 10% of the baseline amount. Here the legacy of £80,000 is more than 10% of £475,000 (£47,500) so the estate qualifies for the reduced rate.
The calculations on COMPASS will apportion the tax between the instalment and non-instalment option property as shown below. Deduct 10% of the tax to allow the reduced rate.

Chargeable estate	£720,000	
Nil rate band	-£325,000	
	£395,000	
Tax at 40%	£158,000	
Apportioned between	NIOP	IOP
	£48,277.77[21]	£109,722.22[22]
Relief against tax (10%)	-£4,827.77	-£10,972.22
Tax due at reduced rate	43,450.00	£98,750.00
Each instalment		£9,875.00

The total tax due at the reduced rate is £142,200 is the same as £395,000 × 36%.

Example
Following on from the above example, assume E also owned a joint account and her share was worth £100,000.
The baseline amount for the general component is calculated following the steps in IHTA/Sch1A/Para 5 as follows

Estate on death	£800,000[23]	
Legacy to charity (donated amount)	-£80,000	
Chargeable transfer	£720,000	(step 1)

20 Authors' footnote: the "proportion" is 100%.
21 (£220,000 ÷ £720,000) × £158,000 = £48,277.77
22 (£500,000 ÷ £720,000) × £158,000 = £109,722.22
23 Authors' footnote: this assumes the estate is £800k.

Less proportion of nil-rate band[24]	- £285,366	
	£434,634	(step 2)
Add back legacy to charity	£80,000	
Baseline amount	£514,634	(step 3)

Again, the legacy of £80,000 exceeds 10% of £514,634 or £51,463, so the general component qualifies for the reduced rate.
The calculations on COMPASS will apportion the tax between the components and the instalment and non-instalment option property as below. Deduct 10% of the tax attributable to the general component to allow the reduced rate.

Chargeable estate		£820,000[25]	
Nil rate band		- £325,000	
		£495,000	
Tax at 40%		£198,000	
Apportioned between	NIOP	IOP	Joint account
	£53,121.95[26]	£120,731.71[27]	£24,146.34[28]
Relief against tax (10%)	-£5,312.19	-12,073.17	0.00
Tax due at reduced/full rate	£47,809.76	£108,658.54	£24,146.34
Each instalment		£10,865.85	

The total tax due on the general component at the reduced rate is £156,468 or the same as £434,634 (the value at step 2 above) × 36%.

25.10 Interaction with partial exemption

Para 6 sch 1A IHTA provides:

> (1) For the purpose of calculating the donated amount and the baseline amount, any amount to be arrived at in accordance with section 38(3) or (5) is to be arrived at assuming the rate of tax is the lower rate of tax (see paragraph 2(6)).
> (2) For the purpose of calculating the donated amount, section 39A does not apply to a specific gift of property in relation to which section 23(1) applies (but that section does apply to such a gift for the purpose of calculating the baseline amount).
> (3) Subject to sub-paragraphs (1) and (2), the provisions of this Act apply for the purpose of calculating the donated amount and the baseline amount as for the purpose of calculating the tax to be charged on the value transferred by the chargeable transfer.[29]

---

24 £720,000 ÷ (£720,000 + £100,000) × £325,000 = £285,366
25 Authors' footnote: this assumes (inconsistently) that the estate is £900k.
26 (£220,000 ÷ £820,000) × £198,000 = £53,121.95
27 (£500,000 ÷ £820,000) × £198,000 = £120,731.71
28 (£100,000 ÷ £820,000) × £198,000 = £24,146.34
29 Para 10 sch 1A IHTA provides "In this Schedule, in relation to D—
"the chargeable transfer" means the chargeable transfer mentioned in paragraph 1(1)".

The IHT Manual provides an example:

IHTM45030: The charitable giving condition or 10% test: grossing up [Aug 2016]

Where the residue of the estate is partially exempt, passing either to the surviving spouse or civil partner or to charity and the Will contains other legacies that are left free of tax, it is necessary to gross up such legacies (IHTM26121). The grossed up value of chargeable legacies will increase the baseline amount (IHTM45009) and where the charitable legacy is of a fixed amount or is a share of residue, this may mean that the estate component fails the 10% test, solely by reason of the grossing up.

To avoid this happening IHTA84/Sch1A/Para 6(1) provides that solely for the purposes of establishing whether or not the charitable giving condition (IHTM45002) is met, the grossing up calculation should use the lower 36% rate. A grossing up calculator that uses a tax rate of 36% is on the HMRC website.

It is important to recognise that there are two distinct stages here

- firstly, working out whether or not the 10% test is met, and
- secondly, calculating the chargeable estate and applying the appropriate rate of tax.

You may need to perform two separate calculations.

Where the reduced rate may be in point, you should always use the 36% rate grossing calculator to see whether the charitable giving condition or 10% test is met - if it is, this one calculation will then provide the values you need for the chargeable estate. (The reason for doing this is that if you used the 40% rate calculator first and the estate met the 10% test; you would then need to perform the calculations again at 36% to arrive at the chargeable estate - so it is easier to use the 36% rate grossing calculator in the first place.)

If the 10% test is not met using the 36% grossing calculator, the estate cannot qualify for the reduced rate and is liable to tax at the full rate, so you should perform the calculations again using the full rate grossing calculator in the normal way.

This issue will not arise where the legacy is worded in such a way that the amount of the charitable legacy must meet the 10% test (IHTM45003). In these cases, you can use the 36% rate grossing calculator to arrive at the chargeable estate without first testing that the 10% test is met.

Example

Stephen died on 11 September 2012 leaving an estate valued at £1,000,000 after deduction of liabilities.

The Will left pecuniary legacies of £245,000 free of tax to his children and 10% of the residue to the RSPCA.

To qualify for the reduced rate of tax, the amount passing to charity must be at least £67,500 (£1,000,000 - £325,000 = £675,000 × 10%).

The HMRC analysis is as follows:

Ignoring grossing up, the residue of the estate is £1,000,000 - £245,000 = £755,000. The donated amount would be £75,500 and so, initially, the estate appears to qualify for the reduced rate. But as there are legacies that are left free of tax, they must be grossed up to reflect the fact that in reality, the residue and so the share passing to charity will be reduced by the tax paid.

If the estate is grossed up at 40%, the calculations are as follows

Initial residue (£1,000,000 - £245,000)	£755,000
less initial exempt residue (£755,000@10%)	£75,500
Initial chargeable residue	£679,500
Initial chargeable estate (£245,000 + £679,500)	£924,500
Tax on initial estate (£924,500 - £325,000)@40%	£239,800
Gross up gifts at estate rate (£245,000 × £924,500 ÷ (£924,500 - £239,800))	£330,805
Final residue (£1,000,000 - £330,805)	£669,195
Donated amount (£669,195@10%)	£66,919

Grossing up the pecuniary legacies at full rate has increased their value for tax to £330,805. This must be fed into the calculation to determine the baseline amount as follows

Estate on death	£1,000,000	
Legacy to charity (donated amount)	-£66,919	
Chargeable transfer	£933,081	(step 1)
Less nil-rate band	£325,000	
	£608,081	(step 2)
Add back legacy to charity	£66,919	
Baseline amount	£675,000	(step 3)

The donated amount (£66,919) is less than 10% of the baseline (£67,500) so the estate does not qualify for the reduced rate when the legacy is grossed up at the full rate.

If the estate is grossed up at 36%, however, the calculations are as follows

Initial chargeable estate - as above (£245,000 + £679,500)	£924,500
Tax on initial estate (£924,500 - £325,000)@36%	£215,820
Gross up gifts at estate rate (£245,000 × (£924,500 ÷ (£924,500 - £215,820))	£319,611
Final residue (£1,000,000 - £319,611)	£680,389
Donated amount (£680,389@10%)	£68,039

Here, the value of the legacies is grossed up to £319,611. The value of the residue is not reduced by quite so much as when the legacies are grossed up at 40%, so the donated amount is slightly higher. The baseline calculation is as follows

Estate on death	£1,000,000	
Legacy to charity (donated amount)	-£68,039	
Chargeable transfer	£931,961	(step 1)
Less nil-rate band	-£325,000	
	£606,961	(step 2)
Add back legacy to charity	£68,039	
Baseline amount	675,000	(step 3)

The donated amount (£68,039) is now greater than 10% of the baseline (£67,500) so the estate qualifies for the reduced rate. The grossed up value of the legacies and the chargeable estate must be calculated using the 36% rate grossing calculator.

25.11 Interaction with BPR & APR

Para 6(2) sch 1A IHTA provides:

> For the purpose of calculating the donated amount, section 39A does not apply to a specific gift of property in relation to which section 23(1) applies (but that section does apply to such a gift for the purpose of calculating the baseline amount).

The IHT Manual gives an example:

> **IHTM45031: The charitable giving condition or 10% test: interaction** [Aug 2016]
>
> Where an estate component contains relievable property and the estate is also partially exempt because assets are passing to charity, it is necessary to apply the provisions of IHTA84/S39A to allocate the relief and exemptions correctly. Whilst this will often work in the taxpayer's favour by reducing - for IHT purposes - the amount of any chargeable specific legacies, it will also reduce the value of specific gifts left to charity. Without specific provision, this may mean that a component would fail the 10% test, because the value of the donated amount is reduced to a value that is less than 10% of the baseline.
>
> To avoid this happening, IHTA84/Sch1A/Para 6(2) disapplies IHTA/S39A so that, for the purposes of the 10% test, the value of a specific gift to charity shall be taken at its unreduced value. This restriction only applies to specific gifts to charity; all other specific gifts are reduced or relieved in the normal way. As with grossing up, (IHTM45030) it is important to recognise that there are two distinct stages:
>
> - firstly, working out whether or not the 10% test is met, and
> - secondly, calculating the chargeable estate and applying the appropriate rate of tax.
>
> If a specific legacy is worded in such a way that the amount of the charitable legacy must meet the 10% test (IHTM45003), the estate will qualify for the reduced rate. Once you have worked out what the figure for the legacy is, you can apply the interaction calculations for the purposes of calculating the chargeable estate in the normal way.
>
> **Example**
>
> Joanna died on 15 June 2012, leaving an estate valued at £1m after deduction of liabilities.
>
> Her Will leaves pecuniary legacies of
>
> £250,000 to her son, bearing its own tax, and
>
> £20,000 to the RNLI.
>
> The residue is left as to
>
> 5% to the Salvation Army and
>
> the remainder to her two daughters equally.
>
> It includes land qualifying for 100% agricultural relief valued at £200,000.

The HMRC analysis is as follows:

> The effect of interaction will normally be to reduce the value of the legacies and calculate the residue after deduction of the agricultural relief. However, in establishing the donated amount, but not the baseline amount, the legacy to the RNLI remains at £20,000.
>
> The interaction calculation for the purposes of the 10% test follows the normal process (IHTM26101)
>
> **Stage 1**
>
> The value transferred is £800,000; being the value of the estate less agricultural relief.
>
> **Stage 2**
>
> There are no specific gifts of relievable property
>
> **Stage 3**
>
> There is other relievable property that is not specifically given. There are specific gifts to charity and to the son which must be reduced by the IHTA84/S39 (4) fraction which is
>
> (£800,000 - nil) ÷ (£1,000,000 - nil) = 0.80 or 80%.
>
> The values of the gifts are reduced to:
>
> Charity: £20,000 × 80% = £16,000
>
> Son: £250,000 × 80% = £200,000
>
> **Stage 4**
>
> No grossing up is required
>
> **Stage 5**
>
> Calculate the residue using the reduced values

Value transferred	£800,000
Less reduced value of gifts	-£216,000
Residue	£584,000
Exempt share of residue (5%)	£29,200

> The donated amount, after interaction, is revised to £29,000 + £20,000 = £49,000
>
> The calculation of the baseline would then be

Estate on death	£1,000,000	
Less agricultural relief	-£200,000	
donated amount	-£49,200	
Chargeable transfer	£750,800	(step 1)
Less nil-rate band	-£325,000	
	£425,800	(step 2)
Add back donated amount	£49,200	
Baseline amount	£475,000	(step 3)

> The charitable giving condition (IHTM45002) or 10% test requires that the donated amount is at least 10% of the baseline amount or £47,500. At £49,200, the donated amount meets this test, so the estate qualifies for the reduced rate of 36%.
>
> If the estate had failed to meet the 10% test, the chargeable estate will be same, but tax is charged at 40%.

IHTM45032: Reduced rate for gifts to charity: the charitable giving condition or 10% test: example with two estate components, a lifetime cumulative total and where grossing up and interaction apply [Aug 2016]
Where both grossing up and interaction apply, the value of any specific gifts left free of tax will affect the calculation of the baseline and since interaction will reduce the value of those gifts before they are grossed up, it is necessary to go through the full set of calculations to arrive at both the baseline and the donated amount.

Example

Roland died on 15 September 2012, leaving an estate valued at £1.5m after deduction of liabilities. His cumulative total of lifetime transfers is £200,000.
His Will leaves legacies of

£300,000 to his son, free of tax,

Unlisted shares to his daughter, valued at £200,000 that qualify for 100% business relief, and

£35,000 to the Scout Association.

The residue is left as to

10% to the National Trust and

the remainder to his children equally.

It includes land that qualifies for 100% agricultural relief valued at £150,000. He is entitled to an interest in possession under his wife's Will valued at £700,000 which passes to his children absolutely.

The HMRC analysis is as follows:

The calculation taking both interaction and grossing up (IHTM26158) into account, is as follows.

Interaction stage 1

Calculate the value transferred after relief

Gross value of free estate	£1,500,000
Less business relief on shares	-£200,000
agricultural relief on land	-£150,000
Value transferred	£1,150,000

Interaction stage 2

There is one gift of relievable property; being the gift of shares to the daughter; this is taken at its value after relief at 100% or £0.

Interaction stage 3

There is other relievable property (the land), so the specific gift to the son must be reduced by the IHTA84/S39(4) fraction, although for the purposes of calculating the donated amount, the gift to the Scout Association remains at full value (IHTM45031). The fraction is based solely on the value of the Free Estate and ignores the cumulative total and settled property.
The fraction (IHTM26103) is
(£1,150,000 - nil) ÷ (£1,500,000 - £200,000)
So the value of gifts is reduced to:
Charity: £35,000 × (£1,150,000 ÷ £1,300,000) = 30,962
Son: £300,000 × (£1,150,000 ÷ £1,300,000) = £265,385

Interaction stage 4

The gift to the son is free of tax and so the reduced value of the gift must be grossed up. As these calculations are being performed to see whether the 10% test is being met, you should use the reduced rate grossing calculator (IHTM45030). The lifetime cumulative total is taken into account; but the settled property is ignored.

Grossing up stage 1

The legacy of £265,385 is grossed up at its own rate. The available nil-rate band is £125,000. The calculation is

Net value of legacy	£265,385
Less available nil-rate band	-£125,000
Excess over nil-rate band	£140,385
Gross up at (100 ÷ 64)	£219,352
Add back nil-rate band	£125,000
Initial grossed up value	£344,351

Grossing up stage 2

Initial determination of the chargeable part of the estate

Value of free estate after relief	£1,150,000
Less grossed up gift to son	-£344,351
unlisted shares to daughter	0
charitable legacy	-£30,962
Residue	£774,687
10% of residue is exempt	-£77,469
Chargeable residue	£697,218

Initial chargeable estate is £697,218 + £344,351 = £1,041,569.

Grossing up stage 3

The son's legacy at its reduced value of £265,385 is grossed up again at the rate appropriate to the initial chargeable estate taking the cumulative total of lifetime transfers into account and tax due at 36%.

Initial chargeable estate	£1,041,569
Tax on initial estate (£1,041,569 - £125,000)@36%	£329,965
Gross up legacy at estate rate (£265,385 × (£1,041,569 ÷ (£1,041,569 9 £328,965))	£388,442

Grossing up stage 4 & Interaction stage 5

Calculate the residue and chargeable estate

Value of free estate after relief	£1,041,569
Less gift to son	-£388,442
gift to charity	-£30,962
Residue	£730,596
Exempt share of residue (10%)	£73,060

The donated amount, after interaction, is revised to £73,060 + £35,000 = £108,060

The calculation of the baseline is then

Estate on death	£1,500,000
Business relief	-£200,000
Agricultural relief	-£150,000
Charitable legacies	-£108,060

Chargeable transfer	£1,041,940	(step 1)
Less apportioned nil-rate band	-£74,697	
	£967,243	(step 2)
Add back legacy to charity	£108,060	
Baseline amount	£1,075,303	(step 3)

The charitable giving condition (IHTM45002) or 10% test requires that the donated amount is at least 10% of the baseline amount or £107,530. At £108,060, the donated amount meets this test, so the estate qualifies for the reduced rate of 36%.

If the estate fails to qualify for the reduced rate, you should recalculate the position from scratch using the full rate grossing up calculator and reducing both chargeable and exempt specific legacies.

25.12 Abatement

The IHT Manual provides:

> **IHTM45033: Abatement: insufficient assets to pay legacies under the Will** [19 Aug 2016]
>
> Where there are insufficient assets in the estate to pay all the legacies bequeathed by Will, the legacies must abate in accordance with the general law (IHTM12086). Where this results in the value of a charitable legacy being reduced in value, you must use this reduced value for the charitable legacy for the purposes of the 10% test.
>
> **Example**
>
> R died on 14 June 2012 leaving an estate valued at £500,000 after deduction of liabilities.
>
> He left a specific bequest of an antique vase worth £120,000 to his daughter and legacies of £150,000 to each of his three sons. He left £20,000 to English Heritage and the residue to be divided between his four children equally.

The HMRC analysis is as follows:

> At first sight, the estate is likely to qualify for the reduced rate; the baseline is £175,000 and £20,000 exceeds the 10% test.
>
> However, R has left legacies totalling £590,000 and his net estate is only worth £500,000. Under the rules of abatement, his daughter receives her legacy of the vase, leaving legacies totalling £470,000 to be paid from an estate worth £380,000. As the legacies are all in the same class of legacy, they will abate rateably so the legacies to the sons will reduce to
>
> £150,000 × (£380,000 ÷ £470,000) = £121,277
>
> and the legacy to the charity will reduce to
>
> £20,000 × (£380,000 ÷ £470,000) = £16,170
>
> The abated value of the charitable legacy does not meet the 10% test, so the estate will not qualify for the reduced rate. In cases where abatement applies you should look carefully at the terms of any Instrument of Variation (IHTM35011) to ensure that abatement does not continue to apply, even after the Will has been varied.

IHTM45034: Reduced rate for gifts to charity: abatement: caused by grossing up [Jun 2016]
The value of the chargeable transfer cannot be more than the value of the estate for Inheritance Tax purposes, so where the grossed value of the estate exceeds that value, IHTA84/S37(2) applies, with the result that the grossed up value is reduced to the value of the estate as described at IHTM12088. You should use this value of the estate to calculate the baseline and apply the 10% test.

25.13 Interaction with quick succession relief

Section 141A IHTA provides:

> (1) This section applies if any part of the value transferred by the later transfer qualifies for the lower rate of tax in accordance with Schedule 1A.
> (2) The amount of the reduction made under section 141(1) is to be apportioned in accordance with this section.
> (3) For each qualifying component, the tax chargeable on so much of the value transferred by the later transfer as is attributable to property in that component ("the relevant part of the tax") is to be reduced by the appropriate proportion of the amount calculated in accordance with section 141(3).
> (4) "The appropriate proportion" is a proportion equal to the proportion that—
> (a) the relevant part of the tax, bears to
> (b) the tax chargeable on the value transferred by the later transfer as a whole.
> (5) If parts of an estate are treated under Schedule 1A as a single component, subsection (3) applies to the single component (and not to individual components forming part of the deemed single component).
> (6) If, after making the reductions required by subsection (3), there remains any part of the tax chargeable on the value transferred by the later transfer that has not been reduced, the remaining part of the tax is to be reduced by so much of the amount calculated in accordance with section 141(3) as has not been used up for the purposes of making the reductions required by subsection (3).
> (7) In this section—
> "component" means a component of the estate, as defined in paragraph 3 of Schedule 1A;
> "the later transfer" has the meaning given in section 141(1);
> "qualifying component" means a component (or deemed single component) for which the donated amount is at least 10% of the baseline amount, as determined in accordance with Schedule 1A.

The IHT Manual provides:

IHTM45050: Other issues: where the estate is entitled to Quick Succession Relief [Aug 2016]

FB12/Sch32/Para 7 inserts a new section 141A that deals with the application of QSR (IHTM22041) where an estate also qualifies for the reduced rate of tax.

Where there is only one estate component, QSR can be applied in the normal way as it is reducing the tax chargeable on the value transferred on death. And it may also be applied in the normal way where there is more than one component of the estate, but all the components are entitled to the reduced rate of tax as the apportionment of the relief by reference to the capital of the estate will produce the same result as that contained in IHTA84/S141A.

But, where the estate contains more than one component and at least one of the components does not qualify for the reduced rate, you must apportion the QSR as set out in IHTA84/S141A.

The reason for this is that QSR applies to reduce the tax chargeable on the value transferred on death, in other words, the tax chargeable on the aggregate estate. Where the reduced rate applies, the total tax chargeable will be lower than that at full rate. Normally QSR is apportioned by reference to the capital value of the components. If this went unchanged it would allow the qualifying component to have the benefit of the QSR it would be entitled to if it were paying tax at the full rate; when it is only paying tax at the reduced rate.

IHTA84/S141A (3) stipulates that for each qualifying component, the tax attributable to that component is to be reduced by the 'appropriate proportion' of the QSR that is due.

IHTA84/S141 (4) specifies that the appropriate proportion is the proportion that the tax attributable to the qualifying component bears to the tax chargeable on death as a whole. In other words, where an estate qualifies for both QSR and the reduced rate, the QSR attributable to each component must be apportioned by reference to the tax due on each component and not its capital value. The result is that the QSR allowed against the qualifying component reflects the fact that it is bearing a slightly smaller portion of the overall tax liability.

COMPASS will be amended so that QSR will be apportioned by reference to the tax payable by each component. Where the reduced rate does not apply, the end result will be the same; but where the reduced rate does apply, the relief will be correctly apportioned. You should continue to enter QSR in the normal way.

Example

Richard died on 14 November 2012 leaving an estate valued at £300,000 from which a legacy of £50,000 was due to charity.

His estate included joint property passing by survivorship valued at £500,000 and a life interest valued at £1,250,000.

His estate was entitled to QSR of £80,000.

The HMRC analysis is as follows:

The tax calculation is as follows

	General	Survivorship	Settled
Value of component	£300,000	£500,000	£750,000
Legacy to charity (donated amount)	-£50,000	0	0
Chargeable transfer	£250,000	£500,000	£750,000

Less proportion of nil-rate band		- £54,167	- £108,333	- £162,500
		£195,833	£391,667	£587,500
Add back charity exemption		£50,000		
		£245,833		
Baseline amount £24,583				
Tax @ 36%/40%		£70,500	£156,667	£235,000
Total tax	£462,167			

The normal calculation for QSR effectively apportions the £80,000 by reference to the capital value of the components. This would result in the following figures to reduce the tax.

General component £250,000 ÷ £1,500,000 × £80,000 = £13,333
Survivorship component £500,000 ÷ £1,500,000 × £80,000 = £26,667
Settled component £750,000 ÷ £1,500,000 × £80,000 = £40,000
So the tax payable by each component would be reduced as follows

Tax above	£70,500	£156,667	£235,000
QSR	-£13,333	-£26,667	-£40,000
Tax after QSR	£57,167	£130,000	£195,000

But as mentioned above, this allocates QSR between the components on the assumption that each component is bearing an equal proportion of the tax – when in fact the general component is benefiting from the reduced rate. The effect of IHTA84/S141A (3) is that the QSR of £80,000 must be apportioned by reference to tax payable by each component. The aggregate tax is £462,167, so the QSR is apportioned as to

General component	£70,500 ÷ £462,167 × £80,000 = £12,203
Survivorship component	£156,667 ÷ £462,167 × £80,000 = £27,119
Settled component	£235,000 ÷ £462,167 × £80,000 = £40,678

So the tax payable by each component would be reduced as follows

Tax above	£70,500	£156,667	£235,000
QSR	-£12,203	-£27,119	£40,678
Tax after QSR	£58,297	£129,548	£194,322

25.14 Woodland/conditional exemption

These topics are too specialist to be considered here, even in a book which seeks to be comprehensive. See IHTM45051 (charges arising following the deferral of tax for woodlands or conditional exemption).

25.15 Election to merge components

Para 7 sch 1A IHTA provides:

(1) An election may be made under this paragraph if, for a component of the estate, the donated amount is at least 10% of the baseline amount.
(2) That component is referred to as "the qualifying component".
(3) The effect of the election is that
  [a] the qualifying component and
  [b] one or more eligible parts of the estate (as specified in the

election)

are to be treated for the purposes of this Schedule as if they were a single component.

(4) Accordingly, if the donated amount for that deemed single component is at least 10% of the baseline amount for it, the property in that component is to be included in the part of TP that qualifies for the lower rate of tax.

Para 7(5) sch 1A IHTA defines "eligible part":

> In relation to the qualifying component—
>
> (a) each one of the other two components of the estate is an "eligible part" of the estate, and
>
> (b) all the property that forms part of the estate by virtue of section 102(3) of the FA 1986 (gifts with reservation) is also an "eligible part" of the estate.

The IHT Manual provides:

> **IHTM45035: Merger of components: aggregate estate contains two components** [Aug 2016]
>
> Where an estate contains more than one component and the donated amount at one of the components is at least 10% of its baseline, IHTA84/Sch1A/Para 7 provides an option for taxpayers to elect to merge two or more components and apply the 10% test as if there was a single component.
>
> For the purposes of merger only, property in which a reservation of benefit subsists may be merged with another component and qualify for the reduced where the 10% test is met.
>
> If the donated amount for the merged components is at least 10% of the baseline amount for that single/merged component, each of the individual components will qualify for the reduced rate. This option is most likely to be relevant where the beneficiaries of the different components of an estate are the same, or largely the same. Note that the merger is only for the purposes of the 10% test and does not otherwise alter the value of the components concerned. In other words, the share of the residue passing to charity remains at the figure calculated by reference to the bequests in the Will, you do not revise the share of residue passing to charity by reference to the merged estate - because that does not reflect what the charity will receive.
>
> The process for making an election is explained at IHTM45041.

The first example is an estate with two components (general and survivorship):

Example

Following the example at IHTM45012,[30] Andrew agrees with the deceased's personal representatives that they will make an election to merge the survivorship component with the general component.

Merged estate	£780,000	
Legacy to charity (donated amount)	-£75,000	
Chargeable transfer	£705,000	(step 1)
Less nil-rate band	£325,000	
	£380,000	(step 2)
Add back legacy to charity	£75,000	
Baseline amount	£455,000	(step 3)

The baseline amount for the merged component is £45,500 and the legacy of £75,000 clearly exceeds this amount; both components will therefore qualify for the reduced rate. As mentioned above, the share of the reside remains at £75,000 and is not increased to £78,000 (being 10% of the merged estate).

The liability attributable to the survivorship component will be reduced from £6,468 to £5,821.20.

The reader is invited to consider whether the £650 IHT saving would cover the costs involved.

The next example is an estate with three components:

IHTM45036: Reduced rate for gifts to charity: merger of components: aggregate estate contains three components [Aug 2016]

Where an estate contains three components, the taxpayers may elect (IHTM45039) to merge any combination of the components to make the best use of the reduced rate that is available. The principles remain the same as those given in IHTM45012 and IHTM45035 and you will need to combine those principles when looking to see if the 10% test is met.

Example

Following the example in IHTM45012, in addition to her estate of £750,000 and the joint bank account of £30,000, E was also the life tenant under her husband's Will Trust. The trust fund was valued at £300,000 and on E's death the trust funds were to be paid as to £20,000 to the RSPCA and the balance to her daughter Jane.

Without an election, the IHT position is as follows

	General	Survivorship	Settled	
Value of component	£750,000	£30,000	£300,000	
Charity legacy (donated amount)	-£75,000	0	-£20,000	
Chargeable transfer	£675,000	£30,000	£280,000	(step 1)
Less proportion of NRB	-£222,716	-£9,898	-£92,386	
	£452,284	£20,102	187,614	(step 2)
Add back legacy to charity	£75,000	0	£20,000	
Baseline amount	£527,284	£20,102	£207,614	(step 3)

30 See the example of Elizabeth at 25.7.2 (Estate with 2 or 3 components).

To qualify for the reduced rate, the donated amount must be equal to or exceed £52,728 for the general component - which it does - and £20,761 for the settled component, which it does not.

As not all of the donated amount has been 'used' by the general component, the taxpayers have the option of merging one or both of the non-qualifying components with the general component. They will need to test the consequences of the election and be confident that the value of the assets comprising each component are unlikely to alter significantly before deciding which components to merge - although it possible to withdraw an election (IHTM45041) or use an Instrument of variation to make a additional charitable bequest should the asset values alter unexpectedly.

The personal representatives agree with the trustees and Andrew to merge all three components, in which case the baseline calculation for the 10% test will be

Merged estate	£1,080,000	
Legacy to charity (donated amount)	-£95,000	
Chargeable transfer	£985,000	(step 1)
Less nil-rate band	-£325,000	
	£660,000	(step 2)
Add back legacy to charity	£95,000	
Baseline amount	£755,000	(step 3)

The baseline amount for the merged component is £75,500 and the donated amount for the merged component is £95,000. The 10% test is met and all three components qualify for the reduced rate.

IHTM45037: Reduced rate for gifts to charity: merger of components: where grossing up and interaction apply [Jun 2016]

Where an election has been made to merge two or more components, the merger is only for the purposes of establishing which components might qualify for the reduced rate. It does not have the effect of merging titles, for example, in terms of calculating the value of a share of residue (IHTM45035) nor does it affect the rule that titles are treated separately for the purposes of grossing up and interaction.

You should continue to perform the appropriate calculations to arrive at the chargeable value for each individual component, then

- merge the relevant components,
- calculate the baseline for the merged estate, and
- test the total sum passing against the baseline for the merged estate to see if the 10% test is met.

The effect of an election under para 7 may be to *remove* entitlement to the relief. For instance, an estate with:

Survivorship property:	100
General component:	100
Total estate	200

Assume for simplicity that the nil rate band has been used, so these figures equal the baseline amounts.

If there is a gift of £10 to charity, the general component qualifies for relief. But if an election is made to merge the two components of the estate, neither component qualifies for the relief. This is why the consent of the executors is needed to make the election.

25.15.1 *Who makes merger election*

Para 7 sch 1A IHTA provides:

> (6) The election must be made by all those who are appropriate persons with respect to the qualifying component and each of the eligible parts to be treated as a single component.
> (7) "Appropriate persons" means—
> (a) with respect to the survivorship component, all those to whom the property in that component passes on D's death (or, if they have subsequently died, their personal representatives),
> (b) with respect to the settled property component, the trustees of all the settled property in that component,
> (c) with respect to the general component, all the personal representatives of D or, if there are none, all those who are liable for the tax attributable to the property in that component, and
> (d) with respect to property within paragraph (b) of subparagraph (5) [GWR property], all those in whom the property within that paragraph is vested when the election is to be made.

25.15.2 *Should parties agree to elect*

The STEP model clause[31] provides:

> I hereby confer on my executors the power in their absolute discretion to make or withdraw an election under paragraph 7 of Schedule 1A IHTA in relation to any other eligible part of my estate whether or not the general component is the qualifying component and to make or withdraw an election under paragraph 8 of that Schedule.

That does no harm, but the power must be implied.

There may be interesting negotiations if the parties making the election are acting at arm's length. Any party is able to veto the election and so prevent the extended relief. There are many permutations, but in general, where an election is beneficial to one party, electing is likely to be neutral for the other parties.

---

31 See 25.17.1 (STEP clause).

Suppose an estate with a general component and a survivorship component, where the gift to charity is sufficient to qualify both components for legacy relief, if an election is made.[32] IHT on the survivor's component is reduced if the PRs agree to make the election. If the survivor is not a beneficiary of the estate, the PRs may reasonably demand some of the tax saving (unless the will directs otherwise).

Suppose:

(1) H dies and his estate is held on trust for W for life, remainder to charity.

(2) W dies and her estate passes to her children so her estate is subject to IHT.

IHT on W's free estate is in principle reduced if the trustees of H's will trust agree to make the election. In principle a fair deal may be that W's PRs pay half the tax saving to the charity. The trustees of H's will trust must act in the interests of their beneficiaries. They should not act gratuitously in favour of W, unless:

(1) the charity consents (which might be possible if the charity senses a public relations or goodwill downside) or

(2) the Will of H directs them to do so.

The same issue could arise in another way, if:

(1) H dies and his estate is held on trust for W for life, remainder to non-charitable beneficiaries..

(2) W dies and her estate passes to charity.

In this case IHT on H's will trust is in principle reduced if the PRs of W agree to make the election. In principle a fair deal may be that the trustees of H's will trust pay half the tax saving to the charity. The PRs of W must act in the interest of the charity. They should not act gratuitously in favour of W, unless:

(1) the charity consents (which might be possible if the charity senses a public relations or goodwill downside) or

(2) the Will of W directs them to do so.

25.15.3 *Time limit for election*

Para 9 sch 1A IHTA provides:

> (1) An election under this Schedule must be made by notice in writing

---

32 As in the example of Elizabeth, see 25.7.2 (Estate with 2 or 3 components).

> to HMRC within two years after D's death.
> (2) An election under this Schedule may be withdrawn by notice in writing to HMRC given—
> (a) by all those who would be entitled to make such an election, and
> (b) no later than the end of the period of two years and one month after D's death.

That is not usually long enough to agree values.

> (3) An officer of Revenue and Customs may agree in a particular case to extend the time limit in sub-paragraph (1) or (2)(b) by such period as the officer may allow.

The IHT Manual provides:

> **IHTM45044: Elections: late claims** [Jun 2016]
> Under IHTA84/Sch1A/Para 9(3), an officer of Revenue & Customs has the discretion to admit a late claim for either an election to merge components (IHTM45035) or to opt out of the reduced rate (IHTM45040). The circumstances in which you may admit a late claim are the same as for a late claim to TNRB and you should follow the guidance at IHTM43009.

25.16 Opt out of IHT legacy relief

Para 8 sch 1A IHTA provides:

> (1) If an election is made under this paragraph in relation to a component of the estate, this Schedule is to apply as if the donated amount for that component were less than 10% of the baseline amount for it (whether or not it actually is).
> (2) The election must be made by all those who are appropriate persons (as defined in paragraph 7(7)) with respect to the component.

The IHT Manual provides:

> **IHTM45040: Elections: election to opt out** [Jun 2016]
> There may be circumstances where the administrative costs, such as valuing assets, outweigh the benefit of the reduced rate of tax. An example might be where an item of land is specifically bequeathed to charity. Whilst there is no need for a precise value to be agreed before the item is exempt from IHT, it will be necessary to agree a value to see whether or not the 10% test is met.
> For this reason IHTA84/Sch1A/Para 8 contains an option for the taxpayers to elect for the estate component concerned to be treated as if the donated amount for the component is less than 10% of the baseline

amount, whether or not it actually is.
Where such an election is made, the component concerned is subject to Inheritance Tax at the full 40% rate.
The process for making an election is explained at IHTM45041.

In practice we doubt if a para 8 election will ever be made.

25.17 Will drafting

25.17.1 *STEP clause*

STEP have published the following model clause:[33]

> I give [name of charity] such a sum as together with any other gifts to charity made under my will or any codicil shall constitute a donated amount equal to ten per cent (10%)[34] of the baseline amount in relation to the general component of my estate.

We refer to this as the **"legacy relief formula"**.

Further thought is needed for an estate holding property qualifying for business or agricultural property relief, because the attribution rules may have unexpected results and there are too many uncertainties as to what the figure will be. The best solution for estates of this kind is a discretionary will trust of the entire estate or at least of the business/agricultural property.

In relation to a simple estate (with no survivorship property and no settled property components) the legacy relief formula will result in a legacy of between 0% and 10% of the net estate:

(1) The legacy will be zero when the baseline amount is zero, which will be:
  (a) if the estate is within the available nil rate band (allowing for transferrable NRB) or
  (b) if the estate (apart from the NRB) qualifies for the IHT spouse exemption.
(2) The legacy will be 10% of the estate if the NRB is not available (due to a failed PET) and the entire estate is otherwise chargeable (ie no

33 STEP UK Technical Committee "Model Clause Where 10 Per Cent Or More of An Estate is Left to Charity: Reduced Rate of Inheritance Tax" (August 2013) *http://www.step.org/sites/default/files/Policy/Model_Clause_August_2013_updated_8.8.2013.pdf*
This is a revised version of the first draft published February 2012. I have slightly amended the model clause for clarity of exposition.

34 The drafting style of giving words and figures is not recommended.

spouse exemption).

STEP offers an alternative clause which includes the survivorship component:

> I give [name of charity] such a sum as, together with any other gifts to charity made under my will or any codicil and also any property passing to charity forming part of such of the survivorship component and settled property component as are comprised in my estate, shall constitute a donated amount equal to ten per cent (10%) of the baseline amount in relation to the aggregate of the general component and [survivorship component] [and] [settled property component] [and reservation of benefit property][35] of my estate.

The legacy relief formula is now less predictable. It is still the case that the legacy could be zero. However there is no maximum. The legacy under the formula may amount to the entire free estate. In other words, the use of the formula will in some cases wholly disinherit other beneficiaries of the will in favour of the charity.

The safe course is not to use the survivorship component in the formula. The scope for disaster is too great. If the individual holds joint property, and wants IHT legacy relief, the better course is to sever the joint tenancy during the lifetime of the individual (so individual's share of the property passes by will.)

Similarly, great care is needed if the formula includes the settled property component.

The STEP clause partly addresses these uncertainties with an optional clause which sets a maximum and minimum amount:

> 1.6. The legacy given by this clause shall in no event:
> 1.6.1 be less than £[•] whether or not the lower rate of tax shall be applicable.
> 1.6.2 exceed £[•] (the upper limit) even if in consequence of this restriction in the value of this legacy the lower rate of tax shall not apply.
>
> If this proviso shall apply and in consequence the lower rate of tax shall not be payable the amount of this legacy shall
> [be equal to the amount of the upper limit] *Or*
> [be reduced to £ •] *Or*
> [lapse].

---

35 It will rarely if ever be the case that the testator is aware of reservation of benefit property, and the words in these brackets should not be used.

Another issue is if the law changes. STEP add a provision to address that:

> 1.2 If relief under Schedule 1A Inheritance Tax Act 1984 (IHTA) shall have been abolished at the time of my death or if inheritance tax shall have been abolished at that time this legacy shall instead of the amount specified in clause 1.1 above be a sum equal to [ ] per cent ([ ]%) of the residue of my estate.

For a recommended clause, see Kessler & John, *Drafting Trusts and Will Trusts* (14th ed, 2019), para 18.25 (Will providing accommodation for relative or cohabitee; residue to spouse or charity).

25.17.2 *HMRC on STEP clause*

The IHT Manual provides:

> **IHTM45008: Charitable giving condition: charitable legacy worded to meet the 10% test** [Aug 2016]
> To avoid the need to continually revise charitable legacies in Wills, a clause may be worded so that a specific legacy to charity will always meet the 10% test. An example is given below and where such wording is used, you can accept that a specific legacy to charity will always meet the 10% test. You should look carefully at clauses where the reduced rate is used but the wording of the clause is different in any way from that shown below, to ensure that the correct effect is given to the wording used.
> **Example**
>
> > I give to [name of charity] such a sum as shall constitute a donated amount equal to 10 (or larger figure) per cent (%) of the baseline amount in relation to the [general component] [aggregate of the general, [survivorship], [settled property] components and [reservation of benefit property]] of my estate.
> > The legacy given by this clause shall in no event:
> > (i) be less than £nn whether or not the lower rate of tax shall be applicable; and
> > (ii) exceed £nn (the upper limit) even if in consequence of this restriction in the value of the legacy the lower rate shall not apply. [If this proviso shall apply and in consequence the lower rate of tax shall not be payable, the amount of this legacy shall [be equal to the amount of the upper limit] [be reduced to £nn] [lapse]].
>
> The clause may include other administrative provisions, but the essential wording to qualify for the reduced rate is that shown above. It follows from the wording of this clause that the amount of the legacy may not

be known until the value of the estate is settled and the amount of charity exemption will change as the value of the estate changes.
The Society of Trust and Estate Practitioners has developed a model clause for Wills. ...
The first paragraph of the clause ensures that the charitable legacy will meet the requirements for the reduced rate. The legacy is set by the reference to the components of the estate listed; but this only fixes the size of the legacy to be paid under the Will - it does not override the requirement for those liable for the tax at the different components to elect for the components to be merged before other components can benefit from the reduced rate.
Proviso (i) ensures that even if the estate is not liable to Inheritance Tax, the legacy is still payable to the charity. Proviso (ii) ensures that charitable legacy does not exceed a fixed amount, even though that may mean the estate does not qualify for the reduced rate.

The IHT Manual gives a worked example:

IHTM45013: Calculating the baseline amount: where the charitable legacy is worded to meet the 10% test [Aug 2016]
Where a charitable legacy is worded to ensure the 10% test is met (IHTM45008), the calculation of the amount of the legacy will be straightforward where there is only one component in the estate. Following the example at IHTM45010, the charitable legacy will be £42,500. If the value of the estate changes, you will need to recalculate the charitable legacy with each change.
But, where there is more than one component to the estate, you should use the charitable legacy calculator to establish the extent of the charitable legacy. The calculator reflects the fact the baseline amount – of which 10% will be left to charity – will vary depending on the allocation of the nil-rate band between the components of the estate. And that in turn depends on the proportion that each component bears to the aggregate estate.
Example (Thomas)
T died on 17 August 2012 leaving an estate valued at £800,000 after deduction of liabilities. His Will contained a clause which left a legacy to the National Trust equal to the amount that is necessary to qualify for the reduced rate.
He was left a life interest in £250,000 under the Will of his wife.

This is not a tax efficient will: T should have left a life interest in the entire estate to his wife. But that does not affect the example.
The HMRC analysis is as follows:

The estate contains two components, a settled component and a general component. The donated amount in the general component ensures that this component will qualify for the reduced rate; the settled component passes to T's' children under his wife's Will trust so it does not qualify. The charitable legacy calculator generates a value for the donated amount at £55,671. The calculations for each component are as follows

Estate on death	£800,000	
Legacy to charity (donated amount)	-£55,671	
Chargeable transfer	£744,329	(step 1)
Less proportion of nil-rate band[36]	-£243,287	
	£501,042	(step 2)
Add back legacy to charity	£55,671	
Baseline amount[37]	£556,713	(step 3)

Tax at 36% = £180,375.12

The tax on the settled component will be

Chargeable transfer	£250,000
Less proportion of nil-rate band[38]	- £81,713
	£168,287

Tax at 40% = £67,314.80

Thus the nil rate band is partly set against property subject to 36% IHT and partly against property subject to 40% IHT. There is a planning point here. If the interest in possession were terminated shortly before death, it would use up the nil rate band so the nil rate band would more effectively be set against 40% IHT property.

25.18 Instrument of Variation

Charity legacy relief is wholly lost if the donated amount does not meet the 10% test. This was deliberate:

> 1.18 Because the benefit of the reduced IHT rate will be dependent on whether or not the amount of the charitable legacy is sufficient for the estate to pass the 10% test there will be a "cliff edge" effect. Where the amount of the charitable legacy is close to the critical 10% point, a small difference to the amount of the legacy could have a much larger impact on the estate's IHT liability. There are no plans to apply any taper or other mechanism to mitigate this.[39]

---

36 744,329 ÷ (744,329 + 250,000) × 325,000 = £243,287

37 556,713 × 10% = £55,671

38 250,000 ÷ (744,329 + 250,000) × 325,000 = £81,713

39 HMRC Consultation Document, "A new incentive for charitable legacies" (2011).

In this situation, deeds of variation[40] have two particular uses:

(1) If an estate makes a charitable gift of slightly below the 10% requirement, a deed of variation can in principle put the matter right and save tax for the residuary legatees in excess of the additional amount given to charities.

(2) The deed will be useful where values are unclear towards the end of the two year period, to ensure that (whatever values are agreed) the relief is applicable. In practice (especially in larger estates) precise values will often not be agreed within two years so it may be unclear whether or not a gift of a specified amount passes the 10% test. In such a case an instrument of variation making the gift to the charity under the legacy relief formula would be advisable, as it avoids the valuation uncertainties (and reduces the amount at stake in a valuation dispute).

HMRC approves of this planning. The IHT Manual provides:

> **IHTM45039: Merger of components: merger following an Instrument of Variation** [Jun 2016]
> An Instrument of Variation can be used to alter the disposition of an estate by:
> - increasing an existing charitable legacy or
> - making a new gift to charity
>
> so that an estate component will qualify for the reduced rate. As shown in the example at IHTM45011[41] the circumstances of an estate may be such that only a small increase in the amount being left to charity is necessary for the component to be eligible for the reduced rate, with the resulting repayment more than offsetting the additional charitable legacy.
> If a beneficiary varies their entitlement so that another component will be able to benefit from the reduced rate, the provisions of s.142(3) [IHTA] will not normally apply as the variation is only bringing about an extra reduction in tax over and above the reduction that would already arise through an increase in the amount qualifying for charity exemption.
> (This content has been withheld because of exemptions in the Freedom of Information Act 2000)

It is correct that s.142(3) IHTA does not apply; the correct reason is that the IHT saving is not "consideration" for the variation.

---

40 See 29.1 (Variation of wills: Introduction).

41 See 25.7 (HMRC examples).

25.19 Administration

HMRC provide an online charitable legacy calculator.[42] We recommend that this is not relied on, particularly in more complex cases.

The IHT Manual provides:

> **IHTM45001: Introduction and conditions: introduction** [Jun 2016]
> ... A new schedule to form IHT400 – IHT430 – will be designed to help taxpayers gather the correct values to calculate whether the charitable giving condition is met, and to reflect the reduced rate when calculating the tax due on delivery of form IHT400.
> An on-line charitable legacy calculator has been developed and is available on the HMRC website. Taxpayers are encouraged to use this calculator, to print out the results sheet and send it to us with form IHT430 when they deliver their account.

25.20 Charity legacy relief: Critique

25.20.1 *Cost of relief*

The consultation paper estimated the cost (lost IHT) as rising to £170m p/a. Any estimate is guesswork[43] but even though that figure seems much too high[44] the figure is certainly substantial.

25.20.2 *Tax complication*

As tends to happen in tax, the idea is simple but its implementation is not. HMRC themselves had to issue a revised consultation paper because of errors in the first version.[45]

---

42 *https://www.gov.uk/inheritance-tax-reduced-rate-calculator*

43 The consultation paper makes the point more tactfully: the impact assessment "is based on a number of assumptions about how people will respond to the new charitable legacy incentive. These include the extent and speed of take-up."

44 The IHT yield in 2009/10 was £2.5 billion. A general reduction in IHT rates from 40% to 36% would only cost £250m; but even the most extreme forecasts should not anticipate 10% incentive relief having anything like that effect. This seems to be a widely held view. HMRC, "A new incentive for charitable legacies A lower rate of inheritance tax when leaving 10% of an estate to charity Summary of Responses", (December 2011) para 2.3 provides: "Many respondents thought that the impact assessment overstated the likely numbers of estates to be affected, the expected take up and additional revenue for charities."

45 HMRC What's New 16 June 2011: "An updated version of this consultation document ... has been published. This version revises example 7 to correct an error in the calculation."

The anomalies - and need for tax planning - are obvious.

25.20.3 *Evaluation*

The object of the relief is to encourage increased testamentary giving to charities. It is therefore relevant to ask whether the scheme will actually have this effect. There has been no research or evidence to suggest that it will: that has been assumed as self-evident.

The view that the relief will have a very significant effect on testamentary charitable giving seems to us implausible.

There are various categories of testator:

(1) Those who already give 10% of their net estate to charity. The new relief does not encourage them to give more.
(2) Those who give 4% or more of their net estate to charity. The relief pays for charity gifts to be upped to reach the 10% limit, and where the testator has not done so, well advised beneficiaries will do the same by deed of variation. The non-charitable beneficiaries will gain by the increase.
(3) Those who give just under 4% of their net estate to charity. The relief will strongly encourage the gift to be upped to reach the 10% limit as the marginal cost of doing so is very low
(4) The important category - the largest - is those who give nothing or significantly less than 4% of the net estate to charity. Will significant numbers of testators increase their charitable giving (presumably up to 10% of the net estate) because of the relief? Those who support the relief must argue that they will. There is no evidence to support that claim and we think it is implausible. The small reduction in the IHT rate is not sufficient to have much impact on the thinking of a rational well informed testator. The factors which influence testamentary behaviour are of course not exclusively rational. The relief may assist legacy fundraising by charities. On the other hand, there may be some who would otherwise have given 10% of their residuary estate who reduce the gift to 10% of the baseline amount, or some who would otherwise have given more than 10%. It is a matter of speculation. A thorough study in a few years time might be able to suggest some answers, though the difficulty of untangling the many causative factors involved means that the answer may never be known.

In assessing the effect of the relief there are other important factors:

(1) In 2015-16 of 588,000 deaths only 4.2% (or 24,500) of estates were

liable to IHT.[46] For the 97%, the relief is in principle[47] of no importance.

(2) Testators (except those with a short life expectancy) may reasonably question whether the relief will still be in existence at the time of their death.

(3) Where the relief is in point, the amounts involved are trivial and out of proportion to the complexity of the relief and the costs.

(4) The relief will sometimes encourage charitable giving to be postponed. Suppose H and W each intended to give between 5% (or any amount less than 10%) of a baseline amount to charity. They would do better to give the entire estate to the survivor, so the survivor could make a gift qualifying for 10% incentive relief. In fact it will never be appropriate for a married couple to make a charity legacy on the first death. Thus the consequence of the relief is to encourage married testators to postpone giving to charity (and of course incurring the risk that the second gift may not be made). The same will generally apply to unmarried cohabitees, because of the nil rate band.

It should not be thought that the cost of the relief to the Revenue (supposedly £170m p/a) equals additional money brought in to charities. The benefit of the relief will enure firstly to non-charitable beneficiaries,[48] secondly to lawyers drafting deeds of variation, thirdly to lawyers suing lawyers who fail to draft deeds of variation, but not to any great extent to charities.

An evaluation of the new relief also raises the more general question of the merits of using the tax system not to raise tax but to influence behaviour. The generally accepted principles of good tax design are:

---

46 HMRC Inheritance Tax Statistics 2015 to 2016 *https://assets.publishing.service.gov.uk/government/uploads/system/uploads/attachment_data/file/731610/Inheritance_Tax_National_Statistics_Commentary.pdf*

47 For completeness: the relief would matter if someone wrongly considered that they might fall within the scope of IHT. The relief might also be regarded as an exhortation addressed to those outside the scope of IHT, but it seems implausible to suppose that that will have much effect.

48 Economists distinguish formal and effective incidence of taxation. For instance the formal incidence of excise duty and VAT is on the supplier but the economic burden may rest on the consumer (who pays higher prices). The same applies in the case of tax reliefs. Here the formal incidence of the relief is enjoyed by the non-charitable beneficiaries and to a large extent so is the effective incidence.

equity, simplicity and administrative workability. All of these are infringed. However even those who are inclined to approve in principle of the use of tax law to motivate behaviour, rather than to raise tax, may conclude that this particular relief is a foolish gimmick.

Charity tax is vulnerable to this sort of tinkering. No doubt it is well meant, though it also reflects the Government's need for a good headline. Another example was SA donate, which also cost more in administration than it brought to charities.[49] Before then we had Millennium Gift Aid relief, which at least raised a laugh in Parliament when the chancellor announced its abolition.[50]

The reader may recall that at the same time as the new relief commenced, the Government proposed a cap on Gift Aid relief,[51] which, had it passed, would have had a much more negative effect on charitable giving than IHT legacy relief.

25.20.4 *HMRC consultation*

The professional bodies response to the consultation was uniformly negative. CIOT said:

> We object to the proposals ... Our objections are:
> - The proposals are complex and run entirely counter to the tax policy objective of simplification;
> - The Consultation process is flawed: it fails to meet the criteria set out in the Tax Consultations Framework;
> - By giving an effective 76% relief from IHT, the proposals may act as a perverse disincentive to lifetime giving;
> - The Consultation completely ignores the burden of additional valuation and compliance costs, which any estate around the 10% threshold will be forced to bear...[52]

The Law Society:

> The Law Society is not convinced that the proposal will encourage

---

49 See the 8th edition of this work para 16.46 (SA donate: giving in tax return).

50 "This Budget abolishes millennium Gift Aid relief which we won't need for another 989 years;" (George Osborne, budget speech 2011). (The relief was not in fact abolished in the budget, it had lapsed some years earlier; but there was no need for that to spoil the joke.)

51 See 1.4.3 (Cap on Gift Aid).

52 CIOT response to consultation paper *http://www.tax.org.uk/Resources/CIOT/Documents/2011/08/Charity_legacies_CIOT.pdf*

> testamentary charitable giving and believes that the administrative burden and the amount of cost involved for HMRC, practitioners and therefore private clients and charities in implementing workable changes to the IHT system may outweigh the perceived benefit of supporting philanthropy.[53]

STEP:

> ... we are aware of a number of concerns that have been raised in relation to the approach adopted. These include the concern that to introduce a new, and possibly complex relief runs counter to the policy being taken forward by the Office of Tax Simplification in rationalising and abolishing reliefs. It has also been suggested that a more effective and indeed simpler way of assisting charities would be to provide for some form of relief such as transitional relief compensating charities for the reduced ability to reclaim tax following the reduction of the basic rate of income tax. There is some force in these comments for which we have sympathy.

ICAEW:

> 10. We support the government's desire to encourage charitable giving, although as a matter of principle we consider that the tax system should be used to raise revenue rather than influence behaviour because using the tax system in this way tends to introduce grey areas and therefore complexity. Leaving aside our reservations, we think that there is a better way of using the IHT system to encourage charitable legacies than the proposals in the condoc which are regressive once the charitable legacy exceeds the 10% threshold and although the proposals in the condoc might nudge people into increasing gifts to charities to the 10% threshold, they may nudge those who contemplated giving above the 10% threshold into giving less.[54]

HMRC summarised:

> Overall ... the responses were broadly supportive of the new incentive.[55]

It is disappointing (an uncharitable commentator would use a stronger expression) to see the professional bodies views (mis)treated in this way.

Charity legacy relief has been defended on grounds that anything that

53 Law Society (2011) *http://www.lawsociety.org.uk*

54 ICAEW Tax Faculty response (2011) *http://www.icaew.com*

55 HMRC, "A new incentive for charitable legacies A lower rate of inheritance tax when leaving 10% of an estate to charity Summary of Responses", (2011) para 2.2.

assists charitable giving is helpful. From the point of view of charities, that is the case, which no doubt explains the welcome that charities have given to the relief. But a consultation is not a poll, and it is not the case that anything that assists charitable giving is helpful. The benefit must be set against the cost.

25.20.5 *Misselling the relief*

The Law Society make an interesting point:

> 41. The Law Society is concerned that over publicising the new rules will result in it being inappropriately targeted to intending testators for whom the new rules are not applicable which will create more work for solicitors in explaining to intending testators why the new rule will not apply to their estate.[56]

25.20.6 *The future*

In the 2017/19 edition we said:

> If studies are carried out in a few years time we expect they will justify the comments of the professional bodies. Hopefully then the charity legacy relief will be scrapped.

But it has not happened, and perhaps never will.

56 Law Society Response to consultation (2011) *http://www.lawsociety.org.uk*

CHAPTER TWENTY SIX

WILL DRAFTING

26.1 IT + IHT relief on gift by Will

On this topic see 28.4 (Obtaining IHT and IT reliefs on gift by will).

26.2 Residue to charity, provision for spouse[1]

A testator may wish their estate to pass to charity after the death of their spouse if they survives them. The Will should direct their estate to be held on trust for their widow or widower for life, with remainder to the charity. There is no inheritance tax charge on the death of the testator, by virtue of the spouse exemption (s.18 IHTA).[2] There is no tax on the death of the spouse, as the charity exemption will then apply.

It may be possible to arrange that the charity bear some of the costs of the upkeep of the testator's estate, during the lifetime of the widow: see 30.6 (Provision for relative/dependant: Lifetime planning).

---

1 References here to spouse include a civil partner (who for tax purposes is treated the same way as a spouse).

2 The spouse exemption does not apply where the testator is, and the spouse is not, domiciled in the United Kingdom. For this situation, see Kessler, *Taxation of Non-Residents and Foreign Domiciliaries* (21st ed., 2022-23), Chapter 91 (Non-Dom-Non-Resident Spouse) online version *https://www.foreigndomiciliaries.co.uk*

It would often be advisable to give the trustees power to apply trust capital (as well as income) for the spouse's benefit (even though to do this would reduce the amount left for the charity). The spouse might find herself in need of the capital.

26.3 Residue to charity, provision for dependant relative

A testator may wish their estate to pass to charity, subject to provision for the lifetime of a relative or a dependant other than their spouse.

The obvious course is to use the same approach as in the case of the charitable Will with provision for surviving spouse. That is, to draft the Will to provide for the estate to be held on trust for the relative for life, with remainder to the charity after her death. This is in principle expensive in tax terms. There would then be an IHT charge on the death of the testator. Tax would be charged on the entire value of their estate. No charity tax relief is given at the time of their death, because the gift to the charity does not take place until the death of the relative.[3]

What can be done? Different considerations apply, depending whether the testator is dealing with a fund of investments, or a residence.

26.3.1 *Investments*

Ideally, the testator would split their money or investments into two separate funds:

(i) One fund would be given to the relative (or to trustees to hold on suitable trusts for her benefit). This fund would be sufficiently large to provide for the relative for the rest of her life.[4]

(ii) The remaindser of the testator's money or investments would be given to the charity.

The first fund would bear IHT on the testator's death. (The tax charge would need to be taken into account in ascertaining how much to give. It is possible but difficult to arrange that tax be borne out of the charity's share; see 27.1 (The *Benham* problem). The second fund would, however, qualify for IHT relief on the testator's death.

Now, this division is well enough in theory: but in practice, when the

---

3 For the possibility of an IoV where the relative dies within two years of the testator, see 29.4 (Gift to L for life, remainder to charity: Variation to charity).

4 In practice, the funds might advantageously be used to purchase an income tax efficient annuity; that is a question of investment and should not be dealt with in the Will.

testator writes their Will, they will not often know what should be the relative size of these two shares. That will depend on values, rates of tax and life expectancies at the time of the death.

The best solution in cases of this kind is to create a short-term discretionary will trust of the investments, under s.144 IHTA. This would enable the precise distribution between the relative and the charity to be determined up to two years after the death of the testator;[5] and the inheritance tax relief will remain available on the funds given directly to charity.

Even when this is done, the estate will still suffer the inheritance tax charge on the relative's share of the investments; so when the amounts involved are sufficiently substantial, consideration should be given to lifetime tax planning, which is considered at 24.30 (Fund for dependant, then charity).

26.3.2 *Dwelling-house*

Suppose the testator owns a dwelling-house which must be retained for the relative for his or her life, but is then intended to pass to the charity. What can be done here?

The obvious course – to give the relative a life interest in the property – results in an inheritance tax charge on the death of the testator.

The position is no better if the relative is given, by Will, a lease of the property, even at a market rent. In order to claim inheritance tax relief, it is necessary to give the entire interest in the property to the charity: see 24.17 (Entire interest rule).

One simple course is to put the house into a two-year discretionary Will trust. In that case, at least if the individual dies within two years of the testator, charity relief can be obtained. If the relative survives the two years, inheritance tax on the value of the property cannot be avoided. (In administering the estate, care must taken to ensure that the discretionary Will trust does not come to a premature end. See SP 10/79. A full discussion of that contentious Statement of Practice is outside the scope of this book; but a lease to the relative at a nominal rent will normally solve the problem.)

Another solution was first suggested at a Key Haven conference by Christopher McCall QC. This is to give the relative a cash sum (free of IHT) of a value equal to a lease for her life, with appropriate provisions to

5 But not within three months of the death: *Frankland v IRC* [1997] STC 1450.

enable the relative, or trustees for her, to purchase a lease for life from the executors. Care would be needed with the drafting.

26.4 Residue to charity, provision within nil rate band

Another approach would be to give an amount to a relative which uses up the available nil rate band and the residue to charity. Such an arrangement, if drafted properly, can result in no IHT being payable at all. It has occasionally been suggested that this kind of planning could be classified as tax avoidance, since it reduces the IHT due to nil, but this is manifestly not the case – it simply uses a relief provided by the statute in the way intended.[6]

On top of *Benham* type issues (see 27.1 The *Benham* problem), care must be taken with this approach to ensure that the gift that is supposed to fall within the nil rate band does so, particularly where the will is more complex than the archetypal example with just two provisions. In *RSPCA v Sharp* [2010] EWCA Civ 1474 the will provided that: (1) an amount equal to the maximum that can be given without attracting IHT be given to two individuals; (2) a property be given to those same individuals, with any IHT on that gift to be paid out of the residue; and (3) the residue to the RSPCA.

The RSPCA argued that this was not, as the High Court had found, a gift to the individuals of an amount equal to the nil-rate band *as well as* the property, but was a gift of the property as well as any extra amount that fell within the nil rate band – resulting in a much larger residue for them. The Court of Appeal noted that the true meaning was difficult to determine but agreed, basing the decision on only a few words in the drafting.

26.5 Agricultural/business property

26.5.1 *The problem*

Agricultural property and business property may qualify for agricultural property or business property relief at the rate of 50% or 100%. The position is relatively simple if all the estate qualifies for 100% business property relief, or if it all qualifies for IHT charity relief. Where part of the estate qualifies for each relief, the question arises of how the two

6 An example can be seen from the Court of Appeal's consideration of the will in issue in *RSPCA v Sharp* [2010] EWCA Civ 1474.

reliefs interact.

Similar rules govern an estate which partly qualifies for the IHT spouse exemption.

This section considers an estate which contains:

(1) business or agricultural property (for convenience we refer to both types of property as "business property") and
(2) non-business property.

We refer to this as a part-business estate.

What is the position if a testator gives part of a part-business estate to charity? Section 4(1) IHTA provides:

> On the death of any person tax shall be charged as if, immediately before his death, he had made a transfer of value and the value transferred by it had been equal to the value of his estate immediately before his death.

This transfer of value is:

> exempt to the extent that the value transferred by it is attributable to property which is given to charity.

See section 23(1) IHTA. The question, therefore, is to ascertain the extent to which the value transferred by the transfer of value on the death of the testator is "attributable" to the property given to charity. The answer is given by section 39A IHTA.

Section 39A(1) begins:

> Where any part of the value transferred by a transfer of value is attributable to—
> (a) the value of relevant business property, or
> (b) the agricultural value of agricultural property ….

These words are satisfied in our example since:

(a) there is a transfer of value immediately before the testator's death; and
(b) part of the value transferred is attributable to business property.[7]

Section 39A(1) continues:

> … then, for the purpose of attributing the value transferred (as reduced in accordance with section 104 or 116 below), to specific gifts and gifts

7 The context shows in our view that these words are satisfied even in the case of 100% relief.

> of residue or shares of residue, sections 38 and 39 above shall have effect subject to the following provisions of this section.

Section 39A contains two rules:
(1) a rule for specific gifts of business property; and
(2) a rule for other specific gifts.

26.6 Specific gift of business property

The rule for specific gifts of business property is set out in subsection (2):

> The value of any specific gifts of relevant business property or agricultural property shall be taken to be their value as reduced in accordance with section 104 or 116 below.

The basic principle is readily intelligible: if a Will contains:
(1) exempt gifts, such as gifts to charity, and
(2) taxable gifts which do not qualify for any exemption,
then one must ensure that as far as possible:
(1) the exempt gifts are of property which would otherwise be taxable at the highest rate, and
(2) the taxable gifts are of property which qualifies for the highest rate of relief.

The simple course is to give:
(1) specific legacies of non-business property to charities (or other exempt beneficiaries, such as spouses); and
(2) business property to other beneficiaries (eg children).

A specific gift of business property to charity wastes the charity exemption. It might nevertheless happen that the testator wishes to give:
(1) business property to charity, and
(2) non-business property to legatees who are not exempt from inheritance tax (say, children).

One solution in such a case is:
(1) to give non-business property to the charity, and
(2) to include a provision in the Will enabling the executors, if they think fit, to use funds comprised in residue to "purchase" the business property. The purchase is not a purchase in the strict sense, as the executors are, during the administration period, the sole owners of the entire estate. Thus, the purchase should have no stamp duty or CGT consequences nor, provided it is made at a proper value, inheritance

tax consequences. The inheritance tax charge is fixed at the date of death. What the personal representatives may or may not do thereafter in the course of administration cannot retrospectively affect it.[8]

Another solution is:

(1) to give a cash sum[9] to the charity equal to the value of the business property, and

(2) authorise the executors to appropriate the business assets to the charity in satisfaction of the legacy.

26.7 Foreign IHT

Similar considerations apply where part of a deceased's estate is subject to death duties in another jurisdiction with a corresponding tax credit against UK inheritance tax. Foreign jurisdictions do not normally allow death duty exemption on the grounds that a gift is made to a UK charity. (In some cases EU member states may allow relief.) For instance, suppose T wishes to makes a will giving foreign property to a UK charity. The gift may bear foreign death duties which are set against UK IHT so the effective IHT burden is reduced or eliminated.[10] It would be better:

(1) to give the foreign property to beneficiaries who are chargeable under UK law.

(2) to give other (perhaps UK) property to the UK charity which would otherwise bear inheritance tax at the full rate.

In some cases the matter could be put right by a deed of variation.

26.8 Pecuniary legacy from part business estate

This section considers a Will of a part business estate with a pecuniary legacy to charity and residue to children.

Section 39A(3) IHTA provides:

---

8 We are assuming that the exercise by the executors of their power to purchase is not pre-ordained. If it were, then one would have to consider whether the arrangement would fall foul of the GAAR and whether the series of transactions could be "collapsed" so as to charge tax as though the business property were given to the charity.

9 But see 26.8 (Pecuniary legacy from part business estate).

10 The position may be complicated further by foreign rules which make the rate of death duty depend on the relationship of the beneficiary to the deceased; forced heirship rules may also need to be considered.

> The value of any specific gifts not falling within subsection (2) above shall be taken to be the appropriate fraction of their value.

This applies to a pecuniary legacy, which is a "specific gift" as defined: see section 42(1) IHTA. So the value of the pecuniary legacy for IHT is taken to be reduced to the "appropriate fraction" of its true value.

The next step is to ascertain the "appropriate fraction" which is defined in section 39A(4):

> In subsection (3) above "the appropriate fraction" means a fraction of which—
>
> (a) the numerator is the difference between the value transferred and the value, reduced as mentioned in subsection (2) above, of any gifts falling within that subsection, and
>
> (b) the denominator is the difference between the unreduced value transferred and the value, before the reduction mentioned in subsection (2) above, of any gifts falling within that subsection;
>
> and in paragraph (b) above "the unreduced value transferred" means the amount which would be the value transferred by the transfer but for the reduction required by sections 104 and 116 below [Business & Agricultural property relief].

It is easiest to explain by example.

Example 1

Suppose:

(1) The total value of the testator's estate (before business property relief) is £9m. This is the "unreduced value transferred".

(2) £6m qualifies for 100% business property relief. The value transferred on death (after the relief) is then £3m.

(3) The will of the testator provides:
- (a) a pecuniary legacy of £3m to charity;
- (b) the residue of their estate to their children;
- (c) there are no specific gifts of business property.[11]

The appropriate fraction, on these facts, is then A ÷ B where

A is the value transferred (after relief), £3m.

B is the unreduced value transferred, £9m.

The appropriate fraction is therefore ⅓. The legacy is treated as a legacy of £1m.

---

11 So section 39A(2) does not apply.

Since, in the example, the value attributed to the charity is £1m, IHT charity relief is limited to £1m and IHT is charged on the death on £2m.

In short, the effect of section 39A is that pecuniary legacies enjoy some of the benefit of business property relief if the residuary estate contains business property.[12] A simple pecuniary legacy to charity is therefore not tax efficient if the residuary estate includes a substantial amount of business property. Some of the relief is wasted. In the example only £1m of the value transferred on the death of the testator qualifies for IHT charity relief, and £2m remains subject to inheritance tax.

26.9 Residuary gift from part business estate

Now take the same facts as *Example 1* but suppose the will of the testator provides:

(a) a pecuniary legacy of £3m to the children;
(b) residue of the estate to charity.

Once again, £1m is attributed to the pecuniary legacy, given to the children. The important question, however, is how much of the value transferred is attributable to the gift to the charity. The answer is given by section 39 IHTA which provides:

> Such part only of the value transferred shall be attributed to gifts of residue or shares in residue as is not attributed under section 38 above to specific gifts.

So £2m is attributable to the gift to charity and IHT is charged on the death on £1m.

26.10 Pecuniary legacy: Solution

One solution is for the will to make specific gifts of all the business and agricultural property to non-charitable beneficiaries as well as the pecuniary legacy to charity. The substantial effect of the will may be the same as in *Example 1*. However the IHT position is much more favourable: the "appropriate fraction" becomes 100%.[13] So the pecuniary legacy does not enjoy any business property relief and that relief is available to the residuary estate.

---

12 A nil rate band gift in common form would be grossed up in order to ascertain the "largest amount of cash" that can be given to the children.

13 Because, applying the fraction in section 39A(4), the denominator equals the numerator.

In a will which makes more than one pecuniary legacy, also watch section 37 IHTA.

26.11 Pecuniary legacies to avoid business fragmentation

The client's major asset may consist of a substantial holding in a private trading company, qualifying for 100% business relief, yet they may wish to make a large number of legacies. The last thing they would want is for the holding to be split up among several beneficiaries, thereby reducing its overall value or depriving their personal representatives of control. What can be done in these cases? One solution is to bequeath the property qualifying for relief upon trust for sale, with the direction to pay pecuniary legacies out of the proceeds of sale and with the further direction that the surplus, if any, is to fall into residue.

26.12 Interaction of excluded property and charity exemption

The relevant IHTA provisions provide:

> **4 Transfers on death**
> (1) On the death of any person tax shall be charged as if, immediately before his death, he had made a transfer of value and the value transferred by it had been equal to the value of his estate immediately before his death. ...
> **5 Meaning of estate**
> (1) For the purposes of this Act a person's estate is the aggregate of all the property to which he is beneficially entitled, except that ... the estate of a person immediately before his death does not include excluded property. ...

Suppose H (not UK domiciled) leaves his UK situate property to a charity only. It is plain the charity exemption applies to give exemption to the entire transfer of value deemed to take place on the death of H.

Suppose H left only his foreign situate (excluded) property to charity. The position is thought to be that the charity exemption does not apply. An instrument of variation could, in principle, be used to put this matter right.

Supposing H leaves a pecuniary legacy to charity. The IHT Manual provides:

> **IHTM11013: Groups of exempt transfers: quantifying the exemption** [19 Aug 2016]
> - Where the will of a person domiciled (IHTM13000) abroad disposes

> of their UK estate and some or all of their world estate, exemption for pecuniary legacies (IHTM12082) should be given against the UK estate in the proportion it bears to the worldwide estate, and not against the UK estate alone. Any case where you have difficulty obtaining details of the world estate, or where our official practice meets resistance, should be referred to Technical.

It is suggested that this is correct in relation to the IHT charity exemption.[14]

26.13 Cost of administration

There is in general no IHT deduction for the cost of administration of an estate. If a testator leaves an estate of £100,000, and administration expenses amount to £10,000, tax is payable on the £100,000 even though only £90,000 is available for the beneficiaries.

A modest but significant advantage of a gift of residue to charity is that the costs of administering the estate – which are deducted from residue – do not suffer tax. This is because the amount of the transfer of value on death attributable to the specific legacies is calculated according to s.38 IHTA; and the balance of the transfer of value is attributed to the residuary gift (s.39 IHTA), and so is exempt. Again, the mistake if made can be corrected by instrument of variation; this would be worthwhile for estates which for any reason have been very expensive to administer.

14 The correctness of this passage in relation to the spouse exemption is highly doubtful but that is outside the scope of this book.

CHAPTER TWENTY SEVEN

SHARE OF ESTATE GIVEN TO CHARITY: *BENHAM* ISSUES

27.1 The *Benham* problem

Suppose a testator wishes to give a share of their estate to charity. The share given to charity qualifies for an IHT exemption and the balance is chargeable. This chapter considers the impact of IHT on calculating the value of shares in the estate in this situation. Identical problems arise if a testator wishes to give a share of their estate to their spouse and the balance to others: the share given to the spouse is in principle exempt from IHT and the balance is chargeable. Similar problems arise in the case of gifts to maintenance funds, and in any situation where there are both exempt and non-exempt gifts.

27.2 An impermissible form

Section 41(b) IHTA provides:

> Notwithstanding the terms of any disposition ... none of the tax attributable to the value of property comprised in residue shall fall on any gift of a share of residue if or to the extent that the transfer is exempt with respect to the gift.

If a Will gives (say) a share of residue to a charity and a share to a child, the following provisions are therefore void:

the IHT burden shall be shared equally between the child and the charity

the IHT burden shall be borne out of the entire estate of the testator

27.3 Gross *v.* net division

Suppose a testator wishes to leave an estate between two children and a charity in equal (one third) shares. In the worked examples it is assumed that the testator has used up the nil rate band in their lifetime, and leaves an estate of £300,000. For convenience the figures are rounded to the nearest £1,000.

Tax borne by reduction of children's share. The testator may expressly provide in their Will that any IHT payable out of residue should be borne by the children's share. That is straightforward. The consequence will of course be that the charity receives more than each of the children, because the charity's share is not reduced by the tax charge.

Example 1 Each beneficiary receives a ⅓ share of the gross estate, with the children's shares bearing IHT, so:

(a) Each child's share (£100,000 gross) bears tax of £40,000 so each child receives £60,000.

(b) The charity's share (£100,000) bears no tax so the charity receives £100,000.

We refer to this as a "**gross division approach**".

Children to benefit equally with charity: increasing share numerically The testator may wish the charity and each child to receive the same amounts *after* tax has been paid. This is more difficult. A simple direction in the Will that the tax burden should be shared equally between each child and the charity is void: see 27.2 (An impermissible form).

In this case the drafter could provide for a gift of *unequal* shares of residue; the shares to be in such proportion that (after tax) each child and the charity receive the same amounts. If the size of the shares is specifically and numerically stated in the Will there could be no possible objection.

Example 2 The testator gives £115,000 (subject to tax) each to the children, residue to charity, so:

(a) each child's share (£115,000 gross) bears £45,000 tax leaving £70,000.

(b) the charity's share (which bears no tax) is £70,000.

We refer to this as "**net division approach**".

Comparing the two approaches it will be seen that the second favours the children (and also HMRC) over the charity.

27.4 Express grossing up clause

Since it is not practical to state the amounts numerically, the drafter will normally use a formula: they will give their estate to the children and charity in unequal shares, directing their executors to compute the shares in such a manner that after deduction of IHT the charity and the children have equal shares. We call this a "**grossing up clause**" (the effect of a grossing up clause will be a net division approach). For example:

> I give my estate to X charity and Y in unequal shares. The share of X charity (which is exempt from tax) will be of the same magnitude as the share of Y after Y's share has borne the tax attributable to it.

Some practitioners suggest that an express grossing up clause is rendered void by s.41 and cannot take effect. The argument is that the practical effect of a grossing up clause is that tax is, in substance, borne by the charity's share; and that the policy of s.41 is to help charities and prevent such a clause. But no-one takes this view seriously. It is contrary to the decision in *Re Benham* and to obiter dicta in *Re Ratcliffe,* but even apart from authority, the view is wrong in principle. A distinction must be drawn between:

(1) arrangements where the tax is in fact directed to be borne out of the charity's share; and
(2) arrangements which increase the size of an individual's share to allow for tax to be paid out of it.

Although in substance the two reach the same result, they do so by a different technique. Section 41 which strikes down one does not strike down the other. The section should not be given an extended reading. It is a general principle of English law that an individual has, subject to limited restraints, freedom of testamentary disposition. Consistent with this principle an individual should be free to make a Will with a grossing up clause.

The contrary argument is based on a misunderstanding of the purpose of s.41. Section 41 is not intended for the protection of charities. The reason for it, we think, is that the rules set out in ss.36–41 IHTA only work if tax is borne by an individual share, and the rules do not work if tax is paid out of a charity share. This is why s.41 prevents tax being paid directly out of a charity share. There is, in our view, no reason to construe it more widely.

27.5 Is express grossing up clause wise

Where a grossing up clause is used in a simple case, the computation of the shares requires only basic maths. However, if the same Will also makes specific legacies which are not exempt and which do not bear their own tax, then the provisions of s.38(4) IHTA would need to be applied and the resulting computations would be very difficult. The computation should be given to aspiring Will drafters so they learn this truth from bitter experience!

27.6 The common form

A common form is to provide that the executors shall pay all debts and administration expenses (which would include inheritance tax) and shall hold the residue on trust for the charity and the children in equal shares absolutely. The wording derives from the form which takes effect on intestacy. Section 33 Administration of Estates Act 1925 provides:

> (1) On the death of a person intestate as to any real or personal estate, that estate shall be held in trust by his personal representatives with the power to sell it.
> (2) The personal representatives shall pay out of
> (a) the ready money of the deceased (so far as not disposed of by his will, if any); and
> (b) any net money arising from disposing of any other part of his estate (after payment of costs),
> all such funeral, testamentary and administration expenses, debts and other liabilities as are properly payable thereout having regard to the rules of administration contained in this Part of this Act...
> (4) The residue of the said money and any investments for the time being representing the same, and any part of the estate of the deceased which remains unsold and is not required for the administration purposes aforesaid, is in this Act referred to as "the residuary estate of the intestate".

"Administration expenses" includes IHT. Section 211(1) IHTA provides (so far as relevant):

> Where personal representatives are liable for tax on the value transferred by chargeable transfer made on death, the tax shall be treated as part of the general testamentary and administration expenses of the estate

Armed with the definition of "residuary estate" we can turn to s.46 AEA 1925 which provides:

> (1) The residuary estate of an intestate shall be distributed in the manner or be held on the trusts mentioned in this section, namely:
>
> (i) If the intestate leaves a spouse or civil partner [and issue] then the residuary estate shall be held—
>
> (a) as to one half upon trust for the surviving spouse or civil partner during his or her life, and, subject to such life interest, on the statutory trusts for the issue of the intestate, and
>
> (b) as to the other half, on the statutory trusts for the issue of the intestate.

This common form is ambiguous and admits three possible constructions.

Construction 1

One might construe the Will to say that:

(a) tax is to be borne by the children's share;

(b) "equal shares" means equal before tax;

(c) one should therefore deduct IHT from the children's share and pay it to the children; paying the remaining share (without any deduction of tax) to the charity.

The result is a gross division approach.

Construction 2

One might construe the Will to say that:

(a) IHT is to be borne by the children's share;

(b) "equal shares" means equal after tax; a grossing up clause is implied;

(c) so each beneficiary receives unequal amounts before tax. Again, one deducts IHT from the children's share alone, paying the remaining share (without any deduction of tax) to the charity. However, the effect of deducting tax is that each beneficiary receives the same at the end of the day.

The result is a net division approach.

Construction 3

One might construe the Will as purporting to direct that IHT is to be borne by the estate before division, ie by both the charity's share and the children's share.

The testator may (wrongly) think that tax could be paid on half the value of the estate, and the balance shared equally between the charity's share and the children's share. Unfortunately s.41(b) IHTA provides that notwithstanding the terms of the Will, none of the tax attributable to residue shall fall on the charity's share of residue. If the terms of the Will conflict with that, s.41(b) prevails. What, then, is to be done if the terms of the Will cannot be applied? Section 41(b) says that the IHT cannot fall on the charity's share: so it must fall on the children's share. Unless a grossing-up clause is also implied. Construction 3 leads to a gross division approach, the same result as Construction 1.

27.7 Analysis of common form

There are two distinct issues here:

(1) *Which funds bear IHT?* Do the words of the Will direct that:
   (a) IHT is payable out of undivided residue (both the charities' share and the children's share); or
   (b) IHT is payable only out of the children's share?

(2) *"Equality" before tax or after tax?* Does the reference to "equal shares" mean:
   (a) equal before tax; or
   (b) equal after tax (so as to imply a grossing up clause)?

The drafter has not addressed either question very clearly and that is why they are imponderable, which is reflected in the inconsistent case law discussed below.

Which funds bear IHT?

The first point might be answered by applying the general principle that the share of an estate which suffers a tax charge will bear the burden of that tax charge[1]. If there were no other indication in the Will, therefore, the burden of the tax charge will be borne by the children's share. But the draft wording requires IHT to be paid before the split into shares, so it *is* implied that tax is to be borne by the entire estate including the charity's share. The fact that the IHT is a testamentary expense means it must be

---

1 Suppose a trust fund were held on trust for A and B contingently upon attaining the age of 25, in equal undivided shares. Suppose A attains 25 and CGT is payable under s.71 TCGA. The tax is in principle payable out of A's share.

borne by both shares of the estate including the charity's share. If so, then the direction that tax be borne by the charity's share is void and the tax is paid out of the children's share alone.

"Equality" before tax or after tax?
The draft wording does not say, expressly, whether the references to shares in the Will means shares before or after tax. But since the tax is expressed to be deducted first, the best answer is that the drafter assumed that the shares would be equal after tax. This does *not* mean that the drafter intended the children's share to be "grossed up" so as to give such amounts as after deduction of tax yield the requisite shares. The drafter intended tax to be paid out first, before the division of the residuary estate, so that grossing up would be unnecessary.

27.8 Case law

The case law consists of three inconsistent first instance decisions.

27.8.1 *Relevance of case law*

In a question of construction, a great deal depends on the precise words used in the Will in question:

> No case on the construction of one document is authority on the construction of another, even if the words are very similar.[2]

But in practice the wording used is fairly standard and court ought to be able to offer a general answer to the question of construction.

27.8.2 *Re Benham*[3]

In *Re Benham* [1995] STC 210 the Will provided:

> 3. I GIVE DEVISE AND BEQUEATH all the residue of my estate both real and personal whatsoever and wheresoever unto my Trustees to sell call in and convert the same into money with power in their absolute discretion to postpone such sale calling in and conversion for so long as they shall think fit without being liable for loss and to hold the net proceeds thereof together with my ready money upon the

---

2 *Deeny v Gooda Walker* [1996] STC 299 at 306. See further Kessler & John, *Drafting Trusts & Will Trusts* (14th ed, 2019), Chapter 4 (Principles of Interpreting Trust Documents).

3 Where you have a *Benham*-type clause, there is a free calculator for calculating the relevant shares at *http://www.actuaries.eu.com/ReBenham2.html*

following trusts namely

(A) upon trust to pay thereout all my just debts funeral and testamentary expenses

(B) as to the residue after such payment aforesaid to pay the same to those beneficiaries as are living at my death and who are listed in List A and List B hereunder written in such proportions as will bring about the result that the aforesaid beneficiaries named in List A shall receive 3.2 times as much as the aforesaid beneficiaries named in List B and in each case for their own absolute and beneficial use and disposal.

The testator then set out in two lists a number of beneficiaries. In the case of List A one was charitable and the rest were non-charitable, and in List B a number were charitable and a number were non-charitable beneficiaries.

It is hard to identify significant difference between the wording used in *Benham* and the wording used in the common form.

The judge accurately identified the three possibilities discussed at 27.6 (The common form):

> 1. that the non-charitable beneficiaries receive their respective share, subject to Inheritance Tax, which would mean they would receive less than the charitable beneficiaries;
> 2. that the non-charitable beneficiaries are entitled to have their respective shares "grossed up" so the net result is that equality is achieved between charitable and non-charitable beneficiaries;
> 3. that the executors should pay the Inheritance Tax as part of the testamentary expenses under clause 3(a) of the will and distribute the balance equally between the exempt and non-exempt beneficiaries.

The judge dismissed possibility (3):

> [Counsel] submitted that the possibility at 3 above is precluded by section 41 of the 1984 Act. I agree.

The error in this approach is rightly identified in *Re Ratcliffe*:

> It is true that s.41(b) prohibits the third of the three possibilities but the fact that the third possibility is prohibited does not mean that that is not what the testatrix was intending.

Having dismissed possibility (3), the judge turned to choose between (1) and (2). Dismissing a debating point in favour of a gross distribution approach,[4] the judge stated his conclusion in favour of a net division approach:

> ... the plain [!] intention of the Testatrix is that at the end of the day each beneficiary, whether charitable or non-charitable, should receive the same as the other beneficiaries in the relevant list. That result is consistent with the express terms of the will and the statutory provisions that apply. I therefore answer the second question in the originating summons in the sense that the non-charitable beneficiaries receive grossed-up shares so that the sum each of the beneficiaries receives as between themselves in the relevant list is the same.

27.8.3 *Re Ratcliffe*

In *Re Ratcliffe* [1999] STC 262 the Will took the standard form:

> I give devise and bequeath all my real and personal estate whatsoever and wheresoever not hereby otherwise disposed of unto my Trustees upon trust to sell and convert the same into money with power at their absolute discretion to postpone any such sale and conversion for so long as they shall think fit without being answerable for any loss and after payment thereout of my debts and funeral and testamentary expenses to stand possessed of the residue
> [a] as to one-half part thereof for John Hugh McMullan and Edward Brownlow McMullan ... in equal shares absolutely and
> [b] as to the remainder of my estate upon trust for the following Charities in equal shares ...

Blackburne J refused to follow *Re Benham* and a gross division was applied. He said:

> Mrs Ratcliffe's disposable residue includes the tax attributable to the McMullans' share. The fact that, under s.200(1) of the 1984 Act, the plaintiffs, as Mrs Ratcliffe's personal representatives, are the persons liable for the tax and that, under s.211(1), they are entitled to recover the payment as a testamentary expense does not alter the fact that the inheritance tax attributable to the McMullans' share is a part of her gift to them and as such is a part of her disposable residue. Nor does the fact that Mrs Ratcliffe has directed a division of what is left after payment

---

4 "... a presumed intention by the Testatrix that her estate should pay as little Inheritance Tax as possible. ... such a construction would accord with the anticipation of the 'ordinary person' that the extent to which each beneficiary receives an equal share will depend on that beneficiary's status as exempt or non-exempt."

of her testamentary expenses.

We confess we find the reasoning is difficult to follow. The judge bolsters his conclusion with reference to the difficult mathematics of grossing up, and similar debating points[5] which had failed to impress the judge in *Benham*.

27.8.4 *Re Hamblett*

Re Hamblett[6] concerned the will of a New Zealand domiciliary. The estate was governed by New Zealand law, except that English law governed the administration of property in England. The Will provided:

> I GIVE the rest of my estate to my Trustees UPON TRUST to pay my debts and funeral expenses my Trustees administration expenses and any other death duties and to hold the balance UPON TRUST to divide as follows:
> (a) a one quarter share for my said wife JUNE HAMBLETT;
> (b) a one quarter share for my daughter SUSAN ELIZABETH HAMBLETT;
> (c) a one quarter share for my son REX HAMBLETT;
> (d) a one quarter share for my said son PAUL HAMBLETT ...

The High Court of New Zealand stated:

> [48] ... The intention of the testator appears to be clear [!]. All expenses of any sort including duties (and it can be inferred taxes) are to be paid before division. ...
> [50] Even if the deceased is to be taken as having been aware of the UK inheritance tax, the wording with its reference to first paying

5 "... if [counsel for the individual beneficiaries] were correct, it would make no difference if the will had omitted any mention of the payment of debts and funeral and testamentary expenses: testamentary expenses would fall to be paid before residue is ascertained and, absent any contrary indication in the will, inheritance tax would continue to be regarded (as a result of s.211(1)) as a testamentary expense. Moreover, the same grossing up would occur if, instead of leaving a will, Mrs Ratcliffe had died intestate leaving a surviving husband (who would be an exempt beneficiary) and children (who would not be): the provisions of the Administration of Estates Act 1925 (as amended) would have to be applied by grossing up the children's half share of residue so as to produce, after deduction of inheritance tax, a net sum equal in amount to the half share in which the surviving husband takes a life interest. See ss.33(2) and 34(3) of the Administration of Estates Act 1925. ... that would be a surprising consequence of the impact of inheritance tax on the operation of the intestacy rules."

6 [2007] 1 NZLR 120; 8 ITELR 9 *http://www.nzlii.org/nz/cases/NZHC/2006/646.html*

> administration expenses shows an intention that there should be a net equal division between all four beneficiaries, after the payment of all taxes. I consider that this included any UK tax that might apply in whole or in part to the shares of the particular individual residuary beneficiaries. I can see no basis for inferring a qualification that in the event of a taxation exemption attaching as a matter of law to just one residuary beneficiary's share, that the exempt beneficiary's share should itself be solely exempt from the payment of tax.

The judge then considered the effect of English law:

> [73][1] Section 41 does not create a restraint or limitation on dispositions. It creates a rule of construction.
> [2] If the Will had to be construed in accordance with UK law, this New Zealand Court would be obliged to recognise the rule of construction contained within s 41 and apply it to this Will. If that were the exercise to be carried out, ... it would be appropriate to construe this Will in the way the Will was construed in *Re Ratcliffe*. Although there is some difference in the wording in the relevant clauses in the Wills, the differences are not sufficiently significant to warrant *Re Ratcliffe* being distinguished.

Point [1] is wrong. Section 41 is not in any normal sense a rule of construction, for rules of construction are to ascertain the intention of the testator, whereas s.41 overrides the intention of the testator.

27.8.5 *Case law: Conclusion*

It is considered that the *Benham* problem has yet to find an entirely satisfactory analysis in the courts, but the result in *Ratcliffe* is to be preferred to that in *Benham.*

27.9 *Benham* approach favours HMRC

The result of using a grossing up approach is that more tax will be paid by the estate to HMRC. Take the following example. An estate (after the nil rate band has been used up) of £300,000 is to be divided between two children and a charity in equal shares. Where the net division approach is applied the tax paid on the estate is £90,000 (£45,000 on each of the children's shares and nothing on the charity's share).

Where the gross division approach is applied the inheritance tax paid is £80,000 (£40,000 on each of the children's shares of £100,000 and nothing on the charity's share of £100,000).

Despite this, where the common form is adopted HMRC accept that *Re*

Ratcliffe is correct and a gross division approach is appropriate (see 27.11 (HMRC View)).

27.10 What should executors/charities do

If all the beneficiaries have legal capacity this is easy. The executors should administer the estate in the manner which is agreed by *all* the beneficiaries.

If the form of the Will is the same as that in *Re Ratcliffe*, the High Court should under the normal rules of precedent follow that decision. Executors may (in the absence of a claim by beneficiaries) properly distribute the estate on that basis.

If there is no agreement and uncertainty, the executors should go to court to ask for directions. There is no alternative to seeking the court's directions, in the absence of certainty or agreement, because any disappointed beneficiary, either an individual or one of the charities, may otherwise sue the executors for wrongly distributing the estate. They may or may not succeed in that action; but in the absence of:

(1) agreement of the beneficiaries; or
(2) a court order,

the executors are at risk. There is no reason why they should take such risks, and no-one would reasonably expect them to do so.

If beneficiaries are minors, an application under s.48 Administration of Justice Act 1985 may be required: it should be a relatively cheap solution, or indemnities may be available.

If a charity is told that it has a share in residue under a Will, it should ask to see the Will and, in a normal *Ratcliffe* case, seek confirmation from the executors that the estate will be administered using the gross division approach. It is much more difficult to put right after an estate has been administered. The executors may also wish to seek clearance from HMRC to distribute on the gross division approach, following *Re Ratcliffe*.

27.11 HMRC view

The IHT Manual provides:

> **IHTM26171**: Step 4 - *Re Benham* type grossing calculations: legal background [Jun 2016]
> The cases of *Re Benham's Will Trusts* [1995] STC 210 and *Re Ratcliffe* (deceased) (1999) STC 262 were concerned with the meaning of a Will (IHTM12041) in which the residuary estate (IHTM26003) was divided

between exempt and chargeable beneficiaries. As it happened the exempt beneficiaries were charities, but the principles will also apply where part of the residue goes to a spouse or civil partner (IHTM11032), or to any combination of exempt and chargeable beneficiaries. The question addressed in each case was whether the testatrix intended the residuary beneficiaries to receive specified proportions of the estate after all Inheritance Tax had been paid.

In *Re Benham*, the judge decided that the words used showed that intention. IHTA84/S41 (b) provides: 'none of the tax attributable to the value of the property comprised in residue shall fall on any gift of a share of residue if or to the extent that the transfer is exempt with respect to the gift.' To give effect to Jane Benham's Will, and at the same time meet the requirements of ,IHTA84/S41 (b), the chargeable shares of residue were 'grossed up' to include the tax payable on them.

The *Re Ratcliffe* (deceased) case concerned the more usual form of Will drafting precedent. The finding was that Mrs Ratcliffe's intentions were that by directing an equal division of residue after payment of her debts and funeral and testamentary expenses (which would include paying Iinheritance Tax) she was simply directing that the disposable residue was to be divided equally.

IHTM26172: Step 4 - *Re Benham* type grossing calculations: practice [27 Jun 2014]

Usually, working out the deceased's intentions from the wording of the Will, or any other evidence, is a matter for the personal representatives (IHTM05012) and their advisors. But, given the doubt caused by the *Re Benham* decision you may have to consider the point. You should read the Will (IHTM12041) carefully to see if it includes an intention for all Inheritance Tax to be paid before the residue (IHTM26003) is ascertained and divided. In the most common cases the Will directs, after distribution of any specific gifts, that the Executors/Trustees are, for example, 'after payment thereout of my debts and funeral and testamentary expenses to stand possessed of the residue as to one-half part thereof for John … and Edward … in equal shares absolutely … and as to the remainder of my estate upon trust for the following charities in equal shares …' These were the terms of Mrs Ratcliffe's Will. You should calculate the residuary estate, deduct the share or proportion passing to an exempt body or person, and levy tax on the balance in the normal way (IHTM26071).

It is perfectly possible, though unusual, for you to come across a Will that has been deliberately drafted to achieve a *Re Benham* result. These would include, for example, a clause along these lines - 'Mindful of the fact that some but not all of the equal shares given by this clause will be exempt from Inheritance Tax because of the identity of the beneficiary I declare that all the shares are to be of equal net value so that (if Inheritance Tax is payable in respect of my estate) the non-exempt shares are to be treated as shares of such grossed up amount as after tax will leave the recipients with a net amount the same as that received by the donees of the exempt shares.' In this situation you should refer the file after all values have been settled, to the Actuarial Team to 'gross up' the chargeable part of the residue. Your note must show the value of any specific bequests (IHTM26011), and say whether they are free of tax (IHTM26123) or not, as well as identifying the net amount of the estate at that particular title. If you need to calculate the tax on the residue you should make this clear in your note.

Any cases of doubt or difficulty should be referred to Technical, after you have an explanation of the interpretation suggested by the taxpayer or agent. If we agree with the personal representatives, or their advisors, but any of the residuary beneficiaries object you should refer the case to Technical.

The important point is that HMRC accept that in practice *Ratcliffe* principles normally apply, to give a gross division approach. Thus HMRC take the view which results in a smaller amount of tax being payable. They will hardly object if the estate is administered on any other basis (but the charity IHT exemption will only apply to the extent that the estate becomes the property of charities).

27.12 Moral for Will drafter

1. Seek express instructions on whether or not to include a grossing up clause.
2. Do not use the ambiguous form: specify expressly whether or not to gross up the non–charitable share.

CHAPTER TWENTY EIGHT

OBTAINING INCOME TAX AND IHT RELIEFS ON GIFT BY WILL OR IoV

28.1 IT + IHT reliefs on gift by IoV

Suppose a beneficiary receives an asset under a Will. The individual may then make a gift of money or qualifying investments to charity and qualify for income tax relief. That gift would not normally constitute an IoV. Alternatively the individual may execute an IoV giving the asset to charity so that the estate qualifies for IHT relief. This section considers whether the beneficiary may make a gift which:

(1) qualifies for income tax relief; and
(2) qualifies as an IoV so the estate qualifies for IHT charity relief.

These are sometimes called "double dip" arrangements.

There are two possible routes to income tax relief: Gift Aid and QIDR. Great care is needed in the execution of these arrangements.

28.2 Arrangement using Gift Aid

28.2.1 *"Payment of a sum of money"*

Suppose, first, the beneficiary has received a pecuniary legacy of £10,000. The beneficiary could simply execute an IoV directing the legacy to pass to charity. This may fail to qualify for Gift Aid relief: one of the conditions of Gift Aid is that the gift must take the form of a payment of a sum of money. See 15.8 (Payment: Gift Aid condition A). To be sure of satisfying this condition it is recommended that:

1. The executors pay the legacy to a segregated account of the beneficiary.
2. The IoV is executed, and at the same time the beneficiary writes a cheque in favour of the charity.

It is then clearer that the gift takes the form of the payment of a sum of money.

Suppose, now, the beneficiary has received not a pecuniary legacy, but the residue of an estate. In that case it is recommended that the executors should pay a cash sum to the beneficiary's own account on account. The IoV can then be executed over the cash sum.

28.2.2 *Benefit obstacle: St Dunstan's*

HMRC take the objection that Gift Aid relief is lost because of the donor benefit rule.[1] It is said that the individual does receive a benefit, namely the IHT relief given to the estate under s.142 IHTA. This was accepted by the Special Commissioners in *St Dunstan's v Major* [1997] STC (SCD) 212, and the argument was rerun with the same result in *Harris v HMRC* [2010] SFTD 1159. That should be assumed for practical purposes to be the law.

The HMRC argument only runs where the increase in the value of the residuary estate is a benefit to the individual or a connected person (eg if the individual is a residuary legatee or "connected"[2] to the residuary legatee). No problem need arise if the residuary estate is settled on discretionary trusts. Another possible solution is for the donor to ensure that the IHT benefit passes to charity or to a person not connected with them. HMRC have in practice accepted that in such circumstances there is no benefit to the donor.

28.3 QIDR

The other course is to use Qualifying Investment Donation Relief. This relief is restricted but not lost if the donor receives benefits. So-called "double dip" arrangements, which were very popular before the *St*

---

1 See 15.20 (Benefit rule: Condition F).

2 See 15.32 (Benefit of connected/associated person).

Dunstan decision have therefore become viable again.

Example
T inherits a residuary estate of £1m from a parent and wishes to give £100,000 to charity.

Route (1) Instrument of variation.
The IHT saving for the estate is £40,000.

Route (2) QIDR gift.
The income tax saving is (say) £40,000.[3]

Route (3) IoV and QIDR gift.
The IHT saving is £40,000. The income tax relief is:

Value of gift	£100,000
Less benefit[4]	- (£40,000)
	£60,000

The income tax saving may therefore amount to £24,000, sufficient to justify the work involved. If the assets give rise to potential chargeable gains, the tax saving may be much greater than this.

This puts the parties in a similar position as if the testator had made a QIDR gift to charity before their death, and might therefore be regarded as acceptable tax mitigation rather than unacceptable (to HMRC) tax avoidance. But care must, of course, be taken to ensure that all the technical conditions for the tax reliefs are satisfied.

28.4 Obtaining IHT and IT reliefs on gift by will

It is possible for a testator to obtain both IHT and IT tax reliefs by an appropriately drafted will, so no IoV is needed. There are many variants of the idea but in outline, in the case of a gift of cash:

1. The testator makes the pecuniary legacy to an individual (the "Beneficiary") and not to the charity. The individual chosen should:
   (1) be likely to have a sufficient income (ie income which exceeds the amount of the legacy or which at least exceeds one half of the legacy); and
   (2) not benefit directly from any increase in the value of the residuary

---

3 Assuming T has income taxable at the 40% rate. If their income is taxable at the dividend upper rate, for instance, the saving is less.

4 IHT saving, applying principle of *St Dunstan's v Major*.

estate (it would not matter in principle that the residuary estate is held on discretionary trusts of which they are merely a discretionary beneficiary).[5]

2. The testator expresses in their Will a non-binding wish that the Beneficiary should give the legacy to a specific charity. (It is not sufficient to say that the sum should be applied for charitable purposes.)
3. The Beneficiary receives the legacy from the estate and gives it to the charity in accordance with the testator's wish. This must be done within two years of the death.

The tax effect of this arrangement is as follows:

1. The testator's estate will qualify for IHT relief on the legacy: see s.143 IHTA. Inheritance tax relief under s.143 does not require a formal deed or a formal claim to HMRC. The time limit should be noted: the gift must be made within two years of the death.
2. The gift will qualify for Gift Aid, so that (a) the charity will reclaim basic rate tax on the gift; and (b) the Beneficiary will enjoy higher rate tax relief on their gift. The fact that the gift is treated for IHT purposes as made by the testator does not affect the income tax position. This is the view HMRC itself maintains in other contexts (such as identifying the settlor of a settlement for income tax purposes).

The benefits of this arrangement are considerable, even when the amounts given to charity are moderate. It would be possible to juggle with the figures to ensure that the tax benefit was entirely enjoyed by the charity (by increasing the gift to charity) or else to arrange that the charity received the basic gift only, leaving more for the other beneficiaries of the testator's estate. This would slightly complicate the arrangement.

There are certain difficulties with this suggestion, but none of them are very serious.

(1) First, from the testator's point of view. There is the risk that the Beneficiary will not carry out their wishes. Sometimes that will rule out the arrangement; but in very many cases a testator will be able to name one or more persons, members of the immediate family perhaps, in whom they have confidence. The Beneficiary might predecease the

5 Thus the *St Dunstan* decision will not be in point provided (in short) the trust fund is not distributed to the beneficiary shortly after the assignment. Contrast 28.2.2 (Benefit obstacle: *St Dunstan's*).

testator. The Will could provide that, in this case, the legacy should pass to another individual or direct to charity.

(2) Second, from the Beneficiary's point of view. Here the Beneficiary could only benefit from the arrangement. If they make the gift to charity they will enjoy relief from the higher rate of income tax on the gift. Care needs to be taken if the amount of the legacy exceeds the Beneficiary's annual income. The donor may need to make the gifts over a period of two or possibly three tax years but must of course complete the gifts within the IHT time limit of two years from the date of death. See 15.47 (Deposited donation: Carry-forward). In cases of this kind the beneficiary may wish to make larger gifts to charity than they normally do from year to year. It is sometimes convenient to direct the gift to the Charities Aid Foundation. The CAF will hold the funds on account; and will pay them subsequently to any charity at the request of the donor.

(3) Third, from the charity's viewpoint. The charity stands to benefit considerably from the arrangement. For the charity will be able to reclaim income tax on the gift. (The receipt under the Gift Aid route is treated as the charity's income. This is not in practice significant for bona fide charities.)

The arrangement may be stifled by anti-avoidance legislation between the date of the Will and the date of death. The fear of new legislation is not a good reason for doing nothing; even if such legislation is enacted (which is, in the authors' view, unlikely) nothing will have been lost in the attempt.

It is considered that the GAAR does not apply to arrangements of this kind.

28.5 Gift of non-cash asset to charity by will

Similar arrangements can be made where a testator wishes to make a gift of a non-cash asset to charity. The position varies according to whether or not the asset is one which qualifies for QIDR.[6]

28.5.1 *Asset not qualifying investment*

The Gift Aid scheme set out above can still be utilised, in a slightly more complex manner. Suppose a testator wishes to give a picture to charity:

6 See 21.4 ("Qualifying investment").

1. The Will should give a cash sum to the beneficiary of an amount equal to the value of the picture. The Will expresses the wish that the beneficiary should give the sum to charity. The Will may even give the charity the option to purchase the picture.
2. The beneficiary gives the cash sum to the charity.
3. The charity then purchases the asset from the estate.

Gift Aid relief is still available on the beneficiary's cash gift to the charity. The anti-avoidance provision relating to acquisition of property[7] will not apply. For the personal representatives of the estate will not be "connected" with the beneficiary, within the statutory definition. This is so even if the personal representatives are in fact connected to the beneficiary in their private capacities.

Similar arrangements can be made where a testator desires to leave residue or a share of residue to charity.

28.5.2 *Asset is qualifying investment*

Similar arrangements can be made where a testator wishes to make a gift of an asset which is a qualifying investment for the purposes of QIDR, but in this case it is better to use QID relief; see 28.3 (QIDR).

28.6 Importance of will drafting

This proposal requires appropriate steps to be taken during the testator's life. If the testator makes a direct gift to charity in their Will, the omission cannot be put right after death.

Where an existing Will makes a gift to charity, it would be a simple matter to execute a codicil to revoke the gift and make a new gift to an individual.

---

7 See 15.19 (Acquisition of property rule).

CHAPTER TWENTY NINE

VARIATION OF WILLS

Cross references

The following topics are considered elsewhere:
28.1 (IT + IHT reliefs on gift by IoV)
IHT 10% charity legacy relief: see 25.18 (Instrument of Variation)

29.1 Variation of wills: Introduction

Section 142(1) IHTA provides:

> [a] Where within the period of two years after a person's death—
> (a) any of the dispositions (whether effected by will, under the law relating to intestacy or otherwise) of the property comprised in his estate immediately before his death are varied, or
> (b) the benefit conferred by any of those dispositions is disclaimed,
> by an instrument in writing made by the persons or any of the persons who benefit or would benefit under the dispositions,
> [b] this Act shall apply as if the variation had been effected by the deceased or, as the case may be, the disclaimed benefit had never been conferred.

Section 142(1)[a] sets out the conditions for s.142 to apply, and s.142(1)[b] sets out the consequences if it does apply.

A document which satisfies the conditions of s.142(1)[a](a) is called an instrument of variation ("**IoV**"). The requirements of s.142(1) are as follows:

(1) It must be made within two years of the death.
(2) It must vary dispositions of the property comprised in the deceased's estate.
(3) It must be in writing.
(4) It must be made by the persons or any of the persons who benefit or would benefit under the dispositions.

CGT has (almost) identical rules in s.62 TCGA.

29.1.1 *Election*

Section 142 IHTA provides:

> (2) Subsection (1) above shall not apply to a variation unless the instrument contains a statement, made by all the relevant persons, to the effect that they intend the subsection to apply to the variation.
> (2A) For the purposes of subsection (2) above the relevant persons are—
> (a) the person or persons making the instrument, and
> (b) where the variation results in additional tax being payable, the personal representatives.
> Personal representatives may decline to make a statement under subsection (2) above only if no, or no sufficient, assets are held by them in that capacity for discharging the additional tax.

This is effectively an election procedure.

29.1.2 *Variation for consideration*

Section 142(3) IHTA provides:

> Subsection (1) above shall not apply to a variation or disclaimer made for any consideration in money or money's worth other than consideration consisting of the making, in respect of another of the dispositions, of a variation or disclaimer to which that subsection applies.

This can raise some interesting issues, but they are not specifically charity tax questions, and so are not discussed here.

29.1.3 *Notification to charity*

Section 142 IHTA provides:

> (3A) Subsection (1) does not apply to a variation by virtue of which any property comprised in the estate immediately before the person's death becomes property in relation to which section 23(1) applies unless it is shown that the appropriate person has been notified of the existence of the instrument of variation.
> (3B) For the purposes of subsection (3A) "the appropriate person" is—
> (a) the charity or registered club to which the property is given, or
> (b) if the property is to be held on trust for charitable purposes or for the purposes of registered clubs, the trustees in question.

Presumably this is intended to stop the unsubtle fraud of a variation in favour of charity followed by not transferring the funds to the charity. This would in principle amount to theft from the charity (assuming the IoV was valid) as well as fraud on the Revenue (if it was not). So one might think that the rule is unnecessary. However it requires just one more piece of paper which does no harm. If the variation creates a charitable trust, under which the executors are trustees, no notice is required.

The IHT Manual provides:

> **IHTM35124: Requirement to notify IoV to charity** [Jun 2016]
> ... This does not impose a requirement for the charity or the trustees to be a party to the IoV, but the taxpayer must provide evidence that the charity or the trustees are aware of fact that property is to be redirected to them. Copies of an exchange of letters between the parties involved that show the charity or the trustees are aware of the arrangements will be sufficient.

29.1.4 *Standard form for chattels*

Form IHT408 (Household and personal goods donated to charity) is a standard form deed of variation. The explanation on the form (09/15 version) provides:

> **When to use this form**
> Fill in this form if the people who have inherited the deceased's household and personal goods:
> - wish to donate some or all of them to a qualifying charity
> - wish to deduct charity exemption against the value of the estate
>
> If you fill in this form you will not have to submit a formal Instrument

of Variation (IOV) to deduct charity exemption for any household and personal goods given to charity by the beneficiaries

The last paragraph is confused, as the form *is* a formal IoV; but the point is that the beneficiaries do not have to draft the IoV themselves.

29.1.5 *The future*

Spring budget 2015 announced that the Government will review the use of deeds of variation. This party political joke[1] was followed by a call for evidence.[2] But the matter was then dropped.

29.2 "Varied"

Section 142(1)[a] requires that the IoV must "vary" some of the "dispositions ... effected by will ..." of the property comprised in the estate of the deceased. What does this mean?

It is easy to understand how one may "vary" certain types of *legal relationship* or *asset*, such as leases and contracts, annuities and life insurance policies which have a continuing nature and a range of terms which may be altered. Likewise one may "vary" a settlement, which constitutes a continuing relationship between trustees and beneficiaries. In this context statutes often use the word "vary".[3]

It is harder to say what exactly is meant by varying a *disposition*. Let us start with the case of a simple one-off disposition, a transfer of property from T (the deceased) to B, effected by T's will. This disposition (the **"original disposition"**) does not create any continuing asset (which can be varied in the manner of a lease, etc.).[4] There are several possible views on what is required to "vary" that disposition (for the purposes of s.142). Assume B wishes to vary the disposition in favour of C.

One extreme view is that B can only "vary" the original disposition effected by T's will if they execute a document which:

(1) transfers the property to C; and
(2) is completely retrospective for all purposes so the original disposition

---

1 The Guardian aptly lead with the headline: "what came first – the policy or the joke?"

2 *https://www.gov.uk/government/consultations/review-of-deeds-of-variation-for-tax-purposes-call-for-evidence*

3 eg in the Variation of Trusts Act 1958.

4 Similar principles apply in the more complicated case where the Will creates a settlement; as the *disposition* made by the Will is a simple one-off disposition, to be distinguished from the ongoing effect of the settlement.

(which had been effected by the will) has effect as if C had always been the recipient under the will.

If this could be done the original disposition would certainly be "varied". But this possibility must be dismissed because it is not usually possible for B to vary the original disposition in this way.[5]

If the first possibility is rejected, what is necessary to amount to a variation? A second possibility is that B can "vary" the original disposition effected by T's will if they execute a document which:

(1) transfers the property to C; and
(2) which as between B and C has retrospective effect.[6] That is, this document would transfer to C the property and all income from the property arising between the date of death and the date of the variation (the "**intermediate income**").

Such a document may well use the word "vary" or some synonym. (No particular word is essential, as the matter can be expressed in various ways, but "vary" would be an apt word.) This solution does not constitute a variation of the original disposition in the very strictest sense. It is a new disposition which varies the result or effect of the old one. It is, however, as near to a variation of a disposition as English law permits.

A third possibility is that B can "vary" the disposition effected by T's will if they execute a document which:

(1) transfers the property to C; and
(2) recites or mentions the earlier disposition by T's will.

Such a document would not transfer the intermediate income to C. Can one describe such a document as a "variation" of that disposition?

(1) The document does not vary all the consequences of the disposition effected by the Will. It only varies some of the consequences of that disposition (the consequences as from the date of the IoV). But this does not matter, since a variation of some of the consequences of a

---

5 It is a basic principle that "No deed can alter the past". See Kessler & John, *Drafting Trusts and Will Trusts* (14th ed, 2019) para 10.6 (Backdating).

6 It is possible for persons to agree that, as between themselves, their respective rights should be ascertained *as if* some earlier disposition had been varied retrospectively. For instance, in *Bradshaw v Pawley* [1980] 1 WLR 10, a lease was granted in 1977 "from 1974 for ten years". This did not retrospectively vest an estate in the lessee. It could not do so. However, on execution of the lease, rent (or a sum equivalent to rent) then became due in respect of the period back to 1974.

disposition is still a variation of the disposition. "Variation" does not require an *entire* rewriting.[7]

(2) In drafting the document one would not necessarily use the word "vary". One might simply say: "B *transfers* the property they received from T's Will to C". But one could (just) use the word "vary" without impropriety.

It seems arbitrary that:

(a) if the document just says "B transfers the property to C" that is not a "variation" of the disposition effected by the Will; but

(b) if the document says "B transfers the property *received under T's Will* to C" that is a "variation" of the disposition effected by the Will.

But if what is a "variation" is hard to define, arbitrary results must be expected to follow in marginal cases.

A fourth possible view is that every disposition of the property by B varies the earlier disposition effected by T's Will. In a loose sense this is so. This solution would have the remarkable consequence that when anyone transfers property they must be said to be "varying" a previous disposition.

The choice therefore comes back to the second and third possibilities.

29.2.1 *HMRC view*

The HMRC view has wavered. In 1984 they took a view which seems to be close to the second view.[8] Following protests they adopted the third view (which is in principle more generous to taxpayers). Perhaps the context of s.142 supports that reading: it is certainly convenient not to have to bother about intermediate income, which in most cases would not amount to much. The IHT Manual provides:

> **IHTM35021: Published guidelines: introduction** [Jun 2016]
> HMRC has published guidelines setting out the requirements which an instrument must satisfy to qualify for IHTA84/S142. They are contained in a letter dated 11th April 1985 sent by Head Office to The Law Society. The text of the letter is given in the Law Society Gazette of 22 May 1985 at page 1454. The published requirements are that the

---

7 Contrast *Re Holt* [1969] Ch 100 at p.116-118 drawing a distinction between a variation of a trust and a completely new settlement.

8 There is a reference to this in the *Law Society's Gazette,* 7 November 1984.

instrument must
- be in writing (IHTM35022) and must be made by the persons or any of the persons who benefit (IHTM35023) or would benefit under the dispositions of the property comprised in the deceased's estate immediately before his death
- be made within two years after the death (IHTM35024)
- clearly indicate the dispositions that are the subject of the instrument, and vary their destination (IHTM35025) as laid down by the deceased's will or under the law relating to intestate estates, or otherwise ...

The IHT Manual provides:

> **IHTM35011: Instruments of Variation: introduction** [Jun 2016]
> ... In our view the word 'disposition' as used in IHTA84/S142 (1) refers
> [a] not to the content of the provision appearing in the will (or other relevant dispositive instrument or statute), but
> [b] to the result of applying that provision
> so that the focus is on the post-death beneficial interest.
> Accordingly the IoV must purport to change the destination of property in the estate from that prescribed by the disposition (however effected) which originally applied on the death to the property.

The IHT Manual provides:

> **IHTM35025: Published guidelines: destination of property must be varied** [Aug 2016]
> The third bullet under the guidelines at IHTM35021[9] sets out two requirements, the
> - identification of the original disposition, and
> - change of destination of the property subject to the specified disposition.
>
> *Original disposition*
> The first requires that the document which constitutes the variation clearly identifies the original dispositions and so establishes the linkage between their dispositive effect and the redistribution now intended.
> *Example*
> A document such as a deed of assignment/assignation which merely

9 The passage referred to reads:
"Strictly speaking however the instrument of variation does not actually vary the will itself, but only the effects of the will. Therefore it does not have retrospective effect as regards third parties, eg HMRC, except to the extent that statute, Section 62 TCGA 1992 or Section 142 IHTA 1984 so provides."

> transfers property in fact received by A under the will of X to the donee B without mention of that will does not satisfy this requirement. However, the more usual deed of gift which recites the derivation of property under a will or intestacy or by survivorship in joint tenancy or under a survivorship destination in Scotland and then in the operative part simply disposes of all or part of that property to its new beneficial destination will qualify both under this and the second requirement detailed below.

For practical purposes this should be taken to be correct. It follows that an IoV made by B in favour of C can meet the conditions of s.142(1)[a] without transferring the intermediate income to C. All that is needed is a document under which B refers to the will and transfers the property to C. In practice we would prefer to use the word "vary" in the drafting. However, B can keep the intermediate income.

29.3 Gift to individual: Variation to charity

The consequences of an IoV which meets the conditions of s.142(1)[a] IHTA are as follows:

Section 142(1)[b] applies:

> this Act [the IHTA] shall apply as if the variation had been effected by the deceased ....

And s.17 IHTA provides:

> None of the following is a transfer of value—
> (a) a variation ... to which s.142(1) below applies;

Suppose:
(1) T's will gives property to B (an individual) absolutely (so that the property is in principle subject to IHT on the death of the deceased ("T").
(2) B varies this disposition in favour of C (a charity) and the IoV gives the intermediate income to the charity.
In this case the IoV clearly causes T's estate to qualify for the IHT charity exemption.

Suppose the IoV varies the will by transferring property to C (a charity) but B *retains* the intermediate income. Does the IoV cause T's estate to qualify for the charity IHT exemption? The conditions of s.142(1)[a] are satisfied, so one must assume that the variation had been effected by the deceased. But if the deceased had provided by their will that an asset should be held on terms that the income was payable to B for a period, then to pass to charity, would IHT charity relief apply? It would not, because of the postponed gift rule and the entire interest rule.[10] However it is considered that an IoV of this kind still causes the estate to qualify for the charity IHT exemption. Either there is an implied exception to these rules, or else s.142(4) IHTA overrides them:[11]

> Where a variation to which subsection (1) above applies results in property being held in trust for a person for a period which ends not more than two years after the death, this Act shall apply as if the disposition of the property that takes effect at the end of the period had had effect from the beginning of the period; ....

Perhaps this is the reason for s.142(4).

29.4 Gift to L for life, remainder to charity: Variation to charity

We can now turn to the case where T left property by will on trust for an individual for life ("L"), with remainder to charity. T's estate is in principle subject to IHT.

29.4.1 *IoV during lifetime of L*

L during their life can vary the will by an IoV which assigns their life interest to the charity. This will cause T's estate to qualify for the charity exemption. It is not necessary for L to give the intermediate income to the charity.

29.4.2 *Expired life interest: Prospective assignment*

What is the position after the death of L? Suppose the personal representatives ("**PRs**") of L execute a deed under which:

(1) The PRs of L (purport to) assign the (expired) life interest to the charity, and
(2) the deed does not affect the intermediate income.

We refer to this as a "**prospective assignment of an expired life**

---

10 See 24.13 (Postponed gift rule); 24.17 (Entire interest rule).

11 This view was accepted (without argument) in *Schnieder v Mills* [1993] STC 430. In that case the effect of a IoV was to give a legacy to the widow of the deceased but not to affect the intermediate income. The judge assumed that the IHT spouse exemption applied to the estate. The IHT charity exemption works in the same way as the spouse exemption.

interest". This does not satisfy the terms of s.142(1)[a] because it does not *vary* any of the dispositions of the property comprised in the estate. Whether or not a disposition is varied is a question of property law, and as far as property law is concerned, such a deed has no effect. It does not vary anything.

Soutter's Executry v IRC [2002] STC (SCD) 385 concerned a prospective assignment of an expired life interest (in Scotland called a liferent) which had belonged to a Miss Greenlees. The Special Commissioner adopted this reasoning:

> The proposition of the Revenue is, devoid of cliché, that there can be no assignation of something which does not exist. The executors of a liferentrix[12] have nothing they can vary. That situation is wholly different from an outright gift because the estate of the second deceased has received benefit and can refund it, presumably if the beneficiary who had received the funds agreed. But Miss Greenlees' executors did not succeed to anything. They had neither right, title or interest to any liferent. The liferent could only come into existence if the liferentrix survived the deceased. Miss Soutter could have varied her will by omitting the liferent altogether and that, it seems, is what the executors of the second deceased seek to create. In my judgment the approach of Knox J where he cautions against an attempt to use the deeming provision as a method of creating a right is apposite and sound. Miss Greenlees' executors could not have continued to receive the liferent so they had nothing to give up or vary. The liferent was not and could not be assigned [by][13] them. It is in that sense that a purported assignation of an expired liferent has no reality.

HMRC agree. CTO Newsletter December 2001 provides:

> [1] It is perhaps not immediately obvious that a variation must be implemented in the real world.
> [2] S.17(a) IHTA expressly provides that a variation or disclaimer to which s.142(1) applies is not a transfer of value, so the instrument in writing must be more than an empty piece of paper.
> [3] That provision and s.142, in previous incarnations, were in effect a form of relief from double charges under the CTT regime.
> [4] It is a pre-requisite if the provisions are to have any impact that a "real life" disposition or transfer took place, so that the transferor can decide whether or not to make an election in order to trigger the

12 A liferenter (liferentrix) is the Scots equivalent of a life tenant.
13 The text erroneously reads: to.

deeming provisions.

[5] As Mr R T Oerton put it in *Capital Tax Planning* July 1992

> "In the real world of property law, where questions about ownership and the transfer of ownership are decided, the deceased does not make the changes: the beneficiaries do. And the deceased cannot be deemed in the true world to bring about effects which the beneficiaries cannot, or do not, bring about in the real world."

These generalities are broadly correct, though one could quibble with the wording and the details. In particular, the reference to the "real world" reflects some confusions, though the present is not the time to explore them.[14] But the CTO Newsletter now comes to the point:

> [6] Let us take the situation in which, under the will of A, B has an interest in possession in settled property, and on its cesser the beneficial interest in possession passes to C. In other words A leaves a life interest in property to B, with remainder to C. Following B's death within two years of A, C makes a deed of variation – still within that two year period – which purports to vary the will of A by redirecting B's interest to C or to extinguish it totally. In the real world B's interest does not exist, *there is nothing for the deed to bite upon,* and so s.142 simply cannot apply.
>
> [7] If the situation had been that it was possible for B's executors to disclaim his life interest as a matter of general law, then that should fall within the protection of s.142.

HMRC are right to say that a prospective assignment of an expired life interest would not satisfy the conditions of s.142(1)[a]. The reason is that an effective variation must (in the statutory words) "vary" something.

Some commentators have argued that although the IoV does not vary anything, it is deemed to have done so under s.142(1)[b]. This is wrong because unless the conditions of s.142(1)[a] are satisfied, the deeming of s.142(1)[b] does not come into effect. (One might also cite *Russell v IRC*[15] against this argument, to say that the deeming does not go so far. This may be why the Special Commissioner mentioned it in *Soutter,* but it is not necessary to rely on *Russell*. The argument does not get off the ground.)

---

14 The Special Commissioner noted this briefly in *Soutter*: "Part of the problem may be a diversion of thought by the use of such terms as 'in the real world'".

15 [1988] STC 195.

29.4.3 *Expired life interest: Retrospective variation*

Suppose, however, an IoV goes further, as between the parties (L's executors and C), and varies the life interest from the date of the death of the testator, dealing with the intermediate income. We refer to this as a "***retrospective* variation of the expired life interest**".

This possibility was not considered in *Soutter* or in the CTO Newsletter statement. The reasoning adopted in *Soutter* (which is, in our opinion, the same as that adopted in the CTO Newsletter statement), which shows that a *prospective* assignment of an expired life interest is outside s.142, does not apply here. One cannot say of the IoV that it is "an empty piece of paper" or that it has "nothing to bite on", assuming that there has been intermediate income.

In such a case the IoV has in our view "varied" the disposition effected by the Will and the conditions of s.142(1)[a] are satisfied.

An IoV only has to vary the *results* of that disposition,[16] and it is hard to deny that the IoV does do that.

This view is consistent with the rule that a disclaimer after expiry of a life interest is effective for IHT. Why is a disclaimer in such a case not "an empty piece of paper" with "nothing to bite on"? Because it operates retrospectively, ie it applies to the intermediate income.

It appears that HMRC do not agree.[17] IHTM para 35044 (October 2007) provides:

> ... you should not accept a variation which seeks to redirect a life interest after the life tenant has died (IHTM35042) as qualifying for relief under Section 142(1) IHTA 1984...

HMRC may riposte that the IoV is a variation, but it does not vary a disposition of property comprised in the estate of the deceased immediately before their death. It only varies the disposition of income accruing after the death. But the concept of "property comprised in the estate of the testator" must be understood to mean the property as a fund, not the individual assets of the estate. For example, if PRs sell property comprised in the estate and purchase replacement property, it is clear that an IoV can be made over the replacement property.[18]

---

16 See 29.2 ("Varied").

17 But HMRC practice has not been consistent (private correspondence).

18 But HMRC do not agree with that. CG Manual para 31601 (Jun 2016) provides: "An instrument of variation may be executed even if the assets involved have

Of course the meaning of the expression "vary a disposition" depends on the context. It is relevant to consider the purpose of s.142. The CTO Newsletter statement argues at [3] that s.142 is "in effect a form of relief from double charges". That is correct as far as it goes, but too narrowly expressed: if T gives property by will to B, and B varies the estate to give it to charity, then there could be no double charge, only a single charge, but this is a paradigm case of an IoV. The purpose is not just to avoid double charges, but also to avoid unfairness for beneficiaries under the will of a testator which does not take advantage of IHT reliefs; and so to avoid the expensive need for testators to regularly amend their wills (because beneficiaries can amend them after their death). But however that may be, the purpose suggests that relief ought to apply in the current situation. Then there is the case where A dies leaving property to B, and B dies leaving the property to C. HMRC accept that C can "vary" the disposition of property in A's estate so that the property passes directly from A to C.[19] In this context HMRC accept (we think, inconsistently)

---

already vested in the legatee. But if the assets have been sold by the legatee before the instrument is executed, there would appear to be difficulties in accepting the instrument's validity as an instrument of variation, on the basis that in general law the instrument takes effect from the date of execution, and no one can make a gift of property which he or she does not have ... ."

19 The IHT Manual provides:

"**IHTM35042: Who should make the instrument? dead beneficiaries** [Aug 2016]
The beneficiaries of a person who has died may make a variation redirecting that person's entitlement on an earlier death. The variation must be within the two-year period following that earlier death. This is particularly popular when husband and wife, or civil partners (IHTM11032), die within two years of each other. You should make sure the files are worked together and note the effect of the IoV on both deaths on form IOV1. It is not essential that a grant of representation has been obtained to either estate, but see IHTM35032.

Example

H dies leaving their estate to W absolutely. W dies 6 months later. The beneficiaries of W's estate can make an IoV within two years of H's death, redirecting property away from W so that it is no longer part of W's estate for IHT purposes. Most commonly this will be of an amount up to the threshold so that the two estates each gain maximum benefit of the nil-rate band.

In such cases, the redirection effected by the IoV made by W's beneficiaries may be to themselves directly or to others. We do not regard a redirection by W's beneficiaries to themselves directly as infringing the requirement to change the destination of the property. (IHTM35025) Though the final destination of the property in the hands of W's beneficiaries may not in fact be changed by the variation, the variation is still regarded as effecting a change in the disposition of the

that an IoV satisfies the requirements of s.142(1)[a] even though it has no effect as a matter of property law (which HMRC like to call the "real world"). This is not quite the same as our case, but it does suggest that the concept of "variation" is not to be construed so strictly.

What happens if the property given in the Will:

(1) produced no income between the death of the testator and the death of the life tenant; and
(2) was not enjoyed *in specie* by the life tenant?

If that is the case, then even a retrospective variation of the expired life interest does not have any effect as a matter of property law. This kind of issue arises elsewhere in inheritance tax where property produces no income and cannot be enjoyed *in specie* (such as an insurance policy). The question arises whether one can have an interest in possession in such property. The view has always been accepted that the answer is, yes. All that is necessary is that, if there were income from the property, it would be held on terms which satisfy the condition.[20] So a retrospective variation would be possible in relation to property which has not in practice yielded income. Although this is a case of a variation which *in fact* has no effect in property law terms, it is (unlike a prospective assignment of an expired life interest) one which is capable of having effect in some circumstances.

A similar question arises where the property in the estate is a residence which produces no income but which was occupied by the life tenant. In that case, the effect of a retrospective variation will be that the estate of the deceased life tenant is retrospectively required to pay rent (or a sum equivalent to rent) in relation to the period of occupation.

---

property in H's estate."

20 IHT Manual 16066 provides:

"**IHTM16066: Interests in possession: what if there is no income?** [Jun 2016]
The most common interest in possession is a life interest, usually in income producing assets such as stocks and shares, or in real property producing rent.
However it is not necessary for the property to produce income. An interest in possession may commonly exist in assets that do not produce income. A right to reside (IHTM16131) in a house is the most common example of enjoyment of property. Similarly, an interest in possession can subsist in chattels such as a painting or a necklace. It is not difficult to see that a life tenant can 'presently enjoy' things of this kind, without getting any money out of them.
An interest in possession can also exist in circumstances where the present 'enjoyment' is harder to identify. This arises in cases of life assurance policies where the beneficiary appears to take nothing until the death of the life assured. ..."

29.4.4 *Disclaimer during life of L*

If L disclaims their life interest, then (subject to the terms of the will) the property passes to the charity absolutely. This causes the estate of T to qualify for the IHT charity exemption. See s.93 IHTA which provides:

> Where a person becomes entitled to an interest in settled property but disclaims the interest, then, if the disclaimer is not made for a consideration in money or money's worth, this Act shall apply as if he had not become entitled to the interest.

During the lifetime of L, it does not in principle matter for IHT whether the matter is dealt with by disclaimer or by IoV.

29.4.5 *Disclaimer after death of L*

A disclaimer is in principle possible even after the death of L. The disclaimer is made by the PRs of L with the consent (or at the direction) of the beneficiaries of the estate of L who were entitled to the income disclaimed. A disclaimer, if possible, is preferable to an IoV as HMRC accept that a disclaimer even after the death of L causes the estate of T to qualify for the IHT charity exemption. However a disclaimer cannot be made after L has received a benefit from their life interest.

29.5 Gift to L for life, remainder to R (not a charity): variation to charity

So far we have been considering a will giving property to L for life with remainder to C, a charity. We have considered whether the will can be varied by L (or by the PRs of L after their death) so as to give L's interest to C, so that the charity becomes entitled to the property, and so that the estate of T qualifies for the IHT charity exemption. In this section we consider the position where the will of T gives property to L for life, with remainder to R (an individual, not a charity).

29.5.1 *Position during lifetime of L*

L and R can in principle together vary the Will (during the lifetime of L) so as to give the entire property (life interest and reversionary interest) to charity. In this case the IoV causes T's estate to qualify for the IHT charity exemption on the death of T.

Of course an IoV by L alone, or by R alone (during the lifetime of L) cannot cause the entire interest in the property to pass to charity, so it cannot cause T's estate to qualify for the IHT charity exemption.

Alternatively, L may disclaim their life interest, so that (subject to the terms of the Will) R becomes absolutely entitled; R can then vary the will so as to give the entire property to charity.

29.5.2 *Position after death of L*

Suppose L dies within two years leaving their residuary estate to Z, an individual. Can there still be an IoV made by (1) the PRs of L (with the consent of Z) and (2) R, so as to give the property to charity?

In this case there are in principle two IHT charges: the charge on the death of T and the charge on the death of L.[21]

If it is possible for the personal representatives of L (with the consent of the beneficiaries of the estate of L) to disclaim L's life interest then this would cancel the charge on the death of L: see s.93 IHTA. Following the disclaimer (and subject to the terms of the will) R would then become absolutely entitled to the property, and R could vary the will so as to give the property to charity (so that T's estate qualifies for the IHT charity exemption on the death of T).

The charge on the death of T can be avoided by an IoV if the view set out above is correct. However the IoV cannot cancel the IHT charge on the death of L which would otherwise arise, because of s.142(5) IHTA which provides:

> For the purposes of subsection (1) above the property comprised in a person's estate includes any excluded property but not any property to which he is treated as entitled by virtue of section 49(1) above ....

29.6 IoV after life tenant death: Conclusion

Where a Will leaves property to L for life, remainder to charity, the position should be reviewed immediately. An IoV during the lifetime of L is likely to save IHT.

If L dies within two years, the PRs of L should first consider a disclaimer (if possible). If a disclaimer is not possible (eg if L has received benefits from the estate) then an IHT saving is still possible by an IoV. The drafting needs care but the *Soutter* case is not the last word on the subject.

Where a Will leaves property to L for life, remainder to Y, an individual, and L dies within two years, the PRs of L and Y may act together to make

21 We ignore here the complication of quick succession relief.

an IoV in favour of charity.

29.7 Gift to foreign charity: IoV

A poorly advised testator may make a gift by Will to a body which is a foreign charity, not qualifying for IHT charity relief.[22] In that case the foreign charity may wish to vary the Will so as to make the gift to a UK charity which does qualify for the relief.

The UK charity may wish to transfer the assets to the foreign charity. In this context note the comment in the IHT Manual:

> **IHTM35123: Redirection to a charity by a non-qualifying body** [Jun 2016]
> The taxpayers may seek charity exemption as a result of an IoV which purports to redirect to a qualifying charity a bequest to a non-qualifying body. If the original non-qualifying beneficiary, whether UK or foreign, has effectively and completely divested itself of any benefit, for example, in the case of a collecting agency making a variation in favour of an independent charity, this may be acceptable providing the requirements of IHTA84/S142 are fully met. ...
> Where the information suggests that the new body is no more than a conduit by which the benefit will filter back to the original beneficiary, the matter should be referred to TG.

The technical basis on which TG (technical group) would attack the arrangement is not specified. "Conduit" is just a metaphor, not an argument.

One possibility is to allege an agreement between the foreign charity and the UK charity, so that the IoV is made for consideration. It is a question of fact but that will not be the case if the IoV has been carried out properly.

Another possibility is that the GAAR applies. But the arrangement is not entirely "circular" provided that the UK charity fulfills its obligations: see 24.12 (Application for charitable purposes).

It is not essential to vary in favour of a UK charity: the variation could be in favour of any EU charity. But the strict obligations imposed by law and regulators on a UK charity make it a suitable vehicle as that helps answer the HMRC conduit argument.

Ideally, care should be taken to avoid provocative arrangements.

---

22 See 3.24 (Non-EU charities).

29.8 Capital gains tax and IoV

Where there is more than one legatee and not all are charities, it would make sense for:

(1) assets pregnant with chargeable gain to be transferred to the charities, not to taxable persons such as UK resident and domiciled individuals; and

(2) assets not pregnant with gains (or at least with the least gains) to be transferred to taxable persons and not to charities.

This can often be done by means of an appropriation under s.41 AEA 1925, but (depending on the terms of the Will) an IoV may be necessary.

The charity would be able to realise the gains free of tax. The tax saving could be shared between the charity and the other beneficiaries by negotiation, or could be allowed to accrue entirely to the charity if the other beneficiaries were so minded.

It would also make sense for assets pregnant with losses to be transferred to taxable persons (who could use the losses) and not to charities, but s.16A TCGA needs consideration. A full discussion would be too lengthy to include here, but a review of the relevant HMRC Guidance Note suggests that this should be possible to arrange.

CHAPTER THIRTY

BENEFITS FOR DONORS

Cross references

The following topics are considered elsewhere:
15.20 (Benefit rule: Condition F)

30.1 Donor benefits: Introduction

This Chapter discusses certain situations where a donor may wish to obtain some benefit in return for a benefit they confer on a charity, albeit not full consideration. As there will be some element of gratuitous intent, we shall refer to the "donor" even though the transactions will not involve pure bounty on their part.

30.2 To gift or not to gift

In terms of IHT, the simplest course is for the donor to retain assets until their death and then to gift them to charity absolutely. The gift will qualify for the IHT charity exemption and the reservation of benefit rules will not apply.

If the property generates income surplus to the donor's requirements, the excess can be gifted by them to charity free from IHT. Gift Aid relief will normally be available.

While there are no IHT or IT problems, there remains a CGT problem. Any disposals made during the life of the donor would be taxable in full instead of being exempt from tax in the hands of the charity.

30.3 Sale for annuity

A donor might consider transferring an asset to charity in return for an annuity, say, for the duration of their life.

The consideration the donor prima facie receives for CGT purposes is the capitalised value of the annuity.[1] CGT would still be payable notwithstanding that the donor had no cash in their hands. Each instalment of annuity would then be taxed again as income in the hands of the donor. As the annuity would not be a "purchased life annuity" for IT purposes (the charity would not be in the business of granting annuities on human life) the "capital element" in the annuity would still be taxable as income.

The charity would be concerned that its payments are sums "applied for charitable purposes only". This would in principle be the case. The charity would also need to be sure that it did not incur non-charitable expenditure.[2] It is a moot point whether payment of instalments of annuity would amount to the investment by the charity of its funds in acquiring the asset originally transferred to the charity. If so, one would have to consider whether the asset was an approved charitable investment.

If the charity did have income which was not exempt from tax, it would not be possible for it to reduce the amount of its taxable income by deducting instalments of the annuity. As the charity would have received "non-taxable consideration", s.1301 CTA 2009 would be in point.

30.4 Sale for instalments of capital

30.4.1 *Distinguished from annuity*

As the sale of an asset to a charity for an annuity would normally be undesirable, the donor might consider selling an asset for a series of instalments of capital.

In order for the payments received by the donor to constitute capital and

1 If this were less than their allowable expenditure, they would be deemed to receive an amount equal to their allowable expenditure: see 23.3 (Donor CGT relief).

2 See 6.1 (Charitable expenditure rules).

not income, the number and date of the payments should be fixed in advance and the payments should continue to fall due notwithstanding the death of the donor. The amount of the payments should be fixed in advance, although there should be no objection to the instalments being index-linked. This arrangement is suitable only where an asset is sold and not where the donor transfers cash.

In calculating a fair price for the asset, the parties and their advisers would take into account current interest rates for the relevant periods. It is important, however, that all the documentation is in terms of instalments of capital. Otherwise each payment may consist of partly capital and partly interest taxable as income.[3] If the instalments are due over a very long period part of the payment may constitute interest even if it is described as capital in the documentation.[4]

30.4.2 *CGT-exempt assets*

The principal advantage is that while the donor will be liable in principle to CGT on any gain arising from the disposal of the asset, any further sum received will not be taxable as it will simply result from the original disposal. The arrangement is relatively straightforward in the case of a transfer of an asset a gain on the disposal of which is exempt from CGT, such as the principal residence or gilts.

30.4.3 *TCGA s.48 trap*

In the case of a sale for instalments of capital the consideration is deemed to be the total amount receivable without any discount for postponement of the right to receive any part of it: s.48 TCGA. This rule could throw up an artificial capital gain. Moreover, it should be remembered that in the case of a gift to charity the donor is deemed to receive market value only if that prevents them realising a loss and they cannot substitute a market value consideration in order to realise no gain or a smaller gain: s.257(2) TCGA. HMRC have some discretion to allow payment of tax by instalments.

30.4.4 *Sale to non-charity*

Where, therefore, the donor would be deemed to realise an artificially high

---

3 See *IRC v Church Commissioners* 50 TC 516.

4 See *Vestey v IRC* 40 TC 112.

capital gain, we suggest that they enter into the transaction with an entity which in the first instance is not a charity. The entity must be a connected person. The entity may be either a trust or a company, which could convert itself into a charity.

A potential cost of a sale to a non-charity is stamp duty. A conveyance to charity is exempt from stamp duty and SDLT. A conveyance to a non-charity may be subject to stamp duty or SDLT.

30.4.5 *Sale for full consideration*

One would then have to decide whether the transfer should be for full consideration or less than full consideration. If it were for full consideration, there would be no transfer of value on the part of the donor and thus no problem arising from the fact that the transferee was a non-charity. On the other hand, as the transaction would be by way of a bargain at arm's length, s.17 TCGA, which substitutes a market value consideration, would not normally apply unless the donor were connected with the transferee, in which case s.18(2) TCGA would bring s.17 into play. If the transferee were a trust, this could be achieved by making the donor a settlor: s.286(3) TCGA. In the case of a company, it would be appropriate for the donor to control it, eg by owning all of the share capital: s.286(6) TCGA.

Provided s.17 TCGA did apply, then the consideration the donor would be deemed to receive would be the market value of the asset and not the total amount of the capital payments. If the asset were in fact sold for market value, the nominal value of the instalments of capital would, of course, be greater, to compensate the donor for delay in payment.

If an interval after the transfer had been made and, perhaps, before the payment of the first instalment, the non-charity may be converted into a charity. Full control of the entity would now (if not already) be vested in an established charity.

The donor could then from time to time make payments to, say, the established charity out of the instalments of capital received from the new charity. It might be possible to ensure that the payments qualified for Gift Aid relief.

The donor could also, without any adverse IHT consequences, release the charity, whether during their lifetime or on their death, from the obligation to make any further instalments. Similarly, they could reduce the amount, frequency or duration of the payments.

30.4.6 *Sale for less than base cost*

It may be that the donor is content to make the transfer for less than full consideration and may wish to do so in order to reduce or eliminate a chargeable gain which would otherwise accrue to them. This could be important where the amount of CGT payable by the donor is greater than the instalments of capital already received by them.

If the total of the instalments of capital the donor wishes to receive is less than their allowable expenditure, then the simple solution is for the donor to enter into the transaction directly with a charity.

30.4.7 *Less than full consideration, more than market value*

If the total of the capital instalments which the donor wishes to receive exceeds the market value of the asset, they will be deemed for CGT purposes to receive market value, if they enter into the transaction with the non-charity. (They need not be "connected" with the non-charity in such a case, as the transfer will be otherwise than by bargain at arm's length.) The difficulty, however, is that they will have made a transfer of value for IHT purposes in respect of which the charitable exemption will not be available. In the case of a company, the transfer of value will be measured by the diminution in the estate of the transferor. This might not be that considerable, having regard to the fact that they also owned the shares in the company. The transfer of value could not qualify as a PET.

It might be preferable, therefore, especially in the case of the company, for the sale to be on an arm's length basis to a connected non-charity and for any bounty on the part of the donor to come at a later stage: see 30.4.5 (Sale for full consideration). This might incidentally help the donor to obtain Gift Aid relief on any subsequent gifts of cash to the charity made out of the instalments received by them.[5]

30.4.8 *Less than full consideration, less than market value*

Suppose, however, that the total of instalments of capital which the donor wishes to receive is less than the market value of the asset. Is there any advantage in making the transfer to a connected non-charity? Often, it would be positively disadvantageous to do so. For the donor will be deemed to have received a greater consideration than if they had made the

---

5 See 15.19 (Acquisition of property rule).

disposal directly to a charity. In the case of a disposal to a connected trust which is a non-charity, however, it would in some circumstances be possible for the donor to elect for hold-over relief pursuant to s.165 TCGA (as extended by sch 7) or s.260.[6] If an election is validly made, the gain the donor would otherwise have realised is reduced by the "held-over gain on the disposal".

Section 165(7) TCGA provides that in any case where:

> (a) there is actual consideration (as opposed to the consideration equal to the market value which is deemed to be given by virtue of s.17(1)) for a disposal in respect of which a claim for relief is made under this section, and
>
> (b) that actual consideration exceeds the sums allowable as a deduction under s.38,
>
> the held-over gain on the disposal shall be the amount by which the unrelieved gain on the disposal exceeds the excess referred to in paragraph (b) above.

At the very worst, the consideration the donor is deemed to receive will be reduced to that which they would have been deemed to receive on a disposal direct to a charity, ie the total nominal value of instalments of capital.

Is the effect of an election to deem the donor to have received for CGT purposes a consideration of such value as equals the true value of the consideration received by them, that is, the actuarial value of the right to receive the series of instalments rather than their total nominal value? While the point is not unarguable, we are pessimistic as to its chances of success. If the words in brackets did not appear in s.165(7), the argument would be very much stronger. Given the words in brackets, however, HMRC could argue with some force that the drafter is using the phrase "actual consideration" in a somewhat unusual sense, namely to mean deemed consideration other than a deemed market value consideration. Even in the case of a transfer which is in reality for a market value consideration, the consideration receivable is deemed to be higher.

In this case too, however, there exist the same potential IHT drawbacks.

---

6 Where the asset gifted is property used for a business of the transferor, shares or securities in a trading company, or an interest in agricultural property; or where the disposal would amount to a chargeable transfer for IHT purposes, whether or not any tax was actually chargeable.

30.5 Gift of home subject to right of residence

30.5.1 *No gift*

We now consider the situation where a person may wish to gift their home to a charity but nevertheless continue to reside there for the rest of their life and receive some other benefit, for example maintenance by the charity. If the donor does not wish to receive any benefit from the charity, then from their point of view they might as well retain the property and gift it to the charity only by their Will. See 30.2 (To gift or not to gift).

30.5.2 *Lease route*

If the donor transfers the freehold but retains a lease, unless they do so for full consideration they will make a chargeable transfer for IHT purposes. For the charitable exemption is not available in relation to a gift of property which is land or a building if the property is given subject to an interest reserved or created by the donor which entitles them or a person connected with them to possession of, or to occupy, the whole or any part of the land or building: s.23(4)(a) IHTA. Although there is an exception where a full rent is paid, this will be of no interest in the circumstances. If the lease is a "lease for life", further interesting questions arise as to whether the whole of the land (not just the lease) would thereby become settled property chargeable to IHT.

30.5.3 *Licence route*

The donor might convey the house to the charity in return for a personal licence of occupation. Extreme care would have to be taken in the drafting of the arrangements to ensure that the licence was not an interest in land and in particular did not constitute a lease or equitable interest in the land. If the licence were a true licence, s.23(4)(a) IHTA would not apply as it would not be an "interest" and the property would not be "subject to" it. Nor would the arrangement create a settlement, so that on termination of the licence on the death of the donor, there would be nothing to be brought into charge to IHT.

While a licence can be tax efficient, it should be brought home to the donor that it is not capable of being turned to pecuniary account in the same way as, say, a lease. If for any reason the donor is unable or unwilling to continue occupying the property, they will simply have to abandon it unless the charity can be prevailed upon to enter into some other arrangement.

The difficulties with the licence route are twofold. First, the licence will give exclusive possession and the courts might well construe such a licence as a lease, no matter what wording is used in the written agreement: *Street v Mountford* [1985] AC 809; *AG Securities v Vaughan* [1988] 3 WLR 1207; *Skipton Building Society v Clayton* 66 P&CR 223. If that hurdle were overcome, it might be held that a licence is an "interest" reserved over the land, construing that word loosely, rather than in its conveyancing sense.

30.5.4 *Deferred sale*

Another possibility is for the donor to enter into a contract to sell the house, completion to take place only after their death. Given the length of time the vendor would remain in possession, more thought than usual would have to be given to the respective rights and duties of the vendor and purchaser during this period, especially as to maintenance of the house. There is no reason in principle why the purchaser should not take upon itself all the obligations of maintenance, provided, of course, this were properly reflected in a decreased price.

This arrangement would not constitute a settlement for IHT purposes. It would be as well to ensure, however, that so far as possible the terms of the contract were similar to those in any standard contract for the sale of land. For it may safely be assumed that HMRC will not argue that every contract for the sale of land gives rise to a settlement for IHT purposes with a resulting transfer of value on completion, notwithstanding that in the meantime the vendor does stand in a fiduciary relationship to the purchaser and the property is, in a loose sense, held on trust for persons by way of succession.

Where the deferred sale is on terms beneficial to the charity, it is arguable that the vendor makes a chargeable transfer of value on entering into the contract. Whether they make a transfer of value at all depends on the extent to which their liability to convey is taken into account in determining the value of their estate immediately after the contract is made. IHTA s.5(5) allows the liability to be taken into account only to the extent that it was incurred for a consideration in money or money's worth. If the vendor does make a transfer of value, the argument that it does not qualify for the charitable exemption is that the property which is "given to charity" to which the transfer is attributable is "an interest in other property", which interest is "less than the donor's", so that s.23(3)(a) IHTA applies.

30.5.5 *CGT considerations*

If the house in question is the donor's principal residence, then normally there will be no question of a charge to CGT resulting from the arrangements. If it is not, however, then the donor could be liable to CGT if the value of the consideration received by them exceeded their allowable expenditure. In the case of a licence to occupy the land during their life, the valuation of the consideration received by them would be relatively straightforward. In the case of a contract for the sale of land with deferred completion, however, the deferred payment will be valued at its nominal value with no discount for postponement: see 30.4.3 (TCGA s.48 trap). If, therefore, the donor is on completion retrospectively deemed to have sold the property at the date of the contract,[7] that could well throw up a chargeable gain. Provided the contract is not completed until after the death of the donor, it is considered that they would not be deemed to have disposed of the asset at the time of the contract, for their personal representatives are the persons who actually dispose of the asset and they are for CGT purposes regarded as a separate entity from the deceased: s.62(1) TCGA. TCGA s.28 affects only the time of disposal, not the person by whom a disposal was made.

It is true that a difficulty then arises in that the personal representatives are prima facie deemed to have disposed of the asset at a time when they did not own it, namely when the contract was made. While there is nothing necessarily absurd in the notion of a person disposing of an asset before they have acquired it, indeed, "selling short" is a fact of modern financial life, there is some absurdity in a person being deemed to dispose of an asset at a time when they were not in existence and therefore, arguably, not within the charge to CGT at all! The difficulty is that the drafter of the TCGA has not given any thought to the situation which arises where an asset is transferred subject to an existing contract of sale (or option to acquire it). The courts are therefore going to have to write something into the Act in order to make it work. In our opinion, all they need do is so interpret s.28 as to deem an asset to be disposed of at the *later* of the time the contract is made or the time when the person disposing of the asset became entitled to it. (A similar interpretation would be needed in the case of time of acquisition where the benefit of a contract to acquire an asset is transferred before completion.)

---

7 See s.28 TCGA.

If our opinion is correct, then the donor will make no disposal of the property during their lifetime. While their personal representatives will dispose of the property shortly after their death, their base cost should be the market value of the house at the time of death. Thus, unless there had been an unexpected fall in property values, normally they would not realise any chargeable gain. If they did, it would be a real gain on which they could not reasonably expect to avoid paying tax. If the charity were the beneficiary of the donor's estate then it would be important that the contract were not completed, as the personal representatives would not enjoy the charitable exemption. It might be appropriate to seek to avoid these difficulties by devising the property to the charity subject to and with the benefit of the contract of sale, so that the contract will never be completed. Care must be taken, however, to ensure there are no IHT complications resulting from the dispositions by associated operations rules.

30.5.6 *Income tax*

If the charity conferred any benefit on the donor which was of a recurrent nature, this could well give rise to further charges to tax on the donor. The simple case is that of an annuity, as to which see 30.3 (Sale for annuity). Similar payments by a charity could also amount to "annual payments" to or for the benefit of the donor and thus give rise to the same tax consequences as an annuity: for example, payment of council tax (which would be the liability of the donor *qua* occupier) or income (as opposed to capital) expenditure in maintaining the premises. It is a moot point the extent to which the provision of an income benefit otherwise than in cash (or, which is equivalent to cash, discharging a liability of the donor) would be taxable as an annual payment.

Whether or not the provision of benefits by the charity is taxable as income of the donor, the value of the right to receive such benefits would be taken into account in quantifying the consideration received by the donor on the original disposal of the property for CGT purposes. In the case where the benefits are to be conferred over a specified period, it is arguable that s.48 TCGA would apply to their valuation, just as much as if they had taken the form of cash payments.[8]

---

8 For the injustice of s.48, see 30.4.3 (TCGA s.48 trap).

30.6 Provision for relative/dependant: Lifetime planning

A person may wish their estate to pass to charity, subject to provision for the lifetime of a relative or a dependant.

The obvious course is to provide in the Will that the estate should be held on trust for the relative for life, with remainder to charity. Where the relative is the surviving spouse or civil partner, this is completely satisfactory.

Suppose, however, that the dependant is a cohabitee, a parent, or any person other than the surviving spouse. In that case there are serious inheritance tax problems which cannot be wholly solved by Will drafting. See 26.3 (Residue to charity, provision for dependant relative).

Lifetime planning can offer a solution. This is not an area where it is necessary to survive seven years to save tax. The following is a brief guide. Capital gains tax questions may also arise, but are not considered here.

The assets involved may be a fund of investments or (very commonly) one is concerned with a private residence.

(1) Investments
As far as the investments go, s.11(3) IHTA provides an important (and somewhat neglected) tax relief:

> A disposition is not a transfer of value if
> [i] it is made in favour of a dependent relative of the person making the disposition and
> [ii] it is a reasonable provision for his care or maintenance.

The important point to note is that this tax relief applies to lifetime gifts, even if made very shortly before death, but the relief does not apply to gifts made by Will. (At least, this is the HMRC view; the contrary is not unarguable.)

So if the testator can be persuaded to make provision for their dependent relative during their life, and not by Will, then the tax problems can be solved completely. And it is never too late – until death – to make the necessary arrangements. For instance, they may use a lump sum to purchase an annuity for the maintenance of the dependant.

(2) The dwelling-house
The testator may during their lifetime grant a lease to the relative or dependant. The lease may give the relative security of tenure. The grant of the lease may not be a transfer of value by virtue of s.11 IHTA. The

testator will then bequeath the reversion to the lease to charity by their Will. That gift will only qualify for charity IHT relief if the lease is not to a connected person or if full rent becomes payable. See 24.19 (Retained interest rule: Land).

Once again, these arrangements can be put into effect at any time before death; it is not necessary to survive the usual seven-year period to qualify for tax relief.

CHAPTER THIRTY ONE

TRUSTS WITH SOME CHARITABLE ELEMENT

31.1 Types of trust

This Chapter considers trusts which are charitable to varying degrees. (Similar considerations can apply to companies, though in practice this does not arise so often.) We also consider an arrangement which may enable a charity to acquire settled property, whether or not the vendor is a charitable trust, in a tax-efficient manner and consequently at a favourable price to the charity.

We coin the following terminology:

"**Exclusively charitable trust**" means a trust under which capital and income can only be paid to a charity or applied for charitable purposes.

"**Partly charitable trust**" means a trust which contain two (or more) separate funds, of which one (or more) would constitute an exclusively charitable trust if it were the only fund.

"**Temporary charitable trust**" means a trust under which all income currently arising must be paid to a charity or applied for charitable purposes only; but the capital might in the future become held on non-charitable trusts. An example is a trust for charity, subject to a wide overriding power of appointment.

"**Mixed charitable trust**" means a trust under which there is a power to pay or apply capital or income to charities or for charitable purposes or to individuals.

31.2 Partly charitable trust

31.2.1 *IHT*

For inheritance tax purposes, there is no difficulty in severing the fund held on exclusively charitable trusts from the rest of the settled property. If property is gifted to such a fund, the IHT charity exemption will apply: see s.23(6) IHTA.

Similarly, the property comprised in the fund will not constitute "relevant property" and so will not be subject to IHT 10 year and exit charges. See s.84 IHTA which provides:

> For the purposes of this Chapter (except sections 78 and 79) where the trusts on which settled property is held require part of the income of the property to be applied for charitable purposes, a corresponding part of the settled property shall be regarded as held for charitable purposes.

The value of the property would, however, be taken into account in calculating IHT charges on the rest of the settled property.

31.2.2 *Income tax and CGT*

A partly charitably trust is not a charity within the tax definition and does not qualify for CGT relief.

Exemption applies to certain types of investment income of partly charitable trusts (in particular, interest and dividends).[1] Other types of income, eg rents, are strictly taxable.[2]

The position has been held to be different in the case of a trust to pay a proportion of the income to charity. *George Drexler Ofrex Foundation v IRC* 42 TC 524 concerned a charitable trust which contained a proviso that the settlor could direct that 60% of the income should be applied for non-charitable purposes. Cross J said at p.536:

> I must take this proviso into account in considering whether or not this trust is a trust established solely for charitable purposes; and, assuming

1 See 4.6 (Investment income: General conditions for relief).

2 This may only be a cash-flow problem, however, provided the income is paid by the trustees to charities rather than being applied for charitable purposes without so being paid. See 31.3 (Temporary charitable trust). HMRC might not take the point.

> for a moment that the proviso is valid, it seems to me that I cannot say that it is.

31.3 Temporary charitable trust

31.3.1 *IHT*

A gift to a temporary charitable trust will not qualify for the IHT charity exemption.

A temporary charitable trust is not subject to the discretionary trust regime of ten year and exit charges. That only applies to "relevant property" and s.58(1) IHTA provides:

> In this Chapter "relevant property" means settled property in which no qualifying interest in possession subsists, other than—
>
> (a) property held for charitable purposes only, whether for a limited time or otherwise ...

However if the property ceases to be held for charitable purposes only (otherwise than by being applied for such purposes or being transferred to a charity) an exit charge is levied at a penal rate: s.70 IHTA.

31.3.2 *CGT*

A temporary charitable trust is a charity for the English law definition of charity[3] and for CGT purposes.[4]

31.3.3 *Income tax*

The same must apply for income tax, especially since the tax definitions are now the same for all taxes. What if income is accumulated and then the trust ceases to be charitable? There is no statutory clawback charge[5] but one could hardly expect the income to be and to remain exempt. There are two ways to reach that result.

---

3 *Re Peel* (1863) 3 Ch App 543; *Gibson v South American Stores* [1950] 177; Picarda, *Law and Practice Relating to Charities* (4th ed, 2010) p.380 "If the trustees of a charitable trust are given a power to revoke the trusts and to declare new non-charitable trusts the mere existence of this unexercised power does not make the original trusts non-charitable." The English law definition since 2006 incorporates the word "only"("established for charitable purposes only") but there are other indications that temporary charities are regarded as "charities".

4 This is assumed in various CGT provisions; see 5.7 (Termination of charitable trust); 5.9 (Rate of tax on gains).

5 The termination of the trust would not involve "expenditure", so the charitable expenditure rules would not have any application: see s.562(4) (5) ITA.

(1) One might say that a temporary charitable trust could only be a charity if income arising during the charitable period could only be applied for charitable purposes (ie if the terms of the trust did not permit trustees to accumulate income and later appoint that the accumulated income should be held on terms under which it later ceases to be charitable).

(2) One might say that such a trust was a charity but accumulated income was not applied for charitable purposes only.

We prefer the first analysis.

31.4 Mixed charitable trust

31.4.1 *Inheritance tax*

A gift to a mixed charitable trust would not qualify for the IHT charity exemption. The settled property would constitute "relevant property" and so would be subject to IHT 10 year and exit charges. If, however, the property ceases to be relevant property by becoming property held for charitable purposes only without limit of time, then in general there is no exit charge: see 24.37 (Charity exit charge relief).

31.4.2 *Income tax*

The trustees of a mixed charitable trust do not qualify for any charity IT exemption even if they apply the trust income for charitable purposes only. The trustees should pay the income to a charity, in which case there should normally be no difficulty in the recipient charity recovering tax borne by the trustees of the mixed charitable trust.[6]

Similar considerations apply to a trust (too rare to consider here in detail) to pay annuities and hold the balance on charitable trusts. The trust is not a charity and does not qualify for any relief even though a part of the trust income is paid to charity; see *Lawrence v IRC* 23 TC 333. But although the trustees cannot claim the income tax relief applicable to charities, it may be that income tax relief may be available in some other way. If trustees hold a trust fund on trust to pay an annuity to charity and the balance to others, then the trustees can in effect deduct the annuity from their income.

Likewise a trust to repay a loan (not incurred for charitable purposes) and to hold the remainder for the charity, or at least, the repayment of the loan

---

6 Section 610 CTA 2010 prevents tax reclaims on payment to a company but charitable companies are excluded.

is not an application for charitable purposes.[7]

31.4.3 *Capital gains tax*

Trustees of a mixed trust do not qualify for the charity CGT exemption in respect of disposals made by them.

If the trust holds an asset pregnant with gain, it might be sensible for this to be transferred to a beneficiary charity.[8]

31.5 Settlor-interested trust

Section 624 ITTOIA provides (in short) that income arising under a settlor-interested settlement is treated as accruing to the settlor. Section 628(1) ITTOIA disapplies this rule for the benefit of mixed and temporary charitable trusts:

> The rule in s.624(1) does not apply to any qualifying income which arises under a UK settlement if—
> (a) it is given by the trustees to a charity in the tax year in which it arises, or
> (b) it is income to which a charity is entitled under the terms of the trust.

The income must be:

(1) "Given by the trustees to a charity in the tax year in which it arises". This would apply to a mixed charitable trust; or

(2) "Income to which a charity is entitled under the terms of the trust". This would apply to a temporary charitable trust.

31.5.1 *Qualifying income*

This relief applies to "qualifying income". This is defined in s.628 ITTOIA:

> (2) In this section "qualifying income" means—
> (a) income which must be accumulated,
> (b) income which is payable at the discretion of the trustees or any other person, or
> (c) income which (before being distributed) is income of any person other than the trustees.
>
> (2A) The cases covered by subsection (2)(b) include cases where the trustees have, or any other person has, any discretion over one or more

7 See 4.21.2 (Income used to repay loan).

8 See 23.15 (Private trust: Disposal to charity).

of the following matters—
(a) whether, or the extent to which, the income is to be accumulated,
(b) the persons to whom the income is to be paid, and
(c) how much of the income is to be paid to any person.

This definition would seem to include all income arising to the trustees. Section 628(3)(4) ITTOIA provides an apportionment rule:

> (3) Subsection (4) applies if in any tax year qualifying income which arises under a UK trust from different sources exceeds the total of—
> (a) the amount of that income which falls within subsection (1), and
> (b) the amount of that income which falls within s.630(1) (comparable exception for income of relevant children of settlor).[9]
>
> (4) The amount of the qualifying income from different sources which falls within subsection (1) above is rateably apportioned between those sources.

This is relevant if some income accruing to trustees is dividend income. Section 628(5) ITTOIA provides:

> This does not affect the operation of any requirement that the whole, or any specified part, of the income from a particular source is to be given to a charity.

It is difficult to see the point of this provision.

31.5.2 *"UK settlement"*

The relief only applies to a UK settlement. Section 628(6) ITTOIA provides a commonsense definition:

> "UK settlement" means a settlement the trustees of which are resident in the United Kingdom.

There is no justification for this requirement, which is presumably due to

---

9 ITTOIA EN explains: "Subsection (3)(b), which includes within the sum paid to a charity sums for which the exemption in s.630 applies, covers the possibility, unlikely though it may be, of a trust changing its nature during a tax year whereby it is no longer a settlor-interested trust and thus one to which s.630 might apply. (A charge under that section will not apply if a charge under s.624 applies.) Any charitable payments exempted from a charge on the settlor under s.629 must be included to give the correct result."

a prejudice against non-resident trusts and the rule is not EU-law compliant. But the point will rarely if ever arise in practice.

31.5.3 *s.628: Critique*

The relief for settlor-interested trusts will rarely if ever be used. It would generally be easier for the settlor to receive the trust income income and make a gift to the charity under the Gift Aid rules. The provision is dead letter tax law and ought to be repealed.

31.6 Income paid to children of settlor

Section 629 ITTOIA provides (in short) that a settlor is taxed on trust income paid to or applied for the benefit of their minor children. Section 630 ITTOIA provides an exception where the income is given to charities. The relief is misconceived because income given to charities cannot be paid to or for the benefit of minor children. ITTOIA EN stated:

> 974. This exemption might apply in the unusual circumstances of a charity benefiting the minor child of a settlor, that is to say that payments out of the settlement to the charity were paid to or applied for the benefit of the settlor's minor child.

But if such payments were made, it is considered that they should not be regarded as payments made to or for the "benefit" of the minor child in the relevant sense.[10]

31.7 Sale from trust to charity: CGT

Suppose a farm is held on common form discretionary trusts for the benefit of private individuals. The trustees are considering making an appointment of the farm to a beneficiary absolutely. A charitable trust is interested in acquiring the farm as an investment. The asset is pregnant with a capital gain.

One scenario would be for the trustees to appoint the asset *in specie* to the beneficiary and for them then to sell it to the charity. CGT would become payable on the appointment and/or the subsequent sale.

A possible arrangement is as follows:

(1) The trustees appoint the asset to the beneficiary absolutely, contingently upon their surviving for 90 days. The appointment expressly does not carry the intermediate income.

---

10 See 12.5 (Charity beneficiaries).

(2) The beneficiary can then negotiate to sell their contingent interest to a charitable trust before the 90 days have expired. The charity would no doubt wish to insure against the risk of death of the beneficiary within the 90 day period.

Provided the beneficiary survived the 90 days, the charity would become absolutely entitled to the asset on the expiration of that period. The purchase is an approved charitable investment under the charitable expenditure rules.[11] The trustees would be deemed to make a disposal under s.71(1) TCGA. The exemption in s.257(3) TCGA would not apply as the charity would have acquired its interest under the settlement for a consideration in money or money's worth, but the trustees would join with the charity in making an election for hold-over relief from CGT.[12]

The disposal by the beneficiary of their beneficial interest would normally be exempt from CGT: s.76(1) TCGA. The charity would be deemed to dispose of its beneficial interest in consideration of acquiring the farm, which would doubtless throw up a chargeable gain which would not be exempt under s.76(1) TCGA: see s.76(2). The CGT charity exemption contained in s.256 TCGA should in principle be available. If the charity were to dispose of the asset in years to come the general charitable exemption from CGT should likewise be available.

While IHT would be payable when the farm ceased to be settled property, the charitable exemption being excluded by s.76(7) IHTA as the charity would have acquired its interest for a consideration in money, the tax due would be no higher than if the farm had vested in the beneficiary absolutely at the end of the 90-day period. In the case of farmland, agricultural property relief may apply.

Consideration must be given to sch 4A TCGA.

It cannot be over-emphasised that a charity should not participate in arrangements of this kind without taking specialist advice.

---

11 See s.558 (Type 5) ITA (or the CT equivalent) which refers to any interest in land.

12 Assuming that the conditions for hold-over relief are satisfied; see in particular para 3 sch 7 TCGA .

CHAPTER THIRTY TWO

PAYMENTS TO CHARITY FROM NON-RESIDENT TRUSTS

32.1 Payment to charity from non-resident trust

This chapter considers the position where a non-resident non-charitable trust makes a distribution to a charity.

32.2 Income/gains arising on disposal by trust

The transfer of an asset from a trust to a non-charitable beneficiary is treated as a disposal at market value, so a chargeable gain will generally arise. However, no chargeable gain arises on a transfer from a trust to a charity.[1] So there will be no charge on the settlor under s.86 TCGA.

Similarly, no offshore income gain arises.[2]

If the asset disposed of is a deeply discounted security, or a security within the accrued income scheme, the disposal may give rise to income which may fall within s.720 ITA (tax on transferor) or s.731 ITA (relevant income). There is no relief for where the transfer is made to a charity.[3] But it may not often happen, or the amounts involved may not be significant.

---

1 See 23.15 (Private trust: Disposal to charity).

2 See 23.6 (Offshore fund).

3 See 23.7 (Deeply discounted security); 23.8 (Accrued income scheme).

32.3 Capital payment rules

On a distribution to a UK resident trust,[4] the rules in s.87 TCGA need consideration. Section 87(2) TCGA provides:

> Chargeable gains are treated as accruing in the relevant tax year to a beneficiary of the settlement who has received a capital payment from the trustees in the relevant tax year or any earlier tax year if all or part of the capital payment is matched (under section 87A as it applies for the relevant tax year) with the section 1(3) amount for the relevant tax year or any earlier tax year.

For a full discussion of s.87, see Kessler, *Taxation of Non-Residents and Foreign Domiciliaries*.[5]

It is assumed that the trust has s.1(3) amounts (informally called "trust gains") which can be matched to a capital payment.[6]

Also see 15.43.6 (CGT interest surcharge (offshore trust)).

32.4 "Capital payment"

"Capital payment" is defined in s.97(1) TCGA. So far as relevant, this provides:

> ... "capital payment"—
> (a) means
> [i] any payment which is not chargeable to income tax on the recipient or,
> [ii] in the case of a recipient who is not resident in the UK, any payment received otherwise than as income...

The position will depend upon whether the distribution is income or capital in the hands of the charity.[7]

If the receipt is income in the hands of the charity, the income (classified as "annual payments") is within the scope of the income tax charge but

---

4 For distribution to a non-resident charity, see 32.10 (Payment to non-resident charity from non-resident trust).

5 (21st ed., 2022-23), Chapter 60 (Capital Payments from Non-resident Trusts: s.87) *https://www.foreigndomiciliaries.co.uk*

6 No chargeable gains arise on the disposal of an asset from the non-charitable trust to the charity: see above. But gains may have accrued on other disposals by the trustees, which were not disposals to charities.

7 As to what is an income/capital receipt from a trust, see Kessler, *Taxation of Non-Residents and Foreign Domiciliaries* (21st ed., 2022-23), para 41.8 (Trust payment: Income/capital) online version *https://www.foreigndomiciliaries.co.uk*

qualifies for exemption.[8] It is considered in the context of the definition of "capital payment" that the income of a charity is "chargeable" to income tax even if it qualifies for exemption. Otherwise wherever a trust distributes income to a charity it makes a "capital payment" (and reduces its s.1(3) amounts); that result would be very odd. A cash payment from a non-resident company to a charity is treated as income of the charity so it is not a capital payment.[9] A non-cash payment may be preferred, in order to have a capital payment which matches trust gains.

A receipt from a trust which is capital in the hands of the charity is a capital payment as it is not chargeable to IT.[10] The question then is whether s.87 TCGA imposes a CGT charge.

32.5 Is charitable *company* a "beneficiary"

Section 87(2) TCGA only applies if a "beneficiary of the settlement" receives a capital payment. It seems clear that a non-charitable company may be a "beneficiary" for the purposes of s.87. In principle the same should apply to a charitable company (which is, in principle, beneficial owner of its assets).

Section 97 TCGA offers a further route to the same result. A charitable company (if it were not a "beneficiary" in the normal sense of the term) would be deemed to be a beneficiary by s.97(8).

32.6 Is charitable *trust* a "beneficiary"

It is helpful first to consider the position if a capital payment is made from a non-resident trust to trustees of a private (non-charitable) trust. Is the recipient trust[11] a "beneficiary" for the purposes of s.87? The term "beneficiary" (in isolation) is ambiguous. The word may or may not include a trustee who has an interest under a trust which is not a beneficial interest.[12] The context must determine the issue. The context shows that

---

8 See 4.11 (Annual payments).

9 See 17.9 (Position of charity receiving gift).

10 There cannot be any liability to income tax under s.731 ITA. See 32.9 (Capital payment: s.731 ITA).

11 Strictly one should perhaps ask whether the trustees are beneficiaries, not whether the trust is a beneficiary, but in practice the two expressions are used synonymously.

12 See Kessler & John, *Drafting Trusts and Will Trusts* (14th ed, 2019), paras 5.17-5.18 (Definition of "Beneficiaries"). Section 22 Trusts of Land and Appointment of Trustees Act 1996 contemplates that the term "beneficiary" can include a person having an interest in settled property as a trustee.

a private trust is not to be regarded as a "beneficiary" of another trust for the purposes of s.87 TCGA:

(1) Section 90 TCGA sets out a code of rules for transfers to trusts. The view that that trust is a "beneficiary" is inconsistent with s.90.
(2) Section 97(10) TCGA also assumes that a trust is not (and directs that it should not be deemed to be) a "beneficiary" for the purposes of s.87.

These are arguments from context. The context of a charitable trust is entirely different and shows that a charitable trust should be regarded as a beneficiary for the purposes of s.87. This would better fit the scheme of the legislation:

(1) This would be consistent with the position for charitable companies. The courts favour a construction which minimises the differences between the two: *Von Ernst & Cie SA v IRC*.[13]
(2) If (contrary to our view) a charitable trust is not a beneficiary, then no charge arises under s.87 on a capital payment to a charitable trust. Instead the s.1(3) amounts (trust gains) of the non-resident trust, or a proportion of them, would be carried across to the charitable trust under s.90 TCGA. Then chargeable gains would be treated as arising to "beneficiaries" of the charitable trust who receive capital payments from it. But a charitable trust does not have "beneficiaries" in the strict sense.[14] So no tax charge would arise. One cannot solve this problem by saying that "beneficiaries" in s.87 is to be construed in a loose sense; the law would be unworkable. How would a large charity like the Charities Aid Foundation and its "beneficiaries" deal with the position?

These considerations show that a charitable trust should be regarded as a beneficiary for the purposes of s.87 TCGA.

32.7 s.87 gain: Charity's CGT exemption

The next question is whether gains deemed to accrue to a charity under s.87(2) TCGA qualify for the charity's CGT exemption.

It would be absurd if charity CGT exemption did not apply on capital payment from non-resident trust, for several reasons:

(1) Charities generally enjoy exemption from CGT so it would be odd if a payment from a non-resident trust were subject to CGT.

---

13 [1980] STC 111.

14 See 12.5.1 ("Beneficiary" of charity).

(2) Payment of an income nature from a non-resident trust would be exempt, so it would be odd if a capital payment were taxable.
(3) It would severely discourage grants to UK charities from offshore charities and non-charitable trusts, which would not be in the public interest.

HMRC formerly argued that the exemption did not apply, but wisely changed their minds in RI 189. This provides:

> **Capital Payments by Offshore Trusts to UK Resident Charities: Change in Inland Revenue Practice**
> ... Under the provisions of s.87 TCGA, where gains have been realised by the trustees of an offshore settlement, chargeable gains may be treated as accruing to beneficiaries who are resident in the UK to the extent that they receive capital payments from the trust.
> Under s.256 TCGA, gains accruing to charities are not chargeable to tax if they are applicable and applied for charitable purposes. Until [1998], however, the Inland Revenue have always taken the view that this exemption is not available for gains which are treated by s.87 TCGA as accruing to a charity as the beneficiary of an offshore settlement.
> Following recent representations on the matter, the Inland Revenue have taken legal advice on the application of these provisions and, in the light of that advice, have now concluded that the better view is that s.256 TCGA may exempt gains which would otherwise be charged on UK charities under s.87 TCGA.
> Consequently, where a UK charity, as beneficiary of an offshore settlement, receives a capital payment, in respect of which a chargeable gain would be treated as accruing to it under [what is now s.87(2)] TCGA, the charity will now be entitled to exemption from tax provided by s.256(1) TCGA to the extent that the capital payment is applicable and applied for charitable purposes.

Note that the RI assumes that a charity is a "beneficiary" within the meaning of s.87. It does not distinguish between charitable companies and charitable trusts. The correctness of our view that charitable companies and trusts are "beneficiaries" for the purposes of s.87 would only become a live issue in practice if (1) a charity lost its CGT exemption (eg by breach of the charitable expenditure rules) or (2) if HMRC changed their present view (which does not seem likely).[15]

---

15 The arguments relating to the charity's CGT exemption are considered in Venables, "Capital Payments to Charities from Offshore Trusts," OTPR, Vol 6, Issue 3

Thus a non-resident trust within s.87 can in principle make capital payments to charitable trusts or companies without risk of a CGT charge.

The position is the same if a non-resident trust with OIG amounts (offshore income gains) makes a capital payment to charity. The charity exemption applies to the charge otherwise arising under s.87 TCGA as applied by reg 20(3) OFTR 2009.[16]

32.8 Does capital payment to charity reduce s.1(3) amounts

If it is correct that a charity is a beneficiary within s.87 then the capital payment will reduce outstanding s.1(3) amounts, and this is the HMRC view. This seems fair.

32.9 Capital payment: s.731 ITA

Section 731 ITA imposes a charge to income tax on individuals who (in short) receive benefits directly or indirectly from offshore trusts.[17] A charity cannot be subject to tax under s.731 as that section applies only to individuals.

If a charity receives a payment from a trust or company within s.731, and the charity in turn makes a payment to a UK resident individual, it is considered that the individual cannot be subject to tax under s.731.

HMRC accept that a payment to a charity may reduce the extent of relevant income for s.731 purposes: RI 201.

32.10 Payment to non-resident charity from non-resident trust

This section considers the position if a distribution is made to a non-resident charity from a non-resident trust.

32.10.1 *Recipient UK tax charity*

The non-resident charity may qualify as a charity under the standard tax definition, if it is an EU or EEA charity.

A non-resident is not in principle subject to CGT, and so it does not matter to the charity whether a chargeable gain accrues under s.87; though the usual CGT exemption would also have applied, had it been needed.

---

http://www.khpplc.co.uk/reviews

16 See 4.15 (Offshore funds).

17 For a detailed analysis of this section, see Kessler, *Taxation of Non-Residents and Foreign Domiciliaries* (21st ed, 2022-231), Chapter 47 (Settlor-Interested Trust Code) online version *https://www.foreigndomiciliaries.co.uk*

A distribution to a non-resident will not usually reduce s.1(3) amounts (trust gains).[18]

32.10.2 *Recipient charity; not UK tax charity*

The non-resident charity will not qualify as a charity under the standard tax definition, if it not is an EU or EEA charity.

A full discussion is not possible here but the following outline points may be mentioned.

A chargeable gain will accrue to the non-resident trust on the disposal of an asset to the non-resident charity.

A non-resident is not in principle subject to CGT, and so it does not matter that a chargeable gain accrues to it under s.87.

The distribution will not usually reduce s.1(3) amounts (trust gains) of the trust.

IHT would also need consideration.

18 Section 87D TCGA.

CHAPTER THIRTY THREE

ESTATES OF DECEASED PERSONS: CGT

33.1 Succession law background

This Chapter considers the CGT position where a charity benefits under the will of a testator. The following chapter considers income tax.

We refer to the deceased as the **"testator"** though similar points will arise on an intestacy if there is an instrument of variation in favour of charity.

We assume the testator was UK resident, and domiciled in England and Wales, at the time of their death

On the death of a person domiciled in England (the "**deceased**"):

(1) Their property passes to their personal representatives ("**PRs**").[1] The property is known as the "**deceased's estate**" which where the context is clear may be abbreviated to "**estate**".

(2) The PRs pay debts of the deceased and taxes. Provided that there are sufficient assets available, they pay pecuniary legacies and transfer property which the deceased has specifically gifted.

(3) Finally, they transfer the residue of the estate to the residuary

---

1 Scots law is in this respect the same: *Cochrane's Executors v IRC* 49 TC 299. Further consideration is needed if a foreign law applies.

legatees. Thus on completion of the administration, the residuary legatees become entitled to the assets of the estate, and any income which the PRs have not spent.

(4) It is possible for PRs to transfer specific assets before completion of administration.[2]

When PRs transfer an asset to a beneficiary, the formal legal terminology is that they "assent to the vesting of the asset in the beneficiary",[3] which may be abbreviated to "**assent**". But outside formal legal contexts, we prefer the word "transfer". That seems clearer to readers unfamiliar with succession law terminology; there are differences between an assent and other types of transfer, but they are not relevant here.

During the period of administration, the PRs alone are said to be entitled to the assets which are comprised in the estate. The beneficiaries of the estate have the right to compel due administration of the estate, but it has repeatedly been held that the beneficiaries have no legal or equitable interest in the assets of the estate.[4]

Special taxation rules apply during this period of administration. The rules produce some curious results where the deceased, or a beneficiary, is a remittance basis taxpayer or non-resident. There can sometimes be considerable scope for tax planning.

I consider CGT and in the following chapter income tax.

The starting point is that PRs are "persons" (though not "individuals") so they are in principle subject to IT and CGT.

Similar issues arise where beneficiaries of estates are non-resident or remittance basis taxpayers. Further consideration is needed if the testator is domiciled or resident outside England and Wales. For these topics see Kessler, *Taxation of Non-Residents and Foreign Domiciliaries*.[5]

33.1.1 *When is estate administration complete*

How long does the administration period last? This is a question of

---

2 CG30920 raises the possibility that this is not the case in Scotland.

3 See s.36 Administration of Estates Act 1925, set out at 34.3 (Income from specific legacy).

4 *Sudeley v Attorney-General* [1897] AC 11; this (rather odd) principle was re-affirmed in *CSD v Livingston* [1965] AC 694; for a survey of the cases, see *Re Hemming* [2009] Ch 313.

5 (21st ed., 2022-23), Chapters 86 and 87 (Estates of Deceased Persons) online version *https://www.foreigndomiciliaries.co.uk*.

succession law, not tax law, but it often arises in tax contexts, including income tax, CGT, and estate duty, and has given rise to a substantial case law.

In *Sudeley v Attorney-General* [1897] AC 11 the Privy Council said:

> The thing that the legatee was entitled to was one-fourth share of a residuary estate, consisting, it may be, of many things; and I think it was fallacious on the part of [counsel] to say that the residue was very nearly ascertained, because the question is not only of amount – although I think that of itself would not be sufficient if it were only of amount – but it is a question of substance as well as a question of amount. It is uncertain until the residuary estate has been ascertained of what it will consist:...
>
> Until the thing has been ascertained, until the trust fund has been constituted, the thing of which the trustees are the trustees has not been ascertained. Whether you treat them, therefore, as trustees or executors, the same consideration arises. Now, if the only thing that the legatee is entitled to is the fourth share of an ascertained residuary estate, I say that to my mind it is impossible to maintain that the character of any part of that estate can be ascertained so as to make it possess a specific locality until that has happened; it is a condition precedent to know what the residuary estate is, and until that has been ascertained you cannot tell of what it will "consist."

In *IRC v Aubrey Smith* the Court of Appeal cited this and said:

> .... I read all those passages because they appear quite clearly to lay down that until the fact is ascertained, or can or ought to be inferred, that the residue has become defined so that the aliquot portion passing to the beneficiary can also be defined, the beneficiary has not, until that time, a definite interest in the sum which will ultimately fall to him. ... it appears to me as Lord Haldane said in the case I first cited that it is largely a question of fact. ...
>
> What has to be determined here ... is: Is it clear that the portion of each of the sons is ascertained, or has been ascertained, or is capable of ascertainment, and that ascertainment has been assented to by the executor-trustees?[6]

The important points which emerge from the case law are that PRs continue to hold an asset as PRs until:

(1) they transfer (assent) an asset to a beneficiary; or

---

6 15 TC 661 at p.672.

(2) the administration of the estate is complete (at which point there is an implied assent). For this purpose:
   (a) The estate must be completely ascertained. It remains in the course of administration even though this work is nearly done.
   (b) The fact that debts of the deceased remain unascertained or unpaid is a relevant factor but not decisive.
   (c) The fact that the PRs regard themselves as still administering the estate (producing "estate accounts" and not trust accounts) is a relevant factor but not decisive.
   (d) In a marginal case the issue is said to be one of fact and there is a fairly broad "grey area" in which the courts will not interfere with a decision of the first-tier tribunal.

The TSE Manual provides:

> **TSEM7360: Definition of period pf administration** [Mar 2017]
> The period during which the personal representatives are settling the estate is called the period of administration. It starts on the day following the date of death of the deceased person and ends when the personal representatives have taken all the steps necessary to complete the administration of the estate.
> The question of when an administration period ends is essentially one of fact and will depend on individual circumstances. It may in some cases coincide with the date when the residue of the estate can be identified. Sometimes the date of issue of the Inheritance Tax clearance certificate is taken as the date the administration was completed.
> You should normally accept that the administration ended on the date the personal representatives tell you it did.

The CG Manual provides:

> **CG30700: Personal representatives: period of administration** [Mar 2017]
> The period during which the personal representatives are settling the estate is called a period of administration. The period starts with the death of the deceased person. The date on which it ends is a question of fact which is often difficult to resolve. During this period the liability for Capital Gains Tax on sales of assets from the estate falls on the personal representatives unless they have taken specific steps to vest the ownership of the assets involved in legatees in advance of the sale, see CG30900.
> When considering when administration is complete the Courts look for a construction of the law that leads to an early conclusion of administration. The leading case in this respect is *CIR v Sir Aubrey Smith* 15 TC 661.
> In his judgement Lord Hanworth MR set out a principle of general application

when he said, at the bottom of page 675, top of page 676

"The question is, in all cases: has the administration of the Estate reached a point of ripeness at which you can infer an assent, at which you can infer that the residuary estate has been ascertained and that it is outstanding and not handed over merely for some other reason."

On this basis we would normally argue that the period of administration ends when residue has been ascertained, see CG30780+.

CG30710: Personal representatives: extended period of administration [24 Mar 2017]

There are some exceptional cases where all the figures are apparently available to enable residue to be ascertained but it has to be accepted that the period of administration is continuing.

One example is where distributing shares in accordance with legatees' fractional entitlements to residue would result in one legatee receiving a majority shareholding whilst the other legatees would only receive minority holdings. Because of the disparity in values between majority and minority holdings it may be necessary for the personal representatives to apply the rule from *Lloyd's Bank v Duker and others* [1987] 3 All ER CH D 193. This would require them to sell these shares rather than distributing them in specie.

The period of administration would continue in such a case until the shares were sold and the Capital Gains Tax liability arising to the personal representatives was quantified.

The rule referred to above is of fairly limited application. The fact that a majority shareholding would be broken into minority holdings on distribution should not be accepted as preventing distribution of shares and thus the ending of the period of administration. Nor should minor valuation differences between minority shareholdings passing to the legatees be accepted as covered by the rule in the *Duker* case.

The period of administration may also be extended where the distribution of the estate is being challenged. The personal representatives may be unable to distribute the estate pending the outcome of litigation.

CG30720: Personal representatives: confusion over terminology [24 Mar 2017]

Even where ascertainment of residue marks the end of the administration period for Capital Gains Tax purposes, assets may remain in the hands of the personal representatives after that date. They may have to carry out administrative acts regarding transfer of assets to legatees. In some cases they may sell assets. If so they will be doing this as bare trustees for the legatees. Personal representatives and their agents sometimes regard these acts as forming part of the period of administration. This may lead to confusion when references are made to the period of administration.

Because of the possible confusion it is important to establish precisely what is meant when a reference is made to a period of administration. From HMRC's side we can try to avoid this confusion for the majority of cases by referring to events as falling before or after residue has been ascertained rather than simply referring to the period of administration.

CG30780: Personal representatives: necessary to establish if residue ascertained [24 Mar 2017]

There are a number of circumstances where it is important to establish whether residue has been ascertained, see CG30700, because it significantly affects the amount of Capital Gains Tax payable. Depending on the circumstances, the personal representatives and legatees may be arguing for residue having been ascertained at an early date or at a late date.

CG30781: Personal representatives: residue: early date [24 Mar 2017]

If there is a will the personal representatives and legatees may claim that administration has ceased and residue has been ascertained at an early date if:

- the legatees would be liable at a lower rate of Capital Gains Tax than the personal representatives on the disposal of assets in the estate
- have any unused annual exemption that could be used to cover the gains
- the legatee is a charity and any gain on the disposal would be exempt.

You will only see claims under the first two bullet points in cases of intestacy as a charity will not qualify as a legatee under the rules of intestacy.

Applying the rule that assets remain vested in the personal representatives until residue has been ascertained unless specific steps have been taken to vest the assets in advance of ascertainment of residue usually defeats unwarranted claims in this area.

CG30790: Personal representatives: residue: late date [24 Mar 2017]

For the years 2008-09 there will be few cases in which it will be to the taxpayers' advantage to argue that there has been an extended period of administration. This is because the rate of Capital Gains Tax payable by personal representatives is either the same as that paid by the legatees or higher. It cannot be lower. There may be a small advantage if the personal representatives have any unused annual exempt amount and the legatee doesn't or the personal representatives may have unused losses that will be lost.

Unless it is an exceptional case where there are good reasons for accepting that the period of administration must be extended beyond the date residue is ascertained, see CG30710, you should seek the full facts to enable you to determine when residue became ascertainable. You should then argue that the beneficial ownership of the assets vested in the legatees at that date. As stated in CG30700 the attitude of the Courts is to look for an interpretation that allows administration to be completed at an early date.

Unquantified debts

One claim that is sometimes met is that there is an unquantified debt preventing residue being ascertained. This may not be sufficient to prevent the administration period being treated as at an end. Such a situation was considered in *CIR v Sir Aubrey Smith* 15 TC 661. Lord Hanworth commented at page 674

> 'For my own part I think the question of a mortgage debt or any other debt must take its proper place in perspective. It may be in some cases that that is a factor from which a strong inference may be drawn. It may be on the other hand that the device of leaving a debt unpaid is resorted to in order to pretend that the residue of the estate has not been ascertained and is not ascertainable. If such a device were resorted to in

any case it ought to be held ineffective'.

When a Solicitor or other professional person is employed by the personal representatives to deal with the administration of the estate, his or her fees will be one of the estate's debts. Sometimes when personal representatives wish to extend the period of administration they arrange that the Solicitor, etc, does not submit a bill in respect of at least some part of his or her fees. They then argue that this has prevented ascertainment of residue and has caused the period of administration to be extended. Any such claim should be resisted on the basis of the above quotation. It should be contended that the information to quantify the bill must be in the Solicitor's records and that administration should therefore be considered to have ended.

CG30800: Personal representatives: how residue is ascertained [24 Mar 2017]

In order to ascertain residue the personal representatives must identify all the assets and liabilities of the estate. They then need to quantify these.

In the case of taxation liabilities this process will start with settling any Income Tax and Capital Gains Tax liabilities to the date of death. If any income arises to the personal representatives or if they realise any chargeable gains during the period of administration they will also need to agree their own liabilities for this period.

As far as Inheritance Tax is concerned the personal representatives will need to inform HMRC - Trusts and Estates IHT whether any liability arises and if so in what amount. As a part of the process of seeking a grant of probate or letters of administration (or, in Scotland, a confirmation) the personal representatives have to supply HMRC - Trusts and Estates IHT with a provisional computation of the Inheritance Tax due. HMRC - Trusts and Estates IHT will review this and, where necessary, check valuations. When the amunt, if any, of Inheritance Tax payable has been quantified HMRC - Trusts and Estates IHT will issue clearance. We would not normally accept that residue had been ascertained at a date before the date of issue of a clearance. See IHTM05001+ for detailed guidance on the Inheritance Tax procedures.

CG30810: Personal representatives: residue: providing funds [24 Mar 2017]

When the assets and liabilities have been quantified the personal representatives have to consider how they can pay

- the estate's liabilities and
- any pecuniary legacies provided for in the will.

If they do not have sufficient liquid funds they will have to sell assets in order to raise funds. Occasionally they may agree with legatees entitled to pecuniary legacies that the legatee should accept an asset in satisfaction or part satisfaction of the pecuniary legacy.

Disposing of assets may give rise to further Capital Gains Tax liabilities which have to be agreed before residue can be ascertained.

Residue is only ascertained when the personal representatives have both established the net worth of the estate and provided the liquid funds to pay liabilities and pecuniary legacies. Once that point is reached residue is ascertained and it is irrelevant that the assets have not been distributed.

> **CG30820: Personal representatives: residue: executor's year** [24 Mar 2017]
> For estates in England and Wales, the personal representatives cannot be compelled to distribute the assets of the estate until at least one year has elapsed from the date of death (Section 44 Administration of Estates Act 1925). This is commonly referred to as the executor's year.
> When dealing with a dispute about whether a disposal was by personal representatives in that capacity or in their capacity as bare trustees for legatees we would not normally contend that the disposal was on behalf of the legatees if it took place during the executor's year.
> Although personal representatives cannot be compelled to distribute assets during the executor's year there is no bar to them doing so. In a simple estate they may have ascertained residue well before the year ends. If there is evidence that they have done and have then distributed assets to the legatees we can accept that the liability relating to disposals during that year but after the date assets were distributed does lie with legatees.
> *Scotland*
> In Scotland the rule is that the personal representatives are entitled to distribute the estate after six months from the deceased's death if they have provided funds for payment of all the estate debts and made reasonable enquiries for claims.

33.1.2 *Importance of assent*

PRs transfer assets to beneficiaries by means of an "assent". The assent is fundamental, since:

(1) a sale after an assent to a non-resident or a remittance basis taxpayer may in broad terms be free of CGT and a sale before assent may not.

(2) Conversely a sale by non-resident PRs or PRs with losses may be CGT free and a sale after an asset may be taxable.

An assent of land in England and Wales must be in writing. An assent of other property may be oral or implied by conduct. No formal written assent is required if (say) shares are simply transferred to the name of a beneficiary by stock transfer form. If shares are registered in the names of PRs (or their nominees), and the legatee wants them to be sold, it may be administratively convenient if an assent is made under which the PRs (or their nominees) become nominees for the legatee. Then the shares can be sold without CGT (assuming a non-resident legatee or if the remittance basis applies) without the formality of a transfer of legal title to the legatee.

Once land has been assented to a charity a subsequent sale must comply with the formalities of s.117 Charities Act 2011[7] (surveyor's report, etc.).

33.2 Acquisition by PRs

For CGT purposes, PRs are regarded as a single and continuing body of persons.[8] They are liable to CGT on all their chargeable gains (less losses). The rate of tax is the same rate as trustees.

Section 62(1) TCGA provides:

> For the purposes of this Act the assets of which a deceased person was competent to dispose—
> (a) shall be deemed to be acquired on his death by the personal representatives or other person on whom they devolve for a consideration equal to their market value at the date of the death, but
> (b) shall not be deemed to be disposed of by him on his death (whether or not they were the subject of a testamentary disposition).

This is the so-called **"CGT forgiveness on death"**.

33.3 Transfer from PRs to beneficiary

33.3.1 *Transfer from PRs to legatee*

Section 62(4) TCGA provides:

> On a person acquiring any asset as legatee (as defined in section 64)—
> (a) no chargeable gain shall accrue to the personal representatives, and
> (b) the legatee shall be treated as if the personal representatives' acquisition of the asset had been his acquisition of it.

33.3.2 *"Legatee"*

The question whether a person acquires as legatee matters for 2 purposes:

(1) There is no disposal by PRs.[9]

(2) A legatee has relief on disposal of a debt.[10]

Section 64(2) TCGA defines legatee:

---

7 See also s.57 Charities Act (Northern Ireland) 2008

8 Section 62(3) TCGA.

9 See 33.3.1 (Transfer from PRs to legatee).

10 Section 251 TCGA.

In this Act, unless the context otherwise requires,

[a] "legatee" includes any person taking under a testamentary disposition or on an intestacy or partial intestacy, whether he takes beneficially or as trustee, and

[b] a person taking under a donatio mortis causa [gift in anticipation of death] shall be treated (except for the purposes of section 62) as a legatee and his acquisition as made at the time of the donor's death.

Para [b] (gift in anticipation of death) is very rare, so the important para is para [a]. Note it is expressed as an inclusive definition.

33.3.3 *Appropriation to legatee*

Section 64(3) TCGA provides:

[a] For the purposes of the definition of "legatee" above, and of any reference in this Act to a person acquiring an asset "as legatee",

[b] property taken under a testamentary disposition or on an intestacy or partial intestacy includes

[c] any asset appropriated by the personal representatives in or towards satisfaction of

[i] a pecuniary legacy or

[ii] any other interest or share in the property devolving under the disposition or intestacy.

In particular, if PRs appropriate assets in satisfaction of a pecuniary legacy, the beneficiary acquires as legatee. This is so even if the appropriation needs the consent of the beneficiary.[11]

---

11 Although for stamp duty purposes the transfer of the asset to a legatee constitutes a conveyance on sale, if the consent of the legatee is required: *Jopling v IRC* [1940] 2 KB 282.

For completeness: CCAB Statement June 1967 provided:

"The Revenue stated that in their view [TCGA s.62(4)] does not apply in all cases where assets are transferred to beneficiaries in specie. Where assets are appointed by personal representatives to satisfy a legacy in circumstances where such appropriation requires the legatee's consent, ie where the personal representatives do not have (whether by the terms of the will or under the Administration of Estates Act 1925 s.41) powers of appropriation without consent, the Revenue are advised that the acquisition of the asset has a contractual basis and is not strictly an acquisition qua legatee. In practice, however, the disposal of appropriated assets by the personal representatives to a legatee in these circumstances is not treated as an occasion of charge on the personal representatives provided that both they and the legatee agree that the legatee should be treated as acquiring the assets concerned as

If the PRs had no power of appropriation, then an "appropriation" could be authorised only on the basis that it was in fact a sale of the asset to a beneficiary coupled with payment of the legacy by way of set-off. In that case, the beneficiary may acquire as purchaser and not as legatee. In practice, PRs do generally have a power of appropriation,[12] so the issue does not often arise.

33.3.4 *Executors appoint to beneficiary*

Where executors exercise a power to appoint trust property to a beneficiary, that beneficiary takes under the appointment "as legatee". This follows from the trust law principle that, for the purposes of the rules relating to perpetuities, where trustees exercise a power of appointment, the deed of appointment is read back into the original trust instrument. It is treated as coming into operation at the date of the instrument that creates the power.[13]

Quite apart from that, the beneficiary would take as "legatee" in the general sense of the expression. The definition in s.64(2) is inclusive and not a comprehensive definition. The reason that the beneficiaries take as legatee is that they acquire under an assent. They acquire from the PRs acting in their capacity as PRs.

This conclusion is consistent with the general scheme of the TCGA. A person who acquires under an appropriation acquires "as legatee". It would be anomalous if a person who acquired under an appointment would not.[14]

HMRC agree. CG Manual provides:

> **CG31430 power to appoint** [Mar 2017]
> Where a deceased person's will directs that when assets of the estate vest they are to be held on trust, then the terms of that trust specified in the will may empower the trustees to appoint assets out of the trust to legatees. This is frequently because IHTA84/S144 (see IHTM35181) in specified cases treats the appointment, provided it is made within 2

---

legatee for the purposes of [TCGA s.62(4)]."

This was written before the enactment of what is now s.64(3) TCGA in 1969. This brought the law into line with what was formerly HMRC practice. so the CCAB Statement is obsolete.

12 Section 41 Administration of Estates Act 1925.

13 *Muir v Muir* [1943] AC 468.

14 A power of appropriation is sometimes regarded as a dispositive power: *Re Freeston* [1978] Ch 741, though I would not regard that as essential to the argument.

years of death, for all IHT purposes as if it had been made in the will. There is no corresponding provision for CGT.

The assets will normally vest in the trustees on the ascertainment of residue, see CG30940+. But, occasionally, specific steps may be taken to vest assets in will trustees in advance of residue being ascertained see CG30900+. Where the trustees exercise their powers of appointment AFTER the assets have vested then the assets concerned will already have passed out of the estate and into the hands of the trustees. In these circumstances the exercise of the power of appointment so that a beneficiary becomes absolutely entitled amounts to a disposal for CGT purposes.

Where the trustees exercise their powers of appointment before the assets have vested in them then the assets are still in the hands of the personal representatives at the time of the exercise. Even though these may be the same individuals as the trustees they are different bodies of persons for CGT purposes, see CG31110+. If, in these circumstances, the trustees make an appointment under the specific powers given to them in the will, then when the asset(s) vest they should be treated as passing direct to the appointee.

The asset(s) appointed should be treated as never becoming subject to the trust. In effect, the appointment is read back into the will. It is treated as though the deceased had intended the assets concerned to pass directly to the legatee rather than into trust. The appointee then takes those asset(s) as legatee and therefore acquires the asset(s) at probate value by reason of TCGA92/S62 (4), see CG31140+. The time limits and procedures in TCGA92/S62(6) and (7) do not apply to this treatment.

33.4 CGT planning for PRs

If PRs sell assets in the course of administration, then any gain will be subject to CGT, even though the net proceeds of sale will in due course pass to a charity. If, by contrast, PRs transfer an asset *in specie* to a legatee, then the PRs will not realise any chargeable gain but the base cost of the beneficiary will be that of the PRs. Where the beneficiary is a charity the charity will be able to dispose of the asset free of CGT.

It is thus a fundamental principle of CGT planning that PRs should generally avoid, wherever possible, making disposals of assets which pass under the will to charities, if a gain arises on the disposal. (Similar points apply to remittance basis taxpayers and non-residents.)

Where a charity receives a share of residue, the PRs may appropriate the assets showing the largest gain in satisfaction of that share.

Where a charity receives a pecuniary legacy, the PRs may appropriate assets showing the largest gain in satisfaction of the legacy.

Suppose a charity receives the whole of the residue, but it is necessary to sell some assets to pay legacies or liabilities of the PRs, and the assets available for sale will give rise to a chargeable gain. One might think that a solution is as follows:

(1) The PRs transfer the asset to the charity subject to a charge for their liabilities under s.36(10) AEA 1925.
(2) The charity sells the asset: any gain on the sale accrues to the charity: s.26(2) TCGA.
(3) Under the charge the proceeds are used to pay the PRs' liability.

This does not work: the proceeds are not applied for charitable purposes, and the charity's CGT exemption does not apply.[15]

Instead the PRs should sell the asset *at base cost* (or less) to the charity.[16] No chargeable gain will arise.[17] The PRs can use the proceeds of sale to pay legacies and liabilities. The charity will qualify for the charities' CGT exemption when it later sells the asset.

33.5 CGT planning by IoV

Where there is more than one residuary legatee and some are charities (or remittance basis taxpayers or non-residents) it would often make sense for assets with inherent capital gains to be transferred to them rather than to UK resident and domiciled individuals. This can often be done by means of an appropriation under s.41 Administration of Estates Act 1925, but (depending on the terms of the will) an instrument of variation may be necessary. The variation must be made within two years of the death of the testator.

In principle the approach should be to redirect assets of the estate with inherent capital gains to the charity. UK resident and domiciled beneficiaries would instead receive cash or assets without inherent gains. The charity can in due course realise the gains free of tax. There would be an overall tax saving, which could be shared between the charity and the other beneficiaries by negotiation, or which could be allowed to accrue entirely to the charity if the other beneficiaries were so minded.

---

15 See 5.2 (Property charged to non-charity).

16 It is assumed that no-one is prejudiced by the sale: in particular, that the sale yields sufficient funds for the PRs' needs.

17 See 23.3 (Donor CGT relief).

33.6 Claim against charity

The family of a testator disappointed by the terms of a charitable Will may attack the Will in one or more of three ways:

(1) They may raise a claim under the Inheritance (Provision for Family and Dependants) Act 1975 on the ground that the testator failed to make reasonable provision for the family.
(2) They may dispute the validity of the Will, for instance on the ground that the testator lacked testamentary capacity.
(3) They may claim an interest in property of the estate on the basis, perhaps, of a proprietary estoppel.

It is rare for such claims to be taken to court: once the strength of the claimant's case is ascertained, the matter is settled. The tax position on a settlement has become extremely intricate. Arrangements with the same practical effect have quite different tax consequences. In estates of any size it would be essential for the charity to seek specialist tax advice. We here outline the principal IHT and CGT implications. Income tax might also need to be considered.

33.7 Inheritance (Provision for Family & Dependants) Act 1975

The tax position depends on how the claim is settled.

33.7.1 *Settlement by court order*

The tax position here is fairly clear.

Inheritance tax

The terms of the Order are dated back to the death for inheritance tax purposes: s.146 IHTA. The effect is the same as an IoV, except that an IoV treatment is optional (it requires an appropriate statement which, like an election, need not be made) but s.146 is compulsory: no election is required.

The effect of a settlement by court order is normally neutral for IHT purposes if the spouse/civil partner receives any part of the estate which is divested from the charity. This route is generally undesirable where the claimant is not a spouse/civil partner as the charity exemption will be lost to the extent that the property passes to the claimant.

The extent of the loss of tax relief depends not only on the value of the claimant's share in the estate, but on the precise form in which the Will is expressed to be varied. This is especially so if the estate includes agricultural or business property. If specific or pecuniary legacies are directed to the claimant, and the residue (less costs of the action) to the charity, then tax relief might be obtainable for those costs. HMRC could possibly argue that administrative expenses incurred in fighting the action, which are normally properly payable from the residue of the estate, are not "given to charity" and are so outside the charity exemption (see s.23(6) IHTA). In the authors' experience, however, HMRC do not take this point.

Capital gains tax

The terms of the court crder are generally read back for CGT purposes also: s.19 Inheritance (Provision for Family and Dependants) Act 1975. HMRC take the view that consent orders are outside s.19. This is not thought to be correct provided that the terms of the consent order are within the jurisdiction of the court. There is scope for planning in arranging that assets which give rise to a chargeable gain are retained by the charity, while other assets are appropriated to the claimant's share.

33.7.2 *Settlement by IoV*

A settlement within two years of the death can, in the authors' view, be achieved by an instrument of variation. A variation of an estate to settle a claim under the I(PFD)A 1975 is a variation of "dispositions effected by will, under the law relating to intestacy *or otherwise*": the last two words cover this case.

33.7.3 *Settlement without court order: IHT*

A charity may apply some of its general funds to make a payment to a claimant to abandon their claim. This was formerly a tax-effective means for a charity to deal with such a claim. The entire estate passed to the charity and qualified for the charity exemption.

Section 29A IHTA now counteracts the tax advantages. Section 29A provides:

> **29A Abatement of exemption where claim settled out of beneficiary's own resources**
>
> (1) This section applies where—
>
> (a) apart from this section the transfer of value made on the death of any person is an exempt transfer to the extent that the value

transferred by it is attributable to an exempt gift, and

Section 29A does not apply to lifetime gifts (even though those may also be set aside under the I(PFD)A 1975).

(b) the exempt beneficiary, in settlement of the whole or part of any claim against the deceased's estate, effects a disposition of property not derived from the transfer.

"Exempt beneficiary" is given a commonsense definition in s.29A(6):

> "the exempt beneficiary", in relation to an exempt gift, means any of the following, namely—
> (a) where the gift is exempt by virtue of s.18 above, the deceased's spouse or civil partner,
> (b) where the gift is exempt by virtue of s.23 above, any person or body—
> (i) whose property the property falling within subsection (1) of that section becomes, or
> (ii) by whom that property is held on trust for charitable purposes,
> (c) where the gift is exempt by virtue of s.24 or 25 above, any body whose property the property falling within subsection (1) of that section becomes,
> (d) where the gift is exempt by virtue of s.24A above, any body to whom the land falling within subsection (1) of that section is given, and
> (e) where the gift is exempt by virtue of s.27 or 28 above, the trustees of any settlement in which the property falling within subsection (1) of that section becomes comprised;

In practice for our purpose this means the charity beneficiaries. "Exempt gift" is also given a commonsense definition:

> "exempt gift", in relation to a transfer of value falling within subsection (1)(a) above, means—
> (a) a gift with respect to which the transfer is (apart from this section) exempt by virtue of the provisions of any of sections 18 and 23 to 28 above, or
> (b) where (apart from this section) the transfer is so exempt with respect to a gift up to a limit, so much of the gift as is within that limit;

Section 29A continues:

(2) The provisions of this Act shall have effect in relation to the transfer as if—

- (a) so much of the relevant value as is equal to the following amount, namely the amount by which the value of the exempt beneficiary's estate immediately after the disposition is less than it would be but for the disposition, or
- (b) where that amount exceeds the relevant value, the whole of the relevant value,

were attributable to such a gift to the exempt beneficiary as is mentioned in subsection (3) below (instead of being attributable to a gift with respect to which the transfer is exempt).

(3) The gift referred to in subsection (2) above is a specific gift with respect to which the transfer is chargeable, being a gift which satisfies the conditions set out in paragraphs (a) and (b) of s.38(1) below.

(4) In determining the value of the exempt beneficiary's estate for the purposes of subsection (2) above—

- (a) no deduction shall be made in respect of the claim referred to in subsection (1)(b) above, and
- (b) where the disposition referred to in that provision constitutes a transfer of value—
  - (i) no account shall be taken of any liability of the beneficiary for any tax on the value transferred, and
  - (ii) sections 104 and 116 below shall be disregarded.

(5) Subsection (1)(b) above does not apply in relation to any claim against the deceased's estate in respect of so much of any liability as is, in accordance with this Act, to be taken into account in determining the value of the estate.

(6) In this section—

...

"gift" and "specific gift" have the same meaning as in Chapter III of this Part; and

"the relevant value", in relation to a transfer of value falling within subsection (1)(a) above, means so much of the value transferred by the transfer as is attributable to the gift referred to in that provision.

Where a charity uses property not derived from an estate to settle a claim against the estate, the charity exemption is restricted. The restriction equals the extent of the sums applied by the charity in settlement of the claim, grossed up for IHT purposes. Section 29A operates, absurdly, to restrict inheritance tax relief even if the claimant is a spouse/civil partner.

No credit is given for the spouse/civil partner exemption. Section 29A will rarely give a favourable result where the estate includes agricultural or business property. A settlement of a claim by use of a charity's free estate, which comes within s.29A IHTA, will generally be expensive in IHT terms and sometimes (eg if the claimant is a spouse/civil partner) disastrously so.

It is then essential to avoid s.29A, and fortunately this may not be too difficult.

Possibly the PRs might transfer an asset from the estate to the charity. The charity may then sell that asset and use the proceeds to pay off the claimant. Section 29A is not applicable: the section only applies to a disposition of property *not* derived from the transfer. Full inheritance tax relief may still be available on the testator's death. (HMRC might object that s.23(5) restricts the charity tax relief, but this argument would render s.29A unnecessary, at least so far as concerns charities.)

Alternatively the charity might transfer a share of its interest in the unadministered estate to the claimant in settlement of the claim. Section 29A is not applicable for the same reason as above. It is considered that the full charity exemption would not be available in these circumstances, though that might not matter where the claimant was a spouse/civil partner.

Capital gains tax

The capital gains tax position where a claim is settled without a court order is uncertain. Take first the simple case where a claim is settled for a cash sum. As a matter of strict law, it is probable that the claimant has disposed of an asset, namely a chose in action, in consideration of the cash payment. The base cost of the asset disposed of will normally be nil (s.17(2) TCGA) so the entire proceeds will be subject to capital gains tax in the claimant's hands. The extra-statutory concession relating to compensation and damages (D33) might apply and allow the claimant to claim a base cost equal to the market value of their (alleged) share in the estate. The terms of the extra-statutory concession are not as clear as one might wish.

The position is more difficult still where the claimant receives an asset from the estate rather than cash. Firstly, as in the case of a cash payment, the claimant will probably dispose of a chose in action. In the authors' view, the claimant would receive the asset from the PRs "as legatee". In the result, the PRs would not realise a chargeable gain on making the assent, and the beneficiary is treated as acquiring from the death of the testator at the then market value. See s.62(4) TCGA. If our view is wrong, and the claimant does *not* acquire "as legatee", then a chargeable gain might accrue to the PRs on making an assent; the base cost of the asset in the hands of the claimant would be its value on the date of the assent.

It may be possible to avoid the CGT difficulties by means of an instrument under s.62 TCGA. It may be advantageous to draft the document so that s.142 IHTA does not apply.

Payment to charity to accept claim

Another solution is that the claimant may make a payment to charity to accept the claim. This is better for capital gains tax. The charity may make a disposal on settling the claim, but will usually qualify for capital gains tax exemption. The claimant would not make a chargeable disposal.

33.8 Claim against charity: Will disputed

A disappointed beneficiary's claim against a charity may be based not on the I(PFD)A 1975, but on an allegation that the testator lacked testamentary capacity or that the Will was invalid for some technicality. If such an action is fought to conclusion, HMRC may be expected to accept the court's determination on the validity of the Will and assess tax accordingly.

If the matter is settled, the tax position is broadly as discussed above in relation to claims settled under the I(PFD)A 1975. It is a moot point whether a claim under a disputed Will is a claim "against" the estate to which s.29A IHTA may apply.

33.9 Claim against estate: Proprietary estoppel

The IHT position here is much more favourable. If the claimant can prove that he was entitled in equity to an undivided share in an asset of the estate, then the value of the deceased's estate (and so the IHT charge) will be reduced to the extent of that share. Section 29A IHTA does not apply: see s.29A(5). It is thought that HMRC could not easily challenge the basis of any claim settled in good faith.

There would be no capital gains tax charge either, if the claim is resolved by transferring a share in the disputed assets to the claimant.

33.10 CGT allowable loss

If a claim of substance is made against an estate but fails, or expenses incurred exceed the amount awarded, the claimant will realise an allowable loss for CGT purposes.

CHAPTER THIRTY FOUR

ESTATES OF DECEASED PERSONS: INCOME TAX

34.1 Introduction

This chapter considers the income tax position where a charity benefits under a will. It is assumed that the testator was domiciled in England and Wales, and resident in the United Kingdom, and that the personal representatives ("PRs") are UK resident. We consider cases where:

(1) The charity receives a pecuniary legacy (a cash sum)
(2) The charity receives a specific legacy (a specific asset)
(3) The charity receives the residue or a share in residue

A full discussion needs a book to itself. We focus on matters closest to the theme of this book, but that can only be done in the context of a more general discussion of the rules.

For the succession law background, see 33.1 (Succession law background).

The starting point is an estate is not a charity, even if the beneficiaries are charities, and the PRs (who are "persons" for tax purposes) pay income tax at the basic rate (or dividend ordinary rate) on the income of the estate.

34.2 Pecuniary legacy to charity

This section considers the position where a testator by their Will gives a sum of money to a charity.

The charity will not have the right to any specific assets of the estate, or to any income of the estate, so it cannot reclaim any tax paid on income of the estate, either before or after payment of the legacy.

34.2.1 *Interest on legacy*

A legacy will normally carry the right to interest if it remains unpaid after one year, but again, the charity is not specifically entitled to the income of any asset or part of the estate.

If the PRs pay interest on a legacy, the position is as follows:

(1) *The charity*
The charity can qualify for the charity income tax exemption and is not in principle subject to tax on the interest.

(2) *The residuary legatee*
For the purposes of income tax, the interest constitutes an 'allowable estate deduction' and is thus deductible in computing the residuary income of the estate.[1] Hence, the residuary legatees are not subject to tax on the income used to pay the interest.

(3) *The PRs*
So far as the PRs arc concerned, however, the payment of the interest is not allowable as a deduction from their income. Thus, if a legatee charity is entitled to £80 of interest and the basic rate of tax were 20%, the PRs will need to receive a gross income of £100 in order to pay the interest.

While the charity should not be taxable on the interest, it will have no right to reclaim the £20 tax paid by the PRs.

This is not, of course, at all tax efficient. Thus, it will normally make sense for pecuniary legacies to be paid before they start to bear interest.

34.2.2 *Interest on legacy: Planning*

Interest will normally be paid at the expense of the residuary legatee. If the charity is also the residuary legatee, it can waive its right to receive interest on a pecuniary legacy. That will normally involve less income tax

---

1 See 34.11.2 ("Residuary income of estate").

being paid because:

(1) The charity is not subject to tax on interest which is waived.[2]

(2) Roughly speaking, the charity will ultimately be able to reclaim tax suffered by the PRs on the income out of which the interest would otherwise have been paid. If the interest is paid, however, no such recovery is possible.

Waiver should be by deed. (Where the legacy is to an individual, waiver by individual may also be tax effective; but bear in mind that such a waiver is a transfer of value for IHT.)

34.3 Specific legacy given to charity

This section considers the position where a testator by their Will gives specific assets to a charity.

In the first instance, the PRs will acquire the assets and they will receive the income arising from them. If they do not need to use the assets or income for the purpose of paying debts, taxes, etc., the PRs will in due course transfer the assets and income to the charity (the formal legal terminology is that the PRs "assent to the vesting of the assets in the charity").

In the first instance, the PRs pay tax at the basic rate (or dividend ordinary rate) on income arising from the assets. If the PRs transfer the asset and its income to the charity, something rather peculiar happens. The beneficiary is deemed to have been the owner of the asset since the death. The assent is said to "relate back" - that is, it operates retrospectively. For personal property this is a common law rule; for land, it is in s.36 Administration of Estates Act 1925 which provides:

> (1) A personal representative may assent to the vesting, in any person who (whether by devise, bequest, devolution, appropriation or otherwise) may be entitled thereto, either beneficially or as a trustee or personal representative, of any estate or interest in real estate to which the testator or intestate was entitled ...
> (2) The assent shall operate to vest in that person the estate or interest to which the assent relates, and, unless a contrary intention appears, the assent shall relate back to the death of the deceased.

This rule operates for income tax purposes: *IRC v Hawley* 13 TC 327. The beneficiary will, retrospectively, be treated as having received the

---

2 *Girvan v Orange Personal Communications Services* 70 TC 602.

income year by year as it arose and the PRs will be treated as if they had not received it. The PRs may have paid UK tax. This will retrospectively be treated as being paid by the PRs on behalf of the beneficiary. Thus a beneficiary who is a charity can reclaim tax paid by the PRs. (A non-resident beneficiary or a remittance basis taxpayer can also reclaim tax if appropriate.)

TSE Manual provides:

> **TSEM7490: Beneficiaries of estates - legacies** [Mar 2017]
>
> ...
>
> *Tax rules for specific legacies.*
>
> A legacy may take the form of an asset that does not produce income – for example a picture or a piece of jewellery. The beneficiary does not receive income and has no tax liability in respect of the legacy.
>
> Other assets can produce income – for example a bank account, shareholding or land. The general rule is that the beneficiary is entitled to the income arising to that asset from the death of the deceased person. Sometimes however the personal representatives may by law be entitled to use the income for some other purpose.
>
> If the beneficiary gets the income it should be treated as his income for the year in which it arises. The authority for this is *CIR v Hawley* 13 TC 327. The beneficiary cannot however be taxed on or given repayment on income that he did not receive.

34.3.1 *Assessment/reclaim: Time limit*

Section 682 ITTOIA provides:

> (1) This subsection applies if after the administration period ends it is apparent that a person is liable for income tax on estate income for any tax year who previously appeared not to be so liable or to be liable for tax on a lesser amount.
>
> (2) If subsection (1) applies—
>
> (a) the person may be assessed and taxed for the tax year, and
>
> (b) any relief or additional relief to which the person may be entitled for the tax year is to be allowed if a claim is made.
>
> (3) This subsection applies if after the administration period ends it is apparent that a person who previously appeared to be liable for income tax on estate income for any tax year is not so liable or is liable for tax on a lesser amount.
>
> (4) If subsection (3) applies—
>
> (a) all necessary adjustments and repayments of income tax for the tax year are to be made, and

(b) if the person has been allowed relief which exceeds the relief that could have been given by reference to the amount actually charged for the tax year, income tax is charged on the person for that year under this subsection on the excess.

(4A) The excess charged under subsection (4)(b) is treated as an amount of income for income tax purposes, except so far as it represents a tax reduction given effect at Step 6 of the calculation in section 23 of ITA 2007.

(5) An assessment or adjustment made for the purposes of this Chapter or a claim made as a result of this Chapter may be made after the end of the period otherwise allowed if it is made on or before the third anniversary of the normal self-assessment filing date for the tax year in which the administration period ends.

The TSE Manual provides:

TSEM7692: Interests in residue: practical and computational aspects time limit [Mar 2017]
The normal four-year time limit applies to any assessments or repayments in respect of income deemed to be that of a beneficiary.
Sometimes the administration period of an estate may take much longer than four years. To cater for this there is a special time limit in ITTOIA/S682(5) for non-corporate beneficiaries, and in CTA 2009/S965(5) for corporate beneficiaries. This time limit allows assessments and repayments to be made for any year. For non-corporate beneficiaries, the assessment or claim must be made within three years of the end of the year of assessment in which the administration of the estate was completed. For corporate beneficiaries, the assessment or claim must be made within three years of the 31 January following the accounting period in which the administration of the estate was completed.

34.4 Residuary estate given to charity

This section considers the position where a testator gives the whole or part of their residuary estate to a charity absolutely.

During the period of administration, the PRs alone are entitled to the assets in the residue of the estate and their income. On completion of the administration, the residuary legatee becomes entitled to the assets which at that time form part of the estate, and any income which the PRs have not expended in the course of administration. It is possible for PRs to transfer specific assets to a beneficiary before completion of administration.

In order to appreciate the income tax law it is helpful to understand its history. In *R v Special Commissioners, ex p. Dr Barnado's Homes* 7 TC 646, the residuary legatee was a charity. Income arose to the PRs during the period of administration on which the PRs paid income tax. The residuary legatee was not entitled to the income of the residuary estate as it arose during the period of administration, so it could not at that time reclaim that income tax. Instead it sought to recover the tax when it actually received the income, on completion of administration. The House of Lords held that although the sum received by the charity represented (or was derived from) the PR's income, it was received by the charity as a capital receipt (like accumulated income of a trust). The payment on the completion of administration did not operate retrospectively, the PR's income could not be treated as arising to the residuary legatee. So income tax paid by the PRs could not be recovered by the charity. The rule that an assent of a specific legacy relates back to death was not extended to gifts of residue. The reader may think that the charity had the better argument.[3] But that is now of academic interest: the law is settled.

That was a victory for the Revenue, who were no doubt unperturbed about the unfairness to the charity. But subsequently, predictably, individual residuary legatees successfully contended that they were not liable to super-tax (which became surtax in 1927 and is now higher rate tax) on the income of a residuary estate arising during the administration period.[4] The Revenue then realised they had made a rod for their own back. Legislation was therefore brought in which is now to be found in Chapter 6 Part 5 ITTOIA for individuals and trusts (including charitable trusts). The corporation tax equivalent for charitable companies is in Chapter 3 Part 10 CTA 2009.

34.5 Absolute/limited/discretionary interest

The legislation distinguishes absolute/limited/discretionary interests in residue. We are concerned with the position where a charity has an

---

3 See Nitikman, "The Forgotten Law of Assent" Trusts & Trustees, Vol. 18, No. 7, August 2012, p.672. Perhaps the House of Lords was motivated by the (unmentioned) policy argument that any other decision would be inconvenient to the point of unworkable in practice. If so they were right, as the tax rules which have replaced their decision do not work: see 34.14 (Reforming the income taxation of estates: Critique).

4 eg *Corbett v IRC* 21 TC 449. There are several income tax cases on the issue of whether administration was completed.

absolute interest. Section 650(1) ITTOIA provides a fairly commonsense definition:

> A person has an absolute interest in the whole or part of the residue of an estate for the purposes of this Chapter if—
> (a) the capital of the residue or that part is properly payable to the person, or
> (b) it would be so payable, if the residue had been ascertained.

In practice a charity is not likely to have a limited interest in residue: the usual example of a limited interest is a life interest. Discretionary interests in residue are not discussed here.

The legislation distinguishes between a "UK estate" and a "foreign estate".[5] We assume in this chapter that the estate is a UK estate.

34.6 "Payment"

The legislation uses the word "payment" but this is widely defined. Section 681 ITTOIA provides:

> (1) For the purposes of this Chapter—
> (a) a transfer of assets, or
> (b) the appropriation of assets by personal representatives to themselves,
> is treated as the payment of an amount equal to the assets' value at the date of transfer or appropriation.
> (2) The set off or release of a debt is treated for the purposes of this Chapter as the payment of an amount equal to it.
> (3) If at the end of the administration period—
> (a) there is an obligation to transfer assets to any person, or
> (b) personal representatives are entitled to appropriate assets to themselves,
> an amount equal to the assets' value at that time is treated as payable then for the purposes of this Chapter.
> (4) If at the end of the administration period—
> (a) there is an obligation to release or set off a debt owed by any person, or
> (b) personal representatives are entitled to release or set off a debt in their own favour,
> a sum equal to the debt is treated as payable then for the purposes of this Chapter.

5 These terms are defined in s.651(1) ITTOIA.

If the will makes a gift to a charity, there is a payment when the PRs transfer the estate or some of its assets to the charity. If the will sets up a charitable trust, there is a payment on the completion of administration, or when the PRs assent to the vesting of assets in themselves in their capacity as trustees.

34.7 Charge on estate income

Beneficiaries are subject to tax on estate income. There are essentially three parts to the legislation:
(1) The charge to tax on estate income.
(2) The definition of when estate income arises.
(3) The quantification of the amount of estate income.
Section 649(1) ITTOIA provides the charge to tax:

> Income tax is charged on estate income.

Section 659 ITTOIA identifies the person liable:

> (1) If the estate income is from a person's absolute interest or limited interest, that person is liable for any tax charged under section 649 unless subsection (3) or (4) provides that another person is liable.[6]

34.8 Estate income

Section 649 ITTOIA provides:

> (2) In this Chapter—
> "estate income" means the income treated under this Chapter as arising from an absolute, limited or discretionary interest in the whole or part of the residue of an estate ...
> (3) Estate income is treated as income for income tax purposes.
> (4) If different parts of an estate are subject to different residuary dispositions, those parts are treated for the purposes of this Chapter as if they were separate estates.

34.8.1 *When estate income arises*

Section 652 ITTOIA provides:

> (1) Income is treated as arising in a tax year from a person's absolute interest in the whole or part of the residue of an estate if—

---

6 Subsections (3)(4) deal with successive interests and are not relevant here.

> (a) the person has an assumed income entitlement for the tax year in respect of the interest (see sections 665 to 670), and
> (b) condition A or B is met.
>
> (2) Condition A is that a payment is made in respect of the interest in the tax year and before the end of the administration period (see section 653).
> (3) Condition B is that the tax year is the final tax year (see section 653).
> (4) Income treated as arising as a result of this section is estate income for the purposes of this Chapter.

These provisions state *when* estate income is treated as arising. The question of the *amount* of estate income is addressed separately.

The key term here is "assumed income entitlement" which is discussed below.

For completeness, s.653 ITTOIA provides commonsense definitions of "administration period" and "final tax year":

> (1) In this Chapter "the administration period", in relation to the estate of a deceased person, means the period beginning with the deceased's death and ending with the completion of the administration of the estate.
> (2) In the application of subsection (1) to Scotland, the reference to the completion of the administration is to be taken as a reference to the date at which, after discharge of, or provision for, liabilities falling to be met out of the deceased's estate, the free balance held in trust for the residuary legatees or for the persons with the right to the intestate estate has been ascertained.
> (3) In this Chapter "the final tax year" means the tax year in which the administration period ends.

34.9 Amount of estate income

There are two aspects to the rules: quantifying the "basic amount", and grossing up. Section 656 ITTOIA provides:

> (1) In the case of a UK estate, tax is charged under section 649 on the amount of estate income treated as arising in the tax year.
> (2) That amount is the basic amount of that income for the tax year (see subsection (4)) grossed up by reference to the applicable rate for that year (see section 663).
> (3) The gross amount is treated as having borne income tax at that rate.

The applicable rate is not discussed here. The key term is the "basic amount" of estate income.

34.10 Basic amount of estate income

The quantum of the"basic amount of estate income" depends on the type of interest in residue, ie whether there is an absolute, limited or discretionary interest, but we are here only concerned with absolute interests. Section 660 ITTOIA provides:

> (1) The basic amount of estate income relating to a person's absolute interest in the whole or part of the residue of an estate for a tax year before the final tax year is the lower of—
> (a) the total of all sums paid in the tax year in respect of that interest, and
> (b) the amount of the person's assumed income entitlement for the tax year in respect of it.
> (2) The basic amount for the final tax year is equal to the amount of the person's assumed income entitlement for that year in respect of that interest.

The next key term is "assumed income entitlement".

34.11 Assumed income entitlement

34.11.1 *"Aggregate income of estate"*

First one calculates the "aggregate income of the estate". This has a broadly commonsense definition in s.664 ITTOIA:

> (1) For the purposes of this Chapter the aggregate income of the estate for a tax year is
> [a] the total of the income and amounts specified in subsection (2), but
> [b] excluding the income specified in subsection (5).
> (2) The income and amounts are—
> (a) the income of the deceased's personal representatives in that capacity which is charged to UK income tax for the tax year,
> (b) the income of the deceased's personal representatives in that capacity on which such tax would have been charged for the tax year if—
> (i) it was income of a UK resident, and
> (ii) it was income from a source in the UK[7]

Paragraphs (c) to (e) deal with somewhat specialist topics:

---

7 I cannot see the point in (ii). If it is income of a UK resident, why does the source matter?

(c) any amount of income treated as arising to the personal representatives under section 410(4) (stock dividends) that would be charged to income tax under Chapter 5 of Part 4 if income arising to personal representatives were so charged (see section 411),

(d) in a case where section 419(2) applies (release of loans to participator in close company: loans and advances to persons who die), the amount that would be charged to income tax under Chapter 6 of Part 4 apart from that section, and

(e) any amount that would have been treated as income of the personal representatives in that capacity under section 466 if the condition in section 466(2) had been met (gains from contracts for life insurance).

Section 664(3)(4) deal with deductions:

> (3) In calculating the amount of the income within subsection (2)(a), any allowable deductions are to be taken into account.
> (4) In calculating the amount of the income within subsection (2)(b), any deductions which would be allowable if the income had been charged to UK income tax are to be deducted from the full amount of the income actually arising in the tax year.

Section 664(5) identifies two categories of income not included in "estate income". The first is income from specific legacies:

> (5) The excluded income is—
> (a) income to which any person is or may become entitled under a specific disposition[8]

That is excluded from estate income as the income is deemed to accrue to the legatee.[9]

> (5) The excluded income is ...

8 Defined in subsection (6): "In subsection (5)(a) 'specific disposition' means a gift of specific property under a will, including—
(a) the disposition of personal chattels by section 46 of the Administration of Estates Act 1925 (c 23) (succession on intestacy), and
(b) any disposition which under the law of another country has a similar effect to a gift of specific property by will under the law of England and Wales,
but excluding real property included in a residuary gift made by will by a specific or general description of it or, in Scotland, heritable estate included in such a gift."

9 See 34.3 (Specific legacy given to charity).

(b) income from property devolving on the personal representatives otherwise than as assets for payment of the deceased's debts.

That would include property which vests in the PRs under the obsolescent settled land act regime.

34.11.2 *"Residuary income of estate"*

Armed with the figure for the "aggregate income of the estate", one next computes the "residuary income of the estate". This brings in rules for "allowable estate deductions". Section 666(1) ITTOIA provides:

> For the purposes of this Chapter the residuary income of an estate for a tax year is
> [1] the aggregate income of the estate for that year, less
> [2] the allowable estate deductions for that year.
> This is subject to section 669 (reduction in residuary income: inheritance tax on accrued income).[10]

There are four categories of deductions. Section 666(2) ITTOIA provides:

> The allowable estate deductions for a tax year are—
> (a) all interest paid in that year by the personal representatives in that capacity (but see section 233 of IHTA 1984: exclusion of interest on unpaid inheritance tax),[11]
> (b) all annual payments for that year which are properly payable out of residue,[12]
> (c) all payments made in that year in respect of expenses incurred by the personal representatives in that capacity in the management of the assets of the estate,[13] and
> (d) any excess deductions from the previous tax year.[14]

---

10 The exception for IHT is not relevant to charities.

11 The exception for interest on IHT is not relevant to charities. In the HMRC view, interest on IT/CGT tax paid late is disallowed by s.869 ITTOIA.

12 Para (c) should be deleted, as annual payments are not generally allowable; but it does no harm.

13 Section 666(5) restricts this to income expenses: "Payments in respect of expenses are only allowable estate deductions if they are properly chargeable to income (ignoring any specific direction in a will)."

14 This is defined in s.666(6):
"In this section 'excess deductions from the previous tax year' means so much of the allowable deductions for the previous tax year as exceeded the aggregate income of the estate for that year."
This allows unused expenses to be carried forward.

This is subject to subsections (3) to (5).

Subsections (3)(4) prevent double allowances:

(3) No sum is to be treated as an allowable estate deduction if it is allowable in calculating the aggregate income of the estate.
(4) No sum is to be counted twice as an allowable estate deduction.

34.11.3 *"Assumed income entitlement"*

Armed with the figure for the residuary income of the estate, we are at last in a position to compute the assumed income entitlement. Section 665 ITTOIA provides:

(1) Whether a person has an assumed income entitlement for a tax year in respect of an absolute interest in the whole or part of the residue of an estate depends on the results of the following steps.
Step 1 Find the amount of the person's share of the residuary income of the estate that is attributable to that interest for that tax year and each previous tax year during which the person had that interest (see sections 666 to 669).
Step 2 If the estate is a UK estate in relation to any tax year for which an amount has been found under step 1, deduct from that amount income tax on that amount at the applicable rate for that year (see section 670).
Step 3 Add together the amounts found under step 1 after making any deductions necessary under step 2.
Step 4 Add together the basic amounts relating to the person's absolute interest in respect of which the person was liable for income tax for all previous tax years (or would have been so liable if the person had been a person liable for income tax for those years).
(2) For the purposes of this Chapter the person has an assumed income entitlement for the tax year if the amount resulting from step 3 exceeds the amount resulting from step 4.
(3) The assumed income entitlement is equal to the excess.
(4) [This deals with successive interests].

34.12 Charity exemption for estate income

Section 537 ITA provides the exemption for charitable trusts:

(1) If the person liable under s.659 of ITTOIA 2005 for any income tax charged under s.649 of that Act (charge to tax on estate income) is the

trustee of a charitable trust, the estate income[15] is not taken into account in calculating total income.
(2) Subsection (1) applies so far as the estate income is applied to the purposes of the charitable trust only.

The CT equivalent is s.489 CTA 2010.

The requirement for exemption is that the estate income is applied to the purposes of the charitable trust. The wording here is the same as the wording of the charity trading exemption.[16]

Estate income is in fact deemed, fictional income, which cannot be applied for charitable purposes. The assets which the charity receive from the PRs must be taken to include or represent the estate income, and if those assets are applied for the purposes of the charitable trust, the requirement is satisfied. So if:
(1) the executors receive income and
(2) the executors transfer the income to the charity,
the charity exemption would apply. The income from the LLP may not be the same as the estate income, but the link from one to the other is a direct one.

If:
(1) the executors receive income and
(2) the executors used it to pay (non-charitable) legacies, or repay loans, or any other liability of the executors
the position is not quite so clear. The satisfaction of an executors' liability is not an application for charitable purposes.[17] But unless the debt was repaid out of the income, other assets of the estate would be used to repay the liability. Because the liability was repaid out of income, those assets are received by the charity from the estate. They should be taken to represent the estate income so the charity exemption should apply. The there is still a close link between what charity receives and the estate income. Relief would only apply so far as there other assets, that is, if, say, the estate income is used to satisfy the liabilities and there is nothing left for the charity, then no relief would apply.

15 Defined in s.537(3): "In this section "estate income" has the same meaning as in Chapter 6 of Part 5 of ITTOIA 2005 (beneficiaries' income from estates in administration) (see section 649(2) of that Act)."
16 See 8.12 (Application for charity purposes).
17 See 4.21.2 (Income used to repay loan).

34.12.1 *Planning for charity beneficiary*

Since a charity can reclaim tax on its estate income, it would be best for sufficient sums to be paid on account each year for the charity to able to recover tax on a current basis. In short, all the income of the residuary estate should be distributed.

The estate income is reduced by PRs' allowable estate deductions, (essentially, interest and income expenses).[18] A charity which is sole residuary legatee of a solvent estate could meet those expenses out of its own funds. This will increase the charity's estate income and so increase the income on which tax can be reclaimed. Sums so expended by the charity are sums applied for charitable purposes only.

34.13 HMRC practice: Conventional basis

The statutory rules are too complicated, and in practice no-one usually takes much notice of them. The TSE Manual first outlines the law:

> **TSEM7655: Limited interests in residue - statutory - conventional basis of taxation** [Mar 2017]
>
> *The statutory basis*
>
> The statutory basis is provided in ITTOIA/Ss654, 656 and 661 for non-corporate beneficiaries, and in CTA 2009/Ss939, 941 and 944 for corporate beneficiaries. This requires all sums paid during or payable on completion of the administration period to be taxed over the course of the administration period. The amounts are allocated to tax years as follows:-
>
> 1. where
> - the interest has not ceased before the beginning of the tax year
> - the administration period continues after the end of the tax year
>   then the amount is the sum paid in the tax year
>
> 2. where
> - the interest has not ceased before the beginning of the tax year
> - the administration period ends in the tax year
>
> then the amount is the total of
>
> [a] any sum paid in the tax year before the end of the administration period plus
>
> [b] any amount still due to the beneficiary at the end of the administration period...
>
> The amounts allocated to each year are then deemed to be the net income of the beneficiary for that year. The amount concerned is

18 See 34.11.2 ("Residuary income of estate").

grossed at the applicable rate...

The TSE Manual then provides a concession:

> *The conventional basis*
> The beneficiary is treated as if he had been entitled to the income of the estate (or an appropriate part of the estate) as and when the income arose to the personal representatives. The basis applies for all purposes including repayments.
> It is unlikely that there will be cases where it is worthwhile insisting on the statutory basis. If the beneficiary asks for the statutory basis to be applied, you should ask for a computation on that basis. If you have any problems with such a computation, ask HMRC Trusts & Estates Edinburgh for advice.

In other words, the estate is treated as transparent for IT purposes.

It is not certain that a charity can take advantage of the conventional basis, as the income arising to the PRs is not applied for charitable purposes unless and until it is transferred to the trustees. Since the conventional basis is concessionary anyway, that should not be an insuperable objection. Nevertheless, we recommend that a charity should confirm the position with HMRC before seeking to take advantage of this.

Where the estate includes trading income, the charity will not want to use the conventional basis, as the charity trading exemption will not apply.

34.14 Reform income taxation of estates: Critique

There could hardly be a stronger condemnation of the current rules than the statement in the Manual that *It is unlikely that there will be cases where it is worthwhile insisting on the statutory basis.* The entire code needs to be rethought and replaced with something simpler. But that is outside the scope of this book.

CHAPTER THIRTY FIVE

VAT: BASIC CONCEPTS

Cross references

The following topics are considered elsewhere:

VAT position of non-charitable trading companies: see 9.17 (VAT)

18.9 (Gift of goods and services: VAT)

We do not discuss the issues of VAT on land, though we hope to address this in a future edition.

We do not consider VAT on the importation of goods from outsider the UK, or the movement of goods between Great Britain and Northern Ireland. We do not discuss the rules on whether a supply is made in the UK.

35.1 VAT: Introduction

A full discussion of VAT needs a library to itself. VAT on charities can only be understood in the context of the provisions as a whole, so we include a general discussion.

The law on VAT derives from Council Directive of 28 November 2006 on the common system of VAT (2006/112/EC) (the "VAT directive") , which is enacted in the UK by way of the VATA). In addition, there are statutory instruments and HMRC publications and guidance (there are, for example, more than 70 VAT Manuals addressed to specific topics).

Because VAT is a creature of EU law, the question arises as to what the position is following Brexit. The answer lies in the European Union (Withdrawal) Act 2018 (the "Withdrawal Act"), s2(1) of which provides that:

> "EU-derived domestic legislation, as it has effect in domestic law immediately before IP completion day, continues to have effect in domestic law on and after IP completion day."

IP completion day was 31 December 2020 at 11:00pm (see s39(1) European Union (Withdrawal Agreement) Act 2020).

The VATA is "EU-derived domestic legislation" (as defined in s1B(7) Withdrawal Act).

S3(1) Withdrawal Act provides that:

> "Direct EU legislation, so far as operative immediately before IP completion day, forms part of domestic law on and after IP completion day."

"Direct EU legislation" (as defined in s3(2) Withdrawal Act) includes "any EU regulation, EU decision or EU tertiary legislation, as it has effect in EU law immediately before IP completion day" (although, in the context of VAT, note also s42 Taxation (Cross-Border Trade) Act 2018). Further, although a court or tribunal "is not bound by any principles laid down, or any decisions made, on or after IP completion day by the European Court", it may nevertheless "have regard to anything done on or

after IP completion day by the European Court, another EU entity or the EU so far as it is relevant to any matter before the court or tribunal" (see s6 Withdrawal Act).
The current position is not substantially different from what it was before Brexit, although it is likely that the further Brexit recedes in the rear view, the more purely domestic VAT laws will come into their own..

This chapter considers VAT charging provisions and the following topics:
(1) supply
(2) consideration
(3) goods and services
(4) taxable supply
(5) taxable person
(6) business
(7) "in the course or furtherance" of a business
(8) VAT groups

35.2 "Charity"

In general, the meaning of a charity for VAT purposes is the general tax definition for a charity.[1]

There is one difference. Charities subject to the jurisdiction of the High Court of the Isle of Man (in addition to the High Court equivalent of a EU Member State or an EFTA State[2]) or the Isle of Man are able to obtain the same charity VAT reliefs as charities in the UK provided they also meet the other conditions in schedule 6 to the Finance Act 2010.[3]

35.3 Three VAT issues

VAT raises 3 broad sets of issues for charities:
(1) Whether the charity is charged to VAT on supplies that it makes to others.
(2) Whether suppliers are charged to VAT on supplies made to the charity.
(3) If VAT is charged on supplies made to the charity, whether the

---

1 See 3.4 (Tax definition of charity).
2 Iceland and Norway are specified in the schedule to the Taxes (Definition of Charity) (Relevant Territories) Regulations 2010, as well as VAT Notice 701/1 (last updated on 31 December 2020), which also refers (in paragraph 2.1) to Liechtenstein; but neither refers to Switzerland.
3 See 3.6 (Jurisdiction condition).

charity can recover that VAT as input tax.

35.4 VAT on supplies

35.4.1 *EU law*

Article 2 VAT directive provides:

> 1. The following transactions shall be subject to VAT:
> (a) the supply of goods for consideration within the territory of a Member State by a taxable person acting as such...
> (c) the supply of services for consideration within the territory of a Member State by a taxable person acting as such...

35.4.2 *UK law*

Section 1(1) VATA provides:

> Value added tax shall be charged, in accordance with the provisions of this Act—
> (a) on the supply of goods or services in the United Kingdom (including anything treated as such a supply)...

Section 4(1) VATA provides:

> VAT shall be charged on any supply of goods or services made in the United Kingdom, where it is a taxable supply made by a taxable person in the course or furtherance of any business carried on by him.

35.5 Supply

The concept of supply is fundamental to VAT:

(1) VAT is charged on supplies.
(2) The concept of supply relates to the concept of a VAT business, as an activity which does not involve supplies is not generally a business for VAT purposes.

Section 5(2) VATA provides:

> Subject to any provision made by [Schedule 4] and to Treasury orders under subsections (3) to (6) below—
> (a) "supply" in this Act includes all forms of supply, but not anything done otherwise than for a consideration;
> (b) anything which is not a supply of goods but is done for a consideration (including, if so done, the granting, assignment or surrender of any right) is a supply of services

Schedule 4 VATA extends the meaning of supply.

35.5.1 *"Taxable supply"*

Section 4(2) VATA provides:

> A taxable supply is a supply of goods or services made in the United Kingdom other than an exempt supply.

"Exempt supply" is a label that brings in a wide range of exemptions, see 37.1.4 (VAT exemption).

35.6 Amount or value of supply

Article 73 VAT directive provides:

> In respect of the supply of goods or services, other than as referred to in Articles 74 to 77, the taxable amount shall include everything which constitutes consideration obtained or to be obtained by the supplier, in return for the supply, from the customer or a third party, including subsidies directly linked to the price of the supply.

Section 19 VATA provides:

> (1) For the purposes of this Act the value of any supply of goods or services shall, except as otherwise provided by or under this Act, be determined in accordance with this section and Schedule 6, and for those purposes subsections (2) to (4) below have effect subject to that Schedule.
> (2) If the supply is for a consideration in money its value shall be taken to be such amount as, with the addition of the VAT chargeable, is equal to the consideration.
> (3) If the supply is for a consideration not consisting or not wholly consisting of money, its value shall be taken to be such amount in money as, with the addition of the VAT chargeable, is equivalent to the consideration.
> (4) Where a supply of any goods or services is not the only matter to which a consideration in money relates, the supply shall be deemed to be for such part of the consideration as is properly attributable to it.
> (5) For the purposes of this Act the open market value of a supply of goods or services shall be taken to be the amount that would fall to be taken as its value under subsection (2) above if the supply were for such consideration in money as would be payable by a person standing in no such relationship with any person as would affect that consideration.

35.7 Consideration

The concept of consideration is fundamental to VAT:

(1) Something not done for consideration is not (in principle) a supply and so not VATable. Conversely, anything which is done for a consideration is a supply and is (in principle) VATable.
(2) The value of the supply (the amount on which VAT is charged) depends on the value of the consideration.

35.8 *"Consideration"*

The word "consideration" has (at least) two distinct meanings:
(1) A general English law meaning[4]
(2) A VAT meaning

The VATSC Manual provides:

> **VATSC05100 - Consideration: Definition of consideration** [Feb 2022]
> Consideration is a payment for the supply of goods or services. It is usually a payment in money, but can also be of a "non-monetary" nature, such as goods or services supplied in return.
> *Consideration and profit*
> Consideration should not be confused with profit. Whether a payment yields profit or loss is immaterial and has no bearing on whether or not it is consideration. This was brought out in *Heart of Variety* (LON/75/15) where the tribunal said that:
> the concept of consideration and profit are wholly different, and the fact that a trader makes no profit on a supply does not, in our view, mean that there is no consideration for it.
> *Legal Definition*
> There is no definition of consideration in the VAT Act 1994. Neither is it defined in the EU Principal VAT Directive. In the UK, the meaning was originally taken from contract law, but after the European Court of Justice (ECJ) confirmed that the term is to be given the Community meaning and is not to be variously interpreted by Member States the UK adopted that approach. The Community definition used in ECJ cases is taken from the EC 2nd VAT Directive Annex A13 as follows even though this Directive is no longer in force:
>
> > The expression "consideration" means everything received in return for the supply of goods or the provision of services, including incidental expenses (packing, transport, insurance etc), that is to say

---

4 See Kessler, *Taxation of Non-Residents and Foreign Domiciliaries* (21st ed, 2022-23) App 4.2 (Consideration).

> not only the cash amounts charged but also, for example, the value of the goods received in exchange or, in the case of goods or services supplied by order of a public authority, the amount of the compensation received.

The phrase in return for the supply is interpreted to mean that there must be a direct link between the supply and the consideration.

Therefore in order that a supply for a consideration can be made, there must be at least two parties and a written or oral agreement between them under which something is done or supplied for the consideration. There is a direct link between the supply and the consideration because the supplier expects something in return for his supply and would not fulfil his obligation unless he thought that payment would be forthcoming.

ECJ cases on direct link between supply and consideration

The requirement for a direct link is brought out in three ECJ cases

The Dutch potato case

The case of *Staatssecretaries van Financien v Cooperatieve Aardapplenbewarr-plaats* ((1981) ECR 445; (1981) 2 CMLR 337) involved a co-operative providing cold storage facilities to its members who had the right to store potatoes because of the share each member held in the co-operative. Charges were normally made to the members for the storage but for two consecutive years no charges were made. This resulted in a drop in the value of the shares (reflecting the co operative's reduced profits because of the lack of storage fee income). The Dutch tax authorities argued that the reduction in value of each members share was effectively consideration for the storage which had been provided for no fee. The ECJ rejected this argument. There was no direct link between the services of storage and the decrease in share values. Additionally the reduction in value of the shares could not be equated directly to the cost or any other measure of the value of the services provided.

BAZ Bausystem Gmbh v Finanzamt München für Körperschaften

Here the ECJ held that interest awarded to an undertaking by a judicial decision was not consideration where the reason for the award was that the balance of the consideration for services was not paid by the due date, because it had no connection with the services provided and did not constitute consideration relating to a commercial transaction - it was simply compensation for the delay in payment.

Apple & Pear Development Council (APDC), ((ECJ (1988) STC 221; (1988) 2 CMLR 394)

The Council is a statutory body formed to promote the sale of apples and pears. Commercial growers were required to register with the council and pay an annual levy. The industry as a whole received the benefit of

> its promotional activities. The point at question was whether the levy was consideration for the promotional activities. The European Court held that there was no direct link between the supply made and the "payment" received, that is benefit, was not directly related to payments made, and individual growers were obliged to pay the levy, regardless of whether they benefited.
>
> The points which demonstrated this were:
>
> - The benefits of APDC's services accrue to the whole industry, individual growers deriving benefits indirectly from those accruing to the industry as a whole.
> - There was no relationship between the level of benefits which individual growers obtained and the amount of charges they were obliged to pay.
> - The charges were always recoverable from each grower as a debt due to APDC regardless of whether or not a given service conferred a benefit to them.
>
> *Tolsma*
>
> Another ECJ case, *Tolsma* C-16/93 (1994 STC 509), confirmed that for us to see a supply there should also be 'reciprocal performance'. See VATSC06110 for details of this case.
>
> *Other points from ECJ cases*
>
> Other points on consideration which can be drawn from these cases are:
>
> - Consideration is to be defined widely to bring within the tax everything which the taxable person receives as consideration for the goods or services supplied;
> - The consideration must be capable of being expressed in money.
>
> In some circumstances a person may pay for a supply to be made to someone else, for example, where a holding company pays for items such as fuel and electricity which are supplied to its associated companies. As long as there is an agreement between the supplier and the recipient there is still a direct link between the supply and the consideration. However, the supply is to the recipient, not to the payer.

The use of a tripartite arrangement as an example is curious, because it is not always clear in such situations who the supply is made to - is it made to the payer of the consideration (with the person actually receiving the benefit being a third party beneficiary) or is it made to the person who received the benefit (with the payer being a payer of third party consideration)?

The relevant legal principles governing the approach to this question were helpfully summarised by Lady Justice Gloster when Airtours Holidays Transport Ltd was in the Court of Appeal [2014] EWCA Civ 1033:

[37] The following propositions as to the correct approach to apply to the determination of the question whether a service paid for by the taxpayer is supplied to the taxpayer can be derived from various cases decided in this area, including the recent Supreme Court decisions of LMUK (SC) and WHA (SC); the judgment of the CJEU in LMUK (CJEU) and, in addition, the Court of Appeal's and House of Lords' judgments in Redrow:

i) "Consideration of economic realities is a fundamental criterion for the application of the common system of VAT" as regards the identification of the person to whom services are supplied: see e.g. per Lord Reed in LMUK(SC) at [56] and [66]; LMUK (CJEU) at [39]; and HMRC v Newey (trading as Ocean Finance (Case C-653/11) [2013] STC to 432 at [42] ("Newey").
ii) Decisions about the application of the VAT system are highly dependent upon the factual situations involved. Thus a small modification of the facts can render the legal solution in one case inapplicable to another: see e.g. per Lord Reed in LMUK(SC) at [68] and in WHA (SC) at [26].
iii) The case law of the CJEU indicates that, when determining the relevant supply in which a taxable person engages, regard must be had to all the circumstances in which the transaction or combination of transactions takes place: see per Lord Reed in LMUK(SC) at [38] and in WHA (SC) at [26]. In cases where a scheme operates through a construct of contractual relationships, it is necessary to look at the matter as a whole in order to determine its economic reality: see per Lord Walker in LMUK(SC) at [114]-[115] and per Lord Reed in WHA (SC) at [26]. Thus the relevant contracts have to be understood in the wider context of the totality of the arrangements between the various participants.
iv) The terms of any contract between the parties, whilst an important factor to be taken into account in deciding whether a supply of services has been made, are not necessarily determinative of whether as a matter of "economic reality" taxable supplies are being made as between any particular participants in the arrangements. However, the contractual position is generally the most useful starting point for the VAT analysis: see per Lord Reed in WHA (SC) at [27]. That may be particularly so where certain contractual terms do not wholly reflect the economic and commercial reality of the transactions: see per the CJEU in Newey at [43]-[44].
v) There may, as a matter of analysis, be two or more distinct supplies within the same transaction: see per Lord Hope at 412F-413A and Lord Millett at 418B-419H in Redrow; per Lord Millett in CCE v Plantiflor Ltd [2002] UKHL 33; [2002] 1 WLR 2287 at [67]; per

Chadwick LJ in the Court of Appeal in LMUK [2007] EWCA Civ 165 at [38] and [43]; and per Lord Hope in LMUK(SC) at [103]-[108]. Moreover, as Lord Millett said in Plantiflor [50]: "a single course of conduct by one party may constitute two or more supplies to different persons." It is useful to set out Lord Millett's analysis in Redrow at 418B-419H, notwithstanding that his approach, and that of Lord Hope in the same case, were to some extent qualified in the subsequent decisions of the Supreme Court in LMUK(SC) and WHA (SC)):

"Once the taxpayer has identified the payment the question to be asked is: did he obtain anything - anything at all - used or to be used for the purposes of his business in return for that payment? This will normally consist of the supply of goods or services to the taxpayer. But it may equally well consist of the right to have goods delivered or services rendered to a third party. The grant of such a right is itself a supply of services.

...

vi) However, the mere fact that the taxpayer has paid for the service does not necessarily mean that it has been supplied to him...

To distil the relevant legal principles even further, the key with tripartite situations is to:

- look at all the facts;
- look at the contract(s); and
- work out what is the economic reality.

Turning back to the more general question whether there is consideration at all in any given case...

VATSC05200 - Consideration: Other indicators to establish whether there is consideration [Feb 2022]

Further useful pointers, identified in the *Apple & Pear Development Council* case, to help establish whether there is consideration are as follows.

Indicators of consideration

- There must be some form of bargain or transaction between the parties.
- A payment should be related to what the payer receives although the fact that people pay the same amount for varying benefits does not stop it from being consideration.

Indicators of no consideration

- The absence of any consensual element on the part of the payer.
- A lack of control by the payer over the services provided.

The test was expressed (in the so-called Dutch potato case) to be whether or not there is a "direct link" between the services and the payment, or (in *Tolsma*) whether there is:

> "... a legal relationship between the provider of the service and the recipient pursuant to which there is reciprocal performance, the remuneration received by the provider of the service constituting the value actually given in return for the service supplied to the recipient."

Whether or not this is the case in reality is a matter of fact and degree.

35.8.1 *Non-monetary consideration*

The VATSC Manual provides:

> **VATSC05300 - Consideration: What is the consideration?** [Feb 2022]
> The consideration for a particular supply is everything that the supplier receives for making that supply. Consideration may be money (MONETARY) or something other than money (NON-MONETARY), or it may be a combination of both.
> *Monetary consideration*
> Monetary consideration includes cash and payment by cheque; credit card; bank transfer deduction from pay, etc.
> *Non-monetary consideration*
> Non-monetary consideration includes goods or services supplied as payment, for example in a "barter" (including part exchange) agreement. Services provided include the giving up of a right, refraining from doing something, agreeing to suffer some loss etc in return for the supply. At first sight these appear to be merely conditions of an agreement but are in fact consideration for the supply. VATAL - VAT Valuation Manual contains detailed guidance on the valuation of non-monetary consideration and details of significant case law in this area. ...
>
> **VATVAL05300 - Non-monetary consideration: establishing the monetary equivalent of a non-monetary consideration** [May 2021]
> There are several principles that have been established by the European Court that assist in determining the monetary equivalent of a non-monetary consideration. These can be found in two key cases Naturally Yours Cosmetics Ltd. (Case 230/87) and Empire Stores Ltd (Case 33/93).*Naturally Yours Cosmetics Ltd*
> Naturally Yours were wholesalers of cosmetics. They sold goods to beauty consultants who then resold them at parties, which the consultants had encouraged hostesses to arrange. The consultants purchased the goods at wholesale prices and sold them at retail prices

recommended by Naturally Yours. Hostesses who arranged parties were given a pot of cream by the consultants as a reward. When a pot of cream was used for this purpose, the consultant could purchase it from Naturally Yours for £1.50 instead of the usual wholesale price of £10.14 that the consultant would otherwise have had to pay. Naturally Yours argued that VAT was only due upon the £1.50 actually paid by the consultant. Customs argued that VAT was due upon the normal £10.14 wholesale price. The ECJ found VAT was due on £10.14. The consultants were providing Naturally Yours with a service in addition to the cash paid. The value of the services was £10.14 less the £1.50 payment.

The Advocate General's opinion, which was followed by the Court, describes in some detail the points that are essential in identifying non-monetary consideration and in placing a value upon it:

- Article 73 (Article 11(A)(1)(a) of the Sixth Directive in force at the time) was not confined to monetary payment but had to be given the broadest interpretation as to what could constitute consideration for determining the taxable amount. Therefore, both goods and services can be consideration.
- In determining the taxable amount, the only advantages received by a supplier that are relevant are those obtained in return for making the supply. This constitutes the direct link that is essential before a service can be regarded as consideration for a supply. In Naturally Yours this requirement was clearly satisfied because, if the consultant had not arranged for a hostess to hold a party, the cream could only be obtained by the payment of £10.14.
- The service had to be capable of being evaluated and expressed in monetary terms before it could constitute a non-monetary consideration.

The Advocate General said that the value had to be "subjective" in that it had to be assigned by the parties to the transaction.

- The fact that the price is reduced only if the party actually takes place, whereupon the pot of cream will be given to the hostess, shows that the parties subjectively assigned to the service provided a value corresponding to that price reduction. Since the portion of the price of the goods which was not paid initially must be paid subsequently if the party is not in fact held, it is clear that, as regards that portion, the goods are paid for either by provision of the service or by a specific sum of money in lieu of that service."

He then went on to express that principle more broadly:

- In a case such as this one, the relationship between the consideration given by one contracting party and that given by the other is such

> that it is possible to discover what value they attributed to the service which constituted part of the consideration. That value is calculated, indirectly, by reference to the normal wholesale price of the product; there too, however, it is not a question of an abstract value but rather of a specific price, applied by the same contracting parties in "normal" transactions, and moreover that price will be charged for the goods in question if the promised service is not provided.

The general rule deriving from this decision therefore, is that a non-monetary consideration has the value of the alternative monetary payment that would normally have been given for the supply. However, because we are required to ascribe a subjective value, we are not simply putting the question: "What would anyone else have paid for this supply in money?"

You could view the proper question as being: "What would this particular recipient have paid this particular supplier for this particular supply had the payment been in money?"

In a "*Naturally Yours*" situation the alternative monetary consideration is not difficult to establish because the normal price chargeable is self-evident from the contractual arrangement between the parties to the transaction. Alternatively, the monetary equivalent may be set out in a catalogue or price-list which shows what the recipient of the supply will have to pay when he provides no non-monetary consideration. The commonest example of this type of arrangement is where persons providing selling or introductory services to a mail-order trader are entitled to receive catalogue goods for a reduced cash payment or no cash payment at all. However, the position is less straightforward when the goods supplied in return for such services are not otherwise sold to the provider of the service at all. This was the situation which the European Court considered in the case of *Empire Stores Ltd.*

Empire Stores Ltd

In the *Empire Stores* case, the European Court was faced with a twofold question:

- Did introducing oneself or others as potential new customers constitute a service capable of being non-monetary consideration for the supply of a "reward good"?
- If it did, how could this non-monetary consideration be valued in respect of those "reward goods" supplied which were not sold at all by Empire Stores?

Empire Stores are a mail order company that sell goods via catalogues. Two schemes were introduced to attract new customers: a "self-introduction scheme" and an "introduce-a-friend scheme". Under the first scheme, a person was entitled to select an item from a list for no extra charge once they had supplied their personal details, been approved as a customer and placed an order for goods from the catalogue. Under the second scheme, established customers could also select an item if they recommended a friend as a potential customer, the friend had been approved and then made a first payment on an order for goods.

The "reward goods" in question were items that were not advertised for sale in Empire's catalogues. Empire had accounted for VAT on the cost price of these goods. Customs argued that VAT was due upon the tax-exclusive cost plus a 50% "mark-up" on the ground that this is what the sale price would have been if the items had been offered for sale in the catalogues. The Court found that VAT was only due upon the cost price of the items. Concluding as follows:

- The introductory service provided by the customer was non-monetary consideration because there was a direct link between its provision and the supply of the "reward good". The link had to be direct because in the absence of the service no "reward good" would be supplied.
- There was no doubt that the value of the services could be expressed in monetary terms because they were remunerated by a supply of goods.
- Where the value was not a sum of money agreed between the parties:

  > "… it must, in order to be subjective, be the value which the recipient of the services constituting the consideration for the supply of goods attributes to the services which he is seeking to obtain and must correspond to the amount which he is prepared to spend for that purpose. Where, as here, the supply of goods is involved, that value can only be the price which the supplier has paid for the article which he is supplying without extra charge in consideration of the services in question."

The important point to note is that, with non-monetary consideration, its value for VAT purposes is the subjective value of the consideration, not its market or similar value; in particular, the "open market value" rules provided for in section 19(5) VATA have no application in this context.

35.8.2 *Labelling*

The VATSC Manual provides:

VATSC05810: **Payments that are consideration: Introduction** [Feb 2022]

Some payments are not consideration because they do not fulfil the conditions set out in VATSC05100 and VATSC05200: either there is no direct link between a payment and the supply or there is no supply made in return for a payment.

The way in which a payment is described may lead to the conclusion that it is not consideration for a supply. A common example is the description of a 'fine' or 'donation' which implies nothing is being received in return for the payment. However, you must look at the underlying conditions which may reveal that something has in fact been provided in return. If something has been provided, then the payment is consideration for that supply.

The following examples represent common problems about whether a payment is regarded as consideration. VATSC06000 gives the most common examples of payments that are not consideration.

35.9 Grants and donations

On this topic, see too 15.33 (Multiple/single/split payments).

The VATSC Manual provides:

VATSC06110 - Consideration: Payments that are not consideration: Donations [Feb 2022]

If a monetary donation is freely given, it is not consideration for any supply and so is outside the scope of VAT. In this situation, the donation has to be unconditional and the following points will help in deciding whether this is the case.

- Does the donor receive anything in return for the payment?
- Are there any conditions attached to the payment that go beyond merely having to mention it in account statements?
- What will the payments be used for?
- If the donor does not benefit directly, does any third party receive a benefit?
- Is there a contract and what are the terms and conditions?

The test case quoted in the majority of arguments is that of Mr Tolsma, which is described below.

It is also necessary to distinguish between monetary donations and sponsorship payments. Whereas a donation means the donor does not expect anything in return, sponsorship involves the sponsor receiving clearly identifiable benefits. These benefits may include advertising, publicity or use of facilities and any sponsorship payment is within the scope of VAT. How to determine whether a payment is sponsorship is covered in VATSC03560 and Notice 701/41 Sponsorship.

*Mr Tolsma ECJ Case C-16/93 (1994 STC 509***)**

Mr Tolsma played a barrel organ on a public highway and invited passers by to leave donations. The Dutch authorities assessed for output tax on these payments since a supply had been made to the passers by.

> The ECJ accepted Mr Tolsma's appeal and ruled that the playing of music on the public highway for which no payment was stipulated did not constitute a supply of services effected for consideration and so it was not within the scope of VAT. This was because there was no agreement between the parties, and there was also no necessary link between the musical service and the payments to which it gives rise. Mr Tolsma played whether the passers by paid him or not and he had not entered into a formal agreement with them for the provision of his services.

The question was whether the donations were "consideration" for services (if they were, they would be subject to Dutch VAT). It was held that they were not consideration:

> [14] It follows that a supply of services is effected "for consideration" within the meaning of art 2(1) of the Sixth Directive [now Article 73 VAT directive], and hence is taxable, only if
> [a] there is a legal relationship between the provider of the service and the recipient pursuant to which
> [b] there is reciprocal performance, the remuneration received by the provider of the service constituting the value actually given in return for the service supplied to the recipient.
> [15] In a case such as that which is the subject of the main proceedings, it is clear that those conditions are not fulfilled.
> [16] If a musician who performs on the public highway receives donations from passers-by, those receipts cannot be regarded as the consideration for a service supplied to them.
> [17] First, there is no agreement between the parties, since the passers-by voluntarily make a donation, whose amount they determine as they wish. Second, there is no necessary link between the musical service and the payments to which it gives rise. The passers-by do not request music to be played for them; moreover, they pay sums which depend not on the musical service but on subjective motives which may bring feelings of sympathy into play. Indeed some persons place money, sometimes a considerable sum, in the musician's collecting tin without lingering, whereas others listen to the music for some time without making any donation at all.

In *Three Counties Dog Rescue v HMRC* [2011] UKFTT 817 (TC), a charity asked for payments which it called "donations" from the people to whom it passed on rescued dogs. The charity sought to register for VAT and reclaim input tax. HMRC rejected the application on the basis that the charity was rehousing the dogs in exchange for a voluntary donation.

However, the FTT found that notwithstanding the labelling of the payments as "donations", they were in fact compulsory:

> [16] We ask first...what was the nature of the payment being made by the owners. Was it or was it not a donation in the proper meaning of that term?...Our view is that the payments made by the owners were neither "freely given" nor were they given with "nothing supplied in return"... There is nothing optional about [the payments] and even if, as an exception, a dog is transferred without payment that does not mean that it is not standard practice to accept payment...there is also the accounting evidence as to how the donations for the dogs were treated. They were kept entirely separate from the charitable donations and also they were not subject to gift aid.
>
> ...
>
> [18] It is clear to us and so we find that...TC were supplying dogs in return for a mandatory payment, termed by TC as a donation but this not in any way altering the nature of the payment...

In *Friends of the Earth Trust v HMRC*,[5] charity chuggers signed up passers-by to make regular direct debit payments to the charity. Anyone who paid more than £3 per month received benefits, including a magazine, a membership card (if that is a benefit), a discount on purchases from the charity's online shop and one free musical download. The question was whether the payments were donations or consideration for a subscription to the magazine and other benefits:

> [51] We summarise the relevant legal principles and observations that may be extracted from the case law … as follows:
> (1) The requirement that there be a legal relationship and reciprocity are necessary but not sufficient conditions for there to be a supply ([60] of [The Serpentine Trust Ltd] referring to various European cases).
> (2) The notion of a payment being "for" something connotes a quid pro quo as distinct from a quid cum quo. (*Church School Foundation* referring to the jurisprudence developed by the European Court in *Apple and Pear Development Council, Naturally Yours, Tolsma and First National Bank of Chicago*)
> (3) The question of whether a payment is "for" a benefit is an objective one of fact (see [61] of [Serpentine] where Judge Mosedale agrees with tribunal in *Church of England Children's Society*).
> (4) Whether supporters chose to pay on the basis the payment was a donation and irrespective of benefits offered or whether they only paid

5 [2016] UKFTT 411 (TC).

because they wished to receive the benefits - i.e. what the supporters thought - is irrelevant as the test is objective. ([70] of *Serpentine*)
(5) Labels and descriptions are not determinative but may be relevant (see [62] and [63] of Serpentine). We also note that the tribunal in *Church of England Children's Society* did (at [50]) examine the language used in the direct debit form.)
(6) Actual cost (as opposed to marginal cost) and perceived value by the supporter are potentially relevant (there is nothing unusual in perceived value exceeding cost.) (See [61] of Serpentine)
(7) Payments in return for very real benefits may be distinguished from gifts with stipulations which permit donors to check what their donation is used for are not supplies ([77] *Serpentine* referring to *Church of England Children's Society*).
[52] What also emerges from the above tribunal decisions is the fact that, beyond emphasising the objective nature of the analysis, the conclusion as to whether a payment was "for" a benefit was very much dependent on the inferences the tribunal drew having assessed the particular facts of the case and that there was not necessarily the same single attribute of the transaction under consideration which is determinative. In *Serpentine*, the conclusion that the payments were "for" the benefits was inferred from the finding that benefits of very real value to the recipient were provided which were likely to exceed the cost of providing them. That makes sense because when a benefit is provided only to a person who has made a payment and in the situation where that person perceives the benefit to be of very real value this set of circumstances is more consistent with the payment being "for" the benefit than not. A further relevant fact was the prominence given to the benefits in the relevant literature. In *Church of England Children's Society* the relevant factors were the documentary evidence which referred to the payment being a "gift", the ability to opt-out of the newsletter, and the fact that for a period even those who did make the minimum payment received the newsletter. …
[85] In our judgment it is quite clear when viewed objectively that the £3 minimum monthly payment was not "for" the magazine and benefits, or in other words a quid pro quo for them. The magazine and benefits were quid cum quo, the transaction being that the payment was a gift to the appellant to be used in its charitable work and that the appellant would send the supporter free copies of [the magazine].
[86] We reach this view taking account of the low likelihood that the magazine and benefits were mentioned at the time the supporter signed up to a direct debit on the street, the low level of prominence of the magazine and benefits, and the way in which the payment and magazine were referred to in the communications with the supporter following that

engagement on the street in the form of the welcome letter and direct debit confirmation form.

[87] That evidence, when viewed in the round, is simply not consistent with the transaction objectively being one where the person was paying a subscription for [the magazine] and other benefits. We are not satisfied that the appellant and the supporter agreed that the payment constituted value given in return for [the magazine] and the other benefits. It was quite clearly a donation to support the appellant's charitable activities.

35.9.1 *Donation or sponsorship*

The VATSC Manual provides:

VATSC06110 - Consideration: Payments that are not consideration: Donations [Feb 2022]

... It is also necessary to distinguish between monetary donations and sponsorship payments. Whereas a donation means the donor does not expect anything in return, sponsorship involves the sponsor receiving clearly identifiable benefits. These benefits may include advertising, publicity or use of facilities and any sponsorship payment is within the scope of VAT. How to determine whether a payment is sponsorship is covered in VATSC03560 and Notice 701/41 Sponsorship ...

HMRC Guidance Note Annex iv provides:

26. VAT: the VAT treatment of business sponsorship and payments for the use of a charity's logo

The VAT treatment is different from the direct tax treatment. Generally, if a charity receives sponsorship or another form of support it will normally be making a taxable supply for VAT purposes if, in return, it's obliged to provide the sponsor or supporter with a significant benefit.

In some cases the benefit may amount to no more than a simple acknowledgment of support and could not be considered to be a supply for VAT purposes. Guidance on what HMRC considers to be significant benefits and what HMRC recognises as insignificant acknowledgments can be found in VAT Notice 701/41 Sponsorship.

Where the benefits are such that they're not simple acknowledgments of thanks but are tangible benefits then the payment is consideration for those supplies and VAT will be due on the full payment received. You'll also find guidance on this in VAT Notice 701/1 Charities.

If a charity grants the right to another party to use the charity's name and logo in return for a payment the charity's making a taxable supply for VAT purposes. It's the granting of the right that's the taxable supply, rather than any activity (or lack of it) undertaken by the charity or the size and/or prominence of the logo. The same principle applies when a

> charity grants the right for a sponsor's logo to appear in the charity's publication or on the charity's website.
>
> **27. VAT: charity apportioning a payment in respect of donation elements for VAT purposes**
>
> VAT law only allows apportionment of single payments when they're made in relation to different supplies of goods or services. Therefore a single payment covering both a right to use a logo and a donation cannot be apportioned because a donation is not a supply for VAT purposes. VAT will be due on the whole of the payment.

This paragraph (27) could be better phrased. Section 19(4) VATA provides:

> Where a supply of any goods or services is not the only matter to which a consideration in money relates, the supply shall be deemed to be for such part of the consideration as is properly attributable to it.

Does this not provide for apportionment between a supply and a "non-supply"?

In *The Serpentine Trust* [2014] UKFTT 876, Mosedale J held:

> [81] …the intention of s 19(4) was not to reverse, or go behind, the rule on the valuation of consideration set out in the [VAT directive] and as explained in cases such as *Naturally Yours Cosmetics*. Applying those principles the entire amount paid for the benefits was the consideration as that was the price that the parties had subjectively attributed to the supply. Once it was established that the payment was 'for' the benefits, even if the supply was grossly overvalued by the parties, and even if the paying party had donative intent, that made no difference.…
>
> [83] I consider the appellant's case on s 19(4) [that it ought to apply to apportion the payment received from supporters between that part that was attributable to the benefits and that part that was in excess, and was a donation] runs totally contrary to the settled case law of the CJEU. If the Trust had offered benefits for a fixed price and specified anything additional was a donation, then clearly the element of donation would not be paid 'for' the benefits. But here the Trust required the full amount to be paid in return for Benefits. There is nothing for s 19(4) to apportion.

The third last sentence of [83] points to at least one scenario in which an apportionment is possible under section 19(4) VATA.

This scenario is alluded to in HMRC Guidance Note Annex iv as follows:

If a sponsor wants to make a voluntary donation in addition to a sponsorship payment, it must be clear from any agreement that the donation is entirely separate from the sponsorship payment (ie, the payment made in return for a supply) and it's freely given. If the donation is freely given but on condition that a further benefit is provided, it's further consideration for a taxable supply for VAT purposes.

28. VAT and direct tax: affinity credit cards

A charity may receive payments from a bank, building society or other financial institution in return for the charity endorsing that institution's credit card and recommending its use to the charity's members or supporters. Such cards are normally referred to as 'Affinity Credit Cards'.

This is a business supply of marketing services by the charity and VAT is due on any amounts they receive in respect of such supplies. However, a charity may have an arrangement with the bank whereby it enters into separate agreements. One agreement could be for the supply of marketing services by the charity to the bank for an agreed consideration. This is a taxable supply on the part of the charity and VAT is due on such payments. The other, separate agreement provides for the bank to make voluntary contributions to the charity. The contributions may often be based on how often the card, usually associated by the bank with the charity's name and logo, is used. In essence, the nature of the second agreement is that the payments are not made in return for a supply. These contributions are outside the scope of VAT.

Treatment for direct tax purposes is likely to be similar to that for VAT purposes. Any payment accepted as a genuine donation for VAT purposes would normally be accepted as a donation for tax purposes. Anything else paid to the charity in relation to the affinity card is likely to be taxable non-charitable trading income. It is recommended that separate payments are made under carefully drafted legal agreements, in order to make the position clear. The commercial payment should be at a market rate.

35.9.2 *Project funding*

The VATSC Manual provides:

VATSC06110 - Consideration: Payments that are not consideration: Donations [Feb 2022]

... **Project Funding**

Sometimes businesses will join with government departments or local authorities to co-sponsor a research and development project with each individual sponsor contributing funds. The amount contributed depends on the cost of the project rather than on any commercial benefit to the individual sponsor.

It could be seen that the sponsors receive benefits (as discussed above). These could include technical reports, rights relating to or restricting the use of the results, a loan of any items developed from the project or a levy on the sale of the project's results (a way of repaying some of the funding).

Benefits such as these are often necessary safeguards to ensure the money is spent correctly and that the end product is put to proper use. They are incidental to the primary purpose of the project and have a minimal relation to the amount of the funding. Since the benefits are incidental, the funding of the project is not seen as a consideration for any supply and so is outside the scope of VAT.

35.9.3 *Donated goods or services*

The VATSC Manual provides:

VATSC06110 -Consideration: Payments that are not consideration: Donations [Feb 2022]

... **Donated goods and services**

The guidelines on monetary donations above should also be considered when specific goods and services are donated. Typical examples of donated goods are computers and other equipment given to schools and universities. Where goods are given for no consideration the rules on business gifts in VATSC03300 must also be considered.[6]

Donated services may include a business donating its staff for a charity event. Since there is no consideration, the provision of such services is not a supply for VAT purposes. However, in some cases the provider of the services may ask for donations to be made to a charity rather than ask for the standard fee. The most common example of this is Will Aid.

Will Aid

This is a national fund raising scheme for charity where a code of practice has been agreed in order to treat the payments as donations for VAT purposes. The scheme involves solicitors offering to write wills and to arrange for their normal fee to be given to charity ...

It was agreed that any payments under this scheme are disregarded for VAT purposes provided the solicitors make it clear to customers that the will can be obtained without the customers being obliged to pay anything. It must be left entirely up to the customers' discretion whether they wish to pay anything to the charity. The fact that the solicitor may recommend an amount equivalent to their fee be paid to the charity does

6 See 18.9 (Gift of goods and services: VAT).

not alter the donation status of the payments.

35.9.4 *Government grant*

The VATSC Manual provides:

> **VATSC06310 -Consideration: Payments that are not Consideration: Grants: Introduction** [Feb 2022]
> We commonly understand a grant to be a freely given payment in return for which no specific services (or goods) are received. Such a payment is therefore not a supply for VAT purposes. However there is no one definition of a grant and so you may come across payments which are described as grants but which are really payments for supplies.
> A grant is money that a government body, or other organisation, give to another body or person to carry out a particular purpose, the National Audit Office define a grant as 'a permanent transfer of funding for a specific purpose and used in accordance with a set of terms and conditions'.[7] This is a reasonable definition but even if a payment meets the definition it does not answer the question 'is that payment consideration for a supply?'
> What matters when determining if there is a supply is the extent to which goods or services are provided in return for the payment? An outside the scope grant could share some features with a supply made for a consideration - such as being funding for a specific purpose, and being governed by a set of terms and conditions. However grants that are not consideration for supplies are freely given and there is no expectation of goods or services being supplied to the funder, or a specified third party, directly in return for the money paid.
> ...
> **VATSC06311 -Consideration: Payments that are not Consideration: Grants: What is a grant?** [Feb 2022]
> Whether something is described as a grant is not relevant to a VAT analysis except in so far as it may be indicative that money is freely given and no supply has occurred. However because definitions of grants vary the label may be misleading and it is therefore important to look at what actually happens when a payment described as a grant is made. This guidance concentrates on the whether a payment is consideration for a supply for VAT purposes. It does not cover payments such as grant-in-aid which represent funding of public sector bodies from their parent central government departments (in Scotland,

---

7 Author's footnote: NAO, "Government grant services" (2014)
https://www.nao.org.uk/report/government-grant-services-2/
This definition is consistent with the Whole of Government Accounts.

Scottish Futures Trust Ltd) for strategic projects such as infrastructure plans. These payments are always outside the scope of VAT.

When an organisation identifies a need it wishes to fulfil, and decides not to do so itself, it may either:

- enter into an agreement with another body to undertake the task, and fund that body's costs through a grant or subsidy; or
- enter into a contract for the procurement of services (and possibly goods) to enable the task to be completed

The former is not a supply for VAT and will commonly be described as a grant. The latter is a supply for VAT but you may see instances where such arrangements are never the less described as a grant.

The majority of grants originate from central or local government and are given to organisations to support specific community activities or initiatives to benefit the public. This type of funding helps government to achieve its aims by enabling others to provide a wide range of activities and avoids government directly managing projects.

Projects will normally be subject to a tendering process on the open market and the strict rules on public procurement where the funder is a public body. Goods or services tendered for in this way will normally have a legally enforceable contract where goods or services are agreed to be supplied in return for payment.

There are other ways of funding a project such as providing sponsorship, a subsidy, an equity investment or a loan (long or short term). The type of funding used will vary depending on requirements of the project and the value for money offered. In all these situations, no matter what label is applied to the funding, you need to consider what if anything is received in return for the payment to determine whether it is consideration for a supply.

Common controls within an outside the scope grant agreement include a fixed (often maximum) time period, approved uses of any assets bought, and an agreed timetable of financial reporting.

When paying a grant, a government department normally does so under its statutory obligations and so must have a legal power to do so. The rules around state aid must still be observed which means a government cannot provide funding that distorts, or threatens to distort, market competition within the UK.

Therefore, two important questions to ask are:

- Does the funder have a legal power to award a grant and which statute contains this power? If a legal power exists this is an indicator that the funding may be a grant and outside the scope of VAT.
- What was the tendering process? Was there an invitation to tender for a public procurement contract, which was advertised and has

> gone through a specific procurement and tendering processes (this is explained on the GOV.UK website). This is an indicator that the funding may be consideration for a supply.
>
> **VATSC06312 -Consideration: Payments that are not Consideration: Grants: HMRC's approach** [Feb 2022]
> When deciding whether a payment is within the scope of VAT you must treat each agreement on its own merits and apply the basic rules of VAT to it...
> For a transaction to fall within the scope of VAT there must always be a supply, a consideration and a direct link between the two. A payment is not consideration for a supply if one of these factors is missing.
> The following points will help in deciding whether a payment is consideration for a supply for VAT purposes:
> - Does the grantor receive anything in return for the payment?
> - Are there any conditions attached to the payment that go beyond merely having to mention it in account statements?
> - What will the payments be used for?
> - If the funder does not benefit directly, does any third party receive a benefit?
> - Is there a contract and what are the terms and conditions?
>
> …
>
> **VATSC06314 -Consideration: Payments that are not Consideration: Grants: Related guidance** [Feb 2022]
> The consideration for a supply is everything received in return for the supply, including subsidies directly linked to the price. If there is no consideration there is no supply.
> The guidance on the definition of consideration in VATSC05000 must also be taken into account and you may wish to familiarise yourself with this before considering the indicators in this part of the guidance.
> Assistance in deciding whether there is a direct link between a supply and consideration can be found in the ECJ judgment in Mr Tolsma (C-16/93), see VATSC06110. You may also encounter issues around sponsorship and whether a payment is consideration for a supply. The specific guidance on how to approach this subject is in VATSC03560.
> Sometimes funding for activities that are carried out by a public body under statutory powers comes from a mixture of grants and statutory contributions by private individuals or businesses. Guidance about how to approach this subject can be found VATGPB3500...

HMRC lists what they consider are relevant factors when assessing whether a payment is a grant that falls outside the scope of VAT or the consideration for a supply. The VATSC Manual provides:

VATSC06316 -Consideration: Payments that are not Consideration: Grants: Payments that are not Consideration: Indicators of the supply position [Feb 2022]

This guidance sets out indicators to consider when deciding whether or not a payment is consideration for a supply which have been taken from precedent decisions.

The following terms are used -

- Funder - the organisation making the payment
- Supplier - the organisation receiving the payment and supplying goods or services to third parties

All factors need to be considered, the more there are from each section the greater the evidence for a decision. However, it is not simply a matter of 'indicators for' exceeding 'indicators against', a balanced view needs to be formed taking all the applicable indicators into account. You must consider the economic reality not just the contractual terms.

The principal factor to consider is if a specific supply is made to the funder or a third party in return for a payment. If so then the payment is consideration for a supply, but if this direct link is not established then the payment can be treated as outside the scope of VAT.

VATSC06317 -Consideration: Payments that are not Consideration: Grants: Factors indicating the payment is a grant [Feb 2022]

The following factors are taken from precedent cases. They are not in any particular order, all factors should be considered when making a decision. The more there are in your situation, the more likely it is that the payment is outside the scope of VAT.

The factors to consider are:

- the payment was made following a grant application process run by an organisation that regularly provides outside the scope grants, such as central or local government
- are the funders the beneficiaries of the project? To be outside the scope of VAT a grant should be freely given. In using the payment, the supplier carries out its own charitable aims and objectives with the assistance of the money which is given with no expectation of direct benefit in return
- the funder will not attempt to control how the money is spent beyond seeing that the funds are properly managed. Any monitoring is no more than simply ensuring the payments are appropriately spent
- the supplier will set its own targets as opposed to the funder imposing specific targets
- the payments are not treated as trading income or expenditure in the accounts of either party
- if the funding is withdrawn there is no legal redress for the supplier

to have the payment reinstated

- funding is drawn down by the supplier as a reimbursement of expenditure incurred, rather than an advance payment for services. Alternatively, there may be a 'deficit funding' arrangement whereby the funder agrees to plug any funding gaps
- the funding is provided under a statutory provision that empowers the funder to make a grant. This would be mainly relevant if the funder is a Government department or local authority
- there is a 'clawback' provision within the agreement. Funders use this method to reclaim their funding in circumstances such as where not all the money was spent or if the terms of the agreement were not complied with. In contrast, a contract for a supply should not contain a 'clawback' clause as there is no automatic right to reclaim any money. The money is consideration for the supply and the solution for reclaiming the payment in any subsequent breach of contract is to sue for damages.

VATSC06318 -Consideration: Payments that are not Consideration: Grants: Factors indicating the payment is consideration for a supply
[Feb 2022]
The following factors are taken from precedent cases. They are not presented in any particular order all factors should be considered when making a decision. The more there are in your situation, the more likely it is that the payment is consideration for a supply. The factors to consider are:

- who initiates the agreement? If the funder is seeking services in return for their payment then this indicates the payment is consideration for supplies made to them if the funder is the direct beneficiary of the supplies. The funder believes they are receiving something in return for the payment.
- the supplier undertakes outsourced activities on behalf of the funder where the services provided are ones ordinarily provided by the funder so the supplier is acting as a subcontractor. Examples include the provision of functions ordinarily undertaken by local authorities that they have a statutory duty to perform and would face sanctions if they did not happen
- the contract is commercial in nature ie it is a legally binding contract connected to a business activity. This means looking for indicators such as penalty clauses being in place if the supplier does not fulfil their responsibilities and so is in breach of contract
- the supplies are undertaken as an economic activity. It is not necessary for the supplier to have a profit motive, but the type of supplies should have the potential to make a profit

- the relationship between the funder and supplier will be at 'arms length' and there will be a clear level of control from the funder in the supplier's decision making process
- the payments made by the funder to the supplier are made specifically for the supplier to provide particular services to its clients. The fact that the funder does not know at the time the service is provided the identity of the client or the even the specific service which is being provided is not relevant
- each activity carried out by the funder gives rise to a specific and identifiable payment. This is an agreed sum, either a single payment or a sum per activity ie the more work done, the greater the payment. For this to happen there is probably a detailed recording system for timekeeping, outputs achieved etc
- the funder will attempt to control how the money is spent, maybe imposing specific targets in terms of quantity, quality, timeframes etc. Any monitoring is more than simply ensuring the payments are spent properly and is to ensure that specific supplies are made
- if the funding is withdrawn there is legal redress for the supplier to have the payment reinstated or claim compensation
- the payments are treated as trading income or expenditure in the accounts of either party.

VATSC06319-Consideration: Payments that are not Consideration: Grants: Factors that are neutral [Feb 2022]

The following factors are taken from precedent cases. The court decisions referring to these factors regarded them as neutral, so their presence in an agreement generally does not indicate either way whether the payment is an outside the scope grant or consideration.

The neutral factors are:

- the payment is described as a grant in the contract and correspondence. Whilst the wording of a contract is important, what the payment is called does not determine its VAT treatment
- the level of detail within the contract/agreement does not point in either direction, ie it is wrong to say that the more detail there is, the more likely there is a contract for a supply the supplier is obliged to provide reports and information to the funder. This is not an indicator either way as a condition in the agreement to report on how the payments are used will be required either to confirm supplies were made or in a grant situation act as good housekeeping to ensure the money is spent for its intended purpose
- the supplier's activities and the number of projects undertaken are influenced by the payment ie they would be significantly curtailed in the event of a withdrawal or reduction in funding. Although this

could indicate there was a supply made to the funder, you must still look at whether a supply is actually made to them, as a withdrawal of a grant may equally mean a reduction in service provision

35.9.5 *Agricultural grant*

On subsidies generally, the VATSC Manual provides:

VATSC06315 -Consideration: Payments that are not Consideration: Grants Subsidies [Feb 2022]

There are two possible types of subsidy:

1. a global subsidy to cover general operating costs, in which case no parties other than the funder and the supplier are affected in any way
2. a subsidy directly linked to the price of a supply, given by the funder to the supplier to enable a third party to obtain a specific service (or to obtain it more cheaply).

In the *Keeping Newcastle Warm* decision…the ECJ commented 'a subsidy is ordinarily understood to mean a sum paid from public funds, usually in the general interest'. But it is possible for it to be subject to VAT if it forms part of the payment for a particular supply. In looking at whether a subsidy is consideration for a supply the ECJ commented 'it is not the form of the subsidy but its economic effect which is the decisive factor'. So like grants the question is whether anything is received in return for a payment.

A common area for subsidies is in the agricultural sector and further information about these is in VATSC06343.

Type 1 - the global subsidy

Usually, subsidies from public funds are made in the furtherance of the public interest, not to procure goods or services for the state. This means that in the majority of these cases there is no supply made to the government department providing the subsidy.

Global subsidies have factors in common with grants, such as being time-limited, and are usually paid to enable an organisation or individual to cover their general overheads. Although not directly linked to reducing the price of a supply a global subsidy may still be restricted to a particular activity, such as undertaking research, but the key is still that the funder or a third party is not receiving a specific supply in return for the payment.

Type 2 - directly linked to the price of a supply

A subsidy forms part of the taxable consideration received by the supplier if it is directly linked to reducing the price to the customer. This is the case when a payment

– is paid to the producer, supplier or provider of goods or services;
– is paid by a third party to the supplier, and;

- constitutes consideration or part of the consideration for a supply of goods or services

Indicators that the payment is this type of subsidy are:

- the payment must be paid in return for specific goods and/or services
- the payment has a direct effect on price or quantity in that the goods or services could not be provided at that price unless there was a subsidy
- the funder is specifically seeking to promote the supply of the particular goods or services
- there is an arithmetical relationship between a progression of the amount of the payment, the quantity produced and progression of the actual price of the goods or services provided
- the price of the goods or services is ascertainable and determined not later than the time of the payment to demonstrate the consumer benefitted from a particular amount being paid

The VATSC Manual refers to certain specific cases that HMRC considers are important authorities in this area. These include:

> **VATSC06334 -Consideration: Payments that are not Consideration: Grants: Office des Produits Wallons ASBL v Belgium** [Feb 2022]
> Court Reference: C-184/00
> This was a referral to the ECJ from Belgium concerning OPW which was a private non-profit-making association carrying out the advertising and sale of Walloon agricultural and horticultural products and agricultural foodstuffs.
> OPW received an annual subsidy from the Walloon Region through a framework subsidy agreement. Under that agreement, it was responsible for activities such as the publication of a catalogue and a magazine, the running of local offices and participating in local events. The payment also covered running costs such as staff wages, renting premises, purchasing equipment etc. The Belgian authorities thought the subsidy was taxable consideration, whilst POW thought it was a grant outside the scope of VAT because it was not directly linked to the price of the goods or services they supplied.
> The decision was based on Article 11A(1) of the Sixth Directive (now article 73 of Dir 2006/112) which set out the basis of liability to VAT on transactions within the territory of the country…
> At para 35, the judgment stated: ‘I consider the decisive factor to be whether the operating subsidies are directly related to a specific economic activity pursued by the beneficiary which consists in the supply of specific goods or services. That will be the case if the subsidies lead to a reduction in the price of goods or services which the

beneficiary supplies to the consumer or if as a result there is an increase in the quantity of the goods or services supplied. An operating subsidy can also lead to the beneficiary's producing an increased quantity, knowing that a proportion of the costs is incurred at the risk of the authority which granted the subsidy'.
The decision was that there was no general subsidy but rather a payment for services supplied to the public authorities, for example the service of publishing a magazine 'at the behest or at any rate on behalf of the Walloon Region'. Therefore the payment was consideration because it consisted of 'the price of the transaction' and was not a subsidy which was linked to the price.

VATSC06335 -Consideration: Payments that are not Consideration: Grants: Keeping Newcastle Warm [Feb 2022]
Court Reference: C-353/00
This was a referral from the UK to the ECJ on whether a payment formed part of the consideration under Art 11A(1)(a) of the Sixth VAT Directive (now Article 73 of the Principal VAT Directive (2006/112))... Whether a payment by the Energy Action Grants Agency (responsible for implementing the Home Energy Efficiency Scheme) to Keeping Newcastle Warm (KNW) was liable to VAT. KNW gave advice on improving energy efficiency in dwellings to householders and sometimes carried out the work. There was a maximum grant of £10 for each piece of energy advice given and in practice that amount was paid for every piece of energy advice given. Output tax had been accounted for on these sums and although KNW agreed the sum was consideration, they argued the amount was not directly linked to the final price and so was outside the scope of VAT.
The contract with the consumer referred to the payment as a grant, but the ECJ found this money was part of the taxable amount in respect of a supply of services as it was included in 'everything which made up the consideration for the service'. It was clear that the sum paid by the agency to KNW was received by the latter in consideration for the service supplied by it to the householders, indeed KNW's right to receive the subsidy only arose where it agreed to provide the energy advice. As consideration in respect of a supply, that sum formed part of the taxable amount within the meaning of the EC legislation. The fact that the payment was capped did not have any relevance as whatever was received was still payment for the supply of advice.
The Advocate General too found that the subsidy was clearly attributable to the supply of energy advice, intended to pay in full or part for the supply and therefore granted by way of third party consideration. In her Opinion she gave some helpful interpretation of when a subsidy can be

subject to VAT. She concluded that a subsidy is generally understood to mean a sum paid from public funds, usually in the general interest. The fact that there was a reference to subsidies in Article 11A(1)(a), established the principle that subsidies can be subject to VAT under certain circumstances. There is, however, a difference between a global subsidy, paid to cover general operating costs, and a subsidy granted by a donor to the recipient to enable a third party to obtain a specific service - or obtain it more cheaply.

As a rule, there can only be a taxable transaction where the subsidy is of the latter type, one granted in the context of a tripartite relationship. The reason for this is that subsidies from public funds are made in the furtherance of the public interest, not to procure goods or services for the State. In order for there to be a supply, and therefore a taxable transaction for the purposes of Article 2 of the Sixth Directive [Article 2 of Principal VAT Directive], the beneficiary of the supply must be a third party.

VATSC06339 -Consideration: Payments that are not Consideration: Grants: Important Court Decisions: Groundwork Cheshire [Feb 2022]

Court Reference: [2012] UKFTT 750 (TC)

Groundwork trusts were set up as a result of government policy towards promoting urban and post-industrial renewal. More information is in VBNB45400.

Groundwork Cheshire was a non-profit making groundwork trust providing health and safety management and environmental consultancy to businesses to help them improve environmental and energy efficiency. It received funding through the Enworks programme, which was in turn funded by the North West Regional Development Agency and the European Regional Development Fund. This payment was made in relation to a service level agreement and was subject to a 'maximum grant'. This meant clients were not required to pay Groundwork Cheshire for their services.

Groundwork Cheshire contended the payments received from Enworks were a subsidy for the work done by them on behalf of clients because the subsidy was directly linked to the price of the supply, it was not a fixed sum and if the services were not delivered to specific businesses then Enworks would not make any payment.

In deciding the payment was consideration, due to the existence of a direct link between it and the services provided, the relevant factors were:

– The payment enabled the service to be provided free of charge. Therefore the payments from Enworks to Groundwork do affect the price charged by Groundwork to its clients; 'as Wallons makes clear, subsidies will nearly always affect the cost price of goods or services supplied by a subsidised body'

- the payments made by Enworks to Groundwork are made specifically for Groundwork to provide particular services to its clients within the Enworks programme. The fact that Enworks does not know at the time the service is provided the identity of the client or the specific service within the Enworks programme which is being provided is not relevant
- the fact that not all overheads are allocated by Groundwork to particular businesses is not relevant because it simply indicates that the price of the services to those businesses has not been fully ascertained (but there is no reason in principle why the overheads incurred each month could not be allocated)
- each activity carried out by Groundwork gives rise to a specific and identifiable payment. Work done for a client pursuant to the Enworks programme can be traced directly to a monthly payment made by Enworks. The more work done for clients, the greater that payment will be. The relationship between the work done and the payment made is clearly identifiable - the grant is by reference to a maximum amount of funding and the funding is calculated each month by reference to specific services provided to specific businesses
- The relationship between the payment from Enworks and the provision of a free service to clients is significant. The payment is not made globally to cover the whole of Groundwork's running costs
- 'No price is payable by clients to Groundwork. It is therefore artificial to consider whether the price is fixed in such a way that it diminishes in proportion to the payment made by Enworks, or that the subsidy constitutes an element of the price charged to clients. Looked at overall the price that would be payable by clients is clearly related to the payment made by Enworks. It is that payment which enables Groundwork to provide a free service. For the same reason the payment made by Enworks can be said to constitute an element of the price that would be charged by Groundwork to its clients'
- Groundwork records the time spent by each member of staff with each client and any disbursements. Members of staff are required to complete project-coded time sheets
- Groundwork also records outputs and outcomes achieved through delivery of the service. Outputs and outcomes include for example the number of businesses assisted to improve performance, jobs created, sales increased and CO_2 reductions. The causal link between funding and outputs/outcomes is documented.

It is interesting to note that, in this case, it was the taxpayer who argued for the funding to be treated as consideration for a taxable supply (this was in order to enable it to recover related input tax from HMRC).

On agricultural grants specifically, the VATSC Manual provides:

> **VATSC06343-Consideration: Payments that are not Consideration: Grants: Important Court Decisions: Agricultural Grants** [Feb 2022]
> The supply position for agricultural grants was reviewed some years ago in the context of the voluntary surrender of rights, such as a farmer surrendering a milk quota in return for a Government grant. The review included consultation with member states and the European Commission and concluded that the treatment of such grants was inconsistent throughout the EU.
> Following the review, Treasury Ministers decided that VAT should not be applied in the UK to 'outgoers' under the milk quota arrangements and set-aside schemes until a common approach was adopted. Since the same conditions applied to other agricultural grant schemes, it was also decided to suspend the application of VAT on them.
> However, this suspension does not apply to supplies of milk quotas between farmers. These remain standard rated, unless supplied as part of a supply of land in which case they follow the same liability as the land. There are also special rules about grant aid for the processing of dried fodder which are described in VATSC06346.
> Our policy on agricultural grants is consistent with the two most important European Court judgements of Mohr VATSC06344 and Landboden-Agrardienste VATSC06345.
>
> **VATSC06344 -Consideration: Payments that are not Consideration: Grants: Important Court Decisions: Mohr** [Feb 2022]
> Court Reference: C-21/94
> In this case, a dairy farmer received 'compensation' from the EU in return for undertaking to discontinue milk production. The German tax authority treated this payment as consideration for a taxable supply since there was an obligation by Mr Mohr to discontinue production in return for the payment.
> The ECJ agreed with Mr Mohr's appeal that the agreement to discontinue milk production was not a supply under Article 6(1) of the Sixth Directive (now Articles 24(1) and 25 of the Principal VAT Directive (2006/112), enacted in the UKby section 5(2) of VAT ACT 1994). They reasoned that by paying grants the EU or an individual member state did not acquire or consume goods or services for its own use. Rather, they acted in the common interest of promoting the proper functioning of the EU's agricultural policy. Therefore the payment did

not provide any direct benefit which would enable the EU to be seen as the consumer of a service and so the payment was outside the scope of VAT.

The VATSC Manual provides further authority:

> **VATSC06345- Consideration: Payments that are not Consideration: Grants: Important Court Decisions: Lanboden-Agrardienste Gmbh & Co KG** [Feb 2022]
> Court Reference: C-384/95
> In this case, a potato farmer refrained from marketing 20% of his crop in return for a payment of a subsidy. The German tax authorities maintained it was consideration for a supply under Article 6(1) of the Sixth VAT Directive (77/388/EEC) (now Articles 24(1) and 25 of the Principal VAT Directive (2006/112)) since the wording of the law was that a supply of services was:
>
>> any transaction which does not constitute a supply of goods within the meaning of Article 5. Such transactions may include, inter alia, obligations to refrain from an act or to tolerate an act or situation.
>
> The ECJ based its decision on the *Mohr* case VATSC06344. It held that the farmer in this case did not provide services to an identifiable customer or provide any benefit capable of being regarded as a cost component of the activity of another person in the commercial chain.
> The judgement also said that the German authority's argument circumvented the rule that only subsidies linked to price form part of the basis of the assessment. To have accepted the German argument would have taxed not only the subsidy but also the increased price of potatoes as a result of the reduction in supply, an increase that might well be greater than the amount of the subsidy. Therefore the payment was not seen as consideration for a supply and so was outside the scope of VAT.

On the VAT treatment of grants paid in relation to dried fodder, the VATSC Manual used to provide:

> **VATSC06346- Consideration: Payments that are not Consideration: Grants: Important Court Decisions: Treatment of Dried Fodder** [Jan 2019]
> These types of grants are paid throughout the EU by governments to producers of dried animal fodder - such as pellets and bales - in order to keep their price competitive with non-EU producers.
> Until 31 December 1999, the UK treated grants paid to processors of dried animal fodder as outside the scope of VAT. However, this did not follow EU policy and so from 1 January 2000 the UK accepted the

grants were within the scope of VAT. However, since animal fodder is zero rated, the related grants followed the same liability. This decision also applied to processors who process the grass of a third party and return it to them after drying, although this is not something that happens frequently in the UK.
However, in 2001 the European Commission took several member states to court for failing to tax the payments, their argument being that the money was taxable being a subsidy directly linked to the price of the fodder. The Commission lost the case (C-381/01), principally because there was no direct link between the subsidy and the final selling price as the subsidy amount was not directly reflected in the market price.
Following this judgment, the European policy is to treat these grants as outside the scope of VAT and so the UK reverted to its original position from 1 April 2005. Therefore the grants are treated as outside the scope of VAT.

This page has now been archived by HMRC on the basis that the content is "no longer applicable".

35.9.6 *Local authority grant*

The VATSC Manual provides:

VATSC06333 -Consideration: Payments that are not Consideration: Grants: Trustees of the Bowthorpe Community Trust [Feb 2022]
Court Reference: LON/94/1276A
The Bowthorpe CommunityTrust was a registered charity and provided work experience for physically handicapped and disabled students.
The question for the Tribunal was about the Commissioners denying input tax reclaimed by the trustees in respect of expenditure on a new workshop.
The decision noted the Trust's fund raising documents where its aim was stated to be providing work experience for daily placements in woodwork mainly but also in pottery and other crafts, developing self-confidence through creative work in a friendly environment. The Trust also had a counselling service and its benefits were aimed at the physically and mentally disabled in the Norwich area and surrounding area. About 55% of the funding was received from Norfolk County Council with the rest being from donations.
There were two types of agreement with the Council, with conditions such as the requirement for the Trust to provide premises suitable for training, to be open for specified periods and to give priority to 20 referrals from social services. If the Trust did not provide the 20 places then, it had to return the money (it is assumed only that proportion money for unused places is returned).

The decision that the money from the Council was a grant rather than consideration for supplies to the Council applied to both types of agreement. The reasons for this were:

- the supplies made by the trust were made to the individuals, never to the Council
- the amount of the grant was determined in relation to the Council's categories of funding. In its internal documentation, the Council rated the Trust as an organisation 'caring for people who otherwise would require the services of the County Council, enabling people to maintain their independence and enhancing the quality of life of vulnerable people'
- although this category was of assistance to the Council, the Trust was not in the two top priority categories in respect of providing a service which demonstrably prevents people being admitted to the Councils' care or is undertaking a task which by statute would fall upon the Council if the organisation ceased to function
- although the Council had priority in deciding who received training and had certain monitoring rights to ensure the Trust fulfilled its obligations, this was not relevant to the decision.

VATSC06336- Consideration: Payments that are not Consideration: Grants: Edinburgh Leisure & Others [Feb 2022]

Court Reference: EDN/03/22, EDN/03/29, EDN/03/30

This was a combined appeal from three leisure operators - Edinburgh Leisure Ltd (ELL), South Lanarkshire Leisure Ltd (SLL) and Renfrewshire Leisure Ltd (RLL) - who were created as Not for Profit Leisure Trusts. They were formed in order to fulfil an obligation to operate sports centres which was incumbent upon their respective Local Authorities (LA).

The sports centres had been previously operated by the LA, but were rented to the Trusts for a nominal rent. The Trusts operated the sports centres under a service level agreement and kept all the income from the sporting activities. Some of these activities were profitable, but others were not and so each Trust received a negotiated payment from their respective LA. The payment was in recognition that the Trusts could not meet their service level agreement with the LA out of income they generated themselves alone.

Through creating Not For Profit Leisure Trusts, the LAs were able to benefit from a saving which arises in relation to non-domestic rates. The court noted the sums were substantial and in themselves would have justified setting up the arrangement irrespective of VAT considerations (although the Trusts and LAs would seek to achieve a VAT saving where possible). There were also other sources of funding in addition to the LAs, for example SLL received money from Health Boards (by way of a GP referral), the Scottish Football Association, lottery money and new opportunity funds.

The court found The Local Government and Planning (Scotland) Act 1982 imposed a 'wide ranging duty' on LAs to ensure not only adequate provision of facilities in the sense of structures and equipment, but also that the inhabitants of their area were provided adequately with facilities. Any failure to carry out these duties would therefore be 'capable of enforcement if the local authority failed'. The decision was that the LAs were not making a grant to the Trusts to enable them to operate for their own purposes. Rather, the payment is so the Trusts may operate in accordance with the wishes of the Councils to properly fulfil their statutory duty and so in that context the Council is the customer. The decision did not identify the statutory duty as conclusive in itself, but referred to it in order to contrast the situation with that of the councils "making a grant to the companies to enable them to operate for their own purposes".

Other factors considered were:

- the Trusts were obliged to provide the Council with audited accounts and, without need for request, true and complete quarterly financial and monitoring reports detailing its income and expenditure as well as annual reports on all aspects of the company.
- there are binding obligations which are being paid for by the Council. These may be enforceable
- the relationship between the Trusts and the LAs is at arms length
- there is an absence of control by the Council in the Trusts' decision-making in that they are at liberty to dispense with Council services wherever possible
- there was no question of deficit funding because the Trusts were not given whatever money turned out to be needed in a particular year, instead a sum was agreed which is the consideration for the service (although it was irrelevant that the consideration was calculated in advance on the basis that the Trusts should not suffer losses)
- it was relevant that the customer thinks they are receiving something.

VATSC06338 -Consideration: Payments that are not Consideration: Grants: Important Court Decisions: Bath Festivals Trust [Feb 2022]

Court Reference: LON 2006/0511

The Trust was a limited company and registered as a charity. It was acquired from the Bath Festival Society in 1993, from which it also acquired the intellectual rights to the Bath International Music Festival which had been in existence from 1948. The Society had previously promoted the music festival but after financial difficulty, the Arts

Council was unwilling to continue its financial support without significant changes being made, both to the running of the festival and the basis of the support given by Bath County Council.
Hence the Trust took over promotion of the festival with a wider remit - a year round festival with a wider range of activities - and received money from the Council under a service level agreement as the Council wished for the festival to continue in line with its cultural/regeneration policies. In addition to the music festival, the Trust was expected to offer services such as 'financial, managerial, programming, promotional, administrative, technical or other assistance' to the Bath Fringe, Literature and Film Festivals.
The service level agreement contained the wording "In consideration of the payment of the Contract Fee by the Council the Organisation agrees to provide and supply the Services to the Council upon the terms and conditions of this Agreement." It went on to say the payment was made "to obtain a range of services which contribute to the delivery of the Council's Corporate Objectives, Community Strategic, Cultural Strategy, and Service Strategies ..."
The decision took a lead from Edinburgh Leisure ... and ruled the payments were consideration for a supply to the Council. This was mainly based on the differences between the Bath Council and Arts Council payments. Relevant factors considered were:

- the presence or absence of a statutory duty (in this case The Local Government Act 2000) to provide services' is irrelevant as to the question whether the requisite "direct link" between the "thing done" and the "consideration received" can be said to exist'. But if the Trust was not providing these services, the Council would itself be required to provide them in some form through its in-house arts department, but as it was unable to attract the Arts Council grant 'it must be assumed that it would be limited in what it provided'. (Also note: this point relates to the recipient of services having a statutory duty, not whether the provider has a statutory duty)
- to obtain an Arts Council grant the applicant had to set out his proposed programme of activities and define his own targets, whereas under the service level agreements the Council approached the Trust and imposed specific requirements for what was provided
- an Arts Council grant would mean the Trust would have to measure itself against its own targets, whereas with the service level agreement the targets were largely set by the Council and it was up to the Trust to decide whether to accept them or not
- the Arts Council would not attempt to control how the money was spent beyond seeing that the funds were properly managed. The Council's monitoring amounted to more than simply ensuring that

the payments were spent properly, it was also to ensure that the Council received the services it expected and to the standard it required.

- if the Arts Council withdrew the funding there would be no further action the Trust could take, whereas if the Council withdrew its funding, the Trust could litigate against it as there was a properly structured, binding, legal agreement between them.
- The Council regarded the provision of tourism and cultural services as essential to its role as a local authority in a locality where these elements are critical for the local economy. They had to assess whether the Trust's project fitted in with its Arts Development Strategy priorities and the new approach was 'very much tailored to its own specific requirements, strategies and policies' ie there were matters which were imposed on the Trust by the Council, rather than being matters which the Trust had itself wished to provide.
- The council outsourced the single largest portion of its cultural provision to the Trust because the Trust could create services that were more effective, more competitive, more creative and more responsive to the market and more efficient than the Council itself could provide.
- It was not the case that if the Arts Council grant increased then the amount of finance provided by the Council would be reduced proportionately
- There was no merit in the argument for the payment that without the funding from B&NES the Trust would still be able to continue operating.

The VATSC Manual provides:

VATSC06331- Consideration: Payments that are not Consideration: Grants: Hillingdon Legal Resource Centre [Feb 2022]
This case was an appeal against an assessment for over claimed input tax as Hillingdon Legal Resource Centre had claimed they were making taxable supplies to their local authority, but Customs and Excise alleged any payments received were outside the scope grants.
The trader was a charity and operated a citizens' advice centre primarily for issues around welfare, housing and immigration. It received funding from their local authority and the London Boroughs Grants Unit. They argued the payments were consideration for a supply on the basis that there was a condition that required a detailed report and accounts be submitted to the local authority to show the grant was being used as originally intended. The local authority also gave evidence that they regarded the Centre as providing its services on behalf of the Council,

but they did not exercise day to day control over the Centre.
In deciding the payments were a grant and outside the scope of VAT, the judgment considered the following factors most relevant:

- the free legal services were supplied by the Legal Resources Centre to the public
- the Council cannot be said in substance and reality to provide any such legal services
- at no time did the Council request the Centre to supply any specific legal services
- the payment was made under the Local Government Act 1972 which empowered the Council to make a grant
- no direct link is created simply by a requirement to submit reports on how money is spent - this is simply good housekeeping to ensure the correct use of the payment

VATSC06332 -Consideration: Payments that are not Consideration: Grants: Wolverhampton Citizens' Advice Bureau [Feb 2022]
Court Reference: MAN/96/1145
Wolverhampton Citizens Advice Bureau (WCAB) provided facilities to give local citizens access to free legal and other advice. it was a limited company and a registered charity, adhering to the principles of the national CAB service, namely, free, independent, impartial and confidential advice.
Wolverhampton Borough City Council agreed to provide funds through an annual payment and the project also received funds from other organisations such as the City Challenge Project. WCAB accepted all but the Council's payment were outside the scope of VAT since the Council required a written service agreement to be in place - therefore that particular payment was consideration for a taxable supply by the Bureau.
Both sides accepted the supplies made qualifying for legal aid and so funded by the Legal Aid Board were taxable, but Customs and Excise viewed the funding from the Council as outside the scope of VAT as it was a non-business activity. The reason for the appeal was a desire to increase the amount of taxable income in order to have a better recovery rate on the renovation of the premises.
WCAB was subject to a service level agreement with the Council, but the Tribunal considered the case to be indistinguishable from Hillingdon Legal Resource Centre since there was nothing in the agreement to support the claim that a supply was being made. The points brought out in the judgment were:

- The supply of advice was not to the funder
- The services provided were not of a type that were subcontracted by

the council

- The factual position was that a grant was given, there was no purchasing of services by the council.

The trader also made an alternative argument that two supplies were being made - one to the council of the provision of the facilities and one of advice given to local citizens. This was based on the arguments in Redrow Group plc (1999 STC 161)VATSC90400, but the Tribunal found as a fact that there were no supplies made to the Council and so there was no similarity between the cases.

For a case held to fall on the other side of the line, see *Woking Museum and Arts and Crafts Centre* [2014] UKFTT 176 (TC). In this case, a local authority paid the appellant museum a fixed annual sum. The appellant charged the authority VAT. HMRC decided that the appellant was in fact supplying no services to the authority, but that the payments made to the appellant were grant funding outside the scope of VAT. The Tribunal considered the wording of the contract between the appellant and the local authority, the history of the museum project, the local authority's statutory powers, its policy initiatives, the financial reality of the relationship between the parties, the appellant's status as a charity, and the context within which the contract was signed. It found that the delivery of the services by the appellant provided a direct benefit to the local authority, and rejected HMRC's submission that the benefit was to the local community. The Tribunal found that there was a commercial relationship between the parties and allowed the appeal.

Other cases that HMRC considers are important authorities in relation to the VAT treatment of grants include:

VATSC06337 -Consideration: Payments that are not Consideration: Grants: University of Southampton [Feb 2022]
Court Reference: [2006] STC 1389
The university appealed against a refusal to allow input tax recovery on research undertaken which was publicly funded. The Tribunal dismissed the appeal and the High Court confirmed this decision concluding the payment was not in respect of a business activity.
The publicly funded research was funded by grants from research councils, government departments or charities. The university also undertook commercial research funded by industry and commerce in the UK and also the European Commission, the US government and NATO. Some research projects had both private and public funding.
The majority of the decisions' points were about entitlement to input tax recovery, but the factors considered relevant in deciding the payment

was not consideration for a supply were:

- evidence from the funders was that the payment was provided either with the aim of advancing knowledge or for the benefit of the community
- whether there is an economic or business activity is a question of fact
- in this case the research was not carried out with the aim of the funder acquiring exploitable Intellectual Property rights - grants were given on the understanding that the research would be published, but 'there was no requirement or expectation that results of industrial or commercial value should be obtained'
- there was no direct and immediate link between VAT incurred in respect of the publicly funded research and any output transactions
- therefore the research was not part of the university's economic activities and was 'completely distinct from its other business activities of education and commercial research and is not part of one single business'

VATSC06340 -Consideration: Payments that are not Consideration: Grants: Important Court Decisions: Hope in the Community Ltd
[Feb 2022]

Court Reference: [2012] UKFTT 498

This appeal followed a refusal by HMRC to repay a voluntary disclosure reclaiming output tax accounted for on payments that were claimed to be outside the scope grants.

The organisation's aims and objectives were stated in its literature as the provision of "an umbrella of support for faith and voluntary sector groups seeking to regenerate the communities which they serve".

The appeal principally concerned four projects including payments related to feasibility studies about regeneration on behalf of the South East England Development Agency (SEEDA) and also management fees on behalf of South East England Faiths' Forum (SEEFF)

Hope in the Community also worked with other voluntary groups regarding social and economic issues which adversely affected communities and the well-being of their residents. It was funded by the 'Championing Neighbourhoods Project' which was in turn supported by the 'Giving Real Opportunities for Work'(GROW) programme through a European Regional Development Funding (ERDF) initiative. The project was administered by SEEDA who was required to commit itself to expenditure out of its own funds. The cost was then claimed back from the GROW programme, which was paid out of grant funding received from ERDF.

The aim was to encourage and enable local residents to establish projects designed to improve local regeneration, employment opportunities and cohesion within community neighbourhoods. The services Hope in the Community provided were assisting other groups in developing a management framework to record and collate information regarding the project, the production of a website and the holding of meetings and conferences.

HMRC considered the payments were in respect of taxable supplies, for example where Hope in the Community was helping the funders fulfil their objectives. At para 41, Mr Mathias who appeared on behalf of the appellant summarised various tests he thought should be applied to any situation to determine whether a payment was a grant or consideration for a supply.

The decision turned 'on a close examination of the agreement or arrangement between the Appellant and the funder in each of the projects' (para 65). In finding that the payments were consideration for a supply, the judge found the following factors to be relevant in para 66 - 68:

- the appellant was not able to show that the relationship between it and the funder was one of informal optional cooperation not giving rise to any transaction capable of recognition as a supply
- the terminology and the terms and conditions embodied in the agreements are indicative only of the true legal nature of payments made to the appellant
- the appellant's modus operandi appears to have been to undertake outsourced activities on behalf of the funder organisations rather than carrying out its own charitable aims and objectives with the assistance of independent unconditional gratuitous payments
- the fact that the general nature of the projects may have complimented the appellant's declared charitable objectives is not relevant in determining whether there has been a supply in consideration of the payments made
- the commercial activity of the appellant and the number of projects undertaken would have been significantly curtailed in the event of a withdrawal or reduction in grant funding. The appellant's methodology appears to have been to undertake only those projects where its applications for grants or gratuitous payments were successful
- grants which were part of a mechanism whereby the Appellant's activities were promoted and generally for the direct, or indirect, benefit of the funder
- the payments were not made casually, without commitment or as acts of benevolence but as part of specific schemes whereby the funder and the appellant collectively intended to carry out specified aims and objectives, albeit charitable in nature

- the payments were made either as a condition of, or in expectation of, services rendered by the appellant
- it is clear from both the evidence and the appellant's own submissions that the appellant would not have committed itself to certain projects without a clear statement of intent and financial support from the funder.

VATSC06341 -Consideration: Payments that are not Consideration: Grants: Important Court Decisions: South African Tourist Board [Feb 2022]

Court Reference: [2014] UKUT 0280 (TCC)

This case was about whether the South African Tourist Board (SATB) was making supplies in return for the payment from the South African government which provided their funding. The SATB and the provision for its funding originated in South Africa's statute and HMRC ruled this meant there was no supplies made to the government, meaning there was no right to input tax recovery in the UK.

The First Tier Tribunal upheld this decision. SATB was subject to a performance agreement with the government and so was obliged to carry out its duties in return for the payment it received. However, the Tribunal's view was that a statutory body in receipt of government funding could not be carrying out an economic activity.

The Upper Tribunal upheld the decision that there was no supply made to the government, saying that the necessary reciprocity was not present in the agreement and there was no direct link between payment and services, meaning there was no supply for VAT purposes. One difference in the judgement was that the Upper Tribunal stated it was not relevant that SATB was a statutory body as it is possible a statutory body discharging their statutory duties could be an economic activity.

This decision does not extend to other sources of funding from private concerns, collected by way of a levy. In those cases there is a direct link between the payments made and the advertising and other benefits provided by SATB. As this would be a taxable supply if performed within the UK this meant input tax could be recovered in as far as it related to those activities.

South African Tourist Board was recently referenced in Colchester Institute Corporation [2020] UKUT 368.

Colchester Institute Corporation ("CIC") was a further education corporation providing further and higher education and vocational training. The appeal before the Upper Tribunal was primarily concerned with whether the provision of education and/or vocational training by CIC free of charge to students and funded by grants from two government funding agencies was a supply of services for consideration.

In its judgment, the Upper Tribunal held:

> [66] …we are faced with two diametrically opposed analyses, each drawing on previous cases which are said to provide a compelling analogy. So far as the authorities are concerned, that exposes the question which lies at the heart of this appeal: on which side of the line does this case fall? Is this a South African Tourist Board case where the payments are a form of funding on conditions? Or is this a Rayon d'Or case where the payments are made pursuant to a reciprocal arrangement for services, and constitute consideration for supplies?
>
> …
>
> [74] …we do not consider that Rayon d'Or can be distinguished; it is analogous on its facts with this case and our analysis must follow that of the CJEU. That is sufficient to dispose of the question before us on this appeal…But the arguments before us ranged more widely, with each side identifying particular factors which were said to support each side's case, and the FTT took a "balance sheet" approach in its judgment at [127] in order to deal with those arguments. So, we address those arguments...
>
> [75] The FTT placed some weight on the statutory background, characterising that as a factor weighing against the payments being consideration. We agree with the FTT that the statutory background is relevant. It opens the door to the "funding with conditions" analysis, because such funding is typically found in the context of bodies carrying out public functions on behalf of government (as was the case in South African Tourist Board). But Rayon d'Or demonstrates that a supply analysis remains possible even where the payments are made pursuant to statute. Thus, we conclude that in this case the statutory background is a neutral factor, consistent with both parties' cases.
>
> [76] The FTT found that the existence of agreements between the funding agencies and CIC was a neutral factor; their existence was consistent with either side's case. The fact that there were agreements might be said to be consistent with either party's case, but the content of those agreements is far from neutral, because the agreements are the starting point in the analysis (see South African Tourist Board and paragraph [55] above). We do not consider them to be evidentially neutral, rather we consider them to be key to the analysis. There are four important features of the agreements, in our judgement, which provide the answer to the question.
>
> [77] First, although the agreements did not state in terms which courses CIC was to provide, they did restrict the funding to courses within a list on the Government's website. The essence was that the funding was for those courses; CIC was not at liberty to do anything else with the money.

> [78] Secondly, the amount paid was by way of formula and not negotiated…The use of a formula is not itself a basis for concluding that the payments are not consideration, as Rayon d'Or shows. But in this case, the components of the formula give clues as to what the grant payment were for…The formula was …highly specific to CIC's outputs - to the number of students, the type of students, the number of courses and the type of courses.
> [79] Thirdly, one way or another, CIC would have to pay back any part of the grant funding which was not used for supplying the courses as anticipated at the beginning of the year…
> [80] Fourth, in order to give the funding agencies full sight of its activities, and to permit accurate application of the relevant funding formulae, CIC submitted an ILR for each student on a monthly basis, comprising over 200 fields of data for each student. The ILRs were required under the agreements. By them, the funding agencies were given detailed information about how the funds are being spent by CIC. With that information, the funding agencies were able to adjust their payments to match that data and according to the standard formula. With that information, the funding agencies were able to see how their grant funding had been spent.
> [81]Taken together, we conclude that these features, all contained within the agreements, seen in context, indicate the existence of a direct link between the grants coming into CIC and the courses provided to CIC's students for free. We accept, of course, that the link could have been more direct than it was: the funding was not specific to any particular course or courses, it did not reflect the specific costs of any particular course, nor did it identify the particular students who would take those courses. But the law does not require such a degree of specificity; the concept of "direct link" encompasses a range of possibilities.
> …

35.10 "Voluntary" donation

In *Glasgow's Miles Better Mid Summer 5th Anniversary Ball*[8] the appellants printed application form for tickets provided:

> Please supply tickets at * £50 for the Mid Summer Ball to be held in the Royal Scottish Automobile Club on Friday June 24, 1988.

The asterisk against the £50 referred to a line of small print at the foot of the form which provided:

8 EDN/89/95, 8 December 1989.

> * Price indication only. *For VAT purposes the entrance fee is £20.* The balance of £30 represents a minimum voluntary donation in aid of hospice funds.
> [Emphasis added]

On the tickets the price was shown as £50 and an asterisk referred to the same wording as in the application form.

This was misconceived because there is no such concept as a price "for VAT purposes". There is only one price, or, in VAT terminology, one consideration for the supply. Thus the application form (and ticket) might be regarded as inconsistent or self-contradictory, stating two different prices. Which was the true price? The Tribunal rightly held that the true price was £50:

> Furthermore, the subsequent words indicate that the balance of £30 is the minimum voluntary donation, and this [i.e. the word "minimum"] indicates an element of compulsion. Indeed, the ordinary man, looking casually at the ticket or at the application form would take the purchase price to be £50 and would not in our opinion get the impression that entrance could be obtained for less. With regret, we must refuse the appeal. If the price on the ticket had been £20, with the footnote indicating a hope that the purchaser would voluntarily donate at least a further £30 for the benefit of the Hospice, we have little doubt that the consideration would have been accepted as being £20, and other forms of wording ... could have achieved the same result.

35.11 No charge and voluntary donation

HMRC Guidance Note Annex iv para 32 states:

> If a charity believes that a particular event or series of events will not fall within the exemptions, it may be possible to organise the event so as to minimise the amount of tax payable.
> For example, the charity might set a basic minimum charge and invite those attending the event to supplement the charge with a voluntary donation. This minimum charge will be standard rated for VAT (unless exempt under another provision) and for direct tax purposes will be taxable trading income.
> The additional contributions won't be taxable income for direct tax purposes and will also be outside the scope of VAT if all the following conditions are met:
> – it's clearly stated on all publicity material, including tickets, that anyone paying only the minimum charge will be admitted without

further payment
- the additional payment does not secure any particular benefit - for example, admission to a better seat in the auditorium. (For direct tax purposes only, the payment may still be treated as non-taxable income if the benefit is within the limits specified in Gift Aid legislation)
- the extent of further contributions is ultimately left to ticket-holders to decide (even if the organiser indicates a desired level of donation) - these further contributions may be made under Gift Aid, subject to them meeting the requirements of the scheme.
- for film or theatre performances, concerts, sporting fixtures and similar events the minimum charge is not less than the usual price for the particular seats at a normal commercial event of the same type
- for dances, dinners and similar functions the total sum of the taxable minimum charge is not less than the total costs incurred in arranging the event.

HMRC Guidance on fundraising events[9] makes a related point (at the last sub-paragraph of para 4.9):

> If the publicity material for a fund-raising event suggests that those paying a recommended extra amount are more likely to be admitted than those paying merely the basic ticket price, then the extra amount becomes part of the consideration for a supply of services, rather than a donation, and as such is subject to VAT at the standard rate.

The HMRC Guidance Note does not altogether approve of the tax planning, and Annex iv para 32 concludes with a threat:

> If trustees are considering making no charge and relying on expected donations to more than cover costs, professional advice is recommended. Donations received in such circumstances may be eligible for Gift Aid. However, any trustees adopting this approach would have to be able to demonstrate that they had made a properly informed and considered decision that a better return on funds laid out could be achieved by not charging for tickets. Failure to do this could result in the costs being treated as non-charitable expenditure and the trustees being personally liable for any loss of funds.

This is true in theory, though in practice we do not think it likely to happen when a charity acts in good faith. The converse is no less true. Trustees who decide to charge full price for tickets (foregoing the Gift Aid

---

9 *https://www.gov.uk/government/publications/charity-fundraising-events-exemptions*

and VAT advantages of donations) should also be able to show that they have made a properly informed and considered decision otherwise they too may incur non-charitable expenditure and be personally liable for any loss. All decisions of charity trustees should be "properly informed and considered".

HMRC accept a basic charge (VATable) and a voluntary donation (free of VAT). Is it possible to go further and provide services for only a nominal charge, or no charge at all, while asking for a voluntary donation? This may be possible but it depends on the circumstances.

The following practice is sometimes adopted:

(1) A charity and the client sign a "client engagement letter" which provides that the charity will provide certain services to the client "free of charge".
(2) At the same time the client enters into a side letter stating "I will … give the charity £[ ]".

This arrangement can prove to be somewhat awkward to operate in practice.

Under this arrangement the charity is certainly making a supply of services to the client. The issue is whether this supply is made "for consideration". It is argued that the payment under the side letter is not consideration for the supply. This is very doubtful.

There is a risk that the court might construe the side letter as currently worded as a binding promise to pay, constituting the consideration (in a contract law sense) in return for which the charity agrees to execute the client engagement letter and provide the services. There is also a risk that a court may regard the arrangement as a "sham" not reflecting the true intention of the parties.

Let us assume, however, that the documentation is to be taken at its face value so that the charity does not have a binding contract with the client and could not sue the client for the sum promised in the side letter if the client chose not to pay. The sum paid is not "consideration" for the supply in the English contract law sense. Nevertheless it is considered that the services are supplied "for consideration" in the VAT sense.

The arrangement set out above falls on the wrong side of the line. It is particularly significant that the charity would decline a potential assignment from a potential client who was not prepared to undertake to make a "donation". Conversely the client would not make the "donation" if the charity refused to supply the services. Further, the charity owes a duty of care to the client, not under a contract but under the tort of negligence. In the circumstances the court is likely to find there is "reciprocal performance". In short, the mere fact that the payment is not paid under an enforceable contract will not stop a payment being "consideration" (for VAT purposes) if all the other usual features of "consideration" (for VAT purposes) are present.

This is particularly the case because, for VAT purposes, economic reality is just as important as (and, in some cases, more important than) the contractual position. As the CJEU notes in *Loyalty Management UK Ltd & Baxi Group Ltd* (Cases C-53/09 & C-55/09):

> It must also be recalled that consideration of economic realities is a fundamental criterion for the application of the common system of VAT...

In *Paul Newey* (Case C-653/11), the CJEU observes (albeit in the context of identifying the recipient of a supply of services):

> ...[43] Given that the contractual position normally reflects the economic and commercial reality of the transactions and in order to satisfy the requirements of legal certainty, the relevant contractual terms constitute a factor to be taken into consideration when the supplier and the recipient in a 'supply of services' transaction within the meaning of Articles 2(1) and 6(1) of the Sixth Directive have to be identified.
> [44] It may, however, become apparent that, sometimes, certain contractual terms do not wholly reflect the economic and commercial reality of the transactions.
> [45] That is the case in particular if it becomes apparent that those contractual terms constitute a purely artificial arrangement which does not correspond with the economic and commercial reality of the transactions...

Or as Lady Justice Gloster puts it in the Court of Appeal judgement in *Airtours Holidays Transport Ltd* [2014] EWCA Civ 1033:

> The terms of any contract between the parties, whilst an important factor to be taken into account in deciding whether a supply of services has been made, are not necessarily determinative of whether as a matter of "economic reality" taxable supplies are being made as between any particular participants in the arrangements. However, the contractual position is generally the most useful starting point for the VAT analysis: see per Lord Reed in WHA (SC) at [27]. That may be particularly so where certain contractual terms do not wholly reflect the economic and commercial reality of the transactions: see per the CJEU in Newey at [43]-[44].

Turning back to the arrangement set out above, the position would be different if the services were of a type that is often given free (eg admission to charity premises).

35.12 Sponsorship

HMRC Notice 701/41 provides:

> **1.2 Definition of sponsorship**
> Sponsorship is a payment to a charity, social project or a business for which the sponsor receives something in return. Payment may be in the form of money, goods and services (commonly referred to as 'barter'), or a combination of money with goods and services.
> Sponsorship is a common feature of artistic, sporting, educational and charitable activities, but it is not restricted to these areas.
> The payments may also be described as something else, for example as a donation. Sponsorship is similar to a donation in that persons sponsoring a charity or social project are usually motivated by a wish to support it. But where the sponsor also receives something in return, this may have VAT implications.
> **2. Supplies**
> **2.1 When you're making taxable supplies if you get sponsorship**
> Where you getsponsorship or some other form of support you will normally be making taxable supplies if, in return, you're obliged to provide the sponsor with a significant benefit. Typically this might include any of the following:
>
> - naming an event after the sponsor (where to do so gives the sponsor a business benefit, such as promoting their brand), this will not generally apply to naming an event after a private individual or entities
> - displaying the sponsor's company logo or trading name- though not where that logo is purely connected with a government agency or charitable foundation, and merely acknowledges generosity
> - participating in the sponsors promotional or advertising activities
> - allowing the sponsor to use your name or logo(see paragraph 2.2 for more information)
> - giving free or reduced price tickets
> - allowing access to special events such as premieres or gala evenings
> - providing entertainment or hospitality facilities
> - giving the sponsor exclusive or priority booking rights (except where HMRC is satisfied that there's no actual benefit in accessing these rights, and that they merely secure the sponsor's income for the charity)

This list is not exhaustive and there are many other situations where your sponsor may be getting tangible benefits. What matters is that the agreement or understanding you have with your sponsor requires you to do something in return.

2.2 Types of support that are not liable to VAT

You may receive financial or other support in the form of donations or gifts. As long as they're freely given and secure nothing in return for the donor they're outside the scope of VAT. A taxable supply is not created where you provide an insignificant benefit such as a minor acknowledgement of the source of the support. Examples of this can include any of the following:

- giving a flag or sticker
- acknowledging the donor in a list of supporters in a programme or on a notice
- naming a building, a wing of a building, an area of a facility, a role or post in the charity (such as first violin of an orchestra), or university chair after the donor
- putting the donor's name on the back of a seat in a theatre or on any part of the fabric for which they have paid or part paid for
- giving a certificate which acknowledges a person's donation
- payments for 'buy-a-brick' campaigns or for buying clothing that supports a campaign, but cannot realistically benefit the donor
- a charity sponsoring another charity in order to merely show shared endeavour or support in a mutually charitable and collaborative area

A donor will be a person who has no, or minimal influence over what's being provided and cannot insist on receiving any acknowledgement.

Where the benefit provided in return for the payment is an exempt supply for VAT purposes, the exemption will apply and the income received will not be taxable, see paragraph 3.2.

2.3 Mixed sponsorship and donation

If a donation is made separately from your sponsorship agreement, or your sponsorship agreement makes clear which part is payment for services and which is a donation, you do not need to account for VAT on any donation or gift (of the kind described in paragraph 2.2). However, it must be clear that any benefits your sponsor receives are not conditional on the making of the donation or gift.

...

2.4 When you make taxable supplies if you sponsor somebody

You may be making taxable supplies if you provide sponsorship in the form of goods or services rather than in money.

If you provide:

- goods or services to somebody who, in return, is making a taxable supply to you (see paragraph 2.1), then you're making a taxable supply of those goods or services

- goods to somebody as a gift or donation (see paragraph 2.2), then you may be liable to account for VAT under the business gift rules - for further information on business gifts see Business promotions (VAT Notice 700/7)
- services to somebody as a gift or donation (see paragraph 2.2), then no VAT is due

3. Accounting for VAT

3.1 Work out the value of the sponsorship you get

If you make taxable supplies in return for sponsorship you must account for VAT on a value that covers everything you get under the sponsorship agreement. If you agree the amount of sponsorship without allowing for VAT you must treat the amount received as VAT inclusive.

You may exclude from the value any additional payment from your sponsor that may be treated as a non-taxable donation (see paragraph 2.3).

You should consider the guidance on valuation in the VAT guide (VAT Notice 700) where you supply goods and/or services in return for non-monetary consideration in the form of the benefits referred to in paragraph 2.1.

3.2 Special rules for charities

If you're a charity making supplies to sponsors as part of a fund raising event your supplies may be exempt. For further information about this see charity fundraising events: exemptions. There's also guidance about donations of goods to charities in How VAT affects charities (VAT Notice 701/1).

3.3 Sponsors that are not in the UK

If you make supplies of advertising services and publicity to overseas sponsors, your services may be outside the scope of UK VAT. You can find more about this in Place of supply of services (VAT Notice 741A).

3.4 Issuing a VAT invoice

You must issue a sponsor with a VAT invoice for your supplies if the sponsor is registered for VAT. A sponsor who provides sponsorship in the form of taxable supplies of goods or services is also required to issue a VAT invoice.

4. Sponsored prizes for competitions

4.1 If you receive prizes to use in competitions

If you receive goods or services to be given away as prizes and:

- are obliged to promote or provide advertising for the donor, then you're making a taxable supply of services to the donor for non-monetary consideration, you'll find guidance on valuing this supply in VAT guide (VAT Notice 700)
- apart from any general understanding that the donor might benefit

from the publicity, you're not obliged actively to promote or advertise the donor, then you're not making a taxable supply

4.2 Providing prizes for a competition

Generally you should follow the guidance in paragraph 2.4 to decide whether you're making taxable supplies. But if you donate a holiday, the special rules of the Tour Operators Margin Scheme may apply. Further guidance on the scheme is in Tour Operators Margin Scheme (VAT Notice 709/5).

If you do not receive a supply in return for the prizes you give, you may be unable to recover tax on the prize if it falls within the business entertainment provisions. You can find further guidance on these provisions in Business entertainment (VAT Notice 700/65).

Specific guidance on the tax value of goods you provide as prizes in return for advertising or promotion services is given in Business promotion (VAT Notice 700/7).

4.3 Claiming input tax on the prizes you receive for competition

If you receive prizes for your competition in the form of goods and services:

- and you're not obliged to provide anything to the donor in return (see paragraph 4.1), there will be no input tax to claim
- in return for supplies of advertising or publicity you're making to the donor (see paragraph 4.1), then generally you can claim input tax on the prizes, subject to the normal rules, however:
- if the prize is a holiday or day trip you will not be able to claim any input tax
- some prizes may be regarded as business entertainment on which you will not be able to claim any input tax (see Business entertainment (VAT Notice 700/65))

5. Crowdfunding

Crowdfunding is the process of raising funds or capital for a specific project through the internet on specifically designed platforms. The VAT treatment of supplies that might potentially be made is no different to similar financing arrangements (for example, sponsorship, donations and investments) made through more traditional routes. Whether a recipient of crowdfunding is liable to charge and pay VAT depends on the facts in each case.

For example:

- where nothing is given in return for the funding, it will be treated as a donation and not liable to VAT - the position is the same where all that the funder receives is a bare acknowledgement, such as a mention in a programme or something similar
- where the funder receives goods or services that have a real value associated with them (for example, clothing, tickets, DVDs, film

viewings), VAT will be due

- where the payment is for a combination of the 2 examples, if it's clear that the donation element is optional then that part of the sponsorship can be treated as a non-taxable donation
- it might be that the funding takes the form of an investment where the funder is entitled to a financial return such as interest, dividends or profit share - in these cases, any payment due to the funder will not be liable to VAT, unless the arrangement is more by way of a royalty based on a supply of intellectual property or some other benefit - in these circumstances the 'profit share' is likely to be consideration for a supply, the reason why most of these arrangements are outside the scope of VAT is that the provision of capital in a business venture is not seen as a supply for VAT purposes

VAT Notice 701/49: finance has more information.

35.13 "Taxable person"

The expression "taxable person" has different definitions in the VAT directive and in UK law (ie, in the VATA).

35.13.1 *"Taxable person" in VAT directive*

Article 9(1) VAT directive provides:

> 'Taxable person' shall mean any person who, independently, carries out in any place any economic activity, whatever the purpose or results of that activity.

35.13.2 *"Taxable person" in UK law*

Section 3(1) VATA provides an artificial definition:

> A person is a taxable person for the purposes of this Act while he is, or is required to be, registered under this Act.

The registration requirements are not discussed here. In short, para 1(1) Sch 1 VATA provides:

> Subject to sub-paragraphs (3) to (7) below, a person who makes taxable supplies but is not registered under this Act becomes liable to be registered under this Schedule—
>
> (a) at the end of any month, if the person is UK-established and the value of his taxable supplies in the period of one year then ending has exceeded £85,000; or
>
> (b) at any time, if the person is UK-established and there are

> reasonable grounds for believing that the value of his taxable supplies in the period of 30 days then beginning will exceed £85,000.

Registration for VAT is distinct from registration with the Charity Commission.

In *Earl Redway t/a Loktonic v HMRC* [2015] UKFTT 418 (TC), the First-tier Tribunal considered the interaction between the two definitions of "taxable person":

> [31] ...the transposition of the EU law's definition of what it means to be a taxable person (Article 9 [VAT directive]) to UK law, with its reliance on registration as the trigger for creating a taxable person, is not straightforward...particularly the way in which the UK law treats a taxable person whose supplies are below the threshold level.
> [32] The question for this Tribunal is whether...the UK's registration thresholds are merely an administrative matter which should have no impact on the nature of the supplies made, or whether registration within the UK VAT code affects the substantive nature of the supplies made.
> [33] It is clear that as far as VAT is concerned EU law is paramount and any conflict between UK law and EU law has to be decided in favour of the EU legislation. The parties agreed that under EU law a taxable transaction was any form of economic activity and was not related to meeting any administrative hurdles...
> [34] ...[Article 286 VAT directive] makes clear that supplies below any applicable threshold are exempt supplies for EU purposes. In the context of Article 286 registration is acting as more than an administrative procedure, it is the trigger which is used to turn exempt into taxable supplies. Article 286 gives the UK the right to determine the nature of supplies depending on whether they are above or below the UK's thresholds.

35.14 Business

35.14.1 *UK law definition*

Section 94(1) VATA provides:

> In this Act "business" includes any trade, profession or vocation.

Everyone agrees that business, in any context, is a word of very wide meaning. No-one would doubt that a trade, profession or vocation constitute a business. So this does not take matters very far.

The word "business" is used quite often in direct tax, and has given rise to a considerable case law. However. business in a VAT context could

have a different meaning from business in direct tax contexts.
The VBNB Manual provides:

> **VBNB11000: VAT Business/Non-Business basics: introduction** [Jan 2021]
> **The purpose of this manual**
> ...Other UK taxes have their own definitions of business including those administered by our direct tax colleagues. However, these do not necessarily correspond with the VAT definition, which must be given a "European" meaning...
> **VBNB15000-VAT Business/Non-Business basics: UK VAT definition of business** [Jan 2021]
> ... The VAT meaning of business has emerged through the judgments of UK courts and the European Court of Justice (CJEU)..
> It is important to note that although the definition is similar to that used for Schedule D Income Tax,[10] the courts have seen that "business" can have a different meaning for VAT purposes. It should not be assumed that direct tax [ie income tax] legal precedent can be directly applied.

Where it is necessary to distinguish, we refer to a business for the purposes of VAT as a **"VAT business"**. But where the context is clear it is sufficient to use the word "business".

35.14.2 *EU-law background*

Although the VAT directive does use the word "businсss", it is used sparingly and the term used for " VAT business" is "economic activity". Article 9(1) provides:

> 'Taxable person' shall mean any person who, independently, carries out in any place any economic activity, whatever the purpose or results of that activity.

The article goes on to explain "economic activity":

> Any activity of producers, traders or persons supplying services, including mining and agricultural activities and activities of the professions, shall be regarded as 'economic activity'.
> The exploitation of tangible or intangible property for the purposes of obtaining income therefrom on a continuing basis shall in particular be regarded as an economic activity.

Institute of Chartered Accountants in England and Wales v C&E

---

10 The reference to schedule D is (very) out of date, but it does not matter.

comments on the relationship between the VATA and the directive:

> There is a difference in the wording between s 4 of the 1994 Act and arts 2 and 4 of the Sixth Directive. Thus the 1994 Act refers to
>
> > 'taxable supply made by a taxable person in the course or furtherance of any *business* carried on by him [emphasis added]'.
>
> The Sixth Directive refers to the supply of services
>
> > 'effected for *consideration* ... by a taxable person acting as such [emphasis added]'
>
> and taxable person means
>
> > a person who independently carries out any *economic activity,* including 'the activities of the professions'.
>
> The 1994 Act must so far as possible be construed so as to give effect to the Sixth Directive...It does not seem to me that there is any difficulty here in doing that and one would expect the same result to follow from the application of either approach.[11]

The VBNB Manual provides:

> **VBNB13000-VAT Business/Non-Business basics: European law** [Jan 2021]
>
> ... These definitions are deliberately designed to be wide and all embracing. They have tended to be interpreted as such by the Courts. Although "business" is, at first sight, different from "economic activity", UK law must be interpreted so it agrees with the Directive. As a result "business" and "economic activity" must be seen to mean the same thing. If an activity falls within the Principal VAT Directive definition of economic activity it must be business in the UK...

That being the case, it would have been easier if the statute had used the terminology of the VAT directive, and not confused matters by bringing in the concept of"business." But the drafting goes back to 1972 when EU legislation was new and not fully understood.

The VBNB Manual provides:

> **VBNB20500 - VAT Business and Non-Business activities: what are business and non-business activities?** [Jan 2021]
>
> Neither UK nor EC law provides an exhaustive definition or test for working out whether an activity is business. As a result the meaning of "business" and "economic activity" has emerged from a body of case law.
>
> If is not one of the deemed businesses under Section 94 of the VAT Act

11 [1999] STC 398 at p.401.

1994 (VBNB24000), you will need to apply the business test to decide if an activity is to be treated as a business. This test comes from decisions of the VAT Tribunals and other courts that have looked at the business question. (VBNB22000).
A number of cases have looked at the meaning of business and given rise to the business test. The two most important UK cases are Morrison's Academy Boarding Houses Association and Lord Fisher. (VBNB72050)
Morrison's Academy is a key case. It marked a shift from defining business purely in terms of profit. It is still frequently quoted. The decision in Morrison's Academy was based on a number of principles which were repeated and added to by Customs' Counsel in the case of Lord Fisher. For this reason the business test that emerged from this case is usually known as the Fisher test.
Another important case is St Paul's Community Project Ltd (VBNB72050). The provision of nursery and crèche facilities by charities, along the same lines as those in St Paul's Community Project Ltd, is not a business activity for VAT purposes
An important case is Vereniging Noordelijke Land-en Tuinbouw Organisatie (VNLTO) (VBNB72050). The European Court of Justice (CJEU) stated that 'business' extends beyond economic activities giving rise to supplies within the scope of VAT. It also includes any activity that forms part of the wider purpose of the taxable person's undertaking or enterprise. This includes even those activities that are not economic activities (such as those outside the scope of VAT), and that are not normally regarded as 'business' for UK VAT purposes.

35.14.3 *Six indicia of a business*

The VBNB Manual provides:

> **VBNB22000-VAT Business and Non-Business activities: the business test** [Jan 2021]
> ... The six questions are:
>
> [1] Is the activity a serious undertaking earnestly pursued?
> [2] Is the activity an occupation or function, which is actively pursued with reasonable or recognisable continuity?
> [3] Does the activity have a certain measure of substance in terms of the quarterly or annual value of taxable supplies made (bearing in mind that exempt supplies can also be business)?
> [4] Is the activity conducted in a regular manner and on sound and recognised business principles?
> [5] Is the activity predominately concerned with the making of taxable supplies for a consideration?

[6] Are the taxable supplies that are being made of a kind which, subject to differences of detail, are commonly made by those who seek to profit from them?

35.14.4 *Indicia 1: Serious undertaking earnestly pursued*

The VBNB Manual provides:

> **VBNB22000-VAT Business and Non-Business activities: the business test** [Jan 2021]
> ... **Is the activity a serious undertaking earnestly pursued?**
> This asks you to think about whether the activity is carried on for business or daily work rather than for pleasure or daily enjoyment.

35.14.5 *Indicia 2: Actively pursued with continuity*

The VBNB Manual provides:

> **VBNB22000-VAT Business and Non-Business activities: the business test** [Jan 2021]
> ... **Is the activity an occupation or function, which is actively pursued with reasonable or recognisable continuity?**
> This question comes from Morrison's Academy (VBNB72050). In that case Lord Cameron said that "the supply must not be merely in sporadic or isolated transactions but continued over an appreciable tract of time and with such frequency as to amount to a recognisable and identifiable activity of the particular person on whom the liability is to fall."
> When thinking about this test you should consider how often the supplies will be made. A supply made only every few years is less likely to be seen as being business than a supply made every day.
> However, with very high value supplies this might be less of a factor, for example where a property developer sells an office block once every 5 years.

35.14.6 *Indicia 3: Supplies of substantial value*

The VBNB Manual provides:

> **VBNB22000-VAT Business and Non-Business activities: the business test** [Jan 2021]
> ... **Does the activity have a certain measure of substance in terms of the quarterly or annual value of taxable supplies made (bearing in mind that exempt supplies can also be business)?**
> Again this is a test from *Morrison's Academy* (VBNB72050).
> You must look at the value of the supplies that are intended to be made. An activity that is intended to bring in £2.50 per week is less likely to be

seen as business than one which brings in over £10,000 a week.

35.14.7 *Indicia 4: Conducted on business principles*

The VBNB Manual provides:

> **VBNB22000-VAT Business and Non-Business activities: the business test** [Jan 2021]
> ... **Is the activity conducted in a regular manner and on sound and recognised business principles?**
> This test again comes from *Morrison's Academy* (VBNB72050). The judge compared the organisation of the charitable boarding house with its more commercial competitors. He said, "It has every mark of a business activity; it is regular, conducted on sound and recognised business principles, with a structure that can be recognised as providing a familiar constitutional mechanism for carrying on a commercial undertaking, and it has as its declared purpose the provision of goods and services which are of a type provided and exchanged in the course of everyday life and commerce"
> Put another way, in providing the accommodation the business may have been motivated by charitable objectives rather than profit. However, they provided a service similar to that provided by a normal business and they were organised in a similar manner.
> Relevant information includes, for example, how orders are processed or how internal decisions are made. Businesses have certain professional and commercial characteristics.
> For example a new, would be jobbing plumber who does not advertise, keep a diary, give estimates or make any attempt to obtain work may find it hard to show that they are in business. Those are not the business principles that plumbers usually operate under.

35.14.8 *Indicia 5: Predominately making supplies for consideration*

An activity is not a business where it does not involve the making of supplies. In *C&E v The Apple and Pear Development Council* [1986] STC 192 Lord Brightman said:

> ... If an activity neither makes nor is intended to make taxable[12] supplies,

---

12 The reference to *taxable* supplies is not altogether apt, since a person making exempt supplies may carry on a business and exempt supplies are not "taxable". While confusing, the term "taxable" has been used in EU jurisprudence to refer to transactions within the scope of VAT (as distinct from transactions outside the scope of VAT, rather than exempt transactions), and that was probably the intended meaning here.

I do not think that the draftsman of the 1972 Act can have contemplated that it was a "business" ...

The VBNB Manual provides:

VBNB22000-VAT Business and Non-Business activities: the business test [Jan 2021]
...**Is the activity predominately concerned with the making of taxable supplies for a consideration?**
This test can highlight problems. Over the years it has become seen as the most important test.
It is clear from the European Court of Justice (CJEU) case of *Apple & Pear Development Council*[13] (VBNB72200) that if an activity involves the making of supplies of services for no consideration that these cannot be seen as taxable supplies. An activity that involves making no taxable supplies cannot be business.
This means that projects entirely funded by outside the scope grants, and where there is no additional consideration (for example a membership fee), will not be business.[14]
The test of predominant concern has in the past often been seen as a test of purpose or motivation. In other words, what motivates the supplies? Such an interpretation does not sit well with Article 9(1) of the Principal VAT Directive. Article 9(1) talks of someone being a taxable person in respect of an activity "whatever the purpose or the result of that activity".
In the High Court appeal of *Institute of Chartered Accountants England and Wales* (VBNB72200) the court found that the test must be read as asking "What is the real nature of the activity". In other words is the real nature of the activity the making of taxable supplies for consideration or is it something else?
Although a business activity must include the making of taxable supplies for consideration, activities carried out in preparation can be seen as business even if, in themselves, they do not involve the making of any supplies.
Provided a business can show it has a clear intention to make taxable supplies it can register for VAT. Further guidance on registration procedures and conditions relating to intending traders is provided in

13 *C&E v The Apple and Pear Development Council* [1988] STC 221.
14 The reference to taxable supplies is not altogether apt, since a person making only exempt supplies may carry on a business and exempt supplies are not "taxable". While confusing, the term "taxable" has been used in EU jurisprudence to refer to transactions within the scope of VAT (as distinct from transactions outside the scope of VAT), and that is how "taxable supplies" should be construed here.

VATREG01000.

35.14.9 *Indicia 6: Common type of trade*

The VBNB Manual provides:

> **VBNB22000-VAT Business and Non-Business activities: the business test** [Jan 2021]
> **... Are the taxable supplies that are being made of a kind which, subject to differences of detail, are commonly made by those who seek to profit from them?**
> Someone who claims to be part of a known trade or occupation is likely to be in business. Someone who claims to be in business doing something completely improbable and unique is less likely to be in business.
> Although not making a profit, or to having the aim of making one, is not in itself a conclusive test the courts have tended to see it as a good sign. Someone who carries out an activity with the aim of making a profit and to earn a living is most likely in business.

The extent to which the business test summarised above is still relevant was considered by the Court of Appeal in *Longridge on the Thames v HMRC* [2016] EWCA Civ 930. The charity in that case provided water-based and other outdoor activities (for both recreational and educational purposes). It made a charge but the charge was sometimes adjusted to meet the ability of the end-user to pay (depending on the level of donations to the charity and receipts from other activities). The question was whether the activities carried on by the charity amounted - as HMRC contended - to business activities for VAT purposes. Both the FtT and the Upper Tribunal ruled against HMRC, with both following:

> [5] …domestic authorities where the courts have looked at the wider context in order to determine whether the provision of services for a money payment constituted an economic activity for VAT purposes.
> [6] The nub of HMRC's case [on the appeal to the Court of Appeal] is that this approach is not consistent with EU law. HMRC contend that the Court of Justice of the European Union ("the CJEU", in which expression I also include its predecessor the European Court of Justice) has recently clarified the test for determining whether there is an economic activity and that this now focuses on whether there is a direct link between the service which the recipient receives and the payment which he makes, not on the wider context in which the payment was made. If the direct link is not present, there is no economic activity.

> [7] To answer this question, this Court needs to examine many authorities. At the end of the day, and for the detailed reasons given below, I consider that HMRC are correct. The correct test is one of direct link...

The key EU case relied on by HMRC was *Commission v Finland* (Case C-246/08). The case concerns the provision by the Member State of free or subsidised legal aid in return for a sum calculated not as a proportion of the true cost but by reference to the aid recipient's means. Overall individual contributions amounted to about 8% of the Member State's total cost of providing the legal aid in question. The CJEU held that the provision of legal aid in such circumstances did not constitute an economic activity.

Before arriving at this conclusion, the CJEU revisited the law on the meaning of "economic activities":

> 'Economic activities' are defined in Article 4(2) of the Sixth Directive as including all activities of producers, traders and persons supplying services, inter alia the exploitation of tangible or intangible property for the purpose of obtaining income therefrom on a continuing basis...
>
> An analysis of those definitions shows that the scope of the term economic activities is very wide and that the term is objective in character, in the sense that the activity is considered per se and without regard to its purpose or results...An activity is thus, as a general rule, categorised as economic where it is permanent and is carried out in return for remuneration which is received by the person carrying out the activity (*Commission v Netherlands*, paragraphs 9 and 15...).
>
> However, it follows from the case-law that the receipt of a payment does not, per se, mean that a given activity is economic in nature...

It then applied the case law to the facts of the *Finland* case:

> ...it is therefore appropriate to consider, in the first place, whether the legal aid services provided by the public offices in legal proceedings in return for a part payment constitute economic activities...
>
> It must first of all be stated that, in view of the objective character of the term 'economic activities', the fact that the activity of the public offices consists in the performance of duties which are conferred and regulated by law, in the public interest and without any business or commercial objective, is in that regard irrelevant...
>
> Moreover, it is established that the public offices provide the legal aid services in question on a permanent basis.?In those circumstances, it is appropriate to ascertain whether those services can be regarded as

> provided by the public offices in return for remuneration.
> In that connection, it is clear from the case-law of the Court that, within the framework of the VAT system, taxable transactions presuppose the existence of a transaction between the parties in which a price or consideration is stipulated…
> ...according to the Court's case-law...a supply of services is effected 'for consideration' within the meaning of Article 2(1) of the Sixth Directive only if there is a legal relationship between the provider of the service and the recipient pursuant to which there is reciprocal performance, the remuneration received by the provider of the service constituting the value actually given in return for the service supplied to the recipient (see, inter alia, Tolsma, paragraph 14…).
> Consequently, according to the case-law of the Court, a supply of services for consideration within the meaning of Article 2(1) of the Sixth Directive presupposes a direct link between the service provided and the consideration received (see, inter alia, Case 102/86 *Apple and Pear Development Council* [1988] ECR 1443, paragraphs 11 and 12…).
> In this instance, the legal aid services with which the present action is concerned are not provided by the public offices free of charge and thus without any consideration, since the recipients of those services are required to make a payment to the public offices.

The question, therefore, was whether there was any link between the legal aid services and the payment and, if so, whether it was sufficient to constitute a supply of services for consideration - and in turn an economic activity - for VAT purposes. The CJEU ruled that:

> …it is established that the payment concerned is only a part payment since it does not cover the whole amount of the fees set by the national legislation...Indeed…the payment consisting in the basic contribution is a percentage, ranging from 20% to 75%, of that amount.
> Although this part payment represents a portion of the fees, its amount is not calculated solely on the basis of those fees, but also depends upon the recipient's income and assets. Thus, it is the level of the latter - and not, for example, the number of hours worked by the public offices or the complexity of the case concerned - which determines the portion of the fees for which the recipient remains responsible.
> It follows that the part payment made to the public offices by recipients of legal aid services depends only in part on the actual value of the services provided - the more modest the recipient's income and assets, the less strong the link with that value will be.
> …the part payments made in 2007 by recipients of legal aid services provided by the public offices...amounted to EUR 1.9 million, whilst the

> gross operating costs of those offices were EUR 24.5 million…such a difference suggests that the part payment borne by recipients must be regarded more as a fee, receipt of which does not, per se, mean that a given activity is economic in nature, than as consideration in the strict sense.
> Therefore, in light of the foregoing, it does not appear that the link between the legal aid services provided by public offices and the payment to be made by the recipients is sufficiently direct for that payment to be regarded as consideration for those services and, accordingly, for those services to be regarded as economic activities for the purposes of Article 2(1) and Article 4(1) and (2) of the Sixth Directive.

The direct link test is clearly different from the business (Fisher) test. As the Court of Appeal notes in *Longridge*:

> [85] …the domestic authorities have developed in a way which means that they now diverge in some respects from the test to be applied in determining whether an activity of providing services to a recipient who makes a payment constitutes an economic activity resulting in a liability to VAT. In *Finland*, for instance, the focus was on whether there was a sufficiently direct link between the payment and the service. The *Fisher* criteria…by contrast omit reference to the connection or proportionality of the payment to the service.
> [86] The *Fisher* criteria direct attention to (a) seriousness of the enterprise (b) the regularity of the activity (c) the substantiality of the activity (d) the organisational features or the enterprise (e) the predominant concern of the activity and (f) a comparison with commercial providers of the same service. These factors may have a role to play but they cannot displace the approach required by CJEU jurisprudence.
> …
> [88] It is clear that even under the direct link test there will be cases where the activities of an organisation, such as a charity, providing services at a concessionary rate, do not amount to economic activity. It was certainly the case in Finland that the activities at a concessionary rate did not constitute economic activity for VAT purposes…
> [89] The differences between the test of direct link and the *Fisher* criteria are material...
> [90] I now turn to consider how the differences in approach in CJEU jurisprudence to that to be found in the domestic authorities impacts on this case.

> *Application of the CJEU case law to this case*
> [91] The starting point has to be the General Rule [ie the rule that an activity will be an economic activity where it is "permanent and is carried out in return for remuneration which is received by the person carrying out the activity"]...The General Rule can be displaced by evidence that there was no direct link between the service and the payment or by other evidence which shows that there was no economic activity. I agree...that evidence can be of varying kinds and involves the FTT when making its factual findings looking widely at the circumstances of the case.
> [92] As to direct link, the FTT made clear findings of fact about the charges which neither party challenges...the amount of the charge was more than nominal in amount and was directly related to the cost of the activity being provided. In those circumstances, in my judgment, the charges did not prevent the application of the direct link test leading to the result that there was an economic activity in this case.
> [93] As to other evidence...the FTT referred to a number of factors. It referred to the internal systems of Longridge: it described Longridge as conducting and seriously pursuing its activities on a regular basis and having prudent financial management. It also referred to the scale of its activities, which was substantial, and the fact that it operated in a market where similar services were supplied on a commercial basis. I accept...that none of these matters can rebut the General Rule. On the contrary they support the impression of economic activity. The concessionary charges were also not an indicator against the existence of an economic activity...
> [94] That leaves the FTT's final point...that Longridge's predominant concern was to further its charitable objectives. That was demonstrated by its considerable use of volunteers...But economic activity is assessed objectively and so the concern of Longridge, which is its reason for providing the services which it does provide, is not enough to convert what would otherwise be economic activity into an activity of a different kind for VAT purposes. The reduction in costs due to the work of unpaid volunteers would also not lead to that conclusion.
>
> ...
>
> [96] Accordingly in my judgment, Longridge conducted an economic activity for VAT purposes...

The conclusion in the *Finland* case was that the link (if any) between the services in that case and the payment in that case was not sufficiently direct for the payment to be regarded as consideration for a supply of services. On that basis, the CJEU held that the services were not economic activities.

In *Longridge*, the Court of Appeal considered that the link between the services in that case and the payment in that case was sufficiently direct for the payment to be regarded as consideration for a supply of services and proceeded on that basis to hold that the services were economic activities.

Although, on its face, the judgment in *Longridge* may be read to suggest that a finding of a supply of services would inevitably lead to a finding of an economic activity, that is not the case under EU law.

In *Gemeente Borsele* (Case C-520/14), a case concerning the provision of school bus services by a local authority (toward which the parents of some schoolchildren were required to contribute, but not others), the CJEU held (after *Longridge* was heard in the Court of Appeal but before the Court of Appeal handed down its judgment) that:

> …it should be noted that the existence of a supply of services for consideration…is not sufficient to establish the existence of an economic activity within the meaning of Article 9(1) of the VAT Directive.
> In that regard, according to the Court's case-law, in order to determine whether a service is supplied 'in return for remuneration', so that the activity in question is to be classified as an economic activity (see, to that effect, the judgment of 26 March 1987 in Commission v Netherlands, 235/85…paragraph 15), all the circumstances in which it is supplied have to be examined (see, to that effect, judgment of 26 September 1996 in *Enkler*, C-230/94…paragraph 27).
> Comparing the circumstances in which the person concerned supplies the services in question with the circumstances in which that type of service is usually provided may therefore be one way of ascertaining whether the activity concerned is an economic activity (see, by analogy, judgment of 26 September 1996 in *Enkler*, C-230/94…paragraph 28).
> Other factors, such as, inter alia, the number of customers and the amount of earnings, may be taken into account along with others when that question is under consideration (see, by analogy, judgment of 26 September 1996 in *Enkler*, C-230/94… paragraph 29).

This echoes to some extent the dicta of Patten J (as he then was) in *C&E v Yarburgh Children's Trust* [2002] STC 207:

> [23] …in my judgment…the tribunal [is not allowed] to disregard the observable terms and features of the transaction in question and the wider context in which it came to be carried out. This is because the transaction if looked at in isolation will not usually enable the court to decide whether it was carried out in the course or furtherance of a business which is the test under s 4(1) of the 1994 Act or to use the

> language of the Sixth Directive whether it was a supply of services effected for consideration by a taxable person acting as such, ie by a person who is carrying out some form of economic activity (see arts 2 and 4(1)). This test necessitates an inquiry by the tribunal into the wider picture. It will need to ascertain the nature of the activities carried on by the person alleged to be in business, the terms upon which and manner in which these activities (including the transaction in question) were carried out and the nature of the relationship between the parties to the transaction. This is not intended to be an exhaustive or particularised list. But it is clear that the questions posed by Gibson J in Lord Fisher's case or by the Court of Session in *Customs and Excise Comrs v Morrison's Academy Boarding House Association* [1978] STC 1, 1977 SC 279 simply could not be answered by reference only to the fact that a service was provided at a price. That is the beginning not the end of the inquiry.

Yarburgh, like *Morrison's Academy* and *Lord Fisher*, is, of course, one of the UK cases associated with the business (Fisher) test, which the Court of Appeal discounted in *Longridge* in favour of the direct link test derived from EU case law.

The impact of the *Borsele* judgement was considered by a differently-constituted Court of Appeal in *Wakefield College* [2018] EWCA Civ 952. In order for a supply to be in scope for VAT, it must be made "for consideration" (Articles 2(1)(a) and (c) of the VAT directive). To be an economic activity, the activity must be carried out "for remuneration". There has been much debate regarding whether the two are the same. In *Wakefield*, the Court of Appeal held that:

> 15. … "consideration" in article 2 means only some value given to the supplier in return for the goods or services by the person to whom they are supplied. It is this amount on which VAT is payable. It need not be full value or indeed bear any particular relation to the value of the goods or services supplied. By contrast, "remuneration" has a broader meaning, and may be said to encapsulate the concept of carrying on an economic activity "for the purposes of obtaining income therefrom on a continuing basis". Those words appear in article 9(1) as qualifying only the exploitation of tangible or intangible property, but it is established that they apply generally to "economic activity": *Landesantalt für Landwirtschaft v Götz* (Case C-408/06) [2007] ECR I-11295 at [18], *Finland* at [37]. It can readily be appreciated that goods or services may be supplied for "consideration" without the supplier doing so as an economic activity or for "remuneration". In that event, the supplier will not be supplying the goods or services as a "taxable person", so that VAT will not be payable on the consideration.

The Court of Appeal considered the Advocate General's opinion from Borsele, noting how she considered:

> 27. ... "a specific, implicit condition that must be satisfied in order for an activity to be carried out for the purpose of obtaining income within the meaning of [art 9]: market participation". Although not explicit in *Finland*, she said that it ultimately informed the court's decision in that case. She concluded that the municipality was not a market participant in *Borsele*. It did not offer any services on the general market in transport services. In fact, it had "the appearance of itself being the final consumer of the services provided by the transport undertakings, whose transport services it makes available to the parents exclusively in the public interest, even though it sometimes levies a financial contribution for so doing." This was borne out by the recovery of only a small percentage of the costs of the service, which "was not the typical conduct of a market participant". There is "a certain link between the level of remuneration and the existence of an economic activity" (original emphasis), a link confirmed in *Finland*.

The CJEU, as the Court of Appeal noted, echoed this in their judgement:

> 35. It should be noted...that the conditions under which the services at issue in the main proceedings are supplied are different from those under which passenger transport services are usually provided, since the municipality of Borsele, as the Advocate General observed in point 64 of her Opinion, does not offer services on the general passenger transport market, but rather appears to be a beneficiary and final consumer of transport services which it acquires from transport undertakings with which it deals and which it makes available to parents of pupils as part of its public service activities.

The Court of Appeal then turned to the CJEU judgement in Finland, in particular the conclusion "at [51]":

> Therefore, in light of the foregoing, it does not appear that the link between the legal aid services provided by public offices and the payment to be made by the recipients is sufficiently direct for the payment to be regarded as consideration [*French version: une rémunération*] for those services and, accordingly, for those services to be regarded as economic activities for the purposes of Article 2(1) and Article 4(1) and (2) of the Sixth Directive.

The Court of Appeal observed:

> 38. The English version of [51], if read alone, is capable of causing some confusion but, with the clarification supplied by the court in *Borsele* and

> reference to the French version, it can be seen that the court was directing itself to the question of economic activity under article 4 and not to the question of the supply of services for consideration under article 2. Reference is made to article 2, as well as to article 4, because the words "by a taxable person acting as such" in article 2 brings in the definition of "taxable person" contained in article 4 which is, of course, dependent on a finding of "economic activity".
> 39. The court's conclusion in *Finland* was therefore that, while there was a supply of legal aid services for consideration to those recipients who made payments for them for the purposes of article 2, the supply did not constitute economic activity for the purposes of article 4 of the Sixth Directive.

It then turned to its own judgement in Longridge:

> 41. ...The Advocate General had given her Opinion in *Borsele* some four months before the hearing of the appeal in *Longridge*, while the CJEU's judgment in *Borsele* was given only three weeks after the hearing and some time before judgment was given. It is unfortunate that the court was not provided with the Advocate General's Opinion or the CJEU's judgment, all the more so as the United Kingdom had submitted observations to the CJEU in *Borsele*.
>
> ...
>
> 44. Arden LJ records HMRC as submitting that any analysis of prices charged by *Longridge*, their method of calculation and their relationship to costs was impermissible because it offended against the principle that activities can be economic even if they are not pursued for profit. HMRC further submitted that "where consideration was paid for services then there was a presumption that there was an economic activity unless there was some unusual feature to rebut the presumption". The key point in HMRC's case was that *Finland* demonstrated that "there will be economic activity unless there is no direct link between the service and the payment that the recipient of the service makes". HMRC further submitted that "remuneration" meant "consideration which is given for the goods and services", reference being made to *Apple and Pear Development Council v Customs and Excise Coms*. Arden LJ's summary of the submissions of HMRC is set out in 15 paragraphs starting at [29]. It is, I think, fair to say that no clear distinction is drawn in HMRC's submissions between "consideration" within the meaning of article 2 and "remuneration" for the purposes of article 9. The two terms are largely used as interchangeable.

The Court of Appeal then addressed what it considered to be the current state of the law:

51. ...What follows is my analysis of the current legal position...
52. Whether there is a supply of goods or services for consideration for the purposes of article 2 and whether that supply constitutes economic activity within article 9 are separate questions. A supply for consideration is a necessary but not sufficient condition for an economic activity. It is therefore logically the first question to address. It requires a legal relationship between the supplier and the recipient, pursuant to which there is reciprocal performance whereby the goods or services are supplied in return for the consideration provided by the recipient: see, for example, the judgment in *Borsele* at [24]. That is what is meant by "a direct link" between the supply of the goods or services and the consideration provided by the recipient: see Borsele at [26] and contrast *Apple and Pear Development Council v Customs and Excise Comrs*. There is no need for the consideration to be equal in value to the goods or services. It is simply the price at which the goods or services are supplied. This requirement was satisfied in both *Finland* and *Borsele*.
53. Satisfaction of the test for a supply for consideration under article 2 does not give rise to a presumption or general rule that the supply constitutes an economic activity. However, as Mr Puzey for HMRC pointed out, the Advocate General remarked in her Opinion in Borsele at [49], "the same outcomes may often be expected".
54. Having concluded that the supply is made for consideration within the meaning of article 2, the court must address whether the supply constitutes an economic activity for the purposes of the definition of "taxable person" in article 9. The issue is whether the supply is made for the purposes of obtaining income therefrom on a continuing basis. For convenience, the CJEU has used the shorthand of asking whether the supply is made "for remuneration". The important point is that "remuneration" here is not the same as "consideration" in the article 2 sense, and in my view it is helpful to keep the two terms separate, using "consideration" in the context of article 2 and "remuneration" in the context of article 9.
55. Whether article 9 is satisfied requires a wide-ranging, not a narrow, enquiry. All the objective circumstances in which the goods or services are supplied must be examined: see the judgment in *Borsele* at [29]. Nonetheless, it is clear from the CJEU authorities that this does not include subjective factors such as whether the supplier is aiming to make a profit. Although a supply "for the purpose of obtaining income" might in other contexts, by the use of the word "purpose", suggest a subjective test, that is clearly not the case in the context of article 9. It is an entirely objective enquiry.
56. In describing the relationship between the supply and the charges made to the recipients in the context of article 9, the CJEU has used the

> word "link". In *Finland* at [51], the court concluded that "it does not appear that the link between the legal aid services provided by public offices and the payment to be made by the recipients is sufficiently direct...for those services to be regarded as economic activities". Likewise, in *Borsele* at [34], the court adopted precisely those words in concluding that the provision of the school transport was not an economic activity.
>
> ...
>
> 58. I regard this as a largely semantic point. The word "link", whether "sufficient" or "direct", is used as no more than shorthand to encompass the broad enquiry as to whether the supply is made for the purpose of obtaining income. It is not a separate test, or one of the factors to be considered when addressing the central question. For my part, I think it is apt to cause some confusion to use the same word for both article 2 and article 9 and I have not myself found it particularly helpful or illuminating in considering whether there exists an economic activity.
>
> 59. Each case requires a fact-sensitive enquiry. While cases concerning the supply of legal aid services or school transport will provide helpful pointers to at least some of the factors relevant to the supply of subsidised educational courses, there is not a checklist of factors to work through. Even where the same factors are present, they may assume different relative importance in different cases. The CJEU made clear in *Borsele* at [32] that it was for the national court to assess all the facts of a case.

The emphasis in *Wakefield College* on a wide-ranging or broad enquiry recalls the *Yarburgh* test which "necessitates an inquiry by the tribunal into the wider picture", a test that was thought by many to be no longer applicable following the Court of Appeal judgement in *Longridge*.

HMRC has not (yet) revised the VBNB Manual to reflect the Court of Appeal judgments in *Longridge* and *Wakefield College*. Although, following these two cases, it is clear that the business (Fisher) test is no longer the right test, it is still set out (and in some detail) in the VBNB Manual. Indeed, in the case of *Greenisland Football Club* (heard on 14 November 2018, with judgement handed down on 18 December 2018), the business (Fisher) test still sat at the heart of the discussion on what constitutes a "business" (with no reference to *Finland*, *Longridge*, *Borsele* or *Wakefield College*).

This may be because the business (Fisher) test has been a fixture in this area for so long. Whatever the reason, there is likely to be some confusion and uncertainty in the medium term, particularly as (as noted by Lord Justice David Richards in *Wakefield College*):

> 8. We were told that [as at early 2018] HMRC know of about 50 cases, involving approximately £120 million of VAT, that will be affected by the result in this case

35.15 Investment activity

In *Wellcome Trust v C&E* [1996] STC 945 the trust sold shares for £2bn. This formed part of the normal management of trust investments. The trust was not a dealer in shares. It was in the same position as a private investor who confined his activities to managing an investment portfolio. This did not constitute a business (on the basis that the "mere exercise of the right of ownership by its holder cannot, in itself, be regarded as constituting an economic activity").

The position is different for dealers in shares but charities will rarely if ever be share dealers.

The VBNB Manual provides:

> **VBNB29000-VAT Business and Non-Business activities: purchase or sale of shares or securities for investment purposes** [Jan 2021]
> In the case of *Wellcome Trust Ltd* (VBNB72900) the European Court of Justice considered the purchase and sale of shares, and other securities, by a trustee that was managing the assets of a charitable trust.
> The Court found that this was not an economic activity within the meaning of Article 4(2) of the Sixth Directive. As a result tax paid on the cost of such disposals could not be claimed as input tax.
> This ruling potentially has widespread application. It could be seen to apply to all businesses, pension funds and other organisations that carry on such activities wholly for investment purposes.
> However HMRC does not wish to draw such a wide interpretation. Instead we only apply the ruling when a business:
> - disposes of its own shares; and
> - uses the income gained for non-business purposes.

35.16 State functions

Article 13 VAT directive provides:

> 1. States, regional and local government authorities and other bodies governed by public law[15] shall not be regarded as taxable persons in respect of the activities or transactions in which they engage as public authorities, even where they collect dues, fees, contributions or payments in connection with those activities or transactions.

---

15 See 37.3 ("Body governed by public law").

> However, when they engage in such activities or transactions, they shall be regarded as taxable persons in respect of those activities or transactions where their treatment as non-taxable persons would lead to significant distortions of competition.
> In any event, bodies governed by public law shall be regarded as taxable persons in respect of the activities listed in Annex I, provided that those activities are not carried out on such a small scale as to be negligible.[16]
> 2. Member States may regard activities, exempt under Articles 132, 135, 136 and 371, Articles 374 to 377, Article 378(2), Article 379(2), or Articles 380 to 390, engaged in by bodies governed by public law as activities in which those bodies engage as public authorities.

In *Institute of Chartered Accountants in England and Wales v C&E* the ICAEW issued licences under statutory authority which permitted the licence holders to conduct investment, audit and insolvency work. It charged fees of an amount set to cover its costs. This was not a business.

The House of Lords decision was premised on what would now be regarded as the business (Fisher) test, and as Lord Slynn noted at the end of his judgment, because the answer to the business question was clear, there was no need to deal with any argument based on what is now article 13 of the VAT directive.[17]

The same approach was adopted by the tribunal in:

(1) *Quarriers* EDN/07/120 (2008), where a charity running a hospital, mostly financed by Scottish health boards, was held not to be carrying on a business.
(2) *Donaldson's College* EDN/05/12 (2005) where a charity running a school for the deaf was held not to be carrying on a business.

What is now article 13 of the VAT directive was also not discussed in these cases. The three cases cited above allpredate *Longridge* and *Wakefield College*, and the business question may well be decided differently now.

Article 13 VAT directive was recently considered in three FtT cases arising from a dispute between local council authorities across the UK and HMRC concerning the VAT liability of charges paid by members of the public for access to sports and leisure facilities provided by those authorities. HMRC's contention was that the charges should bear VAT at the standard rate; the local authorities disagreed. All three cases were

16 This list of 13 activities is not likely to concern charities.
17 [1999] STC 398 at p.404.

heard by the same three judges, and the judgments of which were all delivered on the same day (with substantively identical reasoning). The three cases were Chelmsford City Council [2020] UKFTT 432, Midlothian Council [2020] UKFTT 433 and Mid Ulster District Council [2020] UKFTT 434.

In its judgment in Mid Ulster District Council, having concluded that the provision of the leisure and recreational services in question amounted to a supply of services for remuneration, and thus that supply constituted an economic activity within Article 9 VAT directive, the FtT went on to say:

> [79] The Council submits that its supply of leisure and recreational services constitutes activities in which the Council engages as a public authority [and so it should not be treated as a taxable person carrying out an economic activity]. Further, that its consequent treatment as a non-taxable person would not lead to significant distortions of competition in respect of those activities…
>
> …
>
> [83] In Saudacor the CJEU stated:
>
> > "69. ... only activities carried out by a body governed by public law acting as a public authority are to be exempted from VAT.
> >
> > 70. The court has consistently held that such activities are activities carried out by those bodies under the special legal regime applicable to them and do not include activities pursued by them under the same legal conditions as those that apply to private economic operators. The court has also made it clear that the subject matter or purpose of the activity is in that regard irrelevant and that the fact that the pursuit of the activity at issue in the main proceedings involves the use of powers conferred by public law shows that that activity is subject to a public law regime (see to that effect, inter alia, judgment in Fazenda Publica v Camara Municipal do Porto (Case C-446/98) [2001] STC 560, [2000] ECR I-11435, paras 17, 19 and 22).
> >
> > 71. In that context, the court has stated that the exemption provided for in the first subparagraph of art 13(1) of Directive 2006/112 covers principally activities engaged in by bodies governed by public law acting as public authorities, which, while fully economic in nature, are closely linked to the exercise of powers conferred by public law (judgment in Revenue and Customs Comrs v Isle of Wight Council (Case C-288/07) [2008] STC 2964, [2008] ECR I-7203, para 31)."…
>
> [84] It is clear from those cases, and the other authorities cited to us, that the decision whether art 13 applies in particular circumstances is highly fact-specific…

[89] Turning to the current appeal, the approach we adopt is that stated by the CJEU in Fazenda Publica (summarising the Court's own caselaw):

> "16. ... it is the way in which the activities are carried out that determines the scope of the treatment of public bodies as non-taxable persons (see Ufficio Distrettuale delle Imposte Dirette di Fiorenzuola d'Arda v Comune di Carpaneto Piacentino (Joined cases 231/87 and 129/88) [1991] STC 205 at 235, [1989] ECR 3233 at 3275, para 15, and Comune di Carpaneto Piacentino v Ufficio Provinciale Imposta sul Valore Aggiunto di Piacenza (Case C-4/89) [1990] ECR I-1869 at 1886, para 10).
>
> 17. It is thus clear from the settled case law of the court that activities pursued as public authorities within the meaning of [art 13] are those engaged in by bodies governed by public law under the special legal regime applicable to them and do not include activities pursued by them under the same legal conditions as those that apply to private economic operators (see in particular EC Commission v France (Case C-276/97) (2000) Transcript (Judgment) (Eng), 12 September, para 40, EC Commission v Ireland (Case C-358/97) (2000) Transcript (Judgment) (Eng), 12 September, para 38, EC Commission v United Kingdom (Case C-359/97) [2000] STC 777 at 787-788, para 50, EC Commission v Netherlands (Case C-408/97) (2000) Transcript (Judgment) (Eng), 12 September, para 35, and EC Commission v Greece (Case C-260/98) (2000) Transcript (Judgment) (Eng), 12 September).
>
> ...
>
> 19. In determining whether such an activity is engaged in by [the taxpayer] as a public authority, it must be noted, first, that this cannot depend on the subject matter or purpose of the activity (see Ufficio Distrettuale delle Imposte Dirette di Fiorenzuola d'Arda v Comune di Carpaneto Piacentino [1991] STC 205 at 235, [1989] ECR 3233 at 3275, para 13).
>
> ...
>
> 21. The national court must, in accordance with the case law referred to in paras 16 and 17 above, analyse all the conditions laid down by national law for the pursuit of the activity at issue in the main proceedings, to determine whether that activity is being engaged in under a special legal regime applicable to bodies governed by public law or under the same legal conditions as those that apply to private economic operators."
>
> ...

[90] In determining whether an activity is being engaged in under a special legal regime, the following factors are irrelevant:

(1) the subject matter of the activity (Fazenda Publica at [19]);

(2) the purpose of the activity (ibid); and
(3) the fact that private providers carry out similar activities (Isle of Wight at [33]).
[91] The first step is to identify the applicable legal regime under which the Council engages in the activities...
[92] In the current appeal, the Council maintains that it provides the leisure and recreational services pursuant to Article 10…
…
[94] We reach [the] conclusion…The Council's provision of the facilities is not done because it is "going into business as a matter of choice". On the contrary, given the statutory equality duties…and the onerous consequences for provision of facilities…it is clear to us that the facilities would not be provided absent the power/duty in Article 10. Thus, the applicable legal regime under which the Council engages in the activities is Article 10.
[95] The second step is to determine whether Article 10 constitutes a special legal regime…
[96] We reach [the] conclusion…The Article 10 regime is hedged around by a number of constraints: the statutory equality duties…and the onerous consequences for provision of facilities, including the need for cohesion of diverse communities; the need to set charges by reference to affordability and accessibility, and the consequent deficit against costs of provision; and the inability (prior to April 2015) for the Council to conduct activities by way of a trade. Any private sector business providing leisure and recreational services in the Council's area - even ones indistinguishable to the consumer from the Council's facilities - would be doing so not under the Article 10 regime but instead under the general legal regime applicable to all facilities operators. Accordingly, the legal conditions under which the Council is providing services are different, because of its function as a public authority, from the legal conditions under which its private sector counterparts are providing perhaps indistinguishable services. Thus the Council's provision of the facilities is being engaged in under a special legal regime applicable to a body governed by public law.
…
[98] For those reasons we determine that the first paragraph of art 13 is satisfied in relation to the Council's provision of the leisure and recreational services.
Significant distortions of competition
[99] Moving to the second paragraph of art 13…
…
[101] The CJEU summarised its own caselaw on this provision in NRA:
"…38 Under the second subparagraph of Article 13(1) of the VAT

Directive, those bodies are to be regarded as taxable persons in respect of the activities or operations in which they engage as public authorities, where their treatment as non-taxable persons would lead to significant distortions of competition.

39 According to the Court's case-law on that provision, first, what is envisaged here is the situation in which bodies governed by public law engage in activities which may also be engaged in, in competition with them, by private economic operators. The aim is to ensure that those private operators are not placed at a disadvantage because they are taxed while those bodies are not (see, to that effect, judgment of 25 March 2010, Commission v Netherlands, C-79/09, not published, EU:C:2010:171, paragraph 90 and the case-law cited).

40 Secondly, that limitation of the rule that bodies governed by public law acting as public authorities are treated as non-taxable persons for VAT purposes is only a conditional limitation. Its application involves an assessment of economic circumstances (see, to that effect, judgment of 17 October 1989, Comune di Carpaneto Piacentino and Others, 231/87 and 129/88, EU:C:1989:381, paragraph 32).

41 Thirdly, the significant distortions of competition which treatment as non-taxable persons of bodies governed by public law acting as public authorities would lead to must be evaluated by reference to the activity in question, as such, without that evaluation relating to any particular market, and by reference not only to actual competition, but also to potential competition, provided that the possibility of a private operator entering the relevant market is real and not purely hypothetical (judgments of 25 March 2010, Commission v Netherlands, C-79/09, not published, EU:C:2010:171, paragraph 91 and the case-law cited, and of 29 October 2015, Saudacor, C-174/14, EU:C:2015:733, paragraph 74).

42 The purely theoretical possibility of a private operator entering the relevant market, which is not borne out by any matter of fact, any objective evidence or any analysis of the market, cannot be assimilated to the existence of potential competition (judgment of 16 September 2008, Isle of Wight Council and Others, C-288/07, EU:C:2008:505, paragraph 64).

43 As follows from the wording of the second subparagraph of Article 13(1) of the VAT Directive and from the case-law on that provision, its application presupposes, first, that the activity in question is carried on in competition, actual or potential, with that carried on by private operators and, secondly, that the different treatment of those activities for VAT purposes leads to significant distortions of competition, which must be assessed having regard to

> economic circumstances.
> 44 It follows that the mere presence of private operators on a market, without account being taken of matters of fact, objective evidence or an analysis of the market, cannot demonstrate the existence either of actual or potential competition or of a significant distortion of competition."
>
> ...
>
> [107] Here the activities in question are the facilities provided by the Council within the constraints which hedge around…its obligations under Article 10…We must evaluate whether the treatment of the Council as a non-taxable person when providing the activities in question would lead to more than negligible actual or potential distortion of competition in the market for such activities in Northern Ireland. We conclude from the evidence before us that there is no non-negligible alternative provision of the activities in question; only local authorities are in a position to provide facilities that meet the demanding requirements for community equality…
>
> [108] For those reasons we conclude that the treatment of the Council as a non-taxable person by virtue of art 13 would not lead to significant distortions of competition, within the meaning of art 13…

35.17 Is education a business

VAT Notice 701/30: Education and vocational training (7 August 2019) provides:

> **2.4 When education is a business activity**
> There are 2 normal sources of funding for education. These are:
> – non-business, government grants (usually from a funding agency)
> – business, when a charge is being made for the education provided.
>
> **2.5 VAT treatment of charges for education**
> The VAT treatment is unaffected by who pays the charge whether the student, employer of a LA.
>
> Education is still a business activity even if the charge is not enough to meet the full cost of providing it and it's subsidised from some other source, such as a grant from central government or a bursary or scholarship.
>
> Where education is wholly funded by grants, in general, direct funding by local or central government is not consideration for a supply of education, or a business activity, and is outside the scope of VAT.
>
> Where education is partly funded by grants, if the education provided to an individual is funded by a combination of government grants and by making a charge, it's a supply for VAT purposes. The government funding is a contribution to the business activity and is outside the scope

of VAT.

3 Education providers

3.1 Educational institutions that are in business

These establishments require payment for the education they provide, so their education is a business activity-

- independent fee paying schools, including non-maintained special schools
- universities
- institutions teaching EFL

3.2 Educational institutions that are not in business

These establishments normally make no charge for the education they provide, so their education is not a business activity-

- community schools
- foundation schools
- voluntary aided schools, including former special agreement schools
- voluntary controlled schools
- community special schools
- foundation special schools
- grant maintained (integrated) schools (Northern Ireland)
- self governing schools (Scotland)
- city technology colleges
- free schools
- academies

There are also sixth form, tertiary and further education colleges, which do not charge for students who are 19 years or under (18 years or under in Scotland) at the start of their courses, but charge students over that age and foreign nationals.

Here the age of the student is immaterial. When a charge is made, the education is a business supply.

These establishments may be in business for other activities they carry out (see paragraph 3.1).

There have been developments since 7 August 2019 that qualify those parts of VAT Notice 701/30 cited above (but, as at 24 March 2022, the Notice itself has yet to be updated). These include the Court of Appeal judgment in *HMRC v Wakefield College* [2018] EWCA Civ 952 and the Upper Tribunal judgment in *Colchester Institute Corporation [2020] UKUT 368.*

The College in *HMRC v Wakefield College* [2018] EWCA Civ 952 provides a range of courses. Its students fall within three primary groups:

- the first group comprising those who are wholly grant-funded and pay no tuition fees;

- the second comprising those who are partially grant-funded, where they or their employers are required to pay some fees, which may be wholly or partially remitted in certain circumstances; and
- the third comprising those (mainly from overseas) who had no grant support at all and who are required to pay full fees.

HMRC accepted that the College did not make supplies in the course of any business to the first group of students. The College accepted that it did make supplies in the course of a business to the third group of students.

The Court of Appeal held that:

> 74. The parties were agreed that students paying subsidised fees provided consideration within the meaning of article 2 for the courses provided to them. In the light of the authorities discussed earlier, this is plainly right.
>
> 75. Turning to the contentious issue of economic activity, both parties drew attention to factors taken into account in *Finland* and *Borsele*, while accepting that ultimately each case depends on its own facts. Those factors were, first, that in *Finland* and, to an extent, in *Borsele*, the charges paid were fixed by reference to the means of the recipients. Second, and as a necessary corollary, the charges were only partly fixed by reference to the cost of the service. Third, the total amount raised by charges was insubstantial, both in absolute terms and relative to the cost of the service. Fourth, in Borsele, the municipality did not offer services on the general passenger transport market and appeared more to be the final consumer of the transport services provided by the transport undertakings engaged by it. Fifth, other factors mentioned in those cases were a comparison of the supply in question with the circumstances in which the relevant type of service is usually provided, and the number of customers.
>
> ...
>
> 78. I consider that overall the evidence establishes that the supply of courses to students paying subsidised fees is an economic activity being carried on by the College. I reach this conclusion for a number of reasons.
>
> 79. First, the sole activity of the College, in the most general terms, is the provision of educational courses. It is not comparable to the municipality in *Borsele* for whom the provision of school transport was very much ancillary to its principal activities.
>
> 80. Second, the provision of courses to students paying subsidised fees is a significant, albeit minority, part of the College's total undertaking.
>
> 81. Third, the fees paid by such students are significant in amount...

> 82. Fourth, the subsidised fees made a significant contribution to the cost of providing courses to the students paying those fees, to the extent of some 25-30%.
>
> 83. Fifth, the level of fees was fixed by reference to the cost of the courses...
>
> 84. Sixth, the fees were not fixed by reference to the means of the students or employers or others paying the fees. The fee was a fixed fee for each course, published each year in the College's prospectus. It may be the case that the College charged less than it was entitled to, as a response to the prevailing economic circumstances in its local catchment area, but that is a factor that any economic activity must take into account and is not comparable to an individual means-tested basis for fixing fees.
>
> 85. Seventh, it is undeniable that there is a market in the provision of further and higher education, whose viability is underpinned by a combination of grant aid and fees. There is no reason to suppose that the College is other than a typical participant in that market or that it provides courses to students paying subsidised fees on anything other than a typical basis, allowing no doubt for some variations between different institutions. If the College was in any way in a position that was unique or atypical, it was for the College to put evidence of it before the FTT.
>
> …
>
> 87. …For the reasons given above, the provision of courses by the College to students paying subsidised fees was, in my judgment, an economic activity carried on by it for the purposes of article 9 of the VAT Directive and was therefore a "business"...

See also the Upper Tribunal judgment in *Colchester Institute Corporation* [2020] UKUT 368 (discussed above at 35.9.6).

In Revenue and Customs Brief 8 (2021) (*VAT treatment of public funds received by further education institutions*), published on 26 May 2021, HMRC states:

> **Background**
>
> The primary decision [in *Colchester Institute Corporation*] concerns the VAT treatment of public monies received by further education institutions to fund the provision of education to 16-19-year-old students (and certain other categories of students entitled to full funding). HMRC is of the view that monies received by these institutions from government funding agencies are grants and the activity funded is outside the scope of the VAT system. However, Colchester Institute Corporation successfully argued that the monies represented third party

consideration paid from the public purse to Colchester Institute Corporation to educate a particular group of students.

The Upper Tribunal decision

The decision of the Upper Tribunal, if sustained, means that further education institutions undertaking the activity of educating 16-19-year-old students will be providing education and training which falls within the scope of the VAT system, but will be exempt from VAT (Item 1, Group 6, Schedule 9, VAT Act 1994). A change in status of these activities from outside the scope (non-business) to within scope (business) would also impact on an institution's ability to obtain certain zero-rated reliefs, which are available to certain charities that carry out non-business activities.

HMRC acknowledges the decision of the Upper Tribunal in Colchester Institute Corporation and has not appealed further because it was successful in its alternative arguments. However, HMRC is taking steps to test the primary decision on the treatment of public monies via a new appeal. In the meantime, HMRC's policy concerning grant funded education will remain unchanged and HMRC will not impose the primary decision on any further education institution. This means that it remains open to institutions, that continue to treat such education as non-business, to claim charitable reliefs, where all the relevant criteria have been met.

Institutions can choose to apply the conclusion of the Upper Tribunal in Colchester Institute Corporation, treat the education as exempt and submit error correction notices for any under or overpayment of VAT, including adjustments to previous claims for charitable reliefs. HMRC will protect its position to secure tax revenues, pending the outcome of an appeal.

The VATEDU Manual provides:

VATEDU36900-Group 6 Item 1 Education, research and vocational training provided by eligible bodies: what is education?: preschool education, nurseries, after-school clubs and playgroups [Jan 2019]

...The provision of pre-school education (without charge) is non-business; breakfast clubs and after-school child-minding/homework clubs are also non-business in the local authority sector even when a charge is made. This is on condition that the school offers the service strictly to its own pupils and that the fee charged is designed to no more than cover overhead costs.

The provision of a day-nursery is a business activity. If the provider is registered with OFSTED, which is most likely as there are few exemptions from registration, then the supplies are an exempt supply of

> welfare services, as they are being provided in a state-regulated institution (VAT Act 1994, Schedule 9, Group 7, Item 9 refers). Otherwise, the supplies will normally be standard-rated. However, if the supplier is an eligible body and there is clear evidence that the supplies follow an educational curriculum, exemption under Group 6 may be appropriate. If you come across such cases you should consult the Education Unit of Expertise or VAT Reliefs Policy Team before giving a ruling.
>
> Exemption extends to the supply of meals and drinks for the children, as well as other sundry items provided as part of the children's care such as picture books, crayons and toys. It does not however, extend to supplies such as children's parties or day trips where the supply is advertised as a separate and identifiable package (this is a provision of entertainment rather than care), or to supplies of meals and drinks to staff and visitors.
>
> Where a local authority provides nursery services to children in care under obligations imposed by the Children Act 1989, this is considered to be non-business.
>
> Following the High Court decisions in *Yarburgh Children's Trust* (Ch D 2001, [2002] STC 207) and *St Paul's Community Project* (Ch D 2004, [2005] STC 95; [2004] EWCH 2490 (Ch)) it has been accepted by HMRC that, where a charity supplies nursery and crèche facilities for a consideration that is fixed at a level designed to only cover its costs, this is not a business activity for business purposes ...

Whether HMRC will revisit the last paragraph in light of the Court of Appeal judgments in *Longridge* and *Wakefield College* remains to be seen. That there is no indication at all in the VATEDU Manual is particularly unsatisfactory given how the latest update was in 8 April 2020 (post-dating both judgments).

35.18 Business and non-business activities

A person may carry on more than one activity (to use a neutral word):

(1) A business and a non-business

(2) Two businesses, one exempt and one VATable

(3) Two businesses, both VATable (but in that case one would not usually worry whether there was one business or two).

The VBNB Manual provides:

> **VBNB26000-VAT Business and Non-Business activities: taxable persons with more than one activity** [Jan 2021]
>
> ...A taxable person may undertake more than one activity. Some of these

may be business for VAT purposes and some non-business. The business test (VBNB22000) should be applied to all of a taxable person's activities.

An example of a private or personal non-business activity might involve a builder whose hobby is trading in old stamps and postcards. They make "supplies" by doing this. However, providing the hobby is seen as a non-business activity when the business tests are applied these supplies will not fall within the scope of the tax.

An example of a non-private non-business activity might involve an organisation providing free advice to members. In the absence of any taxable supplies this is a non-business activity for VAT purposes. It is a non-private activity because it is an activity which forms part of the organisation's overall objectives.

You need to apply the business test to each activity to decide whether it is within the scope of the tax.

Tax paid on goods and services used for both business and non-business activities may need to be apportioned. VIT VAT Input Tax VIT25000provides guidance on how to make an apportionment. VIT VAT Input Tax VIT25510 sets out an alternative treatment where full recovery of the VAT incurred can be obtained upfront with payment of an output tax charge to take account of private use.

In *Rainheath Ltd* (VBNB72600) the tribunal found that there was a mixture of business and non-business activities. The case shows that a limited company is not necessarily in business for all of its activities.

In *Leeds Kashrut Commission and Beth Din Administrative Committee* (VBNB72600) the tribunal found that a single legal entity had two separately identifiable business activities.

In *Walker (DA)* (VBNB72600) the tribunal found that there were two business activities; one taxable, the other exempt.

In *Williamson (RW & AAW)* (VBNB72600) the tribunal found that there were two business activities, both of which were taxable. It showed that being registered under a trading name did not keep other business activities carried on by the same legal entity from being part of the overall business activities to be accounted for under the VAT registration.

35.19 Business of membership subscriptions

Section 94(2) VATA provides:

> Without prejudice to the generality of anything else in this Act, the following are deemed to be the carrying on of a business—
>
> (a) the provision by a club, association or organisation (for a subscription or other consideration) of the facilities or

> advantages available to its members...

In *C&E v Yarburgh Children's Trust* the playgroup was an association providing facilities for its members but it was not carrying on a business. The judge said:

> [35] ...I do not accept s 94(2) should be treated as capable of converting into an economic activity a supply of services which would not otherwise be so treated. It seems to me that the legislative purpose of s 94(2) was to ensure that the activities of an association or other organisation which is not a legal person should not be excluded from the VAT regime for that reason alone. Such an association could therefore be treated as a taxable person and be capable of making a taxable supply within the meaning of ss 4 and 5(2) of the 1994 Act. ...
> [36] ...although an unincorporated association can be a 'person' it can only be a taxable person if it is registered for VAT and the basis of registration is the making of taxable supplies (see para 1 of Sch 1). An association can only make a taxable supply if it is treated as separate from its members to whom those supplies are made. The deeming provision in s 94(2), although couched in terms of the carrying on of a business, seems to me to be no more than a legislative shorthand for saying that services provided by an association to its members on an essentially commercial basis should be treated as part of a business notwithstanding that the association has no legal existence beyond the contractual relationship between its members. It does not require a supply of services which is not inherently commercial to be treated as such. I do not therefore accept that s 94(2) has the effect of making the operation of the playgroup an economic activity.

In direct tax, "mutual trading" is not classified as a trade. Section 94(2)(a) VATA on its face (not to mention the very existence of Article 132(1)(f) of the VAT directive) prevents an argument that a mutual trade is not a VAT business; the question needs to be determined by reference to the *Finland* case, *Borsele* and *Wakefield College*.

A mutual trade may benefit from an exemption. Article 132(1)(f) provides:

> the supply of services by independent groups of persons, who are carrying on an activity which is exempt from VAT or in relation to which they are not taxable persons, for the purpose of rendering their members the services directly necessary for the exercise of that activity, where those groups merely claim from their members exact reimbursement of their share of the joint expenses, provided that such

> exemption is not likely to cause distortion of competition;

This Article throws up a number of technical issues that are beyond the scope of this book.

35.20 Admission to premises

Section 94(2) VATA provides:

> Without prejudice to the generality of anything else in this Act, the following are deemed to be the carrying on of a business ...
>
> (b) the admission, for a consideration, of persons to any premises.

The VBNB Manual provides:

> **VBNB72400- Legal history: cases about section 94(2) activities** [Jan 2021]
>
> ... *The Eric Taylor (deceased) Testimonial Match Committee*[18] arranged a one-off football match. To raise funds for the deceased's family spectators were charged for admission to the ground.
>
> The organisation of the match did not amount to a business activity in the ordinary sense of the word. However, the tribunal found that it was business for VAT purposes. This was by virtue of section 45(1)(d) of the Finance Act 1972, now section 94(2)(b) of the VAT Act 1994.

35.21 Admission charges

The HMRC Guidance Note refers to the Gift Aid rule under which a right of admission may be disregarded as a benefit, and provides:

> 3.39.44 There's no equivalent relaxation of VAT rules for payments to gain admission to view charity property.
>
> 3.39.45 The addition of an amount over and above the standard admission charge, including the voluntary 10% donation on top of an admission charge does not therefore make the entire payment a donation for VAT purposes.
>
> 3.39.46 For VAT a donation must be freely given with the donor receiving nothing in return for the donation (except a token item, which has no intrinsic value, such as a lapel sticker or poppy)
>
> 3.39.47 If a charity is VAT registered VAT at the standard rate will still have to be accounted for on the admission charge - unless the cultural exemption applies, in which case the admission charge will be exempt from VAT.
>
> More information about the Cultural Exemption can be found in VAT

---

18 [1975] VATTR 8.

Notice 701/47 Culture.

3.39.48 Where a charity provides benefits as an incentive, to encourage donations in addition to the admission charge, the VAT position changes, whether or not such donations exceed 10% of the admission charge.

3.39.49 VAT becomes due on the amount paid in addition to the admission charge at the rate appropriate to the benefit provided, such as at the zero, standard or reduced rate.

VAT - admission charge standard rated

3.39.50 Where a charity receives a gift aid donation which is in part subject to VAT at the standard rate, the VAT position is as follows:

- that part of the payment representing the normal admission charge is standard rated
- the additional amount is a donation and outside the scope of VAT, provided that it's truly voluntary and gives no additional benefits

3.39.51 In these circumstances the receipt of such donations does not require a business/non-business apportionment.

VAT and vouchers

3.39.52 A charity may decide to offer vouchers as an incentive to customers who make a donation in addition to an admission charge, the vouchers are often redeemable at an outlet within the charity property. There are a number of different ways in which voucher schemes work and special VAT rules apply. One of the more common types of voucher is a 'face value' voucher.

Face value vouchers display a monetary value and are usually sold at or below that monetary value and can be used to obtain goods and services. The provision of a voucher in return for a donation is regarded as supply in return for payment. There's no VAT on a face value voucher when they're sold (unless they're sold for an amount greater than the face value in which case VAT's due on the difference).

However, when redeemed for goods or services these vouchers are treated as consideration (payment) for those goods or services at their full face value.

Further information can be found in VAT Notice 700/7 Business Promotion Schemes.

The VAT treatment of vouchers has changed. A (very) high-level summary of the changes is set out below (by way of a heavily edited extract from VAT Notice 700/7 (Business promotions) [31 December 2020]):

9. Vouchers from 1 January 2019

…

9.3 Issue, transfer and redemption of a voucher

Although the issue and any transfer of a voucher represents the underlying goods or services, the time of supply will depend on the type of voucher issued or transferred - single purpose vouchers paragraph 9.4 and multi-purpose vouchers paragraph 9.5.

9.3.1 Issue of a voucher

By issue we mean the voucher has been given value and is capable of being used to purchase goods or services for that value. The issue of a face value voucher is to be treated as the supply of the relevant goods or services for which it can be redeemed...

9.3.2 Transfer of a voucher

...The transfer of a face value voucher is to be treated as the supply of the relevant goods or services for which it can be redeemed. The VAT treatment depends on whether it's a single purpose voucher or a multi-purpose voucher.

9.3.3 Redemption of a voucher

...The redemption of the voucher as consideration for the supply of the relevant goods or services is not a transfer of the voucher.

9.4 Single purpose vouchers

9.4.1 Definition of single purpose voucher

A single purpose voucher is one where, at the time of issue, the liability to VAT of the goods or services to which it relates, and the place where they will be supplied (either the UK or another country or territory) are known...

...

9.4.4 Deemed supply on redemption

If the single purpose voucher was issued by a different person than the redeemer then there is a deemed supply of the goods or services to which the voucher relates to that issuer...

...

9.5 Multi-purpose vouchers

A multi-purpose voucher is any voucher that is not a single purpose voucher.

9.5.1 Issue or transfer of a multi-purpose voucher

The consideration for the issue or transfer of an multi-purpose voucher is disregarded at every stage. This is because any VAT becomes due when the goods are handed over or the services are provided in return for the voucher.

9.5.2 Value of the multi-purpose voucher on redemption

For the purposes of calculating the VAT due on redemption, the value of the voucher is its face value or the consideration paid at its most recent supply where that is known to the person accepting the voucher

> as consideration…
>
> …
>
> **9.12 Unredeemed vouchers**
>
> **9.12.1 Single-purpose vouchers**
>
> No VAT adjustment can be made if the voucher is not used or not used for its full value, unless a refund is made.
>
> **9.12.2 Multi-purpose vouchers**
>
> If the voucher is never used there is no VAT to be brought to account because the issue of the voucher has been disregarded and there has been no taxable supply of goods or services.

Turning back to the HMRC Guidance Note:

> **VAT effect on partial exemption calculations**
>
> 3.39.53 Where a charity is partially exempt, only the normal admission charge should be included in the partial exemption calculation. Any additional donation should only be included if the charity provides a gift or benefit in return for the extra amount.
>
> 3.39.54 Freely given donations, where the donor receives nothing in return (other than a token item such as a lapel badge), are excluded from the partial exemption calculation.
>
> **VAT business/non-business calculation**
>
> 3.39.55 The receipt of donations does not in itself create a requirement to carry out a business/non-business calculation. Where a business/ non-business calculation is required, dependent on the apportionment method used, the donative elements may have to be included in the calculation. Non-business activity is generally the supply of goods and services for no charge....

See also 36.1.2 (Business/non-business) and the CJEU ruling in *The Chancellor, Masters and Scholars of the University of Cambridge* (Case C-316/18), as discussed in 36.6 (University of Cambridge).

> **VAT examples**
>
> 3.39.56 A VAT-registered charity makes an admission charge of £10 to view charity property. They seek a donation of more than the £10 admission charge to help them pursue their charitable objectives.
>
> **Example 1**
>
> *The charity provides no goods or benefits in return for the additional donation:*
>
> VAT is due at 20% on the £10 admission charge unless the VAT Cultural Exemption applies (supply is exempt)
>
> As no goods or benefits are given any amounts received in excess of the £10 can be treated as donations - outside the scope of VAT.

Example 2

The charity gives a lapel sticker to visitors who make a donation:

VAT is due at 20% on the £10 admission charge

Because a lapel badge is merely a token any additional amounts can be regarded as a donation and therefore outside the scope of VAT.

Example 3

The charity gives a book about the history of the charity property to visitors who make a donation:

VAT is due at 20% on the £10 admission charge unless the VAT cultural exemption applies (supply is exempt).

As books are zero rated any amounts paid in addition to the admission charge, represent a zero-rated consideration for the book

If the customer does not receive the book either because they've paid an additional amount less than 10% of the admission charge or they choose not to take the book, the additional amount is a donation outside the scope of VAT.

Example 4

The charity gives the customer a set of coasters picturing the charity property:

VAT is due at 20% on the £10 admission charge, unless the VAT cultural exemption applies (supply is exempt),

As the coasters are a standard-rated supply any amount paid in addition to the admission charge is a standard-rated consideration for the coasters and VAT will be due at 20% on the additional amount paid.

If the customer does not receive or accept the coasters the additional amount can be considered a donation outside the scope of VAT.

Example 5

The charity gives the customer a token with a face value of £1 to be redeemed at one of the charity's outlets:

VAT is due at 20% on the £10 admission charge, unless the VAT cultural exemption applies (supply is exempt),

If the customer pays an additional £1 no VAT is due on the face value of the token at this point.

VAT is accounted for when the voucher is redeemed, at the rate appropriate to the goods or services purchased. For example, if it's used to buy a book the zero rate will apply, to buy a snack at a café the standard rate of 20% will apply.

If the extra amount paid by the customer is greater than the face value of the voucher (say £1.50) VAT would be due at the standard rate on £0.50 on admission and VAT on the remaining £1 is accounted for when the voucher is redeemed.

If the customer does not receive a voucher, either because they've paid an additional amount less than 10% of the admission charge or they choose not to take the voucher, the additional amount is a donation outside the scope of VAT.

The discussion in relation to the voucher in Example 5 has been superseded by the introduction of the new rules on the VAT treatment of vouchers. The charity now needs first to determine whether the voucher is a single or multiple-purpose voucher.

A voucher can only be a single-purpose voucher if the rate of VAT applicable to the goods or services to which it relates is the same. VAT on such a voucher is accounted for at the time of issue of the voucher.

A multi-purpose voucher is any voucher that is not a single-purpose voucher. VAT on such a voucher is accounted for at the time of redemption of the voucher.

While not expressly stated, the voucher in Example 5 would appear to be a multi-purpose voucher.

35.22 Supply "in the course or furtherance" of business

Section 94 VATA extends the meaning of this expression:

35.22.1 *Offices*

Section 94(4) VATA provides:

> Where a person, in the course or furtherance of a trade, profession or vocation, accepts any office, services supplied by him as the holder of that office are treated as supplied in the course or furtherance of the trade, profession or vocation.

This will not often be relevant to charities.

35.22.2 *Termination and disposal of business*

Section 94 VATA provides:

> (5) Anything done in connection with the termination or intended termination of a business is treated as being done in the course or furtherance of that business.
> (6) The disposition of a business, or part of a business, as a going concern, or of the assets or liabilities of the business or part of the business (whether or not in connection with its reorganisation or winding up), is a supply made in the course or furtherance of the business.

35.23 Single/multiple supplies

VAT Notice 701/5 (31 December 2020) provides:

5.1 How to treat subscriptions for VAT purposes

5.1.1 Single supplies

If your members pay a subscription to obtain or gain entitlement to any substantive benefits of membership, you must calculate the VAT due on the total amount of the subscription as set out in section 4.

The VAT liability of subscriptions depends on the liability of the membership benefits you supply in return. In most cases clubs supply a package of benefits so that your supply will have more than one component under the terms of paragraph 4.2.

But, just because your membership may offer a package of benefits does not necessarily mean that you are making multiple supplies. In most cases there is one principal benefit or reason for joining. For example, being a member of a professional body or trade union allows the member to enjoy the rights that membership may bring. In addition, other benefits, such as the provision of a hand book or newsletters are an integral or incidental part of the main supply.

In these circumstances, your subscription is consideration for a single supply and its liability is determined by the liability of the main benefit. No apportionment may be made.

But, there is an exception for non-profit making bodies, making a single supply which comprises a mixture of benefits with different VAT liabilities. These bodies may apportion their subscriptions to reflect the value and VAT liability of each individual benefit. This is explained in more detail at paragraph 4.2.

It is up to you whether you wish to take advantage of the concession, but you can not apply the concession retrospectively. If you wish to apportion, for example, subscriptions to cover separate benefits such as zero-rated printed matter, you must apportion all types and elements of subscriptions, in other words you cannot 'pick and choose'.

5.1.2 Multiple supplies

In some cases certain elements of the package of membership benefits you receive are clearly not related at all to the main purpose of joining the membership body or club, meaning that you are making multiple supplies. If your subscription is consideration for multiple supplies under the terms of paragraph 4.2, and the separate elements have different VAT liabilities, you must apportion your subscription between those different elements. Brief guidance on how to apportion is shown at paragraph 5.10. Examples of benefits which may need to be apportioned include:

- priority booking rights
- guaranteed seats
- discounts on admission charges

- items with a resale value

These benefits are considered to be substantive regardless of whether there is any cost to your organisation in supplying them and what that cost might be.

But, you can ignore benefits that have a nominal value, such as simple acknowledgements of support in the form of membership badges, flags or stickers, and listing of names in a programme or on a theatre seat or entrance.

VAT Notice 701/1 [31 December 2020] provides:

5.13 Membership

The provision of membership benefits to members of a club or association is a business activity. The VAT liability of a membership subscription will depend on the benefits being supplied.

In most cases a package of benefits is supplied and the provider has to decide whether he is making a single or multiple supply. If there is one principal benefit, to which all of the other benefits are incidental, the whole subscription is treated as a single supply and the VAT liability will follow that of the principal benefit. For example, if the principal benefit offered by a theatre club to its members is free theatre tickets, and other benefits, such as the right to receive copies of advertising literature, are incidental, then the theatre club would treat the subscription as a single supply of the right of admission. This would either be taxable at the standard rate or exempt if the provider was entitled to exempt its admission charges under the cultural exemption, see paragraph 5.1.

But, as a concession, charities and non-profit making organisations can treat their single supplies of membership benefits as multiple supplies. This means that the VAT treatment of each benefit can be considered individually and the subscription charge apportioned. This means that the supply of magazines or handbooks to members can normally be zero-rated. For more information see Clubs and associations' VAT responsibilities (VAT Notice 701/5) and Zero rating books and printed matter (VAT Notice 701/10).

35.23.1 *Subscription include donation*

VAT Notice 701/5 (31 December 2020) provides:

5.2 Subscriptions which are voluntary payments or donations

If the whole of the subscription is an entirely voluntary payment and secures nothing or only nominal benefits in return, then it is all a donation and you must treat it as being outside the scope of VAT...

> **5.3 Subscriptions which may include a voluntary payment or donation**
> You may only treat part of your subscription as a voluntary payment or donation if either:
> - all the substantive benefits provided are available to non-members at no charge or more cheaply than the subscription, you should ignore any nominal benefits, see paragraph 5.1
> - some or all of the substantive benefits are exclusive to members and you are able to demonstrate that the amount paid is higher than the amount that the subscriber would normally have to pay for similar goods or services.
>
> If you meet these requirements paragraph 5.10 explains how you should apportion the subscription.
> A charity or an organisation having objects in the public domain (for example, philanthropic body), may receive a subscription which includes a donational element.

Similarly, HMRC Notice 701/1 provides:

> **5.14 Patron and supporter schemes**
> Many cultural organisations operate patron or supporter schemes, which offer benefits in return for a minimum payment. Benefits may include free admission to special exhibitions, the right to receive regular publications or discounts on shop purchases. The minimum payment is business income and is standard-rated. But, if one of the benefits to patrons or supporters is the right to receive publications you may be able to treat part of the payment as zero-rated.
> If a patron or supporter pays more than the minimum amount you can treat the excess as a donation and outside the scope of VAT as long as the patron or supporter is aware that scheme benefits are available for a given amount, and that anything in excess of that amount is a voluntary donation. This should be explicit in the patron or supporter scheme literature.

35.23.2 *Joining fee, life membership, other types of fee*

VAT Notice 701/5 (31 December 2020) provides:

> **5.5 Additional joining fees**
> You should treat any additional joining fee of a general nature, in the same way as your subscriptions, applying the same apportionment, if any. Where you charge an additional fee for 'obtaining' a particular facility, you must account for VAT based on the liability of the particular service or goods provided.

5.6 Life membership fees
You must also treat fees for life membership in the same way as your annual subscriptions, unless you supply life members with additional benefits not available to ordinary members.

5.7 How to treat a charge to be placed on a waiting list for membership
It will be exempt if it is:

- deducted from the new member's first subscription or entrance fee and the subscription or fee itself will qualify for exemption
- refundable in the event that the candidate fails to become a member for any reason, including voluntary withdrawal.

In all other circumstances the fee is consideration for the right to be on the waiting list and is standard-rated

5.8 Payment by instalments
Where you allow a member to pay a subscription by instalments over the subscription period and the total instalments exceed a single payment subscription, the liability of the additional amount is the same as that of the subscription.

5.9 Deferred payments
Where an organisation offers annual membership and allows members to defer subscription payment for an additional charge over and above the subscription, the charge is consideration for the exempt grant of credit.

35.23.3 *Apportionment*

VAT Notice 701/5 (31 December 2020) provides:

5.10 How to apportion subscriptions
There are no specific rules for making an apportionment. VAT guide (VAT Notice 700) gives general guidance and examples on how to apportion output VAT. It is usually acceptable for a club to apportion its total subscription income to reflect the relative cost of providing the different supplies to its members. You can base your calculations for the current financial year on your accounts for the previous financial year, provided you apply this method consistently. You must keep your calculations for inspection by our VAT assurance staff.

5.11 Subscriptions which include a donation
Provided you satisfy the terms of paragraph 5.3 and correctly calculate the value of any standard-rated, zero-rated and exempt supplies, you can treat the balance of the subscription as a donation and outside the scope of VAT. To do this, you should calculate the value of the substantive benefits (ignoring nominal benefits of the types described in paragraph 5.3), using the price at which they are available to non-members or the

amount the subscriber would normally have to pay for similar goods or services, see paragraph 5.10). The difference between the amount of the subscription and the total value of the benefits is the donation.

5.12 Subscriptions used to purchase zero-rated or exempt supplies from a third party

This will not in itself entitle you to apportion the value of subscriptions. You can only apportion those separately identifiable supplies of zero-rated or exempt goods or services that you make to your members.

35.23.4 *Meaning of "charity"*

The standard tax definition applies.

35.24 VAT groups

Section 43A VATA provides:

(1) Two or more UK bodies corporate are eligible to be treated as members of a group if—

(a) one of them controls each of the others,

(b) one person (whether a body corporate or an individual) controls all of them, or

(c) two or more individuals carrying on a business in partnership control all of them.

...

(4) An individual carrying on a business and one or more UK bodies corporate are eligible to be treated as members of a group if the individual-

(a) controls the UK body corporate or all of the UK bodies corporate, and

(b) is established, or has a fixed establishment, in the United Kingdom in relation to the business.

(5) Two or more relevant persons carrying on a business in partnership ("the partnership") and one or more UK bodies corporate are eligible to be treated as members of a group if the partnership-

(a) controls the UK body corporate or all of the UK bodies corporate, and

(b) is established, or has a fixed establishment, in the United Kingdom in relation to the business.

(6) In this section-

(a) "UK body corporate" means a body corporate which is established or has a fixed establishment in the United Kingdom;

(b) "relevant person" means an individual, a body corporate or a Scottish partnership.

> (7) Section 43AZA contains provision for determining for the purposes of this section whether a body corporate, individual or partnership controls a UK body corporate."
>
> **43AZA Section 43A: control test**
>
> (1) This section applies for the purposes of section 43A (and expressions used in this section have the same meaning as in that section).
>
> (2) A body corporate ("X") controls a UK body corporate if-
>
> (a) X is empowered by statute to control the UK body corporate's activities, or
>
> (b) X is the UK body corporate's holding company.
>
> (3) An individual ("Y") controls a UK body corporate if Y would, were Y a company, be the UK body corporate's holding company.
>
> (4) Two or more relevant persons carrying on a business in partnership ("the partnership") control a UK body corporate if the partnership would, were it a company, be the UK body corporate's holding company.
>
> (5) In this section "holding company" has the meaning given by section 1159 of, and Schedule 6 to, the Companies Act 2006."

A corporate charity which holds a subsidiary controls that subsidiary, and so the two companies form a group and qualify for VAT group reliefs.

A non-charitable company may be grouped with a charity it controls. The same may be true of a charitable *trust*(depending on the precise facts).

Query whether a corporate trustee "controls" its subsidiaries for these purposes. This turns on whether the corporate trustee is the subsidiaries' "holding company" within the meaning of section 1159 and Sch 6 Companies Act 2006.

Section 1159(1) Companies Act 2006 provides:

> A company is a "subsidiary" of another company, its "holding company", if that other company-
>
> (a) holds a majority of the voting rights in it, or
>
> (b) is a member of it and has the right to appoint or remove a majority of its board of directors, or
>
> (c) is a member of it and controls alone, pursuant to an agreement with other members, a majority of the voting rights in it,
>
> or if it is a subsidiary of a company that is itself a subsidiary of that other company.

Sch 6 Companies Act 2006 provides as follows:

"…

Rights held by one person on behalf of another

5 Rights held by a person in a fiduciary capacity shall be treated as not held by him.

6 (1) Rights held by a person as nominee for another shall be treated as held by the other.

(2) Rights shall be regarded as held as nominee for another if they are exercisable only on his instructions or with his consent or concurrence.

As rights held by a trustee qua trustee are normally held in a fiduciary capacity, paragraph 5 Sch 6 Companies Act 2006 means (on its face) that the corporate trustee would not be regarded (for example) as holding a majority of the voting rights in any of its subsidiaries (even if it actually held such rights and no other person had any voting rights in any such subsidiary).

The VGROUPS Manual provides:

VGROUPS02250 - Eligibility for VAT group treatment: control conditions: shares held by nominees and trustees [Sep 2021]

Shares held by a person as a nominee are treated as being held by the nominator, and may not be used by the nominee to prove control of a company.

A bare trust or nominee works as follows: The bare trust or nominee holds the shares on behalf of the beneficiary and must act in accordance with the instructions of the beneficiary. The bare trustee or nominee is the legal owner and the nominator is the beneficial owner.

For example:

- A holds 100 shares in B on a bare trust (or as nominee) for C. Whilst A holds title to the shares, C is entitled to the shares and any benefit arising from them. There would normally be a short trust declaration, but the principal legal point is that A holds the shares on trust for C and C is entitled to the shares rather than A.
- In practice A is C's nominee and is a bare trustee. C is entitled to the dividends, although the company pays them to A, who is on the register of shareholders as the holder of the shares. In view of the fact that A is registered as the holder of the shares, A is the only one allowed to vote at shareholders meetings. However, A must vote in accordance with C's wishes. Under these circumstances, it would not be the trustee (nominee) A who HMRC would see as the controlling body, but the beneficiary (nominator) C.

In trusts other than bare trusts, trustees may exercise control of a company using the shares that they hold as trustees of that trust.

However, they may not add those shares to any that they may hold in a personal capacity or as trustees of another trust to prove control.
For example:

- If A and B are trustees of a trust which has, amongst its assets, 52% of the shares in C (thereby holding 52% of the voting rights in the company), A and B can exercise those voting rights in their capacity as trustees of the trust and can be said to control the company.
- If on the other hand, A and B, as trustees of trust 1, hold 26% of the voting rights in C and, as trustees of trust 2, they hold a further 26% and they jointly own a further 26% of the voting rights themselves, they cannot combine the shares which they hold in a fiduciary capacity for trust 1 with those held for trust 2 with those they hold themselves in a beneficial capacity (those held in their own joint names) to control the company.
- This is largely because, when exercising the voting rights that they hold in a fiduciary capacity, they are bound to act in the best interests of the beneficiaries of the separate trusts. When exercising the voting rights that they hold in their own names they can act in their own best interests. This may lead to a situation where the interests clash.

Although, in the first bullet under the second set of examples, HMRC refers to A and B holding their shares in C "in their capacity as trustees" (rather than "in a fiduciary capacity", as they do in the next two bullets), because rights held by a trustee qua trustee are normally held in a fiduciary capacity, the difference in terminology is a distinction without a difference.

HMRC clearly does not think that holding shares in C as trustees deprives A and B of control of C for the purposes of VAT grouping.

While it is possible that VGROUPS02250 was written in ignorance of the provisions of Sch 6 Companies Act 2006, this seems unlikely as HMRC discusses nominees and bare trustees on the same page. It seems unlikely that the section on nominees and bare trustees would have been penned in ignorance of paragraph 6 Sch 6 Companies Act 2006, and equally unlikely that if HMRC were aware of paragraph 6, they would not have been aware of paragraph 5.

It is possible that HMRC construes paragraph 5 in accordance with its heading ("Rights held by one person on behalf of another") - in effect, reading paragraph 5 as:

> "Rights held by a person in a fiduciary capacity [on behalf of an identified other person (as opposed to a class of unidentified persons, or

> objects, or a purpose)] shall be treated as not held by him",

in which case a corporate trustee would be the "holding company" of its subsidiaries within the meaning of section 1159 and Sch 6 Companies Act 2006 (as so construed).

Section 43 VATA provides:

> (1) Where under [sections 43A to 43D] any persons are treated as members of a group, any business carried on by a member of the group shall be treated as carried on by the representative member, and-
>
> (a) any supply of goods or services by a member of the group to another member of the group shall be disregarded; and
>
> (b) any [supply which is a supply to which paragraph (a) above does not apply and is a supply] of goods or services by or to a member of the group shall be treated as a supply by or to the representative member...
>
> and all members of the group shall be liable jointly and severally for any VAT due from the representative member.

CC35 provides:

> **4.19 Can a charity guarantee the liabilities of a trading subsidiary?**
> ...The registration of a 'VAT group' comprising a charity and its trading subsidiary or subsidiaries means that each entity within the group guarantees the settlement of the VAT liabilities of the other entities within the group. There is no objection in principle to the registration of a charity as part of a VAT group. But before doing so, trustees need to satisfy themselves that the overall benefits of group registration outweigh the risk of loss to the charity's assets, if those assets have to be used to settle a VAT liability of a trading subsidiary.

CHAPTER THIRTY SIX

RECOVERY OF INPUT VAT

36.1 Recovery of input VAT

The right for a charity to recover VAT on supplies to the charity is often more important than the duty on a charity to pay VAT on supplies made by the charity.

36.1.1 *"Input tax"*

Section 24(1) VATA provides:

> Subject to the following provisions of this section, "input tax", in relation to a taxable person, means the following tax, that is to say—
>
> (a) VAT on the supply to him of any goods or services ...
>
> being (in each case) goods or services used or to be used for the purpose of any business carried on or to be carried on by him.

VAT on supplies of goods or services to a charity is only "input tax" where the charity is a taxable person, and the goods or services are used by it for the purposes of a business carried on or to be carried on by it.

A charity may not carry on any business at all, in which case it would incur no VAT that constitutes "input tax". Where it does carry on a business, it may incur both VAT that constitutes "input tax" as well as VAT that does not.

"Business" in a VAT context does not necessarily correspond with business in other (e.g. direct tax) contexts – see 35.14.

36.1.2 *Business/non-business*

Section 24(5) VATA provides:

> Where goods or services supplied to a taxable person … are used or to be used partly for the purposes of a business carried on or to be carried on by him and partly for other purposes-
> (a) VAT on supplies … shall be apportioned so that so much as is referable to the taxable person's business purposes is counted as that person's input tax, and
> (b) the remainder of that VAT ("the non-business VAT") shall count as that person's input tax only to the extent (if any) provided for by regulations under subsection (6)(e).

The VBNB Manual provides:

> **VBNB30500-Apportionment of tax: why is apportionment of tax needed?**
> [Jan 2021]
> This section of the manual gives guidance on what to do when a business pays tax on goods or services that it intends to use for both:
> - business activities; and
> - non-business activities such as charitable activities.
>
> Guidance on what to do when a business pays tax on costs that are put to mixed business/private use can be found in VIT VAT Input Tax VIT25000.
> A business is unlikely to be able to treat all the tax it incurs as input tax if it undertakes both business and non-business activities. Any tax which relates:
> - to goods or services obtained solely for the purposes of the business activity is input tax; and
> - solely to the non-business activity is not input tax.
>
> Tax on goods and services that relates to both activities must be apportioned to identify the part that is input tax. An example of this would be tax paid on overhead costs.
> Section 24 of the Value Added Tax Act 1994 implies that businesses should directly attribute as much tax as possible to business and non-business activities. This should always be done. A business/non-business apportionment is not an alternative to direct attribution.
> After direct attribution there may be a block of costs which cannot be directly attributed to either category. The tax on this non-attributable expenditure has to be apportioned.
> Under VAT Act 1994 Section 24(5) the business has to apportion tax so that only tax which relates to their business purposes is treated as input tax.
> This is a different apportionment from that carried out under the partial exemption rules to work out what percentage of input tax can be recovered. Where a business:
> - has non-business activities for which it has not agreed a method of apportionment with HMRC; and
> - is partly exempt
>
> any apportionment should be done before the partial exemption calculation is

made.
Where:

- a business makes both taxable and exempt supplies; and
- apportionment between business and non-business use is needed under an agreement made before 1 January 2011

the apportionment process must be carried out before any partial exemption calculations. This is because the non-business element is non-business VAT and would have a distorting effect on the partial exemption calculations.
However, from 1 January 2011, if a business makes exempt supplies any new method must be a business/non-business and partial exemption method. See PE Partial Exemption for more on combined business/non-business and partial exemption methods.
A business should not combine a business/non-business and partial exemption calculation unless it has written approval for such a method from HMRC See PE Partial Exemption PE3000 and VBNB31000 for more on this.

VBNB31000-Apportionment of tax: methods of apportionment [Jan 2021]
The law does not ask a business to apportion tax incurred in any set way. Any method may be used if it results in a fair and reasonable apportionment of the tax. When making an apportionment you should keep in mind:

- the various activities of the business; and
- the purposes for which the cost is incurred.

Section 24(5) of VAT Act 1994 says a business should apportion tax to reflect its business and non-business purposes. Defining the purpose of an item of expenditure can be a subjective question. It is one on which different people may take different views.
In practice there is likely to be a range of acceptable apportionment figures. HMRC staff will normally only challenge an apportionment if it is completely outside what they think this range is.
It may be that a single apportionment of all overhead tax does not achieve a fair and reasonable result. Instead you may need to use a range of apportionments of different items of overhead costs.
Where non-business use is regarded as insignificant HMRC may use its discretion to allow a waiver of apportionment. There is no statutory de minimis level in terms of a monetary or percentage figure. It is a matter of judgement whether the benefit in terms of revenue is outweighed by:

- the administration cost to the business: and
- the cost to the Department in checking that an apportionment has been carried out.

If HMRC decides to allow a waiver of apportionment HMRC will write to the business and tell it that the arrangement applies only for as long as the existing low level of non-business use is kept up. If the extent of non-business use goes up to a significant level the business will need to make an apportionment.
A business may make both taxable and exempt supplies and have to make an apportionment between business and non-business use. Unless it has written approval from HMRC the business must carry out the apportionment process before, and quite separately from, any partial exemption calculations. See PE Partial Exemption PE30000.

The calculations must not be combined. This would prevent the business from correctly applying the partial exemption de minimis limit and the Capital Goods Scheme. For more on the Capital Goods Scheme, including what to do if the business has a combined method, see PE Partial Exemption PE67000.
Please note the partial exemption de minimis limit does not apply if a business has a combined method. The business must restrict any input tax recovery suggested by the calculation. This is so even if the result of a combined method calculation falls below the de minimis limit that would apply if the business has a separate partial exemption method.

VBNB33000:-Apportionment of tax: method for apportionment of tax [Jan 2021]

Fixed apportionment

The simplest method of apportionment is for the business to adopt a fixed percentage figure. It then applies this to the total non-attributable VAT it incurs. This can be an acceptable approach in cases where:

- the balance of the activities of the business does not fluctuate; and
- there is a good reason for adopting a particular percentage.

It can also be effective for those who:

- normally only undertake business activities; but
- undertake a one off non-business project involving a specific item of expenditure.

An example of this would be where a company hires an entertainer to provide a free Christmas party to the children of its employees and those from a local school.

Other indicators of non-business activity

The level of business and non-business activities may move up and down. When this happens a business should adopt a method of apportionment which can take account of any changes.
An ongoing apportionment method should reflect changes in the balance of activities. Therefore a method of business/non-business apportionment must be based upon reliable indicators of activity. There are many such indicators and methods based upon them.

Income based methods

Income is an obvious indicator of non-business activity. Income based methods are the most common business/non-business apportionments.
They usually work by the business:

- calling the income it gets from business supplies ‘business income’; and
- calling the income it gets from outside the scope sources such as grants ‘non-business’ income.

The apportionment is calculated each quarter by taking dividing the business income by the total income:

Total Income from business supplies (business income)	2000
Total Income from grants (non-business income)	3000
Total income from all sources	5000
Apportionment 2000/5000	40%

Income methods:

- are simple;
- rely on accounting information that is usually easy to get;
- rely on accounting information that can be easily checked; and
- are easy to work out the result from.

Sometimes they may not give a fair and reasonable result. This will be the case if the balance of activity does not reflect the balance of funding.

For example, an organisation that spends most of its time and resources on non-business activities may still get the majority of its income from business supplies. If this is so an income method would give a result that does not reflect the real non-business purpose behind most of the mixed expenditure.

An income based method will not give a fair and reasonable result if the commercial activities of a business are partly subsidised by grant income. For example, a basic income method would give a misleading result if applied to a heavily subsided transport operator who also ran free community projects.

Sometimes you can adapt income methods so that distortive income is taken out of the calculation. Alternatively you can weight the calculation in some way.

Complex income methods can work well when income is the best indicator on which to base a method. However, sometimes they can lead to a calculation that is over complicated to operate and monitor. When this happens it is usually better to find another, simpler method based on a different indicator.

Although an income based method is given as an example in section 33.5 of The VAT Guide, HMRC does not have an automatic preference for such methods. They are acceptable only if they give a fair and reasonable result and are simple to operate.

Expenditure based methods

These are a mirror of the income based method. In this type of method the business applies the ratio of business/non-business expenditure to the non-attributable tax.

They are only appropriate if the business can:

- attribute most of its expenditure into distinct business and non-business categories; and
- this ratio is a fair reflection of business and non-business activities.

When there is little directly attributable expenditure these methods give a misleading result and should not be used. An example of this would be where most of the tax incurred is non-attributable. When this happens there is unlikely to be sufficient information for the apportionment to be reliable.

Expenditure based methods are also not appropriate if the ratio of attributable expenditure is likely to be different from the extent of business use of the non-attributable goods and services.

For example, a charity with mostly non-business expenditure may buy a computer system to make taxable supplies of publications. It might only use the computer incidentally for non-business activities. When this happens, an expenditure based method could lead to an apportionment that understates the business purpose behind the computer purchase.

Time based methods

Some organisations keep detailed records of the amount of time spent by staff on business and non-business activities. This can provide a useful basis for a method of apportionment if the business/non-business ratio of staff time reflects the extent of business use of non-attributable costs.

In some cases staffing policy does not give a true indication of what VAT bearing goods and services will be used for. This is especially true if:

- the organisation's non-business work is staff intensive; and
- its business activities are goods and services intensive.

For example, an organisation may spend 90% of its staff time making free supplies of verbal advice to members of the public. The remaining staff time is spent making taxable supplies of publications and on paid consultancy services. Unlike the non-business work this business activity involves the charity spending money on goods and services rather than the non-VAT bearing wages of its staff. A simple time based method would lead to an apportionment that understated the true balance of business use of the overhead goods and services.

Transaction based methods

Some methods based upon a record of transactions such as:

- paid admissions to a museum; or
- books loaned out for a charge by a library

may be proposed.

A common difficulty with such methods is that non-business activities often do not involve recordable transactions. In contrast the business activities will involve making charges and making distinct, recordable supplies. In such cases a transactions based method can lead to an unfair result.

HMRC staff will not automatically dismiss transaction based methods. However, we will want to be sure that they are founded on a valid indicator of business and non-business activity.

VBNB34000:-Apportionment of tax: agreeing an apportionment method
[Jan 2021]

Businesses do not have to get HMRC's agreement for apportionment methods although some will ask for it.

However, many businesses do ask for agreement HMRC will consider all such requests and consider whether:

1. The result is fair and reasonable because the indicator of non-business activity on which the method is based gives a fair reflection of the balance between business and non-business activities.
2. The indicator on which the method is based will reflect changes in the extent of the business and non-business activities.
3. The method can be easily applied by the business and monitored by HMRC or is overcomplicated and prone to error.

Agreement will normally be given if HMRC is satisfied that the method is soundly based. Agreement will only be given if the business does not make exempt supplies.

The method will be agreed on the basis of the current levels of business and non-business activities. The method may no longer give an accurate apportionment if these levels change to a large extent.

A business should keep its method under review. It should notify HMRC if there are significant changes in the nature or levels of business/non-business activities. When agreeing methods, especially complex ones, HMRC will send a letter to the business indicating the basis on which we accept the method.

For example, if it is based on income it will be because at the time the agreement is made income provides an accurate indicator of non-business activity. It will be made clear in the agreement letter that the method will need to change if this is no longer the case.

If the method is complex HMRC will record its understanding of what is meant by the various terms and categories used in the method. Over time both HMRC staff and the representatives of the business who agreed the method are liable to change. It is important their successors have an understanding of how those who agreed the method thought it would work.

Any agreement on apportionment should be noted on HMRC's records. We will check that the agreed method has been carried out. We will also check that it still represents a fair and reasonable reflection of the business and non-business use of the relevant supplies.

A method for businesses with regular non-business activity should normally incorporate an annual adjustment calculation. However, if a cost is incurred totally for non-business purposes the recovery of VAT on that cost cannot subsequently be adjusted using an annual adjustment. That tax remains fully irrecoverable.

VBNB35000-Apportionment of tax: retrospective changes of method [Jan 2021]

If a business requests a retrospective change to a previously agreed method of apportionment it will need to demonstrate that:

- the former method did not produce a fair and reasonable result; and
- the proposed method does achieve this objective.

HMRC will normally approve the change provided these criteria are met. We will normally turn down the request if either of the criteria is not met. See Trustees of the Victoria and Albert Museum (VBNB73500).

Where the agreed method of apportionment is part of a combined business/non-business and partial exemption method a retrospective change of method is not normally allowed. Please see PE VAT Partial Exemption Guidance for more about the limited availability of retrospection in partial exemption methods.

VIT62540-Legal history: cases about apportionment [Mar 2022]

Please note that the following material is not a full summary of the case - it merely highlights the principle referred to in the appropriate section of this manual.

Victoria & Albert Museum Trustees 1996 STC1016

HMRC refused to agree a change of method retrospectively. From 1 April 1990 to 31 March 1993 the museum used an income-based method of apportionment. At that time the museum had a manual system of accounting that could not cope with direct attribution of tax incurred to business or non-business.

Such a system was eventually developed and adopted with effect from 1 April 1993. The museum applied the method retrospectively to 1 April 1990. It lodged

a voluntary disclosure which HMRC rejected.
The tribunal found that although the income based method was less favourable to the museum than the direct attribution method, it was a fair and reasonable method in the circumstances prevailing at the time it was used.
Therefore the museum had not made an error within the meaning of Regulation 64 of the VAT (General) Regulations (now Regulation 34). As a result it was not entitled to retrospectively adjust its input tax claim.
When it upheld the tribunal's decision to dismiss the appeal the High Court commented that: "The problem which, as it seems to me, the Museum is unable to surmount is in demonstrating of what the error consisted, that is of fact, law or otherwise ... there was no error of law. No error of fact is asserted other than that a method of assessment was chosen (please note that the judge is here referring to the Museum's chosen method of apportionment) which did not provide the most favourable outcome. It was nevertheless not one which involved an intrinsic error of fact or law."

VBNB36000-Apportionment of tax: errors in methods [Jan 2021]
Where HMRC has agreed a method with a business we will have recorded the proposed workings of the method. We will have shared this record of how the method should work with the business. This should help to reduce the chance of either the business or HMRC misunderstanding how to apply the method correctly.
However, if a business does make a mistake when using an agreed method it can rework the calculation. This will be subject to the normal time limits for making adjustments. (See VR VAT Refunds Manual VR6700)

VBNB37000-Apportionment of tax: challenging apportionments [Jan 2021]
HMRC cannot challenge a method. However, we can challenge the result it gives.
HMRC will not challenge the method immediately if a business proposes a method that:

- we agree currently gives a fair result; but
- we believe is likely to give an inaccurate result in future.

Instead we will:

- tell the business about our concerns now; and
- in the future challenge the misleading result.

HMRC may disagree with the proportion of tax a business treats as input tax. When this happens we will initially bring our concerns to the attention of the business. We will ask the business to alter or justify the result of its method.
If:

- the result is outside the range of what might be considered fair and reasonable; and
- the business will not change the proportion

HMRC will substitute our own judgement. We will then assess for the difference in input tax between our figures and those of the business.

The VBNB Manual provides guidance on a number of specific scenarios (services provided with the recovery of debts, disposal of works of art from historic houses, activities of museums and galleries etc). One example is:

> **VBNB43000-Specific issues: grant funded bodies** [Jan 2021]
> Some organisations get grants to support their activities. Grants are made by a number of bodies including central government, local government and the national lottery.
> Although they are normally outside the scope, sometimes such payments are direct consideration for a supply or third party consideration for a supply. Guidance on this is given at VATSC06300-Consideration: Payments that are not Consideration: Grants: Contents.
> The receipt of outside the scope income does not automatically mean that an activity is not business or lead to apportionment of input tax. You should look at each grant-funded activity separately and apply the business test.
> An activity is non-business if it:
> - involves the making of no taxable supplies for consideration; and
> - is entirely funded by outside the scope income.
>
> No tax incurred on the costs of a non-business activity can be treated as input tax.
> You should apply the business test if an activity involves:
> - the making of some taxable supplies; and
> - the receipt of some outside the scope income.
>
> The receipt of money to act as a subsidy for a loss making commercial activity need not result in input tax restriction. However, in many cases when an organisation gets outside the scope income it shows that there is a non-business activity. When this happens an apportionment is needed.
> Organisations may incur costs in applying for grants and other income that HMRC treats as being outside the scope of UK VAT. This is particularly true of applications for national lottery funding.
> Tax incurred on the process of applying for such funds is input tax if the intended activity the money is being applied for is a business activity. If the activity is not business, for example if it involves the making of no supplies for consideration, the tax incurred on getting the funding is not input tax. It does not matter whether the grant application is successful or not.

36.2 Right to recover input tax

Where the VAT on a supply of goods or services to a charity is input tax, its right to recover the input tax will depend on the nature of the supplies made or to be made by it in the course of the business carried on by it (i.e. whether the supplies are taxable, exempt or outside the scope with recovery).

Section 25 VATA provides:

> (1) A taxable person shall-
> (a) in respect of supplies made by him, ...

> account for and pay VAT by reference to such periods (in this Act referred to as "prescribed accounting periods") at such time and in such manner as may be determined by or under regulations and regulations may make different provision for different circumstances.
> (2) Subject to the provisions of this section, he is entitled at the end of each prescribed accounting period to credit for so much of his input tax as is allowable under section 26, and then to deduct that amount from any output tax that is due from him.
> (3) If either no output tax is due at the end of the period, or the amount of the credit exceeds that of the output tax then, subject to subsections (4) and (5) below, the amount of the credit or, as the case may be, the amount of the excess shall be paid to the taxable person by the Commissioners; and an amount which is due under this subsection is referred to in this Act as a "VAT credit" ...

This takes us to s.26 VATA which provides:

> (1) The amount of input tax for which a taxable person is entitled to credit at the end of any period shall be so much of the input tax for the period (that is input tax on supplies, ... and importations in the period) as is allowable by or under regulations as being attributable to supplies within subsection (2) below.
> (2) The supplies within this subsection are the following supplies made or to be made by the taxable person in the course or furtherance of his business-
> (a) taxable supplies;
> (b) supplies outside the United Kingdom which would be taxable supplies if made in the United Kingdom;
> (c) such other supplies outside the United Kingdom and such exempt supplies as the Treasury may by order specify for the purposes of this subsection ...

36.3 "Output tax"

Section 24(2) VATA provides:

> Subject to the following provisions of this section, "output tax", in relation to a taxable person, means VAT on supplies which he makes ...

36.4 Attribution

The PE Manual provides:

> **PE21000 - Partial Exemption principles: attribution** [Feb 2022]
> **Definition of attribution**
> Attribution is the process of determining how much of the input tax

incurred by a business relates to taxable supplies made or to be made. We attribute supplies received rather than purchase invoices. It should be borne in mind that several supplies can be included on one invoice or a single supply can be split over several invoices.

There are two main stages to this process. These are:

- direct attribution; and
- apportionment of the remaining tax.

Direct attribution

This is the identification of input tax on supplies that are wholly used, or to be used in making taxable supplies or wholly used or to be used in making exempt supplies. The tax used in making taxable supplies can be recovered in full, whereas the tax used or to be used in making exempt supplies cannot. Whatever input tax is non-attributable is carried forward to the next stage of the process. There is no provision for making ad hoc splits at this point, even if the full final use is known.

Whether any particular supply received can be directly attributed is a question of fact to be decided on the particular circumstances of each case. In order to make these decisions it is useful to understand two additional concepts that are used in categorising input tax. The cases discussed in PE21500 - Attribution case law - will further illuminate these issues.

Supplies can be directly attributed to taxable if they have a direct and immediate link to one or more taxable supplies made or to be made, and to neither any exempt supplies made or to be made nor to the business as a whole, so as to be a cost component of those supplies.

Direct and immediate link

This concept covers the degree of nexus required between a supply received and a supply made for the former to be a cost component of the latter.

This prevents any "look through" being applied to intervening transactions in favour of the ultimate purpose of the business involved. VAT is a transaction-based tax and costs incurred must therefore be linked to the immediate supplies made using them. What the business then does with revenues generated by those supplies is irrelevant.

In general there will be a temporal link, with the input coming before, but not greatly before, the output that it is leading towards. It is possible, however, for the input to be incurred either well before the output is made, or after the output is made, and still have a direct and immediate link. The former mostly occurring where goods have been in stock for a long time, the costs were initially speculative or there is a change of use. The latter mostly occurring where there are obligations on the supplier under a contract, which have not been fulfilled when that contract is signed, and which require further costs to be incurred at a

later date.
It is possible for costs incurred to have a direct and immediate link with more than one supply or with one or more supplies and with the business as a whole. General costs have a direct and immediate link to all of a business's supplies as they are cost components of the business as a whole. Unless all supplies that costs incurred have a direct and immediate link with are either taxable or exempt the costs will not be directly attributable.

Cost components

Input tax is deductible in so far as it is incurred on supplies that are cost components of transactions bearing the right to deduct associated input tax.

In normal accountancy practice all costs incurred are set against income receivable to work out a net profit. Thus all business expenses are cost components of some or all of the business's supplies, with general overheads being cost components of all the business's supplies.

Direct costs such as goods for resale, transport of those goods and selling expenses (e.g. salesmen's commissions) are generally set against the sales they relate to in a trading account leading to a gross profit. General overheads are then set against gross profit so as to arrive at net profit (or loss) for the business.

In deciding what supplies received are cost components of what supplies made, and to what degree, commercial reality is always relevant.

Supplies received as a consequence of supplies made

In general, supplies received as a consequence of making an output transaction, rather than as part of the normal cost components of making the supply, are not cost components of that output transaction. There is thus no direct and immediate link and such costs will normally be non-attributable. These costs include such things as defending litigation for alleged shoddy work or poor advice given.

Intention, change of intention and wasted costs

As any entitlement to deduct arises when VAT is incurred, it is the business's intention at that point that determines how it should be attributed. If that intention is subsequently frustrated so that the costs are wasted and put to no use in the business then there is no change to this initial entitlement. If, however, costs are put to another use within the business then the clawback and payback rules may apply. These are fully explained in PE61000 - Changes in intention or use.

36.5 Partial exemption

The PE Manual provides guidance on the recovery of non-attributable (or residual) input tax - i.e. input tax on supplies that are neither wholly used (or to be used) in making taxable supplies nor wholly used (or to be used) in making exempt supplies:

> **PE23000 - Partial Exemption principles: apportionment** [Feb 2022]
> **Introduction**
> Apportionment refers to dividing residual input tax between taxable and exempt supplies. All partial exemption methods will have one or more apportionment calculations.
> Potential alternative methods of apportionment are discussed below. Where businesses wish to use a calculation other than one based on income they will need to demonstrate that it is fair and reasonable (PE24000). This includes the requirement that a calculation which uses a non income based proxy can be guaranteed to be more accurate than one using the default income based methodology.
> **Outputs based apportionment**
> This is apportioning between supplies in the same ratio as the value of taxable supplies bears to the value of all supplies.
> This is the default measure of use, being the mechanism used for the standard method. It is most likely to give a fair and reasonable result where the supplies are made in the same tax year as the costs are incurred, and where the input tax bearing costs used in making a supply increase in proportion to the value of a supply, for instance where a £1,000 supply will use about ten times the costs of a £100 supply.
> Where there is the likelihood of large, distortive supplies that nevertheless use significant amounts of residual input tax, a sensible approach is to 'cap' the value of supplies at a level so that the method still gives a fair and reasonable result. For instance, treating any supply exceeding £10,000 as though it was £10,000 for the purpose of the calculation.
> A common problem encountered is when the input tax used in making supplies increases with the value of supplies made, but more slowly than the value of the supply itself. Often values and transactions may appear the most appropriate methods, but neither is 'accurate'. In such cases, either an alternative calculation must be found, or a judgement made as to which gives a fair and reasonable result.
> **Transaction based apportionment**
> This is apportioning between supplies in the same ratio as the number of taxable transactions made bears to all transactions made.
> Usually this involves counting the number of supplies made, rather than the value of those supplies. However, other 'numbers of things' might also be appropriate to count. For example, when considering residual input tax in respect of a landlord, the number of buildings where a taxable rental is charged divided by total number of buildings rented out.

Transaction counts tend to be appropriate where the supplies and the related input tax are incurred in the same tax year and where the costs involved are fairly constant whatever the value of a supply. It is a commonly used apportionment method in the finance sector. The costs involved are often fairly constant, whatever the value of shares traded, loans made, etc. Similar examples occur throughout the finance sector, and indeed in many other sectors.

When approving a transaction-based method, it is essential that both parties agree what will or will not be treated as a transaction, and that this is set out unambiguously in the special method approval letter. There are no simple answers as to what should be considered a transaction and what should not, it will depend on the supplies made, and how costs are used in making them.

It should be noted that transaction counts can be weighted, such that if, for example, supply A uses four times the input tax bearing costs of supply B, each occurrence of supply A will count as 4 transactions and each supply B will count as 1 transaction.

Staff time and headcount apportionment

These are calculations where the apportionment is made in the same ratio as the staff time spent making taxable supplies bears to all staff time.

Common residual input tax bearing costs are those that support staff, such as computers, lighting, heating, rental, telephones and training. Staff time spent on different activities is in theory a very good method of apportioning these types of costs.

However, staff time based methods are only appropriate where the staff record their time for purposes other than partial exemption calculations and the liability of the supplies they are working on can be identified. For example, solicitors and accountants will record time regularly on time sheets for fee accuracy, but most other businesses will not.

For these reasons, staff time is rarely a fair and reasonable method of attributing input tax, often being both difficult to operate and impossible to verify.

A headcount method is similar to the staff numbers allocation method and has a similar effect to the using of staff time. However, it can be used by a business that does not keep time sheets. It is most likely to give a result that reflects the use of the input tax in the same circumstances as for staff time, but only where a significant proportion of staff are employed in areas that are involved in making supplies of only one liability.

Input tax and inputs based apportionment

These are calculations where the apportionment is made in the same ratio as the costs directly attributable to taxable supplies bear to all directly attributable costs.

These calculations are most commonly used where costs involved in making supplies are normally incurred in a different tax year than the year the supplies are made. To be able to produce a fair and reasonable result:

there must be directly attributable costs incurred relating to both taxable and exempt supplies;

a significant proportion of the costs must be directly attributable; and

the directly attributable costs must be incurred in about the same proportion as the residual input tax is used to make taxable and exempt supplies.

A property developer is a good example of a business for which such a method may produce a fair and reasonable result. The majority of residual input tax is likely to be incurred on staff supporting costs relating to the management of the various projects. The greater the costs relating to a project, the more time is likely to be spent managing it and thus the more residual input tax bearing costs relate to it.

Rather than costs, directly attributable input tax may be a more appropriate calculation, although this will not be the case if there are substantial exempt and / or zero-rated supplies received, or where one or both liabilities of supply is labour intensive.

Floor space apportionment

This is apportionment in the same ratio as the floor space occupied by income generating staff involved exclusively in making taxable supplies bears to the total floor space of income generating staff.

This is most likely to produce a fair and reasonable result where the residual input tax bearing costs relate primarily to buildings, such as taxable rent incurred, heating, lighting, fixtures and fittings. In order to reflect use, it requires that specific areas be used for supplies of a particular liability and that these represent the predominant proportion of the floor area.

Where staff are spread relatively evenly, such as in an office, a floor space calculation will normally produce a similar result to a headcount calculation. However, where the distribution of staff is uneven, a floor space calculation is more likely to reflect use than a headcount one. For instance, consider a business with a warehouse making exclusively taxable supplies and an office above making exclusively exempt supplies. The warehouse will have few staff in it, but use a significant amount of residual costs. Thought will need to be given as to whether input tax incurred on non-building related costs should be apportioned in the same ratio, since it is likely that the office would incur a greater proportion of, for example, telephone and computer related costs.

When considering a floor space calculation, you should satisfy yourself that the business has correctly identified directly attributable floor space. For instance, shops that sell taxable goods and exempt insurance on those goods often claim the display areas relate only to the taxable supplies. In fact, these areas are also used to make exempt supplies, since the intention in displaying the goods is to make both types of supply. The exempt insurance could not be sold if the goods themselves were not displayed. This means that very little floor space is directly attributable and the method is unlikely to produce a meaningful result. Accordingly floor space calculations are rarely fair and reasonable for the retail sector.

This was illustrated in the Tribunal case of Optika Ltd [VTD 18627] and confirmed in Banbury Visionplus & others [VTD 19266 & STC 1568]. Optika, a retail optician appealed against the Commissioners' rejection of their proposed floor area based special method, and the Tribunal agreed that it did not give a fair and reasonable result. The following features from the Optika case demonstrate this.

Notional Splits of 'Mixed Use' Areas - Few areas of Optika's premises were exclusively used for taxable or exempt activities, and the proposals called for notional splits of mixed use floor areas to create a workable calculation. This is unacceptable due to the inherent uncertainties in making and checking them.

Weighting of Floor areas - The proposed method required a weighting of the floor areas with those at the front of the shop having greater impact on the amount of tax deductible. Optika argued that this reflected a series of weightings, known as zoning used by landlords to calculate rents. The Tribunal held that each rental is a single supply covering the entire premises.

Use of Retail Areas - Optika assumed that the use made of the retail area and the shop front related to their taxable products. However the shop front attracted purchasers to purchase all of their products, and much of the selling of the exempt products took place in the retail area. Because the proposals were based on a mistaken assumption, they were unacceptable.

Similar findings were made in the Banbury Visionplus case.

You must not approve any method that includes one or more of the features confirmed as unacceptable in the Optika case. If you discover that a retailer is using such a method, you should contact your local PESO or TAPE officer for advice regarding withdrawal or amendment of the method.

The value to be used for the denominator

With all apportionment calculations, it is worth considering whether a fair and reasonable result is achieved by putting the taxable plus exempt figure or the total figure in the denominator (bottom line of the

> calculation). It is often argued that use of a denominator that includes the residual amount being apportioned is mathematically flawed.
>
> We are concerned with achieving a fair and reasonable result, not with the mathematical purity of calculations. The purpose of a method is to reflect the use of input tax bearing costs in making taxable supplies. If that is best achieved by the inclusion of the residual amount within the denominator then it should be so included.
>
> For example, imagine a situation where 5% of the input tax bearing cost of an organisation is directly attributable to taxable supplies and 20% of the input tax bearing cost is directly attributable to exempt supplies. This means 75% of the input tax is used to support both taxable and exempt supplies although the vast majority of it is used in support of exempt activity (say for example to support the provision of member's facilities at a golf club where some food and alcoholic drinks are sold; this tax is residual following the decision in Bridgnorth Golf Club, [2009] UKFTT 126).
>
> In such a situation a formula of taxable input tax over total input tax is more likely to produce a fair and reasonable result than taxable input tax over taxable plus exempt input tax.
>
> This is because 5/100 or 5% is likely to be closer to the actual use of the costs than 5/25 (5+20) or 20%.

36.6 University of Cambridge

The University of Cambridge is a charity. It provides education (making exempt supplies) and engages in a variety of other activities (such as commercial research, publication, consultancy) (making taxable supplies). It agreed a partial exemption special method (or PESM) with HMRC for the apportionment of its residual input tax.

The University also paysdonations and endowments into an Endowment Fund, the funds of which are then invested, producing an annual income which income is then used by the University then uses to fund its range of (taxable and exempt) activities.

A dispute arose between the University and HMRC over whether VAT the University had incurred in respect of the management of the Fund was recoverable.

As summarised by the Court of Appeal [2018] EWCA Civ 568:

> 7. It is common ground that the investment activity carried out by the managers of the Fund on behalf of the University is not in itself an economic activity so that the transactions carried out by the Fund are outside the scope of VAT. No input tax in the form of VAT payable on the management fees would therefore be recoverable if the fees must be

> treated for VAT purposes as directly and exclusively attributable to the investment activities themselves. But it was contended … on behalf of the University that the purpose of the Fund was to generate income to be used to support the general activities of the University (including the taxable and exempt activities we have mentioned) and that the VAT incurred on the fees should therefore be treated as residual input tax [*with some of it recoverable*] in accordance with the PESM.

The University prevailed in both the First-tier and Upper Tribunals. HMRC appealed to the Court of Appeal, which came to the conclusion that:

> 53. … the correct approach to be taken to the issue of attribution in this case is not acte clair and we propose to refer the matter for guidance to the CJEU under Article 267 TFEU.

Of the four questions referred to the CJEU, the key one was:

> Is any distinction to be made between exempt and non-taxable transactions for the purpose of deciding whether VAT incurred for the purposes of such transactions is deductible?

The CJEU ruled:

> [24] … transactions that do not fall within the scope of the VAT Directive or that are exempt … do not, in principle, give rise to a right to deduct …
>
> …
>
> [28] In the present case, in order to answer the question whether, in circumstances such as those in the main proceedings, it is possible to deduct VAT paid in respect of the costs associated with the investment of donations and endowments in a fund with the aim of generating resources intended to finance the whole range of activities of an educational establishment such as the University of Cambridge, it is necessary to determine, at the outset, whether the collection of those donations and endowments and their investment in a fund constitute an economic activity within the meaning of the VAT Directive and, on that basis, fall within the scope of that directive.
>
> [29] In this respect, it must be found that, in raising and collecting donations and endowments, the University of Cambridge is not acting as a taxable person. In order to be considered to be a taxable person, a person must carry out economic activities, that is to say activities for consideration. As the donations and endowments - which are essentially made for subjective reasons on charitable grounds and on a random basis - are not consideration for any economic activity, the raising and

collection of them do not fall within the scope of the VAT Directive (see, to that effect, judgment of 3 March 1994, Tolsma, C-16/93, EU:C:1994:80, paragraphs 17 to 19) ... it follows that the input VAT paid in respect of any costs incurred in connection with the collection of donations and endowments is not deductible, regardless of the reason why those donations and endowments were received.

[30] Both the activity consisting in the investment of donations and endowments, and the costs associated with that investment activity must be treated in the same way for VAT purposes as the non-economic activity consisting in the collection of donations and endowments and any costs associated with the latter. Not only does such financial investment activity constitute, for the University of Cambridge, much like a private investor, a means of generating income from the donations and endowments raised, but it is also an activity that may be directly linked to their collection and, consequently, is merely a direct continuation of that non-economic activity. Accordingly, input VAT paid in respect of the costs associated with that investment is also non-deductible.

[31] It is true that the fact that costs are incurred in the acquisition of a service in the context of a non-economic activity does not, in itself, preclude those costs giving rise to a right to deduct in the context of the taxable person's economic activity, if they are incorporated into the price of particular output transactions or into the price of goods and services provided by the taxable person in the context of that economic activity (see, to that effect, judgment of 26 May 2005, Kretztechnik, C-465/03, EU:C:2005:320, paragraph 36).

[32] However, in the present case, it is apparent from the documents before the Court that, first, costs relating to the management of donations and endowments invested in the fund concerned are not incorporated into the price of a particular output transaction. Second, as it is apparent from the documents before the Court that (i) the University of Cambridge is a not-for-profit educational establishment and (ii) the costs at issue are incurred in order to generate resources that are used to finance all of that university's output transactions, thus allowing the price of the goods and services provided by the latter to be reduced, those costs cannot be considered to be components of those prices and, consequently, do not form part of that university's overheads. In any event, as there is no direct and immediate link in the present case either between those costs and a particular output transaction or between those costs and the activities of the University of Cambridge as a whole, the VAT relating to those costs is not deductible.

CHAPTER THIRTY SEVEN

VAT: EXEMPTION

37.1 Rates, exemption and zero rating

There are three rates of VAT.

37.1.1 *Standard rate: 20%*

Section 2 VATA provides the standard rate:

> (1) Subject to the following provisions of this section and to the provisions of section 29A, VAT shall be charged at the rate of 20 per cent and shall be charged—
> (a) on the supply of goods or services, by reference to the value of the supply as determined under this Act...

37.1.2 *Reduced rate: 5%*

Section 29A VATA provides:

> (1) (a) any supply that is of a description for the time being specified in Schedule 7A...
> shall be charged at the rate of 5 per cent.

It is therefore necessary to turn to schedule 7A to discover which supplies are charged at the reduced rate of 5%. The schedule is a strange ragbag of categories, divided into the following groups:

Cable-suspended passenger transport systems
Caravans
Children's car seats
Contraceptive products
Domestic fuel or power
Energy-saving materials: installation
Heating equipment, security goods and gas supplies: grant-funded installation or connection
Installation of mobility aids for the elderly
Residential renovations and alterations
Residential conversions
Smoking cessation products
Welfare advice or information
Women's sanitary products

These are not discussed here. They are only occasionally relevant to charities.

37.1.3 *Zero rate*

Section 30 VATA provides:

> (1) Where a taxable person supplies goods or services and the supply is zero-rated, then, whether or not VAT would be chargeable on the supply apart from this section—
> (a) no VAT shall be charged on the supply; but
> (b) it shall in all other respects be treated as a taxable supply;
> and accordingly the rate at which VAT is treated as charged on the supply shall be nil.
> (2) A supply of goods or services is zero-rated by virtue of this subsection if the goods or services are of a description for the time being specified in schedule 8 or the supply is of a description for the time being so specified...

There are 16 groups specified in schedule 8, numbered (non-numerically, as one might expect) to 18. Part 1 of the schedule provides an alphabetical index:

Bank notes	Group 11	Food	Group 1
Books etc	Group 3	Gold	Group 10
Caravans and houseboats	Group 9	Imports, exports etc	Group 13
Charities etc	Group 15	International services	Group 7
Clothing and footwear	Group 16	Protected buildings	Group 6
Construction of buildings etc	Group 5	Sewerage services and water	Group 2
Drugs, medicines and aids for the disabled etc	Group 12	Talking books for the blind and disabled and wireless sets for the blind	Group 4
European Research Infrastructure Consortia	Group 18	Transport	Group 8

Zero rating is discussed in the next chapter.

37.1.4 *VAT exemption*

Exemption must be distinguished from zero rating.
Section 31 VATA provides:

> (1) A supply of goods or services is an exempt supply if it is of a description for the time being specified in Schedule 9 and an acquisition of goods from another member State is an exempt acquisition if the goods are acquired in pursuance of an exempt supply.
> (2) The Treasury may by order vary that Schedule by adding to or deleting from it any description of supply or by varying any description

> of supply for the time being specified in it, and the Schedule may be varied so as to describe a supply of goods by reference to the use which has been made of them or to other matters unrelated to the characteristics of the goods themselves

There are 15 groups specified in schedule 9. Part 1 of the schedule provides an alphabetical index:

Betting, gaming, dutiable machine games and lotteries	Group 4
Burial and cremation	Group 8
Cultural services etc	Group 13
Education	Group 6
Finance	Group 5
Fund raising events by charities and other qualifying bodies	Group 12
Health and welfare	Group 7
Insurance	Group 2
Investment gold	Group 15
Land	Group 1
Postal services	Group 3
Sport, sports competitions and physical education	Group 10
Supplies of goods where input tax cannot be recovered	Group 14
Supplies of services by groups involving cost sharing	Group 16
Subscriptions to trade unions, professional and other public interest bodies	Group 9
Works of art etc	Group 11

37.1.5 *Scope of chapter*

This chapter discusses the exemptions which most concern charities, in the following order:

Exemption	**Group**	**VAT Directive article 132(1)**
Education	6	*(i)*
Welfare	7	*(g)*
Subscriptions	9	*(l)*
Sports	10	*(m)*
Cultural services	13	*(n)*
Fundraising events	12	*(o)*

37.2 Restrictions on exemptions

A number of the exemptions in article 132 VAT Directive are subject to arts 133 and 134 which impose two sets of restrictions on the exemptions. The restrictions apply to all the exemptions discussed in this chapter except for article 132(1)(o) (fundraising events).

Two points should be noted in this respect: the first being that article 132(1)(o) is subject to its own specific restriction in article 132(2):

> For the purposes of point (o) of paragraph 1, Member States may

> introduce any restrictions necessary, in particular as regards the number of events or the amount of receipts which give entitlement to exemption.

Also, article 132(1)(o) only applies where the activities of the organisation in question are exempt under article 132(1)(b), (g), (h) (i), (l), (m) or (n):

> the supply of services and goods, by organisations whose activities are exempt pursuant to points (b), (g), (h), (i), (l), (m) and (n), in connection with fund-raising events organised exclusively for their own benefit, provided that exemption is not likely to cause distortion of competition;

If, therefore, article 133 or 134 applies to exclude (say) the provision of education by a particular body from the exemption provided for under article 132(1)(i), and the provision of education is the only activity carried on by that body, then the supplies made by that body on a fund-raising event would also fall outside the exemption provided for under article 132(1)(o).

However, unlike article 132(1)(o), VATA sch 9 Group 12 (Fund-Raising Events by Charities and Other Qualifying Bodies) does not refer to "organisations whose activities are exempt" by virtue of the relevant provisions, but simply to charities and qualifying bodies (as defined). On its face, therefore, the domestic provision is wider than its equivalent in the VAT Directive.

Where relevant, under CJEU jurisprudence (as cited in *GMAC UK*, Case C-589/12):

> ... a Member State which has not adopted the implementing measures required by a directive within the prescribed period may not plead, as against individuals, its own failure to perform the obligations which the directive entails ...

37.2.1 *Article 133 restrictions*

Article 133 VAT Directive provides:

> Member States may make the granting to bodies other than those governed by public law of each exemption provided for in points (b), (g), (h), (i), (l), (m) and (n) of Article 132(1) subject in each individual case to one or more of the following conditions:
>
> (a) the bodies in question must not systematically aim to make a profit, and any surpluses nevertheless arising must not be distributed, but must be assigned to the continuance or improvement of the services supplied;
>
> (b) those bodies must be managed and administered on an

> essentially voluntary basis by persons who have no direct or indirect interest, either themselves or through intermediaries, in the results of the activities concerned;
>
> (c) those bodies must charge prices
>   [i] which are approved by the public authorities or
>   [ii] which do not exceed such approved prices or,
>   [iii] in respect of those services not subject to approval, prices lower than those charged for similar services by commercial enterprises subject to VAT;
>
> (d) the exemptions must not be likely to cause distortion of competition to the disadvantage of commercial enterprises subject to VAT ...

These restrictions apply to "bodies other than those governed by public law" so they apply to charities.

37.2.2 *Article 134 restrictions*

Article 134 VAT Directive provides two further restrictions:

> The supply of goods or services shall not be granted exemption, as provided for in points (b), (g), (h), (i), (l), (m) and (n) of Article 132(1), in the following cases:
>
> (a) where the supply is not essential to the transactions exempted;
>
> (b) where the basic purpose of the supply is to obtain additional income for the body in question through transactions which are in direct competition with those of commercial enterprises subject to VAT.

The article 134 restrictions are compulsory, whereas the article 133 restrictions apply at the option of the Member State, ie the Member States may choose whether or not to apply those restrictions.

In *London Borough of Ealing*[1], the CJEU considered how article 133 should be construed:

> 29 While Article 133 of [the] directive permits the Member States to subject the grant of that exemption to compliance with additional conditions, it is apparent from the wording of the first paragraph of that article that Member States may apply the conditions specified in that paragraph, namely points (a) to (d), as a general rule, only to bodies other than those governed by public law. As regards bodies governed by public law, the second paragraph of that article confers the right only to

---

1 Case C-633/15.

impose on them the condition laid down in point (d) of the first paragraph of that article, which is designed to ensure that there is no distortion of competition to the disadvantage of commercial enterprises, that right being conferred solely on Member States which applied, on 1 January 1989, VAT to the supplies of services referred to in Article 132(1)(m) of that directive.

30 Accordingly, the possibility made available to Member States of excluding the grant of a VAT exemption with respect to supplies of services closely linked to sport or physical education, within the meaning of Article 132(1)(m) of Directive 2006/112, on the basis of Article 133 of that directive, is more closely circumscribed for non-profit making organisations governed by public law than for other non-profit making organisations. As the Advocate General stated in point 27 of his Opinion, the latter provision is designed to place bodies governed by public law at an advantage as compared with other bodies in relation to the exemption of supplies of services closely linked to sport or physical education made by them.

Following the case, HMRC issued Revenue and Customs Brief 6 (2017): VAT - treatment of sports facilities by local councils [29 December 2017], in which it states:

...

Explanation of change

The effect of the [*CJEU*] judgment is that councils can opt to make a claim for exemption on the sporting services that they supply to members of the public under the European VAT directive. This means that related VAT on inputs will be restricted where it isn't treated as insignificant under paragraph 8.2 of VAT Notice 749: local authorities and similar bodies

The alternative is that they can continue to tax those supplies on the basis of UK law. This means that VAT on inputs will continue to be recoverable where it relates to taxable supplies.

HMRC expects councils to account for VAT on a consistent basis. This means that where councils have opted to make a claim for exemption in respect of past periods, they'll be expected to continue to exempt supplies in subsequent periods. Claims won't be accepted where councils have proceeded on an inconsistent basis.

Background

... local authorities are entitled to recover any net over-declarations they have made as a result of having treated the supplies as taxable rather than exempt. The net over-declarations are calculated after deducting from the over-declared output tax any input tax wrongly claimed by

prescribed accounting period (VAT return) on the assumption that the supplies in question were taxable and not exempt, unless that input tax is treated as insignificant read paragraph 8.2 of VAT Notice 749: local authorities and similar bodies

Outstanding appeals to the First-tier VAT Tribunal

HMRC now intends to process outstanding claims made by local authorities making supplies of services closely related to sport where:

- the local authorities concerned have asserted their right to direct effect of the sporting exemption on the basis of London Borough of Ealing (Case C 633/15) on a consistent basis?
- subject to satisfactory verification of the amounts claimed

This won't include any amounts claimed on other grounds. Where that amount results in an interim net payment to the local authority, then that amount will be credited.

Unjust enrichment

HMRC reserves the right to refuse claims on the grounds of unjust enrichment where they're able to show that the claimant passed the economic burden of the VAT charge on to their customers. The provisions are explained in sections 9 and 10 of VAT Notice 700/45: how to correct VAT errors and make adjustments or claims

HMRC may examine the quantum of the claim, including the requirement to apply revised partial exemption and capital goods scheme calculations to ensure claims are accurate.

…

37.3 "Body governed by public law"

The VATGPB Manual provides:

VATGPB3250-Non-business activities: whether provided as a public authority: other key Tribunal decisions [Feb 2022]

The question of whether a body is governed by public law has been considered by the VAT Tribunal in the following cases.

In the *Arts Council of Great Britain* (VTD 11991) the point at issue was whether the Council, in providing services to the Department of National Heritage and to the recipients of grants that it distributed, was carrying on a taxable business and therefore able to recover input tax. Although the Arts Council is not referred to in section 33 of the VAT Act 1994, the chairman considered that the Council was

> "'a public body, performing a public function, whose costs were paid out of public funds'."

In relation to those activities the Arts Council, an Executive Non-Departmental Public Body)was not, therefore a taxable person for the purposes of the VAT Act or Article 4(5) of the Sixth VAT Directive (now Article 13(1) of the Principal VAT Directive - see VATGPB2100). It was therefore unable to recover input tax.

In the *Royal Academy of Music* (VTD11871) the appeal primarily concerned a refusal to approve the issue of a certificate for the zero rating of alterations to a listed building which formed part of the Academy's premises.

The Academy considered that the alterations to the property were eligible for zero rating on the grounds that the Academy was a registered charity and that the use of the premises was not in the course or furtherance of a business. It was also argued that if the provision of education in return for tuition fees was considered to be a business activity, albeit exempt for VAT purposes, then its status as a body governed by public law enabled it to treat the provision of education as an activity undertaken in its capacity as a public authority. The supply of education, as a result, being a non-business activity.

In dismissing the appeal, the Tribunal held that the Academy was not a statutory body. Its provision of education was not 'in pursuance of any statutory duties' and therefore its activities fell outside the scope of the then Article 4(5) of the Sixth VAT Directive (now Article 13(1) of the Principal VAT Directive and now Section 41A of the VAT Act 1994).

The law was recently considered by the Court of Appeal in *Open University v HMRC.*[2]

The case concerned services comprising the production and broadcasting of television and radio programmes supplied by the BBC to the Open University in relation to the latter's courses. In assessing whether such services were exempt within article 132(1)(i) VAT Directive, the Chancellor (Sir Terence Etherton) noted that:

> 11 The following general principles applicable to the interpretation of Article [132](1)(i) are…common ground. The exemption in Article [132](1)(i), like all exemptions in the [VAT Directive], is an autonomous concept of Community law. It is to be interpreted strictly since it constitutes an exception to the general principle that VAT is to be levied on all services supplied for consideration by a taxable person. Its interpretation must nevertheless be consistent with the objectives pursued by the exemption and must comply with the requirement of fiscal neutrality inherent in the common system of VAT. Accordingly, the requirement of strict interpretation does not mean that the terms used

2 [2016] EWCA Civ 114.

> in Article [132](1)(i) should be interpreted in such a way as to deprive the exemption of its intended effect …
> 12 A strict interpretation in this context does not mean a restricted interpretation …

The issues were whether, as the Chancellor noted, for the purposes of article 132(1)(i):

> 13 … (1) the BBC was a "body governed by public law"; and if so (2) it had the requisite educational aim; and if not satisfying both those conditions, nevertheless (3) the BBC was "defined" by the UK as having "similar objects", and, if it was not so "defined" but did have "similar objects", it can still claim the direct benefit of the Article [132](1)(i) exemption.
> 14 HMRC has always accepted that the [Open University] had the university educational aim required by Article [132](1)(i) and that the services supplied by the BBC to [Open University] during the relevant period were closely related to the university education provided by the [Open University].

On the first issue - whether the BBC was a "body governed by public law" - it was accepted that the concept of such a body had an autonomous meaning under EU law. The Chancellor referred to the case of *Saudaçor* (Case C-174/14), where:

> 69 The ECJ elaborated … (at para 56) that a person which, not being part of the public administration, independently performs acts falling within the powers of a public authority cannot be classified as a body governed by public law, within the meaning of Article 13(1). It said (at para 57) that the court had made it clear that the status of a "body governed by public law" cannot stem from the mere fact that the relevant activity consists of the performance of acts falling within powers conferred by public law. The ECJ went on to say (at para 58), however, that while the fact that the body in question has, under the applicable national law, powers conferred by public law is not decisive for the purposes of the classification, it does constitute a factor of definite importance in determining whether the body must be classified as a body governed by public law.

Applying the principles laid down by the CJEU in *Saudaçor*, the Chancellor found that the BBC was not a "body governed by public law". He then turned to consider whether it had "similar objects" for the purposes of article 132(1)(i):

88 In order to understand the debate on this issue it is necessary to separate the following matters which arise. (1) It is common ground that the first part of Article [132](1)(i) is not satisfied unless the body governed by public law ("the public body") supplies one of the six specified types of education, that is to say children or young people's education, school or university education, vocational training or retraining. It is not sufficient if the public body only aims to supply "services and goods closely related thereto". (2) On the other hand, a public body which supplies and aims to supply one of those six types of education (say, university education) does not fall outside the first part of Article [132](1)(i) if it supplies closely related services to another body which has a different one of the six specified educational aims (say, assisting a school's education programme). (3) There is disagreement between the parties as to what organisational requirements must be met by the public body to enable the supply of education to fall within the first part of Article [132](1)(i). (4) There is disagreement between the parties as to whether the word "similar" in the expression "similar objects" at the end of the second part of Article [132](1)(i) means "the same" or denotes a broader "likeness".

89 HMRC contends that the expression "similar objects" at the end of the second part of Article [132](1)(i) means "the same objects", in the sense that the "other organisations" must have the object of providing one or more of the six specified types of education in the *Horizon College*[3] sense...HMRC's explanation for the use of the word "similar" is that, unlike public bodies or most public bodies, the principal aim of many private bodies is to make a profit and so it would be wrong to say that they have a purely educational aim.

90 The [Open University] contends that "similar" does not mean "the same"...At first sight that argument faces the difficulty that it would be contrary to the principle of fiscal neutrality if entitlement to the exemption in Article [132](1)(i) was different for public bodies, on the one hand, and private bodies, on the other hand. That principle precludes economic operators, who are carrying out the same transactions, from being treated differently in relation to the levying of VAT, and, in particular, treating similar supplies of goods and services, which are in competition with each other, differently for VAT purposes.

The Chancellor rejected the Open University's arguments and held that the expression "similar objects" means the "same objects". Turning then to the parties' dispute over organisational structure, he noted that:

---

3 [2008] STC 2145.

94 ...This issue arises from the decision in the *Horizon College* case. Horizon College was a teaching establishment in the Netherlands, which mainly provided secondary and vocational education. It also seconded teachers in its employment to other educational establishments to meet temporary shortages of teaching staff. Under the contract of secondment it was for those other establishments to define the duties of the teacher concerned. The teacher's salary continued to be paid by Horizon College, which then claimed the cost back from the other establishment, without taking any profit or charging VAT. The Dutch tax authorities considered that the secondment services provided by Horizon College were not covered by the exemption in Article [132](1)(i), and assessed them to VAT. The ECJ held that the provision of teachers in those circumstances did not fall within the expression "children's or young people's education, school or university education, vocational training or retraining" within Article [132](1)(i) but might be exempt from VAT as a supply of services "closely related" to education if such a teacher placement was a means of better enjoying the education deemed to be the principal service - which it was for the national court to decide.
95 The important point ... is that the ECJ held that the transfer of knowledge and skills between a teacher and students as a result of the secondment was not sufficient to amount to a supply of one of the six types of education specified in Article [132](1)(i) and that an organisational framework was also necessary.

...

96 The ECJ...said as follows:

...

> 20 ...the educational activity referred to in Article [132](1)(i) consists of a combination of elements which include, along with those relating to the teacher/student relationship, also those which make up the organisational framework of the establishment concerned."

...

99 It is common ground, and was common ground before the FTT and the UT, that the requisite educational aim (and organisational framework) must be considered in relation to all the BBC's educational activities and not merely those which it provided for the [Open University]. The FTT and the UT nevertheless reached different conclusions on whether the Horizon College requirements were met in the present case, the FTT deciding that they were not and the UT deciding that they were. I find that UT was plainly correct on this issue [in holding that the only reasonable conclusion was that the UK, acting through a combination of the royal prerogative and Parliament, had

> brought about a situation where the BBC was defined by it as an organisation having the requisite educational aim].

On whether the BBC was "defined" by the UK for the purposes of article 132(1)(i), the Chancellor stated as follows:

> 120 I do not consider…that it is either necessary or indeed desirable for this court to reach a concluded view on this important issue, which I do not consider to be "acte clair" since what is plain is that the [Open University] is entitled to rely directly on Article [132](1)(i) in the present case.
>
> …
>
> 123 …Either the UK had defined the BBC as having "similar objects" within Article [132](1)(i) or, if the United Kingdom had not, the BBC and the [Open University] are entitled to rely directly on that Article because the failure of the UK was a failure to implement the [VAT Directive]. The object of the education and training exemption was intended to increase access to the services specified in Article [132](1)(i) by avoiding the increased costs that would result if they were subject to VAT…To exclude the BBC from the exemption would both be contrary to the objective of the [VAT Directive] and contrary to the principle of fiscal neutrality.

Lord Justice Lewison agreed with the Chancellor:

> 125 … that HMRC's appeal should be dismissed. I agree with the Chancellor for the reasons that he gives that the BBC is not a body governed by public law. I agree also that the BBC had the requisite educational aim, although my reasoning differs slightly. In my view the key points which lead to that conclusion are HMRC's acceptance that:
>
> i) The supplies made by the BBC to the [Open University] were supplies "closely related" to the [Open University]'s educational aim of providing university education;
> ii) The supplier's educational aim need not be its sole, or even its principal aim; and
> iii) The supplier need not have an educational aim falling within the same type of education as the educational aim of the recipient of the supply. Provided that its aim fell within one of the specified categories of education the supplier would still have "such" as its aim.
>
> …
>
> 136 I agree also with the Chancellor, for the reasons that he gives, that even if the BBC was not "defined by" the United Kingdom it was entitled to rely on the directly applicable effect of article [132](1)(i). As

the Chancellor has pointed out in the *JP Morgan* case[4] the CJEU held that a member state's discretion to implement a directive was limited by (a) the purpose of the exemption (see [45]) (b) the principle of fiscal neutrality (see [46]) and (c) the elimination of distortion of competition, even if that distortion is not substantial (see [47]). In those circumstances if the United Kingdom, exercising its discretion, had refused to define the BBC as having "similar objects" to those specified in article [132](1)(i) it would have exceeded its discretion. The JP Morgan case also shows that the existence of a discretion conferred upon a member state does not preclude a provision in a directive from being sufficiently precise as to be directly enforceable, at least where the member state could not legitimately have exercised its discretion so as to exclude the claimant from the exemption.

37.4 Distortion of competition

A common requirement of VAT exemptions is that they should not cause distortion of competition. The VATGPB Manual provides:

VATGPB3320:-Non-business activities: distortions of competition: key Tribunal decisions [Feb 2022]
Distortion of competition has been examined on several occasions by the VAT Tribunal. In the *City of Westminster* (or 'Bruce House') case (VTD 3367) it considered whether the provision of very basic accommodation for homeless men at Bruce House formed part of the business activities of the local authority.
The Council was able to demonstrate that it had a statutory obligation to provide the accommodation under the National Assistance Act 1948 and was therefore acting in its capacity as a public authority. There was also a specific identifiable charge made for the supply, although this did not cover the full cost of providing it.
Although the Tribunal accepted that the accommodation was similar to that provided in hotels, inns and boarding houses, it concluded that there was in reality no private sector competition for the particular type of accommodation provided at Bruce House. Consequently no distortion of competition arose from the supply being treated as non-business.
In *Rhondda Cynon Taff County Borough Council* (VTD 16496) the issue was whether the provision of local authority cemeteries was an exempt business supply. It was found that the statutory conditions under which local authorities operate their cemeteries, for example The Local Authorities' Cemeteries Order 1977 (SI 1977/204), mean that they are provided under a special legal regime.

---

4 Case C-363/05.

Furthermore, although there are nearly 3000 cemeteries in the United Kingdom, few are privately operated. Consequently it does not distort competition for local authority cemeteries to be treated as non-business.

VATGPB3330-Non-business activities: distortions of competition: significant distortion [Feb 2022]
Although an activity may be identified as being in competition with the private sector, it can be more difficult to determine whether non-business treatment will lead to a significant distortion of competition.
The off-street car parking case of Isle of Wight Council (see also VATGPB8616) has indicated that the burden of proof lies with HMRC and not the public body to show that significant distortion of competition exists in relation to an activity performed by a public body. The Tribunal referred several questions to the Court of Justice of the European Union(CJEU) (C 288/07) to clarify how this question should be considered.
The CJEU ruled that competition between public bodies and private operators must be considered in terms of the activity that is taking place and that this must be evaluated in national terms rather than in relation to any local market.
This means, for example, that in the Isle of Wight case it is whether there may be significant distortion of competition in relation to the provision of off-street car parking in general that must be decided rather than by reference to the environs of a local area.
The CJEU also ruled that, in relation to Article 13 of the Principal VAT Directive [now covered by Section 41A(3) of the VAT Act 1994], the phrase 'would lead to significant distortions of competition' the words 'would lead to' are

> 'to be interpreted as encompassing not only actual competition, but also potential competition, provided that the possibility of a private operator entering the relevant market is real, and not purely hypothetical'.

In the same ruling, the word 'significant' was to be

> 'understood as meaning that the actual or potential distortions of competition must be more than negligible.'

The last round of *Isle of Wight Council v HMRC* is now reported in [2015] EWCA Civ 1303 (where the Court of Appeal dismissed the council's appeal).

37.5 Education

37.5.1 *EU-law background*

Article 132 VAT Directive provides:

> 1. Member States shall exempt the following transactions...
>
> (i) the provision of children's or young people's education, school or university education, vocational training or retraining, including the supply of services and of goods closely related thereto,
>
> [A] by bodies governed by public law having such as their aim or
>
> [B] by other organisations recognised by the Member State concerned as having similar objects;
>
> (j) tuition given privately by teachers and covering school or university education;

Para (j) is mentioned for completeness but not discussed here.

The exemption is subject to the restrictions discussed in 37.2 (Restrictions on exemptions).

See 37.3 above for a discussion of how the exemption applied to the services supplied by the BBC to the Open University in relation to the latter's courses.

37.5.2 *Exemptions for education*

Group 6 sch 9 VATA provides exemption for:

> 1 The provision by an eligible body of—
>
> (a) education;
>
> (b) ...
>
> (c) vocational training.

Item 1 is the most important for the purposes of this chapter; other items of the group include:

> 2 The supply of private tuition, in a subject ordinarily taught in a school or university, by an individual teacher acting independently of an employer.[5]
>
> 3 [Examination services - not considered here]
>
> 4 The supply of any goods or services (other than examination services) which are closely related to a supply of a description falling within item 1 (the principal supply) by or to the eligible body making the principal supply provided—
>
> (a) the goods or services are for the direct use of the pupil, student or trainee (as the case may be) receiving the principal supply;

---

5 This item is mentioned for completeness but it does not concern charities, and is not fully discussed in this book.

and

(b) where the supply is to the eligible body making the principal supply, it is made by another eligible body.

5 The provision of vocational training, and the supply of any goods or services essential thereto by the person providing the vocational training, to the extent that the consideration payable is ultimately a charge to funds provided pursuant to arrangements made under section 2 of the Employment and Training Act 1973, section 1A of the Employment and Training Act (Northern Ireland) 1950 or section 2 of the Enterprise and New Towns (Scotland) Act 1990.

37.5.3 *"Education"*

The statute wisely does not attempt to define education.

VAT Notice 701/30 Education and vocational training (7 August 2019) provides an answer:

5.1 What the term "education" covers

Education means a course, class or lesson of instruction or study in any subject, regardless of when and where it takes place.

Education includes:

- lectures
- educational seminars
- conferences and symposia
- recreational and sporting courses
- distance teaching and associated materials.

If a separate charge is made for registration, this is part of the provision of education.

Education does not include admission to events such as:

- plays
- concerts
- sports meetings
- exhibitions ...

The Notice continues with comments on when sports coaching is educational, which are not set out here.

37.5.4 *"Vocational training"*

Note 3 group 6 sch 9 VATA defines "vocational training":

(3) "Vocational training" means—

training, re-training or the provision of work experience for—

(a) any trade, profession or employment; or

(b) any voluntary work connected with—

(i) education, health, safety, or welfare; or
(ii) the carrying out of activities of a charitable nature.

37.5.5 *Youth clubs*

Item 6 group 6 sch 9 VATA provides exemption for youth clubs:

> 6 The provision of facilities by—
> (a) a youth club or an association of youth clubs to its members; or
> (b) an association of youth clubs to members of a youth club which is a member of that association.

Note 6 defines "youth club":

> For the purposes of item 6 a club is a "youth club" if—
> (a) it is established to promote the social, physical, educational or spiritual development of its members;
> (b) its members are mainly under 21 years of age; and
> (c) it satisfies the requirements of Note (1)(f)(i) and (ii).

The reference at (c) is a slip for note 1(e)(i) and (ii).

37.5.6 *Closely related*

In *Brockenhurst College* (Case C-699/15), the taxpayer ran courses in various subjects, including catering and hospitality and the performing arts. To teach students practical skills, the college (I) ran a restaurant in which all the catering functions were carried out by students and (ii) staged concerts and performances put on by students. Patrons at the restaurant and the audience at the concerts and the performances were drawn from a selective group of third parties, all of whom would pay (albeit at heavily discounted prices). The issue was whether the restaurant and entertainment services were exempt under the "closely related" limb of article 132(1)(i). The CJEU ruled as follows:

> 24 The term 'closely related', contained in Article 132(1)(i) of Directive 2006/112, is not defined therein. Nevertheless, it is clear from the wording of that provision that it relates to the supply of services which are closely linked to 'children's or young people's education, school or university education, vocational training or retraining'. Thus, a supply of services can be regarded as 'closely related' to those latter services only where they are actually supplied as services ancillary to the education provided by the relevant establishment, which constitutes the principal supply (see, to that effect, judgments of 14 June 2007, *Horizon College*, C-434/05...paragraphs 27 and 28 and the case-law cited, and

25 March 2010, *Commission v Netherlands*, C-79/09, not published… paragraph 50).

25 In accordance with the Court's case-law, a service may be regarded as ancillary to a principal supply if it does not constitute an end in itself, but a means of better enjoying the principal supply (judgment of 25 March 2010, *Commission v Netherlands*, C-79/09, not published… paragraph 51 and the case-law cited).

26 In that regard, the application of the exemption for activities 'closely related' to education is, in any event, subject to three conditions, laid down, in part, in Articles 132 and 134 of Directive 2006/112. In essence, first, both the principal supply and the supplies of services closely related to it must be provided by bodies referred to in Article 132(1)(i) of that directive; secondly, those supplies of services must be essential to the exempt activities; and, thirdly, the basic purpose of those supplies of services must not be to obtain additional income for those bodies by carrying out transactions which are in direct competition with those of commercial enterprises liable for VAT (see, to that effect, judgments of 14 June 2007, *Horizon College*, C-434/05…paragraphs 34, 38 and 42, and 25 March 2010, *Commission v Netherlands*, C-79/09, not published…paragraph 61).

27 In the case in the main proceedings, it is common ground, as regards the first of those conditions, that the College is a body governed by public law with an educational objective and is therefore eligible for the exemption provided for in Article 132(1)(i) of Directive 2006/112.

28 As regards the second condition, it follows from paragraph 39 of the judgment of 14 June in *Horizon College* (C-434/05…), that, in order to be classified as supplies of services essential to the exempt activities, those supplies must be of a nature and quality such that, without recourse to them, there could be no assurance that the education provided by the body referred to in Article 132(1)(i) of Directive 2006/112 and, consequently, the education from which their students benefit, would have an equivalent value.

29 In the present case, it is apparent from the order for reference that the practical training was designed to form an integral part of the student's curriculum and that, if it were not provided, students would not fully benefit from their education.

…

34 … it appears that the supplies of restaurant and entertainment services at issue in the main proceedings must be regarded as essential to guaranteeing the quality of the principal supply of education provided by the College.

35 As regards the third condition, it must be noted that that condition is an express enunciation of the principle of fiscal neutrality, which

precludes, in particular, treating similar supplies of services, which are thus in competition with each other, differently for VAT purposes (see, to that effect, judgment of 14 June 2007, *Horizon College*, C-434/05 … paragraph 34 and the case- law cited).

…

41 … the services offered by the College to a limited number of third parties do not appear to be comparable to those offered by commercial restaurants and theatres, and the exemption from VAT for services supplied by the College does not amount to a difference in tax treatment.
42 Lastly, it must be borne in mind that it is for the national court to ascertain, on the basis of the guidance provided by the Court, that those conditions are indeed satisfied in the light of the factual circumstances of the case before it.

37.6 "Eligible body" for Group 6

This term is elaborately defined in VATA sch 9 Group 6 note 1. There are six categories of eligible body. We consider them in the order set out in the statute. In particular, charities can qualify: see 37.6.3 (Charities and other nonprofit organisations).

37.6.1 *Schools and universities*

Sch 9 Group 6 note 1 provides:

(1) For the purposes of this Group an "eligible body" is—
- (a) a school [in short, of a form recognised under various categories of education law]
- (b) a United Kingdom university, and any college, institution, school or hall of such a university;
- (c) [Further or Higher Education institutions- in short, of a form recognised under various categories of education law]

There have been numerous cases on whether particular institutions should be treated as a "college" of a University for the purposes of note 1(b). The Supreme Court held:

46. … Parliament has chosen to exercise the discretion conferred upon it by exempting from VAT, so far as relevant, the provision of education by a United Kingdom university and any college of such a university. The term "university" is not defined in the VAT Act. However, the conditions under which a body in the United Kingdom is entitled to use the word university in its title are regulated by statute. Over 100 bodies are presently entitled to call themselves a university and they vary greatly in character. A small but nonetheless significant number of them

are private and run for profit. Some, such as the University of London, are collegiate federal universities in which, for many purposes, the constituent colleges operate on an independent basis. Others, such as the University of Oxford and the University of Cambridge, comprise a kind of federal system of colleges, schools and faculties, in which the colleges are generally financially independent and self-governing. These are just examples. Other universities also comprise or have close relationships with colleges, including the University of the Arts London, the University of the Highlands and Islands and Queen's University of Belfast. The connection between each of these universities and its respective colleges has its own particular character and is a reflection of the history of the institutions involved.

47. It is against the background of the range of possible arrangements between universities and their colleges that the meaning of the phrase "college of such a university" in Note (1)(b) falls to be determined. In my judgment the following points are material.

48. First, for its activities to fall within the scope of Item 1(a), any college of a university, as an eligible body, must provide education.

49. Secondly and as we have seen, the supply of educational services is exempt only if it is provided by bodies governed by public law or by other bodies recognised by the member state as having similar objects. Parliament has exercised the discretion conferred upon it by recognising for this purpose the provision of education by universities, and it has done so regardless of whether those universities are charities or are private and run for profit. If, as I believe, the phrase "a United Kingdom university" in Note 1(b) therefore extends to private universities which are run for profit then in my opinion the same must apply to the expression "any college of such a university". There can be no justification for treating the scope of the two expressions differently in this respect …

50. Thirdly, there is in my view nothing in Note 1(b) or the broader context which would justify limiting the scope of the phrase "any college of such a university" to colleges which are a constituent part of a university in a constitutional or structural sense. To the contrary, if satisfaction of such a constituent part test were required, it would effectively exclude commercial providers such as SEL from the exemption for it is a test they will rarely if ever be able to satisfy. That, so it seems to me, would be contrary to the principle of fiscal neutrality in the light of the decision by Parliament not to limit the bodies it has recognised in Note 1(b) to those which do not make a profit.

51. Fourthly, the United Kingdom must be taken to have recognised that a college (or, for that matter, a school or hall) of a university within the meaning of Note 1(b) has similar objects to those of a university which

is governed by public law and which provides education to young people. In my opinion this consideration focuses attention on the objects of the body in issue, the nature of the educational services that it supplies, and how integrated those services are with those of the university. Put another way, it is necessary to examine the characteristics of those educational services and the context in which they are delivered rather than the precise nature of the legal and constitutional relationship between the body that provides them and its university.

…

53. … the presence of a foundation or constitutional document or some other legal relationship establishing the college as a constituent part of the university in a constitutional or structural sense will be sufficient to prove that it is a college of the university within the meaning of Note 1(b), save in an exceptional case. But that is not a necessary condition. In assessing whether a body is a college of a university the following five questions are also likely to be highly relevant: (i) whether they have a common understanding that the body is a college of the university; (ii) whether the body can enrol or matriculate students as students of the university; (iii) whether those students are generally treated as students of the university during the course of their period of study; (iv) whether the body provides courses of study which are approved by the university; and (v) whether the body can in due course present its students for examination for a degree from the university.

54. If a body can establish the presence of each of these five features, focused as they are on the objects of the body, the relationship between the students of the body and the university and the degree to which the activities of the body are recognised by and integrated with the university, then … it is highly likely to be a college of the university within the meaning of Note 1(b) … All will depend on the particular circumstances of the case.

55. However, some … factors are … likely to be of much less assistance … (i) whether the body is independent from the university; (ii) whether the body is financially dependent on the university, or whether the body and the university are financially interdependent; (iii) whether the body generates any distributable profit; (iv) whether the body is entitled to public funding; (v) the presence or absence of permanent links between the body and the university; (vi) the degree of physical proximity between the body and the university; and (vii) whether the body has any an obligation to offer a minimum number of university places. [It is not suggested] that none of these matters will ever have any evidential weight. For example, the duration of the relationship between the body and the university and how long it may be expected to last may have some relevance, if only as part of the background, but these and similar

matters are unlikely to be determinative.
56. … The question is whether the college and the university are so integrated that the entity is imbued with the objects of the university, and that is best answered in the manner … described.

37.6.2 *Public bodies*

VATA sch 9 Group 6 note 1 provides:

(1) For the purposes of this Group an "eligible body" is...
(d) a public body of a description in Note (5) to Group 7 below;

VATA sch 9 Group 7 note 5 provides:

In item 9 "public body" means—
(a) a Government department within the meaning of section 41(6);
(b) a local authority;
(c) a body which acts under any enactment or instrument for public purposes and not for its own profit and which performs functions similar to those of a Government department or local authority.

37.6.3 *Charities and other nonprofit organisations*

VATA sch 9 Group 6 note 1 provides:

(1) For the purposes of this Group an "eligible body" is...
(e) a body which—
(i) is precluded from distributing and does not distribute any profit it makes; and
(ii) applies any profits made from supplies of a description within this Group to the continuance or improvement of such supplies;

We would have thought that charities will necessarily meet condition (i). VAT Notice 701/30 Education and vocational training (7 August 2019) provides:

4.5 The meaning of the term "does not distribute any profit"
[1] Distributing profits does not just include paying a dividend to shareholders.
[2] It also includes making a payment or donation to another body, even where the recipient is a charity.
[3] Management charges or other fees paid to an associated company or individual may also be viewed as a distribution of profits.

We do not consider a donation to another charity would normally be a distribution of profits. Point [3] is only correct if the charges or fees are at an above market rate, which should not happen in the case of a bona fide charity. The following should be noted:

> **VATEDU39700-Group 6 Item 1 Education, research and vocational training provided by eligible bodies: eligible bodies: other organisations** [Apr 2020]:
> ...We are aware of arrangements whereby bodies that would ordinarily make profit from educational courses argue that they meet the terms of Note 1(e) because such sums are passed to associated companies through charges such as rent or management charges, or alternatively, because such profits are covenanted to a parent company. We do not agree with either argument. If you should come across such an argument you should consult your Tax Avoidance Visiting Officer (TAVO)...

VAT Notice 701/30 continues:

> It will be necessary to provide reasonable evidence that the profits cannot be distributed and that if the organisation's activities do generate a profit that they will be recycled back into its education or training activities. For example, the Memorandum and Articles of Association, or some other constitutional document, containing a suitable reference or clause, may be acceptable as evidence of how profits are to be treated, although it's what takes place in practice which will determine whether the exemption applies.

Charities will meet, or can usually arrange to meet, condition (ii) and so will be, or can arrange to be, eligible bodies. Conversely, charities which do not want exemption can usually arrange not to meet condition (ii). However, the following should be noted:

> **VATEDU39700: Group 6 Item 1 Education, research and vocational training provided by eligible bodies: eligible bodies: other organisations** [Jan 2019]:
> ...an organisation that is ostensibly an eligible body may seek to avoid exemption by arranging to make its supplies of education through a related company that doesn't meet eligible criteria, for example because it is not precluded from distributing profits. This may be done because the recipient of the supplies of education is able to recover any VAT charged to it (such as a local authority eligible to reclaim VAT under Section 33 of the VAT Act 1994), and the supplier does not wish to suffer input tax restriction themselves by making exempt supplies. Such

cases should also be referred to your TAVO, who may need to consult the Education Unit of Expertise or VAT Reliefs Policy Team.

37.6.4 *English language schools*

VATA sch 9 Group 6 note 1 provides:

> (f) a body not falling within paragraphs (a) to (e) above which provides the teaching of English as a foreign language.

37.7 Welfare

37.7.1 *EU-law background*

Article 132 VAT Directive provides:

> 1. Member States shall exempt the following transactions ...
>   (g) the supply of services and of goods closely linked to welfare and social security work, including those supplied by old people's homes,
>   [i] by bodies governed by public law or
>   [ii] by other bodies recognised by the Member State concerned as being devoted to social wellbeing;

The exemption is subject to the restrictions discussed in 37.2 (Restrictions on exemptions).

37.7.2 *UK law*

This exemption is found in VATA sch 9 Group 7. Only two paragraphs are specifically relevant to charities (though supplies by charities may also fall within the more general exemptions in Group 7). These are paragraphs 9 and 10. They provide exemption for:

> 9 The supply by—
> (a) a charity,
> (b) a state-regulated private welfare institution or agency, or
> (c) a public body,
> of welfare services and of goods supplied in connection with those welfare services.
> 10 The supply, otherwise than for profit, of goods and services incidental to the provision of spiritual welfare by a religious community to a resident member of that community in return for a subscription or other consideration paid as a condition of membership.

Note 6 provides:

> In item 9 "welfare services" means services which are directly connected with—
> (a) the provision of care, treatment or instruction designed to promote the physical or mental welfare of elderly, sick, distressed or disabled persons,
> (b) the care or protection of children and young persons, or
> (c) the provision of spiritual welfare by a religious institution as part of a course of instruction or a retreat, not being a course or a retreat designed primarily to provide recreation or a holiday,
>
> and, in the case of services supplied by a state-regulated private welfare institution, includes only those services in respect of which the institution is so regulated.

37.8 Subscriptions

This section deals with VAT exemption for subscriptions; for other aspects, see 35.19 (Business of membership subscriptions).

37.8.1 *EU-law background*

Article 132 VAT Directive provides:

> 1. Member States shall exempt the following transactions ...
> (l) the supply of services, and the supply of goods closely linked thereto, to their members in their common interest in return for a subscription fixed in accordance with their rules by non-profit-making organisations with aims of a political, trade-union, religious, patriotic, philosophical, philanthropic or civic nature, provided that this exemption is not likely to cause distortion of competition;

The exemption is subject to the restrictions discussed in 37.2 (Restrictions on exemptions).

37.8.2 *UK law*

VATA sch 9 Group 9 provides exemption for:

> The supply to its members of such services and, in connection with those services, of such goods as are both referable only to its aims and available without payment other than a membership subscription by any of the following non-profit-making organisations ...

There are five classes of what we call **"exempt organisations"** which are considered in more detail below. In short they are:

(1) Trade unions
(2) Professional associations
(3) Learned associations

(4) Representational trade associations
(5) Public interest bodies

VATA sch 9 Group 9Note 1 restricts the exemption:

> Item 1 does not include any right of admission to any premises, event or performance, to which non-members are admitted for a consideration.

VATA sch 9 Group 9 Note 3 extends the exemption to associations of organisations:

> Item 1 shall include organisations and associations the membership of which consists wholly or mainly of constituent or affiliated associations which as individual associations would be comprised in the item; and "member" shall be construed as including such an association and "membership subscription" shall include an affiliation fee or similar levy.

37.8.3 *"Non-profit making"*

VAT Notice 701/5 Clubs and associations' VAT responsibilities (31 December 2020) provides:

> **11.3 Non-profit making**
> We consider, when judging whether an organisation is "non-profit making", the objects for which an organisation has been established, as distinct from the financial policy being pursued. Although the organisation may generate income surpluses from various activities, we will not refuse recognition as a non-profit making organisation simply because these surpluses subsidise other activities.
> If a body has a constitution or articles of association that bars it from distributing surpluses of income over expenditure to its members, shareholders or any other party, other than in the event of a liquidation or cessation of activities, we normally accept it as non-profit making for the purposes of this exemption.
> But the existence of any provision barring distribution will not necessarily be the sole factor in determining whether an organisation is non-profit making.

37.8.4 *Trade unions*

The first type of exempt organisation in VATA sch 9 Group 9 Item 1 is:

> (a) a trade union[6] or other organisation of persons having as its main

6 Defined in VATA sch 9 Group 9 Note 2: "Trade union" has the meaning assigned to it by section 1 of the Trade Union and Labour Relations (Consolidation) Act 1992.

object the negotiation on behalf of its members of the terms and conditions of their employment;

37.8.5 *Professional associations*

The second type of exempt organisation in VATA sch 9 Group 9 Item 1 is:

(b) a professional association, membership of which is wholly or mainly restricted to individuals who have or are seeking a qualification appropriate to the practice of the profession concerned;

VAT Notice 701/5 Clubs and associations' VAT responsibilities (31 December 2020) adds:

> **11.5 Professional associations**
> ... Membership of the association must be obligatory, or at least customary, for those pursuing a career in that profession.

VAT Notice 701/5 Clubs and associations' VAT responsibilities (31 December 2020) goes on to provide the following discussion of relevant terms:

> **11.6 A profession**
> There is no legal definition of a profession. But VAT tribunal and court decisions have restricted the meaning of the words 'profession' and 'professional' to occupations generally understood to be a profession. Factors in judging whether an occupation is generally understood to be a profession include:
>
> - the nature and status of the activity and those engaged in it
> - whether the exercise of the activity requires a qualification
> - whether the persons carrying out the activity are bound by a code of conduct
> - whether the activity entails having a distinctive and broad base of knowledge from which a person may subsequently diversify into more specialised areas
> - the nature of the association's aims and objectives
> - the actual activities carried out by it.
>
> These criteria are neither fixed nor exhaustive. This means for example that some occupations not currently regarded as professions may acquire that status in the future.
>
> **11.7 Restricting the membership of a professional association**
> It must restrict its membership 'wholly or mainly' to those 'who hold or are seeking a qualification appropriate to the profession concerned.' When considering whether your association restricts its membership,

you should look at what is happening in practice. An association that purports to restrict its membership in its constitution or rules, but does not actually impose the restriction, will not satisfy this criterion. Conversely, an association that does not specifically claim to restrict the membership in its rules or constitution, but in reality does impose a restriction, could meet the criterion.

11.8 When a membership is wholly or mainly restricted
We regard any association with a membership comprising of 75% or more of those individuals "who hold or are seeking a qualification appropriate to the profession concerned" as satisfying this criterion.

11.9 A qualification appropriate to the practice of the profession concerned
A "qualification appropriate to the practice of the profession concerned" is

- held or sought by persons wishing to practice a recognised profession
- obligatory or customary to the practice of that profession
- awarded by the association to the person who is qualified or seeking qualification.

37.8.6 *Learned societies*

The third type of exempt organisation in VATA sch 9 Group 9 Item 1 is:

(c) an association, the primary purpose of which is the advancement of a particular branch of knowledge, or the fostering of professional expertise, connected with the past or present professions or employments of its members;

VATA sch 9 Group 9 Note 4 provides:

Paragraph (c) does not apply unless the association restricts its membership wholly or mainly to individuals whose present or previous professions or employments are directly connected with the purposes of the association.

VAT Notice 701/5 Clubs and associations' VAT responsibilities (31 December 2020) provides:

11.12 A 'branch of knowledge'
A 'branch of knowledge' is restricted to a recognised branch of science or the arts and will therefore be more academic than practical in content. Normally it will be included in a degree course or equivalent. Knowledge relating to the confined area of a specific job does not

> constitute a branch of knowledge for this purpose.
>
> **11.13 Professional expertise**
> 'Professional' has the same meaning as in paragraph 11.6, so that 'professional expertise' is restricted to expertise connected with what is generally understood to be a profession.
>
> **11.14 Restricting the membership of a learned society**
> A learned society must restrict its membership 'wholly or mainly' (75%) to those 'whose past or present professions or employments are directly connected with the purposes of the association'.
> Therefore, an association with the primary purpose of advancing a branch of knowledge amongst the public generally would not qualify for exemption if its membership lacked this 'employment connection'. Exemption will still apply where only a small proportion of the membership lacks the 'employment connection'.

For how to ascertain the "aims" or "primary purpose" of an organisation, see 8.8 (Ascertaining primary purposes).

37.8.7 *Representational trade associations*

The fourth type of exempt organisation in VATA sch 9 Group 9 Item 1 is:

> (d) an association, the primary purpose of which is to make representations to the Government on legislation and other public matters which affect the business or professional interests of its members.

VATA sch 9 Group 9 Note 5 provides:

> Paragraph (d) does not apply unless the association restricts its membership wholly or mainly to individuals or corporate bodies whose business or professional interests are directly connected with the purposes of the association.

VAT Notice 701/5 Clubs and associations' VAT responsibilities (31 December 2020) provides:

> **11.15 Representational trade associations**
> ...A representational trade association must restrict its membership 'wholly or mainly to individuals or corporate bodies whose business or professional interests are directly connected with the purposes of the association'.
> This means that representational trade associations must satisfy all the following criteria for exemption to apply:
>
> - the association's primary purpose is 'to make representations'...

- representations 'to the government' are to the UK government
- the representations must relate to legislation or public matters affecting the members' 'business or professional interests'
- the members are 'wholly or mainly individuals or corporate bodies whose business or professional interests are directly connected with the purposes of the association', you should use the 75% criterion referred to in paragraph 11.8 in applying the 'wholly or mainly' criterion

For how to ascertain the "aims" or "primary purpose" of an organisation, see 8.8 (Ascertaining primary purposes).

37.8.8 *Public interest bodies*

The last type of exempt organisation in VATA sch 9 Group 9 Item 1 is:

> (e) a body which has objects which are in the public domain and are of a political, religious, patriotic, philosophical, philanthropic or civic nature

The Association of Graduate Careers Advisory Services v HMRC[7] comments on "civic" nature:

> 137 Both parties referred in their arguments to the decision of the Court of Appeal in *The Expert Witness Institute v Customs & Excise Commissioners* [2001] EWCA Civ 15 1882. In that case, the Court of Appeal decided that the object of The Expert Witness Institute which was "the support of the proper administration of justice and the earlier resolution of disputes through fair and unbiased expert evidence" was an object of a civic nature. In his judgment, Chadwick LJ said at [30]:
>
> > "The remaining question, therefore is whether "the proper administration of justice and the earlier resolution of disputes through fair and unbiased expert evidence" - which is the primary object for which the Institute is incorporated - is an aim of a civic nature, giving the word "civic" the meanings "of, pertaining, or proper to citizens" or "of or pertaining to citizenship" which, as it seems to me, it can properly bear. I do not think that the answer to that question can be in doubt. A proper administration of justice is, as it seems to me, a central element in the social contract between the state and its citizens."
>
> 138 In his judgment, Longmore LJ said at [36]:
>
> > "... the requirement that a body has objects which are of a civic

---

7 [2016] UKFTT 0560.

> nature if it is to be able to claim exemption, means that the body must have objects which promote the relationship of citizens, not among themselves, but with the state of which they are citizens."
>
> He continued at [37]:
>
> "it would be different if the Institute's objectives were solely or even, perhaps mainly for the benefit of its members. In that case, the objects would not be of a civic nature and the body would have to seek exemption, if at all, as a trade union or professional association."
>
> 139 In the present case … the objects of [the taxpayer] relate primarily to its members … and ultimately to graduates and students who benefit from the services provided by the members … It cannot properly be said that those objectives "promote the relationship of citizens, not among themselves, but with the state of which they are citizens". Rather the objectives promote the relationships between citizens themselves…or between members and the graduates and students or ultimately between students and their respective employers.
>
> 140 Any benefit to wider society is, in our view, too remote. In this context, we are mindful of the principle that the exception in Article 132(1)(l) and reflected in item 1(e) is intended to be limited to bodies whose objects are within the wider public interest. In this case, the principal beneficiaries of [the taxpayer]'s services are its members and the students who benefit from their services.

VAT Notice 701/5 Clubs and associations' VAT responsibilities (31 December 2020) paragraph 12.2 also comments on "civic" nature:

> a body which has objects which promote rights and duties of citizens in matters of public interest and public affairs, and whose objects do not solely or mainly benefit its members.

VAT Notice 701/5 Clubs and associations' VAT responsibilities (31 December 2020) also comments on "political", "religious", "patriotic", "philosophical", and "philanthropic":

> 12.2 **The aims of a 'political, religious, patriotic, philosophical, philanthropic or civic' nature**
>
> There are no legal definitions. The following ... describes the everyday meaning of these terms.
>
> **'political'** campaigns for or against legislative and constitutional changes or campaigns in local and central government elections.
>
> **'religious'** includes all denominations, creeds, old and new, that command a following

'patriotic' to do good work for the benefit of a nation state or for those who have served their country and their dependants

'philosophical' bodies whose primary purpose is the advancement of a particular way of thinking but which are not of a political or religious nature. They are very similar to learned societies as described in paragraph 11.10, in that they are of an academic nature.

'philanthropic' to do good work for the direct benefit of the general community or a particular section of the community or designed to promote the well being of mankind

37.9 Sports

37.9.1 *EU-law background*

Article 132(1) VAT Directive provides:

> Member States shall exempt the following transactions …
> (m) the supply of certain services closely linked to sport or physical education by non-profit-making organisations to persons taking part in sport or physical education.

The exemption is subject to the restrictions discussed in 37.2 (Restrictions on exemptions).

In *The English Bridge Union* (Case C-90/16), the question was whether contract or duplicate bridge was a "sport" for the purposes of article 132(1)(m).

The CJEU held that:

> 23. With regard…to the purpose of Article 132(1)(m) of the directive, it should be recalled that the objective of that provision is to encourage certain activities in the general interest, namely, services closely linked to sport or physical education supplied by non-profit-making organisations to persons taking part in sport or physical education, and, therefore, that provision seeks to promote such participation by large sections of the population ...
> 24. …duplicate bridge involves, inter alia, logic, memory, planning and/or lateral thinking, and constitutes an activity beneficial to the mental and physical health of regular participants. However, even if they do prove beneficial to physical and mental health, activities of pure rest or relaxation are not covered by that provision… In those circumstances, the fact that an activity promotes physical and mental health is not, of itself, a sufficient element for it to be concluded that that activity is covered by the concept of 'sport' within the meaning of that same provision.
> 25. The fact that an activity promoting physical and mental

> well-being is practised competitively does not lead to a different conclusion. In fact, the Court has ruled that Article 132(1)(m) of Directive 2006/112 does not require, for it to be applicable, that the sporting activity be practised at a particular level, for example, at a professional level, or that the sporting activity at issue be practised in a particular way, namely in a regular or organised manner or in order to participate in sports competitions … In that respect, it must also be noted that the competitive nature of an activity cannot, per se, be sufficient to establish its classification as a 'sport', failing any not negligible physical element.
>
> …
>
> 27. It follows … that the provision relates only to activities characterised by a not negligible physical element.

Contract or duplicate bridge was not, therefore, a "sport" for these purposes.

37.9.2 *Domestic UK law*

VATA sch 9 Group 10 provides exemption for 3 items. The first two concern sports competitions:

> 1 The grant of a right to enter a competition in sport or physical recreation where the consideration for the grant consists in money which is to be allocated wholly towards the provision of a prize or prizes awarded in that competition.
> 2 The grant, by an eligible body established for the purposes of sport or physical recreation, of a right to enter a competition in such an activity.

The third exemption is wider and more important:

> 3 The supply by an eligible body to an individual of services closely linked with and essential to sport or physical education in which the individual is taking part.

Note 1 restricts item 3:

> (1) Item 3 does not include the supply of any services by an eligible body of residential accommodation, catering or transport.

Note 16 defines some terms. In particular:

> **"sports supply"** means a supply which, if made by an eligible body, would fall within Item 2 or 3.

37.9.3 *Green fees*

Until 2015, where the body in question operated a membership scheme, the third exemption was only available to members (and not non-members). This was challenged and in *The Bridport and West Dorset Golf Club*[8], a case concerning green fees (i.e. payments made by non-members visiting a golf club for the right to play), the CJEU held that sporting services that would be exempt when supplied to members would qualify to be treated as exempt from VAT when supplied to non-members. The necessary amendments were made to the VATA with effect from 1 January 2015.

In the wake of *Bridport*, repayment claims were made by affected sports clubs for a refund of VAT that had been incorrectly charged on supplies they had made to non-members. HMRC disputed how much should be refunded. This eventually led to HMRC Brief 10 (2016), which provides:

> **VAT Unjust enrichment: non-profit making sports clubs**
> **1. Purpose of this brief**
> This brief provides information on how HM Revenue and Customs will treat claims for VAT refunds from sports clubs following the First Tier Tribunal (FTT) decision in Berkshire and Others handed down on 07 December 2015. This brief cancels Revenue and Customs Brief 25/14 and 19/15.
> **2. Readership**
> Members' golf clubs and other non-profit making sports clubs and their advisers.
> **3. Background**
> The Court of Justice of the European Union found, in the case of Bridport and West Dorset golf club, that the UK had incorrectly applied VAT to certain supplies made to visitors of non-profit making clubs. HMRC had subsequently denied repayment of VAT claims for overpaid VAT on the basis they would be unjustly enriched.
> A number of clubs challenged HMRC's refusal to pay out claims and appealed to the FTT. While the FTT found that the clubs would be unjustly enriched if HMRC paid their claims in full, it was not to the extent HMRC had considered. The FTT concluded the clubs would be unjustly enriched by 10% and were therefore entitled to a 90% refund of the VAT incorrectly paid. HMRC has decided not to appeal the decision and will be making VAT refunds, subject to claims meeting the terms of VAT Information Sheet 01/15.
> 4. **Other issues considered by the FTT**
> The FTT also considered the VAT treatment of corporate days and supplies to tour operators. It found that both supplies were taxable at the

8 Case C-495/12.

standard rate of VAT. It also found, on the facts of the cases, that VAT on golf course maintenance costs was an overhead of the clubs and was to be apportioned in accordance with a partial exemption method as appropriate. This may not always be the case, as the onus is on the club to demonstrate a link between its taxable activities and course costs, in order for such costs to be treated as residual.

The FTT determined that corporate days (supplies made to businesses who use them for their own purposes and so are the true beneficiaries), include green fees and any ancillary supplies (such as catering) supplied to the business concerned, irrespective of how they are constituted. Some clubs may refer to these taxable supplies as golf society days or by some other description, which is different from the VAT exempt society days described in VAT Information Sheet 01/15.

...

6. New claims

All new claims will be subject to the 4 year time limit in section 80(4) of the VAT Act 1994.

7. Return adjustments

Members' clubs with over declarations of output tax within certain monetary limits may wish to correct any errors on their VAT returns rather than submit a formal claim under section 80 VATA 94 to HMRC. However, in doing so they would not receive any interest. Further information on the monetary limits and which returns may be adjusted is available in VAT Notice 700/45: How to correct VAT errors and make adjustments and claims.

8. Penalties

In circumstances where members' clubs have not taken due care in submitting valid claims, they may be charged a penalty in relation to prescribed accounting periods starting on or after 1 April 2008, where the return due date is 1 April 2009 or later. For example, a club may incur a penalty if, as a result of a failure to take reasonable care, it shows too little tax due or claims a repayment that is too large on its VAT return.

9. Implications on other taxes

Where amounts of overpaid output tax are repaid and not reimbursed to customers who bore the burden of the tax, there may be direct tax implications. For example, any surplus of trading income from non-members that remains after the deduction of relevant expenses is taxable, for Corporation Tax purposes and a liability may arise.

37.9.4 *Affiliation fees*

HMRC Brief 1 (2018) provides:

VAT - treatment of affiliation fees for sports clubs

...

2. Who should read this brief

This brief should be read by clubs who currently provide standard rated sporting services.

3. Background

A sport's governing body, or similar umbrella organisation, often charges an affiliation fee to individual clubs who make an onward charge to their members. Where the clubs are non-profit making, the supply of this affiliation fee to their individual members is exempt from VAT.

However, if the club is a profit-making commercial club, then the supply to their individual member is standard rated.

The concession [*which HMRC operated prior to 1 April 2018*] aimed to put profit-making commercial clubs in a similar position to non-profit making clubs, so that they didn't need to account for output tax on the fee charged. It achieved this by allowing profit-making commercial clubs to treat these re-charges to their members as though they were disbursements.

However, as such re-charges of affiliation fees aren't legally disbursements, the concession goes beyond HMRC's discretion and is being withdrawn with effect from 1 April 2018 ...

4. Other points

Withdrawal of the concession means that the onward charge of the affiliation fee will be liable to VAT at the standard rate of 20%, unless it meets the conditions of a disbursement. A full explanation of those conditions can be found in paragraph 25.1.1 of Notice No 700.

The withdrawal of the concession has no impact on the VAT treatment of affiliation fees by non-profit making sports governing bodies, or similar umbrella organisations, and on non-profit making sports clubs to their members.

In their case, the charge they make for affiliation fees will continue to be exempt under the law. If they are partly exempt for the purposes of calculating their recoverable input tax, such bodies should ensure that they continue to include affiliation fees in their exempt and total supplies in any appropriate partial exemption calculation ...

37.9.5 *"Eligible body"*

The meaning of "eligible body" for the purposes of Group 10 is not the same as the meaning in the exemption for education. The notes to VATA sch 9 Group 10 provide:

(2A) Subject to Notes (2C) and (3), in this Group "eligible body" means a non-profit making body which—

(a) is precluded from distributing any profit it makes, or is allowed to distribute any such profit by means only of distributions to a non-profit making body;

(b) applies in accordance with Note (2B) any profits it makes from supplies of a description within Item 2 or 3; and

(c) is not subject to commercial influence.

(2B) For the purposes of Note (2A)(b) the application of profits made by any body from supplies of a description within Item 2 or 3 is in accordance with this Note only if those profits are applied for one or more of the following purposes, namely—

(a) the continuance or improvement of any facilities made available in or in connection with the making of the supplies of those descriptions made by that body;

(b) the purposes of a non-profit making body.

(2C) In determining whether the requirements of Note (2A) for being an eligible body are satisfied in the case of any body, there shall be disregarded any distribution of amounts representing unapplied or undistributed profits that falls to be made to the body's members on its winding-up or dissolution.

(3) In Item 3 "an eligible body" does not include—

(a) a local authority;

(b) a Government department within the meaning of section 41(6); or

(c) a non-departmental public body which is listed in the 1993 edition of the publication prepared by the Office of Public Service and Science and known as Public Bodies.

This approach to granting VAT exemptions is, in some respects, unhelpful because the requirements to obtain a VAT exemption do not correspond with any particular exemptions relating to direct taxes. For example, a CASC will not always qualify for the VAT exemption in Group 10. The approach is how the UK has decided to implement the EU concept of a non-profit-making organisation.

As noted in *Stoke by Nayland Golf and Leisure* [2018] UKUT 0308:

> 60. It was common ground that the legal principles to be applied to the question as to whether conditions of being a "non-profit making body" were satisfied in any particular case are those identified in the judgment of the European Court of Justice ("ECJ") in *Kennemer Golf & Country Club v Staatssecretaris van Financiën* (2002) Case C-174/00 [2002] STC 502 ("*Kennemer*").

...

62. ... the essence of the main issue referred to the ECJ was whether the provisions of what is now Article 132(1)(m) of the Principal VAT Directive was to be interpreted as meaning that an organisation which systematically sought to achieve surpluses should, for that reason, be precluded from the exemption in spite of using those surpluses for the provision of its services...

...

64. In its judgment, the ECJ emphasised that the question as to whether an organisation is "non-profit-making" is to be determined by having regard to the aim which the organisation pursues. It held...

> "26. .... it must be observed first of all that it is clear from [*what is now Article 132(1)(m) of the VAT Directive*] that an organisation is to be classed as being "non-profit-making" for the purposes of that provision by having regard to the aim which the organisation pursues, that is to say that the organisation must not have the aim, unlike a commercial undertaking, of achieving profits for its members ...

...

28. Where it is found that this is indeed the case, the fact that an organisation subsequently achieves profits, even if it seeks to make them or makes them systematically, will not affect the original categorisation of the organisation as long as those profits are not distributed to its members as profits. Clearly, [*what is now Article 132(1)(m) of the VAT Directive*] does not prohibit the organisations covered by that provision from finishing their accounting year with a positive balance. Otherwise, as the United Kingdom points out, such organisations would be unable to create reserves to pay for the maintenance of, and future improvements to, their facilities."

65. The ECJ gave further guidance on what was meant by "profit" in this context. It said this at [33]:

> "...it is not profits ("bénéfices"), in the sense of surpluses arising at the end of an accounting year, which preclude categorisation of an organisation as "non-profit- making", but profit ("profit") in the sense of financial advantages for the organisation's members."

66. ... in our view it is clear from the judgment that it is not sufficient that the organisation in question has, for example, entered into contracts which might be said to be otherwise than at market rates, but whether in doing so it had the aim of making a distribution of profits, in the sense of conferring a financial advantage, on those who have a financial interest in the organisation; such an aim might be inferred from such actions, but is not necessarily implicit in them. In that regard, in our view a person who has control of an organisation must be regarded as

having a financial interest in it, because such a person has the power to determine whether any profits that are made by the organisation concerned are distributed to him.

67. It must also be assumed that it is not necessary that the distribution of profits be made, whether covertly or overtly, to a person who is a "member" of the organisation…before it might result in the organisation in question no longer qualifying as "non-profit-making"…it is clear from…the Advocate General's opinion that he had in mind the question of whether the organisation existed to enrich any person who had a "financial interest" in the organisation in question or control of it, a category that obviously goes wider than being a member of the organisation in one form or another...

68. The Advocate General also makes it clear…as does the ECJ…that the assessment of the organisation's aims is a matter for the national court, to be established on a case-by-case basis having investigated all the circumstances of the case. This calls for the tribunal in question to undertake a multifactorial assessment, taking into account all of the evidence and surrounding circumstances, carrying out a balancing exercise by weighing up the various factors which tend to suggest that the aim of the organisation was to enrich those who have a financial interest in the organisation against those which tend to suggest the opposite and coming to a conclusion.

69. It is therefore necessary for the tribunal to commence its assessment by establishing who has a "financial interest" in the organisation in question...

70. It is clear that a "financial interest" can be established by ownership by a profit-making body or by control of a profit-making body over the organisation in question, or where the body in question is subject to common control with other entities who are part of a commercial group so that all the entities concerned amount to a single commercial enterprise.

…

37.10 Local authorities

The effect of VATA sch 9 Group 10 Note 3 is to exclude local authorities and similar from the exemption. The CJEU considered the compatibility of this Note with EU law in *London Borough of Ealing*[9] - see 37.2 (Restrictions on exemptions) above for a discussion of this case and how HMRC responded to the CJEU judgement.

---

9 Case C-633/15.

37.10.1 *"Subject to commercial influence"*

VATA sch 9 Group 10 Note 4 provides:

> For the purposes of this Group a body shall be taken, in relation to a sports supply, to be subject to commercial influence if, and only if, there is a time in the relevant period when—
> (a) a relevant supply was made to that body by a person associated with it at that time;
> (b) an emolument was paid by that body to such a person;
> (c) an agreement existed for either or both of the following to take place after the end of that period, namely—
> (i) the making of a relevant supply to that body by such a person; or
> (ii) the payment by that body to such a person of any emoluments.

The key terms are "relevant period" and"relevant supply".
The notes to VATA sch 9 Group 10 provide:

> (5) In this Group "the relevant period", in relation to a sports supply, means ...
> (b) where that supply is one made on or after 1st January 2003, the period of three years ending with the making of that sports supply.
>
> (6) Subject to Note (7), in this Group "relevant supply", in relation to any body, means a supply falling within any of the following paragraphs—
> (a) the grant of any interest in or right over land which at any time in the relevant period was or was expected to become sports land;
> (b) the grant of any licence to occupy any land which at any such time was or was expected to become sports land;
> (c) the grant, in the case of land in Scotland, of any personal right to call for or be granted any such interest or right as is mentioned in paragraph (*a*) above;
> (d) a supply arising from a grant falling within paragraph (a), (b) or (c) above, other than a grant made before 1st April 1996;
> (e) the supply of any services consisting in the management or administration of any facilities provided by that body;
> (f) the supply of any goods or services for a consideration in excess of what would have been agreed between parties entering into a commercial transaction at arm's length.
>
> (7) A supply which has been, or is to be or may be, made by any person

shall not be taken, in relation to a sports supply made by any body, to be a relevant supply for the purposes of this Group if—

(a) the principal purpose of that body is confined, at the time when the sports supply is made, to the provision for employees of that person of facilities for use for or in connection with sport or physical recreation, or both;

(b) the supply in question is one made by a charity or local authority or one which (if it is made) will be made by a person who is a charity or local authority at the time when the sports supply is made;

(c) the supply in question is a grant falling within Note (6)(a) to (c) which has been made, or (if it is made) will be made, for a nominal consideration;

(d) the supply in question is one arising from such a grant as is mentioned in paragraph (c) above and is not itself a supply the consideration for which was, or will or may be, more than a nominal consideration; or

(e) the supply in question—

  (i) is a grant falling within Note (6)(a) to (c) which is made for no consideration; but

  (ii) falls to be treated as a supply of goods or services, or (if it is made) will fall to be so treated, by reason only of the application, in accordance with paragraph 9 of Schedule 4, of paragraph 5 of that Schedule.

VAT Notice 701/45 (Sport supplies that are VAT exempt) provides:

5.3 A relevant supply

This table explains the meaning of relevant supply:

A relevant supply is a	**Notes**
grant of either any interest in or right over land or licence to occupy any land which at any time in the relevant period was or was expected to become sports land, and in the case of land in Scotland, of any personal right to call for or be granted any such interest or right, or of the use of sports land (that is, where rent is paid) under leases granted, varied or renewed after 31 March 1996	Grant includes an assignment or surrender. Sports land in relation to any body, means any land used or held for use for or in connection with the provision by that body of facilities for use for or in connection with sport or physical recreation, or both.
supply of any services in managing or administering any of its facilities	
supply of any goods or services for more than the normal market price.	

5.4 Exceptions from relevant supplies

This table explains the circumstances in which a supply is not a 'relevant supply' despite meeting the terms of paragraph 5.3:

Supplies will not be relevant supplies if they are	Notes
made by a charity or local authority	
made by a company to a club owned by that company and whose principal purpose is to provide employees of that company with sports facilities	Employees in relation to a person, includes retired employees of that person.
a gift of sports land or of the use of sports land	Sports land in relation to any body, means any land used or held for use for, or in connection with, the provision by that body of facilities for use for, or in connection with, sport or physical recreation, or both.
of sports land and was made in return for a nominal amount	In normal circumstances we will treat any payment below £1000 as nominal and will give careful consideration to claims for higher amounts to be treated as nominal.
of the use of sports land and made in return for a nominal amount, provided that the original grant of land was also for a nominal amount.	

5.5 Meaning of emoluments

Emoluments include all salaries, fees, wages, perquisites and profits calculated or varied wholly or partly, by reference to the:

- profits from some or all of the activities of the body paying the emolument
- level of that body's gross income from some or all of its activities.

Perquisites (perks) are allowances paid, or goods and services provided, over and above a settled wage.

HMRC VAT Notice 701/45 (Sport supplies that are VAT exempt) provides, at paragraph 5:

> Every time you make a sports supply, you must decide whether you are under commercial influence. If you are under commercial influence you are not an eligible body (see section 4) and your sports supplies are standard-rated. A sports supply is a supply, which if made by an eligible body, would fall within the exemption for sporting and physical education services.

> These rules look [(!)] complicated because they are designed to counter complex tax avoidance schemes. Please contact the VAT helpline if you need any help.

It is interesting to contrast the very English law-based approach taken in the UK in relation to the concept of a non-profit-making organisation with the more EU law-based approach summarised in 9.5 ("Eligible body") above.

37.11 Cultural services

37.11.1 *EU-law background*

Article 132 VAT Directive provides:

> 1. Member States shall exempt the following transactions...
>   (n) the supply of certain cultural services, and the supply of goods closely linked thereto,
>   [i] by bodies governed by public law[10] or
>   [ii] by other cultural bodies recognised by the Member State concerned;

The exemption is subject to the restrictions discussed in 37.2 (Restrictions on exemptions).

37.11.2 *UK law*

VATA sch 9 Group 13 provides exemption for:

> 1 The supply by a public body of a right of admission to—
>   (a) a museum, gallery, art exhibition or zoo; or
>   (b) a theatrical, musical or choreographic performance of a cultural nature.
>
> 2 The supply by an eligible body of a right of admission to—
>   (a) a museum, gallery, art exhibition or zoo; or
>   (b) a theatrical, musical or choreographic performance of a cultural nature.

37.12 "Public body" and "eligible body"

The exemption for public bodies (item 1) corresponds to article 132(1)(n)[i] (bodies governed by public law) and the exemption for eligible bodies corresponds to articles 132(1)(n)[ii] (other cultural bodies recognised by the Member State concerned).

---

10 37.3 ("Body governed by public law").

37.12.1 *"Public body"*

VATA sch 9 Group 13 Note 1 defines "public body":

> (1) For the purposes of this Group "public body" means—
> (a) a local authority;
> (b) a government department within the meaning of section 41(6); or
> (c) a non-departmental public body which is listed in the 1995 edition of the publication prepared by the Office of Public Service and known as "Public Bodies".

VAT Notice 701/47 Admission charges to cultural events (31 December 2020) provides:

> **3.1 Types of public bodies that are affected?**
> Local authorities, government departments and those non-departmental public bodies which are listed in the Public Bodies 2017.

37.12.2 *"Eligible body"*

VATA sch 9 Group 13 Note 2 defines "eligible body":

> For the purposes of item 2 "eligible body" means any body (other than a public body) which—
> (a) is precluded from distributing, and does not distribute, any profit it makes;
> (b) applies any profits made from supplies of a description falling within item 2 to the continuance or improvement of the facilities made available by means of the supplies; and
> (c) is managed and administered on a voluntary basis by persons who have no direct or indirect financial interest in its activities.

There are three conditions here which are best considered separately.

37.12.3 *Precluded from distributing profit*

VAT Notice 701/47 Admission charges to cultural events (31 December 2020) provides:

> **4.4 Non-profit making organisation**
> This is an organisation that does not systematically aim to make a profit and which, if profits nevertheless arise, must not distribute them.
> A body whose constitution or articles of association preclude it from distributing surpluses of income over expenditure to its members, shareholders or any other party (other than in the event of a liquidation

> or cessation of activities), and which as a matter of fact does not distribute any profit, will normally be accepted as having satisfied this condition for the purposes of this exemption.
> For the purposes of this exemption, distribution of profit does not include grants or donations made by charities in pursuit of their wider charitable objectives.

Charities will meet this requirement.

37.12.4 *Restricted application of profit*

VAT Notice 701/47 Admission charges to cultural events (131 December 2020) provides:

> **4.5 Satisfying the application of profit condition**
> To qualify for exemption, all profits arising from exempt admission fees must be:
> - used for the continuance or improvement of the facilities made available to the fee-paying public by payment of the exempt admission fees
> - applied in connection with the making of related cultural supplies (such as research or conservation projects).
>
> If profits are applied to any other activities of the body than those above, the body is not eligible for exemption.

37.12.5 *Managed on voluntary basis by person without financial interest*

First one must identify those who manage and administer the body: they will be the charity trustees. Notice 701/47 Admission charges to cultural events (31 December 2020) provides:

> **4.6 Establish whether you're a body managed and administered on an essentially voluntary basis and by people who have no direct or indirect interest in the activities**
> To determine whether this twofold condition is met, you need first to:
> - consider who manages and administers the body - see paragraph 4.7
> - establish that those who are identified as managing and administering the body have no direct or indirect financial interest in the activities of the body - see paragraph 4.8 and establish if they do so on an 'essentially voluntary basis' - see paragraph 4.12
>
> **4.7 Managing and administering the body**
> In determining who manages and administers a body, you should only consider those members who take the decisions of last resort concerning the policy of a body, particularly in the financial and strategic areas, and carry out the higher supervisory tasks. In other words, those who

> determine what a body will do and how it will do it. For the purposes of this condition, persons who carry out purely executory tasks (those who implement, rather than take high level decisions) can be ignored.
> To determine who takes the decisions of last resort, you should consider:
> - the constitution or articles of association to identify the members of the directing organs and their specific tasks
> - what actually happens in fact. In other words, you should also consider those persons who, without being so designated within the constitution, take rather than implement policy decisions at the highest level

Then one asks whether the trustees act on a voluntary basis, and have no direct or indirect financial interest in the activities of the body in question.

VAT Notice 701/47 Admission charges to cultural events (31 December 2020) considers trustee charging provisions:

> **4.11 Persons covered by an 'as of right' provision**
> Some constitutions include an 'as of right' provision. This gives a trustee the right to charge and be paid reasonable remuneration for (typically professional) services within the scope of the body. The right does not depend on the body or its trustees entering into a contract with the trustee affected.
> 'As of rights' provisions are often not exercised for long periods, or are used intermittently. The presence of such a clause in itself (where it has not been exercised) will therefore not disqualify a body from exemption. It is only as and when remuneration is made under this clause that the potential arises for it to cause disqualification from exemption. However, this will depend on the frequency, number and size of any payments made. See paragraph 4.12 for further details.
> **4.12 Check if a body is 'essentially voluntary'**
> To satisfy the condition governing the management and administration of a body, a body need only be essentially, not exclusively, managed and administered on a voluntary basis by persons with no direct or indirect interest in the activities of the body. Therefore, having identified those persons who manage and administer the body, and have a direct or indirect financial interest in its activities, consideration needs to be given to the issue of 'essentially voluntary'.
> The fact that remunerated staff take part occasionally or peripherally in the adoption of the decision of last resort won't, in itself, disqualify a body from exemption.
> However, if one or more persons identified as managing and administering the body at the highest level receives remuneration, then the body won't qualify for exemption.

> In the case of 'as of rights' provisions, the issue is one of degree - that is, the frequency, number and size of any payments made - and each case will turn on its own facts. It is recommended that if you consider that your continued eligibility or otherwise for exemption turns on payments made under an 'as of rights' provision, that you seek a ruling from HMRC. The helpline will be able to provide the address of the office to where the information should be sent

As for how to interpret the term "direct or indirect financial interest", VAT Notice 701/47 Admission charges to cultural events (31 December 2020) provides:

> **4.8 Meaning of direct or indirect financial interest in the activities of a cultural body**
> A person can have a direct or indirect financial interest in the activities of a body if they receive or have a right to remuneration; take up an 'as of rights' provision (as defined in paragraph 4.11), or are in any other way rewarded directly or indirectly by the body, or have any other financial interest in the body. This financial interest has to be actual not potential.
> A person who's managing and administering the cultural body on a voluntary basis can be seen to have an actual financial interest in its activities only when:
> - the person receives any payments for services supplied to the cultural body above the market rate, paid as routine overheads, or the payments made are profit-related (whether below, at or above market rates)
> - there's a link between the payments and the person's participation in the direction of the cultural body's activities
>
> **4.9 Remuneration**
> For the purposes of this notice only, remuneration means a commercial rate of pay or profit-related payment. Hence the making of a token payment only or payments solely to reimburse out-of-pocket expenses would not disqualify a body from exemption provided all other conditions were met.
> **4.10 Direct or indirect financial interest**
> A financial interest does not exist where the only potential is for a financial loss - for example where a risk is underwritten or guaranteed, so that the guarantor only stands to be impoverished and not enriched as a result.
> If a person has a right to a remuneration, but for whatever reason formally opts not to take it, then this 'right' will not disqualify the body from exemption until the person starts exercising their right to a

remuneration.

Similarly, payments to individuals for services of managing and administering the body (within the meaning of the cultural exemption) are not financial interests if:

- they're allowed by the constitution
- the recipient is excluded from any decision making regarding the award of any contract to themselves
- the payments are not above market rates
- are not linked to profits[11]

37.13 Cultural events

37.13.1 *"Museum, gallery, art exhibition or zoo"*

VAT Notice 701/47 Admission charges to cultural events (31 December 2020) provides:

> **2.3 Definition of a museum, gallery, art exhibition or zoo**
> This has to be judged by reference to the normal everyday meaning of the words, taking into account indicative evidence such as the nature of the collections, objects, artefacts, site and exhibits on show. However, for the avoidance of doubt, a botanical garden does not qualify for exemption.

37.13.2 *"Performance of a cultural nature"*

VAT Notice 701/47 Admission charges to cultural events (31 December 2020) provides:

> 2.4 Meaning of theatrical, musical or choreographic performance of a cultural nature?
> Each event has to be judged on its individual merits. However, where live performances of stage plays, dancing or music are considered to be cultural (as they generally are) they'll qualify for exemption.

37.13.3 *Cinema and other cultural events*

The UK law exemption does not include the seventh art. In *British Film Institute v HMRC* the First-tier Tribunal held:

> [68] ... all cultural services qualify for exemption by virtue of [art 132(1)(n) VAT directive] (provided they are "supplied by bodies governed by public law or by other cultural bodies recognised by the

---

11 See also *Bournemouth Symphony Orchestra v C&E, Longborough Festival Opera v HMRC* [2007] STC 198.

> Member State concerned"), and that such exemption took place with direct effect (without the need for any national implementing legislation) once the transitional provisions in art 28(3)(a) [6th VAT directive] expired on 1 January 1990.[12]

The decision was affirmed by the Upper Tribunal, and then the case was referred to the CJEU, which ruled that:

> [14] … the exemption laid down in [article 132(1)(n)] refers to 'certain cultural services'. The provision does not therefore specify which cultural services the Member States are required to exempt. It does not set out an exhaustive list of cultural services to be exempted, or lay down an obligation of the Member States to exempt all cultural services, but refers only to 'certain' of those services. Consequently, the provision leaves it to the Member States to determine the cultural services that are to benefit from the exemption.

The CJEU also disagreed with the UK Tribunals on the question of direct effect:

> [24] In so far as that provision allows the Member States a discretion in determining the exempted cultural services, it does not satisfy the conditions deriving from the case-law…for being capable of being relied on directly before the national courts.
> [25] That finding is not called in question by the considerations in paragraphs 34 to 37 of the judgment of 17 February 2005, *Linneweber and Akritidis* (C-453/02 and C?462/02…), and paragraphs 59 to 61 of the judgment of 28 June 2007, *JP Morgan Fleming Claverhouse Investment Trust and The Association of Investment Trust Companies* (C-363/05…), according to which a discretion that may be allowed to the Member States does not necessarily exclude direct effect of the exemptions concerned.
> [26] As the Commission noted in its written observations, the line of case-law deriving from the judgment of 17 February 2005, *Linneweber and Akritidis* (C-453/02 and C-462/02…), concerns the possibility for the Member States to establish conditions for the application of an exemption, not their discretion to determine the scope of an exemption, such as follows in particular from the words 'certain cultural services' in Article [132](1)(n) of the [VAT] Directive.
> [27] As regards the judgment of 28 June 2007, *JP Morgan Fleming Claverhouse Investment Trust and The Association of Investment Trust Companies* (C-363/05…), it must be noted that Article [132](1)(n) of

---

12 [2013] SFTD 629 at [68].

> the [VAT] Directive may be distinguished from the exemption at issue in that case in that it requires only the exemption of 'certain' cultural services.

37.13.4 *Distortion of competition*

VATA sch 9 Group 13 Notes 3 and 4 restrict the exemption:

> (3) Item 1 does not include any supply the exemption of which would be likely to create distortions of competition such as to place a commercial enterprise carried on by a taxable person at a disadvantage.
> (4) Item 1(b) includes the supply of a right of admission to a performance only if the performance is provided exclusively by one or more public bodies, one or more eligible bodies or any combination of public bodies and eligible bodies.

The Notes only apply to item 1 (public bodies) and not to item 2 (eligible bodies, such as charities).

VAT Notice 701/47 Admission charges to cultural events (31 December 2020) provides:

> **3.2 Supplies by public bodies that aren't exempt**
> Not all supplies are exempt. Exemption does not apply where:
>
> - exemption of admission charges would be likely to distort competition to the disadvantage of a commercial supplier of similar services (paragraph 3.8)
> - the public body enters into a joint venture, profit or income-making arrangement with anyone other than another public or eligible body
>
> An example of a joint venture which would not qualify for exemption is one where the local authority acts as a ticket broker for a commercial promoter or has a profit or income sharing arrangement with that promoter for a qualifying performance.
> An example of a joint venture which would qualify for exemption is one where the local authority sells tickets for a qualifying performance on behalf of an eligible body (the criteria for eligibility are explained in section 4).
> Paragraphs 3.3 to 3.10 explain the arrangements for judging distortion of competition.
> **3.3 Working out if an exemption will distort competition**
> HMRC holds the view that it's entitled to take a national and overall view of competition where admissions to the various cultural activities are supplied by public bodies. It's necessary therefore to establish at the outset whether commercial suppliers of cultural activities may be placed at relative disadvantage if similar supplies made by a particular public

body are treated as exempt. However, once this has been done it isn't necessary to apply this test to each future separate performance.

3.4 Satisfying the non-distortion requirement in order to exempt admissions

You must take steps to notify all identifiable commercial suppliers of related facilities or performances. For example, a local authority will need to identify from its business rating, planning, taxation and other records, any such supplier within its geographical area of responsibility and to notify in writing its intention of introducing exemption to all those suppliers. This could be by individual letter or by public notice in the local press for the authority's geographical area, which will need to specify a date (say 30 days) by which any objection to exemption has to be lodged.

3.5 What to do after the period for objections has expired and none have been received

You can start to exempt the supplies advertised for exemption but must retain copies of the relevant correspondence and advertisements for future examination.

3.6 What to do if you receive objections

If you still wish to exempt and disagree with the objection, you should forward details of the intended exemption together with copies of the relevant correspondence to HMRC. The VAT: general enquiries helpline will be able to provide the address of the office to where the information should be sent. You should not exempt any supplies which are in dispute until the matter has been resolved.

3.7 If you are unable to identify any commercial supplier of similar services

You'll still be able to tax admissions of a qualifying nature. It's our policy that a public body will not have to exempt, if it does not wish to, but this will remain subject to review.

3.8 The meaning of 'similar services'

In identifying commercial suppliers who may be disadvantaged by exemption, a public body will only need to look at museums, galleries, art exhibitions and zoos or theatrical, musical and choreographic performances in isolation. For example, a public body wishing to exempt admission charges to a museum would have to demonstrate that it would not disadvantage commercial museums, galleries, art exhibitions and zoos within its geographical area, but would not have to take account of commercial theatrical, musical and choreographical performances.

Correspondingly, in judging whether exemption of theatrical performances of a cultural nature would disadvantage a commercial supplier, it will be sufficient for the public body to take account of all commercial suppliers of theatrical, musical or choreographic performances within its geographical area - it will not be necessary to take account of commercial museums, galleries, art exhibitions or zoos.

3.9 Theatrical, musical or choreographic performances after you have satisfied the non-distortion requirement

You do not need to check the competitive position of each one. One comprehensive enquiry along the lines of that set out in paragraph 3.4 will be sufficient.

3.10 Periodic checks to make sure that no new commercial supplier of similar services objects to exemption

You do not need to make periodic checks. It will be for that supplier to make a case direct to HMRC as the occasion arises. The helpline will be able to provide the supplier with the address of the office where they should send their information.

37.13.5 *Option to tax*

VAT Notice 701/47Admission charges to cultural events (31 December 2020) provides:

3.7 If you are unable to identify any commercial supplier of similar services

You'll still be able to tax admissions of a qualifying nature. It's our policy that a public body will not have to exempt, if it does not wish to, but this will remain subject to review.

This is a curious application of an exclusion from the exemption - not dissimilar to the approach taken in Revenue and Customs Brief 6 (2017), issued after the *London Borough of Ealing* case, in relation to the VAT treatment of sporting services supplied by local councils - see 37.2 (Restrictions on exemptions) above. The driver (for the taxpayer) is no doubt VAT recovery.

37.14 Fundraising events

37.14.1 *EU-law background*

Article 132 VAT Directive provides:

1. Member States shall exempt the following transactions: ...
   (o) the supply of services and goods by organisations whose activities are exempt pursuant to points (b), (g), (h), (i), (l), (m) and (n), in connection with fund-raising events organised exclusively for their own benefit, provided that exemption is not likely to cause distortion of competition;

...

> 2. For the purposes of point (o) of paragraph 1, Member States may introduce any restrictions necessary, in particular as regards the number of events or the amount of receipts which give entitlement to exemption.

The relief is found in VATA sch 9 Group 12.

Item 1 of Group 12 provides exemption for the following:

> The supply of goods and services by a charity in connection with an event—
> (a) that is organised for charitable purposes by a charity or jointly by more than one charity,
> (b) whose primary purpose is the raising of money, and
> (c) that is promoted as being primarily for the raising of money.

Item 2 provides a similar exemption for a "qualifying body". This term is defined referentially in Note 3 and includes, in short, trades unions and the professional and representational trade associations and public interest bodies that are entitled to exempt subscriptions by virtue of VATA sch 9 Group 9, and the eligible bodies entitled to the sporting and cultural exemptions in Groups 10 and 13. Item 3 of Group 12 provides exemption for fund-raising events organised jointly by a charity and a qualifying body.

The HMRC views are set out in the online Helpsheet "Fundraising events: exemption for charities and other qualifying bodies" [31 December 2020] (the "HMRC Helpsheet").[13] The Helpsheet repeats the material formerly contained in booklet CWL4 (which was formally withdrawn in 2006 though some online references to that booklet are at present still to be found).

37.15 "Event"

VATA sch 9 Group 12 Note 1 defines "event" to include an event accessed wholly or partly by means of electronic communications.

The HMRC Helpsheet para 3.2 provides:

> An 'event' is an incident with an outcome or a result. This means that activities of a semi-regular or continuous nature, such as the frequent operation of a shop or bar, cannot therefore be an event. The relief isn't intended to exempt normal trading activities from VAT.

---

13 The Helpsheet is *https://www.gov.uk/government/publications/charity-fundraising-events-exemptions*

Whether or not one agrees with the first sentence, the rest of the paragraph is clearly correct.

The HMRC Helpsheet continues:

> **3.3 What kind of events are covered by the exemption?**
> The following are examples of different kinds of events which may be held for fundraising purposes:
> - ball, dinner dance, disco or barn dance
> - performance - concert, stage production, and any other event which has a paying audience
> - showing of a film
> - fete, fair or festival
> - horticultural show
> - exhibition: art, history or science
> - bazaar, jumble sale, car boot sale, or a good-as-new sale
> - sporting participation (including spectators): sponsored walk or swim
> - sporting performance
> - game of skill, contest, or a quiz
> - participation in an endurance event
> - fireworks display
> - dinner, lunch or barbecue
> - an auction of bought in goods - an auction of donated goods is zero-rated

37.16 "Charity" for fundraising event exemption

VATA sch 9 Group 12 Note 2 extends the meaning of "charity":

> For the purposes of this Group "charity" includes a body corporate that is wholly owned by a charity if—
> (a) the body has agreed in writing (whether or not contained in a deed) to transfer its profits (from whatever source) to a charity, or
> (b) the body's profits (from whatever source) are otherwise payable to a charity.

HMRC Guidance Note Annex iv para 34 explains:

> ... The statutory VAT exemption for fundraising events also covers fundraising events organised by a corporate body wholly owned by a charity and whose profits (from whatever source) are payable to a charity. This means that a charity's own trading company can hold qualifying fundraising events on behalf of the charity, while still

benefiting from the VAT exemption.

For a draft deed to meet the requirement in Note 2(a), see 9.5.7 (Deed of covenant).

37.17 "Primary purpose is the raising of money"

The HMRC Helpsheet provides at para 3.2:

> ... Social events which incidentally make a profit don't fall within the exemption. People attending or participating in the event must be aware of its primary fund-raising purpose.
>
> ...
>
> **3.6 Events run over several days but at the same location**
>
> ...
>
> The following don't qualify for exemption:
>
> ...
>
> - events which aren't organised and promoted for fund-raising purposes, such as events which form part of a social calendar for members
> - events which are organised and promoted primarily for another purpose, such as an annual general meeting
>
> ...
>
> **3.15 Evidence to show the event was organised and promoted primarily to raise funds**
>
> There's no single document that you must hold to demonstrate that the event was organised primarily to raise funds. Minutes of meetings, costing and similar documents should show that the main purpose for holding the event is to raise funds for charitable purposes or a qualifying body's own benefit.
>
> The event must be promoted in such a way that those attending the event are aware that its main purpose is to raise funds. Publicity material, tickets etc. should therefore clearly refer to fundraising. For example
>
> - fund-raising for
> - in aid of
> - help us to build
> - help us to raise money for.
>
> Examples of publicity material, tickets etc, should be retained to support evidence of exemption.

An AGM may meet the "primary purpose" test if it was just tacked on to a fundraising event. If the intention is to qualify for the relief, the charity literature should make it plain that the primary purpose is raising money.

In *Loughborough Students Union* [2018] UKFTT 0357, the Appellants argued that anything they did that turned a surplus "must be an organised fundraising event". This was (not surprisingly) rejected by the First-tier Tribunal.

The Appellants in the case also challenged "the effectiveness of Group 12, viewed against the [*VAT*] Directive" - in particular, whether Item 1 (and the relevant Notes) were compliant with Article 132(1)(o).

> 85. First, the condition in Item 1(b) that the raising of money must be the primary purpose of the event. While this condition is not explicitly provided in art 132(1)(o), it follows from my conclusions on the meaning of an organised fundraising event … that a primary purpose of fundraising is a fair interpretation of the legislative wording in art 132(1)(o). Accordingly, I conclude that Item 1(b) is not ultra vires art 132(1)(o).
> 86. Secondly, the condition in Item 1(c) that the event must be promoted as being primarily for the raising of money. Again, this is not explicitly provided in art 132(1)(o). I assume (I heard no submissions on this specific point) the purpose of this condition is to ensure that persons attending (or planning to attend) a fundraising event are aware that it is such an event, and so they regard themselves as benefactors of the organisation rather than mere customers of the goods and services provided at the event. If that is the purpose behind the condition then I consider the restriction is unwarranted. If a charity organises a fundraising event (say, a jumble or nearly-new sale of donated items) then the motivation of customers (benefactors or bargain hunters) does not, I consider, affect the character of the event as a fundraiser. Accordingly, I conclude that Item 1(c) is an unwarranted restriction on the availability of the exemption, and thus is ultra vires art 132(1)(o).

Having held that VATA sch 9 Group 12 Item 1(c) - the requirement for the event to be promoted as being primarily for the raising of money - was *ultra vires* Article 132(1)(o) of the VAT Directive, the First-tier Tribunal continued:

> 88. … That nonconformity requires consideration of the Marleasing principle, which requires a national court of a Member State to interpret the national law in the light and wording of the directive …
> 89. It is straightforward for me to read Item 1 so as to be compliant and conforming with art 132(1)(o); the only offending provision is Item 1(c) and Item 1 is coherent with the simple omission of Item 1(c). So, for completeness, I would read Item 1 after such adjustment as being:
> "The supply of goods and services by a charity in connection with an event-

> *(a)* that is organised for charitable purposes by a charity or jointly by more than one charity, and
> *(b)* whose primary purpose is the raising of money."
>
> 90. That reading "cures" Item 1 so that it is fully compliant with art 132(1)(o). Therefore, I do not accept the Appellants' contention that Item 1 cannot be cured under the Marleasing principle.

37.18 More than 15 events

VATA sch 9 Group 12 Note 4 provides a restriction if there are more than 15 events of the same kind in the same location:

> Where in a financial year[14] of a charity or qualifying body there are held at the same location more than 15 events involving[15] the charity or body that are of the same kind, items 1 to 3 do not apply (or shall be treated as having not applied) to a supply in connection with any event involving the charity or body that is of that kind and is held in that financial year at that location.

The HMRC Helpsheet states:

> **3.4 Limits to the number of events held**
> Eligible events are restricted to 15 events of the same kind in your financial year at any one location by a charity (including its trading subsidiary) or qualifying body. The restriction prevents distortion of competition with other suppliers of similar events which do not benefit from tax exemption. If you hold 16 or more events of the same kind at the same location during your financial year none of the events will qualify for exemption.
>
> **3.5 What does 'location' mean?**
> Location means in the same place. Similar kinds of events held in different locations would qualify for exemption provided all other conditions were met. For example, 20 balls held by a national charity each in different towns in the same financial year would all qualify for relief.
>
> Clearly, events which need to be held on special premises, such as a

---

14 There is an appropriate adjustment if the financial year is longer or shorter than a year - see VATA sch 9 Group 12 Note 6.

15 VATA sch 9 Group 12 Note 7 defines "involving":
For the purposes of Notes (4) and (5)–
(a) an event involves a charity if the event is organised by the charity or a connected charity;
(b) an event involves a qualifying body if the event is organised by the body.
In this Note "organised" means organised alone or jointly in any combination ...

sports ground, swimming pool or theatre are easy to define. Each of these will be accepted as a different location.

If the event is held in a complex of cinemas, theatres or concert halls, the location is the specific cinema, theatre or concert hall in which the fundraising event takes place.

HMRC regards a charity's entire website as a location for events held over the internet.

The rule is designed to be generous to charities which may hold a number of events of the same type in different locations, but in the same town. HMRC will not accept arrangements such as weekly boot sales each held in different, but adjacent fields, as constituting a separate location without considering whether such an arrangement is potentially distorting competition.

3.6 Events run over several days but at the same location

Where an event, such as a concert, is repeated on successive evenings each performance is a separate event and counts towards the maximum number of 15 allowed within the exemption. A single event which takes place at the same location for more than 1 day, such as a golf tournament, is accepted as 1 event.

Where a concert or similar event is offered as part of a travel package this may not be exempt.

...

3.8 More than 15 events of the same kind at a location: is VAT charged only from the 16th event?

No. Every event in a programme of 16 or more events will be taxable at the standard rate. The exemption applies up to 15 events of the same kind at a location. To exempt the first 15 events in a longer sequence risks distortion of competition. If you hold 16 or more events of the same kind at the same location during your financial year none of the events will qualify for exemption.

3.9 Frequent small scale events

The 15 event limit doesn't apply to fundraising events where the gross takings from all similar events, such as coffee mornings, are no more than £1,000 per week. Such activities carried out more than once or twice a week are likely to be trading activities and not eligible for exemption ...

3.10 Small scale events: take over £1000 in a week

All the events in that week won't qualify as small scale events and each will count towards the 15 event allowance.

3.11 Can the hire of a room or other costs be offset against the £1,000?

No. The £1,000 limit relates to the income of the events prior to any costs being deducted.

In *Loughborough Students Union* [2018] UKFTT 0357:

> 87. … the Appellants raise a further ultra vires challenge to Item 1 - they assert that the restrictions in Notes 4 (the 15 event limit) and 11 (no distortion of competition) are ultra vires art 132(1)(o). Their first submission on this point is that Note 11 is exhaustive of distortion of competition matters, and so Note 4 cannot co-exist with Note 11. I do not agree; art 132(2) (emphasis added) specifically permits member states to "introduce any restrictions necessary, in particular as regards the number of events... which give entitlement to exemption". I conclude the purpose of that provision is to allow member states to particularise permitted restrictions in addition to the mandatory restriction in art 132(1)(o), "provided that exemption is not likely to cause distortion of competition". That is exactly what the UK has done in Notes 4 & 11. The Appellants' second submission on this point is that the 15 event restriction is unnecessary. As already stated, art 132(2) specifically permits a restriction on the number of events and so I take the argument to be that the UK has imposed an unnecessary restriction on the exemption by stipulating the limit to be 15 events. I heard no argument as to why a limit of 15 events (as opposed to some other number) was unnecessary; I agree with HMRC that that figure may be generous, in terms of the number of events that could be held during a year without distorting competition with VATable traders. For those reasons I conclude that Notes 4 & 11 are not ultra vires art 132(1)(o).

37.19 Accommodation provided

VATA sch 9 Group 12 Notes 8 and 9 provide another exception to the exemption:

> (8) Items 1 to 3 do not include any supply in connection with an event if—
>
> (a) accommodation in connection with the event is provided to a person by means of a supply, or in pursuance of arrangements, made by—
>
> (i) the charity or any of the charities, or the qualifying body, organising[16] the event, or
>
> (ii) a charity connected[17] with any charity organising the

16 VATA sch 9 Group 12 Note 7 defines "organising":

> … In this Note "organised" means organised alone or jointly in any combination, and "organising" in Note (8) shall be construed accordingly.

17 The term "connected" is given a very restricted meaning in VATA sch 9 Group 12 Note 10:

event,

and

(b) the provision of the accommodation is not incidental to the event.

(9) For the purposes of Note (8) the provision of accommodation is incidental to the event only if accommodation provided to the person by such means, or in pursuance of such arrangements, as are mentioned in paragraph (a) of that Note—

(a) does not exceed two nights in total (whether or not consecutive), and

(b) is not to any extent provided by means of a supply to which an order under section 53 applies.

37.19.1 *Interaction with tour operator margin scheme*

The HMRC Helpsheet provides:

> **3.14 Are fundraising holidays or day trips VAT exempt?**
> Any fundraising activity which falls within the Tour Operator's Margin Scheme, such as a package of travel and accommodation, or which includes more than 2 nights accommodation doesn't qualify for the fundraising exemption. Read further information about the scheme in VAT Notice 709/5: Tour Operators Margin Scheme.

37.20 Distortion of competition

VATA sch 9 Group 12 Note 11 provides:

> Items 1 to 3 do not include any supply the exemption of which would be likely to create distortions of competition such as to place a commercial enterprise carried on by a taxable person at a disadvantage.

The HMRC Helpsheet provides:

> **3.13 Why is there an anti-competition clause?**
> The restriction prevents distortion of competition with other suppliers of similar events which don't benefit from tax exemption. HMRC will

---

(10) For the purposes of Notes (7)(a) and (8), two charities are connected if—

(a) one is a charity for the purposes of this Group only by virtue of Note (2) and the other is the charity that owns it, or

(b) each is a charity for the purposes of this Group only by virtue of Note (2) and the two of them are owned by the same charity.

So it may be possible to avoid the problem by arranging for a non-connected charity to supply the accommodation, although as with all "structured" VAT arrangements, the anti-abuse principle should be considered. .

only use this measure where either:

- this relief is likely to distort the market
- there's significant and systematic evidence of commercial distortion.

If a commercial organisation alleged competitive disadvantage, HMRC would look carefully into the matter and any subsequent action would depend upon the particular circumstances. A charity would have the right of appeal against the decision.

See *Loughborough Students Union* [2018] UKFTT 0357 for a case where exemption is denied because of Note 11.

37.21 Extent of exemption

The HMRC Helpsheet provides:

4.7 What income is included in the exemption?

All the income for supplies of goods and services in connection with an event is exempt, for example

- all admission charges
- the sale of commemorative brochures (may be zero rated)
- the sale of advertising space in those brochures (may be zero rated)
- other items sold by the charity such as t-shirts, non-donated auctioned goods etc - where items are normally supplied zero rated such as children's t-shirts, then zero rating rather than exemption can be applied
- sponsorship payments directly connected with a qualifying event

4.8 Income not included in the exemption

Commemorative goods and souvenirs sold for a period after the qualifying fundraising event, eg:

- video and audio recordings of the fundraising event sold after the event has taken place will be standard rated
- surplus commemorative items such as adult t-shirts, mugs etc will be standard rated
- commemorative programmes will remain zero rated
- children's t-shirts will remain zero rated
- donated goods for sale may still be sold VAT free provided the normal conditions are met

37.22 Avoiding exemption

The exemption is compulsory. There is no need for election or provision for disclaimer. The desire may be not to qualify, so the supplies are taxable (if the VAT can be reclaimed by those who receive the supplies). One way to achieve this is to use a non-charitable subsidiary which is not wholly owned by a charity. The charity law aspects of this proposal would need consideration (as would the anti-abuse principle).

37.23 Interaction with zero-rating provisions

HMRC Guidance Note Annex iv para 30 provides:

> **The VAT exemption for fundraising events**
> The statutory provision for the VAT exemption is Group 12, Schedule 9 of the VAT Act 1994. Under this provision, supplies of goods and services by charities and other qualifying bodies in connection with certain fundraising events are exempt from VAT.
> Detailed guidance on the bodies that qualify for the exemption and all the conditions that must be met are contained in the tax and VAT Helpsheet Fund-raising events: Exemption for charities and other qualifying bodies.
> If the conditions for the exemption are met, the supplies made in connection with the event are exempt from VAT. This means that no VAT is due on the supplies and, if not already VAT registered, this income should not be taken into account when considering liability to register.
> There's no entitlement to recover VAT incurred in making the exempt supplies or organising the event. However, if, within a VAT-exempt fundraising event, sales of goods or service are made to which the zero rate normally applies (eg printed matter or children's clothing) then those zero-rated sales can remain taxable at the zero rate despite the fact they're sold in the course of a VAT exempt fundraising event. As these are taxable supplies, any VAT incurred in the making of the zero-rated supplies will be recoverable, subject to normal rules if VAT registered.
> If VAT's incurred on expenses relating to both exempt and taxable supplies a portion of the VAT may be recoverable subject to partial exemption calculations ...

The HMRC Helpsheet provides:

> **3.12 Can zero-rated supplies be made at an exempt event?**
> Yes, the sale of printed matter, such as programmes and commemorative brochures or any other goods which are eligible for the zero rate relief from VAT, may still be zero rated when supplied at a fundraising event. This means that a VAT-registered charity or other qualifying body will be able to recover any input tax which is directly attributable to the taxable supply of those goods.
> Examples of zero-rated items are:
> - the sale of donated goods by a charity

- eligible food
- eligible printed matter
- young children's clothing
- the supply of advertising time or space to a charity
- any other goods which qualify for zero rating.b

CHAPTER THIRTY EIGHT

VAT: ZERO RATING

38.1 Introduction

This chapter considers some supplies which qualify for VAT zero-rating: advertising and donated goods

For an introduction to zero-rating, see 37.1 (Rates, exemption and zero rating).

38.2 Advertising

Under VATA sch 8 group 15 the following items are zero-rated:

> 8 The supply to a charity of a right to promulgate an advertisement by means of a medium of communication with the public.
> 8A A supply to a charity that consists in the promulgation of an advertisement by means of such a medium.
> 8B The supply to a charity of services of design or production of an advertisement that is, or was intended to be, promulgated by means of such a medium.
> 8C The supply to a charity of goods closely related to a supply within item 8B.

The Notes to these items provide:

> (10A) Neither of items 8 and 8A includes a supply where any of the members of the public (whether individuals or other persons) who are reached through the medium are selected by or on behalf of the charity. For this purpose "selected" includes selected by address (whether postal

address or telephone number, e-mail address or other address for electronic communications purposes) or at random.
(10B) None of items 8 to 8C includes a supply used to create, or contribute to, a website that is the charity's own.
For this purpose a website is a charity's own even though hosted by another person.
(10C) Neither of items 8B and 8C includes a supply to a charity that is used directly by the charity to design or produce an advertisement.

The VCHAR Manual provides:

VCHAR5000 - Advertising [Jun 2021]
The supply of advertising by a charity is normally taxable at the standard rate. However there are some exceptions to this rule which are set out in Notice 701/1 (HMRC website) Charities. One exception is the sale of advertising space to another charity. This can be treated as zero-rated if supplied to another UK charity - for details see Notice 701/58 (HMRC Website) Charity advertising and goods connected with collecting donations.

The relief has a long history:

VCHAR11000 - Advertising [Jun 2021]
Background
In 1984 VAT was introduced on newspaper advertising, which had previously been zero-rated. Reliefs for adverts placed by charities were restored in 1986. The relief at that stage was limited to non-classified advertising which was intended either to educate people in the objects of the charity or to encourage fund-raising. The relief was also restricted to adverts placed in a newspaper, periodical or magazine.
Because of the difficulties in determining what was meant by the term 'non-classified' the relief was extended to include classified advertising in April 1989. At the same time the opportunity was taken to extend the range of places in which an advert would qualify to include programmes, annuals, leaflets and similar publications, and on posters.
In April 1991 the relief was extended to zero-rating for airtime purchased on television, radio and cinema for qualifying adverts.
Problems continued with 'dual purpose' advertisements, such as recruitment advertisements with a 'qualifying message' displaying the charity's objects, and in September 1996 the relief for recruitment advertisements was withdrawn. An exception was made for Voluntary Service Overseas (VSO) volunteers and similar adverts.
Following a review of Charity taxation in 1999 a more far-reaching change in reliefs was effected in April 2000. This was done by recasting

the scope of the relief in Item 8 and introducing the current qualifying notes 10A to 10C. All remaining restrictions in the medium used to advertise and the purpose of the advert were removed. The relief for associated design and production costs was extended accordingly where there was an associated supply of advertising.

An extra-statutory concession was also introduced giving relief to the supply of various goods connected with charitable collections (see ESC 3.3 in Notice 48 Extra-statutory concessions or Notice 701/58 (HMRC website) Charity advertising and goods connected with collecting donations). This included relief on certain items contained in direct mailing applications.

UK VAT law

[The VCHAR Manual sets out items 8-8C and continues]:

The word 'promulgate' is used in Items 8, 8A, and 8B. Words carrying a similar meaning are broadcast, propagate, spread, disseminate, circulate and publish. The word carries an active meaning to what constitutes an advertisement. The charity should be paying to use someone else's time or space.

[The VCHAR Manual sets out the notes to the items and continues]

The effect of the notes is to make restrictions in the relief in respect of direct mailshots (see Postal appeals packs), charity websites and in-house supplies (see In-house supplies, below).

What is an advertisement?

There is no statutory definition of the word 'advertisement'. It may be taken as a notice made available to the public in any form with the purpose of making a message known whether commercial or otherwise. The reproduction of a charity logo, even when unaccompanied by any further text, is an advertisement. The supply of advertising is the purchase of somebody else's time or space.

In order for zero-rating to apply the supply must be to a charity. A supply to a charity's subsidiary trading company will not qualify for relief (see VCHAR2100).

In-house supplies

Charities may choose to produce their own advertising material. This may be either by way of a supply used to create or contribute to a website giving information about the charity or by the production of display material which is then put into use directly or by the direction of the charity. Zero-rating does not apply to these supplies – see notes 10B and 10C of the Schedule reproduced above.

Medium of communication

If the public is reached by the message given by the charity then the supply to the charity is zero-rated under Items 8 to 8C. Any medium of communication may be used. New media will be found from time to time but the test is essentially the same one. Means of communication such as signwriting, peelable plastic stickers or banners and repeating loop systems, such as those found in post offices, will all qualify as media.

Communication with the public

It is essential that there is effective contact with the public at large. Hence we would accept a cinema advert as being within Item 8 but not an advert placed on a DVD. By its nature a DVD is normally the property of a single household and does not reach the wider public. This applies both to advertisements inserted on a DVD and a DVD describing the work of a charity, even if the DVD promotes the objects of a charity or serves a fund-raising purpose. A CD-Rom promoting a charity would not attract relief for the same reason.

The liability of the supply can be apportioned if necessary. For example, a charity needs 100 banners for public display but finds that the print run is barely more expensive for 200 and orders the larger amount, using only the first 100 for public display.

The preparation of posters or other items falling outside the reliefs for books, etc for use in-house by a charity (in its own offices) are standard-rated as the public would not have access to these.

What services qualify for relief?

Where there is a single supply of services of preparing and publishing an advertisement the whole supply will qualify for zero-rating under Item 8A. Where the preparatory services/goods are supplied separately they will fall within Items 8B and 8C.

Services or goods which qualify for relief under Items 8B and 8C extend beyond the cost of publishing the advert to the costs of producing the advert.

Supplies which qualify include:

- printing
- design or artwork
- typesetting.

Supplies which do not qualify include:

- courier services
- distribution and mailing services.

This is because the services of distributing a leaflet, poster or other publication are not themselves promulgations of an advertisement.

Postal appeals packs

Many charities send out appeal packs by post. These packs are NOT covered by the relief for advertising as Note 10A specifically excludes direct mail packs.

A printing company normally puts these packs together for the charity. Where there is a multiple supply of a package consisting entirely of items printed on paper or card and the items have a common link, the supplier can use a 'package test' to determine the overall VAT liability. If there are more zero-rated items than standard-rated items then the supplier can zero rate the whole package. See Notice 701/10 (HMRC website) Books etc for more information.

Since August 2003 ESC 3.3 for charity stationery can be used in conjunction with the 'package test'. This means that pre-printed appeals letters and outer and return envelopes will count as zero-rated for the 'package test'. However, printed lapel stickers count as standard-rated for the 'package test' as they are only eligible for zero-rating under the ESC when they are given away in acknowledgement of a donation – if a charity includes them in a postal appeal pack it is giving the sticker away before any donation has been received.

Where an appeals pack contains an item which is not printed on paper or card, each item supplied to the charity must bear its own individual VAT liability – the supplier cannot use the 'package test'. Many charities include 'token' items such as a charity pen, ribbon or bulb. These are taxable at the standard rate when supplied to the charity. We maintain that the supply of the pack to the charity in such instances is a multiple supply of goods and not a single supply with dominant and ancillary elements.

Appeal letters whose primary purpose is to appeal for money

Item (e) in Extra Statutory Concession 3.3 allows relief for pre-printed letters the primary purpose of which is to appeal for money for charity. It includes 'thank you' letters and 'remember us in your will' letters. It does not include lobbying 'write to your MP' letters.

HMRC Brief 25/10 provides:

VAT: pay-per-click charity advertisements

This Revenue & Customs Brief explains our revised policy on the VAT treatment of pay-per-click (PPC) charity advertising on sponsored links and other associated services.

Background

PPC is used by organisations on search engines such as Google to encourage searchers to click on the organisation's link in priority to any other links on the results page following a search. The organisation pays the search engine provider an agreed amount each time their website is accessed through the sponsored link. Supplies of advertisements for charities, when placed on a third party's website, and their design and production costs, attract the zero-rate of VAT under Schedule 8, Group 15, Item 8 and 8A–8C of VATA 1994. We have until now taken the view that a PPC-sponsored link is not an advertisement itself but simply a means of access to the charity's website. As such, we considered the

> costs of providing PPC were excluded from zero-rating by Note 10B to Group 15, Schedule 8 which excludes zero-rating on the costs of providing a charity's website. Following representations from charities that zero-rating should apply to PPC charity advertisements, we have reviewed our approach and concluded we should revise the VAT treatment of PPC advertising supplied to charities.
>
> **Revised policy**
>
> We now accept that PPC-sponsored links appearing on search engine websites are advertisements for the purpose of Item 8 and 8A, and qualify for zero-rating when supplied to a charity. It follows that the supply of copyright and design services associated with such sponsored links fall within the zero-rating. However, we still maintain that services supplied by copywriters and designers for the purpose of search engine optimisation (structuring a website so that it contains as many keywords as possible) do not qualify for relief. We consider that these services entail the optimisation of the charity's own website, and so are specifically excluded from Item 8 by Note 10B to Group 15. The listing of a charity in the results of a search engine ("natural hits") does not constitute the promulgation of an advertisement for the purpose of Item 8 since the charity's name appears automatically, regardless of any action taken by or on behalf of a charity, and merely highlights text from the charity's own website.
>
> **Making claims or adjustments**
>
> Businesses that have accounted for and paid VAT on supplies of charity advertisements that are now considered to be zero-rated may submit claims for overpaid tax. These will be subject to a transitional four year limitation period and "unjust enrichment" provisions. Guidance on how to make claims is contained in VAT Notice 700/45 "How to correct VAT errors or make adjustments or claims".
>
> **Further information**
>
> Detailed guidance on charity advertising can be found in VAT Notice 701/58 "Charity advertising and goods connected with collecting donations". If you are in any doubt about the correct treatment please contact the Charities Helpline on 0845 302 0203.

HMRC have published guidance in VAT Notice 701/58 (Goods or services supplied to charities) (31 January 2019). We here set out only those comments which are not already dealt with in the VCHAR Manual:

2.3 Relief on advertisements

The relief covers all types of advertisements on any subject, including staff recruitment. The name or logo of the charity does not need to be included for relief to be allowed. This relief does not override charity law or the need to meet the British Codes of Advertising or any other relevant regulations.

3 Advertising media

3.1 In what media can charities advertise VAT free?

Any medium which communicates with the public. This includes all the conventional advertising media such as:

- television
- cinema
- billboards
- the sides of vehicles
- newspapers
- printed publications.

If space is sold to a charity for advertising on other items, this will also be covered by the zero rate, examples are:

- beer mats
- calendars
- the reverse of till rolls
- clothing

The sale of the items themselves will not be VAT free, unless they qualify for other reliefs for example as books or children's clothing.

3.2 What does the term "the public" cover

It means the general public, which can be widely interpreted to include businesses and small groups, such as:

- readers of a trade magazine
- readers of a religious magazine
- people in particular parts of the country who may be targeted by a general poster campaign in their area.

It does not include selected individuals or groups.

3.3 Individuals and groups

These are people who are—

- selected by individual home, business or e-mail address whether named or not
- individually named people, all those at the same address such as family groups or everyone in a particular building

  HMRC considers that selected individuals and groups also include people who are selected via their browsing history. This has led to controversy between the charity sector, their advisors and advertisers on the one hand and HMRC on the other. On 8 September 2020, HMRC released Revenue and Customs Brief 13 (2020) : VAT charity digital advertising relief:

  1. Purpose of this brief

  This brief sets out HMRC's policy in different digital advertising situations. It also explains what advertisers and their customers may need to do.

...

3. Background

Zero rate VAT applies for advertising services supplied by a third party to a charity when the services are designed for the general public. The advertisements can be by any method. The zero rate is explained in detail in VAT Notice 701/58: goods or services supplied to charities.

However, advertising services are excluded from the zero rate if a member of the public has been selected by or on behalf of the charity to receive the advertising. In these circumstances 'selected' includes any method of contact, including electronic communications.

It has always been accepted that advertisements supplied by digital methods have the potential to fall within the zero rate. Revenue & Customs Brief 25/10 explains HMRC's policy of pay-per-click charity advertising on sponsored links, including the treatment of 'natural hits' and direct placements on third party websites. However, digital advertising services include a level of selection that can make it difficult to determine if the zero rate can apply.

HMRC has reviewed a range of digital advertising situations. This brief sets out the policy for those and reiterates the treatment previously stated in Revenue & Customs Brief 25/10.

4. HMRC's policy

The VAT treatment of advertisements can vary. Online advertising services are complex and constantly changing, but they are aimed at general audiences rather than at individuals. On that basis, HMRC has accepted that some, though not all, of the situations we have seen are eligible for the zero rate.

The information below gives details of items eligible for the zero rate and those that remain standard rated.

4.1 Zero rated subject to all other conditions being met

Audience targeting

The use of demographic, behavioural and other third-party data to identify a target audience and placing advertisements related to that data as they browse elsewhere.

Behavioural targeting

Using cookies to identify people who have visited websites or made searches related to particular areas of interest and placing advertisements for related goods and services which are displayed as they browse elsewhere.

Channel targeting

The selection of a specific section of a website on which to place advertisements.

Content targeting

Selection of specific content for advertisements to appear alongside.

Daypart targeting
Advertisers choose to target only specific times of day or specific days of the week, without any decisions involving recipients. This is because their advertisements are more relevant to those periods.

Demographic targeting
Use of data from a number of sources, including logged in and behavioural data, to identify target audiences. The advertisements will be related to that data as they browse elsewhere.

Device targeting
Advertisers choose to reach only certain types of device.

Direct placements on third party websites
Placing an advertisement on a website without any decisions involving recipients. The choice of website is the main consideration.

Location targeting
This is similar to behavioural targeting. When individuals opt in to provide location data, this information is collected and combined into large datasets to target audiences who have visited particular areas. Advertisements relating to that data are then displayed as they browse elsewhere. No personal data or survey results are collected.

Lookalike targeting
Using cookies to identify potential new customers by looking at common traits and behaviours of existing customers.

Pay-per-click adverts
Used to encourage people browsing to click on an organisation's link in precedence to other links shown. The search engine receives a fee every time the organisation's website is accessed through the sponsored link.

Retargeting
Use of cookies to track users and find them again when they browse the internet.

4.2 Standard rated

Email advertisements
Advertisements sent to email addresses are targeted at the individual recipient and are therefore excluded from zero rating.

Natural hits
The listing of a charity in the results of a search engine. This happens automatically regardless of any action taken by or on behalf of the charity and just highlights text from the charity's own website. Such results are not considered advertisements for VAT relief.

Social media/subscription website accounts
When individuals log in to their personal pages, sites use tools to apply advertisements to them when they are signed in. The content will be related to the individual's known likes, dislikes, interests or location, as a signed in member of the website.

HMRC will continue to engage with external stakeholders to ensure we understand the VAT treatment of changing advertising practices.

5. Design and production of advertisements

Generally, as long as the advertisement being published qualifies for the zero rate, the copyright, design and production services will also qualify. VAT Notice 701/58: goods or services supplied to charities gives more details.

However, services supplied by copywriters and designers for the purpose of search engine optimisation, structuring a website so that it contains as many keywords as possible, do not qualify for the zero rate. These services involve the optimisation of a charity's own website and are specifically excluded from the relief.

6. Making claims or adjustments

VAT Notice 700/45: how to correct VAT errors and make adjustments or claims gives information on how to make adjustments.

Businesses that have accounted for and paid VAT on supplies of charity advertisements that are now considered to be zero rated can submit claims for overpaid tax.

All claims will be subject to the 4 year time limit in section 80(4) of the Value Added Tax Act 1994. They can also be considered for unjust enrichment.

7. More information

Amendments will be made to HMRC's guidance in VAT Notice 701/58: goods or services supplied to charities and the VAT Charities guidance manual to reflect this information.

If you are in any doubt about the correct treatment of your charity advertising, please contact the Charities Helpline, Telephone: 0300 123 1073.

Returning to VAT Notice 701/58

3.4 Direct mail and telesales

Both are left out of the relief because they're not a supply of advertising time or space but are marketing and advertising addressed to selected individuals or groups. Direct mail includes that sent by post, fax or electronically.

Individual elements of a postal package can still be zero-rated under the concession for appeal letters and envelopes, see section 6, or because they're, for example, brochures or leaflets. For details on zero-rating of printed matter (including the 'package test' concession) see paragraph 6.4.

3.5 'Package test' for printed matter applying to charities' direct mailing

Suppliers can apply the package test for printed matter to charities' direct mailing materials. See paragraph 6.4 for more information.

3.6 Print and mail

See Postage, delivery and direct marketing (VAT Notice 700/24) for details of how to decide the liability of goods that are delivered.

3.7 Information on the internet

Information, whether or not in the form of advertising, placed in, on or through a charity's own internet site, does not qualify for zero-rating. This is because it is not a supply of someone else's time or space whether or not the website is owned, rented or loaned to the charity. Since the information on the website is left out of the relief, it follows that the associated design costs are also left out. An advertisement placed on a third party's internet site does qualify for zero-rating.

3.8 Methods excluded from the relief

Any method that is not the supply of someone else's advertising time or space, or is in the form of general marketing and promotion. The following are left out:

- direct mail and telesales (see paragraph 3.4)
- anything on a charity's own internet website (see paragraph 3.7)
- advertisements where there's no supply of time or space to the charity, for example, an advertisement on a charity's own greeting cards;
- exhibition stands and space
- services of distribution
- commemorative items whether or not they bear the charity's logo, for example, pens and adult clothing

4 Design and production of advertisements

4.1 Relief on the design or production of an advertisement

Provided it's intended that the advertisement will meet the conditions set out in section 2 and section 3, the supply of design or production of the advertisement will qualify for relief. This includes the design of a poster or the filming or recording of an advertisement to be broadcast.

4.2 Relief on goods linked to the design or production of the advertisement

Goods closely related to the design and production, for example:

- a finished article like a film or recorded cassette
- an element to be incorporated in the advertisement such as a photograph, picture or a sound track
- all other versions of an advertisement produced, to see which works best, even if it's the intention that only one version will be used

4.3 Charities creating their own advertisements

There's no relief because this is not a supply to the charity. Therefore, it is not possible for charities to purchase the equipment and raw materials they use in creating these advertisements VAT free.

4.4 Liability of services with advertising agencies

When a charity uses an advertising agency instead of having a contract with the suppliers of advertising or printing, the VAT liability depends on whether the agency is acting as a principal or an agent. The normal VAT rules for agent or principal agreements will apply.

See VAT guide (VAT Notice 700) the VAT guide for further guidance. This mean that where an advertising agency:

- is the principal, its supply of qualifying advertising time or space and associated production costs to the charity will be zero-rated, however, supplies to the agency will be standard-rated
- acts solely as an agent, the agency fees, charged to the charity, will be standard-rated; the supply of the advertising time or space will be direct to the charity and will be allowed for zero rating under this relief in the normal way.

4.5 It looks as if the liability has to be determined backwards

To some extent, it does. It must first be determined whether a proposed advertisement is intended to be supplied in a way which will qualify for zero rating. If it's the preceding design and production work when supplied to a charity, it will also be zero-rated.

4.6 Pay VAT retrospectively on production costs if the advertisement does not get used

A charity will not have to pay, provided it was clearly the charity's intention to use the services for an advertisement which would have qualified for relief, it will not be required to pay the tax in the event of the work being wasted.

4.7 Apply for retrospective relief

A charity cannot apply for retrospective relief on goods or services purchased for another purpose but subsequently used for a qualifying advertisement.

4.8 Advertisements used in qualifying and non-qualifying media

When a charity knows that a proportion of their purchases, such as posters or artwork for magazine advertisements, are going to be used in public places as well as in-house (for example in the charity's own magazine or shop window), this should be reflected in the declaration given to the supplier. The VAT liability should be split in line with this.

[Paragraphs 5-8 set out the ESCs for (1) printed stationery, (2) boxes and receptacles for the collection of money and (3) lapel stickers and similar tokens - see CROSS REFERENCE SECTION 3 (Goods used to collect donations) BELOW.]

9 Other reliefs

9.1 Other reliefs available

The reliefs described in this notice should not be confused with those contained in Zero rating books and printed matter (VAT Notice 701/10). Some goods such as books and leaflets, will be zero-rated to charities under the relief for printed matter as they are when supplied to all other customers.

10 How to claim relief

10.1 Claimr elief if you're a charity

When a charity claims any of the special zero rate reliefs which are not generally available to all customers, suppliers must be sure that all the relevant rules for relief are met. It's recommended that a charity gives its supplier a declaration that the specific rules for the claimed relief are fulfilled.

10.2 Declarations

Declarations are usually but not always. The current law should make it easier for printers, publishers, broadcasters and similar suppliers to judge whether their supplies to charities will be zero-rated. Suppliers will, however, always need evidence that the supply was made to a charity.

An example of where a declaration may not be necessary is when a charity requests repeat orders, has made a declaration for the first one and the information contained in that declaration has not changed.

10.3 Supplier's responsibility

It's the supplier's responsibility to make sure that the correct VAT rate is applied. They must take reasonable steps to check with the charity any thing which they cannot verify for themselves. Any extra verifications carried out should be recorded and kept with the declaration of eligibility.

If a supplier has taken reasonable steps to check the validity of a declaration but fails to identify an inaccuracy and in good faith makes the supplies concerned at the zero rate, HMRC will not seek to recover the tax due from the supplier. It's therefore important that suppliers carefully check declarations received. (See the ESC on incorrect customer declarations in VAT Notice 48: Extra Statutory Concessions.)

10.4 Charity's responsibility

A charity must give its supplier evidence that it's a charity.

For lapel emblems it will be necessary to declare that they keep to the use criteria of the concession. When asked for further evidence the charity must be able and willing to give it before VAT relief can be given.

10.5 Form of declaration

HMRC has suggested a form of declaration, which you may copy and use if you wish. It's strongly recommended that suppliers fill in part 2 of this form. Other types of declaration whether in paper form, faxed or electronic that contains sufficient verifiable information to accurately identify the customer are acceptable to HMRC.

Charity advertising request for zero rating
Part 1 is to be completed by the charity.
(tick as appropriate)
(* delete as appropriate)
................................(full name)
................................(status in organisation)
of...............................(name and address of organisation)
Declare that the above named charity is * buying from/importing from:
.... (name and address of supplier)
The following which *is/are eligible for relief from VAT under item 8 or 8A 8B or 8C of zero rate group 15
or qualify as

printed appeal letters
printed envelopes for use with appeal letters
printed monetary donation collecting envelopes
monetary donation collecting boxes
Lapel stickers or badges or component parts
..............................(signature and date).

Note: it's the supplier's responsibility to ensure that the goods or services supplied are eligible before zero rating them.

Part 2 is to be completed by the supplier
I have read the guidance in VAT Notice 701/58: charity advertising and goods connected with collecting donations and agree that the goods and services described come within the category shown.
(signature and date)...............................
This certificate should be retained by the supplier for production to a VAT officer.
And any notes on steps taken to verify the declared details.

38.3 Goods used to collect donations

ESC 3.3 provides:

> **3.3 VAT: zero rating of supplies of certain goods used in connection with collection of monetary donations**
> This concession applies to supplies to a charity of the following goods:
> (a) lapel stickers or attachments designed to be worn on the lapel, which are of no intrinsic value, low cost to the charity and are given as a token in acknowledgement of a donation
> (b) component parts of items described in (a) above when supplied for self assembly
> (c) any form of receptacle which:
> • is manufactured specifically for the purpose of collecting donated money
> • is used solely for collecting money for charity
> • is, or will be, clearly marked as collecting for a named charity
> • can be secured by lock or tamper evident seal
> (d) bucket lids, designed to fit buckets and provide a secure seal, for use solely in connection with collecting money for charity
> (e) pre-printed letters the primary purpose of which is to appeal for money for charity (not necessarily including the addressees' particulars)
> (f) envelopes used in conjunction with letters described (e) above for forwarding donations, provided that they are over-printed

with an appeal request related to that contained in the letter;

(g) outer envelopes used in conjunction with letters described in (e) above, provided that they are over-printed with an appeal request related to that contained in the letter

(h) pre-printed collecting envelopes appealing for money (of the type used by the welfare charities and which are usually hand delivered to domestic premises)

(i) stewardship envelopes used for planned giving which, as a minimum requirement, are pre-printed with the name of the relevant place of worship or other charity

Where this concession applies, the supply may be treated as if it were a zero-rated supply.

This concession applies from 1 April 2000.

The Comissioners may withdraw or restrict the applications of this concession if they have reasonable cause to believe it is being abused.

The VCHAR Manual provides:

VCHAR11000- Advertising

Appeal letters whose primary purpose is to appeal for money

Item (e) in Extra Statutory Concession 3.3 allows relief for pre-printed letters the primary purpose of which is to appeal for money for charity. It includes 'thank you' letters and 'remember us in your will' letters. It does not include lobbying 'write to your MP' letters.

VAT Notice 701/58 (Goods or services supplied to charities) (31 January 2019) provides:

6 ESC in relation to printed stationery

6.1 Printed stationery that qualifies

The following items can be zero-rated under the ESC when supplied to a charity:

- collecting envelopes which ask for donations of money, and stewardship and similar envelopes used by religious and other organisations in their planned giving schemes
- pre-printed appeal letters primarily aimed at seeking money for the charity
- envelopes used to send out appeal letters and envelopes for sending donations to the charity, provided each type is over-printed with an appeal request related to that contained in the letter, or are distinguishable from the charity's usual stationery

This relief does not cover general stationery supplied to charities.

6.2 Stewardship envelope used in planned giving schemes

Some religious organisations, and other charities, ask "members" to donate money on a regular basis. The people donating the money are given a series of envelopes, known as stewardship envelopes, which they use for their monthly or weekly giving. Stewardship envelopes that are clearly for use in a planned giving scheme and are printed with at least the name of the place of worship or charity can be zero rated.

Money collecting envelopes that have been especially printed for a charity, making it known that they're donation envelopes, but leaving a space for completion of the individual places of worship, or charity branches, also qualify. Plain envelopes bearing only a symbol (such as a cross printed on them), and available from retailers as general stationery, don't qualify.

6.3 An appeal letter

An appeal letter is a single or multiple sheet letter pre-printed with the description of the cause. The primary purpose of the letter must be a request for donations. It must be a letter not just a form to fill in and return with a donation. It does not matter whether the letter has the individual addressees' details included when supplied to the charity. A letter without an individual's details might qualify for zero rating as a leaflet, see Zero rating books and printed matter (VAT Notice 701/10), in which case the purpose of the letter would be unimportant.

6.4 "Package test" applying for printed matter of stationery that is zero-rated under this concession

The package test for determining the VAT liability of a mixed supply of printed items (such as items for a mail shot) is a separate concession described in see Zero rating books and printed matter (VAT Notice 701). With effect from 1 August 2003 the package test concession has been extended so that some of the charity stationery zero-rated under the ESC see see Zero rating books and printed matter VAT Notice 701/10).

6.5 VAT on the whole package if a charity fails to qualify for relief under the "package test"

If the test does not result in zero-rating of the package, a charity will still be able to claim zero-rating on any item which qualifies for relief either under schedule 8, group 3 or the ESC, see section 5.

7 ESC in relation to boxes and receptacles for the collecting of money

7.1 Types of boxes and receptacles that qualify?

All types of boxes and receptacles used for collecting money qualify providing they meet all the following 3 conditions—

Condition 1

They must be secure, that is, capable of being sealed, for example by tamper evident sticker, tape or lock.

Condition 2

They must clearly be charity collecting boxes for a named charity.

Condition 3

The must either bear the name of the charity, for example by indelible printing, embossing or having raised letters, or allow for the charity name to be added later.

7.2 Examples of boxes which might qualify

Some examples are:

- pre-printed card collecting boxes;
- moulded plastic collecting boxes;
- models in any material including hollow plaster, wood, base metal or glass.

These boxes may be hand held, floor standing, wall mounted or for placing on a tabletop or shop counter.

7.3 Boxes which will not qualify

Boxes of greater value, such as those made of precious metal, are not zero-rated.

7.4 Concession for collection buckets

General purpose buckets of the kind available from hardware stores are not covered by the concession.

The following will qualify for relief:

- specially designed tamper proof bucket lids with tamper evident stickers making them suitable for a charity donation;
- bucket shaped receptacles, which cannot be used for anything except collecting donations of money;
- bucket packs for assembly consisting of bucket, money collecting top and tamper evident seals and labels.

7.5 Concession boxes with mechanical parts

Elaborate receptacles which have an extra purpose, such as gaming or quiz machines, or have some form of mechanical entertainment do not come within the concession.

However, receptacles where, for example, a simple balance mechanism moves the money from one level to another or the weight of a coin causes it to roll helter-skelter fashion into the collecting area are included in the relief.

7.6 Concession receptacles

Receptacles that have another purpose while also having a coin slot do not qualify, such as:

- wishing well
- fonts
- furniture, fixtures and fittings

A simple collecting box fixed to any of these items would still qualify.

8 ESC in relation to lapel stickers and similar tokens

8.1 Lstickers and badges that qualify

Only lapel stickers, emblems and badges which are to be given free as an acknowledgement to donors of money, have no intrinsic value and are low cost to the charity will qualify.

The relief is restricted to small items designed to be worn on clothing, of a kind that were traditionally attached to the lapel. Included are:

- paper stickers
- ribbons
- artificial flowers (if these are used as a symbol of the charity)

- metal pins and badges.

Large items for decorating buildings, vehicles and monuments are not included in the relief even if these are just bigger versions of a lapel badge.

8.2 Definition of "no intrinsic value" and "low cost" for lapel attachments

Emblems or badges given in return for any non-specified donation or a suggested donation of up to £1. In practice this would mean that the cost to the charity would be considerably less than £1 per unit.

8.3 Relief on lapel attachments to be sold for a fixed price

There's no relief on lapel attachments, although relief will apply if a charity suggests a donation of £1. If lapel emblems or attachments are offered for a fixed price, even if this is only £1 or less, they don't qualify for relief because the emblems are not given away freely.

8.4 Relief for goods a charity it buys to make its own lapel attachments

Equipment for manufacturing badges is not included in the relief. However if a charity buys identifiable constituent parts, which it will assemble into badges in-house, these come within the concession.

8.5 Tokens that are intended to be given away

The normal VAT liability will apply.

8.6 Relief on containers for holding the lapel attachments

There's no relief for the containers. However if the container is merely normal packaging for the lapel attachments then these and their container are a single zero-rated supply of lapel attachments. The more substantial containers, such as those with a strap to hang around the neck, are items in their own right and cannot be included in the relief. The supply of an empty container is also standard-rated.

8.7 Relief on containers for lapel attachments with an integral collection box

Where a cardboard collecting receptacle is incorporated in a cardboard tray that holds lapel attachments, and it is supplied as a single item (often as a flat pack) there is a single supply for VAT purposes and normal rules apply. Providing the main purpose of the goods can be seen as the collecting receptacle then the whole supply can be zero-rated.

38.4 Donation and sale of donated goods

VATA sch 8 group 15 provides zero-rating for charities:

> 1 The sale, or letting on hire, by a charity of any goods donated to it for—
>
> (a) sale,
> (b) letting,
> (c) sale or letting,
> (d) sale or export,

(e) letting or export, or
(f) sale, letting or export.

VATA sch 8 group 15 extends the relief to a profits-to-charity person:

> 1A The sale, or letting on hire, by a taxable person of any goods donated to him for—
> (a) sale,
> (b) letting,
> (c) sale or letting,
> (d) sale or export,
> (e) letting or export, or
> (f) sale, letting or export,
> if he is a profits-to-charity person in respect of the goods.

VATA sch 8 group 15 provides corresponding relief for donors:

> 2 The donation of any goods for any one or more of the following purposes—
> (a) sale by a charity or a taxable person who is a profits-to-charity person in respect of the goods;
> (b) export by a charity or such a taxable person;
> (c) letting by a charity or such a taxable person.

38.4.1 *Donation for public sale*

VATA sch 8 group 15 Note (1) provides:

> (1) Item 1 or 1A does not apply unless the sale or letting—
> (a) takes place as a result of the goods having been made available—
> (i) to two or more specified persons, or
> (ii) to the general public,
> for purchase or hire (whether so made available in a shop or elsewhere), and
> (b) does not take place as a result of any arrangements (whether legally binding or not) relating to the goods and entered into, before the goods were made so available, by—
> (i) each of the parties to the sale or letting, or
> (ii) the donor of the goods and either or both of those parties.

Notes (1C) provides:

> (1C) In Note (1) "specified person" means a person who—
> (a) is disabled, or

(b) is entitled to any one or more of the specified benefits, or
(c) is both disabled and so entitled.

(1D) For the purposes of Note (1C) the specified benefits are—
(a) income support under Part VII of the Social Security Contributions and Benefits Act 1992 or Part VII of the Social Security Contributions and Benefits (Northern Ireland) Act 1992;
(b) housing benefit under Part VII of the Social Security Contributions and Benefits Act 1992 or Part VII of the Social Security Contributions and Benefits (Northern Ireland) Act 1992;
(c) council tax benefit under Part VII of the Social Security Contributions and Benefits Act 1992;
(d) an income-based jobseeker's allowance within the meaning of section 1(4) of the Jobseekers Act 1995 or article 3(4) of the Jobseekers (Northern Ireland) Order 1995;
(e) any element of child tax credit other than the family element;
(f) working tax credit; and
(g) universal credit under Part 1 of the Welfare Reform Act 2012 or Part 2 of the Welfare Reform (Northern Ireland) Order 2015.

38.4.2 *"Donated for letting"*

Note (1A) defines "donated for letting":

(1A) For the purposes of items 1, 1A and 2, goods are donated for letting only if they are donated for—
(a) letting, and
(b) re-letting after the end of any first or subsequent letting, and
(c) all or any of—
(i) sale,
(ii) export, or
(iii) disposal as waste,
if not, or when no longer, used for letting.

(1B) Items 1 and 1A do not include (and shall be treated as having not included) any sale, or letting on hire, of particular donated goods if the goods, at any time after they are donated but before they are sold, exported or disposed of as waste, are whilst unlet used for any purpose other than, or in addition to, that of being available for purchase, hire or export.

38.4.3 *"Donated"*

HMRC Brief 14/08 provides:

> This brief explains the VAT liability of the sale of abandoned animals by a charity following the Tribunal decision in the case of *Gables Farm Dogs and Cats Home*.[1]
>
> **Background**
>
> Gables Farm Dogs and Cats Home is a charity that rescues lost, unwanted and homeless cats and dogs many of which are subsequently sold to new owners. It receives unwanted cats and dogs from owners as well as strays and abandoned animals given by local authority dog wardens, the police, and members of the public.
>
> Subject to certain conditions the sale of donated goods by a charity is zero-rated and [HMRC's] view was that only animals given to the home by their original owners could be regarded as "donated" within the terms of the legislation.
>
> The Tribunal found that the charity took steps to return genuinely lost animals to their owners and those it offered for re-homing had been deliberately abandoned. In these circumstances the animals given to the charity by the local authority, the police and members of the public were donated and therefore zero-rated when sold.
>
> **HMRC policy following Gables Farm Dogs and Cats Home**
>
> HMRC is not appealing the Tribunal's decision and accepts that charities selling animals in similar circumstances should zero-rate their supplies
>
> ...

38.4.4 *"Profits-to charity" person*

VATA sch 8 group 15 Note 1E provides the definition:

> (1E) For the purposes of items 1A and 2 a taxable person is a "profits-to-charity" person in respect of any goods if—
>
> (a) he has agreed in writing (whether or not contained in a deed) to transfer to a charity his profits from supplies and lettings of the goods, or
>
> (b) his profits from supplies and lettings of the goods are otherwise payable to a charity.
>
> (1F) In items 1, 1A and 2, and any Notes relating to any of those items, "goods" means goods (and, in particular, does not include anything that is not goods even though provision made by or under an enactment provides for a supply of that thing to be, or be treated as, a supply of goods).

The VCHAR Manual provides:

---

1 VTD 20519.

VCHAR7100 - Charity shops and sales of goods
Introduction [Jun 2021]
The sale of donated and bought in goods by a charity or its trading subsidiary is always a business activity. The VAT treatment of the supply will depend on the type of goods and how they are held out for sale.

VCHAR7200 - Charity shops and sales of goods: Sale of donated goods [Jun 2021]
The sale of donated goods by a charity or a 'profits to charity' person is zero-rated.

The relief applies exclusively to goods and does not include items which may be deemed to be goods in other sections of law. For example, the relief does not apply to any land or buildings donated to and sold by a charity.

The goods can be new or second-hand, but must have been donated to the charity.

"Profits-to-charity"

A "profits-to-charity" body is often a charity's trading subsidiary. But regardless of their relationship with a charity, a "profits-to-charity" body is:

(a) one that has agreed in writing (whether or not contained in a deed) to transfer to a charity his profits from supplies and lettings of the goods, or

(b) one whose profits from supplies and lettings of the goods are otherwise payable to a charity.

Must the goods be sold on in the condition they are received?

The goods can be cleaned or repaired as long as this does not alter their structure or original use.

Garments can be washed and pressed, buttons sewn back etc. This will make garments more presentable and achieve a higher sale price. Some larger charities have a central unit where all donations are taken to be prepared for sale. Any expenses incurred in this unit are directly attributable to taxable supplies made in the shops and input tax can be recovered in full.

If the donated item is altered it will cease to qualify for relief, as demonstrated in the following examples:

- A transport company donates wooden pallets to a charity which runs a day-centre for disabled adults. The disabled adults use the wood to make rabbit hutches and hen coops which are sold to raise funds for the day-centre. These sales are liable to VAT at the standard rate as the goods are not being sold on in the same state that they were donated.

- An artist donates an original painting to a charity. The charity has a number of prints made rather than sell the original painting. The prints have not been donated so will not qualify for zero-rating.

Must the donated goods be held out for sale immediately?

Not necessarily. It is what the charity does with the goods before offering them for sale that affects the liability. If the goods are cleaned or repaired, as described above, the sale will still be zero-rated.

If the goods are let on hire for a period before being sold then the eventual sale will still qualify for zero-rating.

However, if the donated goods are used by the charity for any period before being held out for sale they will be liable to tax at the standard rate. For example, an established charity was given paintings by now famous artists which have hung in their offices for many years. The charity decides to sell the paintings to raise funds. Such a sale would be standard-rated (although you should check whether the sale will be covered by the margin scheme for works of art, antiques and collectors' items) – see Notice 718 (HMRC website).

VCHAR7300 - Charity shops and sales of goods - Charity shops [Jun 2021]

Premises

Many charities operate shops in local high streets. These are often acquired on a short lease. If the landlord has opted to tax the charity will have to pay VAT; the option will not be disapplied because the charity is carrying on a business activity. However, the charity can recover the VAT if it is directly attributable to a taxable supplies.

Staff

The staff may be paid or volunteers or a mixture of both and this does not affect the relief.

Stock

Only goods freely given to the charity can be sold at the zero rate. Bought in goods must be sold at the standard rate (unless those goods are zero rate by statute, such as food). Bought in goods may include items bearing the charity's logo eg mugs, aprons etc. These are still liable to VAT.

Some merchandise may appear to be new and available in a range of sizes. However, do not assume that these goods are bought in; manufacturers may have donated end of lines or have goods that they have been unable to sell in their own outlets.

Restricted access

There are a number of shops, mainly those selling second-hand furniture, that restrict sales to certain categories of the public. The sales still qualify for zero-rating as long as the goods are made available to either disabled people or to people entitled to one or more of the following benefits:

- Income Support
- Housing Benefit
- Council Tax Benefit
- Job Seeker's Allowance
- Any element of Child Tax Credit other than the family element
- Working Tax Credit
- Universal Credit

VCHAR7400 - Charity shops and sales of goods - Fairtrade items [Jun 2021]

Many charity shops sell Fairtrade goods, ranging from foodstuffs to toys. Although the Fairtrade organisation is itself a charity whose aim is to ensure that the initial provider of the goods receives an economic return for their labour, the goods are bought in by the charity selling them. This means that the goods will normally be standard-rated, unless the goods are zero-rated by statute (such as tea bags).

VCHAR7500 - Charity shops and sales of goods: Dress exchange schemes [Jun 2021]

Some charities have become involved in a scheme where a person has a garment which they are not willing to donate, but are willing to give a percentage of the sum the garment sells for to charity. The liability of this type of sale depends on how the scheme is set up.

1 Charity accepts garment for sale. When it is sold the garment's owner donates as much or as little of the sum received as they wish to the charity. All transactions are outside the scope of VAT.

2 Charity accepts garment for sale on condition that a set percentage of the sale price is paid to the charity. The charity is effectively charging a commission and the amount the charity receives will be taxable at the standard rate.

3 Charity accepts garment for sale at a set price eg £1 per week. When the garment is sold the owner is invited to make a donation to the charity, but is under no obligation to do so. The charge made by the charity for displaying the garment for sale is taxable at the standard rate. Any donation is outside the scope of VAT.

In all the above cases the ownership of the garment never passes to the charity, so the garment can never be treated as donated goods. It is normal for the charity to only hold the garment out for sale for a limited period. If, at the end of that period, the garment has not sold the owner may then wish to donate the garment to charity. The ownership then passes to the charity and the sale can be treated as one of donated goods and zero-rated.

VCHAR7600 - Charity shops and sales of goods - Other types of sale [Jun 2021]

Auction

As long as the goods to be sold have been donated to the charity the sale can be zero-rated. However, the charity cannot limit access to selected individuals – the sale must be open to the general public. Access should only be limited for health and safety grounds. However the charity can advertise the auction as it sees fit and may choose to limit adverts to those areas where they feel they are likely to attract potential buyers.

Stalls or tables selling goods within another event

As long as all the goods have been donated to the charity the sales will be zero-rated, even if the event qualifies for exemption as a fund-raising event.

Goods not suitable for sale to the public

These are goods which may be such poor quality that the charity cannot sell them in a shop, or that the charity is unable to sell because of trading standards regulations, such as electrical goods. Such goods can be sold to scrap merchants or the like at the zero rate.

ESC 3.21 provides:

3.21 VAT: sales of poor quality goods

By concession, the supply by a charity of any goods which have been donated for sale or the supply of such goods by a taxable person who is covenanted by deed to give all the profits of that supply to a charity, shall be treated as zero-rated, provided that:

(a) the supply is a sale of goods donated to that charity or taxable person, but

(b) the goods, although of a kind which the charity or taxable person makes available to the general public for purchase (whether in a shop or elsewhere) are by reason of their poor quality not fit to be so made available.

CHAPTER THIRTY NINE

STAMP DUTIES

39.1 Stamp duties: Introduction

Stamp duties on land transactions is a devolved matter, so there are three distinct taxes:

Title	Abbreviation	Application	Legislation
Stamp Duty Land Tax	SDLT	England/NI	FA 2003
Land and Buildings Transaction Tax	LBTT	Scotland	LBTTSA
Land Transaction Tax	LTT	Wales	LTTWA[1]

That makes for a complicated position; but devolution and simplicity are incompatible virtues.

We refer to these together as **"land taxes"**.

1 The full title is: Land Transaction Tax and Anti-avoidance of Devolved Taxes (Wales) Act 2017. We abbreviate that to LTTWA.

This chapter also considers:
(1) Stamp Duty
(2) Stamp Duty Reserve Tax
(3) Annual Tax on Enveloped Dwellings (ATED)

39.2 Land tax charity relief

England/NI	Scotland	Wales
Para 1(1) sch 8 FA 2003	*Para 1 sch 13 LBTTSA*	*Para 3(1) sch 18 LTTWA*
A land transaction is exempt from charge if the purchaser is a charity and the following conditions are met.	A land transaction is exempt from charge if the buyer is a charity and the qualifying conditions are met.	A land transaction is relieved from tax where the buyer is a qualifying charity.
Relief under this schedule is referred to in this Part as "charities relief".		

The reliefs in Scotland and Wales are similar, but not identical to England. The Scots and Welsh drafters have also adopted a slightly more plain legal English style.

39.3 Claim for SDLT charity relief

England/NI	Scotland	Wales
s.68(2) FA 2003	*s.27(2) LBTTSA*	*s.30(4) LTTWA*
Any relief under [sch 8] must be claimed in a land transaction return or an amendment of such a return.	Any relief under [sch 13] must be claimed in the **first return** made in relation to the transaction or in an amendment of that return.	Any relief under [sch 18] must be claimed in the **first return** made in relation to the land transaction, or in an amendment of that return.

HMRC comment on the time limits for a claim under SDLT:

> **Time limit for making a claim**
> Section 68 of the FA 2003 provides that claims for charities relief must be made in a land transaction return or in an amendment to a return. Under Paragraph 6 of Schedule 10 to the FA 2003, an amendment can be made no later than 12 months after the filing date for the return. The filing date for a land transaction return is 30 days after the effective date of the transaction (this is normally the completion date). Claims made

after the expiry of the 12 month amendment period will be time-barred.

Procedure for amending a return

Purchasers who wish to make an amendment to their land transaction return should write to: Birmingham Stamp Office, 9th Floor, City Centre House, 30 Union Street, Birmingham, B2 4AR.

Details of the amendment and the unique transaction reference number (UTRN) for the original land transaction return should be included in the letter.[2]

39.4 "Charity"

39.4.1 *"Charity" for SDLT/LBTT/LTT*

Wales adopts the English law definition. Para 2(3) sch 18 LTTWA provides:

> In this Schedule—
> (a) "charity" has the meaning given by Part 1 of Schedule 6 to the Finance Act 2010

England have different definitions:

England/NI/Wales	**Scotland**
Para 1(1) sch 6 F(No.1)A 2010	*Para 15(1) sch 13 LBTTSA*
For the purposes of the enactments to which this Part applies "charity" means a body of persons or trust that— (a) is established for charitable purposes only, (b) meets the jurisdiction condition (see para 2), (c) meets the registration condition (see para 3), (d) meets the management condition (see para 4).	In this schedule, "charity" means— (a) a body registered in the Scottish Charity Register, or (b) a body which is— (i) established under the law of a relevant territory, (ii) managed or controlled wholly or mainly outwith Scotland, and (iii) meets at least one of the conditions in sub-para (2).

39.4.2 *"Charity" Conditions under SDLT/LTT/LBTT*

England/NI/Wales	**Scotland**
sch 6 F(No.1)A 2010 *Jurisdiction condition* 2 (1) A body of persons or trust meets the jurisdiction	*Para 15 sch 13 LBTTSA* (2) The conditions are— (a) the body is registered in

2 *http://taxnews.lexisnexis.co.uk/TaxNewsLive/Members/BreakingNewsFullText.aspx?id=4697&css=1&xml=0* [2013] STI 2884 (Aug 2013).

condition if it falls to be subject to the control of—

(a) a relevant UK court in the exercise of its jurisdiction with respect to charities, or

(b) any other court in the exercise of a corresponding jurisdiction under the law of a relevant territory.

(2) In sub-para (1)(a) "a relevant UK court" means—

(a) the High Court,

(b) the Court of Session, or

(c) the High Court in Northern Ireland,

(and, for enactments relating to value added tax, includes the High Court of the Isle of Man).

(3) In sub-para (1)(b) "a relevant territory" means—

(a) a member State other than the United Kingdom, or

(b) a territory specified in regulations made by HMRC.

...

Registration condition

3 (1) A body of persons or trust meets the registration condition if—

(a) in the case of a body of persons or trust that is a charity within the meaning of s.10 of the Charities Act 2011, condition A is met, and

(b) in the case of any other body of persons or trust, condition B is met.

(2) Condition A is that the body of persons or trust has complied with any requirement to be registered in the register of charities kept under s.29 of the Charities Act 2011.

(3) Condition B is that the body of persons or trust has complied with any requirement under the law of a territory outside England and Wales to be registered in a register corresponding to that mentioned in sub-para (2).

Management condition

4 (1) A body of persons or trust meets the management condition if its managers are fit and proper persons to be managers of the body or trust.

(2) In this paragraph "managers", in relation to a body of persons or trust, means the persons having the general control and management of the administration of the body or trust.

a register corresponding to the Scottish Charity Register,

(b) the body's purposes consist only of one or more of the charitable purposes.

(3) A relevant territory is—

(a) England and Wales,

(b) Northern Ireland,

(c) a member State of the European Union other than the United Kingdom, **or**

(d) a territory specified in regulations made by the Scottish Ministers.

The conditions for defining "Charity" in Wales takes reference from the same conditions that govern England and Northern Ireland under sch 6 F(No.1)A 2010. By contrast, the conditions for "Charity" in Scotland apply only to the **second** Scottish definition of "Charity" under para 15(1)(b) sch 13 LBTTSA.

Taxes (Definition of Charity) (Relevant Territories) Regulations 2010 applying to the whole of the UK except Scotland as well as Land and Buildings Transaction Tax (Definition of Charity) (Relevant Territories) (Scotland) Regulations 2014 specifies 3 relevant territories: Iceland, Liechtenstein and Norway.

39.4.3 *Charitable purposes*

England/NI	**Scotland**	**Wales**
Para 1 sch 6 F(No.1)A 2010	*Para 16 sch 13 LBTTSA*	*Para 2(3) sch 18 LTTWA*
(4) For the meaning of "charitable purpose", see section 2 of the Charities Act 2011 (which— (a) applies regardless of where the body of persons or trust in question is established, and (b) for this purpose forms part of the law of each part of the United Kingdom (see sections 7 and 8 of that Act)).	In this schedule, "charitable purposes" has the meaning given by section 106 of the Charities and Trustee Investments (Scotland) Act 2005.[3]	In this schedule— ... (b) "charitable purpose" has the meaning given by section 2 of the Charities Act 2011.

39.4.4 *"Charity"* under *SDLT/LTT Post-Brexit*

Post-Brexit amendments to the definitions of "Charity" for SDLT and LTT purposes came into force upon the UK's official withdrawal from the EU on 31 January 2020 and the expiry of the implementation period on 31 December 2020 respectively. In relation to SDLT, the Taxes (Amendments) (EU Exit) Regulations 2019, SI 2019/689, reg 19 repealed the words "other than the United Kingdom" within para 2(3)(a) sch 6 F(No.1)A 2010. In relation to LTT, the Welsh Tax Acts (Miscellaneous Amendments) (EU Exit) Regulations, SI 2019/833, reg 3(1)-(4), introduced 4 new paragraphs into sch 18 LTTWA to supplement the definition of "Charity" for the purposes of LTT post-Brexit. A comparison is set out as follows:

---

3 See 3.15 (Scots law definition of charity).

England/NI

sch 6 F(No.1)A 2010

Definition of "charity" etc

1(1) For the purposes of the [SDLT] to which this Part applies "charity" means a body of persons or trust that—

(a) is established for charitable purposes only,

(b) meets the jurisdiction condition (see paragraph 2),

(c) meets the registration condition (see paragraph 3), and

(d) meets the management condition (see paragraph 4).

Jurisdiction condition

2 (1) A body of persons or trust meets the jurisdiction condition if it falls to be subject to the control of—

(a) a relevant UK court in the exercise of its jurisdiction with respect to charities, or

(b) any other court in the exercise of a corresponding jurisdiction under the law of a relevant territory.

(2) In sub-para (1)(a) "a relevant UK court" means—

(a) the High Court,

(b) the Court of Session, or

(c) the High Court in Northern Ireland,

(and, for enactments relating to value added tax, includes the High Court of the Isle of Man).

(3) In sub-para (1)(b) "a relevant territory" means—

(a) a member State, or

Wales

sch 18 LTTWA

Meaning of "charity"

2A For the purpose of this schedule, "charity" means a body of persons or trust that—

(a) is established for charitable purposes only,

(b) meets the jurisdiction condition (see paragraph 2B),

(c) meets the registration condition (see paragraph 2C), and

(d) meets the management condition (see paragraph 2D).

Meaning of "charity": jurisdiction condition

2B (1) A body of persons or trust meets the jurisdiction condition if it falls to be subject to the control of a relevant UK court in the exercise of its jurisdiction with respect to charities.

(2) A "relevant UK court" means—

(a) the High Court,

(b) the Court of Session, or

(c) the High Court in Northern Ireland.

(b) a territory specified in regulations made by HMRC.	
(4) Regulations under this paragraph are to be made by statutory instrument.	
(5) A statutory instrument containing regulations under this paragraph is subject to annulment in pursuance of a resolution of the House of Commons.	
Registration condition	*Meaning of "charity": registration condition*
3 (1) A body of persons or trust meets the registration condition if—	2C (1) A body of persons or trust meets the registration condition if—
(a) in the case of a body of persons or trust that is a charity within the meaning of section 10 of the Charities Act 2011, condition A is met, and	(a) in the case of a body of persons or trust that is a charity within the meaning of section 10 of the Charities Act 2011 (c. 25), condition A is met, and
(b) in the case of any other body of persons or trust, condition B is met.	(b) in the case of any other body of persons or trust, condition B is met.
(2) Condition A is that the body of persons or trust has complied with any requirement to be registered in the register of charities kept under section 29 of the Charities Act 2011.	(2) Condition A is that the body of persons or trust has complied with any requirement to be registered in the register of charities kept under section 29 of the Charities Act 2011.
(3) Condition B is that the body of persons or trust has complied with any requirement under the law of a territory outside England and Wales to be registered in a register corresponding to that mentioned in sub-paragraph (2).	(3) Condition B is that the body of persons or trust has complied with any requirement to be registered in a register corresponding to that mentioned in condition A kept under the law of Scotland or Northern Ireland.
Management condition	*Meaning of "charity": management condition*
4 (1) A body of persons or trust meets the management condition if its managers are fit and proper persons to be managers of the body or trust.	2D (1) A body of persons or trust meets the management condition if its managers are fit and proper persons to be managers of the body or trust.
(2) In this paragraph "managers", in relation to a body of persons or trust,	(2) In this paragraph "managers", in relation to a body of persons or trust,

means the persons having the general control and management of the administration of the body or trust.	means the persons having the general control and management of the administration of the body or trust.
	(3) Sub-paragraph (4) applies in relation to any period throughout which the management condition is not met.
	(4) The management condition is treated as met if WRA consider that—
	(a) the failure to meet the condition has not prejudiced the charitable purposes of the body or trust, or
	(b) it is just and reasonable in all the circumstances for the condition to be treated as met throughout the period.

By contrast, there are no known changes to Scottish LBTT legislation post-Brexit.

39.4.5 *"Charitable trusts"*

England/NI	**Scotland**	**Wales**
Para 4 sch 8 FA 2003	*Para 13 sch 13 LBTTSA*	*Para 9(1) sch 18 LTTWA*
(1) This schedule applies in relation to a charitable trust as it applies in relation to a charity. (2) In this paragraph "charitable trust" means— (a) a trust of which all the beneficiaries are charities, or (b) a unit trust scheme in which all the unit holders are charities.	"Charitable trust" means— (a) a trust of which all the beneficiaries are charities, or (b) a unit trust scheme in which all the unit holders are charities.	This schedule applies to the following trusts as it applies to a charity but subject to the modifications in sub-paragraph (2)— (a) a trust of which all the beneficiaries are charities, or (b) a unit trust scheme in which all the unit holders are charities.

This is an artificial definition so we refer to "charitable trust" with scare quotation marks.

These provisions assume that a "charitable trust" as defined, ie:

(a) a trust of which all the beneficiaries are charities; or

(b) a unit trust scheme in which all the unit holders are charities is not, or may not be, a charity in the usual tax sense.

Point (a) we find hard to understand: we would have said that a trust in which all the beneficiaries are charities is established for charitable purposes only. Even if that were wrong, we are not able to see any practical need for this provision, which has no parallel in other charity tax reliefs? In practice such trusts are not used (except for unit trusts schemes which are covered by (b)).

As to point (b), unit trust schemes in which all the unit holders are charities are themselves capable of being constituted as charities, but may be set up as non-charities.

England/NI	**Scotland**	**Wales**
Para 4(3) sch 8 FA 2003	*Para 14 sch 13 LBTTSA*	*Para 9(2) sch 18 LTTWA*
In this schedule as it applies by virtue of this paragraph—	In this schedule as it applies in relation to a charitable trust—	(2) The modifications to this schedule are—
(a) references to the purchaser in paragraphs (a) and (b) of paragraph 1(2) are to the beneficiaries or unit holders, or any of them;	(a) references to the buyer in paragraph 3(a) and (b) are to the beneficiaries or unit holders, or any of them,	(a) the references in paragraph 2(2) to the charitable purposes of C are to have effect as if they were references to those of the beneficiaries or unit holders, or any of them;
(b) the reference to the purchaser in paragraph 2(3)(a) is to any of the beneficiaries or unit holders;	(b) the reference to the buyer in paragraph 5(a) is to any of the beneficiaries or unit holders,	(b) the references to C in paragraph 2(4), are to have effect as if they were references to any of the beneficiaries or unit holders;
(c) the reference in paragraph 3(2)(b) to the charitable purposes of C is to those of the beneficiaries or unit holders, or any of them.	(c) the reference in paragraph 6 to the charitable purposes of the buyer is to those of the beneficiaries or unit holders, or any of them.	(c) the references in paragraphs 5(2)(b) and 8(2)(b) to the charitable purposes of C are to have effect as if they were references to those of the beneficiaries or unit holders, or any of them.

In essence, the primary difference in the application of charity SDLT relief to a "charitable trust" is that it is necessary to look to the underlying charities, and not the "charitable trust", to determine whether or not the transaction qualifies for SDLT relief. But the point will hardly ever arise, (except in the very specialist case of a non-charitable unit trust held exclusively by charities).

39.5 Charitable purposes condition

England/NI	Scotland	Wales
Para 1(2) sch 8 FA 2003	*Para 2 sch 13 LBTTSA*	*Para 2(1) sch 18 LTTWA*
The first condition is that the purchaser must intend to hold the subject-matter of the transaction for qualifying charitable purposes ...	The qualifying conditions are— (a) that the buyer intends to hold— (i) the subject-matter of the transaction, or (ii) the greater part of that subject-matter, for qualifying charitable purposes ...	In this schedule, a charity ("C") which is a buyer in a land transaction is a "qualifying charity"— (a) for the purposes of paragraphs 3, 4 and 5, if C intends to hold the whole of the subject-matter of the transaction for qualifying charitable purposes; (b) for the purposes of paragraphs 6, 7 and 8, if C intends to hold the whole of its undivided share of the subject-matter of the transaction for qualifying charitable purposes.

39.5.1 *Qualifying charitable purposes*

England/NI	Scotland	Wales
Para 1(3A) sch 8 FA 2003	*Para 3 sch 13 LBTTSA*	*Para 2(2) sch 18 LTTWA*
For the purposes of this schedule, a charity ("C") holds a chargeable interest for qualifying charitable purposes if it holds it—	A buyer holds the subject-matter of a transaction for qualifying charitable purposes if the buyer holds it—	For the purposes of this schedule, C holds the subject-matter of the transaction for "qualifying charitable purposes" if C holds it—
(a) for use in furtherance of the charitable purposes of C or another charity, or	(a) for use in the furtherance of the charitable purposes of the buyer or of another charity, or	(a) for use in furtherance of the charitable purposes of C or another charity, or

(b) as an investment from which the profits are applied to the charitable purposes of C.	(b) as an investment from which the profits are applied to the charitable purposes of the buyer.	(b) as an investment from which the profits are applied to the charitable purposes of C.

We refer to these as the **"charitable purposes condition"**.

This is similar to the rule for rating relief: see 40.7 (Used for charitable purposes). Housing used by employees of a charity may be used for charitable purposes so its acquisition in principle qualifies for relief.[4] HMRC note the point in relation to clergy. The SDLT Manual provides:

> **SDLTM 26010A: Reliefs: Charities relief** [Mar 2018]
> *Detailed rules to qualify for the relief FA03/SCH8/PARA1: Example*
> ... where a church provides a dwelling for a vicar, priest etc. for occupation in the course of his or her duties, this would be considered as land being provided for charitable purposes.
> The role of the vicar is to further the charitable purpose of the church i.e., to advance religion through various pastoral, care and administrative parish duties.

The charitable purposes condition would exclude relief if the charity intended to act in breach of trust, but charity law and criminal law provide enough sanctions against that.

The charitable purposes condition excludes relief if the purchase was a trading transaction (essentially a purchase with a view to a resale at a profit). However that would be rare and would normally be carried out through a non-charitable subsidiary.

39.5.2 *Registered Social Landlord*

The guidance in relation to the charity relief from SDLT is now contained in the SDLT Manual. The guidance was formerly contained in the Stamp Office's "Notes on Disposals and Charities Relief". The Notes provided:

> [1] An example of a disposal made in furtherance of the charity's objectives[5] is if an RSL [registered social landlord] transfers title to a shared ownership property to a tenant who staircases to 100%.

We think this is considering a case where there are two transfers:

(1) A transfer to the charity for consideration

---

4 See 40.7.2 (Occupation by employees of charity).

5 This is a paraphrase of the statutory word "purposes", but nothing turns on that.

(2) A transfer from the charity to a beneficiary (the tenant)

SDLT charity relief applies on the first transfer. The purchase satisfies the first condition for the reason given. The second transfer is not subject to SDLT as there is no consideration. The Notes continue:

> [2] An example of a disposal that is not made in furtherance of the charity's objectives is the RSL disposes of a ground floor unit to a private individual who wants to open a corner shop. Note that even if the RSL uses the proceeds from the disposal to the private individual to further its own charitable aims, it is still not a disposal made in furtherance of the charity's objectives.

39.6 Avoidance purpose

England/NI	Scotland	Wales
Para 1(3) sch 8 FA 2003	*Para 2 sch 13 LBTTSA*	*s.31(1) LTTWA*
The second condition is that the transaction must not have been entered into for the purpose of avoiding tax under this Part (whether by the purchaser or any other person).	The qualifying conditions are ... (b) that the transaction has not been entered into for the purpose of avoiding the tax (whether by the buyer or any other person).	Relief is not available under [LTT] in respect of a land transaction— (a) which is a tax avoidance arrangement, or (b) which forms part of arrangements which are tax avoidance arrangements.

Section 13(2) LTTWA defines "tax avoidance arrangement" for Wales:

> An arrangement is a "tax avoidance arrangement" if—
> (a) the obtaining of a tax advantage for any person is the main purpose, or one of the main purposes, of the buyer in the land transaction entering into the arrangement, and
> (b) the arrangement lacks genuine economic or commercial substance other than the obtaining of a tax advantage.[6]

Para (b) is not in the standard definition of tax avoidance arrangement but it is difficult to see what it adds.

The wording for SDLT/LBTT is derived from the charitable expenditure rules[7] but it only applies if the purpose is to avoid SDLT/LBTT (as

6 Section 13(3) LTTWA provides common form definitions of arrangement and tax advantage.

7 See 6.22 (Other investments:Type 12).

opposed to other taxes). However, s.31(3) LTTWA defines "tax" more broadly:

> In this section ... "tax" ("*treth*") means land transaction tax, income tax, corporation tax, capital gains tax, stamp duty land tax, stamp duty reserve tax or stamp duty

39.7 Charity/non-charity joint purchase

Prior to 2012, HMRC considered that charities relief was only available if all of the purchasers were charities or charitable trusts.

This position was rejected in *Pollen Estate Trustee v HMRC.*[8] The Court of Appeal held that there was no valid policy reason for refusing partial relief. The Court held that para 1 sch 8 FA 2003 should be construed to read:

> A land transaction is exempt from charge [*to the extent that*] the purchaser is a charity...[9]

The reader may think that an excessively purposive construction, crossing the line from construction to legislation. But there it is. The proportion of the beneficial interest which can be attributed to the undivided share held by the charity for qualifying charitable purposes is exempt from SDLT.

In response, the Government introduced a statutory regime for partial relief in FA 2014. This inserted para 3A into sch 8 FA 2003 for England/ Northern Ireland (with the Welsh equivalent introduced in LTTWA):

England/NI	**Wales**
Para 3A sch 8 FA 2003	*Para 6 sch 18 LTTWA*
(1) Sub-paragraphs (3) to (5) apply in any case where–	(1) This paragraph applies where—
(a) there are two or more purchasers under a land transaction,	(a) there are two or more buyers under a land transaction,
(b) the purchasers acquire the subject-matter of the transaction as tenants in common (or, in Scotland, as owners in common),	(b) the buyers acquire the subject-matter of the transaction as tenants in common, and
(c) at least one of them is, and at least one of them is not, a qualifying charity, and	(c) at least one of the buyers is a qualifying charity and at least one of the buyers is another person who is not a

8 [2013] EWCA Civ 753.

9 at para [47].

(d) no purchaser enters into the transaction for the purpose of the avoidance of tax under this Part (whether by that purchaser or another person).	qualifying charity.
(2) A charity ("C") that is a purchaser under a land transaction is a "qualifying charity" in relation to the transaction if C intends to hold its undivided share of the subject-matter of the transaction for qualifying charitable purposes.	(2) The tax chargeable in respect of the transaction is reduced by the amount of the relief under sub-paragraph (3) (but see paragraph 7 (withdrawal of partial relief)).

The reference to Scotland is now otiose.

The meaning of "qualifying charity" is in effect extended by para 3C sch 8 FA 2003/para 8 sch 18 LTTWA, which provides that charities which only use 'the greater part' of their share of the subject matter of the transaction for charitable purposes should be treated as falling with para 3A sch 8 FA 2003/para 6 sch 18 LTTWA, subject only to some further grounds for withdrawing the relief.

'Greater part' is not defined in the legislation, but HMRC/WRA consider it to mean 51% or more, which seems sensible.

39.7.1 *Amount of SDLT charged*

The amount of relief available under the partial relief rules is based on the lower of

(a) the proportion of the total chargeable consideration paid by the charity, or any person connected with them, or
(b) the proportion of the chargeable interest held by the charity.

In addition, the rate of SDLT paid by the non-charity purchasers will be the rate applicable to the total consideration paid for the property, by both the charity and non-charity purchaser or any persons connected with them.

39.7.2 *Scotland*

There is no equivalent amendment to the LBTTA 2013 schedule 13. However, following *Pollen Estate Trustee* Revenue Scotland said:

> Revenue Scotland has revised its view on the application of Schedule 13 of the Land and Buildings Transaction Tax (Scotland) Act 2013 ('LBTTA') to cases where a charity is one of a number of buyers who are or will become common owners. We now accept that Charities relief from LBTT may be claimed for the charity's (or charities') pro indiviso

> share(s) of the relevant land transaction.
>
> In reaching this view, we have considered matters raised in the Upper Tribunal (Tax and Chancery Chamber) and at the Court of Appeal in the case of *Pollen Estate Trustee Co v HMRC ('Pollen')*, in relation to the UK Stamp Duty Land Tax. The *Pollen* judgement raised questions about consistency of policy and how the statute should be interpreted as a result. Although there are similarities between the LBTTA and the UK legislation, we neither accept nor refute the possible application of the *Pollen* judgement to LBTT and consider that remains uncertain. But we have reviewed the potential implications of the matters discussed in *Pollen* and the application of LBTTA Schedule 13 in cases of common ownership.
>
> We have concluded that the preferred reading of Schedule 13 allows the application of its provisions to one or more, but not all, parties entering into common ownership, based on the individual interests of the different parties. Accordingly, we will no longer refuse claims to partial Charities relief in such cases where appropriate criteria are met.
>
> We have amended our guidance to reflect this new position and to explain how to calculate partial Charities relief.
>
> Where partial Charities relief could have been claimed but was not, this may be claimed now. If the relevant return is still available for amendment online (within twelve months), the return may be amended online. If this is not possible, or if relief was claimed and refused, please write to us at, Revenue Scotland, PO Box 24068, Victoria Quay, Edinburgh, EH6 9BR, setting out the circumstances and how much relief is now being claimed. Please remember to quote the RS number of the relevant return in all correspondence.[10]

Revenue Scotland guidance now states:

> Where a charity, or charities, purchase land and buildings jointly with one or more parties who are not charities, Charities relief may be claimed for the element relating to the charity, or charities. Partial Charities relief is calculated as follows:
>
> - Calculate the LBTT on the whole transaction without relief
> - Identify the percentage that is the lower of:
> - The percentage share which the charity holds (or charities hold) in the property, and
> - The percentage of the purchase price paid by the charity (or charities) for its (or their) share in the property

---

10 *https://www.revenue.scot/land-buildings-transaction-tax/guidance/lbtt-legislation-guidance/exemptions-reliefs/lbtt3010/lbtt3035* (July 2017).

- Multiply the LBTT calculated at bullet one by the percentage at bullet two to get the Charities relief to be claimed.[11]

39.7.3 *Non-residents surcharge*

For this surcharge, see Kessler, *Taxation of Non-residents & Foreign Domiciliaries*[12]

HMRC say:[13]

> **Partial charities relief**
> 5.10 Relief from SDLT is available if a charity purchases a property that is to be used for qualifying charitable purposes. Not all charities are eligible to claim the relief. Those charities that are eligible are defined in Schedule 6 Finance Act 2010.
> 5.11 Where an eligible charity purchases property jointly as tenants in common with a non-charity, partial relief is available, with the SDLT reduced by the lower of:
> • the proportion of the property acquired by the charity, or
> • the proportion of the chargeable consideration given by the charity.
> 5.12 Although partial relief is available, for SDLT purposes the charity and non-charity remain joint purchasers of the property, having joint responsibility for any obligations under the SDLT legislation and joint and several liability for any tax charge that arises.
> 5.13 In line with the proposed treatment for joint purchasers, where partial charities relief is available, the surcharge will apply if any of the joint purchasers are non-UK resident (see Chapter 6 for treatment of joint purchasers).

39.8 Withdrawal of relief

39.8.1 *Withdrawal of relief*

England/NI	Scotland	Wales
Para 2 sch 8 FA 2003	*Para 4 sch 13 LBTTSA*	*Para 4 sch 18 LTTWA*
(1) Where in the case of a transaction ("the relevant transaction") that is exempt by virtue	Relief under this schedule is withdrawn, or partially withdrawn,	(1) This paragraph applies where— (a) a land transaction is

11 LBTT3035 - Charities relief.

12 (21st ed., 2022-23), para 95.40 (SDLT non-resident surcharge), online edition *https://www.foreigndomiciliaries.co.uk*

13 HMRC, "SDLT: non-UK resident surcharge consultation" (2019) *https://www.gov.uk/government/consultations/stamp-duty-land-tax-non-uk-resident-surcharge-consultation*

of this schedule —
(a) a disqualifying event occurs—
(i) before the end of the period of three years beginning with the effective date of the transaction, or
(ii) in pursuance of, or in connection with, arrangements made before the end of that period, and
(b) at the time of the disqualifying event the purchaser holds a chargeable interest—
(i) that was acquired by the purchaser under the relevant transaction, or
(ii) that is derived from an interest so acquired,

charities relief in relation to the relevant transaction, or an appropriate proportion of it, is withdrawn and tax is chargeable in accordance with this paragraph.

if—
(a) a disqualifying event occurs—
(i) before the end of the period of 3 years beginning with the effective date of the transaction which was exempt from charge under this schedule ("the relevant transaction"), or
(ii) in pursuance of, or in connection with, arrangements made before the end of that period, and
(b) at the time of the disqualifying event the buyer holds a chargeable interest—
(i) that was acquired by the buyer under the relevant transaction, or
(ii) that is derived from an interest so acquired.

relieved from tax under para 3 ("the relieved transaction"),
(b) a disqualifying event occurs in relation to a charity ("C") which was the buyer under the relieved transaction, and
(c) the disqualifying event occurs in the circumstances required by sub-paras (3) and (4).
(2) Where this paragraph applies, relief under para 3, or an appropriate proportion of it, is withdrawn and tax is chargeable (see sub-para (5)).
(3) The disqualifying event must occur—
(a) before the end of the period of 3 years beginning with the effective date of the relieved transaction, or
(b) in pursuance of, or in connection with, arrangements made before the end of that period.
(4) At the time of the disqualifying event C must hold a chargeable interest that—
(a) was acquired by C under the relieved transaction, or
(b) that is derived from an interest so acquired.

England/NI

Para 2 sch 8 FA 2003

(2) The amount chargeable is the amount that would have been chargeable in respect of

Scotland

Paras 8-9 sch 13 LBTTSA

8 Where relief is withdrawn, the amount of tax chargeable is the amount that would have

Wales

Para 4 sch 18 LTTWA

(5) The amount chargeable is the amount of tax that would have been chargeable but for

that would have been chargeable in respect of the relevant transaction but for charities relief or, as the case may be, an appropriate[14] proportion of the tax that would have been so chargeable.	been chargeable in respect of the relevant transaction but for the relief. 9 Where relief is partially withdrawn, the amount of tax chargeable is an appropriate proportion of the tax that would have been chargeable but for the relief.	para 3 or, as the case may be, an appropriate proportion of that amount.

39.8.2 *"Disqualifying event"*

The key term is "disqualifying event":

England/NI	**Scotland**	**Wales**
Para 2(3) sch 8 FA 2003	*Para 5 sch 13 LBTTSA*	*Para 2(4) sch 18 LTTWA*
For the purposes of this paragraph a "disqualifying event" means—	A "disqualifying event" means—	In this schedule, in relation to C which is a buyer in a land transaction, a "disqualifying event" occurs when—
(a) the purchaser ceasing to be established for charitable purposes only, or	(a) the buyer ceasing to be established for charitable purposes only, or	(a) C ceases to be established for charitable purposes only, or
(b) the subject-matter of the transaction, or any interest or right derived from it, being used or held by the purchaser otherwise than for qualifying charitable purposes.	(b) the subject-matter of the relevant transaction, or any interest or right derived from it, being held or used by the buyer otherwise than for qualifying charitable purposes.	(b) the whole or any part of the subject-matter of the transaction relieved from tax under this schedule, or any interest or right derived from it, is used or held by C otherwise than for qualifying charitable purposes.

Paragraph(a) might apply to a temporary charitable trust (if that is in fact a charity) if it ceases to be charitable. Paragraph(b) would cover an appropriation to trading stock (which is even less likely than an

14 Para 2(4) sch 8 FA 2003/para 10 sch 13 LBTTSA/para 4(6) sch 18 LTTWA elaborates the meaning of "appropriate".

acquisition of trading stock). A sale of land from a charity to another person is *not* a disqualifying event simply because the land then ceases to be held by the "purchaser" (the vendor charity). HMRC agree. The background notes to the Finance Bill 2003 provide:

> 7. This clause provides for a clawback if charities relief is granted but the purchasing charity subsequently ceases to be a charity or uses the property otherwise than for charitable purposes. The relief is only withdrawn if the charity still owns the land at the time of the disqualifying event. Charities will therefore be free to dispose of their land within the three-year period without a clawback applying. They can also allow land to fall vacant without the clawback applying.

The SDLT Manual provides:

> **SDLTM19680: Lease assignations: treated as a new lease** [Jun 2016]
> ... In relation to the withdrawal of charities relief, it should be noted that the removal of a charity from the Scottish Charities Register maintained by the Office of the Scottish Charities Register does not, of itself, amount to a disqualifying event. What matters is whether the charity continues to be established for charitable purposes only within the meaning of the relevant taxation legislation .... Scottish charities which have been removed from the Scottish Charities Register should consult HMRC Charities to establish whether they are still entitled to the charitable tax reliefs.

This is correct for SDLT but not for LBTT.

There are additional disqualifying events that apply only in relation to relief under the partial relief rules:

England/NI	**Scotland**	**Wales**
Para 3C(3) sch 8 FA 2003	*Para 6 sch 13 LBTTSA*	*Para 8(2)(b) sch 18 LTTWA*
The following are "additional disqualifying transactions" if they are not made in furtherance of the charitable purposes of C—	Where the relevant transaction is exempt from charge by virtue of qualifying condition (a)(ii), the following are also disqualifying events—	[F]or the purposes of paragraph 7 [Withdrawal of partial relief] "disqualifying event" includes the following if they are made otherwise than in furtherance of C's charitable purpose—
(a) any transfer by C of a major interest in the whole or any part of the chargeable interest acquired by C under the	(a) any transfer by the buyer of a major interest in the whole or any part of the subject-matter of the relevant transaction,	(i) any transfer by C of a major interest in the whole or any part of the subject-matter of the

relevant transaction; (b) any grant by C at a premium of a low-rental lease of the whole or any part of that chargeable interest.	or (b) any grant by the buyer at a premium of a low-rental lease of the whole or any part of that subject-matter, that is not made for the charitable purposes of the buyer.	relieved transaction; (ii) any grant by C at a premium of a low-rental lease of the whole or any part of that subject-matter.

39.9 Land partly used for charity

39.9.1 *Application of relief*

The SDLT/LBTT/LTT charitable purposes condition would exclude relief where a charity acquired land intending to retain part and sell part, if the sale was a trading transaction. That may not be so unusual. However, para 3 sch 8 FA 2003/para 2 sch 13 LBTTSA/para 5 sch 18 LTTWA provides:

England/NI	**Scotland**	**Wales**
Para 3 sch 8 FA 2003	Para 2 sch 13 LBTTSA	Para 5 sch 18 LTTWA
(1) This paragraph applies where— (a) a land transaction is not exempt from charge under paragraph 1 because the first condition in that paragraph is not met, but (b) the purchaser ("C") intends to hold the greater part of the subject-matter of the transaction for qualifying charitable purposes. (2) In such a case— (a) the transaction is exempt from charge...	The qualifying conditions are— (a) that the buyer intends to hold— (i) the subject-matter of the transaction, or (ii) the greater part of that subject-matter, for qualifying charitable purposes, and (b) that the transaction has not been entered into for the purpose of avoiding the tax (whether by the buyer or any other person).	(1) This paragraph applies where— (a) a land transaction is not relieved from tax under paragraph 3 because the buyer is not a qualifying charity, but (b) the buyer is a charity ("C") which intends to hold the greater part of the subject-matter of the transaction for qualifying charitable purposes. (2) In such a case— (a) paragraphs 3 and 4 have effect as if C were a qualifying charity...

The "greater part" is measured by value and not by area. The SDLT Manual provides:

SDLTM26030A: Reliefs: Charities relief [Jun 2016]
Circumstances where relief is available where a charity or charitable trust holds the greater part of the land FA03/SCH8/PARA3: Examples
A charity buys a five-storey office block, and intends to dispose of the top three floors at the time of acquisition. For whatever reason, the ground and first floors represent 55% of the total monetary value of the block with the remaining upper three floors representing 45%.
The charity would qualify for relief as it intended to hold the greater part of the land, even though in terms of floor space it would have disposed of more than half.

This view is confirmed in *Pollen Estate Trustee Co v HMRC* [2013] STC 1479 at [19](ii).

Where the condition in para 3 sch 8 FA 2003 is met the whole transaction is exempt from SDLT, not just the part that is held for charitable purposes.

39.10 *Withdrawal of relief*

SDLT/LBTT/LTT charity relief applies where a purchaser ("C") intends to hold the greater part of the subject-matter of the transaction for qualifying charitable purposes.

Para 3 sch 8 FA 2003/para 6 sch 13 LBTTSA/para 5 sch 18 LTTWA continues with an anti-avoidance provision for this case. This is done by the technique of extending the definition of "disqualifying event" and then incorporating para 2 sch 8 FA 2003/para 2 sch 13 LBTTSA/para 4 sch 18 LTTWA with amendments. Para 3 sch 8 FA 2003/para 6 sch 13 LBTTSA/para 5 sch 18 LTTWA provides:

England/NI	**Scotland**	**Wales**
Para 3 Sch 8 FA 2003	Para 6 Sch 13 LBTTSA	Para 5 Sch 18 LTTWA
(1) This paragraph applies where— (a) a land transaction is not exempt from charge under para 1 because the first condition in that paragraph is not met, but	Where the relevant transaction is exempt from charge by virtue of qualifying condition (a)(ii), the following are also disqualifying events—	(1) This paragraph applies where— (a) a land transaction is not relieved from tax under para 3 because the buyer is not a qualifying charity, but
(b) the purchaser ("C") intends to hold the greater part of the subject-matter of the transaction for	(a) any transfer by the buyer of a major interest in the whole or any part of the subject-matter of the relevant transaction,	(b) the buyer is a charity ("C") which intends to hold the greater part of the subject-matter of the transaction for qualifying

qualifying charitable purposes. (2) In such a case— (a) the transaction is exempt from charge, but (b) for the purposes of para 2 (withdrawal of charities relief) "disqualifying event" includes— (i) any transfer by C of a major interest in the whole or any part of the subject-matter of the transaction, or (ii) any grant by C at a premium of a low-rental lease of the whole or any part of that subject-matter, that is not made in furtherance of the charitable purposes of C.	or (b) any grant by the buyer at a premium of a low-rental lease of the whole or any part of that subject-matter, that is not made for the charitable purposes of the buyer.	charitable purposes. (2) In such a case— (a) paras 3 and 4 have effect as if C were a qualifying charity, but (b) for the purposes of para 4, "disqualifying event" includes the following if they are made otherwise than in furtherance of C's charitable purpose— (i) any transfer by C of a major interest in the whole or any part of the subject-matter of the relieved transaction; (ii) any grant by C at a premium of a low-rental lease of the whole or any part of that subject-matter.

Para 3 Sch 8 FA 2003/para 7 Sch 13 LTTSA/para 5(5) Sch 18 LTTWA continues:

England/NI	**Scotland**	**Wales**
Para 3 Sch 8 FA 2003	Para 7 Sch 13 LBTTSA	Para 5(5) Sch 18 LTTWA
(3) For the purposes of sub-para (2)(b)(ii)—	A lease—	For the purposes of this paragraph—
(a) a lease is granted "at a premium" if there is consideration other than rent, and	(a) is granted "at a premium" if there is consideration other than rent, and	(a) a lease is granted "at a premium" if there is consideration other than rent, and
(b) a lease is a "low-rental" lease if the annual rent (if any) is less than £1,000 a year.	(b) is a "low-rental" lease if the annual rent (if any) is less than £1,000 a year.	(b) a lease is a "low-rental" lease if the annual rent (if any) is less than £1,000 a year.

The anti-avoidance provision in para 2 Sch 8 FA 2003 /para 2 Sch 13

LBTTSA/para 4 Sch 18 LTTWA reads:

England/NI	**Scotland**	**Wales**
Para 2 Sch 8 FA 2003 (1) Where in the case of a transaction ("the relevant transaction") that is exempt by virtue of this Schedule— (a) a disqualifying event occurs— (i) before the end of the period of three years beginning with the effective date of the transaction, or (ii) in pursuance of, or in connection with, arrangements made before the end of that period, and (b) at the time of the disqualifying event the purchaser holds a chargeable interest— (i) that was acquired by the purchaser under the relevant transaction, or (ii) that is derived from an interest so acquired, charities relief in relation to the relevant transaction, or an appropriate proportion of it, is withdrawn and tax is chargeable in accordance with this paragraph. (2) The amount chargeable is the amount that would have been chargeable in respect of the relevant transaction but for charities relief or, as the case may be, an appropriate proportion of the tax that would have been so	Para 2 Sch 13 LBTTSA The qualifying conditions are— (a) that the buyer intends to hold— (i) the subject-matter of the transaction, or (ii) the greater part of that subject-matter, for qualifying charitable purposes, and (b) that the transaction has not been entered into for the purpose of avoiding the tax (whether by the buyer or any other person).	Para 4 Sch 18 LTTWA (1) This paragraph applies where— (a) a land transaction is relieved from tax under para 3 ("the relieved transaction"), (b) a disqualifying event occurs in relation to a charity ("C") which was the buyer under the relieved transaction, and (c) the disqualifying event occurs in the circumstances required by sub-paras (3) and (4). (2) Where this paragraph applies, relief under para 3, or an appropriate proportion of it, is withdrawn and tax is chargeable (see sub-para (5)). (3) The disqualifying event must occur— (a) before the end of the period of 3 years beginning with the effective date of the relieved transaction, or (b) in pursuance of, or in connection with, arrangements made before the end of that period. (4) At the time of the disqualifying event C must hold a chargeable interest that— (a) was acquired by C under the relieved transaction, or (b) that is derived from an interest so acquired.

chargeable.

(3) For the purposes of this paragraph a 'disqualifying event' means-
(a) the purchaser ceasing to be established for charitable purposes only, or
(b) the subject-matter of the transaction, or any interest or right derived from it, being used or held by the purchaser otherwise than for 'qualifying charitable purposes.

(4) In sub-paras (1) and (2) an "appropriate proportion" means an appropriate proportion having regard to—
(a) what was acquired by the purchaser under the relevant transaction and what is held by the purchaser at the time of the disqualifying event, and
...
(5) In this paragraph "qualifying charitable purposes" has the same meaning as in para 1.

(5) The amount chargeable is the amount of tax that would have been chargeable but for para 3 or, as the case may be, an appropriate proportion of that amount.

(6) An "appropriate proportion" means an appropriate proportion having regard to—
(a) what was acquired by C under the relieved transaction and what is held by C at the time of the disqualifying event,...

The SDLT Manual provides:

SDLTM26030A: Reliefs: Charities relief [Jun 2016]
Circumstances where relief is available where a charity or charitable trust holds the greater part of the land FA03/SCH8/PARA3: Examples
...
A charity buys a housing development with 10 equal residential units for a total of £1m with the intention to dispose of three of these units on the open market.
The charity would initially gain full stamp duty land tax charity relief on the whole £1m purchase price.
When the charity disposes of the three units, a clawback of relief on the £300,000 apportioned value of the three units is made.

> The clawback would be taxed at the rate appropriate to the whole initial consideration i.e. 4% stamp duty land tax on the £300,000 proportion attributed to the units would mean £12,000 clawed-back Tax

The matter is summarised in EN FA 2004:

> The purpose of these amendments [i.e. the introduction of para 3 Sch 8 by FA 2004] is to make it possible for charities to claim partial relief from Stamp Duty Land Tax (SDLT) on certain acquisitions. They ensure that when a charity makes an acquisition, provided that it intends to hold the greater part of the land or property for qualifying charitable purposes, the acquisition will initially attract full relief from SDLT. A clawback of a relevant portion of the relief will occur when the charity disposes of part of that acquisition, or holds part of it other than for qualifying charitable purposes. This ensures that the relief granted is in proportion to the share of the acquisition held by the charity in furtherance of its charitable aims.
> For example, if a charity intends to hold 85% of an acquisition for qualifying charitable purposes, then relief will initially be granted on the entire acquisition. When the charity subsequently disposes of the 15% share of the acquisition, 15% of relief will be clawed back. If instead of a 15% disposal, the charity disposes of a greater or lesser share, then the amount of relief clawed back will be calculated by reference to that greater or lesser share.

39.11 Stamp Duty Reserve Tax

Section 90(7) FA 1986 provides relief from Stamp Duty Reserve Tax:

> Section 87 [which imposes the charge to SDRT] above shall apply as regards an agreement to transfer securities to—
> (a) a charitable company, or
> (b) the trustees of a charitable trust...

39.12 Stamp Duty

Section 129 FA 1982 provides:

> (1) Where any conveyance, transfer or lease is made or agreed to be made to charitable company or to the trustees of a charitable trust or to the Trustees of the National Heritage Memorial Fund or to the National Endowment for Science, Technology and the Arts, no stamp duty shall be chargeable under Part I or II. of Schedule 13 to the FA 1999 on the instrument by which the conveyance, transfer or lease, or the agreement for it, is effected.

> (2) An instrument in respect of which stamp duty is not chargeable by virtue only of subsection (1) above shall not be treated as duly stamped unless it is stamped in accordance with section 12 of the Stamp Act 1891 with a stamp denoting that it is not chargeable with any duty.

39.13 Non-charitable subsidiary

A charity may own a non-charitable subsidiary. The subsidiary does not qualify for charity SDLT or SDRT relief. Land and securities should normally be purchased by the charity and not by the subsidiary.

An exception is if the transaction is one of trading in land, where charity law considerations may require the purchase to be through a subsidiary; but in that case the purchase by the charity would not qualify for SDLT charity relief.

A transfer from a charity to its subsidiary may qualify for group relief if the charity is a company, but not if it is a charitable trust.

39.14 Annual tax on enveloped dwellings

ATED is, in short, a tax on companies, and other (so called) "non-natural" persons, which hold a residential property worth more than £500k.[15]

A charitable trust does not fall within ATED as it is not a "non-natural" person. HMRC agree. HMRC ATED guidance provides:

> 42.8 The trustees of a charitable trust, even where they are bodies corporate, will not meet the ownership condition for any single dwelling interest that they hold for the purposes of the charitable trust. They are therefore outside the scope of ATED. This is because the rules exclude from the meaning of an entitlement to a single-dwelling interest those entitlements that exist because of the person being a trustee (see paragraph 2 of this guidance).[16]

A charitable company would fall within the charge. Relief is available under s.151 FA 2013 (**"ATED charity relief"**).

39.14.1 *ATED charity exemption*

Section 151(1) FA 2013 provides:

---

15 For a full discussion see Kessler, *Taxation of Non-Residents and Foreign Domiciliaries* (21st ed., 2022-23), Chapter 95 (ATED and SDLT) online version *https://www.foreigndomiciliaries.co.uk*

16 *https://www.gov.uk/government/publications/annual-tax-on-enveloped-dwellings-technical-guidance*

> A charitable company[17] that is entitled to a single-dwelling interest is regarded as not meeting the ownership condition with respect to the interest on any day on which the interest is held by the company for qualifying charitable purposes, other than an excluded day.

The consequence of not meeting the ownership condition is that ATED does not apply. There is no need to claim this relief.

Some of the wording which follows is drawn from the tainted donation rules.

HMRC ATED guidance provides:

> 42.2 The exemption will only be available where the single dwelling interest is held solely by the charitable company or is held jointly by one or more charitable companies or charitable companies and charitable trusts.[18]

HMRC ATED guidance correctly provides:

> 42.9 Where there is a company that is owned by a charitable company (or a charitable trust) and that subsidiary company is entitled to a single-dwelling interest that is within the tax, then exemption under the charitable companies provisions is not permitted. This is because such a company is not a charitable company - it is simply owned by a charitable company. However, such subsidiary companies can claim ATED reliefs where the relevant conditions are met.[19]

39.14.2 *Qualifying charitable purposes*

Section 151(2) FA 2013 provides:

> The interest is "held for qualifying charitable purposes" if it is held—
> (a) for use in furtherance of the charitable purposes of the charitable company or of another charity, or
> (b) as an investment from which the profits are (or are to be) applied to the charitable purposes of the charitable company.

39.14.3 *Excluded day*

ATED charity relief does not apply on an "excluded day".

---

17 The standard tax definition of "charitable company" applies: see 3.25 (Classification of charities for tax purposes).

18 *https://www.gov.uk/government/publications/annual-tax-on-enveloped-dwellings-technical-guidance*

19 *https://www.gov.uk/government/publications/annual-tax-on-enveloped-dwellings-technical-guidance*

Section 151(3) FA 2013 provides:

> A day is an "excluded day" if the following conditions are met—
> (a) a person ("the donor") has on or before that day made, or agreed to make, a gift[20] to the charitable company or to a charity that is connected with it,[21]
> (b) there exist on that day arrangements[22] under which or as a result of which a linked individual is permitted, or is to be or may in the future be permitted, to occupy the dwelling, and
> (c) it is reasonable to assume from either or both of—
> (i) the likely effects of the gift and the arrangements, or
> (ii) the circumstances in which the gift was made and the circumstances in which the arrangements were entered into,
> that the gift would not have been made and the arrangements would not have been entered into independently of one another;
> But see the exception in subsection (5).

Section 151(4) FA 2013 provides a wide definition of linked individual:

> In subsection (3)(b) "linked individual" means an individual who—
> (a) is the donor, or
> (b) was, when the arrangements were entered into, an associate of the donor.

Section 151(5) FA 2013 provides three exceptions to the exception:

> A day is not an "excluded day" if the first, second or third condition is met on that day.
> The first condition is that the activities undertaken for carrying out the primary purposes of the charitable company include, or normally include, opening the dwelling to the public.[23]

---

20 Section 152(7) FA 2013 provides a wide definition: "References in section 151 and this section to a gift include the disposal of an asset for consideration of an amount or value which is less than the market value of the asset."

21 Defined (after a fashion) in s.151(8) FA 2013: "For the purposes of subsection (3)(a)—
(a) "connected" means connected in a matter relating to the structure, administration or control of the charitable company, and
(b) section 172 does not apply."

22 Section 152(8) provides the standard (unnecessary) definition.

23 Section 151(6) FA 2013 provides:
(6) In subsection (5)—
(a) "opening the dwelling to the public" means offering the public the opportunity to make use of, stay in or otherwise enjoy, on at least 28 days in any year,

The second condition is that the dwelling is being exploited through commercial activities that involve, or normally involve, opening the dwelling to the public.

The third condition is that steps are being taken—

(a) to secure that the first or second condition will be met without undue delay,[24] or

(b) to secure that the single-dwelling interest will be sold without undue delay.

39.14.4 *"Associate"*

"Associate" is relevant to the definition of linked person. Section 152 FA 2013 provides:

> (1) In section 151 "associate", in relation to the donor, means any of the following—
>
> (a) an individual ("a connected person") who is connected with the donor,
>
> (b) an individual who is the settlor in relation to a settlement of which a trustee is (in the capacity of trustee) connected with the donor,
>
> (c) the spouse or civil partner of a connected person or of a relevant settlor,
>
> (d) a relative of a connected person or of a relevant settlor, or the spouse or civil partner of a relative of a connected person or of a relevant settlor,
>
> (e) a relative of the spouse or civil partner of a connected person or of a relevant settlor, or
>
> (f) the spouse or civil partner of a person falling within paragraph (e).
>
> (2) In subsection (1)—
>
> "relative" means brother, sister, ancestor or lineal descendant;
>
> "settlement" and "settlor" have the same meaning as in Chapter 5 of part 5 of ITTOIA 2005 (see section 620 of that Act).

---

areas that constitute a significant part of the interior of the dwelling or of the dwelling's garden or grounds...

(7) For the purposes of subsection (6)(a), the size (relative to the size of the whole dwelling or of the whole garden or grounds), nature, and function of the areas concerned are to be taken into account in determining whether they form a significant part of the interior of the dwelling or (as the case may be) of the garden or grounds.".

24 Section 151(6) FA 2013 provides an unnecessary definition: "without undue delay" means without delay, except so far as delay is justified by commercial considerations or for the sake of a primary purpose of the charitable company.

> (3) In subsection (1)(b) "trustee" is to be read in accordance with section 1123(3) of CTA 2010 ("connected persons": supplementary).
> (4) For the purposes of section 151 occupation of any part of a dwelling is regarded as occupation of the dwelling.

39.14.5 *2013 transitional rule*

Section 152 FA 2013 provides:

> (5) For the purposes of section 151(3)—
> (a) the making of a gift is disregarded if it is made before the day on which this Act is passed, and
> (b) an agreement to make a gift is disregarded if the agreement is made before that day.
> (6) Arrangements entered into before the day on which this Act is passed are disregarded for the purposes of section 151(3) unless a material alteration has been made to them on or after that date. "Material alteration" means an alteration affecting anything in the arrangements that relates to the individual's having (at any time), or potentially having, permission to occupy the dwelling.

39.14.6 *Critique*

These are absurdly complex rules, but in practice it will be rare for anyone to have to pay attention to them. HMRC ATED guidance gives examples of such improbability that they are not set out here.

CHAPTER FORTY

RATING RELIEF

40.1 Charity rating relief: History

The Report of the Committee on the Rating of Charities and Kindred Bodies (the "**Pritchard Committee report**")[1] contains a brief history of our subject:

> 7. Though there were earlier local taxes, some of them of the nature of rates, it is generally accepted that the modern system of rating owes its origin to the need to provide for the relief of the poor. Originally on the basis of voluntary contributions, the payment of a poor rate was made compulsory in 1597. The subsequent Poor Relief Act, 1601 is commonly regarded as the beginning of the modern rating system. The Act ... 13 November 2012 authorised the overseers to raise weekly or otherwise sums for the relief of the poor "by taxation of every inhabitant, parson,

1 Cmd 831 (1959) *https://www.kessler.co.uk/wp-content/uploads/2012/04/Report-of-the-Committee-on-the-Rating-of-Charities.pdf*

> vicar and other, and of every occupier of lands, houses, tithes impropriate, propriations of tithes, coal mines or saleable underwoods in the said parish."
>
> 8. During the nineteenth century local authorities were empowered or required to provide new services. The expenses of some of these (e.g. education) were made a charge on the poor rate. For others, new rates were levied, the most important of these being the "general district rate" ("special expense rate", later "special rate", in rural districts) to finance expenditure on public health. Section 2 of the Rating and Valuation Act, 1925 merged virtually all of these rates into one general rate, and the borough and urban and rural district councils became the rating authorities...
>
> 12. Thus, after three-and-a-half centuries rates are the main source of revenue within the direct control of local authorities; it is the occupier, rather than the owner, of a hereditament who is rateable in respect of it; it is his occupation of land (using the term in its widest sense) which gives rise to a liability; and his liability is determined by the open market rental value of the land after due allowance for the cost of maintenance and repairs.

The Pritchard Committee report then outlines the history of rating reliefs:

> 15 The nature of the reliefs enjoyed by charities and kindred bodies before 1956 and the reasons from time to time advanced for giving them make a confused history. Some charities have been exempt under the Scientific Societies Act 1843; some have been exempted by rating authorities under the Sunday and Ragged Schools (Exemption from Rating) Act 1869; and some have been exempted under the Voluntary Schools Act 1897, or under the Education Act 1921, or the Education Act 1944, which successively modified the 1897 exemption ... But between 1865 and 1956 most charities were dependent upon sympathetic treatment by rating authorities, for which there was no statutory sanction; before 1865 the rateability of property occupied for charitable purposes was not free from doubt...
>
> 18. Both the statute law and the earlier case law was exhaustively reviewed in *Mersey Docks and Harbour Board Trustees v Cameron* (11 HLC 443) in 1865 .... In his speech Lord Westbury said:
>
>> Trustees who are in law the tenants or occupiers of valuable property upon trust for charitable purposes, such as hospitals ... are in principle, rateable, notwithstanding that the buildings are actually occupied by paupers who are sick or insane...

In practice only limited notice was taken of this decision of the House of Lords and exemption continued on an erratic basis by concession:

> 20 Apparently the new certainty of the law did not result in uniformity of treatment of charities... In general [charitable] properties were undervalued. Their rateable values were generally between 25% and 75% of their true net annual values, the proportion varying between rating areas and some times within individual areas. A few were fully valued and a few were not rated at all ...

The Pritchard Committee report then went on to describe the statutory exemptions for charities. There were, effectively, five heads under which charities were eligible for relief: (1) relief on account of poverty, (2) Sunday and "ragged"[2] schools, (3) voluntary schools (under the Voluntary School Act 1897), (4) societies for science literature and the fine arts (under the Scientific Societies Act 1843), (5) section 8 Rating and Valuation (Miscellaneous Provisions) Act 1955.

The Pritchard Committee report summarises:

> 65. The rating system today provides a practical basis for local taxation. It has evolved, in over three hundred and fifty years, from something akin to an income tax levied to relieve the poor into a tax on the occupation of land levied to pay for a wide range of social and environmental services other than the relief of the poor. It has become a patchwork system which it is easy to denigrate but for which no acceptable replacement has been found. There is much in it that is arbitrary, and perhaps not the least arbitrary feature has been the granting of reliefs. We think that it is impracticable to eliminate all elements of arbitrariness; in considering charities and kindred bodies our object has been to find a reasonable balance of conflicting arguments and interests, consistent with simplicity, certainty and economy in administration.

The Pritchard Committee report went on with an analysis of the issues - it is striking to compare its standard of policy analysis with contemporary consultation papers - and only lack of space prevents us quoting it in full. It concludes with its recommended system which has survived to the present day:

> 153 ...
> (12) The time has come to introduce a measure of uniformity and certainty into the rating reliefs enjoyed by bodies within our terms of

---

2 A ragged school was one "... used for the gratuitous education of children and young persons of the poorest classes ...", the Sunday and Ragged Schools (Exemption from Rating) Act 1869; s.2.

reference. A satisfactory scheme should be simple and economical to administer and should not add materially to the rates borne by other classes of ratepayer. The essential basis should be mandatory relief for the great majority of the classes of organisation which have in the past enjoyed some measure of relief.

(19) There is some justification for the proposal to give a greater measure of relief to "local" bodies than to others, but it is impracticable to draw a clear line between these two classes and, in the interests of simplicity and ease of administration, there should be a single rate of mandatory relief for all charities ...

(21) Local authorities should have power to give further relief to charities at their discretion.

(22) Organisations on the fringe of the field of charity should be eligible for relief at the discretion of the local authorities ... the simplest practical solution is to leave the amount of the relief for these organisations entirely in the hands of the local authorities ...

(24) Rating authorities should be given power to grant relief to a particular body within the field for discretionary relief in any of the following three ways:

(i) For the ensuing rate period only.

(ii) For a specified term of years, not exceeding five, with power to decide at any time, being not more than two years before the expiry of one term, upon the amount of relief for the succeeding term and the length of that term.

(iii) For an indefinite period, subject to notice of not less than one clear financial year to discontinue or reduce the relief ...

40.2 Legislation and guidance

The legislation for England and Wales is in the LGFA 1988.

The Department of the Environment issued guidance in 1989 and 1990. This was updated and re-issued by the Office of the Deputy Prime Minister in a document entitled: "Non-domestic rates: guidance on rate reliefs for charities and other non-profit making organisations".[3] We refer to this as the **"ODPM rates guidance"**. This lapsed when responsibility was moved to the Department for Communities and Local Government. It is not clear whether that was unintentional or as a result of a policy of localism.[4] We set out the guidance here as it is still likely to be the basis

3 *https://www.kessler.co.uk/wp-content/uploads/2013/06/OPDM-rates-guidance.pdf* The document is undated but seems to have been published December 2002.

4 The Department for Communities and Local Government website *http://www.communities.gov.uk/corporate/about/* (November 2012) states:

current practice. Individual local authorities issue their own guidance, in more or less detail.

HMRC does not administer rates; charities will need to deal with Local Authority Finance Departments.

40.3 Charge on ratepayer

Non-domestic rates are charged on units of land called "hereditaments". The issues of what constitutes land and what constitutes a "unit" are not considered here. For present purposes the word may be taken as equivalent to units of land and in this chapter we use the word "property".[5]

Section 43(1) LGFA provides:

> A person (the ratepayer) shall as regards a hereditament be subject to a non-domestic rate in respect of a chargeable financial year if the following conditions are fulfilled in respect of any day in the year-
>
> (a) on the day the ratepayer is in occupation of all or part of the hereditament, and
>
> (b) the hereditament is shown for the day in a local non-domestic rating list in force for the year.

The ratepayer is in short the occupier.

40.4 Amount of charge

Section 43(2) LGFA provides:

> In such a case the ratepayer shall be liable to pay an amount calculated by-
>
> (a) finding the chargeable amount for each chargeable day,[6] and

---

"Localism, localism, localism
The Government is overseeing a fundamental shift of power away from Westminster to councils, communities and homes across the nation. A radical localist vision is turning Whitehall on its head by decentralising central government and giving power to the people.
At the Department for Communities and Local Government we are helping to end big government and create a free, fair and responsible Big Society by ... decentralising power as far as possible...
The Department sets policy on supporting local government; communities and neighbourhoods; regeneration; housing; planning, building and the environment; and fire. The Department is ending the era of top-down government by giving new powers to councils, communities, neighbours and individuals."

5 For the full definition of "hereditament" see s.64(1) LGFA.

6 Section 43(3) LGFA provides a commonsense definition: "A chargeable day is one which falls within the financial year and in respect of which the conditions mentioned

(b) aggregating the amounts found under paragraph (a) above.

The chargeable amount is defined in s.43(4) LGFA:

> Subject to subsections (4A), (5) and (6A) below, the chargeable amount for a chargeable day shall be calculated in accordance with the formula (A × B) ÷ C

A, B and C are defined in s.44(2)-(6) LGFA:

> (2) A is the rateable value shown for the day under section 42(4) above as regards the hereditament...[7]
> (4) Subject to subsection (5) below,[8] B is the non-domestic rating multiplier for the financial year...
> (6) C is the number of days in the financial year.

The basis of the valuation for the chargeable amount was considered in *Stephen G Hughes (VO) v York Museums and Gallery Trust* [2017] UKUT 200 (LC). The Tribunal had to consider whether the properties should be valued on the ordinary basis which is the receipts and expenditure basis of valuation or the contractor's basis:

> 111 The statutory basis on which the rateable value of a non-domestic hereditament is to be determined is prescribed by section 56 of and Schedule 6 to the 1988 Act. In the ordinary case the rateable value is equal to the rent at which the hereditament might reasonably be expected to let from year to year at the material day but having regard to values at the antecedent valuation date. The hereditament is assumed to be in a state of reasonable repair (but excluding any repairs which a reasonable landlord would consider uneconomic), with the tenant undertaking to pay all usual tenant's rates and taxes and to bear the cost of repairs, insurance and any other expenses necessary to maintain the hereditament. For the purpose of the 2005 list the material day was 1 April 2005 and the antecedent valuation date was 1 April 2003; for the 2010 list they were 1 April 2010 and 1 April 2008 respectively.
> 112 Ascertainment of the rent at which premises might reasonably be expected to let on the statutory assumptions is a question of fact, not one of law. The selection of the most appropriate technique to be employed

---

in subsection (1) above are fulfilled."

7 Section 42(4) provides that in the local non-domestic rating list for each day on which an hereditament is listed it must also be accompanied by the rateable value of that property. Therefore A will be determined by the billing authority responsible for the non-domestic rating list.

8 The exception relates to special authorities (population less than 10,000).

> in answering that question is a matter of valuation judgment rather than legal precedent.
> 113 The best evidence of rental value is provided by rents for comparable properties agreed in the open market. The greater the adjustments required to be made to mirror the statutory valuation assumptions or other differences, the less reliable a guide the comparable may be, but valuation by the comparative method always has the advantage over other methods of being rooted in evidence of the behaviour of real landlords and tenants in the market in which it is to be assumed the subject premises are being let. Regard may also be had to evidence of comparable assessments, which in most cases are likely to be based on evidence of lettings in the market.
> 114 Where sufficient evidence of comparable lettings or assessment evidence is not available some other approach to valuation must be employed. Three alternative approaches were relied on by the experts: the contractor's basis, the receipts and expenditure basis, and the "shortened receipts" basis. Given the evidence we have received of some surprising practices in the valuation of historic buildings for rating purposes, we will consider these alternative techniques in a little detail.

After considering the different methods of valuation, the Tribunal did not find either method to be wholly persuasive; however, they found in favour of the charity and determined that the rates should be based on net income, not the cost of rebuilding, which has traditionally been used by the VOA for valuing museums. This meant that the Charity's business rates were significantly reduced. Many museums could benefit from this determination and should consider whether they could argue for reduced rates.

40.5 Mandatory relief

Section 43(6) LGFA provides:

> This subsection applies where on the day concerned
> (a) [i] the ratepayer is a charity or trustees for a charity[9] and
> [ii] the hereditament is wholly or mainly used for charitable purposes (whether of that charity or of that and other charities), or
> (b) [i] the ratepayer is a registered club for the purposes of Chapter

9 The words "trustees of a charity" seem otiose as a charitable trust is itself a charity but it does not matter.

9 of Part 13 of Corporation Tax Act 2010 (community amateur sports clubs) and

[ii] the hereditament is wholly or mainly used -

(i) for the purposes of that club, or

(ii) for the purposes of that club and of other such registered clubs.

This takes us to s.43(5) LGFA:

> Where subsection (6) below applies the chargeable amount for a chargeable day shall be calculated in accordance with the formula—
>
> $(A \times B) \div (C \times 5)$

We refer to this as **"mandatory relief"**. If this is compared with the formula used to calculate the liability of those not entitled to the relief[10] it is clear that a charity pays one fifth of the full rates, ie, mandatory relief is 80% of the full liability

40.6 "Charity"

Section 67(10) LGFA provides:

> A charity is
>
> [a] an institution or other organisation established for charitable purposes only or
>
> [b] any persons administering a trust established for charitable purposes only.[11]

"Charitable purposes" has the meaning given by s.2 Charities Act 2011.

It has been suggested that "charity" (for rating purposes) is by implication restricted to charities subject to the jurisdiction of the English or UK courts.[12] If that were right, UK law would be in breach of EU law and charities established in EU member states (and Iceland and Norway, and arguably other EEA countries) would nevertheless qualify for the relief under the EU or EEA treaties.[13] Other foreign charities could not in principle qualify. The better view is that there is no jurisdiction requirement for the purposes of rating relief so (for instance) an American charity (if its purposes are charitable in English law) would qualify for

---

10 See 40.4 (Amount of charge).

11 Section 67(10) [b] is otiose, as a charitable trust is within [a], but it does not matter.

12 The argument relies on the *Dreyfus* decision but a decision on direct tax legislation is not relevant for rates.

13 See 3.20 (EU law: Introduction).

relief. This is the Government's view.[14] That explains why the standard tax definition of charity in the F(No.1)A 2010 does not apply for rating purposes.

40.7 Used for charitable purposes

Section 43(6) LGFA provides that relief is available where

> the hereditament is wholly or mainly used for charitable purposes (whether of that charity or of that and other charities), ...

There are in fact two overlapping conditions for rating relief:

(1) The charity must occupy the land (as otherwise the charity is not the ratepayer).
(2) The land must be wholly or mainly used for charitable purposes.

In *Merton LBC v Nuffield Health* [2021] EWCA Civ 826, the Court of Appeal confirmed that when assessing 'public benefit' in this context, what matters is the activities and purposes of the charity, not the activities carried out at the site in question. Accordingly, in order to qualify for relief, there is no need for a public benefit to be provided at the site. Rather, all that is required is that the site is being used by the charity for its charitable purposes.

40.7.1 *Use by beneficiary of charity*

Housing used by beneficiaries of a charity may be occupied by the charity and used for charitable purposes.

Soldiers' Sailors' and Airmen's Family Association v Merton Corporation [1967] 1 WLR 127 concerned a charity providing accommodation to dependants of servicemen. The Court of Appeal said:

> We come, therefore, to the age-old question—what constitutes "occupation" for rating purposes? ... This is a case of rival or competing occupations. Each flat is occupied for rating purposes either by the charitable organisation or by the lady resident. The court has to choose between them. It looks to see which is paramount and which is subordinate, and holds that that person is rateable whose occupation is paramount; see *Westminster City Council v Southern Ry Co* [1936] AC 511 at pp 529, 530)... So, as between landlord and lodger, the

---

14 See the Letter dated 10 August 2010 from the Department for Communities and Local Government *https://www.kessler.co.uk/wp-content/uploads/2012/04/RatingRelief01.pdf*

> occupation of the landlord is paramount. As between site operator and caravan owner, the occupation of the caravan owner is paramount over his pitch. In deciding between them, the court looks, not only to the degree of control exercised by each, but also to the purposes of each. Thus in the case of the lodger, although the lodger may have the exclusive use of his rooms, the landlord is held to be in rateable occupation, because he uses the premises for the purpose of his business of keeping lodgers; see *Westminster City Council v Southern Ry Co* [1936] AC at pp 556, 560)...
> In the present case the decisive question is the purpose for which these flats are used. It is plain that each flat is used for charitable purposes. It is the very means whereby this association provides houses for ladies who are in need. Physically no doubt each flat is indistinguishable from a commercial flat. Legally no doubt each flat is let on a tenancy, but the degree of control exercised by the association by means of its regulations is tighter than the degree of control exercised by a commercial landlord; and the purpose is beyond doubt charitable.
> This turns the scale and shows that the association is in paramount occupation. The occupation of each lady resident is subordinate to the occupation of the association.

For other examples, see *Polish Historical Institution v Hove Corporation* (1963) 61 LGR 438; *Forces Help Society v Canterbury City Council* (1978) 122 Sol Jo 760.

40.7.2 *Use by employee of charity*

Housing used by employees of a charity may be occupied by the charity and used for charitable purposes: see *Royal Society for the Protection of Birds v Hornsea Urban Council* 18 RRC 57, where living accommodation on a nature reserve was held to be used for charitable purposes on the following grounds:

> Is the warden by living in the house, better able to perform his duties as a servant to a material degree ... the true answer is that the RSPB satisfies the requirements of section 40 of the General Rate Act 1970 and is entitled to the reduction ...

The same point is made in *Glasgow Corporation v Johnstone* [1965] AC 609:

> The second question is whether the house was wholly or mainly used for charitable purposes within the meaning of section 4(2) Local Government (Financial Provisions, etc.) (Scotland) Act 1962. The

> appellants contended that it was used as a residence and for no other purpose. But, once the [the charity] have been held to be the occupiers, I think that it is their use of the premises that we must consider. They use the house to have a servant on the spot to assist them in the more efficient performance of their charitable activities. I think that it is much too narrow a view simply to see whether any charitable activity is carried on in the house ... If the use which the charity makes of the premises is directly to facilitate the carrying out of its main charitable purposes, that is, in my view, sufficient to satisfy the requirement that the premises are used for charitable purposes.

40.7.3 *Partly used, partly unused*

Public Safety Charitable Trust v Milton Keynes Council[15] concerned a charity which entered into agreements with owners of unoccupied commercial properties in order to avoid rates. The charity took a lease and placed a small transmitter at the premises to provide free wireless internet access to anyone within range and broadcast public safety messages. The provision of such a service was charitable. Apart from this, the buildings were unused.

The Court correctly noted:

> The concept of "occupation" as used in the LGFA...is different from the concept of "use".

The judge then considered the meaning of "wholly...used":

> A building may fairly and properly be described as being wholly used for a particular purpose even though not every square metre of floor space is in constant use all the time. For instance, the whole of a room used as an office can be described as being wholly used as an office, even though it is spacious and not crammed with people working. I also think it can fairly be described as being wholly used as an office, albeit it is closed and left vacant during the night.

The judge concluded that although the charity was in occupation of the buildings, they were not used wholly or mainly for charitable purposes.

The concept of "wholly or mainly used for charitable purposes" seems sufficiently open ended to defeat schemes of this kind.

An independent report commissioned by the Welsh Government from The Business Rates Task and Finish Group and published in April 2013

---

15 [2013] EWHC 1237; see Quint, "Charities and Non-Domestic Rate Relief: Occupation, Use or Purpose" [2013] PCB 286.

suggested limiting the amount of relief available as a means of preventing tax avoidance:

> 55. There is currently an anomalous provision in the rules governing rate relief whereby relief will apply to a vacant property where it appears that it will next be occupied by a charity. This provision has led to certain examples of irregular practice that may be considered in some cases as simply a tax avoidance strategy.
> 56. The provision to allow rate relief to vacant premises where there is a claim that it will next be occupied by a charitable organisation is difficult to justify. Apart from those situations where a registered charity is demonstrably refurbishing or stocking premises ready for imminent occupation it can be difficult for LAs to properly verify future intentions. Ambiguous cases allow a relatively easy loophole for EPR avoidance.
> 57. [Local Authorities] have cited specific examples where large retail outlets and warehouses that have been lying vacant have been occupied by often "unfamiliar" charitable organisations and as a result, have avoided the empty property rate that would otherwise be levied. In some instances there have been serious doubts as to whether the occupation has been genuine.
> 58. Mandatory 80% charitable relief applies where premises are, in the terms of the relevant legislation, "wholly or mainly" occupied by a charitable organisation and for charitable purposes (Community Amateur Sports Clubs or CASCs, are also entitled to this category of relief). We are aware that some LAs have taken action to withdraw the relief, for example where it has been possible to establish that very little of the premises has been actually occupied and the "wholly or mainly" requirement has therefore not been fulfilled. In other cases, despite concerns, the LA has had insufficient grounds to cancel the relief. (The CRA has offered to work with the Welsh Government to explore ways of ensuring that charities are not inappropriately occupying premises.)
> 59. The potential for imposing an upper RV limit to prevent such opportunity for abuse has been considered by the group, but it is not a straightforward issue. There are many instances where premises with very high RVs are occupied by organisations with genuine charitable status. To avoid such organisations being adversely affected it would seem that any upper RV limit for charitable relief would have to be targeted at specific categories of property such as retail and/or storage.
> 60. As regards the issue of tax avoidance we had thought of recommending that an upper RV level of £36K should be applied to large commercial buildings outside town centres - particularly those that are used for storage and are currently being occupied by 'unfamiliar' charitable organisations in order to avoid empty property rates. However,

> we decided that this issue was outside of our remit and we simply take this opportunity to flag up a potential solution to the problem.

More recently, the Charity Commission investigated a business rates relief scheme: the "empty property scheme". The scheme worked by charities occupying empty commercial properties through a tenancy at will for a peppercorn rent in exchange for an agreement to vacate the premiss with 24 hours' notice. The Charity Commission found that the charity which had entered into this scheme did not do so in the best interest of the charity. In terms of advice for other charities the report concluded:[16]

> Trustees must exercise their duty of care and taking proper decisions, and not allow the good name of charity to be abused for the benefit of commercial companies. Charities are held in high esteem by the general public, and trustees must ensure they do not enter into agreements that could jeopardise that public trust.
>
> Before entering into any tenancy agreements to occupy empty properties, charity trustees must:
>
> - be assured that the tenancy agreement is for the exclusive benefit of the charity, will further the charity's purposes and is in its best interests
> - ensure the property is genuinely required and is fit for purpose
> - consider the potential liability of the charity to pay outstanding rates if the local authority disputes use of the premises and refuses rates relief
> - very carefully safeguard the charity's independence and ensure the charity is not being abused for the benefit of a commercial company
> - where appropriate, take suitable professional advice, including legal advice, before entering into a tenancy agreement.
>
> If landlords are perceived to disproportionately benefit from entering into arrangements with charities, this creates a perception that the real purpose is to benefit commercial companies and has the potential to impact on public trust and confidence in the charity concerned and more widely.
>
> Trustees should ensure they maintain a position of accountability and transparency through the implementation of proper governance and regularly review policies and procedures to ensure they are fit for purpose.
>
> The Commission recognises that, on occasions it is possible for the activities of a charity to drift from being exclusively charitable and for

16 *https://www.gov.uk/government/uploads/system/uploads/attachment_data/file/601863/africa_relief_trust_art.pdf*

the public benefit. However trustees should ensure they implement safeguards such as risk assessments and regular reviews of the activities undertaken against the objects of the charity to ensure activities are compatible with those objects and do not expose the charity to unmanaged risks.

40.7.4 *Use for fundraising*

Oxfam v Birmingham City Council concerned charity shops selling (mainly) donated goods. Lord Cross said:

> [the exemption for rating relief] is somewhat curiously worded. No body or trust can be a charity unless its objects are exclusively charitable and if it is using premises of which it is in occupation for purposes for which it is entitled to use them and not in breach of trust it must be using them for some purpose or purposes of the charity. Yet this subsection clearly contemplates that a charity may be properly using premises which it occupies for purposes which are not "charitable" purposes of the charity. A line has therefore to be drawn somehow or other between the user of premises for purposes which are charitable purposes of a charity within the meaning of the subsection on the one hand and their user for purposes which though purposes of the charity are not charitable purposes of the charity on the other.[17]

This line was drawn by distinguishing:
(1) use for "purposes directly related to the achievement of the objects of the charity" and
(2) use for the "purposes of getting in, raising or earning money for the charity".

The latter is not regarded as use for charitable purposes. The distinction is in effect (if not in wording) similar (maybe identical) to the rule that a charity trade is exempt if it is carried on in the course of a primary purpose of the charity. The courts might have construed the rating legislation differently, but the law is now settled.

On this basis the Oxfam shops were not entitled to the relief because the shops were not used directly for the objects of the charity, but merely for fundraising.

40.7.5 *Relief for charity shops*

Section 64(10) LGFA now provides relief specifically for charity shops:

---

17 [1976] AC 126 at p.135.

> A hereditament shall be treated as wholly or mainly used for charitable purposes at any time if at that time it is wholly or mainly used for the sale of goods donated to a charity and the proceeds of the sale of goods (after any deduction of expenses) are applied for the purposes of a charity.

This relief only applies to charity shops selling donated goods and not to shops which buy and resell goods. However, the shop need only be used "wholly or mainly" for the sale of donated goods, and therefore some non-donated goods would not prevent the shop obtaining the relief. A shop which mainly resells goods made by beneficiaries of the charity would be used for charitable purposes and does not need the relief in s.64(10).

CC35 (Trustees, trading and tax) paragraph 4.14 summarises:

> ... the term 'charitable purposes' normally excludes fundraising activities, but includes the sale of donated goods.

For policy aspects of this exemption, see 8.19.1 (Fair competition argument).

The Welsh Government's Business Rates Task and Finish Group report suggests that the relief available to charity shops should be capped. The report sets out suggested levels of relief:

> The review group noted the extent to which the professionalism and commercial focus of the charity shop has increased markedly over the last twenty years. We then questioned whether businesses of the size and commercial sophistication of some of the larger charity shop chains should continue to receive mandatory rate relief of 80% - relief at levels not available to other retailers.
>
> We are therefore recommending new thresholds for charity shop rate relief to help reduce current (and possible future) distortions to which the current mandatory 80% relief for all charity shop properties, irrespective of size, gives rise. The group, therefore, recommends that the amount of rate relief available for larger charity shops occupying premises of higher Rateable Value be restricted to an upper RV limit of £36K and that other thresholds should be introduced as follows:
>
> - The full, mandatory rate relief of 80% will be available on properties with a rateable value (RV) up to £12K (the current upper limit for Small Business Rate Relief). All charity shops will receive 80% rate relief on the first £12,000 of the RV.
> - Charity rate relief will then be reduced from 80% to 50% on the next £24K of rateable value, i.e. up to a maximum RV of £36K. All

charity shops will receive 50% rate relief on the next £24,000 of the RV.

- For RVs in excess of £36K we recommend that the business rate relief falls to zero.

The above reliefs will be tiered, i.e. cumulative...Therefore all charity shops will receive some rate relief from business rates but the amount of relief they receive will be reduced in stages.

...We recommend that, as the economy picks up, consideration should be given to reducing the mandatory 80% rate relief as follows:

- The full, mandatory 80% rate relief will be available on properties with a rateable value (RV) up to £12K (the current upper limit for Small Business Rate Relief). All charity shops will receive 80% rate relief on the first £12,000 of the RV.
- Charity rate relief will then be reduced from 80% to 50% on the next £24K of rateable value, i.e. up to a maximum RV of £36K. All charity shops will receive 50% rate relief on the next £24,000 of the RV.
- For RVs in excess of £36K we recommend that the business rate relief falls to zero.

...When the next Rating List for 2022 is introduced, consideration be given to reducing the mandatory 80% charitable relief to 50% for all charity shops and that as much as possible of charitable reliefs should be left to the discretion of the local authorities.[18]

The responses to the consultation were mixed. Charities were against the changes stating that the changes would reduce charity shop income, lead to closures and, ultimately, reduced support for beneficiaries.[19] This can be contrasted with the views of, for example, the Federation of Small Business Wales who were more supportive of the recommendations as an opportunity to regenerate Wales' town centres.[20] The Welsh Government's Summary of Consultation Responses[21] was published on 17 July 2013 and

---

18 Business Rate Relief for Charities, Social Enterprises and Credit Unions – Recommendations from an independent report to the Welsh Government [April 2013] *wales.gov.uk/docs/det/consultation/130423businessratesen.pdf*

19 See, for example, the response from the Charity Finance Group [June 2013] *https://www.wcva.org.uk/media/419045/cfg_consultation_response_business_rates__welsh_government_.pdf*

20 FSB Wales response to Welsh Government - Business Rate Relief for Charities, Social Enterprises and Credit Unions [June 2013] *https://docplayer.net/15779470-Fsb-wales-response-to-welsh-government-business-rate-relief-for-charities-social-enterprises-and-credit-unions.html*

21 *http://gov.wales/topics/businessandeconomy/how-we-support-businesses/business-rates/brr/?lang=en*

reflected the anxiety in the sector for the suggested reforms with very few actually in favour of the changes.

40.7.6 *Wholly/mainly charitable purposes*

In the case of mixed use, it is necessary to decide if property is:
(1) wholly or mainly used for charitable purposes; or
(2) wholly or mainly used for the sale of goods donated to a charity.

CC35 (Trustees, trading and tax) provides:

> **4.14 Do trading subsidiaries qualify for rate relief?**
> Premises occupied partly by a charity and used for charitable purposes, and partly by a trading subsidiary, qualify for the mandatory charity rate relief only in respect of the part occupied by the charity.
> Charity rate relief may be available if a charity is in occupation of premises even though the premises are used partly for fundraising, provided that they are used 'mainly' for 'charitable purposes'. Even if the fundraising trade is being carried on by a trading subsidiary, the charity may be able to argue that it is occupying the whole of the premises, and using them 'mainly' for charitable purposes.

Fawcett Properties Ltd v Buckingham County Council concerned the phrase "an industry mainly dependent upon agriculture" in s.115 Housing Act 1936. The House of Lords said:

> The word "mainly" at once gives rise to difficulties. Probably it means "more than half" ... Even so, one must ask "more than half of what?"[22]

This is not necessarily applicable in relation to charity rating relief.
CC35 (trustees, trading and tax) paragraph 4.14 provides very tentative guidance:

> There is no statutory definition of 'mainly'. However it is often argued that, if in a particular period the value of the sales of the donated goods exceeds the value of the sales of the bought-in goods, the premises are used 'mainly' for the sale of the donated goods, and thus for charitable purposes. In such cases the trustees should contact the appropriate rating authority, and if necessary their own legal advisers, for further advice.

The ODPM rates guidance provided:

> 6.2.2 Although this is a mandatory relief, billing authorities need guidance as they still have a decision making role to play. Many billing

---

22 [1961] AC 636 at p.669.

> authorities, charities and others have told us that the rules about what constitutes 'wholly or mainly' are not clear, so that there is inconsistent treatment up and down the country. This lack of clarity makes it difficult for charities to comply with the rules and causes problems for billing authorities seeking to apply them. The legislation does not determine what constitutes wholly or mainly for charitable purposes. Whilst we are unaware of any case law that provides guidance on the meaning of 'mainly' in relation to the rating legislation, in other circumstances, 'mainly' has been held to mean 'more than half' (see *Fawcett Properties Ltd v Buckingham County Council* [1961] AC 636 at 669).
>
> 6.2.3 In deciding whether a charity shop is 'wholly or mainly' used for the sale of donated goods, we understand that some billing authorities currently take some or all the following relevant factors into account:
>
> I. The percentage of floor space occupied by donated goods.
>
> II. The percentage of turnover and profit represented by the sale of donated goods.
>
> III. The percentage of individual items sold which are donated goods.

What if the factors point in different directions? The author did not know the answer:

> 6.2.4 The use of the above factors may not, in every case provide billing authorities with the solution for determining eligibility for rate relief. Charity shops often present difficulties for billing authorities in determining eligibility for rate relief because in terms of quantity of goods displayed, most items may be goods donated by the public. However, in terms of value, the donated goods may represent only a small proportion of turnover. In such circumstances, the weight given to the charitable and non-charitable uses of the hereditament may also need to be considered even if the charitable use, which could be the main use, occupies less than half of the floor space. Clearly, the three factors given above can go up or down depending on the prevailing local economy. In the interests of certainty to ratepayers, billing authorities should try to ensure that properties do not move in and out of charitable relief regularly as a result of such minor fluctuations.

40.7.7 *Occupation by trading subsidiary*

Land occupied by a non-charitable subsidiary of a charity does not qualify for rating relief, as it is not occupied by a charity (and not used for charitable purposes).

CC35 (Trustees, trading and tax) paragraph 4.14 provides:

> This mandatory relief is not available in the case of premises occupied

by a trading subsidiary. However rating[23] authorities have discretion to grant rate relief to some bodies which are not charities.

40.8 Discretionary relief

Power to grant discretionary relief is conferred on billing authorities by s.47 LGFA:

> (1) Where the first and second conditions mentioned in subsections (2) and (3) below ...[24] are fulfilled for a day which is a chargeable day within the meaning of section 43 or 45 above (as the case may be)—
> (a) the chargeable amount for the day shall be such as is determined by, or found in accordance with rules determined by, the billing authority concerned, and
> (b) sections 43(4) to (6B) and 44 above, sections 45(4) to (4B) and 46 above, regulations under section 57A or 58 below or any provision of or made under Schedule 7A below(as the case may be) shall not apply as regards the day.
>
> (2) The first condition is that one or more of the following applies on the chargeable day—
> (a) the ratepayer is a charity or trustees for a charity, and the hereditament is wholly or mainly used for charitable purposes (whether of that charity or of that and other charities);
> (b) the hereditament is not an excepted hereditament,[25] and all or part of it is occupied for the purposes of one or more institutions or other organisations none of which is established or conducted for profit and each of whose main objects are charitable or are otherwise philanthropic or religious or concerned with education, social welfare, science, literature or the fine arts;
> (ba) the ratepayer is a registered club for the purposes of Chapter 9

---

23 A note on terminology. The Charity Commission Guidance refers to "rating authorities" though the statutory term in s.67 LGFA is "billing authorities". The terms are synonymous.

24 The words omitted refer to relief in accordance with the rural settlement condition and for former agricultural property.

25 An excepted hereditament is defined in s.47(9) LGFA as:

> A hereditament is an excepted hereditament if all or part of it is occupied (otherwise than as trustee) by
> (a) a billing authority; or
> (b) a precepting authority, other than the Receiver for the Metropolitan Police District or charter trustees; or.
> (c) a functional body, within the meaning of the Greater London Authority Act 1999

of Part 13 of the Corporation Tax Act 2010 (community amateur sports clubs), and the hereditament is not an excepted hereditament and is wholly or mainly used—

(i) for the purposes of that club, or

(ii) for the purposes of that club and of other such registered clubs;

(c) the hereditament is not an excepted hereditament, it is wholly or mainly used for purposes of recreation, and all or part of it is occupied for the purposes of a club, society or other organisation not established or conducted for profit.

(3) The second condition is that, during a period which consists of or includes the chargeable day, a decision of the billing authority concerned operates to the effect that this section applies as regards the hereditament concerned.

...

(4) A determination under subsection (1)(a) above—

(a) must be such that the chargeable amount for the day is less than the amount it would be apart from this section;

(b) may be such that the chargeable amount for the day is 0;

(c) may be varied by a further determination of the authority under subsection (1)(a) above.

(5) In deciding what the chargeable amount for the day would be apart from this section the effect of any regulations under section 57A or 58 below and of any provision of or made under Schedule 7A below shall be taken into account but anything which has been done or could be done under section 49 below shall be ignored.

(6) A decision under subsection (3) above may be revoked by a further decision of the authority.

(7) A decision under subsection (3) above is invalid as regards a day if made more than six months after the end of the financial year in which the day falls.

...

40.8.1 *Guidance on discretion*

The granting of discretionary relief is at the discretion of the billing authority and an application must be made by the ratepayer. The manner of the application may vary between billing authorities.

The ODPM rates guidance discussed the exercise of the discretion in relation to community amateur sports clubs:

5.2 Discretionary relief for non-profit making sports clubs

The issue of discretionary rate relief is a matter for individual local authorities. However, to help achieve more consistency of treatment when considering whether a non-profit making sports club which does not have or decides not to obtain charitable status should receive discretionary relief, authorities may wish to consider the following issues. Authorities may also wish to bear in mind the legal definition of a Community Amateur Sports Club (CASC) ... set out in [now CTA 2010].

5.3 Access to clubs

...5.3.3 Does the organisation actively encourage membership from particular disadvantaged or under-represented groups in the community e.g. young people, women, older age groups, persons with disability, ethnic minorities' etc? An organisation that encouraged such membership might justify more sympathetic consideration than one which made no effort to attract members from groups which the authority considered to be particularly deserving of support.

5.3.4 Are the facilities made available to people other than members e.g. schools, casual public sessions etc? The wider use of facilities should be encouraged and rate relief might be one form of recognition that an organisation was promoting its facilities more widely.

5.4 Provision of facilities

5.4.1 Does the organisation provide training or education for its members? Are there schemes for particular groups to develop their skills e.g. young people, the disabled, retired people? An organisation providing such facilities might deserve more support than one that did not.

5.4.2 Have the facilities available been provided by self-help or grant aid? The fact that a club uses or has used self-help for construction or maintenance of its facilities or has attracted grant aid, might be an indicator that they were more deserving of relief.

5.4.3 Does the organisation run a bar? The mere existence of a bar should not in itself be a reason for not granting relief. The authority should look at the main purpose of the organisation. In sports clubs for example the balance between playing and non-playing members might provide a useful guide as to whether the main purpose of the club is sporting or social activities. A club whose main aim is to bring together people with similar sporting or recreational interests should not be excluded from relief just because of the existence of a licensed bar. Some authorities already include in their decision making criteria how much in percentage terms they would deduct from the overall relief granted to clubs with bar facilities based on how much additional revenue the facility raises.

5.4.4 Does the organisation provide facilities that indirectly relieve the authority of the need to do so, or enhance and supplement those that it does provide? Authorities should not refuse relief on the grounds that an organisation is in competition with the authority itself, but should look at the broader context of the needs of the community as a whole. A new need, not being provided by the authority itself but identified as a priority for action, might be particularly deserving of support.

5.5 Other considerations

5.5.1 Is the organisation affiliated to local or national organisations e.g. local sports councils, county or national representative bodies? i.e. are they actively involved in local/county/national development of their interests?

5.5.2 Is the membership drawn from people mainly resident in the billing authority's area? Although authorities will have in mind that 25% of the cost of any relief given will be borne by the council taxpayers in their area, particular difficulties may arise with hereditaments which straddle or are close to local authority boundaries. In these cases, a proportion of the membership may come from another local authority area. Also, for geographical reasons, or because of the nature of the terrain, particular facilities may be the only ones available for a wide area. In such cases the joint use of facilities by one or more similar organisations is not uncommon. In most cases there will be a measure of reciprocity between the membership of organisations from different areas.

5.5.3 Are members paid to participate? Authorities should consider whether to grant relief where payments or other significant benefits are provided to players. Exceptions could include for example, the reimbursement of reasonable travel expenses for players or officials and reasonable provision and maintenance of club owned equipment necessary for playing the sport. Authorities may choose to look favourably on clubs whose paid players contribute more to the club than just playing, e.g. by coaching younger members.

5.5.4 Authorities may wish to consider the extent to which the activities of the organisation contribute to a local or regional community strategy and/or authority objectives for building neighbourhood identity, community building or social inclusion.

5.5.5 Authorities may wish to add further criteria or substitute relevant alternative criteria that are appropriate to the furthering of their policies and the needs of the community such as development programmes. They should also bear in mind the need to encourage new activities in the wide range of organisations for which relief from rates is available.

5.5.6 Authorities may wish to consider using a points system for the granting of relief which might give greater weight to any particular aspect of the role of community clubs authorities wish to promote. The amount of relief given need not be 100% in all cases, but might be lower

if some but not all criteria are met. Indeed, some local authorities already operate a points system in considering applications.
5.5.7 To assist sports clubs with their long term planning, authorities may wish to indicate in their decisions the likelihood of continued rate relief in future years.

40.9 Unoccupied property

40.9.1 *The charge*

Section 45(1) LGFA sets out the charge on unoccupied property:

> A person (the ratepayer) shall as regards a hereditament be subject to a non-domestic rate in respect of a chargeable financial year if the following conditions are fulfilled in respect of any day in the year -
> (a) on the day none of the hereditament is occupied,
> (b) the hereditament is shown for the day in a local non-domestic rating list in force for the year, and
> (c) the hereditament is shown for the day in a local non-domestic rating list in force for the year, and
> (d) on the day the hereditament falls within a class prescribed by the Secretary of State by regulations.

Regulation 3 Non-Domestic Rating (Unoccupied Property) (England) Regulations 2008[26] provides:

> The class of non-domestic hereditaments prescribed for the purposes of section 45(1)(d) of the Act consists of all relevant non-domestic hereditaments other than those described in regulation 4.

Regulation 4 sets out the following exceptions:

> The relevant non-domestic hereditaments described in this regulation are any hereditament—
> (a) which, subject to regulation 5, has been unoccupied for a continuous period not exceeding three months;
> (b) which is a qualifying industrial hereditament that, subject to regulation 5, has been unoccupied for a continuous period not exceeding six months;
> (c) whose owner is prohibited by law from occupying it or allowing it to be occupied;

26 And the Non-Domestic Rating (Unoccupied Property) (Wales) Regulations 2008, and the Non-Domestic Rating (Unoccupied Property) (Northern Ireland) Regulations 2007

(d) which is kept vacant by reason of action taken by or on behalf of the Crown or any local or public authority with a view to prohibiting the occupation of the hereditament or to acquiring it;
(e) which is the subject of a building preservation notice within the meaning of the Planning (Listed Buildings and Conservation Areas) Act 1990(b) or is included in a list compiled under section 1 of that Act;
(f) which is included in the Schedule of monuments compiled under section 1 of the Ancient Monuments and Archaeological Areas Act 1979(b);
(g) whose rateable value is less than £2,600;
(h) whose owner is entitled to possession only in his capacity as the personal representative of a deceased person;
(i) where, in respect of the owner's estate, there subsists a bankruptcy order within the meaning of section 381(2) of the Insolvency Act 1986;
(j) whose owner is entitled to possession of the hereditament in his capacity as trustee under a deed of arrangement to which the Deeds of Arrangement Act 1914 applies;
(k) whose owner is a company which is subject to a winding-up order made under the Insolvency Act 1986 or which is being wound up voluntarily under that Act;
(l) whose owner is a company in administration within the meaning of paragraph 1 of Schedule B1 to the Insolvency Act 1986 or is subject to an administration order made under the former administration provisions within the meaning of article 3 of the Enterprise Act 2002 (Commencement No. 4 and Transitional Provisions and Savings) Order 2003;
(m) whose owner is entitled to possession of the hereditament in his capacity as liquidator by virtue of an order made under section 112 or section 145 of the Insolvency Act 1986.

40.9.2 *The relief*

Section 45A LGFA provides charity relief for unoccupied property:[27]

> (1) Where section 45 applies in relation to a hereditament, the chargeable amount for a chargeable day is zero in the following cases.
> (2) The first case is where -

27 All unoccupied hereditaments are entitled to an initial rate free period of three months under the Non-Domestic Rating (Unoccupied Property) Regulations 1989, but the mandatory relief for charities may be applicable thereafter.

(a) the ratepayer is a charity or trustees of a charity, and
(b) it appears that when next in use the hereditament will be wholly or mainly used for charitable purposes (whether of that charity or of that and other charities).

(3) The second case is where -
(a) the ratepayer is a registered club for the purposes of Schedule 18 to the FA 2002 (community amateur sports clubs),[28] and
(b) it appear that when the hereditament is next in use
(i) it will be wholly or mainly used for the purposes of that club and that club will be such a registered club, or
(ii) it will be wholly or mainly used for the purposes of two or more clubs including that club, and each of those clubs will be such a registered club.

Ths confers 100% relief, as opposed to the 80% mandatory relief on occupied property.

40.10 Place of public religious worship

Para 11 sch 5 LGFA provides:

> (1) A hereditament is exempt to the extent that it consists of any of the following—
> (a) a place of public religious worship which
> [i] belongs to the Church of England or the Church in Wales (within the meaning of the Welsh Church Act 1914) or
> [ii] is for the time being certified as required by law as a place of religious worship;
> (b) a church hall, chapel hall or similar building used in connection with a place falling within paragraph (a) above for the purposes of the organisation responsible for the conduct of public religious worship in that place.

The property is likely to qualify for 80% charity relief, so the significance is to increase the relief to 100%.

In relation to places of religious worship other than the Church of England or the Church in Wales the certification "as required by law" is certification under the Places of Worship Registration Act 1855. The rating authority is able to challenge the registration of a place of religious worship.[29]

---

28 The drafter of the CTA 2010 overlooked need to update this reference, but it does not really matter.

29 *Church of Jesus Christ of Latter Day Saints v Henning* [1964] AC 420.

40.10.1 *Place of worship*

In *R (oao Hodkin and another) v Registrar General of Births, Deaths and Marriages* [2013] UKSC 77 the Supreme Court considered the meaning of "place of worship" in the context of the Places of Worship Registration Act 1855. Lord Toulson said:

> ...I would describe religion in summary as a spiritual or non-secular belief system, held by a group of adherents, which claims to explain mankind's place in the universe and relationship with the infinite, and to teach its adherents how they are to live their lives in conformity with the spiritual understanding associated with the belief system. By spiritual or non-secular I mean a belief system which goes beyond that which can be perceived by the senses or ascertained by the application of science...Such a belief system may or may not involve belief in a supreme being, but it does involve a belief that there is more to be understood about mankind's nature and relationship to the universe than can be gained from the senses or from science. I emphasise that this is intended to be a description and not a definitive formula.
>
> **[60]** On the approach which I have taken to the meaning of religion, the evidence is amply sufficient to show that Scientology is within it; but there remains the question whether the chapel at 146 Victoria Street is "a place of meeting for religious worship".
>
> ...
>
> **[62]** I interpret the expression "religious worship" as wide enough to include religious services...This broader interpretation accords with standard dictionary definitions. The Chambers Dictionary, 12th ed (2011) defines the noun "worship" as including both "adoration paid to a deity, etc" and "religious service", and it defines "worship" as an intransitive verb as "to perform acts of adoration; to take part in religious service". Similarly, the Concise Oxford English Dictionary, 12th ed (2011), defines "worship" as including both "the feeling or expression of reverence and adoration of a deity" and "religious rites and ceremonies".
>
> **[63]** The broader interpretation accords with the purpose of the statute in permitting members of a religious congregation, who have a meeting place where they perform their religious rites, to carry out religious ceremonies of marriage there. Their authorisation to do so should not depend on fine theological or liturgical niceties as to how precisely they see and express their relationship with the infinite (referred to by Scientologists as "God" in their creed and universal prayer). Those matters, which have been gone into in close detail in the evidence in this

> case, are more fitting for theologians than for the Registrar General or the courts.

The Supreme Court overturned *R v Registrar General, ex p Segerdal* [1970] 2 QB 697 which also considered the meaning of the phrase "religious worship" in the context of Scientology, and in which the Court of Appeal came to the opposite decision on the basis of their judgment that a "religion" recognise a god, who is venerated during "worship".

40.10.2 *"Public" worship*

The property must be a place of *public* worship. In *Church of Jesus Christ of Latter-Day Saints v Henning* [1964] AC 420 a Mormon temple was open only to Mormons of good standing. This was not sufficiently public:

> The defect of this view is that it would have to regard the meeting place of a small esoteric circle of some twenty or thirty persons worshipping secretly behind closed doors as a place of public religious worship, a conclusion which offends against one's common sense ... if the public are excluded from the meeting, then the meeting house is not a place of public religious worship.

The Mormons returned to the courts in *Gallagher v Church of Jesus Christ of Latter-day Saints.*[30] The Local Authority argued that the temple was not entitled to rating relief because it was not a place of "public religious worship" because it was not open to the public. It was not even open to all Mormons. The right of entry was reserved to members who have acquired a "recommend" from the bishop after demonstrating belief in Mormon doctrine, an appropriate way of life and payment of the required contribution to church funds. Such members are called Patrons and the rituals which take place in the temple are exclusive to them. The House of Lords followed the decision in *Henning.* Lord Hoffmann said (at [8]):

> ... this very point was decided more than 40 years ago by this House in *Church of Jesus Christ of Latter-Day Saints v Henning* [1964] AC 420 ... The House... held that the words could not apply to places used for religious worship from which the public was excluded. ...
> Lord Pearce, who gave the leading opinion, said (at pp. 440-441) that Parliament was entitled to take the view that religious services which were open to the public provided a public benefit which justified the exemption. ...

30 [2008] 1 WLR 1852.

> [it was] submitted that the House should depart from *Henning's* case or at any rate not apply its reasoning to Schedule 5 of the 1988 Act. It is true ... the current legislation is not the same as the statute which was construed in *Henning's* case. But the extensions are dependent upon the central concept of a "place of public worship" ... it seems to me inconceivable that Parliament did not intend the phrase to carry the meaning which it had been given in *Henning's* case. The legislature has had at least two opportunities (in 1988 and 1992) to take up Lord Evershed's invitation to reconsider the matter and has not done so. In my opinion, therefore, *Henning's case* is conclusive against the appellants on this point

The Church's second point was based on the right to freedom of religion under the HRA[31]. This too failed. While Lord Scott dissented on the Human Rights issue, the House of Lords were unanimous that the temple was not a place of public worship, and the decision in *Henning* still stands.

40.10.3 *Church halls and similar*

The exemption is extended by para 11(1)(b) sch 5 LGFA to "*a church hall, chapel hall or similar building used in connection with*" a place of public religious worship. The test is not a structural or architectural one, but one of use. In *West London Methodist Mission Trustees v Holborn Borough Council* (1958) 3 RRC 86 a building adjoining a Methodist chapel was held to be a "similar building" qualifying for the relief because it was used for a variety of activities, including as a youth club, for church socials and as a Sunday school and mission office.

40.11 Rating relief in Scotland

40.11.1 *Mandatory relief*

The system for providing rating relief in Scotland is different to the system in England and Wales.

Section 151 LGFA provides:

> (1) Part X of this Act, section 150 above, Part II of Schedule 12 below, and Part IV of Schedule 13 below, extend to Scotland only.
> (2) Sections 133, 135, 137, 143, 144(1), 145, 146(6) and (7), 147, 148 and 149 above, this section, section 152 below, Schedule 10 below, and Part III of Schedule 12 below, extend to England and Wales and Scotland.

31 See further chapter 1, paragraph 1.6.

(3) Subject to subsections (1) and (2) above, this Act extends to England and Wales only

The relief for Scottish charities is contained in s.4 Local Government (Financial Provisions etc.) (Scotland) Act 1962. Section 4(2) provides:

(2) If notice in writing is given to the rating authority that any lands and heritages—

- (a) are occupied by, or by trustees for, a charity and are wholly or mainly used for charitable purposes (whether of that charity or of that and other charities); or
- (aa) are occupied by a registered community amateur sports club and are wholly or mainly used for the purposes of that club (or for the purposes of that and of other clubs which are, or are entitled to be registered as, such clubs);
- (b) are held on trust for use as an almshouse; or
- (c) are within any such category as the Secretary of State may by order specify, being a category of lands and heritages which are not used for profit–making purposes, which are wholly or mainly used as residential accommodation for persons living separately from any family and in which certain facilities are shared by those persons, then, subject to the provisions of this section, any rate leviable in respect of the lands and heritages for a relevant period[32] during which the lands and heritages are within the categories described in -
  - (i) any of paragraphs (a), (aa) and (b) of this subsection, shall not exceed one–fifth
  - (ii) paragraph (c) of this subsection shall not exceed such fraction (and different fractions may be specified for different cases) as the Secretary of State may by the said order specify, of the rate which would be leviable apart from the provisions of this subsection: Provided that where lands and heritages cease to be within the said categories, a previous notice given for the purposes of this subsection shall not have effect as respects any subsequent period

---

32 Subsection 2A explains what is meant by the "relevant period". It provides:
"In subsection (2) of this section "relevant period" means—
(a) in a case where the occupation and use, or as the case may be the holding, commenced on or after the first day of the financial year immediately preceding the financial year in which the notice is given, any period after that commencement;
(b) in any other case, that first day and any period thereafter."

> during which the lands and heritages are within either of those categories.

This sets out slightly different categories of ratepayers to the English legislation, though in practise there is little different in the eligibility for entitlement. The relief is also the same: a charity gets a mandatory relief of 80% of the value of the non-domestic rates. However, subsection (8) brings a further category within the mandatory (and discretionary) relief, providing that:

> Lands and heritages belonging to or held by or on behalf of a religious body, being the residence from which a full–time clergyman or minister of any religious denomination performs the duties of his office, or which are being held available to provide such a residence, shall be treated for the purposes of this section as occupied by a charity and wholly or mainly used for charitable purposes, whether apart from this provision they would be so treated or not.

40.11.2 *Discretionary relief*

The LGFPSA also provides that there can be an additional discretionary relief. Section 4(5) LGFPSA provides:

> Without prejudice to the powers conferred by section 25A of the Local Government (Scotland) Act 1966, a rating authority shall have power to reduce or remit any rate leviable in respect of—
> (a) any lands and heritages within the categories described in paragraph (a) (b) or (c) of subsection (2) of this section;
> (b) any lands and heritages occupied for the purposes of one or more institutions or other organisations (whether corporate or unincorporate) which are not established or conducted for profit and whose main objects are charitable or are otherwise philanthropic or religious or concerned with education, social welfare, science, literature or the fine arts;
> (c) any lands and heritages occupied for the purposes of a club, society or other organisation not established or conducted for profit, and which are wholly or mainly used for purposes of recreation,
>
> for any such period as is mentioned in subsection (6) or, as the case may be, (6A) of this section:
> Provided that any such reduction or remission shall cease to have effect on a change in the occupation of the lands and heritages in respect of which it was granted.

The discretionary relief is available to three categories of organisation in Scotland: (i) those falling within subsection (2) above; (ii) associations established not for profit and whose main objects are charitable; and (iii) not for profit organisations the purpose of which is wholly or mainly recreation. The discretionary relief, is therefore, open to a wider range of organisations than the mandatory relief.

The third category is similar to the category of sports clubs (which includes, but is not limited to, community amateur sports clubs) in England that are eligible for the discretionary relief. No specific guidance as to when a recreational organisation may obtain the discretionary relief is given in relation to the Scottish legislation; it is not stated whether or not the English guidance is also relevant to Scotland.

40.11.3 *Charity shops*

In common with the English rating relief, the Scottish legislation makes provision for charity shops. Section 4(11) LGFPSA provides:

> Without prejudice to the meaning of the expression "wholly or mainly used for charitable purposes", lands and heritages shall be treated as so used, for the purposes of subsection (2) of this section, if—
> (a) they are used wholly or mainly for the sale of goods donated to a charity; and
> (b) the proceeds of sale (after any deduction of expenses) are applied for the purposes of a charity.

Thus charity shops will be eligible for the mandatory relief, but also for consideration for the discretionary relief, provided they meet the criteria of s.4(11).

40.12 Northern Ireland rating relief

The regime for rating relief in Northern Ireland is on a different basis to that in England and Wales (and Scotland). It does not take the form of an 80% mandatory relief for charities and up to an additional 20% discretionary relief, at the discretion of the local authority. In February 2015, the Department of Finance and Personnel concluded a consultation in relation to the non-domestic rating system. The discussion paper regarding charities issued as part of the consultation mooted various changes to the treatment of charities, most of which involved restricting the exemptions. Some suggested reforms included reducing rate relief for charity shops from 100% to 80% and reducing empty property relief from

100% for the first 3 months and 50% thereafter to a flat rate of 25%.[33].

Unsurprisingly, the results of the consultation were unanimously against any charity restrictions, and the report was passed back to the Executive to consider primary legislation. The result is that although there is an upcoming revaluation of rates in Northern Ireland,[34] there are no changes currently proposed to the charity rules.

40.12.1 *Eligibility for relief*

The charitable relief in Northern Ireland is given in Art 41(1) Rates (Northern Ireland) Order 1977, which provides:

> (1) Subject to the provisions of this Article, where the Commissioner or the district valuer is satisfied that a hereditament is a hereditament of a description mentioned in paragraph (2), he shall distinguish the hereditament, or cause it to be distinguished, in the valuation list as exempt from rates in accordance with paragraph (3).

Article 41(2) Rates (Northern Ireland) Order 1977 provides:

> The hereditaments referred to in paragraph (1) are—
> - (a) any hereditament which is altogether of a public nature and is occupied and used for purposes of the public service;
> - (b) any hereditament which consists of either or both of the following—
>   - (i) a church, chapel or similar building occupied by a religious body and used for purposes of public religious worship;
>   - (ii) a church hall, chapel hall or similar building occupied by a religious body and used for purposes connected with that body or for purposes of any charity;
>
>   together, in either case, with buildings ancillary thereto;
> - (c) any hereditament, other than a hereditament to which sub-paragraph (b) applies, which—
>   - (i) is occupied by a charity; and
>   - (ii) is used wholly or mainly for charitable purposes (whether of that charity or of that and other charities);
> - (d) any hereditament, other than a hereditament to which sub-paragraph (b) applies, which is occupied by a body—
>   - (i) which is not established or conducted for profit; and
>   - (ii) whose main objects are charitable or are concerned with

33 *https://www.finance-ni.gov.uk/consultations/review-northern-irelands-non-domestic-rating-system*

34 *https://www.finance-ni.gov.uk/news/work-start-non-domestic-rates-revaluation*

science, literature or the fine arts;

where the hereditament is used wholly or mainly for the purposes of those main objects;

(e) any hereditament which is used wholly or mainly for purposes which are declared to be charitable by the Recreational Charities Act (Northern Ireland) 1958

...

The relief in Northern Ireland extends to a number of religious buildings (used for appropriate purposes) and buildings of a public nature used for public purposes. However, the uses mentioned in (c) to (e) are charitable or quasi-charitable. The property granted the relief in (c) is that occupied by charities and used wholly or mainly for charitable purposes.

Under (d) property which is occupied by a quasi charitable organisation is also eligible for the relief. The property must be occupied for a body not established or conducted for profit and the main objects of which are charitable, or concerned with science, literature or fine arts.

Para (e) provides relief for property used wholly or mainly for purposes which are declared charitable by the Recreational Charities Act (Northern Ireland) 1958. Section 1 provides:

> (1) Subject to the provisions of this Act, it shall be and be deemed always to have been charitable to provide, or assist in the provision of, facilities for recreation or other leisure-time occupation, if the facilities are provided in the interests of social welfare:
>
> Provided that nothing in this section shall be taken to derogate from the principle that a trust or institution to be charitable must be for the public benefit.
>
> (2) The requirement in subsection (1) that the facilities are provided in the interests of social welfare cannot be satisfied if the basic conditions are not met.
>
> (2A) The basic conditions are—
>
> (a) that the facilities are provided with the object of improving the conditions of life for the persons for whom the facilities are primarily intended; and
>
> (b) that either—
>
> (i) those persons have need of the facilities by reason of their youth, age, infirmity or disability, poverty, or social and economic circumstances, or
>
> (ii) the facilities are to be available to members of the public at large or to male, or to female, members of the public at large
>
> (3) Subject to the said requirement, sub-section (1) applies in particular

to the provision of facilities at village halls, community centres and women's institutes, and to the provision and maintenance of grounds and buildings to be used for purposes of recreation or leisure-time occupation, and extends to the provision of facilities for those purposes by the organising of any activity.

40.12.2 *The relief*

Art 41(3) Rates (Northern Ireland) Order 1977 provides:

> 3) The hereditament shall be distinguished—
>
> (a) in the capital value list, if it is used for domestic purposes which are also exempting purposes, as exempt from rates under that list to one-half of the extent to which it is so used;
>
> (b) in the NAV list, as exempt from rates under that list to the whole of the extent that it is used for exempting purposes which are not domestic purposes.
>
> (3A) Where the hereditament is used otherwise than wholly for domestic purposes which are exempting purposes, the capital value of the hereditament shall be apportioned by the Commissioner or the district valuer between—
>
> (a) the use of the hereditament for domestic purposes which are exempting purposes; and
>
> (b) the use of the hereditament for other purposes (so far as relevant to its capital value);
>
> and the apportionment shall be shown in the capital value list.
>
> (3B) Where the hereditament is used otherwise than wholly for exempting purposes which are not domestic purposes, the net annual value of the hereditament shall be apportioned by the Commissioner or the district valuer between—
>
> (a) the use of the hereditament for exempting purposes which are not domestic purposes; and
>
> (b) the use of the hereditament for other purposes (so far as relevant to its net annual value);
>
> and the apportionment shall be shown in the NAV list.
>
> (3C) In paragraphs (3) to (3B) and (4), "exempting purposes" means purposes mentioned in sub-paragraph (a), (b)(i) or (ii), (c), (d) or (e) of paragraph (2).

Thus there is a complete exemption from non-domestic rates for charities and other quasi charitable organisations, to the extent that the property is used for those purposes. The Department of Finance and Personnel policy paper explains at paragraph 24:

As a general rule a secondary activity will be regarded as charitable if it directly facilitates the main charitable activity. Non-charitable purposes might include an activity that is purely for commercial purposes, for example, the leasing of a gable wall for advertising purposes to a private company.

40.12.3 *Charity shops*

While the relief for charity shops is provided along with the relief for other charitable purposes in Art 41 (at Art 41(2)(d)) the application of the relief to charity shops is modified by Art 41(5) which provides:

> (5) Notwithstanding anything in paragraph (4) and without prejudice to the generality of paragraph (2)(c)(ii), a hereditament shall be treated as used for charitable purposes—
>
> (a) to the extent that it is used for the sale of goods donated to a charity, and
>
> (b) if it is mainly used for the sale of goods donated to a charity, to the extent that it is used for the sale of other goods if they are of a description specified in an order made by the Department,
>
> so long as the proceeds of the sale of the goods mentioned in sub-paragraph (a) (after any deduction of expenses) are applied for the purposes of a charity.
>
> (5A) The Department shall not make an order under paragraph (5)(b) unless a draft of the order has been laid before, and approved by resolution of, the Assembly.

The Department of Finance and Personnel policy paper explains:

> A charity shop must be able to show the percentage of donated and non-donated goods sold. It only gains exemption for the percentage of goods sold which are donated goods. This restriction is designed to restrict relief to shops predominantly selling second hand goods. Shops owned by charities, which are to all intents and purposes trading commercially, are not eligible for rate relief.[35]

40.12.4 *Sports clubs*

Article 31 Rates (Northern Ireland) Order 1977 provides:

> 31.—(1) Subject to paragraph (5) and Article 44(2A)(b)(i), the amount which, apart from this Article, would be payable on account of a rate in respect of a hereditament to which this Article applies shall for each year be reduced in

---

35 Non-domestic Charitable Exemptions and Reliefs From Rate Liability in Northern Ireland [February 2005]

accordance with paragraphs (3) and (4).

(2) This Article applies to a hereditament—

(a) which, or any part of which, is used solely for the purposes of a prescribed recreation; and

(b) which is occupied for the purposes of a club, society or other organisation that—

(i) is not established or conducted for profit, and

(ii) does not employ any person to engage in any recreation for reward, except for the instruction of other persons who are themselves engaging or preparing to engage in it otherwise than for reward; and

(c) which is not distinguished in the NAV list as exempt from rates as being a hereditament of a description mentioned in Article 41(2)(e) (recreational charities) or by virtue of Article 12(2), (3) or (4) of the Rates (Capital Values, etc.) (Northern Ireland) Order 2006.

(3) Where the hereditament is shown in the NAV list as used solely for the purposes of a prescribed recreation, the reduction shall be effected by reducing the normal rate by 80 per cent.

(4) Where the hereditament is shown in the NAV list as having part of its net annual value apportioned to a part or parts of the hereditament used solely for the purposes of a prescribed recreation, the reduction shall be effected by computing separately—

(a) so much of the amount payable as is referable to the part of the net annual value shown in the list as so apportioned, and

(b) so much of that amount as is referable to the remainder of the net annual value,

and by reducing the normal rate, for the purpose of the computation mentioned in sub-paragraph (a), by 80 per cent.

(5) Where a hereditament is one to which this Article applies during part only of a year, the reduction shall be made for that part of the year only; and if the reduction, or any adjustment in it, affects the amount levied on account of a rate in respect of the hereditament for that year, the difference—

(a) if too much has been paid, shall be repaid or allowed; or

(b) if too little has been paid, shall be paid and may be recovered as if it were arrears of the rate.

(6) In this Article—

"the normal rate" for any year in respect of any hereditament means the amount which, apart from this Article, would be the amount in the pound of the rate to be levied for that year in respect of the rateable net annual value of that hereditament;

"prescribed recreation" means a recreation, whether conducted indoors or outdoors, which in the opinion of the Department demands an appreciable degree of physical effort and which is of a kind specified by the Department, after consultation with the Sports Council for Northern Ireland and with any association which appears to the Department to be representative of district councils, by an order made subject to affirmative resolution;

"use" in relation to a hereditament or any part of it means use by members of the club, society or other organisation for the purposes of which the hereditament is occupied or by other persons who under the rules of that club, society or organisation are permitted to use the hereditament or that part;

and for the purposes of this Article and Article 44(2A) an area provided as a parking place for vehicles of persons engaging in a prescribed recreation, and any part of a hereditament constructed or adapted for use by such persons (or by persons who have engaged or intend to engage in the recreation) as a bathroom or lavatory or for use wholly or mainly for the storage of their clothing or of equipment used for purposes of the recreation, shall be treated as used solely for the purposes of that recreation (notwithstanding that it is also used by other persons or that at particular times it is used by persons none of whom are engaging in such a recreation).

CHAPTER FORTY ONE

SPORTS CLUBS

Cross references

The following topics are considered elsewhere:
Mutual trading: 42.1

41.1 CASCs: Introduction

In order to understand the taxation of community amateur sports clubs ("**CASCs**") it is helpful to start with the history.

41.1.1 *2002: Introduction of CASCs*

The 2001 Budget provided:

> 5.90 The Government has received a number of representations seeking extension of the reliefs to amateur sports clubs that play a valuable and important role in promoting the health and cohesion of their local communities but do not attract tax relief, because they are not recognised as charitable. Over the next few months the Government will consult on the best way for tax relief to help community amateur sports clubs that make a positive contribution to their local communities.

On 30 November 2001, the Charity Commission published a Guidance Note, following its consultation paper issued earlier in the year, announcing that it would recognise as charitable the "promotion of community participation in healthy recreation by the provision of facilities for the playing of particular sports". So (almost[1] all) community sports

1 For completeness: There were still a few sports which the Charity Commission said were not charitable, as they were not healthy enough. RR11 (Charitable Status and Sport) (2003) provided:
"11. The following sports do not at present appear to us to meet our criteria for

clubs *were* in principle charitable.

A code of tax reliefs for CASCs was introduced in 2002 for the benefit of CASCs unable or unwilling to apply for charitable status.

41.1.2 *2002 - 2009: CASC charitable*

Between 2002 and 2009, a CASC could be a charity, and no doubt many were.

41.1.3 *2009: De-charitisation of CASCs*

Section 6(1) Charities Act 2011 (re-enacting a provision in the CA 2006, which took effect in 2009) provides:

> A registered sports club[2] established for charitable purposes is to be treated as not being so established, and accordingly cannot be a charity.

The intention is to maintain two separate regimes so a sports club can choose to be a (non-charitable) CASC or a charity.

Charity Commission guidance RR11 states that a CASC can be a charity.[3] (RR11 was published 2003 and has not been updated.) This led some clubs to register as a charity whilst still registered as a CASC, which is in breach of the Charities Act 2011! That could raise difficulties, though in practice one would hope that HMRC would simply deregister the CASC while leaving it a registered charity, and not pursue the tax questions which might arise.

Eynsham Cricket Club v HMRC[4] has correctly held that s.6 applies for

---

'healthy recreation': Angling, Ballooning, Billiards, Pool and Snooker, Crossbow, Rifle and Pistol Shooting, Flying, Gliding Motor Sports, Parachuting."

These were (and still are) eligible sports for CASC purposes, so these sports could be CASCs but not charities.

2 Defined s.6(2) Charities Act 2011: In subsection (1), "registered sports club" means a registered club within the meaning of Chapter 9 of Part 13 of the Corporation Tax Act 2010 (community amateur sports clubs).

3 Para 7 provides: **"What sort of CASCs can be charitable?**

7. In practical terms, a CASC can be a charity provided that two criteria are satisfied:

(i) The sport in question must be capable of improving physical health and fitness; and

(ii) The club must have an open membership, that is, access to the club's facilities must be genuinely available to anyone who wishes to take advantage of them."

4 [2021] EWCA Civ 225 rejecting the view of the FTT; in the 12th edition of this work we described the FTT decision as surprising and unconvincing and advised charities not to rely on it.

tax (including VAT) purposes. A club must choose one status or the other.

41.1.4 *Current law and guidance*

Since 2010 it is the usual story of constant amendment (amendments in 2010, 2012, 2013, 2014 and 2015) and ever-increasing complication.

There have been consultation and response documents but these are now of historical interest only.[5]

The law is mostly in Chapter 9 Part 13 CTA 2010 and Community Amateur Sports Clubs Regulations 2015 ("**CASCR**"). HMRC have issued a detailed Guidance Note (the "**CASC Guidance Note**").[6]

41.2 Types of club

Sports clubs fall into three categories:

(1) A CASC
(2) A charity; we refer to this as **"a charitable sports club"**
(3) Neither a CASC nor a charity:
  (a) CASC status is a matter of choice, as even if a club meets the necessary conditions, it may choose not to register.
  (b) A club whose objects are charitable cannot choose not to be a charity[7] but if desired one can arrange for a club to be non-charitable by drafting its constitution to include some non-charitable object or power.

We refer to this as **"a private sports club"**. A private sports club may be(i) a proprietary club or (ii) a members club.

---

5 HMRC, "Community Amateur Sports Clubs Consultation document" (June 2013) *http://www.gov.uk/government/uploads/system/uploads/attachment_data/file/207958/130321_Final_CASC_condoc_v3_0.pdf*
HMRC, "Community Amateur Sports Clubs Summary of Responses (Nov 2013) *https://www.gov.uk/government/uploads/system/uploads/attachment_data/file/260944/CASCs_Consultation_Response.pdf*
HMRC, "Community Amateur Sports Clubs Technical Consultation (October 2014) *https://www.gov.uk/government/uploads/system/uploads/attachment_data/file/364277/Community_Amateur_Sports_Clubs_-_Technical_Consultation.pdf*
HMRC, "Community Amateur Sports Clubs Summary of responses (December 2014) *https://www.gov.uk/government/uploads/system/uploads/attachment_data/file/387636/141201_final_responses_doc.pdf*

6 *https://www.gov.uk/government/publications/community-amateur-sports-clubs-detailed-guidance-notes*

7 Except by registering as a CASC.

In the CTA 2010 the term used for a CASC is "registered club".[8] Other statutes use the more transparent term "registered sports club." In this chapter we use the term **"CASC"** (it is assumed that the CASC is registered, ie we leave the word registered to be understood).

We use the term **"sports club"** to refer to any club, whether a charity or a CASC or a private club.

This chapter discusses the taxation of CASCs. The taxation of members clubs is discussed in the next chapter. Proprietary clubs are treated like any other taxpayer and do not need separate discussion.

41.3 Sports qualifying for CASC/charity

41.3.1 *Eligible sport for CASC purposes*

The CASC provisions apply to "eligible sports". Section 661(1) CTA 2010 provides:

> For the purposes of this chapter "eligible sport" means a sport which is designated for those purposes by an order made by the Treasury.

Relief for Community Amateur Sports Clubs (Designation) Order 2002 provides:

> A sport is designated as an eligible sport for the purposes of Schedule 18 to the FA 2002 [now Chapter 9 Part 13 CTA 2010] where that sport appears on the list maintained by the National Sports Councils[9] of activities recognised by them.

The list of eligible sports is accessible from the UK Sport website.[10] It is set out in App 4.1 (Eligible Sports). This list seems almost comprehensive, but bodies representing sports which are not on the list may apply to UK sports for recognition.

The English Bridge Union have had their claim for judicial review of

---

8 Section 658(6) CTA 2010 provides: "In this Chapter a "registered club" means a club which is for the time being registered as a community amateur sports club under this section." That definition only applies for Chapter 9 Part 13 CTA 2010, but the definition is incorporated by reference elsewhere, eg s.105(3) CTA 2009; s.257(5) TCGA. It would be simpler if this was a taxes-act wide definition.

9 Defined regulation 3: "The National Sports Councils" means UK Sport, Sport England, Sport Scotland, the Sports Council of Wales and the Sports Council of Northern Ireland."

10 *https://www.sportengland.org/our-work/national-governing-bodies/sports-that-we -recognise/*

Sport England's refusal to recognised bridge as a sport dismissed. The question of whether Bridge is a sport for the purposes of the VAT sports exemption was referred to the CJEU, and the CJEU held that in order to be a sport for such purposes, the activity in question must have a "not negligible physical element". Bridge fails in this, and is, therefore, not a sport for the purposes of the exemption.[11]

41.3.2 *Sport qualifying as charitable*

Section 3(1) Charities Act 2011 provides:

> A purpose falls within this subsection if it falls within any of the following descriptions of purposes ...
> (g) the advancement of amateur sport.[12]

This restates and slightly extends the view taken by the Charity Commission in 2003: from 2006 any sports can in principle be charitable – even those which in 2003 were thought not to be charitable as they did not promote physical health and fitness: it is now sufficient if they promote health "by involving physical *or mental* skill or exertion."

The CASC Guidance Note recognises that the objects of a CASC are (more or less) the same as the objects of a charitable sports club:

> 2.19.1 The main purpose of [a CASC] the club must be clearly stated in its governing document, or constitution, and must be to:
> - provide facilities for,
> - encourage participation in
>
> one or more eligible sports.
> This is quite similar to the [Charity Commission approved] version [of objects] acceptable for charities.
> 'The promotion of community participation in healthy recreation by providing facilities for playing particular sports'.

41.4 CASC requirements

The requirements of a CASC are (more or less) the same as those which apply to a charitable sports club, but with greater, or at least more express,

---

11 See *The English Bridge Union Limited v HMRC* Case C-90/16.

12 Section 3(2)(d) Charities Act 2011 defines sport:
"in paragraph (g) "sport" means sports or games which promote health by involving physical or mental skill or exertion."

emphasis on equality issues, a topic which had acquired greater prominence by the time that the CASC rules came to be formulated.

Section 658(1) CTA 2010 provides:

> A club is entitled to be registered as a community amateur sports club if conditions A, B and C are met.

Conditions A – C are (not very convenient) labels for three sets of rules.

41.5 Open to whole community

Section 658(1A) CTA 2010 provides:

> Condition A is that the club is, and is required by its constitution to be, a club which—
> (a) is open to the whole community (see section 659)...

This brings in rules relating to non-discrimination and costs.

41.6 Non-discrimination

Section 659 CTA 2010 provides:

> (1) A club is open to the whole community for the purposes of section 658 if
> (a) its membership is open to all without discrimination,
> (b) its facilities are available to members without discrimination ...
> (3) A club is not prevented from being "open to the whole community" for the purposes of section 658 merely because it charges different fees for different descriptions of person.

41.6.1 *Membership non-discrimination*

The CASC Guidance Note provides:

> 2.3.1 The term 'membership' refers to the people the club recognises as having accepted the rights and liabilities as set out in its governing document.
> 2.3.2 It's up to a club to set out in its governing documents the rights of the members. Usually clubs allow members to attend general meetings and decide resolutions by majority vote. However a club may accept juniors as members without a right to vote until they reach the age of 18. This club would not be discriminating against juniors - membership is open to all even though juniors may have to wait until they are 18 to vote at annual general meetings.
> 2.3.3 Most members clubs in the form of companies are limited by guarantee and the terms of membership are usually clearly defined in their constitutions. These will usually say that when each member joins they're entitled to a single vote at annual general meetings.

2.3.4 Companies limited by shares are different because voting rights are determined by the number of shares held. In the case of members clubs, HMRC would expect to see an equal shareholding for each member but this can be difficult to achieve where members come and go. It can be done by making sure that each member is allocated a single share and that this is reallocated upon leaving.

2.3.5 Most members clubs are unincorporated associations which unlike companies have no legal personality. In these cases membership rights are those which exist under the contract between members. Full membership is determined by the members' rights. HMRC's view is that membership of a club must mean full membership.

2.3.6 Clubs may have different classes of membership based on the age of the member, or whether the member is a student, is waged, is a playing member, or how far from the club the member lives. For example, a club may offer a class of senior membership at reduced rates to people over 65 which isn't open to younger people. This is acceptable, provided that the senior members are not effectively excluded from the club's activities, or prevented from becoming general members if they wish.

2.3.7 A club with limited facilities may have to regulate how many members it has, to enable it to carry out its objectives of providing facilities for, and promoting participation in, eligible sports. This is acceptable as long as the club can demonstrate that it has a fair and open membership process. If a club has a waiting list it should admit members from this list in chronological order only. For example, they should not select members from the waiting list on the basis of sporting ability or how much they will pay for membership.

2.3.8 There must be no discrimination when dealing with applications from potential members. A club must ensure that its membership procedures are open, transparent and objective. For example, they must not have unfair restrictions requiring applications for membership to be proposed and seconded by existing members or displaying applicant details for comment by members on club notice boards.

2.3.9 Some clubs offer honorary or free life memberships (or equivalent) to some members to thank them for serving a club for many years as a coach, committee member, umpire or volunteer. CASCs can offer honorary or life memberships if they continue to be open to the whole community. A CASC cannot restrict applications by new members on the basis that the Club has lots of honorary members and cannot accept any new members. HMRC will consider what criteria a club uses for granting honorary and free life memberships to ensure that a club is open to the whole community and it does not restrict the number of ordinary memberships available.

2.3.10 Clubs which also, for example, insist on prospective members agreeing to carry out services to support the club would not be open to all and so would not qualify to be a CASC. In those clubs membership is only open to those who are prepared to carry out services for the club. When a club wants members to volunteer it can suggest, rather than require, that members who are able to, volunteer to do things at the club but membership must not be refused to applicants who refuse to volunteer.

It is interesting that HMRC felt that they had to make the fairly obvious point in 2.3.9 that a club cannot get around the general rule of being open to the whole community by offering so many lifetime memberships that it becomes impossible to accommodate new members. One can only assume that this is because a CASC tired and failed to circumvent the rule in this way.

41.6.2 *Discrimination*

Section 659(2) CTA 2010 provides:

> For the purposes of this section "discrimination" includes indirect discrimination and (in particular) includes discrimination on the grounds of —
> (a) ethnicity or nationality,
> (b) religion or beliefs,
> (c) sexual orientation,
> (d) sex, age or disability (except as a necessary consequence of the requirements of a particular sport).

The CASC Guidance Note provides:

> 2.3.13 Discrimination isn't limited under the CASC rules to those categories. Any form of discrimination of whatever nature would mean that a club does not meet the qualifying conditions.
> 2.3.14 Discrimination on the grounds of sex, age or disability isn't permitted except as a necessary consequence of the requirements of a particular sport. Some sports are not suitable for certain groups of people. For example, motor racing may not be suitable for the very young, or a sport's governing body may impose restrictions on the age of participation in a particular sport for safety reasons. Neither of these restrictions would be regarded as discrimination. However it would not be acceptable for a club to impose its own restriction, which isn't a necessary consequence of the requirements of the sport. For example, if the members of a club refused to admit children, even if the sport was suitable for them to take part in, that would be unacceptable discrimination.
> 2.3.15 Clubs can refuse or revoke membership on non-discriminatory grounds, where the membership, or continued membership, of the person concerned would be likely to not be in the best interests of the sport or the good conduct and interests of the club. These are internal matters for the club. Such procedures should be open and transparent and include an independent appeals process. HMRC will not become involved in such internal issues. Provided the club has acted openly and followed its CASC-compliant constitution there should be no

effect on the club's CASC status.

41.6.3 *Facilities non-discrimination*

The CASC Guidance Note provides:

> 2.4.1 A club must not discriminate between classes or categories of members, and it must make its facilities available, without discrimination, to all members. There is no difference between the terms "making facilities available" and "providing facilities." These terms are interchangeable. For example, where there are insufficient facilities such as tennis courts for all members to use at the same time, there must be no discrimination in allowing use, for example by giving the senior men's team players preferential treatment. Similarly, a cricket club can't restrict the use of its main pitch to the first team, forcing less skilful players to use pitches of a lower standard. The facilities of the club are those it is required to provide by its constitution.
> 2.4.2 The club can put restrictions on the days or times when different classes of membership have access to the facilities, provided the restrictions don't effectively exclude those members from full participation in the club.
> 2.4.3 A club may provide facilities for single sex members, juniors or disabled people. If others are explicitly prohibited from playing in matches this is only acceptable if it is a necessary consequence of a requirement of the sport. This will often be because it is set out in the rules of the sport's governing body. However there must be no bar to others joining and participating in other ways. For example, a women's football club might also have men who coach teams and referee matches.

41.7 Cap on membership costs

Section 659(1) CTA 2010 provides:

> A club is open to the whole community for the purposes of section 658 if ...
>
> (c) the costs associated with membership of the club for any year do not represent a significant obstacle to membership of the club, use of its facilities or full participation in its activities (see subsection (2A)).

41.7.1 *Flexible cap on costs*

Section 659(2A) CTA 2010 provides:

> For the purposes of subsection (1)(c) the costs associated with

membership of a club for any year represent a significant obstacle to membership of the club, use of its facilities or full participation in its activities if—

(a) those costs exceed the amount specified for the year for the purposes of this subsection in regulations made by the Treasury, and

(b) the club has not made such arrangements as are necessary to secure that those costs do not represent such an obstacle.

Regulation 5(1) CASCR provides:

The amount specified for a year for the purposes of section 659(2A) of CTA 2010 (costs associated with membership of a club) is £520.

41.7.2 *Steps to avoid costs obstacle*

The CASC Guidance Note provides:

2.8.1 Some clubs that offer more expensive sports may have a 'cost associated with membership' that is more than £520 a year. To be eligible for CASC status these clubs will need to demonstrate that they have put in place arrangements that ensure that the club is open to the whole community - including those on low or modest incomes.

2.8.2 The law states that HMRC has to be satisfied any arrangements put in place to bring the costs associated with membership below £520 a year. There is no need to seek HMRC's view on these arrangements. If your arrangements are the same or similar to those given below in the examples, you can assume they are acceptable. If your arrangements are different you can contact HMRC for confirmation they are acceptable.

2.8.3 Any club that has a 'cost associated with membership' of more than £520 a year will need to ensure that those who can't afford to pay can still become a member and fully participate in sport at the club.

2.8.4 All arrangements need to be clearly advertised to the public. HMRC will not accept that an arrangement is acceptable if it can only be found in the small print of a membership form. HMRC would expect the provisions to be advertised widely to members and to anyone who may be considering membership. For example a club could advertise on their website, application form, clearly display the information on a noticeboard, or in a newsletter etc.

2.8.5 There is no set income limit to define who is a member who can't afford to pay more than £520 a year. It is expected this should apply to members who are on a low or modest income. It is up to the club to decide what provisions it makes for members - the important point is that these provisions reduce the costs to £520 (or less) a year whilst still allowing the member to fully participate in the sport.

Examples of acceptable provisions

Example (H)

A club has a cost of membership over £520 a year.

It is open for most of the year and has not opted to use the 'seasonal reduction'.

The club has decided to offer a fixed price annual membership of £520 a year for those who can't afford to pay more.

Included in this is free access to equipment and insurance.

Those members taking advantage of this reduced memberships will not incur any other additional costs.

They advertise the fixed price membership on their application form and website.

Those who want to take advantage of the reduced price membership must apply to the secretary of the club and demonstrate that the full cost of membership would not be affordable to them.

2.8.6 HMRC would accept this as a reasonable provision for those on low or modest incomes and this club would be eligible for CASC status.

Example (I)

A golf club has a cost of membership that is £800 a year, this is mainly made up of an annual membership fee of £770.

This club decides to offer a 4 day membership to all members for £450 a year.

This new membership allows the member to play on 3 week days and either a Saturday or a Sunday.

As this membership is available to all members the club will not need to ask members for evidence that they can't afford the full price membership, this is an acceptable provision for those on a low income.

2.8.7 Alternatively this club could offer free membership to those who can show they can't afford to pay more than £520 a year. Members who took advantage of this would then be charged £10 per round each time they played, which could be on any day of the week. The club could also provide a number of second hand golf clubs for members to hire for no cost. The club's website and notice board invited applications from those who can't afford the full price membership and they were considered by the management committee.

2.8.8 When considering whether this is acceptable HMRC would look at the cost of participating once a week - which in this case would give an annual cost of membership of £520 a year.

Example (J)

A club has opted for the seasonal reduction.

Due to the weather the club is actually only open for 6 months a year and therefore must offer a costs of membership that is no more than £260.

This club allows a 5 day annual membership (including one weekend day) for £250.

This membership is available to all members.

2.8.9 For those members who can't afford their own equipment the club has some available for hire. Usually members have to pay to hire the equipment but those who can't afford the cost can complete a short application form to demonstrate that they can't afford to pay more than the £260 charged for the annual membership. The club allows these members to hire the boat as many times as they like for no cost.

Provisions which would not be adequate for CASC status

2.8.10 To protect those people who can't afford a membership cost that's more than £520 a year, HMRC won't accept any clubs:

- that refuse reasonable applications for a reduced cost of membership when the applicant has clearly shown they can't afford the full cost of participation
- who only offer discounted memberships at times that would prevent some members from participating - for example, if the only discounted membership available was restricted to weekday mornings - as a rule of thumb HMRC would expect the membership to allow playing outside of typical working hours and on at least one day at the weekend
- that don't clearly show they offer reductions for those on low or modest incomes - for example, only mentioning the provisions in the club rule book or hidden somewhere in the small print in the terms of membership - all provisions should be clearly advertised to those considering whether to participate in sport at the club
- who set a limit on the number of members requiring a provision to bring the cost of membership under £520 a year - clubs can't limit these members and can only close membership when the club is full to all types of members

41.7.3 *Cost associated with membership*

Regulation 5 CASCR provides:

> (2) The costs associated with membership of a club for a given year consist of amounts A and B together.
> (3) Amount A is the membership fees for a member for that year (see regulation 8).
> (4) Amount B is the sporting activity costs for that year (see regulation 9).

The CASC Guidance Note provides:

> 2.7.1 Once a club is satisfied that its membership fees are less than £1,612 a year it will then need to work out the costs associated with membership. The costs associated with membership (C) is made up of the most expensive membership (A) plus the costs of sporting activity (B). So A + B = C.
> *To work out the most expensive membership (A)*
> 2.7.2 This is straightforward if a club offers one type of membership as that membership will automatically be the most expensive. However, many clubs offer a range of memberships so you will need to work out which one is the most expensive.
> 2.7.3 The most expensive membership should be worked on an annual basis. For example, if a club offers a 3 month membership for £120 they would need to work out how much this would cost over 12 months (£120 × 4 = £480).
> 2.7.4 If a club offers family memberships or other group memberships it will need

to work out the cost per member. Once you've worked out how much all of your memberships cost (per person) on an annual basis you can then identify the most expensive membership (A).

To work out the costs of sporting activity (B)

2.7.5 The sporting activity costs are the costs that the members are required to pay in order to fully participate in the club's activities for the year. These are the costs that are incurred in addition to the membership fee costs. When you calculate the sporting activity costs, include:

- any additional charges for using the club's facilities - for example pitch hire, flood lighting
- fees charged to play in a match
- any fees charged by the club for hiring specialist equipment (this includes any necessary safety equipment)
- the cost to purchase or hire any specialist equipment that's necessary to participate in the sport (when not provided free of charge by the club)
- the cost to purchase or hire any clothing that the club requires the member to wear (when not provided free of charge by the club)
- insurance costs needed for the member to participate in the sport

2.7.6 When calculating the cost to buy clothing or equipment for the purposes of this test you may use the lowest cost. For example, you can purchase a second hand set of golf clubs for £30 online.

2.7.7 You should calculate these costs on the basis that the member participates on 52 occasions a year (unless you are a seasonal club claiming the seasonal apportionment). Annex 4 gives more details.

2.7.8 Match fees should only be included on the basis that the member takes part on 52 occasions a year if there is a match every week. For example, if your club only holds matches on 40 occasions a year then the cost of playing in a match should be includes on this basis.

2.7.9 If your club is seasonal and chooses to apply the seasonal apportionment the costs should be calculated on the basis that the member participates at least once a week for each week that the club is open.

Working out the costs associated with membership (C)

2.7.10 The costs associated with membership (C) is worked out by adding together the most expensive membership (A) and the sporting activity costs for that year (B).

2.7.11 For most CASCs the costs associated with membership will be £520 a year or less for all members. If this is the case then the club does not need to do anything else because it is already affordable for the whole community.

2.7.12 If a club has a costs associated with membership that are more than £520 a year then it will be required to make provisions for those who can't afford to pay more than £520 a year. If no suitable arrangements are made then this club will not be able to be a CASC because it isn't open to the whole community.

Example (B)

A tennis club has several membership options available.

The most expensive membership is a 3 month membership that costs £100.

The club also charges a £20 joining fee.

The annual cost of the most expensive membership is £420.

As this is under £1,612 the club should now work out the costs associated with membership.

2.7.13 The club does not require any specialist equipment, clothing or insurance. Members must provide their own rackets. Members must book a court and this costs an additional £3.50 per booking. The club is open all year. This club should work out the costs associated with membership as follows:

Cost of most expensive membership	£420
Match fees	£0
Additional charges for facilities £3.50 × 52 =	£182
Fees for hiring specialist equipment from the club	£0
Cost to purchase or hire equipment Cost of second hand racket	£5
Cost to purchase or hire clothing required by the club	£0
Insurance costs required by the club	£0
Total	£607

2.7.14 The costs associated with membership are £607 a year, so the club will need to provide for any members who can't afford to pay more than £520 a year.

Example (C)

A sailing club offers 12 month memberships for £120 a year.

There are no additional costs or other membership options available.

At the club members have free use of a boat owned by the club and there is no specific requirement for clothing or equipment.

All necessary safety equipment is also available for free hire from the club.

This equipment is basic and members can use their own boat or safety equipment if they wish.

Cost of most expensive membership	£120
Match fees	£0
Additional charges for facilities	£0
Fees for hiring specialist equipment from the club	£0
Cost to purchase or hire equipment	£0
Cost to purchase or hire clothing required by the club	£0
Total	£120

2.7.15 The costs associated with membership are less than £520 a year and no provisions are needed.

Example (D)

A rugby club charges £250 a year for 12 months membership.

There are no joining fees and this is the most expensive membership offered by the club.

2.7.16 The club charges £2 for match subs but there is no additional charge for training at the club. The club provides all of the necessary equipment free of charge for members to use. There is no insurance required as this is covered by the membership fee. Members must purchase a club shirt if they want to participate in matches this is available at the club for £20. They must also wear rugby boots to play, which start at £20. The rest of the kit isn't specialist (dark shorts, socks etc).

Cost of most expensive membership	£250
Match fees £2 × 52 =	£104
Additional charges for facilities	£0

Fees for hiring specialist equipment from the club	£0
Cost to purchase or hire equipment	£0
Cost to purchase or hire clothing required by the club	£40
Insurance costs required by the club	£0
Total	£394

2.7.17 The costs associated with membership are less than £520 a year and no provisions are needed.

Example (E)

A squash club offers a number of membership packages.

The most expensive is a 12 month membership costing £360, with a £20 administration fee for joining.

The club does not provide any equipment to members and there is no special requirement for clothing.

There are additional fees for playing squash at the club of £5 per hour and the club is open all year.

Cost of most expensive membership	£360
Match fees	£0
Additional charges for facilities £5 × 52 =	£260
Fees for hiring specialist equipment from the club	£0
Cost to purchase or hire equipment	
second hand racket and balls	£10
Cost to purchase or hire clothing required by the club	£0
Insurance costs required by the club	£0
Total	£630

2.7.18 The costs associated with membership are £630 a year, as a result the club will need to make a provision for any members who can't afford to pay more than £520 a year.

Example (F)

A golf club offers a number of packages, the most expensive is a 12 month membership costing £846.

The club does not provide any equipment to members and they require golf shoes to be worn, costing £10.

There are no additional costs for playing and the club is open all year.

Cost of most expensive membership	£846
Match fees	£0
Additional charges for facilities	£0
Fees for hiring specialist equipment from the club	£0
Cost to purchase or hire equipment	
second hand golf clubs	£20
Cost to purchase or hire clothing required by the club	£10
Insurance costs required by the club	£0
Total	£876

2.7.19 The costs associated with membership are £876 a year, as a result the club will need to make a provision for any members who can't afford to pay more than £520 a year.

Example (G)

Another club has a cost associated with membership of £400 a year.

It is open for 9 months of the year and has opted for the seasonal reduction.
The £520 limit is reduced to 9/12 × £520 = £390.
This club would need to make a provision for members on low or modest incomes.

41.7.4 *Cap on membership fees*

Regulation 6 CASCR provides:

> A club is not entitled to be registered as a community amateur sports club under section 658 of CTA 2010 if it receives membership fees exceeding £1,612 in respect of any member in respect of any year.

The CASC Guidance Note provides:

> 2.5.2 If a club charges any member more than £1,612 a year for membership fees then it would not be considered open to the whole community. The club would not be eligible for CASC status even if they offered discounted or cheaper memberships to other members.
> 2.6 **Does my club charge more than £1,612 a year for membership?**
> 2.6.1 Clubs will need to check whether their membership fees cost less than £1,612 a year. If a club offers more than one type of membership it will need to make sure all of them cost less than £1,612 a year. For example, a club may offer a 12 month full membership, a 6 month membership and a 3 month membership - each of these memberships will need to cost less than £1,612 a year.

41.7.5 *"Membership fees"*

Regulation 8 CASCR provides the definition:

> (1) "Membership fees" means—
> (a) any joining fees, and
> (b) any supplementary fees, subscriptions or other costs,
> charged by the club as a condition of membership.
> (2) In calculating the costs associated with membership—
> (a) where a club charges a membership fee which relates to more than one member, that fee is to be divided the number of members to which it relates, and
> (b) where a club charges membership fees which vary, whether by reference to the duration of the membership or otherwise, the highest fee is to be used.

The CASC Guidance Note provides:

> 2.6.2 To calculate the annual cost of a club's membership fee include

joining fees and any other costs that are a condition of membership. For example, compulsory subscriptions that all members are required to pay. The calculation should only include costs that members are required to pay in order to join the club, not for example, the cost of mandatory equipment.

2.6.3 If a club offers some memberships that are shorter or longer than 12 months then they will need to check how much each of these memberships would cost over a 12 month period.

Example (A)

A club offers an 18 month membership costing £800.

The membership fee would be (12/18) × £800= £533.33 a year for the purpose of this test.

The same club also offers a 3 month membership costing £250.

The membership fee is (12/3) × £250 = £1,000 for this test.

Both of these memberships are under the £1,612 limit.

2.6.4 If a club offers family memberships or other group memberships it will need to work out the cost per member. For example, a family membership for 2 adults costs £900 a year with a joining fee of £140. The cost per member here would be £1,040 divided by 2 = £520. This membership is below the limit of £1,612 per person so the club would be eligible for CASC status.

41.7.6 *"Sporting activity costs"*

Regulation 9 CASCR provides the definition:

> (1) "Sporting activity costs", for a year, means charges, fees or other costs that a member would be required to pay or incur to participate fully in the club's activities for the year (other than membership fees).
>
> (2) Sporting activity costs include, in particular—
>
> (a) any fee that a member is required to pay to use the club's facilities for the purpose of playing an eligible sport;
>
> (b) any fee charged to play an eligible sport in a match;
>
> (c) any fee charged by the club for the use of specialist equipment[13] required to play an eligible sport;
>
> (d) where it is not provided free of charge—
>
> (i) the cost of hiring or purchasing any specialist equipment required to play an eligible sport; and
>
> (ii) the cost of hiring or purchasing any clothing required by

---

13 Regulation 9(3) CASCR provides:

"For the purposes of paragraph (2)(c) and (d)(i) specialist equipment includes equipment required for the purposes of health and safety."

the club to play an eligible sport; and

(e) the cost of insurance cover required by the club to play an eligible sport.

...

(4) Sporting activity costs paid or incurred—

(a) under paragraph (2)(a), (b) or (c); and

(b) where equipment is hired rather than purchased, under paragraph (2)(d),

are calculated by reference to a member participating fully in the club's activities.

(5) For the purposes of this regulation, a member is not to be treated as participating fully in the club's activities unless the member has the opportunity to participate—

(a) where a club chooses to apportion the participation threshold in accordance with regulation 19(1) (apportionment of days of participation: seasonal sports), on at least one occasion in each week the club is open; or

(b) where a club chooses not to apportion the participation threshold in accordance with regulation 19(1), on at least 52 occasions.

41.7.7 *Annualisation of limits*

Regulation 7 CASCR provides:

(1) Where—

(a) the membership fees charged by the club vary by reference to duration of the membership, or

(b) the club offers memberships for periods of greater or less than one year,

the limits specified in regulations 5(1) (costs associated with membership of a club) and 6 (limit on membership fees) are proportionately reduced or increased accordingly.

(2) If a club chooses to reduce the participation threshold (see regulation 19), the limits specified in regulations 5(1) (costs associated with membership of a club) and 6 (limit on membership fees) are proportionally reduced by reference to the number of weeks the club is open.

41.8 Organised on amateur basis

Section 658(1A) CTA 2010 provides:

(1A) Condition A is that the club is, and is required by its constitution to

> be, a club which ...
> (b) is organised on an amateur basis (see section 660)

"Organised on an amateur basis" is a label for four distinct rules. Section 660(1) CTA 2010 provides:

> A club is "organised on an amateur basis" for the purposes of section 658 if—
> (a) it is non-profit making (see subsections (2) and (3)),
> (b) it provides for members and their guests only the ordinary benefits of an amateur sports club (see subsections (4) and (5)),
> (ba) it does not exceed the limit on paid players (see subsection 5A), and
> (c) its constitution provides for any net assets on its dissolution to be applied for approved sporting or charitable purposes (see subsections (6) and (7)).

41.9 Non-profit making

Section 660(1) CTA 2010 provides:

> A club is "organised on an amateur basis" for the purposes of section 658 if—
> (a) it is non-profit making (see subsections (2) and (3))...

That takes us to s.660(2)(3) CTA 2010 which provide:

> (2) A club is "non-profit making" for the purposes of subsection (1) if its constitution —
> (a) requires any surplus income or surplus gains to be reinvested in the club, and
> (b) does not allow the distribution of any of its assets (in cash or in kind) to members or third parties.
> (3) A club is not prevented from being "non-profit making" for those purposes merely because it makes donations to charities or registered clubs.

The CASC Guidance Note provides:

> 2.10.1 The term 'non-profit making' is used for various purposes within tax law - for example, in VAT the term is used to determine eligibility for certain reliefs. But there is a specific definition in relation to the CASC scheme.
> 2.10.2 A club is non-profit making if its constitution:
> - requires any surplus income or gains to be reinvested in the club
> - doesn't permit any distribution of club assets in cash or in kind to

members or third parties

2.10.3 This does not prevent a club making donations to charities or to other clubs that are registered as CASCs. A club which meets this condition will not necessarily be non-profit making for other purposes.

2.10.4 HMRC considers all the facts to decide whether a club meets this requirement. For example, it would not be acceptable for a privately-owned club or business to draw up rules to meet this requirement. HMRC requires detailed evidence to show a club is run as a members' club whose rules require it to be non-profit making. The CASC scheme isn't suitable for proprietary clubs and businesses.

41.10 Ordinary benefits of amateur club

Section 660(1) CTA 2010 provides:

> A club is "organised on an amateur basis" for the purposes of section 658 if ...
>
> (b) it provides for members and their guests only the ordinary benefits of an amateur sports club (see subsections (4) and (5))...

That takes us to s.660(4) CTA 2010 which provides:

> The following are "the ordinary benefits of an amateur sports club for the purposes of subsection (1)—
>
> (a) the provision of sporting facilities,
> (b) the reasonable provision and maintenance of club-owned sports equipment,
> (c) the provision of suitably qualified coaches,
> (d) the provision, or reimbursement of the costs, of coaching courses,
> (e) the provision of insurance cover,
> (f) the provision of medical treatment,
> (g) the reimbursement of necessary and reasonable travel or subsistence expenses incurred by
> [i] players,
> [ii] match officials,
> [iii] coaches,
> [iv] first-aiders and
> [v] accompanying individuals[14]

14 Defined s.660(4A) CTA 2010: "In subsection (4)(g) ...

(b) an "accompanying individual" means an individual accompanying a person who—

(i) has a disability for the purposes of the Equality Act 2010, and

travelling to away matches,

(h) the reasonable provision of post-match refreshments for players and match officials, and

(i) the sale or supply of food or drink as a social benefit which arises incidentally from the sporting purposes of the club.

41.10.1 *Travel + subsistence expenses*

Section 660(4A) CTA 2010 provides:

> "In subsection (4)(g)—
>
> (a) "subsistence expenses" means expenses on food, drink and temporary living accommodation".

Regulation 14 CASCR provides:

> (1) Subsistence expenses are neither necessary nor reasonable for the purposes of section 660(4)(g) of CTA 2010 if the journey is a reasonable daily journey.
> (2) In this regulation, a "reasonable daily journey" means one where the total travel time to and from the match from the club base is no more than four hours.
> (3) In paragraph (2), the "club base" is the address for the club registered with HMRC under section 658 of CTA 2010.
> (4) Travel and subsistence expenses incurred in connection with away matches are neither necessary nor reasonable for the purposes of section 660(4)(g) of CTA 2010 unless the main purpose of the match or matches is the promotion of, and participation in, an eligible sport.

The CASC Guidance Note provides:

> **2.12 What are necessary and reasonable travel and subsistence expenses?**
> 2.12.1 Travel and subsistence expenses are only reasonable when the purpose of the match or sporting event are the promotion of and participation in eligible sport(s).
> 2.12.2 'Reasonable' in this context also means that clubs should not provide excessive levels of benefits. For example, it would not be reasonable for a club to hire cars for each first team player to travel to away matches. However it would be reasonable to provide a mileage allowance or to cover the cost of travel on public transport. Similarly it would not be reasonable to reimburse first class travel costs if standard class transport was cheaper and available.
> 2.12.3 A CASC may only reimburse subsistence expenses when the journey is longer than a 'reasonable daily journey'. A 'reasonable daily journey' is a journey where the total travel time (starting at the club base) to and from the match or

---

(ii) is a player or match official."

sporting event is less than 4 hours. The club base is the address the club has registered with HMRC.

2.12.4 When calculating the journey length HMRC expects clubs to base this on the route and method of transport actually used by the members. If a journey takes longer than usual (due to cancellations or bad weather) HMRC will accept that it is reasonable for the club to make subsistence payments based on the time the journey actually took - the club should keep a record of the delay to demonstrate that the additional subsistence payment was still necessary and reasonable.

2.12.5 As a guide, HMRC will usually accept any amounts paid that are within the benchmark rates to be reasonable as long as they are necessary and have been incurred for the purpose of promoting participation in eligible sport.

2.12.6 Some sports governing bodies produce guidance on members' expenses in relation to maintaining amateur status for the purpose of that particular body. Such rules should not be confused with the CASC conditions. They can include items which would not be acceptable as ordinary benefits and reasonable expenses for a CASC.

Examples of reasonable expenses

Example (K)

A rugby club based has a match which is more than 4 hours away from the club. The total travelling time will be 10 hours and a whole team, plus coach and manager will be travelling to the match. The club hires a coach to make the journey and makes a subsistence payment to each person of £10 (which is within the benchmark rates for a 10 hour day).

Example (L)

A football club arranges for its members to participate in a tournament which is 2 and a half hours away by train. The club agrees to reimburse the cost of the standard price ticket and also provides a £5 payment to each member to cover the cost of lunch.

Example (M)

A cricket team are attending a match which is an hour away. It agrees to reimburse those members who travelled by train for the price of the standard price train ticket. Those who used their own car received HMRC's approved Mileage Allowance payments. The club does not provide any subsistence payment because the match is within reasonable daily travel.

2.13 Tours

2.13.1 Tours are likely to be costly for the club. If a club wants to fund a tour it must be able to demonstrate that the cost incurred is proportionate with meeting its main purpose of providing facilities and encouraging participation.

2.13.2 In most cases HMRC expect members to pay for their own expenses when they travel on a tour with the club. However, not everyone could afford to travel if they had to pay their own expenses so HMRC accept that payments in these circumstances would be acceptable to allow all members to fully participate as long as the main purpose of the tour was to promote participation in sport and not to have a holiday. HMRC will not accept that a luxury/expensive tour was arranged mainly for the purpose of promoting participation. Clubs that wish to contribute to the cost of a tour should ensure that the members are using reasonable standard class accommodation and transport.

2.13.3 To accept that the main purpose of the tour was to promote participation in sport HMRC normally expect to see evidence of matches played, training and other activities that serve to promote participation happening throughout the tour. HMRC accept that members might not be able to participate in sport on the days they travel if the journey takes more than 6 hours. On some tours it may not be practical to participate in sport every day. For example, a tour for junior members or tour for a club that promotes participation in a physically demanding sport. In all other circumstances HMRC expect there to be meaningful participation in the eligible sport. For example, a 30 minute training session followed by a day of sightseeing would not be acceptable.

2.13.4 Tours should be encouraging participation more widely in the sport so HMRC would expect clubs to promote and arrange tours that catered to all members, including juniors and beginners. A tour that was only for the club's first team would not be accepted as promoting participation in the sport.

2.13.5 In some cases a tour may not involve a long trip overseas, these rules also apply to shorter events. For example, attending 3 day sporting event in another city in the UK that required an overnight stay.

2.13.6 If members want to fund a tour/holiday themselves they are able to do this but they should not donate this money to the CASC first. Gift Aid would not be due on the payment because it would be considered a payment for the holiday and not a qualifying gift. Once the CASC has received funds from the members it is required to spend this money on qualifying purposes within the CASC rules.

Examples of tours

Example (N)

A group of football clubs organise a tournament in Spain with games and other activities planned to take place over a week. As well as tournament matches, 2 promotion events are held each day, a coaching session to improve beginners' skills, and another is a taster session to encourage non-participants to play. The matches and other events are timetabled so that every CASC member will play or participate in 2 events per day for each full day away from home.

Example (O)

A similar tournament is run by a group of tennis clubs on a knock out basis and there are no plans to use any spare time for those knocked out for tennis related events or to return home early. This tour does not ensure that there is substantial and meaningful opportunity for all players to participate in sufficient matches or promotion events during the trip. It would not be deemed acceptable under the new rules.

Example (P)

A sailing club arranged for its members to take part in an amateur regatta in France that took place over 6 days. The journey to the regatta took 5 hours and the members spent the second part of the day preparing the boats and taking part in a short classroom-based training exercise. The regatta involved taking part in one race each day and the remainder of the day was spent in training, the most inexperienced members sailed with a coach that was hired for the duration of the regatta. On the final day the members travelled home after the last race.

41.10.2 *Permitted payments*

Section 660(5) CTA 2010 provides:

> A club is not prevented from providing for members and their guests only the ordinary benefits of an amateur sports club for the purposes of subsection (1) merely because—
> (a) a member supplies goods or services to the club on an arm's length basis, or
> (b) the club employs members of the club on an arm's length basis.

One might have thought this unnecessary as arm's length remuneration is not a benefit.

41.11 Limit on paid players

Section 660(1) CTA 2010 provides:

> A club is "organised on an amateur basis" for the purposes of section 658 if ...
> (ba) it does not exceed the limit on paid players (see subsection 5A)...

This takes us to s.660(5A) CTA 2010:

> (5A) A club does not exceed the limit on paid players for the purposes of subsection (1) if—
> (a) the number of persons paid to play for the club does not at any time exceed the specified maximum,
> (b) the number of such persons in any year does not exceed the specified maximum for that year,
> (c) the amount paid to any such person in any year in respect of activities undertaken for the club does not exceed the specified maximum for that year, and
> (d) the total amount paid to such persons in any year in respect of activities undertaken for the club does not exceed the specified maximum for that year.
> "Specified" means specified in regulations made by the Treasury.

41.12 Amount paid to players

Regulation 11 CASCR provides:

> (1) For the purposes of section 660(1)(ba) of CTA 2010 (limit on paid players), a club does not exceed the limit on paid players if the total amount paid to persons paid to play for the club in any year, in respect of activities undertaken for the club, does not exceed £10,000.
> (2) For the purposes of this regulation, "year" means an accounting

period of the club.
(3) But where the club's accounting period is shorter than 12 months the limit in paragraph (1) is proportionately reduced.
(4) If a club is a registered club for only part of an accounting period, this regulation has effect as if that part were a separate accounting period.

41.12.1 *"Paid player"*

Regulation 11(5) CASCR provides:

> An individual is only regarded as a person paid to play for a club ("a paid player") if conditions A to E (see regulation 12) are met.

Regulation 12 CASCR provides:

> (1) Condition A is that the individual is paid to play an eligible sport for the club.
> (2) Condition B is that all amounts paid to the player to play for the club—
> (a) are agreed on an arm's length basis, or
> (b) if not agreed on an arm's length basis, are agreed in circumstances where the features of the agreement which cause it to be otherwise than on an arm's length basis, when taken together, are more advantageous to the club than if the agreement had been on an arm's length basis.
> (3) Condition C is that the individual is not—
> (a) a manager (within the meaning of section 661B(2) of CTA 2010)[15] or an officer of the club, or
> (b) connected with a manager or an officer of the club.
> (4) Condition D is that the individual is not paid by one registered club to play for another registered club.
> (5) Condition E is that the individual is not paid by a person other than the club, or a person connected to the club, to play for the club.

41.12.2 *Calculating amount player paid*

Regulation 13 CASCR provides:

> (1) This regulation makes provision in relation to the calculation of the total amount paid to paid players in any year for the purposes of the limit specified in regulation 11(1).
> (2) Amounts paid to a paid player means any amounts paid to the player for playing for the club which would be—

---

15 See 41.19 (Management condition).

(a) earnings within Chapter 1 of Part 3 of ITEPA 2003, or
(b) treated as earnings under Chapters 2 to 11 of Part 3 of ITEPA 2003 (the benefits code).

(3) Amounts paid to a paid player to play for the club include payments made in respect of the following—
(a) training for the purposes of playing an eligible sport, and
(b) travel for the purposes of playing or training for an eligible sport.

(4) But amounts paid to a player do not include the reimbursement of reasonable and necessary travel or subsistence expenses referred to in section 660(4)(g) of CTA 2010.[16]
(5) Amounts paid to a paid player include any payments made pursuant to an agreement or understanding (whether or not legally enforceable).
(6) For the purposes of this regulation the paid player is to be treated as employed to play for the club and the provisions of ITEPA 2003 referred to in paragraph (2) are to apply accordingly.

The CASC Guidance Note provides:

2.15 Payments to players
2.15.1 For HMRC to accept that a club is organised on an amateur basis they must not pay players more than £10,000 in a 12 month accounting period. There's no limit on the number of players that a club can pay for playing as long as the total amount paid to all players is less than £10,000 a year.
2.15.2 Where an accounting period is shorter than 12 months the £10,000 limit should be proportionately reduced. For example, a club with a 10 month accounting period would only be allowed to pay players up to £8,333 a year.
2.15.3 If a club is registered midway through an accounting period the limit should also be proportionately reduced. A club registered midway through a 12 month accounting period will have a limit of £5,000 for the remainder of that accounting period and then a limit of £10,000 for the next 12 month accounting period.
2.15.4 A CASC can't make payments to a player that plays for another club. Also any cash or benefits provided by third parties connected to the CASC will still count towards the paid player limit.
2.15.5 To work out how much your club can pay players you must also include the value of any non-cash benefits. HMRC expects clubs to follow the benefits code to work out the value of any benefits they offer to paid players. The value of the benefit is worked out on the 'cash equivalent' of the benefit - this is usually the cost to the club less any amount made good by the paid player. In some cases there could be a scale charge (for example car benefits), so to work out the amount of the cash equivalent in each case you'll need to look at the instructions for that particular benefit.
2.15.6 Amounts paid to players must be agreed on an 'arm's length' basis, or on

---

16 See 41.10.1 (Travel + subsistence expenses).

a basis that is in the club's favour. Any payments made to a player more than would be expected if agreed on an 'arm's length' basis, would not be an allowable payment to a player. This would mean that the club was not organised on an amateur basis.

2.15.7 'Arm's length' means that the arrangement should be entered into by both parties as if they were acting independently of each other, in their own self-interest and as if they were in no way connected.

2.15.8 CASCs can only pay players for playing in an eligible sport. HMRC accepts that this can include payments made to a player for:

- training for the purposes of playing an eligible sport
- travel for the purposes of playing or training for an eligible sport (this does not include allowable travel and subsistence payments for away matches or tours)

...

2.16 Paying members for good and services

2.16.1 Payments to members for non-playing services don't count towards the £10,000 limit. Clubs may enter into agreements with members to supply goods or services to the club, or employ members. This means that clubs can pay members for work done on a self-employed basis, or as staff for the club, provided that the arrangements are the same as if the people doing the work were unrelated to the club. Examples would include catering services, bar work, coaching and ground work.

Example (Q)

A cricket club pays a member for his services as a groundsman. The rates of pay are no higher than the local commercial rate. Providing the club can show evidence of having sought quotes from elsewhere and isn't paying in excess this would be acceptable for a CASC.

Example (R)

An amateur football club pays 2 members who also play for them in a local league. They are paid for coaching and development roles with the club's junior squads which are open to all, regardless of ability. They are not paid for playing in the league matches and the rates paid reflect the duties performed. This is acceptable for a CASC.

2.17 Prizes and competitions

2.17.1 Clubs may want to arrange prize competitions where the nature of both the competition and the prize is such as to promote participation in the sport. This is allowed where the value of prizes is in keeping with amateur participation in the particular sport, and would not prevent a club from being registered. Competitions with prizes of sufficient value or of such frequency to attract professionals are not acceptable for a CASC.

Example (S)

A golf club holds a series of competitions for members throughout its season. Although individual events may be limited by gender or golf handicap, all members are able to participate in some of the competitions. Prizes of golf equipment, for example bags, shoes, balls or £50 vouchers redeemable at the club shop are awarded. This is acceptable.

Example (T)

A bowling club organises various competitions during the season for club members with cash prizes subsidised by a brewery. All members are able to enter the competitions and there is no handicap applied which would give most members an average chance of winning. The effect is that a small group of the best players will often win the prizes and so derive significant benefit from these arrangements. A club that subsidised a section of its members in this way would be unlikely to qualify as a CASC.

41.13 Social members

Section 660A(1) CTA 2010 provides:

> A club is not to be regarded as a club that has as its main purpose the provision of facilities for, and the promotion of participation in, one or more eligible sports if the percentage of its members who are social members exceeds the percentage specified for the purposes of this section in regulations made by the Treasury.

Regulation 15 CASCR provides:

> For the purposes of section 660A(1) of CTA 2010 (clubs consisting mainly of social members), the percentage specified is 50%.

41.13.1 *"Social member"*

Section 660A(2) CTA 2010 provides:

> A member is a "social member" for the purposes of this section if the member does not participate, or participates only occasionally, in the sporting activities of the club.

41.13.2 *Cap on social members*

Section 660A CTA 2010 provides:

> (1) A club is not to be regarded as a club that has as its main purpose the provision of facilities for, and the promotion of participation in, one or more eligible sports if the percentage of its members who are social members exceeds the percentage specified for the purposes of this section in regulations made by the Treasury.
> (2) A member is a "social member" for the purposes of this section if the member does not participate, or participates only occasionally, in the sporting activities of the club.

The CASC Guidance Note provides:

> 2.21.1 To meet the main purpose test a club must ensure at least 50% of the members are 'participating members'. To be a participating member they must participate in the sporting activities of the club on a number of occasions that is equal to or more than the club's participation threshold. The participation threshold is based on the number of weeks in the club's

accounting period but there are reduced thresholds for members who join or leave a club at a time other than the start of an accounting period.

2.21.2 For family or other group memberships each individual member will be counted separately for the purposes of this test.

2.21.3 Where a club that originally fulfilled this requirement finds that over half of its members no longer participate in sport then the club will need to take action to encourage existing members to participate or recruit new members who will actively participate. Clubs could also consider restricting the number of social memberships available to ensure the threshold isn't exceeded.

2.21.4 Examples of 'participating in the sporting activities of the club' are:

- participating in an eligible sport organised by the club
- being a match official for an eligible sport for the club
- coaching club members in an eligible sport
- providing first aid to people playing an eligible sport for the club
- being an accompanying individual for the club
- driving a club vehicle, or a vehicle hired by the club, to transport those persons listed above
- preparing or maintaining club sporting facilities or equipment for use in an eligible sport
- being an officer, or a committee member of the club
- undertaking a relevant training course

2.21.5 Clubs will need to keep sufficient records to allow them to work out whether they have met the requirement to have 50% of their members participating in eligible sport.

2.21.6 Examples of records you could keep include:

- a signing-in book for members to use when they participate at the club
- records of training courses attended
- records of membership participation in matches (whether as a participant or as a volunteer preparing facilities or driving the club vehicle)

2.21.7 This isn't a complete list and HMRC is willing to consider other types of evidence as long as the club can show that it is a reliable record of participation. If a club is forced to cancel a planned event due to circumstances outside of their control they should keep evidence of the circumstances and if necessary, contact their sport's governing body or HMRC for advice.

41.13.3 *Participate in sporting activities*

Regulation 16 CASCR provides:

(1) For the purposes of section 660A(2) (definition of social member) of CTA 2010, "participating in the sporting activities of the club" means—

(a) participating in an eligible sport organised by the club;
(b) being a match official for an eligible sport for the club;
(c) coaching club members in an eligible sport;
(d) providing first aid to persons playing an eligible sport for the club;
(e) being an accompanying individual (within the meaning of section 660(4A)(b) of CTA 2010)[17] for the club;
(f) driving a club vehicle, or a vehicle hired by the club, to transport persons listed in sub-paragraphs (a) to (e) or equipment on behalf of the club for the purposes of the participation in activities referred to in those sub-paragraphs;
(g) preparing or maintaining club sporting facilities or equipment for use in an eligible sport;
(h) being an officer, or a committee member, of the club; or
(i) undertaking a relevant training course for the purposes of sub-paragraphs (a) to (d), (g) or (h).

(2) Where an event planned by the club is cancelled due to extreme circumstances outside the club's control then planned participation in that event is deemed to be participation.

41.13.4 *Occasional participation*

Regulation 17 CASCR provides:

(1) For the purposes of section 660A(2) of CTA 2010, a member participates only occasionally in the sporting activities of the club in an accounting period if that member does not meet the participation threshold for that accounting period.

(2) For the purposes of this regulation, the participation threshold is participation in the sporting activities of the club on the required number of days in the accounting period of the club.

(3) The required number of days is determined in accordance with table 1.

Table 1

Accounting period (weeks)	*Participation Threshold (days)*	*Accounting period*	*Participation Threshold*
4 or fewer	1	25 to 28	7
5 to 8	2	29 to 31	8
9 to 12	3	32 to 35	9
13 to 16	4	36 to 39	10
17 to 20	5	40 to 43	11

17 See 41.10 (Ordinary benefits of amateur club).

21 to 24	6	44 or more	12

(4) If the club is registered for only part of an accounting period, that part is to be treated as a separate accounting period for the purposes of this regulation.

41.13.5 *Accounting period*

Regulation 18 CASCR provides:

(1) Where a person is a member of a club for only part of an accounting period, the participation threshold in regulation 17 is determined by using table 2 in place of table 1 for the purposes of that regulation.
(2) For the purposes of calculating weeks of membership for table 2, a person is a member during any given week if that person is a member for any part of that week.
Table 2

41.14 Seasonal sports

Number of weeks of membership	*Participation Threshold (Days)*	*Weeks of membership*	*Participation Threshold*
4 or fewer	1	25 to 28	7
5 to 8	2	29 to 31	8
9 to 12	3	32 to 35	9
13 to 16	4	36 to 39	10
17 to 20	5	40 to 43	11
21 to 24	6	44 or more 12	

Regulation 19 CASCR provides:

(1) Where a club is only open for part of the accounting period, that club may choose to reduce the participation threshold in regulation 17 for all members and use table 3 for the purposes of that regulation in place of table 1.
(2) If a club chooses to reduce the participation threshold under paragraph (1) and a person is a member of a club for only part of an accounting period, then regulation 18 applies to determine the participation threshold for that person and table 2 in regulation 18 is used in place of table 3.
(3) A club is open during any given week if any of the facilities provided by the club are made available to members for any part of that week.
Table 3

The CASC Guidance Note provides:

Club open (weeks)	*Participation Threshold (days)*	*Club open*	*Participation Threshold*
4 or fewer	1	25 to 28	7
5 to 8	2	29 to 31	8

9 to 12	3	32 to 35	9
13 to 16	4	36 to 39	10
17 to 20	5	40 to 43	11
21 to 24	6	44 or more	12

Example (U)

A sailing club is open 26 weeks in an accounting period, they choose to use the seasonal reduction. The members of this sailing club will be participating members if they participate on at least 7 occasions in the period.

Example (V)

A cricket club with a 12 month accounting period has worked out that they are open for 40 weeks a year. They have decided to use the seasonal reduction and as a result its members will need to participate on 11 occasions in the accounting period to be a participating member.

The CASC Guidance Note Annex 4 provides:

Seasonal Sports

1. **Overview**

1.1 HM Revenue and Customs accepts that for some sports it's more difficult to meet the requirement to have at least 50% of your members participating on 12 occasions a year, especially if the club closes for a period during the year when participation is not safe or practical.

1.2 To help seasonal sports qualify for CASC status there's another option open to these clubs. Seasonal clubs that aren't open all year can opt to reduce the participation threshold so that it accurately reflects the number of weeks that the club is actually open. If the club is open on 1 day in a week, it will be considered open for the whole of that week for the purposes of this test.

1.3 If clubs choose to reduce the participation threshold they must also accept that the limit for membership fees is also proportionally reduced. It will be for the club to decide which option is best for them and this will depend on the levels of participation at your club and also how expensive it is to participate.

Example:

A yachting club is open for 30 weeks in a 12 month accounting period. They opt for the seasonal reduction which reduces the participation threshold to 8 days. To meet the participation test the club will need to keep a record that shows that at least 50% of the club's members have participated in yachting on at least 8 occasions during that 12 month period.

They'll also have reduced limits for membership fees 30/52 × £1,612 = £930 and the costs associated with participation 30/52 × £520 = £300. The club will need to keep within these reduced limits to meet the conditions of the CASC scheme.

41.15 Distribution on dissolution

Section 660(1) CTA 2010 provides:

> A club is "organised on an amateur basis" for the purposes of section 658 if ...
>
> (c) its constitution provides for any net assets on its dissolution to be applied for approved sporting or charitable purposes (see subsections (6) and (7)).

That takes us to s.660(6)(7) CTA 2010 which provide:

> (6) In relation to any club, the following are "sporting or charitable purposes" for the purposes of subsection (1)—
>
> (a) the purposes of the governing body of an eligible sport for the purposes of which the club existed, for use in related community sport,
>
> (b) the purposes of another registered club, and
>
> (c) the purposes of a charity.
>
> (7) Purposes of a club are "approved" sporting or charitable purposes for the purposes of subsection (1) if they are approved by—
>
> (a) the members of the club in general meeting, or
>
> (b) the members of the club's governing body.

41.16 Main purpose promotion of sport

Section 658(1A) CTA 2010 provides:

> Condition A is that the club is, and is required by its constitution to be, a club which ...
>
> (c) has as its main purpose the provision of facilities for, and the promotion of participation in, one or more eligible sports (see sections 660A and 661).

For the question of how to identify the main purpose of a CASC, see 8.8 (Ascertaining primary purposes).

The club's purpose must be to provide facilities *and* to promote participation. Merely one or the other is not enough.

The CASC Guidance Note provides:

> 2.20.1 A club must promote participation in an eligible sport and also provide facilities for playing the sport. A club does not necessarily have to own premises to 'provide facilities'; it may, for example, hire premises. Other clubs which simply organise opportunities for members to participate in the sport may qualify. For example, small football clubs

may hire or borrow facilities provided by the local authority. Some cycling clubs have standing arrangements to meet at a particular time and place for club rides; this would amount to providing facilities.

2.20.2 The provision of facilities itself does not amount to the promotion of participation in sport. Clubs must also encourage all members to participate regardless of ability. It's not enough to provide facilities to enable a small number of members who are sports enthusiasts to take part. The emphasis must be on encouraging as many members of different abilities as possible to take part.

2.20.3 Most clubs are able to meet this condition as they are structured in a way that caters for all abilities. For example, a club might field a number of teams ranging in ability from novice players to a high standard. This is acceptable as long as the overall emphasis is on participation. A club that only allows participation at an elite level, with other members being spectators rather than players isn't acceptable.

2.20.4 Some clubs have the main purpose of providing social leisure facilities. If this is the case they will not be able to register as CASCs, because these clubs are principally places for people to meet for social purposes even though some sporting activities take place.

2.20.5 Some social clubs provide sporting facilities and establish teams that help some members to participate in sport, but this isn't enough to be a CASC. A club must be able to demonstrate that it has the promotion of participation in eligible sport as its main purpose. For example, many pubs run Sunday league football teams. This encourages participation in sport, but this isn't the main purpose of the pub, which is to sell food and drink. Therefore this would not qualify as a CASC.

2.20.6 Certain clubs are structured in ways that make it difficult for them to qualify as a CASC. Sometimes there are a number of separate clubs all using the same grounds and club house. Where there is a separate body running the facilities on behalf of the clubs this body will struggle to demonstrate that it is itself promoting participation in sport.

2.20.7 The club that provides the facilities must also fully satisfy all the conditions itself to be registered as a CASC. It can't simply provide the facilities for the other clubs; it must also be a sports club that actively encourages participation for all its members. The fact that it also allows other clubs, whether registered or not as CASCs, to use the facilities as well doesn't prevent it from being a CASC as long as its main purpose is to provide facilities for its own members and to promote participation for these members.

The CASC Guidance Note provides:

2.14.1 Where a club sells food and drink, this should be a social benefit which arises incidentally from the sporting purpose of the club, for example when a bar is open for post-match refreshment. Examples of incidental sale or supply would include the sale of:

- food and drink in a cafeteria to members of a multi-sports club as part of their participation in the sporting experience
- confectionery and snacks etc from a tuck shop to members of a gymnastics club as part of their gym session
- drink to members of a club in the bar before, during and after games and training
- food and drink to non-members in the bar after watching a game and being invited in for a drink by a member
- food and drink to visiting players and spectators using the bar after a game when invited to do so by members
- food and drink as part of a social event designed to encourage participation in the sport or to generate more regular sporting participation by club members

41.17 Multi-sports clubs

The CASC Guidance Note Annex 3 provides:

Multi-Sports Clubs

1. **Overview**

1.1 Clubs that offer more than one sport can still become Community Amateur Sports Clubs (CASCs) as long as all of the sports are all eligible sports. For example a club offering Ju-Jitsu, Karate and Kickboxing would not be eligible because Kickboxing is not an eligible sport.

1.2 Multi-sports clubs will still need to meet the all of the other conditions for CASC status. In particular multi-sports clubs that wish to apply for CASC status will need to ensure that they structure themselves in a CASC compliant way.

1.3 Multi-sports clubs are usually made up of:

- one club offering several eligible sports
- one club made up of different sporting sections
- a group of affiliated clubs

2. **One club offering several eligible sports**

2.1 This is the most straightforward structure for a multi-sports club. There would usually be one company or unincorporated association with one governing document. The club will be run by one management committee who would be responsible for admitting and removing members, organising the sporting activity and managing the property and financial affairs of the club. The club will produce one set of financial accounts. As long as this type of club meets the other conditions of the scheme it would qualify for CASC status.

2.2 If one club offers more than one eligible sport it will need to offer all participating members the same rights. For example, a club offering tennis and squash could not restrict member voting rights to only those who play tennis.

2.3 This type of club may offer individual sporting memberships and also a membership package for all eligible sports. For example, a club offering tennis and squash may offer a tennis membership, a squash membership and a dual membership for tennis and squash. When considering the membership fees and costs of membership the club should look at the most expensive single sport memberships. CASCs are not required to meet the membership requirements on memberships that are for more than one sport.

Example:

A single integrated multi-sport club offers 3 sports - football, rugby and cricket. The membership fee for each sport is £120 a year or you can have a membership for all three sports for £200. The cricket club has the most additional costs on top of the membership fee, making it the most expensive sport.

This club needs to check whether the costs of membership for cricket are more than £520 a year.

In this case the costs of membership for cricket are £190 a year so no provision is needed for those on low or modest incomes.

3. **One club made up of different sporting sections**

3.1 Some clubs offering more than one sport choose to set up sporting sections. For HM Revenue and Customs (HMRC) to register this type of club it needs to make sure that this is really one club and not a group of clubs using the same facilities.

3.2 If there's only one club made up of sporting sections then there should only be one governing document and only one company or unincorporated association registered with HMRC. Each sporting section may have their own management committee, but all members will be a member of the whole club and will be able to vote in member's meetings.

3.3 To accept that this type of club is suitable for CASC status HMRC would need to see evidence that:

- you have a single set of financial accounts for the club - if the sporting sections keep their own accounts they should be consolidated at the end of the year
- this is one club and that there is a central management committee that has overall responsibility for each section
- if the club was closed (or wound up) the assets of one section would be used to cover the debt of another section

- the details of bank statements are available for all accounts held by the club if you have different bank accounts for each section

3.4 If your club is structured this way you must still meet the other conditions of the CASC scheme. It's important you look at the club as a single entity when deciding if you are eligible. For example, the income of each section will be added together for the purpose of the income condition.

3.5 To meet the 50% participating members requirement you must add together the numbers of participating and non-participating members across all sporting sections to check whether the 50% participation threshold has been met. The club will only have one £10,000 a year limit for paying players, so the sections will need to agree how this limit should be allocated across the different eligible sports.

3.6 As with the previous structure, the club should look at the most expensive sport for the purposes of the membership fee and costs associated with membership tests. If the most expensive single sport membership fee is more than £1,612 a year then the club would not be eligible for CASC status.

3.7 If the most expensive single sport had a cost associated with membership that was more than £520 a year, the club would need to make provisions for those who can't afford to pay more than £520 a year.

4. **A group of affiliated clubs**

4.1 Sometimes a group of separate but affiliated clubs will work together and may even share facilities.

4.2 Affiliated clubs can each apply for CASC status, or they can choose not to. If one club is successful in applying for CASC status this does not mean that the other clubs are CASCs and they will not be entitled to any relief unless they are successful in making their own application.

4.3 Each club within this structure will have to decide whether it wishes to apply for CASC status. Applications will be judged independently on the criteria of the CASC scheme.

4.4 Sometimes a group of affiliated clubs will include a club that owns and operates the sporting facilities that are used by the other sports clubs. For example a club running a sports centre that allows use to other affiliated sports clubs. If the main purpose of this club is to provide facilities alone, it won't be eligible for CASC status. These clubs are known as 'mother clubs'.

5. **Mother club with individual members**

5.1 This type of club may own and manage the facilities, allowing affiliated clubs to use its facilities. This type of club may be part of a group of affiliated clubs.

5.2 Often each individual member of an affiliated club is required to become a member of the mother club. They may for example be automatically given membership of the mother club when admitted as a member of an affiliated club.

5.3 The mother club may also admit them as members and then they apply or are allocated to the different affiliated clubs, depending on what sport they wish to play. There may be a subscription to join the mother club or this may be free with subscriptions paid to the affiliated clubs for membership of these.

5.4 To be accepted as a CASC the mother club must itself meet the statutory criteria, regardless of the activities of any affiliated clubs. This means that the mother club must itself actively promote participation in eligible sports and can't merely be a passive provider of facilities.

5.5 Activities that a mother club might engage in to promote participation in sports might include:

- actively engaging with the local community and the sport's governing bodies to widen participation
- publicising its facilities and the sports that it caters for and taking positive action to attract new participants to the club
- organising festivals, tournaments and coaching courses

5.4 A decision will be made for each individual case on whether a club's activities are sufficient to amount to promoting participation. This type of club may struggle to meet the 50% participation threshold.

6. **Mother club with affiliated member clubs**

6.1 Where a mother club has no individual membership, but has affiliated clubs as its members (that is it is a club of clubs), HMRC will not accept that the mother club as a CASC. However the affiliated clubs will be able to apply for CASC status.

6.2 This structure doesn't comply with the CASC requirements as membership is only open to organisations (the affiliated clubs) and not to individuals. It is therefore not open to the whole community.

The mother club may in principle be a charity.

41.18 Location condition

Section 661A(1) CTA 2010 provides:

A club meets the location condition for the purposes of section 658 if—

(a) it is established in a member State or a relevant territory,[18] and

---

18 Section 661A(2) CTA 2010 provides:
In this section "relevant territory" means a territory specified in regulations under paragraph 2(3)(b) of Schedule 6 to FA (No.1) 2010 (definition of "charity" etc). See 3.6 (Jurisdiction condition).

(b) the facilities that it provides for eligible sports are all located in a single member State or relevant territory.

Thus EU sports clubs are eligible for registration as CASCs. However they would be better advised to claim relief as charities.

A sports club will not qualify as a CASC unless it is registered with HMRC.[19] No well advised EU sports clubs is likely to register as a CASC in order to obtain the reliefs available to CASCs because it could claim the reliefs as a charity without doing so.

41.19 Management condition

Section 661B CTA 2010 provides:

> (1) A club meets the management condition for the purposes of section 658 if its managers are fit and proper persons to be managers of the club.
> (2) In this paragraph "managers", in relation to a club, means the persons having the general control and management of the administration of the club.

Section 661C CTA 2010 provides:

> (1) This paragraph applies in relation to any period throughout which the management condition is not met.
> (2) The management condition is treated as met throughout the period if the Commissioners for HMRC consider that—
> (a) the failure to meet the management condition has not prejudiced the purposes of the club, or
> (b) it is just and reasonable in all the circumstances for the condition to be treated as met throughout the period.

For a discussion, see 3.8 (Management condition).

41.20 2015 transitional relief

The CASC Guidance Note provides:

> 6.1.8 CASCs that have always been fully compliant with the rules prior to 1 April 2015 will be given 12 months from the 1 April 2015 to meet the requirements of the new rules. If any of these CASCs are still unable to meet the new conditions after this time they will be deregistered with

---

19 A drafting quirk of the legislation that under the rules for charities, EU charities do have to meet a "registration condition" but do not generally have to register with anyone; whereas under the rules for CASCs, there is no rule called the "registration condition" but CASCs do have to register with HMRC.

effect from 1 April 2016.

41.21 Registration of CASC

41.21.1 *Procedure for registration*

To be eligible for CASC reliefs, a CASC must be registered. The procedure for registration is set out in s.658 CTA 2010, which provides:

> (2) A club may apply to an officer of Revenue and Customs to be registered as a community amateur sports club.
> (3) The officer must register the club as a community amateur sports club if satisfied that the club is entitled to be registered.
> (4) The officer—
> (a) may register the club with effect from such date as the officer may specify (which may be before the date of the application)...

The application form is in the the CASC Guidance Note appendix 1.
The CASC Guidance Note provides:

> 2.1.1 To apply for CASC status you must complete a CASC (A1) application form and provide certain documents to show that your club is suitable. The form must be completed by an authorised official or responsible person from the club. Once an application has been submitted you can't withdraw it.
> 2.1.2 HMRC will review your application to check whether your sports club meets the conditions of the scheme. It's important that your club is already meeting these conditions in practice. It's not enough to explain what you plan to do once you have CASC registration. HMRC can't be satisfied that your club is suitable unless it is already run in a CASC compliant way as described in this guide.
> ...
> 2.26.1 HMRC must be satisfied that a club already meets the conditions of the CASC scheme before it can register them. This means that the club should be acting in a CASC compliant way, run by its members with a CASC compliant governing document.
> 2.26.2 HMRC has the discretion to specify any date for registration, even a date that is before the date of the application. HMRC can register a club from the beginning of the accounting period in which the application was made as long as the club can satisfy HMRC that the scheme requirements were met throughout that period. If a club has changed its constitution to meet the eligibility criteria, HMRC will only register a club as a CASC from the date that new rules were formally adopted by the club's members.

41.21.2 *Registration appeals*

Section 670 CTA 2010 provides:

> An officer of Revenue and Customs must notify the club of any decision—
> (a) to register it as a registered club,
> (b) to refuse to register it as a registered club, or
> (c) to cancel its registration.

Section 671 CTA 2010 provides:

> (1) A club may appeal against a decision of any officer of Revenue and Customs in relation to its application, or registration, as a registered club.
> (2) Notice of the appeal must be given in writing to an officer of Revenue and Customs within 30 days of the date of the notification under section 670.
> (3) The notice must specify the grounds of the appeal.
> (4) If the appeal is against a refusal to register the club, or a decision to register it with effect from a particular date, the tribunal may (if not dismissing the appeal)—
> (a) direct that the club is to be registered with effect from a specified date, or
> (b) send the matter back to any officer of Revenue and Customs for reconsideration.
> (5) If the appeal is against a decision to cancel the registration of the club, or to do so with effect from a particular date, the tribunal may (if not dismissing the appeal)—
> (a) revoke the cancellation,
> (b) direct that the cancellation is to have effect from a specified date, or
> (c) send the matter back to any officer of Revenue and Customs for reconsideration.
> (6) The provisions of TMA 1970 relating to appeals under the Taxes Acts (within the meaning of TMA 1970) apply to an appeal under this section as they apply to those appeals.

41.21.3 *Published list*

Section 658(5) CTA 2010 provides:

> HMRC may publish the names and addresses of registered clubs.

A list is published on the HMRC website.[20]

---

20 *https://www.gov.uk/government/publications/community-amateur-sports-clubs-casc-registered-with-hmrc--2*

41.22 Reliefs for donor

41.22.1 *Gift Aid*

Gift Aid applies to for donations to CASCs.[21]
For individuals, s.430 ITA provides:

> In this chapter "charity" includes ... a club that is registered as a community amateur sports club for the purposes of Chapter 9 of Part 13 CTA 2010.

For companies, s.202 CTA 2010 similarly provides:

> In this Chapter "charity" includes ... (aa) a registered club[22]...

41.22.2 *Inheritance tax*

IHT relief for gifts to charities also applies to CASCs. Section 23(1) IHTA provides:

> Transfers of value are exempt to the extent that the values transferred by them are attributable to property which is given to charities or registered clubs.[23]

Section 23(2)(3)(4) contain anti-avoidance provisions applicable to charities and CASCs, which are discussed in the chapter on IHT reliefs for charities. Section 23(5) contains a rule applicable to charities and section 23(5A) contains the equivalent rule for CASCs:

> In the case of any property which is given to a registered club, subsection (1) above shall not apply in relation to the property if it or any part of it may become applicable for purposes other than—
> (a) the purposes of the club in question;
> (b) the purposes of another registered club;
> (c) the purposes of the governing body of an eligible sport[24] for the purposes of which the club in question exists; or
> (d) charitable purposes.
>
> ...

---

21 See 15.1 (Gift Aid: Introduction).

22 Section 202A CTA 2010 provides the standard definition of "registered club".

23 Section 23(7) IHTA provides a referential definition:
"For the purposes of this section "registered club" ... have the same meaning as in Chapter 9 of Part 13 of the Corporation Tax Act 2010."

24 Section 23(7) provides a referential definition:
"For the purposes of this section ... "eligible sport" have the same meaning as in Chapter 9 of Part 13 of the Corporation Tax Act 2010."

Lastly, s.23(6) IHTA defines "given to registered clubs":

> For the purposes of this section ...
> (b) property is given to registered clubs if
> [i] it becomes the property of registered clubs or
> [ii] is held on trust for purposes of registered clubs only...

Amusingly, a trust for "purposes of registered clubs only" would be void, as registered clubs are not charitable! English trust law does not (in short) allow non-charitable purpose trusts. But s.23(6)(b)[ii] is not entirely otiose since it would apply to trusts governed by Scots law, or foreign (non-UK) trust laws, which may accept that a trust for the purposes of a registered CASC is valid. Perhaps that is what the drafter had in mind.

In short, the IHT relief for CASCs is (more or less) the same as that for charities. For further discussion, see 24.1 (IHT reliefs on transfers to charity).

41.22.3 *CGT donor relief*

This relief applies to CASCs: see 23.3 (Donor CGT relief).

41.22.4 *Other donor reliefs*

Other charity donor reliefs which apply to CASCs are:
(1) gifts of trading stock: s.105 CTA 2009
(2) gifts of plant or machinery: s.63(2) Capital Allowances Act 2001.[25]

41.23 **Tax exemptions for CASC**

The exemptions available to CASCs are as follows:
(1) Trading income
(2) Interest income
(3) Gift Aid income
(4) Property income
(5) Chargeable gains
(6) Rates[26]

41.23.1 *"Qualifying purposes"*

The CASC exemptions require the income or gains to be applied for

---

25 See 18.7 (Gift of trading stock, plant/machinery).

26 A CASC is entitled to the same rating reliefs as a charity. See 40.1 (Charity rating relief: History).

"qualifying purposes". "Qualifying purposes" is defined in s.661(3) CTA 2010:

> For the purposes of this Chapter "qualifying purposes" means—
> (a) the purpose of providing facilities for one or more eligible sports, and
> (b) the purpose of promoting participation in one or more eligible sports.

41.24 Trading and property income

41.24.1 *Trading income exemption*

Section 662 CTA 2010 provides:

> (1) A club which is a registered club throughout an accounting period may make a claim for its UK trading income[27] for that period to be exempt from corporation tax if conditions A and B are met.
> (2) Condition A is that the receipts which would (but for this section) be brought into account in calculating the club's UK trading income for that period do not exceed the relevant threshold.
> (3) Condition B is that the whole of its UK trading income for that period is applied for qualifying purposes.
> ...
> (5) In this section "the relevant threshold" means—
> (a) £50,000 in the case of an accounting period which is 12 months, and
> (b) a proportionately reduced figure in the case of a shorter accounting period.

This exemption is capped at a *turnover* of £50,000 (not a profit of £50,000).

There is a special rule where a CASC is registered for part of an accounting period. Section 662(4) CTA 2010 provides:

> If a club is a registered club for only part of an accounting period, this section has effect as if—
> (a) that part were a separate accounting period, and
> (b) the club's UK trading income and receipts for that separate

---

27 Defined in s.662(6) CTA 2010: "In this section "UK trading income" means profits that (apart from this section) are chargeable under Chapter 2 of Part 3 of CTA 2009 and are—
(a) profits of a trade carried on wholly or partly in the United Kingdom, or
(b) profits of an activity other than a trade."

accounting period were proportionately reduced.

Thus by treating any accounting period in which a club became a CASC as two separate accounting periods, the relief is available for the time which a club is registered as a CASC.

The charity trading exemption is usually better than the CASC trading exemption, as the charity exemption for primary purpose trading income is uncapped and the charity exemption for other income is 25% of incoming resources with a minimum of £5k and a maximum of £50k.[28] It is possible to envisage cases where the CASC exemption is better, but that will be unusual;[29] and if it was worth the trouble, a charity could always use a trading subsidiary to avoid the charge.

41.24.2 *Computing trading income*

CASC Guidance Note Annex 1 provides:

> 3. **What is trading income?**
> 3.1 For income to benefit from the trading exemption it must be trading income. The supply of goods or services with a view to making a profit will amount to trading, and the profits will be liable to Corporation Tax as trading income.
> 3.2 This is not normally the case where a members club makes supplies to its own members.[30] So membership subscriptions paid to a CASC will not be trading income. Similarly, amounts paid by members to use facilities or for bar and catering are unlikely to be trading income.
> 3.3 Supplies made to non-members will normally be trading income. It is essential that all member and non-member income is separately recorded by the club. This information is needed to work out whether the club can claim the trading income exemption or if they have tax to pay.
> 3.4 Receipts from visitors who, in return for payment on a commercial basis, are allowed to use a club's facilities will be receipts from a taxable trade in the club's hands. This applies to individuals who arrive at a club to use its facilities on a casual basis and to groups who may book in advance.
> 3.5 Such visitors may become 'temporary members' of the club. This doesn't prevent receipts from their use of the club's facilities from being taken into account for tax, unless their rights as temporary members (such as rights to vote at meetings, participating in club activities and

---

28 See 8.15 (Small trade).

29 It would involve a CASC with non-primary purpose trading turnover of up to £30k and limited incoming resources outside the non-primary purpose trading.

30 See 42.6 (Social and recreational clubs: membership activity).

exercising control over running the club), are similar to those of full members. In computing the taxable income derived from non-members in this way the related expenses will be deductible.

3.6 Income from 'social members' will also be considered trading income unless they are offered the same rights to vote at meetings, participate fully in club activities and generally exercise control over the running of the club as those of full participating members.

3.7 Sometimes sports clubs engage in what is known as mutual trading. Mutual trading occurs where supplies are made to the members of a club or association and any surplus profit is returned to the members. The profits of mutual trading are not treated as trading profits for tax purposes. However, a club which engages in mutual trading cannot qualify as a CASC, because the return of surpluses to members means that it will not qualify for CASC status.

3.8 In order that they may accurately identify the trading income eligible for exemption, clubs will need to keep accurate records to enable them to distinguish between non-trading supplies and profits from trading activities.

Example

A tennis club provides tennis courts, which can be used by members and non-members. It runs a bar, shop and small café. The club must be able to differentiate between its non-trading transactions and its trading income.

The non-trading income would include payments from members for:

- membership subscriptions
- use of sports facilities
- purchases from bar/café/shop

The trading income would be receipts from non-members for:

- use of sports facilities
- purchases from bar/café/shop

3.8 Where a club has a fairly high turnover it might still be entitled to the trading exemption provided the proportion of that turnover relating to non-members does not exceed the £50,000 limit. It is important for clubs to record their different sources of income properly because there is just one turnover limit which applies to all the various activities. Unless clubs properly monitor their trading income they will not be able to tell when they may become liable to corporation tax and so need to make a return of income.

3.9 If a club has taxable trading income you will need to make sure that you work out your taxable profits correctly. You should work out how much trading income you have received from non-members and then you should deduct expenditure that was incurred in generating this trading income.

3.10 Usually CASCs will have 3 types of expenditure, which will be the costs:

- of providing goods or services to members
- when trading with non-members
- incurred for both of the above

3.11 It is important that the club only deducts expenses that relate to trading with non-members when calculating the level of taxable profit. That means excluding any expenditure that relates to providing members with goods and/or services, you should also apportion the expenses that are relate to both members and non-members.

41.24.3 *Property income exemption*

Section 663 CTA 2010 provides:

> (1) A club which is a registered club throughout an accounting period may make a claim for its UK property income[31] for that period to be exempt from corporation tax if conditions A and B are met.
> (2) Condition A is that the receipts which would (but for this section) be brought into account in calculating the club's UK property income for that period do not exceed the relevant threshold.
> (3) Condition B is that the whole of its UK property income for that period is applied for qualifying purposes.
> (4) If a club is a registered club for only part of an accounting period, this section has effect as if—
> (a) that part were a separate accounting period, and
> (b) the club's UK property income and receipts for that separate accounting period were proportionately reduced.
> (5) In this section "the relevant threshold" means—
> (a) £30,000 in the case of an accounting period which is 12 months, and
> (b) a proportionately reduced figure in the case of a shorter accounting period.

This exemption is capped to £30,000 *turnover* in the relevant accounting period.

CASC Guidance Note Annex 1 provides:

> 4. **Property Income exemption**
> 4.1 There's an exemption on rental income subject to a limit of £30,000 per year. The amount will be apportioned for shorter accounting periods

---

31 Defined s.663(6) CTA 2010: "In this section "UK property income" means income of a UK property business which would (but for this section) be chargeable under Chapter 3 of Part 4 of CTA 2009."

> in exactly the same way as for trading income. If your club is required to submit a Corporation Tax return then exemption must be claimed in the return, and the claim must relate only to income that is applied for qualifying purposes. It doesn't matter who rents the property - rental income from both members and non-members is taken into consideration.
>
> 4.2 Income should only be treated as property income when it's for the use of land or property only – for example the hire of an unstaffed function room with no catering or the rental of the grounds to another club to use. If the club provides staff or other services with the hire then it will be trading income if it is from non-members and non-taxable member income if the arrangement is between the club and one of its members.
>
> 4.3 For example, a rugby club hires out its pitch to a local business (for use when the rugby club is not open) for £8,000 a year they also earn £24,000 hiring out a hall to members and non-members. No staff, catering or security is provided with the hire of the room or pitches. This club has property income of £32,000 and will not be exempt on the profits because this turnover is more than the exemption limit of £30,000.

41.24.4 *Breach of trading/property cap*

The exemptions for property income and trading income are "all or nothing" exemptions, that is, if the trading or property turnover limits are exceeded there is no exception on the income below that amount. Of course, if the CASC were a charity (rather than a CASC) it could avoid charges where its income exceeds the relevant level as the charity exemptions are not capped.

The caps can be avoided by use of a trading or investment subsidiary company. HMRC approve of this:

CASC Guidance Note provides:

> 2.22.5 HMRC would not register a club that doesn't meet the income condition. If your club is already registered and you think you might exceed the threshold, HMRC would expect your club to take steps to reduce the level of non-member trading and property income earned by your club. One way that you could do this is to set up a trading subsidiary which is owned by the CASC. Alternatively you could choose to reduce the income received from non-members and property to ensure your club meets the income condition.

Similarly, the HMRC detailed guidance note provides:

> Charities and CASCs may set up wholly-owned subsidiary companies to carry out trading activities that fall outside the tax exemptions available to them... A CASC may set up a wholly-owned subsidiary for trading income eg for income received from bar takings or the private hire of club facilities.
>
> 3.14.2 These companies often enter into a Gift Aid arrangement with their parent charity, under which they agree or contract to pay to the charity or CASC a sum of money equivalent to some or all of their taxable profits.

41.25 Exemption: Interest/Gift Aid income

Section 664 CTA 2010 provides exemption for Gift Aid income and for interest income, but it is helpful to discuss the exemptions separately.

41.25.1 *Interest income exemption*

Section 664 provides:

> (1) A club which is a registered club throughout an accounting period may make a claim for—
>
> (a) its interest income for that period,
>
> (b) its gift aid income for that period, and
>
> (c) its company gift income for that period
>
> to be exempt from corporation tax if the whole of that interest income gift aid income and company gift income is applied for qualifying purposes.
>
> (2) If a club is a registered club for only part of an accounting period, this section has effect as if—
>
> (a) that part were a separate accounting period, and
>
> (b) the club's interest income for that separate accounting period were proportionately reduced.
>
> (3) In this section—
>
> "company gift income", in relation to a club, means gifts of money made to the club by companies which are not charities..
>
> "interest income", in relation to a club, means interest arising to the club that is not brought into account under section 297 of CTA 2009 (trading credits and debits brought into account under Part 3 of that Act as trading income) and
>
> "gift aid income", in relation to a club, means gifts made by individuals to the club which are qualifying donations for the purposes of Chapter 2 of Part 8 of ITA 2007 (gift aid).

There is no cap on this relief.

Section 664(1) provides that all of the interest and Gift Aid income must be applied for qualifying purposes. In the (somewhat theoretical) event that a CASC had both interest and Gift Aid income, a part of, for example, the Gift Aid income was applied for qualifying purposes, but that the interest income was not, this would prevent the CASC from claiming the relief in respect of all the Gift Aid income as well as the interest.

41.25.2 *Gift Aid income*

Individuals who make donations to CASCs are eligible for Gift Aid relief under Chapter 2 Part 8 ITA.[32]

Section 661D CTA 2010 provides that the gift is treated as income of the recipient CASC:

> (1) This section applies if a gift is made to a registered club by an individual and the gift is a qualifying donation for the purposes of Chapter 2 of Part 8 of ITA 2007 (gift aid).
> (2) The club is treated as receiving, under deduction of income tax at the basic rate for the tax year in which the gift is made, a gift of an amount equal to the grossed up amount of the gift.
> (3) The income tax treated as deducted is treated as income tax paid by the club.
> (4) The grossed up amount of the gift is treated as an amount in respect of which the club is chargeable to corporation tax, under the charge to corporation tax on income.
> But this is subject to section 664 (exemption for interest and gift aid income).
> (5) References in this section to the grossed up amount of the gift are to the amount of the gift grossed up by reference to the basic rate for the tax year in which the gift is made.

Section 661D(1)-(4) is the CASC equivalent of s.520 ITA; see 15.49 (Position of charity). The definition in s.661D(5) is the CASC equivalent of s.415 ITA: see 15.43.1 ("Grossed up amount").

EN FB 2012 explains the background to s.661D:

> 22. HMRC allows registered CASCs to claim Gift Aid repayments on donations made to them provided that the donations are used for qualifying purposes. It is the intention that they should be able to claim Gift Aid in the same way as charitable companies. Owing to an error that occurred when legislation was re-written for Corporation Tax Act 2010,

---

32 See 41.22.1 (Gift Aid).

> CASCs are not treated in the same way as charitable companies for the purpose of the Gift Aid legislation. Schedule 15 [inserting s.661D CTA 2010] amends the legislation to allow CASCs to claim Gift Aid repayments and to put HMRC current practice on to a statutory footing.

Section 661E CTA 2010 makes similar provision for corporate Gift Aid income:

> If a registered club receives a gift of a sum of money from a company which is not a charity, the gift is treated as an amount in respect of which the registered club is chargeable to corporation tax, under the charge to corporation tax on income.

This is the CASC equivalent of s.473 CTA 2010; see 17.9 (Position of charity receiving gift from company).

Gift Aid income qualifies for exemption in s.664 CTA 2010, for which see 41.25.1 (Interest income exemption).

41.26 Exemption from tax on gain

Section 665 CTA 2010 provides:

> A registered club to which a gain accrues may make a claim for the gain not to be a chargeable gain for the purposes of TCGA 1992 if the whole of it is applied for qualifying purposes.

CASC Guidance Note Annex 1 provides:

> 6.1 Capital gains are exempt from the charge to corporation tax provided the whole of the gain is applied for qualifying purposes and the club makes a claim for exemption. The whole of the gain means the whole of the proceeds of the sale, not just the profit.[33]
> 6.2 There is nothing to prevent a club from selling all or part of its land whilst a registered CASC. It may want to do so, for example, to move to better premises. Clubs can continue to provide facilities for, and promote participation in, sport during the transitional period in which they are moving by coming to arrangements with other clubs for their members.

41.27 Anti-avoidance

Tax exemption on income/gains only apply if the CASC applies all that income/gains on qualifying purposes. This is the CASC equivalent of the

---

33 Author's note: More analytically, the gain is an unidentifiable part of the proceeds of sale, so if any part of the proceeds is not applied for qualifying purposes, it is not the case that the *whole* of the gain is applied for qualifying purposes.

application for charitable purposes rule.[34] There are four further anti-avoidance rules:

(1) Deregistration
(2) Qualifying expenditure rules
(3) Tainted donation rules[35]
(4) Charge on ceasing to be a CASC

41.28 Deregistration

Section 658(4) CTA 2010 provides:

> The officer [of HMRC] ...
> (b) may cancel the club's registration with effect from such date as the officer may specify (which may be before the date of the decision to cancel it) if no longer satisfied that the club is entitled to be registered.

For the appeal procedure, see 41.21.2 (Registration appeals).

Para 10 sch 21 FA 2013 provides:

> (1) In a case where a club that was registered as a community amateur sports club before the day on which this Act is passed ceases to be entitled to be registered as such by virtue of this Schedule, an officer of Revenue and Customs may not cancel the club's registration with effect from a date earlier than that day.
> (2) But sub-paragraph (1) does not prevent the cancellation of the club's registration if the officer is satisfied that—
> (a) any information provided by a person ("P") at the time of registration was inaccurate, and
> (b) the inaccuracy was careless (within the meaning of paragraph 3 of Schedule 24 to FA 2007) or deliberate on P's part.

The fact that cancellation is not retrospective is somewhat limited protection. We think charitable sports clubs are less likely to find the requirements for charitable status amended in such a cavalier fashion.

41.29 Qualifying expenditure rules

The rules are modelled on the charitable expenditure rules.[36]

41.29.1 *"Non-qualifying expenditure"*

The legislation uses the expression "non-qualifying expenditure". This is

34 See 4.21 (Application for charitable purposes).
35 See 7.25 (Tainted donation rules: CASCs).
36 See 6.1 (Charitable expenditure rules).

given a commonsense definition in s.661 CTA 2010:

> (4) For the purposes of this Chapter "non-qualifying purposes" means purposes which are not qualifying purposes.
> (5) For the purposes of this Chapter "non-qualifying expenditure" means expenditure which is incurred for non-qualifying purposes.

41.29.2 *Non-qualifying expenditure rule*

Section 666 CTA 2010 provides:

> (1) This section applies if—
> (a) a registered club has relevant income or relevant gains for an accounting period ("the accounting period in question"), and
> (b) the club incurs non-qualifying expenditure in that period.
> (2) For the purposes of this section—
> "relevant income", in relation to an accounting period, means income which is exempt under this Chapter for that period (ignoring the effect of the following provisions of this section),
> "relevant gains", in relation to an accounting period, means gains which are not chargeable gains under this Chapter for the purposes of TCGA 1992 for that period (ignoring the effect of the following provisions of this section), and
> "income receipts and chargeable gains", in relation to an accounting period, means the sum of
> [i] the club's income receipts for that period (whether or not chargeable to tax) and
> [ii] its chargeable gains for the purposes of TCGA 1992 for that period (ignoring the effect of section 665 [CASC CGT relief]).
> (3) If the amount of the non-qualifying expenditure in the accounting period in question is less than the amount of the income receipts and chargeable gains for that period, there is a reduction in the amount of relief given under this Chapter.
> (4) The total amount of the relevant income and relevant gains for that period exempted under this Chapter is reduced by the amount found by the appropriate fraction.
> (5) This is the appropriate fraction—
> RIRG × (NQE/IRCG)
> where—
> "RIRG" means the total amount of the relevant income and relevant gains for that period,
> "NQE" means the amount of the non-qualifying expenditure in that period, and
> "IRCG" means the income receipts and chargeable gains for that period.

(6) If the amount of the non-qualifying expenditure in the accounting period in question is at least equal to the amount of the income receipts and chargeable gains for that period, the exemptions under this Chapter—

(a) do not apply, and

(b) are treated as never having applied,

to any of the relevant income or relevant gains for that period.

(7) If the amount of the non-qualifying expenditure in the accounting period in question is greater than the amount of the income receipts and chargeable gains for that period, there is a reduction in the amount of relief given under this Chapter for previous accounting periods.

(8) The total amount of the relevant income and relevant gains for previous accounting periods exempted under this Chapter is reduced (but not below nil) by the surplus amount.

(9) The surplus amount is the amount by which the amount found by the appropriate fraction exceeds the total amount of the relevant income and relevant gains for the accounting period in question.

Section 667 CTA 2010 provides for the attribution of surplus gains and income to previous accountancy periods:

(1) This section supplements section 666.

(2) An amount exempted under this Chapter for an earlier accounting period is reduced by the surplus amount only if that earlier accounting period ends not more than 6 years before the end of the accounting period in question.

(3) If the condition in subsection (2) is met in the case of more than one earlier accounting period, amounts exempted under this Chapter for later accounting periods are reduced in priority to earlier ones.

(4) If an amount exempted under this Chapter has been reduced under section 666 in respect of non-qualifying expenditure incurred in an accounting period, it may not be reduced again under that section in respect of non-qualifying expenditure incurred in a later accounting period.

(5) Such adjustments must be made (whether by way of the making of assessments or otherwise) as may be required in consequence of section 666(7).

Thus where there is non-qualifying expenditure this can be used to reduce the relief given to the CASC in previous accountancy periods back to six previous years.

It is left to the CASC to determine which previously exempted amounts will be attributed. Section 668 CTA 2010 provides:

(1) A registered club may specify the income and gains to be reduced (in

whole or in part) as a result of section 666.

(2) A specification under subsection (1) is made by notice to an officer of Revenue and Customs.

(3) Subsection (5) applies if—

(a) an officer of Revenue and Customs requires the club to make a specification under this section, and

(b) the club has not given notice under subsection (2) of the specification before the end of the required period.

(4) The required period is 30 days beginning with the day on which the officer made the requirement.

(5) An officer of Revenue and Customs may determine the income and gains to be reduced (in whole or in part).

41.29.3 *HMRC example*

The CASC Guidance Note provides:

> *Example (W)*
> A CASC incurs non-qualifying expenditure of £5,000.
> They need to work out how much CT relief will be restricted.
> They have RIRG of £35,000 and IRCG of £60,000.
> The RIRG is made up of £30,000 trading income which is exempt from CT and £5,000 of donations made under Corporate Gift Aid.
> The IRCG is made up of £30,000 trading income, £5,000 of Gift Aid and £25,000 income from members.
> The reduction in their exemption is worked out as follows: £35,000 × (£5,000/£60,000) = £2,916.67.
> The CASC will have a CT liability and will need to complete a Self Assessment return.

THE CASC Guidance Note formerly gave the following example:

> *Example four. CASC Four is entitled, in a particular accounting period, to exemption on the following sources of income:*

bank interest	*£6,000*
income from property (gross)	*£5,000*
Gift Aid income (gross)	*£15,000*
total	*£26,000*

> *The club also has income of £5,000 membership fees.*
> *During the accounting period the club spends £7,000 on a non-qualifying purpose.*

The authors' analysis

One needs to ascertain
RIRG

NQE
IRCG

Two of these are straightforward:
NQE (the amount of the non-qualifying expenditure) = £7,000
IRCG (here the income receipts[37]) = £31,000.

RIRG (here the total amount of the relevant income[38]) is more difficult. Relevant income is income which is exempt under the CASC exemptions. (Ignoring the qualifying expenditure rules). If any of the income has been used for the non-qualifying purposes it is not exempt. HMRC's analysis assumes that the exemption would (ie all the income has been used for qualifying purposes). That is possible though somewhat far-fetched. On the given facts, one cannot work out the amount of trading income or property income, since we are given the gross receipts but not told what expenses are deductible.

Applying s.666(5) CTA 2010, the reduction in tax relief is given by the fraction RIRG × (NQE/IRCG), that is, RIRG × (7,000/31,000)

HMRC analysis

> *The calculation of the reduction of income, which is available for relief is as follows:*
> *£26,000 × (£7,000/£31,000)[39] = £5,870*
> *So instead of £26,000 being exempt only £20,130 is covered by the exemption and the amount of £5,870 is taxable. In practice HMRC will generally determine which source of income is brought back into charge to Corporation Tax. However, the club can, within thirty days of being notified of the adjustment, specify which income or gains it wants brought back into charge As CASC Four has no other taxable income, the income of £5,870 is charged at the appropriate Corporation Tax rate.*

The professional costs for the CASC (and the administration costs for HMRC) will far exceed the amount of the tax charge. But these rules are not intended to be applied: they are intended to deter.

41.30 Ceasing to be CASC

Section 669 CTA 2010 provides:

> (1) This section applies if a club holds any asset (within the meaning of

---

37 And chargeable gains, but in the example there are no gains.
38 And relevant gains, but in the example there are no gains.
39 The HMRC example erroneously reads: £26,000 - (£7,000/£31,000)

TCGA 1992) and, without disposing of it (within the meaning of that Act)—

(a) the club ceases to be a registered club, or

(b) the club ceases to hold the asset for qualifying purposes.

(2) The club is treated for the purposes of TCGA 1992 as disposing of, and immediately reacquiring, the asset at the time of the cessation for a consideration equal to its market value at that time.

(3) The exemption under section 665[40] does not apply to any gain accruing on that deemed disposal.

(4) So far as any of the asset represents (directly or indirectly) the consideration for a disposal of any other asset by the club, the exemption under that section does not apply, and is treated as never having applied, to any gain accruing on that disposal of that other asset.

(5) Such adjustments must be made (whether by way of the making of assessments or otherwise) as may be required in consequence of this section.

(6) But an assessment in respect of a chargeable gain accruing as a result of this section may not be made more than 3 years after the end of the accounting period in which the cessation in question occurred.

Thus it seems that there will in principle be a charge on ceasing to be a CASC. That is the equivalent of the rule for charities. However, where a CASC ceases to be registered as a CASC, it will in principle become a charity and so be eligible for the charity relief from tax on chargeable gains under s.256(1) TCGA.[41]

41.31 Inflated member-related expenditure

Section 202B CTA 2010 provides a restriction on corporate Gift Aid relief. Section 202B(1) CTA 2010 provides:

Subsection (2) applies if—

(a) one or more qualifying payments are made by a company to a registered club ("the club") in an accounting period ("the current period"),

(b) the company is wholly owned,[42] or controlled, by the club or by a number of charities which include the club, for all or part of that period, and

---

40 See 41.26 (Exemption from tax on gains).

41 See 5.1 (Taxation of charity capital gains).

42 Section 202B(8) CTA 2010 Section 809ZJ(9) ITA provides a referential definition of wholly-owned: "Section 200 (company wholly owned by a charity) applies for the purposes of this section." See 9.4.1 (Meaning of "wholly-owned").

(c) inflated member-related expenditure is incurred by the company in that period.

If these conditions are met, section 202B(2) CTA 2010 imposes the restriction on relief:

> For the purposes of section 189 (relief for qualifying charitable donations), the total amount of those qualifying payments[43] is treated as reduced (but not below nil) by the total amount of that inflated member-related expenditure.

41.31.1 *Surplus expenditure carry-back*

Section 202B CTA 2010 provides for a carry-back of surplus inflated member-related expenditure to earlier periods:

> (3) Subsection (4) applies if—
> (a) the total amount of that expenditure exceeds the total amount of those payments, and
> (b) the company made one or more qualifying payments to the club in an earlier accounting period ending not more than 6 years before the end of the current period.
> (4) For the purposes of section 189, the total amount of the qualifying payments made in the earlier accounting period is treated as reduced (but not below nil) by the amount of the excess.
> (5) If subsection (3)(b) applies in relation to more than one earlier accounting period—
> (a) subsection (4) applies to treat amounts paid in later accounting periods as reduced in priority to amounts paid in earlier ones (until the excess is exhausted or all amounts have been reduced to nil), and
> (b) in applying subsection (4) in relation to an accounting period, the reference to the excess is to be read as a reference to so much of it as exceeds the total amount of qualifying payments which, under that subsection, have previously been reduced to nil by the excess.

The carry-back does not go before 2014. Section 35 FA 2014 (which introduced s.202B CTA 2010) provides:

---

43 The expression is defined in s.202B(6) CTA 2010: "For the purposes of subsections (3) and (4), a reference to the total amount of qualifying payments made in an earlier accounting period is to the total amount of those payments after—
(a) any reduction under subsection (2), and
(b) any previous reduction under subsection (4)."

> (13) The amendments made by this section have effect in relation to payments made on or after 1 April 2014.
> (14) But the amendments made by subsections (1) to (7) are to be ignored for the purposes of section 199 of CTA 2010 (payment attributed to earlier accounting period) if the claim mentioned in subsection (1)(c) of that section is in respect of an accounting period ending before 1 April 2014.
> (15) The earlier accounting periods mentioned in section 202B(3) of CTA 2010 (see subsection (7) of this section) do not include any accounting period ending before 1 April 2014.

As the limit on carry-back is 6 years, this will cease to be relevant in 2020. There is no carry forward rule.

Section 202B(7) CTA 2010 deals with assessment:

> Such adjustments must be made (whether by way of the making of assessments or otherwise) as may be required in consequence of subsections (4) to (6).

Section 202B defines "control":

> (9) For the purposes of this section, the club controls the company if it has the power to secure—
> (a) by means of the holding of shares or the possession of voting power in relation to the company or any other company, or
> (b) as a result of any powers conferred by the articles of association or other document regulating the company or any other company,
>
> that the affairs of the company are conducted in accordance with the club's wishes.
> (10) For the purposes of this section two or more charities (including the club) control the company if, acting together, they have the power to secure, as mentioned in paragraph (a) or (b) of subsection (9), that the affairs of the company are conducted in accordance with the wishes of those charities.
> (11) In this section—
> "charity" has the same meaning as in Chapter 2,
> "qualifying payment" means a qualifying payment for the purposes of Chapter 2, and
> "registered club" has the same meaning as in Chapter 2,
> and any reference to a member of the club includes a reference to a person connected with a member of the club.

41.31.2 *Inflated member-related expenditure*

Section 202C CTA 2010 provides:

> (1) This section applies for the purposes of section 202B.
> (2) "Inflated member-related expenditure" means—
> (a) employment expenditure incurred in respect of the employment of a member of the club, by the company, where that employment is otherwise than on an arm's length basis, or
> (b) expenditure incurred on a supply of goods and services to the club by—
> (i) a member of the club, or
> (ii) a member-controlled body,
>
> otherwise than on an arm's length basis.
> (3) But if the features of an employment or supply which cause it to be otherwise than on an arm's length basis, when taken together, are more advantageous to the company than if the employment or supply had been on an arm's length basis, any expenditure incurred in respect of the employment or on the supply is not inflated member-related expenditure.

The drafter did not have complete confidence in the definition, and conferred a power to amend it by regulations.[44] We doubt if the power will ever be used.

EN FB 2014 provides an example:

> **Example 2**
> 33. A contract agreed between a CASC controlled company and a CASC member provides for two supplies for a total figure of £100,000. An arm's length transaction would have cost £25,000 for each supply. It is impossible to know how the £100,000 is allocated to each supply in this case, therefore the whole of the £100,000 will be treated as Inflated Member Related Expenditure.

---

44 Section 202C CTA 2010 provides:

"(7) For the purposes of subsection (2)(a), the Treasury may by regulations specify—
(a) descriptions of expenditure which is to be treated as employment expenditure incurred in respect of the employment of a member of a club;
(b) descriptions of expenditure which is not to be so treated.
(8) Section 1171(4) (orders and regulations subject to negative resolution procedure) does not apply to any regulations made under subsection (7) if a draft of the statutory instrument containing them has been laid before, and approved by a resolution of, the House of Commons."

41.31.3 *"Member-controlled"*

Section 202C CTA 2010 provides:

> (4) A company is "member-controlled" if a member of the club has (or two or more members acting together have) the power to secure—
> (a) by means of the holding of shares or the possession of voting power in relation to that or any other body corporate, or
> (b) as a result of any powers conferred by the articles of association or other document regulating that or any other body corporate,
> that the affairs of the company are conducted in accordance with the wishes of the member (or, as the case may be, members).
> (5) A partnership is "member-controlled" if a member of the club has (or two or more members acting together have) the right to a share of more than half the assets, or of more than half the income, of the partnership.
> (6) In this section any reference to a member of the club includes a reference to a person connected with a member of the club.

41.31.4 *Critique*

The detailed guidance note provides an example which is presumably the case that HMRC wish to catch:

> **Chapter 3.17: Inflated member-related expenditure by companies that are wholly owned by a CASC**
> ...*Example*
> A company, owned and controlled by a CASC buys supplies from one CASC member and rents property from another. Both of the payments are more than what would be expected under an arm's length arrangement. As a result [two] CASC members benefit financially to the detriment of the company and its parent sports club.
> In the Accounting Period Ending (APE) 31 January 2016, the subsidiary company incurred total costs of £37,500 and £12,500 for the supply of sporting equipment and rent, respectively.
> In respect of the same APE the subsidiary made a qualifying gift of its entire net profit of £75,000 to the CASC.
> Because neither of the arrangements was at arm's length the value of the qualifying gift would be reduced by £50,000 (37,500 + £12,500).
> Accordingly, the subsidiary would become liable to pay corporation tax on the profit of £50,000, rather than nil, despite the company donating its entire net profit to the CASC.[45]

In the example, there seems to be a straightforward fraud on the company,

45 The example is from EN FB 2014.

and the CASC its shareholder. Leaving aside the criminal aspects, the excessive payments should not be deductible in computing the profits of the company. If we ignore that, the payments are taxable income of the two CASC members. Why is the inflated member-related expenditure rule needed here?

In practice we expect the rule will never be invoked.

41.32 VAT position of CASC

Sports clubs qualify for two exemptions: sport and fundraising: see 37.9 (Sports); 37.14 (Fundraising events).

As a CASC is not a charity it will not be entitled to VAT reliefs outside of the above exemption that are available to charities.

Most CASCs will fall below the VAT registration threshold and the lack of these exemptions will not worry them. Where CASCs come above the registration threshold this may disadvantage the CASC (although, of course, making taxable supplies would enable the CASC to recover related input tax). Where a CASC comes above the VAT registration threshold, consideration should be given to converting to charity status, not least because such a CASC is likely to have income exceeding the limited CASC exemptions; see 41.24.1 (Trading income exemption) and 41.24.3 (Property income exemption).

41.33 Planning: CASC or charity

41.33.1 *CASC v charitable status*

The main advantage of CASC status is that it not subject to the jurisdiction of the Charity Commission because it is not a charity.[46]

On the other hand:

(1) The tax reliefs available to CASCs are more limited than those available to charities:
   (a) Larger CASCs may have turnover in excess of the permitted limit.
   (b) Some charity reliefs are not available: SDLT relief, Payroll Giving.

(2) The statutory conditions for tax relief are more onerous. They operate

---

46 The same applies to CASCs in Northern Ireland: s.5(3) Charities Act (Northern Ireland) 2008.
In Scotland, however, there is no equivalent rule so Scots CASCs are generally charities for the purposes of Scottish charity law and should strictly register with OSCR. It appears however that in practice Scots CASCs do not generally register with OSCR.

on an all or nothing basis, eg any facilities other than listed (and list is vague) will be a problem. They depend significantly on HMRC's reasonable administration. Record keeping may be onerous.
(3) Fundraising from charitable trusts may be more difficult.
(4) VAT exemptions that apply only to charities do not apply.

41.33.2 *Planning for new sports clubs*

New organisations should reject the offer of CASC status and register as charities unless they are sure that:
(1) they will never need more than the limited CASC reliefs and
(2) they will always qualify so clearly for CASC status that detailed record keeping will not be needed.

Even smaller organisations are probably better off as charities.

In March 2022 there were 7365 CASCs (up from 6715 in April 2015).[47] Despite the gap between the tax benefits of a charity and a CASC, the CASC regime still appears to be popular. It is possible that the popularity of the CASC regime is because of the potentially lesser administrative burden of being a CASC (not required to register with the Charity Commission and submit annual returns) but we think the likely reason is a lack of awareness of charitable status alternative.

41.33.3 *Planning for existing CASC*

The best option for an existing CASC which has or is likely to exceed the tax reliefs available to it is to
(1) set up a new organisation that is registered as a charity
(2) transfer all its assets to that charity.

It is then able to deregister as a CASC.

41.33.4 *Change of status*

The CASC Guidance Note provides:

> 1.1.4 Once registered as a CASC, a club can't apply to be recognised as a charity. To convert a registered CASC to a charity involves closing down (winding up) the CASC and transferring over the assets and activities to a new charity.
> 1.1.5 If your club is already a charity then CASC status is unlikely to be

47 https://www.gov.uk/government/publications/community-amateur-sports-clubs-casc-registered-with-hmrc--2

of any additional benefit. You may still apply for CASC status, but if your club meets the requirements of the scheme and HMRC registers the club as a CASC, then it would no longer be entitled to be a charity.

41.34 Abolish CASCs: Critique

The CASC regime was based on a mistaken view that sports clubs could not be charities. The current two-tier system is complex, confusing and unnecessary. The rule that CASCs are not charities should be repealed,[48] existing CASCs should (if they choose) be registered as charities and Chapter 9 Part 13 CTA 2010 should be repealed.[49]

That has many advantages. Firstly, it would be a worthwhile simplification. Secondly, it would make CASCs subject to the jurisdiction of the Charity Commission (or Northern Ireland equivalent).[50] At present, the only supervision of a CASC is by HMRC (and only so far as concerns tax).

This change could benefit CASCs since charity tax reliefs are better than CASC tax reliefs but since larger and properly advised CASCs will register as charities anyway, it should have no cost implications.

41.35 Incorporation of CASC

CASC Guidance Note Annex 2 provides:

> 1.1 Many Community Amateur Sports Clubs (CASCs) are unincorporated associations. In small clubs this is often the easiest way to set up a club, but as a club grows you may decide to incorporate in order to limit the liability of the club's members and to enable the club to enter contracts in its own name. Some national governing bodies of sport encourage incorporation. The new company is a separate entity for legal and tax purposes and must reapply for CASC status.
>
> ...

---

48 Devolution makes this more difficult. Amendments are required to the Charities Act (Northern Ireland) 2008 as well as the English Charities Act 2011. But an interim solution allowing some in UK tax and English charity law could take place pending reform in Northern Ireland. No amendment would be needed to the Charities & Trustee Investment (Scotland) Act 2005 because (accidentally? deliberately?) there is no rule that CASCs are not charities in Scotland.

49 In the Parliamentary debate on the Charities Act 2006, Lord Hodgson asked why the CASC regime was being maintained, but did not receive a coherent answer.

50 Although in theory Scots CASCs should register as Scots charities, in practice this is not often done so the effect of the change would be to bring Scots CASCs under the regulation of the OSCR.

4. **CASC status is not transferrable**

4.1 If your club is already registered as a CASC and your members decide they want to incorporate, HM Revenue and Customs (HMRC) can't simply transfer the unincorporated club's CASC status to the new company.

4.2 Once the new company is established you'll need to submit a new application using a CASC application form. HMRC can't then register the new club until the assets and activities have been transferred across.

4.3 There have been some recent changes to the conditions for CASC status and it's important that you read about these changes before deciding whether to incorporate.

4.4 This is important because a registered CASC is not allowed to transfer its assets to a company that is not a registered charity or CASC. If a CASC does transfer its assets to a company that is then refused CASC status, there'll potentially be a capital gains tax charge on the unincorporated club which is based on the value of the chargeable assets that have been transferred.

5. **Checking that the new company is eligible for CASC status**

5.1 If you'd like HMRC to check whether the new company is suitable for CASC status before you make the transfer you should submit a CASC application for the new company with a covering note which:

- explains that your club intends to incorporate
- gives details of the existing unincorporated CASC and provide the last set of financial accounts
- provide a copy of the proposed governing documents (memorandum and articles of association) for the new company

5.2 HMRC will review this application and let you know whether the new company will meet the conditions of the scheme. If the new company meets the conditions of the scheme HMRC will then put the application on hold until the assets and activities are transferred across to the new company.

5.3 Once you've transferred the assets and activities across to the new club you should write to HMRC providing:

- 3 months bank statements in the new company's name
- details of the date the assets and activities were transferred across to the new company

5.4 If the new company doesn't meet the conditions for the scheme then HMRC cannot register the new company as a CASC.

6. **Once you've transferred the assets and activities to the new company**

6.1 You should tell HMRC when the assets and activities of the unincorporated club have been transferred to the new company. HMRC will then deregister the unincorporated association from the scheme and

> register the new company if it is satisfied that it qualifies as a CASC.
> 6.2 If you've not already done so you need to send in a CASC application form for the new company. You'll also need to provide evidence that the assets and activities of the unincorporated club are now part of this new company. When you submit an application for the new company you'll need to provide:
> - 3 months bank statements in the new company's name
> - the last set of financial accounts for the old unincorporated association and the CASC reference for this former unincorporated association
> - an opening statement of affairs of the new company detailing the assets and liabilities
> - the governing document (memorandum and articles of association) for the new company
> - a completed CASC application form
> - the minutes of the meeting where the members voted on decision to incorporate.
>
> 6.3 When the assets of an unincorporated club are transferred to a new company that will carry on the sporting activities of the original club then Capital Gains Tax will not be due. When the transfer of assets from a club to a company meets the conditions within sections 136 and 139 TCGA 1992 then no gain or loss will accrue and the new company will acquire the assets at the historic base cost on the date the assets are transferred.

It would usually make much more sense to incorporate as a charity, not as a CASC.

41.36 Relief for gifts to sports clubs

Finance (no.2) Act 2017 introduced a new Part 6A CTA 2010: Relief for expenditure on grassroots sport. The Explanatory Notes to the Finance Bill March 2017 provides:

> 27. This measure extends the circumstances in which contributions to grassroots sports can be deducted from the taxable profits of corporation tax payers. Companies will be able to make deductions for all contributions to grassroots sports through "qualifying sport bodies" (recognised sport governing bodies, and any body wholly owned by a recognised sport governing body), and deductions of up to £2,500 in total annually for direct contributions to grassroots sports. Qualifying sport bodies will be able to make deductions for all their contributions to grassroots sports, subject to specified conditions.
> 28. This measure will make it easier for corporation tax payers to receive

a deduction for contributions to grassroots sports, thereby encouraging sports participation at a local level, and reducing administrative burdens for some organisations which currently make contributions to grassroots sports.

29. This measure will not affect existing routes for tax-deductible expenditure to support grassroots sports. Currently, deductions can be made as sponsorship or as charitable donations (including payments to Community Amateur Sports Clubs). A deduction cannot be claimed under these new rules where it could be claimed under any existing rules.

41.36.1 *The relief*

Section 217A CTA 2010 provides:

> (1) A payment made by a company which is qualifying expenditure on grassroots sport (and which is not refunded) is allowed as a deduction in accordance with this section from the company's total profits in calculating the corporation tax chargeable for the accounting period in which the payment is made.
> (2) The deduction is from the company's total profits for the accounting period after any other relief from corporation tax other than—
> (a) relief under Part 6,
> (b) group relief, and
> (c) group relief for carried-forward losses.
> (3) If the company is a qualifying sport body at the time of the payment, a deduction is allowed for the amount of the payment.
> See section 217C for the meaning of "qualifying sport body".

41.36.2 *Amount of deduction*

Section 217A CTA 2010 provides:

> (4) If the company is not a qualifying sport body at the time of the payment, a deduction is allowed—
> (a) if the payment is to a qualifying sport body, for the amount of the payment, and
> (b) if the payment does not fall within paragraph (a) (a "direct payment"), in accordance with subsections (7) and (8).
> (5) If at any time on or after 1 April 2017 the company receives income for use for charitable purposes which are purposes for facilitating participation in amateur eligible sport, a deduction is allowed only if, and in so far as, the payment exceeds an amount which is equal to the amount of that income which—
> (a) the company does not have to bring into account for corporation

tax purposes, and

(b) has not previously been taken into account under this subsection to disallow a deduction under this Part of all or any part of a payment.

See section 217B(3) for the meaning of terms used in this subsection.

(6) But in any case, the amount of the deduction is limited to the amount that reduces the company's taxable total profits for the accounting period to nil.

(7) If the total of all the direct payments made by the company in the accounting period is equal to or less than the maximum deduction for direct payments, a deduction is allowed under subsection (4)(b) in respect of that total.

(8) If the total of all the direct payments made by the company in the accounting period is more than the maximum deduction for direct payments, a deduction is allowed under subsection (4)(b) in respect of so much of that total as does not exceed the maximum deduction for direct payments.

(9) The maximum deduction for direct payments is £2,500 or, if the accounting period is shorter than 12 months, a proportionately reduced amount.

41.36.3 *"Qualifying expenditure"*

Section 217B CTA 2010 provides:

(1) For the purposes of this Part, a payment is qualifying expenditure on grassroots sport if—

(a) it is expenditure incurred for charitable purposes which are purposes for facilitating participation in amateur eligible sport, and

(b) apart from this Part, no deduction from total profits, or in calculating any component of total profits, would be allowed in respect of the payment.

For the meaning of charitable purposes, see sections 2, 7 and 8 of the Charities Act 2011.

(2) Where expenditure is incurred for both—

(a) charitable purposes which are purposes for facilitating participation in amateur eligible sport, and

(b) other purposes,

then, for the purposes of subsection (1), it is to be apportioned between the purposes in paragraph (a) and the purposes in paragraph (b) on a just and reasonable basis.

(3) For the purposes of section 217A(5) and subsection (1)(a)—

(a) paying a person to play or take part in a sport does not facilitate participation in amateur sport, but paying coaches or officials for their services may do so, and

(b) "eligible sport" means a sport that for the time being is an eligible sport for the purposes of Chapter 9 of Part 13 (see section 661).

41.36.4 *"Qualifying sport body"*

Section 217C CTA 2010 provides:

(1) For the purposes of this Part, a "qualifying sport body" is—

(a) a recognised sport governing body;

(b) a body which is wholly owned by a recognised sport governing body.

(2) A "recognised sport governing body" is a body which is included from time to time in a list, maintained by the National Sports Councils, of governing bodies of sport recognised by them.

(5) In this section "the National Sports Councils" means—

(a) the United Kingdom Sports Council,

(b) the English Sports Council,

(c) the Scottish Sports Council,

(d) the Sports Council for Wales, and

(e) the Sports Council for Northern Ireland.

41.36.5 *Relationship with co Gift Aid*

Section 217D CTA 2010 provides:

If, but for section 217A, an amount—

(a) would be deductible under Part 6 [corporate gift aid], or

(b) would be deductible under Part 6 but for Chapter 2A of Part 6,

the amount is not deductible under this Part [part 6A, grassroots sport], and nothing in this Part affects the amount's deductibility (or non-deductibility) under Part 6."

41.36.6 *Commencement*

Section 22 of F(No2)A 2017 provides:

(6) The amendments made by this section have effect for the purpose of allowing deductions for payments made on or after 1 April 2017.

(7) Where a company has an accounting period beginning before 1 April 2017 and ending on or after that date, the accounting period for the purposes of the new section 217A(9) is so much of the accounting period as falls on or after 1 April 2017.

CHAPTER FORTY TWO

CLUBS AND MUTUAL CONCERNS

42.1 Mutual concerns: Introduction

This chapter considers:

- **Clubs**, here meaning social & recreational clubs, other than CASCs
- **Mutual concerns** used in commerce
- **Co-operative societies**[1]

These bodies may take the legal form of an unincorporated association, or a company or other body corporate. They will therefore be a company for tax purposes,[2] and subject to CT on their profits.

There are no statutory definitions of mutual concern, or mutual trade, although the terms are occasionally used in tax legislation.[3] The concepts derive entirely from case law.

42.1.1 *Taxable/mutual trade/non-trade*

A body may carry on 3 types of activity:
(1) an activity which is not a trade (**"a non-trade"**)
(2) a trade, which may be:
  (a) a **mutual trade**
  (b) a non-mutual trade, which one may call a **"taxable trade"**

---

1 The full name is "Co-operative & mutual society". Statute uses the term"registered society", and the term formerly used was "industrial and provident society".

2 See 3.25.1 (Charitable company).

3 s.101 CTA 2009, see 42.21 (Distribution on winding up); s.1070 CTA 2010, see 42.20.2(Dividend from mutual).

A body which carries on, or may carry on, a mutual trade is called a **"mutual concern"**, abbreviated to **"mutual"**.

A mutual may carry on more than one of the above activities.

A taxable trade is said to yield a trading **"profit"**, whereas a non-trade or mutual trade may be said to have a mere **"surplus"**. The terminology conveniently indicates that the latter is not taxable. But for accountancy/ non-tax purposes, these terms are, we think, synonymous.

Similarly, a trade is said to yield a trading **"loss"** whereas a non-trade or mutual trade may be said to have a mere **"deficit"**.

An alternative analysis is to say that a mutual trade is not a "trade" at all, in the strict or statutory sense; that is another route to the same destination: non-taxability.

42.1.2 *Mutual trade: Definitions*

"Mutual trade" should be regarded as a technical term.

Rowlatt J gave this explanation in *Municipal Mutual Insurance Ltd v Hills*:

> Now I do not think that one can make cases on this point turn upon an analysis of, the word "mutual" a word that is very much abused as I pointed out, in the argument, in certain very well known instances. Of course the word "mutual" is used in insurance language to describe a certain class of company, and so on. But ... the point is ... whether there is any profit; that is to say, whether you get more than this, that *a certain class of people are associating together to put up money to achieve an object for each other, and divide what is not wanted among themselves in that character, namely, in the character of the persons who put it up*. That is what I understand is at the bottom of it. If you like to call that "mutuality", well, it is a convenient word.[4]

Similarly, Lord Macmillan:

> The cardinal requirement is that all the contributors to the common fund must be entitled to participate in the surplus and that all the participators in the surplus must be contributors to the common fund; in other words, there must be complete identity between the contributors and the participators.[5]

---

4 16 TC 430 at p.437, emphasis added. For discussion of the *Municipal Mutual Insurance* case, see 42.4.1 (Contributors/participators identical).

5 16 TC 430 at p.448.

HMRC identify four requisites of mutual trade:

(1) Source and application of the surplus:
  (a) Identity of contributors/participators
  (b) Surplus returned to contributors
  (c) Return proportionate to contribution

(2) Membership control of the mutual

> **BIM24020 Characteristics Of A Mutual Trade** [Jan 2019]
> For a trade to be a mutual trade there must be:
> [1] complete identity, as a class, between the contributors to the mutual surplus and the participators in it (see BIM24105)[6]; and
> [2] arrangements which ensure that the surplus ultimately finds its way back to the contributors and no arrangements for it to go to anybody else (see BIM24110)[7]; and
> [3] a reasonable relationship between the amount a person contributes to the surplus and the amount distributed to them on winding up (see BIM24115)[8]; and
> [4] arrangements that entitle the contributors to the common fund to control it (see BIM24120)[9].

There is evidently some overlap between these conditions.

42.1.3 *Non-trade v mutual trade*

BIM24025 gives an anodyne example of a mutual concern carrying on a non-trade, a social group's kitty:

> **BIM24025 Origins Of The Concept** [Jan 2019]
> ... An example is a group who, for a social occasion, establishes a 'kitty'. Each member contributes a sum to the kitty. After the event any surplus is returned to the contributors; perhaps in accordance with their contribution and/or the extent to which they have derived benefit from the communal purse. The reason why the surplus is not taxable is not because of mutual trading but because it does not arise from trading at all.

We would have said there were two reasons why the group was not taxable on its profit:

(1) the activity is not (or at least does not appear to be) a trade and

---

6 See 42.4.1 (Contributors/participators identical).

7 See 42.4.2 (No surplus to non-contributors).

8 See 42.4.3 (Return proportionate to contribution).

9 See 42.5 (Membership control).

(2) if it were a trade, it would be a mutual trade.[10]

HMRC say it is important to distinguish a non-trade and a mutual trade. A pragmatic reader may wonder just how important that is. In either case the profit/surplus is not taxable. But it helps analytically to make the distinction; it is good to know what one is talking about. And if an activity is a non-trade, there is no need to consider whether the requirements of mutual trading are satisfied. A charity or CASC, for instance, may conduct a non-trade, though they are not mutual concerns, and often do.

42.1.4 *Taxable trade v mutual trade*

BIM24100 describes the essential requirements of a mutual trade in the following terms:

> **BIM24100 Essential Requirements: Contents** [Jan 2019]
> If an entity has customers, who are not entitled to receive back surplus amounts they have contributed, the entity's transactions with them cannot amount to mutual trading. Tax has to be paid on the surplus arising from those transactions in the usual way. If the amount of trade, which is not mutual, is very small it will not affect the tax treatment of the mutual trading with members. If the amount of any non-mutual trade is substantial it may result in the entity's trade being considered wholly within the charge on trade profits. Where the sums are significant, refer any cases of difficulty to Business Profits.

42.1.5 *Rationale: trading with oneself*

The intuition underlying the mutual trading rule is that a person cannot trade with himself. The principle seems clear. Likewise a person cannot pay interest or rent to herself. Or if one prefers to call the sum interest/rent/profit, it is not taxable.

However this principle is carried much further than one might expect: it applies not only to one person trading with himself, but also to a group trading with themselves; and continues to apply if the group is incorporated into a company, trading with its members; this seems to be an implied exception to the principle of separate legal personality.

There are, perhaps, unarticulated policy reasons operating here. Mutual social clubs (and other mutual concerns) should not pay tax; but mutual

---

10 This assumes that the social group is sufficiently organised that it is an unincorporated association, and so a company for tax purposes, and a mutual concern.

concerns also need to incorporate.

BIM24155 Non-Mutual Insurance Trading Activities: Corporation Water Works [Jan 2019]

One of the earliest judgements that people cannot make a profit by trading with themselves was made by the Lord President in *Harris v Corporation of Burgh of Irvine* [1900] 4 TC 221.

The Corporation owned a water works that supplied its own town and also two neighbouring towns, Stevenston and Saltcoats. All recipients were charged a water rate and the Revenue sought to tax the surplus.

The Court of Session held that the surplus from Stevenston and Saltcoats was assessable but not that from the people of Irvine. The people were the Corporation and it was their water works. So they were supplying water to themselves. The Lord President compared the situation to that of a person laying on a water supply for their own house and allowing for it in their household accounts, 4 TC at page 233:

> 'The provider of the supply and the consumer of the water are one and the same individual, and I have never yet heard that a man can make a profit by taking money out of one pocket and putting it into another.'

The concept that there must be two parties to a trading transaction was heard again in the *Styles v New York Life Insurance Company* [1889] 2 TC 460 (see BIM24035[11]) and *CIR v The Cornish Mutual Assurance Co Ltd* [1926] 12 TC 841 (see BIM24040) cases.

BIM24210 Distinction Between Proprietary And Members Clubs [Jan 2019]

...Lord President Clyde, in *CIR v Stonehaven Recreation Ground Trustees* [1929] 15 TC 419, restated the principle, at pages 426 and 427:

> An ordinary social or playing club to which its members subscribe - and some of whose advantages may perhaps only be enjoyed by members in respect of further payments - presents another instance of a mutual association, whose privileges are confined to the members, and which does not therefore carry on a trade. Any balance to the good on its accounts is really in no different position from a balance shown on the accounts of a housekeeper for a private householder who may happen to have supplied the housekeeper with more cash than the expenses of the year turn out to require.

42.2 History of mutual trading

The topic has a long history. It was discussed as early as the Report of the Departmental Committee on Income Tax (1905)[12] and again in section XII Royal Commission on Income Tax (1920).

---

11 See 42.2.3 (Mutual trade: Early cases).

12 Section VIII (Co-operative Societies) and see the Inland Revenue Memorandum submitted to the committee for "a very clear statement of the actual situation as regards IT".

42.2.1 *Early history*

HMRC's Business Income Manual notes a lack of cohesion in the early cases, as well as the two main 'strands' of case law which ultimately developed:

> **BIM24025 Origins Of The Concept** [Jan 2019]
> ... In the earliest cases the doctrine that has become mutual trading was not fully established. The concept developed through a series of cases. The case law can be confusing and some of the decisions are difficult to reconcile with others. In later cases judges 'clarified' remarks made by their predecessors. Blinkered application of quotations from particular judgments can lead to the incorrect conclusion. The body of case law should be seen in the context of a process leading (not always sure-footedly) to the current state of affairs.
> **BIM24100 Essential Requirements: Contents** [Jan 2019]
> The cases of *Styles v New York Life Insurance Company* [1889] 2 TC 460 and *CIR v The Cornish Mutual Assurance Co Ltd* [1926] 12 TC 841, referred to at BIM24040, belong to the strand of 'mutual' case law involving mutual insurance (the other major strand being social and recreational clubs - see BIM24200 onwards). It was in a series of early insurance cases that the basic principles of mutual trading were developed. But mutual trading is not restricted to the mutual insurance business. The mutual trading principle is concerned with the financial framework for carrying on an activity. This is what counts rather than the subject matter of the activity.

42.2.2 *Attempt to tax mutuals*

Section 31(1) FA 1933 provided:

> *In the application to any company or society of any provision or rule relating to profits or gains chargeable under Case I. of Schedule D (which relates to trades) ...*
> *[a] any reference to profits or gains shall be deemed to include a reference to a profit or surplus arising from transactions of the company or society with its members which would be included in profits or gains for the purposes of that provision ... if those transactions were transactions with non-members,*
> *[b] and the profit or surplus aforesaid shall be determined for the purposes of that provision ... on the same principles as those on which profits or gains arising from transactions with non-members would be so determined...*

BIM24027 Early Attempt At Taxing Surplus [Jan 2019]

...There was a legislative attempt to abolish mutual trading for tax purposes and for corporate taxpayers. S31 Finance Act 1933 (FA 1933) sought to impose a charge to tax on the profits of corporate mutual concerns. The legislation sought to charge surpluses arising from transactions with members as if the transactions were with non-members. *Ayrshire Employers Mutual Insurance Association Ltd v CIR* [1946] 27 TC 331 established that the legislation was defective. It is possible to carry on business with non-members on mutual terms so the distinction in the legislation between members and non-members was irrelevant. Please also see BIM24605.

Although the legislation in question is no more, the case retains its importance. The decision shows that it is not the fact of membership or non-membership that determines immunity from or liability to tax. It is the nature of the transactions themselves. If the transactions are in the nature of mutual trading (be it mutual insurance or some other trading activity) the resulting surplus is not taxable. The transactions can only amount to mutual trading if the contributors are entitled to a return of their share of the surplus contributions (see BIM24110).[13]

The Association was a company limited by guarantee whose members were all colliery owners. The company insured its members against employers' liabilities in case of injury. The company did no business with non-members. Each year, each member was entitled to a bonus of 50% of the excess of their contributions over expenditure. The bonus was credited to a reserve. In a winding up, any surplus of assets was to be distributed among members in proportion to their contributions.

The company was clearly carrying on a mutual trade and the Revenue invoked S31 FA 1933 in an attempt to tax the surplus. The courts found the provision to be ineffective. S31 assumed that surpluses on transactions between a body corporate and its members was not taxable. So S31 required that the surplus be treated as arising from transactions with non-members - the assumption being that such would give rise to taxable profits. The courts did not support this assumption.

In the Court of Session the Lord President, Normand, observed, at page 343 of 27 TC, that on the facts it mattered not that the transactions were with members or with non-members and so the legislation did not impose a charge:

> 'Section 31(1) of the Finance Act, 1933, shortly read, makes surpluses arising from the transactions of an incorporated company or society with its members taxable as if those transactions were transactions with non-members. But if the transactions in this case had been with non-members, the result would have been precisely the same as regards profits. Instead of members sharing losses, non-members would have been sharing losses, and no profit could have resulted. … the Sub-section does not seem to warrant a construction which involves a hypothetical modification of the actual transactions as well as the hypothetical substitution of non members for members as the parties to those transactions.
>
> My conclusion is, therefore, that since those transactions could beget no profit, whether the parties to them were members of the Company or not, there is no hypothetical profit within the meaning of the Sub-section. My opinion is thus in agreement with the opinion delivered by Lord Fleming. But I have thought it right, at the risk of some repetition,

13 See 42.4.2 (No surplus to non-contributors).

to say so much, because I feel great difficulty in stating more positively the intention of the Sub-section, and in defining its ambit. It is not wholly satisfactory to me to say that this Company and others like it lie outside the ambit, while confessing my uncertainty about what companies or societies fall within it. For, take any kind of association of persons whose transactions inter se were outside the scope of Income Tax till 1933, because in the nature of things they could yield no taxable profit, how could a hypothetical profit spring into being from the mere supposition that the same transactions took place between non-members instead of between members of the association? Yet it appears to me that the underlying assumption of the enactment is that somehow the substitution of non-members for members would have just that miraculous result. I seem in the end to be driven to that last refuge of judicial hesitation when confronted with a difficulty of interpretation, the doctrine that no tax can be imposed on the subject without words in an Act of Parliament clearly showing an intention to lay a burden on him. It might be some consolation to reflect that that is a doctrine which might be allowed special force against the Crown's contention that the Act entitled it to treat as profits sums which in reality are not profits at all and which a modification of the Company's book-keeping for future years would entirely eliminate, were it not that, in Income Tax questions, complete equity is mere error unless it is based on a sound construction, however difficult to arrive at, of the statutory provisions.'

The House of Lords agreed that the legislation did not achieve its intended object.

The reader may find the reasoning unconvincing: non-members do not control the organisation, so it cannot be conducting a mutual trade with them.[14] But there it is.

Accepting the technical argument, as under the doctrine of precedent one must, this notorious case was still wrongly decided by subsequent standards of statutory interpretation, not applying a contemporary purposive interpretation, but well before that style of interpretation came to its current height:

> I venture respectfully to suggest that if, as in this case, the courts can identify the target of Parliamentary legislation their proper function is to see that it is hit: not merely to record that it has been missed.[15]

But in the different atmosphere of 1946, Parliament accepted its defeat and did not try again. Section 31 was eventually repealed. The episode is now of historical interest only,[16] though the case is sometimes said to illustrate an important principle, the reader may doubt both the principle

---

14 See 42.5 (Membership control).

15 Diplock, "The Courts as Legislators" (1965) *https://www.kessler.co.uk/wp-content/uploads/2012/05/CourtsAsLegistlators.pdf*

16 However, in *Cooper v Billingham* 74 TC 139 at [35] the Court of Appeal was prepared to say that the same result could happen today (albeit rarely)

and its importance.

42.2.3 *Mutual trade: Early cases*

HMRC's Business Income Manual provides:

BIM24030 Founding Principles [Jan 2019]
The origins of the concept
The basis of mutual trading is the general proposition that no one can trade with themselves or make a profit out of themselves.
One of the earliest references to this concept emerges in *Dublin Corporation v M'Adam* [1887] 2 TC 387. The Corporation was empowered to supply water beyond the city boundaries. The income from this activity was paid into a consolidated fund available for all the Corporation's purposes. The issue was whether the profit from supplying water to others was chargeable to Tax. Palles CB decided it was, saying at page 397 of 2 TC:

> '...what we have to consider, in my opinion, is whether, in relation to the extra-municipal districts, the Corporation of the City of Dublin are carrying on a trade, adventure, or concern in the nature of a trade; for if they are, I am clear that whatever surplus may remain of the receipts incident to that concern over the expenses of that concern is a profit within the meaning of the Act. On the other hand, I think it is perfectly clear that, in order to bring this case within the operation of the Income Tax Act, it is necessary that there shall be this trading in its strict true sense. There must be, at least, two parties - one supplying water, and the other to whom it should be supplied and who should pay for it. If these two parties are identical, in my opinion there can be no trading. No man, in my opinion, can trade with himself; he cannot, in my opinion, make, in what is its true sense or meaning, taxable profit by dealing with himself...'

You should note that the Judge first looked to see if the Corporation was carrying on a trade. Having found that the Corporation was trading, the second question was whether that trade was with itself or included trading with others. On the facts, the Corporation was trading with others and such trading was not mutual trading. This case is an early example of the view that trade involves what may be called a 'customer supplier' relationship (see BIM24045[17] for a description of what is required for activities to amount to a trade). If the customer and the supplier are the same person then any resulting 'profits' are not taxable as trading income.
BIM24035 Two Early Mutual Insurance Cases [Jan 2019]
Lord Radcliffe, referring to [*Last v London Assurance*], said in *Sharkey v Wernher* [1955] 36 TC 275 at page 302:

> 'Later decisions have shown that this simple proposition may cover what are to be regarded as two separate questions, whether a man can trade or deal with himself and whether a man can make taxable profit by so doing.'

These two questions can be restated as providing for the following approach to questions of mutual trading.

1. Whether activities amount to a trade is essentially a question of fact (see BIM24045[18]). That the dealings are limited to one person or to members only does

---

17 See 42.3 (Is there a trade).
18 See 42.3 (Is there a trade).

not preclude trading.

2. Whether a trade is a mutual trade requires that all of the conditions in BIM24020 are satisfied.[19]

42.2.4 *Is there a trade: Early cases*

The Business Income Manual provides:

BIM24030 Founding Principles [Jan 2019]

... A leading early case on mutuality, *Styles v New York Life Insurance Company* [1889] 2 TC 460 seemed to have answered the first of Lord Radcliffe's questions in the negative. New York Life had no shares or shareholders and carried on the business of mutual insurers. The company had a branch in London and had no members other than the holders of participating policies, to whom all the assets of the company belonged. Each policyholder was a member of the company, and was entitled to a share of the assets of the company and liable to all losses and expenses incurred by the company. The majority of any annual surplus of premiums over expenditure was returned to members; either as an increase in the sums for which they were insured or as a reduction in their premiums. Nothing was paid out in cash. Any balance of surplus was carried forward. It seemed that the courts took the view that the company was not trading - the House of Lords taking the view that mutual insurance was not a trade at all. Lord Bramwell said that there could not be a trading profit where there was only one party to a transaction and because of the identity between the company and its members, there was effectively only one party here. *New York Life* distinguished its position from that in the case of *London Assurance Corporation* (see above) citing the following differences.

- London Assurance received premiums in pursuance of and derived profits from contracts between itself and their policyholders who were not members of London Assurance.
- In contrast, the premiums paid to New York Life were contributed by members of the company.
- The quantum of each member's contribution to New York Life was an estimated amount required to cover the risks for the year and the necessary expenses.
- Any surplus or balance remaining over and above the sum that may actually be required for such purposes is not profit or gain liable to assessment, but it is in fact an excess of contribution over expenditure.

The General Commissioners found that:

- No part of the premium income of the company received under participating policies was liable to be assessed.
- The company was, however, liable to be assessed in respect of profits made on annuities granted.
- The company was also liable to be assessed on profits made from premiums paid under non-participating policies.
- The company was liable to be assessed on all income derived by or from investment of all premiums or other money paid to them in the UK and invested in the UK or abroad, and as to the latter when such income is received in the UK.

---

19 See 42.1.1 (Taxable/mutual trade/non-trade).

- The company was liable to be assessed on all profits (if any) derived in any mode other than by the annual premium contributions of the participating policyholders.

The High Court and the Court of Appeal, following the decision in *Last v The London Assurance Corporation*, held that the New York Life was assessable. In the lower courts the Judges seem to have attached importance to the fact that the society was incorporated, and was an entity distinct from the members composing it.

The House of Lords distinguished between policyholders who were members of the company (participating policyholders) and those who were not (non-participating). Lord Watson explained the difference at pages 469-470:

> 'The Appellant Company, so far as regards its membership, is constituted upon the principles of mutual assurance. The Company issues life policies of two kinds, participating and non-participating; but the relations existing between the Corporation and the two classes of insured differ materially. There are no shares and no shareholders in the ordinary sense of the term; but each and every holder of a participating policy becomes, ipso facto, a partner of the Company with a voice in its administration, entitled to a share of its assets and liable for all losses and expenses incurred by it. On the other hand, the holder of a non-participating policy is not a partner of the Company; he is a creditor merely without any interest in its assets and without any liability for its debts.'

The profits on dealings with non-participating members were assessable and this was not disputed in the courts.

Lord Watson went on to find that the mutual insurance activities of the Company did not amount to a trade. At page 471 he said:

> 'When a number of individuals agree to contribute funds for a common purpose, such as the payment of annuities, or of capital sums, to some or all of them, on the occurrence of events certain or uncertain, and stipulate that their contributions, so far as not required for that purpose, shall be repaid to them, I cannot conceive why they should be regarded as traders, or why contributions returned to them should be regarded as profits. That consideration appears to me to dispose of the present case. In my opinion, a member of the Appellant Company when he pays a premium makes a rateable contribution to a common fund, in which he and his co-partners are jointly interested, and which is divisible among them at the times and under the conditions specified in their policies. He pays according to an estimate of the amount which will be required for the common benefit; if his contribution proves to be insufficient he must make good the deficiency; if it exceeds what is ultimately found to be requisite, the excess is returned to him. For these reasons I have come to the conclusion that the transactions of the Appellant Company in so far as these relate to the participating policies, do not constitute the carrying on of a trade within the meaning of the Income Tax Acts, and that the surplus funds returned or credited to its members are not profits.'

BIM24040 Further Early Mutual Insurance Cases [Jan 2019]

The House of Lords approach in New York clarified

In *CIR v The Cornish Mutual Assurance Co Ltd* [1926] 12 TC 841 the company was incorporated under the Companies Acts as a company limited by guarantee (and so had no share capital). The company carried on a mutual fire insurance business. The persons insured and the members of the company being one and the same body of persons. The House of Lords decided unanimously that Cornish Mutual was trading and was liable to the then form of Corporation Profits Tax. At the time the legislation included a provision to the effect that profits shall include in the case of mutual trading concerns the surplus arising from transactions with members.

Whilst the actual result in Cornish Mutual depended on particular legislation which was repealed long ago, the significance is that thereafter (despite what the House of Lords seemed to say in *Styles v New York Life Insurance Company* [1889] 2 TC 460 - see BIM24035[20]) it could no longer be argued that a mutual insurance company did not carry on a trade or business merely because it was mutual. The view taken from Cornish Mutual onwards is that a mutual insurer (and indeed any mutual trader) does carry on a trade but does so on mutual terms - they are mutual traders. There are instances (for example, some five years later, the Lord President in the *CIR v The Stonehaven Recreation Ground Trustees* [1929] 15 TC 419 case - see BIM24210) where judges occasionally took an approach that is hard to reconcile with the current view, but never where it mattered.

In *Cornish Mutual*, at page 867 of 12 TC, Viscount Cave explained what he thought the House of Lords had in mind in their decision in *New York* - see BIM24035[21].

> 'I cannot help thinking that that very learned Lord [Lord Watson] directed his observations only to the real question before the House, namely whether there were taxable profits within the Income Tax Acts; and I cannot believe that he intended to decide that a company of this kind, simply because it was a mutual company, did not carry on any business at all.'

Therefore, as the term implies, and subsequent case law confirms, a prerequisite for mutual trading is that a trade is actually being carried on. Because mutual trading is a trading concept, you should not accept that it has any wider application, for example to income taxable as part of a property business or to savings and investment income. *Salisbury House Estate Ltd v Fry* [1930] 15 TC 266 confirms that the different heads of income in the Tax Acts are mutually exclusive so that any exemption from tax as trading income is not automatically extended to any other head of income...

42.3 Is there a trade

The Business Income Manual provides:

BIM24045 Essential That The Activity Is A Trade [Jan 2019]

What is a trade?

... The subjective test, of whether there was the intention to make a profit, has played a central role in the development of case law ...

The so-called 'badges of trade' (see BIM20200 onwards) can also be helpful indicators in some cases.

Mutual associations are established for a variety of reasons. Many mutual associations have no overt profit-seeking motive or may be required to apply their profits to particular ends. Such a state of affairs does not prevent them from carrying on a trade.

The absence of a profit-seeking motive does not preclude the carrying on of a trade - see

---

20 See 42.2.3 (Mutual trade: Early cases).

21 See 42.2.3 (Mutual trade: Early cases).

for example *Brighton College v Marriott* [1925] 10 TC 213. Brighton College was a company, limited by guarantee. The company was formed to carry on a public school. Under its Memorandum of Association the whole of the company's income and property was applied solely towards the promotion of the objects of the college, including the remuneration of its officers and other persons for services rendered.

The fees charged for attendance at the school exceeded the current expenses. The surpluses were mainly applied in paying interest on, and in reducing, mortgage debts incurred in connection with extensions and improvements of the college.

The Court of Appeal decided that the surplus fees were profits or gains arising from the carrying on of a trade assessable to Income Tax as trade profits notwithstanding that:

- the surplus was applied in a particular way, or
- the college's professed intention was not to make a profit.

The Master of the Rolls, Pollock, explained that what the college did with its surplus did not have a bearing on the taxability of that surplus:

> '...it is clear that under Income Tax law the fact that profits when made are to be devoted solely to the advancement of the charity will not induce an exemption. Profits when made are subject to the tax, and their destination does not secure immunity for them.'

Pollock M.R. goes on at page 221 to quote with approval Cotton L.J. in *Hermann Gusav Erichsen v W H Last* [1881] 4 TC 422, at page 427:

> '...when a person habitually does a thing which is capable of producing a profit for the purpose of producing a profit and enters into a contract habitually, he is carrying on a trade or business...'

The House of Lords unanimously agreed that the college was trading. Lord Blanesburgh made the following points:

- The college did not lose its charitable status by charging fees.
- The charging of fees did not of itself make the college's activities into a trade.
- Whether activities amount to a trade is always a question of fact.
- What the college did with any surplus was irrelevant.
- The important issue was whether the activities were conducted on a commercial basis.

That an entity professes to conduct its affairs on a 'not for profit' basis does not preclude a finding of trading. In *CIR v The Hyndland Investment Co Ltd* [1929] 14 TC 694 at page 699 the judge tells us:

> '...the question is not what business does the taxpayer profess to carry on, but what business does he actually carry on.'

In *Royal Agricultural Society of England v Wilson* [1924] 9 TC 62 at page 67 the judge tells us:

> 'If you do the operations of trading and make a profit, it seems to me that you are carrying on a trade, which in that case becomes taxable, and you are carrying on a trade whether you make a profit or not, and whether you want to make a profit or not, because it is not a mere question of motive.'

42.4 Application of surplus

42.4.1 *Contributors/participators identical*

The Business Income Manual provides:

BIM24025 Origins Of The Concept [Jan 2019]
... The case of *Municipal Mutual Insurance Ltd v Hills* [1932] 16 TC 430 concerned a company limited by guarantee that was set up to enable local authorities to insure against fire and other risks, mainly employers' liability. Over the years the company extended coverage to all forms of insurance except marine and life. By 1922 half of the business was fire insurance and half 'other'. Separate funds were maintained for fire and 'other' business. The company claimed not to distinguish between members of the company and policyholders. But the surpluses on both fire and 'other' business were applied as a reduction of the fire premiums. No such reduction was made in respect of 'other' premiums. The Revenue conceded that the surplus from fire business arose from mutual trading. The company conceded that profits from business done with persons who were neither members of the company nor holders of fire policies were taxable. The point at issue was the taxability of the profits arising from the employers' liability business....
[The Manual set out the two classic definitions of mutual trade[22] and continued] Rowlatt J went on to explain that as there was no return of surpluses to the contributors in their capacity as contributors, there was no mutual trading. Viscount Dunedin in the House of Lords said that the matter depended on to whom the profits went:

- if they go to the insurer (trader), there is a profit; but
- if they go to the insured (contributor), there is not (and it does not matter whether they go in cash, or as an increase in the sum assured or as a reduction of premiums).

... There was no contributor/participator identity in *Municipal Mutual Insurance Ltd* so the surpluses on the 'other' business were taxable.

BIM24105 Contributors To And Participators In A Surplus Must Be Identical [Jan 2019]
An essential requirement is that there is complete identity, as a class, between the contributors to a mutual surplus and the participators therein. [The Manual refers to Lord Macmillan's definition of mutual trade[23] and continues:]

The requirement does not prevent members from coming and going
This does not mean that the individual contributors must always remain participators in a surplus, or that new contributors may not join the group. Upjohn J. commenting on the statement of Lord Macmillan, in the case of *Faulconbridge v National Employers' Mutual General Insurance Association Ltd* [1952] 33 TC 103, made this point when he said, at page 125:

> '...I think it is clear that when Lord Macmillan speaks of the cardinal requirement being complete identity between the contributors and the participators, he is not referring to individual identity but to identity as a class, so that at any given moment of time the persons who are contributing must be identical with the persons who are entitled to participate; whereas it follows, in my judgement, that it matters not that the class has been diminished by persons going out of the scheme or that others may come in in their place in the future.'

The following points emerge from *Faulconbridge*:

- It is not necessary for surpluses to have been applied as reductions in premiums or as bonuses provided that it is intended that they will be so applied one day.

---

22 See 42.1.2 (Mutual trade: Definitions).
23 See 42.1.2 (Mutual trade: Definitions).

> '…the time has not yet arrived when any part of the surplus can be safely returned to the members…'

- A changing and fluctuating individual membership does not matter provided that identity as a class is preserved.
- Being a member of the company per se is not essential provided that the contributors (or the contributors as a class) get their surplus contributions back.

The last point is important. An attempt was made in S31 Finance Act 1933 to bring surpluses from mutual trading by a body corporate into the charge to tax. The section proceeded on the basis that it was membership or non-membership that determined if the activities were a mutual trade. The House of Lords showed in the *Ayrshire Employers Mutual Insurance Association Ltd v CIR* [1946] 27 TC 331 case (see BIM24027)[24] that this was an incorrect view. What matters are the terms on which the transactions are undertaken.

From a practical point of view you may limit consideration to those who have been contributors at any time in the previous five years - see BIM24115.[25]

In *Medical Defence Union Ltd v IRC* [2021] BTC 544, the Upper Tribunal (UT) held that retrospective reductions in insurance premiums paid by a mutual fund were tax-free by virtue of the mutuality principle. The UT regarded it as significant that one of the reductions took effect by way of a payment into the fund from the insurer. Nevertheless, it held that, in context, the payment 'represented' a contribution to the surplus of the fund by the members of the company maintaining it. It made no difference that the members held individual policies with the insurer (rather than the company holding a group policy, for example). Nor did it matter that the membership subscriptions from which the insurance premiums were ultimately paid were collected by a third party acting as agent of both the insurer and the company.

42.4.2 *No surplus to non-contributor*

The Business Income Manual provides:

> **BIM24110 Surplus Must Go Back To Contributors And To No One Else** [Jan 2019]
>
> Arrangements must be in place to ensure that any surplus ultimately finds its way back to the contributors, with no arrangements for it to go to anybody else. Viscount Cave in *Jones v The South-West Lancashire Coal Owners' Association* Ltd [1927] 11 TC 790, said at page 838:
>
> > 'Sooner or later, in meal or in malt, the whole of the association's receipts must go back to the policy-holders as a class, though not precisely in the proportions in which they have contributed to them…'
>
> The company was limited by guarantee. Its only activity was the mutual insurance of colliery owners against liability in respect of accidents to employees.
>
> Viscount Cave's comments concerning the proportions of returned contributions have been clarified in later cases where the courts have indicated that the

24 See 42.2.2 (Attempt to tax mutuals).

25 See 42.4.3 (Return proportionate to contribution).

amounts returned to a contributor should bear a reasonable relationship to the contributions made by that contributor.

This does not mean that the surpluses in the years prior to winding up have to be returned to contributors, either in the form of reduced contributions in the future or as a return of those contributions, merely that the intention is that any surplus will eventually be returned to the contributors. Upjohn J. in the *Faulconbridge v National Employers' Mutual General Insurance Association Ltd* [1952] 33 TC 103 case, rejected the proposition that a requirement of mutuality was that a contributor must be entitled to share in the annual surpluses prior to winding up, when he said, at page 125:

> 'The authorities show that the only essential conditions are that any surplus must ultimately come back to the contributors in meal or in malt on a winding-up or otherwise.'

An entity that includes in its rules/constitution/articles a requirement that in the event of a winding up any surplus is to go to an entity with similar aims or to a charity cannot be carrying on a mutual trade. The surplus at a winding up must go back to the contributors and to no one else. It does not matter that in practice the surplus only goes back to contributors, there must be no possibility of it going to non-contributors.

The requirement that the surplus must go back to the contributors does not preclude a mutual trader from, for example, making a donation out of its surplus to (say) a charity. But to retain mutual trading status such a donation would have to be approved by the contributors. The contributors in effect collectively agreeing to give away some of their own money.

42.4.3 *Return proportionate to contribution*

The Business Income Manual provides:

BIM24115 Return Of Surplus Contributions [Jan 2019]

Need for a reasonable relationship between the contribution and the distributable surplus

Despite Viscount Cave's comments in *Jones v The South-West Lancashire Coal Owners' Association Ltd* [1927] 11 TC 790 (see BIM24110[26]) that the return of a surplus need not be in proportion to the contributions, the weight of judicial authority shows that there must be a reasonable relationship between the amount a person contributes and the amount distributable to them.

There is no requirement that the surplus or part thereof must go back to the contributors as and when the surplus arises. The requirement is that on a winding up the surplus goes back to the contributors. Lord Wilberforce made this point in the case of *Fletcher v ITC* [1972] AC 414 (see BIM24235)[27] when he said:

> 'It may not be an essential condition of mutuality that contributions to the fund and rights in it should be equal; but if mutuality is to have any meaning there must be a reasonable relationship, contemplated or in result, between

---

26 See 42.4.2 (No surplus to non-contributors).

27 See 42.8.3 (Voting rights).

what a member contributes and what, with due allowance for interim benefits of enjoyment, he may expect or be entitled to draw from the funds: between his liabilities and his rights.'

There is no need to work out the exact amount due to all contributors, both current and past. You may accept that an entity satisfies this condition if the return of contributions only takes into account current contributors and those who ceased to be contributors within the last five years.

The proportion returned to each contributor (current and past) must bear a reasonable relationship to the contributor's (or former contributor's) contribution to the surplus. But where the trader offers a variety of goods or services to contributors with different profit margins, a return that simply reflects the amount spent by each contributor may not reflect their contribution to the surplus. A contributor who purchased fewer services but at a higher margin may make an equal or greater contribution than a contributor who made greater volume of purchases at a lower margin. Each case will therefore need to be approached from the viewpoint of the facts that relate to the nature of the transactions that the entity conducts with its own members.

42.4.4 *Capacity of contributor*

The Business Income Manual provides:

BIM24035 Two Early Mutual Insurance Cases [Jan 2019]

The case of *Last v London Assurance Corporation* [1884] 2 TC 100 concerned a proprietary office carrying on an insurance business. The Corporation and its shareholders formed a body quite distinct in personality and in interest from those insured. A member of the Corporation might effect an insurance with it, but that circumstance could neither enlarge or diminish their rights as a partner. The Corporation was not carrying on a mutual trade.

The Corporation, as a branch of its business, dealt in what were called 'participating' policies. These were issued to all persons, whether members or not, who had insurable lives, and were willing to pay premiums on a higher scale than those charged for ordinary or non-participating policies. In consideration of these increased payments the Corporation undertook to return to the holders of participating policies by way of bonus or abatement of premium, two-thirds of any surplus funds applicable to such policies, which were to be ascertained and allotted every five years. The one-third retained by the Corporation admittedly represented business profits; and it was not in dispute that the remaining two-thirds would also have been profits of the Corporation except for its agreement to return that amount to the insured. The point at issue before the courts was whether the two-thirds of surplus payable to the participating policyholders fell to be deducted from receipts in ascertaining the Corporation's trading profits. By a majority of two to one the House of Lords decided that the two thirds of profits paid to participating policyholders was in reality a share of profits. Their Lordships reaffirmed the position that the destination of profits once earned has no bearing on the computation of those profits for tax purposes, Lord Fitzgerald saying at page 129 of 2 TC:

> 'The premiums payable by the participating policy holders come into the coffers of the Company quarterly, half-yearly, or annually in ordinary course, and form part of the annual income of the concern. When received those moneys are probably invested, the profit of the investment also forming a part of the income, and I cannot see that they the less form part of its annual income because that at a subsequent period of time a part of the gross profits (if any) realised may be allotted to certain of the policy holders. It seems to me, on the contrary, to be annual "income" after deducting the proper expenses of earning it, and subject to income tax notwithstanding its subsequent special destination. The prospect of a future participation in profits is held out as an inducement to customers to insure in the participating series, and probably has proved to be successful, but it seems to me, my Lords, to be a very forced interpretation of the contract and position of the parties to put it down as part of the expenses of making the income.'

This may be categorised as a "capacity of contributor" case.

BIM24160 Non-Mutual Insurance Trading Activities: Corn Trading Association [Jan 2019]
In the case of *The Liverpool Corn Trade Association Ltd v Monks* [1926] 10 TC 442 the Revenue successfully argued that the annual surplus was taxable.
The Association was a company limited by shares, its function was to:
- promote or oppose legislation affecting the corn trade,
- provide and maintain a market, and
- establish a clearinghouse for debts.

Members paid an entrance fee and an annual subscription. The articles provided that all the income was the property of the Association and allowed the directors to dispose of it as they thought fit. There was a power for the directors to pay a dividend.
Rowlatt J. observed that there had been no shareholders in the *Styles v New York Life Insurance Company* [1889] 2 TC 460 case (see BIM24035[28]) where policyholders were members of the company and got back what was not wanted. In that event it was possible to ignore the fact of incorporation. But in the Association's case where there was a share capital and a chance of a dividend, the fact of incorporation could not be ignored (see BIM24405). Rowlatt J. indicates that for mutual trading to be present any surplus must be distributed to contributors:
- as of right, and
- as contributors and not as shareholders.

You should be aware that nowadays such an association would most

---

28 See 42.2.3 (Mutual trade: Early cases).

likely be considered to be a trade protection association (see BIM24800).[29]

42.5 Membership control

The Business Income Manual provides:

> **BIM24120 Members Must Control The Common Fund** [Jan 2019]
> In the case of unincorporated associations ownership of the common fund by the contributors is necessary for mutual trading and in the case of corporate bodies, the contributors must control the common fund.
> This point was referred to in *Revesby Credit Union v The Commissioner of Taxation for the Commonwealth of Australia* (112 CLR 564), where McTiernan J. said at page 574:
>
> > 'Where a number of people contribute to a fund created and controlled by them for a common purpose, any surplus paid to the contributors after the use of the fund for a common purpose is not income but is to be regarded as a mere repayment of the contributor's own money. Incorporation of the fund is not relevant. What is required is that the fund must have been created for the common purpose and owned or controlled wholly by the contributors. If it is owned or controlled by anyone else the principle cannot apply.'
>
> See also BIM24225[30] for discussion of the decision in the *Westbourne Supporters of Glentoran v Brennan* (SPC22) case as to what amounts to control.
> The requirement that the contributors control the common fund does not mean that each contributor has to take part in the day to day management of the entity in question.

42.6 Clubs: Outline

42.6.1 *Members club: definition*

HMRC's Business Income Manual defines a members' club in the following terms:

> **BIM24210 Distinction Between Proprietary And Members Clubs** [Jan 2019]
> ... A members club is one where ownership of the club and its assets rests with the general membership who control the club and its dealings.

---

29 See 42.27 (Trade protection association).

30 See 42.8.2 (Temporary members).

> Such control may be exercised through an elected committee...

42.6.2 *Members club: Non-trading*

The Manual goes on to explain that the reason such clubs are not taxed on any surplus arising from any dealing with its own members can be attributed to the absence of 'commerciality':

> **BIM24205 Members' Clubs: Introduction** [Jan 2019]
> A club, established by its members for their own social or recreational objects, is unlikely to be liable to tax on any surplus which arises from transactions with its full members. This is because the surplus from such transactions does not arise from the carrying on of a trade. The club, in its dealings with its members, lacks the necessary element of commerciality.[31]

Whether a club is acting commercially when dealing with its members is a question of fact, but it seems right to say that this is not usually the case.[32] Indeed if it were, a club in the form of an unincorporated association would actually be a partnership (carrying on business in common with a view of profit); and no-one suggests that. But there may also be an unarticulated element of policy in the approach to the facts: HMRC do not wish to tax these clubs.

> If the subscriptions exceed the expenditure in any year, the surplus is just that, a surplus and not a trading profit. Because they are not trading the question of mutual trading does not arise, even in connection with such matters as meals and bar sales. The members are not buying and selling food and alcohol; they own it jointly and are consuming their own property.

The last sentence might surprise a member reaching for their wallet. But there it is.

42.6.3 *Members club: Trading*

The Manual continues:

> However, where the club provides services, on a commercial basis, to outsiders (such as visitors or temporary members) then any surplus made from such transactions is liable to tax as trading income. The issue then is how to allocate the clubs income and expenses between the trade

---

31 See 42.3 (Is there a trade).
32 See 8.2.3 (Uncommercial activity not trading).

carried on with non-members and the provision of non-taxable services to members. Similarly, where the club provides food or drink to non-members for a charge that too may amount to a trade and that is not a mutual trade.

Other income (for example savings and investment income) and gains of members clubs are chargeable to tax in the normal way. Also, if the members club pays interest on loans from brewery companies, or other suppliers, it may need to account for [withholding tax]. You should bear these points in mind when considering the liability of members clubs.

42.6.4 *Proprietary club*

The Business Income Manual provides:

BIM24210 Distinction Between Proprietary And Members Clubs [Jan 2019]

Does the club carry on a trade with its members?

Where the club is a proprietary club, that is the ownership of the club rests other than with the general membership, the profit earned from providing goods or services to its members is not exempt from tax under the rule mentioned in the first paragraph of BIM24205.

Whether a proprietary club is carrying on a commercial activity is strictly a question of fact, but it seems right to say that this is usually the case. Proprietary clubs are not discussed further in this chapter. They are taxed like any other trader.

42.7 Members Club

42.7.1 *Incorporated club*

The Business Income Manual provides:

BIM24210 Distinction Between Proprietary And Members Clubs [Jan 2019]

Does the club carry on a trade with its members?

The case of *CIR v The Eccentric Club Ltd* [1925] 12 TC 669 extended the doctrine that there is no trading in a social context to the activities of a body corporate incorporated for the purpose of operating a members club. The club was a company limited by guarantee. The club was formed to provide a social club and refreshment for payment for members. The club was purely a members club and the members of the club and the members of the company were identical. No non-members were admitted.

Warrington LJ said that the company did not carry on a business with a view to profit as an ordinary commercial concern. In substance the company was an ordinary members club not a proprietary club. Warrington LJ highlighted the distinction between a proprietary club and a members club when he said, at page

696 of 12 TC:

> The club proprietor, whether an individual or a company, carries on a business with a view to profit as an ordinary commercial concern the Company in the present case is a convenient instrument or medium for enabling the members to conduct a social club the objects of which are immune from every taint of commerciality. What is in fact being carried on, putting technicalities aside, is a members club and not a proprietary club,

Warrington LJ draws a clear distinction between a members club and a proprietary club. The Judges comments are simply an extension of the kitty example in BIM24020.[33]

Sargent LJ took the same line. In substance this was an ordinary members club, which existed solely for the supply to their own corporation of the ordinary amenities of a social club. This distinguished the club from a trading concern. Sargent LJ goes on to note, following the *Styles v New York Life Insurance Company* [1889] 2 TC 460 case (see BIM24035[34]), that there was a complete identity between the providers and the receivers of the social amenities. That is to say a complete identity between the members of the company and the members of the club. So, because there was effectively only one party to the transactions, the process of providing social amenities could not be trading. The club was not outside the charge on trade profits because of mutual trading; it was outside the charge because it was not trading at all.

The reader may think this is an eccentric decision, but the law is settled.

42.7.2 *Co-operative society club*

The Business Income Manual provides:

> **BIM24245 Members' Clubs: Incorporated As Industrial And Provident Societies** [Jan 2019]
> If a social or recreational club is incorporated under the Industrial and Provident Societies Acts,[35] the members of the club are required to be the clubs shareholders. No member is allowed to hold a large amount of share capital. A club incorporated under these Acts (for example, a workingmens club) is regarded as a members club for tax purposes.

42.7.3 *Membership activity indivisible*

BIM24210 provides as follows:

> **You cannot isolate particular facilities of a members club**
> In the case of *The National Association of Local Government Officers v Watkins* [1934] 18 TC 499, the trade union bought a holiday camp to be used by

33 See 42.1.1 (Taxable/mutual trade/non-trade).
34 See 42.2.3 (Mutual trade: Early cases).
35 See 42.29 (Industrial & Provident Society).

members and their families. For the 1931 summer only, bookings were accepted from families who had visited it before the union acquired it and who had already booked to return. Union members and their families accounted for about two thirds of the Camp occupancy and non-members one third. The unions rules required that any profits be applied for the benefit of all members, not just those who used the camp. The Revenue argued that all of the profits were taxable; the union, that only the portion derived from non-members was taxable.

Finlay J. accepted the unions contentions. The Judge said that it was of crucial importance that the union was an unincorporated association, which put it in the position of a club. In turn, this meant that there could be no transaction of purchase and sale among the members. Accordingly the surplus from members was not a trading profit. The surplus from non-members was however a trading profit.

The really important point is that the transactions with members were social or recreational in nature so that there was no trading with members. The nature of the body is of secondary importance. The decision would be the same in a case where a body corporate takes the place of the union. You should not place any great reliance on those passages in Finlay's judgement that imply that the decision turned on the status of the association. They should not be quoted or relied upon out of context.

The case also demonstrates that it is not possible to isolate particular activities or facilities that a members club offers to its members, for example a bar, and argue that that element constitutes a trade. Finlay J. made this point, at page 506 of 18 TC:

> I cannot think that you can, in the case of a club, isolate the dining room, the library, or the other various facilities which are offered by the club. The truth of the matter is, I think, that the members own the whole.

42.7.4 *Services to non-member: trading*

The Manual continues:

Members club making its facilities available to non-members

This does not, of course, prevent members clubs from carrying on a taxable trade when they provide facilities to non-members on a commercial basis. This was the case in *The Carlisle and Silloth Golf Club v Smith* [1913] 6 TC 48 & 198. Indeed, the quote of Lord President Clyde in the *CIR v The Stonehaven Recreation Ground Trustees* [1929] 15 TC 419 case, referred to above, actually continued at page 427:

> If, on the other hand, a club admits outsiders to its privileges or some of them for payment, it may lose its character as a mutual association either altogether or at least as regards its receipts from outsiders.

You should note that the Judge also envisages that the admission of non-members to a members club may so change the character of the entity that it altogether loses any mutual element. Such cases are likely to be the exception. The issue being essentially a question of fact.

42.8 Who are the members?

42.8.1 *Junior members*

The Business Income Manual provides:

BIM24220 Members' Clubs: Classes Of Club Membership [Jan 2019]
The rules of a members club may provide for restricted categories of membership. For example, junior members may have rights falling short of the rights of full members to hold office or vote at meetings. If the restricted members subscriptions:

- are fixed at a lower rate than the subscriptions of full members, and
- are not intended to subsidise full members,

you may accept that they are not trading income.
Normally no liability arises where a member pays for their personal guests, even though these may be described as visitors fees. A personal guest would be one where the member bore the costs of the guest visiting the club. A guest who had to pay their own way should be treated as any other visitor - the income arising should be brought into account in computing the clubs trade profit.
Many clubs allow visitors or temporary members to use their facilities on payment of a commercial fee. You should treat such receipts as taxable trading receipts of the club - see BIM24225 to BIM24240[36]. This applies both to individuals who simply arrive at a club to use its facilities on a casual basis and to groups who may book such use in advance.
The description of such visitors as temporary members of the club (for example, temporary membership to a golf club may form part of a holiday package) does not prevent receipts from being taxable. Similar receipts from associate members for their use of the clubs facilities is also trading income unless it can be shown that their rights are equivalent to those of full members. (These rights (might) include the right to vote at meetings, participate in club activities and generally to exercise control over the running of the club).
The expenses incurred in earning the fee income are deductible in computing assessable profits. The deduction extends to the appropriate proportion of the clubs overhead expenses. For example, in the case of golf clubs, a reasonable proportion of the course overheads may be deducted.
You should also quantify other incidental trading receipts, such as non-member catering income, in worthwhile cases.

42.8.2 *Temporary members*

The Business Income Manual provides:

BIM24225 Members Clubs: Temporary Membership [Jan 2019]
Often visitors to members clubs are described as, or become, temporary

---

36 See 42.8.2 (Temporary members).

members. However, this does not alter the commercial nature of their transactions with the club, unless their rights as temporary members are similar to those of full members. The relevant rights to consider might, for example, include:

- being able to participate fully in the clubs activities
- vote at meetings and generally exercise control over the running of the club, and
- share in any distributions on a winding up.

Similarly, receipts from associate members for the use of the clubs facilities will also be trading income, unless they can also show that their rights are equivalent to full members.

The position of associate members was considered by the Special Commissioners (the predecessors to the Tribunal) in the case of *Westbourne Supporters of Glentoran v Brennan* (SPC22). The case involved an unincorporated club, which had two classes of member, ordinary, and associate, both of which paid the same entrance fees and membership subscription. However, only the ordinary members had voting rights.

In finding that the clubs activities with its associate members did not give rise to a taxable profit, the Special Commissioner found that the associate members, who significantly numbered about 70% of all members, exercised informal control over the management of the club. Further, their entitlement to participate in any surplus on dissolution was protected by general law relating to unincorporated associations and clubs. The distinction between the ordinary and associate members originated in the Registration of Clubs Act (Northern Ireland), whose prime object was to ensure the proper conduct of clubs supplying alcoholic beverages. Since associate members rights were basically the same as ordinary members, the economic substance of their transactions with the club were also the same. It was accepted that ordinary members transactions with the club did not constitute trading and it therefore followed that associate members transactions were also not on a commercial basis.

Apart from the fact that this decision is not a legally binding precedent, it should prove possible to distinguish the case on the basis of its particular facts. The decision is of relevance only to unincorporated associations. Incorporated concerns are legal persons separate from their members and different considerations apply - see BIM24240 onwards.

For the text of an article originally published in TB12 discussing this issue see BIM24230.

[The Manual then cites Tax Bulletin 12, not set out here as it adds nothing to what is set out elsewhere]

42.8.3 *Voting rights*

The Manual provides:

BIM24235 Members Clubs: Voting Rights [Jan 2019]

Voting rights not conclusive of mutual trading

The Privy Council case of *Fletcher v ITC* (1972 AC 414) provides a

> useful contrast to the *Westbourne Supporters of Glentoran v Brennan* (SPC22) decision (see BIM24225[37]). In the Fletcher case a members club made its facilities available, on a commercial basis, to the guests of local hotels. It subsequently admitted the hotels as members, with voting rights. The Privy Council found that the profits derived from the provision of services to hotel guests and were taxable as trade profits:
>
> The hotels may have become members in 1963; but side by side with their membership there continued the pre-existing relationship with the ordinary members which was essentially a trading relationship, similar to that with outside visitors. What is, and always has been, of significance is not the fact of membership or non-membership but the nature of the transactions: if these were trading transactions, the addition of membership makes no difference.
>
> The fact that the hotels only had one vote and were an insignificant proportion of the total membership, which meant that their rights to participate in any surplus bore no relationship to their contributions, were clearly factors taken into account as pointing to the continued commercial nature of the transactions.
>
> Privy Council decisions are of persuasive authority only in the UK; this means that courts and tribunals should treat them with respect but are not bound in law to follow them.

See too Harris, "Mutuality and Temporary Membership" [1998] BTR 24.

42.9 Incorporated club

42.9.1 *Company with share capital*

The Business Income Manual provides:

> **BIM24255 Members' Clubs: Incorporated As Limited Company: Not Paying Dividends** [Jan 2019]
>
> A social or recreational club may be conducted through the vehicle of a company. Provided that all of the following conditions are met, you should treat such companies as members clubs (rather than as proprietary clubs) in agreeing trading profits:
>
> - the company does not pay dividends to shareholders, and
> - any share capital is all of one class, and every member (other than a person with restricted membership - BIM24220) is a shareholder, and
> - the intention is that the members and shareholders shall be an identical body, and

37 See 42.8.2 (Temporary members).

- substantial identity actually exists between members and shareholders.

You should ignore the death, resignation or removal of former members in considering whether substantial identity exists. You should consider any inequality of shareholdings in doubtful cases but, in general, such may be ignored as long as dividends are not paid.

42.9.2 *Guarantee co*

The Business Income Manual provides:

> **BIM24405 Incorporation: Difficulties Associated With Having Shareholders** [Jan 2019]
> A number of the early cases on mutuality involved companies limited by guarantee. Being limited by guarantee, the companies had no share capital. The insertion of a company between the contributors and their activities presented no difficulties to the courts when considering the question of mutuality. This is because the contributors were normally identical to the members and got back what was not wanted. The courts felt able to look through the fact of incorporation.

42.9.3 *Company with share capital*

The Manual continues:

> However, as the case of *The Liverpool Corn Trade Association Ltd v Monks* [1926] 10 TC 442 - see BIM24160 made clear, where a company has share capital and the shareholders a chance of a dividend, one cannot ignore the fact of incorporation. As Rowlatt J. said, at page 453:
>
> > When you have got a case where there is not any share capital then it does not matter if there is an incorporation, because the corporation is merely an entity which stands at the back, and all it is doing is to collect from a certain body of people certain funds and hand them back to them as far as they are not wanted. In a case like that it does not matter whether there is an incorporation or not, because there is nothing belonging to the corporation which is severable from what belongs to the aggregation of the individuals - nothing.
> > But in a case where there is share capital, with a chance of dividends, a chance of a right to dividends if declared, upon the share capital, and to one side of that a dealing with people who happen to be the owners of the share capital there is no reason at all for saying that you are to neglect the incorporation, or that you can regard otherwise than as profits the difference which is obtained by

dealings between that corporation and people who happen to be its members.

As explained in BIM24410 a company that trades only with its shareholders is not necessarily carrying on a mutual trade.

42.9.4 *Club paying dividends*

The Business Income Manual provides:

BIM24260 Members' Clubs: Incorporated As Limited Company: Paying Dividends [Jan 2019]

If a company pays dividends, it will normally be liable to tax as a trading concern. However, if the other conditions in BIM24255 are satisfied, there is likely to be liability only where there is a marked inequality of shareholdings and the dividends are substantial.

BIM24410 Incorporation: A Company Trading Only With Its Members May Be Non-Mutual [Jan 2019]

To satisfy the conditions for carrying on a mutual trade the trader must show that any surplus arising from the trade will go back to the contributors and to no one else - see BIM24110.[38] The surplus must go back in the form of returned contributions and not in any other form. This can pose difficulties for a company limited by shares. Rowlatt J. commented on this difficulty, at pages 822-823 in *Jones v The South-West Lancashire Coal Owners Association Ltd* [1927] 11 TC 790 (see BIM24110 [39]):

> The principle laid down in the *New York Insurance Company* [see BIM24035[40]] case is that no one can make a profit out of himself. Now that is very true, but I am not at all certain that it does not confuse us in this particular case. It is true to say a person cannot make a profit out of himself, if what is meant is that he may provide himself with something at a lesser cost than that at which he could buy it, or if he does something for himself instead of employing somebody to do it. He saves money in those circumstances, but he does not make a profit. But a company can make a profit out of its members as customers, although its range of customers is limited to its shareholders. If a railway company makes a profit by carrying its shareholders, or if a trading company, by trading with its shareholders - even if it is limited to trading with them - makes a profit, that profit belongs to the shareholders, in a sense, but it belongs to them qua shareholders. It does not come back to them as purchasers or customers. It comes back to them as shareholders, upon their shares.

You should not interpret Rowlatt J's remarks as always precluding a company limited by shares from carrying on a mutual trade. Rowlatt J makes the point that it makes no difference that a mutual association takes the form of an incorporated body. This is because what was returned to the members of the association was returned to them in their capacity as contributors to a surplus and not as shareholders sharing in a profit. If there is no profit where people do something for themselves, there will be no profit if they

38 See 42.4.2 (No surplus to non-contributors).

39 See 42.4.2 (No surplus to non-contributors).

40 See 42.2.3 (Mutual trade: Early cases).

incorporate a legal entity to do it for them.
Incorporation can present a significant hurdle to be overcome when considering the constitutional and financial framework necessary for mutuality. That is, for mutual trading to be present, the profits/surpluses have to be distributed to the contributors in that capacity, i.e. as contributors, not as shareholders. To achieve mutual trading a company limited by shares may need to override Companies Act provisions.
The normal Companies Act rules provide that in the event of a winding up any surplus available to distribute to members will be distributed pro rata to shareholding. The normal rules also provide that any such distribution will only be to the members on the register at that time. To satisfy the conditions for mutual trading the company's rules/articles will need to specify that:

- on a winding up any surplus available for distribution will be returned to contributors in a reasonable proportion to their contribution to that surplus (to satisfy BIM24115[41]); and
- that any distribution will also need to include contributors who have left in the last five years (also to satisfy BIM24115[42]).

From a practical point of view you may limit consideration to those who have been shareholders at any time in the previous five years - see BIM24115.[43]

42.10 Charities/CASCs: not mutuals

42.10.1 *Charity not mutual*

A charity does not carry on mutual trading. HMRC agree:

> **BIM24320 Members' Clubs: Community Associations** [Jan 2019]
> Community associations provide recreational or similar facilities to local communities in the interests of social welfare. Many of these associations began as village halls and over the years the refreshment facilities provided have grown into permanent licensed bars. They normally have a constitution that enables them to be considered as charities under the Charities Act 2011.
> A community association with charitable objects is not a members club.
> ...

42.10.2 *CASC not mutual*

Similarly, a community amateur sports club cannot be a mutual concern. HMRC agree. CASC Guidance Note Annex 1 provides:

> 3.7 ... a club which engages in mutual trading cannot qualify as a CASC, because the return of surpluses to members means that it will not qualify

41 See 42.4.3 (Return proportionate to contribution).
42 See 42.4.3 (Return proportionate to contribution).
43 See 42.4.3 (Return proportionate to contribution).

for CASC status.

42.11 Activity partly trading

The Business Income Manual provides:

> **BIM24455 Allowable Expenditure: Trades That Are Partly Non-Mutual** [Jan 2019]
>
> **How to apportion between the mutual and non-mutual aspects of the trade**
>
> As explained at BIM24210, the typical members sporting club does not carry on a trade. The activities undertaken by the club lack the required degree of commerciality that case law shows is an essential characteristic of a trade.
>
> The most commonly encountered situation is that a bona fide members club does not trade with its members but that the club may carry on a trade in making sporting or other facilities available to non-members on a commercial basis. The question then arises as to how to apportion the expenses incurred by the club between its non-taxable dealings with members and its taxable dealings with non-members.
>
> A typical club will incur expenses that fall into three broad categories:
>
> - wholly for members
> - wholly for non-members, and
> - both for members and for non-members.
>
> In calculating the amount of the clubs profits taxable as trade profits the expenditure incurred wholly for members (for example the membership secretary's salary, costs of a members only bar) will not be allowable at all. The costs that are incurred wholly for non-members (for example costs of advertising to attract non-member custom) will be allowable provided of course that they otherwise meet the trading deduction rules. Problems can arise with the mixed category of expenditure and this is discussed in the guidance that follows.

42.11.1 *Apportionment of expenditure*

Section 54 CTA 2009 provides:

> (1) In calculating the profits of a trade, no deduction is allowed for—
>
> (a) expenses not incurred wholly and exclusively for the purposes of the trade, or
>
> (b) losses not connected with or arising out of the trade.
>
> (2) If an expense is incurred for more than one purpose, this section does not prohibit a deduction for any identifiable part or identifiable proportion of the expense which is incurred wholly and exclusively for

the purposes of the trade.

BIM24460 Allowable Expenditure: Apportionment Of Mixed Expenditure [Jan 2019]

The statutory rules for calculating the taxable profits of a trade allow for the deduction of any part or proportion of expenses incurred partly for the purposes of the trade and partly for some other purpose which can be identified as incurred wholly and exclusively for the purposes of the trade. This rule has been expressly incorporated in the statute only recently, but is intended to follow existing case law and established practice.

[The Manual cites various cases making this point, not now important, and continues:]

There is no judicial guidance on apportionment of expenditure when an activity is partly mutual and partly not. But there is judicial guidance on apportionment of the expenditure of a members club where an activity is partly within the charge to tax on trade profits and partly outside.

In his opening remarks the Master of the Rolls in the case of *The Carlisle and Silloth Golf Club v Smith* [1913] 6 TC 198 indicates that the club was not formed for the purpose of making profits. In its dealings with its members the club was not carrying on a trade and so this was not a case of mutual trading. The point at issue was to establish the amount deductible where parts of the entity's activities were outside the scope of the charge to tax on trade profits and part within. The Master of the Rolls, on the facts of that case, at page 199 expressed the view that:

> there is a real difference between moneys received from members and applied for the benefit of members, and moneys received by the club from strangers. Whether there have been any profits or gains is a matter of fact; and the answer will depend upon the mode in which the expenses of maintenance and other outgoings ought to be attributed to the visitors. This is really a question of fact for the Commissioners, and not for the Court. I agree, that the particular rule adopted by the Commissioners was wrong.

The Master of the Rolls rejected the Commissioners method of apportioning expenditure (on a pro rata basis according to the comparison between income from members and income from non-members). The Master of the Rolls did not say that no maintenance expenditure should be deducted in computing the profits derived from trading with non-members. You should also note that the Master of the Rolls did not say that the correct basis to adopt was that of marginal cost - that the club would incur maintenance etc expenditure in any event and so none can be said to be wholly and exclusively for the purpose of the trade with non-members. The Master of the Rolls approved Hamilton Js approach in the High Court (see BIM24465).

BIM24465 Allowable Expenditure: Judicial Guidance On Apportionment [Jan 2019]

In the case of *The Carlisle and Silloth Golf Club v Smith* [1913] 6 TC 48 & 198 Hamilton J rejected the so-called marginal cost approach. Addressing the problem of determining the quantum of assessment, Hamilton J tells us at page 58:

> it was suggested that possibly the gross amount of the green fees would be the sum in respect of which the assessment should be made; because there was no finding at any rate that the whole of the items on the debit side would not have been incurred just the same for the members if there had been no visitors. I need not decide that contention, because it does not seem to me to be really before me; but I should hesitate long before I accepted it. It appears to me that the profits must be the real profits, the net profits, and that can only be arrived at after ascertaining whether there is not, as one certainly

> would expect there would be, something to come off the gross before arriving at the net sum.

Hamilton J therefore gives no support to the view that as the costs of providing golfing facilities would have been incurred in any event no allowance for such expenditure is available in computing the amount of the taxable profits arising from the clubs dealings with non-members.

Hamilton J tells us at page 58 of 6 TC that the case has to go back to the Commissioners to ascertain:

> what is the real apportionment of the total expenses of the club on common items which falls to the visitors and does not fall to the members.

Hamilton J also tells us at page 56 of 6 TC:

> I think if it were worth while to incur the expense it would be possible by taking the experience of the working of this or similar clubs over a period of years, and by examining the number of persons of each class using the club and the links and the times of the year at which they do so and the numbers at particular times in which they congregate together, to ascertain with real arithmetical accuracy what proportion of the clubs gross expenditure upon house and grounds is attributable truly to the user by the visitors in respect of which the green fees are receivable.

Clearly Hamilton J sees no difficulty in apportioning common items or expenditure on house and grounds. In practice you will need to establish all the facts as to how the entity in question organises its affairs, what expenses relate solely to members, what expenses relate solely to non-members and how the mixed expenses may reasonably be apportioned.

An approach that has proved useful in the case of members golf clubs is described in BIM24470. The members golf club is not conducting a mutual trade with its members; rather it is not trading at all. But the principles behind the apportionment mechanism are equally applicable to mutual traders who also trade with non-members.

42.11.2 *Application of profit not relevant*

The Business Income Manual provides:

BIM24470 Allowable Expenditure: Members Golf Clubs: Is Intention Relevant?

The case of *Hutchinson & Co (Publishers) Ltd v Turner* [1950] 31 TC 495 shows that the destination of any profits has no bearing on their assessibility. Thus placing any or all of a surplus into a fund for capital expenditure does not secure that the profits remain untaxed.

A members club may seek to attract non-member custom with a view to subsidising members. That non-members in effect subsidise members is of no relevance. Buckley LJ in the Court of Appeal in *The Carlisle and Silloth Golf Club v Smith* [1913] 6 TC 48 & 198 case dealt with this issue in the following terms (6 TC at page 200):

> The fact that in the pocket of the club it [income from non-members] saves the pocket of the member by reducing in his favour the current expenditure which otherwise he would have to bear is not a material circumstance for

the purpose of ascertaining whether the club as a society has made a profit or not.

In some cases the evidence may show that overall the members club seeks to make little or no profit; any profit, in the absence of some specific purpose, only contributing to a reserve distributable to members.

The club may also wish to minimise individual members subscriptions. To that end the club may take steps to generate income. One way of doing so is to offer the use of their facilities, at commercial rates, to outsiders. Carlisle and Silloth established that profits made by a members golf club from the provision of its facilities to visitors in this way was chargeable as trade profits. This is so whether or not the club accounts show an overall surplus.

That is self-evident.

42.11.3 *Apportionment of income*

The Business Income Manual provides:

BIM24485 Allocation Of Income: Nature Of Activities [Jan 2019]

Some of a mutual associations dealings with its members will not amount to trading. Any income or expenses in connection with such activities are neither taxable nor allowable. Other activities will amount to trading. Where the trading is with members and all of the conditions in BIM24020[44] are satisfied any profit or loss is ignored for tax purposes on the basis that it arises from a mutual trade.

From a practical point of view there may be nothing to be gained by distinguishing between an entity's non-trading activities and its mutual trading activities - for on either basis the profits are not taxable and the losses are not allowable.

The commercial activities with non-members (or with members who fall to be treated in the same way - for example temporary members (see BIM24225[45]); or junior/honorary members who pay for facilities on the same basis as everyone else - will gave rise to taxable profits as trading income.

You need to establish the facts in sufficient detail to distinguish the entity's taxable and non-taxable income.

BIM24490 Allocation Of Income: Income From Contributors (Members) [Jan 2019]

Income from members falls into a number of broad categories:

- Subscriptions - for ordinary members this forms part of the non-taxable income arising from the clubs mutual activities; for temporary members or junior/honorary members, whose subscriptions subsidise those of ordinary members and whose rights are not equivalent to full members, this is taxable as trading income - see BIM24220, BIM24225[46] and BIM24240.
- From non-trading activities - this is not taxable as trading income. But remember that non-trading items are taxable in the normal way, for example rental income will be

44 See 42.1.1 (Taxable/mutual trade/non-trade).

45 See 42.8.2 (Temporary members).

46 See 42.8.2 (Temporary members).

taxed under the property income rules.

- From trading activities where the conditions in BIM24020[47] are satisfied, this is not taxable on the basis that it derives from a mutual trade.

BIM24495 Allocation Of Income: Income From Non-Contributors [Jan 2019]

Income from trading with non-members is taxable as trading income. The normal rules apply.

BIM24500 Allocation Of Income: Mixed Income [Jan 2019]

There may be broad categories of income that accrue both from members and from non-members.

A simple example is the takings from a bar that is open to members and non-members of a mutual trading entity.

Takings from external functions such as wedding receptions or conferences held on the mutual traders premises are wholly taxable as trading income. But where members and non-members use the bar then you will need to establish the usage in sufficient detail to allow an apportionment. If members and non-members are charged the same prices then a simple apportionment is all that is necessary. If there are different prices for members and non-members then you will need to weight the apportionment accordingly.

Where the mutual trader has a members-only facility (restaurant, bar, whatever) the profits arising will arise from a mutual trade and not be taxable as trading income. You will need to be satisfied that only members use the facility.

Where it is necessary to determine any apportionment of income we would not expect the mutual trader to keep detailed records of non-member usage. You can accept a split between members and non-members based upon the monitoring of takings for a representative sample period or periods.

BIM24505 Allocation Of Income: Sundry Income

Many sporting clubs operate a variety of fund raising activities including:

- Supporters shops - much of the over the counter trade is likely to be with members. But if the club advertises goods for sale by mail order there are likely to be significant sales to non-members. You will need to examine closely any claim that the profits from mail order sales are derived from mutual trading. Where members are charged different prices you will need to weight the figures accordingly.
- Lotteries, raffles, scratch cards etc - These will be operated in accordance with the Gambling Act 2005. If operated by the club the profit will form part of their trade profits and will need to be apportioned between mutual (with members) and non-mutual (with others). You will need to consider the possible application of SP/C1 - see BIM61600 onwards.
- Sponsorship - receipts from sponsorship are not part of the mutual trade and are to be included as receipts in computing taxable trade profits unless provided personally (not by their company/partnership/business) by a member of the club.
- Hospitality boxes - income from hospitality boxes let to non-members (including drinks and catering) are not receipts of the mutual trade. The profits will be taxable as trade profits.
- Advertising - the income will be from the non-mutual trade and included as receipts in computing taxable trade profits.

---

47 See 42.1.1 (Taxable/mutual trade/non-trade).

- Hire of facilities - this is non-mutual income.
- Programme sales - if produced and sold by the club you will need to split between mutual and non-mutual. If franchised out to a third party then the income will be non-mutual.
- Catering - if provided by the club you will need to split between mutual and non-mutual. If franchised out to a third party then the income will be non-mutual. If there are specific member only facilities then the income will be mutual. If there are specific non-member facilities then the income will be non-mutual.
- Gaming machines - if the machines are located in parts accessible only to members then the income will be part of the mutual trade. If accessible to non-members you will need to apportion, by reference to usage.
- Car parking - if member only, then the income is part of the mutual trade. If available to non-members then you will need to apportion by reference to usage.
- Television income - part of the non-mutual income.
- Grants from governing body, Lottery Commission, whatever - part of the non-mutual income. The treatment will follow the treatment of grants in general - see BIM40450 onwards.
- Donations - gifts are not taxable. You will need to be satisfied that any donation is just that and not a trading receipt - see BIM41800 onwards.
- Commission on sale of debentures - part of the non-mutual income and taxable.

42.12 Cricket club

The Business Income Manual provides:

> **BIM24345 Cricket Clubs** [Jan 2019]
> ... smaller members recreational cricket clubs are unlikely to be carrying on a trade and so the issue of mutual trading will not arise - see BIM24200 onwards.
> A full-blown professional club is likely to be trading but it may organise its affairs in such a manner that the whole or part of its trade is a mutual trade. Where it doesn't then not only will the income it derives from third parties be taxable as trading income but also income from the provision of facilities to members...
> When considering if a cricket club is carrying on a mutual trade you need to establish precisely what the members contribute and what rights, benefits and privileges are conferred upon them. If membership gives little more than free access to all home matches it may be seen to be no more than the purchase of a season ticket and not representative of mutual trading. You need to establish if members are required to pay commercial rates for access to other matches (for example cup or knockout tournaments). Once admittance has been gained, are members treated in the same way as any other paying customer? Are there separate and/or additional facilities and if so how extensive? Is there any distinction between members and non-members at matches where

members have to pay for admission?
Income accruing to a cricket club, that is carrying on a trade, from television rights, sponsorship, a share of ECB (England and Wales Cricket Board) funds will all be taxable as trading income and not covered by mutual trading.

42.13 Golf club

42.13.1 *Computation of profit*

The Business Income Manual provides:

BIM24360 Golf Clubs: Computation Of Profit [Jan 2019]
Apportionment of expenditure
Income arising to a members golf club from the provision of services to non-members is taxable as trade profits where such provision amounts to the carrying on of a trade. What constitutes a trade is described at BIM24045.[48]
The question then arises as to the amount (if any) of the clubs expenses that are to be set against the receipts derived from that source. This point was discussed in the case of *The Carlisle and Silloth Golf Club v Smith* [1913] 6 TC 48 & 198 - see BIM24455. The courts rejected an approach based upon apportioning expenditure in proportion to the income derived from non-trading in comparison to the clubs total income. Instead the courts referred the matter back to the Commissioners (the predecessors to the Tribunal) with instructions to apportion based on the appropriate degree of usage of the various facilities and other matters involved.
You should therefore contend that the allowable proportion of expenditure on course maintenance be based on usage. That is, the proportion which visitors rounds represent of the total of members and visitors rounds.
An apportionment based on income is unlikely to give the correct figure because although the visitors will be charged a commercial rate based on number of rounds played the same is unlikely to be the case with members who pay a fixed subscription irrespective of the use they make of the course. This approach was also specifically rejected by the courts in Carlisle and Silloth.
Computing trading profit
Trading income
Where a members club provides services and facilities to non-members on a commercial basis all transactions between the club and non-members are trading transactions. Green fees are the most obvious source. There may be other items such as bar, catering and gaming machine receipts but see BIM24315. Other income will depend on the facilities available. For example, fees for conferences and wedding receptions may be generated if the club has suitable accommodation. On the distinction between different classes of member and the treatment of so-called temporary members see BIM24220 - BIM24230.
Where the visitor is the personal guest of a member (that is to say, where the member bears the cost) you should accept that no taxable profit arises. Thus the green fees to be

48 See 42.3 (Is there a trade).

included are the net fees being the total receivable from non-members less the amount included therein which was received from members in respect of their personal guests. If bar and related income derived from sales to non-members is small this should be ignored on de minimis grounds. But where the bar and other refreshment facilities provided by the club to non-members are organised on commercial lines or the club brings in expenditure on bar and catering facilities as a deduction the income from those sales should be taken into account in determining the clubs trading income tax liability.

Allowable expenditure

The expenditure shown in the clubs accounts should first be examined on normal lines. The accounts may not have been prepared with tax considerations in mind and it may be worthwhile considering whether there is any capital expenditure included in the profit and loss account. It is also important to establish whether any expenditure relates to items totally divorced from visitors activities. For example, some bars or other areas of the clubhouse may not be open to visitors. Expenditure on their maintenance, repair, etc. should be totally excluded.

Expenditure falls within three broad headings:

- wholly for members
- partly for members, partly for non-members, and
- wholly for non-members.

You should disallow all of the expenditure in the first category. You should allow all of the expenditure in the third category. You will need to apportion expenditure in the second category.

The expenditure on course maintenance should be apportioned according to usage. This requires an apportionment factor, which is:

Number of non-members rounds, divided by:

Total rounds played by members and non-members.

In the absence of specific information you will need to estimate the total number of rounds played by members and non-members during the year, bearing in mind the following:

Number of playing days per annum

Courses are normally open throughout the year. There may be records of the days when they have been closed because closure will require a decision to be taken by the secretary or professional. Developments in golfing clothing and equipment mean that the game can be played in most conditions and the course will only be closed when, for example, it is waterlogged. An independent study for the Sports Council (Study of golf in England, Sports Council, November 1992) showed that the average members club was closed for ten days per year. It would therefore not be unreasonable to assume that 350 days per year are available for play.

Average playing hours per day

The playing hours are largely determined by the hours of daylight. This may be as little as eight hours in the winter and more than 16 hours in the summer. Sufficient time after tee-off is required to complete a round. The time for a round will depend on the number of holes and the nature of the course. In winter the time may be less than in summer because shorter courses may be used and players may play nine holes rather than eighteen. An annual average of 8 to 10 hours per day would appear to be reasonable.

Number of games per hour

The number of games teeing off per hour can be estimated with some accuracy. In competition games start every six minutes, giving ten per hour. At periods of high usage outside competitions this rate may be reached but for calculation purposes nine games per hour is perhaps more typical.

Number of players per game

The number of players per game is likely to be three or four. Very few golfers play alone and the Sports Council survey shows that few pairs play. A figure of 3 to 3.5 would appear reasonable.

Course usage

Multiplying these factors will give the maximum course usage. Conservatively, using the lower of the figures (350 × 8 × 9 × 3) gives a maximum course usage of about 75,000 rounds per year.

In practice courses are not used to the maximum extent. They will typically be very heavily used at weekends and less so in midweek. Similarly there will be lower use in the winter compared to the summer. Visitors will be encouraged to use the course at times of low use so as to minimise disruption to members. If 100% of the maximum is assumed for Friday to Sunday inclusive and 50% for the midweek period in summer, with corresponding figures of 75% and 25% for winter the result is an overall usage of just over 50%. Thus the actual number of rounds may be around 35,000 to 40,000.

This result accords well with the Sports Council study in which members golf clubs estimated total rounds between 27,000 and 43,000 per annum depending on region.

Further support for the figures can be obtained from the number of members and their average number of rounds per year. Both the Sports Council report and a 1990 general household survey found that golfers played about once a week on average. The Sports Council survey suggests that club members play rather more than the general golfing population and may, on average, play between 50 and 60 times per annum.

It should be stressed that some members will play 4 or 5 times a week or more. An average figure of 50 rounds per annum includes both these members and those who play infrequently or not at all.

The number of club members multiplied by a factor of 50 should produce a result consistent with the total number of rounds per annum as calculated above. Due allowance for visitors rounds (see below) will be required.

Within any particular club some evidence of the rounds played by members can be obtained from the competition records. Most clubs hold a variety of league and cup competitions throughout the year.

Details of the numbers of entrants and the numbers of rounds may provide some data although it will still be necessary to estimate the number of casual rounds played by members. The probability is that the majority of rounds played by members will normally fall into this casual category.

Visitors rounds

Visitors rounds will normally be far fewer than those played by members. Although the number of visitors will probably be accurately recorded the number of rounds they play may not always be available. A casual visitor may play a single round while a corporate hospitality event or visiting party may involve the participants playing one round before lunch and a second round in the afternoon. The average is likely to be between one and two.

Some understanding of the type of visitor and the clubs pricing structure may allow this figure to be ascertained more accurately. The prices for a visitors round during the week and at weekends and for a visitors day ticket (two rounds) during the week and at weekends will probably be fixed for the season. Thus the fee paid by a visitor may indicate the number of rounds played by that visitor. Equally, correspondence with visiting parties and other related records may include documents specifying the number of rounds to be played.

Use of apportionment factor

The proportion of course usage as estimated above should be applied to most expenses from which visitors can be said to derive some benefit. But it may be that the facts of a particular case are such that a different proportion of some expenditure should be allowed. Salaries may be especially in point here.

For example, if the club employs a visitors secretary and it can be shown that the secretary's duties are in fact totally concerned with visitors the whole of the salary can be allowed. If this is the case little or no deduction for the club secretary's salary would appear appropriate.

The club professionals contract may specify that some percentage of green fees are payable to him. This can be allowed as a deduction but no further deduction in respect of the professionals salary would be allowable unless the facts warrant it. Such indication may be found in a contract that requires the professional to devote a proportion of their time to visitors.

If any proportion of the salary of a bar steward or catering staff is claimed as a deduction the same proportion of income from that source would normally be brought in as trading income.

Ministerial assurances

Clubs may quote from a letter from the then Chancellor of the Exchequer, Norman Lamont, to Lord Whitelaw:

> where clubs earn such profits, they may set expenses incurred in earning these profits against their liability to tax. the allowable expenditure may include not only the direct costs of providing for non-members, but also a reasonable proportion of general expenditure on the facilities of the club.

There is nothing in the contents of this letter that we dispute. The problem is how to arrive at the reasonable proportion of expenditure to be allowed.

Different patterns of course usage

The question of appropriate estimates has been discussed above but alternative figures, either in detail or summary form, may be put. Usually, all the figures will be based on estimates. In many cases the result of the estimates is to understate the total number of rounds played and overstate visitors rounds while understating members rounds. Consequently the visitors are shown to play an unduly high proportion of all rounds on the course and an unduly high proportion of expenditure is set against the income. A secondary result is that club members are shown as playing a very low average number of rounds per year. It then becomes necessary to consider whether there are special factors explaining why they play so little.

Any claim that the average member of a particular golf club plays less than 50 rounds per year should be viewed critically.

It will be apparent that the apportionment factor can be adjusted by making inappropriate assumptions regarding the number of rounds played by visitors. For reasons discussed earlier the number of visitors rounds is likely to be the number of visitors multiplied by a factor between one and two. The precise factor will depend on the type of visitor at the course.

42.14 Rugby club

The Business Income Manual provides:

> **BIM24370 Rugby Football Union (RFU) Booklet** [Jan 2019]
> In 1997 the RFU provided their members with a booklet setting out guidelines on mutual trading as it applied to RFU members. HMRC was consulted during the production of the booklet and accepted that it established a consistent and easily applied methodology to assist clubs in complying with their tax obligations. HMRC reserved its position as regards the detailed application of legal principles.
> You should refer any case where following the RFU booklet apparently results in an outcome inconsistent with the legal principles underlying mutual trading to Business Profits.

42.15 Hunt meetings

The Business Income Manual provides:

BIM24775 Hunt Point-To-Point Meetings: Trading? [Jan 2019]
For many years HMRC agreed not to seek to tax any profits arising from point-to-point meetings organised by Hunts and held under Master of Foxhounds Association rules. With increasing commercialisation of the events in question the agreement not to tax profits was withdrawn with effect from 1 January 1999. This does not necessarily mean that the profits of every point-to-point are now taxable. You need to establish that the point-to-point in question is organised in such a way as to amount to the carrying on of a trade. As emphasised in BIM24045,[49] whether a trade is being carried on is essentially a question of fact. It may be difficult to establish to the satisfaction of a Tribunal that a small-scale event that only takes place once a year over agricultural land (in contrast to organised regular commercial events run by racecourses) amounts to a trade.
Where a trade is carried on you then need to consider the deductions that are to be allowed in computing the taxable profits. In particular you will need to take into account the approach in *British Legion, Peterhead Branch, Remembrance and Welcome Home Fund v CIR* [1953] 35 TC 509 - see BIM24475. As virtually all of the work involved in organising and carrying out events is done on a

---

49 See 42.3 (Is there a trade).

voluntary and unpaid basis by Hunt members, a significant adjustment may accrue under the so-called Peterhead principle. In addition there may be expenditure on ambulance and medical personnel, police or other security staff.

BIM24780 Hunt Point-To-Point Meetings: Dealings With Members [Jan 2019]

Where the point-to-point is conducted in such a way as to amount to a trade, and provided that the conditions in BIM24020[50] are satisfied, any trading income that arises from dealings with Hunt members is not taxable on the grounds of mutual trading.

42.16 Allotment and garden societies

The Company Taxation Manual provides:

CTM40575 Allotment And Garden Societies [Jun 2016]

Trading surpluses of allotment and garden societies which are registered societies should not be treated as trading income where:

- the services and facilities of the association etc, are available only to members, and
- the rules and practice of the association etc, are consistent with mutuality of trading by the members.

Registered societies will normally satisfy the above conditions. CTIS (Technical) can advise where necessary.

Income arising from investments remains liable to tax. Rents charged by a society to its members for plots that they occupy, however, may in practice include some contribution towards the cost of providing the society's services as a whole. Where this is so, part of the overhead expenses of the association may be set off against the property income. This will normally result in there being no liability but if, exceptionally, the amounts involved are substantial, CTIS (Technical) can advise.

The principles set out above should also be applied to unregistered allotment and garden societies.

42.17 Mutual property business

s.321 ITTOIA	**s.260 CTA 2009**
(1) Nothing in this Part [Part 3 ITTOIA/Part 4 CTA 2009, Property Income] is to be read as applying the rules relating to mutual business to property businesses.	[Identical]

---

50 See 42.1.1 (Taxable/mutual trade/non-trade).

(2) Accordingly, receipts and expenses are to be brought into account in calculating the profits of a person's property business even if a relationship of mutuality exists between that person and another.	(2) Accordingly, receipts and expenses are to be brought into account in calculating the profits of a company's property business even if a relationship of mutuality exists between that company and another person.
	(3) Nothing in this section affects the operation of Chapter 7 of Part 13 of CTA 2010 (co-operative housing associations).

> **BIM24782 Property Management Companies** [Jan 2019]
> In many blocks of flats, services such as security, gardening, external decoration and the cleaning and decoration of common parts of the building are provided by a management company. Each occupant pays a regular charge to the management company.
> If the property management company is carrying on a property business there can be no question of mutual trading. This is because mutual trading is exclusively a trading concept. There is specific statutory confirmation of the non-application of the mutuality principle to a property business at S321 Income (Trading and Other Income) Act 2005, S260 Corporation Tax Act 2009.
> The treatment to be adopted in respect of service charges received by occupier-controlled flat management companies is described at PIM1070.

It is not logical to draw a distinction between mutual trading (not taxable) and mutual property business (taxable); but there it is.

42.18 Mutual concern in commerce

When one moves from social/recreational clubs to mutual concerns used in commerce, further questions arise: is a payment to the mutual concern a deductible expense, and what is the tax treatment of payments made from the concern to its members.

It may be less common that the mutual concern is conducting its affairs non-commercially, so as to carrying on a non-trade; or at least the context in which the commerciality/trading issue arises is different.[51]

The general principle is symmetry: if the payment from the member to

---

51 See 42.6.2 (Members club: Non-trading)

the concern is a deductible expense, the payment from the concern to the member is a trading receipt and so taxable.

42.19 Payment to mutual: Deduction

The Business Income Manual provides:

> **BIM24605 Distributions On Winding-Up: Taxable On First Principles Or Statute** [Jan 2019]
> Traders who are members of a mutual entity may make payments to that entity. These payments are allowable if
> [a] they are not capital (BIM35000) and
> [b] are incurred wholly and exclusively for the purposes of the trade (BIM42100).

These are basic principles.

> **BIM24950 Deductibility Of Payment Made By Contributor To A Mutual Trader** [Jan 2019]
> The case of *Thomas v Richard Evans & Co Ltd* [1927] 11 TC 790 established that a contributors payments to a mutual trader were deductible for tax purposes even if there was the possibility of those payments being returned.
> A colliery company made payments to an association for the mutual insurance of its members against liability for compensation in respect of fatal accidents to their employees. The payments were found to be deductible in full notwithstanding that the payments were partly applied in accumulating a fund that might, in certain events, be returned to members.
> The Master of the Rolls, Lord Hanworth, saw no reason not to allow the deduction of the premiums paid.

We set out here a slightly fuller passage than that cited in the Manual:

> [1] If the business men carrying on the Association thought it safe to say that the accumulated reserve is too large, and that the Association might be able to distribute, or allow a set-off against the premiums, if that contingency were to arise then it would be possible for the Revenue to say: "Well, you have not paid the whole of these premiums." They could point, if and when a distribution was actually made, to the quota received, and say that the sums paid for premiums must be diminished because in fact the members of the Association had not paid their full premium;
> [2] but upon the facts before us it is plain that, these sums are paid for the purpose of obtaining insurance and for nothing more, and that

> there is no reason to cut down the cost of this insurance below the sum which has actually been paid by the members of the Association ... For these reasons, in the first case it appears to me plain that these sums so paid are properly deductible as part of the costs of seeking the profits and gains which are the subject matter of and chargeable to Income Tax.[52]

The Manual continues:

> In suitable cases there is a possibility of challenging the quantum of deductions claimed by a contributor for payments made to a mutual trader on wholly and exclusively lines. Lord Evershed commented at page 335 in the case of *Brogan v Stafford Coal & Iron Co Ltd* [1963] 41 TC 305 that:
> If a mutual insurance company were established as a means to secure the building up of large capital assets, I cannot think that the annual payments would be allowed as a trading expenses because they were called insurance premiums, or at least would not be allowed to the extent that in truth and in fact they were not properly so required.
> Where such a challenge is being considered refer the matter to Business Profits.

42.20 Tax on distribution to members

42.20.1 *Trading receipt*

The Business Income Manual provides:

> **BIM24555 Distributions: The Basic Approach** [Jan 2019]
> Where a trader makes a payment to a mutual concern, whether incorporated or not, and that payment has been allowed as a deduction in arriving at the traders taxable trade profits (for example, insurance premiums see BIM45590) any distribution by the mutual concern (prior to its winding-up) should be regarded as a receipt of the recipients trade etc to the extent that the distribution represents a return of payments made.
> Similar treatment should be applied to sums received by a trader on, or as a consequence of, the winding-up of an unincorporated mutual concern.
> **BIM24605: Meaning of trade: mutual trading and members clubs: distributions on winding-up: taxable on first principles or statute** [Jan 2019]
> Any payments received by a trader from the entity are treated, on first

52 11 TC 790 at p.828.

principles, as a receipt of the recipients trade to the extent that they constitute a return of contributions made.

The following distributions out of the mutual surplus from a mutual business are taxable as receipts from the recipients trade without recourse to legislation:

- from a corporate mutual concern (other than in a dissolution or winding up), or
- from a non-corporate concern in all circumstances.

42.20.2 *Dividend from mutual*

The Manual continues:

> **BIM24605: Meaning of trade: mutual trading and members clubs: distributions on winding-up: taxable on first principles or statute**
> [Jan 2019]
> Anything that is not a return of contributions must have arisen from the mutual entity's non-mutual operations and should therefore have been taxed in the mutual's hands. Hence S1070 Corporation Tax Act 2010 applies the distributions legislation to such sums.

Section 1070 CTA 2010 provides:

> (1) Subsection (2) applies if a company carries on a business ("the mutual business") of—
> (a) mutual trading,
> (b) mutual insurance, or
> (c) other mutual business.
>
> (2) The provisions of the Corporation Tax Acts relating to distributions apply to relevant distributions made by the company only so far as they are made out of—
> (a) profits[53] of the company which are brought into charge to corporation tax, or
> (b) income of the company consisting of exempt ABGH distributions.[54]
>
> This is subject to subsection (4).

---

53 Defined in s.1070(6) 10: "In subsection (2) "profits" means income and chargeable gains."

54 Defined in s.1070(5A) CTA 2010: "In subsection (2) "exempt ABGH distribution" means a distribution which—
(a) is a distribution for the purposes of the Corporation Tax Acts only because it falls within paragraph A, B, G or H in section 1000(1), and
(b) is exempt for the purposes of Part 9A of CTA 2009 (company distributions)."

(3) In subsection (2) "relevant distributions" means distributions which—

(a) are made to persons participating in the mutual activities of the mutual business, and

(b) derive from those activities.

(4) [mutual life assurance business - not discussed here]

(5) Subject to subsections (1) to (4), the fact that—

(a) a distribution made by a company carrying on a mutual business is derived from the mutual activities of that business, and

(b) the recipient is a company participating in those activities,

does not affect the character that the payment or other receipt has for the purposes of corporation tax or income tax in the hands of the recipient.

42.20.3 *Loan from mutual: loan relationship*

Section 298 CTA 2009 provides:

(1) For the purposes of this Part a company is taken to be a party to a creditor relationship for the purposes of a trade it carries on only if it is a party to the relationship in the course of activities forming an integral part of the trade.

(2) For the meaning of "creditor relationship", see section 302(5).

(3) For the purposes of this Part activities carried on by a company in the course of—

(a) any mutual trading, or

(b) any mutual insurance or other mutual business which is not life assurance business

are treated as not constituting the whole or any part of a trade.

(4) Subsection (3) applies for the purposes of any other relevant enactment as it applies for the purposes of this Part.

(5) In subsection (4) "relevant enactment" means so much of any enactment as contains provision by reference to which amounts are to be brought into account for the purposes of this Part.

42.21 Distribution on winding up

The general rule is that a receipt on winding up a company is capital; but statute undoes the rule here, to preserve symmetry of deductible expense/trading receipt:

s.104 ITTOIA	**s.101 CTA 2009**
(1) This section applies if—	(1) This section applies if—
(a) a deduction has been allowed in	(a) a deduction has been made in

calculating the profits of a trade for a payment to a mutual concern for the purposes of its mutual business,	calculating the profits of a trade for a payment to a mutual concern for the purposes of its mutual business,
(b) the concern is being or has been wound up or dissolved,	[identical]
(c) a person ("the recipient") who is carrying on the trade, or was doing so at the time of the payment, receives money or money's worth representing the concern's assets, and	(c) a company ("the recipient") which is carrying on the trade, or was doing so at the time of the payment, receives money or money's worth representing the concern's assets, and
(d) the assets in question represent profits of the mutual business conducted by the concern.[55]	[identical]

42.21.1 *Receipt by trader*

Assuming the conditions in subsection (1) are met, Section 104(2) ITTOIA/s.101(2) CTA 2009 provides the rule:

> If the recipient is carrying on the trade at the time the money or money's worth is received, the amount or value of the money or money's worth

55 Defined s.103(4) ITTOIA/s.101(4) CTA 2009:

(4) For the purposes of this section money or money's worth represents assets of a mutual concern if it— (a) forms part of the assets of the concern, (b) forms part of the consideration for the transfer of the assets of the concern as part of a scheme of amalgamation or reconstruction which involves its winding up, or	[identical]
(c) consists of the consideration for a transfer or surrender of a right to receive anything falling within paragraph (a) or (b) and does not give rise to a charge to income tax on the person receiving it otherwise than as a result of this section.	(c) consists of the consideration for a transfer or surrender of a right to receive anything falling within paragraph (a) or (b) and does not give rise to a charge to corporation tax on the company receiving it otherwise than as a result of this section.

is brought into account as a receipt in calculating the profits of the trade.

42.21.2 *Receipt after trade ceases*

s.104 ITTOIA	**s.101 CTA 2009**
(3) If the recipient— (a) is not carrying on the trade at the time the money or money's worth is received, but (b) was doing so at the time of the payment to the mutual concern,	[identical]
the amount or value of the money or money's worth is treated as a post-cessation receipt (see Chapter 18).	the amount or value of the money or money's worth is treated as a post-cessation receipt (see Chapter 15).

42.21.3 *Transfer of right*

Subsection (5) is an anti-avoidance rule:

s.104 ITTOIA	**s.101 CTA 2009**
(5) If a transfer or surrender of a right to receive anything which— (a) forms part of the assets of a mutual concern, or (b) forms part of the consideration for the transfer of the assets of a mutual concern,	[identical]
is not at arm's length, the person making the transfer or surrender is treated as receiving consideration equal to the value of the right.	is not at arm's length, the company making the transfer or surrender is treated as receiving consideration equal to the value of the right.

42.21.4 *"Mutual concern"*

Subsections (6)(7) provide a commonsense definition of mutual concern:

(6) In this section references to a mutual concern are to a body corporate which has at any time carried on a trade which consists of or includes the conduct of mutual business (whether or not confined	[identical]

to the members of the body corporate).	
(7) For the purposes of this section a trade does not consist of or include the conduct of mutual business if all the profits of the trade are chargeable to income or corporation tax.	(7) For the purposes of this section a trade does not consist of or include the conduct of mutual business if all the profits of the trade are chargeable to corporation or income tax.

42.22 NHS doctors co-operative

BIM24655 gives an introduction to the topic, but it is not necessary to set that out here.

42.22.1 *Is co-operative trading*

The Business Income Manual provides:

> **BIM24660 NHS Doctors Co-Operatives: Essential Pre-Requisite** [Jan 2019]
> Whether particular activities are conducted in such a way as to amount to a trade is essentially a question of fact. There is detailed guidance at BIM20050 onwards. At the margin the issue can call for fine judgement. There are commercial deputising services that do carry on a trade and these can offer comparison.
> At their most rudimentary, some co-operatives appear to have minimal organisation, providing little more than the administrative minimum to achieve reciprocal arrangements between the parties; somewhat like those found in baby sitting circles, at a price designed to do no more than cover costs. You will need to form a judgement as to whether the activities are conducted in such a way that a Tribunal would find them to amount to trading.

42.22.2 *Is there a mutual trade*

On this question, the Manual provides as follows:

> **BIM24665 NHS Doctors Co-Operatives: Does The Trade Meet The Criteria?** [Jan 2019]
> ...The essential features for a trade to be mutual trading are set out at BIM24020.[56] There is no relaxation of these criteria in the case of NHS doctors co-operatives which are providing out-of-hours care on their own

56 See 42.1.1 (Taxable/mutual trade/non-trade).

behalf. You should apply the tests in exactly the same way as you would to an entity carrying on any other activity. In particular you should ensure that any surplus must go back to the contributors and to no one else - see however BIM24675.

42.22.3 *Types of doctors co-operative*

The Business Income Manual provides:

BIM24670 NHS Doctors Co-Operatives: Varieties [Jan 2019]
Many and various
The term doctors co-operative covers organisations which range from those providing little more than the administration of on-call rotas between neighbouring practices, to co-operatives (particularly in big cities) that are large and have negotiated bulk deals with commercial deputising services. The term may also apply both to co-operatives contracting with Primary Care Trusts or Primary Care Organisations to provide out-of-hours care and to a co-operative providing such care on behalf of its members. In the latter case, members pay to benefit from the co-operatives services and are themselves paid for the work that they do for the co-operative. The typical such co-operative is owned and staffed by General Practitioner (GP) principals. A GP using the co-operative to provide out-of-hours cover pays a fee for the service. The doctors working for the co-operative are most often paid a session rate, so much per shift worked.
Local Health Authorities have allocated funds to reimburse any non-doctor costs of a GPs membership of a co-operative. Such costs may, for example, include communication equipment (pagers, telephones, fax machines, etc), premises, non-medical staff costs and so on. Equipment costs are likely to be capital. Capital contributions by the GP to the co-operative will not be allowable.
For administrative convenience, payment may be made direct to the co-operative. But the reality is that the payments belong to the individual GP who may then pay them to the co-operative together with the balance of their contributions for the services that they receive. In strictness the payments from the Local Health Authority should be shown in the GPs own (or partnership) accounts, either as a professional receipt or netted off against payments to the co-operative.
It is essential that you establish all of the facts before venturing an opinion as to whether the co-operative carries on a trade and if such trade is a mutual trade.
BIM24675 NHS Doctors Co-Operatives: National Association Of GP Co-Operatives [Jan 2019]
The National Association of GP co-operatives is a national representative body for GP co-operatives. The Association has produced a model constitution for its members. In its initial form the constitution precluded a co-operative that adopted it from being accepted as carrying on a mutual trade. This was because the constitution required any surplus on winding up or dissolution to go to a successor body or to charity. Such a requirement is contrary to BIM24110nn[57], which requires that any surplus go back to the members and to no one else.
In the case of a recently formed co-operative that:

57 See 42.4.2 (No surplus to non-contributors).

- has adopted a constitution that precludes its trade from being a mutual trade, but
- the clear intention from the outset was that it carry on a mutual trade, and
- there have been no distributions,
- and the doctors who are members of the co-operative have not opted out of providing out-of-hours patient care, see BIM24655,

you may treat the co-operative as a mutual trader from its inception if the constitution is promptly amended to conform to the requirements in BIM24100 onwards.

42.23 Mutual health insurer

The Business Income Manual provides:

BIM24695 Mutual Health Insurers: Are They Trading? [Jan 2019]
Whether particular activities are conducted in such a way as to amount to a trade is essentially a question of fact. There is detailed guidance at BIM20050 onwards. At the margin the issue can call for fine judgement.
The insurer will have been authorised under the Financial Services and Markets Act 2000 to carry on business. It seems unlikely that such business will be conducted in such a way as not to amount to a trade. But you will need to establish the facts in each case and confirm the position.
BIM24700 Mutual Health Insurers: Is The Trade Mutual? [Jan 2019]
The essential features for a trade to be mutual trading are set out at BIM24020.[58] There is no relaxation of these criteria in the case of mutual health insurers. You should apply the tests in exactly the same way as you would to an entity carrying on any other activity. In particular you should ensure that any surplus must go back to the contributors and to no one else - see however BIM24675.
The larger funds tend to be companies limited by guarantee. The presence of a share capital does not, of itself, preclude a finding of mutual trading but it can cause considerable difficulties for the would-be mutual trader - see BIM24405.
The constitutions of a number of mutual health insurers meant that they could not be carrying on a mutual trade. Principally this was because of rules that precluded the contributors from controlling the insurer. Following discussions with the British Health Care Association (the body representing the majority of the insurers involved), it was agreed, that those mutual health insurers (who had hitherto been treated as mutual traders but whose rules on examination were found to be inconsistent with such treatment) could either:

- accept that they were not carrying on a mutual trade (and so accept liability on all of their trading income, including from dealings with members), or
- make the necessary changes to their rules/constitution to comply with the requirements for mutual trading.

HMRC did not seek to apply a change retrospectively or re-open closed years. HMRC also allowed the changeover to take place from a convenient date; for example the beginning of the insurers next accounting period.
A health insurer who adopted the first alternative above may at a future date (and for commercial reasons) wish to amend their constitution/rules to conform to the

---

58 See 42.1.1 (Taxable/mutual trade/non-trade).

requirements for mutual trading. Where there are sound reasons for so doing the change may be accepted without further enquiry. Any case where the change appears to be designed to secure a tax advantage should be critically examined.

42.24 Agricultural co-operative

42.24.1 *Mutual trading*

The Business Income Manual provides:

> **BIM24720 Agricultural Co-Operatives: Three Points To Watch** [Jan 2019]
> In the context of mutual trading you need to consider the following three issues:
> 1 If the co-operative purchases produce from the growers, and sells to third parties, the profits derive from trading with third parties and not from trading with its own members. Those profits do not therefore derive from mutual trading.
> If the co-operative merely finds buyers on behalf of its members and receives a fee from its members for doing so, the surpluses derive from the service supplied to its members and are therefore mutual. Some co-operatives accounts may show purchases and sales, but examination of the members marketing agreement will usually reveal that these figures represent the produce handled as agents by the co-operative on behalf of members.
> 2 Sometimes a co-operative may allow a person (who may or may not also be a contributor as described above) to make use of a part of the facilities (for example - a co-operative which harvests members crops may hire out some machinery when it is not required for the co-operatives own mutual trade).
> Such use of surplus capacity for a fee (whether by a non-contributor to the mutual operation or a contributor):
> - is not within the mutuality arrangements described above,
> - creates a source of income chargeable to tax, and
> - does not render the person concerned a contributor by virtue of that transaction alone.

42.24.2 *Corporate member: Planning*

The Business Income Manual provides:

> **BIM24720 Agricultural Co-Operatives: Three Points To Watch** [Jan 2019]
> ...There used to be a trend for members of co-operatives to attempt to exploit the exemption from tax on profits arising from mutual trading.

A typical arrangement was for

[1] six members of a co-operative to form a company; the company then became the seventh member of the co-operative.

[2] The six members marketed their own produce through the co-operative but the seventh, the company, marketed the produce of non-members.

Alternatively,

[1] the six members made use of the co-operatives facilities for their own produce,

[2] while the seventh undertook to make them available to non-members for their produce.

It was argued that all the co-operatives profits were exempt from tax on the basis of mutual trading, because all trading was done with members. We do not accept this contention.

Where the six members obtained facilities for their own use, or for their own produce, and the seventh obtained them for the use of non-members or for the produce of non-members, HMRC did not accept that the activities were truly being conducted in a mutual spirit. The share of any surpluses returned to the members embraced two elements:

- a share of the surplus derived from payments made by the members as members, and
- a share of the surplus derived from payments made by the seventh member as agent for the non-members.

This means that one of the essential conditions of mutual trading - that what is returned to each contributor is the surplus of their own contribution - was not met.

You should however note that where the seventh member became the owner of the produce so as to put it on an equal footing with the other members, HMRC accepted that the co-operative was operating on a mutual basis providing that the charges imposed on each of the seven members were the same, and that the basis of distribution of surpluses among the members was the same, so that there was no question of surpluses being diverted from the seventh member via the co-operative to the other six members.

42.24.3 *Loan/grant/membership charge*

The Business Income Manual provides:

BIM24725 Agricultural Co-Operatives: Financing [Jan 2019]

Members not allowed to deduct loans made to co-operative

Co-operatives generally derive their funds for capital expenditure from three sources:

- loans from members,

- government or EU grants
- bank borrowing.

A member is not entitled to a deduction in computing the amount of their trading income for a loan they make to a co-operative; this is so even when it is a condition of membership that such a loan be made.
Capital grants may be deducted from the cost of the asset for capital allowances purposes, but such allowances are not available in respect of mutual trading.
Revenue expenditure is generally financed by charges imposed on members, usually in proportion to the amount of produce committed to the co-operative and the use the member makes of its facilities, but grants may also be available from the UK government and the EU towards revenue expenditure. With the exception of a grant towards the cost of formation (which is a non-allowable expense) grants are to be included in computing the surplus or deficit of (non-mutual) co-operatives.

42.24.4 *Tax position of member*

The Manual provides:

BIM24740 Agricultural Co-Operatives: Members Taxation [Jan 2019]
Whether a co-operative is engaged in mutual trading or not, the member is not entitled to a deduction in computing the amount of their trading income for any initial charge or loans made to the co-operative.
But the member is entitled to a deduction for normal recurrent service charges made by the co-operative, even though these may include provision for the replacement of capital assets.
In either case[59] refunds by the co-operative of annual contributions or distributions of profit should normally be regarded as trading receipts of the member.

42.24.5 *Hedging*

The Business Income Manual provides:

BIM24745 Agricultural Co-Operatives: Futures Dealing [Jan 2019]
Some co-operatives are known to carry out hedging transactions in futures to protect the price of the commodity being sold on behalf of members.
Where the scale of the hedging is such that it can genuinely be linked to

---

59 Authors' footnote: We think the meaning is, whether a co-operative is engaged in mutual trading or not.

the sale of the commodity being marketed by the co-operative, you should accept that such dealings are an integral part of that activity, rather than a separate trade. In these circumstances the hedging is being done to benefit the members rather than for the co-operative on its own account. Accordingly the surplus should be regarded as derived from mutual trading.

If however the hedging transactions are carried out in a different commodity, or if the scale of the transactions greatly exceed the transactions carried out on behalf of the members, the co-operative may be carrying on a separate trade and is doing so as a principal rather than as agent for its members. In these circumstances the profit is liable to Corporation Tax under the derivative contracts rules (see CFM50000 onwards).

42.25 Chamber of commerce

The Business Income Manual provides:

BIM24755 Chambers Of Commerce: Trading? [Jan 2019]

... Where the Chamber derives its income solely from members subscriptions and contributions then it is likely to be a non-trading entity - see BIM24001 and BIM24010. The basis of this approach is that these transactions between the Chamber and the members are on a non-commercial or non-trading footing. This is because the object of the Chamber is to support the common purpose of its members rather than to trade with them. But profits derived from transactions with non-members in the ordinary course of a trade are taxable as trade profits.

In addition to acting as a collective voice for the membership, most Chambers also supply a range of services for which they make a commercial charge. These services include such matters as provision of certificates of origin, translation, training, telecoms, etc. Even where these services are supplied to members you will need to carefully examine any claim that such provision amounts to a mutual trade. The surpluses are usually applied for the benefit of all members and not just those who contributed to their creation. Where such is the case, it must follow that the class of beneficiaries is wider than the class of contributors. As explained in BIM24105 such a mismatch precludes mutual trading.

Receipts from outsiders for these services and other receipts such as advertising or commissions will fall outside mutual trading.

If the Chamber has both trading and non-trading activities you will need to apportion income and expenses between the two on a basis that is consistent with the facts. There is general guidance at BIM24450 onwards.

BIM24760 Chambers Of Commerce: A Mutual Trade? [Jan 2019]

The essential features for a trade to be mutual trade are set out at BIM24020.[60]

There is no relaxation of this criteria in the case of Chambers of Commerce. You should apply the tests in exactly the same way as you would to an entity carrying on any other

60 See 42.1.1 (Taxable/mutual trade/non-trade).

activity. In particular you should ensure that any surplus must go back to the contributors and to no one else.

It is usual for UK Chambers of Commerce to be constituted under rules that prohibit the payment or transfer of any part of their income or property to persons who have at any time been members. This rule means that any trade carried on by such a Chamber could not be a mutual trade. The essence of mutuality is that, sooner or later, those who contribute to a surplus must be entitled to receive back a fair proportion of any surplus. Rules and constitutions that specifically prohibit the distribution of surpluses in a winding-up mean that the conditions for mutual trading cannot be satisfied.

The Chambers rules and constitution should specify what happens to any surplus on a dissolution/winding-up and if that surplus is not to be returned to the contributors then it will not be carrying on a mutual trade.

42.26 Bulk buying group

The Business Income Manual provides:

> **BIM24784 Bulk Buying Groups: Introduction And Layout Of Guidance** [Jan 2019]
>
> An entity that provides the services of a central buying organisation in order that purchases may be made for members at an advantageous rate may be regarded as trading mutually with those members provided all the other requirements for mutual trading are met - see BIM24020.[61] In such circumstances there is a banding together to buy a product at one price from outsiders and to distribute it at another to members.
>
> The position is different if the body acts as principal rather than merely as agent in relation to such transactions by:
>
> - taking title to the goods, or
> - manufacturing the product, or
> - growing the product.
>
> **BIM24786 Bulk Buying Groups: Basic Principles** [Jan 2019]
>
> The basic approach for the taxation of bulk buying groups that act as principal rather than merely as agent for the members derives from the decision in a Privy Council case, *English & Scottish Joint Co-operative Wholesale Societies Ltd v The Commissioners of Agricultural Income Tax, Assam* ([1948] AC 405). The utility of Privy Council decisions is described at BIM24235.[62]
>
> The society was incorporated in the UK under the Industrial and Provident Act 1893. The society owned an estate in Assam where it grew and blended tea, virtually all of which was sold to member societies at ruling market prices. The following passage from the judgement describes the position:
>
>> their Lordships are of the opinion that the [mutual trading] principle cannot apply to an association, society or company which grows produce on its own land or manufactures goods in its own factories, using either its own capital or capital borrowed from its members or from others, and sells its produce

61 See 42.1.1 (Taxable/mutual trade/non-trade).

62 See 42.8.3 (Voting rights).

> or goods to its members exclusively. In the present case the appellant company is not bound by its rules to sell its tea only to its members, but it could make no difference if it were. No matter who the purchaser may be, if the society sells the tea grown and manufactured by it at a price which exceeds the cost of producing it and rendering it fit for sale, it has earned profits which are, subject to provisions of the taxing act, taxable profits.

The emphasis on the society's independent status (and in particular the repetition of own) shows that a clear contrast is drawn between a society or company that acts as a principal and one that in the words of the immediately preceding passage is no more than a convenient agent.

BIM24788 Bulk Buying Groups: Two Relationships [Jan 2019]

A person trading with a body of which they are a member and which acts as principal has two distinct relationships with that body:

- there is the buyer-seller (or similar) relationship as regards their trading transactions with the body, and
- a member-society (or similar) relationship as regards their right to a division of the society's distributable surplus.

Any surplus arising to the body from buyer-seller transactions where it acts as principal are profits earned by the body itself. They do not represent the surplus of members funds not required for the realisation of the joint purpose. Such transactions are not mutual trading.

This follows from Lord Normand's remarks in the *English & Scottish Joint Co-operative Wholesale Societies Ltd v The Commissioners of Agricultural Income Tax, Assam* [1948] AC 405 (see BIM24786).

there was a dual relationship between the appellant and its members a mutual creditor debtor relationship and a buyer/seller relationship

Rather than there being a common fund to which the members contributed and in which they participated. Lord Normand went on to say:

> The principles of the *Styles* [see BIM24035[63]] case cannot apply to a body which grows produce on its land or manufactures goods in its own factories and sells its goods to its members exclusively.

42.27 Trade protection association

The Business Income Manual provides:

> **BIM24805 Trade Protection Associations: HMRC Arrangement** [Jan 2019]
>
> Ordinary trade protection associations, formed to protect the common interests of their members and funded by their annual subscriptions, are normally non-trading concerns and so cannot carry on a mutual trade - see BIM24010.
>
> A member of a trade association is entitled to a deduction for that part of their subscription which is applied by the association towards

63 See 42.2.3 (Mutual trade: Early cases).

expenditure which would have been allowable had it been incurred by the member themselves (*Lochgelly Iron & Coal Company Ltd v Crawford* [1913] 6 TC 267). Unless the Tribunal is otherwise satisfied, effect cannot be given to a members right to a deduction without the production of the associations accounts *(Grahamston Iron Company v Crawford* [1915] 7 TC 25). Following these cases the HMRC established its long-standing trade protection association arrangement.

42.27.1 *Trade protection arrangements*

The Manual continues:

A trade protection association, whose members subscriptions are not otherwise chargeable to Corporation Tax, may make an application to adopt the HMRC arrangement. The arrangement amounts to a contractual agreement under which:

- members entrance fees, subscriptions, levies and other payments (other than loans or payments of a capital nature), are allowed in full as deductions,
- payments which the association makes to members (other than loans or payments of a capital nature), are to be treated as their trade receipts,

and

- the association agrees to be assessed to Corporation Tax on any surplus of receipts over expenditure, computed under trade profits rules.

In effect the arrangements honour the *Lochgelly* principle but by a different route.

These arrangements can only be made with associations that have members who are chargeable for trade profits and who would normally be dealt with under BIM47420. However, see BIM47430 about subscriptions to small local associations.[64]

Where an association appears to meet the necessary criteria and has not applied for the arrangements you should send them details of how they work. You should deal with any application according to the instructions given in the first sub-paragraph of BIM24810. When you first contact the association make it clear that any application to adopt the arrangements will be referred to Business Profits for approval.

BIM24810 Procedural Points When Adopting HMRC Arrangement [Jan 2019]

You should explain the arrangement to any trade association that asks about it. Send any applications to Business Profits with a copy of the associations:

- constitution
- rules, and
- accounts.

No deduction is to be made in computing the amount of the associations trading income for any expenditure which the association incurs of a political nature even if it is one of the aims of the association. Expenditure on indirect internal taxes is dealt with at BIM46455.

S1298, S1299 Corporation Tax Act 2009, covered in BIM45000 onwards, apply to calculating the entertainment expenses of any association that has adopted the arrangement. Normally only certain expenses are allowed. These are for entertaining:

- staff of the association (but when staff entertainment is incidental to entertainment of

---

64 This is set out below.

others (disallowed under Section 1298) its cost is disallowed);

- representatives of the members, if the costs to the members themselves would be allowed under Section 1299.

Profits that are legally liable are excluded from the arrangement. This includes any sums chargeable to Corporation Tax as trading income, property income or capital gains or under the loan relationship rules. An association which has adopted the arrangement may, if its expenditure is greater than its income, claim relief in the same way as a company may claim for trading losses. That is, the deficiency is treated as if it were a loss in trade available for set-off under S37 Corporation Tax Act 2010 (CTA 2010) (see CTM04500 onwards) against other profits. If there is a deficiency that cannot be allowed under that Section, the association can claim to have it set off against surpluses, calculated according to paragraph 4 of the arrangement. This applies to the last six years as long as the deficiency has not been allowed already. The set-off should normally be made first against the surplus of the earliest of the last six years. Any balance can be carried forward under S45 CTA 2010 and set off against later surpluses. This is covered in CTM04000 onwards.

For the purpose of group relief (see CTM97000 onwards), any deficiency of the association which may be claimed under the arrangements as if it were a trading loss under Section 37 is available for group relief. Similarly, the surplus of an association that has adopted the arrangement should be regarded as part of its total profits against which group relief may be set off.

Refer any disagreement about assessments for associations who have adopted the arrangement to Business Profits before the appeal procedure under the arrangement is invoked or if they do not pay any tax owed.

BIM24815 Benefits To Members Of Adopting HMRC Arrangement [Jan 2019]

The arrangement allows any payments to members that are treated as trade receipts of the members to be deducted from the surplus the association has made. They are not treated as distributions under S1000 CTA 2010. Apart from this treatment, which is part of the terms of the arrangement, the normal rules apply. Trade protection associations do not usually trade, so S1071 CTA 2010 applies. Payments and benefits to members are not counted as distributions unless they come from:

- profits on which Corporation Tax can be charged or
- franked investment income dividends - this is covered in CTM15550.

Payments to members from accumulated surpluses that have been assessed under the arrangement should not be regarded as distributions either. This is because these surpluses are not liable to Corporation Tax (which is collected only as a result of the contractual arrangement).

BIM24820 Text Of HMRC Arrangement [Jan 2019]

The HMRC arrangement is currently being updated. Until the new version is available for publication you should refer to Business Profits.

BIM47430: subscriptions: trade associations: other [Dec 2016]

Local trade associations

Any legally disallowable part of a fixed annual subscription payable to a local association as a chamber of trade is usually of negligible amount, and the absence of an HMRC arrangement should not be taken as grounds for disallowing the subscription.

Ordinary annual subscriptions by non-members (for example by a jam manufacturer to a grocers' association) are normally admissible as sums laid out wholly for the purposes

of the subscriber's trade with members of the association.
An arrangement for the allowance of the subscriptions is not necessary in such cases, but an association may apply to adopt the official arrangement with a view to securing relief for losses.

Foreign trade associations

Fixed annual subscriptions to an association outside the UK may normally be allowed as a deduction in the absence of any evidence of inadmissibility. Production of the accounts of the association need not be requested.

42.28 Barristers chambers

Bar Council guidance provides:

> **Chambers expenditure**
>
> 148. Whilst it may seem obvious that contributions to chambers expenses should be tax deductible in the accounts of the individual barrister, the matter is not as straightforward.
>
> 149. At its simplest, chambers is no more than a group of individuals who have banded together to share common business expenses. Chambers is not a separate legal entity and therefore the tax treatment of members' contributions will depend on when and how those monies are applied by chambers. That is to say, it is not what the members pay into chambers that determines the tax deduction in their accounts, but rather how chambers uses those contributions or indeed if they do not (thus giving rise to a surplus).
>
> 150. Where some chambers expenditure does not qualify for a tax deduction, or is of a capital nature, then the members need to make adjustments in their own accounts to reflect this.
>
> 151. Chambers must advise each member of their share of non-deductible revenue or capital expenditure. This information must include the date on which the cost was incurred in order that the barrister is able to make the appropriate adjustments.
>
> 152. Chambers must also advise each member of their share of chambers capital expenditure qualifying for capital allowances. Again, this information must include the date on which the cost was incurred. Further, where chambers have surplus funds as a result of members' contributions exceeding chambers' expenditure, this also has to be reflected in the members' accounts. Members' contributions have to have been expended by chambers in order to be tax deductible, and chambers must advise each member of their share of unexpended chambers contributions.
>
> 153. The apportionment of these adjustments can be administratively complex where members have different accounting year ends, and where some members prepare their accounts on the cash basis, whereas others use the earnings basis. Chambers records need to be kept in a manner that permits them to identify the tax adjustments so that the information can be provided to the members.
>
> 154. Barristers need this information if they are to complete their self assessment tax returns correctly. It is open to HMRC to enquire into a barrister's tax return to ensure that the correct tax treatment has been applied. If on enquiry it is found that chambers have not provided this information to a member, there

> is a likelihood that this could trigger enquiries into the tax returns of all the members of that set.
>
> 155. Simply setting up a service company does not circumvent the tax difficulties. Members' contributions to these service companies are treated as mutual income, and the "mutual trading" rules apply. Consequently, the service company is transparent for tax purposes, and the tax deductibility of members' contributions to such companies depends on the end use of those contributions, in exactly the same manner as if the company did not exist.
>
> 156. Chambers organise themselves in widely differing ways, and the function of what is written here is to alert barristers to the problem, rather than to provide solutions for every situation. The apportionment of expenses is dealt with differently in different sets of chambers. Whatever system is used, however, it is important that it aims to charge for a year only the amount actually expended by chambers in the year, and that any deficit or surplus is made up, or returned to members, as soon as possible after the end of the chambers' accounting period.[65]

This is an austere view.

42.29 Industrial & Provident Society

Section 1 Co-operative and Community Benefit Societies Act 2014 has repealed the former Industrial and Provident Societies Act 1965. Industrial and Provident Societies in England and Scotland have become registered societies under the 2014 Act. The HMRC Manuals have not yet been updated for this change. Its references to Industrial and Provident Societies, (except for Northern Ireland) now relate to registered societies.

42.30 Co-operative society

42.30.1 *Co-operative society: Definition*

Section 1 Co-operative and Community Benefit Societies Act 2014 provides the definition for the 2014 Act:

> (1) In this Act "registered society" means a society registered under this Act, that is—
>
> (a) a society registered under this Act on or after 1 August 2014 (the day this Act comes into force), or
>
> (b) (by virtue of section 150(1)) a society that immediately before that date was registered or treated as registered under the 1965 Act.
>
> (2) In this Act "the 1965 Act" means the Industrial and Provident Societies Act 1965.

65 Bar Council, "Taxation and Retirement Benefits Guidance" (2016) *https://www.barcouncilethics.co.uk/documents/taxation-handbook*

Section 379(2) ITTOIA/s.1119(2) CTA 2010 use the term "registered society", which includes similar bodies in Northern Ireland and the EU:

> "registered society" means—
> (a) a registered society within the meaning of the Co-operative and Community Benefit Societies Act 2014,
> (b) a society registered or treated as registered under the Industrial and Provident Societies Act (Northern Ireland) 1969,
> (c) a society registered as a credit union under the Credit Unions (Northern Ireland) Order 1985, or
> (d) an SCE [Societas cooperativa Europaea] formed in accordance with Council Regulation (EC) No 1435/2003 on the Statute for a European Cooperative Society

42.30.2 *Background law*

The Company Taxation Manual provides:

CTM40505 General [June 2016]
The Cooperative and Community Benefit Societies Act 2014 (CCBS14) became law on 1 August 2014 and consolidated all of the legislation relating to Great Britain (GB) Industrial and Provident Societies.
From that date those GB societies will no longer be called industrial and provident societies, rather they will be co-operative or community benefit societies or credit unions, though they are termed registered societies throughout the 2014 Act and the updated tax legislation. In Northern Ireland the societies will continue to be known as industrial and provident societies or credit unions.
All societies which were registered under Industrial and Provident Societies Act 1965 or earlier Acts are now treated as registered under CCSB14.
Throughout this guidance they will all be referred to as registered societies (i.e. including Northern Ireland (NI) societies, unless otherwise indicated).Societies registered under CCSB14 and equivalent NI legislation are bodies corporate. Registered societies are therefore companies for tax purposes and are liable to CT in respect of their profits, which are computed in accordance with normal rules as amended by the Corporation Tax Acts (but see CTM40150 for the treatment of credit unions).
The key differences in treatment between registered societies and other companies are that
- the share interest and loan interest paid by a registered society, and share interest paid by an agricultural co-operative, are treated as interest under a loan relationship and are not treated as distributions within CTA10/PART 23;

and, for those societies carrying on a trade,
- the dividends paid by reference to the transactions a member has with the society (sometimes called the'divi') are deductible and are not treated as distributions within CTA10/PART23.

The legislation governing the tax treatment of the societies and their members was previously to be found in ICTA88/S486 and S487. This is now spread throughout the Taxes Acts. The provisions can be found as follows:

- the treatment of share and loan interest in the hands of both
- the society - treated as a non-trading loan relationship debit CTA09/S499 and
- the recipient - treated as a receipt of interest ITTOIA05/S379 (1);
- the disapplication of the company distribution provisions to payments of share and loan interest by a society, CTA10/S1055;
- no gain/no loss treatment on a transfer of engagements from one society to another TCGA92/S217D;
- the treatment of dividends, bonuses, discounts etc in respect of transactions between the member and the society:
- the society gets a deduction from its profits CTA09/S132,
- the recipient will be taxed or not on the receipt depending on what it represents in their hands though this is not specified in the legislation, and
- the distributions legislation is again disapplied CTA10/S1056;
- payment of the share or loan interest is to be made gross to the recipient ITA07/S887(1), except for non UK residents;
- returns to HMRC of the gross payments made to the members of over £15, ITA07/S887 ((2) and (3));
- societies which fail to make returns to HMRC get no relief for the payments (CTA09/S500).

Examples of the activities of registered societies include:

- retail co-operatives,
- community shops/post offices,
- sports clubs, supporters trusts,
- community associations,
- housing associations / registered social landlords, and
- credit unions.

Close companies

A registered society is not a close company because of CTA10/S442.

42.30.3 *Types of society*

The Company Taxation Manual provides:

CTM40507 Background And Types Of Society [Sep 2018]

Registration etc

All UK industrial and provident societies, credit unions and co-operative and community benefit societies are registered by the Mutual Societies Registration section of the Financial Conduct Authority. They enjoy limited liability in the same way as companies registered under the Companies Acts. The FCA's role as registering authority is separate from its role as conduct regulator, but, depending on the activities of a particular society, it may also be subject to FCA regulation.

A GB society may register under CCSB14 as a co-operative society or a community benefit society if it satisfies either of the two conditions found at section 2 (2) of that Act. The conditions are that:

- the society is a bona fide co-operative society,or
- the business of the society is being, or is intended to be, conducted for the benefit of the community, (a 'bencom').

Bona fide co-operative society

There is no statutory definition of a 'bona fide co-operative' society but there are criteria laid down by the registering authority. These are:

- there is a community of interest - there must be a common economic, social or cultural need or interest among all members,
- conduct of the business must be for the mutual benefit of the members with the benefits they receive deriving mainly from their participation in the business,
- control of the society must be vested in the members equally, the principle of 'one man, one vote' is fundamental,
- interest on share/loan capital shouldnot exceed a rate necessary to obtain and retain sufficient capital to carry out the society's business,
- profits, if distributable amongst the members, will be distributed in relation to the extent members have either traded with the society or taken part in the society's business, and
- there should be open membership, membership must not be artificially restricted with the aim of increasing the value of any proprietary rights and interests.

The aim is to ensure a genuine community of interest amongst a society's members based on something other than the amount of capital they have placed in the society. A society cannot be a co-operative society if it carries on, or intends to carry on, business with the object of making profits mainly for the payment of interest, dividends, or bonuses on money invested or deposited with or lent to, the society or any other person'.

Benefit of the community

A society 'for the benefit of the community' must principally show that:

- the business must be run primarily for the benefit of people who are not members of the society and must be in the interests of the community at large,
- the rules of the society must not allow distribution of profits or assets to the members: profits should be ploughed back into the business, and
- on dissolution the assets of the society must pass to some other body with similar objects, not to the members.

A 'bencom' must also meet the same requirements in respect of interest on share on loan capital as for a bona fide co-operative society.

Subject to the above constraints societies are entitled to carry on any business or trade. A registered society must have at least three members (but this is reduced to two where both are registered societies. There is no equivalent to the authorised share capital of a Companies Act company and therefore no limit to the number of shares that may be issued. There is a maximum withdrawable share subscription limit of £100,000 although this limit does not normally apply to shares held by another registered society . There is no limit on non-withdrawable share capital. The rules of any particular registered society may specify lower limits.

There are different rules about membership and share capital for credit unions, see [CTM40155] (*https://www.gov.uk/hmrc-internal-manuals/company-taxation-manual/ctm40155*).

42.31 Taxation of registered society

The Company Taxation Manual provides:

> **CTM40510 Claims For Exemption** [Dec 2018]
>
> A registered society is not exempt from corporation tax. BAI has seen a number of claims from, for example, community shops arguing that

> they are exempt because they are a registered society and/or a not for profit organisation.

Oh dear.

> As in CTM40505 a registered society is a body corporate and broadly pays tax under the same rules as any other company. Equally a registered society can get the benefit of the same reliefs as any other company, unless the corporation tax acts specifically prevent it.
> A body such as a community shop is trading and is potentially in competition with other shops and businesses. It does not trade with a view to making a loss, rather it will try to make a profit, but, rather than distribute its profits to its members, any profit/surplus is likely to be ploughed back in to the business or to other community projects. That does not however mean that it will be exempt from tax.

We do not discuss the specialist topics of transfers between co-operative societies, and conversion to companies.

42.31.1 *Interest: non-distribution*

Section 1055 CTA 2010 provides:

> (1) Interest paid[66] by a registered society in respect of a mortgage, loan, loan stock or deposit is not a distribution for corporation tax purposes.
> (2) If any dividend, bonus, interest or other sum—
> (a) is paid to a shareholder in a registered society, and
> (b) is payable by reference to the amount of the shareholder's holding in the society's share capital,
> it is not a distribution for corporation tax purposes.
> (3) Subsections (1) and (2) apply even if the amount in question would otherwise be a distribution by virtue of any enactment relating to corporation tax.

Section 1056 CTA 2010 provides:

> (1) This section applies if—
> (a) a dividend or bonus is granted by a registered society, and
> (b) section 132 of CTA 2009 (dividends etc relating to transactions with a registered society)[67] allows the sum representing the dividend or bonus to be deducted in calculating the profits of a trade.

---

66 Defined in s.1055(4) CTA 2010: "For the purposes of this section crediting an amount counts as paying it."

67 See 42.31.6 (Dividend: deductible for society).

(2) The dividend, or the bonus, is not a distribution for the purposes of the Corporation Tax Acts.

42.31.2 *Dividend: deemed interest*

s.379 ITTOIA	**s.499 CTA 2009**
(1) Any dividend, bonus or other sum payable to a shareholder in— (a) a registered society, or (b) a UK agricultural or fishing co-operative,[68]	[identical]
is treated as interest for income tax purposes if it is payable by reference to the amount of the shareholder's holding in its share capital.	is treated for corporation tax purposes as interest under a loan relationship of the society or co-operative if it is payable by reference to the amount of the shareholder's holding in its share capital.
[No equivalent]	(2) If subsection (1) applies— (a) so far as the shareholder's holding is held for the purposes of a trade, the shareholder is treated for the purposes of section 297 as a party to the loan relationship referred to in subsection (1) for that purpose, and (b) so far as the holding is held for any other purpose, the shareholder is treated for the purposes of that section as a party to that loan relationship for that other purpose.

42.31.3 *Withholding tax exemption*

Payment of interest by a company is normally subject to withholding tax: s.874 ITA. Section 887(1) ITA excludes this duty so interest is normally paid gross:

> The duty to deduct a sum representing income tax under section 874 does not apply to either of the following payments if they are payable to

68 See 42.32 (Agricultural/fishing co-operative).

a person whose usual place of abode is in the United Kingdom—

(a) a payment[69] of interest made by a registered society[70] in respect of any mortgage, loan, loan stock or deposit, or

(b) any interest, dividend, bonus or other sum payable to a shareholder of such a society by reference to the amount of the shareholder's holding in the share capital of the society.

42.31.4 *Interest payment: Return*

Instead of withholding tax, there is a duty to make a return. Section 887 ITA provides:

> (2) A registered society must, within 3 months after the end of each of its accounting periods, deliver to an officer of Revenue and Customs a return containing the information mentioned in subsection (3).
> (3) That information is—
> (a) the name and place of residence of every person to whom the society has, as a result of this section, made one or more payments in the period amounting in total to at least £15 without deducting a sum (or sums) representing income tax, and
> (b) the amount so paid in the period to each of those persons.

The penalty for failure to make the return is that the interest is non-deductible. Section 500 CTA 2009 provides:

> (1) This section applies if for any accounting period a registered society is obliged to make a return under section 887(2) of ITA 2007.
> (2) If the society has not made the return within 3 months after the end of the period, no interest paid by it in the period is to be brought into account for the period for the purposes of Part 5.
> (3) It does not matter for the purposes of subsection (2) whether the payment would be interest apart from section 499.
>
> **CTM40525 Returns Of Gross Payments** {Jun 2016]
> Payments of share and loan interest within ITA07/S887 and payments in respect of transactions with the so-ciety are made gross.
> The society should make a return of the gross payments of share and loan interest. ITA07/S887 requires the society to make a return within 3 months of the end of each accounting period of all payments over £15 made to any person. In practice returns are required only for payments of £250 and over to any person.

---

69 section 887(6) ITA defines payment: "For the purposes of this section crediting interest (or amounts treated as interest) counts as paying it."

70 Section 887(5) ITA provides the standard definition.

The return should include the name and address of each person to whom such a gross payment of £250 or more has been made and the amount paid to each. The returns should be sent to:
HM Revenue and Customs
Centre for National Information
Ground Floor, Government Buildings, Ty Glas, Llanishen, Cardiff, CF14 5ZG
There is information on how the process works for registered societies at:
http://www.gov.uk/government/publications/notes-for-submitting-a-return-under-section-887-of-the-income-tax-act-2007-on-a-spreadsheet-industrial-and-provident-society-ips-5fa
There is similar guidance for credit unions at:
https://www.gov.uk/government/publications/notes-for-submitting-a-return-under-section-887-of-the-income-tax-act-2007-on-a-spreadsheet

42.31.5 *Position of payee*

The Company Taxation Manual provides:

CTM40530 Payment Of Share And Loan Interest And Other Payments: Treatment Of Recipient
A member may be in receipt of various payments from a registered society, all of which are paid gross by the society.
Interest
A society may pay interest in respect of any mortgage, loan, loan stock or deposit, This is a receipt of gross interest for the recipient and is part of his total income. It should either be coded out through his PAYE tax code or included on his tax return as untaxed income as appropriate.
Any interest, dividend, bonus or other sum payable to a shareholder of such a society by reference to the amount of the shareholder's holding in the share capital of the society is also treated as a receipt of gross interest in the hands of the recipient (ITTOIA05/S379) and the member is responsible for ensuring that tax is paid on it as above.
Some members who have low incomes will have no tax to pay.
Other payments
A registered society, in particular a co-operative society, may also pay a discount, bonus, dividend or rebate to its members based on the level of their transactions with the society. Whether or not this is taxable in the hands of the member depends on the nature of the transaction on which the dividend is based and the nature of the relationship between the member and the society.
For example in a retail co-operative where the member is simply buying retail goods from the company, then any dividend based on the amount of purchases made is effectively a discount on the purchase price of the goods and as such is not taxable income in the hands of the member.
However where the dividend is based on trade transactions with a member, for

example in an agricultural co-operative where a farmer member is supplying say vegetables to the co-operative, then the dividend is a trading receipt of the member and should be included in his trading income.

BIM24560 Distributions: Dividends From A Co-Operative Etc Society [Jan 2019]
... Dividends on purchases received by a trader from a co-operative society should be regarded as discounts and taken into account for tax purposes to the extent to which those purchases qualify for a tax deduction or allowance. (See *Pope v Beaumont* [1941] 24 TC 78.)
Dividends on sales made by a trader to or through co-operative societies (for example, egg packing stations and auction societies) should be treated as additions to the sale proceeds and, therefore, as trading receipts.
Dividend in this context means any sum that the society would be entitled to deduct as an expense under S132 CTA 2009[71] if it were an IPS, that is any discount, rebate, dividend or bonus granted by the society to members in respect of their transactions with it. A bonus satisfied in whole or in part by the allotment of shares in the society is within this definition whether or not the member is given the option of taking cash instead of shares (see *Staffordshire Egg Producers Ltd v Spencer* [1963] 41 TC 131). Where, in such a case, a trader receives an allotment of shares, the amount to be included as a receipt of their trade is the nominal value of the shares. A deferred bonus, that is a bonus treated as an interest-bearing loan repayable at some future date, should, where the recipient is a trader, be included as a receipt of the trade when it is recognised under generally accepted accounting practice - see BIM31015.

42.31.6 *Dividend: Deductible for society*

Section 132 CTA 2009 provides a statutory trading deduction for the society:

(1) This section applies if a trade is carried on by a registered society and—
- (a) the society does not sell to persons who are not its members, or
- (b) the number of shares in the society is not limited by the society's rules or practice.

(2) In calculating the profits of the trade, a deduction is allowed for sums which meet conditions A and B.
(3) Condition A is that—
- (a) the sum represents a discount, rebate, dividend or bonus granted by the society to a member or other person ("the recipient"),
- (b) the discount, rebate, dividend or bonus is in respect of—
  - (i) amounts paid or payable by the recipient, or
  - (ii) amounts paid or payable to the recipient,

71 See 42.31.6 (Dividend: deductible for society).

on account of the recipient's transactions with the society, and

(c) those transactions are taken into account in calculating the society's profits chargeable under this Part.

(4) Condition B is that the sum mentioned in subsection (2) is calculated by reference to—

(a) the amounts paid or payable by or to the recipient, or

(b) the size of the transactions,

and not by reference to the amount of any share or interest in the capital of the society.

In *Staffordshire Egg Producers v Spencer*:[72]

> what Parliament had in mind when enacting [s.132] was to make it clear that the dividend on purchases returned to their members by cooperative societies, and other similar sums, should be deductible expenses when computing the societies' profits from trading. Before 1933 they were largely exempt, the view being taken that a transaction between members of a mutual society was not trading. The pressure of private trading interests caused an alteration in the law. Hence, Section 31 of the Finance Act, 1933...[73] But it was obviously desirable in the same legislation to make it clear that dividends on purchases and suchlike, allowed by these societies, should not be regarded merely as distributions of profit to members but as expenses deductible in the computation of those profits. Hence, [s.31(3) FA 1933, now s.132 CTA 2009].

> **BIM24735 Agricultural Co-Operatives: Not Conducting A Mutual Trade** [Jan 2019]
> If the co-operative is an IPS [now, a registered society] then Section 132 provides that such things as discounts, rebates and dividends paid in respect of the members dealings with the society are to be allowed as a deduction in computing its trade profits. These payments should normally be included as a trading receipt in the recipients accounts.[74]

> **CTM40515 Carrying On Trade - Dividends Etc** [Mar 2020]
> CTA09/S132 ... applies equally to loyalty or reward card-type schemes, where points are earned for each transaction, as it does to the traditional 'divi'.
> The amount to be deducted is the full amount of dividend, bonus etc granted, whether or not the full amount is immediately released to members. Thus a bonus satisfied in whole or in part by
> [1] the allotment of paid-up shares in the capital of the society or
> [2] a 'deferred bonus', that is, a bonus treated as an interest-bearing loan repayable at some future date,[75]

---

72 41 TC 131 at p.144.

73 See 42.2.2 (Attempt to tax mutuals).

74 Authors' footnote: it is assumed here that the recipient is trading.

75 Authors' footnote: A lawyer would more accurately describe [2] as an issue of a debenture, rather than a "deferred bonus".

becomes deductible as soon as it is granted - see *Staffordshire Egg Producers Ltd v Spencer* (1963) 41 TC 131.

The sums deductible are in strictness the amounts granted in respect of the transactions of the accounting period. The amounts shown by the society's accounts as having been paid or credited in the accounting period may be used, even though these may in some cases include late payments of 'divi' for earlier periods.

In the common case of a society which makes an 'interim' distribution at the end of the first three months of a half-year, and a 'final' distribution after making up its accounts for the half year, the 'interim divi' added to the 'final divi' may be taken as the appropriate deduction for the half-year...

Worker Co-operatives

A bonus in respect of the services of a worker member is not within the definition of a bonus in respect of transactions with the society, i.e. it will not fall within CTA09/S132. Such a bonus will usually be employment income and PAYE/NIC should be applied to it as normal.

42.31.7 *Losses*

The losses of a registered society which are carried forward under CTA10/S45 may be relieved against the following items of income for the purposes of CTA10/S46 (trade-related interest etc - see CTM04250):

- interest brought into the computation of CT profits as a trading loan relationship credit
- foreign investment income.

These sums must be income from investments which would have been taken into account as trading income but for the fact that they are charged under other Parts of CTA09.

42.31.8 *Conversion to/from company*

The CT Manual provides:

CTM40550 conversion to a Companies Act company and vice versa [Feb 2020]

Where a registered society converts to a Companies Act company under CCBS14/S112, or a Companies Act company converts to a registered society under CCBS/S115, this does not cause one entity to cease and another to come into being. They are treated as the same legal entity both before and after the conversion. No change of UTR should be necessary.

... such conversions do not generally give rise to any deemed or actual disposal of chargeable assets or distributions and there is no cessation and recommencement of the business...

42.32 Agricultural/fishing co-operative

42.32.1 *Definition*

Section 499 CTA 2009 provides:

> (3) In subsection (1) "UK agricultural or fishing co-operative" means a co- operative association—
> (a) which is established in the United Kingdom and UK resident, and
> (b) whose primary object is assisting its members in—
> (i) carrying on agricultural or horticultural businesses on land occupied by them in the United Kingdom, or
> (ii) carrying on businesses consisting in the catching or taking of fish or shellfish.
> (4) In subsection (3) "co-operative association" means a body with a written constitution from which the Secretary of State considers that it is in substance a co-operative association.[76]

As this definition applies for s.499, it is repeated verbatim in s.379 ITTOIA.

> **BIM24735 Agricultural Co-Operatives: Not Conducting A Mutual Trade** [Jan 2019]
> A UK agricultural or fishing co-operative is a co-operative association which is established and resident in the UK and whose primary objective is assisting its members in carrying on agricultural or horticultural business on land in the UK or business consisting in catching or taking fish or shellfish. A co-operative association for this purpose is a body with a written constitution from which the Secretary of State (or Northern Ireland Department of Agriculture and Rural Development) considers that it is in substance such an association.

42.32.2 *Agricultural co-operative: dividend to member*

Section 1057 CTA 2010 provides:

> (1) Interest paid by a UK agricultural or fishing co-operative in respect of a mortgage, loan, loan stock or deposit is not a distribution for

---

76 Section 499 continues:
"(5) For the purposes of subsection (4), the Secretary of State must have regard to the way in which the body's constitution provides for its income to be applied for its members' benefit and all other relevant provisions.
(6) In the application of subsections (4) and (5) in Northern Ireland for "the Secretary of State" substitute "the Department of Agriculture and Rural Development".

corporation tax purposes.

(2) If any dividend, bonus, interest or other sum—

(a) is paid to a shareholder in a UK agricultural or fishing co-operative, and

(b) is payable by reference to the amount of the shareholder's holding in the co-operative's share capital,

it is not a distribution for corporation tax purposes.

(3) Subsections (1) and (2) apply even if the amount in question would otherwise be a distribution by virtue of any enactment relating to corporation tax.

(4) For the purposes of this section crediting an amount counts as paying it.

42.32.3 *Dividend from co-operative*

The Business Income Manual provides:

BIM24565 Distributions: S1070 Corporation Tax Act 2010 [Jan 2019]
S1070 Corporation Tax Act 2010 (CTA 2010)
Where a company carrying on a mutual trade (or other mutual business) makes a distribution to its members you need to establish if that distribution comes from the surplus from the company's trading with its members or from trading with non-members or a mixture of both.

- Distributions out of a mutual surplus give rise to taxable receipts.
- Distributions out of taxable income give rise to non-taxable receipts.

Section 1070(2) ensures that the normal Corporation Tax provisions (see CTM15120) only apply to distributions deriving from:

- profits that have been brought into charge to Corporation Tax, or
- income of the company that consists of exempt ABGH distributions (defined by section 1070(5A)) or, prior to 2016/17, franked investment income.

Section 1070(3) restricts the effect of Section 1070(2) to distributions made to a person participating in the mutual activities of the mutual business and deriving from those activities.
In the case of a mutual insurance business, Section 1070(4) provides that the Corporation Tax provisions concerning distributions do not apply to distributions made to persons participating in the mutual activities of the life insurer and derived from those activities.
Section 1070(5) notes that the fact that a distribution by a company carrying on a mutual business to a person participating in those activities is derived from the mutual activities does not change the character of the distribution for Corporation Tax or Income Tax in the hands of the recipient.
The result is that Section 1070 applies the normal Corporation Tax provisions concerning distributions to a mutual trader (and to companies carrying on mutual insurance or other mutual business). In effect the provisions make clear, for example, that distributions to trading members out of mutual surpluses are trading receipts in the hands of the recipient to the extent that the distribution represents a return of payments made.
The reasoning behind this is that anything which is not a return of contributions must have arisen from the concerns non-mutual operations and will have been taxed in the

hands of the concern.

Section 1070 applies if a company has carried on a mutual trade or has never carried on a trade or a business of holding investments. In both cases, the distributions legislation is limited to such distributions as are made out of profits brought into charge to Corporation Tax or out of franked investment income, that is income not derived from mutual trading.

The legislation is not specific as to the source of the sums to be distributed. The point is whether they have been subject to Corporation Tax or not. Hence, any sums exempted from Corporation Tax under the Substantial Shareholdings Exemption (see CG53005 onwards) would not be subject to the provisions of the distributions legislation.

A company that is limited by guarantee has no share capital. Where such a company makes a distribution to its members on a winding-up, the distribution is not excluded from the definition of distribution by S1030 CTA 2010 because it is not a distribution made in respect of share capital in a winding-up. To secure that companies limited by guarantee receive comparable treatment to companies limited by share capital, you should treat distributions in a winding-up by a company limited by guarantee as capital distributions.

42.33 Agricultural marketing board

Statutory agricultural marketing boards are a somewhat specialist topic; but we set out the legislation for completeness.

Section 153 CTA 2009 provides:

> (1) This section applies to a statutory body if its object (or one of its objects) is—
> (a) marketing an agricultural product, or
> (b) stabilising the price of an agricultural product.
>
> (2) Subsections (3) and (4) apply if the body is required, by or under an approved scheme or arrangement ("the scheme"), to pay the whole or part of any trading surplus into a reserve fund meeting the conditions specified in section 154.
>
> (3) Any sums which the body is required by or under the scheme to pay into the fund out of the profits of its trade are allowed as deductions in calculating the profits of the trade.
>
> (4) Any sums withdrawn by the body from the fund are taken into account as trading receipts, except so far as—
> (a) they are required, by or under the scheme, to be paid to a Minister or department,
> (b) they are distributed to producers of the product in question, or
> (c) they are refunded to persons who pay any levy or duty.
>
> (5) In this section—
> "approved scheme or arrangement" means a scheme or arrangement approved by, or made with, a Minister or department,
> "producers of the product" includes persons producing the product

from another product,
"statutory body" means a body established by or under an enactment,
"trading surplus" means a surplus from the body's trading operations or other trade receipts.

Section 154 CTA 2009 provides:

(1) These are the conditions to be met by the reserve fund (see section 153(2)).
(2) The first condition is that no sum may be withdrawn from the fund without the authority or consent of a Minister or department.
(3) The second condition is that if—
  (a) money has been paid to the body by a Minister or department—
    (i) in connection with arrangements for maintaining guaranteed prices, or
    (ii) in connection with the body's trading arrangements, and
(b) the money is repayable to the Minister or department,
sums standing to the credit of the fund are required to be applied (in whole or in part) in repaying the money.
(4) The requirement mentioned in subsection (3) must be imposed by or under the scheme or arrangement mentioned in section 153(2).
(5) The third condition is that—
  (a) the fund is reviewed by a Minister at intervals fixed by or under the scheme or arrangement mentioned in section 153(2), and
  (b) if the fund appears to the Minister to exceed what is reasonably required by the body, the excess is withdrawn from the fund.

Section 155 CTA 2009 provides definitions of "Minister" and "department" which need not be set out here.

CHAPTER FORTY THREE

POLITICAL PARTIES

43.1 Political parties

Political parties are not, of course, charities: their objects do not qualify as charitable.[1] They do benefit from some reliefs similar to those available to charities. However the reliefs given to political parties are not as extensive as those for charities.

We do not discuss taxation of income or gains accruing to political parties.

43.2 IHT political party exemption

43.2.1 *IHT party exemption*

Section 24 IHTA provides:

> (1) Transfers of value are exempt to the extent that the values transferred by them—
>
> (a) are attributable to property which becomes the property of a political party qualifying for exemption under this section.

The exemption for gifts to political parties applies to lifetime gifts, as well as gifts on death.

In the case of a gift to one of the smaller parties, a testator at the time of

---

1 See 3.2 (Charitable purpose: English law).

making a will, cannot know whether or not the party will qualify for IHT relief at the time the will takes effect, and the drafter should consider both possibilities.

43.2.2 *"Becomes property of party"*

The IHT Manual provides:

> **IHTM11193: requirements for exemption** [June 2016]
> For a gift to be exempt underIHTA84/S24, the relevant property has to become the property of a qualifying (IHTM11196) political party
> Where it is not clear that the relevant property 'becomes the property' of the political party itself, you should refer the case to Litigation. Examples where this might be the case are gifts to
> - a local association, or
> - another body connected with a political party.

Care is needed for gifts to local constituency parties.
The IHT Manual continues:

> **IHTM11194: gifts to the Conservative party** [Jun 2016]
> You should accept that gifts to The Conservative Party Foundation Ltd. have become the property of the Conservative Party, unless there are conditions attached to the gift that specify how it should be used. This may be an 'express trust'.
> You should refer the case to Technical if:
> - conditions are attached to the gift that may indicate that an express trust applies.
> - you have any doubt that the gift will become the property of the Conservative Party.
> - the gift is by will (IHTM12041)(or exceptionally, under a settlement) and is to the Conservative party, itself or to the Central Office Fund or its treasurers, exemption has been claimed, and the net cumulation would exceed the nil-rate band if that exemption were not available. This is because dicta in the case of *Conservative and Unionist Central Office v Burrell* [1982] 2 AER 1 throws doubt on the legal validity of such a gift.
>
> (This content has been withheld because of exemptions in the [FOI] Freedom of Information Act 2000)
> **11195: gifts to the Liberal Democrats** [10 Jun 2016]
> You should accept that gifts to The Liberal Democrats (Trustees) Ltd. have become the property of the Liberal Democrats, unless there are conditions attached to the gift that specify how it should be used. This may be an 'express trust'.

You should refer the case to Technical if

- conditions are attached to the gift that may indicate that an express trust applies.
- you have any doubt that the gift will become the property of the Liberal Democrats.

A gift to a trust under which property may be applied for charitable purposes or paid to a political party does not qualify for IHT relief. It does not qualify under s.24 because it does not become the property of a political party. It does not qualify under s.23 because s.23(6) IHTA provides:

> For the purposes of this section property is given to charities if it becomes the property of charities or is held on trust for charitable purposes only, and "donor" shall be construed accordingly.

43.2.3 *Qualifying political parties*

Section 24(2) IHTA provides:

> A political party qualifies for exemption under this section if, at the last general election preceding the transfer of value,—
> (a) two members of that party were elected to the House of Commons, or
> (b) one member of that party was elected to the House of Commons and not less than 150,000 votes were given to candidates who were members of that party.

After the 2017 election, qualifying parties are:

Party	***Seats***	
Conservative	317	
Labour	262	
SNP	35	
Liberal Democrat	12	
DUP	10	
Sinn Féin	7	
Plaid Cymru	4	
Green	1	(524,604 votes)

This test has mostly excluded UKIP, who prior to the 2015 general election, where they won one seat and over 3 million votes, had not had any MPs elected to the commons in a general election. This despite the fact that they did have European MPs and they had also won a by-election in the period. Since the 2017 election, where they again failed to win a seat despite gathering over 500,000 votes, UKIP once again do not count as a political party for the purposes of section 24.

In *Arron Banks v HMRC* [2018] UKFTT 0617 (TC), businessman Arron Banks challenged this result in the FTT on the basis that it was contrary to both his right to non-discrimination on the grounds of political belief under Article 14 ECHR and EU law. The tribunal dismissed the EU point, but did agree both that there was discrimination under Article 14 and that the provision could not be justified as proportionate. It concluded, however, that it did not have room to interpret the section differently, and since it could neither issue a declaration of incompatibility the appeal was dismissed.

In relation to a gift to a political party of another EU member state, there must nonetheless be an argument that section 24 is in breach of EU law, since the statute does not allow relief for non-UK political parties. It is considered that a gift to foreign political parties which meet equivalent requirements in their own countries would qualify for IHT relief.[2]

43.2.4 *Anti-avoidance*

Section 24 IHTA provides:

> (3) Subsections (2) to (5) of section 23 above shall apply in relation to subsection (1) above as they apply in relation to section 23(1).
> (4) For the purposes of section 23(2) to (5) as they apply by virtue of subsection (3) above property is given to any person or body if it becomes the property of or is held on trust for that person or body, and "donor" shall be construed accordingly.

See 24.11 (Anti-avoidance: introduction).

43.3 Gift to party: CGT hold-over relief

Section 260 TCGA provides:

> (1) If—
> (a) an individual or the trustees of a settlement ("the transferor") make a disposal within subsection (2) below of an asset,
> (b) the asset is acquired by an individual or the trustees of a settlement ("the transferee"), and
> (c) a claim for relief under this section is made by the transferor and the transferee or, where the trustees of a settlement are the transferee, by the transferor alone,

---

2 See 3.20 (EU law: Introduction).

> then, subject to subsection (6) below and sections 169, 169B, 169C and 261, subsection (3) below shall apply in relation to the disposal.
> (2) A disposal is within this subsection if it is made otherwise than under a bargain at arm's length and—
> ...
> (b) is an exempt transfer by virtue of—
> (i) section 24 [IHTA] (transfers to political parties),

Subsection (2) clearly assumes that relief is available on a gift to a qualifying political party. Subsection (1) taken literally does not confer relief since a gift to a political party does not meet the condition in (1)(b) that the asset is acquired by an individual or the trustees of a settlement. But the subsection should be construed to include a gift where the asset is acquired by a political party though not an individual or a trust.

Section 260(3) provides the relief:

> (3) Where this subsection applies in relation to a disposal—
> (a) the amount of any chargeable gain which, apart from this section, would accrue to the transferor on the disposal, and
> (b) the amount of the consideration for which, apart from this section, the transferee would be regarded for the purposes of capital gains tax as having acquired the asset in question,
>
> shall each be reduced by an amount equal to the held-over gain on the disposal.
> (4) Subject to subsection (5) below, the reference in subsection (3) above to the held-over gain on a disposal is a reference to the chargeable gain which would have accrued on that disposal apart from this section ...

Thus the availability of hold-over relief, in the case of a political party, is linked to the inheritance tax relief in s.24 IHTA.

43.4 Reorganisation of constituency boundary

There are CGT and SDLT reliefs for transfers on the reorganisation of local constituency boundaries; s.264 TCGA and s.67 FA 2003. These reliefs are not discussed here.

43.5 Gift to political party: IT relief

Gift Aid relief does not apply as a political party is not a charity.

The Business Income Manual provides:

> **BIM42528: political and propaganda expenses** [Jun 2016]
> You should disallow payments to political funds, contributions to party funds, and expenses of candidates at elections etc.

> As regards propaganda of a political nature carried on by a trader, see *Boarland v Kramat Pulai Ltd* [1953] 35 TC 1 (see BIM37035).
> The cost of propaganda undertaken by a trader wholly and exclusively to prevent him from losing his business and to preserve its assets is admissible (*Morgan v Tate and Lyle Ltd* [1954] 35 TC 367, see BIM35570).

See 18.2 (Charity gift: Deductible expense).

Matthew Paris puts the case for allowing Gift Aid:

> We could offer tax relief ... like the gift aid enjoyed by charities, to small-to-medium-sized donations to political parties. ... Not only would this augment party funds, but my guess is that it would increase people's willingness to give. I'm much encouraged to donate when I know this will force the chancellor to chip in too.[3]

43.6 Planning

A donor who owns a suitable company might arrange that:

(1) The donor gives the company to the political party.
(2) The political party extracts the funds by way of dividend.

The gift at stage (1) qualifies for CGT hold-over relief; and the distribution at stage (2) would not be taxable assuming the party is a company for tax purposes.

It seems that Labour arranged this in 2013, giving rise to a fit of indignation, or purported indignation, from the Conservatives. An open letter from George Osborne to Ed Milliband provided:

> Dear Ed,
> You said in April last year that 'tax avoidance is a terrible thing'. ...
> Yet ... the Labour Party has gone to great lengths to help your biggest donor, Mr John Mills, avoid paying tax on a political donation. ...
> The Labour Party registered a donation of shares in JML worth £1.65 million in January 2013, from Mr John Mills. By making a donation in shares rather than as a single cash dividend, it has been reported that Mr Mills managed to avoid a potential tax charge of £724,710. ...
> As leader of the Labour Party, and given your previous statements on tax avoidance, such actions by your party appear to be directly at odds with your public statements.
> Most importantly, will you now pass the amount of tax that has been

3 The Times, 6 June 2015. The relief would have to apply to EU charities, though it could be restricted (like IHT) to parties which have attained widespread support..

> avoided to the Exchequer? As you say, this is money that is needed to fund vital public services such as the health service and our schools.
> Yours sincerely,
> George Osborne[4]

What is one to make of this? We think any practitioner, or anyone who understood the tax background, would regard this as in the category of "sensible tax planning" a long way from an avoidance, and miles from the sort of abusive transactions which might be castigated as immoral.[5] The letter could be seen as just an example of debased or meaningless political debate, whose object is just to knock the opposition. However, it may be regarded as an illustration of the difficulties which inevitably arise if one regards taxation as governed by moral principles distinct from black letter tax law. The letter might then be regarded as a rather subtle and well aimed contribution to a political debate which is beyond the scope of this book. Perhaps there are elements of both.

---

4 6 June 2013 *http://eastmidslibdems.org.uk/en/article/2013/0694861/george-osborne-letter-to-ed-miliband-over-donor-s-taxes*

5 See Kessler, *Taxation of Non-Residents and Foreign Domiciliaries* (21st ed., 2022-23), Chapter 2 (Tax Avoidance)
online version *https://www.foreigndomiciliaries.co.uk*

CHAPTER FORTY FOUR

HOUSING ASSOCIATIONS

44.1 Housing associations: Introduction

The CT Manual provides:

> **CTM40405: housing associations: introduction** [Jun 2016]
> Housing associations are 'non-profit making' organisations which aim to provide for people in housing need.
> Some housing associations rely on the work of a committee of (usually unpaid) volunteers; others employ staff. Most associations provide rented accommodation, including houses, flats and hostels. Some also provide homes for sale through low cost home ownership schemes, such as shared ownership which is part sale, part rent. Some associations buy sites or properties for redevelopment. Others take over existing tenanted housing from local authorities or other public sector landlords under voluntary transfers.
> Housing associations registered with the appropriate authority are variously known as Registered Social Landlords (RSL), Registered Providers and, more recently, Private Registered Providers of Social Housing (PRP). The terms RSL and PRP may both be encountered, but housing association is still the usual term and is widely used.
> The Homes and Communities Agency (HCA) provides subsidies for new housing and regulates housing associations in England (except in London where the responsibility is that of the Greater London Authority). From 1 April 2012 the HCA is the regulatory authority for housing associations in England. The HCA's responsibility was formerly that of the Housing Corporation.

Arrangements are different in Northern Ireland (Northern Ireland Housing Executive), Scotland (Scottish Housing Regulator) and Wales (Welsh Government responsibility).

The fact that housing associations are often described as 'non profit making' means, in broad terms, that it is not their primary purpose to make a commercial profit which can be distributed to their investors. Any profits that do in fact arise are, subject to the guidance contained in this section, subject to CT in the normal way. Housing associations' day to day activities are funded by rent and service charges and in this sense they are commercial entities.

There has been debate about the public/private status of housing associations. They are regarded as public for some EU purposes and have been held subject to judicial review as public bodies are.

How housing associations are constituted

Most housing associations are 'registered societies' in Great Britain – formerly industrial and provident societies, see CTM40505 – and their treatment is set out in this section at CTM40400 onwards. There are also housing association Companies Act companies and trusts. which may (or may not) have charitable status. The normal company, trust and charity rules apply to all of these.

44.2 IHT housing association exemption

Section 24A IHTA provides:

> (1) A transfer of value is exempt to the extent that the value transferred by it is attributable to land in the United Kingdom given to a body falling within subsection (2) below.
>
> (2) A body falls within this subsection if it is—
>
> (za) a non-profit registered provider of social housing;
>
> (a) a registered social landlord within the meaning of Part I of the Housing Act 1996;
>
> (b) a registered housing association within the meaning of the Housing Associations Act 1985; or
>
> (c) a registered housing association within the meaning of Part II of the Housing (Northern Ireland) Order 1992.

The bodies which can qualify for the s.24A exemption in England are non-profit registered providers of social housing and registered housing associations. In Wales the exemption applies to registered social landlords and registered housing associations. These are all terms defined in other acts.

The IHT Manual explains the history of the terminology:

> **IHTM11212: Gifts to registered housing associations: registered social landlords (RSLs)** [Jun 2016]
> Under the Housing Act 1996 the concept of a registered housing association was replaced by that of a 'registered social landlord' (RSL). Consequential changes to IHTA84/S24A (1) and IHTA/S24A (2) by paragraph 12 Schedule 2 of the Housing Act 1996 (Consequential Provisions) Order 1996 S.I. 1996/2325 are, with effect from 1 October 1996 in IHTA84/S24A (1) the phrase 'registered housing association' is replaced by 'body falling within subsection IHTA84/S24A (2) below.'

It is considered that a gift to foreign housing associations which meet equivalent requirements in their own countries qualify for IHT relief under EU law.[1]

The exemption is subject to restrictions very similar to the IHT charity exemption. Section 24A(3) IHTA provides:

> Subsections (2) to (5) of section 23 and subsection (4) of section 24 above shall apply in relation to subsection (1) above as they apply in relation to section 24(1).

44.3 Capital gains

44.3.1 *Relief for gift to housing association*

Section 259(1) TCGA provides:

> Subsection (2) below shall apply where-
> (a) a disposal of an estate or interest in land in the United Kingdom is made to a relevant housing provider otherwise than under a bargain at arm's length, and
> (b) a claim for relief under this section is made by the transferor and the relevant housing provider.

Section 259(2) TCGA provides the relief:

> Section 17(1) shall not apply; but if the disposal is by way of gift or for a consideration not exceeding the sums allowable as a deduction under section 38, then-
> (a) the disposal and acquisition shall be treated for the purposes of this Act as being made for such consideration as to secure that neither a gain nor a loss accrues on the disposal, and
> (b) where, after the disposal, the estate or interest is disposed of by

1 See 3.20 (EU law: Introduction).

> the relevant housing provider, its acquisition by the person making the earlier disposal shall be treated for the purposes of this Act as the acquisition of the relevant housing provider.

This is the same as the CGT relief for gifts to charity; see 23.3.3 (Position of donor).

Section 259(3) TCGA defines "Relevant housing provider":

> In this section "relevant housing provider" means-
> (a) a non-profit registered provider of social housing,
> (b) a registered social landlord within the meaning of Part I of the Housing Act 1996,
> (c) a body registered in the register maintained under section 20(1) of the Housing (Scotland) Act 2001, or
> (d) a registered housing association within the meaning of Part 2 of the Housing (Northern Ireland) Order 1992...

Part 1 of the Housing Act 1996 now relates only to registered social landlords in Wales, which must be on the register kept by the Welsh Ministers in accordance with s.1 Housing Act 1996.

The phrase "non-profit registered provider of social housing" refers to housing associations in England. The definition is in sch 1 Interpretation Act 1978:

> "Registered provider of social housing" has the meaning given by section 80(2) of the Housing and Regeneration Act 2008 (and "non-profit" and "profit-making" in connection with a provider have the meanings given by section 115 of that Act).

Section 80 Housing and Regeneration Act 2008 provides:

> (1) In this Chapter a reference to the provider of social housing is to be construed as follows.

Type of social housing	*Provider*
Low cost rental accommodation	The Landlord
Low cost home ownership accommodation:	
shared ownership	The Landlord
equity percentage	The "seller" within the meaning of section 70(5)(a)
shared ownership trust	The "social landlord" within the meaning of paragraph 7(3) of Schedule 9 to the Finance Act 2003

> (2) Chapter 3 provides for the establishment of a register of providers of social housing: persons listed in the register—
> (a) may be referred to in an enactment or other instrument as "registered providers of social housing", and
> (b) are referred to in this Part as "registered providers".

(3) Persons listed in the register who are not local authorities—
   (a) may be referred to in an enactment or other instrument as "private registered providers of social housing", and
   (b) are referred to in this Part as "private registered providers"...

The CG Manual provides:

> CG**66635: Gifts of land to housing associations** [Jun 2016]
> TCGA92/S259 brings the Capital Gains Tax treatment of gifts of land to non-charitable registered housing associations into line with the rules which apply to gifts of land to charitable housing associations. The provisions apply to disposals made on or after 14 March 1989 and a claim to the relief has to be made by the donor and the association.
> If the land is given or transferred at less than market value to a registered housing association the market value rule (TCGA92/S17) does not apply. The transfer is not treated as taking place at market value.
> If the consideration for the transfer is greater than the sums allowable as a deduction under TCGA92/S38, which do not include the indexation allowable, then you compute the chargeable gain in the normal way using the actual consideration received as the disposal proceeds. This is also the housing association's acquisition cost. As with a charity the housing association is treated as having the original owner's date of acquisition.
> If the consideration does not exceed the amount of the TCGA92/S38 expenditure the person making the disposal will be treated as making neither a gain nor a loss after any indexation allowance. This is also the housing association's acquisition cost. As with a charity the housing association is treated as having the original owner's date of acquisition.

44.4 Relief for housing association income/gains

44.4.1 *Relief for housing association income*

Section 642 CTA 2010 provides:

> (1) Subsections (2) and (3) apply if a housing association makes a claim under this section for an accounting period or part of an accounting period during which the association was approved for the purposes of this Chapter.
> (2) Rent to which the association was entitled from its members for the accounting period or part of an accounting period is ignored for tax purposes.
> (3) The association is treated for corporation tax purposes as if any interest payable by it for the accounting period or part of an accounting period were not payable.
> (4) But subsection (3) does not apply so far as the interest is attributable

to property that is not subject to a tenancy.

44.4.2 *Relief for housing association gains*

Section 643 CTA 2010 provides:

(1) This section applies if-
- (a) chargeable gains accrue to a housing association on a disposal by way of sale of any property which has been occupied, or is occupied, by a tenant of the housing association,
- (b) the gains accrue in an accounting period or part of an accounting period during which the association was approved for the purposes of this Chapter, and
- (c) the association makes a claim under this section for that period or part of a period.

(2) No liability to corporation tax arises in respect of the gains.

44.4.3 *"Approved" housing association*

Section 644 CTA 2010 provides:

(1) In the case of a housing association in Great Britain, the power to approve housing associations for the purposes of this Chapter-
- (a) is exercisable by the Scottish Ministers if the association has its registered office in Scotland,
- (b) is exercisable by the Welsh Ministers in relation to Wales, and
- (c) is otherwise exercisable by the Secretary of State.

(2) In the case of a housing association in Northern Ireland, the power to approve housing associations for the purposes of this Chapter is exercisable by the Department for Social Development.

(3) An approval given for the purposes of this Chapter-
- (a) has effect from the date specified by the approving authority (which may be earlier or later than the date on which the approval is given), and
- (b) may be revoked by the approving authority.

(4) See also paragraph 80 of Schedule 2 (concurrent exercise by the Secretary of State of certain functions exercisable by the Welsh Ministers)

Section 645 CTA 2010 sets out the requirements for approval:

(1) The authority mentioned in section 644(1) or (2) must not approve a housing association unless it is satisfied that the association satisfies each of tests A to E.

(2) Test A is that the association is—
- (a) a housing association within the meaning of the Housing Associations Act 1985 (see section 1(1) of that Act), or

(b) a housing association within the meaning of Part 2 of the Housing (Northern Ireland) Order 1992 (SI 1725 (NI 15)) (see Article 3 of that Order).

(3) Test B is that the association is a society—

(a) a registered society within the meaning of the Co-operative and Community Benefit Societies Act 2014, or

(b) a society registered or treated as registered under the Industrial and Provident Societies Act (Northern Ireland) 1969.

(4) Test C is that the rules of the association—

(a) restrict membership to persons who are tenants or prospective tenants of the association, and

(b) preclude the granting or assignment of tenancies to persons other than members.

(5) Test D is that the association satisfies any other requirements prescribed by-

(a) the Secretary of State as regards England and Scotland,

(b) the Welsh Ministers as regards Wales, or

(c) the Department for Social Development as regards Northern Ireland.

(6) Test E is that the association will comply with any conditions that may be prescribed by—

(a) the Secretary of State as regards England and Scotland,

(b) the Welsh Ministers as regards Wales, or

(c) the Department for Social Development as regards Northern Ireland.

Section 646 CTA 2010 provides:

(1) In relation to a housing association which is a registered provider of social housing (see section 80(2) of the Housing and Regeneration Act 2008) the Secretary of State may delegate to the Regulator of Social Housing any of the Secretary of State's functions under section 644 or 645.

(2) The functions may be delegated—

(a) to any extent that the Secretary of State specifies, and

(b) subject to any conditions that the Secretary of State specifies.

44.5 *Claim for relief*

Section 647(1) CTA 2010 provides a time limit:

A claim under section 642 or 643 must be made-

(a) within two years after the end of the accounting period to which it relates, or

(b) if it relates to part of an accounting period, within two years after the end of that accounting period.

Section 647 CTA 2010 introduces further requirements:

(2) A housing association must not make a claim under section 642 or 643 for an accounting period or part of an accounting period unless-
- (a) the requirements in subsection (3) were complied with during that period or part, or
- (b) the association reasonably considers that those requirements were substantially complied with during that period or part.

(3) The requirements are that-
- (a) no property belonging to the association was let otherwise than to a member of the association,
- (b) only persons who were then members of the association occupied (whether solely or jointly with another person) any property, or any part of any property, let by the association,
- (c) the association satisfied each of tests A to C in section 645 and complied with any conditions that were in force by virtue of section 645(6), and
- (d) any covenants required to be included in grants of tenancies by those conditions were observed.

(4) If a member of a housing association dies and another person occupies a property, or part of a property, in accordance with the member's will or the provisions applicable on the member's intestacy, that person's occupation during the first 6 months after the death does not infringe the requirement in subsection (3)(b).

44.6 CT Manual

The CT Manual (not yet written up for the CTA 2010) provides:

CTM40415: Co-operatives: background [Jun 2016]
The aim behind co-operative, or 'co-ownership', housing associations is to give tenant-members some of the benefits enjoyed by owner-occupiers by treating them collectively as such. It is a relatively small sector. There are only about 10,000 cooperative housing associations compared to some 1.6m other housing associations. A co-ownership housing association normally consists of a number of persons who collectively own a group of houses or flats, the cost of which has been financed on mortgage. The association holds the legal title to the land and is mortgagor; the members occupy the dwellings under short tenancy agreements or leases from the association. All members of the association have to be tenants or prospective tenants and all tenants have to be members of the association. Rents payable to the association are fixed at a figure to cover the member's share of the total annual

outgoings, including mortgage interest payments and repayments of capital.

On joining the association, a member will normally have purchased a share of nominal value and sometimes also repayable loan stock to the value of, say, 5% of the cost of the house or flat. On leaving, the tenant surrenders the lease to the association and is repaid any loan capital. If the property was occupied by the tenant for not less than three years, the tenant will also receive a premium which takes into account his share of the capital repayment made by the association and any increase in the market value of his property at the date of leaving. The premium is regarded as consideration for the disposal of an interest in the property previously occupied by the outgoing member and therefore within the scope of chargeable gains. In most cases, however, exemption will be due under TCGA92/S222 (private residence relief – see CG64200 onwards).

CTM40420: Co-operatives - nature of relief and claim [Jun 2016]

CTA10/PART13/CHAPTER7

S642 (for income) and S643 (for gains) within CTA10/PART13/ CHAPTER7 provide reliefs to approved co-operative housing associations (CTM40425) as follows:

1. rents paid to the association by members are disregarded for tax purposes
2. interest payable by the association is disregarded
3. the association is exempt from CT on chargeable gains on the disposal of any property which has been or is occupied by a tenant of the association (see CG12624).

Where relief is allowable under CTA10/S642 the association is still liable to CT on any investment income not specifically exempted by the section such as, for example, interest received on a bank deposit account. It is also liable to CT on other chargeable gains that do not fall within (c) above.

A co-operative housing association will not normally make distributions within the meaning CTA10/PART23. CTA10/S1064 cannot apply because a 'registered society' in Great Britain – formerly industrial and provident society, cannot be a close company (see CTM40505).

(This content has been withheld because of exemptions in the Freedom of Information Act 2000)

CTM40425: Co- operatives: approval [Jun 2016]

To obtain relief under CTA10/PART13/CHAPTER7 (CTM40420), an association must be approved by the Secretary of State (or Scottish or Welsh Ministers) – CTA10/S644. In practice the power of delegation to the relevant regulator of social housing is exercised – CTA10/S654.

It is a condition of approval that the association is a 'registered society' in Great Britain (formerly a registered industrial and provident society – see CTM40505 onwards) and is a housing association within the meaning of the Housing Associations Act 1985. When the relevant authority approves an association, it receives an official letter of approval with instructions to send one copy to the HMRC office that deals with the association's accounts.

CTM40430: Co-operatives - interest paid [Jun 2016]

ITA07/S887 (1) provides that any share or loan interest paid by a registered society (see CTM42405) may be paid in full, except where the interest is payable to a person whose usual place of abode is outside the UK.

As such a registered society, any other interest of such a housing association will be paid in full.

An association which claims under CTA10/PART13/CHAPTER7 and supplies the information required on Form 75 (which includes details of all interest paid, whether in full or under deduction of tax) should not also be required to render separate returns of interest paid. (This content has been withheld because of exemptions in the Freedom of Information Act 2000)

First year of claim

On the first occasion on which a housing association wishes to make a claim under CTA10/PART13/CHAPTER7 the Office responsible should issue Form 75, which requires the association to submit:

- a copy of the rules, a copy of the relevant authority's letter of approval (CTM40425),

and

- a copy of the accounts.

A duplicate form may be issued for retention by the association.

CTM40435: Co-operatives - unlet properties [Jun 2016]

Interest paid by a housing association (CTM40405) in respect of properties that are in course of building, or which are completed but not yet let, cannot form part of the claim under CTA10/S642 (CTM40420) as there is no tenancy – see CTA10/S642 (4). The interest should be excluded when calculating the relief allowable to members. The interest to be excluded can be determined by any reasonable method of apportionment, for example, by reference to the approximate amounts of the capital expenditure on the respective properties.

Example

Total rents receivable by the association	£25,000
Add notional rent for one unlet property (six months)	£1,250
	£26,250
Total interest paid by association	£15,000

Less treated as paid by members	
(£25,000/£26,250 × £15,000)	£14,290
Balance to be treated as paid by association	£710

The balance treated as paid by the association rather than the members will be allowable to the association under the normal rules for 'registered societies' in Great Britain – formerly industrial and provident societies - see CTM40570.

CTM40440: Co-operatives: disqualifying letting [Jun 2016]

CTA10/S647 (3)

A housing association (CTM40405) may be disqualified from relief under CTA10/S642 (CTM40420) if there is letting:

1. by the association to non-members, or
2. by a member to a non-member.

In the case of 1. above, the association should be asked for an explanation if, as is likely, such letting is not permitted by its rules. A report should then be made to CTIS (Technical) including an estimate of the probable rental income arising on the rents from non-members.

In the case of 2. above, the official letter of approval issued to the association (CTM40425) specifies the limited extent to which sub-letting by members will be permitted. If this limit is exceeded advice should be sought from CTIS (Technical).

Where it is agreed that the requirements of CTA10/S647 (3) have been substantially complied with the rents from non-members will be taxable under the normal property income rules. The interest paid in respect of a property let to a non-member will not be within CTA10/S642 and the loan relationship provisions will apply.

CTM40445: Co-operatives: death of a member [Jun 2016]

CTA10/S647 (4)

Where a member of a co-operative housing association dies, rights under the lease (CTM40415) will pass to the personal representative for a limited period. CTA10/S647 (4) provides that, for the first six months after the death of a member, occupation by non-members in accordance with the will, or under the provisions applicable on intestacy, will be treated as though it were occupation by a member.

40460: Charity aspects [Jun 2016]

Charitable housing associations (identifiable normally by the adoption of model charitable rules published by the National Federation of Housing Societies) do not normally involve any identity between tenants and members. Consequently, they do not qualify for relief under CTA10/PART13/CHAPTER7 (CTM40420), but charity relief may be due under CTA10/PART11/CHAPTER3 (and TCGA92/S256 for capital gains). ...

44.7 Management co-operative

The CT Manual provides:

> **CTM40465: Management co-operatives** [Jun 2016]
> Management co-operatives are a type of housing association (CTM40405) which enables tenants of local authorities to participate in managing their housing accommodation. Such management co-operatives may acquire a lease from the local authority and sub-let the houses to members, or they may merely manage the houses on behalf of the local authority, which remains the landlord of the members. There are no special tax reliefs for such co-operatives and they are taxed in the normal way. Exactly how a management co-operative will be taxed will depend on what its activities are.
> Where a co-operative does not acquire a lease or other interest in land the question is whether the management service it provides to the local council falls within trading income. Like other housing associations, management co-operatives are normally 'registered societies' in Great Britain, formerly industrial and provident societies, see CTM40505. One of the conditions for registration is that a society must not trade for profit. There are similar prohibitions in the statute relating to housing associations. These rules are not decisive and the question is what the society actually does as a matter of fact. A copy of the agreement between the local authority and the co-operative should be obtained and examined before reaching a decision. If the co-operative is not a 'registered society' (see above) a copy of the deed setting up any trust should be examined.
> In general, the management of a co-operative activity is unlikely to amount to the carrying on of a trade. This is because the agreement between a management co-operative and a local authority usually provides that the local authority re-imburses the co-operative's expenses. Although a surplus may arise in any given accounting period, this is likely to be the result of timing differences rather than a genuine profit from trading activity. Where the facts in a particular case support this view, no tax liability will arise on the management activity. Liability to CT is therefore only likely to arise on investment income and chargeable gains.

44.8 Self-build society

The CT Manual provides:

> **CTM40470: Self-build societies** [Jun 2016]
> *CTA10/S651*
> Self-build housing societies are usually formed to build houses for sale

to members. As each house is completed the member moves in, as tenant or licensee, and pays a rent. When all the houses are completed, they are conveyed to individual members and the society is wound up.

A self-build society approved under CTA10/S651 is exempt from tax in respect of rents paid to the society by members and from CT on chargeable gains on disposals to members.

To qualify for approval under CTA10/S651 a self-build society must exist for the purpose of building or improving dwellings, mainly by use of its members' own labour, for eventual sale to its members for their occupation, and be a 'registered society' in Great Britain – formerly industrial and provident society, see CTM40505.

Applications for and notifications of approval are handled by the relevant regulator of social housing – see CTM40425.

Where a self-build society first wishes to claim relief under CTA10/S651 form 75 (CTM40430) should be issued in duplicate so that the society may retain a copy. The form calls for:

1. confirmation that no land or house was occupied other than by a member of the society,
2. confirmation that the conditions for approval were observed,
3. a copy of the relevant authority's letter of approval,
4. a copy of the rules of the society,
5. a copy of the accounts.

The claim should be made within two years of the end of the accounting period to which the claim relates (CTA10/S655).

Where the claim is acceptable, the reliefs mentioned above may be allowed and any other profits as shown by the accounts assessed in the normal way. For years subsequent to the first year of claim form 75 should be issued annually until the society is wound up. (This content has been withheld because of exemptions in the Freedom of Information Act 2000)

Where a member has died, occupation by non members in accordance with the will or intestacy provisions is treated as satisfying the membership requirement for six months. See CTM40445.

HMRC has discretion to admit claims where the statutory requirements are substantially complied with. Such cases should be reported to CTIS (Technical).

CHAPTER FORTY FIVE

LOCAL AUTHORITIES

45.1 Local authorities: Introduction

Local authorities are not charities and do not qualify for charity tax reliefs. They do qualify for a number of other reliefs.

45.2 "Local authority"

Section 999 ITA provides:

> (1) In the Income Tax Acts "local authority", in relation to England and Wales, means-
> (a) a billing authority as defined in section 1(2) of the Local Government Finance Act 1992,
> (b) a precepting authority as defined in section 69(1) of that Act,
> (c) a body with power to issue a levy (by virtue of regulations under section 74 of the Local Government Finance Act 1988),
> (d) a body with power to issue a special levy (by virtue of regulations under section 75 of that Act),
> (e) a fire and rescue authority in Wales constituted by a scheme under section 2 of the Fire and Rescue Services Act 2004 or a scheme to which section 4 of that Act applies,
> (f) an authority with power to make or determine a rate,[1] or

---

1 Defined in s.999(4): In this section "rate" means a rate—
(a) whose proceeds are applicable for public local purposes, and
(b) which is leviable by reference to the value of land or property."

> (g) a residuary body established by order under section 22(1) of the Local Government Act 1992.
>
> (2) In the Income Tax Acts "local authority", in relation to Scotland, means-
>
> (a) a council constituted under section 2 of the Local Government etc (Scotland) Act 1994,
>
> (b) a joint board or committee within the meaning of the Local Government (Scotland) Act 1973, or
>
> (c) an authority with power to requisition any sum from a council such as is mentioned in paragraph (a).
>
> (3) In the Income Tax Acts "local authority", in relation to Northern Ireland, means a district council constituted under section 1 of the Local Government Act (Northern Ireland) 1972).

Section 1130 CTA 2010 sets out the same definition for Corporation Tax verbatim.

Section 288 TCGA incorporates the IT definition for CGT purposes:

> In this Act, unless the context otherwise requires—
> "local authority" has the meaning given by section 999 of ITA 2007;

Section 272 IHTA incorporates the CT definition for IHT purposes:

> In this Act, except where the context otherwise requires,—
> "local authority" has the meaning given by section 1130 of the Corporation Tax Act 2010.

It would take too much space to set out all the provisions referred to in s.999 ITA/1130 CTA 2010. Among the most important, s.1(2) LGFA 1992 provides:

> (2) In this Part "billing authority" means—
>
> (a) in relation to England, a district council or London borough council, the Common Council or the Council of the Isles of Scilly, and.
>
> (b) in relation to Wales, a county council or county borough council

Section 2 Local Government etc (Scotland) Act 1994 provides:

> (1) For every local government area there shall be a council consisting of a convener and councillors...
>
> (3) The council for each local government area shall be a body corporate by the name "The Council" with the addition of the name of the particular area...

Section 1 Local Government Act (Northern Ireland) 1972 provides:

> (1) For every local government district established in pursuance of section 1 of the Local Government (Boundaries) Act (Northern Ireland) 2008 or the succeeding provisions of this Act there shall be a district council ...
> (2) A council shall be a body corporate with perpetual succession, and, subject to the provisions of this Act,—.
> (a) the name of the council shall be the name of the district with the addition of words "district council"...

The CT Manual provides:

> **CTM40860: Local authorities: definition** [Jun 2016]
> For the purposes of the Corporation Tax Acts, 'local authority' is defined at CTA10/S1130. That definition includes all bodies which have the statutory power to bill, precept or make other demands for money from other local authorities where those powers are derived from those sections of the relevant Local Government Finance Acts specified at S1130. This means that it includes town and parish councils in England (in Wales, Community Councils).
> The definition also includes local education authorities in England, Wales and Scotland, education and library boards in Northern Ireland, and schools and colleges that are under local authority control (see CTM40895 for more on this aspect).
> Where a body first makes a claim that it is a local authority within the exemptions (see CTM40855) it should be asked to provide details of the legislation under which it was established and/or gave it the powers to precept, bill or issue a levy as required in CTA10/S1130. A report should be made to CTIS (Technical) if there is any concern about a claim. See 'Technical Help' on the left bar.
> In recent years a number of activities previously carried out by local authorities have been transferred into separate limited companies. Examples of this are waste disposal activities. Such companies are not within the definition of a local authority and are liable to CT in the normal way. This is so even where all or part of the company's share capital remains in the ownership of the local authority.
> Similarly since 2002 many local authorities/councils have set up arm's length management organisations (ALMOs). These not for profit organisations are meant to deliver better social housing. The typical ALMO set up by a council is a company limited by guarantee without share capital but with the council as its sole member. ALMOs manage, repair, improve and maintain the council's housing stock, while ownership of the housing stock remains with the council. See

BIM58210 for more details of their tax treatment. They are not local authorities.

45.2.1 *"Local authority association"*

A local authority association is defined in s.1000 ITA, which provides:

> (1) In the Income Tax Acts "local authority association" means any incorporated or unincorporated association which meets conditions A and B.
> (2) Condition A is that all of its members are local authorities, groups of local authorities or local authority associations.
> (3) Condition B is that its purpose, or primary purpose, is to protect and further the general interests of local authorities or any description of local authorities.
> (4) For the purposes of condition A, if a member ("M") of a local authority association is a representative of, or is appointed by, a local authority, group of local authorities or a local authority association, the authority, group or association concerned (rather than M) is to be treated as a constituent member of the local authority association.

Section 1131 CTA 2010 sets out the same definition for Corporation Tax verbatim.

45.3 Income tax exemption

The income tax position of local authorities is straightforward because they are wholly exempt from income tax. Section 838 ITA provides:

> (1) A local authority in the United Kingdom is not liable to income tax in respect of its income.
> (2) A local authority association in the United Kingdom is not liable to income tax in respect of its income.
> (3) Tax is repayable as a result of subsection (1) or (2) only if a claim for repayment is made

45.3.1 *Deduction at source from interest*

The CT Manual provides:

> **CTM40855: Local authorities: introduction** [Jun 2016]
> ...The only liability to tax of a local authority may be on IT deducted from payments it makes of yearly interest under ITA07/PART15/CHAPTER3 or as a deposit taker within the tax deduction scheme for interest (see SAIM9035, CTM35050 and CTM40870).
> FA02/S94 introduced legislation whereby certain payments made or received by a local authority on or after 1 October 2002 can be made without deduction of tax – see CTM40870 for further details...

CTM40870: Receipt or payment of gross interest [Jun 2016]

Certain payments made or received by a local authority are outside the rules for deduction of tax. This was done to align the withholding tax obligations of a local authority with those of a company.

Payments made by local authorities of yearly interest and other amounts listed at CTM35215 may be made without deduction of tax if the authority reasonably believes that the recipient falls within the relevant categories.

With effect from the same date, payments within the CTM35215 categories received by local authorities may also be made without deduction of tax if the payment is made by:

- a company,
- another local authority, or
- a partnership, if any member of the partnership is a company or a local authority,

and the reasonable belief test (see above) is satisfied in the eyes of the payer.

SAIM9035 gives details of local authorities' remaining duty to deduct tax from interest payments.

CTM40875: Income tax deducted from payments made [Sept 2011]

Since 1991 local authorities have had to account under two different regimes for tax deducted from interest and certain other payments made.

ICTA88/S349 and ICTA88/S350

Local authorities are not within the Taxes Acts definition of a company at ICTA88/S832 (1). Unless the payment falls within the tax deduction scheme for interest (TDSI) scheme (covered below), IT deducted under ICTA88/S349 should therefore be collected by way of assessment under ICTA88/S350 rather than under the ICTA88/SCH16 form CT61 procedure. Any Section 350 assessments should be made from an IT file. Local authorities are not however within ITSA. As such, the file should be set up under clerical control. The file should be set up by the office which processes assessments or repayments for the geographical area in which the authority is situated, or, if the authority operates from a number of sites, the area in which its main office is situated.

Assessments under Section 350 should be made under the SA facility – see CO3150 onwards. Details of the form of assessment to be raised are at AP160. The procedure to be followed is as follows.

The authority should be asked to submit details of any Section 349 liability as soon as possible following the end of the tax year to 5 April. If the information has not been provided within a reasonable period (normally, by the following 31 May) you should raise an estimated assessment.

The assessment should be made in the full amount of the interest etc paid or estimated to be paid under deduction of tax by the authority, a deduction being made of the IT suffered, or estimated to have been suffered, at source.

Assessments under Section 350 issued after 31 January 2001 for 1999–2000 and later years carry interest under TMA70/S86 where the payment of IT is made after 31 January following the end of the year of assessment. Section 350 assessments for the years 1998–99 and earlier, issued at any time, and assessments for 1999–2000 and 2000–01 issued on or before 31 January 2001, do not carry S86 interest.

Tax deduction scheme for interest

Local Authorities were brought within the TDSI, in respect of interest paid or credited on 'relevant deposits' on or after 6 April 1991, by ICTA88/S481 (2)(ca).

Local authorities paying interest on 'relevant deposits' under TDSI have to complete forms CT61 as if they were a company. This is because ICTA88/S480A (3) applies ICTA88/SCH16 to all deposit takers regardless of whether or not they are a company for tax purposes.

Where a local authority pays interest on relevant deposits under the TDSI scheme a CT file will be required solely to deal with the issue of forms CT61.

You should note that, in practice, the majority of local authorities are not involved in raising finance from individuals in this way.

Note also that ICTA88/S480A (4)(a) amends ICTA88/SCH16 for those deposit takers (such as local authorities) that are not companies. Importantly, it disapplies ICTA88/SCH16/PARA5 so that a local authority is not entitled to set off tax suffered on interest received against its liability to deduct tax on interest paid. Thus IT suffered can only be set off against tax due under ICTA88/S349, or repaid.

(Note that CTM40870 gives guidance on circumstances in which tax need not be deducted from payments of interest etc by local authorities.)

...

CTM40880: Income tax deducted from payments received [Jun 2016]

Local authorities are entitled to repayment of any IT borne by deduction, for example on interest received. In practice, tax repayable should be set off against any tax deductible (see SAIM9035), leaving the authority to account for the balance.

Where there is an excess of tax deducted from income received by the authority over tax deducted by the authority from payments it has made, the balance of tax should be repaid to the authority.

The tax affairs of local authorities are usually dealt with by the Individuals and Public Bodies team in LC.

Repayment claims by local authorities should be made in writing. There is no standard claim form and claims should therefore be made on headed letter paper. Such claims should:

- state the gross amount of income and the tax deducted,
- state the amount of repayment claimed,
- contain the words 'to the best of my knowledge and belief the particulars given in this claim are correct and complete',
- be signed by a senior official of the authority.

The frequency of claims is a matter for negotiation. However, no objection should be raised to claims at monthly intervals if significant sums are involved.

CTM40885: Interest paid in full between authorities [17 Feb 2006]

Payments of interest before 1 October 2002 between local authorities that are exempt under ICTA88/S519 (see CTM40855) could be paid in full, subject to the following conditions:

a. The onus was on the borrowing authority to ascertain whether or not the body receiving the interest was exempt under Section 519.

b. If, exceptionally, interest was paid in full to a body that was not exempt under Section 519, the Revenue reserves the right to look to the paying authority for the tax if necessary.
c. After the end of each financial year the authority paying the interest should have provided details of the amount paid in full to each other authority.

The arrangements for the payment of interest in full applied also to loans between health service bodies within ICTA88/S519A (see CTM40350 onwards) and to loans between local authorities and health service bodies.

From 1 October 2002 payment of interest between local authorities can be made without deduction of tax as long as the conditions of ICTA88/S349A and ICTA88/S349B are satisfied (CTM40870).

45.4 Corporation tax

Section 984 CTA 2010 provides exemption:

> (1) A local authority in the United Kingdom is not liable to corporation tax.
> (2) A local authority association in the United Kingdom is not liable to corporation tax.

However, s.1121 CTA 2010 provides:

> In the Corporation Tax Acts "company" means any body corporate or unincorporated association, but does not include a partnership, a local authority or a local authority association.[2]

Section 2(1) CTA 2009 provides:

> Corporation tax is charged on profits of companies for any financial year for which an Act so provides.

Since a local authority is not a company, it cannot be subject to corporation tax and the exemption is not necessary.

45.5 Capital gains tax

Local authorities are exempt from CGT. Section 271(3) TCGA provides:

> A local authority, a local authority association and a health service body shall be exempt from capital gains tax.
> In this subsection-
> "health service body" has the meaning given by section 986 of CTA 2010, and
> "local authority association" has the meaning given by section 1000 of ITA 2007.

---

2 The IT equivalent is s.992 ITA.

A local authority is a company for CGT purposes and so may form a member of a CGT group for group relief purposes.

45.6 Inheritance tax

Gifts to local authorities qualify for the IHT exemption for "national purposes". See 24.35 (IHT exemption for gifts to national institutions).

45.7 SDLT

SDLT is dealt with more fully in Chapter 34, but there are in addition specific exemptions for local government in certain circumstances.

45.7.1 *Exemption for planning obligation*

Section 61(1) FA 2003 provides:

> A land transaction that is entered into in order to comply with a planning obligation or a modification of a planning obligation is exempt from charge if-
> (a) the planning obligation or modification is enforceable against the vendor,
> (b) the purchaser is a public authority, and
> (c) the transaction takes place within the period of five years beginning with the date on which the planning obligation was entered into or modified...

Section 61(3) FA 2003 defines public authorities:

> The following are public authorities for the purposes of subsection (1)(b)-
> Government ...
> Local government: England
> A county or district council constituted under s.2 Local Government Act 1972
> The council of a London borough
> The Common Council of the City of London
> The Greater London Authority
> Transport for London
> The Council of the Isles of Scilly
> Local government: Wales
> A county or county borough council constituted under section 21 Local Government Act 1972
> Local government: Northern Ireland
> A district council within the meaning of the Local Government Act (Northern Ireland) 1972 ...

Section 61(2) FA 2003 defines "planning obligation":

> In this section-
> (a) in relation to England and Wales-
> "planning obligation" means either of the following-
> (a) a planning obligation within the meaning of section 106 of the Town and Country Planning Act 1990 that is entered into in accordance with subsection (9) of that section, or
> (b) a planning obligation within the meaning of section 299A of that Act that is entered into in accordance with subsection (2) of that section; and
> "modification" of a planning obligation means modification as mentioned in section 106A(1) of that Act;"
> (b) in relation to Scotland, "planning obligation" means an agreement made under section 75 or section 246 of the Town and Country Planning (Scotland) Act 1997;
> (c) in relation to Northern Ireland-
> "planning obligation" means a planning agreement within the meaning of section 76 of the Planning Act (Northern Ireland) 2011 that is entered into accordance with subsection (10) of that section, and
> "modification" of a planning obligation means modification as mentioned in section 77(1) of that Act.

45.7.2 *Public bodies reorganisation*

Section 66 FA 2003 provides a relief for reorganisation of public bodies. This is too specialist to be discussed here.

45.8 Company held by local authority

A company held by a local authority is subject to corporation tax in the usual way.

The company qualifies for corporate Gift Aid, so corporation tax may be avoided by gifts to charities carrying out activities in the local area which the local authority wishes to support. The planning is similar to that for companies held by charities but there are differences. Since the local authority is not itself a charity, the donations must not be to the local authority itself (though the local authority may make suggestions). The company is not wholly-owned by charities, so donations must be made in each tax year and cannot be carried back to an earlier year.[3] Morever charities set up trading subsidiaries for tax reasons (as the charity may not

3 See 9.4 (Carry-back relief).

qualify for tax relief on its trading income).

There is no tax reason for a local authority to use a subsidiary: it is exempt from tax on all its income. There may be non-tax reasons for a local authority to use a subsidiary. But a LLP (which is transparent for CT) may be better than a company.

45.8.1 *Group relief*

The CT Manual provides:

> **CTM40855: Local authorities: introduction** [Jun 2016]
> ...Local authorities are not within the Corporation Tax Acts definition of a company at CTA10/S1121. They are, however, persons for the purposes of the Taxes Acts (Interpretation Act 1978 Sch 1 says that 'person' includes a body of persons corporate or unincorporate). It is therefore possible for a local authority to control other companies within the meaning of CTA10/S449 and for those companies to be associated with one another within the meaning of CTA10/S25.
> From 1 April 2000 it is also possible for subsidiary companies of a local authority to form a group for group relief purposes in some circumstances. This is because a local authority that is also a body corporate satisfies the definition of 'company' in CTA10/S188 (1) (any body corporate) introduced by FA00. This means that it is possible for two subsidiaries to be in a group relationship with each other because they are both 75 per cent subsidiaries of a third company – CTA10/S152 (b). So the subsidiaries can claim and surrender group relief between one another. It is not, however, possible for a local authority to surrender any 'losses' or other excess amounts to its subsidiary companies, as the authority itself is not within the charge to CT. So it has no amounts eligible for relief from CT as required by CTA10/S99.
> This applies only for the purposes of group relief and does not affect the CG position. Different criteria will apply for CG (see CG45000 onwards).

45.9 Annual tax on enveloped dwellings

Section 153 FA 2013 provides ATED relief for public bodies, including local authorities, and for companies owned by public bodies.

45.10 LEAs, schools/colleges

The CT Manual provides:

> **CTM40895: LEAs, schools and colleges** [Jun 2016]
> *Local education authorities (LEAs)*
> LEAs are the bodies responsible for the local administration of state sector

education services in England, Wales and Scotland. Education and library boards are the equivalent bodies in Northern Ireland. Both are within the definition of local authority for tax purposes.

Schools

When a local authority controls a school (or college or polytechnic) its income is covered by the local authorities' exemption (see CTM80455).

Under the Schools Standards and Framework Act 1998 there are three categories of mainstream maintained school:

- community,
- foundation,
- voluntary (divided into aided and controlled).

Community and foundation schools replaced the previous categories of county, special agreement and grant maintained. Schools in all three categories have much in common and all work closely with the LEA and receive most of their funding from the LEA. However, only community schools are controlled by the local authority and therefore covered by the authority's own exemption.

Foundation and voluntary schools are outside the control of local authorities and are not therefore covered by Section 519. Such schools are, however, charities within the meaning ofFA10/SCH6/PARA1 (and briefly before that CTA10/S467) and will be entitled to the exemptions in CTA10/PART11/CHAPTER3. Any claim for charitable exemption or evidence that a taxable source of income or a chargeable gain has arisen should be submitted to HMRC Charities with a copy of the latest accounts (if available). Do not ask for a copy of the instrument creating the body.

School funds

The Education Reform Act 1988 set up the local management of schools scheme for schools which continue to be controlled by LEAs. This gives school-governing bodies a limited degree of financial independence and discretion through what amounts to a form of delegated budgeting. Individual schools may open bank accounts under these arrangements and receive interest. HMRC takes the view that the funds in local management of schools bank accounts remain in the beneficial ownership of LEAs and any interest received is therefore exempt under their exemption. Accordingly interest should be credited to these bank accounts without IT being deducted (CTM40880).

Many schools will also hold accounts with other items, reflecting for example funds collected for a school trip, donations raised to buy an expensive piece of equipment and so forth. Generally such funds are held on charitable trusts and the income is exempt. But if there is any doubt about this, or if repayment is claimed, submit the file to HMRC Charities.

It is common for schools to be involved in fund raising operations through parent teacher associations and income will normally fall within the charitable exemption. On the other hand where it appears that governing bodies of local authority schools are engaging in adventurous or entrepreneurial fund raising schemes themselves, or have sold off some or all of the school premises, and significant amounts of tax could arise on the profits, establish the facts and seek advice from CTIS (Technical) before seeking liability to tax.

Colleges

Further education corporations are bodies corporate set up under the Further and Higher Education Act 1992 to take over the running of institutions such as colleges of further education. The kinds of establishment covered by this category are:

- general Further Education Colleges.
- sixth Form Colleges.
- voluntary Aided Sixth Form Colleges.
- voluntary Controlled Sixth Form Colleges.
- tertiary Colleges.
- agriculture and Horticulture Colleges.
- art and Design Colleges.
- designated Colleges (other than Voluntary Aided Sixth Form Colleges).

Higher education corporations are bodies corporate set up under the Education Reform Act 1988, which have taken over the running of polytechnics and colleges of higher education. This status was not affected by the renaming of polytechnics as universities.

Further and higher education corporations are charities. Submit any case where a corporation claims to be a charity to HMRC Charities. Do not ask for a copy of the instrument creating the body.

CHAPTER FORTY SIX

SOCIAL INVESTMENT RELIEF

46.1 Introduction

This chapter considers social investment relief ("**SI relief**").[1] This is one of a set of reliefs: EIS, SEIS, VCTs, but these are not discussed here. The legislation is in Part 5B ITA.

We first consider definitions; then the operation of the relief itself and the conditions for the relief.

HMRC have published some guidance but this is just a precis of the legislation and so of limited importance.

46.2 Social enterprise

Section 257J(2) ITA provides:

> In this Part "social enterprise" means–
> (a) a community interest company,
> (b) a community benefit society (see section 257JB) that is not a charity,
> (c) a charity,
> (d) an accredited social impact contractor (see section 257JD), or
> (e) any other body prescribed, or of a description prescribed, by an order made by the Treasury.

I abbreviate social enterprise to "**SE**".

46.3 "Community benefit society"

The definition matters as a community benefit society is a social

---

1 The term is statutory: s.257J(1) ITA provides:
> This Part provides for income tax relief for social investments ("SI relief"), that is, entitlement to tax reductions in respect of amounts invested in social enterprises by individuals.

enterprise. Section 257JB(1) ITA provides:

> In this Part "community benefit society" means a body that–
> (a) is registered as a community benefit society under the 2014 Act,
> (b) is a pre-commencement society (within the meaning of the 2014 Act) that meets the condition in section 2(2)(a)(ii) of the 2014 Act, or
> (c) is a society registered, or treated as registered, under section 1 of the Industrial and Provident Societies Act (Northern Ireland) 1969 in the case of which the condition in section 1(2)(b) of that Act is fulfilled,
> and in respect of which the condition in subsection (2) is met.

This takes us to Section 257JB(2) ITA which provides:

> The condition is that–
> (a) the body is of a kind prescribed by regulation 5 of, and
> (b) the body's rules include a rule in the terms set out in Schedule 1 to,
> [i] the Community Benefit Societies (Restriction on Use of Assets) Regulations 2006 (SI 2006/264) or
> [ii] the Community Benefit Societies (Restriction on Use of Assets) Regulations (Northern Ireland) 2006 (S.R. 2006/258).

Regulation 5 Community Benefit Societies (Restriction on Use of Assets) Regulations 2006 provides:

> **5 Prescribed community benefit societies**
> All kinds of community benefit societies except--
> (a) a community benefit society that is a registered social landlord; and
> (b) a community benefit society that is a charity.
> are prescribed pursuant to section 1(1) of the 2003 Act.

Schedule 1 Community Benefit Societies (Restriction on Use of Assets) Regulations 2006 provides:

> The rule included in a prescribed community benefit society's rules must be in the following terms--
> "Restriction on use
> Pursuant to regulations made under section 1 of the Co-operatives and Community Benefit Societies Act 2003:
> (1) All of the society's assets are subject to a restriction on their use.
> (2) The society must not use or deal with its assets except--

(a) where the use or dealing is, directly or indirectly, for a purpose that is for the benefit of the community;
(b) to pay a member of the society the value of his withdrawable share capital or interest on such capital;
(c) to make a payment pursuant to section 24 (proceedings on death of nominator), 25 (provision for intestacy) or 26 (payments in respect of mentally incapable persons) of the Industrial and Provident Societies Act 1965;
(d) to make a payment in accordance with the rules of the society to trustees of the property of bankrupt members or, in Scotland, members whose estate has been sequestrated;
(e) where the society is to be dissolved or wound up, to pay its creditors; or
(f) to transfer its assets to one or more of the following–
  (i) a prescribed community benefit society whose assets have been made subject to a restriction on use and which will apply that restriction to any assets so transferred;
  (ii) a community interest company;
  (iii) a registered social landlord which has a restriction on the use of its assets which is equivalent to a restriction on use and which will apply that restriction to any assets so transferred;
  (iv) a charity (including a community benefit society that is a charity); or
  (v) a body, established in Northern Ireland or a State other than the United Kingdom, that is equivalent to any of those persons.

(3) Any expression used in this rule which is defined for the purposes of regulations made under section 1 of the 2003 Act shall have the meaning given by those regulations."

46.4 "Company"

Section 257JC ITA provides:

> In this Part (except section 257JD),[2] a reference to a company includes a reference to a charity that is a trust.

46.5 "Social impact contractor"

The definition matters as an accredited social impact contractor:
(1) is a social enterprise

---

2 See 46.5 ("Social impact contractor").

(2) is exempt from many SI conditions

Social Investment Tax Relief Guidance Concerning the Accreditation of Social Impact Contractors [3] provides:

> 27. Social Impact Contractors are, in principle, subject to the broader SITR criteria set out in Chapter 3 and Chapter 4, and the conditions for claims for relief in Chapter 6, of Part 5B of the Act. However, the provisions below have been modified or not applied for Social Impact Contractors:
> - Section 257LB (2) – (4) is not applied.
> - Section 257MJ is not applied (and as a consequence, section 257MK is not relevant)
> - Section 257ML is not applied.
> - Section 257MM applies with modification, as described in subsection (7).
> - Section 257MN is not applied.
> - Section 257P applies with modification, as described in subsection (2).
> - Section 257PB applies with modification, as described in subsection (4).
>
> 28. There are specific confidentiality provisions that apply to Social Impact Contractors: see section 257SI.

46.5.1 *"Accredited SI contractors"*

Section 257JD ITA provides:

> (1) In this Part "accredited social impact contractor" means a company limited by shares that is accredited under this section as a social impact contractor.
> (2) Applications for accreditation as a social impact contractor must be made to a Minister of the Crown in the form and manner specified by a Minister of the Crown.
> (3) A Minister of the Crown is to accredit a company if, but only if, that Minister is satisfied that–
> (a) the company has entered into a social impact contract (see section 257JE),
> (b) the company is, and at all times since its incorporation has been, established–
> (i) for the purpose of entering into and carrying out a social

3 *https://www.gov.uk/government/uploads/system/uploads/attachment_data/file/492974/SITRAccreditationGuidanceVersion2forpunlicationJan16V2.pdf* Jan 2016

impact contract, or for that purpose and purposes incidental to it, but

(ii) for no other purpose, and

(c) the activities of the company in carrying out that contract will not consist wholly, or as to a substantial part, in excluded activities (see section 257MQ).

(4) If a Minister of the Crown is satisfied that the condition in subsection (3)(b) or (c) has ceased to be met in relation to a company that is an accredited social impact contractor, that Minister is to withdraw the company's accreditation with effect from the time the condition ceased to be met or a later time.

46.5.2 *Social impact contract*

Section 257JE ITA provides:

> (1) In this Part "social impact contract" means a contract that meets such criteria as may be specified in regulations made by the Treasury.
> (2) The criteria which may be specified under subsection (1) include, in particular, criteria as to a party to the contract other than the company seeking accreditation.
> (3) Criteria may be specified in regulations under subsection (1) by reference to material published by, or on behalf of, a Minister of the Crown after the making of the regulations (as well as by reference to material published before the making of the regulations).
> (4) Regulations under subsection (1) may make different provision for different cases or circumstances or in relation to different areas.

See App 46.5 (Accreditation of social impact contractors).

46.6 Minor definitions

46.6.1 *"Debenture"*

The SI code provides a commonsense, pointless definition. Section 257KB(6) ITA provides:

> For the purposes of subsections (3) to (5) "debenture" includes any instrument creating or acknowledging indebtedness.

This only applies for s.257KB, but the same definition is repeated verbatim elsewhere: s.257L(6), s.257LA(4), s.257LDA(4) ITA.

46.7 SI relief

Section 257JA(1) ITA provides

> If an individual–
> (a) is eligible for SI relief in respect of any amount, and
> (b) makes a claim in respect of all or some of the amount,
> the individual is entitled to a tax reduction for the tax year in which the amount was invested.
> This is subject to the provisions of this Part.

46.8 *Claim*

A claim for relief by an investor is made in the same way as for EIS and SEIS relief. HMRC say:

> The company will send you a compliance certificate that shows they've met the conditions of the scheme and how long you will need to hold the shares for.
> You must have received this certificate before you can claim tax relief.
> If you want to claim in the current tax year you can request:
> a change to your PAYE tax code
> an adjustment to any Self Assessment on account that's due
> If you want to claim for the previous tax year, make your claim on your Self Assessment tax return.[4]

46.8.1 *Amount of relief*

Section 257JA(2) ITA provides:

> The amount of the reduction to which an individual is entitled under this Part for any particular tax year is the amount equal to tax, at the SI rate for that year, on–
> (a) the amount or, as the case may be, the sum of the amounts invested in that year in respect of which the individual is eligible for and claims SI relief, or
> (b) if less, £1 million.
> (3) The tax reduction is given effect at Step 6 in section 23.
> ...
> (5) In this Part "the SI rate" means 30%.

46.8.2 *Carry back of relief*

Section 257JA ITA provides:

> (4) If an individual–

---

4 HMRC, "Tax relief for investors using venture capital schemes" *https://www.gov.uk/guidance/venture-capital-schemes-tax-relief-for-investors*

> (a) is eligible for and claims SI relief in respect of an amount, and
> (b) makes a claim for part of that amount to be treated for the purposes of subsections (1) and (2) as if it had been invested not in the tax year in which it was actually invested but in the preceding tax year,
>
> those subsections apply, and the individual's liability to tax for both tax years is determined, in accordance with the claim.

46.9 "Eligible for SI relief"

Section 257K ITA provides:

> (1) An individual ("the investor") who invests in a social enterprise is eligible for SI relief in respect of the amount invested if–

Three conditions, or sets of conditions, follow:

> (a) the investment is made–
> (i) by the investor on the investor's own behalf,

I do not understand what this means, especially as nomineeships are expressly permitted. Section 257K(4) ITA provides:

> Investments made by, subscribed for, issued to, held by or disposed of for an individual by a nominee are treated for the purposes of this Part as made by, subscribed for, issued to, held by or disposed of by the individual.

46.9.1 *Date of investment*

The next condition concerns date of investment:
Section 257K ITA provides:

> (1) An individual ("the investor") who invests in a social enterprise is eligible for SI relief in respect of the amount invested if–
> (a) the investment is made...
> (ii) on or after 6 April 2014, and
> (iii) before 6 April 2021 (but see subsection (5)),[5] and

46.9.2 *SI conditions*

Section 257K ITA provides:

> (1) An individual ("the investor") who invests in a social enterprise is

5 (5) The Treasury may by order substitute a later date for the date for time being specified in subsection (1)(a)(iii).

> eligible for SI relief in respect of the amount invested if ...
>
> (b) the conditions set out in Chapters 3 and 4 are met.

We refer to the **"SI conditions"**.

The rules are relaxed for a accredited social impact contractor. Section 257K(2) ITA provides:

> Subsection (1)(b) is subject to the provisions in sections 257LB and 257MJ to 257MN which provide for conditions set out in those sections not to apply where the social enterprise is an accredited social impact contractor.

46.9.3 *Double relief*

Section 257K(3) ITA provides:

> The investor is not eligible for SI relief in respect of the amount invested if–
>
> (a) the investor has obtained in respect of that amount, or any part of it, relief under–
>
> (i) Part 5 (enterprise investment scheme),
>
> (ii) Part 5A (seed enterprise investment scheme), or
>
> (iii) Part 7 (community investment tax relief), or
>
> (b) that amount, or any part of it, has under Schedule 5B to TCGA 1992 (enterprise investment scheme: reinvestment) been set against a chargeable gain.

46.10 Definitions

Section 257KA ITA provides:

> In the following provisions of this Part (except section 257N), a reference to–
>
> "the amount invested",
>
> "the investment",
>
> "the investor", or
>
> "the social enterprise",
>
> is to be read in accordance with section 257K(1).

46.10.1 *Investment date*

Section 257KB ITA provides:

> (1) For the purposes of this Part "the investment date" means the date on which the investment is made.
>
> (2) So far as the investment is in shares, for the purposes of this Part it

is made when the shares are issued to the investor by the social enterprise.

(3) If the investment, so far as it is in qualifying debt investments (see section 257L), involves making the only advance covered by the debenture or debentures concerned, for the purposes of this Part it is made–

(a) when the social enterprise issues the debenture or debentures to the investor, or

(b) in a case where there is to be no such issuing, when the debenture or debentures, so far as relating to the advance, take effect between the social enterprise and the investor.

46.10.2 *Multiple advances*

(4) If the investment, so far as it is in qualifying debt investments, involves making the first of multiple advances covered by the debenture or debentures concerned, for the purposes of this Part it is made-

(a) when the social enterprise issues the debenture or debentures to the investor, or

(b) in a case where there is to be no such issuing, when the debenture or debentures, so far as relating to all of those advances, take effect between the social enterprise and the investor.

(5) If the investment, so far as it is in qualifying debt investments, involves making the second of multiple advances covered by the debenture or debentures concerned, or a subsequent one of those advances, for the purposes of this Part it is made-

(a) when the amount of that advance is fully advanced in cash, or

(b) if later–

(i) when the social enterprise issues the debenture or debentures to the investor, or

(ii) in a case where there is to be no such issuing, when the debenture or debentures, so far as relating to all of those advances, takes effect between the social enterprise and the investor.

46.10.3 *Applicable periods*

Section 257KC ITA provides:

(1) In this Part "the shorter applicable period" and "the longer applicable period" have the meaning given by this section.

(2) The shorter applicable period begins with the investment date.

(3) The longer applicable period begins with–

(a) the day on which the social enterprise is–
    (i) incorporated (if it is a body corporate), or
    (ii) established (in any other case), or
(b) if later, the day whose first anniversary is the investment date.

(4) Each of the periods ends with the third anniversary of the investment date.

46.11 Investment in shares

Section 257L(1) ITA provides:

> At all times during the shorter applicable period, the investment must be in–
> (a) shares that meet conditions A and B and are issued to the investor by the social enterprise in return for the amount invested ...

We refer to "**Share conditions A and B**".

In the case of a charity, the issue of shares is not likely to be an option: the investment will be by way of loan.

46.11.1 *Condition A: Equity return*

Section 257L(2) ITA provides:

> Condition A is that the shares must carry none of the following–
> (a) a right to a return which, or any part of which, is a fixed amount;
> (b) a right to a return which, or any part of which, is at a fixed rate;
> (c) a right to a return which, or any part of which, is otherwise fixed by reference to the amount invested;
> (d) a right to a return which, or any part of which, is fixed by reference to some other factor that is not contingent on successful financial performance by the social enterprise;
> (e) a right to a return at a rate greater than a reasonable commercial rate.

46.11.2 *Condition B: winding up*

Section 257L(3) ITA provides:

> Condition B is that, for the purpose of determining the amounts due in respect of the shares to their holder in the event of the winding-up of the social enterprise–
> (a) those amounts rank after all debts of the social enterprise except any due to holders of qualifying debt investments in the social

enterprise in respect of their qualifying debt investments, and

(b) the shares do not rank above any other shares in the social enterprise.

46.12 Qualifying debt investments

Section 257L(1) ITA provides:

At all times during the shorter applicable period, the investment must be in ...

(b) qualifying debt investments of which the investor is the holder in return for advancing the amount invested to the social enterprise.

Section 257L ITA provides:

(4) In this Part "qualifying debt investments", in relation to the social enterprise, means any debentures of the social enterprise in respect of which the following conditions are met–

46.12.1 *No priority*

(a) neither the principal of the debt concerned, nor any return on that, is charged on any assets,

46.12.2 *Reasonable consideration*

(b) the rate of any such return is not greater than a reasonable commercial rate of return, and

46.12.3 *Winding up*

(c) in the event of the winding-up of the social enterprise and so far as the law allows, any sums due in respect of the debt (whether principal or return)–
   (i) are subordinated to all other debts of the social enterprise except sums due in the case of other unsecured debentures of the social enterprise which rank equally,
   (ii) rank equally, if there are shares in the social enterprise and they all rank equally among themselves, with amounts due to shareholders in respect of their shares, and
   (iii) rank equally, if there are shares in the social enterprise and they do not all rank equally, with amounts due in respect of their shares to the holders of shares that do not rank above any other shares.

(5) The condition in subsection (3)(a) or (4)(c)(i) is met even if the sums concerned do not rank after debts which are postponed–

(a) by rules under section 411 of the Insolvency Act 1986, or
(b) by or under any other enactment.

46.13 Investment paid up

46.13.1 *Paid up shares*

Section 257LA(1) ITA provides:

> So far as the investment is in shares–
> (a) the shares must be subscribed for wholly in cash, and
> (b) must be fully paid up at the time they are issued.

46.13.2 *Paid up debentures*

Section 257LA(2) ITA provides:

> If the investment, so far as it is in qualifying debt investments, involves making-
> (a) the only advance covered by the debenture or debentures concerned, or
> (b) one of multiple advances covered by the debenture or debentures concerned,
>
> the full amount of that advance must have been advanced wholly in cash by the time the investment is made.

46.13.3 *"Paid up"*

Section 257LA(3) ITA provides:

> For the purposes of this section–
> (a) shares are not fully paid up, or
> (b) the full nominal amount of qualifying debt investments has not been advanced,
>
> if there is any undertaking to pay cash to any person at a future time in respect of the acquisition of the shares or investments.

46.14 Exit arrangements

46.14.1 *Arrangement to realise investment*

Section 257LB(1) ITA provides:

> There must not at any time in the shorter applicable period be any arrangements in existence for the investment to be redeemed, repaid, repurchased, exchanged or otherwise disposed of in that period.

46.14.2 *Arrangement to cease trading*

Section 257LB ITA provides:

> (2) The issuing arrangements for the investment must not include–
> (a) arrangements for or with a view to the cessation of any trade which is being or is to be or may be carried on by the social enterprise or a person connected with the social enterprise, or
> (b) arrangements for the disposal of, or of a substantial amount (in terms of value) of, the assets of the social enterprise or of a person connected with the social enterprise.
>
> (3) The arrangements referred to in subsection (2)(a) and (b) do not include any arrangements applicable only on the winding-up of a company except in a case where–
> (a) the issuing arrangements include arrangements for the company to be wound up, or
> (b) the arrangements are applicable on the winding-up of the company otherwise than for genuine commercial reasons.
>
> (4) In this section "the issuing arrangements" means–
> (a) the arrangements under which the investor makes the investment, and
> (b) any arrangements made before, and in relation to or in connection with, the making of the investment by the investor.
>
> (5) Subsections (2) to (4) do not apply if the social enterprise is an accredited social impact contractor.

46.15 Risk investment

Section 257LC ITA provides:

> (1) There must not at any time in the shorter applicable period be any arrangements in existence the main purpose or one of the main purposes of which is (by means of any insurance, indemnity, guarantee, hedging of risk or otherwise) to provide partial or complete protection for the investor against what would otherwise be the risks attached to making the investment.
>
> (2) The arrangements referred to in subsection (1) do not include any arrangements which are confined to the provision–
> (a) for the social enterprise itself, or
> (b) if the social enterprise is a parent company that meets the trading requirement in section 257MJ(2)(c) or is a parent company that is an accredited social impact contractor–
> (i) for the social enterprise itself,
> (ii) for the social enterprise itself and one or more of its

subsidiaries, or

(iii) for one or more of the subsidiaries of the social enterprise,

of any such protection against the risks arising in the course of carrying on its business as might reasonably be expected to be provided in normal commercial circumstances.

46.16 Linked loan

Section 257LD(1) ITA provides:

> No linked loan is to be made by any person, at any time in the longer applicable period, to the investor or an associate of the investor.

Section 257LD(2) ITA defines "linked loan"

> In this section "linked loan" means any loan[6] which–
> (a) would not have been made, or
> (b) would not have been made on the same terms,
> if the investor had not made the investment, or had not been proposing to do so.

46.17 Existing investment

Section 257LDA(1) ITA provides:

> If at the time immediately before the investment is made the investor holds any shares in or debentures of—
> (a) the social enterprise, or
> (b) a company which at that time is a qualifying subsidiary of the social enterprise,
> those shares or debentures must be risk finance investments or (in the case of shares) permitted subscriber shares.

46.17.1 *"Risk finance investment"*

Section 257LDA(2) ITA provides:

> A share or debenture is a "risk finance investment" for the purposes of this section if—
> (a) it is a share that was issued to the investor, or a debenture of

---

6 Loan is widely defined in s.257LD(3): "References in this section to the making by any person of a loan to the investor or an associate of the investor include–
(a) references to the giving by that person of any credit to the investor or any associate of the investor, and
(b) references to the assignment to that person of a debt due from the investor or any associate of the investor."

which the investor is the holder in return for advancing an amount, and

(b) at any time, a compliance statement under section 205, 257ED or 257PB is provided in respect of it or of shares or investments including it.

46.17.2 *Compliance statement*

There are three types of compliance statement:

Section	**Relief**
205	EIS
257ED	SEIS
257PB	SI

Section 205 ITA provides:

> (1) A "compliance statement" is a statement, in respect of an issue of shares, to the effect that, except so far as they fall to be met by or in relation to the individuals to whom shares included in that issue have been issued, the requirements for EIS relief (see section 157)—
> (a) are for the time being met in relation to the shares to which the statement relates, and
> (b) have been so met at all times since the shares were issued.
> (2) In determining for the purposes of subsection (1) whether the requirements for EIS relief are met at any time in relation to the issue of shares, references in this Part to "the relevant shares" are read as references to the shares included in the issue.
> (3) A compliance statement must be in such form as the Commissioners for Her Majesty's Revenue and Customs direct and must contain—
> (a) such additional information as the Commissioners reasonably require, including in particular information relating to the persons who have requested the issue of compliance certificates,
> (b) a declaration that the statement is correct to the best of the issuing company's knowledge and belief, and
> (c) such other declarations as the Commissioners may reasonably require.
> (4) The issuing company may not provide an officer of Revenue and Customs with a compliance statement in respect of any shares issued by it in any tax year—
> (a) before the requirement in section 176(2) or (3) (trade etc must have been carried on for 4 months) is met, or
> (b) later than two years after the end of that tax year or, if that requirement is first met after the end of that tax year, later than two years after the requirement is first met.

Section 257ED ITA provides:

> (1) A "compliance statement" is a statement, in respect of an issue of shares, to the effect that, except so far as they fall to be met by or in relation to the individuals to whom shares included in that issue have been issued, the requirements for SEIS relief (see section 257AA)—
>
> (a) are for the time being met in relation to the shares to which the statement relates, and
>
> (b) have been so met at all times since the shares were issued.
>
> (2) In determining for the purposes of subsection (1) whether the requirements for SEIS relief are met at any time in relation to the issue of shares, references in this Part to the relevant shares are read as references to the shares included in the issue.
>
> (3) A compliance statement must not be made in respect of an issue of shares before at least one of the following conditions is met—
>
> (a) at least 70% of the money raised by the issue has been spent for the purposes of the qualifying business activity for which it was raised;
>
> (b) the new qualifying trade which constitutes the qualifying business activity or to which that activity relates has been carried on by the issuing company or a qualifying 90% subsidiary of that company for at least 4 months.
>
> (4) A compliance statement must be in such form as the Commissioners for Her Majesty's Revenue and Customs direct and must—
>
> (a) state which of the conditions in subsection (3) is met at the time the statement is made,
>
> (b) contain such additional information as the Commissioners reasonably require, including in particular information relating to the persons who have requested the issue of compliance certificates,
>
> (c) contain a declaration that the statement is correct to the best of the issuing company's knowledge and belief, and
>
> (d) contain such other declarations as the Commissioners may reasonably require.]

Section 257PB ITA provides:

> (1) For the purposes of this Part, a "compliance statement" in respect of the investment is a statement by the social enterprise to the effect that, except so far as they fall to be met by or in relation to the individual, the requirements for SI relief—
>
> (a) are for the time being met in relation to the investment (or in relation to investments that include the investment), and
>
> (b) have been so met at all times since the investment was made.

(2) A compliance statement must be in such form as the Commissioners for Her Majesty's Revenue and Customs may direct and must contain—

(a) such additional information as the Commissioners may reasonably require, including in particular information relating to the persons who have requested the issue of compliance certificates,

(b) a declaration that the statement is correct to the best of the social enterprise's knowledge and belief, and

(c) such other declarations as the Commissioners may reasonably require.

(3) The social enterprise may not provide an officer of Revenue and Customs with a compliance statement in respect of the investment—

(a) before the requirement in section 257MM(2) (trade must have been carried for 4 months) is met, or

(b) later than 2 years after the end of the tax year in which the investment is made or, if that requirement is first met after the end of that tax year, later than 2 years after the requirement is first met.

(4) If the social enterprise is an accredited social impact contractor, subsection (3) applies with the omission of its paragraph (a).

HMRC say:

Complete a separate statement for each share or debt issue.

If you've got advance assurance, provide copies of any documents that have changed since HMRC gave you advance assurance.

If you've not got advance assurance, provide the following information for your social enterprise and any of its subsidiaries:

- the business plan and financial forecasts
- a copy of the latest accounts if available
- which enterprises or companies will use the investments
- details of all trading and activities to be carried out, and how much you expect to spend on each activity
- a list of the amounts, dates and venture capital schemes under which you've previously received an investment
- copies of any documents you use to explain your proposal to your investors
- details of any other agreements between the enterprise and the investors
- a signed letter from one of your directors or trustees if you're allowing an agent to act on your behalf
- the certificate of incorporation of your company or charity

- the memorandum and articles of association of your company or the equivalent governing documents of your charity, such as a trust deed
- the loan agreement or debt instrument, if the investment is through qualifying debt
- any other documents to show you meet the qualifying conditions for the scheme.[7]

Following the receipt of the compliance statement HMRC will issue a compliance certificate:

> If your application is successful, HMRC will send you a letter and compliance certificates (form SITR3) to give to your investors.
> The letter will include a unique investment reference number. You must include this on the compliance certificates you give to investors. Investors need the compliance certificate and reference number to be able to claim tax relief.
> If HMRC decides the investments do not meet SITR requirements, we'll write to you explaining why. If you disagree, you can ask HMRC to review the decision, or appeal against it.
> You must follow the scheme rules for at least 3 years after the investment is made - otherwise tax relief will be withdrawn from your investors. You must tell HMRC if you no longer meet the conditions within 60 days.
> All money raised from the investment must be used within 28 months of the date of the investment.[8]

46.17.3 *"Subscriber shares"*

Section 257LDA ITA provides:

> (3) Subscriber shares are "permitted subscriber shares" for the purposes of this section if—
> (a) they were issued to the investor and have been continuously held by the investor since they were issued, or
> (b) they were acquired by the investor at a time when the company which issued them—
> (i) had issued no shares other than subscriber shares, and
> (ii) had not begun to carry on or make preparations for carrying on any trade or business.

7 *https://www.gov.uk/guidance/venture-capital-schemes-apply-to-use-social-investment-tax-relief#how-to-apply*

8 *https://www.gov.uk/guidance/venture-capital-schemes-apply-to-use-social-investment-tax-relief#how-to-apply*

46.18 SI TAAR

Section 257LE ITA provides:

> The investment must not be made as part of any arrangements the main purpose or one of the main purposes of which is the avoidance of tax.

Section 989 ITA provides:

> The following definitions apply for the purposes of the Income Tax Acts-
> "tax", if neither income tax nor corporation tax is specified, means either of those taxes

46.19 Disqualifying arrangements

Section 257LEA(1) ITA provides:

> The investment must not be made, and money raised by the social enterprise from the making of the investment must not be employed,—
> (a) in consequence or anticipation of disqualifying arrangements, or
> (b) otherwise in connection with disqualifying arrangements.

It is difficult to see what (a) adds to (b), but there it is.

46.19.1 *"Disqualifying arrangement"*

Section 257LEA(2) ITA provides:

> Arrangements are "disqualifying arrangements" if—
> (a) the main purpose, or one of the main purposes, of the arrangements is to secure both that an activity is or will be carried on by the social enterprise or a 90% social subsidiary of the social enterprise[9] and that—
> (i) one or more persons (whether or not including any party to the arrangements) may obtain relevant tax relief[10] in respect of a qualifying investment[11] which raises money for the purposes of that activity, or
> (ii) shares issued by the social enterprise which raise money

9 Section 257LEA(6) provides: "In this section "90% social subsidiary" is to be read in accordance with section 257MV.

10 See 46.19.4 ("Relevant tax relief").

11 Section 257LEA(6) provides: In this section ... a "qualifying investment" means—
(a) shares in the social enterprise, or
(b) a qualifying debt investment in the social enterprise (see section 257L)".

for the purposes of that activity may comprise part of the qualifying holdings[12] of a VCT,

(b) that activity is the relevant qualifying activity,[13] and

(c) one or both of conditions A and B are met. ...

We refer to **"disqualifying conditions A and B"**.

Section 257LEA(5) ITA provides:

> (5) For the purposes of this section it is immaterial whether the social enterprise is a party to the arrangements.

46.19.2 *Payment to relevant person*

Section 257LEA(3) ITA provides:

> Condition A is that, as a (direct or indirect) result of the money raised by the investment being employed as required by section 257MM, an amount representing the whole or the majority of the amount raised is, in the course of the arrangements, paid to or for the benefit of a relevant person[14] or relevant persons.

46.19.3 *Condition B: other traders*

Section 257LEA(4) ITA provides:

> Condition B is that, in the absence of the arrangements, it would have been reasonable to expect that the whole or greater part of the component activities[15] of the relevant qualifying activity would have been carried on as part of another business by a relevant person or relevant persons.

46.19.4 *"Relevant tax relief"*

Section 257LEA(7) provides:

---

12 Section 257LEA(6) provides: "In this section ... "qualifying holdings", in relation to the social enterprise, is to be construed in accordance with section 286 (VCTs: qualifying holdings)".

13 Section 257LEA(6) provides: "In this section ... "relevant qualifying activity" means the qualifying trade or activity mentioned in section 257ML(1) for the purposes of which the investment raised money".

14 Section 257LEA(6) provides: "In this section ... "relevant person" means a person who is a party to the arrangements or a person connected with such a party".

15 Section 257LEA(6) provides: "In this section ... "component activities" means the carrying on of a qualifying trade or preparing to carry on such a trade, which constitutes the relevant qualifying activity".

"Relevant tax relief"—

(a) in relation to a qualifying debt investment, means SI relief in respect of that investment;

(b) in relation to shares, means one or more of the following—

(i) SI relief in respect of the shares;

(ii) EIS relief (within the meaning of Part 5) in respect of the shares;

(iii) SEIS relief (within the meaning of Part 5A) in respect of the shares;

(iv) relief under Chapter 6 of Part 4 (losses on disposal of shares) in respect of the shares;

(v) relief under section 150A or 150E of TCGA 1992 (EIS and SEIS) in respect of the shares;

(vi) relief under Schedule 5B to that Act (EIS: reinvestment) in consequence of which deferral relief is attributable to the shares (see paragraph 19(2) of that Schedule);

(vii) relief under Schedule 5BB to that Act (SEIS: reinvestment) in consequence of which SEIS reinvestment relief is attributable to the shares (see paragraph 4 of that Schedule).

46.20 Working for SI

Section 257LF ITA provides:

(1) This section applies–

(a) to the investor, and

(b) to any individual who is an associate of the investor.

(2) An individual to whom this section applies must not at any time in the longer applicable period be–

(a) an employee of–

(i) the social enterprise,

(ii) any subsidiary of the social enterprise,

(iii) a partner of the social enterprise, or

(iv) a partner of any subsidiary of the social enterprise,

(b) a partner of–

(i) the social enterprise, or

(ii) any subsidiary of the social enterprise,

(c) a trustee of–

(i) the social enterprise, or

(ii) any subsidiary of the social enterprise, or

(d) a remunerated director of–

(i) the social enterprise, or

(ii) a linked company.

We refer to this as the "**SI work rule**".

46.20.1 *SI working definitions*

Section 257LF(3) ITA provides:

> In this section–
> "linked company" means–
> (a) a subsidiary of the social enterprise,
> (b) a company which is a partner of the social enterprise, or
> (c) a company which is a partner of a subsidiary of the social enterprise;
> "related person" means–
> (a) the social enterprise,
> (b) a person connected with the social enterprise,
> (c) a linked company of which the individual is a director, or
> (d) a person connected with such a company;
> "subsidiary", in relation to the social enterprise, means a company which at any time in the longer applicable period is a 51% subsidiary of the social enterprise (and such a company is therefore a subsidiary of the social enterprise for the purposes of this section even at times when it is not a 51% subsidiary of the social enterprise).

46.20.2 *"Remunerated"*

Section 257LF ITA provides:

> (4) For the purposes of subsection (2)(d), an individual who is a director of the social enterprise or a linked company is "remunerated" if the individual (or a partnership of which the individual is a member)–
> (a) receives at any time in the longer applicable period a payment from a related person, or
> (b) is entitled to receive a payment from a related person in respect of any time in the longer applicable period.
> (5) For the purposes of subsection (4) the following are ignored–
> (a) any payment or reimbursement of travelling or other expenses wholly, exclusively and necessarily incurred by the individual in the performance of the individual's duties as a director,
> (b) any interest which represents no more than a reasonable commercial return on money lent to a related person,
> (c) any dividend or other distribution which does not exceed a normal return on the investment,

(d) any payment for the supply of goods which does not exceed their market value,
(e) any payment of rent for any property occupied by a related person which does not exceed a reasonable and commercial rent for the property,
(f) any necessary and reasonable remuneration which–
 (i) is paid for services, rendered to a related person in the course of a trade or profession, that are not secretarial services and are not managerial services and are not services of a kind provided by the person to whom they are rendered, and
 (ii) is taken into account in calculating for tax purposes the profits of that trade or profession

46.20.3 *Reasonable remuneration*

Section 257LF ITA provides:

(5) For the purposes of subsection (4) the following are ignored ...
 (g) if condition A is met and (where applicable) condition B is also met, any other reasonable remuneration (including any benefit or facility) received by the individual, or to which the individual is entitled, for services rendered by the individual–
  (i) to the company (whether the social enterprise or a linked company) of which the individual is a director, and
  (ii) in the individual's capacity as a director of that company.

We refer to **"remuneration conditions A and B"**.

46.20.4 *Remuneration condition A*

Section 257LF(6) ITA provides:

Condition A is that the investor made the investment, or previously made another investment meeting the requirement in section 257L(1), at a time ("the qualifying time") when–
(a) the requirements of this section and sections 257LG and 257LH (even if the three sections were not then in force) would have been met even if each other reference in the three sections to any time in the longer applicable period were a reference to any time before the qualifying time, and
(b) the investor had never been involved in carrying on (whether on the investor's own account or as a partner, director or employee) the whole or any part of the trade, business or profession carried on by the social enterprise or a subsidiary of

the social enterprise.

46.20.5 *Remuneration condition B*

Section 257LF ITA provides:

> (7) Condition B is that–
> (a) the investment did not meet condition A (but a previous investment did), and
> (b) the investment was made before the third anniversary of the date when the investor last made an investment in the social enterprise which met condition A.
> (8) References in this section to an individual in the individual's capacity as a director of a company include, if the individual is both a director and an employee of the company, references to the individual in the individual's capacity as an employee of the company but, apart from that, an individual who is both a director and an employee of a company is treated for the purposes of this section as a director, and not an employee, of the company.
> (9) In subsections (2), (4) and (5) "director" does not include a trustee of a charity that is a trust.

46.21 Control

46.21.1 *"Related company"*

Section 257LG(2) ITA provides:

> In this section "related company" means–
> (a) the social enterprise, or
> (b) a company which at any time in the longer applicable period is a 51% subsidiary of the social enterprise (and such a company is therefore a related company for the purposes of this section even at times when it is not a 51% subsidiary of the social enterprise).

46.21.2 *Control rule*

Section 257LG ITA provides:

> (1) This section applies–
> (a) to the investor, and
> (b) to any individual who is an associate of the investor. ...
> (3) There must not be any time in the longer applicable period when an individual to whom this section applies has control of a related company.

(4) There must not be any time in the longer applicable period when an individual to whom this section applies directly or indirectly possesses or is entitled to acquire–

(a) more than 30% of the ordinary share capital of a related company,

(b) more than 30% of the loan capital of a related company, or

(c) more than 30% of the voting power in a related company.

(5) For the purposes of subsections (3) and (4) ignore any shares in a related company held by the individual, or by an associate of the individual, at a time when that company–

(a) has not issued any shares other than subscriber shares, and

(b) has not begun to carry on, or make preparations for carrying on, any trade or business.

(6) For the purposes of this section, the loan capital of a company–

(a) is treated as including any debt incurred by the company–

(i) for any money borrowed or capital assets acquired by the company,

(ii) for any right to receive income created in favour of the company, or

(iii) for consideration the value of which to the company was (at the time when the debt was incurred) substantially less than the amount of the debt (including any premium on it),[16] and

(b) is treated as not including any debt incurred by the company by overdrawing an account with a person carrying on a business of banking if the debt arose in the ordinary course of that business.

(7) For the purposes of this section–

(a) an individual is treated as entitled to acquire anything which the individual is entitled to acquire at a future date or will at a future date be entitled to acquire, and

(b) there is attributed to any individual any rights or powers of any other person who is an associate of the individual.

We refer to this as the **"SI control rule"**.

46.22 Non-qualifying investment

Section 257LH ITA provides:

There must not at any time in the longer applicable period be any arrangements–

---

16 The wording is takenf rom the definition of loan creditor in s.453 CTA 2010.

(a) as part of which–
  (i) the investor makes the investment, or
  (ii) the investor, or an individual who is an associate of the investor, makes any other investment in the social enterprise,

(b) which provide for a person to make an investment in a company other than the social enterprise, where that person is not the individual ("A") who invests as mentioned in paragraph (a), and

(c) to which there is a party (whether or not A) who is an individual in relation to whom not all of the requirements in sections 257LF [SI work rule] and 257LG [SI control rule] would be met if–
  (i) references in those sections to the investor were read as references to that individual, and
  (ii) references in those sections to the social enterprise were read as references to the company mentioned in paragraph (b).

46.23 Ongoing social enterprise

Section 257M ITA provides:

> The social enterprise must be a social enterprise throughout the shorter applicable period.

46.24 Gross asset cap

Section 257MC ITA provides:

> (1) If the social enterprise is a single company, the value of its assets–
> (a) must not exceed £15 million immediately before the investment is made, and
> (b) must not exceed £16 million immediately after the investment is made.
>
> (2) If the social enterprise is a parent company, the value of the group assets–
> (a) must not exceed £15 million immediately before the investment is made, and
> (b) must not exceed £16 million immediately after the investment is made.
>
> (3) For the purposes of subsection (2), the value of the group assets is the sum of the values of the gross assets of each of the members of the group, ignoring any assets that consist in rights against, or shares in or securities of, another member of the group.

HMRC's current guidance does not define 'gross assets', but the original guidance for SI relief says:

> For further information on how HMRC interprets the term 'gross assets' for SITR purposes, please see the corresponding Statement of Practice for the Enterprise Investment Scheme (EIS) - the same interpretation applies to both EIS and SITR.
> VCM13110 - EIS: income tax relief: the issuing company: gross assets requirement[17]

46.25 Unquoted company

Section 257MD ITA provides:

> (1) At the beginning of the shorter applicable period–
> (a) the social enterprise must not be a quoted company,
> (b) there must be no arrangements in existence for the social enterprise to become a quoted company, and
> (c) there must be no arrangements in existence for the social enterprise to become a subsidiary of a company ("the new company") by virtue of an exchange of shares, or shares and securities, if arrangements have been made with a view to the new company becoming a quoted company.
> (2) For the purpose of this section, a company is a "quoted company" if any shares, stocks, debentures or other securities of the company are–
> (a) listed on a recognised stock exchange,
> (b) listed on a designated exchange in a country outside the United Kingdom, or
> (c) dealt in outside the United Kingdom by such means as may be designated.
> (3) In subsection (2)(b) and (c) "designated" means designated by an order made by the Commissioners for Her Majesty's Revenue and Customs for the purposes of that provision.

Section 257MD(5) ITA provides relief for a reorganisation:

> The arrangements referred to in subsection (1)(b), and the second arrangements referred to in subsection (1)(c), do not include arrangements in consequence of which any shares, stocks, debentures or other securities of the social enterprise or the new company (as the case may be) are at any subsequent time–

17 HMRC, "Social Investment Tax Relief (SITR): guide for social enterprises" (2014)

(a) listed on a stock exchange that is a recognised stock exchange by virtue of an order under section 1005(1)(b), or
(b) listed on an exchange, or dealt in by any means, designated by an order made for the purposes of subsection (2)(b) or (c),

if the order was made after the beginning of the shorter applicable period.

46.26 Independence of SE

46.26.1 *Company controlled by SE*

Section 257ME(1) ITA provides:

> The social enterprise must not at any time in the shorter applicable period control (whether on its own or together with any person connected with it) any company which is not a qualifying subsidiary of the social enterprise.

46.26.2 *Control of SE*

Section 257ME(2) ITA provides:

> The social enterprise must not at any time in the shorter applicable period–
> (a) be a 51% subsidiary of a company, or
> (b) be under the control of a company, or under the control of a company and a person connected with that company, without being a 51% subsidiary of the company.

46.26.3 *Arrangements*

Section 257ME(3) ITA provides:

> No arrangements must be in existence at any time in the shorter applicable period by virtue of which the social enterprise could fail to meet either or both of subsections (1) and (2) (whether during that period or otherwise).

46.27 Subsidiary of SE

46.27.1 *Qualifying subsidiary*

Section 257MF ITA provides:

> Any subsidiary that the social enterprise has at any time in the shorter applicable period must be a qualifying subsidiary of the social enterprise.

46.27.2 *Property-managing subsidiary*

Section 257MG ITA provides:

> (1) Any property-managing subsidiary that the social enterprise has at any time in the shorter applicable period must be a 90% social subsidiary of the social enterprise.
> (2) In subsection (1) "property-managing subsidiary" means a subsidiary of the social enterprise whose business consists wholly or mainly in the holding or managing of land or any property deriving its value (directly or indirectly) from land.

46.28 Cap on employees

Section 257MH ITA provides:

> (1) If the social enterprise is a single company, the full-time equivalent employee number for it must be less than 250 when the investment is made.
> (2) If the social enterprise is a parent company, the sum of–
> (a) the full-time equivalent employee number for it, and
> (b) the full-time equivalent employee number for each of its qualifying subsidiaries,
> must be less than 250 when the investment is made.

46.28.1 *Number of employees*

Section 257MH(3) ITA provides:

> The full-time equivalent employee number for a company is calculated by taking the number of full-time employees of the company and adding, for each employee of the company who is not a full-time employee, such fraction as is just and reasonable.

HMRC say:

> To work out the number of FTEs, calculate the number of hours a year a full time employee in your business would normally work, and then divide that into the total number of hours per year worked by all your employees (you can find some examples of how to calculate the FTE figure in the explanatory notes to completing the Compliance Statement).

46.28.2 *"Employees"*

Section 257MH(4) ITA provides:

In this section "employee"–
(a) includes a director, but
(b) does not include–
(i) an employee on maternity or paternity leave, or
(ii) a student on vocational training.

HMRC say:

> You don't have to count staff on maternity or paternity leave, apprentices or students on vocational training. [18]

46.29 No partnership

Section 257MI ITA provides:

> (1) The requirements in this section apply during the shorter applicable period.
> (2) The social enterprise must not be a member of any partnership.
> (3) Each 90% social subsidiary of the social enterprise must not be a member of a partnership.

46.30 Financial health

Section 257MIA ITA provides:

> (1) The social enterprise must meet the financial health requirement at the beginning of the shorter applicable period.
> (2) The financial health requirement is that the social enterprise is not in difficulty.
> (3) The social enterprise is "in difficulty" if it is reasonable to assume that it would be regarded as a firm in difficulty for the purposes of the Community Guidelines on State Aid for Rescuing and Restructuring Firms in Difficulty (2004/C 244/02).

The guidelines (which should not be confused with the similar and more recent guidelines in relation to non-financial firms[19]) say:

> 9. There is no Community definition of what constitutes 'a firm in

---

18 HMRC, "Social Investment Tax Relief (SITR): guide for social enterprises" (2014) *https://www.gov.uk/government/uploads/system/uploads/attachment_data/file/378085/se-guide.pdf*

19 Community Guidelines on State Aid for Rescuing and Restructuring Firms in Difficulty (2014/C 249/01) *http://eur-lex.europa.eu/legal-content/EN/TXT/HTML/?uri=CELEX:52014XC0731(01)&from=EN*

difficulty'. However, for the purposes of these Guidelines, the Commission regards a firm as being in difficulty where it is unable, whether through its own resources or with the funds it is able to obtain from its owner/shareholders or creditors, to stem losses which, without outside intervention by the public authorities, will almost certainly condemn it to going out of business in the short or medium term.

10. In particular, a firm is, in principle and irrespective of its size, regarded as being in difficulty for the purposes of these Guidelines in the following circumstances:

(a) in the case of a limited liability company, where more than half of its registered capital has disappeared and more than one quarter of that capital has been lost over the preceding 12 months;

(b) in the case of a company where at least some members have unlimited liability for the debt of the company, where more than half of its capital as shown in the company accounts has disappeared and more than one quarter of that capital has been lost over the preceding 12 months;

(c) whatever the type of company concerned, where it fulfils the criteria under its domestic law for being the subject of collective insolvency proceedings.

11. Even when none of the circumstances set out in point 10 are present, a firm may still be considered to be in difficulties, in particular where the usual signs of a firm being in difficulty are present, such as increasing losses, diminishing turnover, growing stock inventories, excess capacity, declining cash flow, mounting debt, rising interest charges and falling or nil net asset value. In acute cases the firm may already have become insolvent or may be the subject of collective insolvency proceedings brought under domestic law. In the latter case, these Guidelines apply to any aid granted in the context of such proceedings which leads to the firm's continuing in business. In any event, a firm in difficulty is eligible only where, demonstrably, it cannot recover through its own resources or with the funds it obtains from its owners/shareholders or from market sources.

12. For the purposes of these Guidelines, a newly created firm is not eligible for rescue or restructuring aid even if its initial financial position is insecure. This is the case, for instance, where a new firm emerges from the liquidation of a previous firm or merely takes over such firm's assets. A firm will in principle be considered as newly created for the first three years following the start of operations in the relevant field of activity. Only after that period will it become eligible for rescue or restructuring aid, provided that:

> (a) it qualifies as a firm in difficulty within the meaning of these Guidelines, and
> (b) it does not form part of a larger business group except under the conditions laid down in point 13.
>
> 13. A firm belonging to or being taken over by a larger business group is not normally eligible for rescue or restructuring aid, except where it can be demonstrated that the firm's difficulties are intrinsic and are not the result of an arbitrary allocation of costs within the group, and that the difficulties are too serious to be dealt with by the group itself. Where a firm in difficulty creates a subsidiary, the subsidiary, together with the firm in difficulty controlling it, will be regarded as a group and may receive aid under the conditions laid down in this point.

46.31 Trading rule

Section 257MJ(1) ITA provides:

> The social enterprise must meet the trading requirement throughout the shorter applicable period, but this does not apply if the social enterprise is an accredited social impact contractor.

46.31.1 *"Trading requirement"*

Section 257MJ(2) ITA provides:

> The trading requirement is that–
> (a) the social enterprise is a charity,
> (b) the social enterprise is a single company that is not a charity, and its business–
> (i) does not, if things done for incidental purposes are ignored, consist to any extent in the carrying-on of non-trade activities, and
> (ii) does not consist wholly, or as to a substantial part, in the carrying-on of excluded activities, or
> (c) the social enterprise is a parent company that is not a charity, and the business of the group does not consist wholly, or as to a substantial part, in the carrying-on of non-qualifying activities.

The effect of (a) is that the rule effectively does not apply to charities.

46.31.2 *Proposed acquisition*

Section 257MJ(3) ITA provides:

> If the social enterprise intends that one or more companies should

become its qualifying subsidiaries with a view to their carrying on one or more qualifying trades–[20]

(a) the social enterprise is treated as a parent company for the purposes of subsection (2)(b) and (c), and

(b) the reference in subsection (2)(c) to the group includes the social enterprise and any existing or future company that will be its qualifying subsidiary after the intention in question is carried out,

but this subsection does not apply at any time after the abandonment of that intention.

46.31.3 *"Business of the group"*

Section 257MJ ITA provides:

(4) For the purposes of subsection (2)(c) "the business of the group" means what would be the business of the group if the activities of the group companies taken together were regarded as one business.

(5) For the purposes of determining the business of a group, activities of a group company are ignored so far as they are activities carried on by a mainly trading subsidiary otherwise than for its main purpose.

(6) For the purposes of determining the business of a group, activities of a group company are ignored so far as they consist in–

(a) the holding of shares in or securities of a qualifying subsidiary of the parent company,

(b) the making of loans to another group company, or

(c) the holding and managing of property used by a group company for the purpose of one or more qualifying trades carried on by a group company.

46.31.4 *Definitions*

Section 257MJ(1) ITA provides:

(7) In this section–

"incidental purposes" means purposes having no significant effect (other than in relation to incidental matters) on the extent of the activities of the body in question;

"mainly trading subsidiary" means a qualifying subsidiary which, apart from incidental purposes, exists wholly for the purpose of carrying on one or more qualifying trades,[21] and

any reference to the main purpose of such a subsidiary is to be read

20 See 46.39 ("Qualifying trade").

21 See 46.39 ("Qualifying trade").

accordingly, and
"non-qualifying activities" means–
(a) excluded activities, and
(b) activities, other than activities carried on by a charity, that are carried on otherwise than in the course of a trade, and
"non-trade activities" means activities which are neither of the following–
(a) activities carried on in the course of a trade, and
(b) activities carried on in the course of preparing to carry on a trade.

46.31.5 *Administration or receivership*

Section 257MK ITA provides:

> (1) The social enterprise is not regarded as ceasing to meet the trading requirement merely because of anything done in consequence of the social enterprise or any of its subsidiaries being in administration or receivership, but this is subject to subsections (2) and (3).
> (2) Subsection (1) applies only if–
> (a) the entry into administration or receivership, and
> (b) everything done as a result of the company concerned being in administration or receivership,
> is for genuine commercial reasons, and is not part of any arrangements the main purpose or one of the main purposes of which is the avoidance of tax.
> (3) The social enterprise ceases to meet the trading requirement if before the end of the shorter applicable period–
> (a) a resolution is passed, or an order is made, for the winding-up of the social enterprise or any of its subsidiaries (or, in the case of a winding-up otherwise than under the Insolvency Act 1986 or the Insolvency (Northern Ireland) Order 1989 (SI 1989/2405 (NI 19)), any other act is done for the like purpose), or
> (b) the company or any of its subsidiaries is dissolved without winding-up,
> but this is subject to subsection (4).
> (4) Subsection (3) does not apply if the winding-up or dissolution is for genuine commercial reasons, and is not part of any arrangements the main purpose or one of the main purposes of which is the avoidance of tax.

46.32 Money for qualifying trade

Section 257ML ITA provides:

(1) The social enterprise must be a party to the making of the investment (so far as not in bonus shares) in order to raise money for the carrying-on, by the social enterprise or a 90% social subsidiary of the social enterprise, of–

(a) a qualifying trade[22] which on the investment date is carried on by the social enterprise or a 90% social subsidiary of the social enterprise, or

(b) the activity of preparing to carry on (or preparing to carry on and then carrying on) a qualifying trade–

(i) which on the investment date is intended to be carried on by the social enterprise or a 90% social subsidiary of the social enterprise, and

(ii) which is begun to be carried by the social enterprise or such a subsidiary within 2 years after that date.

(2) In this Chapter–

(a) the purpose within subsection (1) for which money is raised is referred to as "the funded purpose",

(b) the qualifying trade mentioned in subsection (1)(a) or (b) is referred to as "the chosen trade", and

(c) if the funded purpose is the carrying-on of the activity mentioned in subsection (1)(b), "relevant preparation work" means preparations that form the whole or part of the activity.

(3) In determining for the purposes of subsection (1)(b) when a qualifying trade is begun to be carried on by a 90% social subsidiary of the social enterprise, any carrying-on of the trade by it before it became such a subsidiary is ignored.

(4) The reference in subsection (1)(b)(i) to a 90% social subsidiary of the social enterprise includes a reference to any existing or future body which will be such a subsidiary at any future time.

(5) This section does not apply if the social enterprise is an accredited social impact contractor.

46.33 Required trading period

Section 257MM ITA provides:

(1) All of the money raised by the social enterprise from the making of the investment must, no later than the end of 28 months beginning with the investment date, be employed wholly for the funded purpose.

(2) The chosen trade must have been carried on for a period of at least 4 months ending at or after the time the investment is made and,

---

22 See 46.39 ("Qualifying trade").

throughout that period, the trade–

(a) must have been carried on by the social enterprise or a 90% social subsidiary of the social enterprise, and

(b) must not have been carried on by any other person.

(3) Employing money on the acquisition of shares or stock in a body does not of itself amount to employing the money for the funded purpose.

(3A) Employing money on the repayment of a loan does not amount to employing the money for the funded purpose.

(4) Subsection (1) does not fail to be met merely because an amount of money which is not significant is employed for other purposes.

(5) If–

(a) merely because of the social enterprise or any other company being wound up, or dissolved without winding-up, the qualifying trade[23] is carried on as mentioned in subsection (2) for a period shorter than 4 months, and

(b) the winding-up or dissolution–

(i) is for genuine commercial reasons, and

(ii) is not part of any arrangements the main purpose or one of the main purposes of which is the avoidance of tax,

subsection (2) has effect as if it referred to that shorter period.

(6) If–

(a) merely because of anything done as a result of the social enterprise or any other company being in administration or receivership, the chosen trade is carried on as mentioned in subsection (2) for a period shorter than 4 months, and

(b) the entry into administration or receivership, and everything done as a result of the company concerned being in administration or receivership–

(i) is for genuine commercial reasons, and

(ii) is not part of any arrangements the main purpose or one of the main purposes of which is the avoidance of tax,

subsection (2) has effect as if it referred to that shorter period.

46.33.1 *Social impact contractor*

Section 257MM(7) ITA provides:

If the social enterprise is an accredited social impact contractor, the preceding provisions of this section apply with the following modifications–

---

23 See 46.39 (“Qualifying trade”).

(a) in subsection (1), for "28 months" substitute "24 months",
(b) in that subsection, for "the funded purpose" substitute "the carrying out of the social impact contract concerned", and
(c) omit subsections (2), (3), (3A) (5) and (6).

46.34 SE is trader

Section 257MN ITA provides:

> (1) There must not be a time in the shorter applicable period when–
> (a) the chosen trade, or
> (b) relevant preparation work,
> is carried on by a person who is neither the social enterprise nor a 90% social subsidiary of the social enterprise.

There is an exception for preparatory work:

> (2) If relevant preparation work is carried out in the shorter applicable period by the social enterprise or a 90% social subsidiary of the social enterprise then, for the purposes of determining whether the requirement in subsection (1) is met, ignore any carrying-on of the chosen trade that takes place in that period before the trade begins to be carried on by a person who is the social enterprise or a 90% social subsidiary of the social enterprise.

There is an exception for winding up:

> (3) The requirement in subsection (1) is not regarded as failing to be met if, merely because of any act or event within subsection (4), the chosen trade–
> (a) ceases to be carried on in the shorter applicable period by the social enterprise or any 90% social subsidiary of the social enterprise, and
> (b) it is subsequently carried on in that period by a person who is not any time in the longer applicable period connected with the social enterprise.
> (4) The acts and events within this subsection are–
> (a) anything done as a consequence of the social enterprise or any other company being in administration or receivership, and
> (b) the social enterprise or any other company being wound up, or dissolved without being wound up.
> (5) Subsection (4) applies only if–
> (a) the entry into administration or receivership, and everything done as a consequence of the company concerned being in administration or receivership, or

(b) the winding-up or dissolution,

is for genuine commercial reasons, and is not part of any arrangements the main purpose or one of the main purposes of which is the avoidance of tax.

(6) This section does not apply if the social enterprise is an accredited social impact contractor.

46.35 Investment within 7 years: Cap

Section 257MNA(1) ITA provides:

> This section applies where—
> (a) the investment is made before the end of the period of 7 years beginning with the relevant first commercial sale, or
> (b) the investment is made after that period but—
> (i) a relevant investment was made in the social enterprise before the end of that period, and
> (ii) some or all of the money raised by that relevant investment was employed for the purposes of (or of part of) the qualifying activity for which the money raised by the investment is employed.

If this condition is satisfied, we turn to the rule in subsection (2):

> (2) Where this section applies, the total amount of relevant investments made in the social enterprise[24] on or before the date when the investment is made must not exceed £1.5 million.

We refer to this as the **"7 year rule"**.

46.35.1 *"Qualifying activity"*

Section 257MNA ITA provides:

> (4) In this section—
> "qualifying activity" means—
> (a) a qualifying trade[25] within paragraph (a) of section 257ML(1) carried on by the social enterprise or a 90% social subsidiary of the social enterprise, or
> (b) an activity within paragraph (b) of section 257ML(1) so carried on;

24 Subsection (3) provides: "The reference in subsection (2) to relevant investments "made in the social enterprise" is to be read with section 257MNB." See 46.36 (Investment "in SE").

25 See 46.39 ("Qualifying trade").

"the relevant first commercial sale" has the meaning given by section 175A(6), reading—

(a) references to the issuing company as references to the social enterprise,

(b) references to the issue date as references to the investment date, and

(c) references to money raised by the issue of the relevant shares as references to money raised by the investment;

"relevant investment" has the meaning given by section 173A(3) (reading references in section 173A(3) to a company as including any social enterprise).

(5) Section 173A(4) and (5) apply to determine for the purposes of this section when a relevant investment is made.

(6) Where the social enterprise is an accredited social impact contractor—

(a) the reference in subsection (1)(a) to the relevant first commercial sale is to be read as a reference to the date on which the social enterprise first entered into a social impact contract;

(b) the reference in subsection (1)(b) to the qualifying activity mentioned there is to be read as a reference to the carrying out of the social impact contract for which the money raised by the investment is employed.

46.36 Investment "in SE"

Section 257MNB ITA provides:

(1) In section 257MNA(2) the reference to relevant investments "made in the social enterprise" includes—

(a) relevant investments made in a company which, at the material date, is or has been a 51% subsidiary of the social enterprise,

(b) any other relevant investment made in a company to the extent that the money raised by that relevant investment has been employed for the purposes of a trade carried on by another company ("company X") which, at the material date, is or has been a 51% subsidiary of the social enterprise, and

(c) any other relevant investment made in a company if—

(i) the money raised by that relevant investment has been employed for the purposes of a trade carried on by that company or another person, and

(ii) after that relevant investment was made, but on or before the material date, that trade became a transferred trade (see subsection (5)).

46.36.1 *Company becomes/ceases to be subsidiary*

Section 257MNB ITA provides:

> (2) The investments within paragraph (a) of subsection (1)—
> (a) include investments made in a company mentioned in that paragraph before it became a 51% subsidiary of the social enterprise, but
> (b) where a company mentioned in that paragraph is not a 51% subsidiary of the social enterprise at the material date, do not include any investments made in that company after it last ceased to be such a subsidiary.
> (3) For the purposes of subsection (1)(b), where company X is not a 51% subsidiary of the social enterprise at the material date, any money employed after company X last ceased to be such a subsidiary is to be ignored.

46.36.2 *Transferred trade*

Section 257MNB ITA provides:

> (4) Where only a proportion of the money raised by a relevant investment is employed for the purposes of a trade which becomes a transferred trade, only the corresponding proportion of that relevant investment is to be treated as falling within subsection (1)(c).
> (5) For the purposes of this section, if—
> (a) on or before the material date a trade is transferred—
> (i) to the social enterprise,
> (ii) to a company which, at the material date, is or has been a 51% subsidiary of the social enterprise, or
> (iii) to a partnership of which the social enterprise, or a company within sub-paragraph (ii), is a member, and
> (b) the trade or part of it was at any time before the transfer carried on by another person,
>
> the trade or part mentioned in paragraph (b) becomes a "transferred trade" when it is transferred as mentioned in paragraph (a).
> (6) The cases within subsection (5)(a)—
> (a) include the case where the trade is transferred to a company within subsection (5)(a)(ii), or a partnership of which such a company is a member, before the company became a 51% subsidiary of the social enterprise, but
> (b) where a company within subsection (5)(a)(ii) is not a 51% subsidiary of the social enterprise at the material date, do not include the case where the trade is transferred to that company,

or a partnership of which that company is a member, after that company last ceased to be such a subsidiary.

(7) In this section—

"the material date" means the date on which the investment is made;

"relevant investment" has the meaning given by section 173A(3) (reading references in section 173A(3) to a company as including any social enterprise).

(8) Section 173A(4) and (5) apply to determine for the purposes of this section when a relevant investment is made.

(9) Section 173A(6) and (7) (meaning of "trade" etc) apply also for the purposes of this section.

46.37 Investment after 7 years: Cap

HMRC say:

> The rules for the de minimis SITR scheme will be amended to reflect all the above changes, other than the requirement for the first risk finance investment to be received no later than 7 years after the first commercial sale. This means that older social enterprises that would otherwise meet the rules of the enlarged scheme will be able to receive investments of up to €344,000 over a 3 year rolling period.[26]

Section 257MNC ITA provides:

> (1) This section applies where—
> (a) the investment is made at any time after the period mentioned in section 257MNA(1)(a), and
> (b) it is not the case that the conditions in section 257MNA(1)(b)(i) and (ii) are met [series of investments][27].

In short, this is a case where the 7 year rule does not apply. If so, we move on:

> (2) Where this section applies—
> (a) the total amount of relevant investments made in the social enterprise on or before the date when the investment is made must not exceed £1.5 million, and
> (b) the amount invested must not be more than the amount mentioned in subsection (3).

---

26 HMRC, "Enlarging Social Investment Tax Relief (Jan 2017) *https://www.gov.uk/government/publications/income-tax-enlarging-social-investment-tax-relief/income-tax-enlarging-social-investment-tax-relief*

27 See 46.35 (Investment within 7 years: Cap).

Para (a) is the 7 year cap. Para (b) is an additional cap:

> (3) That amount is the amount given by the formula—
>
> $$\frac{€200{,}000 - M}{RCG + RSI} - T$$

In short:
T is **t**otal investment
M is the de **m**inimis amount
RCG is the **r**ate of **CG**T
RSI is the **r**ate of **SI** relief

In full:

> T is the total of any relevant investments made in the social enterprise in the aid period,
> M is the total of any de minimis aid, other than relevant investments, that is granted during the aid period—
> (a) to the social enterprise, or
> (b) to a qualifying subsidiary of the social enterprise at a time when it is such a subsidiary,
> RCG is the highest rate at which capital gains tax is charged in the aid period, and
> RSI is the highest SI rate in the aid period.
> (4) In subsection (3) "the aid period" means the 3 years—
> (a) ending with the day on which the investment is made, but
> (b) in the case of that day, including only the part of the day before the investment is made.
> (5) In this section "de minimis aid" means de minimis aid which fulfils the conditions laid down—
> (a) in Commission Regulation (EU) No. 1407/2013 (de minimis aid) as amended from time to time, or
> (b) in any EU instrument from time to time replacing the whole or any part of that Regulation.
> (6) For the purposes of subsection (3), the amount of any de minimis aid is the amount of the grant or, if the aid is not in the form of a grant, the gross grant equivalent amount within the meaning of that Regulation as amended from time to time.
> (7) For the purposes of subsection (3), if—
> (a) the investment or any relevant investment is made, or
> (b) any aid is granted,
> in sterling or any other currency that is not the euro, its amount is to be converted into euros at an appropriate spot rate of exchange for the date

on which the investment is made or the aid is paid.
(8) In this section "relevant investment" has the meaning given by section 173A(3) (reading references in section 173A(3) to a company as including any social enterprise).
(9) Section 173A(4) and (5) apply to determine for the purposes of this section when a relevant investment is made.
(10) Section 257MNB (which expands the meaning of "relevant investments made in the social enterprise") applies for the purposes of each of subsections (2) and (3) above as it applies for the purposes of section 257MNA(2).

46.38 Investment cap: Shorter applicable period

Section 257MND ITA provides:

> (1) This section applies where condition A or condition B is met.
> (2) Condition A is that—
> (a) a company becomes a 51% subsidiary of the social enterprise at any time during the shorter applicable period,
> (b) all or part of the money raised by the investment is employed for the purposes of a qualifying activity which consists wholly or partly of a trade carried on by that company, and
> (c) that trade (or part of it) was carried on by that company before it became a 51% subsidiary as mentioned in paragraph (a).
> (3) Condition B is that all or part of the money raised by the investment is employed for the purposes of a qualifying activity which consists wholly or partly of a trade which, during the shorter applicable period, becomes a transferred trade (see subsection (9)).

Assuming these conditions are met, we move on to the rule:

> (4) Where this section applies, at each time in the shorter applicable period ("the relevant time") the total of the relevant investments made in the social enterprise before that time must not exceed £1.5 million.
> (5) In subsection (4) the reference to relevant investments "made in the social enterprise" includes—
> (a) relevant investments made in a company which at any time before the relevant time has been a 51% subsidiary of the social enterprise,
> (b) any other relevant investment made in a company to the extent that the money raised by that relevant investment has been employed for the purposes of a trade carried on by another company ("company X") which at any time before the relevant time has been a 51% subsidiary of the social enterprise, and

(c) any other relevant investment made in a company if—
   (i) the money raised by that relevant investment has been employed for the purposes of a trade carried on by that company or another person, and
   (ii) after that relevant investment was made, but before the relevant time, that trade (or part of it) became a transferred trade.

(6) The investments within paragraph (a) of subsection (5)—
   (a) include investments made in a company mentioned in that paragraph before it became a 51% subsidiary of the social enterprise, but
   (b) where a company mentioned in that paragraph is not a 51% subsidiary of the social enterprise at the relevant time, do not include any investments made in that company after it last ceased to be such a subsidiary.

(7) For the purposes of subsection (5)(b), where company X is not a 51% subsidiary of the social enterprise at the relevant time, any money employed after company X last ceased to be such a subsidiary is to be ignored.

(8) Where only a proportion of the money raised by a relevant investment is employed for the purposes of a trade which becomes a transferred trade, only the corresponding proportion of that relevant investment is to be treated as falling within subsection (5)(c).

(9) For the purposes of this section, if—
   (a) before the relevant time, a trade is transferred—
      (i) to the social enterprise,
      (ii) to a company which, at the relevant time, is or has been a 51% subsidiary of the social enterprise, or
      (iii) to a partnership of which the social enterprise, or a company within sub-paragraph (ii), is a member, and
   (b) the trade or part of it was at any time before the transfer carried on by another person,

the trade or part mentioned in paragraph (b) becomes a "transferred trade" when it is transferred as mentioned in paragraph (a).

(10) The cases within subsection (9)(a)—
   (a) include the case where the trade is transferred to a company within subsection (9)(a)(ii), or a partnership of which such a company is a member, before the company became a 51% subsidiary of the social enterprise, but
   (b) where a company within subsection (9)(a)(ii) is not a 51% subsidiary of the social enterprise at the relevant time, do not include the case where the trade is transferred to that company,

or a partnership of which that company is a member, after that company last ceased to be such a subsidiary.

(11) In this section—

"qualifying activity" has the same meaning as in section 257MNA (see subsection (4) of that section);

"relevant investment" has the meaning given by section 173A(3) (reading references in section 173A(3) to a company as including any social enterprise).

(12) Section 173A(4) and (5) apply to determine for the purposes of this section when a relevant investment is made.

(13) Section 173A(6) and (7) (meaning of "trade" etc) apply also for the purposes of this section.

46.39 "Qualifying trade"

"Qualifying trade" matters as money raised must be used in a qualifying trade.[28]

Section 257MP ITA provides:

(1) For the purposes of this Chapter, a trade is a qualifying trade if–

(a) it is conducted on a commercial basis and with a view to the realisation of profits, and

(b) it does not at any time in the shorter applicable period consist wholly or as to a substantial part in the carrying-on of excluded activities.

(2) References in this section and sections 257MQ to 257MT (excluded activities) to a trade are to be read without regard to the definition of "trade" in section 989.

46.40 "Excluded activity"

Excluded activities are (in short) not a qualifying trade. Section 257MQ ITA provides:

(1) The following are excluded activities for the purposes of sections 257JD, 257MJ and 257MP–

There are 14 categories of excluded activity:

(a) dealing in land, in commodities or futures or in shares, securities or other financial instruments,

(b) banking, insurance, money-lending, debt-factoring, hire-purchase financing or other financial activities,

---

28 See 46.32 (Money for qualifying trade).

(ba) leasing (including letting ships on charter or other assets on hire),
(bb) receiving royalties or licence fees,
(bc) operating or managing nursing homes[29] or residential care homes[30] or managing property used as a nursing home or residential care home (see section 257MQA),[31]
(bd) generating electricity, exporting electricity (see subsection (3)) or making electricity generating capacity available,
(be) generating heat,
(bf) generating any form of energy not within paragraph (bd) or (be),
(bg) producing gas or fuel,"
(c) property development (see section 257MR),
(d) activities in the fishery and aquaculture sector that is covered by Council Regulation (EC) No 104/2000 of 17 December 1999 on the common organisation of the markets in fishery and aquaculture products,
(e) the primary production of products listed in Annex I to the Treaty on the Functioning of the European Union (agricultural etc products), with the exception of products covered by Council Regulation (EC) No 104/2000 (fishery and aquaculture products),
(f) road freight transport for hire or reward, and
(g) providing services or facilities for a business carried on by another person (other than a company of which the provider of

---

29 Section 257MQA ITA provides a commonsense definition:
(1) This section supplements section 257MQ(1)(bc).
(2) "Nursing home" means any establishment which exists wholly or mainly for the provision of nursing care—
(a) for persons suffering from sickness, injury or infirmity, or
(b) for women who are pregnant or have given birth.

30 Section 257MQ(3) ITA provides:
"Residential care home" means any establishment which exists wholly or mainly for the provision of residential accommodation, together with board and personal care, for persons in need of personal care because of—
(a) old age,
(b) mental or physical disability,
(c) past or present dependence on alcohol or drugs,
(d) any past illnesses, or
(e) past or present mental disorder.

31 Section 257MQ(4) ITA provides:
The activities of a person are not to be taken to fall within section 257MQ(1)(bc) unless that person has an estate or interest in, or is in occupation of, the nursing home or residential care home in question.

the services or facilities is a qualifying subsidiary) if–

(i) the business consists wholly or as to a substantial part of activities falling within any of paragraphs (a) to (g), and

(ii) a controlling interest (see section 257MT) in the business is held by a person who also has a controlling interest in the business carried on by the provider of the services or facilities.

(3) For the purposes of subsection (1)(bd) electricity is exported if it is exported onto a distribution system or transmission system (within the meaning of section 4 of the Electricity Act 1989).

46.41 Advance clearance

The same system of advanced clearance operates for SI as it does for EIS and SEIS. HMRC say:

> You can ask HMRC if they agree that an investment would meet the conditions of a scheme before you apply. This is called advanced assurance. You can use this to show your potential investors that your proposed investment may qualify for a scheme.
> Advance assurance will not tell you if an investor would meet the conditions of the scheme.
> You'll need to make separate applications for each proposed investment that you want advance assurance for.
>
> **What you'll need to apply for advance assurance**
> For all schemes, you must include the following information for your company and its subsidiaries:
>
> - how much you hope to raise
> - the business plan and financial forecasts
> - a copy of the latest accounts if available
> - which companies will use the investments
> - details of all trading and activities to be carried out, and how much you expect to spend on each activity
> - a list of the amounts, dates and venture capital schemes under which you've previously received an investment
> - an up to date copy of the memorandum and articles of association and details of any changes you expect to make
> - a copy of the register of members from the date you apply for advance assurance
> - the latest draft of any documents you use to explain your proposal to potential investors
> - details of any other agreements between the company and the shareholders or VCT

- a signed letter from one of your directors or trustees if you're allowing an agent to act on your behalf
- any other documents to show you meet the qualifying conditions for the scheme

If you've used a venture capital scheme before, you do not have to provide details of your potential investors, however it will help your application.[32]

32 *https://www.gov.uk/guidance/venture-capital-schemes-apply-for-advance-assurance*

CHAPTER FORTY SEVEN

ADMINISTRATION: TAX RETURNS AND CLAIMS

47.1 Introduction

This chapter deals with the following topics:

(1) HMRC/charity relationship

(2) Registration with HMRC

(3) Form ChV1 (change of details)
(4) Form 64-8: Authorising an agent
(5) Tax returns by charities
(6) Claims by charities:
 (a) for charity tax relief
 (b) for repayment of tax from HMRC
(7) Assessment and collection of tax from charities
(8) Charity audits

47.2 Charity/HMRC relationship

The relationship between charities and HMRC is unlike other taxpayers. In *Mountstar v Charity Commission*:

> Mountstar as charity trustee owes obligations of disclosure and co-operation to the [Charity] Commission qua charities' regulator, and HMRC qua tax collector, which are of a different order to those which ordinary taxpayers such as the donors might owe to HMRC. It may well be legitimate for a private taxpayer or donor to be economical and tactical with the provision of information and data to HMRC or cause delays to stretch things out for as long as possible: such is his choice and he takes any consequences.
> Charities, however, are in a different position. They must act as an ordinary prudent man of business would act, independently of the interests of others. Also, and importantly, charities are established for public benefit and enjoy special privileges, advantages and tax exemptions which carry with them (in our view) an obligation to be open and transparent in the provision of information to the Commission which, we judge, extends to the provision of information to HMRC
> Thus there may come times when the Charity acting properly should be providing information to the Commission and to HMRC which it would be in the interests of the private donors to delay or not provide at all.[1]

47.3 Registration with HMRC

This was formerly done by form ChA1, but registration is now online.[2] HMRC say:

---

1 CA/2013/0001 at [150]-[152]. *https://www.judiciary.gov.uk/wp-content/uploads/JCO/Documents/Judgments/mountstar-charity-commission-decision-17102013.pdf*

2 *https://www.gov.uk/charity-recognition-hmrc*

> The HMRC Charities Application Form (ChA1) is for use by charities that wish to make claims for repayment of UK Income Tax, including Gift Aid, or where HMRC asks the organisation to demonstrate it is eligible to claim the charity tax reliefs and exemptions available in the UK. Please don't complete this form unless you want to register for the Gift Aid scheme or HMRC has asked you to complete it. HMRC will use this form to determine whether your organisation satisfies the definition of a charity for UK tax purposes.[3]

Similarly, the HMRC Guidance Note provides:

> 2.1.8 For a charity to be able to take advantage of the Gift Aid scheme, other giving schemes and the charitable tax exemptions, and to be able to make claims for repayment of tax, it must register online [link provided] so that HMRC Charities can decide whether it satisfies the relevant conditions and set up the appropriate records.

This is an administrative rather than a statutory requirement but in practice charities will have to register when HMRC require it.

There is substantial overlap with the application for registration with the Charity Commission, OSCR or CCNI which (almost) all new charities also have to complete.

The FPP guidance[4] discusses form ChA1 and provides:

> **Charities with an existing HMRC charity reference**
> Charities that already have an HMRC charity reference aren't normally[5] be asked tregister with HMRC online [an 'HMRC Charity Application Form' (ChA1)] to confirm their eligibility to charity tax reliefs.
> They don't need to do anything until they need to notify changes to the charity's details, such as their address, or changes in the people who deal with HMRC on a day to day basis (authorised officials, other officials or nominees) or the charity's agent (see below).
> **Charities without an existing HMRC charity reference**
> The first time a charity claims a tax relief or exemption HMRC may ask them to register their details online [complete an 'HMRC Charity Application Form' (ChA1)].

---

3 HMRC "How to complete Form ChA1 HMRC Charities Application Form" *https://www.gov.uk/government/publications/charities-hmrc-charity-application-form-cha1*

4 HMRC, "Guidance on the fit and proper persons test" (9 March 2017) *https://www.gov.uk/government/publications/charities-fit-and-proper-persons-test/guidance-on-the-fit-and-proper-persons-test*

5 The word "normally" was not in earlier versions of the FPP guidance.

HMRC asks all charities claiming Gift Aid repayments of tax for the first time to register with them.
If you are asked to register your charity's details you will need to provide information about the authorised officials, other officials and nominees.
Once HMRC is content that a charity is entitled to claim tax reliefs and exemptions they will issue it with an HMRC Charities reference. This is a reference number starting with 2 letters followed by some numbers such as QQ123456A.

47.3.1 *Trust registration service*

For a discussion of TRS, see Kessler, *Taxation of Non-Residents and Foreign Domiciliaries* (21st ed., 2022-23), chapter 125 (Trust Registration).[6]

A charitable trust is an exempt trust under para 5 sch 3A Money Laundering, Terrorist Financing and Transfer of Funds (Information on the Payer) Regulations 2017 which sets out the categories of exempt trust. Para 5 sch 3A provides:

> A trust for charitable purposes which—
> (a) in Scotland or Northern Ireland, is registered as a charity; or
> (b) in England and Wales, is registered as a charity or not required to register by virtue of section 30(2)(a) to (d) of the Charities Act 2011.

TRS Manual provides:

> **TRSM23060: charitable trusts** [May 2021]
> **Practicalities of charity registration**
> In practice, it can take time for a charity registration to be approved in the UK. To avoid unnecessary registrations on TRS, HMRC don't require trusts pending approval of registration as a UK charity to register on TRS in the interim, so long as the trustees have a genuine expectation that the trust will be accepted for registration as a charity.

The Manual provides an example to hammer the point home:

> **Example**
> A charitable trust is set up in Wales to provide new household items for those struggling financially in the local area. For the first two years the income of the charity remains below £5,000. The charity is therefore not

6 Online edition *https://www.foreigndomiciliaries.co.uk*

required to register with the Charities Commission in England and Wales. It is not required to register on TRS either.
In its third year the work of the charity expands considerably and its gross income is £50,000. The charity therefore applies for registration with the Charities Commission in England and Wales which the trustees have a genuine expectation will be accepted.
The application takes several months to be processed and accepted. The trust is not required to register on TRS, neither during the period when waiting for the request to be processed nor going forward.

In short, exempt trusts are only required to register if they incur a tax liability. Of course, a charitable trust will not normally incur a tax liability.

TRS FAQs provides:

O. REGISTERING A CHARITABLE TRUST
Do charitable trusts need to register?
The two conditions for registration are:
Condition A: is the trust in question either a UK express trust or a non-UK express trust with either UK source income or UK assets; and,
Condition B: have the trustees incurred a liability to pay any of the relevant UK taxes.
If the answer to both of these questions is "yes" then the trustees need to register.
Will charitable trustees need to follow this process every tax year?
Yes. The trustees will need answer each of these two questions/ conditions each tax year as registration is linked to when the trustees incur a liability to pay any of the relevant UK taxes...
Which charitable trusts need to register?
A charitable trust will need to register when the trustees have incurred a liability to any of the relevant UK taxes in a given tax year in relation to the trust income or assets. Therefore, a charitable trust will only need to comply with the legislation if their activities generate a tax liability that falls outside the scope of the charity exemptions, for example, where a charity incurs non-charitable expenditure and/or is in receipt of non-exempt income.
How does a charitable trust register?
The TRS is not currently available for charitable trusts. Those charitable trusts that need to complete the Trusts Register should contact HMRC by telephone on 03000 123 1072 and request a copy of a paper form.
What happens if I have a large number of beneficiaries do I need to register the details of each and every beneficiary?
To help keep administrative burdens to a minimum for trusts with

particularly large numbers of beneficiaries (such as ... charitable trusts ...) the trustees will only be asked to identify the class of beneficiary if the number of named beneficiaries exceed ten. ...

Are donors to a charity to be treated as settlors and therefore his or her details need to be registered?

We do not consider donors to be settlors and therefore the details of a donor does not need to be included on the TRS as long as he or she has no influence or control over the trust nor receives a financial benefit from the trust.

Do the trustees of all charitable trusts need to maintain accurate and up to date written records of beneficial owners under regulation 44(1) of the legislation?

Yes. We expect the trustees to maintain accurate and up to date written records of all beneficial owners of the trust as set out under regulation 44(1) of the legislation. This information should be held because under the legislation any law enforcement authority can make a request directly to the trustees for information about the beneficial owners of that trust including from a trust which does not incur a liability to any of the relevant UK taxes.[7]

47.4 ChV1: Charities variations form

47.4.1 *Change of charity name*

The HMRC Guidance Note provides:

> 2.6.1 If the charity changes its name, the trustees must notify HMRC Charities as soon as possible using form ChV1 HMRC Charities change of details form.[8] If the charity is a company it should include a copy of the Certificate of Incorporation of Change of Name. If the charity isn'tt a company it should include the minutes of the meeting of the trustees at which the name change was adopted.

This is not statutory but it would be sensible to follow HMRC's practice. In any case, a change of name is not common.

47.4.2 *Change of trustee/bank account*

The HMRC Guidance Note provides:

> 2.6.2 If the charity trustees or managers change or if the bank account

---

7 *https://www.step.org/sites/default/files/Policy/TRS_Guidance_FAQ_-_22_November_2017.pdf*

8 *https://www.gov.uk/government/publications/charities-change-of-details-form-chv1*

> details change, HMRC should be notified as soon as possible using form ChV1.
> 2.6.3 It's important that any relevant changes are notified to us on form ChV1 at least 1 month before a claim using the new details is made so that we can change your charity's records and make any repayment using the new details.

This is not statutory but it would be necessary to inform HMRC of changes in details of the bank account or the nominee dealing with HMRC.

This passage suggests that a charity should inform HMRC of every change in charity trustee. There is no statutory duty to do so and in practice we doubt if that should be regularly done.

The FPP guidance provides:

> **Managers charities need to tell HMRC about**
> As explained above the definition of 'managers' covers a potentially wide range of persons. HMRC need to ensure that the managers making tax claims and receiving tax payments are authorised to do so by the charity and are fit and proper persons.
> HMRC may ask a charity about any of its managers but, unless specifically asked to provide more details, charities should only tell HMRC when they appoint or change certain categories of managers:
> **The authorised official**
> This is the person within your charity you have told HMRC is authorised to deal with your tax affairs, make Gift Aid or other repayment claims and Gift Aid Small Donations Scheme (GASDS) claims and, where necessary, sign and submit tax returns. They will also be the person HMRC will contact if they have any questions about your charity. Charities can appoint 2 authorised officials and where they do so they need to inform HMRC of both
> **The other officials**
> These will normally be trustees or directors of the charity (if the charity is a company), or CASC officials. You need to nominate a minimum of 2, maximum of 4, other officials
> Charities may also appoint a nominee or nominees, who are individuals or organisations outside your charity who you have authorised to submit Gift Aid claims, other repayment claims and GASDS claims to HMRC on your behalf. They might just make the claims for your charity or they might make the claim and receive the repayment or payment for your charity and other charities. Although nominees aren't 'managers' for the purposes of the fit and proper persons test, you do still need to notify

HMRC if you appoint a nominee or that nominee changes.
HMRC will only act on information about changes to the authorised official, other officials and nominees (and agents – see below), and changes to the charity's details such as their address and bank account if the notification is made by existing authorised officials or other officials.

Telling HMRC about changes
HMRC asks all charities to let it know when **certain** managers change. Charities **don't** need to inform HMRC of **all** changes to managers.
Notification of changes should be made on the 'HMRC Change of Details Form' (ChV1) which is also the form for charities to notify HMRC of certain other changes to their organisation.
Charities only need to inform HMRC when the following people change:
• authorised officials (charities can have 2 of these)
• other officials
• nominees
• agents
You should use form ChV1 to notify HMRC about such changes – except agents. You don't have to tell HMRC about changes of other managers unless you wish to do so. If you do wish to do so then you should use form ChV1 to explain what other managers have left and what new ones have arrived.[9]

Form ChV1 provides:

> I confirm I have read the HMRC Fit and Proper Persons guidance which is available on the GOV.UK website

There was a similar requirement in the former Form ChA1 which probably survives in its successor. There is no statutory requirement to do this and we speculate that in practice the requirement may be more honoured in the breach than the observance; though of course charities do need to consider the issue.

47.5 Form 64-8: Authorising agent

HMRC only deal with a taxpayer's agent if the taxpayer authorises that, and form 64-8 (Authorising your agent) confers that authority.

---

9 HMRC, "Guidance on the fit and proper persons test" (9 March 2017) *https://www.gov.uk/government/publications/charities-fit-and-proper-persons-test /guidance-on-the-fit-and-proper-persons-test*

FPP guidance provides:

> **Agents acting on behalf of your charity**
> An agent is an individual or organisation outside your charity who acts on your behalf, such as an accountant or lawyer. You don't have to have an agent but if you do they can submit tax returns, prepare accounts or exchange information with HMRC on your behalf. There is a separate process for informing HMRC that you have appointed an agent using autorisation form 64-8. Form 64-8 is available on the GOV.UK website and you must send HMRC a completed form whenever you appoint a new agent.
> However there are specific situations where, in addition to the form 64-8 you must send a completed ChV1 regarding an agent if:
> - you appoint an agent as a nominee for your charity
> - they cease to act as a nominee
>
> The only time it's possible for an agent to be the 'authorised official' is if the agent is already a 'manager' of your charity. This would normally apply where the agent is a trustee or director of the charity. If an agent is not already a 'manager' then they can't be the authorised official for your charity. You need to tell HMRC when an agent is appointed as your authorised official, or when they cease to be, on the ChV1
> Don't send your completed form 64-8 to the Central Authorisation Team, send it to: Charities, Savings and International 2, HM Revenue and Customs, BX9 1BU[10]

47.6 Tax returns

47.6.1 *When tax return required*

HMRC Guidance Note provides:

> **6.7 Self Assessment**
> 6.7.1 All charities are subject to the self assessment legislation and must submit a tax return if either they:
> - are asked to do so
> - believe that they may have tax to pay
>
> 6.7.2 Charities set up as trusts are within the self assessment regime. Their tax affairs are dealt with on a tax year basis.
> 6.7.3 All other types of charities (for example companies limited by guarantee, bodies created by Royal Charter or Act of Parliament,

---

10 HMRC, "Guidance on the fit and proper persons test" (9 March 2017) *https://www.gov.uk/government/publications/charities-fit-and-proper-persons-test /guidance-on-the-fit-and-proper-persons-test*

> Industrial and Provident societies or unincorporated associations) are within the Corporation Tax Self Assessment(CTSA) regime. Their tax affairs are dealt with on an accounting period basis.

Elsewhere, HMRC say:

> Some charities have to make a tax return every year but most only have to from time to time. If you're asked by HMRC to make a return you must do so.
> Even if you're not asked, you must make a tax return if your charity has:
> - income, gains or profits that are not covered by a tax exemption or relief, for example income generated from trading that wasn't within your charity's primary purpose (the method or trade by which the charity achieves its charitable objectives)
> - used income or gains for non-charitable purposes - known as non-charitable expenditure
>
> You must tell HMRC when you:
> - receive - or think you may receive - income or gains that are taxable
> - use any income or gains on non-charitable expenditure
> - make any non-qualifying investments or loans
>
> HMRC will then usually send you a tax return so you can make a formal declaration of your charity's taxable income or non-charitable expenditure.
> If your charity doesn't declare how much tax it owes correctly and on time, HMRC may charge a penalty.[11]

It is clearly envisaged that tax returns will not be put in where all the income is covered by a charity tax exemption, even though the tax relief claim which is formally required is not made.

In practice it will be very rare for a charity to have taxable income so it will be rare to put in a tax return.

47.6.2 *Charitable trust return*

HMRC say:

> Charitable trusts pay tax under Self Assessment. So as a trustee of your charitable trust you'll have to fill in a Trust and Estate tax return - form SA900.
> You'll also need to fill in the supplementary page SA907 which asks you for details of:
> - any claim for tax exemptions on income, profits or gains that your

11 *https://www.gov.uk/charities-and-tax/pay-tax.*

charity received in the period covered by the tax return
- any non-charitable expenditure or investments

You should also send in a copy of your accounts for the period covered by the tax return.

If you prefer, you can complete and file a Trust and Estate Return online using commercial software.[12]

47.6.3 *Charitable company return*

HMRC say:

> CASCs, and charities that aren't trusts, are treated as companies for tax purposes. This means your CASC or charity may be liable for Corporation Tax and you'll need to file a Company Tax Return and supporting documents to account for any tax you owe.
>
> You'll also have to complete the supplementary charities page which asks you for details of:
>
> - any claim for tax exemptions on income, profits or gains that your charity or CASC received in the period covered by the Company Tax Return
> - any non-charitable expenditure or investments[13]

47.7 Claims

Charities may make various types of claim. This chapter considers two sorts of claim:

(1) **Tax relief claim**: A claim for charity tax relief

(2) **Tax repayment claim**: A claim for repayment of tax to a charity

These are distinct claims. If a charity receives income gross (without deduction of tax) it should strictly make a tax relief claim; if it receives net income (after deduction of tax, such as Gift Aid) should strictly make two claims: a tax relief claim and a tax repayment claim.

In practice the position is different:

(1) HMRC do not require tax relief claims when income is paid gross. We have never heard of HMRC complaining that no claim is made, and in practice they are content not to be bothered by routine claims from charities which do not reclaim tax. However if there were a

---

12 Tax returns for charities and Community Amateur Sports Clubs *https://www.gov.uk/charities-and-tax/pay-tax#4*

13 Tax returns for charities and Community Amateur Sports Clubs *https://www.gov.uk/charities-and-tax/pay-tax#4*

dispute, a claim would be formally made and refused, allowing an appeal to proceed.

(2) When income is paid net of tax, a claim is made for tax repayment, now through Charities Online, which (if it mattered) may be regarded as a tax relief claim as well as a tax repayment claim.

47.8 Tax relief claims

We set out the procedure for tax relief claims though, as noted, they are not usually made in practice, or at least, they are not made formally.

47.8.1 *Need for IT relief claim*

Section 538 ITA provides:

> (1) The exemptions under this Part [Part 10 ITA] require a claim.
> (2) Subsection (1) does not apply to an exemption under—
> (a) section 534 (exemption for transactions in deposits), or
> (b) section 535 (exemption for offshore income gains).

The exceptions in s.538(2) are accidents of history. It is a pity that the ITA did not tidy up. Subsection (2) should be repealed, but it is not sufficiently important to bother, except, perhaps, in the context of a wider review.

Thus a charitable trust which receives income is required by statute to make a claim for income tax relief, and if they do not do so, the income is strictly taxable.

47.8.2 *Need for CT relief claim*

A claim must also be made in order to obtain almost every type of charity corporation tax relief. Unfortunately the requirement is set out separately in every section conferring a relief, about 15 times in all:

Topic	**Claim under CTA 2010**
Gift Aid gifts from individuals	s.472(4)
Payroll giving gifts from individuals	s.472A(3)
Gifts from a company	s.473(3)
Payments from another charity	s.474(5)
Trading exemptions	s.478(5), s.480(6)
Miscellaneous income	s.481(6)
Fundraising events	s.483(4)
Lotteries	s.484(4)
Property income	s.485(5)
Investment income	s.486(6)

Public revenue dividends	s.487(3)
Annual payments etc	s.488(4)
Estate income	s.489(3)

It could have been drafted more concisely, but that is the style of the tax law rewrite.

47.8.3 *Charitable trust: making tax relief claim*

For IT, claims are mostly governed by s.42 TMA, and are made in tax returns:

> (1) Where any provision of the Taxes Acts provides for relief to be given, or any other thing to be done, on the making of a claim, this section shall, unless otherwise provided, have effect in relation to the claim.
>
> ...
>
> (2) Subject to subsections (3) to (3ZB)[14] below, where notice has been given under section 8 [personal return], 8A [trustee return] or 12AA [partnership return] of this Act, a claim shall not at any time be made otherwise than by being included in a return under that section if it could, at that or any subsequent time, be made by being so included.[15]

Charitable trusts do not usually receive a notice to submit a return under s.8A. Even if they do, s.42(3ZA) TMA takes tax relief claims out of s.42(2):

> Subsection (2) above shall not apply in relation to any claim by the trustees of a charitable trust for an amount to be exempt from tax by virtue of—
>
> (a) s.521(4) of ITA 2007 (gifts entitling donor to gift aid relief: charitable trusts),
>
> (b) s.532 of that Act (exemption for savings and investment income),
>
> (c) s.533 of that Act (exemption for public revenue dividends),
>
> (d) s.536 of that Act (exemption for certain miscellaneous income), or
>
> (e) s.537 of that Act (exemption for income from estates in administration).

---

14 These exceptions are not applicable to charities.

15 Section 42(5) TMA extends "included in a return": "The references in this section to a claim being included in a return include references to a claim being so included by virtue of an amendment of the return."

Instead, s.538A ITA provides a special procedure for making a tax relief claim:

> (1) This section also applies to claims for amounts to be exempt from tax by virtue of—
> (a) s.521(4) (gifts entitling donor to gift aid relief: charitable trusts), or
> (b) any of the provisions mentioned in subsection (A1)(b).
> (2) A claim to which this section applies may be made—
> (a) to an officer of Revenue and Customs, or
> (b) by being included in a return under section 8A of TMA 1970 (trustee's self-assessment return).

So tax relief claims by charitable trusts are free-standing claims, ie not made in a return. The practical significance is that the claims procedure is governed by sch 1A TMA (Claims etc not included in a return), rather than the procedure in Part 2 TMA (Returns of income and gains).

47.8.4 *Charitable co: making tax relief claim*

Section 477A CTA 2010 provides:

> (1) This section also applies to claims for amounts to be exempt from tax by virtue of—
> (a) section 472 (gifts qualifying for gift aid relief: charitable companies), or
> (b) section 475 (gifts qualifying for gift aid relief: eligible bodies).
> (2) A claim to which this section applies may be made—
> (a) to an officer of Revenue and Customs, or
> (b) where the claimant is a company, by being included in the claimant's company tax return.

Section 491A CTA 2010 extends this:

> (1) Subsections (2) to (5) of section 477A (claims in relation to gift aid relief) apply to—
> (a) claims for amounts to be exempt from tax by virtue of a provision listed in subsection (2), and
> (b) claims for repayment of income tax deducted at source from income which is exempt from tax by virtue of such a provision,
> as they apply to claims to which that section applies.
> (2) The provisions are—
> (a) s.486 (investment income and non-trading profits from loan relationships),

(b) s.487 (public revenue dividends),
(c) s.488 (certain miscellaneous income), and
(d) s.489 (income from estates in administration).

Section 665A CTA 2010 makes equivalent provision for CASCs.

47.9 Charitable trust: Tax repayment claims

47.9.1 *Right to reclaim tax*

The right to a tax repayment is normally governed by s.59B TMA:

> (1) Subject to subsection (2) below, the difference between—
> (a) the amount of income tax and capital gains tax contained in a person's self-assessment under section 9 of this Act for any year of assessment, and
> (b) the aggregate of
> [i] any payments on account made by him in respect of that year (whether under section 59A of this Act or otherwise)
> [ii] and any income tax which in respect of that year has been deducted at source,
> shall be payable by him or (as the case may be) repayable to him as mentioned in subsection (3) or (4) below[16]

However a charity's right to a tax repayment is taken out of s.59B by s.59B(7) TMA:

> In this section any reference to income tax deducted at source is a reference to income tax deducted or treated as deducted from any income or treated as paid on any income. But such a reference does not include income tax repaid on a claim for repayment of income tax which—
> (a) is treated as having been paid by virtue of section 520(4) of ITA 2007 (gift aid relief: income tax treated as paid by trustees of charitable trust), or
> (b) has been deducted at source from income to which section 532, 533, 536 or 537 of that Act (certain sources of income exempt

---

16 For completeness, s.59B(1) continues:
"... but nothing in this subsection shall require the repayment of any income tax treated as deducted or paid by virtue of
[i] section 246D(1) of the principal Act [ICTA 1988],
[ii] section 626 of ITEPA 2003 or
[iii] s.399(2) or 530(1) of ITTOIA 2005."
But this does not concern charities.

from income tax) applies.

Section 42(3ZB) TMA takes tax repayment claims out of the usual s.42(2) rule (claims made in tax return):

> Subsection (2) also does not apply in relation to any claim for repayment of an amount of income tax which—
> (a) is treated as having been paid by virtue of s.520(4) of ITA 2007 (gift aid relief: income tax treated as paid by trustees of charitable trust), or
> (b) has been deducted at source from income to which any of the provisions mentioned in paragraphs (b) to (e) of subsection (3ZA) applies.

Instead, s.538A ITA provides a special procedure for making a tax repayment claim:

> (A1) This section applies to claims for—
> (a) repayment of income tax treated as having been paid by virtue of section 520(4) (gift aid relief: income tax treated as paid by trustees of charitable trust), or
> (b) repayment of income tax deducted at source from income to which any of the following applies—
> (i) s.532 (exemption for savings and investment income),
> (ii) s.533 (exemption for public revenue dividends),
> (iii) s.536 (exemption for certain miscellaneous income), or
> (iv) s.537 (exemption for income from estates in administration).

The rules for claims are set out in s.538A(2) ITA:

> A claim to which this section applies may be made—
> (a) to an officer of Revenue and Customs, or
> (b) by being included in a return under section 8A of TMA 1970 (trustee's self-assessment return).

47.10 Freestanding claim procedure

The claims procedure takes us to Para 1 sch 1AB TMA which provides:

> (1) This paragraph applies where—
> (a) a person has paid an amount by way of income tax or capital gains tax but the person believes that the tax was not due, or
> (b) a person has been assessed as liable to pay an amount by way of income tax or capital gains tax, or there has been a determination or direction to that effect, but the person believes

> that the tax is not due.
> (2) The person may make a claim to the Commissioners for repayment or discharge of the amount...
> (6) The Commissioners are not liable to give relief in respect of a case described in sub-paragraph (1)(a) or (b) except as provided—
> (a) by this Schedule and Schedule 1A (following a claim under this paragraph), or
> (b) by or under another provision of the Income Tax Acts or an enactment relating to the taxation of capital gains.
> (7) For the purposes of this Schedule, an amount paid by one person on behalf of another is treated as paid by the other person.

Para 3(4) sch 1AB TMA deals with the procedure for a tax reclaim:

> A claim under this Schedule may not be made by being included in a return under section 8, 8A or 12AA of this Act.

47.10.1 *Sch 1A rules*

This takes us to sch 1A TMA (Claims etc not included in returns). Para 2 sch 1A TMA provides:

> (1) Subject to any provision in the Taxes Acts for a claim to be made to the Board, every claim shall be made to an officer of the Board.
> (2) No claim requiring the repayment of tax shall be made unless the claimant has documentary proof that the tax has been paid by deduction or otherwise.
> (3) A claim shall be made in such form as the Board may determine.
> (4) The form of claim shall provide for a declaration to the effect that all the particulars given in the form are correctly stated to the best of the information and belief of the person making the claim.
> (5) The form of claim may require—
> (a) a statement of the amount of tax which will be required to be discharged or repaid in order to give effect to the claim;
> (b) such information as is reasonably required for the purpose of determining whether and, if so, the extent to which the claim is correct; and
> (bb) the delivery with the claim of such accounts, statements and documents, relating to information contained in the claim, as are reasonably required for the purpose mentioned in paragraph (b) above.

47.10.2 *Record keeping*

Para 2A sch 1A TMA provides:

(1) Any person who may wish to make a claim in relation to a year of assessment or other period shall—

(a) keep all such records as may be requisite for the purpose of enabling him to make a correct and complete claim; and

(b) shall preserve those records until the end of the relevant day.

(2) In relation to a claim, the relevant day for the purposes of sub-paragraph (1) above is whichever of the following is the latest, namely—

(a) where enquiries into the claim or any amendment of the claim are made by an officer of the Board, the day on which, by virtue of paragraph 7(1) below, those enquiries are completed; and

(b) where no enquiries into the claim or any amendment of the claim are so made, the day on which such an officer no longer has power to make such enquiries.

(2A) HMRC may by regulations—

(a) provide that the records required to be kept and preserved under sub-paragraph (1) include, or do not include, records specified in the regulations, and

(b) provide that those records include supporting documents so specified.

(3) The duty under sub-paragraph (1) to preserve records may be discharged—

(a) by preserving them in any form and by any means, or

(b) by preserving the information contained in them in any form and by any means,

subject to sub-paragraph (3A) and any conditions or further exceptions specified in writing by HMRC.

(3A) Sub-paragraph (3)(b) does not apply in the case of records of the kinds specified in section 12B(4A) or paragraph 22(3) of Schedule 18 to the FA 1998.

(4) Subject to sub-paragraph (5) below, any person who fails to comply with sub-paragraph (1) above in relation to any claim which is made for a year of assessment or accounting period shall be liable to a penalty not exceeding £3,000.

(5) Sub-paragraph (4) above does not apply where—

(a) the records which the person fails to keep or preserve are records falling within paragraph (a) of section 12B(4A) of this Act or paragraph 22(3) of Schedule 18 to the FA 1998; and

(b) an officer of the Board is satisfied that any facts which he reasonably requires to be proved, and which would have been proved by the records, are proved by other documentary evidence furnished to him...

(7) In this paragraph "supporting documents" includes accounts, books, deeds, contracts, vouchers and receipts.

47.10.3 *Amendment window*

Para 3 sch 1A TMA provides:

> (1) Subject to sub-paragraph (2) below—
>
> (a) at any time before the end of the period of nine months beginning with the day on which a claim is made, an officer of the Board may by notice to the claimant so amend the claim as to correct any obvious errors or mistakes in the claim (whether errors of principle, arithmetical mistakes or otherwise); and
>
> (b) at any time before the end of the period of twelve months beginning with the day on which the claim is made, the claimant may amend his claim by notice to an officer of the Board.
>
> (2) No amendment of a claim may be made under sub-paragraph (1) above at any time during the period—
>
> (a) beginning with the day on which an officer of the Board gives notice of his intention to enquire into the claim, and
>
> (b) ending with the day on which the officer's enquiries into the claim are completed.

47.10.4 *Giving effect to claim*

Para 4 sch 1A TMA provides:

> (1) Subject to sub-paragraphs (1A), (3) to (5) below, an officer of the Board or the Board shall, as soon as practicable after a claim other than a partnership claim is made, or such a claim is amended under paragraph 3 above, give effect to the claim or amendment by discharge or repayment of tax.
>
> (1A) [This concerns PAYE, not relevant here]
>
> (2) [This concerns partnership claims, not relevant here]
>
> (3) Where any such claim or amendment as is mentioned in sub-paragraph (1) or (2) above is enquired into by an officer of the Board—
>
> (a) that sub-paragraph shall not apply until the day on which, by virtue of paragraph 7(1)] below, the enquiry is completed; but
>
> (b) the officer may at any time before that day give effect to the claim or amendment, on a provisional basis, to such extent as he thinks fit.
>
> (4) Nothing in this paragraph applies in relation to a claim or an

amendment of a claim if the claim is not one for discharge or repayment of tax.

(5) This paragraph has effect subject to any provision in the Taxes Acts that—

(a) requires or allows effect to be given to a claim by other means, or

(b) provides that an amount is not to be discharged or repaid.

47.10.5 *Enquiry into claim*

Para 5 sch 1A TMA provides:

(1) An officer of the Board may enquire into—

(a) a claim made by any person, or

(b) any amendment made by any person of a claim made by him,

if, before the end of the period mentioned in sub-paragraph (2) below, he gives notice in writing of his intention to do so to that person or, in the case of a partnership claim, any successor of that person.

(2) The period referred to in sub-paragraph (1) above is whichever of the following ends the latest, namely—

(a) the period ending with the quarter day next following the first anniversary of the day on which the claim or amendment was made;

(b) where the claim or amendment relates to a year of assessment, the period ending with the first anniversary of the 31st January next following that year; and

(c) where the claim or amendment relates to a period other than a year of assessment, the period ending with the first anniversary of the end of that period;

and the quarter days for the purposes of this sub-paragraph are 31st January, 30th April, 31st July and 31st October.

(3) A claim or amendment which has been enquired into under sub-paragraph (1) above shall not be the subject of—

(a) a further notice under that sub-paragraph; or

(b) if it is subsequently included in a return, a notice under section 9A(1) or 12AC(1) of this Act or paragraph 24 of Schedule 18 to the Finance Act 1998.

HMRC v Tooth explains the relationship between:

(1) An enquiry into a claim under para 5 sch 1A TMA and

(2) An enquiry into a return under s.9A TMA

7. A "discovery assessment" is not the only way in which HMRC can go behind past assessments to tax or claims to relief. HMRC can launch an

enquiry into a claim for relief under Schedule 1A TMA. They can also launch an enquiry into a return under section 9A TMA. Schedule 1A and section 9A TMA are mutually exclusive mechanisms. Each has a prescribed time limit within which HMRC must take action.

8. Under Schedule 1A, HMRC can only enquire into a claim which is not included in a return, and the time limit is, in broad terms, 12 months from the date of the claim. By contrast, where a claim is included in a return made under section 8 or 8A TMA, the enquiry must be under section 9A. Enquiries under section 9A extend to anything contained in the return or required to be contained in the return, including a claim or election included in the return. The time limit for section 9A enquiries is, again in broad terms, 12 months from the filing of the return.

9. Schedule 1A paragraph 3 contains a power for HMRC to amend a claim, but that power is not exercisable during the period when a claim is being enquired into. Section 9ZB contains a power to amend a return, which must be exercised within 9 months of the delivery of the return or a relevant amendment.

10. Where an enquiry is launched into a claim under Schedule 1A, paragraphs 4(1) and (3) of that Schedule provide that HMRC are not required to give effect to the claim until the enquiry is completed.

11. It can therefore be of some importance to decide whether or not a claim is included in a return. This question was considered by the Supreme Court in *Revenue and Customs Commissioners v Cotter,*[17] where it held that a return did not include the entirety of the information set out in the return, but only that information which was submitted for the purpose of establishing the amount to which a person is chargeable to tax for a year of account.[18]

47.10.6 *Completion of enquiry*

Para 7 sch 1A TMA provides:

> (1) An enquiry under paragraph 5 above is completed when an officer of the Board by notice (a "closure notice") informs the claimant that he has completed his enquiries and states his conclusions.
> (2) In the case of a claim for discharge or repayment of tax, the closure notice must either—
> (a) state that in the officer's opinion no amendment of the claim is required, or
> (b) if in the officer's opinion the claim is insufficient or excessive,

17 [2013] UKSC 69.
18 [2019] EWCA Civ 826.

amend the claim so as to make good or eliminate the deficiency or excess.

In the case of an enquiry falling within paragraph 5(1)(b) above, paragraph (b) above only applies so far as the deficiency or excess is attributable to the claimant's amendment.

(3) In the case of a claim that is not a claim for discharge or repayment of tax, the closure notice must either—

(a) allow the claim, or

(b) disallow the claim, wholly or to such extent as appears to the officer appropriate.

(4) A closure notice takes effect when it is issued.

(5) The claimant may apply to the tribunal for a direction requiring an officer of the Board to issue a closure notice within a specified period.

(6) Any such application is to be subject to the relevant provisions of Part 5 of this Act (see, in particular, section 48(2)(b)).

(7) The tribunal shall give the direction applied for unless satisfied that there are reasonable grounds for not issuing a closure notice within a specified period.

(8) In relation to a partnership claim, references in this paragraph to the claimant are to the person who made the claim or his successor.

47.10.7 *Giving effect to amendments*

Para 8 TMA provides:

(1) An officer of the Board or the Board shall, within 30 days after the date of issue of a closure notice amending a claim other than a partnership claim under paragraph 7(2) above, give effect to the amendment by making such adjustment as may be necessary, whether—

(a) by way of assessment on the claimant, or

(b) by discharge of tax or, on proof to the satisfaction of the officer or the Board that any tax has been paid by the claimant by deduction or otherwise, by repayment of tax.

(2) An officer of the Board or the Board shall, within 30 days after the date of issue of a closure notice amending a partnership claim under paragraph 7(2) above, give effect to the amendment, as respects each of the relevant partners, by making such adjustment as may be necessary, whether—

(a) by way of assessment on the partner, or

(b) by discharge of tax or, on proof to the satisfaction of the officer or the Board that any tax has been paid by the partner by deduction or otherwise, by repayment of tax.

(3) An assessment made under sub-paragraph (1) or (2) above shall not

be out of time if it is made within the time mentioned in that sub-paragraph.

Para 9 deals with appeals against amendments.

47.10.8 *Assessment after enquiry closed*

After an enquiry into a claim is closed, an assessment can only be made under the provisions of s.29 TMA on the basis that "a relief which has been given is or has become excessive".

47.11 Future reforms

Further reform has been proposed. Section 538A ITA provides:

> (3) In this section—
> "free-standing claim" means a claim made as mentioned in subsection (2)(a), and
> "tax return claim" means a claim made as mentioned in subsection (2)(b).
> (4) HMRC may by regulations make provision—
> (a) limiting the number of free-standing claims that may be made by a person in a tax year, or
> (b) requiring a claim for an amount below an amount specified in the regulations to be made as a tax return claim.
> (5) The regulations may make different provision for different cases or purposes.

However there are as yet no regulations under this section.

The CT equivalent is s.477A(3)(4)(5) CTA 2010 which repeats s.538A(3)(4)(5) verbatim.

47.12 Charitable company tax repayment

Claims in relation to CT are governed in general by Part 7 sch 18 FA 1998. In *Champions Fun v HMRC* the Tribunal said:

> 65. We do not think that these provisions [Part 7 Schedule 18 FA 1998] apply to a repayment of income tax to a company in respect of tax treated as paid by virtue of s 471 CTA 2010. Section 471 does not provide for a "claim" for repayment of income tax. No other provision of Schedule 18 FA 1998, CTA 2009 (including in particular s 3) or CTA 2010 does so.[19]

---

19 [2018] UKFTT 516 (TC). The taxpayer appeared in person, and HMRC were not represented by Counsel.

But we think the right to a repayment of income tax is under s.477A CTA 2010 which provides:

> (A1) This section applies to claims for repayment of income tax treated as having been paid by virtue of—
> (a) section 471 (gifts qualifying for gift aid relief: charitable companies), or
> (b) section 475 (gifts qualifying for gift aid relief: eligible bodies)...
> (2) A claim to which this section applies may be made—
> (a) to an officer of Revenue and Customs, or
> (b) where the claimant is a company, by being included in the claimant's company tax return.

47.13 Quantification of claim

Section 42(1A) TMA provides:

> Subject to subsection (3) to (3ZC) below,[20] a claim for a relief, an allowance or a repayment of tax shall be for an amount which is quantified at the time when the claim is made.

47.14 Time limit for claim

Para 3 sch 1AB TMA sets out the time limit for a tax repayment claim:

> (1) A claim under this Schedule may not be made more than 4 years after the end of the relevant tax year.
> (2) In relation to a claim made in reliance on paragraph 1(1)(a),[21] the relevant tax year is—
> (a) where the amount paid, or liable to be paid, is excessive by reason of a mistake in a return or returns under section 8, 8A or 12AA of this Act, the tax year to which the return (or, if more than one, the first return) relates, and
> (b) otherwise, the tax year in respect of which the payment was made.

A charitable trust must make any claim within four years of the end of the year of tax to which it relates.[22]

A charitable company must make any claim within four years from the

20 The exceptions are not applicable to charities.
21 See 47.10 (Freestanding claim procedure).
22 Section 43 TMA. Late claims are permitted in some circumstances under s.43A TMA.

end of the accounting period to which the claim relates.[23] The HMRC Guidance Note summarises the time limits for making a claim:

> **6.5 Time limit for making claims**
> 6.5.1 Claims must be made within 4 years of the end of the tax year (for charitable trusts) or the accounting period (for other charities and CASCs) to which they relate. Claims made late won't be paid.
> 6.5.2 For example, for a charity that is a trust a donation on 1 December 2010 falls in the tax year 6 April 2010 to 5 April 2011. So a Gift Aid claim would have to be made in respect of that donation by 5 April 2015.
> 6.5.3 If the charity or CASC is a company with an accounting period ending on 31 December, a donation on 1 December 2012 would fall in the accounting period ended 31 December 2012 and so the Gift Aid claim would have be made by 31 December 2016.

47.15 "Charities online" repayment system

The system for charities and CASCs to make repayment claims is known as "Charities Online".

The former R68 repayment form has been abolished.

HMRC's have issued guidance **("Charities Online Guidance")**.[24]

Charities Online Guidance provides:

> From 22 April 2013, Charities and CASCs can make Gift Aid repayment claims, and claim for other repayments on taxed income online, through the new Charities Online service. You must also use Charities Online to claim top-up payments under the Gift Aid Small Donations Scheme (GASDS).

Charities Online provides two methods of making online claims.

47.15.1 *Option 1: <1000 donors*

Charities Online Guidance provides:

> *Option one: claim using an online form*
> Option one can be used to submit a claim with up to 1,000 Gift Aid donors by completing and attaching a schedule spreadsheet to the online claim form.
> There is no limit to the numbers of claims you can submit. If for example you normally send one annual claim with say 6,000 donations, you can

---

23 Para 55 sch 18 FA 1998.

24 *https://www.gov.uk/guidance/claim-tax-back-on-donations-using-charities-online*

submit six claims online with up to 1,000 donations on each claim form. For many this might be preferable to option two, which is aimed at very large charities who submit significantly more than 1,000 donations.

The Online claim forms will have fields you must fill in, and will automatically check that the information has been entered in the correct format.

To make Gift Aid repayment claims using the online form you need to sign up to use HMRC's Online Services, and enrol for Charities Online.

47.15.2 *Option 2: >1000 donors*

Charities Online Guidance provides:

> *Option two: claim through your own database*
>
> This option is for those who file Gift Aid claims for more than 1,000 donors, although it can also be used to make smaller claims.
>
> Those choosing this option will be able to send one claim per day directly from their own internal database or system, with details for up to 500,000 Gift Aid donors. Charities and CASCs wishing to use this system will either need to develop their own compatible software package or purchase a suitable package from a software provider.
>
> If your charity is thinking of buying software to make a claim using the Charities Online service, HMRC has published a list of commercial software and suppliers that have tested their products and provided evidence that they interact with the Charities Online Service.

The list can be found at *https://www.gov.uk/government/ publications/charities-online-commercial-software-suppliers/charities-online-commercial-software-suppliers*

47.15.3 *Paper claims*

Charities Online Guidance provides:

> *Option three: claim using a paper form*
>
> This option is for those who don't have access to the internet.
>
> A new paper repayment claim form, called a ChR1, will replace all existing R68 claim forms. If you choose this option, you can order ChR1 forms from the HMRC Charities Helpline from 25 March 2013.
>
> You will then need to complete the form and return it by post to HMRC. The form is designed so that HMRC can automatically scan the information into the new system, so payments can be made quicker. Old R68 forms or photocopies of the ChR1 will not be accepted because the new system will not be able to scan the information.
>
> There will be no limit to the number of claims that can be submitted on

the ChR1. Continuation sheets for the form (called ChR1CS) can be requested so you can send in the details up to 90 Gift Aid donors with each individual claim.

47.15.4 *Charities Online: Registration*

Charities Online Guidance provides:

> To use Charities Online, your charity needs to sign up for HMRC Online Services, and enrol for Charities Online.
> If your charity already has an HMRC Online Services account, for example for filing Self Assessment, Corporation Tax or VAT Returns, you need to enrol for the Charities Online service so that you can use it. This will add the service to your existing account.

47.15.5 *Gift Aid tax reclaim*

To use Charities Online to make repayment claims for Gift Aid, charities will need to create "Gift Aid Schedule Spreadsheets". These can be downloaded from the HMRC website. Charities Online Guidance provides:

> You can use the HMRC Charities Online service to make a Gift Aid repayment claim on donations your charity has received. To do this, you need to record your donations on a schedule spreadsheet and attach it to your online claim.
> You can use the schedule to record donations from individuals, or from sponsored events. You can also add together or 'aggregate' donations of £20 or less from different donors and show them as a single entry on the spreadsheet, provided that the total donation on one line is not more than £1000.
> You must have valid Gift Aid declarations for all the donations shown in this schedule spreadsheet, which you should retain for your records.
> **What to put on the spreadsheet**
> Complete the Gift Aid schedule spreadsheet to show the donations you have received for which you are claiming a repayment of Gift Aid.
> Enter the name of each individual donor, using up to a maximum number of characters per line:
> Title: 4 characters First name: 35 characters Last name: 35 characters
> All claims will have to include the following minimum donor information that's already required on the valid donor Gift Aid declaration form. Unless it says otherwise, all the following information is required:
> - title (optional)
> - first name

- last name
- donor's address; this should be the house name or number and the postcode - see below if you don't have the postcode or if the address is abroad
- donation date
- amount

Address details

Providing the donor's house name or number and the postcode is the quickest and easiest way of providing the donor's address. It also helps your claim to be paid quickly. ... Please note that from April 2014 you will need to find the postcodes for UK addresses either direct from the donor or, for example, by using the Royal Mail's free online postcode finder, and note them in your records.

The address information you provide can be in a number of formats:

UK address where you have a postcode

Enter the house name or number and postcode. If it's easier, you can enter the first line of the address, or as much of the address as will fit in the space (there is space for 40 characters using charities online) and the postcode.

UK address where you do not have a postcode

Enter as much of the address as will fit in the space provided, but make sure this includes the house name or number, first line of the address and postal town/city (there is space for 40 characters using charities online) and leave the postcode box blank.

If you don't include a postcode for UK addresses your claim could take longer to handle and HMRC is more likely to review the claim or ask you to provide full address details for the donors.

Non-UK address

Enter as much of the address as will fit in the space provided, but make sure this includes the house name or number, first line of the address and country (there is space for 40 characters using charities online) and leave the postcode box blank.

Aggregated donations

You can add together donations of £20 or less from different donors and show them as one entry provided that the total included in one line is not more than £1,000. The total must not include any donations associated with admissions to charity visitor attractions.

To claim Gift Aid on aggregated donations, do not enter the name and address of the donors. Instead, enter in the 'Aggregated Donations' box a simple description such as, 'April gifts' or 'Thursday club donors', using a maximum of 35 characters. Enter the date of the last donation and the total amount raised.

Only add together donations that were made within the same accounting period. Your accounting period ends on the date to which you prepare accounts, unless your organisation was set up by a trust deed or will or was established outside the UK. In those cases, your accounting period runs to 5 April.

Sponsored events

If you are claiming Gift Aid on donations from a sponsored event, you do not need to include individual donor details except for donations over £500. Instead, you should enter the name and address of the participant in the sponsored event using up to a maximum number of characters per line:

Title: 4 characters First name: 35 characters Last name: 35 characters

Enter 'yes' in the sponsored event box and enter the date the sponsorship payments were received by the charity and the total amount raised from all donations by this participant.

If any of the donations are over £500 these should be shown as if they were normal Gift Aid donations rather than donations from sponsored events. Do not enter 'yes' in the sponsored event box.

Donation Date

For a single donation this is the date the donation was received. Where the charity receives a series of donations or you are aggregating donations, you should enter the date of the last donation received. However, you may need to show a different date if these donations cover more than one accounting period.

Accounting Period

If regular donations are made by one person these can be shown on one line, added together and just the latest date in the series can be entered in this box. But only add together donations that were made within the same accounting period.

Your accounting period ends on the date to which you prepare accounts, unless your organisation was set up by a trust deed or will or was established outside the UK. In those cases, your accounting period runs to 5 April.

To enable transitional relief to be calculated if your accounting period covers 5 April 2011 you would also need to split the donations in that year to before and after 5 April 2011.

Previously over-claimed amount box

This allows you to amend an error which was made in a previous claims which caused you to receive an overpayment to which you are not entitled including a claim under the Gift Aid Small Donations Scheme. The over-claimed amount will, where possible, be deducted from this claim. Where this is not possible, if for example the overpaid amount is

more than the repayment claim you are making, then you will need to make an additional payment to HMRC. Please note you should enter the amount of tax over-claimed, not the value of the donation. This amount will then be deducted from the claim you are in the process of submitting.
Do not complete this if you have already completed the adjustment box for your claim or the over-claimed amount will be deducted twice.

47.15.6 *Aggregated small claim*

When charities record their Gift Aid donations, they are able to aggregate donations under £20 in order to make recording easier. Previously, the total permitted for aggregate donations was capped at £500. With the introduction of Charities Online, this is increased to £1,000.

Higher limit for aggregated donations
The rules for aggregating Gift Aid donations will change for Charities Online, allowing you to add together more small donations. The current limit of £500 will be increased and claimants will be able to aggregate individual Gift Aid donations of £20 or less, up to a total of £1,000 per entry.
This will reduce the number of donations you have to provide details for, but you don't have to aggregate payments if the way you record donations makes it easier to list them individually. You'll still need to keep details of all donations in case HMRC needs to check your claim.

47.15.7 *Sponsored events*

All donations for someone taking part in a sponsored event can be made in a single entry under the name of that participant.
Charities Online Guidance provides:

Easier Gift Aid records for sponsored events
For claims made using Charities Online, all the donations for someone taking part in a sponsored event can be put as one entry under the name of that participant.
This means you won't need to list every individual donor who sponsored the person, which is what happens now for fewer than ten donors. Only individual donations from a donor of £500 or more shown on individual sponsor sheets will need to be separated out and listed individually on the claim form.
You don't have to include sponsored events in this way: if the way you keep your records makes it easier to list each individual donation separately, then that's fine.

In the past HMRC has agreed with some charities that certain other claims could be included under this modified claims basis, (also known as 'special modified claims') as a way of making claims easier for charities. The changes to sponsored events, and the increases explained below in 'Higher limit for aggregated donations' to the aggregated claims limits, cover most of these other arrangements. These arrangements will end when Charities Online begins.

47.15.8 *Repayment claim for other income*

Charities Online Guidance provides:

> You can use the HMRC Charities Online service to claim tax back on any income your charity has received that has had tax deducted (taken off). To do this, you need to fill in an Other Income schedule spreadsheet and attach it to your online claim.
>
> Examples of income your charity receives that may be taxed include:
>
> - Bank and building society interest
> - Interest from government stocks
> - Royalties
> - Other types of annual payment
> - Estate income
> - Discretionary trust income
>
> *What to put on the spreadsheet*
>
> On the Other Income schedule spreadsheet, enter the following details:
>
> - name of the payer, using a maximum of 40 characters
> - date of the payment DD/MM/YY
> - amount of the gross payment
> - amount of the tax deducted
>
> You must have written confirmation from the payer showing the tax that has been deducted from the income received.
>
> *Adjustment box*
>
> This allows you to amend an error which was made in a previous claim which caused you to receive an overpayment to which you are not entitled including a claim under the Gift Aid Small Donations Scheme. The over-claimed amount will, where possible, be deducted from this claim. Where this is not possible, if for example the overpaid amount is more than the repayment claim you are making, then you will need to make an additional payment to HMRC. Please note you should enter the amount of tax over-claimed, not the value of the donation. This amount will then be deducted from the claim you are in the process of submitting.
>
> Do not complete this if you have already completed the adjustment box for your claim or the over-claimed amount will be deducted twice.

> *Download an Other Income schedule spreadsheet for HMRC Charities Online*
> You can use the HMRC Charities Online service to claim tax back on other income your charity has received that has had tax deducted, for example bank interest, legacies and royalties. To do this, you must record this information on an Other Income schedule spreadsheet, and attach it to your online claim.

47.15.9 *GASDS: Building top-up claim*

Charities Online should also be used for claiming top-up payments under GASDS for donations collected in community buildings. Charities Online Guidance provides:

> To claim a top-up payment on small charitable donations collected in community buildings under the Gift Aid Small Donations Scheme (GASDS), you need to use the HMRC Charities online service. To do this you need to record the donations you collected in community buildings on a Community Buildings schedule spreadsheet, and attach it to your online claim.
> A community building is a building, or those parts of it, which the public have access to at some or all times. If you collect donations whilst your charity is carrying out charitable activities in a community building, your charity may be able to claim more under the GASDS.
> **What to put on this schedule spreadsheet**
> Enter the community building name, address and postcode using up to the maximum number of characters per line:
> Building name - 160 characters First line of address - 40 characters Post code - mandatory field
> If you do not know the postcode, you can find it out from the Royal Mail postcode finder website. If, exceptionally, the building does not have a postcode, enter the postcode of the nearest building to the community building.
> Enter the end of the tax year for which you are claiming under the GASDS. The earliest year that you can claim for is the tax year ending on 5 April 2014.
> Enter the amount of all small donations of £20 or less collected in each community building that you are for claiming under this scheme.

47.15.10 *GASDS: Connected charities*

The amount that can be claimed under the GASDS may be reduced if the charity in question is "connected" to another charity. Charities Online therefore makes provision for disclosing such connections. Charities

Online Guidance provides:

> If your charity or CASC is connected to other charities or CASC, the amount you can claim under the GASDS may be reduced...
> Connected organisations that claim a top-up payment for the year will share the maximum £5,000 donations limit between them.
> If you want to claim a top-up payment under the GASDS, you need to record the names of connected charities on a Connected Charities schedule spreadsheet and attach it to your online claim.

47.15.11 *Time for repayment*

HMRC say:

> Claims made via Charities Online are normally paid within 20 working days of HMRC receiving the claim. HMRC will send you a written confirmation that a payment has made into your bank account.[25]

47.16 Interest on tax repayment

The HMRC Guidance Note provides:

> 6.6.4 Repayment interest may be due and payable on a Gift Aid claim. Interest is calculated as follows:
> - for a Charitable Trust - from 1 February next following the year of assessment to which the income relates
> - for a Charitable Company or CASC - from the day after the end of the accounting period to which the income relates
>
> If repayment interest is due, HMRC Charities will calculate the amount due and will pay the total tax claimed plus interest due together as a single payment to the charity or CASC.

The repayment rate is the higher of 0.5% p/a or the percentage per annum found by subtracting 1 from the Bank of England rate.[26]

47.17 Assessment and collection of tax

47.17.1 *Collection by assessment*

Section 30(1) TMA provides:

> Where an amount of income tax or capital gains tax has been repaid to any person which ought not to have been repaid to him, that amount of

---

25 *https://www.gov.uk/guidance/claim-tax-back-on-donations-using-charities-online #make-a-claim*

26 Regulation 4 Taxes and Duties, etc (Interest Rate) Regulations 2011.

tax may be assessed and recovered as if it were unpaid tax.

47.17.2 *Collection by set-off*

HMRC may set money owed to a taxpayer against money owed by the taxpayer to them. That conveniently saves HMRC from the trouble of collecting the tax, and gives them priority in the event of insolvency. Section 130 FA 2008 provides:

> (1) This section applies where there is both a credit and a debit in relation to a person.
> (2) The Commissioners may set the credit against the debit (subject to section 131 and any obligation of the Commissioners to set the credit against another sum).
> (3) The obligations of the Commissioners and the person concerned are discharged to the extent of any set-off under subsection (2).

Section 130 continues with the definitions:

> (4) "Credit", in relation to a person, means-
> (a) a sum that is payable by the Commissioners to the person under or by virtue of an enactment, or
> (b) a relevant sum that may be repaid to the person by the Commissioners.
> (5) For the purposes of subsection (4), in relation to a person, "relevant sum" means a sum that was paid in connection with any liability (including any purported or anticipated liability) of that person to make a payment to the Commissioners under or by virtue of an enactment or under a contract settlement.
> (6) "Debit", in relation to a person, means a sum that is payable by the person to the Commissioners under or by virtue of an enactment or under a contract settlement.
> (7) In this section references to sums paid, repaid or payable by or to a person (however expressed) include sums that have been or are to be credited by or to a person.

This may apply to Gift Aid tax reclaims. But there has to be a "debit", ie, a sum payable by a taxpayer. This will be the case if an assessment is made and not appealed, or if an assessment is appealed and tax is not postponed pending the outcome of the appeal. But there is no debit just because HMRC dispute the claim in correspondence, or where there is an assessment and an appeal and tax is postponed. There is no general power to withhold tax reclaimed because a charity is under investigation. The DMB Manual provides:

> **DMBM700050: S130 FA2008: when we can set-off** [Jun 2016]
> ...
> The debit and credit must both be properly quantified and already payable: that is
> - the debit established (where the amount has been agreed or the time for appeal has either passed or the appeal has been determined)
> - the credit must have cleared all necessary credibility and verification checking.

Lastly, for completeness, s.130(8) FA 2008 provides:

> This section has effect without prejudice to any other power of the Commissioners to set off amounts.

47.17.3 *Set-off in Scotland*

Section 130(10) FA 2008 provides:

> Subsections (1) to (8) extend to England and Wales and Northern Ireland only.

The DMB Manual provides:

> **DMBM700010: Set-offs - S130 FA2008: background** [June 2016]
> ...The power to set-off applies only in England, Wales and Northern Ireland and aligns with existing common law in Scotland.

47.17.4 *Set-off under s.967 CTA 2010*

For completeness: Section 967 CTA 2010 provides:

> (1) Subsection (2) applies if a UK resident company receives a payment on which it bears income tax by deduction.
> (2) The income tax on the payment is to be set off against any corporation tax assessable on the company for the accounting period in which the payment falls to be taken into account for corporation tax, or would fall to be so taken into account but for any exemption from corporation tax.
> (3) Subsection (2) is subject to the provisions of the Corporation Tax Acts.
> (4) The reference in subsection (1) to a payment received by a company—
> (a) includes a reference to a payment received by another person on behalf of or in trust for the company, but
> (b) does not include a reference to a payment received by the company on behalf of or in trust for another person.

> (5) The reference in subsection (1) to a payment received by a company does not include a reference to a payment which is exempt from tax by virtue of any of the following—
> section 472 (gifts qualifying for gift aid relief: charitable companies);
> section 475 (gifts qualifying for gift aid relief: eligible bodies);
> section 486 (investment income and non-trading profits from loan relationships);
> section 487 (public revenue dividends);
> section 488 (certain miscellaneous income);
> section 489 (income from estates in administration);
> section 664 (exemption for interest and gift aid income: community amateur sports clubs).

The s.967 set-off rule does not apply to Gift Aid repayments, and most other types of charity tax reclaim, so it will rarely if ever apply to charitable companies.

47.18 Gift Aid audit

The HMRC Guidance Note provides:

> **3.7 Recording and audit of Gift Aid declarations**
> 3.7.1 HMRC is required to ensure that any tax repaid to a charity is properly due and correctly calculated. HMRC does this by carrying out inspections to check that Gift Aid claims are made for the correct amounts and are backed by valid Gift Aid declarations and clear audit trails in respect of donations received.
> 3.7.2 A charity must maintain a clear auditable record of declarations and of the making of those declarations, so that it's able to demonstrate that a donor has in fact made an appropriate declaration.

The HMRC Guidance Note provides:

7.1 Introduction
7.1.1 HMRC Revenue and Customs (HMRC) selects a number of charities and CASCs for audit to ensure that the Gift Aid scheme is being used properly and that any repayment claims made are accurate. If your 19 May 2013 claim is selected for a review, it doesn't necessarily mean that HMRC believes the claim is wrong or that there's suspicion about anything to do with the claim or your charity or CASC.
HMRC wants to help you to get things right and will help your charity or CASC to make further repayment claims if it is found that less tax has been claimed than was due
7.1.2 HMRC auditors aren't evaluated on the level of adjustments made or rewarded for the amount of tax they recover.
7.1.3 Charity trustees are ultimately responsible for ensuring that all claims are correct so they have an obligation to ensure that appropriate systems are in place to achieve that result. It's also important that they're aware of any review being undertaken by HMRC,

and if it isn't necessary for them to deal with the auditor directly they, should nominate a suitable charity official to do so in writing.

7.1.4 Chapter 3 of the Detailed Guidance Notes for Charities explains the requirements of the Gift Aid Scheme and the records you should keep and how long you need to keep them.

7.2 How a charity is chosen for audit

7.2.1 Claims for audit are generally selected for review on a 'risk' basis which takes into account a wide range of factors. HMRC also select a number of claims for review on a random basis.

7.2.2 If your charity's repayment claim is selected for a review, it doesn't necessarily mean that HMRC believes the claim is wrong or that they're suspicious about anything to do with the claim or your charity.

7.3 What happens when a charity is selected for audit?

7.3.1 HMRC will issue you with a questionnaire to help the auditor to get a better understanding of the relevant issues and the areas that'll need to be covered during the review.

7.3.2 The main part of any audit is a detailed review of the documentation associated with a claim, including Gift Aid declarations and banking records. You'll be advised in advance about:

- the records the auditor will need to see during the review
- whether the auditor intends to review all of the records supporting a claim or a sample of those records

The auditor may request sight of the Gift Aid declarations and audit trails for a number of donors included in your repayment claim along with the issue of the questionnaire. The auditor will then decide whether the review can be undertaken by correspondence, or whether a visit is required. If you're asked to send your records to HMRC but would prefer our auditor to visit please let them know.

7.3.3 If a visit is required, a member of the audit team will contact you, giving as much notice as they reasonably can, to arrange a convenient date and venue for the audit.

7.3.4 If the proposed review date isn't convenient or if you have any problems providing the records requested, you should discuss this with the auditor as soon as possible.

7.3.5 The auditor will work with you to help resolve any difficulties and to schedule appropriate dates for the review.

7.3.6 Where a charity can show that it has embarked on a programme to identify donors for whom Gift Aid declarations are missing or not appropriate (and to obtain declarations from them) this work may be continued to an agreed deadline and the auditor will take this into account when considering whether a full review is necessary.

7.3.7 Normally, the auditor will visit the place where the charity's records are kept. When confirming arrangements for a review visit, please ensure the auditor knows where your records are kept. If any of your records are stored elsewhere or held by a third party, please tell the auditor and agree on arrangements for those records to be made available. If your records are kept on a computer, it may be necessary to allow the auditor to access hard copies of the records, which may determine where the review will take place.

7.4 What the audit review involves

7.4.1 HMRC auditors will check records supporting a tax repayment claim including donation records, Gift Aid declarations and banking/cash records.

The auditors will generally base every review as follows:

If the charity is a trust for tax purposes, the auditors will review claims submitted that cover the last full tax year, that is, claims submitted in respect of donations received between 6 April and 5 April.

If the charity is a company for tax purposes, the auditors will review claims submitted that cover the year up to the last Accounts Period Ended (APE), for example, a charity has an APE of 30 September - claims will therefore be reviewed in respect of donations received between 1 October and 30 September.

Where there's a specific reason for reviewing earlier claims the review may extend beyond the periods referred to above

7.4.2 The audit will involve reviewing the charity's accounting records, systems and procedures.

7.4.3 During the course of this work HMRC may also identify other potential tax risks, such as non-charitable expenditure, employer compliance and VAT issues.

7.4.4 Where potential problems are identified, the auditor may:

- advise the charity on accounting improvements that should be made
- take action to recover tax that HMRC considers to have been incorrectly repaid
- arrange a further payment by way of a further claim where the charity has claimed less than was due
- refuse to authorise payment of a proposed claim that HMRC consider to be incorrect
- refer matters for further consideration to other HMRC departments
- provide any advice necessary to help reduce the burden of record keeping for the charity

7.5 What the auditor be looking for

7.5.1 Essentially, the auditor will need to be satisfied that the charity's records properly support the tax repayment claims.

7.5.2 The auditor will make checks such as ensuring that tax repayment forms (R68i) have been properly completed from the charity's records.[27]

7.5.3 The auditor will seek to confirm the validity of Gift Aid claims by ensuring that:

- appropriate Gift Aid declarations are held for all donations on which a Gift Aid tax repayment is claimed
- donations meet the requirements of the relevant legislation - for example that gifts aren't subject to a condition as to repayment
- any benefits provided for Gift Aid donors do not exceed statutory limits

7.5.4 The auditor will need to see that an acceptable audit trail exists to link tax repayment claims to individuals, their donations and to their Gift Aid declarations.

7.5.5 The auditor will also need to see that an acceptable audit trail exists to show that the repayment under review has been received by the charity and been correctly banked into the appropriate account.

7.6 What constitutes an acceptable audit trail

7.6.1 Usually an acceptable audit trail is easily established for donations received by cheque, standing orders, direct debits, debit card or credit card.

Cheque payments should be detailed on the paying in slips when banked by the charity,

---

27 Repayment claims will now be made through Charities Online as set out above. This guidance has not been updated to reflect that and so still refers, erroneously, to R68(i).

or can be included on a banking breakdown sheet if there are numerous cheques.
Standing orders and direct debit payments can be fully reviewed directly from the charity's bank statements.
Card payments can be traced through the verification and confirmation provided to the charity by the card issuer.
However, there can be difficulties in:

- linking a particular cash donation to an individual who has given a valid Gift Aid declaration
- tracking that donation from the time it is made to the time it is banked by the charity

7.6.2 A charity must therefore ensure it maintains suitable records when claiming Gift Aid on cash donations. This may include an envelope giving scheme (see 6.4), or the issuing of receipts for every cash donation received.
7.6.3 It is not acceptable for a pool of cash collected on an unattributable basis to be arbitrarily allocated to individuals for whom a Gift Aid declaration is held and claims made on that basis.
7.6.4 As an example, a tried and tested record system that meets HMRC requirements involves:

- an individual sealing a cash donation in an envelope with a pre-printed Gift Aid declaration on it and putting his/her name and the amount given on the outside
- the envelopes being opened in the presence of at least two charity officials with the amount contained in each being checked against the statement on the outside and attributed to the named individual
- a record being kept of the name and amount given by each donor for whom a valid Gift Aid declaration has been received
- the envelopes that incorporate the Gift Aid declarations for one off donations being retained for 4 years from the date that the donation is included in a charity repayment claim
- a record being kept of the total cash collected and how it is banked

7.6.5 This isn't the only system that will meet HMRC requirements but it illustrates what they're looking for.
7.6.6 An envelope might, instead of a declaration, incorporate a reference that links the named donor to a declaration given earlier, covering all donations to the charity. In such circumstances, the charity is advised to keep a minimum of one month's envelopes per tax year, covering a period of 4 years. For example, a church may decide to keep every general giving envelope received throughout the month of August. After a period of four years the church will have in place a total 4 months envelopes, all received during August for the preceding 4 years.
7.6.7 HMRC is happy to review and comment on any system you have in place or are thinking of introducing in your charity.

7.7 Other 'risks' will the auditor be looking for

7.7.1 The auditor will consider whether there's anything that would bring into question entitlement to exemptions from tax available to charities - such as pursuit of non-charitable activities or applying funds for non-charitable purposes.
7.7.2 The auditor may also check that donors, who have provided Gift Aid declarations, have in fact paid the relevant amount of tax to cover the Gift Aid claimed on their donations. This will involve taking the names and addresses of some of the donors included in claims so that their tax records can be checked.

7.7.3 Any problems identified by such a review will be a matter between the individual donor and HMRC. For reasons of taxpayer confidentiality, HMRC won't be able to identify the particular donors concerned to the charity. It will be up to the donors whether or not they wish to discuss such matters with the charity.

7.7.4 If HMRC find an unacceptable proportion of Gift Aid donors can't be traced this may suggest poor record keeping by a charity, inadequate communication with donors or, exceptionally, fraud - these issues would be discussed further with the trustees of the charity.

7.7.5 In the course of their work, the auditor may sometimes come across evidence that a charity is failing to fulfill responsibilities with regard to other tax obligations (for example, in the operation of PAYE or VAT). Any such issues will be brought to the attention of the trustees and may be followed up by other HMRC offices.

7.8 Statistical sampling

7.8.1 Where the number of documents supporting a repayment claim is too large to review in total within a reasonable period of time, HMRC will use statistical sampling techniques to consider the overall accuracy of the claim. This will help to ensure that the time spent carrying out the audit is acceptable and cost effective for both the charity and for HMRC.

7.8.2 These techniques involve:

- identifying all relevant 'populations' of income sources for example, sponsored events, membership subscriptions, one off donations within the tax claim being reviewed
- taking a representative sample of relevant records from each population - the number of records sampled will depend on the size of the population and is fixed by a standard statistical formula
- reviewing the sample records and establishing the extent of any errors
- calculating the error rate for the sample (that is, the proportion of the amount claimed for which supporting records were not provided or weren't acceptable)
- for example - a sample of 475 Gift Aid declarations is selected for review - upon review, 20 declarations were found to be missing or not acceptable - the potential error rate is:

  20/475 x 100 = 4.2%
- applying the error rate for the sample to the relevant population as a whole and using it to compute an estimate of the tax repaid with respect to that population that cannot be substantiated for the year of review

7.8.3 If you're uncertain about any aspect of this procedure, please ask to discuss it with your auditor before the review.

7.9 Sampling populations

7.9.1 Usually, all the donations included in a single claim will constitute a single 'population'.

7.9.2 Where donations are processed in significantly different ways, there may be a case for treating them as distinct populations. For example:

- donors giving more than a particular amount may be treated in a different way
- donations relating to a particular sponsored event may be handled differently
- different branches of a charity may have different record keeping procedures
- some donations may be handled by a third party using different processes

7.9.3 Where some donations are processed in significantly different ways, you should advise the auditor before the review visit.

7.9.4 It's possible that the review itself may reveal unexpectedly significant variations in the treatment of different groups of donations. In such circumstances, another review may be necessary. The auditor will discuss this with the trustees and/or senior management for a larger charity.

7.10 Application of results to earlier periods

7.10.1 If HMRC identify errors in relation to a particular donor population, they will assume that the same error rate is likely to apply to all similar claims for the same population.

7.10.2 If earlier claims were handled in a significantly different way to the one reviewed in the audit, please discuss this with the auditor - ideally before the review visit.

7.10.3 It may, for example, be the case that:

- records for earlier claims are maintained on paper instead of computer
- a member of staff identifiably responsible for flaws in the preparation of a particular claim was not involved in the preparation of other claims

7.10.4 HMRC may need to look at a claim (or part of it) separately if they agree that the sample used is not representative for that claim.

7.11 When the audit is finished?

7.11.1 On the day the audit ends, the auditor will talk to you about exactly what has been reviewed and the results of that review.

7.11.2 The same information will be included in a letter to the charity summarising the audit findings and what action the charity may need to consider.

7.11.3 If HMRC find that less tax has been claimed than was due, the auditor will help you to make a further repayment claim.

7.11.4 If HMRC can't substantiate a tax repayment claim and, as a result, they have paid you too much, the auditor will:

- explain in detail what HMRC believe the problem is and the formal process they need to follow to recover the tax involved
- provide a summary of the amounts of tax recoverable for all relevant years
- provide a computation of interest due, up to a projected settlement date;
- where appropriate, discuss the basis for any penalties HMRC believes are due and explain HMRC policy on mitigation of the maximum penalty payable
- offer to negotiate a settlement with the trustees by way of a suitably worded letter of offer, which when accepted by HMRC would constitute a binding agreement, or raise formal assessments/determinations to recover the tax identified as repayable to HMRC at the review.
- discuss any payment difficulties (where appropriate, HMRC can agree an instalment programme but the effect of interest means that this is likely to increase the total amount payable)

Usually, HMRC won't recover tax for more than 4 years prior to the year under review. However, there are circumstances when this period may be extended. If this is being considered, the auditor will provide a full explanation to the trustees.

7.11.5 In the majority of cases, concerns arising from an audit will be resolved by discussion and an appropriate settlement will be agreed with the trustees.

7.11.6 If it proves impossible to settle the matter in this way, HMRC will start formal recovery action.

7.11.7 Trustees will have the opportunity to appeal against any formal assessments/ determinations HMRC make.

7.11.8 Any wider potential risks identified during the audit will be discussed with the charity trustees and/or senior management, who will be advised how matters will be taken forward either within HMRC Charities or by another HMRC office.

7.12 Putting right problems identified by the auditors

7.12.1 The charity will have at least 30 days from the date of the letter summarising the audit findings to resolve any problems identified. This may involve the charity having to obtain new appropriate declarations from donors.

This 30 day period will also apply to charities where the auditor has undertaken a sample review. Charities and CASCs can repair errors identified in a population within an audit sample, and HMRC will extrapolate the repaired error rate across the population (rather than the error rate found in the first instance).

Repaired means that the charity finds the missing declaration, or obtains a new (or fully completed) declaration from the taxpayer.

7.12.2 Also, HMRC will operate a de minimis limit when looking at error rates and tax recovery. An error rate of four per cent or less, calculated after the charity has had opportunity to repair the sample, for charities that claim under £2,500.00 Gift Aid per tax year or APE, will mean that the charity is not penalised for errors in their Gift Aid claims. The size of the error rate, and the amount of subsequent tax repayable to HMRC in respect of the year of review will affect how the auditor seeks to conclude the case. The following parameters will be followed:

Repaired error rate	**Amount at stake**	**Action at Audit 1**
Less than 4%	Less than £100	No recovery in year of audit or earlier years. No card issued.
Less than 4%	Less than £500	Recovery in year but not earlier years. No card issued.
Less than 4%	More than £500	Recovery in year but not earlier years. 'Yellow' card issued.
More than 4%	Less than £500	Recovery in year but not earlier years. 'Yellow' card issued.
More than 4%	More than £500	Recovery in year and earlier years

'Yellow Card' warnings

7.12.3 Where either the amount or level of errors is small HMRC will also introduce an optional 'yellow card' warning system to apply to earlier years rather than make recoveries for those years (see table above). 'Yellow cards' will be accompanied by advice on remedial action as to how the charity/CASC should prevent errors in its record keeping in the future. This will support charities and CASCs in understanding Gift Aid and rectifying errors for future claims.

The issue of a 'yellow card' has to be agreed by both HMRC and the charity involved. HMRC commits to only recover the tax due in respect of the year of review while the charity commits to take any remedial action HMRC think necessary to improve their record keeping. If agreement can't be reached, HMRC will recover tax for both in year and earlier years based on the identified error rate.

If agreement is reached, but the remedial action hasn't been taken the next time HMRC examine the claims of the charity/CASC, they will go back and recover any earlier years that are still in date.

A further examination of the records following the issue of a 'Yellow card' will be discussed with the charity by the auditor at the conclusion of the original review. The period between the original review and the further examination (if required) will not usually be longer than 36 months, and may well be shorter depending on the circumstances.

7.12.4 Where errors have been identified and a settlement has been concluded on that basis, it may be possible for the charity to make new claims.

For example:

During an audit a charity may find that Gift Aid declarations are missing for some of the donations under review. The charity may review some or all of its records and identify donations for which no valid Gift Aid declaration is held. The charity may secure new declarations from donors to cover the donations in question and submit a new claim with respect to those donations.

7.12.5 Generally, a charity is able to claim a repayment of tax for four years prior to the current tax year. Such new claims are not restricted to the amount of the original estimate of the error.

7.12.6 Following an audit, a charity is not required to review declarations in respect of periods covered by claims that were the subject of the review - but the charity should make no further Gift Aid claims without first ensuring that a declaration is in place for each donor to be included in the claim.

7.12.7 Charities should ensure that any problems identified are properly addressed so that they don't recur.

7.12.8 HMRC are happy to work with charities to improve systems for processing donations and maintaining records.

APPENDIX ONE

INTERNATIONAL ENTITY SECURITIES: APPROVED CHARITABLE INVESTMENTS

Council Directive 2003/48/EC provides the list of international entities whose securities are approved charitable investments.[1]

Council Directive (EU) 2015/2060 repealed directive 2003/48/EC with effect from 2016. It was replaced by directive 2014/107/EU which implements the OECD common reporting standard known as CRS. The new directive does not have any equivalent list of securities. But the list in the annex to the former directive will continue to have effect for the definition of approved charitable investments.

The list is as follows:

Belgium

Vlaams Gewest (Flemish Region)
Région wallonne (Walloon Region)
Région bruxelloise/Brussels Gewest (Brussels Region)
Communauté française (French Community)
Vlaamse Gemeenschap (Flemish Community)
Deutschsprachige Gemeinschaft (German-speaking Community)

Bulgaria

Общините (municipalities)
Социалноосигурителни Фондове (Social Security Funds)

Spain

Xunta de Galicia (Regional Executive of Galicia)
Junta de Andalucía (Regional Executive of Andalusia)
Junta de Extremadura (Regional Executive of Extremadura)
Junta de Castilla-La Mancha (Regional Executive of Castilla-La Mancha)
Junta de Castilla-León (Regional Executive of Castilla-León)
Gobierno Foral de Navarra (Regional Government of Navarre)
Govern de les Illes Balears (Government of the Balearic Islands)
Generalitat de Catalunya (Autonomous Government of Catalonia)
Generalitat de Valencia (Autonomous Government of Valencia)

---

1 See 6.12 (International securities). The text can be found at *http://eur-lex.europa.eu/legal-content/EN/TXT/?uri=CELEX:02003L0048-20140415*

Diputación General de Aragón (Regional Council of Aragon)
Gobierno de las Islas Canarias (Government of the Canary Islands)
Gobierno de Murcia (Government of Murcia)
Gobierno de Madrid (Government of Madrid)
Gobierno de la Comunidad Autónoma del País Vasco/Euzkadi (Government of the Autonomous Community of the Basque Country)
Diputación Foral de Guipúzcoa (Regional Council of Guipúzcoa)
Diputación Foral de Vizcaya/Bizkaia (Regional Council of Vizcaya)
Diputación Foral de Alava (Regional Council of Alava)
Ayuntamiento de Madrid (City Council of Madrid)
Ayuntamiento de Barcelona (City Council of Barcelona)
Cabildo Insular de Gran Canaria (Island Council of Gran Canaria)
Cabildo Insular de Tenerife (Island Council of Tenerife)
Instituto de Crédito Oficial (Public Credit Institution)
Instituto Catalán de Finanzas (Finance Institution of Catalonia)
Instituto Valenciano de Finanzas (Finance Institution of Valencia)

Greece

Οργανισμός Τηλεπικοινωνιών Ελλάδος (National Telecommunications Organisation)
Οργανισμός Σιδηροδρόμων Ελλάδος (National Railways Organisation)
Δημόσια Επιχείρηση Ηλεκτρισμού (Public Electricity Company)

France

La Caisse d'amortissement de la dette sociale (CADES) (Social Debt Redemption Fund)
L'Agence française de développement (AFD) (French Development Agency)
Réseau Ferré de France (RFF) (French Rail Network)
Caisse Nationale des Autoroutes (CNA) (National Motorways Fund)
Assistance publique Hôpitaux de Paris (APHP) (Paris Hospitals Public Assistance)
Charbonnages de France (CDF) (French Coal Board)
Entreprise minière et chimique (EMC) (Mining and Chemicals Company)

Italy

Regions
Provinces
Municipalities
Cassa Depositi e Prestiti (Deposits and Loans Fund)

Latvia

Pašvaldības (local governments)

Poland

gminy (communes)
powiaty (districts)
województwa (provinces)
związki gmin (associations of communes)
powiatów (association of districts)
województw (association of provinces)
miasto stołeczne Warszawa (capital city of Warsaw)
Agencja Restrukturyzacji i Modernizacji Rolnictwa (Agency for Restructuring and Modernisation of Agriculture)
Agencja Nieruchomości Rolnych (Agricultural Property Agency)

Portugal

Região Autónoma da Madeira (Autonomous Region of Madeira)

Região Autónoma dos Açores (Autonomous Region of Azores)

Municipalities

Romania

autorităţile administraţiei publice locale (local public administration authorities)

Slovakia

mestá a obce (municipalities)

Železnice Slovenskej republiky (Slovak Railway Company)

Štátny fond cestného hospodárstva (State Road Management Fund)

Slovenské elektrárne (Slovak Power Plants)

Vodohospodárska výstavba (Water Economy Building Company)

International entities

European Bank for Reconstruction and Development

European Investment Bank

Asian Development Bank

African Development Bank

World Bank/IBRD/IMF

International Finance Corporation

Inter-American Development Bank

Council of Europe Soc. Dev. Fund

Euratom

European Community

Corporación Andina de Fomento (CAF) (Andean Development Corporation)

Eurofima

European Coal & Steel Community

Nordic Investment Bank

Caribbean Development Bank

The provisions of Article 15 are without prejudice to any international obligations that Member States may have entered into with respect to the abovementioned international entities.

Entities in third countries

Those entities that meet the following criteria:

1. the entity is clearly considered to be a public entity according to the national criteria;
2. such public entity is a non-market producer which administers and finances a group of activities, principally providing non-market goods and services, intended for the benefit of the community and which are effectively controlled by general government;
3. such public entity is a large and regular issuer of debt;
4. the State concerned is able to guarantee that such public entity will not exercise early redemption in the event of gross-up clauses.

APPENDIX TWO

MODEL GIFT AID DECLARATIONS

App. 2.1 Model Gift Aid declarations

This appendix contains the text of HMRC's model Gift Aid declarations. The forms were published 2011 and amended in 2015 in the light of HMRC research.[1]

App. 2.2 Gift Aid declaration: single donation

Charity Gift Aid Declaration – single donation
Boost your donation by 25p of Gift Aid for every £1 you donate
Gift Aid is reclaimed by the charity from the tax you pay for the current tax year. Your address is needed to identify you as a current UK taxpayer.
In order to Gift Aid your donation you must tick the box below:
☐ I want to Gift Aid my donation of £______________ to:
Name of Charity

____

I am a UK taxpayer and understand that if I pay less Income Tax and/or Capital Gains Tax in the current tax year than the amount of Gift Aid claimed on all my donations it is my responsibility to pay any difference.
My Details
Title _________________
First name or initial(s) _______________________________
Surname____
Full Home address____
Postcode ______________________
Date ____________________________________

1 HMRC Research Report 334 "Gift Aid: Understanding donor behaviour" (Oct 2014) *https://www.gov.uk/government/uploads/system/uploads/attachment_data/file/372221/report344.pdf*

Please notify the charity if you:
. want to cancel this declaration
. change your name or home address
. no longer pay sufficient tax on your income and/or capital gains
If you pay Income Tax at the higher or additional rate and want to receive the additional tax relief due to you, you must include all your Gift Aid donations on your Self-Assessment tax return or ask HM Revenue and Customs to adjust your tax code.[2]

In practice we doubt if this form will often be used; the form for multiple donations would be as good and maybe better.

App. 2.3 Gift Aid declaration: multiple donation

Charity Gift Aid Declaration – multiple donation
Boost your donation by 25p of Gift Aid for every £1 you donate
Gift Aid is reclaimed by the charity from the tax you pay for the current tax year. Your address is needed to identify you as a current UK taxpayer.
In order to Gift Aid your donation you must tick the box below:[3]
☐ I want to Gift Aid my donation of £______ and any donations I make in the future or have made in the past 4 years[4] to:
Name of Charity

____

I am a UK taxpayer and understand that if I pay less Income Tax and/or Capital Gains Tax than the amount of Gift Aid claimed on all my donations in that tax year it is my responsibility to pay any difference.
My Details
Title ________________
First name or initial(s) ______________________________
Surname ____
Full[5] Home address

____
Postcode ______________________
Date[6] ___________________________________
Please notify the charity if you:
. want to cancel this declaration
. change your name or home address[7]

2 The form is accessible *https://www.gov.uk/government/publications/charities-gift-aid-declaration-form-for-a-single-donation*
3 Authors' note: the 5 lines to here may be omitted.
4 Authors' note: Some may prefer the form "I want to Gift Aid any donations I make now or in the future or have made in the past 4 years" which makes it unnecessary to specify the amount of the gift in the form, so making the form easier to complete.
5 Authors' note: the word *full* may be omitted.
6 Authors' note: the date may be omitted..
7 Authors' note: this line and following may be omitted.

. no longer pay sufficient tax on your income and/or capital gains
If you pay Income Tax at the higher or additional rate and want to receive the additional tax relief due to you, you must include all your Gift Aid donations on your Self-Assessment tax return or ask HM Revenue and Customs to adjust your tax code.[8]

App. 2.4 Gift Aid declaration: Sponsored gifts

Sponsorship and Gift Aid declaration form
Please sponsor me (name of participant)____

To (name of event) ____

In aid of (name of charity or CASC)________________________________

If I have ticked the box headed 'Gift Aid? ✓', I confirm that I am a UK Income or Capital Gains taxpayer. I have read this statement and want the charity or Community Amateur Sports Club (CASC) named above to reclaim tax on the donation detailed below, given on the date shown. I understand that if I pay less Income Tax / or Capital Gains tax in the current tax year than the amount of Gift Aid claimed on all of my donations it is my responsibility to pay any difference. I understand the charity will reclaim 25p of tax on every £1 that I have given.[9]

Remember: You must provide your full name, home address, postcode & '✓' Gift Aid for the charity or CASC to claim tax back on your donation.

	Sponsor's Full Name *(First name & surname)*	**Sponsor's Home Address** *Only needed if are Gift Aiding your donation. Don't give your work address if you are Gift Aiding your donation.*	Post-code	Donation Amount £	Date Paid	Gift Aid '✓'
1						
2						
3						
		Total donations received	**£**			

8 The form is accessible *https://www.gov.uk/government/publications/charities-and-casc-gift-aid-declaration-forms-for-multiple-donation*

9 The form is accessible *https://www.gov.uk/government/uploads/system/uploads/attachment_data/file/473639/Sponsorship_and_Gift_Aid_declaration_form_-_Nov_2015.pdf.*

Total Gift Aid donations	**£**			
Date donations given to Charity or CASC				

APPENDIX THREE

RETAIL GIFT AID: TEMPLATE LETTERS

This appendix sets out the test of HMRC's template letters for use with the retail Gift Aid scheme: see 15.40 (Retail Gift Aid).

App. 3.1 Method A template letters: standard method

App. 3.1.1 *Gift Aid Letter at end of tax year*

HMRC say:

> This template is for charity shops to use to advise donors of the proceeds of sale under the Standard Method. For guidance on when to use this letter and how to operate the retail Gift Aid Scheme, follow the link at the end of the letter.
>
> Please note- *the text in italics is compulsory.*
>
> Dear (name of supporter),
> Thank you for bringing your goods to (name of charity) for sale. *You agreed that we would contact you to advise you how much we raised from the sale of your goods.*
> *I am pleased to tell you that proceeds from selling your goods have raised £XX.XX (net of commission and VAT). To donate this sum of £XX.XX to our charity you need do nothing further. This will allow the Charity to reclaim an additional £YY.YY in Gift Aid in the tax year to 5 April YYYY.*

If we do not hear from you within 21 days of the date of this letter, we will assume that you wish to donate the money raised to our charity and, once again, we thank you for your support.

Please also contact us within 21 days if:

a) you expect to pay less than £ZZ.ZZ (cumulative gift aid claimed in tax year) in UK Income and / or Capital Gains Tax in this tax year to meet the Gift Aid amount claimed back by the charity or

b) your personal details, such as name and address, have changed, oryou wish to cancel your gift Aid declaration.

If you have paid insufficient tax to meet the Gift Aid claimed by the charity HMRC may seek to recover this sum from you direct, as it is your responsibility to pay any difference.

Yours faithfully/sincerely/truly,

App. 3.1.2 *In-Year letter for Gift Aid notifications for sale that exceeds £100 and subsequent sales*

HMRC say:

This template is for charity shops to use to advise donors if the proceeds of sale under the Method A are more than £100 and they make subsequent sales. For guidance on when to use this letter, follow the link at the end of the letter.

Please note- *the text in italics is compulsory.*

Dear (name of supporter),

Thank you for bringing your goods to (*name of charity*) for sale. *You agreed that we would contact you if your goods sell for more than £100 and each time further goods are sold within the tax year.*

I am pleased to tell you that proceeds from selling your goods raised a further £XX.XX in excess of £100 (net of after commission and VAT). *This will allow the Charity to reclaim an additional £YY.YY in Gift Aid. To donate this amount to our charity you need do nothing further. If we do not hear from you within 21 days of the date of this letter, we will assume that you wish to donate the £XX.XX raised to our charity* and, once again, we thank you for your continued support.

Please also contact us within 21 days if:

a) you expect to pay less than £ZZ.ZZ (the cumulative gift aid claimed year to date) in UK Income and / or Capital Gains Tax in this tax year to cover the Gift Aid amount claimed back by the charity or

b) your personal details, such as name and address, have changed or if you wish to cancel your Gift Aid declaration..

If you have paid insufficient tax to meet the Gift Aid claimed by the charity, HMRC may seek to recover this sum from you direct, as it is your responsibility to pay any difference.

App. 3.2 Method B template letters

App. 3.2.1 *Gift Aid Letter at end of tax year*

HMRC say:

This template is for charity shops to use to advise donors of the proceeds of sale under the Method A at the end of the tax year including cases where net sales proceeds are more than £100 and charities choose to notify donors at year end to confirm that donors wish to donate the excess over £100. For guidance on when to use this letter, follow the link at the end of the letter.

Please note- *the text in italics is compulsory.*
Dear (name of supporter),
Thank you for bringing your goods to (name of charity) for sale. *You agreed that we would contact you at the end of the tax year, which runs from 6 April to 5 April the following year, and let you know how much we raised from selling your goods.*

Wording to be used where net sales proceeds are less than or equal to £100.
I am pleased to tell you that proceeds from selling your goods have raised £XX.XX (net of commission and VAT) which will allow the Charity to reclaim Gift Aid of £YY.YY in the tax year to 5 April YYYY.

Wording to be used where net sales proceeds are more than £100.
I am pleased to tell you that proceeds from selling your goods have raised £XXX.XX (net of commission and VAT) which will allow the Charity to reclaim Gift Aid of £YY.YY in the tax year to 5 April YYYY.

Since the total proceeds are in excess of £100, we agreed that we would write to you to confirm that you wish to donate the additional sum of £ZZ.ZZ over and above the amounts in excess of £100 that you may have been notified of during the tax year and already agreed to donate to the charity.
To donate this amount to our charity you need do nothing further. If we do not hear from you within 21 days of the date of this letter, we will assume that you wish to donate the money raised to our charity and , once again, we thank you for your continued support.
We appreciate that your status as a taxpayer making Gift Aid donations can change from one tax year to the next.
Please contact us within 21 days if:

a) you have paid less than £YY.YY in UK Income and/or Capital Gains Tax in this tax year to meet the Gift Aid amount claimed back by the charity or

b) your personal details, such as name and address, have changed or if you wish to cancel your Gift Aid declaration.

If you have paid insufficient tax to meet the Gift Aid claimed by the charity, HMRC may seek to recover this sum from you direct, as it is your responsibility to pay any difference.

Yours faithfully/sincerely/truly,

App. 3.3 In-Year letter for Gift Aid notifications for sale that exceeds £1,000 and subsequent sales

HMRC say:

This template is for charity shops to use to advise donors if the proceeds of sale under the Method B are more than £1,000 and they make subsequent sales. For guidance on when to use this letter, follow the link at the end of the letter.

Please note- *the text in italics is compulsory.*

Dear (name of supporter),

Thank you for bringing your goods to (name of charity) for sale. *You agreed that we would contact you if your goods sell for more than £1,000 and each time further goods are sold within the tax year.*

I am pleased to tell you that proceeds from selling your goods raised a further £XX.XX in excess of £1,000 (net of after commission and VAT). *This will allow the Charity to reclaim an additional £YY.YY in Gift Aid in the tax year 5 April YYYY.*

To donate this amount to our charity you need do nothing further. If we do not hear from you within 21 days of the date of this letter, we will assume that you wish to donate the £XX.XX raised to our charity and, once again, we thank you for your continued support.

Please also contact us within 21 days if:

a) you expect to pay less than £ZZ.ZZ (the cumulative gift aid claimed year to date) in UK Income and / or Capital Gains Tax in this tax year to cover the Gift Aid amount claimed back by the charity or

b) your personal details, such as name and address, have changed or if you wish to cancel your Gift aid declaration..

If you have paid insufficient tax to meet the Gift Aid claimed by the charity, HMRC may seek to recover this sum from you direct, as it is your responsibility to pay any difference.

Yours faithfully/sincerely/truly,

App. 3.3.1 *Gift Aid Letter at end of tax year*

HMRC say:

This template is for charity shops to use to advise donors of the proceeds of sale under the Method B at the end of the tax year including cases where net sales proceeds are more than £1,000 and charities choose to notify donors at year end to confirm that donors wish to donate the excess over £1,000. For guidance on when to use this letter, follow the link at the end of the letter.

Please note- *the text in italics is compulsory.*

Dear (name of supporter),
Thank you for bringing your goods to (name of charity) for sale. *You agreed that we would contact you at the end of the tax year, which runs from 6 April to 5 April the following year, and let you know how much we raised from selling your goods.*

Wording to be used where net sales proceeds are less than or equal to £1,000.
I am pleased to tell you that proceeds from selling your goods have raised £XXX.XX (net of commission and VAT) which will allow the Charity to reclaim Gift Aid of £YYY.YY in the tax year to 5 April YYYY.

Wording to be used where net sales proceeds are more than £1,000.
I am pleased to tell you that proceeds from selling your goods have raised £X,XXX.XX (net of commission and VAT) which will allow the Charity to reclaim Gift Aid of £YYY.YY in the tax year to 5 April YYYY.

Since the total proceeds are in excess of £1,000, we agreed that we would write to you to confirm that you wish to donate the additional sum of £ZZ.ZZ over and above the amounts in excess of £1,000 that you may have been notified of during the tax year and already agreed to donate to the charity.
To donate this amount to our charity you need do nothing further. If we do not hear from you within 21 days of the date of this letter, we will assume that you wish to donate the money raised to our charity and, once again, we thank you for your continued support.
We appreciate that your status as a taxpayer making Gift Aid donations can change from one tax year to the next.
Please contact us within 21 days if:

a) you have paid less than £YY.YY in UK Income and / or Capital Gains Tax in this tax year to meet the Gift Aid amount claimed back by the charity or
b) your personal details, such as name and address, have changed or you wish to cancel your Gift Aid declaration..

If you have paid insufficient tax to meet the Gift Aid claimed by the charity, HMRC may seek to recover this sum from you direct, as it is your responsibility to pay any difference.

Yours faithfully/sincerely/truly,

APPENDIX FOUR

CASCs: ELIGIBLE SPORTS

App. 4.1 Eligible Sports

This is the list of eligible sports for the purposes of CASC relief:[1]

Aikido
Air Sports
  Flying
  Aerobic Flying
  Aero Model Flying
  Ballooning
  Gliding
  Hang/Paragliding
  Microlight
  Parachuting
  Popular Flying
American Football
Angling
  Federation
  Coarse
  Game
  Sea
Aquathlon
Archery
  Target
  Field
Arm Wrestling
Artistic Skating
Athletics
  Mountain/Fell
  Road
  Track and Field
  Cross Country
Australian Rules Football
Badminton
Ballooning
Ballroom Dancing
Baseball
Basketball
Baton Twirling
Biathlon
Bicycle Polo
Billiards and Snooker
Bobsleigh
Boccia
Bowls
  Crown
  Federation
  Short Mat
Boxing
Camogie
Canoeing
  Marathon
  Polo
  Wild Water Racing
  Freestyle
  Sea Kayaking
  Slalom
  Surfing
  Canoeing
Caving
  Cave Diving
  Pot Holing
  Mine Exploration
Chinese Martial Arts
  See below
Clay Pigeon Shooting
Climbing
Cricket
Croquet
Curling
Cycling
  BMX
  Mountain Biking
  Road
  Cycle Speedway
  Track
Cyclo Cross
  Downhill
  Stunt
Dance Sport
Darts
Disability Sport
  See end
Diving
Dodgeball

1 See 41.3.1 (Eligible sport for CASC purposes) and *https://www.sportengland.org/our-work/national-governing-bodies/sports-that-we-recognise/*.

Dragon Boat Racing
Duathlon
Equestrian
  Dressage
  Horse Driving
  Endurance
  Vaulting
  Show Jumping
  Harness Racing
  Polocrosse
  Eventing
  Reigning
  Mounted Games
  Horseball
  Carriage Driving
Exercise, Movement and Dance
  Keep Fit
  Medau
  MargaretMorris Movement
Dance
  Ballroom
  Latin
  Highland Dancing
  Scottish Country
  Folk Dance
Fencing
Fives
  Eton
  Rugby
Floorball
Football
  Futsal
Gaelic Games
  Handball
  (non Olympic)
  Football
  Hurling
Golf
Gymnastics
  Artistic
  Recreational
  Rhythmic
  Team Gym
  Sports Acrobatics
  Sports Aerobics
  Trampolining
  Tumbling
Handball
  Olympic
Highland Games
Hockey
  Field
Horse Racing
Horse Riding
Hovering
Hurling
Ice Hockey
Ice Skating
  Short Track
  Figure
  Synchronised
Judo
Ju Jitsu
Kabbadi
Karate
Kendo
  Iaido
  Jodo
Kite Surfing
Kneeboarding
Korfball
Lacrosse
Land-sailing/yachting
Life Saving
Luge
Model aircraft flying
Modern Pentathlon
Motor Cycling
  Road Racing
  Trials
  Enduro
  Motorcross
  track Racing
  super Moto
  Drag/Sprint
  Speedway
  Rallying
  Sidecar Racing
  Hill Climbing
Motor Sports
  Autotests
  Autosolo
  Autocross
  Circuit Racing
  Drag Racing]
  Cross Country
  Hill Climbing
  Karting
  Rallycross
  Rallying
  Sprints
  Time Attack
  Trials
Mountaineering
  Abseiling
  Bouldering
  Climbing
  Trekking
Movement and dance
Netball
Octopush
Orienteering
Parachuting
Parkour
Petanque
Polo
Polocrosse
Pool
Powerboating
Powerlifting
Puck hockey (roller)
Quoits
Rafting
Rackets
Rambling
  Long Distance
  Walking
Real Tennis
Roller derby
Roller Sports
  Speed
  Inline Hockey
  Artistic
  Skater Hockey
  Freestyle
  Roller Hockey
  Roller Derby
Rounders
Rowing

Rugby League
Rugby Union
  Tag
  Sevens
  Touch
Sailing and yachting
  Sailing
  Sportsboats
  Powerboating
  Windsurfing
  Personal Watercraft
  Motor Cruising
  Inland Boating
Sand and Land Yachting
Shinty
Shooting
  Federation
  Clay Target
  Pistol
  Small-bore Rifle
  Rifle
  Muzzle Loaders
Showjumping
Skateboarding
Skater hockey (roller)
Skipping
Snowsport
  Skiing
  Snowboarding
Telemark
Softball
Sombo
Squash
  Squash Racketball
Stoolball
Sub-Aqua
  Underwater Hockey
Surfing
  Short Board
  Kneeboard
  Long Board
  Body Board
Surf Life Saving
Swimming
  Swimming
  Diving
Synchronised
  Water Polo
  Open Water
  Long Distance
Table Tennis
Taekwondo
Tang Soo Do
Tenpin Bowling
  Skittles
Tennis
Triathlon
Trampolining
Tug of War
Ultimate (frisbee)
Volleyball
Water Polo
Water Skiing
  Barefoot
  Cable Ski
  Kneeboard
  Racing
  Tournament
  Wakeboarding
Weightlifting
  Olympic
  Powerlifting
Wheelchair basketball
Wheelchair rugby
Windsurfing
Wrestling
  Olympic Freestyle
Yoga
Disability Sport

APPENDIX FIVE

DEEMED CHARITIES AND NATIONAL BODIES

App. 5.1 Introduction

This appendix considers some specific institutions:

(1) Non-charities deemed charities for tax purposes
(2) Four national bodies (also called "eligible bodies")
(3) Educational establishments
(4) CDC Group (formerly the Commonwealth Development Corporation)

App. 5.2 War Graves Commission Fund

Section 123 F(no.1) A 2015 provides:

> In the enactments to which Part 1 of Schedule 6 to FA 2010 applies, any reference to a charity includes—
> (a) the Commonwealth War Graves Commission, and
> (b) the Imperial War Graves Endowment Fund Trustees.

HMRC explain:

> The CWGC is responsible for the commemoration and maintenance of the graves of Commonwealth forces who died in the First and Second World Wars. The Commission was established by Royal Charter in

> 1917 and was set up as a "not for profit" organisation. ...
> The CWGC has a separate Endowment Fund (The Imperial War Graves Endowment Fund) which was created by Act of Parliament in 1926.
> When the CWGC was created it did not register as a charity but it was entitled to charitable exemptions from tax until the law was changed in 2010.
> This amendment is necessary to continue CWGC's entitlement to claim charity tax reliefs.[1]

Why these bodies would not otherwise qualify as charities is not clear. We would be grateful if any reader could explain.

App. 5.3 National/eligible bodies

Section 468 CTA 2010 provides:

> Each of the following is an eligible body for the purposes of this Part—
> (a) the Trustees of the National Heritage Memorial Fund,
> (b) the Historic Buildings and Monuments Commission for England,
> (c) the Trustees of the British Museum,
> (d) the Trustees of the Natural History Museum, and
> (e) the National Endowment for Science, Technology and the Arts.

Section 154 FA 2013 describes these as "bodies established for national purposes". We refer to them as **"national/eligible bodies"** which seems a clearer (if clumsier) expression.[2]

These bodies fall into two categories:

(1) Non-charitable bodies:
   (a) National Heritage Memorial Fund
   (b) Historic Buildings and Monuments Commission for England[3]

1 HMRC, "Status for tax purposes of certain bodies" (2015) *https://www.gov.uk/government/uploads/system/uploads/attachment_data/file/413932/TIIN_1035_status_for_tax_purposes_of_certain_bodies.pdf*

2 The term "eligible bodies" is used with a different meaning in VAT but we are not concerned with VAT here.

3 This title was too long to be used, and it was popularly known as English Heritage. In 2015 its sites were transferred to a charity, reg no. 1140351, which retains the name English Heritage. Other functions relating to the protection of the historic environment carry on being provided by the pre-2015 English Heritage organisation but under a new name, Historic England. Statutory references have not changed; presumably because the "Historic Buildings and Monuments Commission for England" remains the correct formal name for this organisation.

(2) Charitable bodies:
  (c) British Museum
  (d) Natural History Museum

We understand that the fifth body, National Endowment for Science, Technology and the Arts, no longer operates; it has been replaced by NESTA which is a charity.[4]

For the 2 charitable bodies (the British and Natural History museums) the status as eligible bodies makes little practical difference, though tax reliefs as eligible bodies may be slightly wider than tax reliefs of charities.

For the non-charitable bodies (NHMF and English Heritage) the status as eligible bodies is important as charity tax reliefs only apply so far as they are expressed to apply to eligible bodies.

App. 5.3.1 *Income tax exemption*

Eligible bodies are governed by slightly different rules from other charities: see ss.475, 476, 490 CTA 2010. This is too specialist to consider in full detail, even in a book which seeks to be comprehensive.

App. 5.3.2 *CGT exemption*

Section 271 TCGA provides:

> (6) The following shall, on a claim made in that behalf to the Board, be exempt from tax in respect of all chargeable gains—
> (a) the Trustees of the British Museum and the Trustees of the Natural History Museum; and
> (b) an association (in the sense that word has in section 469(1)(a) of CTA 2010) which meets conditions A and B in that section (conditions for qualifying as a scientific research association).
>
> (7) The Historic Buildings and Monuments Commission for England, the Trustees of the National Heritage Memorial Fund and the National Endowment for Science, Technology and the Arts shall be exempt from tax in respect of chargeable gains.

---

4 Nesta's 2014 accounts state: "Nesta was established and registered as a charity in 2011 to act as successor body to the National Endowment for Science, Technology and the Arts ("NESTA").NESTA was a non-departmental public body established in 1998 with a statutory remit to promote talent, creativity and innovation in science, technology and the arts ... All NESTA activities, staff, assets and liabilities were transferred on 1 April 2012 to Nesta and to the Nesta Trust (the "Trust"). The Trust holds the expendable endowment and Nesta, its sole trustee, uses returns from the Trust to pursue the charitable objects of the Trust.

This is wider than the charity CGT exemption. It is not likely to make any difference, but if it did, there is no good reason why these bodies should be singled out for special treatment.

App. 5.3.3 *Gift Aid small donation scheme*

Section 3(3) SCDA provides:

> Subsection (2)[5] does not apply to—
> (a) the Trustees of the National Heritage Memorial Fund;
> (b) the Historic Buildings and Monuments Commission for England;
> (c) the Trustees of the British Museum;
> (d) the Trustees of the Natural History Museum.

It is possible to see the logic but we have reached an absurd level of micro-detail. Perhaps the Parliamentary Counsel's Office ran a sweepstake for the most pointless tax provision.

App. 5.3.4 *Stamp duties*

Section 69 FA 2003 provides:

> A land transaction is exempt from charge if the purchaser is any of the following—
> (a) the Historic Buildings and Monuments Commission for England;
> (b) the National Endowment for Science, Technology and the Arts;
> (c) the Trustees of the British Museum;
> (d) the Trustees of the National Heritage Memorial Fund;
> (e) the Trustees of the Natural History Museum.

Section 90(7) FA 1986 provides relief from stamp duty reserve tax:

> Section 87 [which imposes the charge to SDRT] above shall not apply as regards an agreement to transfer securities to ...
> (c) the Trustees of the National Heritage Memorial Fund, or
> (d) the Historic Buildings and Monuments Commission for England or
> (e) the National Endowment for Science, Technology and the Arts.

Section 46 FA 1983 provides:

5 See 16.10 (Applied for charitable purposes).

(3) For the purposes of the enactments set out below, the Historic Buildings and Monuments Commission shall be treated as [a charitable company]:—

(c) ... section 129 of the FA 1982 (reliefs from stamp duty).

App. 5.3.5 *Annual Tax on Enveloped Dwellings*

Section 154 FA 2013 provides exemption for the four national/eligible bodies:

(1) A body listed in subsection (2) is not regarded as a company for the purposes of this Part [part 3, ATED].

(2) The bodies are—

the Historic Buildings and Monuments Commission for England;
the Trustees of the British Museum;
the Trustees of the National Heritage Memorial Fund;
the Trustees of the Natural History Museum.

App. 5.3.6 *Critique*

It is considered that the special provisions relating to national/eligible bodies ought to be repealed.

The British and Natural History Museums should qualify for normal charity reliefs like any other charities.

The National Heritage Memorial Fund and(if thought appropriate after the 2015 reorganisation) the Historic Buildings and Monuments Commission for England should be deemed to be charities for tax purposes.

That would be right in principle and a small but worthwhile simplification.

App. 5.4 Educational establishments

Educational establishments qualify for 3 minor charity reliefs. See:

(1) 18.7 (Secondment of employees)
(2) 18.8.7 (Stock gift to charity)
(3) 18.8.8 (Gift of plant/machinery)

They do not qualify for other reliefs unless actually charitable. Once again, it would be simpler to provide that they are charities for all tax purposes.

App. 5.5 CDC Group

CDC Group PLC (formerly the Commonwealth Development

Corporation) qualifies for reliefs in sch 3 Commonwealth Development Corporation Act 1999. This is too specialist to discuss even in a book which seeks to be comprehensive.

APPENDIX SIX

ACCREDITATION OF SOCIAL IMPACT CONTRACTORS

App. 6.1

This appendix sets out the test of the Guidance Concerning the Accreditation of Social Impact Contractors.[1]

PART 1
INTRODUCTION
Content

1. This guidance is issued by the Cabinet Office on behalf of the Minister for the Cabinet Office (the "Minister"). It provides guidance on, and to a limited degree specifies, the criteria by which the Minister makes decisions with respect to companies seeking accreditation as Social Impact Contractors.[2] It also gives guidance on the accreditation process. This material has the effect and purpose conferred by, and must be read in conjunction with, Part 5B of the Income Tax Act 2007, and the Tax Relief for Social Investments (Accreditation of Social Impact Contractor) Regulations 2014 (the "Regulations").

2. Under this legislation, investments by individuals into a social impact contractor can be eligible for Social Investment Tax Relief (SITR), and "Social Impact Contractor" means a Company Limited by Shares that has been accredited by the Minister.

3. In addition to the requirements of accreditation, investments must comply with the broader requirements of SITR listed in the Income Tax Act 2007 (in so far as they are applicable – see Part 4 of this guidance, SITR for Social Impact Contractors) and the Social Investment Tax Relief (Accreditation of Social Impact Contractors) Regulations 2014.

4. While Cabinet Office manages the accreditation, HMRC is responsible for administering the tax relief scheme overall. ...

---

1 *https://www.gov.uk/government/uploads/system/uploads/attachment_data/file/492974/SITRAccreditationGuidanceVersion2forpunlicationJan16V2.pdf* Jan 2016.

2 The section of the guidance which specifies criteria is Part 2B – see further paragraph 13 below.

Background on Social Investment Tax Relief can be found here:[3]
More information about social impact bonds can be found here:[4]

PART 2A

CRITERIA FOR ACCREDITATION

5. References below to "the Act" refer to the Income Tax Act 2007, as amended by the Finance Act 2014.

6. Cabinet Office will accept applications from special purpose vehicles (SPVs) that are companies limited by shares for accreditation as a social impact contractor. At the time of application, the SPV must hold a signed contract with a Contracting Authority.

7. In order to accredit an SPV as a Social Impact Contractor, the Minister will need to be satisfied that the SPV fulfils the following criteria (specified in section 257JD of the Act):

- the SPV is, and has been at all times since its incorporation, established for the purpose of entering into and carrying out a "social impact contract" (or for that purpose and for purposes incidental to it), and for no other purpose, (where "social impact contract" is defined as in section 257JE of the Act and in the Regulations – see further below);
- the SPV's activities in carrying out that contract will not consist wholly, or as to a substantial part, in excluded activities (see section 257MQ of the Act).

8. The Minister will therefore need to be satisfied that the contract held by the SPV fulfils the criteria to qualify as a social impact contract according to the Regulations.[5] Those criteria are:

- at least one counterparty to the contract is a Contracting Authority, which means any body which is a Contracting Authority for the purposes of regulation 2(1) of the Public Contracts Regulations 2015 (SI 2015/102);
- the contract sets out "defined outcomes" that are intended to be achieved under the contract. These outcomes must have a social and/or environmental purpose;
- the defined outcomes must be capable of being objectively measured and the method of measurement must be set out in the contract;
- progress towards achieving the defined outcomes must be assessed at

3 *https://www.gov.uk/government/uploads/system/uploads/attachment_data/file/279864/SITR_Pack.pdf*

4 *https://data.gov.uk/sib_knowledge_box/*

5 Section 257JE(1) of the Act says that a "social impact contract" is a contract that meets such criteria as may be specified in regulations made by the Treasury. Section 257JE(3) says that the criteria may, in particular, be specified by reference to material published by, or on behalf of, a Minister. The Regulations are the regulations that have been made for these purposes: they specify the relevant criteria, in part, directly and, in part, by reference to Part 2B of this guidance – see paragraph 13 below.

intervals which the Minister for Cabinet Office is satisfied are appropriate;
- of the total payments that could be made under the contract by the Contracting Authority to the company, at least 60% by value must be conditional on achieving the defined outcomes.

9. The Regulations define social or environmental purposes as meaning one or more of the following:
- the relief of those in need by reason of youth, age, ill-health, disability, financial hardship or other disadvantage,
- the relief of prevention of poverty,
- the promotion of employment, culture, heritage or sport,
- the advancement of training and education,
- the prevention of crime,
- environmental protection,
- social housing and the relief of homelessness,
- the provision of community facilities,
- the promotion of social inclusion and cohesion,
- the advancement of citizenship or community development,
- the improvement of physical and mental health,
- the provision of long-term care in relation to any infirmity, or
- any other areas that may reasonably be regarded as analogous to, or within the spirit of, any of the areas listed above.

10. For examples of SIB contracts that fulfil a social or environmental purpose, please see case studies of existing UK SIBs here:[6]

11. Many of these examples fulfil several of the purposes listed above in paragraph 9. For example, the Greater London Authority SIB fulfils the following social purposes: the relief of those in need, the relief of homelessness; the promotion of social inclusion; the promotion of employment; the advancement of training and education; and the improvement of physical and mental health.

12. Likewise, the It's All About Me Adoption Bond serves the following purposes (or, at the very least, purposes analogous to these): the relief of those in need by reasons of youth or other disadvantage; the promotion of social inclusion; and the improvement of physical and mental health.

13. Regulation 3(1)(c)(ii) of the Regulations specifies that, as well as pursuing a social and/or environmental purpose, the defined outcomes under the contract must meet the further conditions set out in next section of this Guidance - Part 2B (further conditions for defined outcomes).

14. Except in the case of second and subsequent call off contracts for spot purchase SIBs (see below), the assessment of whether or not a contract meets the criteria for being a social impact contract will be made by the Minister on a

---

6 *https://data.gov.uk/sib_knowledge_box/case-studies-existing-sibs.*

case-by-case basis, in response to a specific application for accreditation (or reaccreditation) (see paragraphs 39-40 below).

Spot Purchase SIBs

15. In a spot purchase SIB, an SPV will enter into any number of contracts, in substantially the same form, with different Contracting Authorities. All the contracts will commit the SPV to deliver the same outcome(s) for a set price. This means that Contracting Authorities are able to 'buy' outcomes for as few as one beneficiary, whereas in most SIBs they will agree to buy outcomes for relatively large numbers of beneficiaries.

16. In the case of spot purchase SIBs, the Minister will look at the first call off contract under a particular framework agreement, to assess whether the relevant SPV can be accredited. If the Minister finds the criteria to be met for that particular contract then he may:

- set the duration of accreditation by reference to (or by specifying a date expected to coincide with) the end of the term of the last call off contract expected to be made under the relevant framework agreement; and
- specify, as a condition of accreditation, that the SPV must, throughout the period of accreditation, be party to one or more contracts with Contracting Authorities in materially identical terms (so far as relevant to the criteria for accreditation), to the first call off contract (the "no gaps condition").

17. During the specified period of accreditation, so long as the no gaps condition, and all other conditions of accreditation are met, then the SPV will remain an accredited social impact contractor; in other words, it will not be necessary for the SPV to re-apply for accreditation in respect of each new call off contract that it enters into.

18. For example, if an SPV had put in place a framework agreement in 2016 and expected to have five different call off Social Impact Contracts, with five different local authorities over the following five year period:

- the SPV would seek accreditation when the first call off contract was put in place;
- assuming the criteria for accreditation were met in relation to that contract, the Minister might grant accreditation for a period beginning with the commencement of the first call off contract and ending in 2021 (or at the point at which the last call off contract was expected to terminate);
- if he did so, then the Minister would impose the no gaps condition, i.e. the Minister would make it a condition of accreditation that the SPV was party to one or more contracts with Contracting Authorities, in materially identical terms (so far as relevant to the criteria for accreditation) to the terms of the first call off contract, throughout the period of accreditation.

19. In this way, the SPV would maintain its accreditation on a rolling basis: it would continue to be an accredited social impact contractor as long as it had no gaps between its 5 call off contracts (assuming all other conditions of

accreditation remain met).

20. If the SPV were no longer party to a relevant contract, so the no gaps condition was breached, then the Minister would consider withdrawing accreditation in accordance with regulation 9 of the Regulations.

PART 2B

FURTHER CONDITIONS FOR DEFINED

21. This Part of the guidance has the effect, through section 257JE(3) of the Act and regulation 3(1)(c)(ii) of the Regulations, of specifying further conditions which a contract must meet in order to be a "social impact contract" for the purposes of SITR.

22. When assessing whether accreditation should be granted, the Minister will need to be satisfied that the following further conditions are fulfilled with respect to the defined outcomes of the contract:

(a) by undertaking to deliver the defined outcomes in the contract, the SPV is tackling a complex issue; (condition (a)) and

(b) achieving the defined outcomes would:

  (i) deliver significant improvements in the social or environmental well-being of one or more disadvantaged or high needs groups (the "target group"); and

  (ii) result in long term positive social and/or environmental impacts (these impacts may be on the target group specifically, or they may be more wide-reaching) (respectively, conditions (b)(i) and (b)(ii)).

23. The following examples illustrate how the further conditions for defined outcomes apply in practice:

- Defined outcomes for reducing re-offending by ex-offenders and getting them into employment: address a complex issue, i.e. recidivism, (condition (a)) and are likely to deliver significant improvements in the social or environmental well-being of a disadvantaged group (ex-offenders) (condition b(i)); and result in long term positive social impacts for that group and (by reducing crime) for society more generally (condition b(ii)).
- On the other hand, a contract to reduce litter within a certain area, would not typically contain defined outcomes that would meet these conditions. For example, the contract might include a defined outcome that litter dropped in the relevant area will have been collected within 24 hours. While this outcome can be said to have an environmental purpose, delivering it: does not address a complex issue (condition (a)); and does not result in significant improvements in the social or environmental well-being of one or more disadvantaged or high needs groups (condition (b)(i)); nor does it result in long term positive environmental impacts (because achieving the outcome while the contract is on foot is not likely to lead to any enduring reduction in littering) (condition (b)(ii)).
- If a particular contract aimed to reduce the number of young people not in

employment or education training after leaving school:

1. a robust outcome metric could be 'securing and sustaining a full time paid job' with payments triggered against securing the job, and sustaining it for a specified period of time; achieving such an outcome addresses a complex issue, i.e. youth unemployment (condition (a)); it delivers a significant improvement in the social well-being of the target group (condition (b)(i)); and those impacts, together with beneficial impacts for society more generally (at the least, increased tax revenues and reduction in benefits payments) are likely to endure in the long term (because the employment has already been sustained for a significant period);
2. other acceptable metrics might be 'improving attendance at school to at least the school average attendance level' or achieving certain defined qualifications, because these outcomes can be shown to have a close link to the longterm outcome of a young person securing a job.
3. however, 'securing the appointment of more teaching assistants' would be unlikely to meet the further conditions for defined outcomes, because achieving this outcome would not, of itself: address a complex issue (condition (a) not fulfilled - more teaching assistants will not necessarily lead to a reduction in youth unemployment, for instance); or be likely to result in significant improvements in the social or environmental well-being of the Target Group (condition (b)(i) not fulfilled), even if the appointment of more teaching assistants could be shown to deliver positive social impacts more generally, that would be likely to endure long term (for the purposes of condition (b)(ii)).

24. When considering, for the purposes of condition (b)(i), what constitutes a significant improvement in the social or environmental well-being of one or more disadvantaged or high needs groups, the Minister may factor in the cohort size, and the scale and size of the programme, in addition to the overarching social purpose and outcomes metrics of the contract.

25. When considering whether the SPV is tackling a complex issue, the Minister will look to see whether it is addressing a social issue that has proved intractable and/or which requires coordinated effort by a number of different bodies to address it. For example, if the issue is "reducing numbers of children in care", there are many public bodies that would be supporting the troubled family, including schools, local authorities, and potentially others, like the Department for Work and Pensions (through payment of social security benefits), the Ministry of Justice (through the justice system and the National Offender Management Service), and the National Health Service.

26. When evaluating the long-term positive impact of the contract, the Minister will look for evidence that the impact of the programme will last significantly beyond the length of the contract. In most cases, the Minister will expect to see

evidence to show that positive impacts are likely to endure for at least 12 months after the contract comes to an end.

...

PART 4

TERMS AND CONDITIONS OF ACCREDITATION

Requirements of Accreditation

29. Accreditation is conditional on the SPV complying with:

- the requirements set out in regulations 10-13 of the Regulations (which are summarised below); and
- such other requirements as the Minister may impose.

30. The requirements of accreditation set out in the Regulations are as follows:

- The accredited SPV must remain a party to a social impact contract at all times after entering the contract.

31. The accredited SPV is required to give notice to the Minister for the Cabinet Office by emailing Applications must be made in writing by a director of the SPV via email to the Centre for Social Impact Bonds in the Cabinet Office at *centreforsocialimpactbonds@cabinetoffice.gov.uk* within 30 days of the following:

- o any material change to the social impact contract (including the termination of the social impact contract); and/or
- o any material change to the name, address, aims or business operations of the accredited Social Impact Contractor

32. The accredited Social Impact Contractor is required to send an annual report every year within one month of the anniversary of the date accreditation was granted (or such other date as is agreed with the Cabinet Office). This must be sent by email to *centreforsocialimpactbonds@cabinetoffice.gov.uk* and must provide, at a minimum, the information specified in Annex B.

33. The accredited Social Impact Contractor, or any other party to the social impact contract, must, if requested, provide the Minister with such information as the Minister reasonably requires for the purpose of his functions under the Act and/or the Regulations.

34. In addition, the accredited SPV must continue to fulfil the conditions in section 257JD(3) of the Act (see paragraphs 7 and 8 above). For example, if the Minister were satisfied that the SPV and the Contracting Authority had varied the terms of their contract in such a way that it no longer met the criteria to be a social impact contract, then he would have to withdraw accreditation from the SPV for breach of the condition in section 257JD(3)(b).

35. In the case of spot purchase SIBs (see paragraphs 8 to 14 above), an SPV may be party to several social impact contracts simultaneously. The requirements of accreditation will need to be satisfied in respect of all relevant contracts.

Notification of changes to contract and breach of conditions for approval

36. The accredited SPV shall as soon as reasonably possible give notice to the Minister by emailing the Centre for Social Impact Bonds in Cabinet Office at *centreforsocialimpactbonds@cabinetoffice.gov.uk* where it fails to comply or it is likely to fail to comply with any requirement of accreditation or any of the conditions of accreditation in section 257JD(3)(b) and (c) of the Act.

37. This notice must specify

a. the circumstances that caused or are likely to cause any requirement or condition to cease to be met or not to be met;
b. state the extent to which any requirement or condition has ceased or will cease to be met; and
c. where the company considers that any requirement or condition is likely not to be met on or by a date after the date of the notice, specify (if possible) that future date.

38. In addition, the accredited SPV must give notice to the Minister (by emailing the Centre for Social Impact Bonds in Cabinet Office at *centreforsocial impactbonds@cabinetoffice.gov.uk*) of any material change to a social impact contract, any change of name of the SPV or of its business address within 30 days of the relevant change.

State aid de minimis

39. The SITR scheme is subject to state aid de minimis rules. It is the social enterprise receiving tax-advantaged investment (i.e. the SPV) which is considered to be the beneficiary of the State aid, rather than the investors receiving tax relief. A qualifying social enterprise is limited in the amount of de minimis state aid from all sources which it may receive in any rolling 3 year period.

40. The SPV must notify HMRC of all de minimis state aid it has received in the 3 years up to and including the date of the relevant SITR investment. The UK Government does not keep a central record of de minimis state aids. If a social enterprise has received any publicly-funded aid and is not clear whether that aid is de minimis state aid, it should seek advice from the administrator of the aid.

41. If it is subsequently discovered that aid has been granted which causes the limit to be exceeded then the SPV must notify HMRC within 60 days. HMMRC will then recover tax relief from investors.

For more guidance regarding state aid de minimis regulations, please see HMRC's SITR website.

PART 5

APPLYING FOR ACCREDITATION

Timing

42. An SPV that is a company limited by shares can make an application for accreditation to the Cabinet Office after it has signed a contract with a Contracting Authority.

43. An application should be made by completing the form, and providing the

further information detailed, at Annex A of this Guidance. The same form should be completed when an SPV that has previously been accredited is applying for (re)accreditation, relying on a different contract.

44. Accreditation can be granted retrospectively (but may not take effect earlier than 6 April 2014).

45. If granted, the accreditation will specify:

- the date it is granted;
- the date on which the period of accreditation begins; and
- the period of the accreditation (or how the period is to be determined).

46. Typically, the Minister will set the period of accreditation to begin from when the contract was commenced; and to end when the final outcomes payments are paid by the Contracting Authority. In the case of a spot purchase SIB, the Minister may set the duration of accreditation by reference to (or by specifying a date expected to coincide with) the end of the term of the last contract under the spot purchase SIB; if he does, then he will specify, as a condition of accreditation, that the SPV must, throughout the period of accreditation, be party to one or more contracts with Contracting Authorities in materially identical terms, so far as the criteria for accreditation are concerned, as the first call off contract.

47. If the Minister makes accreditation conditional on meeting additional requirements (additional to those requirements that have to be met by virtue of the Regulations and section 257JD(3) of the Act), then these requirements will be set out in the accreditation.

48. After an SPV receives accreditation, eligible investors must submit a compliance statement to HMRC for tax relief. This must be submitted within two years of the end of the tax year that the relevant investment was made. For investors in Social Impact Contractors, this means that a compliance statement must be made for every year an investment was drawn down into the SPV.

49. Investments must be held for 3 years to be eligible for SITR (see section 257L of the Act).

Application process

50. Applications must be made in writing by a director of the SPV via email to the Centre for Social Impact Bonds in the Cabinet Office at *centreforsocialimpactbonds@cabinetoffice.gov.uk*

51. Applications must be made within one year of signing the social impact contract.

52. Applications for accreditation may be made once the contractual documents are signed and applicants must provide the information specified in Annex A and any additional information which is requested by the Cabinet Office, after initial consideration of the application.

53. Prospective applicants can contact the Centre for Social Impact Bonds in advance of submitting an application for informal guidance. In particular,

applicants considering submitting an application for accreditation for a spot purchase SIB may wish to contact the Centre for Social Impact Bonds for informal guidance.

Right to request more information

54. The Minister can require any accredited SPV, or any other party to the relevant social impact contract or contracts, in the case of a spot purchase SIB, to provide additional information beyond that supplied in the application for accreditation.

Notification of accreditation or refusal

55. Notification of accreditation or refusal will generally be made within three weeks of receipt of a fully documented application.

56. Where a body has been refused accreditation, feedback will be provided on the main reason or reasons why the application was unsuccessful. If a body that has been refused accreditation believes that it is in a position to provide for consideration further information that addresses the issues raised in the feedback it may do so. Such a body may also reapply at any time if it wishes to do so.

Withdrawal of accreditation

57. The Minister for the Cabinet Office may withdraw an accreditation where there is: a failure to comply with any requirement of the accreditation (e.g. failure to submit an annual return); or the conditions in s. 257 JD(3)(b) or (c) of the Act (see paragraphs 7 and 8 above) have ceased to be met.

58. In the case of a spot purchase SIB, the Minister for the Cabinet Office may make it a condition of accreditation that the SPV is party to one or more contracts with Contracting Authorities in materially identical terms (so far as relevant to the criteria for accreditation) to the terms of the first call off contract, through the period of accreditation. Therefore, if at any time the SPV is not party to a contract with a Contracting Authority, the Minister for the Cabinet Office may withdraw accreditation

59. If accreditation is withdrawn, the Minister for the Cabinet Office will give notice specifying the date from which accreditation is withdrawn and the reasons for the withdrawal.

60. The SPV must give notice within 30 days to any affected investors, who received compliance statements for investments made within the three years immediately preceding the date that accreditation was withdrawn. This notice must state that accreditation has been withdrawn and specify the date from which accreditation was withdrawn.

Appeals

61. The SPV may appeal, by following the process outlined in regulation 16 of the Regulations, against any of the following decisions of the Minister:

- to refuse accreditation;
- to impose an additional requirement of accreditation; or
- to withdraw accreditation.

APPENDIX SEVEN

SUBSTANTIAL DONOR RULES

App. 7.1 Substantial donor rules

The substantial donor rules were introduced in 2006 and (more or less) repealed from 1 April 2013. There remain some (somewhat unusual) circumstances in which the rules may still apply. That is discussed here, but the rules themselves are not discussed; see the 9th edition of this work (2013/14) appendix 3.

App. 7.2 Repeal of substantial donor rules

Para 13 sch 3 FA 2011 provides:

> Sections 549 to 557 (substantial donor transactions) are repealed.[1]

This would repeal the substantial donor rules. However para 27(2) sch 3 FA 2011 provides:

> The repeals made by paragraphs 12 to 14, 16, 18 and 22 to 25 [repeal of the substantial donor rules and consequential amendments] have effect in relation to any transaction, other than an excluded transaction, occurring on or after 1 April 2013.

Thus:

(1) The substantial donor rules are repealed from 1 April 2013.
(2) In relation to "excluded transactions" the substantial donor rules continue to apply even after 1 April 2013. Thus the rules will never

1 The CT equivalent is para 23 sch 3 FA 2011.

become formally obsolete, though after a sufficiently long period – roughly by 2020 – they will be effectively obsolete and perhaps by 2030 a consolidation or tax simplification project might be bold enough to repeal them from the statute book.

App. 7.2.1 *"Excluded transactions"*

Para 27(3) sch 3 FA 2011 provides:

> A transaction is "excluded" if it is entered into in pursuance of a contract made before 1 April 2013, other than in pursuance of a variation of the contract made on or after that date.

EN FB 2011 provides:

> This Schedule provides for the repeal of the existing substantial donor rules, in respect of transactions taking place on or after 1 April 2013, subject to a specific exclusion. The current substantial donors to charity legislation will continue to apply after 1 April 2013 if a substantial donor enters into a contract before 1 April 2013 and a transaction under that contract is entered into on or after 1 April 2013. The effect of this is to ensure that ongoing payments made under a contract that is caught by the substantial donors to charity legislation continue to be caught by those rules. However, if the terms of the contract are varied on or after 1 April 2013 the substantial donors to charity legislation will no longer apply and the situation will fall to be considered under the new rule. Therefore, this situation should only apply to a very small minority of substantial donors.

It is possible to vary contracts in order to disapply the substantial donor rules, but in practice that seems unlikely ever to be necessary.

App. 7.2.2 *Relief for non-tainted transactions*

Para 29 sch 3 FA 2011 provides:

> (2) Sub-paragraphs (3) and (4) apply where—
> (a) a substantial donor transaction is entered into before, or on or after 1 April 2011, and
> (b) that transaction is not tainted.
>
> (3) Where a payment made on or after 1 April 2011 by a charitable trust to a substantial donor in the course of, or for the purposes of, the substantial donor transaction would (in the absence of this sub-paragraph) be treated under section 551(1) or (5) of ITA 2007 as non-charitable expenditure, that payment is not to be so treated.

> (4) Where, as a result of the substantial donor transaction, non-charitable expenditure would (in the absence of this sub-paragraph) be treated as incurred under section 551(2) of that Act on or after 1 April 2011, that expenditure is not to be treated as so incurred.

Thus sub-para (3) and (4) effectively undo the substantial donor rules as long as the transaction is not tainted.

The key term is "tainted".

Para 29(5) sch 3 FA 2011 provides:

> A substantial donor transaction is "tainted" if (and only if) it is reasonable to assume from—
> (a) the likely effects of the relevant relievable gifts and the substantial donor transaction, and
> (b) the circumstances in which the relevant relievable gifts were made and the circumstances in which the substantial donor transaction was entered into,
>
> that the relevant relievable gifts (or one or more of them) would not have been made and the transaction would not have been entered into independently of one another.

The wording is based on the wording of the tainted donation rules.[2]

Para 29(6) sch 3 FA 2011 provides some commonsense subsidiary definitions:

> In this section—
> "relevant relievable gifts", in relation to the substantial donor transaction, means the relievable gifts by reason of which a person is a substantial donor and the transaction is a substantial donor transaction;
> "relievable gift" has the meaning given by section 550 of ITA 2007;
> "substantial donor" and "substantial donor transaction" have the meaning given by section 549 of that Act.

EN FB 2011 provides:

> A transitional provision has been introduced that relaxes the substantial donors to charity rules in relation to certain transactions on or after 1 April 2011. Where a pre-existing substantial donor enters into a transaction caught by the substantial donors to charity rules, but that transaction is not "tainted" then no charge to tax will arise. A substantial donor transaction is "tainted" if it is made as part of an arrangement that would not have occurred independently of the associated donation. The

2 See 7.8 (Donation-dependent arrangement).

effect of the provision is to ensure that transactions that would not have formed part of an arrangement under the new anti-avoidance rule will not attract a tax charge under the substantial donors to charity rules. Charities will therefore need to monitor only those transactions with existing substantial donors where the donations and arrangements were not independent of each other and even then, only for two years rather than the five years under the current substantial donors to charity legislation.

EN FB 2011 provides an example:

Example 5
Donor A donated £30,000 to charity B on 1 May 2010 which means that donor A is a substantial donor of charity B.
Under the existing substantial donors to charity legislation the charity would need to monitor any transactions it enters into with donor A for five years after the tax year 2010/11 (i.e. to 30 April 2016).
A person connected with donor A enters into a transaction with charity B in June 2012; for example, donor A's son is employed by charity B after a recruitment process, to fill a vacancy that had arisen in the charity and receiving remuneration at a rate that is commensurate to the work they are carrying out. Under the substantial donors to charity legislation this would be treated as a caught transaction and charity B would be charged to tax in respect of the value of the remuneration paid.
However, the new rule introduces transitional provisions which mean that the transaction will only continue to be caught (between 1 April 2011 and 31 March 2013 inclusive) if the donation by donor A and the transaction entered into between charity B and donor A's son, would not have taken place independently of one another.
From the facts in this scenario, it is clear that there is no link between the donation and the transaction. Charity B had a vacancy that it needed to fill, the donation did not lead to donor A's son being given the job and the remuneration received reflects the value of the job being carried out. Therefore, the substantial donors to charity legislation will not apply to this transaction.

The proposition that "there is no link between the donation and the transaction" does not seem altogether "clear" but the point is that HMRC do not want to use the rules in this situation.

However, if donor A's son were employed (between April 2011 and March 2013) because of the donation (regardless of whether the remuneration was well above what would be expected for the work they were doing) it could not be argued that the donation and the transaction were entered into independently of one another, and the transitional provision would not relieve a charge under the substantial donors legislation.

If the transaction were caught under the existing substantial donors to charity legislation, because the contract for employment was entered into before 1 April 2013 and would create ongoing obligations on the part of the charity to pay the remuneration, those payments would continue to be non-charitable expenditure of the charity under the existing legislation. However, if the terms of that contract are varied on or after 1 April 2013 (e.g. to ensure that the remuneration is consistent with the market rate for that type of work) then future payments will no longer be caught under the substantial donors to charity legislation.

App. 7.3 What went wrong: Critique

The critique of the substantial donor rules is not set out here as it is not longer relevant; see the 8th edition of this work para 6.16. It is however desirable to note the cause of the failure of the substantial donor legislation in the hope of avoiding the same mistakes in the future. The problem is not difficult to identify. The substantial donor rules:

(1) were introduced without any published statement of the types of avoidance which required new anti-avoidance rules;
(2) were enacted without consultation and without the opportunity for a proper public debate. (No substantial changes were made or could be made between publication of Finance Bill and the Finance Act.)

The debacle illustrates - if illustration is necessary - the importance of:

(1) proper analysis of the problems, and
(2) effective consultation,

in the preparation of tax legislation, including (perhaps especially) anti-avoidance legislation.

The 2011 tainted donation rules suggest that the lesson has not been learnt; though optimists may draw comfort from the decision in 2014 not to proceed with the proposals on charities involved in tax avoidance.[3]

3 See 2.3.1 (Reform of definition of charity?)

APPENDIX EIGHT

HOW TO IMPROVE THE TAXATION OF CHARITIES

Part 1: Low lying fruit
Part 2: Reforms with losers or politically contentious
Part 3: Reforms involving avoidance rules

"To tax and to please, no more than to love and to be wise, is not given to men."[1] The following programme of tax reform is therefore split into three parts. Part 1 is a list of short technical improvements with no significant tax cost, no significant winners or losers, and not politically contentious. It represents some cheap and easy improvements to charity tax to which no-one should object or find difficult, the "low lying fruit" of charity tax reform.

Part 2 sets out some more fundamental reforms which would be significant improvements but may not be universally welcomed.

Part 3 touches on tax avoidance on which HMRC are very sensitive.

Part 1: Low lying fruit

Proposal	Outline
The definition of charity for tax purposes should accept as charitable any objects which are charitable in the law of Scotland or Northern Ireland. (One UK wide definition of charity is better, but devolution makes this difficult to achieve.)	See 3.19 (UK-wide definition of charity: Critique) *Also proposed by:* Calman Commission on Scottish Devolution; Joint Committee on the Draft English Charities Bill

1 Edmund Burke, Speech on Conciliation with America (1774).

Align taxation of charitable trusts and companies	Charitable trusts should be subject to corporation tax (or charitable companies could be subject to income tax). See 3.26 (Alignment of charitable trusts/companies: Critique)
Align exemptions for dividends, interest etc with other charity exemptions	See 4.6.3 (Align exemptions: Critique)
Abolish rule that losses are non-charitable expenditure	See 6.32 (Trading loss of non-primary purpose trade)
Abolish beneficiary worker exemption for trading income	See 8.9.2 (Worker exemption: Critique)
Repeal s.527(2) ITA and its CT equivalent	See 8.15.2 (Miscellaneous income)
Extend small trade exemption	The complexity of the reliefs in s.526–528 ITA is out of proportion. See 8.19 (Charity trade exemptions: Critique)
Relief for all trading income	See 8.19 (Charity trade exemptions: Critique)
Repeal estimated donation relief; extend carry-back relief to 12 months	See 9.5.8 (Estimation relief: Critique)
Abolish reliefs for employees of charities	See 12.1 (Employees of charity)
Abolish fixed cap on Gift Aid benefits	The proportional cap is sufficient. See 15.34.4 (Fixed benefit cap: Critique) *Also proposed by:* McGregor report.
Abolish Annualisation rules	The rules do not strike the right balance between simplicity and fairness. No-one takes any notice of them in practice. See 15.38.4 (Critique) *Also proposed by*: Tax law rewrite project

Abolish relief for settlor-interested trusts	This relief is not useful and not used. See 15.38.4 (Critique)
Repeal carry-back relief; but if retained, simplify election rules	See 15.45.5 (Carry-back relief: Merits); 15.45.5 (OTS reform proposals)
Ignore incidental costs in computation of QIDR	See 21.9 (Incidental costs of disposal)
Repeal s.257(2)(b) TCGA	This has no purpose; see 23.3.4 (Position of charity)
CGT relief for loss accruing on gift to charity	See 23.14 (Asset of inherent loss)
Abolish overlap between s.23, 25 IHTA	See 24.35.2 (Definition of national institutions: Critique)
Repeal s.628, 630 ITTOIA	See 31.5 (Settlor-interested trust); 31.6 (Income paid to children of settlor)
Abolish CASC regime	The rule that CASCs are not charities should be repealed, existing CASCs should be registered as charities and chapter 9 part 13 CTA 2010 should be repealed. See 41.34 (Abolish CASCs: Critique) *Also proposed by:* CLA
Abolish reliefs for "eligible bodies"	These bodies should be taxed on the same basis as other charities; see App 5.3 ("Eligible bodies")

Part 2: Reforms with losers or politically contentious

Move to deduction system of Gift Aid relief	See 15.50 (Gift Aid: Critique)
Minimum amount for Gift Aid relief	See 15.50 (Gift Aid: Critique)

Repeal payroll giving scheme	Gift Aid is sufficient; see 19.11 (Payroll giving: Critique)
Repeal IHT 10% legacy relief	A foolish gimmick; see 25.20 (Charity legacy relief: Critique)
Repeal Gift Aid Small Donation Scheme	Not worthwhile, at least as currently formulated; see 16.24.4 (GASDS: Evaluation)

Part 3: Reforms involving avoidance rules

Abolish application for charitable purposes rule: This is superceded by subsequent anti-avoidance rules; see 4.21.14 (Application for charitable purposes rule: Critique).

The tainted donations rules need review; see 7.26 (Tainted donation: Critique).

The topic of taxation of non-resident charities needs review, especially the management condition; see 3.10.10 (Management condition: Critique).

APPENDIX NINE

BIBLIOGRAPHY

Background to FA 2000 charity tax reforms

HM Treasury, *Review of Charity Taxation: a consultation document*, (1999) *http://webarchive.nationalarchives.gov.uk/20100407120701/http://hmrc.gov.uk/consult/rct.htm*

Inland Revenue, *Review of Charity Taxation: Summary of Responses to the Government's Consultation Document*, (1999) *http://webarchive.nationalarchives.gov.uk/20140109143644/http://www.hmrc.gov.uk/feedback/charity.htm*

Inland Revenue, *Research briefing charity tax review*, (2000) *http://webarchive.nationalarchives.gov.uk/20140109143644/http://www.hmrc.gov.uk/feedback/research.htm*

A review of this background (descriptive, not analytical or critical) can be found in *Taxation of Charities* House of Commons Research Paper 01/46 (2001) *http://www.parliament.uk/briefing-papers/rp01-46.pdf*

UK policy background

Individuals' Donations to Charities and their Use of Tax Relief Deborah Smeaton, Alan Marsh, Ruth Rajkumar & Andrew Thomas *http://webarchive.nationalarchives.gov.uk/20091103064833/http://www.hmrc.gov.uk/research/rep9-main.pdf*
A study of UK giving patterns and attitudes to tax relief. Of interest to policy makers and lobbyists, but not relevant to practitioners.

Comparative studies and resources

Taxation of Non-Profit Organisations - Cahiers de droit fiscal international, Vol 89 (1999) Kluwer. A very brief survey of charity tax in 30 jurisdictions.

The Tax Treatment of NGOs, ed. Paul Bater, Frits Hondius and Penina Kessler Lieber (no relation), Kluwer Law International 2004. Includes a thoughtful discussion of the rationale of charity tax exemption by Prof. Rab. Atkinson.

http://www.icnl.org The International Centre for Not-for-profit Law. Includes a useful directory of resources from countries around the world.

Index

This is mainly an index to chapter numbers. The start of each chapter has a full list of headings and cross references.

TAXATION OF CHARITIES AND NONPROFIT ORGANISATIONS

JAMES KESSLER QC
ETIENNE WONG
and
JON-SELOUS BORLACE

VOLUME ONE

THIRTEENTH EDITION

Key Haven Publications Ltd
P. O. Box 669, Oxford, OX3 3AU
Tel: 01865 352121
http://www.khpplc.co.uk

INTRODUCTION AND WHAT'S NEW

Scope of this book

The subject of this book is the taxation of:
(1) charities
(2) other nonprofit organisations[1]
(3) their donors and supporters

The importance of tax, and the tax cost of ignoring tax law, will be obvious to all our readers. It is the duty of charity trustees – and their professional advisers – to ensure that a charity's tax affairs are properly managed.

The years 2020-2022 in review

HMRC have reversed their longstanding view and now accept that waiver of a debt qualifies for Gift Aid relief; an unexpected consequence of the Covid pandemic. In *Eynsham Cricket Club v HMRC*, the Court of Appeal confirmed that a registered club cannot be a charity. *Re Webster* illustrated the importance of inserting the correct figures in a tax return when claiming Gift Aid carry-back relief.

The years 2020-2022 in review

On VAT, the last couple of years saw the Court of Justice of the European Union deliver its ruling in University of Cambridge (on VAT recovery) and the Supreme Court hand down its judgment in SAE Education Limited (on the education exemption). They also saw new HMRC guidance on the VAT treatment of digital advertising, and the culmination of the dispute between local authorities across the UK and HMRC regarding the VAT liability of charges for access to sports and leisure

1 A note on terminology: The term "not for profit entity" is sometimes used. "Public benefit entity" has the same meaning; though it is more formally defined in FRS 100 as "an entity whose primary objective is to provide goods or services for the general public, community or social benefit and where any equity is provided with a view to supporting the entity's primary objectives rather than with a view to providing a financial return to equity providers, shareholders or members."

facilities (in Chelmsford City Council, Midlothian Council and Mid Ulster District Council).

There have been many revisions to the HMRC Guidance Note, as usual, and new guidance from the Charity Commission. Many other parts of the book have been rewritten in an attempt to analyse the problems more deeply and more clearly.

Thanks...

We are very grateful to Robert Venables QC, joint author of the first two editions of this book, for enjoyable discussions on many aspects of tax, and to Setu Kamal, Harriet Brown, Mary Ashley and Ross Birkbeck, co-authors of previous editions. Yanpei Zhang as research assistant resolved many puzzles. We owe a great debt to Jane Hunt and Ruth Shaw who work diligently on this challenging text throughout the year.

... and request for help

Comments from readers would be of the greatest value and interest to the authors. The pleasure in writing this book consists in the interest of the questions which it raises and the success which it may have achieved in answering them. On the basis of what is known at 1 April 2022, it seeks to state the law for 2022/23.

James Kessler QC
Etienne Wong
Jon-Selous Borlace

15 Old Square
Lincoln's Inn
London WC2A 3UE

kessler@kessler.co.uk
Ewong@15oldsquare.co.uk
jon-selousborlace@15oldsquare.co.uk

OBTAINING FURTHER ADVICE - AND DISCLAIMER

Further advice

If you want advice on which you are legally entitled to rely you can obtain it - but not from this work.

In particular you may instruct any of the authors to advise. We enjoy writing, but spend most of our time giving independent specialist professional advice, including, in particular, advice on the taxation of charities. For further details see *https://www.taxationofcharities.co.uk*.

In cases where a charity which we wish to support cannot be expected to pay a commercial fee, we will consider acting for less than a commercial fee or pro bono. If a matter is not suitable, for reasons of cost or any other reasons, we will give recommendations.

Taxation of Charities Online

ToC Online is an online version of Taxation of Charities, and more. It can be used:

(1) to search the text of this book or to access it online.
(2) to see if the book has been updated.
(3) to correct or contribute to the book.

ToC Online is available as a free service to individuals and firms who have purchased the current edition of this book.

To access ToC Online, go to *https://www.taxationofcharities.co.uk*. The authorisation code is on the inside cover of this volume, and is valid until publication of the next edition.

Disclaimer

Edition history

1st Edition 1989 Robert Venables QC & James Kessler
2nd Edition 1994 James Kessler

3rd Edition 2000	James Kessler
4th Edition 2003	James Kessler
5th Edition 2005	James Kessler QC
6th Edition 2007	James Kessler QC & Setu Kamal
7th Edition 2009	James Kessler QC & Harriet Brown
8th Edition 2011	James Kessler QC & Harriet Brown
9th Edition 2013	James Kessler QC & Oliver Marre
10th Edition 2015	James Kessler QC & Oliver Marre
11th Edition 2017	James Kessler QC, Etienne Wong & Mary Ashley
12th Edition 2019	James Kessler QC, Etienne Wong & Ross Birkbeck

This work was entitled "Tax Planning and Fundraising for Charities" for the first three editions, "Taxation of Charities" for the next four editions, and renamed "Taxation of Charities and Nonprofit Organisations" in the 8th edition.

CONTENTS IN BRIEF

CONTENTS IN DETAIL

Chapter 7
Tainted Donation Rules

Chapter 18
Giving by Businesses to Charity

Chapter 19
Payroll Giving

Chapter 20
Interest-free Loans to Charity

Chapter 21
Gifts of Shares/Land to Charity

Chapter 24
Inheritance Tax Reliefs for Charities

Chapter 25
Charity Legacy Relief

Chapter 26
Will Drafting

Chapter 27
Share of Estate Given to Charity: *Benham* Issues

Chapter 46
Social Investment Relief

Chapter 47
Administration: Tax Returns and Claims

TABLE OF CASES

TABLE OF STATUTES

TABLE OF STATUTORY INSTRUMENTS

TABLE OF ABBREVIATIONS

Statutes and Regulations

CA 2011:	Charities Act 2011
CASCR:	Community Amateur Sports Clubs Regulations 2015
CTA:	Corporation Tax Act 2009
CTISA:	Charities and Trustee Investment (Scotland) Act 2005
DCGADR:	Donations to Charity (Gift Aid Declarations) Regulations 2016 ("DCGADR")
FA:	Finance Act
FSMA:	Financial Services and Markets Act 2000
GRA:	General Rate Act 1967
ICTA:	Income and Corporation Taxes Act 1988
IHTA:	Inheritance Tax Act 1984
ITA:	Income Tax Act 2007
ITEPA:	Income Tax (Earnings and Pensions) Act 2003
ITTOIA:	Income Tax (Trading and Other Income) Act 2005
LBTTSA:	Land and Buildings Transaction Tax (Scotland) Act 2013
LGFA	Local Government (Finance) Act 1988
LGFPSA:	Local Government (Financial Provisions etc) (Scotland) Act 1962
LTA:	Landlord and Tenant Act 1987
LTTWA:	Land Transaction Tax and Anti-avoidance of Devolved Taxes (Wales) Act 2017
OFTR:	Offshore Funds (Tax) Regulations 2009
SCDA:	Small Charitable Donations Act 2012
SCDR:	Small Charitable Donations Regulations 2013
TCGA:	Taxation of Chargeable Gains Act 1992
TFEU:	Treaty on the Functioning of the EU
TMA:	Taxes Management Act 1970
VATA:	Value Added Tax Act 1994

Periodicals

BTR:	British Tax Review
CLPR:	Charity Law and Practice Review
OITR:	Offshore & International Taxation Review (formerly OTPR)

OTPR: Offshore Tax Planning Review[1]
PCB: Private Client Business
PTPR: Personal Tax Planning Review

Other

CASC: Community Amateur Sports Club
CCNI: Charity Commission Northern Ireland
CG: Capital gains
CGT: Capital Gains Tax
CIOT: Chartered Institute of Taxation
CLA: Charity Law Association
CT: Corporation tax
DTA: Double Taxation Arrangement
DCMS: Department for Culture, Media and Sport
ECHR: European Convention on Human Rights
EN: Explanatory Notes
ESC: Extra Statutory Concession
HMRC: Her Majesty's Revenue and Customs
ICAEW: Institute of Chartered Accountants in England & Wales
IHT: Inheritance Tax
IIP Interest in Possession
IoV: Instrument of Variation
IPS: Industrial and provident society
IT: Income tax
NPO: Non-profit organisation
OSCR: Office of the Scottish Charity Regulator
PET: Potentially Exempt Transfer
PRs: Personal Representatives
QIDR: Qualifying Investment Donation Relief
SORP: Accounting and Reporting by Charities: Statement of Recommended Practice (FRS 102)
SP: Statement of Practice
STEP: Society of Trust & Estate Practitioners
TD: Tainted donation

HMRC & Charity Commission Publications

CC35: "Charities and Trading" (April 2007)
HMRC Guidance Note: Charities: detailed guidance notes[2]

1 OTPR (1992-1996) was renamed "Offshore Taxation Review" (1997-1998) and renamed OITR from 1999.
2 *https://www.gov.uk/government/publications/charities-detailed-guidance-notes.*

VATEDU:	VAT on Education Manual
VATGPB:	VAT Government & Public Bodies Manual
VATSC:	VAT Supply and Consideration Manual
VBNB:	VAT Business/Non-Business Manual
VIT Manual:	VAT Input Tax Manual

CHAPTER ONE

POLICY ISSUES IN CHARITY TAXATION

1.1 Introduction

This chapter considers the history of charity tax relief and its policy and human rights issues. It concludes with a look into the future.

1.2 Brief history of charity tax

Tax relief for income of charities goes back to the origin of income tax, being found in the 1799, 1803 and 1842 Income Tax Acts, and was controversial from the beginning.[1] An Inland Revenue memorandum prepared for the 1920 Royal Commission on Income Tax explains the 19th century history of the subject:

> In 1863 Mr Gladstone proposed to repeal the income tax exemption in favour of charities, on the ground that the exemption amounted to a grant of public money without public control, and a large number of charities, especially the "dole" charities, were not beneficial to the community. ... The proposal was strongly opposed and was eventually

---

1 This chapter only considers the UK position, but the issues are international: see Chia "Charitable Treatment?—a Short History of the Taxation of Charities in Australia" *https://law.unimelb.edu.au/__data/assets/word_doc/0006/1977270/2.-TaxingCharitiesFINAL2.doc*
For more historical background see Daunton, Trusting Leviathan (2001) p.210-217.

dropped, although the matter went so far as the introduction of a repealing clause in the Customs and Inland Revenue bill of the year 1863.[2]

Again in 1871, in relation to the Charity Commission, a resolution was passed in the House of Commons to the effect that "discontinuing the exemption of endowed charities from income tax is a suitable method of carrying out the decision of this House against the payment of the expenses of the Charity Commission out of public funds". [3] No action was, however, taken to put the resolution into effect.[4]

No-one more recently has seriously proposed the complete abolition of charity tax relief.[5]

This chapter focuses on IT relief; see too:

For the history of specific types of charity tax relief, see:

Topic	**See para**
Gift Aid	15.2
Corporate Gift Aid	17.2.1
IHT charity relief	24.5
Charity rating relief	40.1

1.3 Reform of tax definition of charity

1.3.1 *Single definition: problems*

At present (more or less) the same definition of charity is used for different purposes:

(1) Tax reliefs

(2) Charity law, which provides special rules governing registration, administration and duration of charities.

Lord Cross pointed out the problems which arise from using the same definition for both purposes:

2 See Hansard, [Bill 91] Committee (4 May 1863) *http://hansard.millbanksystems.com/commons/1863/may/04/bill-91-committee#S3V0170P0_18630504_HOC_45*

3 HC Deb 21 April 1871 vol 205 cc1505-14 *http://hansard.millbanksystems.com/commons/1871/apr/21/the-charity-commission-exemption-of*

4 Royal Commission on Income Tax, 6th instalment of the Minutes of Evidence, Cmd. 288-6, Appendix 31.

5 However a minority in the 1955 Royal Commission on the Income Tax proposed that charities should be taxed at a lower rate: Report Cmd. 615 p.352 & 417.

> It is, of course, unfortunate that the recognition of any trust as a valid charitable trust should automatically attract fiscal privileges, for the question whether a trust to further some purpose is so little likely to benefit the public that it ought to be declared invalid and the question whether it is likely to confer such great benefits on the public that it should enjoy fiscal immunity are really two quite different questions. The logical solution would be to separate them and to say - as the Radcliffe Commission proposed[6] - that only some charities should enjoy fiscal privileges.

It would be better to have two distinct definitions.[7]

1.3.2 *Reform proposals*

Proposals for reform generally involve leaving the charity law definition alone, and providing a separate (usually narrower) definition for tax purposes. But that cannot be done unless one can come up with a better definition of what should be a charity for tax purposes. While the current definition of charity is not ideally suited to identify the causes for which tax relief is appropriate, it is difficult to come up with a better one.

The Inland Revenue invited the 1920 Royal Commission to narrow the definition of charity for tax purposes:

> It might perhaps take the form of confining the relief from income tax:-
> (a) to charities concerned primarily to benefit classes of persons with small incomes which, if not below the limit of exemption, are subject to little or no tax after allowance of all reliefs, and
> (b) to other charities not falling under (a), but conforming to the popular conception of the term, ie, to charities for the relief of physical distress.
>
> Under a restricted exemption of this nature, charities for the relief or education of the poor, hospitals and other charities for the relief of physical distress (such as the National Life-Boat Institution) will continue to enjoy the relief. On the other hand, charities for the education of the well-to-do, religious bodies, and the miscellaneous charities which are not infrequently for the benefit of the well-to-do in

6 See 1.2 (Brief history of charity tax).

7 The trust law problems raised by non-charitable purpose trusts would best be resolved not by a wider definition of "charity" but by a regime which allows such trusts, subject to safeguards, as exists in many trust law jurisdictions. But in practice this problem may not be very important.

> part, or are for the dissemination of some particular doctrine, religious or secular, would no longer be entitled to claim relief.
> ... there is no doubt that there would be strong opposition to the proposal
> ...

The 1920 Royal Commission concluded that "charity" should be redefined for tax purposes[8] but it did not say what the new definition should be!

The 1955 Royal Commission (the Radcliffe Commission) again proposed that "charity" should be narrowly defined for tax purposes.[9] It put forward a definition: "the relief of poverty, the prevention of or relief of distress, the advancement of education, learning and research, and the advancement of religion". This would exclude the fourth class of charity (other objects beneficial to the community). The Commission recognised that under its proposal "exemption would be denied to a number of praiseworthy activities which at present enjoy it" and nothing was done.

The Charities Act 2006 (now the CA 2011) provided a statutory definition of charitable purpose. However the definition of charity has not materially changed. Everything (or virtually everything) which was charitable before 2006 is charitable now. Unlike earlier proposals to reform the definition of charity, the 2006 Act was not a reform much motivated by tax considerations.

1.3.3 *Single definition: consequences*

The present situation of a single definition has some impact on the way the courts approach the question of what is charitable. Lord Cross continues:

> But, as things are, validity and fiscal immunity march hand in hand and the decisions in the *Re Compton* [1945] Ch 123 and *Oppenheim* [1951] AC 297 cases were pretty obviously influenced by the consideration that if such trusts as were there in question were held valid they would enjoy an undeserved fiscal immunity.[10]

Although other judges expressed the view that tax advantages should not be a relevant consideration in determining whether an object is charitable, that must inevitably play a role in judicial thinking. This issue was reviewed in *Independent Schools Council v Charity Commission* which

8 Report of the Royal Commission on the Income Tax Cmd. 615 p.67.
9 Royal Commission on the Taxation of Profits and Income Final Report, 1955, Cmd. 9497, p.57.
10 *Dingle v Turner* [1972] AC 601 at p.625.

reached the same conclusion:

> ... the fact that fiscal privileges are given underlines the need for genuine public benefit.[11]

1.4 Charity reliefs: Policy

Almost all western countries (and many underdeveloped countries)[12] recognise the desirability of supporting nonprofit organisations by granting tax exemptions to charities and to donors. The details differ but there is a broad international consensus that some reliefs are in principle justified.

For a discussion of the policy issues the starting point should be Melbourne Law School (2011) "Taxing Not-for-profits: a Literature Review".[13]

1.4.1 *Reliefs of charity*

The case for tax reliefs on a charity's income and gains is that it facilities the work of charities. The benefit to the public from (most) charitable activity is perhaps self-evident, but if one wishes to be more analytic, the arguments include the following:

(1) Charities offer a means of delivering services:
  (a) which may not be provided by private businesses
  (b) which may be more effectively or cheaply provided than by the state (given a charity's special relationship with the community)
  (c) the cost of which may otherwise fall on the State.
  Hence some traditionally government activities are being outsourced to charities.

(2) Charities promote important values, including voluntarism, self-responsibility, and participative democracy.

---

11 [2012] Ch 214 at [176].

12 See eg the Katz Commission report in South Africa http://www.polity.org.za/polity/govdocs/commissions/1999/katz9_2.htm.

13 Melbourne Law School (2011) *https://law.unimelb.edu.au/__data/assets/word_doc/0006/1977270/2.-TaxingCharitiesFINAL2.doc* See too:
Fleisher, "How is the opera like a soup kitchen?" in Bhandari, ed, *Philosophical Foundations of Tax Law* (2017).
Koele *International Taxation of Philanthropy* para 2.3 (Political philosophy of preferential tax status)
https://dspace.library.uu.nl/handle/1874/23627

(3) Charities constitute an important mechanism for encouraging philanthropy.

HMRC publish data on the tax cost of charity reliefs,[14] but raw statistics require interpretation. For instance, local authorities are exempt from taxation; if they spin off activities into charities there is no net tax cost, (unless you count in the cost of local authorities tax relief too) but additional figures enter into the HMRC data. Similarly for national government. The amount involved here may be substantial and may not be easy to measure. The charts are highly misleading as they do not adjust for inflation.

1.4.2 *Reliefs of donor*

Donor tax reliefs raise slightly different issues.

Some donor reliefs prevent a charge which would otherwise arise on a gift to charity (such as CGT and IHT relief on lifetime gifts). It is self-evident that these reliefs encourage philanthropy, and that few donors would make voluntary gifts to charity if the making of the gift gave rise to a tax charge.

Other donor reliefs (corporate Gift Aid, QIDR and higher rate relief for individual Gift Aid) confer an income tax deduction on the donor. We refer to these as **"donor-deduction reliefs"**. The case for donor-deduction reliefs is similarly self-evident, but if one wishes to be analytic, the arguments include the following:

(1) A pragmatic argument: donor-deduction reliefs encourage philanthropy and so benefit charities and the public generally
(2) Fairness arguments

As to the pragmatic argument, it is relevant to ask whether donor deductibility does increase philanthropy? and if so by how much: are the reliefs value for money, ie, does the additional amount received by charity exceed the tax foregone? Commonsense and anecdotal evidence suggest that the answer to the first question must be yes; but that will not answer the second question: the extent to which donor deductibility leads to greater donations is not easy to measure. As a starting point, it depends

14 HMRC, "UK Charity Tax Relief Statistics 1990-91 to 2016/17" (2017) *https://www.gov.uk/government/uploads/system/uploads/attachment_data/file/532722/UKCharityTaxReliefStatisticsCommentary.pdf*

on:

(1) The price elasticity of charitable giving (what donations would be made if there were fewer or no tax reliefs?)[15]
(2) The value of the tax relief (which in turn depends on the marginal tax rates).
(3) The administrative cost and hassle involved.
(4) Donor's perceptions: incentive effects of reliefs may be diminished if donors underestimate the value of relief, or it may be increased if donors overestimate it.[16]

A full deduction for charitable donations offers the highest level of benefit to top rate taxpayers. If tax rates increase, the value of the incentive rises so if the incentive is effective, charity giving by top rate taxpayers ought to increase. That seems to offer scope for measurement. But an increase in tax rates reduces taxpayers' available income and with it the funds needed to make charitable contributions. In addition, philanthropy depends on unmeasurable donor perceptions of fairness: pragmatic and fairness considerations interact. It seems to us unrealistic to expect that the many causative factors can be untangled: most of what can be said on the effect of donor relief on the motivation of donors remains in the realm of conjecture in psychology and must remain there. But this does not stop economists from trying. *Taxing Not-For-Profits*[17] summarises the American economic literature:

> ... early accusations that the charitable contribution deduction was

15 There is also the question of to what extent donors could continue to find ways to obtain relief for charitable support if the current reliefs such as Gift Aid were abolished.

16 This factor is hard to measure: for discussion in a US context, see Listokin, "Tax Expenditure Salience" [2014] American Law and Economics Review p.144.

17 Melbourne Law School (2011) p.30 *https://law.unimelb.edu.au/__data/assets/word_doc/0006/1977270/2.-TaxingCharitiesFINAL2.doc* in reviewing the US material it is of course necessary to consider to what extent the position in the UK is the same as in America. For a UK study, see Smith, "Increasing Charitable Giving: What Can We Learn from Economics?" (2012), Fiscal Studies, 33: 449–466.
See too See Feldstein (1975) "Income tax and charitable contributions: Aggregate and distributional effects", National Tax Journal 28(1) 81-100; Brown(1987) "Tax incentives and charitable giving – evidence from new survey data", Public Finance Quarterly 15(4) 386-396.

inefficient as it did not induce more giving than it 'lost' in revenue[18] stimulated the growth of a voluminous econometric literature on the relationship between tax incentives and charitable giving... The research focuses on whether tax incentives are economically efficient ways of driving charitable giving,[19] based on their '**price elasticity**'. Price elasticity measures the increase in aggregate giving in response to a decrease in after-tax cost, and a price elasticity figure greater than 1 indicates that is a '**treasury efficient**' measure.

Such literature has demonstrated strong independent links between levels of giving and changes in the "price of giving", being the net, out of pocket cost of giving a dollar to charity.[20] A major review by Clotfelter in 1985 found a notable consistency in the findings, with the consensus being that the price elasticity for the population of taxpayers was probably greater than 1, with a range of -0.9 to -1.4, and taxes also influence giving through changing the income. As well, it was observed that the price elasticity appeared to rise with income; there are substantial lags in giving behaviour; and there is little effect of 'crowding out' individual contributions through government contributions.[21] While there were tax effects on corporate giving, this

18 Footnote original: See, eg, Taussig, 'Economic Aspects of the Personal Income Tax Treatment of Charitable Contributions,' (1967) 20 National Tax Journal 1; Schwartz, 'Personal Philanthropic Contributions,' (1970) 78 The Journal of Political Economy 1264.

19 Footnote original: For summaries, see Charles T Clotfelter, *Federal Tax Policy and Charitable Giving* (University of Chicago Press, 1985); J Johnson, 'The Determinants of Charitable Giving with Special Emphasis on the Income Deduction Under the Income Tax—A Survey of the Empirical Literature' (1981) 3 *Canadian Taxation* 258; Scharf, Hogg, and Cherniavsky, *Tax Incentives for Charities in Canada*, (Working Paper No CPRN, No 03, Canadian Policy Research Networks, 1997).

20 Footnote original: See the overviews in John Peloza and Piers Steel, 'The Price Elasticities of Charitable Contributions: A Meta-Analysis' (2005) 24 *Journal of Public Policy and Marketing* 260; Scharf, Hogg, and Cherniavsky, *Tax Incentives for Charities in Canada*, above. See also Clotfelter, *Federal Tax Policy and Charitable Giving*, (University of Chicago Press, 1985); Gerald E Auten, Holger Sieg and Charles T Clotfelter, 'Charitable Giving, Income, and Taxes: An Analysis of Panel Data' (2002) 92 *American Economic Review* 371. The basic economic model used is explained in Charles T Clotfelter and Lester M Salamon, 'The Impact of the 1981 Tax Act on Individual Charitable Giving' in Susan Rose-Ackerman (ed), *The Economics of Nonprofit Institutions: Studies in Structure and Policy* (Oxford University Press, 1986) 207, 211–212.

21 Footnote original: Clotfelter, *Federal Tax Policy and Charitable Giving*, (University of Chicago Press, 1985), 274–275.

> appeared to be less than for individual contributions, and there was also evidence that corporations time-shift their donations.[22]
> The literature has examined both the 'price effects' (including tax rates), which influence the cost of giving, and the 'income effects', such as inflation or economic growth, that affect the income available for charitable giving.[23] Newer methodologies used in more recent studies have reported much lower price elasticities.[24] Nevertheless, a recent meta-analysis of the 40 years of research in this field concluded that tax deductions were treasury efficient, and (surprisingly) that the price elasticity was not significantly higher for high-income earners.[25]

Similarly, in the US context, Lester Salamon has concluded:

> Whether such tax incentives actually induce taxpayers to make charitable contributions or merely influence the timing and amount of such gifts is open to debate, but there appears to be compelling evidence that they have some effect at least on the timing and amount of gifts.[26]

A second and in our view no less important justification for donor-deduction reliefs is fairness or (more precisely expressed) horizontal equity, the view that people who are relevantly equal should pay the same amount of tax. This turns on the question of whether two taxpayers with the same income are relevantly equal, if one does and the other does not make a gift to charity. In our view, charitable giving is different to any other personal expenditure. Those who give to charity are making a payment for the public benefit, just as taxes are a payment for the public benefit, so it is just and reasonable to allow some tax relief for charitable donors. Thus the pragmatic argument that donor-deduction reliefs increase charitable giving (while valid) is not the only or even the main justification for the reliefs.

---

22 Footnote original: Ibid 275.

23 Footnote original: Clotfelter and Salamon, 'The Impact of the 1981 Tax Act,' in Susan Rose-Ackerman (ed), The Economics of Nonprofit Institutions: Studies in Structure and Policy (Oxford University Press, 1986) 210.

24 Footnote original: See, eg, Richard Steinberg, 'Taxes and Giving: New Findings' (1990) 1 *Voluntas: International Journal of Voluntary and Nonprofit Organizations* 61; William C Randolph, 'Dynamic Income, Progressive Taxes, and the Timing of Charitable Contributions' (1995) 103 *Journal of Political Economy* 709.

25 Footnote original: Peloza and Steel, 'The Price Elasticities of Charitable Contributions: A Meta-Analysis' (2005) 24 Journal of Public Policy and Marketing 267–268.

26 Salamon, The International Guide to Nonprofit Law (1997).

A third justification for donor-deduction reliefs is that charitable giving is a good *per se*: an act of civic participation which strengthens the fabric of the community, and so is to be encouraged for its own sake.

If one accepts that charity reliefs encourage charitable activity, there is still the question of whether charities make better use of funds than the State. (One might similarly ask whether some bodies not within the current definition of charity may make better use of funds than the State, if they qualified for exemption.) This raises deep issues on the role of the State. Those who take the view that governments know better than individuals how resources should be applied will naturally find charity reliefs unpalatable.[27] Those with animosity towards government spending will tend to support the reliefs.[28]

Smith summarises the issue this way:

> In providing tax relief, the government forgoes its own spending to subsidise privately-funded public goods and this has implications for the mix of public good provided. The type of good that individuals choose to allocate money to may be different in terms of efficiency of provision and the types of goods provided. In some of the media, this was summarised fairly crudely as a choice between funding the National Health Service or the Royal Opera House. The White Paper is relatively silent on the issue of whether causes matter, focussing only on the overall level of giving, yet it is potentially an important issue.
> There is relatively little evidence on the types of charities supported by different donors that would be particularly relevant to the debate on the cap on tax relief...

Smith refers to data from data from the Individual Giving Survey.[29] The relevant figures are those specifying the total amounts given, not the total

27 "Critics charge ... that such incentives are undemocratic since they vest in the hands of private persons, decisions over how to allocate revenues that would otherwise come to the government in the form of taxes." Salamon, *The International Guide to Nonprofit Law* (1997).

28 A careful discussion of these issues also needs to scrutinise the distinction between government and the charitable sector, which can become blurred; see Galbraith, *The Economics of Innocent Fraud*, (2004) chapter 7 (The Myth of the Two Sectors).

29 An overview of charitable giving in the UK (2018) *https://www.cafonline.org/docs/default-source/about-us-publications/caf-uk-giving-2018-report.pdf*

number of donors. I here set out the most recent graph:[30]

Figure 5: Proportion of total donation amount received by each cause in 2017

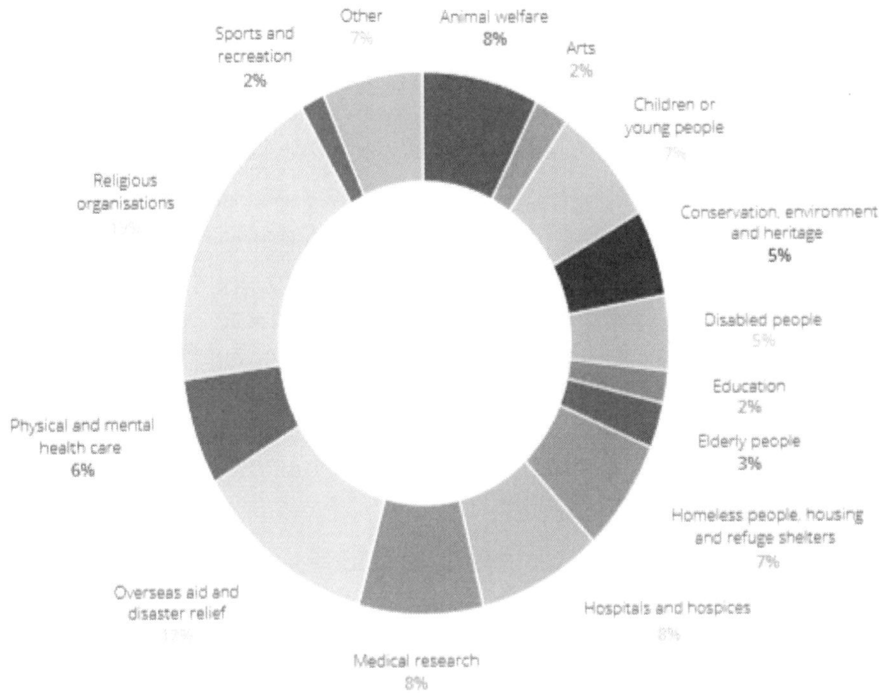

Base: All adults 16+ who have donated directly to a charity in the last four weeks (n=4,028)

In this graph, religious organisations recieve the largest share of donations in terms of total monetary value (19%). If the process of secularisation in the UK continues at its current rate,[31] the case for tax relief for religious charities may come under scrutiny (though conversely, the sums given for religious charities would decline).[32] But medical charities are by far the most popular cause and receive almost one-quarter of all donations, if one regards medical and hospitals (including hospices) as a single item. It is clear that "choice between funding the National

30 The proportion of donors do not add up to 100% due to the fact that a donor can choose more than one cause. The category of 'other' has been excluded from the table and for this reason neither does the proportion of total amount donated sum to 100%.

31 For the sociological background, see Bruce *Secularization* (2011).

32 The case against tax relief is set out by Edge, "Charitable Status for the Advancement of Religion: An Abolitionist's View" (1995) 3 CLPR 29.

Health Service or the Royal Opera House" is a tendentious way of summarising the issue, though if one did put it that way, donors greatly favour health over the arts.

Smith concludes:

> Looking at this allocation raises some fairly important questions about whether it is optimal in any sense - for example, whether the money is going to the most effective charities, or to the areas of greatest need, or indeed to match donors' preferences over the allocation of total giving.[33]

Once again the raw data needs interpretation. The issues are more complicated than this table suggests in (at least) three ways:

(1) The statistics do not easily cater for gifts to grant making charities (including the CAF) or the grants made by them.

(2) Governments may (and no doubt to some extent do) mitigate what they regard as an imbalance by reducing their own allocation to causes which are considered sufficiently well funded by charitable giving.

(3) This table measures charitable giving: some of that giving would not qualify for charity tax relief.

The statistical problems may be insoluble but at the least it should be noted that raw data gives an impression of accuracy which is entirely spurious.

Although the public debate has focussed on donor-deduction reliefs (primarily, Gift Aid) similar issues would arise if there were a debate on the merits of reliefs enjoyed by charities themselves. Here too the debate should consider not just the total cost of the relief, but the way in which the relief is distributed round different parts of the charitable sector: which sectors have the most investment income and so benefit most from the reliefs? We are not aware of data relating to this issue.

For the question of whether charity tax relief constitutes unfair competition for non-charities, see 8.19.1 (Fair competition argument).

1.4.3 *Proposed cap on donor reliefs*

Gift Aid originally had a (somewhat theoretical) limit of £5m, and at one time deeds of covenant had a much lower limit for higher rate relief.[34]

33 Smith, "Increasing Charitable Giving: What Can We Learn from Economics?" (2012), Fiscal Studies, 33: 449–466.

34 See 15.2 (Gift Aid: History).

Some other countries impose a limit of some kind.[35] In the 2011/12 edition of this work, we dealt with this issue quite briefly, saying:

> If it is accepted that gifts to charity are in principle to be encouraged, it is difficult to see why more substantial gifts should be discouraged by a cap on the tax relief, so the UK system is to be preferred.

However, the "omnishambles" budget of 2012 provided:

> 2.40 **Cap on unlimited reliefs** – The Government will, from 6 April 2013, introduce a new cap on income tax reliefs to ensure that those on higher incomes cannot use income tax reliefs excessively. For anyone seeking to claim more than £50,000 of relief, a cap will be set at 25% of income (or £50,000, whichever is greater).

The statement added somewhat lamely:

> The Government will explore with philanthropists ways to ensure this new limit of uncapped reliefs will not impact significantly on charities that depend on large donations.

The impact of the cap on large donations was self-evident: donations would not be made in excess of the cap; donors would instead spread gifts to ensure that the donation of each year did not exceed the cap for tax relief.[36]

At first sight it seems unlikely that significant charity donations come from individuals giving more than 25% of their income to charity.[37] However one must take into account capital gains and inheritances. In the year that an individual sells their business, they may realise a large gain and may well feel it appropriate to give the entire income of the year to

35 Ireland has a compromise limit of 10% of an individual's total income applicable to gifts to connected charities. This may be designed to stop members of religious charities giving all their earnings back to their order which supports them. Hong Kong restricts relief to 25% of a person's income: s.16D Inland Revenue Ordinance. In the US there is a general limit of 50% of adjusted gross income.

36 Evidence is also available: Smith,"Increasing Charitable Giving: What Can We Learn from Economics?" (2012), Fiscal Studies, 33: 449–466: "Changes in tax relief are likely to trigger sizeable adjustments in contributions and the charitable sector would stand to lose more from the proposed cap on tax relief than the government would gain in tax revenue. On this evidence, the government's proposal to cap tax reliefs on donations was considering cutting incentives for precisely the group for whom such incentives are likely to matter most for giving..."

37 If that were true it cuts both ways on the policy issues. If there were no limit, it would not make much difference to the tax take.

charity.

The editor of Taxation summarised the debate which followed:

> There was no worthwhile detail provided in the Budget documentation, which suggests that it was a policy cooked up before the now obligatory deliberate leaking of all the Chancellor's proposals to the Sunday Times on Friday night and the actual delivery of the speech on Wednesday lunchtime. The pressures of working in a coalition meant that there had to be a payback for the reduction of the highest rate of tax from 50% to 45%.
>
> The government was not sure whether it was an attack on tax avoiders or the introduction of something like a minimum tax rate. Initially the narrative focused on the former. There were off-the-record briefings about donations into Romanian charitable trusts which would end up back with the donor. If that had been the target, the phrase 'sledgehammer to crack a nut' would never have been more appropriate. It appears that at least one such scheme does exist, but it equally does not appear to be a widespread problem, and could have been stopped by the existing rules if only HMRC had put some manpower into investigating those running such "charities". Conscious that the argument was getting away from it, the government tried to regain some ground, explaining that the Chancellor had seen anonymised tax returns of high-earning individuals who had significantly reduced their tax bills by offsetting ... charitable donations. ... there could have been no way of knowing whether .. any charitable donations were genuinely made for truly charitable purposes, so what the Chancellor saw was meaningless. Only recently has a more realistic line of argument surfaced, which was (ironically) best put in that bastion of Conservative journalism, the Guardian:
>
>> 'There is an entirely reasonable principle behind limiting the relief on donations: namely that people should pay their taxes… No one would openly suggest that the rich should be given special power to divert some large chunk of scarce public funds towards their pet priorities. But that is what happens where donations can be deducted from taxable income without any limit.'[38]
>
> If this was the real motivation, it would have been possible to deliver it in a way which was consistent with the new approach to making tax policy.[39] ... Instead, ... we are back to the 'rabbit out of a hat' approach. If so, the government has only itself to blame for the firestorm it has

38 See 1.4 (Policy reasons for reliefs for charities and donors to charity).

39 HMRC, "Tax policy making: a new approach" (2010).

created.[40]

It has become standard practice that the government proposing a reform offers every possible reason, good bad and indifferent, in its support. So in the absence of a proper policy paper, it is impossible to ascertain what were the actual policy reasons behind the proposed reform, if indeed there were any. But whatever the reasons, the charity lobby had the better of the argument, and public support; and after floating a compromise of increasing the cap to 50%, the government abandoned the proposal.[41]

In all the public debate there was no mention of the history of income tax reliefs; though this issue has arisen many times before.[42] For those who support a principles-based approach to tax reform, the story is a depressing one, though not unfamiliar. But at the end of the day, the right result was reached, and the issue is probably settled for the medium term.

1.5 Matched funding incentives

An alternative to tax reliefs for charity donations is an arrangement under which if an individual gives, the state also makes a payment to same charity. We refer to this as **"matched funding"**. This has not traditionally been a significant feature of UK legislation, but it has occasionally been used. The transitional relief on the reduction of the basic rate of income tax[43] is not a valid example as its purpose was to avoid a sudden drop in charity income, not to encourage charitable giving. An example is the 10% matched funding supplement to encourage the payroll giving scheme, which was in effect from 2000/01 to 2003/04. We are not aware of any serious study, and the raw data published by HMRC needs to be treated with considerable care, but it is possible that this was effective in its aim of increasing payroll giving. Certainly the withdrawal of the matched payment lead to a significant drop in giving; perhaps

40 Mike Truman, Taxation Magazine, 3 May 2012.

41 HMRC, "Delivering a cap on income tax relief: a technical consultation" (2012) para 2.13.

42 The consultation paper which followed misrecords the debate with a chutzpah which deserves to be recorded: "At the Budget, the Government was clear that it does not want donations to charity to be affected by the relief cap. Therefore, following extensive engagement with the charity sector, the Government has excluded the following from the cap: Gift Aid; Relief for gifts of land and shares; Payroll Giving; and Community Investment Tax Relief."
See 15.2 (Gift Aid: History).

43 See the 7th edition (2009/10) of this work para 15.40.

donors brought their giving forward to take advantage of the last year of the relief, and then reduced their giving in the following year.

GASDS is a long term matched funding scheme introduced in 2012.

For basic rate taxpayers[44] (who are no doubt the large majority of donors by number) there is no practical difference between the Gift Aid system (a rebate of basic rate relief to the charity) and GASDS matched funding (payment to the charity regardless of tax status of the donor).

The difference does however cross a recognised line. The 1995 European System of Accounts provides:

> 4.28. The total value of the taxes which should be recorded ... is reduced by the amount of any tax rebates made by general government as a matter of economic policy and any tax refunds made as a result of over-payments.[45]

This may be paraphrased by saying that a payment would be classified as negative taxation in national accounts if:

(1) the benefit to the individual taxpayer did not exceed the amount of tax paid by them,
(2) it was made as a matter of economic policy; and
(3) the allowance was an integral part of the tax system.

The repayment of basic rate tax under Gift Aid rebate is classified as negative taxation; the GASDS top-up payment is classified as a government grant. GASDS is not part of the tax system, since there is no requirement that the donor should be a taxpayer.

1.6 Human rights

Association Les Temoins de Jehovah v France[46] concerned French gift tax on gifts to the French association of Jehovah's Witnesses. The rate of tax was 60%. French law provides relief for gifts to associations for worship but the association had not obtained the necessary authorisation to benefit from the exemption. The association relied on the gifts for its survival.

Article 9 of the European Convention on Human Rights provides:

---

44 Including higher rate taxpayers who do not bother to claim higher rate Gift Aid relief, which is common for smaller donations.

45 Council Regulation (EC) No 2223/96 of 25 June 1996 on the European system of national and regional accounts in the Community.

46 Application number 8916/05 *https://jwleaks.files.wordpress.com/2012/07/association-les-tmoins-de-jhov.pdf*

> Everyone has the right to freedom of thought, conscience and religion; this right includes freedom to ... manifest his religion or belief, in worship, teaching, practice and observance.
> Freedom to manifest one's religion or beliefs shall be subject only to such limitations as are prescribed by law and are necessary in a democratic society in the interests of public safety, for the protection of public order, health or morals, or the protection of the rights and freedoms of others.

The ECHR held that the application of gift tax to the association was a limitation on freedom of religion, because the association faced closure as a result of the tax demand. The court noted a comment by the French Minister of the Budget that tax audits of the sort carried out on the Jehovah's Witnesses "can be the first step in a process that profoundly disrupts a sect or leads to its dissolution". The power to tax includes the power to destroy.[47]

It is well established that for a limitation to be "prescribed by law", a degree of clarity is necessary in that law. In this case, it was insufficiently clear that French gift tax applied to associations at all; the association could not have been expected to know that it was caught. The court therefore concluded that the limitation on freedom of religion was not "prescribed by law". It did not need to go on to consider whether the "necessity" test was met.

Although taxation of religious charities is capable of giving rise to a breach of Article 9,[48] UK tax rules should usually meet the requirement of being "prescribed by law".

In the context of a less destructive tax demand, a charity's human rights argument based on freedom of expression was summarily dismissed in Canada:

> With respect to the Charter argument based on alleged infringement of freedom of expression, the basic premise of the appellant is untenable. Essentially its argument is that a denial of tax exemption to those wishing to advocate certain opinions is a denial of freedom of expression on this basis. ... The appellant is in no way restricted by the Income Tax Act from disseminating any views or opinions whatever. The guarantee of freedom of expression in paragraph 2(b) of the Charter is not a

47 This aphorism derives from Marshall J in *McCulloch v Maryland* 17 U.S. 327 (1819).

48 And, in some circumstances, article 14: see *Religionsgemeinschaft der Zeugen Jehovas v Austria* 40825/98, [2008] ECHR 762 .

> guarantee of public funding through tax exemptions for the propagation of opinions no matter how good or sincerely held.[49]

In *Gallagher v Church of Jesus Christ of Latter-day Saints* a local authority argued that a Mormon temple was not entitled to rating relief because it was not a place of "public" religious worship. The right of entry was reserved to Mormons who have acquired a "recommend" from the bishop after demonstrating belief in Mormon doctrine, an appropriate way of life and payment of the required contribution to church funds. Such members are called Patrons and the rituals which take place in the temple are exclusive to them. The church argued that the exclusion of all but Patrons is a manifestation of their religion. Therefore, to deny them exemption on that ground would be to discriminate against them on grounds of religion, contrary to articles 9 and 14 of the Convention.

Lord Hoffmann said:

> [13] In order to constitute discrimination on grounds of religion, however, the alleged discrimination must fall "within the ambit" of a right protected by article 9, in this case, the right to manifest one's religion. In the present case, the liability of the Temple to a non-domestic rate (reduced by 80% on account of the charitable nature of its use) would not prevent the Mormons from manifesting their religion. But I would not regard that as conclusive. If the legislation imposed rates only upon Mormons, I would regard that as being within the ambit of article 9 even if the Mormons could easily afford to pay them. But the present case is not one in which the Mormons are taxed on account of their religion. It is only that their religion prevents them from providing the public benefit necessary to secure a tax advantage. That seems to me an altogether different matter ...
>
> [15] ... I think that even if this can be regarded as a case of indirect discrimination, it was justified. Parliament must have a wide discretion in deciding what should be regarded as a sufficient public benefit to justify exemption from taxation and in my opinion it was entitled to take the view that public access to religious services was such a benefit.[50]

In our view human rights law is unlikely to be a factor in most aspects of UK charity tax, and HR issues will only occasionally arise.[51]

49 *Human Life International in Canada v MNR* [1998] 3 FC 202; 52 DTC 6196.

50 [2008] 1 WLR 1852. See 40.10.2 ("Public" worship) for other aspects of this case.

51 Eg in the fit and proper persons test: see 3.10.8 (Human rights); see too 16.22 (Human rights).

1.7 Future developments

1.7.1 *Rewrite of HMRC guidance*

In 2011 HMRC said:

> **Improving HMRC guidance - next steps**
> HMRC recognises that some published guidance is targeted at certain groups within the charity community and can be difficult for people who are not tax professionals to use. HMRC are determined to make guidance accessible to the whole of the charities community, from volunteers to professionals.
> To achieve this HMRC will review all charities guidance. This will be a significant undertaking and HMRC will contact many groups and individuals to understand their issues and concerns. HMRC will also consider how to help charities reduce their administrative burdens by, for example, reducing common errors which would save charities time and resources.
> Over the course of the next few months HMRC will be:
> - exploring how better to engage and interact with customers
> - assessing and prioritising all existing charities guidance
> - scoping, developing, designing and piloting some different ways of presenting guidance to see if customers find them more helpful
> - developing a more detailed timetable for this work
> - setting up arrangements to discuss specific topics and issues with customers
>
> This will be a large undertaking, in the interim HMRC will produce a number of short guides on specific topics to support charities.[52]

There was presumably some high level lobbying here. We would not ourselves have identified existing HMRC guidance as a significant problem in charity tax, but it is easier to review guidance than address harder problems embedded in flawed legislation.

In the 2011/12 edition of this work we said:

> It is hard to predict what will come out of this; most probably nothing more important than a few more HMRC "toolkits".

In practice nothing much seems to have happened. Charity tax guidance continues to be rewritten from time to time, but no more so than on any other topic. Perhaps the idea has been quietly dropped.

52 *http://webarchive.nationalarchives.gov.uk/20140109143644/http://www.hmrc.gov.uk/charities/improving.htm*

Those pressing for more guidance should bear in mind that HMRC guidance cannot be relied on:

> **Taxpayers who used HMRC's previous guidance**
> HMRC does not accept that its published guidance alone can necessarily create a 'legitimate expectation' for a taxpayer. ... Chargeable gains and allowable losses included in returns or claims should be calculated on the correct statutory basis, which HMRC now understand to be as described in HMRC Brief 30/09. HMRC's primary responsibility is to apply the law correctly and collect underpaid or under-declared tax. However, in some limited circumstances, to apply the statute may be so unfair as to amount to an abuse of power by HMRC and in these circumstances HMRC may [!] be bound by its previous guidance. ... it is not sufficient to have merely suffered disappointment or upset.[53]

And again:

> **ADML1605** [Apr 2012]
> ...Only in exceptional circumstances will HMRC be bound by incorrect advice.

CIOT warn their members:

> Whilst it is reasonable *in most circumstances* to rely on HMRC published guidance, a member should be aware that the Tribunal and the courts will apply the law even if this conflicts with HMRC guidance.[54]

The promise of guidance re-emerged in 2016:

> 5.6 ... the government is committed to updating and improving the guidance on the donor benefit rules that is available online from HMRC. Given the feedback received from respondents, the government intends to broaden this work. The government will form a working group comprised of HMRC, HM Treasury and charity sector representatives, to consider both guidance and also HMRC's interpretation and application of legislation relating to donor benefits, including with reference to relevant tribunal decisions. The aim of this work will be to provide consistency of understanding across the charity sector and

---

53 HMRC Brief 60/09. Similarly Enterprise Investment Scheme Technical Note (2009): "HMRC has revised its view... where, by the date of this notice, shares have not been issued then, *irrespective of whether the company has had an advance assurance,* we will apply our understanding of the law as set out in this Note."

54 CIOT and others, *Professional Conduct in Relation to Taxation* (2016), para 3.21 *https://www.tax.org.uk/professional-standards/professional-rules/professional-conduct-relation-taxation*

HMRC.[55]

1.7.2 *Charitable Remainder Trusts*

McGregor calls for tax relief for Charitable Remainder Trusts:

> It is estimated that 40% of the value of the endowments of academic, medical and cultural institutions in the US are made by Lifetime Legacies. They form an essential plank of American planned-giving endowment campaigns. The attraction from an endowment perspective is that the gift is irrevocable and yet donors can benefit from the income or asset for the rest of their lives; this addresses concerns over personal financial security. It also allows donors to be thanked and recognised during their life. As with tax relief for gifts of objects this mechanism encourages donors to engage with the museum over the long-term, helping to build a philanthropic culture.[56]

The challenges in introducing an effective CRT relief into the UK tax system are considerable but not impossible;[57] given the scope for fundraising and the US precedent, we think it likely to happen sooner or later.

---

55 *https://www.gov.uk/government/consultations/simplifying-the-gift-aid-donor-benefits-rules-further-consultation* (Nov 2016)

56 Report on the Role Endowments Could Play in DCMS Funded Museums and Galleries. Dec 2010 *https://www.gov.uk/government/uploads/system/uploads/attachment_data/file/77725/Endowments_paper_20101208.pdf*

57 See Kessler, "Charitable Remainder Trusts: A Proposal", Charity Law & Practice Review Vol 8, Issue 2, p.1 (2005).

CHAPTER TWO

TAX AVOIDANCE AND EVASION

2.1 Avoidance, abuse, evasion

This chapter considers the topics of tax avoidance and evasion.

One should not use the complicated, emotionally charged, and constantly abused term **"tax avoidance"** without some explanation of its meaning.[1]

"Tax evasion" is a relatively straightforward concept. It means conduct which constitutes a criminal offence (fraud on HMRC or similar offences). This normally involves dishonest submission of an incorrect tax return. Dishonesty is essential to the offence.

The topics of avoidance and evasion, though often branded together, have nothing in common. We deal with them in the same chapter as there is not enough to say about evasion to give it a chapter of its own.

Charities have often been used for tax avoidance.[2] Hence the long history of charity tax anti-avoidance provisions.

Charities have been used to hold "orphan" companies, where it was desired that the sponsor or arranger of the company did not have ownership or control. That might be for regulatory or tax planning reasons, or for some other reason. Chadwick LJ, writing extra-judicially

---

1 For which see 6.26.1 (Avoidance).

2 For instance, see *IRC v Universities Superannuation Scheme*: "Charities ... often participated in schemes for dividend stripping relying upon their exemption from tax;" 70 TC 193 at p.212.

in 2007, saw nothing wrong with that.[3] But charity regulators today might not agree, and we think that the practice is best avoided. If used, the charity trustees need to consider what reward benefit hat the charity should expect for acting.

Charities are sometimes used for tax evasion and there have been some prosecutions.

2.2 Reasonable tax planning

The Charity Commission say:

> Charity trustees are under a fiduciary duty to act exclusively in the best interests of their charity in the management of its affairs and the application of its property to further the charity's purposes for the public benefit. In so doing, they must exercise reasonable care and skill and act to the standard of an ordinary prudent business person in the conduct of their own affairs. This duty makes it appropriate for them to engage in reasonable and prudent tax planning and to take advantage of available statutory tax reliefs relating to charities where these will assist the work of the charity, encourage genuine donations and coincide with the purposes for which these reliefs were created. In addition, trustees may properly seek to organise their charity's affairs when carrying out particular activities or transactions in a way which minimises the charity's liability to tax...
>
> **5. The Charity Commission's regulatory position**
>
> The commission encourages charities to take advantage of specific charity tax reliefs, for example Gift Aid and recognises that reasonable and prudent tax planning is consistent with the trustees' fiduciary duties to the charity they manage. In certain circumstances the commission may authorise certain arrangements to this effect if judged expedient in the interests of the charity.[4]

---

3 Chadwick, "Control of Special Purpose Vehicles" Jersey & Guernsey Law Review 2007 *https://www.jerseylaw.je/publications/jglr/Pages/JLR0706_Chadwick.aspx*
"The constitution of the SPV company must ensure that the sponsor does not have legal control. That precludes the sponsor from having a legal or beneficial interest in a controlling shareholding. It is probably safer that the sponsor has no interest as shareholder. The structure in *Mahonia* – where the shares in the SPV company were owned by a charitable trust – provides an obvious way in which this requirement can be met. "

4 Charity Commission, "Charity tax reliefs: guidance on Charity Commission policy" (January 2015)
https://www.gov.uk/government/publications/charity-tax-reliefs-guidance-on-charity-commission-policy/charity-tax-reliefs-guidance-on-charity-commission-policy

In the past the Charity Commission put the point rather more forcefully:

> Trustees ... may be personally liable to account for taxation liabilities which are unnecessarily incurred directly or indirectly as a result of the inefficient administration of the charity. It makes no difference whether the liabilities may arise not from the disqualification of the investment made by the charity, but from the disallowance to the associated trading company of corporation tax relief.[5]

The risk to trustees of personal liability for tax blunders has receded in practice, but it remains in theory and may return.

2.3 Avoidance and charitable status

The ire of the Public Accounts Committee was raised by an abusive tax avoidance scheme involving a charitable trust claiming Gift Aid relief.[6] They thought that the trust should not have been registered as a charity:

> 4. In our view it is absolutely clear that the Trust's purposes were not 'exclusively charitable' since its purpose was also tax avoidance. Neither did it provide public benefit. The Gift Aid received by the Trust and the tax relief given to 'donors' would far exceed any grants for charitable purposes and would be a diversion of taxpayers' money from other projects.[7]

In our view:
(1) A tax avoidance purpose does not prevent funds from being applied for charitable purposes only.
(2) A tax avoidance purpose does not prevent what would otherwise be a charitable body from being a charity.

Campbell v IRC 45 TC 427 was such a case. Moreover, the charitable expenditure rules clearly assume that a payment made with a tax avoidance motive may be an application for charitable purposes.[8]

---

5 Charity Commissioners Report 1988 para 44; the same point was made in CC35 (Charity and Trading) April 2000 para 5 but it is not in the current guidance.

6 For the scheme, see 15.5 (Gift in tax avoidance context).

7 Public Accounts Committee, "Charity Commission: the Cup Trust and tax avoidance" (May 2013) *http://www.publications.parliament.uk/pa/cm201314/cmselect/cmpubacc/138/138.pdf*

8 See 6.26 (Tax avoidance condition). See too *Altus Group v Baker Tilly* [2015] STC 788 at [124](2):
"...expenditure does not fail the 'wholly and exclusively' test simply because the taxpayer has arranged its business in a manner specifically and deliberately designed

One might as well say that a trust was not "exclusively charitable" because its purposes included tax mitigation, or "sensible tax planning", which would rule out many if not most family charities.

The Public Administration Select Committee has also addressed this issue. It did not purport to state what the charity law currently is, but it had no doubt as to what the law should be:

> 21. Charities should not be used as a tax avoidance vehicle. ... Having reviewed [the cup trust] case, if the Commission still feels that it was restricted in its legal abilities to prevent such organisations from obtaining charitable status, we would welcome its proposals for a change in the law on the criteria for registering as a charity.[9]

The Cup Trust scheme was on any view abusive, and in principle[10] such schemes should not succeed. The fact is however that the scheme did not succeed, and was judged to have little if any prospect of success. The remedy for tax avoidance schemes is best placed in tax legislation and not charity legislation; and the administration of tax (including combatting tax avoidance) is best conducted by HMRC and not by the Charity Commission. On this occasion neither the legislation nor its administrators seem to have badly failed the test of practice. HMRC also now have the weapon of the GAAR. We do not see any need for charity law reform. We do not share the view of William Shawcross, Chair of the Charity Commission 2012-2018, who described the issue of the Cup Trust as "a disaster for the charity sector"[11] even if it were the case that the charity concerned should have been investigated more promptly. It was, perhaps, a public relations disaster.

> to involve deductible expenditure. ... many companies structure their affairs in ways specifically designed to be tax-efficient; this is not usually taken to indicate duality of purpose as regards section 54 CTA 2009 [expenses incurred wholly and exclusively for trading purposes]."

The position will need to be reviewed when the case is final, but an appeal is not likely to upset that point.

9 Public Administration Select Committee "The role of the Charity Commission and "public benefit": Postlegislative scrutiny of the Charities Act 2006" (May 2013).

10 We say "in principle" because we respect the view of Lord Simon in *Ransom v Higgs* 50 TC 1 at p.94: "Disagreeable as it may seem that some taxpayers should escape what might appear to be their fair share of the general burden of national expenditure, it would be far more disagreeable to substitute the rule of caprice for that of law."

11 Oral evidence before the Public Accounts Committee, 7 March 2013, HC (2012-13) 1027-i, Q 13.

2.3.1 *Reform definition of charity*

A short, shallow discussion paper was published in March 2014 entitled "Approaches to preventing charities being set up to avoid tax".[12] The idea was that bodies established for a tax avoidance purpose should not qualify as charities within the tax definition. But in July 2014 the proposal was dropped. A press release at the time provided:

> **Government decides against charities anti-avoidance legislation**
> Following consultation, the government has decided not to legislate in Finance Bill 2014 on a new test allowing HMRC to deny recognition to charities being established for tax avoidance purposes.
> ... Based on responses to that discussion paper and engagement with the sector, the Government has decided not to legislate in Finance Bill 2014. Feedback confirmed that the 2 approaches outlined in the paper would have a disproportionate and unacceptable effect upon the charity sector and legitimate donors. Possible damage to innocent charities and our existing and new controls mean that changing the law is not justified at this point.
> HMRC already has a wide range of tools available to tackle avoidance and has recently had considerable success in the courts in challenging certain schemes....[13]

This was the right decision for the right reason. Proposed tax avoidance measures are not usually abandoned just because they incur unanimous disapproval of tax practitioners and affected taxpayers. The explanation may be that HMRC were not much in favour of the proposal, and the purpose of the consultation paper was internal government politics; HMRC needed to be seen to be addressing the criticism from politicians on the Public Accounts and Public Administration Select Committees. But that is a matter of speculation.

2.4 Duties of charity involved in avoidance

2.4.1 *Independent advice*

Charities involved in a tax avoidance scheme must take independent advice (ie advice from someone other than those acting for the scheme promoter). In *Mountstar v Charity Commission*:

---

12 *https://www.gov.uk/government/uploads/system/uploads/attachment_data/file/327853/avoid-tax-charities.pdf*

13 [2014] STI 2283.

> If considering embarking upon an untested tax avoidance fundraising scheme, the charity trustee must carefully examine all aspects of it, fully understand it, require all directors to properly and fully disclose and declare their interests and take any necessary independent advice.[14]

The Charity Commission say:

> **2.1 Trustees' responsibilities**
> Where trustees seek to enter into tax planning arrangements they must satisfy their duty of prudence and ensure:
> [1] the arrangements are lawful
> [2] they have power to enter into the arrangements in question
> [3] they are neither conflicted nor have the potential to benefit personally from any arrangement
> [4] they take and consider appropriate independent specialist advice about obtaining fiscal relief or minimising tax in the context of their responsibilities, such advice being independent of both the charity and the promoter of any proposed arrangements[15]
> [5] a record is kept of their decision-making including any tax law, tribunal decision or professional advice upon which they are relying
> [6] they take into account and consider any published guidance and advice as to the lawfulness of the proposed arrangements offered or available from HMRC
> [7] by entering into the arrangement, that they do not expose any of the charity's property to undue risk
> [8] that the proposed transactions will not damage the reputation of the charity and that they have considered how the character of the arrangement fits with the aims of the charity and the ethos of its donors and beneficiaries
> [9] overall, that the arrangements are in the best interests of the charity[16]

---

14 CRR/2013/0001 at [246]
http://www.judiciary.gov.uk/judgments/mountstar-charity-commission-decision-18102013
The same point is made in *Mountstar v Charity Commission* CA/2013/0001 at [170]
https://www.judiciary.gov.uk/wp-content/uploads/JCO/Documents/Judgments/mountstar-charity-commission-decision-17102013.pdf
The Mounstar cases illustrate a catalogue of problems which arose in the absence of independent advice.

15 Authors' footnote: Of course the advice should be independent of the promoter, who has a conflicting interest, but we do not understand why or indeed how the advice could be independent of the *charity*.

16 Charity Commission, "Charity tax reliefs: guidance on Charity Commission policy" (2015)

2.4.2 *Entering into avoidance scheme*

The Charity Commission discourage tax avoidance:

> **1. Trustees' fiduciary duty**
> ... Trustees will however risk scrutiny and potential investigation by the commission if they engage in tax arrangements which exploit tax legislation artificially, particularly where they serve to benefit private interests, as well as those of the charity. The use of such arrangements is likely to be in breach of trustees' duties and responsibilities to act prudently and in the best interest of the charity. Reputational damage to the charity is highly likely to arise from their involvement in such arrangements...
>
> **3. Tax avoidance involving charities**
> Tax avoidance is challenged by HMRC and can be subject to regulatory scrutiny by the commission...

The Charity Commission give examples of schemes and then set out four objections:

> [1] The principal aim of such arrangements is to confer advantage on private businesses or individuals with any benefit to the charity being a by-product of the scheme rather than its principal aim.
> [2] Apart from being subject to a challenge from HMRC, such arrangements are not consistent with trustees' duties to act prudently and to further the charity's purposes in its best interests for the public benefit.
> [3] The risks to the charity involved include damage to their reputation.
> [4] Of great concern to the commission are the risks of wider damage to the reputation of the charity sector in the eyes of the general public and Parliament, and the potential loss of other tax reliefs to the sector as a result of, or as a necessary by-product of, action to stop or close such schemes...

Objection [1] is a question of fact, and not the case for every tax avoidance scheme. Moreover the issue is not the aim of the arrangements (if such a thing can be identified) but the aim of the trustees in participating in them. Objection [2] is likewise a question of fact and not the case for every avoidance scheme. But see 3.10.5 (Tax avoidance behaviour).

---

https://www.gov.uk/government/publications/charity-tax-reliefs-guidance-on-charity-commission-policy/charity-tax-reliefs-guidance-on-charity-commission-policy

What is one to make of objections [3] and [4], that a charity should not enter a tax avoidance arrangement because of the effect on the reputation of (a) the specific charity and (b) the charity sector?

> CASSIO: Reputation, reputation, reputation! Oh, I have lost my reputation! I have lost the immortal part of myself, and what remains is bestial. My reputation, Iago, my reputation!
> IAGO: ... Reputation is an idle and most false imposition, oft got without merit and lost without deserving. You have lost no reputation at all unless you repute yourself such a loser.

Iago is not, admittedly, a role model; but like all Shakespearian villains, he makes a good point. Reputation - largely measured by disapproval in newspapers - is important for charities which raise funds from the public, such as Oxfam.[17] Reputation of that nature may be unimportant for other charities.

Over-emphasis on reputation moves charity regulation from the courts and the charity commission and gives undue power to the press and public-relations people. It is perhaps worth noting at this point that William Shawcross, the chair of the Charity Commission 2012-2018, was a former journalist.

The reputation of the charity sector in the eyes of the general public is indeed a matter for the Charity Commission. The same may apply to potential loss of charity tax reliefs as a result of action to stop avoidance; though one might say that the correct response is to lobby for properly targeted anti-avoidance rules. As far as we are aware the Charity Commission have left tax avoidance issues to HMRC, and they are right to do so. But individual charities should have regard to the interests of their own beneficiaries, not the interests of other charities. The issue arose in *Charity Commission v Mountstar* which supports the same conclusion:

> ... the real argument against pursuing the appeal [the charity's appeal in support of its abusive avoidance scheme] ... is the potential damage it would inflict on the charitable sector as a whole. So the question becomes whether it is legitimate either for the Interim Managers [of the charity], or for the Charity Commission in giving them advice, to take

17 Fortunately no-one suggested that Oxfam lost reputation when it argued, unsuccessfully, twice, that it should not pay the tax imposed by parliament and by law. *Oxfam v HMRC* [2010] STC 686; or (in an earlier generation) that the Church of England lost reputation by entering into an avoidance scheme in *IRC v Church Commissioners* (1976) 50 TC 516.

> account of these wider considerations when taking a decision in relation to this particular charity.
>
> [Counsel] ... indicated that when it came to taking a decision of this sort, he thought that any charity trustee would be entitled to say that his priority had to be the interests of his own charity, and that it was the Charity Commission which had overall responsibility for the well-being of the charity sector as a whole.[18]

We would agree with that. But see 3.10.10 (Trustee disqualification).

> **5. The Charity Commission's regulatory position**
>
> ...The commission considers, tax fraud, tax evasion and tax avoidance to fall within an area of regulatory concern. In addition the commission expects charities to fulfil their obligations under tax law fully and to take every reasonable step to ensure that the charity is not a party to, and does not enter into, any tax planning arrangements that are imprudent in the ways described above or could bring the charity or the charitable sector into disrepute.
>
> The commission will consider investigatory and/or other regulatory action for example where:
>
> [1] the income or assets of a charity is put at significant or undue risk
>
> [2] [a] trustees or related parties are using a charity to obtain significant private benefit or
>
> [b] are obtaining remuneration in cash or kind by acting either directly as an intermediary or a tax advisor to assist individuals or corporations to avoid tax or indirectly by 'common purse' or receipt of consideration in gifts, cash or kind
>
> [3] trustees or related parties are using the charity as a vehicle for their own private benefit to minimise tax
>
> [4] [a] the charity is a sham or
>
> [b] is not operating for the public benefit
>
> [5] trustees have not considered the impact on the charity's reputation and finances from the charity's involvement in a tax planning scheme that afforded third parties significant private benefit
>
> [6] trustees are involved in tax fraud (including the making of fraudulent Gift Aid claims), tax evasion or tax avoidance
>
> [7] [a] trustees have not taken appropriate tax advice and
>
> [b] have incurred non-charitable expenditure giving rise to a material tax liability or charge to the charity or
>
> [c] have incurred tax penalties through non-compliance with legal requirements

---

18 [2016] EWHC 876 (Ch) at [39] - [40].

> In these circumstances the details of any complaint and any information already obtained from the trustees or the charity will be assessed to decide if further action is justified. The commission will share all relevant details or facts with HMRC where appropriate and may report publicly on the outcome.[19]

Likewise CC20 provides:

> **11.13 Fundraising issues that may be serious enough to trigger commission intervention**
> These include ... arrangements which ... seek to exploit tax legislation artificially, including tax avoidance schemes[20]

In practice, instances of abusive (egregious) tax avoidance schemes are not likely after the GAAR, so the issue of Charity Commission intervention is unlikely to arise.

2.5 Successful avoidance

The NAO say:

> 1.27 HMRC has identified tax at risk totalling £240 million through marketed avoidance schemes that use reliefs on donations. This is the total tax revenue HMRC assesses might be lost should it not be successful in challenging what it considers to be avoidance activity related to marketed schemes. This figure has fallen as users, in part prompted by HMRC's investigations, have withdrawn 200 claims with a total value of £23 million. The tax at risk relates to ongoing investigations dating back to 2004.[21]

Tax is only "at risk" in any meaningful sense if the schemes have a chance of success. That seems unlikely, as HMRC agree:

> 2.40 There are 1,800 open cases of people using marketed avoidance schemes which seek to exploit reliefs on donations. This is around 5 per cent of all marketed avoidance cases that HMRC has under investigation,

---

19 Charity Commission, "Charity tax reliefs: guidance on Charity Commission policy" (January 2015)
https://www.gov.uk/government/publications/charity-tax-reliefs-guidance-on-charity-commission-policy/charity-tax-reliefs-guidance-on-charity-commission-policy

20 Charity Commission CC20 "Charity fundraising: a guide to trustee duties" (2016)
https://www.gov.uk/government/publications/charities-and-fundraising-cc20/charities-and-fundraising

21 National Audit Office "Gift Aid and reliefs on donations" (November 2013)
http://www.nao.org.uk/wp-content/uploads/2013/11/10302-001-Gift-Aid-Book1.pdf

> and accounts for around 2 per cent of the value of all open cases. It will take HMRC many years to resolve its investigations of the eight marketed schemes that use reliefs on donations. HMRC identified the earliest scheme under investigation in 2004 and the latest in 2011. HMRC do not expect any of the schemes to succeed when heard at tribunal.

The NAO say:[22]

> 2.7 HMRC estimates that £110 million was lost in 2012-13 through avoidance using reliefs on donations.

The reader wondering what the successful schemes were, or how they succeeded, is left unsatisfied. But we can give some examples of unsuccessful schemes.

2.6 Avoidance by QIDR

2.6.1 *"Avoidance": Overstating donation*

The NAO give an example involving a gift of shares to charity:[23]

> 1 The scheme user buys £10,000 worth of shares in a company that are valued at 10p each.
> 2 The promoter floats the company on a stock exchange, manipulating trading activity to inflate the value of each share to £1.
> 3 The scheme user gifts their shares to a charity, stating a value of £100,000. In practice, the real value of the shares is much lower.
> 4 The scheme user then claims relief from HMRC on the £100,000 donation to charity [ie on the gift of shares whose value was claimed to be £100k].

HMRC described this as a complex scheme[24] but the essence is simple. As the market value of the shares is lower than that stated on the tax return, the taxpayer is claiming relief to which they are not entitled. If those involved know that the figure stated on the tax return is wrong, they are guilty of (criminal) tax evasion. Two accountants were convicted for

---

22 National Audit Office "Gift Aid and reliefs on donations" (November 2013) *http://www.nao.org.uk/wp-content/uploads/2013/11/10302-001-Gift-Aid-Book1.pdf*

23 National Audit Office "Gift Aid and reliefs on donations" (November 2013) *http://www.nao.org.uk/wp-content/uploads/2013/11/10302-001-Gift-Aid-Book1.pdf*

24 HMRC "Levelling the tax playing field: Compliance progress report" (2013) p.16 *http://webarchive.nationalarchives.gov.uk/20131212020409/http://www.hmrc.gov.uk/budget2013/level-tax-playing-field.pdf*

arranging a scheme on these lines, and received sentences of 4 years imprisonment and 18 months imprisonment.

2.6.2 *Gift of gilt subject to option*

The NAO give an example of gifts of gilts to charity:[25]

> 1 The promoter provides a scheme user with an interest free loan through an offshore trust.
> 2 The user buys gilts that they then donate to the charity. Gilts are not subject to capital gains tax.
> 3 The charity receives a fee for participating in the scheme. It sells the gilts at a fraction of market value to the offshore trust, which cancels the loan to the scheme user.
> 4 The scheme user claims relief on the value of the £100,000 donation.

This seems to be a (slightly garbled) version of the scheme in *Ferguson v HMRC*.[26] In essence:

(1) A charity enters into a contract with a (non-charitable) trust on terms that if an individual gives a gilt to the charity, the trust may purchase it for 1% of its value.
(2) The individual gives the gilt to the charity.
(3) The option is exercised.

The individual claimed QIDR for the gift, but was not successful.[27]

2.7 "Avoidance": Extracting value from charity

The NAO give some examples:[28]

> **Donor controlled charities**
> Companies or individuals may try to exploit reliefs on donations where they control a charity
> *How a charity controlled by a company may be used to exploit Corporate Gift Aid*
> [1] The management of the company and the charity overlap, or the company owners effectively control the trustees.

---

25 National Audit Office "Gift Aid and reliefs on donations" (2013) *http://www.nao.org.uk/wp-content/uploads/2013/11/10302-001-Gift-Aid-Book1.pdf*

26 [2014] SFTD 934. This was known as the "Blue Box" scheme. The name seems to be arbitrary, though we should be grateful to any reader who can explain it.

27 For the reasons, see 21.2.2 (Disposal to charity).

28 National Audit Office "Gift Aid and reliefs on donations" (November 2013) *http://www.nao.org.uk/wp-content/uploads/2013/11/10302-001-Gift-Aid-Book1.pdf*

[2] The company donates profits to the charity and receives a reduction in its corporation tax bill through Corporate Gift Aid.

[3] The charity provides a loan to the donor company or to companies owned by the trustees. The company does not repay the loan.

[4] The charity may also distribute some money to causes fulfilling charitable obligations.

Example of a charity controlled by an individual and abuse of Higher Rate relief on Gift Aid

[1] An individual has control over the management of a charity as a trustee or has influence over the trustees.

[2] The individual makes a donation to the charity and claims Higher Rate relief on the donation. The charity also claims Gift Aid on the donation.

[3] The individual receives benefit from their donation. This could be in the form of an interest free loan from the charity.

These two examples are basically the same. Other variants are mentioned:

> It may also be in the form of disguised non-charitable expenditure, such as entertaining,

The NAO report does not give any legal or tax analysis. But the schemes actually set out never could be successful (and as far as we know, never have been successful).

(1) They involve a breach of charity law for which there are charity law remedies:
   (a) the trustees can be required to reimburse the charity;
   (b) The Charity Commission can appoint new trustees

(2) They involve an application of funds for non-charitable purposes so tax reliefs are lost.

Lastly a variant of the above:

> The individual receives benefit from their donation. It may also be in the form of disguised non-charitable expenditure, such as paying substantial salaries to family members.

Actually there should be no tax saving here since tax (including NICs) on the substantial salaries is likely to exceed Gift Aid relief on the gift. But if (as is implied) "substantial" salaries means excessive salaries, then the donation does not qualify for Gift Aid relief.

See too 15.5 (Gift in tax avoidance context); 21.22 (QIDR "avoidance" schemes).

2.8 Fraudulent tax reclaims

A tax reclaim by a charity is fraudulent if the charity knows that it is not entitled to the money claimed. That may be for various reasons, most obviously:

(1) No gift to charity is actually made.[29]

(2) A gift is made to charity, but the donor subsequently steals the amount of the gift back from the charity (so the tax reclaim is invalid as the funds are not applied for charitable purposes).

As far as HMRC are concerned, there is no difference between (1) and (2). The NAO say:[30]

> 2.4 HMRC estimates that £15 million was lost through fraudulent claims in 2012-13.

We wonder how reliable this figure is. The amounts involved in successful fraud must generally be unknown.

> Fraudsters have targeted Gift Aid relief paid to charities. Unlike other reliefs on donations, Gift Aid claims from charities generate a cash repayment rather than reducing a claimant's tax liability.
> 2.5 HMRC have identified a number of ways in which fraudsters may operate. They may set up charities to facilitate fraud or hijack the details of a charity. They may then falsify donations in order to try and generate a repayment of Gift Aid relief. Fraudsters have also attempted to change the bank details of genuine charities held by HMRC by claiming to represent the charity. This would allow them to redirect payments of Gift Aid to a bank account they control.

In our view the best solution to this problem, and probably the only solution, is to move to a deduction system of Gift Aid relief: see 15.50.1 (Gift Aid v deduction relief).

29 Since the tax is repaid to the charity, the fraudster must then steal the tax reclaimed from the charity, if they are to obtain any personal benefit; though charitably minded fraudsters may allow the charity to keep the proceeds of the fraud.

30 National Audit Office "Gift Aid and reliefs on donations" (November 2013) *http://www.nao.org.uk/wp-content/uploads/2013/11/10302-001-Gift-Aid-Book1.pdf*

CHAPTER THREE

DEFINITIONS OF "CHARITY"

Cross references

The following topics are considered elsewhere:
1.3 (Reform of tax definition of charity)

3.1 Definitions of charity

This chapter considers definitions of charity and classification of charities.

The UK has (at least) four definitions of "charity":

(1) General law definitions, ie "charity" as defined:
  (a) in English law (**"English law definition"**)
  (b) in Scots law (**"Scots law definition"**)[1]
  (c) in Northern Ireland law (**"Northern Ireland law definition"**)[2]

(2) "Charity" as defined for UK tax law (**"tax definition"**)

The UK has three definitions of "charitable purpose":
  (a) in English law and in UK tax law (**"English law definition"** or **"CA 2011 definition"**)
  (b) in Scots law (**"Scots law definition"**)
  (c) in Northern Ireland law (**"Northern Ireland law definition"**)

3.2 Charitable purpose: English law

Before looking at the definitions of "charity" we need to consider the definition(s) of "charitable purpose".

Section 2(1) Charities Act 2011 provides:

> For the purposes of the law of England and Wales, a charitable purpose is a purpose which—
> (a) falls within section 3(1), and
> (b) is for the public benefit (see section 4).

Section 3(1) CA 2011 provides a list of 13 charitable purposes:

> A purpose falls within this subsection if it falls within any of the following descriptions of purposes—
> (a) the prevention or relief of poverty;
> (b) the advancement of education;

1 See 3.15 (Scots law definition of charity).
2 See 3.16 (NI law definition of charity).

(c) the advancement of religion;
(d) the advancement of health or the saving of lives;
(e) the advancement of citizenship or community development;
(f) the advancement of the arts, culture, heritage or science;
(g) the advancement of amateur sport;
(h) the advancement of human rights, conflict resolution or reconciliation or the promotion of religious or racial harmony or equality and diversity;
(i) the advancement of environmental protection or improvement;
(j) the relief of those in need because of youth, age, ill-health, disability, financial hardship or other disadvantage;
(k) the advancement of animal welfare;
(l) the promotion of the efficiency of the armed forces of the Crown or of the efficiency of the police, fire and rescue services or ambulance services;
(m) any other purposes—
  (i) that are not within paragraphs (a) to (l) but are recognised as charitable purposes by virtue of section 5 (recreational and similar trusts, etc.) or under the old law,
  (ii) that may reasonably be regarded as analogous to, or within the spirit of, any purposes falling within any of paragraphs (a) to (l) or sub-paragraph (i), or
  (iii) that may reasonably be regarded as analogous to, or within the spirit of, any purposes which have been recognised, under the law relating to charities in England and Wales, as falling within sub-paragraph (ii) or this sub-paragraph.[3]

A discussion of this requires a book to itself. It is not discussed here. The topic may be classified as charity law, rather than tax law (though the question often arises in a tax context); and it is fully covered in charity law textbooks.

3.3 English law definition of charity

Section 1(1) CA 2011 provides:

> For the purposes of the law of England and Wales, "charity" means an institution which—
> (a) is established for charitable purposes only, and

3 Section 3(2)(3) CA 2011 provide further definitions which are not considered here.

(b) falls to be subject to the control of the High Court in the exercise of its jurisdiction with respect to charities.

Section 1(2) CA 2011 anticipates other definitions:

> The definition of "charity" in subsection (1) does not apply for the purposes of an enactment if a different definition of that term applies for those purposes by virtue of that or any other enactment.

3.4 Tax definition of charity

Para 1(1) sch 6 F(No.1)A 2010 provides the tax definition of charity:

> For the purposes of the enactments to which this Part applies "charity" means a body of persons or trust that—
> (a) is established for charitable purposes only,
> (b) meets the jurisdiction condition (see paragraph 2),
> (c) meets the registration condition (see paragraph 3), and
> (d) meets the management condition (see paragraph 4).

The definition is limited to the "enactments to which this Part applies" but in fact it applies for just about all tax purposes. Para 7 sch 6 F(No.1)A 2010 provides:

> The enactments to which this Part applies are the enactments relating to-
> (a) income tax.
> (b) capital gains tax,
> (c) corporation tax,
> (d) value added tax,
> (e) inheritance tax,
> (f) stamp duty,
> (g) stamp duty land tax,
> (h) stamp duty reserve tax,
> (i) annual tax on enveloped dwellings and
> (j) diverted profits tax.

The tax definition does not apply for rating relief.

Para 1(3) sch 6 F(No.1)A 2010 provides for exceptions:

> Sub-paragraphs (1) and (2) are subject to any express provision to the contrary.

For examples, see App 5.1 (Deemed Charities and National Bodies).

A charity within the English law definition of charity does not necessarily qualify as a "charity" within the tax definition.

3.4.1 *Recognition by HMRC*

HMRC say:

> To get tax relief your charity must be:
> - based in the UK, EU, Iceland, Liechtenstein or Norway
> - established for charitable purposes only
> - registered with the Charity Commission or another regulator, if this applies to you
> - run by 'fit and proper persons'
> - recognised by HMRC.[4]

However recognition by HMRC is not a separate requirement to be a charity within the tax definition; it is just an administrative procedure under which HMRC consider whether the other requirements are satisfied.[5]

3.4.2 *F(No.1)A 2010: Critique*

The manner of the enactment of the 2010 Act deserves to be recorded. It was enacted in three working days.[6] The professional bodies called in vain for delay and reflection.[7] In its single three hour debate, some half dozen MPs (5 Conservative, one SNP) understood what that timetable entailed:

> **Mark Hoban:** This Finance Bill contains much that is controversial, much that could be improved by scrutiny and much that could be amended, but Parliament has been denied that opportunity ...
> **John Redwood:** ... none of these clauses has been properly tested. We have not had the chance to consult experts outside on whether each of the clauses will do what the Government intend, and we have not been able to consult people who will experience the impact of those clauses to see whether what the Government intend is fair and reasonable...
> **Stewart Hosie:** We would normally have about three months, but today we have about three hours.
> **William Cash:** I have never witnessed before what we have seen today....... we are not going to be able to examine things in Committee; and this is pure, unadulterated absurdity.
> **Charles Walker:** It is absolutely impossible, even for well-educated people who

4 *https://www.gov.uk/charities-and-tax/get-recognition*

5 See 47.3 (Registration with HMRC).

6 The Bill was published (appropriately) on 1 April and passed on 8th April.

7 "Good tax law requires close examination and detailed scrutiny, from parliamentarians and from outside experts" (Letter CIOT to Alistair Darling, 12 March 2010).

> think they might have an understanding of these things, to penetrate the complexity of this document...
> **David Gauke:** The Bill could have taken the minimalist approach and focussed only on matters that needed to be addressed urgently. The Chartered Institute of Taxation made that point in a hurried but none the less professional submission, saying that "the challenge to the Government is, quite simply, why any clauses more than those necessary to provide for the continuation of income tax and setting of duty rates should be passed."[8]

The tax definition of charity is complex, controversial and unsuitable for rushed enactment. Readers may think it pointless to cry "foul" in a game which has no referee, and whose result was long ago declared. We think the history deserves to be recorded, both as an object lesson in how not to legislate and as an explanation of some of the difficulties in the current law. But there it is.

3.5 Charitable purposes condition

Para 1(1) sch 6 F(No.1)A 2010 provides:

> For the purposes of the enactments to which this Part applies "charity" means a body of persons or trust that—
> (a) is established for charitable purposes only ...

We refer to para (a) as the **"charitable purposes condition"**.

3.5.1 *Established*

One could identify two requirements in para (a): the charity must be
(1) established, as well as
(2) established for "charitable purposes only".

But the better view is that this is a composite phrase, and the word "established" does not bring in any additional requirement. An individual who carried out charitable activities is not a charity (and could not claim relief for their expenses) and the same would apply to an informal group of individuals who have not taken the steps to constitute an unincorporated association (a body of persons). But the reason that an individual or individuals do not constitute a charity is not (just) that a charity has not been "established" but that there is no "body of persons or trust". Any body of persons or trust must necessarily be "established".

In *IRC v Glasgow Music Festival Association* 11 TC 154 Lord Blackburn

8 Hansard 7 April 2010.

took the view that a body could not be a charity unless it was "endowed with a fund protected by a trust of a permanent character". This view, founded on the word "established", was rejected by the majority of the Court of Session. It is considered that the phrase "established for charitable purposes only" means no more than "formed for charitable purposes only".

3.5.2 *How to ascertain purpose*

In *Bowman v Secular Society*:[9]

> Neither the documents preliminary to the incorporation of a company registered with a memorandum of association, nor the action of directors after a company has been formed, can properly be received in evidence for the purpose of determining what the objects of the company may be.[10]

HMRC Guidance Note provides:

> 2.1.2 A 'body of persons or trust' is established for 'charitable purposes only' if it was set up by a governing, or founding, document that restricts its purposes to those detailed in [what is now section 3 CA 2011]. ...
> 2.1.3 For an organisation to be 'established for charitable purposes only' it must be restricted by its governing document to using all its income and assets for its stated charitable purposes.

Thus the purpose(s) of an institution are to be identified from its constitution.[11]

The *activities* of an institution are not relevant for the purpose of identifying its purpose(s). Activities may be considered for the purpose of deciding whether those purposes are charitable, if that is unclear;[12] but this should not often arise because:

(1) A well drafted charity constitution will generally have objects which leave no room for doubt as to whether the objects are charitable.

---

9 [1917] AC 406 at p.468.

10 This was cited in a charity tax context in *Tennent Plays v IRC* 30 TC 107 at p.121.

11 If further authority is needed, see *Derby Teaching Hospitals NHS Foundation Trust v Derby City Council* [2019] EWHC 3436 (Ch) at [53]: "in a case like the present, the purpose for which an institution is established will be defined by the instrument which establishes the institution."
See too 8.8 (Ascertaining primary purposes).

12 See *Tudor on Charities* 10th ed, 7-029 (relevance of activities). Activities are also relevant to determine whether a charity is a sham.

(2) Once an English charity is registered, its objects are deemed to be charitable, so for an English charity, the issue should only arise prior to registration.

3.5.3 *Effect of English registration*

Section 37 CA 2011 provides:

> (1) An institution is, for all purposes other than rectification of the register, conclusively presumed to be or to have been a charity at any time when it is or was on the register.
> (2) For the purposes of subsection (1) an institution is to be treated as not being on the register during any period when the entry relating to it is in suspense under section 36(4).

It seems unlikely that anyone would suggest that a registered charity is not established for charitable purposes only. But if the question is asked, the answer is that under s.37(1) CA 2011 a body entered on the English register is conclusively presumed to be an English law charity, so it must be presumed to satisfy the charitable purposes condition. It therefore must be a tax law charity, unless it fails the management condition.[13] Similarly, if it applies its income/gains properly according to its constitution, it presumed be taking as having applied them for charitable purposes only.

An institution can be removed from the register but this does not operate retrospectively, except in rather limited circumstances: s.34 CA 2011.

3.5.4 *Charitable purpose: Scotland/NI*

Para 1(4) sch 6 F(No.1)A 2010 provides:

> For the meaning of "charitable purpose", see section 2 of the Charities Act 2011 (which—
> (a) applies regardless of where the body of persons or trust in question is established...

13 Ireland adopts a different approach. Section 7 [Ireland] Charities Act 2009 provides:
"(1) Nothing in this Act shall operate to affect the law in relation to the levying or collection of any tax or the determination of eligibility for exemption from liability to pay any tax.
(2) The Revenue Commissioners shall not be bound by a determination of the [Charities Regulatory] Authority as to whether a purpose is of public benefit or not in the performance by them of any function under or in connection with [specified tax provisions]."
The English law approach seems better. It avoids duplication of regulation: the issue of charitable status is decided once and once only, through the registration process.

This applies the English law/CA 2011 definition of charitable purpose[14] for the tax definition of charity, even in relation to Scottish,[15] Northern Ireland,[16] and EU charities.

Para 1(4)(b) sch 6 F(No.1)A 2010 provides:

> For the meaning of "charitable purpose", see section 2 of the Charities Act 2011 (which ...
>
> (b) for this purpose forms part of the law of each part of the United Kingdom (see sections 7 and 8 of that Act)).[17]

Thus the relevant provisions of the CA 2011 take effect as part of Scots and Northern Ireland domestic law; the significance of this is that any dispute is determined by the Scots or Northern Ireland courts as an issue of domestic law, it is not regarded as an issue of foreign law (which may need expert evidence to determine).[18]

It follows that it is not strictly correct to refer to the CA 2011 definition of charitable purpose as the "English law" definition. It also forms part of the law of Scotland and Northern Ireland. Outside the context of English law, it would be more accurate to refer to it as the **"CA 2011 definition."** But it comes to the same thing.

3.5.5 *Charitable purpose: foreign charity*

An EU body may qualify as a charity within the tax definition. This remains the case following Brexit. However, in order to qualify as a charity, the objects of the body must be charitable under the CA 2011 definition of charitable purposes. This raises two sets of issues:

(1) to identify the objects of the foreign body, a matter of foreign law
(2) to determine whether those objects are wholly charitable, a matter of English law

Consider, for instance, a common form Irish charity whose objects are defined as including anything that is charitable under the law of the Republic of Ireland. Ireland is a common law jurisdiction and the Irish

---

14 See 3.2 (Charitable purpose: English law).
15 See 3.15 (Scots law definition of charity).
16 See 3.16 (NI law definition of charity).
17 For sections 7, 8, see 3.15 (Scots law definition of charity); 3.16 (NI law definition of charity).
18 This is a statutory restatement of the earlier case law: *City of Glasgow Police Athletics Association v IRC* 34 TC 76.

definition of charity is very similar to that in England.[19] However the question (strictly) is whether there is *anything* in Ireland which is not charitable in England. If one looks hard enough one might be able to identify something. For instance:

(1) It might be argued that closed monastic orders and the celebration of Masses are not charitable in England[20] but are charitable in the different culture of Ireland.
(2) It might be argued that the promotion of the efficiency of the armed forces of Ireland is not a charitable purpose in England though no doubt it is charitable in Ireland.[21]

If any distinctions like these can be identified, it would allow HMRC to argue that a gift to an Irish charitable trust does not qualify for UK tax relief wherever the terms of the Irish charitable trust (as is no doubt common form) allow it to apply funds on anything which is charitable for the purposes of Irish charity law.

Now consider the same question in relation (say) to a gift to a Maltese church or a Greek school. Issue (1) (ascertaining the objects) will be harder because of the difficulties of language and the greater differences of legal culture, but the approach will be the same.

These difficulties were anticipated in 1936:

> ... the great administrative difficulty which must inevitably attend the world-wide application of the [charity] exemption. If any institution in any part of the world can lay claim to the exemption on the ground that it is established for exclusively charitable purposes, adjudication upon foreign claims for exemption will... involve the two-fold process of ascertaining the relevant foreign law as to the purposes which the institution concerned is empowered to pursue and then determining whether those purposes, considered, I suppose, in relation to the manners, customs, beliefs and social conditions obtaining in the foreign country concerned, are charitable purposes within the meaning of our law. This would be liable to give rise in many cases to an abstruse and controversial inquiry, hardly to be answered short of litigation in the Courts.[22]

---

19 See s.2 [Ireland] Charities Act 2009. From the earliest times to Irish independence, no-one doubted that an Irish charity qualified for UK tax relief; see *Dreyfus v IRC* 36 TC 126. Presumably that must have included one governed by Irish law.

20 *Gilmour v Coats* [1949] 1 AC 426.

21 See the Court of Appeal in *Dreyfus v IRC* 36 TC 126 at p.136.

22 *Dreyfus v IRC* 36 TC 126 at p.150.

A practical way to solve the problem may be to draft the constitution of the foreign body so as to restrict its objects to those which are charitable in both English law and the foreign law.

3.6 Jurisdiction condition

Para 2(1) sch 6 F(No.1)A 2010 provides:

> A body of persons or trust meets the jurisdiction condition if it falls to be subject to the control of—
> (a) a relevant UK court[23] in the exercise of its jurisdiction with respect to charities, or
> (b) any other court in the exercise of a corresponding jurisdiction under the law of a relevant territory.

This is needed because the word "charity" in an ordinary context in an English Act of Parliament means an institution regulated by, and subject to the jurisdiction of, the laws or the courts of the UK.[24]

Para 2(3) sch 6 F(No.1)A 2010 provides a definition of "relevant territory":

> In sub-paragraph (1)(b) "a relevant territory" means—
> (a) a member State, or
> (b) a territory specified in regulations made by HMRC.

Iceland, Norway and Liechtenstein have been specified as relevant territories.[25]

For VAT purposes, the Isle of Man receives special VAT treatment.[26]

3.6.1 *Subject to court: Statutory body*

In *Construction Industry Training Board v AG*:

---

23 Para 2(2) sch 6 F(No.1)A 2010 provides a straightforward definition of "relevant UK court":
In sub-paragraph (1)(a) "a relevant UK court" means—
(a) the High Court,
(b) the Court of Session, or
(c) the High Court in Northern Ireland
and, for enactments relating to value added tax, includes the High Court of the Isle of Man.

24 *Derby Teaching Hospitals NHS Foundation Trust v Derby City Council* [2019] EWHC 3436 (Ch) at [101].

25 The Taxes (Definition of Charity) (Relevant Territories) Regulations 2010.

26 See 35.2 ("Charity").

> where a charity is established by an Act of Parliament, the court will not exercise its jurisdiction in any way which will conflict with the provisions of the Act ... but this does not mean that in such a case the jurisdiction of the court is entirely ousted....If the Attorney-General were to institute proceedings against the board, alleging misapplication of its funds, I feel no doubt that the court would have jurisdiction to entertain the proceedings. So also, if the board wished to have the directions of the court in respect of the conduct of its affairs, I can see no reason why they should not be able to apply to the court for directions just as any other charity trustees could do. The fact that the Act confers upon the Minister the right to control the board in certain specified respects, such as investment, and that the court could not properly seek to interfere with any decision of the Minister with respect to any such matter, cannot, in my opinion, result in the board not being subject to the control of the court in the exercise of its jurisdiction in respect of charities.[27]

Accordingly, the Training Board was subject to the jurisdiction of the English court.

3.6.2 *Subject to court: Foreign body*

Whether a body is subject to the control of a UK court raises issues of private international law. *Gaudiya Mission v Brahmachary* concerned an Indian charitable company. It was administered in India but conducted activities and held assets (a temple) in England. It was not within the jurisdiction of the English court:

> The [Charities Act] is neither intended, nor apt, to apply to an institution established for charitable purposes outside England and Wales, ie an institution constituted in accordance with the law of a foreign state. ... the power of the court to direct schemes, one of the most distinctive powers of the court with respect to charities, can only be exercised in relation to a charity established in, and in accordance with the law of, England and Wales.[28]

---

27 [1973] Ch. 173 at p.187, 188.

28 [1998] Ch 341 at p.350, 352 following the approach of *Dreyfus Foundation v IRC* 36 TC 126. But in Ireland, an American charitable company running a nursing home in Ireland was held, following comments in *Dreyfus*, to have sufficient "establishment" in Ireland to constitute a charity for Irish tax purposes: *Revenue Commissioners v Sisters of Charity of the Incarnate Word* [1998] IEHC 24 [1998] 2 IR 553 *http://www.bailii.org* We also mention for completeness *Civil Engineer v IRC* [2002]

The charity was no doubt under the control of the Indian courts, but was not under the control of the English courts, and so would not meet the jurisdiction condition.

One might think from this that a charitable trust governed by a foreign proper law is outside the jurisdiction of the English High Court. But other passages approved in the same case suggest that in the case of a charitable *trust*, where the trustees are in England, the court has jurisdiction. The court approved these passages from earlier cases:

> *if the trustee is abroad* there is no power in the court to direct a scheme to be settled, and the practice in such a case is to hand over the fund to the trustee to be applied according to the trusts of the will without directing a scheme. ...
> The objection, in the ordinary case, to administering a foreign charity under the superintendence of the court, is this: *those who are engaged in the actual execution of it, are beyond the court's control*, and those who are within the jurisdiction are answerable to the court for the acts of persons as to whom they can derive no aid from the court.[29]

Thus in *IRC v Gull* 21 TC 374, a will trust governed by the law of Ontario with one trustee in the UK and one outside it was held to be a charity for tax purposes; this was apparently approved in *Dreyfus Foundation v IRC* 36 TC 126.

In *Manoogian v Sonsino*:[30]

> It is not essential to a valid charitable trust that there be a trustee within the jurisdiction. Would, for instance, a charitable trust with resident trustees cease to be charitable simply because the trustees went abroad, whether temporarily or permanently? The answer to my mind is obviously no. Of course if the trustees went abroad permanently and the objects and assets of the trust were all abroad, the trust might cease to be within the remit of the Charity Commissioners.

The position is changed, arguably, by the Recognition of Trusts Act 1987. This provides that the duty of trustees to account for their administration is governed by the proper law: see The Hague Convention, Article 8(j). Arguably this excludes the jurisdiction of other courts. Certainly a place

STC (SCD) 72 which follows *Dreyfus* but adds nothing to it.

29 At pages 351 and 352; our emphasis.

30 [2002] EWHC 1304 (Ch) at [34].

of jurisdiction clause may do so.[31]

The Charity Commission guidance says:

> The following factors can indicate that your organisation falls within the High Court's charity law jurisdiction:
>
> - your governing document adopts the law of England and Wales to govern it
> - most of your trustees live in England and Wales
> - most of your organisation's property is in England and Wales
> - your organisation's centre of administration is in England and Wales.[32]

While the question is one for Scots lawyers, it seems to us that Scots law trusts, subject to supervision by the OCSR, are subject to the jurisdiction of the Court of Session, pursuant to the CTISA 2005. Various provisions of this Act[33] give the Court of Session jurisdiction to act in relation to Scots law trusts.

The safe course may be to arrange that the charity is indisputably subject to the control of a UK court. If a trust, the charity should be subject to a UK proper law and have at least one UK trustee. (If appropriate this can be achieved by use of a corporate trustee.) If a company, the charity should be incorporated under the Companies Acts and have at least one director here.

3.6.3 *Swiss charity*

Switzerland is not a member of the EEA. Nevertheless, prior to the UK's withdrawal from the EU, Switzerland entered into bilateral treaties with the EU under which freedom of establishment and free movement of capital rules apply. It is therefore surprising that the tax definition of charity includes charities in Norway, Iceland and Liechtenstein, but not Switzerland. It is noteworthy that the Irish response to the EU issues made provision for Swiss charities.[34]

The manner of enactment of the F(No.1)A 2010 precluded debate but

31 See Kessler & John, *Drafting Trusts and Will Trusts* (14th ed, 2019), para 30.6 (Exclusive jurisdiction clause).

32 CC4, "What makes a charity?" *https://www.gov.uk/government/publications/what-makes-a-charity-cc4/what-makes-a-charity-cc4#part-5*

33 For example, ss.34 and 78 CTISA 2005.

34 See s.24 [Ireland] FA 2010.

there is a hint of HMRC's thinking in the EN to the Taxes (Definition of Charity) (Relevant Territories) Regulations 2010:

> 7.5 UK charity tax reliefs are being extended to EEA countries where sufficient information exchange and collection of tax arrangements are in place to ensure the reliefs can be administered properly, including the ability to obtain information about individuals and organisations in those countries, and to recover overpaid tax.
> 7.6 HMRC have established efficient information exchange and tax collection arrangements with Iceland and Norway...

Similar points should apply to Switzerland under the 2011 Swiss/UK Tax Agreement and the Common Reporting Standard. Switzerland has ratified the Convention on Mutual Administrative Assistance in Tax Matters, which took effect in Switzerland on 1 January 2017.[35]

3.7 Registration condition

Para 3(1) sch 6 F(No.1)A 2010 provides:

> A body of persons or trust meets the registration condition if—
> (a) in the case of a body of persons or trust that is a charity within the meaning of section 10 of the Charities Act 2011, condition A is met, and
> (b) in the case of any other body of persons or trust, condition B is met.

We refer to **"registration conditions A and B"**.

This is required because a body which fails to register may still be a charity in the general law definition.

Section 10 CA 2011 provides the standard English charity law definition of charity with the exclusion of certain Church of England charities:

> (1) In the rest of this Act, "charity", except in so far as the context otherwise requires, has the meaning given by section 1(1).
> (2) But in the rest of this Act (apart from Chapter 3 of Part 17) "charity" is not applicable to—
> (a) any ecclesiastical corporation in respect of the corporate property of the corporation, except a corporation aggregate having some purposes which are not ecclesiastical in respect of its corporate property held for those purposes,

35 *http://www.oecd.org/ctp/exchange-of-tax-information/convention-on-mutual-administrative-assistance-in-tax-matters.htm*

(b) any Diocesan Board of Finance, or any subsidiary of such a Board, in respect of the diocesan glebe land of the diocese, or
(c) any trust of property for purposes for which the property has been consecrated.[36]

In short, English law charities must meet registration condition A (apart from certain Church of England charities).

3.7.1 *English charity*

Para 3(2) sch 6 F(No.1)A 2010 provides:

> Condition A is that the body of persons or trust has complied with any requirement to be registered in the register of charities kept under section 29 of the Charities Act 2011.

Section 29 CA 2011 explains what the register is:

> (1) There continues to be a register of charities, to be kept by the Commission in such manner as it thinks fit.
> (2) The register must contain—
> (a) the name of every charity registered in accordance with section 30, and
> (b) such other particulars of, and such other information relating to, every such charity as the Commission thinks fit.

What is needed to comply with "any requirement to be registered"? The answer must be found in the Charities Act.

The expression *"any* requirement" means "the requirement (if any)". If there is no requirement to register (eg in the case of an exempt charity) then the registration condition is met.[37]

What about a charity which is required to be registered? The wording of registration condition A does not mesh neatly with the wording of the Charities Act,[38] because the Act imposes two requirements relating to the register.

The first requirement is in s.30(1) CA 2011 which provides:

> Every charity must be registered in the register unless subsection (2)

36 Section 10(3)(4) contain definitions for the purpose of s.10(2) but that need not be considered here.

37 This is self-evident, but if authority is needed, see *Eynsham Cricket Club v HMRC* [2019] UKUT 47 (TCC) at [127].

38 No doubt due to the haste in which it was enacted; see 3.4.2 (F(No.1)A 2010: Critique).

applies to it.[39]

This is the duty of the Charity Commission (who keep the register).

The second requirement is in s.35(1) CA 2011 which provides:

> If a charity required to be registered by virtue of section 30(1) is not registered, the charity trustees must--
> (a) apply to the Commission for the charity to be registered, and
> (b) supply the Commission with the required documents and information.

This is the duty of the charity.

There are different possible views of the registration condition.

(1) The first view is that the requirement to which the registration condition refers is the requirement under s.35(1) to *apply* to be registered. On this view, once a charity has applied to the Charity Commission, the registration condition is met. The duty to make an entry on the register is a duty of the Charity Commission, not the charity.

(2) The second view is that the requirement to which the registration condition refers is the requirement under s.30(1) to *be* registered.

It cannot be correct that *no* relief ever applies before the actual date of registration. If one adopts the second view, the question whether the registration condition is satisfied should be decided when the claim for relief is decided. The condition need not be met in the year that the income or gains arise. In other words, registration operates retrospectively.

On this analysis, in most cases there is not a great deal of practical difference between the two views and it would not usually matter which is the better view.

HMRC (more or less) adopt the second view:

> On the new requirement to register then I assume you mean the registration condition at paragraph 3(2) of Schedule 6 to FA 2010 and whether that means that a charity is not entitled to tax reliefs in respect of income/donations etc arising/made before the charity was actually registered by the regulator. In general terms I do not think there is a problem here. The key point is that if it is required to be registered, then the charity must be registered at the time the relief is claimed. It is then possible to look back and give relief in respect of income/donations etc

39 Section 30(2) sets out the list of charities which do not have to register; this is not considered here.

> made before the charity was registered, provided there were no significant changes, such as an amendment to its founding document, between the date of donation etc and the date of registration.[40]

The context shows that a "significant change" is one which turns a non-charitable entity into a charitable one. The entity is not a tax charity during the non-charitable period, not because of the registration condition[41] but because of the charitable purposes condition. The HMRC statement continues:

> In other words, provided the charity:
> - met the definition of a charity in Schedule 6 to FA 2010, other than the registration condition, at the time of the donation etc; and
> - it is registered at the date of claim; and
> - it took steps to register with the regulator as soon as it became clear that it should be registered; and
> - all other conditions are met;
>
> then the claim will succeed.
>
> So in practical terms where there is a gap between a charity being formed and a charity regulator registering it does not mean the charity does not qualify for tax reliefs until the date of registration. The charity will need to take steps to register as soon as it becomes clear it should be registered and it therefore follows that if they don't then eligibility for reliefs will not necessarily follow. However we would consider a charity is complying with the registration condition when it starts the process of registration with, say, the Charity Commission. The Charities Act obliges the charity to register, and by applying for registration, it has started this process. As you suggest, HMRC would not seek to penalise the charity if the process of registration was unduly extended.
>
> For example if
>
> [1] a new charity was set up on 14 May 2010,
>
> [2] it applied to OSCR for registration on 20 June 2010 and
>
> [3] OSCR confirmed it had registered the charity on 18 August 2010.
>
> If all the other conditions were satisfied any income or gains arising after 14 May 2010 would qualify for tax relief but in practice HMRC would not be able to give the relief until after 18 August 2010.

The period before the charity made the application to be registered is in principle exempt, following registration, at least if the charity took prompt

40 Informally circulated correspondence.

41 A non-charitable entity is not required to register, so it meets the registration condition.

steps to register.

> On the other hand if
> [1] a new charity was set up on 14 May 2010,
> [2] it applied to OSCR[42] for registration on 20 June 2010 but OSCR would not register it due to a problem with its founding documents.
> [3] The charity amended the documents on 12 September and reapplied to OSCR who then confirmed it had registered the charity on 4 November 2010.
> In this case only income or gains arising after 12 September 2010, which was the date of the amendment to the governing document that put it into a form acceptable to OSCR, would be eligible for tax relief, subject to the other conditions being satisfied. Again in practice HMRC would not be able to give the relief until after 4 November 2010.

HMRC conclude with comments on students unions and churches:

> - For the Students' Unions, as it has been agreed with the Charity Commission that registration would be phased over time, then we would obviously need to accommodate that and unless it appeared that a particular Students' Union was unlikely to be registered we would allow relief to continue. In effect the Students Unions have started the registration process and simply agreed to extend it to help the phasing of the work.
> - For churches then again this seems to be a temporary problem and so long as the Church "took steps to register with the regulator as soon as it became clear that it should be registered" then relief would be given assuming all other conditions were met.[43]

The HMRC Guidance Note provides:

> 2.2.6 Once an organisation has registered with an appropriate regulator it can make an application to HMRC for recognition as a charity for tax purposes.

See 47.3 (Registration with HMRC).

HMRC will not consider the position until registration has been granted. This may be for one of two reasons:

(1) Prior to registration, HMRC may not be satisfied the body is a charity;

42 Authors' footnote: The fact that this example concerns a Scots law charity could complicate matters, due to differences in charity law; but it is not necessary to pursue that here.

43 Informally circulated correspondence.

or

(2) Prior to registration, the registration condition is not met (adopting the second of the two views considered above).

It is convenient for HMRC to defer consideration of a charity's tax status until registration. That may cause difficulties for the charity: registration often takes a considerable time. But a charity has no practical alternative but to wait for registration. In the meantime, a solution may sometimes be to make gifts to existing charities which then lend or give to the charity whose registration is pending.

3.7.2 *Date registration required*

Section 30 CA 2011 provides:

> (1) Every charity must be registered in the register unless subsection (2) applies to it.
> (2) The following are not required to be registered...[44]
> (d) a charity whose gross income[45] does not exceed £5,000.
> (3) A charity within ... (b) subsection (2)(d),
> must, if it so requests, be registered in the register.

In the absence of a Charity Commission direction under s.30(4)(b), an English law charity is not required to register in its first year, no matter how large its income, because in the previous year it had no income at all.

---

44 Exceptions (a) to (c) are not considered here. For completeness, they are:
(a) an exempt charity (see section 22 and Schedule 3),
(b) a charity which for the time being—
(i) is permanently or temporarily excepted by order of the Commission, and
(ii) complies with any conditions of the exception,
and whose gross income does not exceed £100,000,
(c) a charity which for the time being—
(i) is, or is of a description, permanently or temporarily excepted by regulations made by the Minister, and
(ii) complies with any conditions of the exception,
and whose gross income does not exceed £100,000.

45 Section 20(4) CA 2011 provides:
In this section any reference to a charity's gross income is to be read, in relation to a particular time—
(a) as a reference to the charity's gross income in its financial year immediately preceding that time, or
(b) if the Commission so determines, as a reference to the amount which the Commission estimates to be the likely amount of the charity's gross income in such financial year of the charity as is specified in the determination.

It would normally be wise to apply promptly for voluntary registration, if it is anticipated that income of the first year will exceed £5,000, rather than waiting until the second year when registration becomes compulsory.

3.7.3 *Registration of CIO*

Different registration rules apply to a CIO. A CIO is required to register even if it has income of less than £5k.[46] In practice small charities (income less than 5K) are likely to be unincorporated associations or trusts.

3.7.4 *Non-English charity*

Para 3(3) sch 6 F(No.1)A 2010 provides:

> Condition B is that the body of persons or trust has complied with any requirement under the law of a territory outside England and Wales to be registered in a register corresponding to that mentioned in sub-paragraph (2).

There are charity registers:
(1) in Scotland, administered by OSCR[47]
(2) in Northern Ireland, administered by CCNI[48]

These registers correspond to the English Charity Commission register, but there are some differences. For instance, these jurisdictions have no minimum income requirement so even the smallest charities must register. In England (in short) charities with income under £5,000 do not need to register though they may be registered if they wish.

The HMRC Guidance Note provides:

> 2.2.3 The Office of the Scottish Charity Regulator (OSCR) has responsibility for the regulation of charities in Scotland. All bodies wishing to act as charities in Scotland must register with OSCR....
> 2.2.4 The Charity Commission for Northern Ireland (CCNI) is responsible for the regulation of charities in Northern Ireland and began registering charities in December 2013. Charities in Northern Ireland must first register with CCNI before applying to HMRC....

Section 39 [Ireland] Charities Act 2009 establishes a charity register in

46 Reg 6 Charitable Incorporated Organisations (General) Regulations 2012.

47 *http://www.oscr.org.uk*

48 *http://www.charitycommissionni.org.uk/charity-search*
However the NI charity register is not yet complete.

Ireland.[49]

For elsewhere in the EU, the HMRC Guidance Note offers no guidance (presumably they do not know):

> 2.2.5 Other relevant countries (EU member states and those listed in regulations) may have their own charity regulators and it's the responsibility of the organisation to ascertain whether registration is required.

There are various surveys of European foundations which may offer a starting point for research; see the survey of literature in the Feasibility Study on a European Foundation Statute at p.48.[50] The Feasibility Study addresses the question whether foundations are required to register with a public authority, to which the answer is yes, in almost all jurisdictions.[51] However whether that involves a register corresponding to the register under the Charities Act 2011 would need further research. We would be interested to hear from readers with expertise in this area.

In the Netherlands, the Dutch Tax Authorities administer a public register for Algemeen Nut Beorgende Instelling (Public Benefit Organisations). This has been said to correspond to the English Charities Act register.

3.8 Management condition

Para 4(1) sch 6 F(No.1)A 2010 provides:

> A body of persons or trust meets the management condition if its managers are fit and proper persons to be managers of the body or trust.

HMRC have published:

- guidance on the fit and proper person test **("FPP guidance")**[52]
- summary guidance the **("FPP Helpsheet")**[53]

49 *https://www.charitiesregulator.ie/en/information-for-the-public/search-the-charities-register*

50 *https://lawlegal.eu/european-foundation-statute/#The_Feasibility_Study_on_a_European_Foundation_Statute_Comparative_overview*

51 At p.81.
The Liechtenstein *Stiftungsaufsichtsbehörde* (Foundation Supervisory Authority) supervises Liechtenstein charitable foundations; see *http://www.stifa.li/home-3/*

52 HMRC, "Guidance on the fit and proper persons test" (March 2017) *https://www.gov.uk/government/publications/charities-fit-and-proper-persons-test/guidance-on-the-fit-and-proper-persons-test*

53 *https://www.gov.uk/government/publications/charity-tax-relief-model-declaration*

- a model declaration (with the FPP Helpsheet)

3.9 "Managers"

The definition of "managers" is crucial. Para 4(2) sch 6 F(No.1)A 2010 provides:

> In this paragraph "managers", in relation to a body of persons or trust, means the persons having the general control and management of the administration of the body or trust.

This definition is taken from (what is now) s.177 CA 2011:

> In this Act, except in so far as the context otherwise requires, "charity trustees" means the persons having the general control and management of the administration of a charity.[54]

In the following discussion:
"Managers (for tax purposes)" means persons who are managers within the definition set out above.
"Charities-Act trustees" means persons who are "charity trustees" within the Charities Act definition.

Although the label is different, the content of the definition is the same and it is considered that anyone who is a Charities-Act trustee is a manager (for tax purposes), and vice versa.

HMRC do not agree:

> [1] The definition of a manager in paragraph 4 stands alone and should not be interpreted in the context of the Charities Act 1993.
> [2] If we had wanted to adopt the Charities Act definition we should have included a cross reference to that Act (for example there is a specific cross reference to the Charities Act 2006 in paragraph 1(4) of the Schedule, applying the Charities Act definition of charitable purpose to the new rules in Schedule 6).
> [3] We appreciate that this has the potential to cause confusion [!].[55]

As to [1], if parliament intended two definitions to have different meanings, it would be strange to define them in exactly the same words. It is true that in one case the label used is "charity trustees" and in the other case the label used is "managers" but that does not suggest that the definition is different: the drafter probably took the view that their

54 The same wording is found in s.106 Charities and Trustee Investment (Scotland) Act 2005; s.180 Charities Act (Northern Ireland) 2008.

55 Informally circulated correspondence.

terminology was an improvement as the term "trustees" is somewhat inapt when applied to a charity which may be a company or an unincorporated association.

The position would be different if there were anything in the context of the Charities Act or the F(No.2)A 2010 to suggest that the words of the definition did not carry their natural meaning, but that is not the case.

As to point [2], it is quite understandable to repeat verbatim the short definition of charity trustees but to incorporate by reference the lengthy definition of charitable purpose (any other course would have been bizarre).

Control and management of a charitable company normally subsists at shareholder level and at board level. In our view the relevant test here is control at board level. Thus the managers and the only managers are the trustees of a charitable trust, the directors of a charitable company, and the governing committee of a charitable unincorporated association.

The FPP guidance provides:

> This [definition of managers] can apply to
> [1] the trustees of charities,
> [2] directors of corporate charities,
> [3] directors of corporate trustees,
> [4] CASC officials, and
> [5] any other persons having general control and management over the running of the charity or the application of its assets.

[1] and [2] are not controversial.

Para [3] is not strictly correct (it involves piercing the corporate veil) but where the directors of a corporate trustee are not fit and proper, then the corporate trustee itself is not a fit and proper person, so it comes to the same thing. Likewise if the corporate trustee is beneficially owned (directly or indirectly) by a person who is not fit and proper, the trustee is not fit and proper, at least if the ultimate beneficial owner might exercise their power of control.

[4] and [5] are not controversial, though slightly vaguely expressed.

The FPP guidance continues:

> The term 'general control and management' has a wider scope than that found in the Charities Act 2011, which applies only to trustees of a charity.
> For example:
> [1] in a typical small local charity a manager for the purposes of the fit and proper persons test could include the Chairperson, Treasurer,

> Secretary and the rest of the management committee who would have control over expenditure

Point [1] would be correct if (as is perhaps assumed) the "typical small local charity" is an unincorporated association, since the members of the "management committee" would be Charities-Act trustees.

> [2] In a larger charity a manager, would include all trustees or directors of a corporate charity but may also extend to certain employees who are able to determine how a significant proportion of the charity's funds are spent.

Point [2] steps back from the first version of the FPP guidance (which said that anyone who could exert influence over a charity was a manager) but it is still wrong so far as it considers those who are not trustees (in the Charities Act sense) can be managers. If it were correct, "larger charities" (whatever that means) would not be able to identify who their managers are, because what is meant by a "significant proportion" is impossible to say.

> [3] Most large charities have a Board of Trustees and an Executive Board of senior employees. In such a case the trustees and members of the Executive Board would be managers of the charity.

Large UK charities no doubt usually have a Board of [Charities-Act] Trustees, as do all corporate charities, but we do not think it is usual to have a separate Executive Board of senior employees. Large charities may have a Chief Executive (who is typically an employee but not a member of the Board of Trustees) but a Chief Executive of that type would not be a manager for tax purposes. Para [3] makes same point as [2] and is equally doubtful.

3.9.1 *Manager: Financial responsibility*

The FPP guidance provides:

> **How HMRC applies discretion in practice**
> When considering the application of the fit and proper persons test to particular managers, HMRC takes account of the likely impact on the charity's tax position. The position that the person holds within the organisation is very important as those with greater control over how the charity tax reliefs are claimed, processed and used will clearly present a greater risk than those with no such control. As a result, the checks HMRC applies vary from case to case, depending on individual circumstances.

HMRC considers that any person who has no dealings with HMRC and no control over financial issues or spending charity funds, even if the person is not a fit and proper person, is unlikely to affect the charity's eligibility to tax reliefs and the charity is therefore likely to meet the management condition.

As an example, charities concerned with the rehabilitation of offenders may knowingly appoint ex-offenders to management positions within the charity. In such a case HMRC applies the fit and proper test flexibly:

- If a person might not be considered to be a fit and proper person but is not able to exert control over the charity's finances and tax affairs then HMRC will consider that the person can't affect the charitable purposes of the charity and the charity would be treated as meeting the management condition. For example this would happen if the person was on the management committee but not on the finance committee of the charity, had no access to charity funds and couldn't authorise expenditure without the approval of the full management committee and wasn't in a position to otherwise unduly influence financial decision making
- If the charity wishes to give the person some financial responsibility, such as making claims to tax relief on behalf of the charity then, provided the charity puts in place adequate controls, HMRC may accept the person as being a fit and proper person for the purposes of the management condition. However in such cases the charity should advise HMRC of the circumstances when they notify HMRC of the appointment. In appropriate cases HMRC will work with the charity in an attempt to ensure that eligibility for the charity tax reliefs continues.

3.10 Fit and proper

3.10.1 *"Fit and proper"*

"Fit and proper" is a vague test to be determined in the light of all the circumstances. It is impossible to define.

The FPP guidance provides:

> Examples of factors that may lead to HMRC deciding that a manager isn't a fit and proper person include, but aren't limited to, where individuals:
>
> [1] have been involved in tax fraud
>
> [2] have been involved in other fraudulent behaviour including misrepresentation and/or identity theft
>
> [3] are known by HMRC to have involvement in attacks against, or abuse of, tax repayment systems

[4] have been removed from acting as a charity trustee by a charity regulator or been disqualified from acting as a charity trustee or company director

[5] have used arrangements notified under the Disclosure of Tax Avoidance Schemes (DOTAS) rules in Part 7 Finance Act 2004 in respect of which a reference number has been issued under section 311 of Finance Act 2004, and the arrangements featured charitable reliefs or which used a charity, and their tax position has been adjusted by HMRC to wholly or partly remove the tax advantage generated by the arrangements and such adjustments have become final

[6] have used tax arrangements which have been successfully counteracted under the general anti-abuse rules (see Part 5 of Finance Act 2013 or section 10 National Insurance Contributions Act 2014, as enacted or as amended from time to time) and such counteraction has become final

[7] have been actively involved in designing and/or promoting tax avoidance schemes featuring charitable reliefs or which used a charity, and they are:

[a] a promoter named by HMRC under the Promoters of Tax Avoidance Schemes (POTAS) legislation in Part 5 of Finance Act 2014

[b] a promoter of any tax arrangements designed or intended to obtain for any person a tax advantage and such tax advantage has successfully counteracted by HMRC under the general anti-abuse rule (see Part 5 of Finance Act 2013 and section 10 National Insurance Contributions Act 2014 as enacted or as amended from time to time) and such counteraction has become final

[c] a promoter of arrangements notified under DOTAS, in respect of which a reference number has been issued under section 311 of Finance Act 2004, and the tax position of all or any of the users of the arrangements has been adjusted by HMRC to wholly or partly remove the tax advantage generated by the arrangements and such adjustments have become final

Factors [1] through [4] seem self-evident.

Factors [5] through [7] were inserted in 2017 replacing the previous individuals covered by tax avoidance.

The FPP guidance provides:

> For these purposes adjustments or counteraction becomes final when an appeal against such adjustments or counteraction is no longer possible.

For the purpose of this test an individual will not be considered to be actively involved in designing or promoting tax avoidance schemes merely because they work for or in the same organisation or partnership as an individual who has been actively designing or promoting schemes. However, just because a person has been, say, barred from acting as a charity trustee or one of the other points above applies, it doesn't follow that the charity will always fail the management condition. In all cases HMRC will consider all the relevant circumstances. For example if manager has used a tax avoidance scheme involving charitable tax reliefs HMRC will consider all the relevant circumstances such as the nature and size of the scheme, the extent of the manager's involvement and the likelihood of future participation in such schemes.

The Bank for International Settlements makes some general observations on the expression when used in a regulatory context:

Principal elements of fit and proper criteria

7. Fitness tests usually seek to assess the competence of managers and directors and their capacity to fulfil the responsibilities of their positions while propriety tests seek to assess their integrity and suitability. To determine competence, formal qualifications, previous experience and track record are some of the elements focussed on by supervisors. To assess integrity and suitability, elements considered include: criminal records, financial position, civil actions against individuals to pursue personal debts, refusal of admission to, or expulsion from, professional bodies, sanctions applied by regulators of other similar industries, and previous questionable business practices.

8. Factors relative to the assessment of the fitness, propriety or other qualifications of key shareholders include business repute and financial position, and whether such ownership would adversely affect the regulated entity.

9. It is recognised that in addition to the factors identified in the previous paragraphs, the assessment of fitness, propriety and other qualifications is a judgmental matter and that supervisors may have additional information at their disposal that they can consider on a case-by-case basis....

13. The application of fitness, propriety or other qualification tests to managers, directors and key shareholders may vary depending on the degree of their influence and on their responsibilities in the affairs of regulated entities. It is recognised that an individual considered fit for a particular position within an institution may not be considered fit for another position with different responsibilities or for a similar position within another institution, and conversely, an individual considered

> unfit for a particular position in a particular institution may be considered fit in different circumstances.
>
> 14. There are significant differences in legislative and regulatory frameworks across countries as regards the functions of the board of directors and senior management. In some countries, there is a two tier board system consisting of a supervisory board which has the main, if not exclusive, function of supervising the executive body (the management board) to ensure that the latter fulfils its tasks. This means that the board has no executive functions. In other countries, with a unitary board system, the board has a broader competence in that it lays down the general framework for the management of the institution. In this regard, fitness, propriety or other qualification tests should be applied to directors in light of their role and responsibilities.[56]

In *Hunt v HMRC*[57] the First-tier tribunal refused to register an individual under Money Laundering Regulations which contain a comparable FPP test. The taxpayer had been convicted of fraud. This was not, on its own, sufficient to bar him automatically from registration, but it was not a promising start. On the facts, HMRC were entitled to decide that he was not fit and proper.

3.10.2 *HMRC checks*

The FPP guidance provides:

> Where a charity is regulated by a charity regulator in its home country HMRC also takes into account the checks that the regulator has carried out on any managers, to ensure that checks are not duplicated.

The FPP guidance does not indicate what checks charity regulators carry out and we doubt if much is done. In England, the Charity Commission does not carry out routine checks on trustees, though they do say that they carry out annual checks on a random sample of trustees to establish that charities themselves have carried out trustee eligibility checks.

> However, if the person has not been subject to previous checks, or is based in a country where there is no other regulation of the organisation then, depending on the potential risks presented, the checks that HMRC carries out may need to be extensive. As a result such checks may take some time to complete.

56 Fit and Proper Principles Paper (February 1999) *http://www.bis.org/publ/bcbs34.pdf*

57 [2014] UKFTT 1094 (TC).

HMRC refer to "Checking against criminal databases and other sources of intelligence."[58]

3.10.3 *What should charity do*

Charities cannot ask HMRC for help. The FPP guidance provides:

> HMRC doesn't offer a clearance service for charities to confirm that particular managers are fit and proper persons.

That is understandable.

The FPP guidance provides:

> **Complying with the fit and proper persons test**
> HMRC assumes that trustees of a charity wouldn't knowingly appoint someone who wasn't a fit and proper person. HMRC's general presumption is that all managers are fit and proper persons and HMRC won't routinely ask charities to demonstrate that their managers are fit and proper persons. ...
> However, HMRC will expect charity trustees to be able to show, if asked, that they have given proper consideration to the suitability of people they appoint to positions of trust or influence in the charity, where they are able to exert control over the charity's finances and tax affairs.
> It's up to charities to decide how they will be able to demonstrate that they have given proper consideration to the suitability of managers, and that the managers are fit and proper persons.
> Some, but not all, charities will already have procedures in place, such as records of following up references for the person on their appointment. Charities may wish to devise their own procedures or, if they wish, they can follow the suggested procedure below.
> ***Suggested procedure for charities when they appoint new managers***
> **There is no statutory requirement for charities to follow this suggested procedure**[59] but asking managers to read the helpsheet[60] and sign a declaration based on the model declaration included in the helpsheet is one way the charity can demonstrate to HMRC that it has taken the necessary steps to reassure itself its managers are fit and proper.
> Using the helpsheet and model declaration in the way suggested will mean that a charity can assume that they meet the management condition

58 Impact Assessment of Extending Charity Tax Reliefs to Certain Organisations in Europe, 24 March 2010.

59 Bold text is original.

60 *https://www.gov.uk/government/publications/charity-tax-relief-model-declaration*

at all times unless

[a] they knowingly appoint a manager who isn't a fit and proper person to a position from which the person is able to influence the charitable purposes of the charity or the application of its funds[61] or,

[b] exceptionally, they are challenged by HMRC.

1. Charities should ask all newly appointed managers to read the helpsheet and sign a declaration based on the model declaration. ...

2. Assuming the manager signs the declaration then the charity should keep that declaration in case HMRC asks to see it. The declaration should be kept for the duration of the manager's engagement with the charity, and for 4 years after the manager has departed...

4. The charity can then assume that they meet the management condition unless HMRC contacts them

The FPP guidance then considers what to do if the manager qualifies the certificate but is unable to give any actual guidance:

> 5. If the manager refuses to sign the declaration (and refuses to comply with any other attempts by the charity to verify their suitability as a fit and proper person) then the charity should decide for themselves whether that person should be appointed as a manager of the charity and what financial responsibilities they should be given
>
> 6. If the person signs the declaration but adds additional information, the charity will need to consider that information and decide whether to seek advice from HMRC on what to do

3.10.4 *HMRC model declaration*

The HMRC Model Declaration for Fit and Proper Persons is set out at the end of the FPP helpsheet. It now provides:

> [1] I am not disqualified from acting as a charity trustee
>
> [2] I have not been convicted of an offence involving deception or dishonesty (or any such conviction is legally regarded as spent)
>
> [3] I have not been involved in tax fraud or other fraudulent behaviour including misrepresentation and/or identity theft
>
> [4] I have not used arrangements notified under the Disclosure of Tax Avoidance Schemes ("DOTAS") rules in Part 7 Finance Act 2004 in respect of which a reference number has been issued under section 311

61 Actually a manager by definition must have general control and management, which is a stronger requirement than ability to influence; the wording reflects the first version of the guidance where HMRC argued that anyone able to influence a charity was within the definition of "manager".

of Finance Act 2004, where the arrangements featured charitable reliefs or which used a charity, and where my tax position has been adjusted by HMRC to wholly or partly remove the tax advantage generated by the arrangements and such adjustments have become final.

[5] I have not used tax arrangements which have been successfully counteracted under the general anti-abuse rules (see Part 5 of Finance Act 2013 or section 10 National Insurance Contributions Act 2014, as enacted or as amended from time to time) where such counteraction has become final.

[6] I have not been actively involved in designing and/or promoting tax avoidance schemes featuring charitable reliefs or which used a charity, and I am not:

- [a] a promoter[62] named by HMRC under the Promoters of Tax Avoidance Schemes (POTAS) legislation in Part 5 of Finance Act 2014, or
- [b] a promoter of any tax arrangements designed or intended to obtain for any person a tax advantage and such tax advantage has successfully counteracted by HMRC under the general anti-abuse rule (see Part 5 of Finance Act 2013 and section 10 National Insurance Contributions Act 2014 as enacted or as amended from time to time) and such counteraction has become final, or
- [c] a promoter of arrangements notified under DOTAS, in respect of which a reference number has been issued under section 311 of Finance Act 2004, and the tax position of all or any of the users of the arrangements has been adjusted by HMRC to wholly or partly remove the tax advantage generated by the arrangements and such adjustments have become final

[7] I am not an undischarged bankrupt

[8] I have not made compositions or arrangements with my creditors from which I have not been discharged

[9] I have not been removed from serving as a charity trustee, or been stopped from acting in a management position within a charity

[10] I have not been disqualified from serving as a Company Director

[11] I will at all times seek to ensure the charity's funds, and charity tax reliefs received by this organisation, are used only for charitable purposes

62 [Footnote original] The meaning of a 'promoter' in this context is explained in the Promoters of Tax Avoidance Schemes guidance: *https://www.gov.uk/government/uploads/system/uploads/attachment_data/file/313987/Promoters_of_Tax_Avoidance_Schemes_Guidance_v1_0.pdf*

The drafter used (what is now) s.178 CA 2011 as a precedent, adding item [3] to [6] to reflect HMRC's special interests and item [11] as a catchall.

The drafter was perhaps unaware that the Charity Commission offer their own overlapping form which they recommend charities to use.[63] See the Charity Commission guidance CC30 "Finding New Trustees" section 5.2 (How should charities check on prospective trustees?).[64]

Should a charity choose one form or the other or both to be on the safe side? It is difficult to imagine that either form is likely to do much good though neither can do any harm. While it might be best practice for a charity to complete both forms, failure to do so should not by itself matter.

In Scotland, OSCR do not provide a similar form, but recommend that "prospective charity trustees sign a declaration before their election or appointment to confirm they are not disqualified from acting as a charity trustee."[65]

A person who has committed some tax offence or perceived misdemeanour in the distant past may be in some difficulty here.

Disclosure to the charity will be embarrassing. On the other hand it is absurd if someone convicted of an offence can ignore it once the relevant period has elapsed, under the Rehabilitation of Offenders Act, but someone not convicted has no such protection.

The HMRC form also asks the individual signing to supply:

- Previous address if moved in past 12 months
- Date of birth
- National Insurance number
- National Identity Card Number (if you have one)

The first three of these are unnecessarily intrusive; the National Identity Card scheme was scrapped in 2011 and the government destroyed the personal details of everyone who had an identity card.[66] It is suggested that trustees should not be asked for any of this (though some of the data will be needed for a charitable company's register of directors).

63 Declaration of eligibility *https://www.gov.uk/government/publications/confirmation-of-charity-trustee-eligibility*
This form is not compulsory and we wonder how much it is used in practice.

64 (2018) *https://www.gov.uk/government/publications/finding-new-trustees-cc30*

65 OSCR, "Guidance and Good Practice for Charity Trustees" *https://www.oscr.org.uk/media/2728/v10_guidance-and-good-practice-for-charity-trustees.pdf*

66 *https://www.gov.uk/identitycards*

3.10.5 *Tax avoidance behaviour*

A person may also be in difficulty if they fall within [5] through [7]:

> [5] have used arrangements notified under the Disclosure of Tax Avoidance Schemes (DOTAS) rules in Part 7 Finance Act 2004 in respect of which a reference number has been issued under section 311 of Finance Act 2004, and the arrangements featured charitable reliefs or which used a charity, and their tax position has been adjusted by HMRC to wholly or partly remove the tax advantage generated by the arrangements and such adjustments have become final
>
> [6] have used tax arrangements which have been successfully counteracted under the general anti-abuse rules (see Part 5 of Finance Act 2013 or section 10 National Insurance Contributions Act 2014, as enacted or as amended from time to time) and such counteraction has become final
>
> [7] have been actively involved in designing and/or promoting tax avoidance schemes featuring charitable reliefs or which used a charity, and they are:
>
> > [a]a promoter named by HMRC under the Promoters of Tax Avoidance Schemes (POTAS) legislation in Part 5 of Finance Act 2014
> >
> > [b] a promoter of any tax arrangements designed or intended to obtain for any person a tax advantage and such tax advantage has successfully counteracted by HMRC under the general anti-abuse rule (see Part 5 of Finance Act 2013 and section 10 National Insurance Contributions Act 2014 as enacted or as amended from time to time) and such counteraction has become final
> >
> > [c] a promoter of arrangements notified under DOTAS, in respect of which a reference number has been issued under section 311 of Finance Act 2004, and the tax position of all or any of the users of the arrangements has been adjusted by HMRC to wholly or partly remove the tax advantage generated by the arrangements and such adjustments have become final

The FPP guidance goes on to define tax avoidance in this context:

> Tax avoidance is an attempt to exploit legislation to gain a tax advantage that Parliament never intended. This often involves contrived or artificial transactions that serve little or no purpose other than to produce a tax advantage. However, tax avoidance is not the same as tax planning, which involves applying tax legislation in the way it was intended - for example making a donation to charity under Gift Aid.

While such actions may reduce the total amount of tax paid, they are not tax avoidance, because they involve using tax reliefs in the way that Parliament intended when it passed the relevant legislation.

...

To encourage charitable endeavour the government allows charities a number of valuable tax reliefs. Using these in the ways intended is tax planning. For example:

- encouraging eligible donors to use Gift Aid when making cash donations to charity
- giving advice on legacy gifts to charity in a will that will attract tax relief from Inheritance Tax
- encouraging higher rate tax payers to claim the higher/additional rate relief (the difference between their marginal rate tax and the basic rate of tax) on their cash donation and adjust the amount they donate to charity as a result of the overall cost to them of the donation being lower

3.10.6 *Waiver of management condition*

Para 5 sch 6 F(No.1)A 2010 confers power on HMRC to waive the management condition:

> (1) This paragraph applies in relation to any period throughout which the management condition is not met.
> (2) The management condition is treated as met throughout the period if HMRC consider that—
> (a) the failure to meet the management condition has not prejudiced the charitable purposes of the body or trust, or
> (b) it is just and reasonable in all the circumstances for the condition to be treated as met throughout the period.

EN FB 2010 para 43 provides:

> For example, some charities appoint ex-offenders to positions of trust within a charity. If the ex-offender is not involved in the financial administration of the charity then sub-paragraph (2)(a) may apply and the charity may be treated as meeting the management condition...

The FPP guidance provides:

> **When it may be reasonable to treat the management condition as being met**
> Where a charity unknowingly appoints a person who isn't a fit and proper person to a position where they have dealings with HMRC, or control over spending charity funds, the charity won't necessarily lose

access to charity tax reliefs.

For example, if HMRC identified a manager who wasn't a fit and proper person to hold a position giving them influence over the finances of the charity, and the charity does either of the following:

- moves that person from that role to, say, another role where they wouldn't have influence; or
- puts in place close supervision of the person's activities in relation to their financial activities on behalf of the charity

then HMRC has the discretion to treat the charity as having met the management condition throughout the period of the manager being in office. As a result the charity won't lose its entitlement to the charity tax reliefs during that period. However, if a charity doesn't amend its organisation in response to an approach from HMRC then HMRC may refuse the charity's claims to reliefs.

If a charity has unknowingly appointed a manager who isn't a fit and proper person, and that person has misapplied some of the charity's funds without the charity's knowledge, the charity won't necessarily be denied charity tax reliefs and exemptions. Where the charity can demonstrate that it had taken reasonable steps and wasn't party to the misapplication of funds then HMRC will work with the charity in an attempt to correct the position.

3.10.7 *Administration*

EN FB 2010 provides:

> A charity may challenge a decision by the Commissioners for HMRC not to apply paragraph 5 by appealing against the refusal of a claim to a tax Tribunal.

The question arises whether the Tribunal decide for themselves whether the individual is fit and proper or whether the test is merely one of judicial review (whether HMRC are reasonably entitled to form their view). The former must surely be correct, for if the law is the latter, then the law is essentially that charity tax relief is available "if and only if HMRC like you" and very clear wording would be required to have such a result.

The FPP guidance provides:

> HMRC takes the view that charities will have given proper consideration to the suitability of their managers to act in such capacity, and that consequently those managers are normally fit and proper persons. However, where HMRC becomes aware of information that suggests that a charity's managers aren't fit and proper persons, HMRC will normally raise its concerns with the manager initially and later, if

> appropriate, with the charity. This will be the case even if the charity regulator hasn't identified the manager as not being a fit and proper person. HMRC may become aware of such information either from information that it already holds or that is passed to it. For example, HMRC may be aware that a certain individual has been involved in fraudulently claiming tax credits. If that same individual appointed to the management committee of a small local charity, HMRC would want to explore the extent to which that individual was able to exert control over the charity's finances and tax affairs.

The FPP guidance provides:

> **If a manager isn't considered a fit and proper person**
> HMRC would always encourage a person who is appointed as a manager of a charity to be open and honest with the charity to prevent problems arising.

Unfortunately for the person applying to be a manager, the charity would usually avoid hassle and prevent problems arising by looking for other applicants.

> If the charity knows a person may fail the fit and proper persons test they can seek early advice from HMRC about what to do to prevent any loss of tax reliefs.
> Where the charity hasn't already approached HMRC but HMRC is concerned that a manager may not be a fit and proper person HMRC will normally notify that person of the grounds for concern and give them the opportunity to challenge HMRC's view. The person may wish to include the charity in the discussions but there is no obligation to do so.
> If following the discussions HMRC continues to consider the person isn't a fit and proper person, and also considers that it wouldn't be appropriate to exercise its discretion in relation to the management condition, HMRC will notify the person in writing of their decision.

The first version of the guidance stated at this point:

> There is no direct right of appeal by a person against HMRC's decision that they are not a fit and proper person.

This was (and still is) correct, but following protests by charities the sentence was omitted from the guidance. Instead it provides:

> If the person is dissatisfied with HMRC's decision that they are not a fit and proper person they can ask for that decision to be reviewed by a senior manager in HMRC Charities. The person should write to:
> Charities, Savings and International 2

> HM Revenue and Customs
> BX9 1BU
> Which senior manager reviews the case will depend on who in HMRC took the decision the person wasn't 'fit and proper'. The decision would normally (!) be reviewed by a manager not involved in the original decision.
> If the reviewing manager considers the original decision was correct and the person is still dissatisfied with the decision that they aren't a fit and proper person they can ask for that decision to be reviewed again by the Head of HMRC Charities. The person should write to the Head of HMRC Charities, at the address shown above.
> If the Head of HMRC Charities upholds the decision and the person is still dissatisfied then they can ask the Adjudicator to look into the case. The Adjudicator is a fair and unbiased referee, and the service is free.[67]

The Adjudicator is no doubt fair and unbiased, but it is misleading to call her a "referee". The Adjudicator's role is not to consider whether HMRC have made the right decision, but whether they have made a reasonable decision, which is a different matter.

The FPP guidance continues:

> **What happens to the charity if a person is not fit and proper**
> Where HMRC has found someone isn't a fit and proper person then, as explained above, HMRC will normally advise the person of its decision and the person may ask for that decision to be reviewed. If, after those reviews, HMRC still considers the person isn't fit and proper HMRC will normally ask them if they intend remaining as a manager of the charity. If the person stands down as a manager HMRC won't normally inform the charity; however, if they remain as a manager HMRC will notify the charity that it considers that the manager is not a fit and proper person, if the charity is not already aware. HMRC isn't normally able to disclose specific concerns about the person to the charity without the person's permission but they will need to explain that, because the manager isn't a fit and proper person, the management condition isn't met and so tax relief may not be given.

The confidentiality issues are not easy. The unfitness is the unfitness of the manager, but the tax liability is that of the charity or the donor to charity who seeks charity tax relief. One point is clear. Only in a totalitarian state could an official say to a taxpayer (charity or donor) that

67 The text continues with a description of the Adjudicator's procedures not set out here.

it must pay tax, or sack an employee, for reasons that it is not prepared to inform the taxpayer. In practice a tribunal should order disclosure to the charity or donor concerned (if appropriate on confidential terms) because otherwise a fair trial of the tax dispute cannot take place.[68]

> HMRC will also, where appropriate, advise the charity what it must do, and by when, if HMRC is to apply its discretion to treat the charity as having met the management condition throughout the period of the person's term in office. For instance, the conditions may require the charity to move the manager from a particular role within a specified period or ensure that person has no access to, or control of, charity funds or put in place close supervision of the person's activities.

The earlier version of the guidance was brutal but more honest:

> *For instance, the conditions may require the charity to remove the manager within a specified period.*

In practice a charity would generally have to sack an employee who HMRC identify as not fit and proper (though employment law considerations may make this expensive) and certainly no such person could expect to find employment in the charitable sector.

> [1] A charity's tax reliefs and exemptions won't normally be withdrawn during an enquiry into whether it meets the management condition.
> [2] HMRC may however decide not to make repayments of tax during an enquiry, depending on the circumstances.

There seems to be a contradiction between these two sentences but perhaps the point is that the reliefs will not be withdrawn, but merely suspended pending investigation.

> Where the management condition is found to be satisfied, or HMRC treats the management condition as being met, throughout the period then the charity will qualify for tax reliefs and exemptions throughout the period. HMRC will make any outstanding repayments at the conclusion of that enquiry.
> If, in exceptional cases, the charity doesn't make any changes HMRC may reject the charity's claim to tax relief. The charity would have a right of appeal through the normal procedures, either by way of appealing against HMRC's refusal of the claim or against an amended assessment to tax, depending on whether the claim to relief was included

68 *WEA Records v Visions Channel 4* [1983] 1 WLR 721 at 724G, 726G, 728D; *Mantovanelli v France* 24 EHRR 370.

in a tax return.

It is interesting to compare the lack of appeal with the provisions for appealing against HMRC's determination that a pensions administrator is not a fit and proper person. This is not the place for a detailed consideration of the legislation, but HMRC's Guidance[69] is instructive:

> **What if I don't agree with HMRC?**
> *Appeals and penalties - registration*
> If HMRC decides not to register a scheme for any reason, including because we do not believe you are a fit and proper person to be the scheme administrator, you can appeal within 30 days of being notified of the decision. [Section 156 FA04]...
> *Appeals and penalties – de-registration*
> If HMRC decides to de-register an existing scheme for any reason including because we do not believe you are a fit and proper person to be the scheme administrator, you can appeal within 30 days of being notified of the decision. [Section 159 FA04]

3.10.8 *Human rights*

Article 6(1) ECHR provides:

> In the determination of his civil rights and obligations ... everyone is entitled to a fair and public hearing within a reasonable time by an independent and impartial tribunal established by law.[70]

The determination that a person is not fit and proper is a determination of their civil rights since it effectively determines whether they are able to act as a charity manager. The determination procedure does meet the requirements of article 6. The adjudicator is not a tribunal and the adjudicator's review does not constitute a fair or a public hearing.

HMRC senior staff no doubt take the view that they can be trusted to use their draconian powers wisely. It makes no difference to the Human Rights argument, but it is worth noting that this confidence is not widely held within HMRC. Only 30% of its staff agreed with the statement that "Overall, I have confidence in the decisions made by HMRC's senior managers".[71]

---

69 *http://www.hmrc.gov.uk/pensionschemes/fitproper-guidance.pdf*

70 Similarly article 47 EU Charter of Fundamental Rights.

71 2016 survey report for HMRC (based on 45, 259 Returns, Response rate: 69%) *https://www.gov.uk/government/uploads/system/uploads/attachment_data/file/575526/HM_Revenue_and_Customs_-_Civil_Service_People_Survey_2016.pdf*

However that may be, the law is not human rights compliant. The point should be raised in any case where a charity manager wishes to dispute a suggestion by HMRC that they are not a fit and proper person, and the authors would be willing to act *pro bono* in an appropriate case.

3.10.9 *Validity of appointment*

An appointment of a trustee of a charitable trust who is not a fit and proper person might be held invalid under the rule in *Pitt v Holt* [2013] UKSC 26, if the appointors were mistaken as to the implications of appointing the new trustee.

3.10.10 *Management condition: Critique*

While no-one would deny that charity managers should be fit and proper persons, there are grave objections to the management condition.

1. It is vague. It gives HMRC a discretion who can and who cannot be a charity trustee. This allows them to attack more or less any charity with a manager that they do not like, eg one who has or has had a revenue investigation.

HMRC response to complaints of vagueness is to provide guidance. Guidance is not a satisfactory answer to this problem: it is and must necessarily be vague and in most respects non-binding. Also it has been issued without any parliamentary oversight or even consultation.

The power to waive the management condition is not a satisfactory answer.

The management condition is a tax equivalent of the former Sus law: power to impose tax (or disapply a tax exemption) by suspicion alone is as objectionable as power to search and arrest by suspicion alone.

2. The penalty for having a manager who is not a fit and proper person is loss of all tax relief, which is disproportionate.

3. The problem which this provision seeks to address is primarily dealt with by the charitable expenditure rules, in short, that all income and gains must be applied for charitable purposes only. If the income and gains are so applied, then relief should be available whether or not the trustees include a person not fit and proper. If they are not, then tax relief is not available.

4. The tax consequences of a charity appointing an unfit person (or a fit person becoming unfit) have not been thought through. Would CGT and

IHT exit charges apply?

5. The public cannot know whether a charity has "fit and proper" managers. Eg, if an individual makes a gift to a foreign church (let us assume in principle a charity) must they review the status of the trustees before assuming that they qualify for Gift Aid relief, and how could they do so?

6. There is no remedy for a person if HMRC determine that they are or may not be fit and proper (one can hardly expect a charity to appoint such a person trustee if there is any doubt) and the confidentiality problems are severe. The charity may not want to - indeed it would generally be improper - to use its resources to clear an individual's name. Suppose HMRC say that it won't withhold a charity's tax relief as long as the individual steps down as a Trustee. It is not in the charity's interest to fight the claim but the individual's reputation is ruined - effectively they are disqualified from acting as a charity trustee. Directors of companies cannot be disqualified in this arbitrary fashion. The law is not human rights compliant.[72]

7. The rule is a breach of Hampton principles,[73] since it is essentially a matter of charity regulation. That ought (at least for UK charities) to fall within the remit of the Charity Commission, (or CCNI or OSCR) firstly to avoid duplication and secondly as charity regulation is a task for which the Charity Commission are better qualified than HMRC to carry out.

This provision is intended to address fraudulent charities making false claims, which is a serious concern, but there are other solutions to the problem which do not confer wide powers on HMRC and which may in fact offer better protections against fraud. One is to apply the objective

---

72 Contrast the criticisms made of senior accounting officer regime, *Thathiah v HMRC* [2017] UKFTT 601 (TC) at [76].

73 Hampton, *Reducing administrative burdens: effective inspection and enforcement,* (2000) *https://webarchive.nationalarchives.gov.uk/20090609014248/http://www.berr.gov.uk/files/file22988.pdf* The principles include:

- Businesses should not have to give unnecessary information, nor give the same piece of information twice;
- When new policies are being developed, explicit consideration should be given to how they can be enforced using existing systems and data to minimise the administrative burden imposed;
- Regulators should be of the right size and scope, and no new regulator should be created where an existing one can do the work.

rules of s.178 CA 2011. Another is the route of s.93 FA 2009 (senior accounting officers of qualifying companies). A third is the rules (such as are found in VAT) requiring security or suspending relief pending introduction of procedures to prevent fraud.

The most serious problems relate to Gift Aid repayment claims, which can also be mitigated by shifting to or towards a deduction system of relief.[74] The Irish system whereby a charity must be in existence for two years before submitting repayment claims is also an interesting weapon in the battle against fraud.

The reader may think it is unfortunate that there was no opportunity to consider these points between the publication of the Finance Bill 2010 on 1st April 2010 and its enactment on 8th April.

HMRC reported on their use of the fit and proper person test in 2013:

> HMRC have identified around 200 cases in which they questioned if the managers are 'fit and proper', refusing to recognise a charity for tax purposes or pay a Gift Aid claim until the charities answer relevant questions. None of the charities concerned have done so.[75]

The fit and proper person test is used as a simple means of challenging fraudulent charities but it should not be needed for that purpose.

This view is evidently not shared by HMRC, as a similar rule has subsequently been adopted in pension taxation. HMRC may refuse to register a pension scheme if (in short) the scheme administrator is not a fit and proper person to be a scheme administrator.[76] It is possible that case law or other developments in that area may have some relevance for taxation.

3.10.11 *Trustee disqualification*

Section 181A CA 2011 (inserted by the Charities (Protection and Social Investment) Act 2016) gives the Charity Commission power to disqualify charity trustees.

Section 118A(6) CA 2011 provides:

> The Commission may make an order disqualifying a person under this section only if it is satisfied that—
>
> (a) one or more of the conditions listed in subsection (7) are met in

74 See 15.50 (Gift Aid: Critique).

75 National Audit Office "Gift Aid and reliefs on donations" (2013) para 2.15 *http://www.nao.org.uk/wp-content/uploads/2013/11/10302-001-Gift-Aid-Book1.pdf*

76 Section 153 FA 2004, as amended in 2014.

relation to the person,

(b) the person is unfit to be a charity trustee or trustee for a charity (either generally or in relation to the charities or classes of charity specified or described in the order), and

(c) making the order is desirable in the public interest in order to protect public trust and confidence in charities generally or in the charities or classes of charity specified or described in the order.

The conditions in (7) are wide, including:

C that the person has been found by HMRC not to be a fit and proper person to be a manager of a body or trust, for the purposes of paragraph 4 of Schedule 6 to the FA 2010 (definition of charity for tax purposes), and the finding has not been overturned.

F that any other past or continuing conduct by the person, whether or not in relation to a charity, is damaging or likely to be damaging to public trust and confidence in charities generally or in the charities or classes of charity specified or described in the order.

It is not sufficient to meet the conditions in (7): the person must also be unfit to be a trustee. But a finding by HMRC that a person fails the FPP test is likely to lead to disqualification proceedings.

3.11 Recognised foreign charity

3.11.1 *Published list*

Para 6 sch 6 F(No.1)A 2010 provides:

> HMRC may publish the name and address of any body of persons or trust that appears to them to meet, or at any time to have met, the definition of a charity in paragraph 1.

The HMRC list could not be relied on because it would not bind HMRC. EN FB 2010 provides:

> Paragraph 6 allows HMRC to publish a list of the names and addresses of organisations that have claimed, and appear to be eligible to, charitable tax reliefs. The list would be a guide only to an organisation's eligibility, which may change from time to time, depending upon whether it meets all the conditions in paragraph 1 at any given time. The omission of an organisation will not necessarily signify that the organisation is not eligible to charitable tax reliefs; it is possible that an organisation that is eligible for charitable tax reliefs will not have made a claim for relief or exemption from tax to HMRC.

In practice no list has been published. Para 6 ought to be repealed.

3.11.2 *Unpublished list*

In practice it has proved difficult for foreign charities to be accepted as charities by HMRC. In a Freedom of Information request in 2019, HMRC stated that 167 overseas organisations had applied to HMRC for recognition as charities for tax purposes since 2010, but only 25 of these had been successful.[77]

3.12 UK/foreign tax relief on disposition

An intriguing possibility arising from the new law is that gifts to charity may qualify for double reliefs, both UK and foreign charity tax reliefs. Sometimes this will be right. Suppose an Irish resident and domiciled individual (within the scope of Irish CAT (gift tax)) makes a gift of UK land to an Irish or a UK charity. Obviously the gift ought to qualify for IHT charity relief and for CAT charity relief. Sometimes however this may seem unduly generous. Suppose the same person had UK and Irish source income and made a gift of cash to charity. Could the gift qualify for Gift Aid relief in the UK and any Irish equivalent? It will be necessary to consider this in the context of the rules of all 27 EU states (and Iceland, Norway and Liechtenstein).

3.13 The future

Para 29(1) sch 6 F(No.1)A 2010 provides:

> HMRC may by order make such further consequential, incidental, supplemental, transitional or transitory provision or saving as appears appropriate in consequence of, or otherwise in connection with, Part 1.

This confers power on HMRC to deal with errors and afterthoughts. In the 2013 edition of this work we said:

> When the issues come to be examined properly, it should become apparent that the extension of charity reliefs to EU charities will require a wholesale review and amendment of the current law. Primary legislation will be needed. Major changes should be anticipated in a few years time.

But this did not happen, and maybe we will continue to muddle through.

77 Private correspondence.

3.14 Foreign charitable objects

An institution may be a charity (under the English/Scots/Northern Ireland and tax definitions) even though its objects are outside the UK and outside the EU.[78] For instance, the relief of poverty in Africa is a charitable purpose, even though no person in the UK may benefit directly. Such charities qualify for the same[79] tax relief as charities whose objects relate to the UK.

Some countries, mostly but not exclusively less economically developed countries, take a different view on this policy issue.[80] There are however powerful arguments in favour of the current UK rules:

(1) There may be important indirect benefits to the UK. Leaving aside reputational benefits, charity giving can help address cross-border problems such as health pandemics, nonstate terrorism, ecological

---

78 *McGovern v AG* [1992] Ch 321 at p.327: "The mere fact that the trust was intended to be carried out abroad would not by itself necessarily deprive it of charitable status." Likewise *Routier v HMRC* [2016] EWCA Civ 938 at [14]: "it matters not that those [charitable] purposes are to be carried out outside the United Kingdom."

79 For one anti-avoidance provision see 6.6 (Foreign body rule).

80 We are not in a position to draw up a full list, but this includes the following countries:

Hong Kong: Section 88 [Hong Kong] Inland Revenue Ordinance restricts charity relief if the profits are expended substantially outside Hong Kong: see Hong Kong Revenue, "Tax Information: Charitable Donations and Tax-Exempt Charities: A Tax Guide for Charitable Institutions and Trusts of a Public Character" *http://www.ird.gov.hk/eng/tax/ach_tgc.htm*

India: Section 11 [India] Income Tax Act 1961 generally restricts Indian charity tax exemption to purposes in India; there is also an exemption for charitable purposes "which tends to promote international welfare in which India is interested" even though the income is applied to purposes outside India, which perhaps illustrates the difficulty of drawing strict geographic restrictions. An updated version of the Indian ITA is available at *https://indiankanoon.org/doc/789969/*

Australia: section 50-5 of the [Australia] Income Tax Assessment Act 1997 restricts Australian charity tax relief (broadly) to charities which incur expenditure and pursue objectives principally in Australia.

New Zealand: Section CW 42 [New Zealand] Income Tax Act 2007 restricts exemption for business income to charities which carry out their charitable purposes in New Zealand.

Singapore: Regulation 3(1)(c) [Singapore] Charities (Registration of Charities) Regulations requires registered charities (which qualify for tax relief) to have purposes which are "beneficial wholly or substantially to the community in Singapore". The Minister has power to waive that requirement.

disasters, and refugees.[81]

(2) There may be mutual benefits from other countries which take the same policy approach. Thus the UK may not benefit much if at all from UK tax relief for, say, gifts to charities in the form of "friends of American universities" or similar charities. However the UK does benefit correspondingly if US taxpayers likewise give to "American friends" of UK universities or similar charities.[82] This benefit may arise even in the absence of formal treaties or mutual agreements.

The IHT Manual provides:

> **IHTM11128. Procedure: beneficiaries outside the UK** [March 2022]
> The primary purpose of some large, well-known, qualifying charities such as Oxfam and Christian Aid is the relief of poverty and humanitarian aid, internationally. This does not prevent a gift to such a charity (IHTM11112) being exempt, even if it is stated that the gift is for the work of the charity in a specific foreign country that is not in the European Union (EU) or is not a specified country (IHTM11116).
> **Example**
> A legacy of £10,000 to Oxford Famine Relief (better known as 'Oxfam') absolutely for the charity's work in Ethiopia. The legacy is exempt under IHTA84/S23 (1). If the charity exemption is sought for property held on trust for charitable purposes which include bodies or objects outside the UK EU or other specified country you should refer the case to Technical.

The IHT Manual also provides:

> **IHTM11132. Procedure: the Charities Aid Foundation** [March 2022]
> The Charities Aid Foundation is an organisation which, as well as managing other charities, is also a charity in its own right (IHTM11112). A bequest to the Foundation which is not conditional or was accompanied merely by a wish that it be used in a certain way will be exempt. But, if the bequest is accompanied by a direction that it is to be used for purposes outside the EU or other specified country, you should refuse the exemption.
> You should refer any similar case relating to other charities to

81 The White Paper on International Development (2009) notes this point: "Poverty breeds extremism, incubates disease and drives migration and conflict. Instability around the world threatens us all".

82 There is also the special case of UK resident US citizens, who are within both tax regimes and may need both sets of reliefs for a single gift.

Technical.

Where a gift to charity is accompanied by a direction that the funds be used for non-charitable purposes, charity relief does not apply. However, a direction to use funds for "purposes outside the UK" may be a charitable purpose and may qualify for relief. The author of the Manual does not, we think, mean to say otherwise. The point is that these cases are thought to need investigation, and relief should not be granted until that has been done.

3.14.1 *"Friends" of foreign charity*

Where a direct gift to a foreign charity does not qualify for relief, an arrangement may be made under which:
(1) A gift is made to a UK charity the ("intermediary")
(2) The UK charity makes a grant to the foreign charity.

A number of questions arise:
(1) Does the intermediary qualify as a charity within the tax definition
(2) Charity law requirements the intermediary must satisfy to properly make the payment
(3) Tax issues:
  (a) Whether the gift to the intermediary qualifies for tax relief
  (b) Whether the intermediary qualifies for relief on its income (does it apply its income for charitable purposes only)

Whether or not the intermediary actually qualifies as a charity within the tax definition depends on the documentation and facts. Additionally, the intermediary must comply with its duty to take reasonable care.[83] But subject to that, HMRC regard this arrangement as acceptable.[84]

EU charities may in the past have set up UK associated charities in order to qualify for UK tax reliefs. If the EU charity qualifies as a charity within the tax definition, these are not now needed, so far as tax is concerned, and if there is no other need for them, they could be allowed to become dormant.[85] We suspect that it may often be easier to retain a UK charity or to set up a new one, rather than go through the hoops for an EU charity to qualify for UK tax relief.

83 See 6.6 (Foreign body rule).
84 See 7.18.1 (Applied for charitable purposes).
85 But not wound up, as then legacies to the charities might lapse.

3.15 Scots law definition of charity

3.15.1 *English/Scots definition compared*

Section 7 CTISA 2005 contains a "charity test" . This is expressed to apply for the purposes of the CTISA 2005, but is incorporated by reference in other contexts, such as LBTT, so it may be taken as the general definition of charity for the purposes of Scots law.

The definition is very similar to the English law definition of charity, but not identical. It was in fact intended that the definitions should be the same, and the Scottish definition was based on the draft English Charities Act.[86] Unfortunately the English Act was subsequently amended.

The differences include the following:[87]

(1) CA 2011 speaks of the "advancement of amateur sport", whereas CTISA speaks of the "advancement of public participation in sport".

(2) CTISA includes the "provision of recreational activities" which s.5 CA 2011 expresses slightly differently.

(3) CA 2011 includes the "promotion of the efficiency of the armed forces of the Crown, or of the efficiency of the police, fire and rescue services or ambulance services" which CTISA does not.

(4) Section 7(4) CTISA 2005 provides:

> A body which falls within paragraphs (a) and (b) of subsection (1) does not, despite that subsection, meet the charity test if—
>
> (a) its constitution allows it to distribute or otherwise apply any of its property (on being wound up or at any other time) for a purpose which is not a charitable purpose,
>
> (b) its constitution expressly permits the Scottish Ministers or a Minister of the Crown to direct or otherwise control its activities, or
>
> (c) it is, or one of its purposes is to advance, a political party.

But English law has similar rules, even if not expressed in the statute.

(5) There are differences in the wording of the public benefit test.[88] In particular, the Scots definition is not tied to case law, and states expressly that "unduly restrictive" charges or fees can fail the test.

---

86 Scottish Executive, *Draft Charities and Trustee Investments (Scotland) Bill: Consultation* (2004) para p.8 *http://www.scotland.gov.uk/Resource/Doc/47251/0030333.pdf*

87 Serving Scotland Better: Scotland and the UK in the 21st Century - Final Report (2009).

88 Section 8 CTISA 2005.

The CA 2011 definition of charitable purposes applies for the purposes of the tax definition of charity, even in the case of a Scottish charity.[89] Section 7 Charities Act 2011 provides:

> (1) This Chapter [ss.1 - 9 CA 2011] affects the law of Scotland only in so far as it affects the construction of references to—
> (a) charities, or
> (b) charitable purposes,
> in enactments which relate to matters falling within Section A1 of Part 2 of Schedule 5 to the Scotland Act 1998 (reserved matters: fiscal policy etc.).
> (2) In so far as this Chapter affects the law of Scotland—
> (a) references in sections 1(1) and 2(1) to the law of England and Wales are to be read as references to the law of Scotland, and
> (b) the reference in section 1(1) to the High Court is to be read as a reference to the Court of Session.

Amended as directed, s.1 and s.2 CA 2011 provide for UK tax purposes as follows:

> **1 Meaning of "charity"**
> (1) For the purposes of the law of ~~England and Wales~~ Scotland, "charity" means an institution which--
> (a) is established for charitable purposes only, and
> (b) falls to be subject to the control of the ~~High Court~~ Court of Session in the exercise of its jurisdiction with respect to charities...
> **2 Meaning of "charitable purpose"**
> (1) For the purposes of the law of ~~England and Wales~~ Scotland, a charitable purpose is a purpose which--
> (a) falls within section 3(1), and
> (b) is for the public benefit (see section 4).
> (2) Any reference in any enactment or document (in whatever terms)--
> (a) to charitable purposes, or
> (b) to institutions having purposes that are charitable under the law relating to charities in England and Wales,
> is to be read in accordance with subsection (1)....

3.15.2 *Scots charity: Status in UK*

It appears at first sight that there may be purposes which are charitable in the CTISA definition but not in the CA 2011 definition. If that is right,

89 See 3.5 (Charitable purposes condition).

then a Scots charity is not established for charitable purposes only (within CA 2011 definition), and does not qualify for UK tax relief, if:

(1) its objects include those specific purposes; or
(2) it has general Scots charitable objects (objects including anything which is charitable within the Scots law definition).

We prefer the view that notwithstanding differences of wording, everything charitable under CTISA is also charitable under the CA 2011. But that has yet to be established (and may never be).

A joint statement from OSCR and HMRC is intended to address this problem:[90]

> **Defining the phrase 'charitable purpose' or the word 'charitable' in the constitutions of Scottish Charities**
> OSCR and HMRC have clarified the requirement for 'definition clauses' (defining the meaning of the words 'charitable', 'charitable purpose' or 'charity') in constitutions of bodies on the Scottish Charity Register that also wish to seek tax relief from HMRC.
> The agreement reached between OSCR and HMRC was informed by the knowledge that there is very little divergence between the concept of what is 'charitable' etc in terms of the Charities and Trustee Investment (Scotland) Act 2005 and what is 'charitable' etc for the purposes of the Taxes Acts and the mutual desire to maintain that position going into the future. The objective of the agreement has been to arrive at an operational arrangement that has a minimum impact on Scottish charities.
> HMRC and OSCR have therefore agreed as follows:
> 1. Not all charities on the Scottish Charity Register that have been established under Scottish law need a definition of the terms 'charitable' or 'charitable purpose' to be included in their constitution in order to be able to meet the requirements of HMRC and qualify for tax reliefs. A definition clause is not needed if:
>
> a. The terms 'charitable' or 'charitable purpose' are not used in the constitution; or
> b. The constitution does not contain a reference to general 'charitable purposes', nor a dissolution clause which allows the distribution of assets for 'any charitable purpose'.

In practice, charity governing documents do usually use the word

90 19 February 2008 *http://webarchive.nationalarchives.gov.uk/20140109143644/http://www.hmrc.gov.uk/charities/oscr-hmrc-statement082202.pdf*

"charitable" so we read on:

> 2. Any charities on the Scottish Charity Register that may have adopted a definition or interpretation clause published by OSCR prior to February 2008, that was different from those contained in this statement, do **not** need to change this in order to be able to benefit from tax relief

It may not be easy now to ascertain what were the clauses published by OSCR prior to February 2008, but it does not matter since pre-2008 charities will normally fall within the next paragraph:

> 3. Scottish charities **already on the Register** and which are already registered with HMRC which do not have a 'definition clause' in their constitution will **not** be required by HMRC to change their constitutions in order to qualify for tax relief. (However, HMRC stress that it would be good practice to make such a change if the constitution were updated for another reason).

In short, for Scots charities registered before 19 February 2008, HMRC will ignore the problem.

The position is different for charities registered after that date:

> 4. Scottish charities to be entered **new** on the Register by OSCR (and that use the terms charitable etc in their draft constitutions), will be advised (both by OSCR and HMRC) that, should they at any point wish to claim tax relief, they will probably need to define the terms 'charitable' or 'charitable purpose' (where used) in a way acceptable to HMRC, i.e. by inserting the model definitions clause(s) (see below).
> 5. HMRC and OSCR wish to maintain the working practice (of HMRC) that entry on the Scottish Charity Register would, in the vast majority of cases, satisfy HMRC for the purposes of granting tax relief (and that separate submission of a constitution to HMRC will not usually be necessary).[91] OSCR will therefore bring to the attention of HMRC any charities that are entered on the Register without a definition clause in the constitution, where exact drafting of the constitution would need this for HMRC purposes. (OSCR will also inform the relevant charity if this is the case). This will allow HMRC to make separate, individual assessments of these cases should these charities request tax relief.
> **Example definition clauses:**
> These clauses can be amended or adjusted as appropriate and necessary within the context of the exact drafting of the constitution concerned.

91 This sensible working practice was abandoned (or overlooked) in the 2010 reforms; see 47.3 (Registration with HMRC).

What is to be achieved is a definition which unambiguously defines the terms 'charitable purpose', 'or 'charitable' in terms of the 2005 Act as well as the Tax legislation. Which one of the example clauses should be used depends on the drafting of the constitution.

To define the term 'charitable purpose':

> *The expression 'charitable purpose' shall mean a charitable purpose under section 7 of the Charities and Trustee Investment (Scotland) Act 2005 which is also regarded as a charitable purpose in relation to the application of the Taxes Acts.*

To define the term 'charity' or charitable body', charitable institution', charitable organisation (etc):

> *UK Charitable body', 'charitable institution', 'charitable organisation'* [as applicable in the context of the constitution] *and charity' shall mean a body on the Scottish Charity Register which is also regarded as a charity in relation to the application of the Taxes Acts.*

We wonder whether this will be enforced in practice. The IHT Manual provides (inconsistently, but sensibly):

> **IHTM11129. Procedure: selection trusts** [March 2022]
> ***...A trust or bequest directing the trustees to appoint or distribute to bodies described as 'charities' or 'charitable'.***
> These can be immediately accepted as qualifying for charity exemption without identifying the recipients if the Will (IHTM12041) has effect under UK law.... *In practice 'charitable' can be taken as having the same meaning under the law in Scotland and Northern Ireland.*

3.15.3 *English charity: Status in Scotland*

Similar problems arise for English law charities in Scotland. It appears at first sight that there may be purposes which are charitable in English law but not within CTISA. If that is right, then an English charity is not established for charitable purposes only (within the Scots law definition), if:

(1) its objects include those specific purposes; or
(2) it has general English charitable objects (objects including anything which is charitable within the CA 2011 definition).

We prefer the view that notwithstanding differences of wording, everything charitable under the CA 2011 is also charitable under the CITSA. But that has yet to be established (and may never be).

This matters for:

(1) Tax reliefs restricted to charities whose purposes are exclusively charitable in Scots law: rating relief in Scotland and LBTT charity tax relief.
(2) English charities which wish to register as Scots charities for any other reason.

Here it seems that there is no transitional relief on offer for pre-2008 charities. The Charity Commission offers the following guidance:

> Any E&W [England & Wales] charity that wishes to refer to itself as a charity and occupies any land or premises in Scotland or carries out activities in any office, shop or similar premises in Scotland, needs to apply for registration as a charity with OSCR. If the charity meets the Scottish charity test contained in the 2005 Act, it will be entered on the Scottish Charity Register. ...The test requires that the charity's objects are charitable under section 7 of the 2005 Act and that the charity cannot distribute or apply any of its property for purposes which are not charitable under section 7.
>
> The governing documents of charities established under the law of E&W are interpreted according to that law. However, the terms "charitable" or "charitable purposes" do not have precisely the same meaning under the 2005 Act as it does under E&W law.
>
> The effect of the difference between E&W law and Scots law is that where an E&W charity's governing document makes reference to "charitable" or "other charitable purposes" in its objects and/or dissolution clause, it is not clear that the organisation can only use its assets for purposes which are exclusively charitable in accordance with the 2005 Act. This means that it will fail the Scottish charity test.
>
> **6. What can we do to enable these charities to register in Scotland?**
>
> E&W charities that have applied for registration with OSCR and have been asked to make an amendment to their governing documents before they can be registered, will generally need to contact the Commission. In most cases, an amendment to a charity's purposes or objects can only be made with our consent. Often an amendment to a dissolution clause will also need the consent of the Commission and/or a parent body.
>
> The standard wording we have agreed with OSCR is set out below:
>
> (a) Where a charity is established in England & Wales and undertakes significant activities in Scotland and its objects clause makes reference to "charitable" or "other charitable purposes", this form of wording will be suitable for use as an interpretation clause for the governing document:
>
> ***Throughout this*** [insert type of GD [Governing Document] e.g. Trust Deed]***, "charitable" means charitable in***

accordance with the law of England and Wales provided that it will not include any purpose which is not charitable in accordance with section 7 of the Charities and Trustee Investment (Scotland) Act 2005. For the avoidance of doubt, the system of law governing the constitution of the charity is the law of England and Wales.

(b) This clause is intended to be used where the **objects** clause is acceptable as charitable both in England & Wales and in Scotland but the charity does not meet the distribution test (i.e. its dissolution clause makes reference to "charitable" or "other charitable purposes") in section 7 of the 2005 Act:

> ***Nothing in this*** [insert type of GD e.g. trust deed] ***shall authorise an application of the property of the charity for purposes which are not charitable in accordance with section 7 of the Charities and Trustee Investment (Scotland) Act 2005.***[92]

It would not generally be convenient to have a body which was a charity under Scots law but not a charity for tax purposes. However it might be convenient to have a body which is a charity for tax purposes but not a charity under Scots law; such a body would escape the regulatory burden of the OSCR but still qualify for UK tax relief. The HMRC Guidance Note recognises that this is possible:

> 2.4.1 Because the definition of charitable purposes for tax purposes is the one set down by the Charities Act (England and Wales) 2006 it's possible that an organisation refused registration by a charity regulator outside England and Wales may still be able to satisfy the conditions in the Taxes Acts and be recognised as a charity for tax purposes.

3.16 NI law definition of charity

Section 1 Charities Act (Northern Ireland) 2008 provides a definition of "charity" in (effectively) the same terms as s.1 [English] Charities Act 2011:

> (1) For the purposes of the law of Northern Ireland, "charity" means an institution which—

92 Guidance for English and Welsh charities that wish to register in Scotland can be found at: *https://webarchive.nationalarchives.gov.uk/20140505230922/http://www.charitycommission.gov.uk/detailed-guidance/protecting-your-charity/charities-working-internationally/english-and-welsh-charities-working-in-scotland/*

(a) is established for charitable purposes only, and
(b) falls to be subject to the control of the Court in the exercise of its jurisdiction with respect to charities.

(2) The definition of "charity" in subsection (1) does not apply for the purposes of a statutory provision if a different definition of that term applies for those purposes by virtue of that or any other statutory provision.[93]

However the definition of "charitable purposes" is not identical to the English (or Scots) law definitions, though it is broadly similar. In Northern Ireland (unlike England) the advancement of peace and good community relations is in the list of charitable purposes, and promoting the efficiency of the armed forces is not. The public benefit test was rewritten (with retrospective effect) by the Charities Act (Northern Ireland) 2013, and follows the English wording, though regard is had to Northern Ireland case law, which could therefore differ from English case law (particularly in relation to religious purposes).

The CA 2011 definition of "charity" applies for tax purposes even in Northern Ireland. Section 8 CA 2011 provides:

(1) This Chapter [s.1 - s.9 CA 2011] affects the law of Northern Ireland only in so far as it affects the construction of references to—
(a) charities, or
(b) charitable purposes,
in enactments which relate to matters falling within paragraph 9 of Schedule 2 to the Northern Ireland Act 1998 (excepted matters: taxes and duties).

(2) In so far as this Chapter affects the law of Northern Ireland—
(a) references in sections 1(1) and 2(1) to the law of England and Wales are to be read as references to the law of Northern Ireland, and
(b) the reference in section 1(1) to the High Court is to be read as a reference to the High Court in Northern Ireland.

We expect that a practice similar to Scotland will be applied in Northern Ireland.

93 See Kessler & Grattan, *Drafting Trusts and Will Trusts in Northern Ireland* (4th ed, 2019), Chapter 25 (Charitable trusts). Up to date versions of the 2008 Act and the (amending) 2013 Act are at:
https://www.charitycommissionni.org.uk/about-us/charity-legislation/

3.17 HMRC/charity regulator relations

3.17.1 *Generally*

The FPP guidance states:

> HMRC works closely with the UK charity regulators and where HMRC identifies a manager who isn't considered to be a fit and proper person HMRC will advise the relevant charity regulator of the concerns where permitted by law to disclose the information.

Investigation into charity malpractice may be carried out by charity regulators or HMRC.

3.17.2 *HMRC/Charity Commission*

Sections 54-59 CA 2011 provide a complex set of confidentiality rules, not discussed here, which override the usual duty of confidentiality in s.18 Commissioners for Revenue and Customs Act 2005. HMRC has a memorandum of understanding with the Charity Commission to facilitate the sharing of information. The memorandum was revised in 2013 to widen the information shared.[94] This document is not publically available, unlike the OSCR/HMRC memorandum of understanding.[95] As it is not likely that there is any significant difference in the content of the documents, one may infer that the culture of secrecy is more deeply embedded in the old English bureaucracy than the new Scottish one.

3.17.3 *HMRC/OSCR*

Similar but slightly wider powers are provided in relation to OSCR and CCNI.

A Memorandum of Understanding Between OSCR and HMRC[96] has some interesting comments on the way in which the two bodies aim to work together. In particular, this discusses confidentiality:

---

94 National Audit Office "Gift Aid and reliefs on donations" (November 2013) para 2.22, 2.23 *http://www.publications.parliament.uk/pa/cm201314/cmselect/cmpubacc/792/792we01.htm*

95 The Charity Commission claim, perhaps implausibly, that the MOU is exempt from disclosure under section 31(1)(g) Freedom of Information Act 2000, which provides that information is exempt if its disclosure would be likely to prejudice the exercise by any public authority of its functions; and that the public interest does not favour disclosure. (Private correspondence).

96 *https://www.oscr.org.uk/media/1892/hmrc-mou-web.pdf*

> 4.4 Section 18(1) of the CRCA 2005 ("CRCA") lays down the general principle that HMRC may not disclose information that it holds in connection with its functions. However, subsection 3 of section 18 of the CRCA provides that subsection 1 is subject to any other enactment permitting disclosure. Section 3 of the Charities and Trustee Investment (Scotland) 2005 Act (Consequential Provision and Modification Order) 2006 states that for the purposes of enabling and assisting OSCR to exercise its functions, HMRC may disclose to OSCR any information concerning a charity which they have acquired in the performance of their functions. It is considered that any disclosure by an official of HMRC made in accordance with section 3 of the Charities and Trustees Investment (Scotland) 2005 Act (Consequential Provision and Modification Order) 2006 will not constitute a breach of the confidentiality requirement imposed by section 18(1) of the CRCA.
> 4.5 Neither OSCR nor HMRC will disclose information received under the terms of this Memorandum to any other person or body without first consulting the disclosing party.
> 4.6 Any onward disclosure of HMRC information without the consent of HMRC may constitute a criminal offence.

3.17.4 *HMRC/CCNI*

In Northern Ireland the provisions relating to disclosure of information between are found in the Charities (Disclosure of Revenue and Customs Information to CCNI) Regulations 2010.

3.18 Relief without charity regulator

Before the F(No.1)A 2010, a body which wanted UK tax reliefs had to be a UK charity and regulated by the English Charity Commission (or its Scots or NI equivalents). For most charities this was not, we think, too burdensome but some had a difficult relationship with the regulator, for instance those whose activities were borderline charitable. Now a body can in principle escape the burden of Charity Commission regulation by incorporating in another EU jurisdiction (it still has HMRC regulation so far as UK tax is an issue but avoids one regulatory layer).

This may also be useful in (perhaps only theoretical) cases where English charity law is wider than that in Scotland, Northern Ireland, or the Republic of Ireland. HMRC accept this. The HMRC Guidance Note provides:

> 2.4.1 Because the definition of charitable purposes for tax purposes is the one set down by the Charities Act (England and Wales) 2006 it's

possible that an organisation refused registration by a charity regulator outside England and Wales may still be able to satisfy the conditions in the Taxes Acts and be recognised as a charity for tax purposes.

3.19 Definition of charity: Critique

The Joint Committee on the Draft [English] Charities Bill recommended that the definitions of charity should be the same throughout the UK (Report para 40):

> It would be an issue of some consternation if UK based charities were required to meet different criteria for achieving charitable status in different parts of the UK, or if some organisations were considered charities in one part of the UK but denied charitable status in another.

The Calman Commission on Scottish Devolution agreed:

> There should be a single definition of each of the expressions "charity" and "charitable purpose(s)", applicable for all purposes throughout the United Kingdom.[97]

This reform would be an important simplification and reduce the problem of jurisdiction-shopping discussed above.[98] But simplification is incompatible with devolution.

The Hodgson review rejected the proposal, though not for a good reason:

> **Establishing a UK-wide definition of charity?**
> 4.17 ... It is worth noting at the outset that any difference in definitions across the UK will only affect those charities operating across more than one jurisdiction.

This is not correct, because of the tax issues. The mistake, the reader may think, invalidates or substantially weakens the conclusion which follows:

> However, for those charities, there are some resulting challenges and administrative burdens. The views of charities affected on whether change should actually be attempted are, however, mixed. Many would welcome a UK-wide definition as simpler to administer. However, the significant minority were of the view that some administrative irritation was a small price to pay for diversity, flexibility, and the upholding of principles of devolution (one respondent also added that the sector was already so complex and diverse anyway that a bit more complication

97 *http://researchbriefings.files.parliament.uk/documents/SN04744/SN04744.pdf* June 2009 Recommendation 5.2.

98 See 3.18 (Relief without charity regulator).

> mattered little!).
> 4.18 From a logical point of view, in terms of administrative efficiency and consistency, and of minimising confusion and difficulty for charities across the UK, a single definition of charity would be desirable. ... However, even among those in favour of change, the difficulty of agreeing a shared definition and the challenge and disruption of implementation were highlighted. Bearing in mind these challenges, together with the lack of appetite in the devolved administrations for any change and the state of legal flux in Northern Ireland, the least worst option must be to maintain the status quo, at least for the time being.[99]

There is no current prospect of reform of the definition of charity: the three jurisdictions of the United Kingdom cannot agree on a single definition. On that basis, charity tax reliefs should be extended so that they apply to charities as defined in each jurisdiction.

3.20 The impact of Brexit

When the tax definition of "charity" in sch 6 F(No.1)A 2010 was enacted, the UK was a member of the EU. At the time, although direct taxation fell within the competence of individual member states, the UK was under an obligation to exercise its competence consistently with Community law.

The 2010 definition was intended to meet various objections that the previous rules had discriminated against non-UK EU charities. In 2006 the European Commission sent the UK a formal request in this regard.[100] The Commission complained that UK domestic law restricting charity tax relief to UK charities contravened EU law relating to:

(1) Free movement of capital.
(2) Freedom of establishment.
(3) Free movement of persons.

The Explanatory Memorandum to The Taxes (Definition of Charity) (Relevant Territories) Regulations 2010 SI 1904 explains the official

99 Hodgson report "Trusted and Independent: Giving charity back to charities - Review of the Charities Act 2006" (2012) *https://www.gov.uk/government/uploads/system/uploads/attachment_data/file/79275/Charities-Act-Review-2006-report-Hodgson.pdf*

100 IP/06/964. The text is set out in the 2009/10 edition of this work. The requests were sent in the form of Reasoned Opinions, the second step in the infringement procedure (Art.258 TFEU). If there were no satisfactory reaction within 2 months, the Commission may refer the matter to the ECJ. The text of the request was not published but its content is not hard to guess.

HMRC position:

> 7.2 Until the beginning of 2009 the UK Government held the view that UK tax reliefs for donors and charities applied only in relation to UK charities. However, this view has changed following a decision in the European Court of Justice in January 2009 (*Persche v Finanzamt Lüdenscheid)* which held that tax reliefs and exemptions for charities and their donors may not be limited to charities within a member State of the EU. ...

In fact after *Stauffer* in 2006 the HMRC official view up until 2009 could be described as wishful thinking.[101] But however that may be, the law was duly amended in 2010 to afford tax relief to EU charities.

Post-Brexit, the tax definition of "charity" has remained essentially unchanged. In particular, the 'jurisdiction condition' continues to be satisfied when the body of persons or trust is subject to the control of a member state. The only change in this regard is a small alteration to the wording of para 2(3)(a) sch 6 F(No.1)A 2010, designed to reflect the fact that the UK itself is no longer a member state[102].

3.20.1 *Primacy of EU law*

Prior to Brexit, the primacy of EU law was well established. Following Brexit, the basic position is that the primacy of EU law does not apply to any enactment or rule of law passed or made on or after the expiry of the implementation period. However, it continues to apply "so far as relevant to the interpretation, disapplication or quashing of any enactment or rule of law passed or made before IP completion day". [103] Accordingly, EU law remains relevant.

3.21 EU charity cases

There are four ECJ charity cases in the light of which the EU-law position is reasonably clear.

In *Stauffer*[104] an Italian charity (tax exempt in Italy) received rent from

101 See the Feasibility Study on a European Foundation Statute at p.142: "We can hardly see a convincing justification why *Pershe* should be decided differently from *Stauffer*".

102 *The Taxes (Amendment) (EU Exit) Regulations 2019* (SI 2019/689), regs. 1.19(2).

103 Section 5 European Union (Withdrawal) Act 2018.

104 *Centro di Musicologia Walter Stauffer v Finanzamt München für Körperschaften* [2008] STC 1439.

property in Germany. German law allowed charity tax exemption only for charities established in Germany.

In *Persche*[105] the taxpayer gave towels, toys and zimmer frames to a charitable retirement and children's home in Portugal but was refused a deduction in Germany.

In *Missionswerk*[106] a Belgian succession duty relief was restricted to Belgian NPOs.

In *European Commission v Republic of Austria*[107] a deduction for gifts to research institutions was limited to institutions established in Austria.

In each case the domestic law was held to be an unlawful restriction on free movement of capital.

It is difficult to see why the same points have been argued so many times. We addressed the cases in more detail in the 2019/20 edition of this work, para 3.20-3.25 but omit this material now as it is of diminished importance.

3.22 Free movement of capital

Article 63 TFEU provides:

> 1. Within the framework of the provisions set out in this Chapter, all restrictions on the movement of capital between Member States and between Member States and third countries shall be prohibited.
> 2. Within the framework of the provisions set out in this Chapter, all restrictions on payments between Member States and between Member States and third countries shall be prohibited.

3.22.1 *"Movement of capital"*

Movement of capital includes:

(1) Investments in real estate, as in *Stauffer*.
(2) Gifts and endowments. In *Persche* one question was whether gifts of goods in specie fall within the rules relating to the free movement of capital. Of course they do:

> [25] Where a taxpayer of a member state seeks the deduction for tax purposes of a sum reflecting the value of gifts to third persons resident in another member state, it does not matter, in order to determine whether the national legislation in question is covered by the Treaty

105 *Persche v Finanzamt Lüdenscheid* [2009] STC 586.
106 *Missionswerk Werner Heeukelbach eV v État belge* Case C-25/10.
107 Case C-10/10.

provisions on the movement of capital, whether the underlying gifts were made in money or in kind.

(3) Inheritance, as in *Missionswerk.*

3.22.2 *Restriction on free movement*

In *Stauffer*[108] the ECJ held that the differing tax treatment for German and non-German charities did constitute a restriction on free movement of capital (which one might have thought obvious).

Similarly in *Persche*, the second question was whether the German rules constituted a restriction on free movement of capital. This was just a rerun of the arguments in *Stauffer* and the conclusion was inevitable.

The point was followed yet again in *Missionswerk* at [24]- [26] where the Belgian succession duty relief restricted to Belgian NPOs was held to be a restriction on free movement of capital.

3.22.3 *Free movement: Non-EU countries*

Free movement of capital applies not just between member states but also between member states and non-EU countries.

In *Routier v HMRC,*[109] the court was concerned with a gift made before the UK's withdrawal from the EU. A testatrix died in 2007, leaving UK assets on trust for purposes which were charitable under English law. The trustees were domiciled in Jersey, and the proper law of the trust was the law of Jersey. HMRC argued that relief under section 23 of the Inheritance Tax Act 1984, which provides relief in respect of gifts made to charities, was not available. They did this by relying on the earlier case of *Dreyfus Foundation v IRC,*[110] in which the House of Lords had held the phrase "trust established for charitable purposes only" in section 37 of the 1918 Act must be interpreted as implicitly limited to trusts which are governed by the law of some part of the UK and subject to the jurisdiction of UK courts. By drawing a link between the wording of that earlier provision and section 23 of the 1984 Act, HMRC argued that the same implicit restriction (referred to in the judgment as the '*Dreyfus* gloss') must apply in circumstances such as those in *Routier*. It was acknowledged that, if this view was correct, there would have been a clear restriction on the free

108 *Centro di Musicologia Walter Stauffer v Finanzamt München für Körperschaften* [2008] STC 1439.

109 [2019] UKSC 43.

110 36 TC 126.

movement of capital. However, HMRC sought to circumvent that issue by arguing that Jersey should not be regarded as a non-EU state for these purposes.

HMRC's argument was rejected by the Supreme Court, which held that Jersey was to be regarded as a third country in this context. Since the restriction imposed by *Dreyfus* was incompatible with the prohibition on restrictions on the free movement of capital, the Supreme Court held that it should be disapplied.

Of course, *Routier* concerned a transfer of capital before the UK's withdrawal from the EU. The question arises as to how a transfer of capital to a non-EU state would be treated now. On one hand, the Supreme Court in *Routier* appeared to confine its decision to circumstances falling within the scope of article 56 of the Treaty Establishing the European Community (i.e. the predecessor of article 63 TFEU):

> the *Dreyfus* gloss…cannot be applied to section 23 in situations falling within the scope of article 56[111]

In turn, that treaty article is expressed in terms of transfers of capital between 'Member States' and third countries. Given that the UK is no longer a member state, the argument could be made that the decision does not apply to transfers of capital made following the UK's withdrawal from the EU.

However, Section 4 of the European Union (Withdrawal) Act 2018 serves to preserve rights and restrictions which were available in UK domestic law by virtue of EU treaties prior to the completion of the implementation period. Crucially, it is the rights and restrictions which are preserved, rather than the wording of relevant treaty articles. Accordingly, Section 4 of the 2018 Act serves to ensure that the free movement of capital remains a part of UK domestic law. In turn, section 5(2) of the 2018 Act provides that the primacy of EU law continues to apply "so far as relevant to the interpretation, disapplication or quashing of any enactment or rule of law passed or made before IP completion day".It therefore follows that the *Dreyfus* gloss on section 23 of the Inheritance Tax Act 1984 (and other provisions) remains disapplied.

3.23 Justification

In relation to transfers of capital made before the UK's withdrawal from

111 at [52].

the EU, some restrictions on free movement of capital may still be regarded as lawful. *Stauffer* indicates where the ECJ draw the line:

> 32. According to the case law, for national tax legislation such as that at issue in the main proceedings, ... to be regarded as compatible with the Treaty provisions on the free movement of capital, the difference in treatment must concern situations which are not objectively comparable or be justified by overriding reasons in the general interest, such as the need to safeguard the coherence of the tax system or effective fiscal supervision ... In order to be justified, moreover, the difference in treatment between charitable foundations with unlimited tax liability[112] in Germany and foundations of the same kind established in other member states must not go beyond what is necessary in order to attain the objective of the legislation in question.[113]

3.23.1 *Charity purpose: Domestic law*

The ECJ held that for a restriction on free movement of capital to arise (or for a restriction to be unjustified) the objects of the foreign charity had to be charitable under domestic law:

> 39. ... it is not a requirement under Community law for member states automatically to confer on foreign foundations recognised as having charitable status in their member state of origin the same status in their own territory. Member states have a discretion in this regard that they must exercise in accordance with Community law ... In those circumstances, they are free to determine what the interests of the general public they wish to promote are by granting benefits to associations and foundations which pursue objects linked to such interests in a disinterested manner.
> 40. Nevertheless, the fact remains that where a foundation recognised as having charitable status in one member state also satisfies the requirements imposed for that purpose by the law of another member state and where its object is to promote the very same interests of the general public, which it is a matter for the national authorities of that other state, including its courts, to determine, the authorities of that member state cannot deny that foundation the right to equal treatment solely on the ground that it is not established in its territory.[114]

112 A note on terminology "unlimited tax liability" means the German charities are potentially subject to tax on German source and foreign source income.

113 *Stauffer* at [32].

114 The ECJ made the same point when the issue was rerun in *Persche*: see at [43]-[48]

Stauffer argued that it met this requirement, ie its objects met the German law requirements of charity; the ECJ referred the issue back to the German courts.

3.23.2 *Difficulty of administration*

In *Stauffer*, Germany (supported by the UK and Ireland) argued that the practical difficulty of administration justified the difference in treatment. This was only accepted halfway:

> 47. The court has, on many occasions, held that effectiveness of fiscal supervision constitutes an overriding requirement of general interest capable of justifying a restriction on the exercise of the fundamental freedoms guaranteed by the Treaty ...
> 48. Thus, before granting a foundation a tax exemption, a member state is authorised to apply measures enabling it to ascertain in a clear and precise manner whether the foundation meets the conditions imposed by national law in order to be entitled to the exemption and to monitor its effective management, for example, by requiring the submission of annual accounts and an activity report. Admittedly, where foundations are established in other member states, it may prove more difficult to carry out the necessary checks. Nevertheless, these are disadvantages of a purely administrative nature which are not sufficient to justify a refusal on the part of the authorities of the state concerned to grant such foundations the same tax exemptions as are granted to foundations of the same kind, which, in principle, have unlimited tax liability [ie tax exemption] in that state ...
> 49. There is nothing to prevent the tax authorities concerned from requiring a charitable foundation claiming exemption from tax to provide relevant supporting evidence to enable those authorities to carry out the necessary checks. Further, national legislation which absolutely prevents the taxpayer from submitting such evidence cannot be justified in the name of effectiveness of fiscal supervision ...

The ECJ reverted to the point again later in its judgment:

> 60 Fourthly, it was argued at the hearing, in particular by the Finanzamt and the German Government, that it is not inconceivable that criminal gangs and terrorist organisations may assume the legal status of a foundation for the purposes of money-laundering and the illegal transfer of funds from one Member State to another.
> 61 Even if, by granting a tax exemption only to charitable foundations that are established in its territory, the authorities of a Member State seek to combat crime, the fact remains that the fact that a foundation is

> established in another Member State cannot give rise to a general assumption of criminal activity. Moreover, to preclude such foundations from entitlement to a tax exemption when a number of measures are available to monitor their accounts and activities may be considered to be a measure which goes beyond what is necessary to combat crime.[115]

The practical difficulties (at least in the UK) of conferring charity relief on foreign charities are formidable, and the ECJ may have underestimated them; it makes a change for HMRC to be on the receiving end of an authority not always concerned with the practical difficulty of the rules which it promulgates.

3.23.3 *Free movement restriction: Yield*

The ECJ did not think much of this as a justification for a restriction on free movement of capital. In *Stauffer* the ECJ said:

> 58 Thirdly, the German Government states that the refusal to grant the tax exemption to foundations with limited liability to tax [ie subject to tax] is justified by the need to protect the basis of tax revenue.
> 59 Whilst, for the Federal Republic of Germany, recognition of the right to exemption from corporation tax for non-resident charitable foundations would entail a reduction in its corporation tax receipts, it has been consistently held in the case-law that reduction in tax revenue cannot be regarded as an overriding reason in the public interest which may be relied on to justify a measure which is, in principle, contrary to a fundamental freedom.[116]

Persche just reran the arguments in *Stauffer* with the minor difference that the charity tax relief was claimed by a donor to charity and not the charity itself. The same decision was reached again in *Missionswerk.*

3.23.4 *Reciprocity of exemption*

The EC say:

> The Commission has requested Italy to amend its inheritance tax legislation, which discriminates against bequests to non-profit organisations in another EU Member State or EEA State. Under Italian law, legacies to non-profit organisations pursuing public and social

115 The ECJ refers to Case C-243/01 *Gambelli and Others* [2003] ECR I-13031, paragraph 74).

116 The ECJ referred to: *Verkooijen,* at [59]; Case C-136/00 *Danner* [2002] ECR I-8147, at [56]; *X and Y* at [50]; *Manninen*, at [49].

goals are exempt from tax. However, similar legacies to non-profit bodies established elsewhere in the EU/EEA are only granted an exemption if there is reciprocity from that Member State (i.e. that the country in question gives an exemption to Italian non-profit organisations). If there is not this reciprocity, then the legacy is taxed at 8% of its value. As a result, the taxation of bequests to foreign non-profit entities is frequently higher than bequests to their Italian counterparts. In addition, Italian legislation excludes Italian bonds and public securities from the inheritance estate, while bonds and public securities issued by other EU and EEA States are not allowed this exclusion.

The Commission considers such provisions to be discriminatory and to constitute unjustified restrictions on the free movement of capital. The requests sent to Italy take the form of two reasoned opinions. If Italy does not comply within two months, the Commission may refer the case to the Court. (ref.:2012/2156 and 2012/2157)[117]

3.24 Non-EU charities

If a non-EU charity has UK sources of income and does not qualify for tax relief, the most convenient course may be to set up an associated charity in the UK or elsewhere in the EU.

This may also be advantageous for a foreign charity with no UK-source income, if it wishes to take advantage of double tax treaties.[118]

Difficulties arise where a charity needs to satisfy the requirements of UK tax law (to secure UK tax relief) and also the requirements of another country's tax code. These cases will need to be considered in the light of their particular circumstances.[119]

3.25 Classification of charities

The tax definition of charity requires that it must be a body of persons or trust.[120]

Para 1(2) sch 6 F(no.1)A 2010 provides standard tax definitions of the terms "charitable company" and "charitable trust":

For the purposes of the enactments to which this Part applies—

---

117 MEMO/14/537 25/09/2014
http://europa.eu/rapid/press-release_MEMO-14-537_en.htm

118 See 14.1 (Double Taxation Treaties and Charities).

119 For a structure which constitutes a charity under UK and foreign law, see 14.7 (Dual jurisdiction charity).

120 See 3.4 (Tax definition of charity).

> "charitable company" means a charity that is a body of persons;
> "charitable trust" means a charity that is a trust.

Tax law classifies every charity as a charitable company or a charitable trust.

3.25.1 *Charitable company*

In practice, a charitable company will take one of the following forms:

(1) A body corporate. This includes:
   (a) A company incorporated under UK company acts, by statute or by royal charter
   (b) A charitable incorporated organisation[121]
   (c) A Scottish charitable incorporated organisation[122]
   (d) A co-operative and community benefit society[123]

(2) An unincorporated association (classified as a company, see below).

"Company" is widely defined for tax purposes and includes any body corporate or unincorporated association.[124]

A charitable company (being a body of persons) will be a company within this definition. A charitable company is therefore a company for tax purposes and treated as any other company, except so far as specific charity exemptions or other provisions apply.

3.25.2 *Unincorporated association*

Conservative and Unionist Central Office v Burrell 55 TC 671 at p.699 considered the meaning of "unincorporated association":

> I infer that by "unincorporated association" in this context Parliament meant two or more persons bound together for one or more common purposes, not being business purposes, by mutual undertakings, each having mutual duties and obligations, in an organisation which has rules which identify in whom control of it and its funds rests and on what terms and which can be joined or left at will. The bond of union between

121 Section 205(1) CA 2011 provides: "A CIO is a body corporate."

122 Section 49(2) CTISA 2005 provides: "A SCIO is a body corporate..."

123 Section 3 Co-operative and Community Benefit Societies and Credit Unions Act 2014 provides: "A registered society shall by virtue of its registration be a body corporate..."

124 Section 992(1) ITA; s.1121 CTA 2010; s.288(1) TCGA. For a full discussion of the meaning of "company" see Kessler, *Taxation of Non-residents and Foreign Domiciliaries*, (21st ed., 2022-23), para 88.3 (Definition of "company"); online version *https://www.foreigndomiciliaries.co.uk*

the members of an unincorporated association has to be contractual.

EN CTA 2009 chapter 2 provides:

> The HMRC view of unincorporated associations differs from this in two main respects. These are that
> [1] the union between the members need not be legally enforceable and that
> [2] there is no reason why an unincorporated body should not have trading or business objectives or carry on significant commercial activities.

Point [1] is odd but perhaps it does not arise in practice.

The point behind [2] is that if the association is carrying on a business with a view to profit, it is classified as a partnership. But that probably cannot apply to a charitable association.

An unincorporated association is treated as a company for tax purposes, under the definition set out above, though it is not a company in the normal sense of the word.

An unincorporated association may be a body of persons "established for charitable purposes only" and so qualify as a charity within the tax definition. See 3.27.1 (Unincorporated association).

3.25.3 *Charitable trust*

A charitable trust is a trust for tax purposes and treated as any other trust, except so far as specific charity exemptions or other provisions apply.

3.25.4 *Incorporated trustee*

This section considers the position where trustees of a charitable trust have incorporated under s.251 CA 2011. The property law consequences of this are set out in ss.251 and 252 CA 2011:

> **251 Incorporation of charity trustees**
> (1) The Commission may grant a certificate of incorporation of the charity trustees of a charity as a body corporate if-
> (a) the charity trustees of the charity, in accordance with section 256, apply to the Commission for such a certificate, and
> (b) the Commission considers that the incorporation of the charity trustees would be in the interests of the charity...
> (4) On the grant of such a certificate-
> (a) the charity trustees of the charity become a body corporate by such name as is specified in the certificate, and
> (b) any rights or liabilities of those trustees in connection with any

property vesting in the body under section 252 become rights or liabilities of that body.

Paragraph (b) does not affect the operation of section 254 (liability of charity trustees not affected by incorporation).

(5) After their incorporation the charity trustees-

(a) may sue and be sued in their corporate name, and

(b) have the same powers, and are subject to the same restrictions and limitations, as respects the holding, acquisition and disposal of property for or in connection with the purposes of the charity as they had or were subject to while unincorporated;

and any relevant legal proceedings[125] that might have been continued or commenced by or against the charity trustees may be continued or commenced by or against them in their corporate name.

252 Estate to vest in incorporated body

(1) The certificate of incorporation vests in the incorporated body all real and personal estate, of whatever nature or tenure, belonging to or held by any person or persons in trust for the relevant charity.

(2) On the vesting of all real and personal estate under subsection (1), any person or persons in whose name or names any stocks, funds or securities are standing in trust for the relevant charity must transfer them into the name of the incorporated body.

(3) Subsections (1) and (2) do not apply to property vested in the official custodian.

The trustees of the charitable trust become a "body corporate" and are therefore classified as a company for tax purposes: see s.992 ITA or 1121 CTA 2010. However, it is reasonably clear from s.50(4) that this body corporate is not regarded as beneficial owner of the charity's assets. The tax classification of a charitable trust which is incorporated under the Charities Act is therefore the same as any other charitable trust with a sole corporate trustee. Thus if a charitable trust with an incorporated trustee becomes subject to tax (eg because it receives trading income outside the trading exemption), it pays income tax like a charitable trust, at trust rates; it does not pay corporation tax.

3.26 Charitable trusts/companies: Critique

At present we have two tax regimes for charities:

(1) Charitable trusts are subject to IT/CGT rules.

125 Defined in ss(6): "In subsection (5) "relevant legal proceedings" means legal proceedings in connection with any property vesting in the incorporated body under section 252."

(2) Charitable companies are subject to corporation tax.

Thus the 30 pages of legislation in part 10 ITA are repeated (more or less verbatim) in the CTA 2010. It is suggested that the position should be simplified: so the same tax regime applies to all charities. There is no reason to have two! This would be a painless and worthwhile simplification in the law, with no significant tax cost.

The question arises whether charitable trusts should be brought within the corporation tax regime or charitable companies should be brought within the IT/CGT regime. The practical differences between the two regimes are marginal so that it does not make a great deal of difference which way the reform goes. On some minor points the charity corporation tax regime is better in that it allows exemption where exemption ought to be allowed.[126] So the better solution is to move charitable trusts into the corporation tax regime. There is no difficulty in that. Contrast the rule that unit trusts are treated as companies. Charitable trusts are already treated as companies in some cases:

(1) Some accounting rules devised for companies apply to charitable trusts.

(2) Charitable trusts are treated as companies for some purposes of the Gift Aid Small Donations Scheme; see 16.12 ("Connected").

3.27 Temporary charity

In this section we consider the status of bodies whose purposes are wholly charitable for a period, but which may in the future cease to be charitable. We refer to these as "**temporary charities**". For temporary charitable trusts, see 31.3 (Temporary charitable trusts).

3.27.1 *Unincorporated association*

A difficulty arises from the relatively informal nature of an unincorporated association. An association is governed by rules formed by a contract, and the rules of the association can be changed by the members. Any charitable unincorporated association is a "temporary charity": it may cease to be a charity.

In the early history of income tax, it was argued that for this reason an unincorporated association could not be a charity (at least, under the tax

126 See 4.18.2 (Swaps: Non-trading); 5.6.4 (Section 3 planning). This would also avoid the problems of an unintended charge on loans from close companies to charitable trusts.

definition) but that was rejected:

> It may be said of every voluntary society that, ... it may be by adding to its objects, objects which are non-charitable, or by substituting for its objects an object which is non-charitable instead of a charitable object. But if it does so, then it appears to me that the Society will cease to be a society established for a charitable purpose, and its funds presumably will not he devoted to charitable purposes only. But until it does do so it appears to me to be the same question of whether it was established for a charitable purpose and whether you can find that it is still operating in that sphere, and that is the position. As I have said, if in fact it did choose to adopt as its purpose some additional and non-charitable purpose, the position would be that its income derived after that time would not be subject to the obligation to expend it for a charitable purpose, but its income acquired while it professed to be a society for a charitable purpose only would have to be so applied. It seems to me immaterial to consider what the precise remedies are, either to the Attorney-General as representing the public, or to the individual members, for the purpose of establishing that obligation, but the obligation plainly exists, and to my mind plainly enforceable. [127]

So an unincorporated association in principle qualifies as a charity provided:

(1) The objects of the association are wholly charitable.
(2) The present income of the association can only be expended for a charitable purpose even if the association changes its objects as regards future income.

The association's constitution should expressly so provide; but the courts may infer this intention even if it is not expressed.

Accordingly, a temporary charitable association is in principle be a charity within the tax definition.

3.27.2 *Temporary charitable company*

A temporary charitable company may be a charity for tax purposes. Indeed, between 1948 and the reforms of the Companies Act 1989 and the Charities Act 1992, most charitable companies were in principle temporary charities, since they had power to alter their objects, a power belatedly restricted by law reform in ss.197, 198 CA 2011.

This was recognised in the Nathan Report:

127 See *IRC v Yorkshire Agricultural Society* 13 TC 58 at p.78.

> 573 ... If however a company is incorporated under the Companies Act, 1948... for the purpose of starting and carrying on a new charity, it will conduct the affairs of the charity under the powers conferred by its Memorandum of Association, which may be altered by the members by special resolution under the provisions of section 5 of the Act for the purposes mentioned in that section. The funds may, then, not be held upon any trusts but may constitute assets of the company applicable for the purposes authorised by the memorandum and be subject to the debts and liabilities of the company. Such a company may resolve to alter its Memorandum and a question may arise how this alteration affects the application of its funds. As the company is not obliged to obtain the sanction of the Court to an alteration of its Memorandum, it may well become possible for a company formed in this manner to carry no charitable activities, to divert some or all of the funds to purposes which are not charitable.[128]

Similarly, the Charity Commission explained:

> 30. A more general point arises where a charity company wishes to change the objects clause of its memorandum of association and holds substantial property for its general purposes ... The possibility that this might happen is the greater because the objects clause of a company can now be changed very easily particularly when there are only a handful of company members, as is frequently the case with the charity company.[129]

The position now is that an English charitable company cannot change its objects without the consent of the Charity Commission.[130] The Commission are unlikely to consent to a charitable company acquiring non-charitable objects so most English charitable companies are no longer temporary charities. However, temporary charitable companies may still exist. A company may adopt objects which are limited so as to be charitable for a period, and which then cease to be charitable. Since there is no alteration of the memorandum of the company, the law does not prevent this.

The position of such a company is analogous with that of a temporary charitable trust. It is considered that it does in principle qualify as a

128 Nathan Report (MD8710).

129 Charity Com. Report 1971.

130 Section 198 CA 2011. In relation to other UK companies, see s.21 Companies Act 2006; Article 9 Charities (Northern Ireland) Order 1987; s.112 Companies Act 1989 and s.16 CTISA 2005.

charity within the tax definition.

The restrictions in ss.197, 198 CA 2011 do not apply to a charitable co-operative and community benefit society, but it is considered that such a society could not change its objects so as to cease to be a charity.[131]

At one stage it seemed to be settled law that a temporary charity was charitable. However the contrary was argued in *Derby Teaching Hospitals NHS Foundation Trust v Derby City Council*[132] where the judge left the point open:

> [The rating authority] submitted that it is a fundamental requirement for a charity that its assets be dedicated to charitable purposes in perpetuity. Thus ... it was not possible to have a trust for charitable purposes for a fixed period or until the happening of an event. Further, she said, it was not possible for a corporation to be a charity if on dissolution its assets could be distributed amongst its members and used for non-charitable purposes.
>
> [The Trust] submitted that, in the case of a corporation, that the corporation had to be "established" for charitable purposes only. The purposes for which a corporation was established were the purposes which it could pursue while it existed. The distribution of its assets on its dissolution was not a purpose for which it was established and so the destination of its assets on a dissolution was irrelevant.
>
> ... In view of the difficulty of reconciling all of the authorities, and because to do so will not affect the outcome of this case, I have concluded that the prudent course is not to express any views on this question which would be obiter dicta only and might not be considered to be helpful in another case where the point does need to be decided.

3.28 Mixed charitable institution

This section considers the status of a body whose objects at any one time are partly charitable and partly not charitable. We shall refer to these bodies as **"mixed charitable institutions"**.[133]

An unincorporated association or company whose objects include charitable and non-charitable purposes is not a "charity" and does not qualify for any charity tax relief. The best course for such institutions is to split up into two parts: a charitable arm, restricted to charitable purposes only, which will qualify for tax exemption; and a non-charitable

131 Ssee *Hole v Garnsey* [1930] AC 472 at p.500.
132 [2019] EWHC 3436 (Ch) at [108] ff.
133 For mixed charitable trusts see 31.4 (Mixed charitable trust).

arm, unrestricted in its activities. The latter will not qualify for tax relief, but may obtain relief by giving funds to the charity (by Gift Aid).

If an unincorporated association or company holds two identifiably separate funds, one of which is to be applied for charitable purposes only, then what is the position? Unless the association or company holds the charitable fund as trustee, one cannot say that there is any body of persons established for charitable purposes only, and it is therefore not a charity within the tax definition. It is necessary to arrange a complete separation between charitable and non-charitable purposes.

3.29 Charity in course of liquidation

In *Re Arms*:

> The description of the company as [a "charity"] is not inaccurate as a matter of law, because, although it is in insolvent liquidation, it can remain registered with the Charity Commission (although I understand that it is the normal practice of the Charity Commission to remove a charitable company from the register if it goes into insolvent liquidation). Furthermore, it is hard to contend that the description of the company, even after it has gone into insolvent liquidation, as a "charity" is inaccurate, bearing in mind that [what is now s.113 CA 2011] ... clearly treats a company established for charitable purposes as a charity at all times until it is actually dissolved.[134]

Deregistration of insolvent charities should not prevent the charity from qualifying as a charity under the tax definition, as the requirement is not that they must be registered, but they comply with the requirement to be registered if any. However if it is possible not to deregister, then this issue would not arise.

134 *In re Arms Ltd* [1997] 1 WLR 877 at p.882.

CHAPTER FOUR

TAXATION OF CHARITY INCOME

Cross references

The following topics are considered elsewhere:
8.1 (Trading by charities)
34.12 (Charity exemption for estate income)
47.7 (Claims for income tax relief)

4.1 Meaning of "income"

The question sometimes arises as to what is the "income" of a charity or whether any particular receipt is "income". This question arises in various circumstances:

(1) For accountancy purposes
(2) For charity law purposes, eg:
  (a) Registration and audit requirements depend on the amount of a charity's income;
  (b) a charity's constitution may require income to be dealt with in a different way from capital
(3) For tax purposes

Accountancy principles generally govern the definition of income for (1) and (2). Accountancy principles apply for some tax purposes, eg relating to trading income[1] but not for other tax purposes.

4.2 Are gifts "income"

The starting point is that gifts are not in principle "income" for tax purposes and are not subject to Income Tax. This rule applies whether the gift is to a charity or a non-charity.

In *Graham v Green*:

> a mere gift is not a profit or gain,[2] and I hardly feel any doubt about that.[3]

HMRC agree. The Business Income Manual provides:

> **BIM80101: Scope of the provisions: Overview** [May 2011]
> ... Although the Miscellaneous Income provisions [s.687 ITTOIA] are

---

1 Section 25 ITTOIA.

2 The expression "profits or gains" in an income tax context was synonymous with "income" though this usage is now out of date.

3 9 TC 309 at 312. Likewise *Stedeford v Beloe* 16 TC 505 at 520:
"... it has been held again and again that a mere voluntary gift is not ... in the true sense of the word, income. It is merely a casual payment which depends upon somebody else's goodwill."

> "sweep up" sections, this does not mean that these provisions tax **all** profits that fall outside the other charging provisions of the Taxes Acts. The Miscellaneous Income provisions **do not** tax:
> ...voluntary receipts such as gifts and gratuities...

Likewise gifts by will and government grants do not in principle constitute income.

By contrast, the accountancy rule is that voluntary income is generally to be included in the statement of financial activities.[4] How does one reconcile what appears to be a contradiction? The answer is, the word "income" is imprecise and may have different meanings in different contexts. On this point tax and accountancy concepts simply differ.[5]

Corporation tax is a tax on profits, but profits means income and chargeable gains,[6] so the same principles apply.

The general rule that gifts are not income for tax purposes is subject to many exceptions:

(1) Gifts to a charity are treated as taxable income in the following cases:
   (a) Gift Aid payment from individuals[7]
   (b) Gift of money from companies[8]
   (c) Payroll giving scheme gift[9]
   (d) Inter-charity payment[10]
(2) Where the recipient is trading/an employee, a gift may constitute a trading receipt/earnings[11]

4.2.1 *Types of gift*

The Charities SORP distinguishes various types of gift: donations (restricted or unrestricted), and grants (for general or specific purposes, and unrestricted or performance-related):

---

4 See Charities SORP *http://www.charitiessorp.org/download-a-full-sorp*

5 One could reconcile the conflict in this way, by saying that gifts are income of a charity, but that income is not subject to income tax because income tax is in general charged only on income deriving from specified sources. A simple gift has no source (or its source is the benevolence of a donor which is not a source for IT purposes). But the cases do not take this approach.

6 See s.2(2) CTA 2009.

7 See 15.49 (Position of charity).

8 See 17.9 (Position of charity receiving gift).

9 See 19.6 (Position of charity receiving donation).

10 See 4.3 (Inter-charity payment).

11 See 12.7.2 (Charity grant: Trading receipt); 12.7.1 (Charity grant: Employment income).

Donations:

> **Donations** comprise gifts that will not provide any economic return to the donor other than the knowledge that someone will benefit from the donation.

Donations may be restricted or unrestricted:

> Income from donations includes gifts that must be spent on some particular area of work (i.e. restricted income funds) or given to be held as endowment funds...

Grants:

> **Grant income** is any voluntary income received by the charity (or other transfer of property) from a person or institution. The income or transfer may be for the general purposes of the charity, or for a specific purpose. It may be unconditional or be subject to conditions which, if not satisfied by the recipient charity, may lead to the grant property acquired with the aid of the grant or part of it being reclaimed by the grant-maker.

Grants may be performance-related:

> **Performance-related grant** is the term used to describe a grant that has the characteristics similar to those of a contract, in that:
> - the terms of the grant require the performance of a specified service that furthers the objectives of the grant maker; and
> - entitlement to the grant receivable is conditional on a specified output being provided by the grant recipient.
>
> Donations, for accounting presentation purposes, exclude any gifts such as performance-related grants where entitlement is dependent on the performance of a particular level of service or units of output being delivered.

All these categories of gift constitute gifts, and so are not income, for tax purposes, though the accounting treatment may differ.

These types of gift may be distinguished from contract income:

> **Contract income** is income received by a charity for the purpose of providing the goods or services under the terms of a legal contract. Indicators of a contract for the supply of services are:
> - the payer, rather than the recipient charity, has taken the lead in identifying the services to be provided; and/or
> - the arrangement provides for damages to be paid in the case of a breach of its terms, rather than, for example, for total or partial

refund of the payment made.

If there is no contract, the rights and obligations of the parties will depend primarily on the law of trusts and conditional gifts, rather than on the law of contract; such arrangements are termed performance-related grants by the SORP. A contractual payment to the charity will normally be unrestricted income of the charity.

The same or very similar distinctions are drawn:

- For direct tax: contract income would constitute a trading receipt, and taxable subject to the reliefs for trading income
- For VAT: supplies for services are VATable[12]

Of course, these particular distinctions are not the only ways to slice the cake,[13] but these are the distinctions which matter for UK tax and general law.

4.3 Inter-charity payment

s.523(1) ITA	**s.474 CTA 2010**
This section applies to payments which—	Subsection (2) applies if
(a) are received by charitable trusts from other charities,	a charitable company receives from another charity a payment which—
(b) are not made for full consideration in money or money's worth,	(a) is not made for full consideration in money or money's worth,
(c) are not charged to income tax, apart from this section, and	(b) is not chargeable to corporation tax apart from this section, and
(d) are not of a description which (on a claim) would be exempt from income tax under any of the exemptions conferred by this Part [Part 10, Charitable Trusts].	(c) is not of a description which (on a claim) would be exempt from corporation tax under any of the exemptions conferred by this Part [Part 11 Charitable Companies].

In the following discussion:

(1) The **"payor charity"** is the charity which makes a payment to another

12 See 35.10 (Grants and donations).

13 Shona distinguishes between a free gift (*handwa*) and a gift given to predispose the receiver in the giver's favour (*tsinzo*); Riddell, *Does Foreign Aid Really Work* (2007), p.1.

charity.

(2) The **"payee charity"** is the charity which receives the payment.
(3) The **"inter-charity payment"** is the payment to the payee charity.

Section 523 ITA/s.474 CTA 2010 then set out the treatment of inter-charity payments:

s. 523 ITA	**s.474 CTA 2010**
(3) Income tax is charged under this section on the payments.	(2) The payment is treated as an amount in respect of which the charitable company is chargeable to corporation tax, under the charge to corporation tax on income.
(4) It is charged on the full amount of the payments arising in the tax year.	
(5) But a payment is not taken into account in calculating total income so far as it is applied to charitable purposes only...	(3) But the payment is not taken into account in calculating total profits so far as it is applied to charitable purposes only.
(7) The trustees of the charitable trust are liable for any tax charged under this section.	

It is arguable that the transfer of an asset other than money does not constitute a "payment". At first sight it seems anomalous that there should be a distinction between money and non-money transfers. In such cases the word "payment" is capable of being understood widely to include non-money transfers. But if (as is generally thought the case) the requirement to deduct basic rate tax from annual payments applies only to money payments, then it makes sense that the charge on inter-charity payments (which is historically though not presently linked to annual payment) should be restricted to money payments.

4.3.1 *Discretionary trust rules*

s. 523(6) ITA	**s.474(4) CTA 2010**
The amount charged under this section in the case of certain payments made by the trustees of a	In the case of a payment to which section 494 of ITA 2007 (discretionary payments by trustees)

charitable trust in the exercise of a discretion is subject to section 494 (grossing up of discretionary payments from trusts).

applies, the references in subsections (2) and (3) to the payment are to be read as references to the grossed up amount of the discretionary payment within the meaning of that section.

Sections 493 and 494 ITA apply a deduction of tax regime where a non-charitable trust makes income payments. These sections do not apply to charitable trusts[14] so s.523(6) ITA/s.474(4) CTA 2010 are misconceived.

4.3.2 *Territorial limitation*

The charge on inter-charity payments only applies when both payor and payee are UK tax charities; so the provision does not apply where:

(1) a charity which is not a UK tax charity (eg a foreign (non EU) charity) makes a payment to a UK charity; or
(2) a UK tax charity makes a payment to a charity which is not a UK tax charity (eg a foreign (non EU) charity) .[15]

Section 523(2) ITA provides:

> This section does not apply to a payment which arises from a source outside the United Kingdom.

Before 2010, only a body established in the UK could be a UK tax charity, and we observed "It is difficult to see how a payment from a UK tax charity could have a foreign source, so these words are not strictly necessary." But now it will be needed since a non-resident charity could be a UK tax charity. There is no charge on a payment from a non-resident UK tax charity to a UK resident charitable trust.

Corporation Tax has no equivalent to this provision. Before the 2010 reforms that made no difference. EN CTA 2010 provides:

> 1453. Earlier drafts of subsection (1) added to the conditions (now paragraphs (a) to (c)) a further condition (paragraph (d)) that payment should not arise from a source outside the United Kingdom. This requirement has now been removed. It was unnecessary and subsection (1) now rewrites the law accurately as it stands. CTA 2009 replaced the reference to Schedule D Case III in section 505(2) of ICTA with a

14 See 12.5 (Charity beneficiaries).
15 But see 6.6 (Foreign body rule) below for tax considerations in such cases.

reference to the charge to corporation tax on income. The amendment made it clearer that the charge under section 505(2) is not limited to payments from a source in the United Kingdom.

No thought was given in 2010 to the implications of the reforms in this context. It is suggested, however, that the usual territorial limitations will apply, so a payment from a non-UK resident charity should be regarded as foreign source income and outside the scope of UK tax if received by a non-resident UK charitable company.

4.4 Taxable charity income

A charity may be subject to tax on its income in two circumstances. The charity may fail to satisfy some of the conditions for exemption, such as charitable expenditure rules. There are also some forms of income which do not qualify for tax relief. Examples are:

(1) Trading income outside the statutory exemptions
(2) Miscellaneous income outside the small misc income exemption[16]
(3) Employment income

4.5 Rate of tax on income

In practice most charitable income does qualify for tax relief. If charity income is taxable, the rates of tax are as follows. For UK resident charities:

(1) A charitable trust is subject to income tax at the basic or dividend ordinary rates (depending on the type of income). The trust is not subject to tax at the higher or additional rates, or dividend upper or additional rates, as these rates apply only to individuals, not to trustees. The trust is not subject to tax at the trust rate or the dividend trust rate. Section 479 ITA normally imposes these rates on discretionary trusts, but s.481(1)(c) ITA provides exemption for a charitable trust.
(2) A charitable company is subject to corporation tax at the corporation tax rate.

4.6 Investment income: General conditions for relief

4.6.1 *Investment income exemptions*

Sections 532 and 536 ITA contain reliefs for 10 categories of income, of

---

16 See 8.15.2 (Small misc income exemption).

which the most important are dividends, interest and annual payments. We refer to these as "**investment income exemptions**". This not an entirely accurate label, but it is difficult to think of better.

Section 532(2) ITA sets out six types of income which qualify for exemption and s.536(3) ITA sets out four types of income which qualify for exemption. The CT equivalents are s.486(2) and s.488(3) CTA 2010. The categories of income which are exempted for CT are slightly different, reflecting differences between CT and IT. In short, the exemptions are as follows:

Section 532 ITA exemptions	*Section 486 CTA 2010 exemptions*
(a) interest	(a) non-trading profits loan relationships
(b) dividends/distributions: UK resident co.	(b) dividends/distributions
(c) dividends: non-UK resident company	
(d) purchased life annuity	
(e) deeply discounted securities	
(f) unauthorised unit trusts	(c) unauthorised unit trusts

Section 536 ITA exemptions	*Section 488 CTA 2010 exemptions*
(a) royalties	(a) non-trading gains on intangible fixed assets
(b) telecommunication rights	(b) annual payments
(c) annual payments	(c) income from intangible fixed assets.
(d) relevant foreign distributions	

The investment income reliefs all share the standard condition that:

> Subsection (1) applies so far as the income is applied to charitable purposes only.[17]

See 4.21 (Application for charitable purposes).

4.6.2 *Exemptions requirements*

The investment income exemptions have one feature in common which is convenient to consider here.

s. 523(1) ITA	**s. 486 CTA 2010**
The income mentioned in subsection (2) is not taken into account in calculating total income if—	[identical]

---

17 Sections.532(4) and s.536(2) ITA; and for CT, s.486(5) and s.488(2) CTA 2010.

(a) it is income of a charitable trust, or	(a) it is income of a charitable company, or
(b) it is required, under an Act, court judgment, charter, trust deed or will, to be applied to charitable purposes only.[18]	(b) it is required, under an Act (including an Act of the Scottish Parliament), court judgment, charter, trust deed or will, to be applied to charitable purposes only.[19]

Thus the general condition for the investment income exemptions is that the income is either:

(1) income of a charitable trust or charitable company, or

(2) the income, under the provisions of the relevant constitution, is applicable to charitable purposes only.[20]

Requirement (1) is the standard requirement.[21] The alternative requirement (2) requires:

(1) an institution established by Act, court judgment, charter, trust deed or will, and

(2) under the constitution of the institution, income is applicable for charitable purposes only.

The terminology was explained by Jenkins LJ in *Dreyfus v IRC*: "charter" means royal charter granted by the Sovereign;"trust deed", and "will", refer to trusts and wills taking effect and enforceable under the law of the UK.[22] The reference to acts of parliament and charters reflects the state of company law in 1842, a time before companies could be incorporated under the companies acts.[23]

---

18 Section 536(1) ITA is the same:

"The income mentioned in subsection (3) is not taken into account in calculating total income if—

(a) it is income of a charitable trust, or

(b) it is required, under an Act, court judgment, charter, trust deed or will, to be applied to charitable purposes only."

19 Section 488(1) CTA 2010 imposes the same requirements.

20 This is clear in the statutory provisions but (if authority is necessary) the point was made in *George Drexler Ofrex Foundation v IRC* 42 TC 524 at p.543.

21 See 3.4 (Tax definition of charity).

22 36 TC at p.152. This should now be read as extending to EU laws, to be EU law compliant.

23 See Avery Jones, "Bodies of Persons" [1991] BTR 453 at p.455.

The IT provision refers to an Act, and the CT provision adds "including an Act of the Scottish Parliament" but that is not a real difference, as the ITA has a definition of the word "Act".

Income which falls into category (2) will generally fall within (1) as income of a UK tax charity. What is the reason for alternative (2)? *Dreyfus v IRC* explains:

> The alternative was added in order to cover those cases in which only a part of the income is, by virtue of the Act of Parliament or other instrument named, applicable to charitable purposes, in contradistinction to those bodies of persons or trusts which are exclusively established for such purposes.[24]

Category (2) only applies to income falling within the investment income exemptions, that is, in short, distributions, interest and annual payments. Such income will qualify for relief in the hands of temporary charitable bodies and partly charitable bodies even if such bodies are not "charities" for UK tax purposes. Other forms of income are not so favourably treated, and enjoy charity relief only if the recipient is a UK tax charity.

4.6.3 *Align exemptions: Critique*

Sections 532(1)(b) and 536(1)(b) ITA (and the CT equivalents, s.486 and s. 488 CTA 2010) should be repealed so that the investment income exemptions only applies to charities. This would bring the investment income exemptions into line with all other charity exemptions.

In practice no-one takes any notice of this historical clutter, and eventually, perhaps, someone will take the opportunity to rationalise and simplify.

4.6.4 *Restriction on s.532 exemptions*

For completeness, s.532(3) ITA (no CTA equivalent) provides:

> Subsection (1) applies only so far as the income falls within, and is dealt with under, Part 4 of ITTOIA 2005 (see s.366 of that Act as to provisions given priority over Part 4).

This takes us to s.366 ITTOIA:

> (1) Any income, so far as it falls within—

24 36 TC 126 at p.137.

(a) any Chapter of this Part, and
(b) Chapter 2 of Part 2 (receipts of a trade, profession or vocation),
is dealt with under Part 2.
(2) Any income, so far as it falls within—
(a) any Chapter of this Part, and
(b) Chapter 3 of Part 3 so far as the Chapter relates to a UK property business,
is dealt with under Part 3.
(3) Any income, so far as it falls within—
(a) any Chapter of this Part other than Chapter 3 or 6, and
(b) Part 2, 9 or 10 of ITEPA 2003 (employment income, pension income or social security income),
is dealt with under the relevant Part of ITEPA 2003.

Thus if (say) a charity is trading in shares, and receives dividend income which is a trading receipt, the rules for trading income take priority. In practice this will not often if ever arise.

4.7 Dividends and distributions

4.7.1 *Outline*

In outline:

(1) Charitable companies:

(a) Exempt distributions are not subject to corporation tax, so charity tax relief is not needed

(b) Non-exempt distributions qualify for charity tax relief: s.486 CTA 2010

(2) Charitable trusts:

(a) Distributions from UK companies qualify for charity tax relief: s.532 ITA

(b) Distributions from non UK companies qualify for charity tax relief: s.536 ITA

The end result is that charities should not pay tax on dividends or other distributions.

There are two reasons for the complexity:

(1) Charity tax reliefs must fit into the existing (complex) rules for taxation of distributions.
(2) There are different rules for charitable companies and for charitable trusts

The second set of complications could easily be avoided;[25] but there it is.

4.7.2 *Co: Exempt distribution*

Section 931A(1) CTA 2009 provides:

> The charge to corporation tax on income applies to any dividend or other distribution of a company, but only if the distribution is not exempt.

A full discussion of the relief for exempt distributions is outside the scope of this book. In outline, there are two sets of rules in Part 9A CTA 2009: Chapter 2 provides the rules where the recipient is a "small company" and Chapter 3 provides the rules for other companies.

A charitable company may need to know if it is a small company in order to know which set of rules applies. Section 931S(1) CTA 2009 provides a referential definition:

> For the purposes of this Part a company is a "small company" in an accounting period if it is in that period a micro or small enterprise, as defined in the Annex to Commission Recommendation 2003/361/ EC of 6 May 2003.

A full discussion of this definition is also outside the scope of this book but one point is worth noting. In order to be a small company, a charity must be an enterprise. As to when a charity is an enterprise, see 9.16.1 (When is charity affected). Many charitable companies which are in fact small will not count as "small companies" for these purposes so will be governed by the rules which regulate large companies. However in most cases this will not make any difference, as dividends will generally qualify for exemption whether or not a charitable company is "small."

4.7.3 *Charitable trust: UK distribution/Co: Non-exempt distribution*

s.532 ITA	**s.486 CTA 2010**
(1) The income mentioned in subsection (2) is not taken into account in calculating total income ...[26]	(1) The income mentioned in subsection (2) is not taken into account in calculating total profits...
(2) The income referred to in	[identical]

25 See 3.26 (Alignment of charitable trusts/companies: Critique).

26 For the words which follow here, see 4.6.2 (Exemption requirements).

subsection (1) is...	
(b) a dividend[27] or other distribution of a UK resident company ...	(b) a dividend or other distribution of a company...

Section 486(3) CTA 2010 deals with the case where a dividend/ distribution is also a receipt of a trade or property business, but that is not likely to apply to charities.

4.7.4 *Trust: Foreign distribution*

For income tax, s.532 ITA provides relief for foreign dividends:

> (1) The income mentioned in subsection (2) is not taken into account in calculating total income ...[28]
> (2) The income referred to in subsection (1) is ...
> (c) a dividend of a non-UK resident company,

Section 536 ITA provides relief for other foreign distributions:

> (1) The income mentioned in subsection (3) is not taken into account in calculating total income ...[29]
> (3) The income referred to in subsection (1) is
> (d) relevant foreign distributions.[30]

4.7.5 *Dividend income: Planning*

It is in principle better for a charity to invest in direct investments, and not to receive dividend income from a company within the charge to corporation tax.[31]

---

27 Section 532(5) ITA defines dividend by reference:
"'dividend', in relation to a UK resident company, has the same meaning as in Chapter 3 of Part 4 of [ITTOIA] (dividends etc from UK resident companies etc) (see s.382(4) of [ITTOIA])."

28 For the words not printed here, see 4.6.2 (Exemption requirements).

29 For the words not printed here, see 4.6.2 (Exemption requirements).

30 Section 536(4) ITA defines "relevant foreign distribution":
"relevant foreign distribution" means a distribution of a non-UK resident company which—
(a) is not chargeable to tax under Chapter 4 of Part 4 of ITTOIA 2005 (dividends from non-UK resident companies), but
(b) would be chargeable to tax under Chapter 3 of that Part of that Act (dividends etc from UK resident companies etc) if the company were a UK resident company.

31 For the situation where a charity owns all or a substantial part of a company, see 9.3 (Extracting profit by Gift Aid) .

It is better for an individual to retain shares and give a cash sum equal to the dividend income to a charity (under Gift Aid) rather than to give the shares to the charity; assuming
(1) QIDR does not apply; and
(2) The individual pays sufficient tax to frank the Gift Aid payment.

4.8 Interest

s.532 ITA	s.486 CTA 2010
(1) The income mentioned in subsection (2) is not taken into account in calculating total income ...[32]	(1) The income mentioned in subsection (2) is not taken into account in calculating total profits...
(2) The income referred to in subsection (1) is—	(2) The income referred to in subsection (1) is—
(a) interest.[33]	(a) profits which are charged to tax under section 299 of CTA 2009 (non-trading profits from loan relationships)[34]...

4.9 Deeply discounted securities

For income tax, s.532 ITA provides:

> (1) The income mentioned in subsection (2) is not taken into account in calculating total income ...[35]
> (2) The income referred to in subsection (1) is ...
> (e) profits on the disposal of deeply discounted securities.

For charitable companies, such profits fall within the Loan Relationship rules and so are exempt.[36]

4.10 Unauthorised unit trusts

s.532 ITA	s.486 CTA 2010
(1) The income mentioned in	(1) The income mentioned in

32 For the words not printed here, see 4.6.2 (Exemption requirements).
33 Section 532(5) ITA defines "interest" by reference:
"'interest' includes anything treated as interest for the purposes of Chapter 2 of Part 4 of [ITTOIA] (interest)".
34 See 11.5 (Loan relationships).
35 For the words not printed here, see 4.6.2 (Exemption requirements).
36 See 11.5 (Loan relationships).

subsection (2) is not taken into account in calculating total income ...[37]	subsection (2) is not taken into account in calculating total profits...
(2) The income referred to in subsection (1) is ...	[identical]
(f) income treated for the purposes of Chapter 10 of Part 4 of ITTOIA 2005 (distributions from unauthorised unit trusts) as received by a unit holder from a scheme to which s.547 of that Act applies (unauthorised unit trust schemes).	(c) income treated for the purposes of Chapter 5 of Part 10 of CTA 2009 (distributions from unauthorised unit trusts) as received by a unit holder from a scheme to which section 972 of that Act applies (unauthorised unit trust schemes)...
	(4) Subsection (1) applies, in relation to the income mentioned in subsection (2)(c), only so far as the income falls within, and is dealt with under, Part 10 of CTA 2009 (see section 982 of that Act as to provisions given priority over Part 10).

4.11 Annual payments

"Annual payment" is a technical term: it is an opaque label for a category of income whose meaning is discussed in a large body of case law. The most important type of annual payment now is income payments from a discretionary trust.

s. 536(3) ITA	**s. 488 CTA 2010**
(1) The income mentioned in subsection (3) is not taken into account in calculating total income...[38]	(1) The income mentioned in subsection (3) is not taken into account in calculating total profits...
(3) The income referred to in subsection (1) is ...	[identical]

37 For the words not printed here, see 4.6.2 (Exemption requirements).
38 For the words not printed here, see 4.6.2 (Exemption requirements).

(c) annual payments charged to tax under Chapter 7 of Part 5 of ITTOIA 2005.

(b) annual payments charged to tax under Chapter 7 of Part 10 of CTA 2009

For completeness, s.532 ITA provides:

> (1) The income mentioned in subsection (2) is not taken into account in calculating total income ...[39]
> (2) The income referred to in subsection (1) is ...
> (d) an annuity payment under a purchased life annuity

In practice charities will not usually purchase a life annuity.

Under CTA 2010, the exemption applies to annual payments having a UK or a foreign source.

Profits of a trade are not "annual payments", so a charity's trading income is not exempt from tax under these sections.[40]

4.12 Royalties

In this section we use the term **"royalty income"** to mean royalties and other receipts from intellectual property (defined s.579 ITTOIA).

Royalty income is classified for tax purposes in one of three ways. Statute does not provide much terminology, so we coin the following terms:

(1) **Trade royalties**: royalties which constitute a receipt of a trade or profession (including a post-cessation receipts).

(2) **Non-trade royalties**: royalties which are not trade royalties. These may be:

(a) **Annual payment royalties**: royalties which are annual payments

(b) **Non-annual payment royalties**.

The three categories are recognised in *Noddy Subsidiary Rights v IRC* 43 TC 458 at p.474:

> It seems to me that, where you have this position, that a person owns an asset of any kind, whether physical or not, and grants licences under it, the activities which he carries on in connection with the grant of those licences may amount to a trade and then Case I of Schedule D applies.

---

39 For the words not printed here, see 4.6.2 (Exemption requirements).

40 This now seems self-evident, but in the early history of income tax it seemed arguable: see *Trustees of Psalms and Hymns v Whitwell* 3 TC 7, followed (despite some criticism) in *R v Special Commissioners ex p. Shaftesbury Homes and Arethusa Training Ship* 8 TC 367.

> On the other hand, at the other end of the scale, the activities may amount to the mere holding of an investment, so that the receipt of income is in the nature of pure income profit and then Case III of Schedule D applies. There may be intermediate cases in which Case VI of Schedule D might apply.

ITTOIA has changed the terminology but not the underlying categorisation.

s. 536(3) ITA	**s. 488 CTA 2010**
(1) The income mentioned in subsection (3) is not taken into account in calculating total income...[41]	(1) The income mentioned in subsection (3) is not taken into account in calculating total profits...[42]
	(2) Subsection (1) applies so far as the income is applied to charitable purposes only.
(3) The income referred to in subsection (1) is ...	[identical]
(a) royalties and other income from intellectual property[43] that do not fall within Chapter 2 of Part 2 of ITTOIA 2005 (receipts of a trade etc),	(a) non-trading gains on intangible fixed assets ...
(b) income derived from a relevant telecommunication right[44] that is not income falling within Chapter 2 of Part 2 of ITTOIA 2005 (receipts of a trade etc),	(c) qualifying income from intangible fixed assets...

The exemption applies to all royalty income taxable under Chapter 2 Part 5, ie it does not matter whether or not the royalties are "annual payments".[45] It is however essential that the royalties are not trading

41 For the words not printed here, see 4.6.2 (Exemption requirements).
42 For the words not printed here, see 4.6.2 (Exemption requirements).
43 Section 536(4) ITA defines "intellectual property" by reference.
44 Section 536(4) ITA defines "relevant telecommunication right" by reference.
45 This was also the position under the ICTA rules which applied to charitable trusts before 2005 and charitable companies before 2009: *Lawrence v IRC* 23 TC 333.

income, since trading income does not qualify for the s.536 exemption, and would be taxable (unless the very limited trading income exemption applied.) For the trade/non trade dividing line, in the context of royalties, see *Noddy Subsidiary Rights Co Ltd v IRC* 43 TC 458 AT p.474.

Section 488(5) CTA 2010 provides supplemental definitions:

> In this section—
> "intangible fixed asset" has the same meaning as in Part 8 of CTA 2009 (see section 713 of that Act),
> "non-trading credit" has the meaning given by section 301 of CTA 2009,
> "non-trading gain" has the meaning given by section 751 of CTA 2009,
> "pre-FA 2002 asset" has the meaning given by sections 881 and 892 to 895 of CTA 2009, and
> "qualifying income from intangible fixed assets" means income which—
> (a) is in respect of intangible fixed assets which are pre-FA 2002 assets,
> (b) is of a kind which, if the intangible fixed assets were not

---

ITA EN change 96 considered (probably wrongly, but it does not matter) that royalties of charitable trusts did not qualify for exemption between the introduction of ITTOIA in 2005 and the introduction of ITA in 2007, unless they were annual payments (ie non annual payment royalties did not qualify). However HMRC did not take that point and it is now academic. ITA EN provided:

Change 96: Charitable trusts: exemption for income from intellectual property etc: s.536

This change provides an exemption from income tax for certain royalties and other income from intellectual property and certain income derived from a relevant telecommunication right, whether or not the income is annual in nature.

Section 488 CTA 2010 provides for an exemption from tax in respect of (among other things) income chargeable under s.579 of ITTOIA and income chargeable under Chapter 4 of Part 5 of ITTOIA. But only, in each case, to the extent that the income relates to annual payments.

Section 579 of ITTOIA charges royalties etc from intellectual property and Chapter 4 of Part 5 charges certain telecommunication rights. In each case the charge to tax is on income that does not arise from the carrying on of a trade. So the income chargeable under the provisions referred to can be annual in nature, but need not be so. Prior to ITTOIA, income of this sort was chargeable under Schedule D Case III if annual in nature, and under Schedule D Case VI if not. So the exemption applied only to Case III income. But in practice HMRC allow an exemption for income chargeable under s.579 or under Chapter 4 of Part 5 whether or not it is annual in nature. This change is in line with that practice, and reflects the unity of the charging provisions post-ITTOIA.

pre-FA 2002 assets, would fall to be brought into account under Chapter 6 of Part 8 of CTA 2009 as non-trading credits, and

(c) does not fall within subsection (3)(a) or (b).

4.13 Property income

s. 531 ITA	**s.485 CTA 2010**
(1) Income which is chargeable to income tax under Part 2 of ITTOIA 2005 (trading income) as a result of s.261 of that Act is not taken into account in calculating total income so far as—	(1) Income which is chargeable to corporation tax under Part 3 of CTA 2009 (trading income) as a result of section 287 of that Act is not taken into account in calculating total profits so far as—
(a) it arises in respect of rents or other receipts from an estate, interest or right in or over land, and	[identical]
(b) the estate, interest or right is vested in any person in trust for a charitable trust or for charitable purposes.	(b) the estate, interest or right is vested in any person for charitable purposes.
(2) Income which is chargeable to income tax under Part 3 of ITTOIA 2005 (property income) is not taken into account in calculating total income so far as—	(2) Income which is chargeable to corporation tax under Part 4 of CTA 2009 (property income) is not taken into account in calculating total profits so far as—
(a) it arises in respect of an estate, interest or right in or over land, and	[identical]
(b) the estate, interest or right is vested in any person in trust for a charitable trust or for charitable purposes.	(b) the estate, interest or right is vested in any person for charitable purposes.
(2A) Distributions to which section 548 of CTA 2010 (Real Estate Investment Trusts: distributions) applies and which are chargeable to income tax under Part 2 or Part 3 of ITTOIA 2005 are not taken into account in calculating total income	(3) Distributions to which section 548 (Real Estate Investment Trusts: distributions) applies and which are chargeable to corporation tax under Part 4 of CTA 2009 are not taken into account in calculating total profits so far as they arise in respect

so far as they arise in respect of shares vested in a person in trust for a charitable trust or for charitable purposes.	of shares vested in any person for charitable purposes.
(3) Subsection (1) to (2A) apply so far as the income is applied to charitable purposes only.	(4) Subsections (1) to (3) apply so far as the income is applied to charitable purposes only.
	(5) The exemptions under this section require a claim

Property income is normally exempt under s.531(2) ITA. Section 531(1) ITA is needed for the rare case where property-type income is charged as trading income.[46]

The requirement that land must be vested in a person for charitable purposes is satisfied when land is vested in any charity, whether a trust, company or an unincorporated association. The requirement is also satisfied where the land is vested in a nominee for a charity. The income arises from an equitable interest vested in the charity.

Rent to a charitable trust for the use of furniture in a furnished letting is (in the absence of a trade) charged as property income. See Part 3 of ITTOIA or s.248 CTA 2009. Sections 531 ITA or s.485 CTA 2010 do not strictly provide exemption since such rent is not from land. HMRC may not take the point. HMRC Guidance Note at Annex i3.2 previously stated that the exemption included income from furnished lettings. HMRC Guidance Note has now been amended and this is not mentioned, but this is no reason to assume that the position has in fact changed.

The exemption extends to land outside the United Kingdom.

As to the border between property/trading income, see 8.2.2 (Rent or trading income?).

46 Section 261 ITTOIA provides:

"**Provisions which must be given priority over Part 3**

Any receipt or other credit item, so far as it falls within-

(a) Chapter 3 of this Part so far as it relates to an overseas property business or Chapter 8 or 9 of this Part (rent receivable in connection with a UK s.12(4) concern or for UK electric-line wayleaves), and

(b) Chapter 2 of Part 2 (receipts of a trade, profession or vocation),

is dealt with under Part 2."

The exemption covers income arising from the lease premium provisions.

4.13.1 *Transactions in land*

The transactions in land provisions[47] impose an IT/CT charge on a variety of capital gains arising from a disposal of land.[48] They can apply in many cases where there is no intention of tax avoidance. An example is overage (where the sale price depending on the price received from a subsequent sale by the purchaser).

s.517C(1) ITA	**s. 356OC(1) CTA 2010**
The profit or gain is to be treated for income tax purposes as profits of a trade carried on by the chargeable person.	The profit or gain is to be treated for corporation tax purposes as profits of a trade carried on by the chargeable company (see section 356OG).

As the trade is not a primary purpose trade, the charity trading exemption does not apply. The profit does not qualify for charity relief.

The solution may be

(1) a subsidiary company holds the land. The subsidiary may sell the land.
(2) subsidiary company holds a sub-subsidiary which holds the land

Diagrammatically:

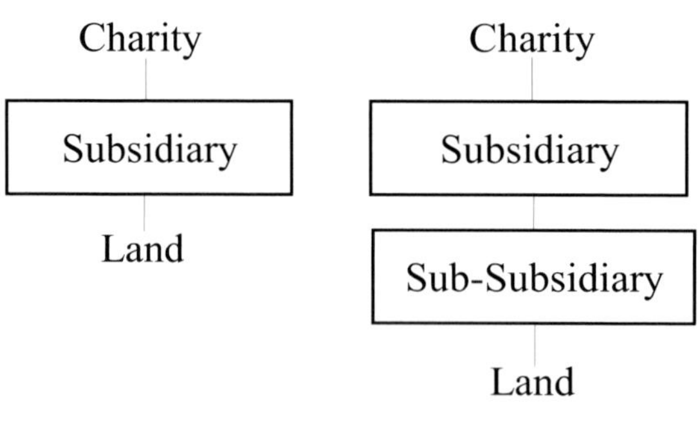

The profit on the sale may be taxable under the TiL rules; but the vendor may then make a qualifying donation to the charity.

47 For a discussion of these provisions, see Kessler, *Taxation of Non-Residents and Foreign Domiciliaries* (21st ed, 2022-23), para 22.5 (Transactions in land: Introduction) online version *https://www.foreigndomiciliaries.co.uk*

48 Section 752 ITA; the CT equivalent is s.815 CTA 2010.

4.14 Life policies/annuities

4.14.1 *Introduction*

This section considers gains from:

(1) a policy of life insurance,
(2) contract for life annuity, or
(3) capital redemption policy.

We refer to these as "policies". They fall within the scope of provisions known as the "chargeable event provisions". For charitable trusts they are found in Chapter 9 Part 4 ITTOIA. A full discussion of these provisions needs a book to itself.[49]

In outline, there are three stages to the application of these provisions. The first is to ascertain whether there is a "chargeable event". The second stage is to compute the gain arising on the chargeable event. The third stage is to ascertain the method of charging the gain to tax.

A "qualifying policy" (elaborately defined) will not normally give rise to a chargeable event, unless it has been acquired for consideration, and charitable trusts currently enjoy a limited exemption from the tax charges imposed on some policies. However, the return on the funds invested in the policy (whether qualifying or not) will reflect the fact that the life company (if UK resident) will itself normally be subject to tax on its investments. Accordingly, policies are not appropriate investments for any charity.

4.14.2 *Charitable expenditure rules*

Policies are approved charitable investments (for the charitable expenditure rules) if a claim is made under s.558 ITA or, for corporation tax, s.511 CTA 2010. (This assumes no tax avoidance, but it is difficult to see how there could be any.) HMRC Guidance Note Annex vi.2 provides:

> **Premiums paid**
> vi.2 Premiums paid
> vi.2.1 HMRC can't accept premiums paid by charities on insurance policies (including policies assigned in favour of charities) as qualifying [ie approved charitable] investments within type 12 of section 558

---

49 For a general introduction see Kessler, *Taxation of Non-Residents and Foreign Domiciliaries* (21st ed., 2022-23), Chapter 65 (Life Policies and Contracts) online version *https://www.foreigndomiciliaries.co.uk*

Income Tax Act 2007 or type 12 of section 511 Corporation Tax Act (CTA) 2010 (previously Paragraph 9(1) Schedule 20 Income and Corporation Taxes Act 1988). Further, HMRC don't accept such payments as qualifying expenditure within the previous definition in S506 ICTA1988. That is, HMRC regard the payment of premiums by a charity as non-charitable expenditure within section 543(f) ITA 2007 or section 496(d) CTA 2010.
vi.2.2 While section 558 ITA 2007 and section 511 CTA 2010 (previously paragraph 9(1)) gives HMRC the power to consider investments other than those specified at types 1 to 11 of those Acts (previously Schedule 20), such investments should be of the same kind as those specified. HMRC don't consider that premiums paid under an insurance policy have the same character as those specified investments. Such premiums are payment of consideration for entering into a contractual relationship. Further, regular premiums are paid in discharge of obligations under such a contractual relationship. The policy holders acquire or maintain rights under the contract; they don't acquire any entitlement to an interest in the underlying investments. The underlying investments remain the property of the insurer.
vi.2.3 HMRC don't consider amounts paid as premium under insurance policies to be qualifying expenditure (previously within section 506 Income and Corporation Taxes Act (ICTA) 1988) but as non- charitable expenditure within section 543(f) ITA 2007 or section 496(d) CTA 2010, as they're not laid out in furtherance of a charity's charitable objects.

We cannot agree: a policy may in principle be an "investment" which falls within s.558 ITA or s.511 CTA 2010. The fact that the charity/insurance company relationship is contractual is neither here nor there. A charity/banker relationship is also contractual but a bank deposit is an approved charitable investment. As noted above, however, a policy is not an appropriate investment for a charity, so in practice it does not matter.

4.14.3 *Charitable trust*

For charitable trusts the gain is subject to tax: s.467(2) ITTOIA. Tax is charged at the savings rate: s.467(7)(a) ITTOIA. In the case of a UK or EU policy, the trustees would in principle be entitled to a corresponding (non-repayable) credit so no tax becomes payable: ss.530–534 ITTOIA.

The HMRC view is set out in HMRC Guidance Note Annex vi.5 to vi.8. This is not set out here as in practice it should not arise.

4.14.4 *Charitable company*

The FA 2008 brings all life insurance policies and life annuity contracts to which a company is a party, other than protection-type policies, within the loan relationships legislation, so charitable companies do not generally have to consider the chargeable event rules. The profit under the loan relationship rules qualifies for exemption.[50] HMRC agree. HMRC Guidance Note provides:

> **Accounting periods beginning on or after 1 April 2008**
> VI.5.5 Sections 541, 546 and 547 ICTA 1988 were repealed by Schedule 14 Finance Act (FA) 2008 and the treatment for investment life assurance contracts (includes capital redemption products) was replaced by Schedule 13 of that Act (see also section 36 FA 2008) and then incorporated into sections 560 to 569 CTA 2009.
> Such policies (contracts) were deemed to be loan relationships with effect from accounting periods beginning on or after 1 April 2008. Exemption from tax on non- trading profits in respect of loan relationships is available under section 486 CTA 2010 ... provided the income is applied to charitable purposes only.

4.15 Offshore funds

Offshore funds are in principle approved charitable investments for the charitable expenditure rules, if the necessary claim is made.[51]

A gain arising on the disposal of an offshore fund (an offshore income gain) is normally taxed as income.

s. 535 ITA	**Reg 31(1) Offshore Funds (Tax) Regulations 2009 ("OFTR")**
(1) Offshore income gains[52] accruing to a charitable trust are not taken into account in calculating total income.	A charitable company[53] shall be exempt from corporation tax in respect of an offshore income gain

50 See 11.5 (Loan Relationships) .
51 See 6.22 (Other investments:Type 12) .
52 Defined by reference in s.535(3) ITA:
"In this section 'offshore income gain' has the same meaning as in Chapter 5 of Part 2 of the OFTR."
53 Regulation 31(6) OFTR provides the definition by reference: "In this regulation "charity" and "charitable company" have the same meaning as in section 506 of ICTA." The reference is obsolete (the policy of the tax law rewrite was not to update statutory instruments). However the legislation still works, because the continuity provisions in (for example) para 5 sch 2 CTA 2010 require old references to take effect as references to the rewritten provisions.

(2) Subsection (1) applies if the gain is applicable and applied to charitable purposes only.	if the gain is applicable and applied for charitable purposes.

The wording of the exemption is similar to the charity's CGT exemption.[54]

Regulation 101 OFTR provides exemption for the charge (in reg.94) on undistributed income of reporting funds:

> (1) This regulation applies if—
> (a) a charitable company[55] is a participant in a reporting fund, or
> (b) the trustees of a charitable trust are participants in a reporting fund.
> (2) No liability to tax arises in respect of any amount which, under regulation 94(1), is treated as distributed to a charitable company or the trustees of a charitable trust.

For completeness, reg. 94(3) disapplies the CGT relief which prevents a double charge to tax where the regulation 94 charge applies. In practice this is of theoretical interest only since any gains accruing to charity will be exempt:

> Paragraph (2) of regulation 99 (read with paragraphs (3) and (4) of that regulation) does not apply to the disposal of an interest in a reporting fund by a charitable company or the trustees of a charitable trust.

4.15.1 *Cross references*

Regulation 31(1) OFTR provides a clawback charge which is discussed at 5.7 (Termination of charitable trust).

For relief on an offshore income gain arising on a gift of an offshore fund to charity, see 23.6 (Offshore fund) and for QIDR, see 21.4 ("Qualifying investment").

For the taxation of offshore funds generally, see *Taxation of Non-Residents and Foreign Domiciliaries* (20th ed., 2021-22), Chapters 63 - 65 (Offshore Funds) online version *https://www.foreigndomiciliaries.co.uk*

4.16 Miscellaneous minor exemptions

A miscellany of minor charging provisions make a specific exemption for

---

54 See 5.1 (Charity's CGT relief) .

55 Regulation 31(6) OFTR again provides the standard (obsolete) definition discussed in the footnote above: "In this regulation "charity" and "charitable company" have the same meaning as in section 506 of ICTA."

charity.

(1) *Certificates of Deposit.* Charities are exempt from the charge relating to certificates of deposit and deposit rights if the profits or gains on disposal are applied to charitable purposes only: s.534 ITA and, for corporation tax, s.486 CTA 2010.

(2) *Accrued Income Scheme.* Charitable trusts are exempt from the accrued income scheme: see s.645 ITA. There is, as with offshore income gains, a clawback provision if a temporary charity ceases to be charitable.[56] There is no requirement that any sum should be applied for charitable purposes; though this is of little practical significance if the view which we have taken of this expression is correct; see 4.21 (Application for charitable purposes). Charitable companies do not need this exemption as the accrued income scheme does not apply to companies; instead the loan relationship rules apply.

(3) *Charity Pension Schemes.* An income tax charge normally arises where an authorised surplus payment is made to a sponsoring employer by an occupational pension scheme. This charge does not apply when the employer is a charity: s.207(6) FA 2004. There is no requirement that the sums repaid must be applied to charitable purposes only. There is no exemption for the charge on unauthorised payments made by a registered pension scheme.

(4) *Non-trading gains on intangible fixed assets.* The charge in Part 8 CTA 2009 (formerly in sch 29 FA 2002) does not apply.

(5) *Miscellaneous income*: see 8.15.2 (Small misc income exemption).

4.17 Disguised interest

Disguised interest is covered in Chapter 2A Part 4 ITTOIA.

Section 381A ITTOIA imposes the charge to tax:

> (1) This Chapter applies where a person is party to an arrangement[57] which produces for the person a return in relation to any amount which is economically equivalent to interest.
> (2) Income tax is charged on the return if the return is not charged to income tax under or as a result of any other provision of this Act or any other Act.

---

56 See 4.15 (Offshore funds) and 31.3.2 (Temporary charitable trust: income tax and CGT) .

57 Section 318A(6) provides the standard definition: "In this Chapter "arrangement" includes any agreement, understanding, scheme, transaction or series of transactions (whether or not legally enforceable)."

Section 381A(3) ITTOIA provides that other charging provisions have priority even if they qualify for exemption from tax:

> Subsection (2) does not apply to a return that would be charged to income tax under or as a result of another provision but for an exemption.

These terms are elaborately defined, but this is not considered here.

Since there is a charity tax exemption for interest, there ought to be a charity exemption under these provisions.

The provisions do not apply to charitable companies. There is comparable corporation tax legislation, but if this applied (which is not likely) it brings in the loan relationships rules, where a charity exemption applies.[58]

The conclusion is that charitable companies may invest in this class of asset but charitable trusts should not do so.

If (as recommended in this book) charitable trusts were brought into corporation tax, this problem would cease to arise.[59]

In practice however disguised interest is not likely to arise.

4.18 Swaps

4.18.1 *Swaps: Trading or non-trading*

The first question is:

(1) whether the charity is trading, and if so

(2) whether the swap is held for the purposes of the trade (ie as trading stock).

The two questions normally come to the same thing.

HMRC comment in RI 263:

> 17. The question of whether a swap is held for the purposes of a trade is one of fact. Where a swap transaction by an approved pension scheme[60] appears to fall close to the trading/investment borderline, the Revenue will look at the case on its merits.
>
> 18. However, where an approved pension scheme uses interest rate swaps, currency swaps, equity swaps, credit derivatives or similar instruments –

---

58 See 11.5 (Loan relationships).

59 See 3.26 (Alignment of charitable trusts/companies: Critique).

60 Authors' footnote: Although this refers to a pension scheme, the same would apply to a charity.

> - to hedge risks inherent in its existing investment portfolio of shares, bonds or similar securities; or
> - as part of an investment strategy to enhance the return from its existing investment portfolio; or
> - to create a synthetic exposure to investments of a particular type or in a particular market, in line with the fund's normal policies of investing directly in such instruments,
>
> the Revenue will normally regard such swaps as investments. ...
>
> 20. As outlined above in relation to approved pension schemes, "investment" takes its normal commercial meaning. It is capable of including a swap. While we cannot give advance confirmation that a particular swap will be a qualifying investment we can confirm that we will follow the Charity Commission guidance in their leaflet CC14 in deciding whether a particular swap is an investment.[61]

If the charity is carrying on a trade, the profits will be dealt with as other trading profits: see 8.1 (Trade carried on by charity).

4.18.2 *Swaps: Non-trading*

There are three issues:

(1) whether expenditure on acquisition of the swap (or payment of liabilities under the swap) is non-charitable expenditure under the charitable expenditure rules

(2) whether profit from the swap is in principle taxable

(3) if so whether charity exemption applies.

RI 263 notes but has nothing to say on the first issue:

> ... There is guidance in Annex III to the Detailed Guidance notes in the charities pages on the Inland Revenue website that sets out the approach we adopt in deciding whether or not a particular investment is [an approved charitable investment].
>
> 21. However, even where the Board is satisfied that a swap contract held by a charity is [an approved charitable] investment, profits arising on the swap will only be exempt from income or corporation tax if they fall within one of the categories [qualifying for charity tax relief].

It is necessary to consider charitable companies and trusts separately. For charitable companies, RI 263 continues:

---

61 Authors' footnote: CC14 (Charities and investment matters: a guide for trustees) makes only general comments, and does not refer specifically to swaps.

> 22. The types of swap in normal commercial use will fall within [what is now Part 7 CTA 2009] derivative contracts regime ... where the charity concerned is a company or unincorporated association. In such cases, profits from the swap will normally give rise to non-trading loan relationship credits, taxable under [now s.299 CTA 2009]. The exemption [now s.486 CTA 2010] will apply.

So far so good. For charitable trusts, however, the position is different:

> 23. Where the swap is held by a charitable trust, however, profits will in many instances fall within Case VI[62] ...

Assuming the profit is taxable in principle, the question arises whether any charity exemption applies.

> Case VI income from such a source does not fall within any of the [now Part 10 ITA] exemptions. But there is a *de minimis* exemption in [s.527 ITA] which exempts most Case VI income of charities below £5,000. It also exempts the lesser of £50,000 or the income if it is less than 25% of the charities' incoming resources for the chargeable period.[63]

The conclusion is that charitable companies may invest in swaps, but in order to avoid a dispute, charitable trusts should not do so unless the small misc income exemption applies (but this is likely to be too small to solve the problem). However if the instrument is a future or option it is not a swap for this purpose, and (provided it does not produce disguised interest) there is no IT charge: s.143 TCGA.

If (as recommended in this book) charitable trusts were brought into corporation tax, this problem would cease to arise.[64]

4.19 Public revenue dividends

s. 533 ITA	s. 487 CTA 2010
(1) Public revenue dividends on securities which are in the name of trustees are not taken into account in calculating total income so far as the dividends are applicable and	(1) Public revenue dividends on securities which are in the name of trustees are not taken into account in calculating total profits so far as the dividends are

62 For income tax purposes, Case VI sch D is replaced with Chapter 8 Part 5 ITTOIA. The circumstances in which profits from swaps are income rather than capital are discussed in para 1-13 of the RI, not set out here.

63 See 8.15.2 (Small misc income exemption).

64 See 3.26 (Alignment of charitable trusts/companies: Critique).

applied only for the repair of—	applicable and applied only for the repair of—
(a) a cathedral, college, church or chapel, or	[identical]
(b) a building used only for the purposes of divine worship.	[identical]
(2) In this section "public revenue dividends" means—	[identical]
(a) income from securities which is payable out of the public revenue of the United Kingdom or Northern Ireland, or	[identical]
(b) income from securities issued by or on behalf of a government or a public or local authority in a country outside the United Kingdom.	[identical]

Income from public revenue dividends will qualify for the normal exemption for interest accruing to charities. The only circumstances in which the relief could ever be needed would be if the dividends accrued to a trust under which:

(1) the dividends were applicable only for the repair of a church (or similar building); and
(2) at the same time the trust was not a charity in the UK tax sense (ie it was not established for charitable purposes only).

In practice it is unlikely that there are any trusts of this kind in existence. This is exactly the sort of clutter which the Tax Law Rewrite should have deleted.[65] But there it is.

---

65 The exemption is derived from the 1842 Act. Before the decision in *Pemsel's case* 3 TC 53, it was not clear what constituted a "charity" for the purposes of the general tax exemption for charities and it was sensible in 1842 to make the express provision which became unnecessary in 1891. Lord Herschell recognised this:

> "With regard to the specific exemptions in favour of the British Museum and of the repairs of churches, it is not the first time we have seen tautology in an Act of Parliament. When the Act was introduced in 1842 its passage would have been much facilitated by the Church party seeing that repairs of churches and cathedrals

4.20 Charitable unit trust

Regulation 7 Income Tax (Definition of Unit Trust Scheme) Regulations 1988 provides the definition:

> (1) A unit trust scheme is a charitable unit trust scheme if it is of one of the descriptions specified in paragraph (2) below.
>
> (2) Those descriptions are—
>
> (a) a common investment fund established under section 22 of the Charities Act 1960 or section 25 of the Charities Act (Northern Ireland) 1964 [now s.96 CA 2011 and s.43 Charities Act (Northern Ireland) 2008];
>
> (aa) a common deposit fund established under section 22A of the Charities Act 1960 [now s.100 CA 2011];
>
> (b) an investment fund or a deposit fund within the meaning of the Scheme scheduled to the Church Funds Investment Measure 1958 or of the scheme contained in the First Schedule to the Methodist Church Funds Act 1960;
>
> (c) a fund held by the Church of Scotland Trust under the provisions of section 15 of the Church of Scotland Trust Order 1932 or under the provisions of the Church of Scotland (Properties and Investments) Order 1994;
>
> (ca) a fund held by the Church of Scotland General Trustees or the Church of Scotland Investors Trust under the provisions of the Church of Scotland (Properties and Investments) Order 1994;
>
> (d) a unit trust scheme under the terms of which—
>
> (i) the scheme property is held by the trustee on trust for charitable purposes only, and
>
> (ii) the participants are required to be bodies of persons established for charitable purposes only or trustees of trusts so established;
>
> and the income of the participants in which is in either case applied to charitable purposes only.

The term unit trust scheme is abbreviated here to unit trust.

The requirement that scheme property is held on trust for charitable purposes raises some interesting questions which cannot be addressed here.

4.20.1 *Treatment of unit trust*

Regulation 3 Income Tax (Definition of Unit Trust Scheme) Regulations

---

were in terms exempted. The insertion of these clauses arose simply from abundant caution" (3 TC at p.61).

1988 provides:

> Subject to the provisions of these Regulations, a unit trust scheme which is ...
>
> (b) a charitable unit trust scheme...
>
> shall be treated as not being a unit trust scheme for the purposes of section 354A [ICTA 1988, now s.504 ITA and s.621 CTA 2010].

The significance of this is that a charitable unit trust is transparent for IT. The income accrues to the unitholders, and so should qualify for charity exemption. The unit trust distributes its income without deduction of tax.

There is no equivalent rule for CGT in the Capital Gains Tax (Definition of Unit Trust Scheme) Regulations 1988 because authorised unit trusts are not subject to CGT: s.100 TCGA.

4.21 Application for charitable purposes

It is (almost) always[66] a requirement for charity tax exemption that the charity's income must be *applied to charitable purposes only* (or some very similar form of words).[67]

4.21.1 *Legitimate application of income*

If a charity applies its income in a manner permitted by its constitution then the income is necessarily applied for charitable purposes only.

> If the first requirement is satisfied [ie income accrues to a charity] then ... the second requirement [that the income be applied for charitable purposes] must equally be satisfied if the application is within the powers of the charity.[68]

A body established for charitable purposes only, which applies income according to its constitution, must apply that income for charitable purposes. Any other view requires that the word "charitable" has two different meanings in the same section. A charity's income is necessarily applied for charitable purposes unless:

(1) it is applied for non-charitable purposes (as discussed above); or
(2) it is not "applied" at all, ie surplus income is left uninvested.

---

66 For exceptions see 4.16 (Miscellaneous minor exemptions).

67 The trading exemptions have a variant form of words, see 8.12 (Application for charity purposes).

68 *IRC v Educational Grants Association* 44 TC at p.107.

In either case the charity is acting in breach of its constitution.

In *Campbell v IRC*[69] a non-charitable company carried on an educational business (Davies's, then a well-known institution). The shareholders could have given or sold the company to a charity, but that would not have qualified for income tax relief. Instead:

(1) The company covenanted to make payments to a charity. (This was before Gift Aid, but covenanted payments to charity could qualify for a form of tax relief).
(2) There was an understanding[70] that the charity would use the money to purchase the educational business from the company at market value.
(3) In due course the charity used the money to acquire the educational business from the company.[71]
(4) The charity sought to recover income tax deducted from the covenanted payments.

The charity had to show it had applied its income (the covenanted payments) for charitable purposes only. For an educational charity to purchase a school at market value[72] seems an obvious application for charitable purposes. HMRC argued that the income was not applied for charitable purposes *only* because there was an incidental benefit to the donor; or because the charity was obliged to use the income in this way. The House of Lords dealt with the point quite briefly:[73]

> The purchase by the [charity] trustees of the business of Davies's is charitable. The whole of the £21,900 has been applied for that charitable

---

69 45 TC 427.

70 In more detail: Some judges found that this was a binding understanding. However as far as application for charitable purposes is concerned, the outcome would be the same whether or not the charity was under a legally binding obligation to purchase the business.

71 In more detail: the charity advanced the money to a trading subsidiary, which purchased the educational business in part. But nothing turned on that.
A successor to the charity still exists, the Vernon Educational Trust, which runs Danes Hill School. Other parts of the former Davies Educational group seem to be in different ownership.

72 It would be different if the charity paid an inflated price. That is self-evident but if authority is needed, see *Campbell v IRC* 45 TC 427 p.467.

73 The charity also had to show that the covenanted payments were "annual payments". As the charity lost on that point, the question of application for charitable purposes only did not strictly need to be answered, but in HL, 4 out of 5 judges considered it. The annual payment issue is no longer important for charity tax and is not considered here.

> purpose ... It is not ... necessary or permissible to consider
> [1] what reason or motive the trustees may have had for their method of applying the money, or
> [2] whether they were under any obligation to adopt that method, or
> [3] whether it may have conferred some incidental benefit[74] on someone else.[75]

In *IRC v The Helen Slater Charitable Trust*[76] one charity transferred funds to another. HMRC contended that this did not constitute application for charitable purposes only, because (i) the money was not spent "in the field"; or (ii) because the money passed without change of "beneficial ownership". These contentions were rejected by the Court of Appeal.

It follows that money properly spent in the administration of a charity (including expenses of preparing accounts, dealing with tax and fundraising) is applied for charitable purposes only. HMRC agree. HMRC Guidance Note Annex ii provides:

> 2.1 Charitable expenditure is expenditure that the charity has incurred for charitable purposes only. It includes such items as ... expenditure incurred on the administration of the charity.

For instance, legal expenses properly incurred by a charity for defending its president from criminal charges are applied for charitable purposes.[77]

Rating cases draw a distinction between purposes of the charity and charitable purposes within the meaning of the relevant rating legislation, but
the distinction depends on the "curiously worded" section which has no parallel in the present context.[78]

The existence of a tax avoidance motive does not by itself prevent income from being applied for charitable purposes.[79]

4.21.2 *Income used to repay loan*

What is the position when a charity uses income to repay a loan or meet

74 It is open to question whether the purchase of an asset at market value is aptly described as an "incidental" benefit to the vendor; but the point does not matter here, and was not investigated.

75 45 TC 427 at p.464 (Lord Dilhorne, Lord Upjohn agreeing); see too p 467 (Lord Hodson), and Lord Donovan agreeing at p.475.

76 55 TC 230.

77 *Ananda Marga Pracharaka Sangha v CIT* [1994] 76 Taxman 88 (Cal).

78 See 40.7.4 (Use for fundraising).

79 See 2.3 (Tax avoidance and charitable status).

some other liability?

In *Guild v IRC* 66 TC 1:

(1) A non-charitable trust[80] borrowed money.
(2) The terms of the trust were amended to direct the trustees to:
   (a) sell the trust property (shares)
   (b) repay the loan (and satisfy any other trust liabilities)
   (c) subject to that, the trust fund was held for a charity.
(3) The trustees used income[81] to repay the loan.

The question was whether the income was applicable and applied for charitable purposes. Was the repayment of the debt a charitable purpose? The Court of Session held the income was not applicable or applied for charitable purposes:

> There is no indication in clause 11 that the duty at this stage was to preserve the trust funds in the interests of the charity, or that it was in the charity's interest that their duty was to be performed. The trustees were not bound to consult the charity before selling the shares or repaying the loan, nor were they obliged to accept any direction from the charity in these matters. This is a clear indication that the right of the charity was merely to receive what might be found to remain after the antecedent purposes of clause 11 had been implemented.
>
> Their position seems to us to be analogous to that of a residuary beneficiary, where assets sold by trustees for the purpose of fulfilling antecedent purposes of the trust settlement are held not to form part of the residue... In terms of clause 11 the right of the [charity] was to receive only "the balance of such price and any other money or funds" in the hands of the trustees, and in our opinion it was only when the balance had been ascertained that the charity became absolutely entitled to payment of it from the trustees.
>
> This interpretation of clause 11 is, in our view, confirmed by a closer analysis of the provisions in regard to the sale of the shares. ... There is no indication here that it was any part of the duties of the Trustees to obtain the best possible price for the shares in the interests of the charity.
>
> ...
>
> As for the obligation on the trustees to repay to the company the amount then outstanding on the loan, it appears to us that this obligation was plainly dispositive, not administrative, in character. It was an essential

80 The trust was an Employee Share Scheme Trust, but nothing turned on that.
81 The trust property was shares, and the income arose on a sale of the shares back to the company; but nothing turns on the nature of the income.

> part of the winding-up of the scheme in the best interests of the company, not something which the trustees were required to do in order to maintain the trust estate for the benefit of the charity.

A variety of reasons are to be found here. One sufficient objection to the charity's case was that the trustees were under no duty to the charity, to obtain for the charity the best price on the sale of the shares.

A second objection was that (more or less) all the trust income and capital was needed to repay the loan, so the charity obtained (more or less) nothing. The Court of Session did not need to rely on that, and did not even mention it, but it must be wrong to say that £200k is applicable for charitable purposes when the charity receives (more or less) no benefit from it.

Suppose different facts: (1) the trust owed their duties solely to the charity from the outset and (2) the trust had sufficient capital to repay the loan (so that even though income was used to repay the loan, the charity does receive the benefit of the income, by receiving the trust capital which would otherwise be used.) The above objections would not apply. However it is suggested that the income is applied for charitable purposes only where the debt or other liability was incurred for charitable purposes; where funds are borrowed for non-charitable purposes, the repayment of the loan is not an application of funds for charitable purposes. Thus even on better facts than those of *Guild*, the charity exemption would not apply. The point has not been decided, but the last paragraph in the passage cited above tends to support that view.

4.21.3 *Misapplication of income*

If a charity applies its income in a way not permitted by its constitution, then the income will not usually be "applied for charitable purposes".

An obvious example is if the trustees misappropriate the charity funds by transfer or interest free loan to themselves: (amongst other consequences) the funds are not applied for charitable purposes, and the charity will forfeit its tax relief.

A charity which expends income on political activities would forfeit its tax relief as political activities are in principle non-charitable.

A charity which made a grant to a non-charity will be misapplying its income unless it has a specific charitable purpose in making the grant. For an example, see *Nuffield v IRC*.[82]

---

82 28 TC 479.

In *Simpson v HMRC*[83] a body whose formal objects and constitution were wholly charitable was formed for the purpose of making a grant to a non-charity. The Special Commissioners held that the body was not a charity. It is considered that the correct analysis was that the body was a charity but incurred non-charitable expenditure. It made no difference in that particular case which analysis was correct, but it would matter in other cases.

Misapplication of charitable income may be of a more subtle nature. For example, the concept of charity requires that money must be spent for *public* benefit; a trust for the benefit of a private class of individuals (such as employees of a company, small or large) is not normally charitable. So, in one case when a charity spent money on a playing field open only to employees of Electrolux Ltd, the money was not applied for charitable purposes, any more than if the trustees had pocketed the money themselves: see *Werner's Charitable Trust v IRC*.[84] Likewise, in *IRC v Educational Grants Association*,[85] an educational charity applied most of its income for the education of children of senior employees of Metal Box Ltd. This was education by way of private benefit, not public benefit; that money was not applied for charitable purposes and tax relief was lost.

It is considered that the test is an objective one: the fact that a charity believes it is acting properly is not sufficient if in fact the funds are not applied for charitable purposes.

4.21.4 *Charity Commission consent*

The Charities Act offers two ways to proceed:

(1) The Charity Commission may formally authorise an action: s.105 CA 2011. If this is done, the act is deemed to be proper. No tax problems can arise, since even if the Charity Commission were wrong, income applied pursuant to the Order is deemed to be applied for charitable purposes only.

(2) The trustees may seek the advice of the Charity Commission: s.110 CA 2011. The trustees may rely on such advice and act without risk of personal liability. The position here is unlike that where there has been an Order under s.105. Section 110 does not deem an act in accordance with the Commission's advice to be proper for all

83 [2009] UKSPC SPC00732.

84 21 TC 137.

85 44 TC 93 analysed in *Independent Schools Council v Charity Commission* [2011] UKUT 421 at [154].

purposes. Thus HMRC are in theory free to seek to raise tax on the basis that the Charity Commission's advice is wrong, and charitable income has been misapplied. In practice it seems most unlikely that the HMRC would take this course. It is considered that a charity acting in accordance with the Charity Commission's advice under s.110 will not in practice be at risk of losing its tax relief even if the Charity Commission's advice is wrong.

4.21.5 *Stolen income*

Is income applied for charitable purposes if it is stolen from a charity, or obtained by deception? Technically, it does seem hard to say that such income has been applied for charitable purposes. However, it seems unjust that a charity which is the victim of theft or fraud should then lose its tax relief. The authors consider it possible to argue that income is applied for charitable purposes wherever a charity has taken reasonable care in the handling and application of its funds. This view is perhaps supported by the approach of the foreign body rule,[86] and it appears to be accepted by HMRC, as the FPP Guidance provides:

> If a charity has unknowingly appointed a manager who isn't a fit and proper person, and that person has misapplied some of the charity's funds without the charity's knowledge, the charity will not necessarily be denied charity tax reliefs and exemptions.[87]

4.21.6 *Ex gratia payment*

A charity may make an ex gratia payment out of motives of self-interest. It may, for instance, be in a charity's best interest to give a member of staff a pension on retirement in excess of that to which they are contractually entitled. That would be for charitable purposes only.

A charity may make payments out of moral considerations, and not out of pure self-interest. For instance, a charity may receive property from an estate where the testator intended some other person to receive the funds; the testator may have intended to revoke the gift to charity, but which failed to do so because of some legal technicality. In such cases the charity may transfer the property to the individual who was intended to have it. That is permitted with the Charity Commission consent.[88] Is this sort of ex

---

86 See 6.6 (Foreign body rule).

87 See 3.10.6 (Waiver of management condition).

88 Section 106 Charities Act 2011; Charity Commission, "Ex gratia payments by charities (CC7)". The Northern Ireland equivalent is s.47 Charities Act (Northern

gratia payment applied for charitable purposes? Perhaps the question never arises, since it is always in accordance with a charity's best interest to act morally. If it did arise, it is suggested that the payment is for charitable purposes. In *Re Snowden*[89] an ex gratia payment was justified as being in the best interest of the charity. The judge noted that charities depend for their continued existence on the recognition by members of the public of a moral obligation to give to charity, so they should have regard to moral obligations themselves. It is difficult to see why a charity which complies with its moral obligations and with the terms of the Charities Act should lose its tax relief. So it is considered that ex gratia payments properly made are applied for charitable purposes.[90]

One can imagine a case in which the relations subsisting between the charity and the person who is asking that the voluntary payment be made to them are such as to make it expedient for the charity with a view to its future prosperity to comply with the request. But this may not be an application for charitable purposes *only*.

4.21.7 *Withholding tax*

There is a theoretical difficulty in satisfying the *applicable for charitable purposes* requirement when a charity receives income from which tax has been deducted at source. Suppose a charity receives a Gift Aid payment of £80 (£20 being deducted at source assuming 20% basic rate). The charity can only claim a complete refund on the basis that the entire £100 has been applied for charitable purposes only. How can the charity comply with this requirement when it has received only £20? One answer is that £20 is deemed (provisionally) to be applied for charitable purposes, since the £20 is treated as income tax paid by the charity. The £20 has then been applied for charitable purposes just like any other administrative expense of the charity, such as the payment of rates. Another answer is that the requirement is that only income in the hands of the charity need be applied for charitable purposes only.[91]

In practice HMRC make repayment to charities in good standing.

Ireland) 2008. Different considerations apply in Scotland: A charity governed by Scots law may take a commercial view, but cannot make an ex gratia payment on moral grounds alone.

89 [1970] Ch 700 .

90 For IHT issues, see 24.32 (Charity makes ex gratia payment).

91 The view taken in *Commissioner of Income-tax v Jayashree Charity Trust* [1986] 159 ITR 280 (CAL).

4.21.8 *Accumulated income*

This section considers whether income is applied for charitable purposes if:

(1) it is accumulated; or

(2) it is retained for future use, without being "accumulated" in the trust law sense of being added to trust capital.[92]

For convenience we refer to both (1) and (2) as "accumulation".

It was formerly suggested that accumulated income would not be "applied for charitable purposes" since it was not "applied" in any way.[93] In some circumstances accumulation is obviously necessary for sensible charity administration (eg to raise funds for a specific project). The Court of Appeal have decided that accumulated income is applied for charitable purposes:

> Charitable trustees who simply leave surplus income uninvested cannot, I think, be said to have 'applied' it at all ... But if the income is reinvested by them and held, as invested, as part of the funds of the charity, I would be disposed to say that it is no less being applied for charitable purposes than it is if it is paid out in wages to the secretary.[94]

Thus the law is settled that income lawfully accumulated is applied for charitable purposes. This view is consistent with the treatment of Gift Aid payments and inter-charity payments. These are treated as income for tax purposes;[95] but everyone agrees that such payments are applied for charitable purposes, so as to qualify for tax relief, even if they are retained by the charity and so in a (non-technical) sense accumulated. This view is also consistent with the CGT position, for everyone agrees that gains are applied for charitable purposes, so as to qualify for tax relief, even if they are retained by the donee and so in a sense accumulated.

HMRC agree. HMRC Guidance Note Annex ii para 8 provides:

> Where a charity accumulates income, or builds up reserves, HMRC needs to decide if this is within the meaning of the phrase 'applied to charitable purposes only'. HMRC will challenge accumulations of

---

92 For the Charity Commission view see CC19 (Retention of Income Reserves).

93 In *General Nursing Council for Scotland v IRC* 14 TC 645 Lord Blackburn took that view, though Lord Sands disagreed; the other two judges expressed no view.

94 *IRC v Helen Slater Charitable Trust* 55 TC 230 at p.250. This view was followed in *Nightingale v Price* [1996] STC (SCD) 116; *Sheppard v IRC (No 2)* 65 TC 724 at p.731.

95 See 4.2 (Are gifts"income").

income on the grounds that the income hasn't been applied to charitable purposes, for example if:

[1] if income isn't invested at all but kept in cash or in a current account; or

[2] if it becomes apparent that investment decisions aren't made exclusively for the benefit of the charity, for example, where accumulated income is being invested in a project in which there's a potential conflict between the interest of the charity and the interest of the trustee or provider of the charity funds.

The Charity Commission correctly say:

> If trustees have a power to accumulate income, that power must be consciously exercised in a proper way and with the good of the charity's beneficiaries in mind. A failure to consider the matter and simply to allow the income to accumulate without good reason amounts to a breach of trust. There are also possible tax consequences. Where we have reason to believe a charity may be pursuing that course, we shall seek explanations from the trustees and will then take appropriate action if we are not satisfied by the responses received.[96]

This is supported by the passage from *Helen Slater* cited above. Income retained without proper reason is not "applied for charitable purposes" and tax relief may therefore be lost. But see 4.21.10 (When must income be applied for charitable purposes).

Income accumulated with a view to committing a breach of trust later is not applied for charitable purposes and example [2] from HMRC Guidance Note set out above is an example of that.

The same position applies in Australia:

> 220. An institution can be charitable even though it has a power to accumulate profits.
>
> 221. In *Word Investments*[97] the High Court said at paragraph 22:
>
> a power to retain profits conferred on directors of a company which has charitable purposes cannot negate its character as a charitable institution. Its exercise, while it may delay the moment when assets are applied to charitable purposes, also increases the chance that more assets will eventually be so applied.
>
> 222. This does not mean that excessive or indefinite accumulation is

96 Report for 1992, para 98.

97 *Federal Commissioner of Taxation v Word Investments Limited* (2008) 236 CLR 204; [2008] HCA 55.

acceptable. The charitable status of an institution for tax purposes is a year by year assessment. An institution that accumulates a significant proportion of its profits over a number of years needs to be able to show on a year by year basis that accumulation is still consistent with it having a charitable purpose.[98]

4.21.9 *Breach of trust*

Suppose income is invested in breach of trust. Is the income applied for charitable purposes? The answer depends on the breach of trust involved.

Suppose a charity uses its funds for charitable purposes but not those specified in its constitution, eg a charity for the advancement of education expends its funds on the relief of poverty. The income is nevertheless applied for charitable purposes.[99]

Suppose charity trustees make an investment in an asset which is outside the range of their powers of investment.[100] It is considered that the income is still applied for charitable purposes, being retained and invested for future charitable use, even though the trustees are in technical breach of trust.

Suppose trustees invest in assets within a category of permitted investments, but the trustees failed to take proper care in choosing the investments, or the investments are unduly speculative. The breach of trust may well lead to losses to the charity. It is considered that as long as the trustees act in good faith, the income is applied for charitable purposes. The purposes of the trustees are wholly charitable, even if the manner of application is wrong.

---

98 Australian Taxation Office TR 2011/4
http://law.ato.gov.au/atolaw/view.htm?docid=TXR/TR20114/NAT/ATO/00001
This view is also adopted by the Australian Administrative Appeal Tribunal in *TACT v Commissioner of Taxation* [2008] AATA 275. Mr. P.W.Taylor SC held at [46]:
"Although the issue in the *Helen Slater Charitable Trust Ltd* case was the application of income, Oliver LJ's reasoning has equal force in answering the question whether the fund itself was applied for the required purpose. Indeed Oliver LJ's view is essentially the same as that expressed by Owen J in *Mahoney v Commissioner of Taxation of the Commonwealth* (1965) 39 ALJR 62 at 63. The reasoning of both judges supports the view that a fund may still be regarded as being applied for its nominated purposes even if, during particular accounting periods, the fund accumulated its income for the general purpose of augmenting the value of the fund."

99 This is self-evident, but if authority is needed see *George Drexler Ofrex Foundation v IRC* 42 TC 524 at p.537.

100 This is less likely to arise after the Trustee Act 2000 extended powers of investment.

Suppose the trustees invest in a transaction in which they are interested. The charity might purchase an asset of the trustees, or lend to a company in which a trustee is interested. This is in principle a breach of trust but if the terms of the transaction are favourable to the charity, no-one may object. No tax problem arises. This is confirmed by *Nightingale v Price* [1996] STC (SCD) 116. This case concerned (inter alia) a loan (on terms which favoured the charity) from a charity to a private company connected with a charity trustee. HMRC argued that the loan was a benefit to the private company, so the loan was not an application of funds for charitable purposes *only*. The argument was dismissed. The loan was not a benefit at all; if it was a benefit, that was merely incidental, and the loan was still for charitable purposes only. A similar conclusion was reached by the Special Commissioner in *Sheppard v IRC (No 2)* [1993] STC 240 at p.245; no appeal was made on this point.

Contrast the position where a charity applies its income by investing in a manner which is not a technical, but a substantive breach of trust; for instance, a loan on unfavourable terms to a private company in which the trustees are interested. Here the income is not applied for charitable purposes at all (eg an interest-free loan) or is not applied for charitable purposes only (eg a loan giving charity less than commercial rate of interest).

4.21.10 *Applied by charity: Time limit*

Statute does not lay down a time limit within which the income must be applied for charitable purposes. It is considered that income must be applied for charitable purposes by the time the claim for exemption is determined.[101] This (seemingly generous) rule would not cause difficulties to HMRC, since a charity's income is strictly taxable until a valid claim is made.[102]

In practice no difficulty arises. The Trust and Estate Charities return (form SA907, 2021) requires the charity to answer the question:

> Have all income and gains that you are claiming to be exempt from tax been, *or are they to be* applied for charitable purposes?[103]

---

101 See 47.7 (Claims).

102 See too 5.4 (When must gain be applied for charitable purposes).

103 The same question is put in the Company Tax Return Form for Charities & Community Amateur Sports Clubs form CT600E.

So HMRC allow exemption provided the charity states that it will apply its income for charitable purposes.

4.21.11 *Income misapplied later*

Suppose trustees invest income properly in authorised investments; and at a later date apply it for non-charitable purposes. It is considered that the position is as follows:

(1) The income is not applied for charitable purposes if the non-charitable application was intended at the time the investment was made.
(2) The income has been applied for charitable purposes if at the time of the investment it was intended to apply the funds for charitable purposes, and there was some change of plan.

The charitable expenditure rules and tainted donation rules would need to be separately considered.

4.21.12 *Which funds must be applied for charitable purposes*

The application for charitable purposes rule only requires that a charity must apply its income (and chargeable gains) on charitable purposes. The rule is not broken if a charity applies any of its funds on non-charitable purposes, so long as all its income of the year (and chargeable gains) is so applied. The question may arise whether any particular funds which have not been applied for charitable purposes only represent the income of the year. There is no reported case on this point, but it is thought that the usual tracing rules must be applied, based on the rule in *Clayton's Case*.

Where capital has been applied for purposes which are not charitable, and income is used to replenish the capital, it is considered that the income has, technically, been applied for charitable purposes. Where, however, there is a close link between the expenditure of capital and its replacement by income, there is a risk that the sums misapplied might be held to represent income ("in reality") and not capital, so that income tax relief will be lost.

Similar considerations apply where income is used to repay a debt owed by the charity. The income is applied for charitable purposes so long as the debt is incurred for charitable purposes. If the money borrowed has been applied for non-charitable purposes, income used to repay that debt might be held not to be applied for charitable purposes. This is even more likely to be the case if the borrowing and repayment were part of a pre-planned arrangement.

4.21.13 *Statutory (fictional) income*

Sometimes the amount of income received by a charity may be less than the amount of income computed for tax purposes; context shows that the requirement is only to apply income actually received for charitable purposes.[104]

It sometimes happens that a charity's income from a source (computed on accountancy principles, or in a commonsense way) may be greater or lesser than its income as computed for tax purposes. Before 1996, this was almost always the case for trading income, under the preceding year basis. It may now apply to a charity holding any unauthorised UK resident unit trust: s.504 ITA or s.621 CTA 2010. Is the deemed income applied for charitable purposes?

In practice HMRC do not take this point and sensibly grant exemption provided all the trading receipts actually received by a charity are applied for charitable purposes only.

Deemed disposals of assets under the CGT rules give rise to similar problems. See 5.5 (Deemed gain).

4.21.14 *Applied for charitable purposes: Critique*

There is an overlap between two sets of anti-avoidance rules:

(1) The requirement in income and CGT exemptions that income/gains should be applied for charitable purposes only (the "application for charitable purposes rule").
(2) The charitable expenditure rules (which require that a charity must not incur non-charitable expenditure).

There is no need now for the first set of rules, since in any case where a charity fails to apply its income or gains for charitable purposes only, the charitable expenditure will disallow charity relief. The abolition of the application for charitable purposes rule would not have any practical effect but would be a logical and worthwhile simplification.

4.22 Deduction at source

Since a charity does not usually pay tax, it is in principle entitled to reclaim the tax which is deducted from its income. In some cases a charity is exempt from the deduction at source rules.

---

104 Contrast *Commissioner of Income-tax v Programme for Community Organisation* [1997] 228 ITR 620 (KER).

A bank normally deducts interest at source from a "relevant investment", s.851 ITA. This term is defined in s.856 ITA:

> (1) An investment is a relevant investment for the purposes of this Chapter if it meets—
> (a) the individual interest condition (see subsection (3)),
> (b) the Scottish partnership condition (see subsection (4)),
> (c) the personal representative condition (see subsection (5)), or
> (d) the settlement condition (see subsection (6)).

These conditions are as follows:

> (3) An investment meets the individual interest condition if the only persons beneficially entitled to interest on the investment are individuals.
> (4) An investment meets the Scottish partnership condition if—
> (a) a Scottish partnership is beneficially entitled to all interest on the investment, and
> (b) that partnership consists only of individuals.
> (5) An investment meets the personal representative condition if personal representatives are entitled to any interest on the investment and they receive it in that capacity.
> (6) An investment meets the settlement condition if all interest on the investment is income arising to the trustees of a discretionary or accumulation settlement and they receive it in that capacity.
> For the meaning of "discretionary or accumulation settlement", see s.873(1).

Thus an account held by a charitable company is not a relevant investment, since none of the conditions are met. An account held by a charitable trust does not fall within s.856 ITA. In particular, the settlement condition is not satisfied. Section 873 ITA provides:

> (1) A settlement is a discretionary or accumulation settlement for the purposes of this Chapter if any income arising to the trustees would (unless treated as income of the settlor) be to any extent income within subsection (2) for the tax year in which it arises.
> (2) Income is within this subsection so far as it is—
> (a) accumulated or discretionary income as defined in s.480 (other than income arising under a charitable trust or an unauthorised unit trust in relation to which s.504 applies), or
> (b) an amount of a type set out in s.482 (unless the trust is a unit trust scheme or the amount is income arising under a charitable trust or is excluded by s.481(5)).

Charitable trusts are expressly excluded from this definition.

ITA EN Change 129 explains the change in procedure:

> **Change 129: Deduction of tax: deposit-takers and building societies: investments to be treated as being or as not being relevant investments: s.857**
>
> ...
>
> As part of the alignment of the building society regime and deposit-takers regime, it is necessary to have one common basis for determining when an investment should be treated as being a relevant investment. This involves changes to the rules regarding the way that building societies check whether a particular payment should be made gross.
>
> For example, regulations 11(1), (2), (2A) and (4) of the Income Tax (Building Societies) (Dividends and Interest) Regulations 1990 (SI 1990/2231) (the building society regulations) state that a building society cannot treat a payment as being within one of the gross payment categories found in regulation 4(1)(a) to (g), (k) or (r) unless it has a declaration to that effect. But once it has that declaration, it can continue to treat such payments as gross until it has information that regulation 4(1) of the building society regulations may not apply.
>
> For deposit-takers, declarations are only required for persons falling in the equivalent of regulations 4(1)(a) to (c). As deposit-takers do not have to obtain declarations in respect of regulation 4(1)(d) to (g), (k) or (r), once the two regimes are aligned, building societies will no longer have to obtain declarations for payments previously caught under regulations 4(1)(d) to (g), (k) and (r). Building societies will have to check only that the payment is not caught in one of the four categories and, if it is not, no further checks or declarations will be required.

4.23 Registered social landlord

Property Income Manual provides:

> **PIM1070. Flat management companies** [June 2016]
>
> **.. Registered social landlords (RSLs) and other 'exempt landlords'**
>
> RSLs are, in England and Wales, independent, private sector, non- profit making bodies whose main purpose is to provide decent quality, affordable housing for people on low incomes. About three-quarters of them are charities.
>
> LTA87/S42 does not apply to tenants of exempt landlords (LTA87/S42 (1)). In accordance with LTA87/S58 (1)(g) a RSL is an exempt landlord. There are other exempt landlords defined in LTA87/S58 (1) & (1A) such as district councils and certain development corporations. ...

Whilst LTA87/S42 does not apply to RSLs and other exempt landlords, as explained below, the terms under which sinking funds and/ or service charge funds are held by exempt landlords may still create a trust.

Thus, in summary, reference must be made to the terms of the lease to determine the application of LTA87/S42. A statutory trust will arise where the tenants of two or more dwellings are required under the terms of their leases to contribute to the payment of variable service charges to the landlord or other persons to whom such charges are payable under the terms of the leases. However, LTA87/S42 does not apply where the landlord is an exempt landlord.

Funds not within LTA87/S42

Where a fund exists but it is not within LTA87/S42, for example where freehold owners of property decide to create a sinking fund, or because the landlord is an RSL or other exempt landlord, then the treatment of that fund will depend on what structure is used:

- Where an individual holds the funds: the individual could be an employee, trading as a maintenance contractor or they could hold funds as trustee for the freeholders. If the latter then the sort of trust depends on the terms of the trust, not on LTA87/S42.
- Where a company holds the funds: assuming the company was formed to hold funds for the freeholders who created it, then it could hold the funds as trustee. Alternatively it could trade as a flat management company receiving payments under a contractual arrangement to supply services and pay CT. The status of the fund will depend on the terms under which the payments are made and the terms under which the company holds the funds.
- Where a trust holds the funds: it could be any sort of trust depending on the terms of the deed but it would not be within LTA87/S42.
- Where an unincorporated association holds the funds: such as a residents' association. It would be liable to CT unless it was acting as a trustee. Again any trust would not be within LTA87/S42.

Any funds held by trustees would be subject to the normal trust rules. It is possible for the funds to be held under a bare trust, interest in possession trust, discretionary trust or accumulation trust arrangement. The exact status will depend on the terms and nature of the trust agreement.

What trustees should do

As the TB37 article made clear, in the past some flat management companies have been permitted to make returns in respect of investment income, arising on service charge funds and sinking funds, as part of their CT returns. That is no longer appropriate where trustees hold funds as trustees under LTA87/S42. Likewise where LTA87/S42 does not apply but the terms under which the funds are held creates a trust. Trustees should write to the appropriate trust office, address below, enclosing a completed form 41G (Trust), ...

4.24 Contemplative religious community

508A ICTA provides:

(1) Subsection (2) applies in a case where members of a qualifying contemplative religious community transfer all their income and assets, or covenant all their income, to the community ("the independent community") (and for this purpose it is irrelevant whether or not the community is part of an order or religious institution).
(2) As respects each chargeable period of the independent community, and each person who is a qualifying member of the independent community at any time in that period, the independent community shall be treated for the purposes of corporation tax as if an amount of its profits for the chargeable period equal to the relevant amount (see subsections (5) to (7)) were income of the qualifying member.
(3) Subsection (4) applies in a case where—

- (a) one or more qualifying contemplative religious communities ("constituent communities") are part of an order or religious institution ("the parent body"), and
- (b) members of the constituent communities transfer all their income and assets, or covenant all their income, to the parent body.

(4) As respects each chargeable period of the parent body, and each person who is a qualifying member of a constituent community at any time in that period, the parent body shall be treated for the purposes of corporation tax as if an amount of its profits for the chargeable period equal to the relevant amount (see subsections (5) to (7)) were income of the qualifying member.
(5) For the purposes of subsections (2) and (4), the relevant amount, in relation to a chargeable period, is the amount of the annual personal allowance for persons under 65 (see section 35 of ITA 2007) for—

- (a) the tax year which begins in the chargeable period, or
- (b) if no tax year begins in the chargeable period, the tax year which is current when the chargeable period begins.

(6) But, if the chargeable period is less than 12 months, the relevant amount is
$(P / 365) \times A$ where—
P is the number of days in the chargeable period;
A is the amount determined under subsection (5) in relation to the chargeable period.
(7) If, during the chargeable period, an individual ceases to be a qualifying member of the independent community or a constituent community (otherwise than on death), the relevant amount, in relation to the chargeable period and that qualifying member, is
$(Q / P) \times B$ where—
Q is the number of days in the chargeable period for which the individual is a qualifying member of the independent community or constituent community;
P is the number of days in the chargeable period;
B is the amount determined under subsection (5), or subsections (5) and (6), in relation to the chargeable period.
(8) So far as the exemption from corporation tax conferred by this section calls for

repayment of tax, no repayment shall be made except on a claim made by the independent community or parent body.

(9) In a case where a member of an independent community or constituent community—

(a) has transferred or covenanted income to the community (in the case of an independent community) or the parent body (in the case of a constituent community), and

(b) has income for a tax year which does not exceed 20% of the annual personal allowance for persons under 65 (see section 35 of ITA 2007) for that tax year,

the member is, for the purposes of this section, to be taken to have transferred or covenanted all his or her income for that tax year to the community or parent body.

(10) For the purposes of this section a contemplative religious community is a "qualifying" contemplative religious community if—

(a) the community is established in the United Kingdom,

(b) the members of the community live and practise their religion in a communal establishment, and

(c) the community is not a charity, but the religion that is professed by the members of the community does not prevent the community from being a charity.

(11) In this section—

"member", in relation to a religious community, means an individual who—

(a) is living in the community, and

(b) has taken vows or made equivalent commitments (whether probationary or not);

"qualifying member", in relation to a religious community, means a member of the community who—

(a) has been a member of the community for a period of at least six months, and

(b) has transferred all his or her income and assets, or covenanted all his or her income, to the community (in the case of an independent community) or the parent body (in the case of a constituent community).

508B ICTA provides:

(1) Subsection (2) applies if, as respects a chargeable period—

(a) section 508A(2) applies in relation to an independent community,

(b) the profits of the independent community in the chargeable period are less than the total of the amounts that fall to be treated as income of the qualifying members of the community in accordance with section 508A(2), and

(c) the independent community has chargeable gains in the chargeable period.

(2) As respects the chargeable period and each qualifying member of the independent community, the community shall be treated for the purposes of corporation tax as if the relevant amount of its chargeable gains for that period were income of the qualifying member.

(3) Subsection (4) applies if, as respects a chargeable period—

(a) section 508A(4) applies in relation to a parent body,

(b) the profits of the parent body in the chargeable period are less than the total of the amounts that fall to be treated as income of the qualifying members of the constituent communities in accordance with section 508A(4), and

(c) the parent body has chargeable gains in the chargeable period.

(4) As respects the chargeable period and each qualifying member of a constituent community, the parent body shall be treated for the purposes of corporation tax as if the

relevant amount of its chargeable gains for that period were income of the qualifying member.

(5) For the purposes of subsections (2) and (4), the relevant amount, in relation to a qualifying member of the independent community or a constituent community, is the smaller of—

(a) the shortfall in profits, and

(b) the average gain.

(6) The shortfall in profits is the difference between—

(a) the relevant amount determined under section 508A(5) to (7) in relation to the qualifying member, and

(b) the amount that has actually been treated as the income of the qualifying member.

(7) The average gain is G / N where—

G is the amount of the chargeable gains which the independent community or parent body has in the chargeable period;

N is the number calculated by adding together the relevant value for each qualifying member of the independent community or constituent communities who, under section 508A(2) or (4), falls to be treated as having income.

(8) For the purposes of calculating "N" in subsection (7)—

(a) the relevant value for a qualifying member is 1;

(b) but, if section 508A(7) applies in relation to the qualifying member, the relevant value for that member is 1 × (Q / P)

where Q and P have the same meanings as in section 508A(7).

(9) So far as the exemption from corporation tax conferred by this section calls for repayment of tax, no repayment shall be made except on a claim made by the independent community or parent body.

These are reliefs of narrow interest, which may explain why they are not written into ITA and CTA where they belong.

CHAPTER FIVE

TAXATION OF CHARITY GAINS

Cross references

The following topics are considered elsewhere:

For the position on capital payment to a charity from a non-resident trust see 32.1 (Payment to charity from non-resident trust).

For the CGT relief on gifts *to* a charity (when a gain accrues to the donor) see 23.3 (Donor CGT relief). We refer to that as the **"Donor CGT relief"**.

5.1 Charity's CGT exemption

This chapter discusses the relief for gains accruing to a charity, ie when a charity disposes of assets and realises a gain.

In principle, charitable trust are subject to CGT on chargeable gains and charitable companies are subject to corporation tax. For present purposes (more or less) the same rules apply and we refer for simplicity to CGT.

Charity relief has applied since the inception of CGT. As charities have always qualified for IT relief, it would have been illogical to impose CGT.

The relief is now in s.256(1) TCGA which provides:

> Subject to the following provisions of this section, a gain shall not be a chargeable gain [and so is exempt from CGT] if it accrues to a charity and is applicable and applied for charitable purposes.

We refer to this as "**the charity's CGT exemption**".

Four conditions (or sets of conditions) must be satisfied for the relief to apply:

(1) The gain must accrue to a charity. The standard tax definition applies.

(2) The gain must be applicable for charitable purposes. At first sight this condition appears to be otiose. However, it is (just) possible to envisage circumstances where a gain fails this condition while satisfying the other conditions for relief.[1]

(3) The gain must be applied for charitable purposes. This rule is derived from the income tax rule. It is considered that "applied for charitable purposes" has in general the same meaning as "applied to charitable purposes only" in the income tax code, notwithstanding the slight difference in language. This view was accepted in *IRC v Helen Slater Charitable Trust* 53 TC 230. This rule is discussed in 4.21 (Application for charitable purposes).[2]

(4) The charitable expenditure rules[3] and tainted donation rules[4] must be satisfied. These rules apply to charity's CGT exemption in a manner similar to income tax.

There is no requirement to make a formal claim for the charity's CGT exemption (unlike income tax reliefs) but that makes no difference in practice.

5.2 Property charged to non-charity

An interesting question arises where a charity owns an asset subject to a mortgage, and the mortgagee exercises their power of sale. The gain on the sale accrues to the charity: s.26(2) TCGA. Is the gain applicable and applied for charitable purposes? Where the charge was granted to secure a liability incurred by the charity, it is considered that the gain is applied for charitable purposes; in other circumstances it is not.

Particular care is needed where property subject to a charge is given to charity. For instance, executors might be tempted to transfer property from an estate to a charity subject to a charge for their expenses under s.36(10) Administration of Estates Act 1925. See 33.4 (CGT planning for PRs).

---

1 See 5.6.3 (Charity's CGT exemption); 33.4 (CGT planning for PRs).

2 See too 6.27 (Meaning of "approved charitable loan").

3 See 6.1 (Charitable expenditure Rules).

4 See 7.1 (Tainted donation rules).

5.3 Identifying the gain

Section 256 provides relief where the "gain" is applied for charitable purposes.

The question of identifying the gain is problematic. Strictly speaking, a gain is not an item of property: like trading income, it is a figure resulting from a mathematical computation. The quantum of a gain (generally) depends (in part) on the amount or value of the proceeds of a disposal, but that does not entail that the gain is a part of the proceeds. The proceeds of a disposal are not the gain. But notwithstanding the jurisprudential nature of a gain, context shows that the proceeds of a disposal for full consideration should be regarded as constituting or including the gain for the purposes of the application for charitable purposes rule.

Suppose:

(1) A charity sells for £100 an asset with a base cost of £50, thus realising a gain of £50. The £100 receipt represents one half gain and one half base cost.

(2) Out of the £100 proceeds of sale, a proportion (say £50) is not applied for charitable purposes.

There would seem to be three possibilities:

(1) the misapplied £50 represents base cost and not gain; thus the *gain* is applied for charitable purposes, and the charity qualifies for CGT exemption under s.256;

(2) the £50 represents gain and not base cost; the charity is then disqualified from tax relief;

(3) the £50 represents partly gain and partly base cost.

It is considered that option (3) is to be preferred. In addition, of course, charitable expenditure rules would come into play.

5.4 Applied by charity: Time limit

Statute does not say when the gain must be applied for charitable purposes. It is considered that strictly the relief applies if the gain is applied for charitable purposes at any time before an assessment on the gain is finally determined. In practice no difficulty arises: see 4.21.10 (Income applied by charity: Time limit).

5.5 Deemed gain

There are a number of circumstances where a gain is deemed to accrue. Deemed gains do not often arise for charities, but examples are:

(1) A charity may dispose of an asset by way of gift to a beneficiary of the charity. The charity will be deemed for CGT purposes to have disposed of the asset at market value and so the transfer may give rise to a deemed gain.[5]

(2) A charity may appropriate an asset to trading stock.[6]

Is tax relief available for a deemed gain?

It might at first sight be thought that a deemed gain can never be applied for charitable purposes. But the deeming should be understood in a sensible, purposive manner, and it is clearly possible for a deemed gain to be applied for charitable purposes. This is assumed in s.256(2) TCGA which provides:

> If property held on charitable trusts ceases to be subject to charitable trusts—
>
> (a) the trustees shall be treated as if they had disposed of, and immediately reacquired, the property for a consideration equal to its market value, any gain on the disposal being treated as not accruing to a charity, and
>
> (b) if and so far as any of that property represents, directly or indirectly, the consideration for the disposal of assets by the trustees, any gain accruing on that disposal shall be treated as not having accrued to a charity.

It is considered that a deemed gain is regarded as applied for charitable purposes if the property from which the gain arises is so applied.

5.6 Section 3 TCGA

5.6.1 *The charge*

Section 3 TCGA provides:

> (1) This section applies if—
>
> (a) a chargeable gain accrues at any time to a non-UK resident close company,[7]

5 Section 17 TCGA. This arises when a UK charity transfers an asset to an individual or to a body which is not a charity within the tax definition. (No chargeable gain accrues on a disposal by one charity to another tax charity because that disposal will itself qualify for relief under s.257 TCGA). Similar points arise in any transaction other than a bargain at arm's length.

6 But see 8.5 (Appropriation to/from trading stock).

7 Section 3(11) TCGA provides the standard definition: "In this section "a non-UK resident close company" means a company-

> (b) the gain is connected to avoidance (see section 3A),
> (c) the gain is not connected to a foreign trade or other economically significant foreign activities (see section 3A), and
> (d) apart from this section, some or all of the gain would not be chargeable to corporation tax on the company.
>
> (2) So much of the gain as would not otherwise be so chargeable is apportioned among participators, or indirect participators, in the company—
> (a) who are resident in the UK at that time, or
> (b) who are trustees of a settlement and are not resident in the UK at that time.
>
> (4) The amount apportioned to each person is treated as a chargeable gain accruing to the person.

In short, gains accruing to a non-resident close company (the **"non-resident company"**) are attributed to shareholders and other participators of the company.[8]

5.6.2 *Exemptions*

Section 3(6) TCGA provides a *de minimis* exemption:

> No apportionment of any part of a gain is made to a person if the total amount that would, apart from this subsection, be apportioned to-
> (a) the person, and
> (b) persons connected to the person,
> is 25% or less of the amount of the gain falling to be apportioned.

Section 3(1)(c) TCGA disapplies the charge if the non-resident company carries on "economically significant activities" (defined in s.3A).

Section 3(1)(b) TCGA provides a motive defence, defined in s.3A(1) TCGA:

> A gain accruing to a company on the disposal of an asset is taken to be "connected to avoidance" unless it is shown that neither-
> (a) the disposal of the asset by the company, nor
> (b) the acquisition or holding of the asset by the company,

---

(a) which is not resident in the UK, and
(b) which would be a close company if it were resident in the UK."

For the definition of close company see 11.3 (Close company: Introduction).

8 For a discussion of s.3 see Kessler, *Taxation of Non-Residents and Foreign Domiciliaries* (21st ed., 2022-23), Chapter 63 (Gains of Non-Resident Companies) online version *https://www.foreigndomiciliaries.co.uk*

formed part of a scheme or arrangements of which the main purpose, or one of the main purposes, was avoidance of liability to capital gains tax or corporation tax.

We do not discuss these reliefs here as they are more fully considered in Kessler's *Taxation of Non-residents and Foreign Domiciliaries*.[9]

Because of the motive defence, de minimis rule, and and economically significant activity test, a charity is not likely to come within s.3.

5.6.3 *Charity's CGT exemption*

The HMRC view is that if a gain does accrue to a charity under s.3 it does not qualify for the charity's CGT exemption. The charity does not apply the gain for charitable purposes as it does not actually receive anything. The non-resident company would not normally apply the gain for charitable purposes, but even if it did, the gain is not "applicable" for charitable purposes. It is considered that the HMRC is correct, though surprising. The contrary view is faintly arguable on a purposive interpretation. But anything is arguable on a sufficiently purposive interpretation.

If the non-resident company is held by a non-resident trust which makes a capital payment to the charity, then CGT relief is applicable as the charge comes under s.87, not s.3.[10]

5.6.4 *s.3 planning*

Charities should consider s.3 issues before acquiring interests in non-resident close companies (including non-resident close unit trusts) if their interest (including connected persons within s.3) exceeds 25%.

If s.3 issues arise, one solution may be to utilise allowable losses; see 5.8 (Loss accruing to charity). Another may be to hold the non-resident company in a UK resident non-charitable subsidiary of the charity; that company may then obtain tax relief as necessary by Gift Aid donations. Another solution may be to procure the non-resident company to transfer its assets to the charity, since no chargeable gain arises on that disposal.

If the non-resident company is situate in a country with an appropriate Double Taxation Arrangement, double taxation relief may override the charge. The relief will apply if the charity is a charitable company but not

---

9 (21st ed., 2022/23), chapter 63 (Gains of Non-resident Companies) online version *https://www.foreigndomiciliaries.co.uk*

10 See 32.7 (s.87 gain: Charity's CGT exemption).

if it is a charitable trust: see s.79B TCGA. A solution for a charitable trust which needs DT relief may be to vest its interest in the non-resident company in a subsidiary or to set up a corporate sister charity. If (as recommended in this book) charitable trusts were brought into corporation tax, this problem would cease to arise.[11]

Another possible solution is to arrange that the shares in the non-resident company are held by a non-resident charity.

5.7 Termination of charitable trust

This section considers the various anti-avoidance provisions that apply where property ceases to be subject to charitable trusts.

In practice this almost never happens, so the topic is largely of theoretical interest.

5.7.1 *CGT deemed disposal*

Section 256(2) TCGA provides:

> If property held on charitable trusts ceases to be subject to charitable trusts—
>
> (a) the trustees shall be treated as if they had disposed of, and immediately reacquired, the property for a consideration equal to its market value, any gain on the disposal being treated as not accruing to a charity...

We call this the **"CGT deemed disposal"**.

5.7.2 *CGT exemption: Clawback*

Section 256(2) TCGA provides:

> If property held on charitable trusts ceases to be subject to charitable trusts ...
>
> (b) if and so far as any of that property represents, directly or indirectly, the consideration for the disposal of assets by the trustees, any gain accruing on that disposal shall be treated as not having accrued to a charity,

We call this the **"CGT clawback charge"**. An assessment may be made on the persons who were trustees at the time when the disposals were made.

This provision is apparently aimed at temporary charitable trusts. It

---

11 See 3.26 (Charitable trusts/companies: Critique).

seems right that such trusts should suffer a clawback charge on charity relief formerly granted to them, when they cease to be charities.

Section 256(2) continues:

> and an assessment to capital gains tax chargeable by virtue of paragraph (b) above may be made at any time not more than 3 years after the end of the year of assessment in which the property ceases to be subject to charitable trusts.

A trustee who retires from a temporary charitable trust may need to take an indemnity against the possibility of a CGT clawback charge.

The clawback charge may arise at any time so that gains may be taxed decades after they were originally realised.

A CGT charge may arise even though the trust has become non-resident.

5.7.3 *Offshore income gain: Clawback*

There is a similar rule for offshore funds, so it is convenient to deal with here (though strictly an offshore income gain is income for tax purposes, not a chargeable gain subject to CGT).

Regulation 31 Offshore Funds (Tax) Regulations 2009 provides:

> (3) Paragraphs (4) and (5) apply if—
> (a) property held on charitable trusts ceases to be subject to charitable trusts, and
> (b) that property represents directly or indirectly an offshore income gain.
> (4) The trustees are treated as if they had disposed of and immediately reacquired that property for a consideration equal to its market value.
> (5) An offshore income gain accruing on the disposal arising under paragraph (4) is treated as an offshore income gain not accruing to a charity.

This is based on s.256(2)(b) TCGA.

For offshore funds, there is no express equivalent of s.256(2)(a). It is not needed, as the OFTR incorporates the relevant CGT rules. The Offshore Funds Manual gives an example which assumes that s.256(2)(a) applies for the purposes of offshore fund taxation:

> **OFM16600: Investors in non-reporting funds: exceptions to the charge to tax: charitable companies & charitable trusts – Regulation 31** [June 2016]
>
> ...
>
> [1] If interests in non-reporting offshore funds held by charitable

companies or charitable trusts cease to be subject to charitable trusts (note that property held by charitable companies is subject to a trust arrangement)[12], and an offshore income gain would arise on accrued gains on a disposal at that time, then the trustees are treated as if they had disposed of and immediately reacquired that property for a consideration equal to its market value. An offshore income gain accruing on the disposal arising under this paragraph is treated as an offshore income gain not accruing to a charity, and is subject to corporation tax or income tax accordingly.

[2] Property will 'cease to be subject to charitable trusts' when a charity loses its charitable status, for example if the charity is a 'time charity', i.e. an arrangement such as that where assets are held on charitable trusts under the terms of a will and the income applied for charitable purposes until such time as a minor reaches a particular age; when the assets are passed to the ultimate beneficiary chargeable gains, or here an offshore income gain, would arise on the transfer of the assets.

5.7.4 *Hold-over relief*

The termination of a temporary charitable trust will generally give rise to a charge to IHT under s.70 IHTA. In such circumstances an election can be made to hold over the chargeable gain on the deemed disposal: s.260 TCGA. This would avoid a CGT charge under s.256(2)(a), though it would not avoid the same charge on offshore income gains (to which hold-over relief does not apply).

Hold-over relief would not avoid the clawback charge under s.256(2)(b) A charity may also have allowable losses to set against the charge.

5.7.5 *Charitable trusts cease*

When does property "cease to be held on charitable trusts"? An obvious case is where a temporary charitable trust ceases to be a charity but the property remains held in trust.

A second case is where property ceases to be held in a temporary charity and becomes the absolute property of a beneficiary. In this case it is not necessary for s.256(2)(a) to provide for a deemed disposal as there is a deemed disposal under s.71 TCGA; but the CGT clawback charge could still apply.

Another case is if a charity which is entitled to an equitable interest under

12 Authors' footnote: The OFM suggests that a charitable company is regarded as a charitable trust for the purposes of s.256(2): that view is difficult to defend, but in practice the point is not likely to arise.

a trust (of which all the beneficiaries are charities) disposes of its interest to a non-charity.

Suppose a charitable trust disposes of an asset by virtue of an application for charitable purposes. A trust for the benefit of the homeless may, for instance, assign a lease of a property to a homeless person. One might have thought that a tax charge must arise: the asset, formerly held on charitable trusts, has indeed ceased to be subject to charitable trusts. Yet this cannot be what the section is intended to cover, and it is considered that the courts would not construe it to apply to such circumstances.

Likewise if an asset is sold for full consideration, the section does not apply because a trust fund has a continuing identity.

Suppose a charitable trust fails. That might happen if the original purpose cannot be fulfilled. It might, exceptionally, happen where the original purpose ceases to be charitable and the Charity Commission removes the charity from the register. In such cases the charity trustees must seek to have the property applied to other charitable purposes under the cy-près rules.[13] Accordingly the property never ceases to be held on charitable trusts.

The section is limited to charitable *trusts:* it does not in terms apply to charitable companies or associations. The drafter may (rightly) have considered that the CGT holdover relief scheme which s.256(2)(a) was intended to block only needed to be blocked for charitable trusts; or else perhaps overlooked the possibility that companies and associations may be temporary charities. HMRC do not agree: see the OFM passage quoted above.

There was formerly a concession relating to the Reverter of Sites Act, (ESC D47). This was withdrawn from 1 April 2010, but had only been used twice so the topic is of specialist interest only.[14]

5.7.6 *Critique*

These rules have been part of the CGT code since the inception of CGT in 1965. The reason for the CGT deemed disposal is presumably a concern that temporary charities may qualify for CGT on their gains, and then cease to be charities and apply the gain for non-charitable purposes.[15]

---

13 See s.62 Charities Act 2011; s.26 Charities Act (Northern Ireland) 2008

14 HMRC Technical Note, "Withdrawal of Extra-statutory Concessions" April 2009.

15 We had wondered whether the reason might be to prevent hold-over relief schemes under which a donor might give property to a temporary charity, claiming Donor CGT relief, and the trust later ceased to be charitable. But that cannot be the original

One might have though that the simpler and better way to deal with temporary charitable trusts would be to treat them as non-charities for tax purposes, and deny them CGT and IT relief at the outset, rather than allowing them relief subject to a clawback on ceasing to be non-charitable.

But as ESC D47 recognises, there are a number of important charities (schools subject to the Reverter of Sites Acts) which may cease to be charitable, though the possibility of that happening may be low. Consequently the approach of the TCGA - to claw back relief if necessary - seems the only practical solution.

5.8 Loss accruing to charity

Allowable losses may be deducted from chargeable gains in calculating CGT liabilities. Section 16(2) TCGA defines allowable loss:

> Except as otherwise expressly provided, all the provisions of this Act which distinguish gains which are chargeable gains from those which are not, or which make part of a gain a chargeable gain, and part not, shall apply also to distinguish losses which are allowable losses from those which are not, and to make part of a loss an allowable loss, and part not; and references in this Act to an allowable loss shall be construed accordingly.

Most assets, of course, may give rise to chargeable gains ("chargeable assets") and losses on such assets are allowable losses. It appears at first sight that losses on disposals of chargeable assets which accrue to a charitable trust are allowable losses. Gains accruing to a charitable trust are admittedly not (usually) chargeable if they are applied for charitable purposes only. But it is not possible to apply a loss for charitable purposes only, so s.16(2) does not classify a loss accruing to a as a non-allowable loss. We call this the "wide view". If this were right, most *bona fide* charitable trusts could[16] gradually build up a reserve of allowable losses: their losses will be allowable, their gains should be exempt.

An argument against the wide view is this: although s.256 refers to a *gain* being applied for charitable purposes, what is actually applied for charitable purposes is the consideration for disposal of the assets, which represents the gain. By parity of reasoning, the consideration for an asset may also represent the loss which has accrued on the disposal of the asset.

---

reason for the CGT deemed disposal rule, as that rule dates back to the FA 1965, and Donor CGT relief only came later, in 1972.

16 If a claim is made: see below.

In this sense a loss may be applied for charitable purposes, and s.16(2) prevents the loss from being an allowable loss.

This leads to the view (the "narrow view") that an allowable loss only arises on a disposal if or to the extent that:

(1) the proceeds of the asset are not applied for charitable purposes; or
(2) the charitable expenditure rules would have given rise to a tax charge had a gain arisen on that disposal.

The argument in favour of the narrow view is weak. For while the proceeds of a disposal do in principle represent a gain, this is not so in the case of a loss. The plainest case is a complete loss, such as the destruction of an uninsured asset. So it is considered that the wide view is correct. This means that charitable trusts could in principle gradually build up a reserve of allowable losses, which they will not normally need to use, since their gains are normally exempt.

Losses from 1996/97 are not allowable unless a claim is made: s.16(2A) TCGA. In practice charitable trusts will not usually need their losses. Except in unusual circumstances, it is suggested that charitable trusts may safely adopt a course of not making claims for loss relief.

It is considered that losses accruing to charitable companies are not in principle allowable. Section 8(2) TCGA is differently worded:

> For the purposes of corporation tax in respect of chargeable gains, "allowable loss" does not include a loss accruing to a company in such circumstances that if a gain accrued the company would be exempt from corporation tax in respect of it.

5.9 Rate of tax on gains

5.9.1 *Charitable trust*

Section 1H TCGA provides:

> (7) Residential property gains accruing in a tax year to the trustees of a settlement are charged to capital gains tax at a rate of 28%.
> (8) Other chargeable gains accruing in a tax year to the trustees of a settlement are charged to capital gains tax at a rate of 20%.

UK trusts are treated as higher rate taxpayers.
So the rate of tax on gains is 28% or 20%. The rate can be higher than the rate of income tax, so a charity may do better to realise taxable income than chargeable gains. But the point has little practical importance since income and gains should in principle qualify for exemption.

A trust enjoys a CGT annual exemption, normally one half of the individual's exemption. See s.1K and sch 1C TCGA. This is shared where a settlor has made more than one trust, but the restriction only applies to qualifying settlements. Para 7 sch 1C TCGA provides:

> (1) In this Schedule "qualifying UK settlement", in relation to a tax year, means any settlement in relation to which both of the following conditions are met—
>
> (a) the trustees of the settlement are resident in the United Kingdom during any part of the tax year, and
>
> (b) the property comprised in the settlement is not held for a charitable or pensions purpose.
>
> (2) Property comprised in a settlement is held for a charitable purpose if (and only if)—
>
> (a) it is held for charitable purposes only, and
>
> (b) it cannot become applicable for other purposes.

So in the case of a permanent charity (but not a temporary charity) the annual CGT exemption is not affected by the provisions relating to groups of settlements. The rule was no doubt designed to ensure the sensible result that a settlor who created a charitable trust did not restrict the annual exemption for their private trust or trusts. A consequence is that one settlor might (subject to the GAAR) create any number of permanent charities each of which could qualify for the annual exemption. But the point has little practical importance.

5.9.2 *Charitable company*

A charitable company which forfeits the charity's CGT exemption will pay corporation tax on its gains at the appropriate CT rate.

CHAPTER SIX

CHARITABLE EXPENDITURE RULES

6.1 Charitable expenditure rules

Charity tax relief has always required that a charity's income or gains must be applied for charitable purposes only.[1] That rule has two defects:

(1) The rule only requires the application of a charity's income or gains for charitable purposes. If a charity misapplied other funds then tax relief would be unaffected.[2]

(2) The concept of "application for charitable purposes" is wide, and arguably includes expenditure which should not qualify for charity tax relief. The difficulty here is to find a way to identify types of expenditure which should disqualify tax relief, which is workable and gives better results.

The charitable expenditure rules, introduced in 1986, deal with the first of these problems but only touch lightly on the second.

The substantial donor rules, introduced in 2006, and (more or less) repealed in 2011, should be seen as an unsuccessful attempt to grapple with the second point.[3] The tainted donation rules are the third attempt. That topic is discussed in the following chapter.

Until ITA 2007 the rules were written out only once. The rules are now set out three times: separately for IT, CT and CGT.

s.539 ITA	**s.492 CTA 2010**	**s.256 TCGA**
(1) This section applies if a charitable trust has a non-exempt amount for a tax year (see s.540).	(1) This section applies if a charitable company has a non-exempt amount for an accounting period (see s.493).	(3) Subsection (4) below applies if a charitable trust has a non-exempt amount under s.540 of ITA 2007 for a year of assessment. (3A) Subsection (4) below also applies if a charitable company has a non-exempt amount

1 See 4.21 (Application for charitable purposes).

2 Interesting questions of tracing could in theory have arisen when a charity applies part but not all of its funds for non-charitable purposes, but in practice the courts never had to consider the point.

3 See App. 7.3 (What went wrong: Critique).

		under s.493 of CTA 2010 for an accounting period.
(2) The exemptions under this Part [Part 10 ITA] do not apply, and are treated as never having applied, to so much of any income of the charitable trust for the tax year as is attributed under s.541 to the non-exempt amount.	(2) The exemptions mentioned in subsection (3) do not apply, and are treated as never having applied, to so much of any income of the charitable company for the accounting period as is attributed under s.494 to the non-exempt amount.	(4) Gains accruing— (a) to the charitable trust in the year of assessment, or (b) to the charitable company in the accounting period, are treated as being, and always having been, chargeable gains so far as they are attributed to the non-exempt amount under s.256A (in the case of a charitable trust) or s.256C (in the case of a charitable company).
	(3) Those exemptions are— (a) the exemptions under this Part [Part 11 CTA 2010], and (b) the exemption under regulation 31(1) of the Offshore Funds (Tax) Regulations 2009 (exemption from corporation tax in respect of certain offshore income gains).	

The task is, therefore, to identify the non-exempt amount. (Having done that, the attribution of the non-exempt amount to income and gains is relatively straightforward.)

6.2 Non-exempt amount

s.540 ITA	**s.493 CTA 2010**
(1) A charitable trust has a non-exempt amount for a tax year if it has—	(1) A charitable company has a non-exempt amount for an accounting period if it has—
a) non-charitable expenditure for	[identical]

the tax year (amount A), and (b) attributable income and gains for the tax year (amount B).	
(2) The non-exempt amount for the tax year is—	(2) The non-exempt amount for the accounting period is—
(a) amount A, or (b) if less, amount B.	[identical]

In short, the non-exempt amount is the lower of non-charitable expenditure and attributable income/gains.

6.3 Attributable income/gains

s.540(3) ITA	**s.493(3) CTA 2010**
For the purposes of this Part— (a) a charitable trust's "attributable income" for a tax year is the charitable trust's income for the tax year that is exempt from income tax as a result of any of the exemptions under this Part,	For the purposes of this Part— (a) a charitable company's "attributable income" for an accounting period is the charitable company's income for the period that is exempt from corporation tax as a result of any of the exemptions mentioned in s.492(3),
(b) a charitable trust's "attributable gains" for a tax year are any gains accruing to the charitable trust in the tax year that as a result of s.261[4] of TCGA 1992 are not chargeable gains, and	(b) a charitable company's "attributable gains" for an accounting period are any gains accruing to the charitable company in the period that as a result of s.261[5] of TCGA 1992 are not chargeable gains, and
(c) a charitable trust's "attributable income and gains" for a tax year is the sum of its attributable income for the tax year and its attributable gains for the tax year...	(c) a charitable company's "attributable income and gains" for an accounting period is the sum of its attributable income for the period and its attributable gains for the period.

4 This is an error for s.256(1) TCGA. It is considered that this can be corrected under the slip rule.

5 This is an error for s.256(1) TCGA. It is considered that this can be corrected under the slip rule.

The HMRC Guidance Note Annex ii, paragraph 3 provides:

> Attributable income and gains means the amount of income and gains that are eligible for tax relief or exemption. It includes Gift Aid donations, payroll giving donations, income such as rental income, interest received, profits from a charity's primary purpose trading activity, and capital gains. Income which doesn't qualify for tax exemption, such as the profits of non-charitable (non-primary purpose) trading or amounts taxable under anti-avoidance provisions isn't included.

Income such as legacies and donations not qualifying for donor reliefs (Gift Aid, payroll giving, QIDR) are also excluded.

6.3.1 *Dividend income of charitable co*

In the case of a charitable company, a dividend or other distribution from a UK or non-resident company is not normally attributable income. Section 931A(1) CTA 2009 provides:

> The charge to corporation tax on income applies to any dividend or other distribution of a company, but only if the distribution is not exempt.

The effect of this is that an exempt distribution will not be attributable income, but where (exceptionally) the distribution is not exempt, it will be attributable income. As to what are exempt distributions, see 4.7.2 (Co: Exempt distribution).

6.4 "Non-charitable" expenditure

The central concept of the charitable expenditure rules is "non-charitable" expenditure. This term is elaborately defined.

6.4.1 *Expenditure on non-charitable purpose*

s.543(1)(f) ITA	**s.496(1)(d) CTA 2010**
For the purposes of this Part a charitable trust's non-charitable expenditure for a tax year is ...	For the purposes of this Part a charitable company's non-charitable expenditure for an accounting period is ...
(f) any expenditure incurred by the charitable trust in the tax year ... which is not incurred for charitable purposes only ...	(d) any expenditure incurred by the charitable company in the accounting period which is not incurred for charitable purposes only ...

HMRC Guidance Note Annex ii, paragraph 7 provides:

> 7. **Payments outside the terms of the charity's governing document**
> 7.1 If a charity's governing document specifically prohibits or restricts certain expenditure, it'll be treated as non-charitable expenditure.
> 7.2 If expenditure is clearly of a charitable nature, but it's not specifically authorised by the terms of the governing document of the charity, it won't necessarily be treated as non-charitable expenditure. HMRC may seek the views of the relevant charity regulator in considering the tax treatment.

If the expenditure is charitable, it does not become non-charitable just because it is outside the specific charitable objects of the charity. But in practice this issue will rarely if ever arise.

6.4.2 *Other non-charitable expenditure*

There are 9 more categories of non-charitable expenditure:

Topic	**ITA**	**CTA 2010**	**See**
Trade losses	s.543 (a)-(e)	s.496 (a)-(c)	6.32
Substantial donors (obsolete)	s.543 (g)(h)	s.496(e)(f)	App 7.1
Investments	s.543 (i)	s.496(g)	6.8
Loans	s.543 (j)	s.496(h)	6.27

Section 543 ITA/s.496 CTA 2010 conclude:

> But anything which falls within more than one of the above paragraphs counts as non-charitable expenditure only once.

6.5 "Expenditure"

Unless a charity incurs "expenditure" it cannot incur "non-charitable expenditure" under s.543(1)(f) ITA/s.496(1)(d) CTA 2010. Accordingly for that purpose it can matter whether or not something is "expenditure". However the issue is only of limited importance, because losses, payments or amounts within other paragraphs of s.543(1) ITA/s.496(1) CTA 2010 are deemed to be "non-charitable expenditure" whether or not they constitute "expenditure" in the normal sense of the word.

Nevertheless, there is a partial definition of "expenditure". Section 545(1) ITA/s.498(1) CTA 2010 provide an inclusion:

s. 545(1) ITA	**s.498 CTA 2010**
For the purposes of s.543(1)(f) "expenditure" includes expenditure of a capital nature.	For the purposes of s.496(1)(d) "expenditure" includes expenditure of a capital nature.

It seems unlikely that anyone would have doubted that, but the provision does no harm. Section 545(2) ITA/s.498(2) CTA 2010 then provide three exclusions:

s. 545(2) ITA	**s.498(2) CTA 2010**
None of the following is "expenditure" for those purposes—	None of the following is "expenditure" for those purposes—
(a) the investment of any of the charitable trust's funds,	(a) the investment of any of the charitable company's funds,
(b) the making of a loan by the charitable trust, or	(b) the making of a loan by the charitable company, or
(c) the repayment by the charitable trust of the whole or a part of a loan made to it.	(c) the repayment by the charitable company of the whole or a part of a loan made to it.

Points (a) and (b) are misleading as while approved charitable investments and loans are not "expenditure", non-approved investments and loans are deemed (non-charitable) expenditure. Point (c) might sometimes be relevant.

6.6 Foreign-body rule

s.547 ITA	**s.500 CTA 2010**
A payment made, or to be made[6], to a body situated outside the UK is non-charitable expenditure under s.543(1)(f)[7] if—	A payment made, or to be made, to a body situated outside the United Kingdom is non-charitable expenditure under s.496(1)(d) if—
(a) it is incurred for charitable purposes only, but	[identical]
(b) the trustees of the charitable trust have not taken such steps as HMRC consider are reasonable in the circumstances to ensure that the payment will be applied for charitable purposes.	(b) the charitable company has not taken such steps as HMRC consider are reasonable in the circumstances to ensure that the payment will be applied for charitable purposes.

6 The words "to be made" are appropriate when expenditure is treated as incurred when committed, not when actually incurred: see 6.33 (Timing of expenditure).

7 The words "under s.543(1)(f)" are meaningless and must be disregarded.

We refer to this as the "**foreign-body rule**".

At first sight it seems odd that the foreign-body rule disapplies tax relief when expenditure *is* incurred for charitable purposes only: s.547(a) ITA/s.500 CTA 2010. But this allows HMRC to act where:

(1) expenditure is not yet applied for non-charitable purposes (eg it is for the time being invested) but

(2) there is a likelihood, or at least a risk, that it may be applied for non-charitable purposes in the future.

What if the charity does take reasonable steps, but nevertheless the foreign body does not apply its payment for charitable purposes only? In these cases the charity does incur charitable expenditure, but if a donor and the foreign body are linked persons, the tainted donation rules need consideration.[8]

6.6.1 *Body situated outside UK*

"Body" is not defined. It includes anything within the more common legal terms "body of persons" and "body corporate or unincorporate", but it may be wider. A partnership is a body.[9] HMRC Guidance Note Annex ii provides:

> 9.3 ...Payment(s) to an overseas body and payment(s) to a body outside the UK ... include monetary payments sent outside the UK to charities, companies, agents, partners and individual persons outside the UK.

The term "body" is not apt to describe an individual, but the issue is not likely to arise.

The body must be situated outside the UK. This expression is not defined. There are rules of private international law which determine the situs of an asset (eg shares) but not the situs of a body (eg a company). The situs may be the place of residence or (in the case of a body corporate) the place of incorporation. In practice the two tests are likely to lead to the same result, in which case no difficulty arises, and the position is clear.

In relation to bodies outside the UK but in the EU, the foreign-body rule appears to breach EU law and is not enforceable, but the issue is not likely to arise.

---

8 See 7.18.1 (Applied for charitable purposes).

9 See Kessler, *Taxation of Non-Residents and Foreign Domiciliaries* (21st ed., 2022-23), para 83.14 (Partnership: Body/office); see 34.3.1 (Offices) online version *https://www.foreigndomiciliaries.co.uk*

6.6.2 *"Payment"*

"Payment" is not defined. A transfer of assets other than money is not a payment in the strict sense. However, the word can be used more widely to include the transfer of a non-cash asset, and the context suggests that is the case here.

HMRC do not agree. HMRC Guidance Note Annex ii provides:

> 9.3 ... Payment(s) to an overseas body and payment(s) to a body outside the UK mean any monetary payment to any body outside the UK...

The context shows that the section is not concerned with a payment for full consideration. The section must be construed in this way to avoid absurdity. For instance, suppose a church makes a payment to a Dutch organ building company for a new organ. It can hardly be intended that payments of that sort are to be applied for charitable purposes by the Dutch company.

6.6.3 *Reasonable steps*

What constitutes "reasonable steps" will depend on the circumstances. HMRC Note Annex ii provides:

> **9. Payments to overseas bodies**
>
> ...
>
> 9.2 A charitable payment made to a body outside the UK will only be charitable expenditure for UK tax purposes by the charity provided the charity can clearly demonstrate to the Commissioners for HMRC that it has taken steps that the Commissioners consider are reasonable in the circumstances to ensure that the payment is applied for charitable purposes.
>
> If that condition isn't met, the payment is treated as non-charitable expenditure by the charity for UK tax purposes.
>
> 9.3 Applied for charitable purposes means applied for purposes which are regarded as charitable within Section 2 of the Charities Act (England and Wales) 2006. The same definition of charitable purpose applies for all charities claiming UK tax reliefs and exemptions whether the charity is in the UK or another member state of the EU, Iceland or Norway...
>
> 9.4 Trustees are required to carry out appropriate research in relation to the overseas body, followed by monitoring and evaluation, and to avoid or minimise risk to the charity's finances to meet their legal duty as trustees. The charity trustees must be able to describe the steps they take, explain how those steps ensure charitable application of funds, demonstrate that those steps were reasonable and produce evidence that

the steps were, in fact, taken.

It's not sufficient for the charity to simply establish that the overseas body is a charity under the domestic law of the host country. Nor is it enough to keep records of how things are spent. These are important but for overseas payments trustees must do more. The rest of this chapter deals with the situation where the charity makes a payment for which it must take steps to ensure that the payment is applied for charitable purposes.

9.5 When considering whether the steps taken by the charity were 'reasonable in the circumstances', HMRC will have regard to:

- the charity's knowledge of the overseas body
- previous relations with the overseas body
- previous history of the overseas body
- the amounts given in both absolute and relative terms
- the charity's observance of its own internal financial, management and decision making procedures, and whether or not these were adequate

9.6 When reviewing payments made to overseas bodies HMRC will generally ask the charity trustees to provide information and supporting documentation about:

- the person or persons to whom the payment was given
- the specific charitable purpose for which the payment was given, the reasons, and how the decision to provide the payment was arrived at
- the guarantees or assurances that have been obtained from the overseas body that the payment will be applied for the purpose for which it was given (such as a partnership or other written enforceable agreements), and what financial controls were in place, including sufficiently detailed financial records providing robust audit trails
- the steps the trustees took to ensure the payment will in fact be applied for charitable purposes (such as safeguards, monitoring and oversight)
- the follow-up action taken by the trustees to confirm that payments were applied properly

The Commissioners for HMRC must be satisfied that the steps taken by the trustees are reasonable in the circumstances. If HMRC Charities isn't provided with sufficiently detailed evidence of the steps taken it may not be able to accept the expenditure as charitable expenditure. This may give rise to a liability to tax. The steps to be taken will depend upon the nature and circumstances of the expenditure, for example, whether the recipient body may pass on the funds to a connected person who may use the funds for non-charitable purposes. The rest of this section explains what sorts of steps would be reasonable depending on the circumstances

> of both the donating charity and receiving bodies.
> 9.7 Trustees are expected to make adequate enquiries to find out such information as is reasonably available about the overseas body, and establish what evidence will be provided or made available by that body to show that the payment(s) will or have been applied for charitable purposes. The nature of the steps will depend upon the scale of operations, the size of the sums involved and the relevant circumstances. Enquiries should also be made to identify risks relating to connections between the body and other organisations. Where visits are required proper documentation is needed to show the checks carried out. Trustees should also identify any specific risks for certain projects especially in remote areas where language literacy and banking might be issues. Properly documented systems should be put in place if necessary to manage these. Where payments are to be made to overseas branches/partners, funds should be held in properly operated accounts by authorised persons.

The last sentence is correct, though a payment to an overseas branch of an UK body is not in fact a payment to a foreign body.

6.6.4 *Small payments*

HMRC Guidance Note Annex ii provides:

> 9.8 In the case of small one-off payments, an exchange of correspondence between the charity and the overseas body will normally be sufficient. Where possible, the correspondence should be on headed paper and it should:
> - give details of the payment and the purpose for which it was given
> - provide confirmation that the sum has or will be applied for the purpose given

We do not see why more than an email exchange should be necessary. The guidance is dated: how much is headed paper used nowadays?

> **Example 1**
> A situation where a thank you note on headed notepaper will be sufficient evidence.
> A pastor from a church outside the UK visits a partner parish in the UK. On his return home he discovers that the church building in his home town has burned down. When writing to the UK church to thank them for his visit he mentions this and the UK church decide to donate £500 to help rebuild the church. The overseas church sends a thank you note and a picture of the new building when it is complete.
> This is a situation where the local pastor is known to the UK charity, the

amount is a small, one-off payment and there are likely to be good connections between the charity and the overseas church. In this case a thank you note on headed paper is sufficient.

The relatively small amount of the donation affects the level of evidence required. In a situation like this HMRC would accept that the trustees' personal knowledge of the pastor and his connection with the overseas church is sufficient evidence.

Where there was no history of personal contact and knowledge with the pastor more evidence would be needed, for example press reports confirming that the building had, in fact burnt down, and was, in fact, a church and had been rebuilt.

9.9 More thorough work by the trustees will be required where the sums involved are larger or where a transfer of funds is to form part of an ongoing commitment. This might include independent verification of the overseas body's status and activities, along with reporting and verification of the manner of application of resources provided. The steps required can be reviewed in the light of evidence of proper use of funds and resources from recent earlier involvement on a particular project.

6.6.5 *Medium size payments*

HMRC Guidance Note Annex ii provides:

Example 2

A situation where further evidence of action taken, is required.

A UK charity becomes aware of a small overseas hospital that's struggling to afford drugs to treat a local epidemic. They agree to provide funding for 6 months supplies at the cost of £10,000 and enter into an arrangement with a pharmaceutical supplier close to the hospital. The supplier provides the necessary drugs to the hospital and invoices the UK charity.

In this situation the invoices from the drugs company aren't sufficient on their own. The trustees must be able to produce sound evidence to show what they did to verify that the hospital warranted the funding. This might include evidence of governance arrangements, financial controls and alternative available funding. In addition as things progress the trustees should check that the correct drugs are actually being delivered to the hospital in the amounts invoiced. A letter from the hospital confirming that they've received what the charity purchased would be acceptable evidence.

The larger level of the donation, a lack of detailed knowledge of the recipient charity and the existence of a third party means that more evidence is required than for example 1. In a situation like this the evidence to verify the suitability of the expenditure is likely to include:

- records to demonstrate the research undertaken, including the process in relation to the trustees' decision to provide funding
- records of meetings or teleconferences with the overseas body
- exchanges of correspondence
- detailed financial records
- a copy of any agreement between the third party and the charity

If the charity was supporting a particular project being carried out by an overseas body, official project documentation and literature.

6.6.6 *Funding agreements*

HMRC Guidance Note Annex ii provides:

> 9.10 The steps taken are to 'ensure' that the payment to the overseas body will be applied for charitable purposes. If the recipient body isn't bound by its own domestic law to apply all of its income for charitable purposes, then the trustees of the paying charity should consider seeking a legally binding and enforceable agreement to ensure that their payment will be applied charitably. If the overseas body declines to enter into such an agreement, the trustees of the paying body may have difficulty ensuring that the payment is applied for charitable purposes. If an agreement's entered into the trustees will need to have a means of establishing whether the agreement has been complied with.

The Guidance rightly says that the UK charity should *consider* a legally binding agreement, ie a contractual agreement. It may not be appropriate or necessary to have an agreement. A payment made for a purpose will generally be held on trust so that it can only be used for that purpose, so that a contract may not be necessary. The value of a contract may be overestimated for it is one thing to have a contract with an overseas body and another to enforce it. But a formal grant agreement is best practice, where the amounts involved are sufficient to justify it.

6.6.7 *Large payments*

HMRC Guidance Note Annex ii provides:

> 9.11 Where a charity makes a series of payments to the same overseas body for the same charitable purpose, it's not necessary for fresh enquiries to be made in respect of each new payment. If the trustees have recently checked the overseas body is applying its charitable funding properly, for example within the last year, and they're satisfied that the overseas body has an ongoing need for funding and is bound to apply payments from the charity for charitable purposes, then it's not unreasonable for the trustees to rely on the results of this review for a

payment shortly afterwards.

9.12 However, reliance on the overseas body's integrity may diminish with the passing of time and the trustees should be able to demonstrate that they are making enquiries of a sufficiently searching nature at regular intervals to ensure that the funds are being properly applied for charitable purposes.

Situations where more positive action is needed.

Example 3a

A charity's approached by an overseas body to provide support for a school building project. This is scheduled to take 18 months to complete. The proposed project is evaluated by the trustees who consider this to be within their charitable objects. They agree to provide staged funding totalling £250,000.

In this case the trustees must be able to produce evidence to demonstrate the research carried out in advance of any funds being made available and detailed financial and other records of how the grants were actually spent.

In a situation that involves large sums of money and a long term commitment, which could involve several overseas contractors, HMRC would expect to see comprehensive evidence of the trustees' considerations. This might include:

- a detailed project plan
- a formal funding application from the overseas body
- records of the evaluation and decision making procedures carried out by the trustees

In addition HMRC would expect the funding to be dependent on the overseas body entering into a formal agreement with the charity providing for:

- the payment of grants in stages based on specific targets
- a series of reviews to monitor project delivery
- claw back provisions should the project fail or the building is not used as intended

The trustees should also be able to produce evidence of ongoing evaluation as the project advanced including recommendations in relation to further funding.

Example 3b

A charity wishes to endow an overseas body with £1,000,000 to be used for charitable purposes at the body's own discretion. The research to be carried out by the trustees should include obtaining sufficiently detailed financial records to provide robust audit trails in support of their decision. Further, they'll need to either:

- obtain detailed and legally binding assurances from the recipient

body that the money will be applied for purposes that are charitable for UK purposes
- satisfy themselves that the body is established in such a manner that it's subject to regulation in the overseas country that will ensure its funds can only be applied for purposes that are charitable for UK purposes

If the charity is seeking binding assurances it will need to:
- obtain the assurances in a form that's legally binding and enforceable in the overseas country, ideally this will be in writing
- ensure, taking specialist advice if necessary, that it will be able to take enforcement action against the overseas body in case funds are not applied as intended
- ensure that it and the overseas body have a clear understanding what expenditure the funds provided are intended to meet and over what time scale
- ensure that effective monitoring arrangements are agreed with the overseas body

If the charity is relying on the manner of establishment of the overseas body and local regulation it will need to:
- ensure, taking specialist advice as necessary, that the overseas body is established in such a way as to ensure that it can only apply its funds for purposes that are charitable within the meaning of English law; in practice this will be set out in its governing document
- ensure, taking specialist advice as necessary, that the domestic legislation and regulatory structure in the overseas country are such that the overseas body will be effectively monitored, and the controlling individuals held to account, if it fails to apply its funds in accordance with its governing document

6.6.8 *Emergencies*

EN FB 2010 provides:

> 58. In practice that means charities will be required to maintain records of how charitable funds are spent overseas and be able to produce evidence of charitable works undertaken. The level of recordkeeping required will depend upon the circumstances relating to the expenditure. For example, it may not be possible for a charity providing aid during an emergency to maintain the same level of record-keeping as for routine overseas expenditure.

Similarly, HMRC say:

> It should be noted that charities will not be required to submit the

evidence to satisfy HMRC that internationally distributed funds are being spent on legitimate charitable activities as a matter of course. Instead, it is to be made available if HMRC requires it. The charity must take sufficient reasonable steps to ensure that the funds distributed overseas would be applied for charitable purposes. HMRC will take account of the circumstances under which the funds were spent. Routine spending of funds should be evidenced to a higher standard than, for example, spending during an international emergency.[10]

6.6.9 *Charity law duty of care*

Reasonable care is required as a matter of charity law quite regardless of tax.[11] We refer to this as the "**charity law duty of care**".

Charity law guidance is therefore relevant for the foreign-body rule.

The Charity Commission published guidance they issued to the Joseph Rowntree Charitable Trust. This charity made a£300k grant to CAGE, a non-charitable UK organisation, whose objects included to "highlight and campaign against state policies pertaining to the War on Terror" (a non-charitable object). Clearly in such a case some care is needed to ensure that grants are not used for non-charitable objects:

> ... the trustees should have requested written annual update reports in respect of the grants to Cage, especially as the charity was funding a non-charitable organisation, to complement the receipt of annual accounts, closing grant reports and face-to-face discussions. ... the charity needed to strengthen its monitoring processes so that it could reduce the future risk of its charitable funds being spent in furtherance of non-charitable purposes and that the trustees should have exercised closer scrutiny of expenditure and activities undertaken by the grant recipient in areas where the boundaries between what may be regarded as charitable, or not, may not be straightforward.
>
> The trustees were advised to take the following steps to improve their internal procedures:
>
> - Strengthen the charity's grant application terms to cover the

---

10 Impact Assessment of Extending Charity Tax Reliefs to Certain Organisations in Europe, 24 March 2010 (this is no longer available online).

11 See the Charity Commission guidance "Charities: how to manage risks when working internationally" (2013)
https://www.gov.uk/guidance/charities-how-to-manage-risks-when-working-internationally

possibility - when giving to non-charitable entities - that funds may be spent in furtherance of non-charitable purposes. Terms should cover the issue of how the recipient should ensure charitable funds are applied only for charitable purposes, and not for the general/non-charitable purposes of the non-charity. They should also cover 'claw back' arrangements, where the charity can take steps to recover funds where evidence is not provided by the recipient that such funds have been spent exclusively on activities in furtherance of a charitable purpose.

- Strengthen their monitoring processes to include adopting a dip-testing policy to monitor grants more effectively - particularly where funds have been provided to non-charitable entities - so they can have greater assurance that funds have been properly applied. This monitoring should be risk-based so that, where the risks are higher, more steps are taken to verify explanations and expenditure.
- Consider drawing up a specific policy for funding recipients where the charitable purpose is linked to the advancement of human rights. This area can be more difficult than other types of funding and the commission's recommendation was that, if the charity plans regular funding of projects in this field, the charity would be best served by a statement of policy to provide clarity for the future.[12]

6.6.10 *"As HMRC consider reasonable"*

The F(no.1)A 2010 extended the foreign-body rule from a requirement that the charity must take (objectively) reasonable steps to a requirement that the charity must take such steps as HMRC consider reasonable.

The wording, if taken at face value, might be read so as to deprive a charity of tax relief in circumstances where a tribunal accepted that it took reasonable steps but HMRC disagreed, but that would be extraordinary. It is considered that the Tribunal have jurisdiction to allow an appeal if they find the steps taken were reasonable, and so the 2010 amendment did not make a great deal of difference.

6.6.11 *Purpose of foreign-body rule*

There is a large overlap between
(1) the charity law duty of care and

---

12 Charity Commission, "Regulatory Case Report The Joseph Rowntree Charitable Trust" (May 2016) accessible *https://assets.publishing.service.gov.uk/government/uploads/system/uploads/attachment_data/file/521350/joseph_rowntree_charitable_trust.pdf*

(2) the tax law foreign-body rule

The difference between the charity law requirement and the foreign-body rule is, we think, a matter of emphasis rather than substance.

It follows that there is strictly little if any real need for the foreign-body rule. But even if it is otiose, it is no doubt helpful for HMRC to be able to point to a specific tax provision, where they may suspect arrangements under which:

(1) A gift is made to a UK charity (which claims Gift Aid relief).
(2) The UK charity makes a grant to an offshore body for purportedly charitable purposes.
(3) The offshore body fails (or may in the future fail) to apply the funds for charitable purposes. It may return the grant, no doubt after taking a commission, to the donors, or connected persons, or apply it for their benefit. Or the funds may be applied for non-charitable purposes, such as political purposes or for terrorism. The trustees may be fraudulent or simply negligent.

The foreign-body rule is also relevant where HMRC anticipate that funds may be applied for non-charitable purposes in the future, but that has not yet happened.

To police such arrangements effectively requires international co-operation which will be difficult. But a balance still needs to be found between the needs of the state to detect fraud, and the needs of taxpayers to operate with reasonable certainty, and the rule of law. The debate is longstanding,[13] and it is unfortunate that the precipitous enactment of the F(no.1)A 2010[14] precluded any opportunity to consider the issue.

6.7 Approved charitable investment/loan

s.543(1) ITA	**s.496(1) CTA 2010**
(1) For the purposes of this Part a charitable trust's non-charitable expenditure for a tax year is ...	(1) For the purposes of this Part a charitable company's non-charitable expenditure for an accounting period is ...
(i) the amount of any of the charitable trust's funds that is invested in the tax year in an	(g) the amount of any of the charitable company's funds that is invested in the accounting period in

13 The cause célèbre is *Liversidge v Anderson* [1942] AC 206.
14 See 3.4.2 (F(No.1)A 2010: Critique).

investment which is not an approved charitable investment (see s.558), and	an investment which is not an approved charitable investment (see s.511), and
(j) any amount lent in the tax year by the charitable trust, if the loan is neither an investment nor an approved charitable loan (see s.561).	(h) any amount lent in the accounting period by the charitable company, if the loan is neither an investment nor an approved charitable loan (see s.514).

The penalty for making a non-approved charitable investment or loan is severe: the entire amount invested or lent is non-charitable expenditure. If a charity were to pay another person to make the non-approved loan then at most the payment made by the charity to that person would be non-charitable expenditure.

If a charity makes a non-approved loan or investment, the position cannot be set right by repayment of the loan or realising the investment. The non-charitable expenditure is not extinguished. Perhaps the reason was a fear that a tax avoidance advantage would be obtained by the investment and not lost by the sale of the investment, we are unable to think of a practical example of how this might happen.

Section 548 ITA/s.501 CTA 2010 a relief against double counting which is so limited it hardly seems worth paper and ink:

s.548 ITA	**s.501 CTA 2010**
(1) Subsection (2) applies if in a tax year a charitable trust—	(1) Subsection (2) applies if in an accounting period a charitable company—
(a) realises the whole or part of an investment which was made in the tax year and is not an approved charitable investment (see s.558), or	(a) realises the whole or part of an investment which was made in the period and is not an approved charitable investment (see s.511), or
(b) is repaid the whole or part of a loan which was made in the tax year and is neither an investment nor an approved charitable loan (see s.561).	(b) is repaid the whole or part of a loan which was made in the period and is neither an investment nor an approved charitable loan (see s.514).
(2) Any further investment or	(2) Any further investment or

lending in the tax year of the sum realised or repaid, so far as it does not exceed the sum originally invested or lent, is not non-charitable expenditure as a result of s.543(1)(i) or (j).	lending in the accounting period of the sum realised or repaid, so far as it does not exceed the sum originally invested or lent, is not non-charitable expenditure as a result of s.496(1)(g) or (h).

This only provides relief if the sum realised or repaid is reinvested in the same chargeable period.

6.8 Investment

Two questions arise:

(1) *Has the charity made an "investment"?* If so the investment must be an approved charitable investment (or else charity tax relief is lost).

(2) *If a charity does not make an investment, has it incurred expenditure?* If so, the expenditure must be incurred for charitable purposes or else charity tax relief is lost.

In practice, it does not often matter whether or not something constitutes an "investment".

(1) If it is an investment, it must (usually) meet the Type 12 condition, in particular it must be for the benefit of the charity.

(2) If the charity incurs expenditure without making an investment, the expenditure must be for charitable purposes only.

In most cases, the two requirements come to the same thing.

So far as the requirements are different, however, it is necessary to consider what is or is not an investment. The term "investment" is not defined. It will bear its usual meaning, which has often been discussed in a trust law context.

6.9 "Approved charitable investment"

The investment of funds is deemed to be non-charitable expenditure unless the investments are "approved charitable investments".

Section 558 ITA/s.511 CTA 2010 sets out an exhaustive list of approved charitable investments.

s.558 ITA	**s.511 CTA 2010**
An investment is an approved charitable investment for the purposes of s.543 (meaning of "non-	An investment is an approved charitable investment for the purposes of s.496 (meaning of

charitable expenditure") if it is an investment of any of the following types	"non-charitable expenditure") if it is an investment of any of the following types.

In this work, a **"non-approved investment"** is an investment not falling within the list (and so not an approved charitable investment).

The list derives from the former Trustee Investments Act 1961, but that is now of historical interest only.

6.10 Type 1: Securities

Section 558 ITA/s.511 CTA 2010 continues:

s.558 ITA	**s.511 CTA 2010**
Type 1 An investment to which s.559 applies.	*Type 1* An investment to which s.512 applies.

Section 559 ITA/s.512 CTA 2010 sets out 9 categories of securities which fall within Type 1.

6.11 EU/International securities

Section 559 ITA/s.512 CTA 2010 :

> (1) The investments to which this section applies are investments in securities—
> (a) issued or guaranteed by the government of a member State of the European Union

6.12 International securities

Section 559 ITA/s.512 CTA 2010 :

> (1) The investments to which this section applies are investments in securities ...
> (b) issued or guaranteed by the government or a governmental body of any territory or part of a territory,
> (c) issued by an international entity listed in the Annex to Council Directive 2003/48/EC (directive on taxation of interest payments),[15]
> (d) issued by an entity meeting the four criteria set out at the end of that Annex

15 See App 1 (International Entity Securities).

Section 560 ITA/s.513 CTA 2010 :

s.560 ITA	**s.513 CTA 2010**
(1) Section 559 does not apply to an investment by virtue of subsection (1)(b), (c) or (d) of that section unless—	(1) Section 512 does not apply to an investment by virtue of subsection (1)(b), (c) or (d) of that section unless—
(a) condition A is met in relation to the securities, and	[identical]
(b) if the securities are shares or debenture stock, condition B is met in relation to the securities.	[identical]
But see subsection (3) of this section.	[identical]

We refer to **"ACI conditions A and B"**; see below.

6.13 Building society/credit institution

Section 559 ITA/s.512 CTA 2010 :

> (1) The investments to which this section applies are investments in securities ...
> (e) issued by a building society,
> (f) issued by a credit institution which operates on mutual principles and which is authorised by an appropriate governmental body in the territory in which the securities are issued

6.14 Open-ended investment co

Section 559 ITA/s.512 CTA 2010 :

> (1) The investments to which this section applies are investments in securities ...
> (g) issued by an open-ended investment company,[16]

6.15 Unlisted securities

Section 559 ITA/s.512 CTA 2010 :

16 Section 559(3) ITA/s.512 CTA 2010 provides a referential definition: "'open-ended investment company' is to be read in accordance with ss.613 and 615 of CTA 2010."

(1) The investments to which this section applies are investments in securities ...

(i) issued by a company but not listed on a recognised stock exchange.

Section 560 ITA/s.513 CTA 2010 :

s.560 ITA	**s.513 CTA 2010**
(2) In the case of an investment in securities issued by a company which is incorporated, s.559 does not apply to the investment by virtue of subsection (1)(i) of that section unless—	(2) In the case of an investment in securities issued by a company which is incorporated, s.512 does not apply to the investment by virtue of subsection (1)(i) of that section unless—
(a) condition A is met in relation to the securities,	[identical]
(b) if the securities are shares or debenture stock, condition B is met in relation to the securities, and	[identical]
(c) condition C is met in relation to the company.	[identical]
But see subsection (3) of this section.	[identical]

We refer to **"ACI conditions A and B"**.

6.16 ACI conditions

6.16.1 *ACI condition A: traded*

Section 560(4) ITA/s.513(4) CTA 2010 :

Condition A is that the securities are traded or quoted on—

(a) a recognised investment exchange (as defined in s.285(1) of FISMA 2000), or

(b) an investment exchange which constitutes the principal or only market established in a territory on which securities admitted to official listing are dealt in or traded.

6.16.2 *ACI condition B*

Section 560(5) ITA/s.513(5) CTA 2010 :

Condition B is that—

(a) the securities are fully paid up,

(b) the terms of the issue of the securities require them to be fully paid up within the period of 9 months beginning with the day after the day on which they are issued, or

(c) the securities are shares issued with no nominal value.

6.16.3 *Exception to conditions A/B*

Section 560(3) ITA/s.513(3) CTA 2010 :

> Conditions A and B need not be met if the securities are traded or quoted on a money market supervised by the government or a governmental body of any territory or part of a territory.

6.16.4 *ACI condition C*

Section 560(6) ITA/s.513(6) CTA 2010 :

Condition C is that—

(a) throughout the last business day[17] before the investment day,[18] the company has total issued and paid up share capital of at least £1,000,000 (or the equivalent of £1,000,000 in some other currency),[19] and

(b) in each of the five years immediately before the calendar year in which the investment day falls, the company paid a dividend on all the shares issued by the company (excluding any shares issued after the dividend was declared and any shares which by their terms of issue did not rank for dividend for that year).

Section 560 ITA/s.513(8) CTA 2010 goes on to provide a reorganisation relief:

(8) For the purposes of subsection (6)(b) a company formed—

---

17 Section 560(10) ITA/s.513(10) CTA 2010 gives a commonsense definition: "'business day' means, in relation to an investment, a business day in the place where the investment is made."

18 Section 560(10) ITA/s.513(10) CTA 2010 gives a commonsense definition: "'the investment day' means, in relation to an investment, the day on which the investment is made."

19 Section 560(7) ITA/s.513(7) CTA 2010 provides: "For the purposes of the words in brackets in subsection (6)(a) use the exchange rate prevailing in the UK at the close of business on the last business day before the investment day."

(a) to take over the business of another company or other companies, or

(b to acquire the securities of, or control of, another company or other companies,

is treated as having paid a dividend in any year in which a dividend has been paid by the other company or all of the other companies (as the case may be).

(9) It is irrelevant that the company is formed for other purposes in addition to those mentioned in paragraph (a) or (b) of subsection (8).

6.17 Types 2 - 4: Charity funds

Section 558 ITA/s.511 CTA 2010 continues:

Type 2 An investment in a common investment fund established under—

(a) s.22 of the Charities Act 1960 [now repealed][20],

(b) s.24 of the Charities Act 1993,

(bb) s.96 of the Charities Act 2011, or

(c) s.25 of the Charities Act (Northern Ireland) 1964 [now repealed][21].

Type 3 An investment in a common deposit fund established under—

(a) s.22A of the Charities Act 1960 [now repealed][22],

(b) s.25 of the Charities Act 1993, or

(c) s.100 of the Charities Act 2011.

s.558 ITA	**s.511 CTA 2010**
Type 4 An investment in a fund which—	[identical]
(a) is similar to a fund mentioned in relation to Type 2 or 3, and	[identical]
(b) is established for the exclusive benefit of charities by or under a provision relating to any particular charities or class of charities contained in an Act.	(b) is established for the exclusive benefit of charities by or under a provision relating to any particular charities or class of charities contained in an Act (including an Act of the Scottish Parliament).

20 See s.96 Charities Act 2011.

21 See s.43 Charities Act (Northern Ireland) 2008.

22 See s.100 Charities Act 2011.

6.18 Type 5: Land

Section 558 ITA/s.511 CTA 2010 continues:

> *Type 5* An interest in land, other than an interest held as security for a debt.

6.19 Types 6 - 7: Government securities

Section 558 ITA/s.511 CTA 2010 continues:

> *Type 6* Any of the following issued by Her Majesty's Government in the UK—
> (a) bills,
> (b) Certificates of Tax Deposit,
> (c) Savings Certificates, and
> (d) Tax Reserve Certificates.
>
> *Type 7* Northern Ireland Treasury Bills.

6.20 Type 8: Unit trusts

Section 558 ITA/s.511 CTA 2010 continues:

> *Type 8* Units[23]
> [1] in a unit trust scheme (as defined in s.237(1) of FISMA 2000) or
> [2] in a recognised scheme (as defined in s.237(3) of FISMA 2000).

For completeness: the definition of "unit trust scheme" for the purposes of the Income Tax Acts is in s.1007 ITA. This definition is disapplied for the purposes of s.558 ITA: see s.1007(4) ITA. But s.1007 only incorporates the s.237 FISMA definition, so it makes no difference. If that is right, the repeal of s.1007(4) would be a sensible simplification, but the change is too small to be worthwhile except in the context of a more widely ranging review.

6.21 Types 9 -11: Bank deposits

Section 558 ITA/s.511 CTA 2010 continues:

s.558 ITA	**s.511 CTA 2010**
Type 9 A deposit with a bank (as defined in s.991)—	*Type 9* A deposit with a bank (as defined in s.1120)—
(a) in respect of which interest is	[identical]

23 The section adds: "'Units' is defined in s.237(2) of FISMA 2000."

payable at a commercial rate, and (b) which is not made as part of an arrangement under which a loan is made by the bank to some other person.	
Type 10 A deposit with— (a) the National Savings Bank, (b) a building society, or (c) a credit institution which operates on mutual principles and which is authorised by an appropriate governmental body in the territory in which the deposit is taken.	[identical]
Type 11 Certificates of deposit (including uncertificated eligible debt security units as defined in s.986(3)).	*Type 11* Certificates of deposit (including uncertificated eligible debt security units as defined in s.986(3) of ITA 2007).

6.22 Other investments: Type 12

Section 558 ITA/s.511 CTA 2010 includes within the definition of an "approved charitable investment":

s.558 ITA	**s.511 CTA 2010**
Type 12 A loan or other investment as to which an officer of Revenue and Customs is satisfied, on a claim, that	[identical]
[1] it is made for the benefit of the charitable trust and	[1] it is made for the benefit of the charitable company and
[2] not for the avoidance of tax (whether by the trust or any other person).	[2] not for the avoidance of tax (whether by the company or any other person).

There are two conditions, both of which must be satisfied:

(1) the investment is made for the benefit of the charity (the "**benefit condition**")

(2) the investment is not for the avoidance of tax (the "**tax avoidance**

condition")

6.23 Made for benefit of charity

It is well established that "benefit" is a word of wide import.

The words do not mean "in a manner which proves ultimately to be for the benefit of the charity". The ultimate result can only be discovered with the benefit of hindsight, perhaps years after the investment is made. One needs to know at the outset whether an investment is an approved charitable investment. So the test of benefit should be applied at the time that the expenditure is incurred, and without the benefit of hindsight.

The question may arise whether one should apply:

(1) an objective test: ie whether an objective observer would regard the investment as "for the benefit of the charity", having regard to the circumstances at the time it was made; or

(2) a subjective test: ie whether the charity subjectively considered the investment to be for its benefit at the time it was made (applying the appropriate company law principles to attribute the views of the trustees or senior management of the charity to the charity itself); or

(3) a mixture of objective and subjective tests.

The question only arises in the (hopefully) unusual situation where trustees invest in good faith but imprudently or otherwise in breach of charity law. It is suggested that the test should be along the lines of those which apply to directors' duties to a company[24] and trustees' duties to a trust.[25] This involves a combination of objective and subjective requirements which is fairest as between the charity, the charity trustees or directors, and HMRC, and consistent with the background law under which the charity (trust or company) operates. If that is right, a failure to comply with the investment duties of trustees does not necessarily entail that the investment falls outside type 12.

HMRC Guidance Note provides at Annex iii:

> **iii.4 Interpretation of 'for the benefit of the charity'**
> 4.1 There are limited ways in which charities may apply their funds; broadly they may either apply them in carrying out their charitable objects or they may invest their funds to generate income to fund their charitable activities. So, investments and loans made by charities may be made for:

---

24 Chapter 2 Part 10 Companies Act 2006.

25 Section 1 Trustee Act 2000.

> - The financial benefit of the charity, to generate income or gains to enable the charity to carry out its objects, or
> - The charitable benefit of the charity - carrying out its charitable objects
>
> HMRC has long held the view that an investment or loan must be either for financial benefit or for charitable benefit. However HMRC increasingly recognise that charity trustees need greater flexibility in making investment decisions and a rigid distinction is no longer necessarily appropriate
>
> 4.2 HMRC accepts that in considering whether an investment or loan has been made for the benefit of the charity a broad view should be taken of how the charity benefits. This doesn't mean that 'anything goes'; trustees must be able to justify their investment and loan making decisions and demonstrate how the loan benefits the charity. HMRC may ask to see evidence of the trustees' decision-making process and the information considered as part of that process.

Charities should keep the relevant records.[26]

6.23.1 *Loan by way of investment*

HMRC Guidance Note provides at Annex iii:

> 4.3 Type 12 investments include loans made by way of investment as well as other investments not included in type 1 to 11 investments. This kind of investment will normally be made to generate a flow of income or capital appreciation to enable the charity to deliver its charitable objectives. Where this is the case 'for the benefit of the charity' is most likely to mean for the financial benefit of the charity. In this sort of case HMRC would expect to see evidence of trustees having made a properly considered investment decision. This would include
>
> [a] taking properly qualified, and preferably independent, advice as necessary,
>
> [b] the seeking of a commercial rate of return in relation to risk,
>
> [c] taking reasonable steps to limit the charity's overall exposure to risk including securing loans where possible, and
>
> [d] consideration of available alternatives

Charities should keep the relevant records.[27]

> 4.4 There's no one test of commercial soundness and each case must be viewed on its own facts. Where the loan is an investment loan, HMRC

---

26 See 6.28 (Record keeping).

27 See 6.28 (Record keeping).

will normally accept it's for the financial benefit of the charity where it:
[a] carries a commercial rate of interest which is paid and actively pursued
[b] is adequately secured
[c] is made under a formal written agreement which includes reasonable repayment terms
In considering the individual elements above HMRC will look at the arrangement in the round. For example, does the rate of return reasonably reflect the security and repayment terms? Have the trustees made proper enquiries into the credit worthiness of the borrower and do the terms reflect that? Have the agreed terms of the loan been applied in practice?

If the loan is to a person unconnected with the charity, this is a sound approach. If the loan is to a wholly owned trading company, the position is different. An interest free and unsecured loan to a wholly owned company is in principle a simple commercial transaction, indeed a common one:[28]

[1] There is no need for a commercial rate of interest since the return can be taken out by Gift Aid.
[2] There is no need for security if there is no real possibility of the trading company losing money.
[3] [a] A formal written agreement is doubtless desirable but not essential when the parties are parent and subsidiary.
[b] There is no need to specify reasonable repayment terms.

The authors have known HMRC to object, but this is quite misconceived. As far as security is concerned, HMRC recognise that it may be unobtainable:

III.5 Investments and loans to trading subsidiaries
III.5.1 Many charities have subsidiary companies that pass their taxable profits to the parent charity. Where an investment, including an investment loan, is made in such a subsidiary company, the charity is unlikely to be able to obtain normal security for the investment. In such cases HMRC may ask to see the business plans, cash-flow forecasts and other business projections which informed the charity's decision to make the investment.

In CC35 (Charities trading and taxation) para 4.11 the Charity Commission

---

28 This is self-evident but if authority is needed, see *IRC v Levy* 56 TC 68 at p.87.

make some comments on what they take to be the HMRC view:

> Trustees might wish to provide a trading subsidiary with
> [a] an interest-free loan, or
> [b] a loan which is secured only by the contractual undertaking of the subsidiary, and not by a charge over assets of the subsidiary.[29]
> However HMRC Charities takes a critical view of loans which are not made on proper commercial terms (see 4.12). In particular:
> [1] it is unlikely that interest-free loans to a trading subsidiary could be justified as an investment, unless the amount of the loan was small
> [2] whilst the creation of a charge over property of the trading subsidiary to secure a loan involves expense, it is unlikely that a loan secured only by the contractual undertaking of the trading subsidiary could be justified as an investment, unless
> [a] the amount of the loan is small, or
> [b] the value of the security which is available in the subsidiary is limited.

The CC say that HMRC regard interest as (more or less) essential, and security as essential if available.[30] But this does not correctly state HMRC practice as set out in the HMRC Guidance Note at iii.4.3.

The Guidance continues:

> 4.5 As noted above, HMRC will take a broad view of how an investment benefits a charity. For example, a commercial investment might yield a highly advantageous return for the charity, but be so contrary to the charity's objects that it can't be properly considered to be for the benefit of the charity. Conversely, an investment may yield a relatively modest rate of return, but may help directly carry out the charity's objects. In such a case the trustees may be able to demonstrate that overall, there is an acceptable level of benefit to the charity for the amount invested.
> 4.6 A loan not made as an investment does not need to provide a financial benefit and would normally only be 'for the benefit of the charity' if it's made for the charitable benefit of the charity. HMRC would expect to see evidence that the trustees had given proper consideration to how the loan would carry out the charity's objects. This would include taking account of the balance between public benefit and any private benefit to the recipient of the loan. However, a broad assessment has to be made of the benefit provided by such a loan and if

---

29 In ordinary parlance this would be called an unsecured loan.

30 But in practice the exemption in [2][b] will apply. The security available will be limited, so security is not then required.

it provides some financial return this should be taken into account. Section 514(3)(d) CTA 2010 and section 561(3)(d) ITA 2007 apply only to loans not made as investments.

4.7 Guidance published by The Charity Commission for England & Wales identifies a distinction between 'Financial Investments' and 'Programme Related Investments and also recognises the concept of 'Mixed Motive Investments'.

4.8 Investments recognised by the Charity Commission as Financial Investments should be investments in the strict sense - funds invested to generate a flow of income or gains to enable the charity to carry out its objects. Where an investment's a financial investment HMRC would expect trustees to be able to demonstrate that the investment was made for the financial benefit of the charity.

6.23.2 *Ethical investment*

HMRC Guidance Note provides at Annex iii:

4.9 The Charity Commission guidance recognises that a charity can take an ethical approach to its financial investments:

Ethical investments

4.10 Ethical investments may also be known as sustainable or socially responsible investments. While these are still financial investments and must be demonstrably made for the financial benefit of the charity they're likely to be made in accordance with the charity's values and ethos and may yield a lower return than the best performing commercial alternatives. Trustees may be able to demonstrate benefit to the charity, despite this lower performance, by reference to the positive effect on the charity's objects, the avoidance of conflict with those objects or the impact of the investment decision on supporter perceptions.

6.23.3 *Programme related investment*

HMRC Guidance Note provides at Annex iii:

4.11 Programme Related Investments aren't investments in the strict sense.

While such investments may take the form of subscribing for shares in a company they're not made with a view to generating a flow of income or gains to carry out the charity's objects. Indeed, such investments may not offer any realistic prospect of a commercial investment return. Instead, these investments are properly viewed as application of funds to further the purposes of the charity. Where the trustees are able to demonstrate that proper consideration has been given to such an investment and how it's expected to further the charity's objects HMRC is likely to accept that it's been made for the benefit of the charity.

6.24 Mixed motive/social investment

6.24.1 *Definition of social investment*

Section 292A Charities Act 2011 provides a definition:

> (1) This section applies for the purposes of this Part [Part 14A Charities Act 2011].
> (2) A social investment is made when a relevant act[31] of a charity is carried out with a view to both—
> (a) directly furthering the charity's purposes; and
> (b) achieving a financial return for the charity.

The Charities Guidance Note describes this as mixed motive investment.

> (5) An act mentioned in subsection (4)(a) is to be regarded as achieving a financial return if its outcome is better for the charity in financial terms than expending the whole of the funds or other property in question.
> (6) A commitment mentioned in subsection (4)(b) is to be regarded as achieving a financial return if—
> (a) it is not called upon; or
> (b) it is called upon without resulting in the expenditure of the whole of the funds or other property put at risk.
> (7) The fact that a relevant act may also have results other than those mentioned in subsection (2)(a) and (b) does not prevent the carrying out of that act being regarded as the making of a social investment.

Power for a charity to make investments of this kind, described as social investment, is confirmed by s.292A-292C Charities Act 2011, inserted by the Charities (Protection and Social Investment) Act 2016.

6.24.2 *Is "social investment" an investment*

Section 292A(8) Charities Act 2011 provides:

> The fact that carrying out a relevant act of a charity is regarded as the

---

31 Defined s.292A CA 2011:
> (3) References to an act of a charity are, in the case of an unincorporated charity, to an act of the charity trustees.
> (4) A relevant act of a charity is—
> (a) an application or use of funds or other property; or
> (b) taking on a commitment in relation to a liability of another person (such as a guarantee) that puts the charity's funds or other property at risk of being applied or used.

> making of a social investment for the purposes of this Part does not of itself make the act an investment for any other purpose.

Nevertheless a social investment is in principle an investment in the general sense, and so an investment for the purposes of the charitable expenditure rules. The Law Commission say:[32]

> 3.34 The trustees' intention is relevant to whether something is an "investment".[33] Something can be an investment even if the financial return is not the principal purpose of the outlay of funds.[34] Similarly, something can be an investment even if it does not achieve a market rate of return.[35]

6.24.3 *Is Social Investment an approved charitable investment*

HMRC Guidance Note provides at Annex iii:

> 4.12 *Mixed Motive Investments*. Some charity investments will be made on terms that deliver insufficient financial return for them to be accepted as financial investments. At the same time they deliver insufficient charitable benefit to be accepted as being programme related investments. However, trustees may be able to demonstrate that, taken together, the combination of financial return and carrying out of charitable objectives is sufficient for the investment to be made for the

---

32 Law Commission Consultation Paper "Social Investment by Charities" (2014). The same point is made, in less detail, in the final report at 1.12. See *https://www.lawcom.gov.uk/project/charity-law-social-investment-by-charities/*

33 The Law Commission refer to *Re Power* [1947] Ch 572 at p.575.

34 Footnote original: For example, in *Cook v Medway Housing Society* [1997] STC 90, the court considered whether the Medway Housing Society was an "investment company" under s.130 ICTA 1988 so as to entitle it to a certain tax relief. The statutory definition required consideration of whether the company's business involved "the making of investments". The company's objects were to provide housing to people in need at low rents. The housing portfolio "was intended over time to produce a profitable capital and income return" and was therefore an "investment". Lightman J said "it seems to me perfectly possible for a property at the same time to be held to provide affordable housing and to provide a profitable return, and for the Society's business to be the provision of affordable housing and to be that of holding such housing to achieve a profitable return": at 98.

35 Footnote original: In *Cook v Medway Housing Society* [1997] STC 90, Lightman J said that "the critical question is whether the holding of assets *to produce a profitable return* is merely incidental to the carrying on of some other business, or is the very business carried on by the taxpayer. In this case the very business of the Society is the provision of housing at a return below the market return, but nonetheless a return producing a profit" (emphasis added): at 101.

> benefit of the charity.
> For example, trustees of an overseas development charity may decide to invest £25,000 in a fair trade tea production and marketing venture. The agreed rate of return on the investment is only 2% at a time when the trustees could reasonably expect 5% from conventional investment of that amount. However, the trustees are able to demonstrate that the social benefits in the target population are such as would have justified an application of charitable funds to the value of £15,000. Taking account of this, a 2% return on the amount invested looks more reasonable and HMRC would be likely to accept this as being for the benefit of the charity.

The Law Commission make the same point:

> 6.7 The law recognises a number of investments that will automatically be regarded as approved investments and loans for tax purposes. Concerns have been raised that many social investments do not fall neatly within these recognised categories, which means that they can only be approved on an ad hoc basis by HM Revenue and Customs, causing uncertainty to charity trustees.[36]
> 6.8 These concerns may be overstated. Some social investments will fall within the categories of investments that are automatically approved, such as
> [a] investments in any company (whether listed on a stock exchange or not),[37]
> [b] investments in land, investments in unit trusts, or
> [c] loans to beneficiaries of the charity.
> Indeed, those seeking to attract social investment from charities may choose to structure the social investment in such a way as to ensure that the investment is automatically approved. For social investments that are not automatically approved, the charity must satisfy HMRC that the investment or loan is "for the benefit of the [charity] and not for the avoidance of tax". Quite apart from tax considerations, charity trustees ought to be satisfied that a social investment is for the benefit of the charity before committing to it in any event. If the charity trustees are so satisfied, and provided they can give their reasons as to why the social investment was considered to be appropriate, it is difficult to see how HMRC could say that the social investment was not for the benefit of the charity and therefore does not have approved status. We accept,

36 Hodgson review of the Charities Act 2006 (2012) para 9.13; Finch, "Mixed messages on mixed motives" Civil Society (11 December 2013).

37 But see 6.15 (Unlisted securities).

however, that the possibility of an assessment and determination of this point by HMRC may create some uncertainty for charity trustees and perhaps some additional administrative burden or cost.[38]

6.24.4 *Programme related investment*

Programme-related investment ("PRI") may not be "investment" at all, in the sense of financial investment. It is a method of carrying out the objects of a charity, even though the way in which this is done may resemble "investment" by the charity. If so, PRI is treated for tax purposes in a similar way to a grant - charitable expenditure as long as it is in furtherance of the charity's objects.

This is because the word "investment" is used with two meanings. In trust law and tax law, investment means the use of money to gain money. In a looser sense, especially in political discourse, "investment" means any beneficial use of money, such as investment in schools and hospitals, even though that does not produce an identifiable financial return.[39]

There is useful discussion in Charity Commission, "Social Investment by charities - the new power introduced by the Charities (Protection and Social Investment) Act 2016: interim guidance".

6.25 Charity law aspects of investment

The HMRC Guidance Note also makes some comments on charity law aspects of investment. For the Charity Commission views on investment in wholly owned trading companies, see 9.11 (Financing trading company).

HMRC Guidance Note provides at Annex iii:

---

38 Law Commission, "Social Investment by Charities A Consultation Paper" (2014) *http://www.lawcom.gov.uk/wp-content/uploads/2015/06/cp216_charities_social_investment.pdf* Some footnotes are omitted from this quote.

39 The same distinction is made for accounting purposes: The Charities SORP FRS 102 provides:

> "21.9. A programme related investment is an asset held by a charity that provides investment funding to individuals or organisations in order to directly further the charitable purposes of the investing charity; any financial return obtained is not a primary reason for making the investment.
> 21.10. A programme related investment is made exclusively to further the charitable aims of the investing charity by funding specific activities or related tangible fixed assets of a third party which, in turn, contribute to the investor's own charitable purposes.
> 21.21. Programme related investments must be disclosed either as a separate line on the face of the balance sheet or identified as a separate class of investment in the notes to the accounts, depending on the materiality of the holding."

iii.6 Probity of investments and loans.
6.1 When deciding whether to make an investment charities should bear in mind the requirements of charity law relating to:

- objectivity in the selection of investments
- the need to avoid undue risk or speculation
- the need for a proper spread of investments

6.2 Charities should also of course bear in mind the scope of the requirements of the Trustee Act 2000 as well as their own investment powers as set out in the charity's governing document

Also at Annex iv, para 51:

> Investments will be regarded as made for the benefit of the charity if they're commercially sound and meet the requirements of English charity law. Usually, charities should ensure that investments are secure, carry a fair rate of return (actually paid) and, in the case of loans, provide for recovery of the amount invested.

CC35 (Trustees, trading and tax) para 4.12 provides:

> An investment would not be considered to be "for the benefit of the parent charity", if, for example, the investment was
> [1] speculative, or
> [2] driven by a desire to keep the trading subsidiary going, regardless of the prospects of economic return to the parent charity.

As to point [1], what is "speculative"? Fred Schwed Jr gives the best explanation:

> Investment and speculation are said to be two different things, and the prudent man is advised to engage in the one and avoid the other. This is something like explaining to the troubled adolescent that Love and Passion are two different things. He perceives that they are different, but they don't seem quite different enough to clear up his problems. Investment and speculation have been so often defined that a couple more faulty definitions should do no harm, the science of economics having reached a point where further confusion is impossible. Thus,
>
> > Speculation is an effort, probably unsuccessful, to turn a little money into a lot.
> >
> > Investment is an effort, which should be successful, to prevent a lot of money from becoming a little.
>
> If you take a thousand dollars down to Wall Street and attempt to run it up to $25,000 in the course of a year, you are speculating. If you take $25,000 down there and attempt to earn a thousand dollars a year with it (by buying twenty-five four per cent bonds) you are investing. The

> odds against your being successful in the first venture are roughly 25-1. The odds against the success of the second venture are odds on, or something like 1-25. These odd are, of course, only vague approximations. But here is an attractively unfair wager if you care to make it and can find the necessary sucker: challenge an investment man to write down a list of the twenty-five safest corporate bonds he knows (each on a different corporation). The bet is that they won't all pay their interest for the next five years.[40]

As to point [2], the reputational damage to the charity from the failure of its trading company may be considerable, and that must be factored into the decision. It is not just a matter of money. But of course the time eventually comes when a trading subsidiary must be allowed to fail.

6.26 Tax avoidance condition

Section 558 ITA/s.511 CTA 2010 requires that an approved charitable investment type 12 is:

s. 558 ITA	**s.511 CTA 2010**
A loan or other investment... that ... is ... not for the avoidance of tax (whether by the trust or any other person).	A loan or other investment... that ... is ... not for the avoidance of tax (whether by the company or any other person).

Section 989 ITA/s.1119 CTA 2010 provide:

s.989 ITA	**s.1119 CTA 2010**
The following definitions apply for the purposes of the Income Tax Acts... "tax", if neither income tax nor corporation tax is specified, means either of those taxes.	The definitions referred to in s.1118(2) [the list of definitions for the purposes of the Corporation Tax Acts] are ... [identical]

So "tax" means income tax or CT.

"Tax" does not include CGT. One might have expected CGT to be included in the expression "tax" since the charitable expenditure rules apply to a charitable trust's CGT exemption. Would a court find that "tax" includes CGT, on a purposive construction? The better view is that it should not, but legal realism suggests that the outcome will depend

---

40 Fred Schwed Jr *Where are the Customers Yachts?* (1940) chapter 8.

partly on whether the appeal concerns a tax avoidance scheme.

"Tax" does not include IHT.

6.26.1 *Avoidance*

"Tax avoidance" means "contrary to the evident intention of parliament".[41]

Avoidance of tax by a person other than the charity and its wholly owned companies is a comprehensible if problematic notion.

The idea of avoidance of tax by the charity itself is more difficult. Charities benefit from so many exemptions from tax that they can be expected to and generally do arrange their affairs so that income and gains which accrue to them are of a type which is tax exempt. Thus some tax planning strategies adopted by charities are so widespread and so well established that parliament can be said to acquiesce in their acceptability.

The idea of avoidance of tax by a wholly owned subsidiary of a charity is equally difficult. Parliament encourages subsidiaries to gift-aid up all their profits so as to escape paying tax.[42] The most obvious example is the use of trading subsidiaries but the reliefs apply to all companies. This saves tax being paid by the charity (because income accrues to the trading company) and it saves tax being paid by the subsidiary (because profits are Gift Aided back to the charity). Parliament did not intend, in introducing the charitable expenditure provisions, to counteract this and it is considered that it has not done so. An arrangement which for decades has been carried on with the approval of HMRC can hardly be regarded as avoidance. The purpose of limiting the charity trading exemption (and so requiring charities to trade through trading companies) is not to raise tax.[43]

6.26.2 *"For" avoidance*

Whether an investment is "for" the avoidance of tax depends on the object or purpose of the charity making the investment: the charity's object or purpose (we use the words as synonyms) must not be the avoidance of tax.

It is helpful to contrast the wording of other anti-avoidance tests. The wording of the transfer of assets motive test is whether the purpose of

---

41 *Willoughby v IRC* 70 TC 57. For the meaning of "tax avoidance" see Kessler, *Taxation of Non-Residents and Foreign Domiciliaries* (21st ed., 2022-23), para 52.8 (Meaning of "avoidance") online version *https://www.foreigndomiciliaries.co.uk*

42 See 9.4 (Carry-back relief).

43 See 8.19 (Charity trade exemptions: Critique). Of course, a charity may be able to say that its trading company is needed for commercial purposes other than tax planning, but that is not always the case.

avoiding liability to taxation was the purpose *or one of the purposes* for which the relevant transactions were effected;[44] similarly the transactions in securities motive test is whether enabling tax advantages to be obtained is the main object *or one of the main objects* of the transaction.[45] Here we have only "for" the avoidance of tax. It is considered that one must identify the charity's main or principal purpose and if the main or principal purpose was not tax avoidance then the investment may be an approved charitable investment. It would not matter that tax avoidance was one of a number of purposes if it was not the main or principal purpose. In practice this point is not likely to matter very often.

The wording of other anti-avoidance provisions such as s.137 TCGA 1992 is whether the relevant transaction "forms *part of a scheme or arrangements* of which the main purpose, or one of the main purposes, is avoidance of liability to tax" Here the question is whether the *investment* is for the avoidance of tax. It does not matter if the investment forms part of a scheme or arrangement whose purpose is the avoidance of tax – provided that the investment itself is not for the avoidance of tax. However an investment or loan in isolation would not normally give rise to *any* tax saving. It is considered that the charitable expenditure avoidance condition is satisfied if and only if the investment is an essential step in procuring the tax saving even if the tax saving in fact arises from some other step.

The avoidance condition only applies to investments of Types 11 and 12. In other cases, investments are approved charitable investments even if there is a tax avoidance motive.

6.26.3 *Back-to-back loans*

Loans to banks are approved investments even if they are made with a tax avoidance motive, so long as there is no back-to-back arrangement.

Suppose a deposit with a bank is part of a back-to-back arrangement. This does not fall within Type 9. May the back-to-back loan qualify by virtue of Type 12? The answer is yes. Section 558 ITA/s.511 CTA 2010 state that an investment will constitute an approved charitable investment if it falls within any of the listed "Types".

A charity should not make a back-to-back loan to a bank unless it is satisfied that a claim under Type 12 will succeed. There are various

---

44 Section 737 ITA 2007.

45 Section 734 CTA 2010.

alternative possibilities. The charity may acquire a certificate of deposit in connection with a back-to-back arrangement. The certificate of deposit is an approved charitable investment: see above. It may be possible to make a back-to-back loan through a building society, the charity's loan to the building society being an approved charitable investment. Arrangements may be made where the charity lends money to one bank, and then another company in the same group lends the money to a third party. Lastly, it may be possible to make arrangements which do not involve a "loan".

6.27 "Approved charitable loan"

Section 561 ITA/s.514 CTA 2010 :

s.561 ITA	**s.514 CTA 2010**
(1) A loan is an approved charitable loan for the purposes of s.543 (meaning of "non-charitable expenditure") if it meets conditions A and B.	(1) A loan is an approved charitable loan for the purposes of s.496 (meaning of "non-charitable expenditure") if it meets conditions A and B.
(2) Condition A is that the loan is not made by way of investment.	[identical]
(3) Condition B is that either—	[identical]
(a) the loan is made to another charity for charitable purposes only,	
(b) it is made to a beneficiary of the charitable trust in the course of carrying out the purposes of the charitable trust,	(b) it is made to a beneficiary of the charitable company in the course of carrying out the purposes of the charitable company,
(c) it consists of money placed on current account with a bank[46] otherwise than as part of an arrangement under which a loan is made by a bank to some other	[identical]

46 Defined by reference in s.561(4) ITA/s.514(4) CTA 2010: "In this section 'bank', has the meaning given by s.991/s.1120."

person, or	
(d) an officer of Revenue and Customs is satisfied, on a claim, that the loan is made for the benefit of the charitable trust and not for the avoidance of tax (whether by the charitable trust or by some other person).	(d) an officer of Revenue and Customs is satisfied, on a claim, that the loan is made for the benefit of the charitable company and not for the avoidance of tax (whether by the charitable company or by some other person).

Loans by way of investment have been considered above: we are now concerned with loans which are not "by way of investment", eg an interest-free loan or a loan on uncommercial terms. If a charity makes a non-approved loan then it is treated as incurring non-charitable expenditure.

"Loan" is not defined. Contrast other anti-avoidance provisions such as s.455 CTA 2010 (close companies) or s.173 ITEPA (Employment-related loans). If a charity sells an asset to a person but leaves the purchase price outstanding the debt is not in principle a loan; likewise if a charity allows a donor to delay making payments due under a covenant: see *Ramsden v IRC* 37 TC 619. But if a charity sells to a person and leaves the purchase price outstanding on non-arm's length terms, it may be that the gain on the disposal is not applied for charitable purposes only, and so does not qualify for the charity's CGT exemption.

It is considered that any loan made in good faith to another charity for the purposes of that charity is made for charitable purposes only. It does not matter if the borrower charity intends to incur non-charitable expenditure, or intends to retain and invest the sum loaned, so long as it is not intended to make a breach of trust. Compare the *Helen Slater* case, which held that a bona fide inter-charity payment is a payment for charitable purposes only.

6.28 Record keeping

The Guidance Note provides at Annex iv para 51:

> All investment decisions, including a decision to invest in a subsidiary company, should be properly minuted, including the factors on which the decisions were based. Depending on the size of a proposed investment, the decision may be based on the following:
>
> - business plans
> - cashflow forecasts

- projections of future profits.

A standard HMRC enquiry is to require copies of the relevant correspondence in respect of the loan/investment including minutes of trustees' meetings. Proper records of trustees' meetings and investment decisions will be essential. In particular, where an investment or loan is made to a trading subsidiary, the trustees must be in a position to show that its trading company was reasonably efficiently run and had a reasonable expectation of making a profit: that the trustees took proper care in carrying out their investment duties.

6.29 Type 12: Claims

A claim is in strict law essential.[47] The usual time limit applies.[48] In the absence of a claim an investment is strictly a non-approved investment even though a claim would have been acceptable.

The method of making claims is explained in HMRC Guidance Note Annex III para 10 which provides:

> **Where a charity receives a tax return**
> 10.1 If a charity is satisfied that all of its investments or loans fall within [type] 1-11 and its non-investment loans are charitable loans, it should tick the box on its tax return for a:
> - company return box E26 of the charity supplementary page (CT600E)
> - trust return the question 'were all investments qualifying ('approved charitable') investments, and were loans made qualifying loans, within section 558 and section 561 ITA 2007?'on the charity supplementary page (SA 907)
>
> The charity need do nothing more.

No claim is needed for types 1-11. The guidance then turns to type 12:

> 10.2 If the charity is satisfied that any other investment or loan still qualifies as an approved investment or loan because it's made for the benefit of the charity and not for avoidance of tax, there are 2 options:
> [1] tick the box on the appropriate return page (as indicated above) and be prepared to make a formal claim in respect of the relevant investment if requested by HMRC
> [2] or make a formal claim with the return. Charitable trusts only may make a separate claim

---

47 See 47.7 (Claims).
48 See 47.14 (Time limit for claim).

> **Claims**
> 10.4 Where a charity wants to make a formal claim or if a formal claim's requested by HMRC that claim must be in writing and must specify:
> - the nature of the investment (loan, shares etc)
> - the amount involved
> - the accounting period in which the loan or investment was made
> - whether the claim is made under section 511 CTA 2010 or section 558 ITA 2007 (both type 12 investments) or section 514 (3)(d) CTA 2010 or section 561 (3)(d) ITA 2007 (both charitable loans)
>
> It's also helpful if any other relevant information's supplied at the time of the claim, for example, details of the terms of a loan, copy of any loan agreement or prospectus.
> Where a charity has been required by HMRC to give a company tax return for the accounting period to which the claim relates and the claim can be made by either including it in, or by amending, that return, the claim must be so made.

The HMRC Guidance Note continues:

> **Unapproved investments or loans**
> 10.5 Where a charity has purchased investments or entered into loan arrangements which don't satisfy the requirements to be approved investments or loans the total of such loans or investments must be entered for a:
> - company return, box E27 of the charity supplementary pages CT600E
> - trust return, box 7.38 of the charity supplementary page

This is somewhat theoretical.

6.30 Clearance procedure

There is no formal clearance procedure.

In practice HMRC might give an informal intimation of whether a proposed transaction will be regarded as an approved charitable investment or loan. If the correspondence is suitably worded this would bind HMRC. But HMRC may simply refuse to answer. HMRC Guidance Note Annex III para 10 provides:

> 10.3 A formal claim for determination of whether an investment or loan qualifies as an approved charitable investment or loan can be made at any time after the investment or loan has been entered into. There's no provision in the Taxes Acts for HMRC approval to be given in advance of transactions being carried out.

The Law Commission have recommended a clearance procedure:

> We recommend that HM Treasury introduce a procedure by which charities can obtain prior clearance from HMRC as to the tax treatment of a proposed social investment.[49]

If there was to be a clearance procedure, it should apply generally, not just to social investment. HMRC understandably expressed concern about the resource implications, for if there were a clearance procedure, caution would require it to be used just in case. It is difficult to imagine that is the best use of resources. Whatever the reason, no-one has taken any notice of the Law Commission's recommendation.

6.31 Trading loss: Primary purpose trade

6.31.1 *Loss of primary purpose trade*

HMRC Guidance Note Annex iv para 41 provides:

> Charities can make trading losses. If the trading is within the charitable objects of a charity (charitable trading), losses will be charitable expenditure.

That must in principle be right. For completeness: a primary purpose activity which only makes losses does not actually constitute a trade[50] but it will not usually matter whether it is a trade or not.

"Trading within the charitable objects" will include any primary purpose trade.[51] It is possible that losses may be due to incompetence or some other breach of trust, in which case there would be non-charitable expenditure, but that would not usually be the case.

6.31.2 *Relief for primary purpose trade loss*

In principle a charity could (if necessary) qualify for relief on its primary purpose trading losses. However, s.66 ITA/s.44 CTA 2010 prevents loss relief unless the trade is carried on on a commercial basis and with a view to profit. It is possible for a primary purpose trade to meet this condition: it is a question of fact. But in practice a charity will not normally need to claim loss relief on a primary purpose trade.

---

49 Law Commission, "Social Investment by Charities" The Law Commission's Recommendations

50 See 8.2.3 (Uncommercial activity not trading).

51 The wording will include a trade within the purposes of the charity which is not a *primary* purpose, but in practice that is not likely to arise. However the Guidance Note assumes that any trade not "within the charitable objects" is a "non-primary purpose trade".

6.32 Trading loss: Non-primary purpose trade

6.32.1 *Trading loss*

Section 543(1) ITA/s.496(1) CTA 2010 :

s.543(1) ITA	**s.496(1) CTA 2010**
For the purposes of this Part a charitable trust's non-charitable expenditure for a tax year is—	For the purposes of this Part a charitable company's non-charitable expenditure for an accounting period is—
(a) any loss made in the tax year in a trade carried on by the charitable trust unless—	(a) any loss made in the accounting period in a trade carried on by the charitable company unless—
(i) the trade is a charitable trade in relation to the tax year, or	(i) the trade is a charitable trade, or
(ii) the trade is not a charitable trade[52] in relation to the tax year but profits of the trade arising in the tax year would be exempt from income tax as a result of one of the exemptions in ss.526, 529 or 530 [small-scale trades, fund-raising events and lotteries].	(ii) the trade is not a charitable trade but profits of the trade arising in the period would be exempt from corporation tax as a result of one of the exemptions in section 480, 483 or 484 [small-scale trades, fund-raising events and lotteries].

6.32.2 *Post-cessation loss*

Section 543(1)(b) ITA/s.496(1)(b) CTA 2010 provide the equivalent rule for post-cessation losses:

For the purposes of this Part a charitable trust's non-charitable expenditure for a tax year is...	(1) For the purposes of this Part a charitable company's non-charitable expenditure for an accounting period is—(b) any loss made in the accounting period in a trade, or in a UK property business or an overseas property business, carried on by the charitable company, if—
(b) any payment made in the tax	(b) any loss made in the accounting

52 For this term see 8.7 (Charitable trade).

year by the charitable trust in connection with a trade in circumstances where relief is available under s.96 (post-cessation trade relief) unless—	period in a trade, or in a UK property business or an overseas property business, carried on by the charitable company, if—
(i) the trade was a charitable trade in relation to the tax year in which the cessation occurred, or	(i) the loss relates to land, and
(ii) the trade was not a charitable trade in relation to that tax year but profits of the trade arising immediately before the cessation would have been exempt from income tax as a result of one of the exemptions in ss.526, 529 or 530.	(ii) profits of the trade, or income of the business, generated from the land in the period would not be exempt from corporation tax as a result of the exemptions in section 485,

6.32.3 *Property business loss*

Section 543(1)(c) ITA/s.496(1)(b) CTA 2010 the equivalent rule for property business losses:

s.543(1)(c) ITA	**s.496(1)(b) CTA 2010**
For the purposes of this Part a charitable trust's non-charitable expenditure for a tax year is...	For the purposes of this Part a charitable company's non-charitable expenditure for an accounting period is...
(c) any loss made in the tax year in a trade, or in a UK property business or an overseas property business, carried on by the charitable trust, if—	(b) any loss made in the accounting period in a trade, or in a UK property business or an overseas property business, carried on by the charitable company, if—
(i) the loss relates to land, and	[identical]
(ii) profits of the trade, or income of the business, generated from the land in the tax year would not be exempt from income tax as a result of the exemptions in s.531.	(ii) profits of the trade, or income of the business, generated from the land in the period would not be exempt from corporation tax as a result of the exemptions in s.485.

Loss relief will not be available as the relief applies only to trading losses.

Section 543(1)(d) ITA provides the equivalent rule for post-cessation losses of a property business:

> For the purposes of this Part a charitable trust's non-charitable expenditure for a tax year is...
> (d) any payment made in the tax year by the charitable trust in connection with a trade or UK property business in circumstances where relief is available under s.96 or 125 (post-cessation trade or property relief), if—
> (i) the payment relates to land, and
> (ii) profits of the trade, or income of the business, generated from the land immediately before the cessation would not have been exempt from income tax as a result of the exemptions in s.531.

6.32.4 *Miscellaneous transaction loss*

Section 543(1)(e) ITA/s.496(1)(c) CTA 2010 the equivalent rule for miscellaneous transaction losses:

s.543(1)(e) ITA	**s.496(1)(c) CTA 2010**
For the purposes of this Part a charitable trust's non-charitable expenditure for a tax year is...	For the purposes of this Part a charitable company's non-charitable expenditure for an accounting period is ...
(e) any loss made in the tax year in a miscellaneous transaction entered into by the charitable trust otherwise than in the course of carrying out a charitable purpose.	(c) any loss made in the accounting period in a miscellaneous transaction entered into by the charitable company otherwise than in the course of carrying out a charitable purpose.

Section 544(3) ITA/497(2) CTA provide:

A transaction is a miscellaneous transaction if it is of such a nature that, if income or gains had arisen from it— (a) ignoring section 527 (exemption from charges under provisions to which section 1016 applies), it would have been charged to income tax under or by virtue of any provision to which	A transaction is a miscellaneous transaction if it is of such a nature that, if income or gains had arisen from it (ignoring section 481 (exemption from charges under provisions to which section 1173 applies)), it would have been charged to corporation tax under or by virtue of any provision to which section 1173 applies.

section 1016 applies,[53] and
(b) the trustees of the charitable trust would have been liable for any tax so chargeable.

6.32.5 *Loss relief*

The HMRC Guidance Note provides at Annex iv para 41:

> However, the fact that a loss arising from non-charitable trading is treated as non-charitable expenditure may not result in a net tax liability. The trading loss itself may be available for set-off against the amount that would otherwise be chargeable to tax resulting from the restriction on exemptions by section 492 CTA 2010 or section 539 ITA 2007. The effect can, therefore, be self-cancelling, as shown at B in the table below. The trading loss will only be unavailable for set off against the amount chargeable if the trading isn't on a commercial basis and either there is no reasonable expectation of gain (Corporation Tax) or the trading is not carried out with a view to the realisation of profit (IT).

Where loss relief is available, it will not usually matter whether the loss is non-charitable expenditure, because no tax charge will arise. Where loss relief is not available (eg no reasonable expectation of profit) then the loss is probably not charitable expenditure. So the correctness of the HMRC view would only arise in a very unusual case where the loss relief is needed for some other form of chargeable income.

The Guidance Note continues with some comments on loss relief:

> The table below gives an overview of the main possibilities, though each case depends on its own facts:
> Quick guide to the Treatment of taxable non-primary purpose trading by charities

Table A

Tax profit/ loss	**Basis of Trading**	Is it charitable expenditure?	Tax position
Loss	**Not on a commercial basis:** No reasonable expectation of gain (CT). Not with a view to the realisation of profit (IT)	No. Loss is Non Charitable Expenditure charge (NCE)	NCE results in a loss of tax exemption by reason of s492 CTA 2010/s539 ITA 2007. The resulting tax charge is not cancelled by loss relief*

53 See 8.15.2 (Small misc income exemption),

Table B

Tax profit/ loss	Basis of Trading	Is it charitable expenditure?	Tax position
Loss	Reasonable expectation of tax exemption by gains (CT) With a view to the realisation of profit (IT)	No. NCE.	NCE results in loss of reason of s492 CTA 2010/s539 ITA 2007. The resulting tax charge is typically cancelled by loss relief*

Table C

Tax profit/ loss	Basis of Trading	Is it charitable expenditure?	Tax position	
Profit	Reasonable expectation of gain (Corporation Tax). With a view to the realisation of profit (IT)	NCE results in loss of tax exemption by reason of section 492 CTA 2010/ section 539 ITA 2007. |The resulting tax charge is typically cancelled by loss relief *.	NA	Profits are taxable

*** Restrictions on the use of losses that apply to other taxpayers also apply to charities.**

42. Direct Tax: The commerciality test

Paragraph 41 above covers the need to ascertain whether trading is on a commercial basis, with a reasonable expectation of gain (Corporation Tax) or with a view to the realisation of profit (for charitable trusts liable to Income Tax). This 'commerciality test' should initially be applied to the taxable deemed trade (non-charitable trade), after the split created by s.479(2) and (3) CTA 2010 or s.525(2) and (3) ITA 2007.

If the taxable trade is, on the facts of the case, not commercial, it is then necessary to consider whether the 'larger undertaking' of which it is a part is both commercial and 'with the intention of making a profit.

Guidance on the meaning of 'larger undertaking' can be found in the Company Taxation Manual for Corporation Tax and BIM 75720 for Income Tax.

If the taxable trading source is part of a 'larger undertaking', then it may be that the commerciality test is applied before the split created by section 479(2) and (3) CTA 2010 or section 525(2) and (3) ITA 2007 so that the loss is allowable. Each case must, however, be decided on its own merits

43. Direct Tax: What should a charity with trading losses show in its tax return?

In paragraph 41 Table C scenarios, the charity is being taxed just like any other person or business which carried on the same trade and should fill in its tax return accordingly.

For Table B, assuming that an equivalent amount of tax-exempted income has been received, charities might show in their computations

Income liable to assessment by virtue of s.505(4) ICTA 88	X
Relief for trading losses*	-X
Profit	Nil

*** Restrictions on the use of losses that apply to other taxpayers also apply to charities.**

This would be reflected in a charity's tax return. The loss has been used and should therefore not be shown on the return as available to carry forward. This may cause difficulties if a charity's loss making non-charitable trade later moves into profit. However, if a charity wishes to pursue such trading, this can be done using a subsidiary company, which can mitigate its tax liability by Gift Aiding its profits to its parent charity.

44. Direct Tax: trading losses - further considerations

The paragraph 41 Table A scenario may present the most difficulty. The charity may find that its non-charitable trading creates a cash surplus over direct costs but there is no realistic expectation of tax profit or gain. The loss cannot be set off against the section 492 CTA 2010 or section 539 ITA 2007 charge, because the trading is not carried on on a commercial basis and with a reasonable expectation of gain/a view to the realisation of profits.

What constitutes non-charitable expenditure is, however, as much a matter of charity law as of tax law, and charities may wish to obtain professional advice if they find themselves in this situation. In general, non-charitable trading is better situated in a trading subsidiary.

In all cases, it should be noted that it is up to the charity whether to claim capital allowances in relation to its non-charitable trade. In reviewing whether a commercial basis and a 'view to the realisation of profits'/'reasonable expectation of gain' exists, HM Revenue & Customs will take into account depreciation (apportioned on reasonable grounds) on assets purchased wholly or partly for the non-charitable trade. If an asset was originally bought wholly for use for a primary purpose, then it is not taken into account.

For any given charity, the facts can change and as a result the tax treatment of the losses may also change. For example, scenario A in paragraph 41 table A may apply - a charity may have a non-charitable activity which yields a cash surplus over direct costs, but which, year after year, shows losses for tax purposes once overheads are allocated. In these circumstances, the loss could not be set off against the tax charge resulting from loss of exemption by reason of sections 492/539 but it could be carried forward and set off against later year profits of the deemed trade. However, from the date that a realistic approach to putting the activity on both a commercial and profitable basis is adopted, scenario B in paragraph 41 Table B would then apply and the loss could be set off against the section 492 or section 539 charge. It is recommended that in such a case an explanation is provided with the return. Charities can pool unused non-charitable trading losses brought forward. These losses will be available to carry forward against profits from non-charitable trading. Computations and returns can be completed on this basis.

HMRC say:

> **2.11 Potential restriction on availability of trading losses**
> 2.11.1 Tax legislation gives relief for losses arising on trading activities under the provisions of part 4 of CTA2010. Under s37 the university can deduct trading losses from total profits (including the taxable profit arising from the NCE) arising in the same accounting period. However s44 requires that in order for a loss to be available, the trade which gives rise to the loss must be carried-on on a commercial basis, and with a view to the making of a profit in the trade or so as to afford a reasonable expectation of making such a profit. This can be either as a standalone activity or as part of a larger-undertaking of which the trade forms part.
> 2.11.2 HMRC's manuals explain that taxpayers must apply this two part test to evaluate whether a loss is restricted under s44 – and guidance can be found on how to do this at CTM 0460016 and CTM04620. It is expected that most universities should be able to satisfy the requirements, and there should be no restriction under s44.
> 2.11.3 s37 CTA2010 requires the taxpayer to make a claim to offset trading losses against other profits arising (NCE in this case). The claim would normally (but not necessarily) be made in the corporation tax return, and the time limit for making the claim is within the period of two years after the end of the loss-making period, or within such further period as an officer of Revenue and Customs may allow.[54]

Although this statement was made to universities, the approach ought to be applied to charities generally.

6.33 Timing of expenditure

Section 546 ITA/s.499 CTA 2010 :

s.546 ITA	**s.499 CTA 2010**
(1) This section applies for the purposes of s.543(1)(f).	(1) This section applies for the purposes of s.496(1)(d).

54 The Corporation Tax Treatment of UK Universities Guidance Note Revised and agreed June 2014 *https://www.bufdg.ac.uk/ViewDocument.aspx?t=1&ID=2362&GUID=5411732f-0599-45f6-8390-9c4c17ae92bd&dl=*1

(2) Subsection (3) applies to expenditure which is referable to commitments (whether or not of a contractual nature) that the charitable trust has entered into before or during a tax year.	(2) Subsection (3) applies to expenditure which is referable to commitments (whether or not of a contractual nature) that the charitable company has entered into before or during an accounting period.
(3) The expenditure is treated as incurred in the tax year if, had the charitable trust been required to draw up accounts that met the requirements mentioned in subsection (4), the expenditure would have been required to be taken into account in preparing those accounts.	(3) The expenditure is treated as incurred in the accounting period if, had the charitable company been required to draw up accounts that met the requirements mentioned in subsection (4), the expenditure would have been required to be taken into account in preparing those accounts.
(4) The requirements referred to in subsection (3) are—	(4) The requirements referred to in subsection (3) are—
(a) that the accounts are drawn up for the tax year, and	(a) that the accounts are drawn up for the accounting period, and
(b) that UK generally accepted accounting practice applies with respect to them.	[identical]

ITA EN Change 99 provides:

> **Change 99: Charitable trusts: tax year in which certain expenditure treated as incurred: s.546**
> This change makes it explicit that the time when expenditure is treated as incurred depends on UK generally accepted accounting practice (UK GAAP)….
> Section 506(2) [ICTA] was first enacted in FA 1986 and advanced the time that certain expenditure is recognised, on the basis that charitable trusts may have some flexibility in this regard. As a result of subsequent developments in accounting practice, the legislation now implicitly mirrors UK GAAP.
> Section 546 is based on s.506(2) of ICTA, and makes the reference to UK GAAP explicit. Section 997(2) [ITA] defines UK GAAP for the Income Tax Acts.
> Section 546 is drafted in terms of the position if UK GAAP had applied

> because there is no legal or other obligation requiring all charitable trusts to prepare their accounts in accordance with UK GAAP. In particular "Accounting and Reporting for Charities: Statement of Recommended Practice (revised 2005)", which imposes a requirement to account in accordance with UK GAAP on charitable trusts (with certain exceptions), is not mandatory in Scotland and Northern Ireland. Neither does it apply to charitable trusts which are able to prepare accounts on a "receipts and payments" basis rather than an "accruals" basis.
>
> This approach ensures parity of treatment as between charitable trusts operating in different parts of the UK or adopting different bases of accounting.

The charity's accounts would no doubt record its commitments in the year in question in accordance with the charities SORP.

The timing of charitable expenditure does not matter but the timing of non-charitable expenditure would affect the question of which year the charity tax relief is disallowed. In practice, we doubt if this provision will ever make any difference.

6.34 Attribution to non-exempt amount

Once one has ascertained the non-exempt amount, one needs to attribute it to a charity's income or gains.[55] Section 541 ITA/s.494 CTA 2010 provide:

s.541 ITA	**s.494 CTA 2010**
(1) This section applies if a charitable trust has a non-exempt amount for a tax year.	(1) This section applies if a charitable company has a non-exempt amount for an accounting period.
(2) Attributable income of the charitable trust for the tax year may be attributed to the non-exempt amount but only so far as the non-exempt amount has not been used up.	(2) Attributable income of the charitable company for the accounting period may be attributed to the non-exempt amount but only so far as the non-exempt amount has not been used up.
(3) The non-exempt amount can be used up (in whole or in part) by—	[identical]
(a) attributable income being	

55 See 6.1 (Charitable expenditure rules).

attributed to it under this section, or	
(b) attributable gains being attributed to it under s.256A of TCGA 1992.	(b) attributable gains being attributed to it under s.256C of TCGA 1992.
(4) The whole of the non-exempt amount must be used up by—	[identical]
(a) attributable income being attributed to the whole of it under this section,	
(b) attributable gains being attributed to the whole of under s.256A of TCGA 1992, or	(b) attributable gains being attributed to the whole of it under s.256C of TCGA 1992, or
(c) a combination of attributable income being attributed to some of it under this section and attributable gains being attributed to the rest of it under s.256A of TCGA 1992.	(c) a combination of attributable income being attributed to some of it under this section and attributable gains being attributed to the rest of it under s.256C of TCGA 1992.
(5) See s.542 for the way in which income is to be attributed to the non-exempt amount under this section.	[no equivalent provision]

The CGT equivalent is s.256A TCGA.

6.34.1 *Power of selection*

The amount of the charity's income and gains may exceed the non-exempt amount. The charity then has power to select which items of its income or gains should be attributed to its non-exempt amount (and so lose the benefit of charity tax relief).

Section 542 ITA/s.495CTA 2010/s.256B TCGA provide:

s.542 ITA	**s.495 CTA 2010**	**.s.256B TCGA**
(1) This section is about the ways in which attributable income can be attributed to a non-exempt amount under s.541.	(1) This section is about the ways in which attributable income can be attributed to a non-exempt amount under s.494.	(1) This section is about the ways in which attributable gains can be attributed to a non-exempt amount under s.256A.

(2) The trustees of the charitable trust may specify the attributable income that is to be attributed to the non-exempt amount.	(2) The charitable company may specify the attributable income that is to be attributed to the non-exempt amount.	(2) The trustees of the charitable trust may specify the attributable gains that are to be attributed to the non-exempt amount.

If the charity does not make the choice then HMRC will do so. Section 542 ITA/s 495 CTA 2010/s.256B TCGA set out the procedure:

s.542 ITA	**s.495 CTA 2010**	**s.256B TCGA**
(3) A specification under subsection (2) is made by notice to an officer of Revenue and Customs.	[identical]	(3) A specification under subsection (2) is made by notice to an officer of Revenue and Customs.
(4) Subsection (6) applies if—	(4) Subsection (6) applies if—	(4) Subsection (6) applies if—
(a) an officer of Revenue and Customs requires the trustees of a charitable trust to make a specification under this section, and	(a) an officer of Revenue and Customs requires a charitable company to make a specification under this section, and	(a) an officer of Revenue and Customs requires the trustees of a charitable trust to make a specification under this section, and
(b) the trustees have not given notice under subsection (3) of the specification before the end of the required period.	(b) the charitable company has not given notice under subsection (3) of the specification before the end of the required period.	(b) the trustees have not given notice under subsection (3) of the specification before the end of the required period.
(5) The required period is 30 days beginning with the day on which the officer made the requirement.	[identical]	[identical]
(6) An officer of Revenue and Customs may determine the attributable income that is to be attributed to the non-exempt amount.	[identical to ITA]	(6) An officer of Revenue and Customs may determine the attributable gains that are to be attributed to the non-exempt amount.

There are many situations where it is material which items of income or gains lose tax relief. A charity may have losses to set against its chargeable gains and so wish to select that its gains should be disallowed charity relief. A charitable trust would prefer to pay tax on its income and not its gains as the rate of tax is much lower.
A charitable company cannot select its dividend income, because its dividend or distribution income is not normally attributable income.[56] A charitable trust could do this so the income is taxable at a slightly lower rate.

6.35 Non-charitable expenditure: Carry-back

Sections 562 and 563 ITA provide a carry-back rule for the case where non-charitable expenditure exceeds attributable income and gains. The provisions use a number of elaborately defined terms.
The CT equivalents are s.515 - 517 CTA 2010.

6.35.1 *"Non-taxable sums"*

Section 562(5) ITA/s.515(5) CTA 2010 provide:

s.562(5) ITA	**s.515(5) CTA 2010**
In subsection (4) "non-taxable sums" means donations, legacies and other sums of a similar nature which, ignoring exemptions from income tax under this Part and from capital gains tax under s.256 of TCGA 1992, are not liable to income tax or capital gains tax.	In subsection (4) "non-taxable sums" means donations, legacies and other sums of a similar nature which, ignoring exemptions from corporation tax under this Part and under s.256 of TCGA 1992, are not liable to corporation tax.

Donations under the payroll giving scheme were non-taxable sums until 24 March 2010. Money borrowed is not within the charge to tax, and not "of a similar nature" to donations and legacies. So it is not a non-taxable sum. Non-taxable sums matter because non-charitable expenditure is not carried back to the extent of any non-taxable sums.

6.35.2 *"Available income and gains"*

Section 562(4) ITA/s.515(4) CTA 2010 provide:

56 See 6.3.1 (Dividend income of charitable company).

s.562(4) ITA

For the purposes of this Part a charitable trust's "available income and gains" for a tax year is the sum of—

(a) the charitable trust's total income for the tax year (ignoring any restrictions on the exemptions under this Part which result from ss.539(2) and 541),

(b) any chargeable gains accruing to the charitable trust in the tax year (ignoring any restriction on the exemption under s.256(1) of TCGA 1992 which results from s.256(4) of that Act),

(c) the charitable trust's attributable income and gains for the tax year (see s.540), and

(d) any non-taxable sums received by the charitable trust in the tax year.

s.515(4) CTA 2010

For the purposes of this Part a charitable company's "available income and gains" for an accounting period is the sum of—

(a) the amount in respect of which the charitable company is chargeable for the period under the charge to corporation tax on income after giving effect to any exemption under this Part,

(b) any chargeable gains accruing to the charitable company in the period,

(c) the charitable company's attributable income and gains for the period (see s.493), and

(d) any non-taxable sums received by the charitable company in the period.

6.35.3 *"Excess expenditure"*

Section 562 ITA/s.515 CTA 2010 :

s.562 ITA

(1) This section applies if a charitable trust's non-charitable expenditure for a tax year exceeds its available income and gains for the tax year.

(2) The excess is the charitable trust's "excess expenditure" for the tax year.

s.515 CTA 2010

(1) This section applies if a charitable company's non-charitable expenditure for an accounting period exceeds its available income and gains for the period.

(2) The excess is the charitable company's "excess expenditure" for the accounting period.

Armed with these definitions, we can now turn to the carry-back rule. Section 562(3) ITA/s.515(3) CTA 2010 provide:

s.562(3) ITA	**s.515(3) CTA 2010**
The charitable trust's excess expenditure for the tax year is treated for the purposes of this Part as non-charitable expenditure for earlier tax years so far as it can be attributed to earlier tax years under s.563.	The charitable company's excess expenditure for the accounting period is treated for the purposes of this Part as non-charitable expenditure for earlier accounting periods so far as it can be attributed to earlier accounting periods under s.516.

So we turn to s.563 ITA/s.516 CTA 2010:

s.563 ITA	**s.516 CTA 2010**
(1) The rules in this section apply for attributing a charitable trust's excess expenditure for a tax year to earlier tax years under s.562.	(1) The rules in this section apply for attributing a charitable company's excess expenditure for an accounting period to earlier accounting periods under s.515.
(2) The excess expenditure for a tax year may be attributed to an earlier tax year if—	(2) The excess expenditure for an accounting period may be attributed to an earlier accounting period if—
(a) the earlier tax year ends not more than 6 years before the end of the tax year in question, and	(a) the earlier period ends not more than 6 years before the end of the period in question, and
(b) the charitable trust's available income and gains for the earlier tax year exceed its non-charitable expenditure for the earlier tax year.	(b) the charitable company's available income and gains for the earlier period exceed its non-charitable expenditure for the earlier period.
(3) If the conditions in subsection (2) are met in the case of more than one earlier tax year, the excess expenditure is to be attributed to a later tax year in priority to an earlier tax year.	(3) If the conditions in subsection (2) are met in the case of more than one earlier accounting period, the excess expenditure is to be attributed to a later accounting period in priority to an earlier accounting period.

(4) The amount of excess expenditure that is to be attributed to an earlier tax year must not be greater than the amount by which the charitable trust's available income and gains for the earlier tax year exceed its non-charitable expenditure for the earlier tax year.

(4) The amount of excess expenditure that is to be attributed to an earlier accounting period must not be greater than the amount by which the charitable company's available income and gains for the earlier period exceed its non-charitable expenditure for the earlier period.

(5) For the purposes of subsections (2)(b) and (4) the charitable trust's non-charitable expenditure for the earlier tax year includes any excess expenditure attributed to the earlier tax year as a result of a previous operation of this section, but ignores the attribution in question.

(5) For the purposes of subsections (2)(b) and (4) the charitable company's non-charitable expenditure for the earlier accounting period includes any excess expenditure attributed to the earlier period as a result of a previous operation of this section, but ignores the attribution in question.

CHAPTER SEVEN

TAINTED DONATION RULES

7.1 Tainted donation rules

In accordance with the drafting style of the tax law rewrite, the tainted donation rules are set out twice:

IT: Chapter 8 Part13 ITA (s.809ZH to s.809ZR)[1]
CT: Part 21C CTA 2010 (s.939A to s.939I)

HMRC guidance is in HMRC Guidance Note Annex viii.[2]
The layout of this chapter is as follows:

(1) Definitions
(2) Tainted donation conditions A and B (which are the main conditions)
(3) Examples
(4) Reliefs and tainted donation condition C
(5) Consequences of tainted donations rules, if they ever do apply

7.2 "Tainted donation"

This central term is elaborately defined. Section 809ZJ(1) ITA/ s.939C(1) CTA 2010 provide:

> For the purposes of this Chapter/Part[3] a relievable charity donation is a tainted donation if (and only if) Conditions A, B and C are met.

We refer to **"TD conditions A, B and C"**.
This definition applies for Chapter 8 Part 13 ITA/Part 21C CTA 2010, so it has to be incorporated by reference elsewhere.[4]

7.3 "Relievable charity donation"

This expression is used in the definition of "tainted donation".
Section 809ZI(1) ITA/s.939B(1) CTA 2010 provide a commonsense definition:

> In this Chapter/Part[5] "relievable charity donation" means a gift or other disposal which—
> (a) is made by a person to a charity, and
> (b) is eligible for tax relief.

In the following discussion:

---

1 The idiosyncratic numbering is because the sections are slotted in after s.809ZG and before s.809A. See Kessler, *Taxation of Nonresidents & Foreign Domiciliaries* (21st ed., 2022-23) App.14.3 (Section numbering system).
2 The development of the guidance can be traced through EN FB 2011 and draft guidance (2013), but that is now of historical interest only.
3 That is, Chapter 8 Part 13 ITA/Part 21C CTA 2010.
4 See s.257A(2)(a) TCGA.
5 That is, Chapter 8 Part 13 ITA/Part 21C CTA 2010.

The "**donation**" means the gift or other disposal.
The "**donor**" is the person who makes the donation.
The "**donee-charity**" is the charity which receives the donation.

7.4 "Eligible for tax relief"

This expression is used in the definition of relievable charity donation. Unless a donation is "eligible for tax relief", it is not a relievable charity donation and so not a tainted donation.

Section 809ZI(2) ITA/s.939B(2) CTA 2010 provide:

> A gift or other disposal is eligible for tax relief if one or both of the following apply—
> (a) (ignoring the tainted donation provisions) tax relief would be available in respect of it under a relevant relieving provision[6];
> (b) the charity is entitled to claim a repayment of tax in respect of it.

Para (a) is relatively straightforward.

Para (b) envisages a disposal under which tax relief is not available under a relevant relieving provision, but the charity is entitled to claim repayment of tax. Examples are:

(1) A Gift Aid donation. A gift aid donation is taxable income of a charity which qualifies for relief,[7] but this particular relief is not included in the list of relevant relieving provisions, so the gift does not fall within para (a).
(2) A payment of income from a discretionary trust to a charity.

The definition of "eligible for tax relief" requires that tax relief under a relevant relieving provision would be "available". What is the meaning of this?

If an individual gives an asset on which no chargeable gain arises, because the base cost equals or exceeds market value, it is suggested CGT relief is not "available" (though it could have been, if a gain had arisen).

Suppose Charity A transfers a chargeable asset[8] to Charity B. Section 257 TCGA prevents a gain from accruing to Charity A. That appears strictly to be a relievable charity donation. But assuming that relief did not apply, the gain on the disposal would in principle qualify for charity's

---

6 See 7.4.2 ("Relevant relieving provisions").
7 See 15.49.2 (Gift Aid charge & relief).
8 That is, an asset on which a chargeable gain may accrue, not cash.

CGT relief under s.256 TCGA.

A charity will know whether a Gift Aid gift made by an individual is eligible for tax relief (since it reclaims basic rate tax). It will not always know if other gifts are eligible for tax relief. It may need to enquire.

7.4.1 *"Tainted donation provisions"*

This expression is used in the definition of "eligible for tax relief". Section 809ZI(3) ITA/s.939B(3) CTA 2010 provide a commonsense definition:

s. 809ZI(3) ITA	**s.939B(3) CTA 2010**
"The tainted donation provisions" are—	[identical]
(a) this Chapter [Chapter 8 Part 13],	(a) this Part [Part 21C],
(b) section 257A of TCGA 1992 (tainted charity donations: disapplication of section 257), and	[identical]
(c) Part 21C of CTA 2010 (tainted charity donations: removal of corporation tax reliefs).	(c) Chapter 8 of Part 13 of ITA 2007 (tainted charity donations: removal of income tax relief etc).

7.4.2 *"Relevant relieving provisions"*

This expression is used in the definition of "eligible for tax relief".

There are seven sets of relevant relieving provisions. Section 809ZI(4) ITA\s.939B(4) CTA 2010 provide:

The following are "relevant relieving provisions"—[9]

Section	**Topic**
s.257 TCGA	Donor CGT relief
s.63(2)(a)(aa)(ab) CAA	Gift of plant and machinery
Part 12 ITEPA	Payroll giving
s.108 ITTOIA	Gift of trading stock
Chapters 2 & 3 Part 8 ITA	Gift Aid and gift of shares/land
s.105 CTA 2009	Gift of trading stock
Part 6 CTA 2010	Corporate Gift Aid and gift of shares/land

9 For clarity, I set this out in a table format, and abbreviate the section descriptions. The drafting is based on the definition of "relievable gifts" in s.550 ITA (with stylistic improvement in the drafting).

An interest-free loan is not a relievable charity donation. A gift for which a trader obtains a trading deduction[10] is not a relievable charity donation.

7.5 "Linked person"

The expression "linked person" is used in:

(1) TD condition A (donor/linked person enters into arrangements)
(2) TD condition B (purpose of donor/linked person to obtain financial advantage for donor/linked persons)

Section 809ZJ(3) ITA/s.939C CTA 2010 provide an ultra-wide definition, as one might expect:

> "Linked person" means—
> (a) the person who made the donation ("the donor"), or
> (b) a person connected with the donor at a relevant time.[11]

"Linked" means linked (as defined) to the charity donation. For clarity, we use the expression "**donor/linked person**".

Strictly speaking, one should not use the term "linked person" in the abstract. A linked person exists in relation to a specific donation, (or as far as para (b) is concerned, in relation to a specific donor). Just as a person may be a donor in relation to one donation but not another, a person may be linked person in relation to one donation but not to another donation. But where the context is clear it is permissible to refer to a donor/linked person in isolation (leaving the words "in relation to a donor and a donation" and the identity of that donor and donation to be inferred).

"Relevant time" is widely defined. Section 809ZJ(4) ITA/s.939C(4) CTA 2010 provide:

> In subsection (3) "relevant time" means a time during the period which begins with the earliest, and ends with the latest, of the following times—
> (a) the time when the arrangements are entered into as mentioned in subsection (2);
> (b) the time when the relievable charity donation is made;
> (c) the time when the arrangements are first materially implemented.

---

10 See 18.2 (Charity gift: Deductible expense) .

11 This definition only applies for the purposes of s.809ZJ so it has to be incorporated by reference in s.809ZK(5) ITA.

7.5.1 *"Connected person"*

The expression "connected person" is used in:
(1) The definition of "linked person"
(2) The (less important) definition of "qualifying charity-owned company"

The standard definition of the term is in s.993 ITA/1122 CTA 2010. That is an ultra-wide definition.[12] Section 809ZQ(1) ITA/s.939H(1) CTA 2010 incorporate that definition with amendments which give it an even wider meaning:

s. 809ZQ(1) ITA	**s.939H(1) CTA 2010**
Section 993 (meaning of "connected" persons) applies for the purposes of this Chapter [Chapter 8 Part 13]—	Section 1122 (meaning of "connected" persons) applies for the purposes of this Part [Part 21C]
(a) subject to section 809ZP,[13] and	(except section 939G),
(b) as if, after subsection (7) there were inserted the provision in subsection (2).	but subject to the following modification.

Section 809ZQ(2) inserts s.993(8)-(9) ITA and s.939H(2) inserts s. 1122(9)-(10) CTA 2010.
The inserted s.993(8) ITA/s.1122(9) CTA 2010 provide:

> A person who is a beneficiary of a settlement is connected with—
> (a) a person in the capacity as trustee of the settlement, and
> (b) the settlor in relation to the settlement.

"Beneficiary" is not defined.

s.993(9) ITA	**s. 1122(10) CTA 2010**
For the purposes of this section—	For the purposes of this section—

---

12 See Kessler, *Taxation of Non-Residents and Foreign Domiciliaries* (21st ed., 2022-23), para 101.12 (Connected person)
online version *https://www.foreigndomiciliaries.co.uk*

13 The point of para (a) is that the standard (s.993) definition does not apply to the term "connected charity" which has a different definition in s.809ZP: see 7.6 (Connected charity).

(a) a man and woman living together as husband and wife are treated as if they were husband and wife, (b) two people of the same sex living together as if they were civil partners of each other are treated as if they were civil partners of each other	(a) two people living together as if they were a married couple or civil partners are treated as if they were spouses or civil partners of each other...

To treat cohabitees as spouses is standard in anti-avoidance legislation since at least 2008.[14]

Lastly, the inserted s.993(9) ITA/s.1122(10) CTA 2010 provide:

> (c) "close company" includes a company that would be a close company if it were resident in the United Kingdom.

This is otiose: non-resident close companies are already covered by s.993(3)(d) ITA/s. 1122(6)(d) CTA 2010.

7.6 "Connected charity"

The expression "connected charity" is used:

(1) In TD condition B (financial advantage from the donee-charity or a connected charity)

(2) In two less important contexts:

   (a) The definition of "qualifying charity-owned company"

   (b) The Gift Aid rules and trust donation rules (both referring to the charity to which the ... donation is made, or any connected charity)

Section 809ZP ITA/s.939G CTA 2010 provide:

> For the purposes of this Chapter/Part[15] a "connected charity" in relation to another charity means a charity which is connected with that other charity in a matter relating to the structure, administration or control of either charity.

---

14 See Kessler, *Taxation of Non-Residents and Foreign Domiciliaries* (21st ed., 2022-23), App 3.4.1 (Cohabitee treated as spouse) online version *www.foreigndomiciliaries.co.uk*

15 That is, Chapter 8 Part 13 ITA/Part 21C CTA 2010.

The definition derives from the former substantial donor rules.[16]

It is poor drafting to use the expression "connected" with a non-standard meaning, especially as the standard meaning is also used in the same code,[17] but it does not greatly matter.

The definition of "connected" in this context is almost hopelessly vague. Two charities are connected if they have identical trustees because there is a link of administration/control. Are they connected if they have just one trustee in common? Presumably not. Where does the dividing line come? Presumably if they have a majority of trustees in common.

We do not know what is meant by the "structure" of a charity. It is probably meaningless or otiose.[18]

The CTA 2010 (Factors Determining Substantial Commercial Interdependence) Order 2011 represents a more thoughtful way of dealing with this type of issue, in the context of the former small profits relief.

7.7 "Potentially advantaged person"

This term is used in:

(1) TD condition C (charity-owned company)[19]

(2) Liability to the tainted donation charge[20]

Section 809ZJ(5) ITA/s.939C CTA 2010 provide the definition:

> Condition B is that the main purpose, or one of the main purposes, of the [donor/] linked person[21] in entering into the arrangements is to obtain a financial advantage—
>
> (a) directly or indirectly from the charity to which the donation is made
>
> (b) for one or more [donor/]linked persons who are not charities (each of whom is referred to in this Chapter/Part[22] as "a potentially advantaged person").

7.8 Donation-dependent arrangement

Armed with these definitions, we proceed to consider TD conditions A

---

16 Section 556(2) ITA (now repealed).

17 See 7.5.1 ("Connected person").

18 The only reference to "structure" in charity legislation is in the phrase "organisational structure".

19 See 7.19 (Charity-owned company).

20 See 7.21.3 (Recovery of Gift Aid tax reclaim); 7.23 (Payment from trust).

21 See 7.5 ("Linked person").

22 That is, Chapter 8 Part 13 ITA/Part 21C CTA 2010.

and B.

7.8.1 *"Arrangement"*

Section 809ZJ(2) ITA/s.939C(2) CTA 2010 sets out two requirements for condition A. First:

> Condition A is that—
> (a) a [donor/] linked person enters into arrangements (whether before or after the donation is made)

The statute uses the plural but there is no difference between arrangement (singular) and arrangements (plural) so we refer to the word in the singular.

"Arrangement" is a word of wide meaning.[23]

The donor/linked person must enter into the arrangement: it is not sufficient that the charity does so.

Annex viii HMRC Guidance Note provides:

> **6 What is an arrangement?**
> 6.1 The action of a donor making a simple donation to charity isn't in itself entering into an arrangement.

More analytically, a donation is an arrangement, even though it is a single transaction; but we need to identify (1) a donation and (2) an arrangement, in order to decide whether the donation and the arrangement are mutually dependent. The arrangement will usually consist of a number of steps, and may include the donation itself, but the arrangement cannot be the donation alone, or the question of mutual dependency cannot be asked.

7.8.2 *Mutual dependency*

Section 809ZJ(2) ITA/s.939C(2) CTA 2010 provide:

> Condition A is that ...
> (b) it is reasonable to assume from either or both of—
> (i) the likely effects of the donation and the arrangements, and

---

23 Section 809ZR(1) ITA provides the standard (though unnecessary) commonsense definition: "In this Chapter "arrangements" includes any scheme, arrangement or understanding of any kind, whether or not legally enforceable, involving a single transaction or two or more transactions".
See Kessler, *Taxation of Non-Residents and Foreign Domiciliaries* (21st ed., 2022-23), App 2.2 (Arrangement)
online version *https://www.foreigndomiciliaries.co.uk*

> (ii) the circumstances in which the donation is made and the circumstances in which the arrangements are entered into,
>
> that the donation would not have been made and the arrangements would not have been entered into independently of one another.

We need terminology to describe the cases where a donation and an arrangement would (or would not) have been "entered into independently of one another". We refer to them as **"mutually dependent"** (or not) and the test is one of **"mutual dependency"**.

We refer to an arrangement within condition A as **"a donation-dependent arrangement"**.

7.8.3 *Reasonable to assume*

Is there any difference between the convoluted wording of s.809ZJ(2)(b) ITA/s.939C(2)(b) CTA 2010 and the simple requirement that:

> the donation would not have been made and the arrangements would not have been entered into independently of one another.

That is, could there be a case where (1) the donation would *not* in fact have been made independently of the arrangements, but (2) it *is* reasonable to assume from:

(i) the likely effects of the donation and the arrangements, and
(ii) the circumstances in which the donation is made and the circumstances in which the arrangements are entered into,

that it would?

Or vice versa: could there be a case where (1) the donation *would* have been made independently of the arrangements, but (2) it is *not* reasonable to assume from:

(i) the likely effects of the donation and the arrangements, and
(ii) the circumstances in which the donation is made and the circumstances in which the arrangements are entered into,

that it would?

It is considered that such cases are not possible. The extra words are just verbiage.[24] They are however common form in modern anti-avoidance provisions.

---

24 See Kessler, *Taxation of Non-Residents and Foreign Domiciliaries* (21st ed., 2022-23), App 2.20 (Reasonable-to-assume)
online version *https://www.foreigndomiciliaries.co.uk*

7.8.4 *Mutual dependency*

Section 809ZJ(2) ITA/s.939C(2) CTA 2010 provide:

> Condition A is that ...
> (b) ... the donation would not have been made and the arrangements would not have been entered into independently of one another.

This is novel wording in tax legislation. It is suggested the condition requires that:

(1) The donation would not have been made unless the arrangement had been made; *and*
(2) The arrangement would not have been made unless the donation had been made.

7.9 Financial advantage purpose

Section 809ZJ(5) ITA/s.939C(5) CTA 2010 provide:

> Condition B is that the main purpose, or one of the main purposes, of the [donor/] linked person[25] in entering into the arrangements is to obtain a financial advantage—
> (a) directly or indirectly from the charity to which the donation is made or a connected charity,
> (b) for one or more [donor/]linked persons who are not charities...

Identifying the main purpose of the donor/linked person is a subjective test. It is frequently a source of difficulty.[26]

If the TD conditions are met, the entire donation is tainted even if the financial advantage is only small. But if the advantage is small, it is not likely to be a "main purpose" to obtain it.

The scope of condition B is increased by the deemed financial advantage rule, and (slightly) curtailed by the financial advantage disregards, which we consider below.

In the case of a Gift Aid donation, condition B overlaps with the Gift Aid benefit rule. Where a main purpose is to obtain a financial advantage, there is likely to be a benefit which disqualifies Gift Aid relief.

---

25 See 7.5 ("Linked person").

26 See Kessler, *Taxation of Non-Residents and Foreign Domiciliaries* (21st ed., 2022-23), paras 3.9 (How to identify purpose); 3.11 (Foresight/purpose distinction); 49.12 (Consequence/purpose distinction); 3.10 (Purpose: Adviser/agent) online version *https://www.foreigndomiciliaries.co.uk*

7.9.1 *"Financial advantage"*

"Financial advantage" is an unusual expression in tax or other statutory drafting. The usual word is "benefit". Perhaps the drafter wished to stress that non-financial advantages (eg reputational) did not count. Or perhaps there was no reason and the drafter just used the first expression that came to mind.

7.10 Deemed financial advantage

7.10.1 *"Linked transaction"*

Section 809ZK ITA/s.939D CTA 2010 provide:

> (1) This section applies for the purposes of Condition B.[27]
> (2) Subsection (3) applies where the arrangements entered into by the [donor/]linked person[28] (as mentioned in Condition A) involve a transaction[29] to which—
> (a) that or any other [donor/]linked person ("X"), and
> (b) another person ("Y"),
> are parties.

We refer to a transaction within (2) as a **"linked transaction"**.

A mutually dependent arrangement will generally involve one or more linked transactions. The purpose of (2) is to identify the transactions which are referred to in s.809ZK(3) ITA/s.939D(3) CTA 2010:

> X obtains a financial advantage from the charity to which the donation is made or a connected charity if—

---

27 For completeness: Section 809ZK(5) ITA provides some routine definitions:

> "In this section "Condition A" and "Condition B" have the same meaning as in section 809ZJ".

This is needed since the definitions of conditions A and B were not expressed to be for the purposes of the tainted donation rules generally.

28 See 7.5 ("Linked person").

29 Section 809ZK(5) ITA provides an inclusive definition: 'transaction' includes (for example)—

> (a) the sale or letting of property,
> (b) the provision of services,
> (c) the exchange of property,
> (d) the provision of a loan or any other form of financial assistance, and
> (e) investment in a business.

Paragraphs (a), (c), (d) and (e) are all unnecessary; but the provision of services for no consideration would not be a transaction in the normal sense of the expression, so the definition is not wholly otiose.

(a) the terms of the [linked] transaction are
  [i] less beneficial to Y or
  [ii] more beneficial to X (or both)
  than those which might reasonably be expected in a transaction concluded between parties dealing at arm's length, or
(b) the transaction is not of a kind which a person dealing at arm's length and in place of Y might reasonably be expected to make.

The drafting is based on s.10 IHTA, but that does not shed much light on the issues here.

Para (3)(a)[ii] is relatively straightforward: X (the donor/linked person] obtains a benefit (financial advantage) but does so from a third party, Y, not from the donee-charity (or a connected charity). In short, it extends the expression "obtains a financial advantage from the charity" to include cases where a person obtains a financial advantage from someone other than the charity.

Para (3)(a)[i] is considering a case where X (the donor/linked person] does not obtain a benefit, but Y (the third party) suffers some burden or disbenefit. We are unable to think of an example of what this is intended to catch.

Para (3)(b) applies where there is an unexpected transaction. It need not confer any benefit or disbenefit on anyone. We are unable to think of an example of what this is intended to catch.

In short, para 3 extends the expression "obtains a financial advantage from the charity" to include cases where:

(1) the donor/linked person obtains a financial advantage, but not from the charity; and
(2) the donor/linked person does not obtain a financial advantage but some other person suffers a disbenefit.

We refer to these as **"deemed financial advantages"**. However, the fact that someone obtains a deemed financial advantage does not matter unless it is a main purpose of the donor/linked person to obtain it.

The purpose of the deemed financial advantage rule is to extend the scope of what is a financial advantage, and not to narrow it. For the avoidance of doubt, s.809ZK(4) ITA and s.939D(4) CTA 2010 provide:

s.809ZK(4) ITA	**s.939D(4) CTA 2010**
Nothing in this section is intended to limit the circumstances in which a [donor/]linked person may be	Nothing in this section is intended to limit the circumstances in which a [donor/]linked person may be

regarded as obtaining a financial advantage for the purposes of section 809ZJ.	regarded as obtaining a financial advantage for the purposes of section 939C.

7.11 Tainted donation issue list

To summarise the discussion so far. The correct way to approach the TD rules in any particular case is to ask the following questions:

(1) **The donation**
- (a) Is there a donation
- (b) Is it a *relievable charity donation*

(2) **TD condition A**
- (a) *The arrangement:* Does a donor/linked person enter into an arrangement (and what is the arrangement)
- (b) *Dependency:* Are the donation and the arrangement mutually dependent:
  - (i) Would the donation be made without the arrangement
  - (ii) Would the arrangement be made without the donation

(3) **TD condition B**
- (a) *Financial advantage:* Does a donor/linked person obtain:
  - (i) a financial advantage or
  - (ii) a deemed financial advantage
- (b) *Purpose:* is a main purpose of a donor/linked person to obtain that financial advantage

We refer to these eight conditions as the **"tainted donation issue list"**. It will be apparent that a rigorous application of the issue list is a labourious exercise. With this in mind we turn to consider some examples.

7.12 Gift for priority treatment

Annex viii HMRC Guidance Note provides:

> 5.3 ... For example, a charitable health provider may offer donors a priority treatment service if their donations exceed £100.

The HMRC analysis is as follows:

> A donor who gives more than £100 with a view to making use of this priority treatment service would be caught by 'Condition A' as the donor would have made a donation as part of an arrangement to make use of the charity's priority treatment service.

We apply the tainted donation issue list:[30]

(1) **The Donation**

(a) *There is a donation.*

(b) *No relievable charity donation.* The donation does not qualify for Gift Aid relief because of the benefit rule.[31] The priority promise is a benefit received as a result of the gift.

As there is no relievable charity donation, it is not strictly necessary to consider TD conditions A and B. But let us consider the issues anyway.

(2) **TD condition A**

(a) *The donor enters into an arrangement.* The arrangement is
   (i) the charity's promise of priority treatment (the "priority promise")
   (ii) the donor's gift

(b) *The donation and the arrangement are likely mutually dependent*:
   (i) The donation would not be made without the priority promise.[32]
   (ii) The priority promise would not be made without the donation.

So if it mattered, TD condition A would be satisfied.

(3) **TD condition B**

(a) (i) *Financial advantage*: Priority treatment is an advantage, but is it a *financial* advantage? It is tentatively suggested not.
   (ii) There is no deemed financial advantage.

(b) *Purpose:* If there were a financial advantage, it may or may not have been a main purpose of the donor to obtain the advantage. The donor may have made the donation anyway. The example posits that the donor made the gift with a view to making use of this priority treatment service, because if that were not the case, TD condition B would not apply.

So if there were a relievable charity donation, it would be unclear whether TD condition B would be met.

In conclusion, the tainted donation rules do not apply on the facts of this

---

30 See 7.11 (Tainted donation issue list).

31 and because the (so called) "donation" is not a gift. The example assumes the value of the benefit exceeds the Gift Aid small benefit limit.

32 The point does not seem to be certain, from the brief facts given. It is possible that the donation would be made regardless of the priority service. After all, £100 is not a large sum. But we may consider it a reasonable inference.

example.

7.13 Gift in thanks for medical care

Annex viii HMRC Guidance Note provides:

> A donor gives £100,000 to a hospital (a charity) in recognition of the excellent treatment received by his son during his stay.
> The hospital subsequently writes to thank the donor for the unexpected donation.[33]

The HMRC analysis is as follows:

> 6.3 In this example the donation won't be caught by the tainted charity donations rules. There was no arrangement in place for the hospital to provide any services in connection with the donation, so 'Condition A' does not apply.

Turning to the tainted donation issue list:[34]

(1) **The donation**

(a) *There is a donation.*

(b) *The donation is a relievable charity donation.*

(2) **TD condition A:**

(a) *The arrangement:* Does a donor/linked person enter into an arrangement and what is the arrangement?.

There are (at least) two arrangements, or possible arrangements, which need to be considered separately:

• A donor/linked person (the donor's son, or, if the son is a minor, the donor himself) enters into an arrangement for the son's medical treatment (the "treatment-arrangement").

• It would be unusual for a donor to give as much as £100,000 without discussing with the charity how the gift would be used (the "funds-use arrangement").

7.13.1 *Treatment-arrangement*

(b) *The arrangement and the donation are not mutually dependent.* Note that there is in fact a partial dependency here. The donor would *not*

---

33 The thank-you letter is not relevant to the tax analysis; perhaps it is included to emphasise that the donation is unexpected. It is unlikely that a charity would fail to thank its donors, whether they give £100k or much smaller sums.

34 See 7.11 (Tainted donation issue list).

have made the donation were it not for the medical treatment. But that is not sufficient. The charity would have provided the medical treatment without the donation.

This is (or should be) the basis of the HMRC analysis. If HMRC mean to say there is no arrangement at all, the HMRC analysis cannot be justified except on the basis that what HMRC dislike is an arrangement, and what HMRC accept is not an arrangement.

(3) TD condition B:
As TD condition A is not met, it is not strictly necessary to consider TD condition B. But let us consider the issue anyway. Is condition B met?

(a) The medical treatment is not a financial advantage. However it may be a deemed financial advantage, because:
   (i) It is a service, and so a transaction, and,
   (ii) Probably, it is not one which would be provided at arm's length[35].
(b) It is the purpose of the donor/linked person (both father and son) to obtain that deemed financial advantage.

So (if it mattered) condition B would be satisfied.

7.13.2 *Funds-use arrangement*

We turn to the analysis on the basis that there is a funds-use arrangement.

(2) **TD condition A**
(a) There is an arrangement.
(b) *The arrangement and the donation are mutually dependent.* The arrangement (use of the donated funds) would not be entered into in the absence of the donation, and (let us assume) vice versa.

On this basis, TD condition A would be satisfied.

(3) **TD condition B**
(a) *Financial advantage:* A donor/linked person (the son) obtains a benefit (the medical treatment) which is a deemed financial advantage.
(b) It is not be the principal purpose of the donor in entering into the funds use arrangement to obtain *that* tax advantage.

So TD condition B is not satisfied.

35 This is however arguable: arm's length is not a precise expression.

7.13.3 *Further treatment*

The HMRC example continues:

> Even if his son (or any other person connected to[36] the donor) were to receive further ongoing treatment at the hospital, a lack of an arrangement means that the donation will not be caught.

The HMRC analysis is as follows:

> 6.4 The making of a donation is not in itself an arrangement and this legislation clearly refers to both concepts separately. In this example, there is a donation, but there are no arrangements and the hospital may spend the donation as it sees fit.

More analytically, there is a further arrangement (the son's further treatment). However this further arrangement and the donation are not mutually dependent.

The author does not address the problem which may arise if the father decided to make a further donation. On the basis that the patient would have received the treatment anyway, it is still not a mutually dependent arrangement.

HMRC note:

> It [the charity] is not under any obligation to provide the donor (or any member of his family) with specific medical treatment.

If it were, the gift would not qualify for Gift Aid and would not be a relievable charity donation.

7.14 Purchase of gilt + "gift" to charity

Annex viii HMRC Guidance Note provides:

> 6.2... For example, an individual may be sold some Government securities at substantial undervalue on the understanding that within a specified period they will either return them or sell them and make a payment to a charity out of the proceeds. That would be an arrangement for these purposes.

This is a slightly garbled version of the Blue Box scheme.[37] The scheme failed for other reasons. It is not possible to carry out a Tainted Donation

---

36 The statutory term is connected *with*. Nothing turns on the preposition, but it is better to adopt the statutory term.

37 See 2.6.2 (Gift of gilt subject to option).

analysis without specifying in full detail the actual transactions under consideration.

7.15 Matched funding

Suppose there is an arrangement under which a company agrees to make a donation to a charity equal to the amount given by its employees. Pursuant to this arrangement:

(1) An employee gives £10 to a charity (the "employee donation").
(2) The company gives £10 to the charity (the "company donation").

There are two donations, an employee donation and a company donation. They need to be considered separately.

7.15.1 *Employee donation*

We begin with the employee donation. Applying the tainted donation issue list:[38]

(1) **The donation**
(a) *There is a donation*
(b) It is a *relievable charity donation* as it qualifies for Gift Aid.

(2) **TD condition A**
(a) *The arrangement:* The employee is the donor, and so a donor/linked person, and enters into an arrangement (agreeing to the company offer of matched funding).
(b) *Dependency:* The employee donation may or may not have been made but for the arrangement. That is a question of fact. The employee might have given £10 anyway. But it is likely that the company's offer incentivises the employee donation. That is the point of matched funding.
The arrangement (which includes the company donation) would not have been made without the employee donation

So TD condition A (donation-arrangement) is satisfied.

(3) **TD condition B**
(a) *Financial advantage:* No-one benefits from the arrangement (except the charity). The employee does not obtain an actual financial advantage within condition B, and at first sight TD condition B is not met.

38 See 7.11 (Tainted donation issue list).

However if the company and the employee are linked persons, the position needs further thought. The company's gift is transaction to which the company and the charity are parties. In the terminology of s.809ZK ITA/s.939D CTA 2010, the company is X and the charity is Y. That transaction is not beneficial to the company, or prejudicial to Y. However it is probably not a transaction of a kind which a person acting at arm's length would make. Persons acting at arm's length do not usually make gifts. So by making a gift to the charity, the company (X, a linked person) is deemed to receive a financial advantage from the charity.

(b) *Purpose*: One then has to ask whether it is the main purpose of the linked person to obtain that financial advantage. There are two linked persons, the company and the employee. This is a difficult question. If a person obtains a benefit, one can ask whether it is the person's purpose to obtain it. But how does one ask if the purpose is to obtain a deemed benefit when entering into a non-arm's length transaction is a deemed benefit. If it is the main purpose of the employee to encourage the company to make the gift, that would appear to suffice.

So TD condition B is met, and matched funding may be caught, unintentionally, by the tainted donation rules.

In practice no doubt HMRC will turn a blind eye.

7.15.2 *Company donation*

If the company's gift qualifies for a trading deduction, it is not a relievable charity donation. But in other cases, by parity of reasoning, the company's gift may also be caught, if the company and the employee are linked persons.

7.16 Sponsored walk

Suppose D promises to make a gift to charity if W goes on a sponsored walk. Applying the tainted donation issue list:[39]

(1) **The donation**

(a) *There a donation*

(b) It is a *relievable charity donation*

---

39 See 7.11 (Tainted donation issue list).

(2) **TD condition A**

(a) *The arrangement:* There is an arrangement (the sponsored walk). The donation would not be made but for the arrangement. On the other hand, W would probably have gone on the sponsored walk even without D's gift.

So TD condition A is probably not satisfied.

TD condition B

As TD condition A is not met, it is not strictly necessary to consider TD condition B. But let us consider the issue anyway. Is condition B met?

D does not obtain a financial advantage in the normal sense. On this occasion, there is no deemed financial advantage, because W's walk is not a "transaction". So TD condition B is not satisfied.

The conclusion is that the tainted donation rules do not apply.

7.17 Charity dinner

Suppose:

(1) A charity hosts a fundraising dinner, for which potential donors do not pay.

(2) D makes a donation which would not have been made but for the dinner.

We apply the tainted donation issue list:[40]

(1) **The donation**

(a) *There a donation*

(b) It is a *relievable charity donation*

(2) **TD condition A**

(a) *The arrangement:* The donor/linked person enters into an arrangement (coming to the dinner)

(b) *Dependency:* Are the donation and the arrangement mutually dependent:

(i) Would the donation be made without the arrangement?

(ii) Would the arrangement be made without the donation?

D's gift would not be made but for the arrangement. But the arrangement would have been made even without the gift. So it is considered that the donation and the arrangement are not mutually dependent, so TD condition A is not satisfied.

---

40 See 7.11 (Tainted donation issue list).

(3) **TD condition B**:

(a) *Financial advantage:* Is the dinner a financial advantage? The point is arguable.[41]

Is there a deemed financial advantage? If the dinner is a "transaction" there is, since giving a free dinner is not a transaction which persons dealing at arm's length would make. One might think that the dinner is not a transaction, but the expression includes the provision of services. So there is a deemed financial advantage.

(b) *Purpose* : It is not the main purpose of the linked person to obtain that advantage. So TD condition B is not satisfied.

7.18 Disregarded financial advantages

Section 809ZL(1) ITA/s.939E(1) CTA 2010 provide four reliefs (**"TD reliefs"**):

> When determining whether a relievable charity donation is a tainted donation, a financial advantage within subsection (2), (3), (4) or (5) is to be ignored.

7.18.1 *Applied for charitable purposes*

Section 809ZL(2) ITA/s.939E(2) CTA 2010 provide:

> A financial advantage is within this subsection if the person for whom it is obtained applies the advantage for charitable purposes only.

Annex viii HMRC Guidance Note gives an example involving a gift to foreign charities routed through a UK charity.[42] We amend the text slightly for clarity:[43]

> **9.2 Example 4**
> A US citizen lives and works in the UK (receiving UK-source income

---

41 See 15.22 (Acknowledgement and advertising).

42 This is standard planning; see 3.24 (Non-EU charities).

43 The text in its original form reads: "A US citizen lives and works in the UK (receiving UK-source income subject to UK tax) and decides she wants to make a relievable charity donation of £10,000 to a charitable organisation in the US. The donor is linked to the US organisation. The donor arranges to make her donation to a UK agency charity recognised by HMRC and, on making the donation, applies Gift Aid so the agency receives £12,500 (£10,000 donation plus a £2,500 Gift Aid repayment) to distribute on the donor's behalf. The donor requests the agency charity to pass the funds to the US organisation that undertakes charitable activities, and the US organisation spends the charitable funds on activities recognised as charitable under the law of England and Wales."

> subject to UK tax).
> She wants to make a relievable charity donation of £10,000 to a charitable organisation in the US.
> The donor is connected with the US organisation so the US organisation is a linked person.
> The donor enters into the following arrangement:
> (1) She makes a donation to a UK agency charity recognised by HMRC.[44]
> (2) She makes a Gift Aid declaration so the agency charity receives £12,500 (£10,000 donation plus £2,500 Gift Aid repayment).
> (3) She requests the agency charity to pass the funds to the US organisation, which is done.
> (4) The US organisation spends the charitable funds on activities recognised as charitable under the law of England and Wales.[45]

The HMRC analysis is as follows:

> 9.3 In this example the donation won't be caught by the tainted charity donations rules.
> The donor enters into arrangements with the agency charity to ensure that her donation, once made, will be routed on to the US charitable organisation. The donation wouldn't have been made to the agency charity in the absence of this arrangement ...

In addition it is relevant to note that the arrangement would not have been made in the absence of the donation.

> ... so 'Condition A' is clearly satisfied.
> 9.4 The main purpose for entering into the arrangement is to increase the funds of the US charitable organisation (a financial advantage) and this organisation is linked to the donor.

More analytically, it is a linked person.

> 9.5 ITA 2007[46] provide for certain financial advantages to be ignored. One such advantage is where the body that receives the financial

---

44 What is intended by specifying that the UK charity is "recognised by HMRC"? Presumably the point is that it is a charity within the tax definition: see 3.4.1 (Recognition by HMRC).

45 The agency charity could only make the payment to the US organisation if satisfied that the US organisation would apply the funds for purposes which are charitable in the English law sense.

46 The HMRC Guidance Note adds: "and section 939E CTA 2010" but this would only be relevant in the case of a corporate donor.

advantage (in this case the US charitable organisation) applies the financial advantage for charitable purposes only. The effect of section 809ZL ITA 2007 ... mean[s] that 'Condition B' can't be met in this case, and therefore the donation isn't tainted.

7.18.2 *Small benefit rule*

The next TD relief concerns small benefits disregarded for Gift Aid purposes.[47]

s. 809ZL(3) ITA	**s.939E(3) CTA 2010**
A financial advantage is within this subsection if (ignoring the tainted donation provisions)[48] it is—	[identical]
(a) a benefit associated with a gift[49] which is a qualifying donation for the purposes of Chapter 2 of Part 8 [Gift Aid for individuals], or	(a) a benefit associated with a gift which is a qualifying donation for the purposes of Chapter 2 of Part 8 of ITA 2007 (gift aid), or
(b) a benefit associated with a payment[50] which is a qualifying payment for the purposes of Chapter 2 of Part 6 of CTA 2010 [corporate gift aid].	(b) a benefit associated with a payment which is a qualifying payment for the purposes of Chapter 2 of Part 6 (charitable donations relief: payments to charity).

At first sight it is difficult to see how this could apply, for the permitted benefits under the small benefits rule are so small that no-one could make the gift with the main purpose of obtaining them. However that is not necessarily true of rights of admission (which may be of a value equal or greater than the amount of the gift).

Annex viii HMRC Guidance Note provides:

---

47 See 15.34 (Small benefits).

48 Section 809ZL(6) ITA/s.939E(6) CTA 2010 provide that "the tainted donation provisions" has the meaning given by section 809ZI(3)/s.993B(3).
The words "ignoring the tainted donation provisions" are otiose, but it does not much matter.

49 Section 809ZL(6) ITA/s.939E(6) CTA 2010 provide that "benefit associated with a gift" has the meaning given by s.417 ITA.

50 Section 809ZL(6) ITA/s.939E(6) CTA 2010 provide that "benefit associated with a payment" has the meaning given by s.196 CTA 2010.

> **17.2 Example 7**
> An art conservation charity offers donors who make donations of £5,000 or more a special membership package called Gold membership. This entitles members to a benefits package including free admission to permanent exhibitions, private viewings, the right to attend an annual 'Curator's Reception', which includes refreshments, an opportunity to meet other major supporters and hear a prominent expert delivering a talk about current art conservation issues, plus 12 monthly newsletters. The charity has agreed with HMRC that the value of the benefits package is £250.
> 17.3 The receipt of a benefits package as a result of making a donation is an arrangement caught by 'Condition A' of the new legislation; the circumstances are such as to suggest the donation would not have been made without the benefits package.

In addition, it is relevant to note that the benefits would not be provided without the donation.

> 17.4 It's likely that 'Condition B' would apply as the donor's main purpose in making the donation in the amount given is likely to be to obtain the benefits package. The donor is caught by 'Condition [B]'[51].

The author needs to say this for the example to work, though in our view it is not at all likely. But it does not matter:

> 17.4[52] However, these packages are designed to incentivise the donor to make a larger donation and ensure that the benefits provided fall within the Gift Aid benefit limits. In this case, the free admission to permanent exhibitions can be disregarded under normal Gift Aid rules. The newsletters are regarded as having negligible value. Private viewings and the right to attend the reception is within the Gift Aid benefit limits. Consequently, the value of the benefits package is ignored as a financial advantage for the purposes of the tainted charity donations rules.

7.18.3 *Qualifying investment relief*

The next TD relief concerns QIDR.

s. 809ZL(4) ITA	**s.939E(4) CTA 2010**
A financial advantage is within this	[identical]

51 The original erroneously refers to condition C.
52 The HMRC Guidance Note has two paragraphs numbered 17.4.

subsection if (ignoring the tainted donation provisions)—	
(a) the relievable charity donation is a disposal in respect of which tax relief would be available under [i] Chapter 3 of Part 8 of this Act (gifts of shares, securities and real property to charities etc) or [ii] Chapter 3 of Part 6 of CTA 2010 (charitable donations: certain disposals to charity), and	(a) the relievable charity donation is a disposal in respect of which tax relief would be available under [i] Chapter 3 of Part 8 of ITA 2007 (gifts of shares, securities and real property to charities etc) or [ii] Chapter 3 of Part 6 (charitable donations: certain disposals to charity), and
(b) the advantage is a benefit the value of which would be taken into account in determining the relievable amount in respect of the disposal for the purposes of the Chapter in question.	[identical]

7.18.4 *Gift of trading stock to charity*

The last TD relief concerns the relief for gifts of trading stock. Section 809ZL(5) ITA/s.939E(5) CTA 2010 provide:

> A financial advantage is within this subsection if (ignoring the tainted donation provisions)—
> (a) the relievable charity donation is a gift in respect of which tax relief would be available under section 108 of ITTOIA 2005 or section 105 of CTA 2009 (gifts of trading stock to charities etc), and
> (b) the advantage is a benefit attributable to the making of the gift in respect of which an amount would be brought into account under section 109 of ITTOIA 2005 or section 108 of CTA 2009 (receipt of benefits by donor or connected person).

See 18.7.7 (Relief for gift of trading stock).

7.19 Charity-owned company

TD condition C is designed for the special case of charity subsidiaries. Section 809ZJ(6) ITA/s.939C(6) CTA 2010 provide:

> Condition C is that the donor is not—
> (a) a qualifying charity-owned company ...

7.19.1 *Qualifying charity-owned co*

Section 809ZJ(8) ITA/s.939C(8) CTA 2010 provide the definition:

> In this section—
> "qualifying charity-owned company", in relation to a relievable charity donation, means a company which—
> (a) is wholly owned[53] by one or more charities, at least one of which is the charity to which the donation is made or a connected[54] charity, and
> (b) has not previously been under the control of, and does not carry on a trade or business previously carried on by, one or more of the following—
> (i) a potentially advantaged person;[55]
> (ii) a person (other than a charity) who, at any time within the period of 4 years ending with the day on which paragraph (a) was first satisfied, was connected[56] with a person who is a potentially advantaged person;

7.19.2 *Housing provider*

Section 809ZJ(6) ITA/s.939C(6) CTA 2010 provide:

> Condition C is that the donor is not ...
> (b) a relevant housing provider linked with the charity to which the donation is made.

Section 809ZJ ITA/s.939C CTA 2010 provide the necessary definitions:

> (7) For the purposes of subsection (6)(b) a relevant housing provider is linked with the charity if (and only if)—
> (a) one is wholly owned, or subject to control, by the other, or

---

53 Section 809ZJ(9) ITA/s.939C(9) CTA 2010 provide a referential definition of wholly-owned:

Section 200 of CTA 2010 (company wholly owned by a charity) applies for the purposes of subsection (8), and for those purposes references in that section to "charity" include a registered club within the meaning of section 658(6) of that Act.

Section 200 (company wholly owned by a charity) applies for the purposes of subsection (8), and for those purposes references in that section to "charity" include a registered club within the meaning of section 658(6).

See 9.4.1 ("Wholly-owned").

54 See 7.6 ("Connected charity").

55 See 7.7 ("Potentially advantaged person").

56 See 7.5.1 ("Connected person").

(b) both are wholly owned, or subject to control, by the same person.

(8) In this section ...

"relevant housing provider" means a body which is—

(a) a non-profit registered provider of social housing, or

(b) entered on a register maintained under section 1 of the Housing Act 1996, section 20 of the Housing (Scotland) Act 2010 or Article 14 of the Housing (Northern Ireland) Order 1992.

7.20 Tainted donation: Loss of reliefs

The tainted donation rules apply where a gift meets the conditions for tax relief, and tainted donation conditions A-C apply. In practice that will rarely if ever happen. However we move on to consider the position if it does.

7.20.1 *No relief on donation*

Section 809ZM/s.939F CTA 2010 first disapply IT/CT reliefs on the tainted donation:

s. 809ZM ITA	**s.939F CTA 2010**
(1) This section applies where a tainted donation is made by a person.	(1) This section applies where a tainted donation is made by a company.
(2) Where (ignoring this Chapter [Chapter 8 Part 13]) income tax relief would be available in respect of the tainted donation, that relief is not available.	(2) Where (ignoring this Part [Part 21C]) corporation tax relief would be available in respect of the tainted donation, that relief is not available.

7.20.2 *No relief on associated donation*

Section 809ZM/s.939F CTA 2010 also disapply IT/CT reliefs on associated donations:

s. 809ZM(3) ITA	**s.939F(3) CTA 2010**
Where—	[identical]
(a) (ignoring this Chapter [Chapter 8 Part 13]) income tax relief would be available in respect of an associated donation, and	(a) (ignoring this Part [Part 21C]) corporation tax relief would be available in respect of an associated donation, and

(b) entitlement to that relief is not withdrawn by subsection (2), that relief is not available.	[identical]

The definition of associated donation is as follows:

s. 809ZM(4) ITA	**s.939F(4) CTA 2010**
In this section—	[identical]
"associated donation", in relation to a tainted donation, means a relievable charity donation made—	[identical]
(a) in accordance with the relevant arrangements, and	[identical]
(b) by a person, other than—	[identical]
(i) a qualifying charity-owned company[57] in relation to that relievable charity donation, or	[identical]
(ii) a relevant housing provider[58] linked (within the meaning of section 809ZJ(7)) with the charity to which that donation is made;	(ii) a relevant housing provider linked (within the meaning of section 939C(7)) with the charity to which that donation is made;
"the relevant arrangements", in relation to a tainted donation, means the arrangements by reference to which Conditions A and B in section 809ZJ are met.	"the relevant arrangements", in relation to a tainted donation, means the arrangements by reference to which Conditions A to C in section 939C are met.

This definition only applies for Section 809ZM ITA/s.939F CTA 2010 so

---

57 This is defined by reference:

s. 809ZM(4) ITA	**s.939F(4) CTA 2010**
"qualifying charity-owned company" has the meaning given by section 809ZJ(8) (except that paragraph (b) of that definition does not apply);	"qualifying charity-owned company" has the meaning given by section 939C(8) (except that paragraph (b) of that definition does not apply);

58 **Section 809ZM(4) ITA/s.939F(4) CTA 2010 provide that** "relevant housing provider" has the meaning given by section 809ZJ(8)/s.939C(8).

it has to be incorporated by reference elsewhere.[59]

7.20.3 *List of disapplied reliefs*

Section 809ZM(4) ITA/s.939F(4) CTA 2010 provide a list of the reliefs which are disapplied, in the form of a definition of "income tax/corporation tax relief":

s. 809ZM(4) ITA	**s.939F(4) CTA 2010**
In this section—	[identical]
... "income tax relief" means relief under—	... "corporation tax relief" means relief under—
(a) section 63(2)(a), (aa) or (ab) of CAA 2001 (gifts of plant and machinery), so far as it applies in relation to income tax,	(a) section 63(2)(a), (aa) or (ab) of CAA 2001 (gifts of plant and machinery), so far as it applies in relation to corporation tax,
(b) Part 12 of ITEPA 2003 (payroll giving),	
(c) section 108 of ITTOIA 2005 (gifts of trading stock),	(b) section 105 of CTA 2009 (gifts of trading stock), or
(d) Chapter 2 of Part 8 of this Act (Gift Aid), or (e) Chapter 3 of that Part (gifts of shares etc);	(c) Part 6 of CTA 2010 (charitable donations relief) [corporate gift aid & qualifying investments];

This is the same as the list of relevant relieving provisions[60] except this list omits donor CGT relief, which is dealt with elsewhere.[61]

7.21 Tainted Gift Aid

The loss of relief rules set out above do not disapply the relief for gift aid donations, as that relief is not in the list of disapplied relief.
Instead, s.809ZM(5) ITA provides:

> Where entitlement to relief is withdrawn under this section in respect of a donation—
>
> (a) subsections (6) and (7) apply if the relief is under Chapter 2 of

---

59 Section 257A(2)(b) TCGA.

60 See 7.4.2 ("Relevant relieving provisions").

61 See 7.24 (Tainted donation: CGT).

> Part 8 (Gift Aid)...

This applies where:
(1) An individual makes a gift which meets the conditions for Gift Aid
(2) The conditions of the tainted donation rules apply

In practice that will rarely if ever happen. However we move on to consider the position if it does.

These rules only apply to a gift made by an individual: they do not apply to a gift by a company which qualifies for corporate Gift Aid. However the rules apply whether the gift is to a charitable trust or to a charitable company.

We refer to such a gift as a **"tainted Gift Aid donation"**.

7.21.1 *Effect on personal allowances*

For completeness: s.809ZM(6) ITA provides:

> For the purposes of Step 2 in section 58(1), the donation is not a qualifying donation for the purposes of Chapter 2 of Part 8.

This prevents the gift from reducing the restriction on personal allowances.[62] That may be strictly logical. As this rule is unlikely ever to apply, and if it did the amount involved is trivial, one might reasonably question whether this strikes the right balance between the need for simplicity as against fairness; but simplicity was not an important consideration to the author of the tainted donation rules.

7.21.2 *Grossing up rules retained*

More importantly, s.809ZM(7)(a) ITA provides that the usual Grossing Up and Gift Aid tax reclaim rules apply:

> But—
> (a) the donation remains a qualifying donation for the purposes of—[63]

Provision	**Topic**	**See**
Part 10 ITA *in particular:*		
s.520, 521	Gift is income of charitable trust	15.49.1
s.538A	Claim to recover Gift Aid tax	47.8.3

62 See 15.43.7 (Personal allowance taper).

63 For clarity I have set this out in tabular form, clarified the references (using italics), and use my own terminology, rather than a precise quote of the statute.

s.899(5) ITA	Annual payment withholding tax[64]	
Chap 2 Part 11 CTA 2010 *in particular:*		
s.471, 472	Gift is income of charitable co	15.49.1
s.664 CTA 2010	CASCs	41.25.2

Section 809ZM(7)(b) ITA provides:

> accordingly, section 414(2)(a) (donation treated as made after deduction of basic rate income tax)[65] applies for the purposes of section 520(4) (income tax treated as deducted to be treated as income tax paid by charitable trust).

The effect is that:

(1) A tainted Gift Aid donation is grossed up (like a normal Gift Aid donation)

(2) A charity may reclaim basic rate tax on a tainted Gift Aid donation;[66] though in most cases the charity is likely to incur non-charitable expenditure, and so lose its tax relief, and so not be entitled to reclaim the tax.

(3) The donor is liable if they pay insufficient tax to frank the Gift Aid donation (as is the case for a normal Gift Aid donation).[67]

Presumably the reason is that it is envisaged that in some cases the charity may be unaware that the gift is a tainted donation.

7.21.3 *Recovery of Gift Aid tax*

After preserving the charity's right to recover tax on a tainted Gift Aid donation, the legislation then recovers it by a special tax charge:

Section 809ZN ITA provides:

> (1) Income tax is charged under this section if—
> (a) a person makes a tainted donation in a tax year,
> (b) (ignoring this Chapter [Chapter 8 Part 13]) relief would have been available under Chapter 2 of Part 8 [Gift Aid] in respect of the tainted donation or an associated donation ("the Gift Aid donation"), and

---

64 For this topic see Kessler, *Taxation of Non-Residents and Foreign Domiciliaries* (21st ed, 2022/23), para 31.10.2 (Annual Payments outside WHT). This is not likely to arise in practice, and is included for historical reasons.
But it is not likely to arise in practice.

65 See 15.44.1 (Tax deemed deducted from gift).

66 See 15.49 (Position of charity).

67 See 15.44 Donor pays insufficient tax).

> (c) the charity to which the Gift Aid donation is made is entitled to claim a repayment of tax in respect of that donation.
>
> (2) The amount of the tax charged under this section is equal to the amount of the repayment of tax which the charity is entitled to claim in respect of the Gift Aid donation (whether or not such a claim is made).

We refer to this as the **"special Gift Aid tax charge"**.

This charge applies to a charitable company and a charitable trust, so there is no CTA 2010 equivalent.

7.21.4 *Liability for special charge*

Section 809ZN ITA provides:

> (3) Each of the persons mentioned in subsection (4) is liable for any tax charged under this section, and the liability of those persons is joint and several.
>
> (4) The persons are—

There are four categories of chargeable person. The first three are:

> (a) the donor in respect of the Gift Aid donation,
> (b) if different, the donor in respect of the tainted donation,
> (c) each potentially advantaged person[68] under the relevant arrangements relating to the tainted donation...

7.21.5 *Liability of charity*

Section 809ZN ITA provides:

> (3) Each of the persons mentioned in subsection (4) is liable for any tax charged under this section, and the liability of those persons is joint and several.
>
> (4) The persons are...
>
> (d) any charity to which the Gift Aid donation or (if different) the tainted donation is made, or any connected[69] charity, which falls within subsection (5).

Section 809ZN(5) ITA provides:

> A charity falls within this subsection if the charity—
>
> (a) is or was party to the relevant arrangements relating to the tainted donation, and

68 See 7.7 ("Potentially advantaged person").
69 See 7.6 ("Connected charity").

(b) was aware,[70] at the time it entered into those arrangements, that a linked person was entering (or had entered or was likely to enter) into the arrangements in circumstances falling within Condition B in section 809ZJ.

Annex viii HMRC Guidance Note provides:

> **14 Meaning of a charity being 'party to' and 'aware of' the tainted charity donation arrangements**
> 14.1 ...In order for a charity to be caught by this provision it must also have been aware, at the time it entered into those arrangements, that the arrangements were for the donor or a person connected with the donor to obtain a financial advantage, directly, or indirectly from the charity. A charity would be 'aware' of the arrangements where the managers or persons in a position of authority or control of the charity had knowledge of the arrangements. Merely receiving a tainted donation would not on its own mean that a charity was 'party to' or 'aware of' such an arrangement.

7.21.6 *Avoidance of double charge*

Section 809ZN(6) ITA provides:

> No liability to income tax arises under this section in respect of a repayment of tax, if (and to the extent that) the repayment is itself repaid to HMRC under any other provision of the Tax Acts.

Annex viii HMRC Guidance Note provides:

> **13 Tainted charity donations and Gift Aid**
> 13.1 If the donation would have been a qualifying donation under the Gift Aid scheme if it weren't a tainted donation, the charity will continue to be entitled to make a repayment claim to HMRC in respect of Income Tax. However an Income Tax charge will arise in connection with this repayment. The amount of the Income Tax charge is equal to the amount of the repayment of tax that the charity would be entitled to claim in respect of the Gift Aid donation (whether or not the charity makes the repayment claim).
> The tax charge may fall on the donor, a connected person or any other potentially advantaged person under the relevant arrangements in

---

70 EN FB 2011 provided: No charge will arise on the charity unless, exceptionally, the charity was party to, and fully aware of the arrangements."
Although the word fully was not in the legislation, this suggests that the word "aware" should be broadly understood.

> relation to the tainted donation, or the charity (or any connected charity). In practice HMRC will look to the donor and any other financially advantaged person first. In any event, HMRC wouldn't seek to charge the charity unless the charity was party to, and aware of, the arrangements to obtain financial advantage.
> 13.2 There will be no liability to Income Tax where the repayment is repaid to HMRC under some other provision, for example if the charity is charged to tax on non-charitable expenditure in relation to the donation.

Section 809ZN(7) ITA provides some referential definitions:

> In this section—
> "associated donation" has the same meaning as in section 809ZM;
> "linked person" has the same meaning as in section 809ZJ;
> "the relevant arrangements" has the same meaning as in section 809ZM.

These are needed since the definitions were not expressed to be for the purposes of the tainted donation rules generally.

7.21.7 *"Entitled" and "liable"*

s. 809ZR(2) ITA	**s.939I(2) CTA 2010**
In this Chapter [Chapter 8 Part 13], in the case of a charitable trust, references to a charity being entitled to a repayment of, or liable to pay, tax are to be read as references to the trustees of the trust being so entitled or liable.	In this Part [Part 21C], in the case of a charitable trust, references to a charity being entitled to a repayment of tax are to be read as references to the trustees of the trust being so entitled.

This provision is unnecessary but it does no harm.

7.22 Tainted payroll giving

Section 809ZM(5) ITA provides similar rules for the payroll donation scheme:

> Where entitlement to relief is withdrawn under this section in respect of a donation ...
> (b) subsection (8) applies if the relief is under Part 12 of ITEPA 2003 (payroll giving).

So we turn to s.809ZM(8) ITA which provides:

> The donation remains a donation for the purposes of Part 12 of ITEPA

2003 for the purposes of—

(a) section 521A (gifts under payroll deduction scheme: income tax liability and exemption), and

(b) section 472A of CTA 2010 (gifts under payroll reduction scheme: corporation tax liability and exemption).

The effect is that although relief is denied, the donation is still income of the charity and (if the charity loses tax relief) it is taxable. It would have been sufficient to deny relief rather than imposing this (potential) double charge to tax.

7.23 Payment from trust

The definition of relievable charity donation in s.809ZI(1) ITA/s.939B(1) CTA 2010 provide:

> In this Chapter/Part[71] "relievable charity donation" means a gift or other disposal which—
>
> (a) is made by a person to a charity, and
>
> (b) is eligible for tax relief.

There is a relievable charity donation where a non-charitable discretionary trust distributes income to a charity beneficiary. The distribution is not a gift, but it is probably an "other disposal". However s.809ZI(5) ITA/s.939B(5) CTA 2010 put the point beyond doubt:

> For the purposes of this Chapter/Part[72] an amount of income which
> [1] arises under a UK settlement[73] and
> [2] to which a charity is entitled under the terms of the settlement
> is to be regarded as an amount gifted to the charity by the trustees of the settlement.

The distribution is "eligible for tax relief" so the condition in para (b) is met.[74]

Section 809ZO ITA provides:

> (1) Income tax is charged under this section if—
>
> (a) a person makes a tainted donation in a tax year,
>
> (b) the tainted donation or an associated donation is a payment by

---

71 That is, Chapter 8 Part 13 ITA/Part 21C CTA 2010.

72 That is, Chapter 8 Part 13 ITA/Part 21C CTA 2010.

73 The second paragraph of s.809ZI(5) provides: "UK settlement" has the same meaning as in section 628 of ITTOIA 2005. See 31.5.2 ("UK settlement").

74 See 7.4 (Eligible for tax relief).

the trustees of a settlement of income arising under the settlement ("the trust donation"), and

(c) the charity to which the trust donation is made is entitled to claim a repayment of tax in respect of that donation.

(2) The amount of the tax charged under this section is equal to the amount of the repayment of tax which the charity is entitled to claim in respect of the trust donation (whether or not such a claim is made).

(3) Each of the persons mentioned in subsection (4) is liable for any tax charged under this section, and the liability of those persons is joint and several.

(4) The persons are—

(a) the trustees of the settlement who made the trust donation,

(b) if different, the donor in respect of the tainted donation,

(c) if section 628[75] or 630[76] of ITTOIA 2005 (gifts from settlor interested trusts etc) applies in relation to the income out of which the trust donation is made, the settlor in relation to the settlement,

(d) each potentially advantaged person[77] under the relevant arrangements relating to the tainted donation,

(e) any beneficiary of the settlement who is party to those arrangements, and

(f) [i] any charity to which the trust donation or (if different) the tainted donation is made, or
[ii] any connected charity,[78]
which falls within subsection (5).

(5) A charity falls within this subsection if—

(a) the charity is or was party to the relevant arrangements relating to the tainted donation, and

(b) the charity was aware, at the time it entered into those arrangements, that a linked person was entering (or had entered or was likely to enter) into the arrangements in circumstances falling within Condition B in section 809ZJ.

(6) No liability to income tax arises under this section in respect of a repayment of tax if that repayment is itself repaid to HMRC under any other provision of the Tax Acts.

(7) In this section—

"associated donation" has the same meaning as in section 809ZM;

"linked person" has the same meaning as in section 809ZJ;

---

75 See 31.5 (Settlor-interested trust).

76 See 31.6 (Income paid to children of settlor).

77 See 7.7 ("Potentially advantaged person").

78 See 7.6 ("Connected charity").

"the relevant arrangements" has the same meaning as in section 809ZM;
"settlement" and "settlor" have the same meaning as in Chapter 5 of Part 5 of ITTOIA 2005 (see section 620 of that Act).

Annex viii HMRC Guidance Note provides two examples. The first concerns a discretionary trust including a charitable beneficiary. The facts (omitting irrelevant details)[79] are as follows:

15.4 Example 5
Mr A settles property worth £20 million on a non-charitable trust (the B Trust).[80]
There is an arrangement under which:
(1) The B trust makes a discretionary income payment of £1 million out of its income to the C Charitable Trust.
(2) The payment is treated as if it were made after deduction of income tax at the trust rate of 50%.[81] The trustees of the C Charitable Trust are treated as receiving a gross payment of £2 million on which £1 million tax has been suffered. They claim exemption from income tax under section 536 ITA 2007 and claim a repayment of £1 million.
(3) The trustees of the C Charitable Trust make a loan to D Ltd (a company connected with A) of £1.9 million at a less than commercial rate of interest.[82]

---

79 The example in full (including its irrelevant detail) is as follows:
"Mr A settles a rental property worth £20 million on a non-charitable trust (the B Trust). The trustees have discretion to apply the income arising for the benefit of the employees of D Industries Ltd as they consider to be appropriate. D Industries Ltd is controlled by Mr A and his immediate family. A discretionary payment of £1 million is made out of the rental income by the B Trust to the trustees of the C Charitable Trust, whose trustees include Mr A. The C Charitable Trust has broad charitable objects, which it exercises in the towns in which D Industries Ltd is based. The payment by the trustees of the B Trust to the C Charitable Trust is treated as if it were made after deduction of income tax at the trust rate of 50%. The trustees of the C Charitable Trust are treated as receiving a gross payment of £2 million on which £1 million tax has been suffered. They claim exemption from income tax under section 536 ITA 2007 and claim a repayment of £1 million. The trustees of the C Charitable Trust are immediately approached by the directors of D Industries Ltd requesting a loan. The trustees agree to make an unsecured loan to D Industries Ltd of £1.9 million at a favourable rate of interest and repayable on demand."
80 This is implausible because of the IHT charge which arises, but we must ignore that in order to follow the example.
81 The text has not been updated for the reduction in the trust rate to 45% in 2013.
82 This example has been edited slightly by the author for greater clarity.

The loan is in fact a breach of trust and non-charitable expenditure, the repayment at (2) should not have been made[83], and the Charity Commission should intervene in the charity.

The HMRC analysis is as follows:

> 15.5 The discretionary payment of £1 million to the C Charitable Trust is a 'relievable charity donation'.
> The donation is 'tainted' because a linked person, Mr A, has entered into arrangements – the discretionary payment and the subsequent advantageous loan – the purpose of which is to obtain a financial advantage from the charity i.e. an advantageous loan of the gross amount of the discretionary payment.
> Consequently, an income tax charge of £1 million can be charged on the trustees of the B Trust, or any of the other persons identified in section 809ZO ITA 2007, which may include the trustees of the C Charitable Trust.

The second example concerns a trust under which a charity has an interest in possession. The facts (omitting irrelevant details)[84] are as follows:

> **15.6 Example 6**
> Mr E settles property worth £40 million on a non-charitable trust, the F Trust.[85]
> The G Charitable Trust is entitled, under the terms of the F trust, to 50% of the income arising to the F Trust. During the tax year 2014-15 the G Charitable Trust is entitled to rental income of £1 million.
> After paying basic rate tax the trustees of the F Trust pay £800,000 to

---

83 Except, perhaps, in relation to the £100k difference between the £2m income and the £1.9m misapplied.

84 The example in full (including its irrelevant detail) is as follows:
"Mr E settles a rental property worth £40 million on a non-charitable trust, the F Trust. One of the beneficiaries is the G Charitable Trust of which Mr E is a trustee. The G Charitable Trust is entitled, under the terms of the settlement, to 50 per cent of the rental income arising to the F Trust. During the tax year 2014-15 the G Charitable Trust is entitled to rental income of £1 million. After paying basic rate tax the trustees of the F Trust pay £800,000 to the charity.
The charity claims exemption from Income Tax and claims repayment of the tax credit £200,000. [Authors' note: The term *tax credit* is not strictly correct, but we may ignore that.] Shortly afterwards H Ltd, a company controlled by Mr E, enters into an agreement with the charity to provide services to the charity on terms that are unduly favourable to H Ltd."

85 As in the previous example, this is implausible because of the IHT charge which arises, but we must ignore that.

> the charity. The charity claims exemption from Income Tax and claims repayment of the £200,000 tax.
> Shortly afterwards H Ltd, a company connected with Mr E, enters into an agreement with the charity to provide services to the charity on terms that are unduly favourable to H Ltd.

This involves a breach of charity law, a likely criminal offence, and non-charitable expenditure. The repayment of the £200k tax should not have been made; and the charity commission should intervene in the charity. However the HMRC analysis is as follows:

> 15.7 The payment of income to which the G Charitable Trust is entitled, under the terms of the settlement of the F Trust, is a 'relievable charity donation'.
> The donation is 'tainted' because a linked person, Mr E, has entered into arrangements, the main purpose of which is to obtain a financial advantage from the charity i.e. the unduly favourable contract.
> So Income Tax of £200,000 can be charged on the trustees of the F Trust to recover the tax repaid, or any of the other persons identified in section 809ZO ITA 2007, which may include the trustees of the G Charitable Trust.

7.24 Tainted donation: CGT

Section 257A(1) TCGA provides:

> Section 257 does not apply in relation to—
> (a) a tainted donation made by a person, or
> (b) any associated donation.[86]

This disapplies donor CGT relief.[87]

7.25 Tainted donation: CASCs

The tainted donation rules apply to CASCs as they do to charities. This is economically achieved by s.809ZR(1) ITA/s.939I[88] CTA 2010, which provide:

> In this Chapter/Part[89]—
> "charity" includes a registered club within the meaning of section 658(6) of CTA 2010 (meaning of "community amateur sports club"

86 See 7.20.2 (No relief on associated donation).
87 See 23.3 (Donor CGT relief).
88 That is 939 with a capital *i*, not 9391.
89 That is, Chapter 8 Part 13 ITA/Part 21C CTA 2010.

and "registered club").

7.26 Tainted donation: Critique

We do of course need provisions to prevent abuse of charity tax reliefs. There are a number of such provisions, in particular:

(1) The application for charitable purposes rule (that relief is only available for income and gains applied for charitable purposes)
(2) The qualifying expenditure rules
(3) The benefit rules for Gift Aid and QIDR
(4) Charity law (under which defaulting trustees are liable for breach of trust)
(5) Criminal law

The question is whether these rules leave any gaps for which the tainted donation rules (or their predecessor, the substantial donor rules) are (or were) needed.

Annex viii HMRC Guidance Note sets out examples including some where the tainted donation rules are said to apply. Here we might expect the reason for the rules to be found.

> **6.2... Example one**
> A donor gives £100,000 to a hospital (a charity) in recognition of the excellent treatment received by his son during his stay.
> The hospital subsequently writes to thank the donor for the unexpected donation.[90]

This is by way of introduction, and we now turn to the point of the example. The HMRC Guidance Note continues:

> **6.5 Example 2**
> The position set out in example 1 would be different if the donor had agreed with the hospital that in return for a Gift Aid donation of £100,000 the hospital would provide treatment that would ordinarily cost £125,000. In this instance, there is clearly an arrangement in place. Further, the circumstances and likely effects are such that it is reasonable to assume that the donation wouldn't have been made, and the arrangements wouldn't have been entered into, independently of each other. There is a connection between the donation and the terms of the arrangement. Consequently, 'Condition A' would be satisfied.

The original HMRC analysis in the EN to the tainted donation draft

---

90 This example is discussed at 7.8.4 (Mutual dependency).

clauses was as follows:

> *Because of the effect of grossing up the donation (under the Gift Aid scheme) of £100,000 the hospital would still receive £125,000.*

This is obviously wrong.[91] On that mistaken assumption, the original HMRC analysis explained how the tainted donation rules were intended to operate:

> *Condition A would apply because the donor would have entered into an arrangement to obtain an advantage from the hospital.*
> *The advantage would arise from a transaction under which treatment was provided by the hospital on terms that would not be available to a party dealing at arm's length, so Condition B would apply.*

Annex viii HMRC Guidance Note acknowledges the error:

> 6.6 It is worth noting that, in this modified example, the first principles of the Gift Aid rules would apply. The payment of £100,000 was clearly not a gift, having been made to secure treatment at a reduced rate, and therefore no tax relief would be available. There wouldn't be any need to consider the tainted charity donations rules in this instance.

So why are the tainted donation rules needed?

> However, if the donor entered into more circuitous arrangements in order to distance the Gift Aid donation from the benefit of medical treatment, the Gift Aid rules may not operate to deny relief. The tainted charity donations rules would then have to be considered.

Analysis is not possible without knowing the precise transactions, but this does not deter HMRC:

> 6.7 'Condition A' would apply because the donor would have entered into an arrangement (now more complicated and contrived than the original scenario) in connection with their donation. If conditions B and C were also satisfied, the donation would be tainted and the tax relief denied.
> 6.8 If 'Condition A' is not satisfied (that is, there is no interdependence between the donation and arrangements entered into) the donation is not a tainted charity donation. Conditions B and C can be ignored.

The HMRC Guidance Note does not offer an example of an "artificial avoidance arrangement" which "distances" the donor from the Gift Aid

---

91 The author had overlooked the Gift Aid benefit rule.

donation or the benefit. We are unable to think of any, and are in some doubt whether HMRC could do so.

Annex viii HMRC Guidance Note continues:

> 8.3 Example 3
> Mr A is a trustee of 2 charities, charity B and charity C. Charity B is responsible for running a college and Charity C provides financial support for the college.
> Mr A also controls company D which runs a leisure facility (swimming pool, gym, squash) which is used by the students of the college during school hours and fee-paying members of the public outside school hours.
> Company D wants to expand the leisure facility to allow opening to the public in the day and to provide more up-market facilities. In other words, this is a wholly commercial development.
> To fund this, company D offers interest-free loan stock.
> Mr A makes a Gift Aid donation of £100,000 to charity B.
> Company D issues interest free loan stock of £125,000.
> Charity B subscribes for £125,000 of the loan stock and requests it be issued in the name of charity C.

The short facts, ignoring the irrelevancies, are that the donor makes a gift to the charity and the charity makes an interest-free loan to the company. Nothing turns on the additional complications.

The HMRC analysis is as follows:

> 8.4 In this example the donation is a tainted charity donation. There's an arrangement in place that, in connection with the donation, the charity will provide an interest free loan (by buying loan stock) to a company connected with the donor and the donation wouldn't have been made and the arrangements would not have been entered into independently of one another. Therefore, 'Condition A' of the new legislation will be satisfied.
> 8.5 A main purpose of entering into the arrangement is for the donor to obtain a financial advantage, in this instance, an interest-free loan for his company, enhanced by the Gift Aid repayment claimed by Charity B, and therefore 'Condition B' is satisfied. The donor isn't a charity-owned company or relevant housing authority so 'Condition C' is satisfied and the donation is therefore a tainted charity donation.

This arrangement is obviously caught by the charitable expenditure rules. The £125k is not applied for charitable purposes only. Accordingly it is non-charitable expenditure under s.543(1)(f) ITA, and the charitable expenditure rules apply.[92]

There is also a benefit to the company as a result of the gift. The subscription of the interest free debenture is as clear a case of a benefit as one could wish for. The company (being controlled by Mr A) is a connected person. Accordingly Gift Aid does not apply to the gift by Mr A.

Further, the payment by charity C is a self-evident breach of trust. HMRC should report that to the charity commission who should:

(1) take proceedings on behalf of the charity to recover the loss caused by the breach of trust, and
(2) in the absence of mitigating circumstances, which we think unlikely, remove the trustees of the charities.

7.26.1 *Conclusion*

HMRC firmly believed that tainted donation rules were needed. However they have been unable to provide any example of what they actually are needed for.

Evasion or avoidance should be countered by enforcing the law, not by introducing new laws.

If any gap in existing legislation could be identified (which we would not rule out, though so far it has not been done) the first step should be to see if existing legislation can conveniently be amended to cover it. The starting point should not be to devise a new and complex anti-avoidance code which is added to existing anti-avoidance codes.

In failing to approach the matter this way, the legislation is in breach of Hampton principles.[93]

We take the view that there is no need for the rules; though it is difficult to prove a negative, it is at least clear that no case for the rules has ever been made out.

HMRC may take the view that it is convenient to have tainted donation

---

92 The better view is also that charity C's transaction is a loan within s.543(1)(j) ITA, which would bring the charitable expenditure rules into effect; though it is not necessary for HMRC to rely on that.

93 Hampton, "Reducing administrative burdens: effective inspection and enforcement" (2000) *https://webarchive.nationalarchives.gov.uk/20090609014248/http://www.berr.gov.uk/files/file22988.pdf*
The principles include: "When new policies are being developed, explicit consideration should be given to how they can be enforced using existing systems … to minimise the administrative burden imposed."

rules and since they do no harm, and may help them in cases of abuse, it is not necessary to demonstrate need. The reader who has labouriously worked through this chapter is not likely to agree. The burden for those in the charity sector who take the law seriously is considerable. If one takes them seriously, the rules are baffling, if not incomprehensible, and constitute the "red tape" that the government have said they are trying to avoid.

7.26.2 *Consultation*

Prior to the introduction of the tainted donation rules there was an informal and confidential consultation with charities. The unsatisfactory nature of confidential consultation was recognised in the Tax Consultation Framework:

> Where possible, the Government will[94] ... minimise the occasions on which it consults only on a confidential basis.[95]

Nothing confidential was actually disclosed in the course of the consultation.

The paper adds:

> Where confidential consultation has been necessary the Government will be as transparent as possible about its outcome and consult openly if pursuing the policy change further.

That did not happen. Official government policy on consultation is that:

> 6.1 All responses ... should be analysed carefully, using the expertise, experiences and views of respondents to develop a more effective and efficient policy. The focus should be on the evidence given by

---

94 A footnote adds: "Subject to the exceptions set out at 8 and 9." These provide: "8. The Government will generally not consult on straightforward rates, allowances and threshold changes, or other minor measures; recognising, however, that even in these cases some level of consultation can often be informative. It may also adopt a different approach for revenue protection or anti-avoidance measures where following this Framework could present a risk to the Exchequer. In other circumstances where the Government decides not to consult during tax policy development it will explain the reasons for that decision.
9. There will be times when it will be necessary to deviate from this Framework. In these circumstances the Government will be as open as possible about the reasons for such deviations."

95 *http://webarchive.nationalarchives.gov.uk/20110615132304/http://www.hmrc.gov.uk/consultations/tax-consultation-framework.pdf* (March 2011)

> consultees to back up their arguments. Analysing consultation responses is primarily a qualitative rather than a quantitative exercise...
> 6.4 Following a consultation exercise, the Government should provide a summary of who responded to the consultation exercise and a summary of the views expressed to each question. A summary of any other significant comments should also be provided. This feedback should normally set out what decisions have been taken in light of what was learnt from the consultation exercise. This information should normally be published before or alongside any further action, e.g. laying legislation before Parliament.[96]

This did not happen. The rules could probably not have been enacted if it had been.

It is easier to announce good intentions than to abide by them.

It is no answer to say, as does EN FB 2011, that the "vast majority of donors do not need to consider these new rules." That is no doubt true. However since most of the population of the UK give to charity, the remaining tiny minority is a very large number; moreover donors and their advisers need to keep the rules in mind in order to know whether or not they need to consider them.

No lessons were learnt from the debacle of the former substantial donor rules[97] so it should not be surprising to find the same mistakes repeated.

---

96 Better Regulation Executive Department for Business, Enterprise and Regulatory Reform "Code of Practice on Consultation" (July 2008) *http://www.bis.gov.uk/files/file47158.pdf*

97 See App 7.3 (What went wrong: Critique).

CHAPTER EIGHT

TRADING BY CHARITIES

Cross references

The following topics are considered elsewhere:

6.31 (Trading losses of primary purpose trade)

Trading companies held by charities are considered in the next chapter.

8.1 Trade carried on by charity

A charity's activities may constitute a trade:

> Now it is perfectly clear that a body like this, which is a charity, may trade ... As good an illustration as any of a trade which is carried on by a Society which was not a trading society, if I may use that expression, is the Religious Tract Society's case.[1] That was a Society for the dissemination of religious literature and that is all, but, incidentally and subsidiarily, they did keep a shop where they sold religious literature in a commercial way and made a profit, and the profit was applied, of course, to the general funds of their Society, and it was not questioned and could not be questioned that the profits of that shop were taxable.[2]

It does not matter that it is not the charity's intention to make a profit:

> Then it appears to me also that it does not prevent operations amounting to a trade if they are not undertaken with the intention of making profits. ... If you do the operations of trading and make a profit, it seems to me that you are carrying on a trade, which in that case becomes taxable, and you are carrying on a trade whether you make a profit or not, and whether you want to make a profit or not, because it is not a mere question of motive.[3]

It does not matter that the charity applies the profit for charitable purposes:

> Another thing that must be borne in mind is that it is quite clear that the application of the profits, when they are made, does not affect Income Tax. Everybody agrees to that. I say "when made." One has to see first of all, as I understand it, whether, in the case of a body which is not a commercial body or a trading body, you can find embedded in their activities something which is a trade, and if you do, and there is a profit, the tax attaches to that profit, although at a later stage its use is in furtherance of the objects of the Society which are not commercial. ...[4]

These points were reaffirmed in *Brighton College v Marriot* 10 TC 213 and the law has long been settled.

8.2 What is a trade

The rule that a profit motive is not required for a trade does not answer the

---

1 *Religious Tract and Book Society of Scotland v Forbes* 3 TC 415.

2 *Royal Agricultural Society of England v Wilson* 9 TC 62. This was before the introduction of the exemption for primary purpose trading.

3 *Royal Agricultural Society of England v Wilson* 9 TC 62.

4 *Royal Agricultural Society of England v Wilson* 9 TC 62.

question of what *is* required for an activity to constitute a trade.[5]

Examples of trading activities carried on by charities include:

(1) A restaurant[6]
(2) Publishing and selling books[7]
(3) A school[8]
(4) Public shows and festivals[9]
(5) Regular public dances[10]

The question whether some specific activities are trades is discussed elsewhere, see:

Topic	**See para**
Swaps	4.18
Lotteries	8.10.2
Fundraising events	8.14.1
Sponsorship	10.2

In *Church Body of the Hong Kong Sheng Kung Hui v IRC*[11] a charity developed an orphanage into residential property. It ceased to use the building as an orphanage. It instructed architects and obtained planning permission. It instructed lawyers and obtained a surrender and regrant of its lease. It marketed the land by approaching developers for offers. The Hong Kong Court of Final Appeal, applying UK case law,[12] held that the charity, which was clearly not originally a trader, had not commenced a trade.

8.2.1 *Sale of donated goods*

HMRC Guidance Note Annex iv provides:

> 17. Many charities raise funds by selling donated goods (items gifted to a charity which the charity sells on its own behalf), such as clothes, books or bric-a-brac. This may be a regular activity carried on at a shop

---

5 See too Kessler, *Taxation of Non-Residents and Foreign Domiciliaries* (21st ed., 2022-23) para 21.2 (Charge on trading income).

6 *Grove v YMCA* 4 TC 613.

7 *Religious Tract and Book Society v IRC* 3 TC 415; *Trustees of Psalms and Hymns v Whitwell* 3 TC 7.

8 *Brighton College v Marriot* 10 TC 213.

9 *Royal Agricultural Society of England v Wilson*; *IRC v Glasgow Music Festival Association* 11 TC 154.

10 See 8.14.1 (Are fundraising events a trade).

11 FACV 16/2015 see *http://www.info.gov.hk/bor/en/court-judgments.htm*

12 including *Taylor v Good* 49 TC 277 and *Lionel Simmons v IRC* 53 TC 461.

> or it may be an occasional activity carried on at a jumble sale or auction. At first glance this may appear to be a trade similar to the retail sale of goods by other commercial businesses. But the way in which the goods are acquired makes it different from most retail trades.
>
> Traders usually sell goods that they've manufactured, or have purchased for resale they don't usually receive goods by way of donation as charities do. For the charity the sale proceeds are simply a realisation of the value of a gift. For this reason the sale of donated goods is generally not regarded as a trade for tax purposes.
>
> This is so even where the donated items are sorted, cleaned and given minor repairs. If the goods are subjected to significant refurbishment or to any process which brings them into a different condition for sale purposes than that in which they were donated, the sale proceeds may be regarded as trading income. For example, where donated cloth is made into garments for sale this will amount to a trade.

This is correct. The Charities SORP takes the same view referring to secondhand goods donated for resale:

> 6.27. In accepting donated goods for resale, the charity is receiving a gift in kind on trust for conversion into cash to fund the charity's activities. Where practicable, donated goods for resale are measured at fair value on initial recognition, which is the expected proceeds from sale less the expected costs of sale.[13]

Similarly the sale of other donated assets (including land and shares qualifying for IT relief) is not a trade.

8.2.2 *Rent or trading income?*

HMRC Guidance Note Annex iv provides:

> 19. All rental income received by a charity from land or buildings is exempt from tax provided the profits arising are applied for charitable purposes. ...
>
> However, if services are provided along with the use of the land or buildings, for example, provision of a caretaker, food or laundry, these services in themselves might amount to trading. Letting activity will itself constitute a trade where the owner remains in occupation of the property and provides services over and above those usually provided by

---

13 Charities SORP FRS 102. See too *Ransom v Higgs* 50 TC 1 at p.98 where Lord Cross noted that "a man who expended time and trouble in establishing an ascendancy over a wealthy relative with the object of causing him to settle some property on him and his family", in modern terms, a legacy hunter, is not carrying on a trade.

> a landlord. Essentially the distinction lies between the hotelier (who is carrying on a trade) and the provider of furnished accommodation (who isn't). An important difference is that in a hotel etc. the occupier of the room doesn't acquire any legal interest in the property. Each case must be considered on its own facts.

This only summarises the distinction between a property business and a trade. For the HMRC view in slightly more detail see Property Income Manual para 4300 [July 2017]. A discussion is outside the scope of this book.

8.2.3 *Uncommercial activity not trading*

An activity which cannot be carried on at a profit is not a trade. An activity not conducted in a commercial manner is not in principle a trade.

Religious Tract and Book Society of Scotland v Forbes concerned the activity of colportage (bible selling by door-to-door salesmen):

> the colportage agency could not be carried on at a profit as a commercial undertaking, and is persevered in merely because the Society find that by appealing to the religious public they are able to obtain subscriptions which enable them to fill up the deficit. When we turn to the methods of the colportage it appears that they are not commercial methods, that is to say, that the business carried on is not purely that of pushing the sale of their goods, but that on the contrary the duty of the salesman is to dwell over the purchase and make it the occasion of administering religious advice and counsel. Now, under these conditions it seems to me to be impossible to hold that this is a business, trade, or adventure, which is unfortunately resulting in loss. It is really a charitable mission in which the sale of the Scriptures is made the occasion for doing something more than merely effect the sale of books.[14]

If the activity does not produce income, it may not matter whether or not it is classified as a trade. The reported cases arose before the introduction of the exemption for primary purpose trades, when the issue was important, because the charity (unsuccessfully) sought to include the losses in computing the taxable profits of (what was held to be) a separate, profitable trade. It would still matter now in the (rare, perhaps theoretical)

---

14 3 TC 415 at p.418; also see 8.4.2 (Trading/non-trading activities).
Similarly, in *Grove v YMCA* 4 TC 613 the YMCA's educational, gymnasium and publication departments (the fees for which were insufficient to cover expenses) were not trading activities, though the (profitable) YMCA restaurant was a trade.

case where a charity was taxable on its trading profits, or if the loss was non-charitable expenditure; and in the case of clubs and mutual concerns, who may be carrying on a non-trade activity and a trade.[15]

8.3 Charity power to trade

CC35 (Trustees, trading & tax) para 3.2 provides:

> Charity law allows charities to trade provided that the trading falls into one of the following categories:
> [1] 'primary purpose trading' (see 3.6)
> [2] 'ancillary trading' (see 3.7)
> [3] non-primary purpose 'trading' that does not involve significant risk to the resources of the charity (see 3.8)
> Note that the third category of trading listed above, 'non-primary purpose trading' that does not involve significant risk to the resources of the charity, is normally understood to include:
> [4] the conduct of lotteries, subject to conditions (see 3.11)
> [5] trading within the terms of the 'small scale exemption' (see 3.12)
> But it may also include other types of trading: it depends on the circumstances.[16]

The Charity Commission say:

> Our view is that any charity may trade within the limits of this exemption, provided that the governing document does not generally prohibit non-primary purpose trading. The familiar provision[17] which, in the context of conferring a power to raise funds, prohibits "substantial" trading should not be treated as prohibiting trading which falls within this exemption.[18]

8.4 Computing charity trade profit

8.4.1 *GAAP*

Originally the Courts sought to lay down the principles for computing trading profits. But accountants are better suited to this task than lawyers,

15 See 42.6 (Social and recreational clubs: membership activity).

16 The Charity Commission (rightly) disregard an *obiter* comment to the contrary in *Tennent Plays Ltd v IRC* 30 TC 107 at p.125.

17 This is a reference to the Charity Commission's model charitable trust, which confers power to raise funds but subject to the restriction that: "In exercising this power, the Trustees must not undertake any substantial permanent trading activity."

18 OG 63 B2 para 2.

and since 1998, accountancy principles are applied. Older cases need to be reviewed with that in mind:

s.25 ITTOIA	**s.46 CTA 2009**
(1) The profits of a trade must be calculated in accordance with generally accepted accounting practice, subject to any adjustment required or authorised by law in calculating profits for income tax purposes.	(1) The profits of a trade must be calculated in accordance with generally accepted accounting practice, subject to any adjustment required or authorised by law in calculating profits for corporation tax purposes.
(2) This does not— (a) require a person to comply with the requirements of the Companies Act 2006 or subordinate legislation made under that Act except as to the basis of calculation, or (b) impose any requirements as to audit or disclosure.	[identical]
(3) This section is subject to section 25A (cash basis for small businesses).	[Cash basis not applicable to companies]

Thus charitable trusts may qualify for the cash basis, but charitable companies do not; however the point is not likely to arise.

8.4.2 *Trading/non-trading activities*

In order to ascertain the trading profits, one needs to identify what is the trade.

Business Income Manual provides:

> **BIM20415: intention - dual motive transactions - links to non-trading undertakings or charities** [10 Jun 2016]
> Operations carried on in connection with non-trading or charitable activities constitute a trade if they can be segregated and in themselves fulfil the conditions of trading.
> In *Religious Tract and Book Society of Scotland v Forbes* [1896] 3 TC 415, the Society was founded for the diffusion of religious literature and ran a shop for the sale of bibles etc. This shop was carried on along commercial lines and made profits.
> In addition the Society sent out colporteurs whose duties were to sell the

literature and act as cottage missionaries. These latter activities sustained large losses, were not commercial and were not capable of making profits.

The court found that the colportage activities were not a trade and not carried on as part of the business of bookselling. The losses could not be set against the shop profits, which were separately assessable. The Lord President said at page 419:

> "...while I completely assent to the view that the establishment and conduct of the shops and the establishment and conduct of the `colportage all rest upon the same ultimate motive, yet at the same time the two operations seem to be essentially distinguished. The shops are simply bookseller's shops - the other is a combination of the sale of books with a missionary enterprise...".

See also *Brighton College v Marriott* [1925] 10 TC 213, *Earl of Jersey's Executors v Bassom* [1926] 10 TC 357, *Earl of Derby v Bassom* [1926] 10 TC 357 and *British Legion, Peterhead Branch, Remembrance and Welcome Home Fund v IRC* [1953] 35 TC 509.

Once such a trade has been identified, you should ensure that income and expenditure attributable to non-commercial operations is excluded from the computation of trading profit.

The manner in which profits from a trading activity are applied does not have any bearing in deciding whether that activity amounts to trade.

Voluntary organisations, such as local committees or Round Tables, may have activities that amount to trading, such as occasional sales of goods from shops or stalls, running donkey derbys, fireworks displays, carnivals and other events. BIM24792 onwards give guidance on the treatment of the profits of such a trade. The online detailed guidance note Charities - Trading and business activities sets out the guidelines on the tax treatment of trades carried on by charities.

8.4.3 *Allocation to deemed trade*

Where a charity is deemed to carry on two trades (one primary purpose and one not) it must somehow allocate expenses and receipts between them. Similarly, allocation of overheads is required where a charity incurs overheads partly for trading and partly for non-trading charitable purposes. HMRC Guidance Note Annex iv provides:

> **37. Direct tax: what profits are taxable?**
>
> Trading receipts should be allocated to the sources listed in paragraph 4 above on a reasonable basis. The profits of taxable non-charitable trading, including capital allowances if applicable, should be calculated in the same way as for any other trader. This may involve apportioning

what was originally charitable trading expenditure to a non-charitable or deemed non-charitable trade. Any such apportionment will apply only for tax purposes.

For most charities the challenge will be to maintain adequate accounting systems to properly identify the separate charitable and non-charitable deemed trades, in order to allocate and where necessary apportion costs to each. Charities are strongly recommended to do this. The approach may vary. For example, there could be a 'high level' approach of identifying the trading activity of a particular department, division or building, etc. as charitable or non-charitable. Alternatively, there might be a 'middle level' approach of, for example, identifying particular contracts or projects, or the work of individuals as charitable or non-charitable. At the most detailed level, charities might identify each individual piece of work done, flag it charitable or non-charitable in the accounting system, and allocate costs accordingly

HMRC's view is that a high or medium level approach may be justified on the facts – a department or a project may be identifiable as wholly charitable or wholly non-charitable. However, this approach would be inappropriate for mixed charitable/non-charitable activity. In HMRC's view, a detailed or 'low level' approach to accounting for charitable and non-charitable activity will be more appropriate. This will give the greatest accuracy and take the least risks with charity law, which places a responsibility on trustees to identify charitable purpose trading carried on by the charity for which they bear responsibility.

There are further factors, discussed below, that may be particularly relevant when calculating the profits of a trade carried on by a charity.

The Guidance Note Annex iv provides:

38. Direct tax: allocation of Indirect Overheads and Costs

For a non-charitable trade s.479(4) CTA 2010 and s.525(4) ITA 2007 requires that there be a 'reasonable apportionment of expenses and receipts'. This will involve taking into account direct expenditure and a reasonable proportion of indirect expenditure such as overheads, whether or not these were originally incurred for charitable purposes.

For example, if a non-charitable trading activity is the charity's only trading activity, is carried on in the charity's premises and takes 30% of the floor area, it might be proper to allocate to the non primary purpose trade 30% of the costs of the premises such as:

[1] heat and light

[2] rent

[3] building repairs and maintenance.

Apart from the use of premises, other indirect overheads that may be

partly attributable to the trade are:
[1] employee salaries
[2] computer costs
[3] telephone charges
[4] postage costs
[5] accountancy and legal fees
[6] general administration.
The proper basis of apportionment of indirect costs will depend on the facts. In the case of the use of premises, the apportionment might be based on:
[1] the size of floor space allocated to the trade.
[2] where student accommodation is let to tourists out of term, the number of days in the year when the premises are allocated to the trade, and actively marketed.
[3] in the case of employee salaries, the amount of employee time devoted to the trade compared to total employee time.

The principles of cost apportionment are discussed in Chapter 3 of The Corporation Tax Treatment of UK Universities Guidance Note Agreed Guidelines[19] (though necessarily at a fairly high level of generality, and it all comes down to common sense.) However since charities should arrange that taxable trades are carried on in subsidiaries, it should not often be necessary to consider this.

8.4.4 *Provision to trader at undervalue*

The Guidance Note Annex iv provides:

39. Direct Tax: goods or services provided at undervalue
It is common for charities to receive goods or services in their trades at no cost, or at less than their full market price. For example:
[1] a supplier might sell trading stock or equipment to a charity at cost price
[2] a professional adviser might provide services for no charge
[3] helpers and beneficiaries might do work on a voluntary basis.
Where a charity (but not a charity subsidiary company) receives goods or services free, or at less than their full market price, the charity may deduct a notional cost/market price when computing the profits of the trade. Notional costs/market price should be calculated on a reasonable basis. For example, were a celebrity to act as a volunteer waiter at a gala

---

19 *https://www.bufdg.ac.uk/ViewDocument.aspx?t=1&ID=2362&GUID=5411732f-0599-45f6-8390-9c4c17ae92bd&dl=1*

dinner, the notional cost would need to be restricted to the going rate for the employment of a waiter, not that of the celebrity.[20] Market price will be the wholesale or trade price at which the charity could reasonably have expected to buy the goods or services in, not the retail value of those goods or services.

In relation to a charity trader, this follows the approach of *British Legion, Peterhead Branch v IRC* 35 TC 509.

The Business Income Manual provides:

BIM24475: Meaning of trade: mutual trading and members clubs: allowable expenditure: the 'Peterhead' principle [Jun 2016]
In the case of *British Legion, Peterhead Branch, Remembrance and Welcome Home Fund v. IRC* [1953] 35 TC 509 the weekly holding of public dances was held to amount to a trade within Case I of Schedule D.
The Fund, a local committee of the British Legion, held public dances weekly from June, 1944, to June, 1947, in the local drill hall.
The Fund only paid a nominal sum for use of the facilities. All management services were given gratuitously by members of the Legion. The charge for admission was 2s. 6d. per head, but considerably more was often given by those who could afford it...
The question then arose as to the amounts properly deductible in computing the profits of the Fund's trade. The court decided that the Fund should be allowed a deduction for the expenses that would have been incurred if the Legion had not provided facilities and services on a gratuitous or nominal basis.
...
At a practical level you should also bear in mind that the application of the principle approved of in the *Peterhead* decision can have a substantial effect in decreasing taxable profits where significant facilities or services have been provided gratuitously or at considerable undervalue – in Peterhead it was accepted the taxable profits were only just over one third of the declared surplus. This principle only applies in cases of the type considered in *Peterhead*.

BIM24796. Voluntary organisations & charities: Trading profits: Donations etc – not assessable [Dec 2013]
The 'Peterhead' principle
Where profits arise to a voluntary organisation or a charity from

20 The example is somewhat fanciful, but a gala dinner is in principle exempt as a fundraising event so the question of computing trading profits would not arise.

> activities that do not satisfy the conditions in BIM24794, such as weekly dances organised to raise funds to build a village community centre, the taxable profits should be limited to the profits computed on a commercial basis. Any donations should accordingly be excluded from receipts. And if a hall or room, or the services of officials, are obtained free (or at reduced rates), you may deduct (in arriving at the profits to be assessed) an amount to give the equivalent deduction to the commercial value of the facilities or services so obtained (see the remarks of the Lord President in *British Legion, Peterhead Branch, Remembrance and Welcome Home Fund v. IRC* [1953] 35 TC 509).

In relation to a non-charitable trading subsidiary, the position according to the HMRC Guidance Note is different. Whether or not this is right must strictly depend on accountancy practice. We think it unlikely that accountancy practice would draw a distinction between the method of computing trading profits of a charity and the method of computing trading profits of a charity subsidiary. In practice the point may not often arise because the profits will pass to the charity by way of corporate Gift Aid. In addition, where the charity subsidiary receives services from the parent charity, these services should normally be paid for at cost.

HMRC Guidance Note at Annex iv para 50 provides:

> [1] If a charity's premises, staff and services are shared with its trading company an appropriate allocation of the costs should be included in the company's accounts. The amount charged by the charity for the shared resources should generally not exceed the cost.
> [2] [a] However, where the charity is demonstrably trading in the services etc which it's providing, then there should be an appropriate mark-up.
> [b] Any profit in the hands of the charity may be taxable as non-exempt trading income.

We are doubtful about point [2][a], but in practice it will be unusual for a charity to be "demonstrably trading in the services which it is providing".

8.5 Appropriation to/from trading stock

8.5.1 *Appropriation to trading stock*

Section 161(1) TCGA provides:

> Subject to subsections (3) to (3ZB) below, where
> [a] an asset acquired by a person otherwise than as trading stock of a trade carried on by him is appropriated by him for the purposes of the

trade as trading stock (whether on the commencement of the trade or otherwise) and,

[b] if he had then sold the asset for its market value, a chargeable gain or allowable loss would have accrued to him,

he shall be treated as having thereby disposed of the asset by selling it for its then market value.

It is doubtful whether this applies to charities, as the condition in s.161(1)[b] is not met: a sale for market value would normally qualify for the charity's CGT exemption. If this does apply, the deemed gain may qualify for relief.[21]

8.5.2 *Election out of deemed disposal*

For completeness: s.161(3) TCGA provides:

> [A] Subject to subsection (4) below, subsection (1) above shall not apply in relation to a person's appropriation of an asset for the purposes of a trade if
>
> (a) he is chargeable to corporation tax in respect of the profits of the trade under Chapter 2 of Part 3 of CTA 2009 and the trade is carried on wholly or partly in the United Kingdom, or
>
> (b) he is chargeable to income tax in respect of the profits of the trade under Chapter 2 of Part 2 of ITTOIA 2005 and the trade is carried on wholly or partly in the United Kingdom,
>
> and he elects that instead the market value of the asset at the time of the appropriation shall, in computing the profits of the trade for purposes of tax, be treated as reduced by the amount of the chargeable gain or increased by the amount of the allowable loss referred to in subsection (1),
>
> [B] and where that subsection does not apply by reason of such an election, the profits of the trade shall be computed accordingly.

8.5.3 *Appropriation from trading stock/cessation of trade*

Section 161(2) TCGA provides:

> If at any time an asset forming part of the trading stock of a person's trade
>
> [a] is appropriated by him for any other purpose, or
>
> [b] is retained by him on his ceasing to carry on the trade,
>
> he shall be treated as having acquired it at that time for a consideration

---

21 See 5.5 (Deemed gain).

equal to the amount brought into the accounts of the trade in respect of it for tax purposes on the appropriation or on his ceasing to carry on the trade, as the case may be.

The remaining subsections of s.161 deal with specialist topics which need not be discussed here: ATED, procedure for elections, and Transactions in Land rules.

8.6 Trading income exemptions: Outline

There are six exemptions. Trading income outside the exemptions is taxable. The exemptions are:

(1) Charitable Trades:
  (a) Trade which is a primary purpose of the charity (**"Primary Purpose Trade"**)
  (b) Trade carried out by beneficiaries of the charity (**"Beneficiary Worker Trade"**)
(2) Lottery
(3) Fundraising event
(4) Small trade
(5) Agricultural show

These are considered in turn.

8.7 Charitable trade

Section 524 ITA provides:

> **524 Exemption for profits etc of charitable trades**
> (1) The income mentioned in subsection (2) is not taken into account in calculating total income if conditions A and B are met.

We refer to **"trading conditions A and B"**.

> (2) The income referred to in subsection (1) is
> (a) the profits of a trade carried on by a charitable trust,
> (b) amounts treated as adjustment income of a charitable trust under s.228 of ITTOIA 2005 in respect of a trade carried on by the trust, and
> (c) post-cessation receipts arising from a trade carried on by a charitable trust which are received by the trustees of the trust or to which they are entitled.

Section 524(3) ITA provides:

> Condition A is—

> (a) in the case of the profits of a trade, that the profits are profits of a tax year in relation to which the trade is a charitable trade,
> (b) in the case of an amount treated as adjustment income, that the amount arises in a tax year in relation to which the trade is a charitable trade, and
> (c) in the case of a post-cessation receipt, that the trade was a charitable trade in relation to the tax year in which the cessation occurred.

The key term here is "charitable trade" which takes us to s.525(1) ITA:

> For the purposes of this Part a trade carried on by a charitable trust is a charitable trade in relation to a tax year if throughout the basis period for the tax year—
> (a) the trade is exercised in the course of carrying out a primary purpose of the charitable trust, or
> (b) the work in connection with the trade is mainly carried out by beneficiaries of the charitable trust.

The CT equivalent is s.478 CTA 2010 which is slightly differently worded but effectively the same:

> (1) The income mentioned in subsection (2) is not taken into account in calculating total profits if the condition in subsection (3) is met.
> (2) The income referred to in subsection (1) is—
> (a) profits of a charitable trade carried on by a charitable company, and
> (b) post-cessation receipts arising from a charitable trade carried on by a charitable company which are received by the company or to which it is entitled.
> (3) The condition is that the profits are, or (as the case may be) the post-cessation receipt is, applied to the purposes of the charitable company only.
> ...
> (5) The exemption under subsection (1) requires a claim.

Section 479 CTA 2010 defines "charitable trade":

> (1) For the purposes of this Part a trade carried on by a charitable company is a charitable trade if—
> (a) the trade is exercised in the course of carrying out a primary purpose of the charitable company, or
> (b) the work in connection with the trade is mainly carried out by beneficiaries of the charitable company...

8.8 Ascertaining primary purposes

The primary purpose of a charity matters for:

Topic	**See para**
Exemption for trading income	*Discussed here*
VAT exemption for subscriptions	37.8
CASC status	41.16

The wording varies somewhat:

Trading exemption	**VAT subscription exemption**	**CASC status**
trade exercised in the course of carrying out a primary purpose of the charitable company	an association, the primary purpose of which is the advancement of a particular branch of knowledge, or the fostering of professional expertise	the club is, and is required by its constitution to be, a club which ... (c) has as its main purpose the provision of facilities for, and the promotion of participation in, one or more eligible sports

But the differences are not material, or at most, are only differences of nuance, so we deal with all three topics here.

Some help may be found from discussion of the expression "primary purpose" elsewhere, or similar expressions such as "main object" or "aim" subject of course to context in each case.[22]

Primary purpose is also relevant for the definition of "public benefit entity" in FRS 102.[23]

---

22 See Kessler, *Taxation of Non-Residents and Foreign Domiciliaries* (21st ed., 2022-23) para 3.17.6 (A choice principle?)
online version *https://www.foreigndomiciliaries.co.uk*

23 The definition is:

> "An entity whose primary objective is to provide goods or services for the general public, community or social benefit and where any equity is provided with a view to supporting the entity's primary objectives rather than with a view to providing a financial return to equity providers, shareholders or members."

FRS provides:

> "The term 'public benefit entity' does not necessarily imply that the purpose of the entity is for the benefit of the public as a whole. For example, many PBEs exist for the direct benefit of a particular group of people, although it is possible that society as a whole also benefits indirectly. The important factor is what the primary purpose

There could be two distinct questions: what are the purpose(s) of the charity and (if more than one) which are the primary purpose(s)? In practice the two questions tend to coalesce.

HMRC Guidance Note Annex iv para 6 gives six uncontentious examples of primary purpose trading.[24]

CC35 para 3.6 provides:

> 'Primary purpose trading' is trading which contributes directly to one or more of the objects of a charity as set out in its governing document.

The purposes of a charity should be, and normally will be, set out in its constitution.[25] HMRC Guidance Note Annex iv para 6 states that the primary purposes of a charity "can be identified from the charity's trust deed, constitution or other governing document".

The constitution may identify primary and non-primary purposes but that will be unusual. If the purposes are focussed and reasonably expressed, they should be the only (and hence the primary) purposes.

If the governing document is unclear (eg expressed in very general terms or lost) regard must necessarily be had to the views of the charity trustees

---

of such an entity is, and that it does not exist primarily to provide economic benefit to its investors. Organisations such as mutual insurance companies, other mutual co-operative entities and clubs that provide dividends or other economic benefits directly and proportionately to their owners, members or participants are not PBEs. Some PBEs undertake certain activities that are intended to make a surplus in order to fund their primary activities. Consideration should be given to the primary purpose of an entity's (or group's) activities in assessing whether it meets the definition of a PBE. PBEs may have received contributions in the form of equity, even though the entity does not have a primary profit motive. However, because of the fundamental nature of public benefit entities, any such contributions are made by the equity holders of the entity primarily to enable the provision of goods or services to beneficiaries rather than with a view to a financial return for themselves. This is different from the position of lenders; loans do not fall into the category of equity."

https://www.frc.org.uk/Our-Work/Publications/Accounting-and-Reporting-Policy/FRS-102-The-Financial-Reporting-Standard-applicab.pdf

24 [1] provision of educational services by a school or college in return for course fees
[2] holding of an exhibition by an art gallery or museum in return for admission fees
[3] sale of tickets for a theatrical production staged by a theatre
[4] provision of health-care services by a hospital in return for payment
[5] provision of serviced residential accommodation by a residential care home in return for payment
[6] sale of certain educational goods by an art gallery or museum

25 See 3.5.2 (How to ascertain purpose).

and the charity's activities.

The meaning of "primary purpose" is discussed in the context of the VAT exemption for subscriptions. HMRC notice 701/5 clubs and associations[26] provides:

> **11.11 A primary purpose**
> A 'primary purpose' is not necessarily the sole purpose of a society but is the main or principal purpose. An association can only have one primary purpose. The primary purpose should be clear from the following:
> [1] the objects and objectives set out in the association's Memorandum and Articles of Association or constitution
> [2] the powers and actual activities of the association
> [3] what the association itself considers its primary purpose to be.

This is based on *Bookmakers' Protection Association (Southern Area) Ltd v C&E*:

> In our view, in order to determine the "primary purpose" of the [taxpayer]..., we must have regard to the objects set out in its Memorandum and its various activities to determine what its directors and members consider to be the most important matter it is seeking to achieve or doing in return for membership subscriptions. The words "primary purpose" indicate to us that the test is subjective and not purely objective.[27]

British Association for Shooting and Conservation v HMRC endorses point [2] in this list: what matters is the actual activities and not just what the constitution says:[28]

---

26 Published 2013, last updated Dec 2020.

27 [1979] VATTR 215 at p.224. HMRC quote this passage with approval in the Trade Unions and Professional Bodies Manual para 5400 (Primary Purpose). See too *British Association of Leisure Parks, Piers and Attractions v HMRC* [2013] STC 1410.

28 Contrast *IRC v Eversden (Greenstock's Executors)* [2002] STC 1109 at [25] (in the context of s.12 Trusts of Land and Appointment of Trustees Act 1996):

> "The 'purposes' of a trust are primarily to be found in the trust instrument, but may in appropriate cases be found outside it: such purposes may however be expected to be consistent with the contents of the trust instrument."

The point was not discussed in the Court of Appeal. Likewise *City of Glasgow Police Athletic Association* 34 TC 76 at p.98:

> "... in order to ascertain what the purposes of an association are, the Court is not limited to consideration of its rules or its constituent documents. They are very important, and it would be difficult for an association to say that something

> How are you to ascertain the "aims" of an organisation?... the professed aims of an organisation must be tested against what happens in reality.[29]

In relation to the CASC requirement, this is expressed in the statute which requires that the club "*is, and is required by its constitution to be* a club which has as its main purpose" the promotion of sport.[30] In other cases this particular wording is not used, but the position is the same because it is implicit that what matters is not only what is meant to be done but what is actually done.

In practice, the main (perhaps the only) example of non-primary purpose trading is trading carried out not in order to carry out the charitable objects, but to raise funds to carry out the charitable objects.[31]

8.8.1 *More than 1 primary purpose*

The wording in the definition of charitable trade is "a" primary purpose. That shows a charity can have more than one primary purpose.

HMRC say in the context of the VAT exemption for subscriptions that "an association can only have one primary purpose". The wording is different in that context ("the" primary purpose); but even there we consider that an association may have more than one primary purpose, because the singular includes the plural. But in practice the issue will not often arise.

8.8.2 *Ancillary trade*

HMRC Guidance Note Annex iv provides:

> 7. Exemption from tax is also extended to other trading which, although not overtly primary purpose in nature, is ancillary to the carrying out of a primary purpose of a charity. This trading can still be said to be exercised in the course of the carrying out of a primary purpose of a charity and is, therefore, part of a primary purpose trade. Examples of trading which qualifies as primary purpose because it is ancillary to the carrying out of a primary purpose are:

---

declared in its rules to be its object was not one of its purposes. But it is quite in order for the association to prove by parole evidence that it had other purposes than that set down in the rules."

29 [2009] STC 1421.

30 See 41.16 (Main purpose promotion of sport).

31 The courts have imposed a similar rule for rating relief: see 40.7 ("Used for charitable purposes").

[1] the sale of relevant goods or provision of services, for the benefit of students by a school or college (text books, for example)

[2] the provision of a crèche for the children of students by a school or college in return for payment

[3] the sale of food and drink in a cafeteria to visitors to exhibits by an art gallery or museum (although sale to the general public, as opposed to exhibition visitors, is non-primary purpose trading)

[4] the sale of food and drink in a restaurant or bar to members of the audience by a theatre (although sale to the general public, as opposed to the audience, is non-primary purpose trading)

[5] the sale by able bodied staff of items produced by the disabled in a disabled workshop

[6] the sale of confectionery, toiletries and flowers to patients and their visitors by a hospital.

It is helpful to see this confirmed as the HMRC view.

The distinction between:

(1) trading which is "not overtly primary purpose in nature but which is ancillary to the carrying out of a primary purpose"; and

(2) trading which is "partly primary purpose and partly non-primary purpose"

is a fine one.

CC35 para 3.7 explains the distinction neatly:

> 'Ancillary trading' contributes indirectly to the successful furtherance of the purposes of the charity.

8.8.3 *Trade partly primary purpose*

Section 525(2) ITA provides:

> For the purposes of subsection (1)(a), if a trade is exercised partly in the course of carrying out a primary purpose of the charitable trust and partly otherwise, each part is to be treated as a separate trade...

The deemed separate trade that is not carried on for primary purposes of the charity will be taxable unless it qualifies for the small trade exemption. Section 525(4) ITA explains how to compute its profits:

> If different parts of a trade are treated as separate trades under subsection (2) or (3), a just and reasonable apportionment is to be made for that purpose of—
>
> (a) expenses and receipts of the trade, and
>
> (b) any amounts which are treated as adjustment income under

> s.228 of ITTOIA 2005 in respect of the trade, or which are post-cessation receipts arising from the trade for the purposes of Chapter 18 of Part 2 of that Act.

The corporation tax equivalent is s.479 CTA 2010.
HMRC Guidance Note provides:

> 8. Under general case law charities will have only 1 trade. For some charities the trade will be a combination of a charitable trade (primary purpose or carried out by beneficiaries) and partly non-charitable trade (non-primary purpose and not carried out by beneficiaries). For example, the trade might deal in a range of goods or services only some of which are within, or ancillary to, a primary purpose. Or the trade might deal with some customers who cannot properly be regarded as beneficiaries of the charity. Examples of such trading include:
> a shop in an art gallery or museum which sells a range of goods, some of which are related to a primary purpose of the charity (direct reproductions of exhibits with no other function, (therefore excluding for example, mugs and postcards), catalogues, etc), and some of which aren't (promotional pens, mugs, tea towels, stamps, all postcards, etc)
> the letting of serviced accommodation for students in term-time (primary purpose), and for tourists out of term (non-primary purpose), by a school or college
> the sale of food and drink in a theatre restaurant or bar both to members of the audience (beneficiaries of the charity - ancillary) and the general public (non-beneficiaries - not ancillary)
> the operation of a café by a 'relief of the disabled' charity where only 50% of the staff are disabled (beneficiaries) and the other 50% are not charitable beneficiaries
> In these circumstances, the charitable part and the non-charitable part of the trade are deemed to be 2 separate trades - sections 479(2) and (3) CTA 2010 (for corporate charities) and sections 525(2) and (3) ITA 2007 (for charitable trusts) apply. The profit from the deemed charitable trade is exempt from tax, as long as it is used for charitable purposes. The profit from the deemed non-charitable trade is taxable unless it's exempt under the small scale trading exemption (see paragraph 13).
> Any receipts or expenses relating to the overall trade should be apportioned to the separate trades on a reasonable basis.
> These rules apply for chargeable periods, that is, tax years for charitable trusts and accounting periods for other charities, beginning on or after 22 March 2006. Charities should ensure they have accounting systems that permit the identification of charitable and non-charitable trading, and the proper allocation of receipts and expenses to each.

The splitting of a trade in this way will not always help charities. For example, suppose a college makes losses on the accommodation it provides for its students. During vacations, it may host conferences at a profit. Before 2006 the two activities could properly be regarded as part of one overall trade, which would not be taxable as it made no profit. But now, the profitable part will be taxed.

Where a trade is partly primary purpose, it may be advantageous to arrange that the primary purpose part is carried on by the charity and the rest is carried on by a non-charitable subsidiary. In some cases it may be convenient for the subsidiary to act as undisclosed agent of the charity, but the documentation would need some care.

Because of this rule, it makes little difference whether a charity actually carries on one trade or two or more distinct trades.

8.8.4 *HMRC clearance*

For registered social landlords, HMRC give guidance on the scope of the trading exemption. The HMRC Guidance Note provides:

> **vii.3 Clearance by HMRC**
> vii.3.1 Before undertaking any housing development, RSLs need to be certain that their property sales will be treated as charitable or non-charitable trading. For smaller and more straightforward developments, this should be obvious. But HMRC recognises that some social housing developments are big, financially complex, or take a long time to complete, for example because of land assembly or planning discussions.
> vii.3.2 In these exceptional cases, RSLs may want reassurance about the likely tax position, either at an early stage or if the scope of the development changes, to help inform their decisions.
> vii.3.3 This clearance process isn't required for every scheme, but provides certainty in those cases where there may be doubt that an intended activity is charitable.
> vii.3.4 Any advice given in response to these requests is governed by HMRC's guidance on Clearances and Approvals CAP1.

The HMRC Guidance Note then rightly provides:

> vii.3.5 This is a formal clearance process and you can rely on the advice of HMRC provided that your written application for advice sets out all the relevant facts and issues. This should include the:
> - total number of dwellings in the development
> - number of dwellings for outright sale
> - number for sale on a shared ownership basis

- number for social renting

Written clearance requests should be sent to the Charities Technical team at HMRC.

The Charity Commission Guidance Notes add:

> C7.6. So it is in your interests, as a charitable RSL, to complete the clearance form as fully and accurately as possible, giving full details of:
>
> - homes being developed; and
> - how these are split between rented and home ownership provision; and
> - which homes are likely to be sold to charitable beneficiaries and on what terms.
>
> Any failure to do so may be regarded as evasion.[32] If the scope of a development changes later, you should make a fresh application.
>
> C7.7. The clearance process aims to provide certainty on the tax treatment of trading by charitable RSLs. With proper consideration, it should be possible to plan housing developments to comply with the principles of primary purpose trading in charity tax law. Sometimes, activity on a particular development may not be as charitable as you originally intended. The clearance process may help to show where you could take compensatory action elsewhere. In some circumstances, you may decide that it is more straightforward or administratively cheaper to accept at the outset that a development is non-primary purpose trading and therefore taxable.[33]

This text is not in the HMRC Guidance Note, though the reason for the omission is not clear.

It is hard to see why this practice should be limited to RSLs and presumably that just reflects effective lobbying on their behalf. Other charities could seek similar guidance. para 3.6 (Further information) provides:

> HMRC Charities will advise trustees whether, in their opinion, a particular activity is within the definition of primary purpose trading.

---

32 [Footnote added] This sentence is very heavy handed. It should state only that material non-disclosure will invalidate any clearance.

33 Affordable Home Ownership – Charitable Status and Tax - Joint guidance from HMRC, the Charity Commission and the Housing Corporation *https://www.gov.uk/government/uploads/system/uploads/attachment_data/file/355526/Affordable_home_ownership_charitable_status_and_tax.pdf*

8.9 Beneficiary worker trade

Section 525(1) ITA provides:

> For the purposes of this Part a trade carried on by a charitable trust is a charitable trade in relation to a tax year if throughout the basis period for the tax year ...
>
> (b) the work in connection with the trade is mainly carried out by beneficiaries[34] of the charitable trust.

The corporation tax equivalent is s.479(1)(b) CTA 2010.

This is a rare case. Trades of this kind would generally qualify for the "primary purpose" exemption: the trades are one of the primary purposes of the charity. There are two reported cases where a claim for this narrow exemption has succeeded. These concerned the period 1921 – 1927, where charities enjoyed only the beneficiary workers exemption. The cases now are of little interest, and are mentioned only for completeness. In *IRC v Glasgow Music Festival Association* 11 TC 154 the Association qualified for the exemption, the (volunteer) choirs being the beneficiaries of the charity. In *Convent of the Blessed Sacrament, Brighton v IRC* 18 TC 76 the school run by the convent qualified for the exemption, the nuns who were teachers being the beneficiaries. In both cases, the trade would now qualify for exemption under the primary purpose exemption.

HMRC Guidance Note Annex iv provides:

> **10. Trading where the work is carried out by beneficiaries of the charity**
>
> Charities can claim exemption from tax on the profits of a trade where the work in connection with the trade is mainly carried out by beneficiaries of the charity and the profits from the trade are used for the purposes of the charity.
>
> Examples of trades carried on by charities where the work is mainly carried out by beneficiaries are:
>
> - a farm operated by students of an agricultural college
> - a restaurant operated by students as part of a catering course at a further education college
> - the sale of goods manufactured by disabled people who are beneficiaries of a disability charity.

In all these cases the trade would qualify for the primary purpose exemption.

---

34 On this terminology, see 12.5.1 ("Beneficiary" of charity).

> **11. What if not all the work is carried out by beneficiaries?**
> Some of the work of a trade may be carried out by employees, contractors or volunteer workers who won't rank as beneficiaries of the charity. In these circumstances tax exemption will still be available for the whole profit arising from the trade provided it can be shown that the greater part of the work in connection with the trade is carried out by beneficiaries of the charity. ...
> **12. What happens if the beneficiaries are also paid employees?**
> A charity may wish to pay salaries to beneficiaries who work in a trade carried on by the charity. This means that the beneficiaries are employees of the charity. PAYE must be operated on the earnings of beneficiaries who are employed by a charity in the same way as for other employees, and national minimum wage rules must be applied. The payment of wages to a beneficiary doesn't affect the balance between charitable and non-charitable trading. For example, if a charity for the relief of disabled people pays disabled people for the manufacture of goods the trade will still be a charitable trade.

This is correct.

8.9.1 *Trade partly carried on by beneficiaries*

Section 525(3) ITA provides:

> For the purpose of subsection (1)(b), if work in connection with a trade is carried out partly but not mainly by beneficiaries, the part in connection with which work is carried out by beneficiaries and the other part are to be treated as separate trades.

The corporation tax equivalent is s.479(3) CTA 2010.

8.9.2 *Worker exemption: Critique*

It is suggested that the beneficiary worker exemption should be abolished. It has not been needed since 1927. This would be a modest but worthwhile simplification.

8.10 Lottery

Lotteries by charities (which include raffles and tombolas) will usually take the form of:

(a) incidental non-commercial lotteries, defined in part 1 of schedule 11 Gambling Act 2005;
(b) private lotteries, defined in part 2 of the schedule; or
(c) small society lotteries, defined in part 4 of the schedule.

A discussion of the gaming law which regulates lotteries is beyond the scope of this book. CC35 para 3.11 summarises the position, but while the law relating to lotteries has not changed substantially the terminology used in the 2005 Act is different to that used in the previous act, and unfortunately this guidance is no longer particularly helpful.

It is important that a charity should seek advice before organising a lottery; to carry out a lottery except within the narrowly defined exemptions is a criminal offence.

Lotteries of these kinds are exempt from pool betting duty: s.6(3) Betting and Gaming Duties Act 1981. Lotteries are in general exempt from VAT: Group 4 sch 9 VATA 1994.

8.10.1 *Lottery exemption*

Section 530 ITA provides:

> (1) The profits accruing to a charitable trust from a lottery are not taken into account in calculating total income if conditions A and B are met.
> (2) Condition A is that—
> (a) the lottery is an exempt lottery within the meaning of the Gambling Act 2005 by virtue of Part 1 or 4 of Schedule 11 to that Act,
> (ab) the lottery is promoted in accordance with a lottery operating licence within the meaning of part 5 of that Act,[35] or
> (b) the lottery is promoted and conducted in accordance with Article 133 or 135 of the Betting, Gaming, Lotteries and Amusements (Northern Ireland) Order 1985 (SI 1985/1204 (NI 11)).
> (3) Condition B is that the profits are applied to the purposes of the charitable trust only.

The corporation tax equivalent is s.484 CTA 2010.

8.10.2 *Non-exempt lottery income*

The statutory lottery exemption would not apply to:

(1) Lotteries carried out by bodies which are not charities, such as non-charitable subsidiaries of charities or political organisations.
(2) Lotteries which did not qualify for statutory exemption because the lottery was not carried out in accordance with general lottery law.

---

35 *http://www.gamblingcommission.gov.uk/Gambling-sectors/Lotteries/Getting-a-licence/Applying-for-a-licence/How-do-I-apply/How-do-I-apply.aspx*

(3) Private lotteries within part 2 of schedule 11 of the Gambling Act. (It will be rare for charities to run private lotteries.)

In such cases the income is taxable if the lottery is a trade. A lottery is not necessarily a trade, and it is considered that in many cases lotteries of charitable or non-profit making bodies will not be a trade. Since the question will now only rarely arise for charities, the point is not considered here.[36]

Income from a lottery incidental to a charitable event may qualify for the exemption for charitable events even if it does not qualify for the lottery exemption.

8.11 Betting Duty

A discussion of betting duty is beyond the scope of this book. in short, the FA 2014 introduced new rules for Pool Betting Duty, which is the duty paid by UK pool betting promoters, or operators of a totalisator in the UK. Section 153 FA 2014 provides an exemption from Pool Betting Duty for bets made through a promoter which is itself a "community society" (which is a defined term meaning, essentially, a charity or a CASC). This provides:

> (1) For the purposes of this Part (but subject to any direction under subsection (3)), a bet is made "for community benefit" if—
> (a) the promoter of the betting concerned is a community society or is bound to pay all benefits accruing from the betting to such a society, and
> (b) the person making the bet knows, when making it, that the purpose of the betting is to benefit such a society.
> (5) In this section "community society" means—
> (a) a society established and conducted for charitable purposes only, or
> (b) a society established and conducted wholly or mainly for the support of athletic sports or athletic games and not established or conducted for purposes of private or commercial gain.
> (6) In this section "society" includes any club, institution, organisation or association of persons, by whatever name called.

8.12 Application for charity purposes

Section 524(4) ITA sets out trading condition B (which must be satisfied for the exemption for charitable trades):

36 There is a discussion in the 2nd edition of this work para 13.2.4.

> Condition B is that the profits are, or the amount or post-cessation receipt is, (as the case may be) applied to the purposes of the charitable trust only.

The same wording is found in the small trade exemption: s.526(5) ITA. Similarly (with minor variations to suit the context) in the other IT trading exemptions.[37]

Most charity exemptions apply "so far as the income is applied to charitable purposes only". There is a theoretical difference between these forms of words. Suppose an educational charity wrongly applied its income for the relief of poverty. Property income, dividends and interest income would be exempt. But trading income would be taxable: though applied for charitable purposes it would not be applied for the purposes of *the* charity. In practice this will not be important; it is surprising that the Tax Law Rewrite did not align the exemptions.

For CT, the equivalent provision is s.484 and 478 CTA 2010.

8.13 Post-cessation receipt

8.13.1 *Income tax*

The s.524 ITA exemption applies expressly to adjustment income and post-cessation receipts. Adjustment income (arising on a change of accounting basis) is of no practical importance (though it is right that it should be covered). Post-cessation receipts[38] might (just) be important. ITA EN Change 92 provides:

> **Change 92: Charitable trusts: exemption for adjustment income and post-cessation receipts of certain trades and property businesses: ss.524, 525, 526, 531 and 539**
> This change introduces an exemption from income tax, in the case of charitable trusts, for the adjustment income and post-cessation receipts of trades whose profits are exempt, or would be exempt if the trade had not ceased. It also introduces an exemption for the adjustment income and post-cessation receipts of property businesses, and of trades in cases where such income or receipts arise

---

37 For completeness: the same wording is found in the charity exemption for estate income.

38 Section 524(6) defines "post-cessation receipt" by reference: "In this section "post-cessation receipt" means an amount that is a post-cessation receipt for the purposes of Chapter 18 of Part 2 of ITTOIA 2005 (post-cessation receipts) (see ss.246 to 253 of that Act)."
For completeness, s.524(5) provides: " Sections 232(1) and (2), 235 and 236 of ITTOIA 2005 (when adjustment income is treated as arising) apply for the purposes of subsection (3) as they apply for the purposes of Chapter 17 of Part 2 of that Act."

from land.
The general rule for calculating the profits of a trade for tax purposes is that the profits must be calculated on the basis of accounts drawn up in accordance with generally accepted accounting practice (see s.25 of ITTOIA). But an adjustment will be required if there is a change of basis in circumstances where the old basis accorded with law or practice in one period of account and the new basis accords with law and practice in the next period of account (see s.227 of ITTOIA). If the adjustment is positive, it is called adjustment income.
Adjustment income is charged to tax as trading income under s.228 of ITTOIA. There is no exemption for adjustment income in the source legislation for charitable trusts. But HMRC practice is to treat adjustment income in the same way as other trading income. That is, to treat it as exempt if it arises from a trade that benefits from the exemption in s.505(1)(e) of ICTA (rewritten as s.524 ITA and section 478 CTA 2010S), or if it arises in a small-scale trade where the income limits in s.46 of FA 2000 (rewritten as s.528) are not breached.
This change provides an exemption for adjustment income of a charitable trade or a smallscale trade. If a trade is treated as two separate trades in accordance with s.525(2) any adjustment income will be apportioned to the two parts (and this could mean completely apportioned to just one part if relating only to that part) and an exemption will then be available for the adjustment income apportioned to the charitable part.
Post-cessation receipts are taxed under Chapter 18 of Part 2 of ITTOIA. There is no exemption for post-cessation receipts in the source legislation for charitable trusts, other than the exemption in s.46 of FA 2000 (rewritten in ss.526 to 528) which applies only if the receipts are below a certain level. But HMRC practice is to treat post-cessation receipts as exempt from income tax if they arise from a trade that benefited from the exemption in s.505(1)(e) of ICTA (rewritten as s.524 ITA and s.478 CTA 2010).
This change provides an exemption for post-cessation receipts from a charitable trade. If a trade is treated as two separate trades in accordance with s.525(2) any post-cessation receipts will be apportioned to the two parts (and this could mean completely apportioned to just one part if relating only to that part) and an exemption will then be available for the receipts apportioned to the charitable part.
The source legislation (s.505(1)(a) of ICTA, rewritten in s.531) provides an exemption from tax under Parts 2 and 3 of ITTOIA in respect of any profits or gains arising in respect of rents or other receipts from an estate, interest or right in or over any land. The exemption is available only to the extent that the profits or gains arise from land vested for charitable purposes and the profits or gains are applied for charitable purposes. HMRC practice is to treat associated adjustment income and post cessation receipts as eligible for exemption. This change provides such an exemption.
This change is in taxpayers' favour in principle. But it is expected to have no practical effect as it is in line with current practice.

The exemptions for lottery income and fundraising events do not refer expressly to post-cessation receipts or (for completeness) adjustment income but it is considered that the exemption could apply if needed. In practice the point is not likely to arise.

8.13.2 *Corporation tax*

For corporation tax, the s.472 CTA 2010 exemptions apply to "tax under Part 3 of CTA 2009 in respect of the profits of any trade carried on by the charitable company". Do the s.472 CTA 2010 exemptions for charitable companies extend to post-cessation receipts chargeable under s.188 CTA 2009? This section applies where:

> **188 Charge to tax on post-cessation receipts**
> The charge to corporation tax on income applies to post-cessation receipts arising from a trade.
> **189 Extent of charge to tax**
> (1) A post-cessation receipt is chargeable to tax under this Chapter only so far as it is not otherwise chargeable to corporation or income tax.

Whilst there are exceptions under s.189(3) and (4), there is no express exemption for charities.

It is arguable that a trade which is a primary purpose, beneficiary worker trade is not one the profits of which are *chargeable* to tax. Contrast 14.6 ("Subject to tax") where HMRC accept that income qualifying for the charity exemption is not "subject to tax" for DTA purposes. It is considered that the statutory exemption in s.472 CTA 2010 applies here. The charge on post-cessation receipts applies to sums *arising from* the carrying on of the trade before the discontinuance. The relief applies to "tax ... *in respect of* the profits of the trade". Although the charge is not a charge *on* the profits of the trade it may be described as a charge "in respect of" those profits. The expression "in respect of" is vague and takes its meaning from context. In the present context it would be absurd if profits which qualified for relief during the continuance of the trade became taxable after the cessation.

In practice HMRC accept this view. The Tax Law Rewrite states in its comment on the proposed statutory exemption for post-cessation receipts:

> Inland Revenue practice is to treat post-cessation receipts as exempt from income tax if they arise from a trade which benefited from the exemption in s.478 CTA 2010.

8.14 Fundraising event

8.14.1 *Are fundraising events a trade*

One of the most common ways of fundraising is the charitable event, in the form of a bazaar, whist drive, dance, dinner, etc. A charity which organises such an event infrequently or on an irregular basis is not carrying on a trade. The profits will not then be subject to tax. In *British Legion, Peterhead Branch v IRC*:

> In my view, a person cannot be said to be engaged in carrying on a trade or a concern in the nature of trade within the meaning of the Income Tax Acts unless, in a reasonable sense, he is conducting business on commercial principles. If he is so conducting business, it matters not from what motive he acts nor to what purpose he devotes the profits, if any. If he is not so conducting the business, enterprise or adventure – if, for example, he is merely using some of the trappings of trade as a means of procuring subscriptions or donations not properly related to any service he renders or to any commodity which he supplies – he may be wearing an easily penetrated disguise which deceives nobody, but he is not trading. Instances of the latter type of operation which readily occur to the mind are the hawking of flags, the conducting of occasional bazaars and sales of work and whist drives, and the showing of private gardens for an admission fee, usually exorbitant.[39]

In the *British Legion* case the taxpayer *was* held to be trading by the Commissioners when it carried on one dance per week over a period of three years. Even this was a marginal case. The Court of Session held that the Commissioners' decision could not be challenged; but the Lord President expressed regret and said that he might have come to a different decision had he been a Commissioner himself.

The Business Income Manual provides:

> **BIM24475: Meaning of trade: mutual trading and members clubs: allowable expenditure: the 'Peterhead' principle** [Jun 2016]
> *To compute equivalent commercial profit*
>
> ...
>
> You should recognise that this case involved unusual circumstances - a significant number of dances (more than 150) held weekly over a three-year period. Notwithstanding the number of events and the time period involved, the judges indicated that the case was borderline; some expressing the view that they would have gone the other way but, unable to say that the Commissioners had erred sufficiently, felt constrained to

39 35 TC 509 at p.513. For completeness: The taxpayer in this case was a non-profit unincorporated organisation but not a charity, because its objects were not wholly charitable: see p.512, 513. But the question of what is a trade is the same for charities and other NPOs.

go along with their findings. Unless there is some other significant factor (for example commercial sponsorship, media funding, etc) it is unlikely that a Tribunal could be persuaded that a local annual fund raising event amounted to a trade.

8.14.2 *Relief for fundraising events*

For income tax, s.529 ITA provides:

> (1) The profits of a trade carried on by a charitable trust are not taken into account in calculating total income so far as they arise from a VAT-exempt event.
> (2) Subsection (1) applies so far as the profits are either applied for charitable purposes or transferred to another charity.
> (3) An event is a VAT-exempt event if the supply of goods and services by the charitable trust in connection with the event would be exempt from value added tax under Group 12 of Schedule 9 to the Value Added Tax Act 1994 (fund-raising events by charities and other qualifying bodies).

The CT equivalent is s.483 CTA 2010.

For the VAT exemption, see 37.14 (Fundraising events).

The relief only applies to the profits from the event. The Business Income Manual provides:

> **BIM24795. Voluntary organisations & charities: Trading profits: ESCC4 conditions** [Aug 2016]
> *Conditions (1) and (2)*
> ...
> [1] The exemption [now the statutory provision] applies to all the profits of the event - and extends not only to the admission charges but also ancillary sources of income such as:
> - sale of refreshments
> - sale of raffle tickets
> - sale of programmes
> - sale of advertising space.
>
> [2] Each ancillary source of income must properly form part of the event and must not constitute a separate profit-making activity. If a programme or brochure is primarily a vehicle for advertisements rather than a way of informing people about the event, you should treat it as a separate profit-making activity.

We find point [2] surprising but perhaps no-one takes much notice of it in practice. In most cases the small trade exemption would plug the gap, if there really is one.

8.15 Small trade

This section considers two modest exemptions:
(1) An exemption for small trades.[40]
(2) An exemption for limited and disparate categories of income sometimes called miscellaneous income.

The two exemptions share some common conditions, so it is convenient to consider them together, even though the latter does not strictly belong in a chapter on the topic of charity trading.

8.15.1 *Small trade exemption*

Section 526 ITA provides:

> (1) The income mentioned in subsection (2) is not taken into account in calculating total income if conditions A and B are met.

We refer to this as the **"small trade exemption"** and refer to conditions A and B as **"small trade conditions A and B"**.

> (2) The income referred to in subsection (1) is—
> (a) the profits of a trade carried on by a charitable trust,
> (b) amounts treated as adjustment income of a charitable trust under s.228 of ITTOIA 2005 in respect of a trade carried on by the trust, and
> (c) post-cessation receipts arising from a trade carried on by a charitable trust which are received by the trustees of the trust or to which they are entitled.

This is the same wording as the charitable trade exemptions.[41]

Section 526(3) ITA disapplies the small trade exemption when a better exemption applies:

> Subsection (1) does not apply in respect of—
> (a) profits of a trade that are, apart from this section, exempt from income tax chargeable under Part 2 of ITTOIA 2005,
> (b) amounts treated as adjustment income that are, apart from this section, exempt from income tax chargeable under Chapter 17 of Part 2 of that Act, or
> (c) post-cessation receipts that are, apart from this section, exempt

---

40 The ITA uses the term "small-scale trades" and the CTA uses the term "small trades". The meaning is the same and this book adopts the CT terminology.

41 See 8.7 (Charitable trade).

> from income tax chargeable under Chapter 18 of Part 2 of that Act.

8.15.2 *Small misc income exemption*

Section 527(1) ITA provides:

> Any income or gains of a charitable trust that is or are chargeable to income tax under or by virtue of any provision to which s.1016 applies is not or are not taken into account in calculating total income if conditions A and B are met.

We refer this as the **"small misc income exemption"** and conditions A and B are **"misc income conditions A and B"**: these are the same as small trade conditions A and B.

Section 1016 ITA lists about 40 provisions to which it applies.

Section 527(2) ITA sets out five categories of income which are in the s.1016 list, but which do not qualify for the small misc income exemption:

> Subsection (1) does not apply in respect of any income or gains chargeable to income tax by virtue of any of—
> (a) s.1086(2) CTA 2010 (chargeable payments connected with exempt distributions),
> (b) [repealed]
> (c) Chapter 9 of Part 4 of ITTOIA 2005 (gains from contracts for life insurance etc),
> (d) Chapter 5 of Part 5 of that Act (settlements: amounts treated as income of settlor),[42] and
> (e) [repealed]
> (f) any other enactment specified in an order made by the Treasury.[43]

It is difficult to see the reason for this, particularly given the limited scope of the small misc income exemption. The repeal of s.527(2) would be a small but sensible simplification.

Section 527(3) ITA is the equivalent of s.526(3); it disapplies the small misc income exemption when a better exemption applies:

> Subsection (1) does not apply in respect of any income that is, or gains that are, apart from this section, exempt from income tax chargeable

---

42 How could the drafter have thought that a charity could come within the scope of Chapter 5 Part 5 ITTOIA (the settlement provisions)?

43 No order has been made.

under or by virtue of any provision to which s.1016 applies.

After one has allowed for the exceptions in s.527(2)(3), and the many types of income in the s.1016 list which are not applicable to charities, there is not much left. An example is the charge under chapter 8 part 5 ITTOIA (income not otherwise charged) which includes casual income. In practice the small misc income exemption will rarely if ever apply.

8.15.3 *Income limit: Condition A*

For the small trade exemption, s.526(4) ITA provides:

> Condition A is—
> (a) in the case of the profits of a trade, that the profits are profits of a tax year in relation to which the condition specified in s.528 (condition as to trading and miscellaneous incoming resources) is met,
> (b) in the case of an amount treated as adjustment income, that the amount arises in such a tax year, and
> (c) in the case of a post-cessation receipt, that it is received in such a tax year.

Likewise for the small misc income exemption, s.527(4) ITA provides:

> Condition A is that the income is, or the gains are, for a tax year in relation to which the condition specified in s.528 is met.

So we turn to s.528 ITA which provides:

> (1) The condition in this section is met in relation to a tax year if—
> (a) the sum of the charitable trust's trading incoming resources and miscellaneous incoming resources for the tax year does not exceed the requisite limit for the tax year, or
> (b) the trustees of the charitable trust had, at the beginning of the tax year, a reasonable expectation that it would not do so.[44]

8.15.4 *"Incoming resources"*

Section 528 ITA provides:

> (2) The charitable trust's "trading incoming resources" for the tax year are—
> (a) the incoming resources which are required to be taken into account in calculating the profits of, or losses made in, the basis

44 The CT equivalent is s.482 CTA 2010.

> period for the tax year of any non-exempt trade carried on by the charitable trust, and
>
> (b) the incoming resources which are treated as adjustment income under s.228 of ITTOIA 2005 in respect of such a trade, or which are post-cessation receipts arising from such a trade.
>
> "Post-cessation receipt"has the meaning given by s.526(7).
>
> (3) For the purposes of subsection (2) a trade is a "non-exempt trade" if any profits of the trade would not, apart from s.526, be exempt from income tax chargeable under Part 2 of ITTOIA 2005.
>
> (4) The charitable trust's "miscellaneous incoming resources" for the tax year are the incoming resources which are required to be taken into account in calculating non-exempt miscellaneous income or non-exempt miscellaneous losses for the tax year.
>
> (5) In this section—
>
> "non-exempt miscellaneous income" means income or gains chargeable to income tax under or by virtue of any provision to which s.1016 applies that is not, or are not, apart from s.526 or 527, exempt from income tax chargeable under or by virtue of that provision, and
>
> "non-exempt miscellaneous losses" means losses arising from a transaction which is of such a nature that if income or gains had arisen from it the income would have been non-exempt miscellaneous income.

"Incoming resources" is an accountancy term explained in the Charities SORPs. Before the ITA, the term used was "gross income". ITA EN Change 94 comments on the change:

> The condition operates by reference to the incoming resources associated with the trading activity and miscellaneous transactions whose profits are not exempt under other provisions. The expression "incoming resources" is used instead of "gross income" because this accounting term is a more direct and accessible way of capturing the meaning of "gross income" as defined in the source legislation.
>
> The source legislation aimed to bring in turnover for trading activity and gross receipts for Schedule D Case VI transactions. But these terms are not used in charity accounting. "Incoming resources" is familiar to those involved in preparing or working with charity accounts. And since charity accounting does not allow offset between income and expenditure in determining disclosure (in contrast with the disclosure in the accounts of commercial organisations), it is relatively easy to check the limits.
>
> It is not clear in s.46 of FA 2000 whether "gross income" includes incoming resources from an activity which gives rise to a loss, in cases where a profit would be taxable. But incoming resources from an activity

are included irrespective of whether there is a profit or a loss. Charitable trusts do not in practice include balancing charges in "gross income". And balancing charges do not come within the meaning of incoming resources.

8.15.5 *"Requisite limit"*

Although the figures have just been increased, the requisite limit is small. Section 528(6) ITA provides:

> The requisite limit—
> (a) is 25% of the charitable trust's total incoming resources for the tax year, but
> (b) must not be less than £8,000 or more than £80,000.

The corporation tax equivalent is s.482(6) CTA 2010.

So for a substantial charity (with incoming resources exceeding £320,000) the requisite limit is £80,000. The *maximum* tax saving the small trade exemption allows is tax on that amount, (2022/23, 20%) = £16,000.[45] In practice the tax saving will be far less as expenses (maybe considerable) can be deducted from the £80k gross turnover.

If the profits exceed the "requisite limit" the exemption is withdrawn in its entirety.

8.15.6 *Reasonable expectation test*

The Guidance Note provides at Annex iv:

> **16. The reasonable expectation test**
> If the total turnover of taxable trading exceeds the small scale trading limits, profits from a non-charitable trade may still be exempt if the charity can clearly demonstrate that, at the start of the relevant accounting period, it was reasonable for it to expect that the turnover would not exceed the limit. This might be because:
> - the charity expected the turnover from the non-charitable trade to be lower than it turned out to be, or
> - the charity expected that its total incoming resources would be higher than they turned out to be.
>
> HMRC Charities will consider any evidence the charity may have to satisfy the reasonable expectation test.
> Examples:
> - the charity may have carried on the activity for a number of years and

45 In 2022/23 the basic rate (paid by charitable trusts) is 20% and the corporation tax rate (paid by charitable companies) is 19%.

may therefore be able to show that the turnover increased unexpectedly compared with earlier years

- the charity might have started carrying out the trading activity during the year in question and might be able to show that the turnover was higher than forecast
- the charity's total incoming resources might be lower than it forecast, for example, because the charity did not receive a grant for which it had budgeted.

The type of evidence needed to demonstrate the levels of turnover and incoming resources which were expected might include:

- minutes of meetings at which such matters were discussed,
- copies of cash flow forecasts,
- business plans and previous years' accounts.

A well organised charity will produce minutes in accordance with this guidance. The HMRC Guidance Note continues with some tax planning advice:

> If the charity expects to be regularly trading at or around the small trading exemption limits, it might be better for the charity to consider using a trading subsidiary company see the guidance at paragraphs 45-50 'using a trading company'.

8.15.7 *Application for charity purposes*

Section 527 (5) ITA provides:

> Condition B is that the income is, or the gains are, applied to the purposes of the charitable trust only.

See 8.12 (Application for charity purposes).

8.15.8 *HMRC examples*

HMRC Guidance Note provides some straightforward examples in para 15:

> A charity sells greetings cards to raise funds and applies all its income charitably. This is not charitable trading, but the sale of cards. The message on the cards does not alter this and so for example, a Christian church, selling cards with a religious message would still be carrying out a non-charitable trade.
>
> *Example 1*
>
> - assume this is the only taxable trading activity
> - the turnover from the cards amounts to £4,500 in the year
> - any profits will be exempt from tax, because the turnover does not exceed £8,000 (the minimum small scale trading turnover limit)

Example 2

- a charity has a turnover from non-charitable trading of £40,000 for the year
- its total incoming resources for the year are £160,000 (including the £40,000 turnover)
- the income from non-charitable trading (£40,000) is not more than 25% of total income (£160,000) and less than £80,000
- profits are exempt from tax because the turnover from the non-charitable trading does not exceed the small scale trading turnover limit

Example 3

- a charity has turnover from non-charitable trading of £40,000 for the year
- its total incoming resources are £150,000 (including the £40,000 turnover)
- the £40,000 turnover exceeds the annual turnover limit (£150,000 @ 25%= £37,500) - so profit from the whole of the £40,000 is taxable
- however, the profits on sales may still be exempt from tax for this year if the charity could demonstrate that it had a reasonable expectation at the start of the year that the turnover would not exceed the small scale trading limit

Sections 480-482 CTA 2010 provides the CT equivalent exemptions.

8.15.9 *Small income exemptions: Critique*

The reader who has studied the text to this point may well agree with the authors that the complexity of the small trading and misc income reliefs in s.526–528 ITA is out of proportion to the amount of tax at stake, which is a maximum of £10,000 p.a. Why not just give relief for the first £50k (or if that is too generous, £25k or even £10k) for trading income, or, better, for every type of income which does not qualify for a fuller relief?

8.16 Planning for non-exempt trade: Outline

We discuss four techniques of tax planning for non-exempt trades. In order of importance:

(1) Trading companies (see the next chapter)
(2) Charge and voluntary donation[46]
(3) Franchising
(4) Trading trusts

46 This topic overlaps with VAT planning, see 35.9 (Charge and voluntary donation).

8.17 Franchising

"Franchising" is a term applied to a variety of commercial arrangements. In short, a franchise is a contractual arrangement under which one person (the "franchisee") carries on a business under a licence authorising them to use the name, goodwill, and maybe other support, of another person (the "franchisor").

Franchising may be appropriate for a charity which raises funds by the sale of Christmas cards, gifts or souvenirs. The goods will be stamped with the charity's name and purchasers will be inclined to purchase the goods because of the charitable connection. The charity is essentially raising funds by exploiting the goodwill associated with its name. The charity may not have the resources to devote to the production or distribution of its goods; a franchise is then a convenient commercial framework. The charity will license a franchisee to sell goods in the charity's name, and will receive payments in the form of a licence fee.

The tax treatment of franchising is more favourable than that of a direct trading operation. The income will in principle qualify for charity tax relief.[47]

If a charity adopts this course it is important to ensure that the charity is not trading.[48] There are two possible difficulties. First, the charity might be carrying on a trade on its own account; secondly, the charity might be carrying on a trade in partnership with the franchisee. In either case, the charity will receive trading income and it is unlikely that any tax relief would be available.

A charity will be trading if, in addition to franchising, it sells some of its products directly. If the charity wishes to sell products directly it should do so as agent for the franchisee. A charity might be trading if it performs other services for the franchisee's benefit, for which it receives an additional fee. That should not normally be a problem: the charity will normally be content to provide the franchisee with a membership list and to leave the franchisee to its own devices.

There may be a greater risk that the charity and the franchisee are carrying on business in partnership. If the charity's royalties are based on the *gross* takings of the franchisee then there will not normally be a partnership. If the royalties are calculated as a percentage of the profits of the franchisee,

---

47 See 4.12 (Royalties).

48 Unless the exemption for small trades applies.

there may well be a partnership.[49] It is considered possible, without creating a partnership, to arrange an intermediate position where the royalty fee is calculated according to a more sophisticated formula and does not depend on gross takings alone.

8.18 Convert trade to annual payment income

Trading income can be converted into income of the form of annual payments by the interposition of a trust.

The trust would not in principle be a charitable trust, as carrying on a non-primary purpose, fundraising trade is in principle regarded as a non-charitable activity even though the profits are intended for charity.

If the trust is a common form discretionary trust, the payments to the charity will carry a tax credit and the charity can reclaim all the tax paid by the trustees.[50]

Alternatively the terms of the trust may require the trustees to make annual payments to a charity. Then the charity will receive income in the form of annual payments (subject to deduction of tax at the basic rate) which qualify for charity tax relief.[51] The trustees of the trust will in effect be able to deduct the annual payments from their taxable income, so the interposition of a trust obviates the tax charge.

A trust under which the charity has an interest in possession would not do, as the charity would be treated for tax purposes as receiving the non-exempt trading income.[52]

The trust would be subject to IHT 10 year charges, but IHT business

---

49 See s.2 Partnership Act 1890.

50 For an outline of the income taxation of discretionary trusts, see Kessler, *Taxation of Non-Residents and Foreign Domiciliaries* (21st ed., 2022-23), Chapter 41 (Discretionary Trust: Income Tax)
online version *https://www.foreigndomiciliaries.co.uk*
For the charity exemption see 4.11 (Annual payments).

51 See *R v Special Commissioners ex p. Shaftesbury Homes and Arethusa Training Ship* 8 TC 367.

52 To decide whether a charity's income from a trust consists of trading income or annual payments under a trust, it is necessary to construe the trust documents: the question depends on the drafting. In *Shaftesbury Homes,* trustees were directed to carry on a trade and pay the yearly balance of income to a charity. The court held that the payments made to the charity were annual payments and so qualified for tax relief. But this was far from clear and following *Archer-Shee v Baker* 11 TC 749, which decided that English law interest in possession trusts were transparent for IT purposes, the decision today may not stand. Nevertheless if the wording is clear enough, a charity will receive annual payments and not trading profits.

property relief should be available.

Funding (if needed) could be from the charity by way of loan or limited recourse loan; of course the charity could only provide funding if its investment was a sound one, but that consideration applies equally to trading companies held by charities.

Which is better: use of a trading trust or a company subsidiary? The company route offers three advantages:

(1) The company route is standard: practitioners and HMRC and the Charity Commissioner are familiar with it.
(2) A company offers limited liability. The trustees would be personally liable for the debts of the trust. (But that may not matter in many cases.)
(3) 9-month carry back relief applies only to companies: see 9.4 (Carry-back relief).

The trust route offers three possible advantages:

(1) The charity avoids auditing and other costs of a company (though the trust would still need accounts and tax returns, so there should not be a great difference).
(2) A trust does not have the restrictions on distributions which apply to a company: See 9.7 (Donation exceeding distributable profits).
(3) There is no need for the trust to publish its accounts.

In practice, charities generally prefer the company route to the trading trust, and that seems the better course, unless points (2) or (3) above are particularly important.

8.19 Charity trade exemptions: Critique

The exemptions for trading income are limited in scope and much charitable trading activity could still be subject to tax. The origin of this rule may be a 19th century prejudice against trade, or even an accidental drafting error.[53] In practice, with the approval of HMRC and parliament,[54]

---

53 "I think it not at all unlikely" said Stephen J in *Psalms and Hymns* (3 TC 7) "that the intention of the legislature was to exempt trading income"; though he held that the language used by parliament, exempting "annual payments", had failed to achieve this aim. But when the present trading exemptions were introduced in 1921, and extended in 1927, 1995, 2000 and 2006, the decision was taken by parliament that trading income outside the narrow exemptions should continue to be taxable.

54 By enacting (what is now) s.199 CTA 2010 to help trading companies held by charities.

the tax charge on non-exempt trading income can be and always is avoided by the use of non-charitable trading subsidiaries.[55] This does however impose a significant administrative cost for charities which could be avoided by extending the charity trading exemption to all trading income. We here consider the arguments for and against this reform.

8.19.1 *Fair competition argument*

The Federation of Small Businesses argue that charity tax reliefs prevent or distort free competition on fair and equal terms.[56] We refer to this as the **"fair competition argument"**.

The argument focuses on charity shops, where the distortion is perhaps strongest. Charity shops selling primarily donated goods have three tax exemptions that do not apply to ordinary businesses:

(1) Rating relief[57]
(2) Effective direct tax exemption[58]
(3) VAT relief[59]

Similar arguments may be applied to other charity enterprises. Charities carrying on primary purpose trades will qualify for rating relief[60] and direct tax exemption, though they may enjoy no special VAT relief. Thus it might be said there is unfair competition between charitable schools and colleges, and theatres, compared to those in the private sector. Other charity enterprises may not qualify for rating relief but will at least qualify for effective direct tax exemption.[61]

The fair competition consideration is at present recognised in some VAT

---

55 An incidental advantage of the present system is perhaps to remind charities otherwise exempt from direct taxation of some realities of taxation. A recent development is campaigning by some charities, such as Christian Aid, against the "tax dodging"; the term is used without much explanation or definition, but it would seem to be wide enough to extend to the use of non-charitable trading subsidiaries.

56 Memorandum from Federation of Small Businesses (DCH 69) Ev 137 *http://www.publications.parliament.uk/pa/jt200304/jtselect/jtchar/167/4062323.htm* The discussion always focusses on taxation, because that is something which parliament could change; but in assessing the competition issues there are other relevant factors. Charity shops also have non-tax advantages: they may be given stock free, and may not pay most of their staff.

57 See 40.7.5 (Relief for charity shops).

58 Because sale of donated goods is not a trade: see 8.2.1 (Sale of donated goods).

59 See 38.4 (Donation and sale of donated goods).

60 See 40.5 (Mandatory relief).

61 Either under one of the statutory trading exemptions or by use of a trading subsidiary.

exemptions,[62] but not in other charity tax exemptions.

The economic assumption behind the fair competition argument is doubtful:

> These predictions of unfair competition were rarely subjected to close analysis, and we know of no empirical examination of the results of [acquisitions of trades by charities].[63] In particular, it was never made clear why the price level that had maximised both the pretax and after-tax profits of the enterprise before the change of ownership would not continue to maximise its profits thereafter.[64] Equally mysterious was the unarticulated but widely accepted assumption that charities would compete unfairly with their taxable rivals in "active" manufacturing and mercantile pursuits, but not in "passive" investment areas. No one suggested, for example, that charities would lend their endowment funds or rent their real estate for less than the going rate, and thus drive private investors in these areas out of business; it was assumed, rather, that "passive" investments by charities were no threat to taxable enterprise.[65] Nor was there any discussion of the possibility that, if charities increased their ownership of active business enterprises, they would correspondingly reduce their ownership of marketable securities and other passive investments and, hence, compete less vigorously with taxable

62 See 37.20 (Distortion of competition); 37.9 (Sports).

63 Footnote original: For anecdotal material, see Mansfield, *Some Aspects of Taxation of Business Income of Exempt Organisations*, in 3 Tax Revision Compendium 2067 (House Comm. of Ways & Means 1959); Sugarman, *Business Income of Exempt Organisations,* in *id.* at 2115. *See generally* Ely, *Federal Taxation of Income of States & Political Subdivisions*, in *id.* at 2091; Dunham, *Business Activities of exempt Scientific Research Organisations,* in *id.* at 2127; Gilpin, *Business Income of Exempt Organisations–Tax Equalisation–Electric Utility Service Organisations*, in *id.* at 2077; Harris, *Tax Exempt Organisations,* in *id.* at 2101.

64 Footnote original: At least in the short run, no reason for a change in pricing policies is apparent, and the long run results of shifting a business from taxable to tax-exempt status are had to predict except on an unrealistic assumption of perfect competition in a state of equilibrium. See Comment, *Colleges, Charities, and the Revenue Act of 1950*, 60 Yale L.J. 851, 876 (1951); Klein, *Income Taxation and Legal Entities* 20 UCLA L. Rev. 13 (1972).

65 Footnote original: But see Break & Pechman, *Relationship Between the Corporation and Individual Income Taxes*, 28 Nat'l Tax J. 341, 344 (1975), proposing that the tax on the unrelated business income of charitable organisations be extended to their investment income; though recognising that this would reduce their ability to finance their activities, the authors say nothing about the relation of the proposed tax to the charitable beneficiaries' ability to pay, evidently because they view the tax as a method of subjecting the charitable institution itself to a "market test of the value or its activities".

investors for these assets.[66]

Australia's Future Tax System Review (the Henry Report) reached the same conclusion:

> Samuelson's invariant valuations theorem (1964) provides a conceptual framework for assessing the impact of the income tax exemption for NFP organisations on resource allocation. The application of the theorem to NFP organisations assumes that these organisations seek to maximise profits in the same way as other businesses; however, this may not be true of all NFP organisations.
>
> The theorem states that where taxable income is the same as economic income, the discounted present value of a stream of cash flows is independent of the tax rate. In other words, the maximum amount that an individual is prepared to pay for an asset is independent of the tax rate. Consequently, a tax on economic income will not create arbitrage opportunities between taxpayers on different rates and will not affect either relative or absolute asset values. Accordingly, it will not distort the composition or level of investment in the economy. Thus, providing that economic income is taxed, the existence of concessionally taxed NFP organisations should not distort asset allocation (or the level of investment) in the economy.
>
> However, as the current income tax base differs considerably from economic income, and as the tax concessions for NFP organisations are linked to particular activities regarded as providing a public benefit, the concessions are likely to distort investment decisions. However, to the extent that the concessions address a market failure (that is, the under-provision of social services), they may still increase wellbeing.
>
> In relation to pricing, NFP organisations, like for-profit organisations, will seek to maximise their profits in support of their philanthropic activities. Accordingly, it appears that the income tax exemption does not provide an incentive for NFP organisations to undercut the prices of their for-profit competitors; rather, NFP organisations follow the same pricing policies as their competitors to maximise their profits.
>
> **Finding**
>
> The NFP income tax concessions do not generally violate the principle of competitive neutrality where NFP organisations operate in commercial markets.[67]

---

66 Bittker & Rahdert, "The Exemption of Non-profit Organizations from Federal Income Taxation", Yale Law Journal, Vol 85: 299; 1976 at p.319. See too S. Rose-Ackerman "Unfair Competition and Corporate Income Taxation" (1982) 34 Stanford Law Review 1017.

67 *http://www.taxreview.treasury.gov.au* para B3-2 (December 2009).

"Taxing Not-For-Profits" summarises the American economic literature:[68]

> Early debate focused on economic analysis of the alleged **competitive advantage** of tax exemptions. Economists overwhelming rejected the arguments offered by Congress that NFPs would gain an advantage as they could offer their products at a lower price or that NFPs could expand faster because of their greater after-tax income,[69] although the analyses leading to this result have become increasingly complex over time.[70]

More fundamentally, the fair competition argument is not an argument against the reform of extending charity trading exemption. If (which we think unproven) the fair competition argument is valid, it is an argument against the present status quo. That is, charity shops *already* have the advantage of rating, VAT and direct tax reliefs. The extension of the charity trading exemption would not alter the competition situation one way or another.

8.19.2 *Charity administration argument*

"Public Action, Private Benefit" (Strategy Unit, 2002) recommended exempting all trading income. But the Blair/Brown administration rejected this on the grounds that the present system encouraged the separation of trades into trading companies which was better charity administration.[71]

The matter was discussed by a Joint Committee on the Draft Charities Bill. The Association of Chief Executives of Voluntary Organisations critique of the Governments arguments in favour of the status quo is in the authors' view unanswerable and deserves citation in full:

> *"That there could be increased risks to charity assets. Charities' assets would be available to creditors to meet trading liabilities. In extreme cases this could force charities to reduce their services to users and beneficiaries, since assets used in the course of charitable work might have to be diverted into paying off the debts of failed trading ventures;"*

---

68 Melbourne Law School (2011) *http://www.law.unimelb.edu.au/notforprofit1#Project Overview* p.33.

69 Footnote original: Michael S Knoll, 'The UBIT: Leveling an Uneven Playing Field or Tilting a Level One' (2007) 76 *Fordham Law Review* 857, 860.

70 Footnote original: William A Klein, 'Income Taxation and Legal Entities' (1972) 20 *UCLA Law Review* 13, 64–66; Richard L Kaplan, 'Intercollegiate Athletics and the Unrelated Business Income Tax' (1980) 80 *Columbia Law Review* 1430, 1465–1466; Rose-Ackerman, 'Unfair Competition and Corporate Income Taxation,' above n 17, 1029; Hansmann, 'Unfair Competition and the Unrelated Business Income Tax,' (1989) 75 Virginia Law Review 610–611.

71 "Charities and Not for Profits: A modern legal framework", July 2003 para 3.28.

The duty of care proposed by the strategy unit included "a duty to give proper consideration to the need to structure the trade in a way which does not expose the assets of the charity to significant risk". This duty of care would make it good practice for charities to continue to isolate untested, speculative, or risky ventures through a trading subsidiary.

The recommendation would in no way compel charities to undertake risky trading within the charitable structure. The recommendation would, however, enable charities to undertake low-risk, well-established trading activity more efficiently, by bringing it within the charitable structure.

If the recommendation is reinstated, those charities that wish to limit risk by continuing to conduct trade through trading subsidiaries should be allowed to do so.

Financial risk is not the only risk involved in trading. Where a small trading subsidiary fails, the parent charity can experience considerable reputational damage. This risk is compounded by the present difficulties associated with building working capital within a subsidiary. Reinstating the recommendation would enable charities to manage this risk more effectively.

"That the boards of many charities presently lack trustees with the commercial experience and acumen to establish and conduct trading operations;"

The Charity Commissioner recommends that trustees "be selected on the basis of their relevant experience and skills." Charities that wish to undertake trading should therefore recruit trustees with the relevant commercial experience and acumen.

The present requirement to establish trading subsidiaries does not ensure that their directors have the relevant skills. In many cases the trading subsidiary is simply a "shell organisation", and the trustees or senior managers of the charity are also directors of the subsidiary.

"That trustees of unincorporated charities might be more exposed to personal liability, since their liability would also extend to trading debts;"

In general, charities should incorporate where there is a risk of personal liability to trustees. The proposed "charitable incorporated organisation" legal form should remove some of the barriers to incorporation.

That some charities might develop trading to such an extent that they became to all intents and purposes trading operations with a charitable sideline. This would not only bring their charitable status into question but, if widespread, it could erode in the public eye the present clear distinction between charities and commercial organisations. This could damage public confidence in charities.

Many charities already conduct considerable non-primary purpose trading through subsidiaries, under a brand name clearly associated with the charity. The public recognises this as fundraising activity by the charity, rather than as a separate commercial operation, without suffering the feared erosion of confidence. Conducting trading within the charity would provide greater transparency, making the purpose and nature of trading activity clearer to the charity's stakeholders.

Many other charities already derive much or most of their income through primary purpose trading, particularly those selling social, educational, or health services to government. It might be argued that such trading blurs the distinction between

> charities and commercial organisations, but it is a large and growing area of charitable activity. There has been a 40% increase in government funding of voluntary organisations (excluding housing) in real terms since 1982.
> The concern that non primary purpose trading might render charitable activity a sideline could be met by retaining a ceiling for trading, but making it more flexible. For example, trading "incidental" to the charity could be permitted within the charitable structure. The threshold could be defined for all charities as it currently is for those with a turnover of between £20,000 and £200,000, as "less than 25% of the charity's total incoming resources".

The (alleged) benefit from the current rules is a regulatory benefit. The question is therefore not whether charities are better off if they are forced to use trading companies. No doubt some are. The question is whether the benefit of forcing charities to use trading companies justifies the cost of the current rules. The issue is one of regulation or deregulation. Looked at in that light, it is very difficult to defend the current rules.

The Joint Committee recommended a compromise solution under which the current £50k turnover limit for small trades should be increased. But even that was rejected. In fact, the decision not to increase the limit since 2000 amounts to a significant reduction in its real value.

Perhaps in tacit acknowledgement of the defeat of the charity administration arguments, the Government fell back on the fair competition argument:

> The level of the statutory exemption for small trading is a matter for Finance Bill legislation rather than for the Charities Bill and any changes would be considered as part of the normal Budget process. But any increase in the overall limit would give charities a greater advantage over private sector businesses, especially small and medium sized enterprises. The Government regards the current exemption, together with the extra statutory concession on fundraising events, as sufficient to allow charities to engage in small amounts of trading without the extra administration costs of setting up a subsidiary, but does not give charities a significant advantage over other commercial businesses. An increased limit would mean that considerably more trading could be carried out by charities tax free, giving them a greater competitive advantage over small businesses which are taxed on their profits. Trading companies have the option to donate their profits to charity, and so start from a similar position whether they are subsidiaries of charities or not. It would be unfair to give charities greater exemptions from the requirements normal commercial businesses have to meet. Charities already enjoy advantages over commercial businesses, with relief from tax on profits of primary purpose and ancillary trades as well as the exemption for small trading, and we need to consider the overall impact for businesses.[72]

---

72 The Government Reply to the Report from the Joint Committee on the Draft Charities Bill (December 2004) Cm 6440

The current position will continue for the time being, but eventually, hopefully, a government will come to see the strength of the arguments.

Note that no-one cites tax as a reason for the current rules. An extension of the charity trading exemption would not cost any significant amount of tax, as the current regime confers effective exemption. An extension of the charity trading relief would not affect the position as regards rates, that is, the rating position is the same whether the trade is carried on by a charity or a charity subsidiary. In either case (except for charity shops) a fundraising trade does not qualify for rating relief.

http://www.archive2.official-documents.co.uk/document/cm64/6440/6440.pdf

CHAPTER NINE

COMPANIES HELD BY CHARITIES

Cross references

The following topics are considered elsewhere:
6.22 (Other investments: Type 12)
8.4 (Computing charity trade profit)
8.16 (Trading stock sold to subsidiary)
8.19 (Charity trade exemptions: Critique)
11.2 (Group relief)
13.1 (Acquisition of company)

9.1 Company held by charity

This chapter considers non-charitable companies held by charities.

The company is typically a trading company, but similar issues arise for investment companies. We refer to it as the "subsidiary company" (or sometimes the "trading company" or the "donor company" according to context).

The company is typically held by one charity, or occasionally by more than one charity. In this chapter the **"parent charity"** is the charity which owns the company.

This chapter also considers some issues for companies held Suj jointly by charities and non-charities.

9.2 Why use trading companies

HMRC Guidance Note provides:

> **3.14: Companies wholly owned by a charity or CASC**
> 3.14.1 ...Charities and CASCs may set up wholly-owned subsidiary companies to carry out trading activities that fall outside the tax exemptions available to them. For example, a charity may set up a wholly-owned subsidiary to operate a retail trade through a network of charity shops. A CASC may set up a wholly-owned subsidiary for trading income eg for income received from bar takings or the private hire of club facilities.
> 3.14.2 These companies often enter into a Gift Aid arrangement with their parent charity, under which they agree or contract to pay to the charity or CASC a sum of money equivalent to some or all of their taxable profits.
> 3.14.3 When a company owned by a charity or CASC makes such a payment it may not be treated as a distribution of profit, but as a qualifying charitable donation under the company Gift Aid rules...
> 3.14.5 Since 1 April 2006, companies wholly owned by a single charity and Companies owned by two or more charities can use Gift Aid donations to donate in this way.

> 3.14.6 Since 1 April 2014, companies wholly owned by one or more CASCs can also use Gift Aid donations to donate in the same way.

HMRC Guidance Note Annex iv provides:

> 45. Charities carrying out trading to which the statutory tax exemptions don't apply may arrange for a trading activity to be carried on by a wholly owned subsidiary trading company. Using this approach it's possible for some or all of the subsidiary company's trading profits to be passed to the charity using the company Gift Aid scheme.
> Companies owned by charities are liable to pay tax on trading profits in the same way as other non-charitable companies. But, like other companies, they can get tax relief for charitable payments to a charity under the company Gift Aid scheme. Subject to certain restrictions outlined at section 191 CTA 2010 and subsequent sections, a company donating all of its taxable profits to charity will get a tax deduction equal to the amount of the profits, so that no Corporation Tax will be payable. In the hands of the charity the donation isn't trading income. The donation is taxable as income but is exempt from tax provided it is applied for charitable purposes (section 473(1) CTA 2010 and section 522 ITA 2007 refer).

Trading companies involve significant administrative costs (including management time) and should only be used:

(1) Where:
  (a) other tax reliefs for charity trading income are not available, and
  (b) the tax saving exceeds the administrative cost; or
(2) Where the charity needs the benefit of limited liability.

9.3 Extracting profit by Gift Aid

Trading profits must be extracted by using Gift Aid. The company will make a gift of an amount equal to its profits to the charity (or any other charity), and will obtain tax relief on the gift.

The HMRC Guidance Note correctly warns at Annex iv:

> 50. Gift Aid payments must be made as a payment of money from the company to the charity. The company and charity should avoid sharing one bank account so that this transfer can be seen to have taken place.

9.3.1 *Dividend*

By contrast, the distribution of profits by the company by way of dividend will always be less tax effective. The distributing company would be bound to pay corporation tax on its profits without deduction for the dividend. The recipient charity would not be subject to tax on the dividend.[1] The result is that where a charity extracts taxable profit from a company by way of dividend it will indirectly bear tax at the company's rate.

9.3.2 *Liquidation*

Liquidation of a company and the return of accumulated profits to the charity by way of capital should result in no additional charge to tax; see 9.18 (Liquidation). However, it will not enable any tax otherwise payable by the company to be recovered.

9.4 Carry-back relief

If the company does not know the exact amount of its profits, it will not know how much to give. If it gives too little, then it will still have some profits which remain subject to tax. To ease this problem, Gift Aid payments by wholly-owned subsidiaries may be made up to 9 months after the end of the accounting period.

Section 199(1) CTA 2010 sets out the requirements for the relief:

> This section applies if—
> (a) a company makes a qualifying payment,
> (b) the company is wholly owned by a charity, and
> (c) the company makes a claim for the payment (or part of it) to be treated as a qualifying charitable donation made in an accounting period falling wholly or partly within the period of 9 months ending with the date of the making of the payment.

Section 199(2) CTA 2010 sets out the relief:

> The payment (or part) is to be treated for corporation tax purposes as a qualifying charitable donation made in that accounting period and not in any later period.

We refer to this as "**carry-back relief**", and the company which makes the gift is the **"donor company"**.

The relief applies to all wholly-owned companies, not just trading companies, though in practice the donor company will usually be trading.

The 9 month time limit matches the filing deadline of the company for the previous accounting period.

The HMRC Guidance Note correctly states that carry-back relief is not

---

1 See 4.7 (Dividends and distributions).

available when a company is not wholly-owned at Annex iv para 48:

> In general, a company can only deduct a company Gift Aid donation (a charitable deduction) from its profits for the accounting period in which the monetary donation is actually made. It's not possible to carry back the deduction into an earlier period or to carry it forward into a later period.

It is difficult to see why carry-back relief should be restricted to wholly-owned companies; perhaps the law reflects effective lobbying on the part of the charitable sector rather than an attempt to found the law on sound principles; but there it is.

The donor company must be wholly-owned at the time the donation is made. Thus a charity could acquire shares in a company and the company could then make a donation and claim carry back relief. However in such a case one would need to consider the acquisition of property rule[2] and the transactions in securities code.[3]

9.4.1 *"Wholly-owned"*

Section 200 CTA 2010 defines "wholly-owned". There are separate definitions for companies limited by shares and companies limited by guarantee. Section 200(1) CTA 2010 provides:

> For the purposes of this Chapter a company is wholly owned by a charity if condition A or B is met.

We refer to **"wholly-owned conditions A and B"**.

9.4.2 *Condition A: Share capital*

Section 200 CTA 2010 provides:

> (2) Condition A is that—
> (a) the company has an ordinary share capital, and
> (b) every part of that share capital is owned by a charity (whether or not the same charity)....
>
> (4) Ordinary share capital of a company is treated as owned by a charity if a charity—
> (a) directly or indirectly owns that share capital within the meaning of Chapter 3 of Part 24, or

2 See 15.19 (Acquisition of property rule).
3 See 13.3 (Transactions in securities).

> (b) would be taken so to own it if references in that Chapter to a body corporate included references to a charity which is not a body corporate.
>
> (4A) In the case of a charity which is a registered club, ordinary share capital of a company is treated as owned by a charity if the charity beneficially owns that share capital.

9.4.3 *Condition B: Guarantee company*

Section 200 CTA 2010 provides:

> (3) Condition B is that—
> (a) the company is limited by guarantee, and
> (b) every beneficiary of the company is or must be a charity or a company wholly owned by a charity....
>
> (5) A beneficiary of a company is a person who—
> (a) is beneficially entitled to participate in the company's divisible profits, or
> (b) will be beneficially entitled to share in any of the company's net assets available for distribution on its winding up.

This is only relevant to non-charitable guarantee companies which are wholly-owned by charities. That is rare.

9.4.4 *Claim for carry-back relief*

Section 199(3) CTA 2010 provides:

> A claim must be made within the period of two years immediately following the accounting period in which the payment is made or such longer period as an officer of Revenue and Customs may allow.

In practice the donor company will make the claim by putting in its tax return.

9.4.5 *Company administration*

The former HMRC booklet CS2 (Trading and Charities) observed at para 12:

> To assist in estimating the trading profits companies should have good up-to-date records. Some companies also prepare part-year accounts ahead of the end of the accounting period so that they can make the estimate more accurately.
>
> In the case of a seasonal trade (for instance, the sale of Christmas cards) it will often be useful if the company's accounting date can be arranged to fall during the quiet part of the trading year ...

It may assist the cash flow of charities if the trading company makes regular payments during the accounting period rather than waiting until just before the end of the accounting period.

Most of CS2 has now been incorporated into the HMRC Guidance Note. This passage was omitted, perhaps because the need for it is reduced by the introduction of carry-back relief, but it remains sound advice.

9.5 Estimated donation

9.5.1 *Need for estimation*

The deadline date for donations is:

(1) 9 months after the accounting period, if carry-back relief applies, or

(2) the end of the accounting period if the relief does not apply (non-wholly-owned companies).

If at that date the donor company is still unsure of its profits, it should make a payment of an estimated amount of profits. This is especially important for companies not wholly-owned, which do not qualify for carry-back relief.

9.5.2 *Problems of estimation*

An underestimate will give rise to a tax charge in the donor company, so the company will prefer to err on the side of caution and overestimate its profits. If it turns out that the donor company has overestimated its profits, and so made a donation in excess of its profits, the question arises whether the charity can return the excess.

In the following discussion:

The "**estimated gift**" means the donation from the donor company to the charity.

The "**refund**" means the refund from the charity to the donor company.

The possible difficulties are:

(1) The refund may be regarded as non-charitable expenditure: that would affect the charity's tax exemption.

(2) (a) The estimated gift may be regarded as made subject to a condition as to repayment: that would disqualify Gift Aid relief on the estimated gift.

(b) The refund may be regarded as a benefit received by the donor company in consequence of the estimated gift: that would disqualify Gift Aid relief on the estimated gift.[4]

In our view, where the donor company expresses the intention to give its profits and no more, over-estimates its profits and so makes too large a donation, and the charity makes a refund, then:

(1) The charity does not incur non-charitable expenditure by making the refund. The reason is that the charity is (normally) under an obligation to repay. (If, exceptionally, that is not the case, the payment can in principle also be defended as for the benefit of the charity.)

(2) The estimated gift is not subject to a condition as to repayment and the refund is not a benefit. The reason is that the estimated gift should be regarded as a split payment:
   (a) the intended donation, equal to the trading profits, which is given unconditionally; and
   (b) the excess, which is returned, but for which no Gift Aid relief is claimed.

9.5.3 *HMRC guidance*

The HMRC Guidance Note provides:

> 3.15.1 Charity or CASC owned companies can estimate their expected Corporation Tax profits and make a qualifying donation based on that estimate with the intention of reducing any Corporation Tax liability to nil. Where the estimated qualifying donation to its parent charity or CASC is more than its actual profits, then the excess part of the donation may be repaid by the charity or CASC. The original donation is not regarded as being made with 'a condition as to repayment' and the amount repaid will not be treated as non-charitable expenditure by the charity or CASCs provided the:
>
> - company is wholly-owned by the charity, or by a number of charities that include the charity
> - charitable payment is an amount which the company estimates to be the amount that will reduce the company's taxable total profits for the accounting period in which the payment is made ('the relevant period') to nil.
> - only reason that the charity or CASC makes the repayment is to adjust the amount of the company's donation so that it is an amount that will reduce the company's taxable total profits for the relevant period to nil

---

4 It is assumed that the amount of the refund exceeds the small benefit limit.

- repayment is made no later than 12 months after the end of the relevant period

There are two valid legal bases for payment of the refund from the charity to the donor company:

(1) a legal obligation (evidenced by correspondence, board minutes or deed that the intention was to pay over only the taxable profits and that excess had to be refunded);

(2) need to repay (in the absence of legal obligation) ie the refund was for the benefit of the charity because the donor company needed the funds.

In practice when profits are estimated there should be correspondence, a board minute or a deed of covenant to meet points [2] and [3]. It does not strictly matter which, but we think a deed of covenant is to be preferred and a draft is set out below.

Even when accounts are final and profits are not estimated, it is best practice to have a deed of covenant, since from time to time errors are later discovered and profits recalculated; this avoids problems if a Gift Aid donation unexpectedly turns out to be excessive.

It can be inferred from the guidance that HMRC did not take any point about the repayment rule or the benefit rule.

While HMRC guidance still remains, wholly-owned charitable companies that do not qualify for estimated donation relief (discussed below) should argue that the guidance still applies (eg if the one year deadline is missed).

9.5.4 *HMRC statement 2009*

The reasonably satisfactory position set out above was thrown into confusion by the consultation document "Extra-statutory Concessions – Second Technical Consultation on Draft Legislation" (2009). This described the HMRC practice as an extra statutory concession, (though the HMRC Guidance Note categorised its guidance as practice, not concession). The Consultation Document provided:

> Companies that are wholly owned by a charity (or one or more charities) typically pay up all of their corporation tax profits as 'company Gift Aid' donations to their parent charity or charities, and claim a deduction thereby ensuring that the subsidiary has no corporation tax liability.
> A deduction is allowed only in respect of payments made by the company in the accounting period concerned - subject to express exceptions. To satisfy this condition companies that are wholly owned by a charity make estimated payments to that charity during the accounting period before

> the final corporation tax liability for that accounting period has been calculated. As it is made before the accounts are finalised, this donation is a best estimate of the taxable profits for the accounting period that would be liable to corporation tax and is made with the intention of reducing the company's tax liability to zero.

So far this is broadly correct, though - despite the reference to "exceptions" - it seems likely that the author overlooked carry-back relief. The statement now becomes contentious:

> These estimated donations carry an option for partial repayment (to the extent that the full amount is not needed to 'cover' the company's profits).

We do not expect that "option" is intended in its strict sense, but merely suggests that the donor company would normally have a right to repayment of the surplus, and (while a question of fact in each case) that would normally be right.

> [1] As a result of this inherent "condition as to repayment", the donations would not legally qualify as company Gift Aid donations within the [current] rules.
> [2] Any repayment by the charity to the donor company would therefore be non-charitable expenditure and a tax charge may arise.
> [3] The concession however permits that where such estimated donations are made, any repayment by the charity is not to be treated as non-charitable expenditure.
> The intention of the draft legislation is to put this extra statutory concession on a legislative footing.

The author muddles two distinct rules, the repayment rule and the charitable expenditure rules, and while a condition as to repayment (if there were one) would indeed disqualify Gift Aid relief, it would not give rise to non-charitable expenditure.

9.5.5 *Estimation relief*

The legislation proposed by the consultative document is now found at s.192 CTA 2010, which provides:

> (1) If—
> (a) a company makes a payment to a charity (the "charitable payment"),
> (b) the charity makes a payment to the company (the "repayment"), and

(c) each of conditions A to D is met,
the charitable payment is not subject to a condition as to repayment.

We refer to this as **"estimated donation relief"** and we refer to the conditions as **"estimated donation conditions A to D"**.

(2) Condition A is that the company is wholly owned[5] by the charity, or by a number of charities that include the charity.
(3) Condition B is that the charitable payment is of an amount which the company estimates to be the amount necessary to reduce to nil the company's taxable total profits for the accounting period in which the payment is made (the "relevant period").

Where carry-back relief applies, the payment is treated as made in the earlier accounting period and not the period it was actually made, so condition B is satisfied.

(4) Condition C is that the only purpose for which the charity makes the repayment is to adjust the amount of the charitable payment so that it is of the amount actually necessary to reduce to nil the company's taxable total profits for the relevant period.
(5) Condition D is that the repayment is made no later than 12 months after the end of the relevant period.

Assuming the estimated donation conditions are satisfied, there are two reliefs. First, s.192(1) CTA 2010 states that the estimated donation is not subject to a condition as to repayment. Secondly, s.192(6) CTA 2010 provides:

If subsection (1) applies—
(a) the repayment is not non-charitable expenditure for the purposes of section 493 or 515 of this Act or section 543(1)(f) of ITA 2007,
(aa) the repayment is not non-qualifying expenditure for the purposes of Chapter 9 of Part 13 (see section 661(5)),[6]...

9.5.6 *Claim estimation relief*

Section 192(6) CTA 2010 provides:

If subsection (1) applies ...
(b) paragraphs 56 and 62 (but not 64) of Schedule 18 to FA 1998 (supplementary claims or elections) apply to the repayment.

5 For the definition see 9.4.1 ("Wholly-owned").
6 This relates to the CASCs: see 41.29 (Qualifying expenditure rules).

The relevant paragraphs of sch 18 provide:

> 56 A company which has made a claim or election under any provision of the Corporation Tax Acts (by including it in a return or otherwise) and subsequently discovers that a mistake has been made in it may make a supplementary claim or election within the time allowed for making the original claim or election...
>
> 62 (1) A claim, election, application or notice to which this paragraph applies—
>
> (a) may be made or given at any time within one year from the end of the relevant accounting period, or
>
> (b) if previously made or given may at any such time be revoked or varied—
>
> (i) in the same manner as it was made or given, and
>
> (ii) by or with the consent of the same person or persons who made, gave or consented to it (or, if a person has died, by or with the consent of his personal representatives),
>
> unless, by virtue of any enactment, it is irrevocable.
>
> (1A) This paragraph applies to a claim under paragraph 51 relating to the accounting period in respect of which the amendment or assessment is made.
>
> (2) This paragraph applies to any other claim, election, application or notice—
>
> (a) relating to the accounting period in respect of which the amendment or assessment is made, or
>
> (b) made or given by reference to an event occurring in that period,
>
> whose making, giving, revocation or variation has or could have the effect of reducing a relevant liability of the company.
>
> (3) The following are relevant liabilities of the company for this purpose—
>
> (a) the increased liability to tax resulting from the amendment or assessment;
>
> (b) any other liability to tax of the company—
>
> (i) for the accounting period to which the amendment or assessment relates, or
>
> (ii) for any subsequent accounting period ending not later than one year after the end of the relevant accounting period.
>
> (4) Where a claim, election, application or notice is made, given, revoked or varied by virtue of this paragraph, all such adjustments shall be made, whether by way of discharge or repayment of tax or the making of amendments, assessments or otherwise, as are required to take account of the effect of the taking of that action on any person's liability to tax for any chargeable period.
>
> (5) The provisions of the Taxes Management Act 1970 relating to appeals against decisions on claims apply with any necessary modifications to a decision on the revocation or variation of a claim by virtue of this paragraph.
>
> (6) This paragraph has effect subject to—
>
> paragraph 63 (consequential claims etc affecting tax liability of another person), and
>
> paragraph 64 (consequential claims etc not to give rise to reduction in liability).

9.5.7 *Deed of covenant*

The purpose of this draft deed is to satisfy the following requirements:

- HMRC practice relating to estimated donations by trading companies: see 9.5.3 (HMRC guidance) - Estimated donation relief: see 9.5.5 (Estimation relief)
- VAT fundraising relief: see 37.16 ("Charity" for fundraising events exemption)

It is assumed that the company is wholly-owned by the charity.
The drafting is based on the statutory provisions.

This deed of covenant is made [date] between:
(1) [Name of company] of [address] (the "Covenantor") and
(2) [Name of charity] of [address] (the "Charity").
Whereas:
(A) The Covenantor has agreed to transfer its profits (from whatever source) to the Charity.
(B) The Covenantor is wholly-owned by the Charity.
Now this deed witnesses as follows:
1. In this Deed:
  (1) **"Accounting Period"** means:
    (a) the accounting period of the Covenantor for the purposes of the Corporation Tax Acts beginning with the accounting period [specify] and
    (b) subsequent accounting periods beginning before the termination of this covenant.
  (2) **"Payment Deadline"** means 9 months after the end of the Accounting Period.
2. The Covenantor covenants to pay to the Charity an amount equal to the total taxable profits of each Accounting Period.
3. If the Covenantor anticipates that the total taxable profits of an Accounting Period (**"the relevant Accounting Period"**) will not be ascertained before the Payment Deadline the Covenantor will estimate the amount necessary to reduce to nil the Covenantor's total taxable profits for the relevant Accounting Period and pay the estimated amount.
4. If payment is made after the end of the relevant Accounting Period, the Covenantor will make a claim under s.199 Corporation Tax Act 2010 that the payment will be treated as a qualifying charitable donation made in the relevant Accounting Period.
5. Payment shall be made before the Payment Deadline for that Accounting Period.
6. If the amount paid by the Covenantor to the Charity exceeds the amount necessary to reduce to nil the Covenantor's total taxable profits for the relevant Accounting Period, the Charity shall repay the excess to the Covenantor no later than 12 months after the end of the relevant Accounting Period.

7. The Covenantor may terminate this covenant by giving 12 months notice in writing to the Charity or such shorter notice as the Charity may agree.
In Witness *etc*

9.5.8 *Estimation relief: Critique*

The 12 month time limit for estimated donation relief scarcely exceeds the 9 month period for carry-back relief. This makes no sense and we suspect that the relief was enacted because someone overlooked the existence of carry-back relief.

A simple reform would be to repeal estimated donation relief and extend the period for carry-back relief to 12 months. That would be a simplification with no loss of tax.

9.6 Maximum donation

HMRC Guidance Note Annex iv para 47 provides:

> When deciding how much of its profits to give to its parent charity, a trading company will need to take account of the following:
> [1] any limitations imposed by the Insolvency Act 1986 on the amount it can pay out

This applies to anyone making a gift, whether a company or an individual. In practice a difficulty here would be unusual.[7]

> [2] retention of sufficient profits to avoid a cash drain

See 9.15 (Returning Gift Aid payment: Circularity).

> [3] any restrictions imposed by the Memorandum and Articles of Association of the company

In practice a difficulty here would be unusual.

> [4] and any other requirements that may be imposed upon the directors.

9.7 Donation exceeds distributable profit

9.7.1 *Mismatch problem*

It may happen that:
(1) a company wishes to give all its taxable profit to its parent, but
(2) the company's taxable profits (for corporation tax purposes) exceed its

---

7 See 15.16 (Repayment rule: Condition B)).

accounting profits (profits available for distribution for company law purposes).[8]

Taxable profits may exceed accounting profits for various reasons, for example:

(1) Some items are deductible for accounting purposes but not for tax; for instance, depreciation.
(2) Timing differences may arise, for instance benefit pension contributions may be deductible for tax purposes on payment but deducted for accounting purposes much earlier.

The subsidiary company would typically be carrying on a non-exempt trade, that is, the trade would not qualify for tax exemption if carried on directly by the charity; but the same issue will apply for a non-trading company, or a company carrying on a trade which could qualify for charity tax exemption.

9.7.2 *Restrictions on distribution*

There are two overlapping rules which restrict distributions from UK companies.[9] We call these the statutory rule and the common law rule. Section 830 Companies Act 2006 provides the statutory rule:

> A company may only make a distribution out of profits available for the purpose.

The common law rule preceded the introduction of the statutory rule[10] but the statutory provisions preserve the common law rule. Section 851 Companies Act 2006 provides:

> (1) Except as provided in this section, the provisions of this Part are without prejudice to any rule of law restricting the sums out of which, or the cases in which, a distribution may be made.
> (2) [The exception in s.851(2) is not relevant here.]
> (3) In this section references to distributions are to amounts regarded as

---

8 We gratefully acknowledge our debt to Mary Stokes, Barrister, for her advice to ICAEW on this topic.

9 Different rules may apply to foreign companies. Tax haven jurisdictions are not likely to have the same rules. In what follows it is assumed that the company is governed by UK law.

10 The common law rule can be traced to *Trevor v Whitworth* (1887) 12 App Cas 409; the statutory rule originated in s.39 Companies Act 1980, implementing EC Directive 1977/91.

> distributions for the purposes of any such rule of law as is referred to in subsection (1).

The two rules largely overlap, though there are minor differences.[11]

9.7.3 *"Distribution"*

Section 829(1) CA 2006 defines distribution for the purposes of the statutory rule:

> In this Part "distribution" means every description of distribution of a company's assets to its members, whether in cash or otherwise ...[12]

The definition is not helpful, as it uses the term "distribution", but "every description of distribution" does suggest that the word is not to be narrowly understood.

The concept of "distribution" is (more or less) the same for both rules. Thus *Clydebank Football Club v Steedman*, a case on the statutory rule, was cited in *Progress Property Company v Moorgarth Group,*[13] the leading case on the common law rule.

In *Clydebank Football Club v Steedman*:

> "Distribution" is not further defined than by [s.829 CA 2006] but it would appear that generally a distribution will be a transfer without consideration given by the recipient. The object of the statutory code is to prohibit the (gratuitous) return to shareholders, other than by specified means, of subscribed capital or assets representing the same. However, ... a transfer involving the passing of some consideration may in certain circumstances give rise to a distribution. That is because a transfer, albeit some consideration is given, may involve in substance a gift of capital to the transferee.[14]

---

11 (1) Under the statutory rule, profits available for distribution are (in short) determined by reference to profits (less realised losses) up to the last annual (or interim) accounts of a company. Under the common law rule one has regard to events occurring after the date of the last accounts. Thus if a company has realised losses after the last accounts, a distribution which is lawful under the statutory rules could still be unlawful under the common law rule.
(2) The statutory rule apply to all companies; the common law rule applies only to limited companies with a share capital.

12 The section continues with exceptions not relevant here.

13 [2010] UKSC 55.

14 [2002] SLT 109 at [55] approved in *Progress Property v Moorgarth Group* [2011] 2 All ER 432.

Aveling Barford v Perion[15] is an example of a transfer at an undervalue that was a distribution. But a transaction at an undervalue is not necessarily a distribution. The question is whether the transaction is entered into by the company because the other party is a shareholder. In short, is it a "company-shareholder transaction".[16] If so, the transaction will be classified as a distribution.

Whether a transaction amounts to a distribution is a matter of substance not form. The label the parties give to the transaction (eg sale, remuneration, or charitable donation) is not decisive.

In some cases the parties state of mind is irrelevant; and in other cases subjective intentions are relevant (e.g. sale of property by a company to a shareholder at an undervalue is not a distribution if the parties considered it to be for full value.)

A gift by a company to a charity (the "donee charity") would not be a distribution if the donee charity is not a shareholder or ultimate beneficial owner. That would be the case even if the donee charity had charitable objects which were the same as the parent charity. (It may be different if there were an arrangement under which the donee charity transferred the funds back to the parent, or used them in some way to benefit the parent.)

A gift by a company to a charity which is a shareholder, but where the reason for the gift has nothing to do with the charity being a shareholder, would not be classified as a distribution. This might be the case where, for example, the charity held only a small number of shares in the company, or the company made gifts to a number of charities and there were reasons why a gift to this particular charity was selected, independent of its status as a shareholder.

All this is clear. Views have however differed on the case where a company is a 100% subsidiary and habitually gives all its taxable profits to its charitable parent. There is no case where the courts had been asked to consider whether a gift from a company to its charitable parent is a distribution.

9.7.4 *Charity commission view(s)*

Until 2015, the Charity Commission stated that giving to the charitable parent company was permitted. The Charity Commission has changed its mind, and the current edition of CC35 (2016) provides:

---

15 [1989] BCLC 626.

16 See *Jenkins v Harbour View Courts* [1966] NZLR 1 at p.23.

4.5 Can trustees expect their charity's wholly-owned trading subsidiary to always Gift Aid all the profits shown in the profit and loss account to its parent charity?

Note: this section was revised on 24/02/2016. It is based on an updated legal view and replaces section 4.5 which was withdrawn on 31/10/2014.

No. Company law makes it unlawful for any company to make distributions in excess of distributable profits. If the accounting profit is higher than the value calculated for distributable profits, only the lower figure can be paid across under Gift Aid.

A consequence of this is that when the taxable profits of the trading subsidiary are greater than its distributable profits, the trading subsidiary may have a tax liability. HMRC's guidance on charities and trading contains advice on the tax treatment of this issue...

The Institute for Chartered Accountants in England and Wales (ICAEW) has issued a 'technical release' Guidance on donations by a company to its parent charity [TECH 16/14BL][17] which provides a more detailed explanation. It is based on legal advice provided to them.

ICAEW's technical release also provides guidance on potential ways of addressing likely accounting issues that may arise when rectifying the position. This includes an option to write off all or part of a loan made to a wholly-owned trading subsidiary in connection with this situation. If trustees are considering this option, they would need to be able to show that:

1. The decision is genuinely in the charity's interests, using the principles in It's your decision.
2. The only purpose of the write-off is to rectify a technical problem resulting from the need to align the arrangements with this clarified company law position.
3. The relationship with the trading subsidiary is itself a legitimate and justifiable arrangement that is clearly operating in the charity's interests.
4. There has not been a previous history of the writing-off of loans advanced by the charity to its trading subsidiary due to the subsidiary's non-performance in repaying loans.
5. The trading subsidiary is otherwise financially viable and a going concern.

---

17 ICAEW, "Guidance on donations by a company to its parent charity" TECH 16/14BL (2014, updated 2016)
http://www.icaew.com/~/media/corporate/files/technical/technical%20releases/legal%20and%20regulatory/tech16%2014bl%20guidance%20for%20donations%20by%20a%20company%20to%20its%20parent%20charity.ashx

> If the conditions listed are fulfilled then trustees do not need to seek any waiver or prior agreement from the commission. If these conditions are not all fulfilled then the commission will not issue any waiver or approval except under the most exceptional circumstances and only after the trustees have taken professional advice and made a case outlining all relevant facts including a reasoned justification for their request.

HMRC agree. Para 45 Annex iv HMRC Guidance Note provides:

> As set out in a Technical Release issued by the ICAEW (TECH 16/14BL), donation payments by a subsidiary company to its parent charity are typically considered to be distributions and therefore subsidiary companies must not pay more to the charity than the level of profits available for distribution, even if the level of taxable profits is higher. Any part of a payment from a subsidiary company to a charity which exceeds the subsidiary company's profits available for distribution is therefore unlawful under the Companies Act 2006.

A gift to a charitable parent is a distribution for company law purposes, because the company law context is focused on identifying a dressed up return of capital, and a gift to a charitable parent may be seen in that light. This is consistent with the object of the rule, which is to protect creditors. This consideration applies even though:

(1) Charity subsidiaries normally have only a nominal share capital, so there is no share capital to protect.
(2) There are rules of insolvency law which constrain making of gifts and which would protect creditors.
(3) The subsidiary company has no creditors at the time of the gift, or no creditors apart from the parent charity.

The former Charity Commission view is not wholly indefensible,[18] but in practice companies should adopt the cautious course and follow this guidance: a subsidiary company should not make a gift to its parent in excess of profits available fo distribution.

9.7.5 *Unlawful distribution: Tax*

Gift Aid relief only applies if there is a "payment".[19] On making an unlawful distribution, the subsidiary company in principle acquires two

---

18 The gift is not a distribution for tax purposes: *Noved Investment Co v HMRC* [2006] STC (SCD) 120 at [55]. But on this point the tax definition may be different from the company law definition.

19 See 15.8 (Payment: Gift Aid condition A).

rights against the parent charity:

(1) A claim *in personam* for an amount equal to the sum distributed; and
(2) A claim *in rem* for the funds transferred, which the charity parent holds on constructive trust for the company.

Because of the constructive trust, there is no "payment" for Gift Aid purposes. In *Ridge Securities v IRC*, a company claimed to fall within (what was then) s.169 ITA 1952 which applied if it made a "payment". The company had made an unlawful distribution, in breach of the common law rule. The court determined that the company did not fall within s.169 because the unlawful distribution was not payment in the relevant sense. It was "a nullity" which had "no legal operation".[20]

HMRC agree. Para 45 Annex iv HMRC Guidance Note provides:

> The company will not get a tax deduction for any unlawful distributions for accounting periods commencing on or after 1 April 2015.

If a charity makes a payment which is in part a lawful distribution and in part an unlawful distribution, the payment qualifies for Gift Aid relief on the part which is a lawful distribution (regardless of whether or not there is a repayment later of the unlawful distribution).

9.7.6 *Unlawful distribution: Repayment*

In some cases the parent charity may repay unlawful distributions to the subsidiary company. A repayment may be treated as income for accountancy purposes, but it is not taxable income. Income tax and corporation tax are charged on specified sources (interest, dividends etc) and repayment of unlawful distributions is not income from a specified source. Accordingly there is a repayment of an unlawful distribution is not subject to CT.

The repayment is in satisfaction of a liability of the charity parent, and not a misapplication of charity funds or a breach of trust, so it has no tax implications for the charity parent.

HMRC agree. Para 45 Annex iv HMRC Guidance Note provides:

> If unlawful distributions have been paid by a subsidiary company to a charity in earlier accounting periods, TECH 16/14BL sets out that

20 See 44 TC 373 at p.395-396. Likewise in *Russell Baker v HMRC* [2013] UKFTT 394 (TC) a company's purchase of its own shares in breach of company law was void, and the purported payment of the purchase price (held on constructive trust for the company) was not a distribution under the standard tax definition.

(subject to time limits) the parent charity has a liability to repay the unlawful distributions and the company has a right to receive the sums. The repayment of such prior unlawful distributions by the charity to the company will not be taxable income in the hands of the company.

9.7.7 *Avoiding accounting profit exceeding taxable profit*

Some steps may prevent the company from generating accounting profits in excess of taxable profits. In particular, so far as a mismatch arises from assets which would be depreciated for company law purposes but which do not qualify for capital allowance for tax purposes, the assets could be purchased by the charity and let at a rent to the company.[21] Then the depreciation is not a deduction in the company's accounting profits.

9.7.8 *Avoiding distribution in excess of distributable profit*

In some cases, subsidiary companies may be able to prepare informal interim accounts as at the time they have profits (and wish to make the distribution), rather than using earlier annual accounts (where there were insufficient distributable profits). Payments may be made up to nine months post-year end and still be carried back for Gift Aid relief to the earlier year. This is unlikely to be a permanent solution unless the company's distributable and taxable profits are expected to come back into line over a period of a few years.

The company subsidiary may make charitable gifts to non-shareholder charities which had appropriate charitable objects (objects which were also within the charitable objects of the parent charity). However the payment would be an expense on the profit and loss account and this would diminish its distributable profits going forward, which would raise a problem if the company later wished to make gifts to its parent.

9.8 Gift aid: Accountancy aspects

The Charities SORP (2nd ed, 2019) provides:

> B.26. FRS 102 requires payments by subsidiaries to their charitable parents that qualify for gift aid to be accounted for as distributions to owners, and treated akin to dividends.
> Section 23 of FRS 102 requires dividends to be recognised when the shareholder's right to receive payment is established. The parent

21 If VAT is an issue, it may be convenient for the parent and the subsidiary to become a VAT group.

charity's right to receive payment is established when the subsidiary has a legal obligation to distribute its profits to its owners at the reporting date.

Therefore, a gift aid payment shall not be recognised as a liability in the individual accounts of a subsidiary unless a legal obligation for the subsidiary to make the payment exists at the reporting date.

9.9 Loan from subsidiary co to charity

Section 455(1) CTA 2010 provides:

> This section applies if a close company makes a loan or advances money to—
>
> (a) a relevant person[22] who is
> [i] a participator in the company or
> [ii] an associate of such a participator,
>
> (b) the trustees of a settlement one or more of the trustees or actual or potential beneficiaries of which is
> [i] a participator in the company or
> [ii] an associate of such a participator, or
>
> (c) a limited liability partnership or other partnership one or more of the partners in which is an individual who is—
> (i) a participator in the company, or
> (ii) an associate of an individual who is such a participator.

If these conditions are met, we read on to s.455(2) CTA 2010 :

> There is due from the company, as if it were an amount of corporation tax chargeable on the company for the accounting period in which the loan or advance is made, an amount equal to 25% of the amount of the loan or advance.

A loan from a close company to a charitable company is not caught, as a company does not fall within paragraphs (a)-(c).

A loan from a close company to a charitable trust could be caught, under para (b), but s.456(2A) CTA 2010 provides relief:

> Section 455 does not apply to a loan or advance made to a trustee of a charitable trust if the loan or advance is applied to the purposes of the charitable trust only.

---

22 Section 455(6) CTA 2010 provides: "In this Chapter, "relevant person" means—
(a) an individual, or
(b) a company receiving a loan or advance in a fiduciary or representative capacity."

9.10 GAAR

One might have thought that the use of a trading company to avoid taxation on trading profits would fail as an abusive scheme rendered ineffective under the GAAR. This would be on the basis that the company is inserted solely to avoid taxation. In practice there should not be a problem here. The arrangement is not abusive, since:

(1) HMRC have indicated that they do not take any objection, in a straightforward case.[23] On the contrary, HMRC Guidance Note encourages charities to use trading companies.

(2) If necessary, in most cases, the charity may be able to argue that the use of the trading company is for bona fide commercial reasons. The Charity Commission prefers or requires charities to operate in this way, taking the view that charity law does not permit a charity to operate a trade for the substantial purpose of fundraising.

A *Furniss v Dawson* attack failed in *Nightingale v Price*.[24]

9.11 Financing trading company

This topic raises tax and charity law issues. The Charity Commission views are in CC35 (Charities, Trading and Tax) and are discussed in this chapter. For tax issues so far as they concern the charitable expenditure rules see 6.22 (Other investments: IT type 12). Since one of the requirements of an approved charitable investment is that the investment is for the benefit of the charity, and an investment made in accordance with charity law is likely to be for the benefit of the charity (the purpose of charity law regulation of investment is to ensure that investment is for the benefit of the charity) the two issues overlap, but they are not identical.

This is an area in which charities will need to act on advice if they are not later to find themselves subject to criticism.

There are several ways to finance a trading company:

(1) Gratuitous support from the charity
(2) Retention of profits in the trading company
(3) Gratuitous support from benefactors
(4) Share subscription from the charity
(5) Loan from the charity
(6) Banks or other arm's length commercial investors

---

23 See the passage cited in 9.15 (Returning Gift Aid payment: Circularity).

24 See 9.15 (Returning Gift Aid payment: Circularity).

9.11.1 *Gratuitous support from charity*

CC35 provides:

> **4.6 How should trading subsidiaries be funded**
> Parent charities must not provide support to trading subsidiaries, on terms which involve a greater or lesser element of gift. For example:
> [1] a parent charity must not make donations to the trading subsidiary, in cash or in kind, whether by purchasing stock for the subsidiary, and donating that stock to the trading subsidiary, or otherwise;
> [2] a parent charity must not settle the debts of a trading subsidiary
> [3] a charity must, if allowing the use of its staff, buildings or equipment by a trading subsidiary, make fair charges for those uses (see 4.21 and 4.22).

This is not true where the activities of a wholly-owned trading company directly further the charitable purposes of the charity.

We do not consider that it is true generally. In the case of a wholly-owned company, there is no difference between a gift and a subscription for share capital. Where one is permitted, so is the other. But in practice this advice is usually followed. Para D6 sums up:

> A trading subsidiary's need for funding will therefore, in most cases, be met mainly out of share capital and/or loan capital. This capital is normally, though not always, provided by the parent charity.

9.11.2 *Trading company retains profit*

CC35 provides:

> **4.7 Can a trading subsidiary fund itself by the retention of profits?**
> As noted in 4.4 above, if all the trading subsidiary's distributable profits are paid to the parent charity as Gift Aid, the trading subsidiary's liability to corporation tax is reduced or eliminated. However, the trading subsidiary's needs for finance then have to be met entirely out of capital. Some parent charities prefer to accept the corporation tax consequences of the trading subsidiary retaining distributable profits. Indeed such retention may be required, where funding by way of loan has been obtained from commercial banks or other third parties, in order to service the loan. This approach:
> [1] enables the trading subsidiary to fund itself by a combination of capital and retained profits in a way which is closer to ordinary commercial practice
> [2] may also make it easier for the parent charity to justify investments in the trading subsidiary, especially where significant equity finance is

required to fund ongoing trading activities; ...

Neither point [1] not point [2] are cogent arguments for retention of profits when set against the cost of the CT charge. We think no sensible charity would or should prefer to leave taxable profits in a trading company if there was an alternative. Para 4.7 continues:

> however, such retention of profits by a trading subsidiary can also prejudice VAT reliefs which would otherwise be available (see 4.13)

VAT zero rating (if applicable)[25] is another reason not to retain relevant profits (as if corporation tax was not enough).

This is because, under VATA sch 8 group 15 Item 1A:

> The sale, or letting on hire, by a taxable person of any goods donated to him for:
> (a) sale,
> (b) letting,
> (c) sale or letting,
> (d) sale or export,
> (e) letting or export, or
> (f) sale, letting or export,
> [*is only zero-rated:*]
> if [*the taxable person*] is a profits-to-charity person in respect of the goods

and a trading subsidiary would only be a "profits-to-charity person" (under VATA sch 8 group 15 Note (1E)) in respect of any goods if:

> (a) [*it*] has agreed in writing (whether or not contained in a deed) to transfer to a charity [*its*] profits from supplies and lettings of the goods, or
> (b) [*its*] profits from supplies and lettings of the goods are otherwise payable to a charity.

9.11.3 *Investment criteria*

CC35 provides:

> **4.8 What are the legal obligations of trustees investing charity funds in a trading subsidiary?**
> The same considerations apply to an investment by a parent charity in a

25 See 38.4 (Donation and sale of donated goods).

trading subsidiary, as to any other investment of a charity's resources. Trustees must, whenever investing a charity's resources:
[1] be certain that the investment is within the charity's investment powers
[2] exercise such care and skill in the investment process as is reasonable in the circumstances
[3] have regard to the suitability to the charity of investments of the same kind as the particular investment which it is proposed to make
[4] have regard to the suitability of the particular investment in question, as an investment of the kind which it seems appropriate to make
[5] have regard to the need for diversification of investments, as appropriate to the circumstances of the charity
[6] ordinarily obtain and consider advice about the investment from a person reasonably believed by the trustees to be qualified to give it by his or her ability in and practical experience of financial and other matters; the advice needs to have regard to the suitability and diversification points previously mentioned
In the context of a proposed investment in a trading subsidiary which is used to carry on a non-primary purpose trade, this means that:
[7] the trustees must reasonably consider that it is in the charity's interests to make the investment, after making a fair comparison of this form of investment with other forms of investment which might be selected
[8] this fair comparison must involve an objective assessment of the trading subsidiary's business prospects
[9] the trustees must be satisfied as to the financial viability of the trading subsidiary, based on its business plan, cash flow forecasts, profit projections, risk analysis and other available information
[10] the trustees must ordinarily take appropriate advice on the investment, and the financial viability of the trading subsidiary. What is "appropriate" will depend on the circumstances: the cost of taking the advice is a relevant factor, and the cost should be commensurate to the size of the proposed investment
Trustees should also:
[11] pay attention to the length of time over which funds may be tied up in an investment in a trading subsidiary, since funds needed in the short to medium term may not be easily realised when invested in this way
[12] consider, and take suitable advice on, the possibility of obtaining independent funding as an alternative to funding by the charity; see 4.9
Precisely how the investment in the trading subsidiary is structured is a decision for which the parent charity's trustees (with professional advice) are responsible, having regard to the trustee investment duties summarised. Trustees must also consider periodically whether or not an

existing investment should be retained or disposed of. When reviewing investments, duties similar to those outlined apply. Trustees must also take into account section 506(4) of, and schedule 20 to, the 1988 act. These provisions can create a tax effect where loans to, or equity investments in, trading subsidiaries are inappropriate. This subject is summarised in 4.12.

9.11.4 *Investment from benefactors*

CC35 provides:

> **4.9 Can a charity seek outside investment in a trading subsidiary?**
> [After some basic comments, CC35 provides:]
> Share capital investment in a charity's trading subsidiary will usually, therefore, be unattractive to outside financiers motivated by profit.

Quite so.

> However a share capital investment in a trading subsidiary could be marketed to supporters of the parent charity, who might not be looking for a commercial return.

We think this unlikely. In particular, it is not generally desirable for supporters of the charity to make gifts to the trading company to provide finance: such gifts will not qualify for Gift Aid or other charity tax reliefs. Gifts should be made to the charity itself, which will then finance the trading company. Interest-free loans to the trading company raise the issues discussed in 20.2 (IT settlement provisions). But gifts to a trading company may be possible for traders who can obtain a trading deduction, or by way of sponsorship.

9.11.5 *Bank loan or arm's length investor*

CC35 para 4.9 continues:

> In most cases, outside investment in a charity's trading subsidiary will be in the form of loan capital, since interest payments on loans and repayments of the principal will take place before any Gift Aid payments to the parent charity. Loan finance may be available from banks, and from other private lenders, including supporters of the charity.
> Trustees should pay close attention to the terms on which loan capital is acquired since interest payments could significantly reduce the level of trading profit in the subsidiary. Even if the subsidiary's trading operation is profitable before loan charges, it may not be so after them. Charities should consider the possibility of obtaining loan capital from their

supporters, who may be prepared to provide finance on preferential terms.

When entering into a joint venture of this nature, it is important that the investment is in the charity's interests. As an aspect of considering the appropriateness of the joint venture, the trustees should consider whether any due diligence checks should be made regarding the financial status of the other partner(s), and should be satisfied that they share with their joint venture partner(s) similar views regarding the scale of investment required, the level of trading risk accepted, the mechanism for setting the direction of the trading activity and for reconciling for any disagreements between the partners.

When entering into a joint venture, whilst all parties will anticipate a successful outcome, it is also important to consider the 'exit strategy', should insuperable difficulties arise.

It is considered that one of the main underlying causes of joint venture failures is an irreconcilable difference in the understanding of the partners about the direction the joint venture is taking. Consequently it is recommended that all partners should consider and agree the objectives of the joint venture, should ensure that all of the necessary documentation is completed, and that a business plan has been agreed. Trustees are recommended to take further professional advice, where appropriate.

Trustees contemplating a joint venture of this nature need to bear in mind the following 2 tax points:

(1) Unless the joint-venture company is wholly-owned by one or more charities, any payments made to a charity as Gift Aid must actually be made during the financial year in which the payments are to offset the company's taxable profits. The facility to make Gift Aid payments up to 9 months after the end of the relevant financial year (see 4.4) is only available to companies which are wholly-owned by one or more charities.

(2) Where the commercial partner receives a distribution of profit from the company, HMRC may challenge the use of Gift Aid to make a corresponding payment to the charitable partner.

9.11.6 *Charity subscribes share capital*

CC35 provides:

4.10 What considerations apply to a charity's investment of share capital in a trading subsidiary?

[After some basic observations, CC35 provides:]

However, there are valid reasons why a parent charity might choose to capitalise a trading subsidiary by means of share capital rather than loan capital. For example:

> [1] the subscription by a parent charity of substantial share capital in its trading subsidiary can give confidence to suppliers, customers, creditors, prospective creditors and others with whom the trading subsidiary has a business relationship
>
> [2] where a trading subsidiary would be exposed to the risk or actuality of insolvency if it were to be capitalised by loan, trustees will have little choice but to invest share capital (subject to the considerations set out in 4.8, above).
>
> The fact that share capital subscribed by the parent charity in a trading subsidiary might not be repaid in full, or even in part, on the dissolution of the subsidiary, is only one factor which the charity's investment adviser should consider when deciding whether to recommend the trustees of the parent charity to subscribe for share capital. The adviser would have to consider the overall economic return to the charity, balancing Gift Aid payments and any anticipated distributions against the risk of capital loss.

Note that anticipated Gift Aid payments are as relevant as any other anticipated distributions in ascertaining whether the investment is a wise one. This must be so since in practice all return on the investment will be by way of Gift Aid and none by way of dividend.

9.11.7 *Charity makes loan*

CC35 provides at 4.4:

> Where a parent charity provides loan capital to a trading subsidiary, the trading subsidiary must, of course, make interest payments and repayments of principal in accordance with the terms of the loan agreement with the charity.

Similarly, at 4.11:

> If a charity makes a loan to a trading subsidiary, trustees must decide on the terms as regards the interest rate and repayment of principal. They must also decide how the loan is to be secured. These decisions are part of the duties of trustees as set out in 4.8.

It is no doubt generally sound advice to require the trading company to pay interest. However that is not always the case. There may be sound commercial reasons for leaving loans outstanding interest free, and this is often done within groups of companies or when the loans are due to 100% shareholders.

To require the trading company to repay capital of loans raises the question of how it could do so except out of retained profits, which would be taxable. It would be better to leave the loan outstanding.

CC35 then turns to the issue of solvency:

> **4.11 What considerations apply to a charity's investment of loan capital in a trading subsidiary?**
> [After some basic observations, CC35 provides:]
> However the amount of any loan capital held by a company is taken into account when determining its solvency. A company must not trade whilst insolvent. Trustees should not, therefore, invest loan capital in a trading subsidiary, if it is reasonably foreseeable that the subsidiary may not be able to service the loan or repay it when the term expires. In such cases trustees should:
> [1] consider whether it is in the charity's interest to maintain the company at all, or whether it is best to dissolve it or to sell it as a going concern (based on the principles set out in 4.8 (see also 4.16)
> [2] provide the investment as share capital (see 4.10), if it is indeed in the charity's interest to provide additional finance
> The provision of loan capital can inadvertently create insolvency in a trading subsidiary even where it is trading profitably. This is because, in order to eliminate corporation tax liability, a trading subsidiary will often pay to its parent charity as Gift Aid all its profits which would otherwise be liable to corporation tax (see 4.4). As a result the trading subsidiary may retain insufficient resources for it to repay loans made by the charity as and when due. That would render the trading subsidiary insolvent, in that it would be incapable of paying its debts.

We do not agree with this. Wrongful trading arises "if there is no reasonable prospect that the company would avoid going into insolvent liquidation."[26] If the charity is prepared to subordinate its debt to the other debts of the company, there may be no prospect of insolvent liquidation.

CC35 then considers HMRC's view of the tax implications of making the loan, see 6.22 (Other investments: IT Type 12).

9.11.8 *Staff of charity/trading co*

CC35 provides:

> **4.15 Can charity trustees and employees also work for a trading subsidiary?**
> In order to ensure that the trading subsidiary is managed in the interests of the parent charity, and to monitor its performance, some of the

26 See s.214 Insolvency Act 1986.

trustees and/or employees of the charity often become directors of the trading subsidiary. However, they must bear in mind that the charity and the trading subsidiary are different entities. Anyone involved with the administration of both has 2 distinct responsibilities, and it can at times be difficult to balance conflicting pressures.

A charity trustee cannot be paid for his or her services as a director or employee of the charity's trading subsidiary unless either:

[1] the governing document of the charity specifically provides for this

[2] there is some other specific authority, such as an order from the commission

The establishment of a trading subsidiary, where the directors of that subsidiary are the same people as the trustees of the parent charity, cannot be used as a means of paying the charity's trustees 'by the back door'

As a matter of good governance, there should be both:

[3] at least one person who is a trustee, but not a director or employee of the trading subsidiary

[4] at least one person who is a director of the trading subsidiary, but not a trustee or employee of the charity.

These people are described as 'unconflicted' as they have no conflict of interest in their roles. These unconflicted trustees and directors should advise their colleagues as to the proper course of action where the duties of those with dual responsibilities are in conflict. This reduces the risk of any transaction between the parent charity and the trading subsidiary being challenged or questioned.

If trustees have delegated responsibility for monitoring the operation of the trading subsidiary to a committee made up entirely of people who are directors or employees of the subsidiary, they should ensure that systems are in place for ensuring that advice is obtained from an unconflicted trustee wherever appropriate.

9.11.9 *Trading co in financial difficulty*

CC35 provides:

> **4.16 What should trustees do if the trading subsidiary is in financial difficulty?**
> If the trading subsidiary has been running at a loss for a significant time, without any special short-term factors in play, trustees must consider the trading subsidiary's viability. Trustees must minimise any losses to the charity, regardless of any sense of moral obligation the trustees may feel towards the trading subsidiary, its directors and employees.

One hopes that the guidance not to feel *any* sense of moral obligation to employees is not taken too literally.

> If the trustees sink further funds into supporting an ailing trading subsidiary at a time when it was reasonably clear that the failure of the subsidiary was likely, this could constitute a breach of trust on their part, putting them at personal risk to make good any losses to the charity. Trustees facing these circumstances should take advice from their professional advisers.
> If a trading subsidiary defaults on a loan agreement with the charity, the trustees must consider enforcing the charity's rights under the agreement. In deciding on their precise course of action, trustees must exercise their commercial judgement, based on appropriate professional advice. Their decision needs to be based on the best interests of the charity which owns the trading subsidiary.
> Trustees have similar responsibilities where the charity has invested share capital in the trading subsidiary, even though share capital is not liable to repayment. The ultimate response for the parent charity - in its role as shareholder - to the trading subsidiary's trading failure is either to procure the subsidiary's termination or to sell the business as a going concern to a third party.
> Trustees might fear that allowing a trading subsidiary to go into insolvent liquidation would adversely affect the charity's reputation. This might seem to justify making a further investment, and/or retaining existing investments in the subsidiary, to prevent or reduce losses to the subsidiary's creditors.
> However the main point of carrying on a trade through the trading subsidiary is to protect the charity's assets from the risks of the trade (see D1). To use those assets to protect the subsidiary's creditors is the very outcome which charity law restrictions on trading by a charity itself are designed to prevent. If trustees act to keep the trading subsidiary in business, regardless of the interests of the charity, they may be personally liable for any consequential loss in the value of the charity's investment in the trading subsidiary.

These are only generalities.

9.11.10 *Monitoring trading company*

CC35 provides:

> **4.17 What duties do charity trustees have in regard to trading subsidiaries?**
> Trustees must review regularly the relationship between the parent charity and the trading subsidiary. The purpose of establishing a trading

subsidiary is normally to raise funds for the charity, and its effectiveness in doing this should be monitored. Investment review must not await a specific trigger, such as the discovery that a trading subsidiary is in financial difficulty.
The parent charity's trustees must also exercise the charity's rights as shareholder in the trading subsidiary so as to promote the charity's interests. The directors of the trading subsidiary are responsible for its management, but other major decisions are for the trustees, as representatives of the parent charity. For example, trustees are responsible for:
[1] the appointment/removal of the directors of the trading subsidiary
[2] the directors' terms of service, including any remuneration
[3] the continuation, or dissolution, of the trading subsidiary

9.11.11 *Guarantees*

CC35 provides:

4.19 Can a charity guarantee the liabilities of a trading subsidiary?
A parent charity or its trustees may be invited to guarantee liabilities of a trading subsidiary. For example, the trading subsidiary's bank may be reluctant to provide overdraft facilities to the trading subsidiary unless the parent charity (or its trustees) guarantees the trading subsidiary's obligation to repay.
If such a guarantee is given by trustees of a parent charity, and liability under the guarantee is enforced by a creditor of the trading subsidiary, trustees are unlikely to be entitled to an indemnity from the charity, and will have to settle the liability personally, where:

- the liability arises out of a failure of a trade carried on by a trading subsidiary
- the parent charity could not itself properly have carried on that trade

The effect of allowing the guarantee to be enforced at the expense of the charity would simply be to frustrate the purpose of the charity law restriction on the carrying on of the trade by the charity itself.
If such a guarantee is given by an incorporated parent charity, it may not be valid at all. The validity of such a guarantee will depend on:

- the provisions of the charity's constitution
- the provisions of section 42 of the Companies Act 2006

If liability under the guarantee is enforceable, and 'is' enforced by the creditors of the trading subsidiary, the trustees may be personally liable to make good the corporate charity's liability under the guarantee, where:

- the liability arises out of a failure of a trade carried on by a trading subsidiary'
- the parent charity could not itself properly have carried on that

> trade'.
>
> In addition, payments made by a parent charity under a guarantee of the liabilities of a trading subsidiary may be considered to be non-charitable expenditure, creating a potential adverse tax effect for the charity...[27]
>
> In general, trustees must aim to ensure that all arrangements are demonstrably on commercial terms and for the benefit of the charity, and do not give rise to the difficulties previously mentioned.

This is not a very balanced account, but charities should certainly not guarantee trading company debts without proper advice.

9.11.12 *Shared bank account*

CC35 provides:

> **4.20 Can a parent charity and its trading subsidiary consolidate their bank accounts?**
>
> The bank accounts of a charity and its trading subsidiary or subsidiaries may be consolidated so long as:
>
> [1] a proper record is kept of the state of the balances on the individual accounts which have been consolidated
>
> [2] the benefits and burdens of the consolidated account are fairly apportioned between the parent charity and the trading subsidiary or subsidiaries, having regard to the state of the individual accounts
>
> [3] the consolidation does not result in the charity incurring non-charitable expenditure, creating in turn a potential tax effect, or otherwise suffering a tax disadvantage

In practice separate bank accounts are needed for Gift Aid purposes. See 9.3 (Extracting profit by Gift Aid).

9.11.13 *Use of charity land*

CC35 provides:

> **4.21 Can a trading subsidiary use its parent charity's land and buildings?**
>
> Any use of the parent charity's land and buildings by a trading subsidiary should be covered by a formal lease or licence of the property concerned from the charity to the subsidiary. The trading subsidiary must pay a rent or fee which is comparable to that which would be payable for letting the property on the open market.
>
> The granting of a lease will, and the granting of a licence may, constitute

27 For the omitted text, see 35.24 (VAT groups).

> a disposition of the charity's land. Any such disposition will need to be authorised by the commission because the trading subsidiary is a 'connected person' in relation to the charity. If a charity purchases land for use by a trading subsidiary, this must be justifiable as an investment of the charity's resources in terms of the commercial return received.

So far as this relates to a lease, it is correct, though surprising: s.117(1) Charities Act 2011.[28] (So far as it relates to a *licence*, it is not correct: the granting of a licence does not require any consent. However, the Commission may be trying to make the point that a document called a licence may in fact be a lease and not a licence: the lease/licence distinction is fraught.) Where a lease is mistakenly granted without consent, it may nevertheless be valid if the trading company has acted in good faith: s.122 Charities Act 2011. There is a substantial case law on the meaning of "good faith" but a discussion would be beyond the scope of this work.

Thought should be given to the SDLT implications:

> Charities enjoy an exemption from stamp duty land tax on their purchases of land (which includes buildings). However, the relief does not apply to purchases by trading subsidiaries.

This is correct: see 39.13 (Non-charitable subsidiary).

> The exemption will be lost if the purchase of the land and buildings cannot be justified as an investment of the charity's resources; or is made in order to avoid tax by the trading subsidiary.

This is not quite correct. The exemption will not be lost if the subject-matter is not held as an investment as long as it is held for use in furtherance of the charitable purposes of the purchaser or of another charity: see 39.5 (Charitable purposes condition).

9.11.14 *Use of charity staff/facilities*

CC35 provides:

> **4.22 Can a charity invest indirectly in a trading subsidiary?**
> Indirect investment[29] in a trading subsidiary can be as important to the

---

28 This is also correct in Northern Ireland, see s.57(1) Charities Act (Northern Ireland) 2008

29 CC35 has struggled slightly with the terminology. The pre-2007 CC35 referred to "non-financial support" but finance is involved here. "Indirect investment" is no better. CC35 is using the word investment in a very loose sense, meaning any

trading subsidiary's viability as capital formally provided by the charity. Allowing the trading subsidiary the use of the charity's land and buildings has already been mentioned (see 4.21). Indirect investment may also take the form of the parent charity allowing the trading subsidiary to use the charity's staff and equipment.

However the indirect investment must not involve any element of subsidy of the trading subsidiary, as that would prevent the objective evaluation of the subsidiary's performance as an investment. Arrangements which involve a subsidy by the charity to the trading subsidiary can also have an adverse tax effect as, in general, such subsidies are unlikely to be 'charitable expenditure' under the 1988 act.

The parent charity should therefore charge for any services and facilities which it provides to the trading subsidiary. Accordingly:

[1] where staff employed by the charity do some work for the trading subsidiary, or where the trading subsidiary uses facilities owned by the charity, appropriate charges must be made by the charity

[2] such charges must be paid within a reasonable period of time; unpaid charges can become a significant form of long-term financing, and amount to a form of subsidy of the trading subsidiary by the charity

[3] such charges should not normally go beyond the reimbursement of the charity's costs; if they do, they will be considered to be a receipt of trading carried on by the charity, the profits of which may not qualify for exemption from tax

Cost-sharing arrangements could be subject to challenge by HMRC Charities, if the costs are not calculated in an acceptable way or shared appropriately.

Such arrangements should be used only where staff and facilities are shared between the parent charity and the trading subsidiary. Where staff are employed exclusively on the trading subsidiary's business, the trading subsidiary should employ the staff. Where equipment is used exclusively by the trading subsidiary, the trading subsidiary should own the equipment.

Sharing arrangements between the parent charity and the trading subsidiary need to be carefully considered, with a view to ensuring that they do not damage the charity's ability to carry out its objects. Trustees wishing to enter into such arrangements should seek advice

---

expenditure or support for a worthwhile purpose. This usage of "investment" is popular usage rather than legal usage, but it does not matter as the meaning is reasonably clear.

from their own professional advisers and contact the commission at an early stage.

9.12 Transfer of asset to subsidiary

A charity may transfer an asset in specie to its subsidiary. The tax position depends on whether the asset is a capital asset or trading stock in the hands of the charity and in the hands of the subsidiary, so there are four possibilities:

Case	**Parent**	**Subsidiary**
1	Cap	Cap
2	Cap	TS
3	TS	Cap
4	TS	TS

Key:
Cap: Capital asset
TS: Trading stock

The position also depends on whether the parent is a charitable company (group relief may apply)[30] or a charitable trust (no group relief).

I here consider CGT and IT issues, but VAT, stamp duty and SDLT may also need consideration.

9.13 Capital asset

The transfer is a disposal for CGT purposes.

9.13.1 *Charitable trust*

If the charity is a charitable trust, it is deemed to receive the market value of the asset and so a gain may arise.

(1) If the charity receives full consideration, there should be no difficulty in applying the consideration for charitable purposes, and the gain should qualify for the charity's CGT exemption.

(2) If the charity receives no consideration, there is still a deemed gain which ought to qualify for the charity exemption, though the point is not quite clear.[31]

9.13.2 *Charitable company*

If the charity is a charitable company, the transfer qualifies for CG group

---

30 See 11.2 (Group relief).
31 See 5.5 (Deemed Gain).

relief, and no gain accrues to the charity.

If the asset is trading stock in the hands of the subsidiary, note s.173 TCGA:

> (1) Where
> (a) a company ("company A") acquires an asset as trading stock of a trade to which this section applies,[32]
> (b) the acquisition is from a company ("company B") that at the time of the acquisition is a member of the same group of companies, and
> (c) the asset did not form part of the trading stock of any such trade carried on by company B,
>
> company A is treated for the purposes of section 161 as having acquired the asset otherwise than as trading stock and immediately appropriated it for the purposes of the trade as trading stock.

9.14 Trading stock relief

Suppose a charity is carrying on a non-exempt trade, and holds trading stock. It may be possible to avoid a taxable profit by

(1) ceasing to trade:

(1) selling the trading stock to its trading subsidiary

(2) the trading subsidiary realises the profit (and makes a qualifying donation to charity)

Section 162 CTA 2009 provides:

> (1) If a company permanently ceases to carry on a trade, in calculating the profits of the trade
> (a) trading stock belonging to the trade at the time of the cessation must be valued, and
> (b) the value must be determined in accordance with sections 164 to 167 (bases of valuation).

Subsections (2)-(2C) deal with the interaction with transfer pricing. Subsections (3)(4) deal with changes to partnerships. It is not necessary to consider these topics here.

9.14.1 *Trading stock*

Section 163 CTA 2009 provides a wide definition:

---

32 Subsection (3) provides: "The trades to which this section applies are
(a) any trade carried on by a company resident in the United Kingdom, and
(b) any trade carried on in the United Kingdom through a permanent establishment by a company not so resident."

(1) In this Chapter "trading stock" means

(a) any property (whether land or other property) which is sold in the ordinary course of the trade or would be so sold if it were mature or its manufacture, preparation or construction were complete, or

(b) materials used in the manufacture, preparation or construction of any property mentioned in paragraph (a).

(2) In this Chapter "trading stock" includes also any services performed in the ordinary course of the trade

(a) the performance of which is wholly or partly completed at the time of the cessation, and

(b) for which it would be reasonable to expect that a charge would be made if there were no cessation and, in the case of partly completed services, their performance were fully completed,

and any article produced, and any material used, in the performance of any such services.

(3) In this Chapter references to the sale or transfer of trading stock include the sale or transfer of any benefits and rights which accrue, or might reasonably be expected to accrue, from the performance of any such services.

9.14.2 *Connected person sale: MV*

Section 166 CTA 2009 provides:

(1) The value of trading stock is determined in accordance with this section if

(a) it is sold to a person who carries on, or intends to carry on, a trade, profession or vocation in the United Kingdom and is entitled to deduct the cost of the stock as an expense in calculating the profits of that trade, profession or vocation for corporation or income tax purposes,

(b) the buyer is connected with the seller, and

(c) no election is made under section 167 (election by connected persons).

(2) The value is taken to be the amount which would have been realised if the sale had been between independent persons dealing at arm's length.

A charity is connected with its trading subsidiary (as one would expect).[33]

---

33 Section 168 CTA 2009 provides a wider than standard definition:

"For the purposes of sections 164 to 167 two persons are connected with each other if any of the following tests is met

9.14.3 *Election out of MV rule*

Section 167 CTA 2009 provides:

> (1) The value of trading stock is determined in accordance with this section if
> (a) it is sold to a person who carries on, or intends to carry on, a trade, profession or vocation in the United Kingdom and is entitled to deduct the cost of the stock as an expense in calculating the profits of that trade, profession or vocation for corporation or income tax purposes,
> (b) the buyer is connected with the seller, and
> (c) an election is made under this section.
> (2) The parties to the sale may make an election under this section if the value of the stock determined under section 166 exceeds both
> (a) its acquisition value,[34] and
> (b) the amount in fact realised on the sale.
> (3) If an election is made, the value is taken to be
> (a) its acquisition value, or
> (b) if greater, the amount in fact realised on the sale.
> (4) An election under this section must be made by both parties not later than two years after the end of the accounting period in which the cessation occurred.

Section 167(6) CTA 2009 deals with apportionment in a commonsense way:

(a) they are connected with each other within the meaning of section 1122 of CTA 2010,
(b) one of them is a firm and the other has a right to a share of the assets or income of the firm,
(c) one of them is a body corporate and the other has control over that body,
(d) both of them are firms and some other person has a right to a share of the assets or income of both of them, or
(e) both of them are bodies corporate, or one of them is a firm and the other is a body corporate, and in either case some other person has control over both of them."

34 Defined subsection (5): "(5) The "acquisition value" of trading stock means the amount which would have been deductible as representing its acquisition value, in calculating the profits of the trade, on the following assumptions
(a) that the stock had been sold in the course of the trade, immediately before the cessation, for a price equal to the value of the stock determined under section 166, and
(b) that the period for which those profits were to be calculated began immediately before the sale."

If the stock is sold together with other assets, so much of the amount realised on the sale as, on a just and reasonable apportionment, is properly attributable to each asset is treated as the amount realised on the sale of that asset.

9.14.4 *Trading subsidiary position*

Section 169 CTA 2009 provides:

(1) This section applies for the purpose of calculating the profits of the trade carried on by the buyer of trading stock.
(2) If the value of the stock is determined in accordance with
  (a) section 164(3) or sections 165 to 167 (sale basis of valuation), or
  (b) section 175(3) or sections 176 to 178 of ITTOIA 2005 (corresponding income tax rules),
the cost of the stock to the buyer is taken to be the value as so determined.

9.15 Returning Gift Aid payment: Circularity

We have already noted that it is essential to strip out the profits of the company and transfer them to the charity. This must be done in the year the profits accrue, or within nine months thereafter.[35] This gives rise to difficulties if the charity wishes to retain the profits in the company so as to expand its trade. The obvious course would be:
(1) The donor company makes a Gift Aid payment to the charity.
(2) The charity immediately returns them back to the company, by way of loan or subscription for new shares (in either case on arm's lenth terms).
Alternatively:
(1) The charity makes a payment to the company, by way of loan or subscription for new shares.
(2) The company immediately makes a Gift Aid payment back to the charity.
We refer to these as **"circular arrangements"**.

HMRC found this objectionable even before the introduction of the charitable expenditure rules in 1986.[36] However HMRC's attack on

35 See 9.3 (Extracting profits by Gift Aid).
36 The pre-1986 HMRC guidance is discussed in the 10th edition (2015-16) of this work para 9.10 (Circular arrangements). It is omitted here as it is now of historical interest only.

circular arrangements failed in *Nightingale v Price* [1996] STC (SCD) 116. Here a trading company made covenanted payments to the charity, and the charity lent them back to the company. HMRC had two arguments:

(1) The payments were not genuinely "made". This failed for the reasons set out in 15.13 (Charity pays donor: Circularity).
(2) *Furniss v Dawson.* This also failed; see 9.10 GAAR).

The assessments concerned years before 1986, so the charitable expenditure rules were not discussed. In the authors' view the charitable expenditure rules will not help HMRC here. A *loan* back to the company is a qualifying loan: see 6.22 (Other approved charitable investments: Type 12). This might have been the subject of further litigation, but nothing has happened since *Nightingale v Price.* Nevertheless HMRC continue to rattle this sabre. The HMRC Guidance Note provides at Annex iv para 52:

> **Direct Tax. Investing in a company which sheds its profits to the charity**
> Most commercial companies keep part of their profits to provide them with funds for day-to-day expenses, working capital and normal development of their business. However, companies which intend to donate all of their profits to charity every year may not be able to retain the funds they need to carry on in business. Charities may therefore want to ensure when a company is set up that it's provided with enough capital to enable it to shed its profits every year **and** stay in business.
> Although the 9 month rule ... should assist with cash flow, the passing of profits up to the parent charity may result in a serious drain on the company's cash. If so, care should be taken to avoid a pattern of frequent injections of funds by the charity in order to keep the company in business. Such a practice might put at risk both the charity's tax exemptions and the company's deductions for its Gift Aid payments. In some cases where there's a serious cash drain in the company, it will be necessary for the company to change its practice so that it keeps part of its profits. In these circumstances some tax will become payable by the company.

It would where possible be wise to avoid a strategy of extracting profits each year and returning the same amount. For any substantial charity this should generally be possible to arrange without either incurring substantial tax charges or unnecessarily restricting the operation of the trade.

9.15.1 *Critique*

While HMRC do appear to oppose circular payments, the reason why has never been articulated, and it is suggested that there is no valid objection on the policy level. The object of forcing charities to trade through trading companies is not to raise tax. It is (supposed) to improve charity administration.[37] It is after all accepted that a charity may accumulate its income without a tax charge, as the accumulation is an application for charitable purposes. So it is hoped that *Nightingale v Price* will be the last word on the matter.

9.16 Transfer pricing

A full discussion of transfer pricing needs a book to itself. We focus here on the issues most relevant to charities.

The transfer pricing provisions of part 4 TIOPA (in short) deem transactions between persons under common control to be at arm's length prices. Transactions between a charity and a subsidiary company can therefore fall within the scope of the transfer pricing rules.

9.16.1 *When is charity affected*

HMRC sets out its view of the transfer pricing rules in the International Manual:

> **INTM412020: rules: the basic transfer pricing rule** (Jun 2016)
> *Overview*
> TIOPA10/S147(3) and (5) contains the basic transfer pricing rule, which is founded on the arm's length principle (see INTM412040). The rule requires a person's or persons' profits and losses to be calculated for tax purposes by substituting an arm's length provision for an actual provision if certain criteria are met, which are that
> - a 'basic pre-condition' is satisfied (TIOPA10/S147(2)(a)) and
> - the actual provision confers on the person or persons a potential advantage in relation to UK taxation (TIOPA10/S147(2)(b) and (4)(b)).
>
> The meaning of provision is at INTM412050, and the meaning of person is covered at INTM412060.
> **The 'basic pre-condition'**
> is defined by TIOPA10/S147(1) as being where

37 See 8.19.2 (Charity administration argument).

- an actual provision (see INTM412050) has been made or imposed between any two affected persons by means of a transaction or series of transactions (see INTM412050 and TIOPA10/S147(1)(a))
- the 'participation condition' is met (TIOPA10/S147(1)(b))
- the actual provision is not within TIOPA10/S147(7) which relates to oil transactions (TIOPA10/S147(1)(c)), as they have their own rules, see INTM412120; and
- there is a difference between the actual provision and the arm's length provision, i.e. that which would have been made between independent enterprises (TIOPA10/S147(1)(d)).

The 'participation condition'

is defined in TIOPA10/S148 and is met when one of the two affected persons was directly or indirectly participating in the management, control or capital of the other, or a third person was participating in the management, control or capital of both the affected persons (see INTM412060).

Considering the provision between two connected persons extends to asking whether such provision 'would' have been made between independent enterprises. However, this can only be done to the extent recommended in OECD guidelines; see INTM440200.

Potential advantage

TIOPA10/S155 provides that there is a potential advantage in relation to UK taxation if a person's:

- taxable profits for a chargeable period are reduced, or
- tax losses for a period are created or increased
- as an effect of the provision not being on an arm's length position.

Where there is a potential advantage, it should be addressed in the return relating to the period in which it arises.

Often only one party to the transaction will be potentially advantaged by the actual provision. However, if both parties to the transaction are potentially advantaged by it, then both would need to make an adjustment.

Previously, the HMRC Guidance accepted that the rules applied only to "enterprises" and would therefore not apply to the majority of charities. This is no longer the case. The Guidance now refers only to "people". We agree that charities fall within this definition:

INTM412030 - Transfer pricing: legislation: rules: meaning of 'person'

Meaning of "person" in TIOPA10

TIOPA10/S147 refers to provision made or imposed between any two

> (connected) persons, suggesting a broad scope for the schedule, as the term persons includes bodies corporate, partnerships and individuals. The reference in S147(1)(d) requires the actual provision to be compared with the arm's length provision that would have been made between independent enterprises. This merely requires that the comparison is with the transaction that would be entered into by independent enterprises; it does not require that the persons themselves must be enterprises.
> Consequently, for example, charities will meet the basic pre-condition of TIOPA10/S147(1)(a) - see INTM412020 - as they are 'persons' within the meaning of TIOPA10/S147 regardless of the fact that they will not usually be enterprises.
> The basic transfer pricing rule of TIOPA10/S147(3) or (5) will not apply to charities in respect of any of their profits which are exempted from tax (under, for example CTA10/S478) as they will then fail to meet the 'potential advantage' requirement of TIOPA10/S147(2)(b) or (4)(b).
> A person includes both individuals and legal persons such as companies. Person also includes a body of persons.
> TIOPA10/S164 requires Part 4 to be construed in accordance with OECD Model Tax Convention, as interpreted by OECD Transfer Pricing Guidelines. Article 9 of the convention sets out the arm's length principle by reference to conditions made or imposed between enterprises. Article 3 defines enterprise as "the carrying on of any business".

We agree that the basic transfer pricing rule cannot apply in respect of charities' profits which are exempt from tax as they would necessarily not meet the "potential advantage" requirement.

9.16.2 *Small/medium enterprise*

The transfer pricing rules do not apply to small enterprises (in short, up to 50 employees and annual turnover or total assets of up to €10m).[38] Although there are exceptions these will not usually apply to charities. Thus charities can ignore the rules if they and their trading subsidiaries are small enterprises.

The rules generally do not apply to medium enterprises (in short, up to 250 employees and annual turnover up to €50m or total assets up to €43m). HMRC can give notice requiring the provisions to be applied to

38 ss.166 and 167 TIOPA.

a medium size enterprise.[39] In practice we have never heard of this happening to charities.

9.16.3 *Large enterprise*

Large charities (ie larger than medium as defined) need to consider and if applicable operate the transfer pricing rules though we have never heard of a case where HMRC have taken this point in practice.

The International Manual provides:

> **INTM440260: Types of transactions: charities** (Sept 2016)
> *Funding of charities and their associates*
> In principle, the funding by UK charities of their UK trading affiliates falls to be considered under TIOPA10/Part 4. When reviewing the funding of charities and their associates it should be recognised that they are expected to follow the general advice and guidelines of the Charity Commission in considering the nature of their investments in trading affiliates. This is consistent with paragraph 1.73 of OECD Transfer Pricing Guidelines. Where, exceptionally, charities enter into financial arrangements which are other than in accordance with the Commission's advice or guidelines, or where avoidance may be present, the provisions of TIOPA10/Part 4 could be in point. This is an area on which advice should be sought from CTIAA Business International.

CC35 provides at 4.22:

> Some very large charity groups may also need to consider the implications of transfer pricing legislation. Where applicable, this requires 'arms-length' pricing of transactions within the charity group for tax purposes, regardless of the terms of the actual agreement between the parent charity and the trading subsidiary. The substitution of an arms length price for the actual price (for tax purposes) may increase the receipts of a trade, increasing the profits of the trade, and so give rise to a tax liability.

We think the substitution of an arm's length price is more likely to reduce the receipts of the trade, but that depends of course on the facts.

> It should be noted that [1] HMRC Charities do not normally expect charities to commission expensive transfer pricing reports, but that [2] charities should be in a position to demonstrate that arrangements are

---

39 ss.168 to 171 TIOPA.

> on commercial (arm's length) terms.

The reader may like to contemplate the contradiction between the two parts of this sentence. In fact, in accordance with Charity Commission guidelines, charity and trading company arrangements are not on commercial arm's length terms, but on terms that the charity is reimbursed its costs and no more. Fortunately the International Manual passage above suggests that this is not caught, having regard to OECD Transfer Pricing Guidelines.

9.17 VAT

The HMRC Guidance Note Annex iv para 46 provides:

> **Tthe VAT position**
> It is important to remember that a charity's trading subsidiary company is not a charity. For VAT purposes a trading subsidiary is treated in the same way as a normal commercial enterprise. Most of the VAT reliefs for charities are not available to their trading subsidiaries. However, some VAT relief, such as zero rating the sale of donated goods and the VAT exemption for certain fund raising events, do extend to charities' trading subsidiaries.

On VAT group registration see 35.24 (VAT groups).

9.18 Liquidation

If the company holds an asset on capital account, then the main aim will be for the company to transfer the asset to the charity without suffering any CT on chargeable gains. One possibility would be for the charity to liquidate the company and for the liquidator to transfer the assets of the company in specie to the charity. That transfer gives rise to two disposals, a disposal by the charity-shareholder, and a disposal by the company in liquidation.

9.18.1 *Disposal by charity-shareholder*

Section 122(1) TCGA provides (so far as relevant):

> Where a person receives or becomes entitled to receive in respect of shares in a company any capital distribution from the company ... he shall be treated as if he had in consideration of that capital distribution disposed of an interest in the shares.

The gain which accrues to the charity on the deemed disposal of its shares under s.122 will in principle be exempt from CGT by virtue of the charity's CGT exemption.

9.18.2 *Disposal by co in liquidation*

Section 17(1) TCGA provides (so far as relevant):

> Subject to the provisions of this Act, a person's ... disposal of an asset shall for the purposes of this Act be deemed to be for a consideration equal to the market value of the asset—
> (a) [i] where he ... disposes of the asset otherwise than by way of a bargain made at arm's length,
> [ii] and in particular where he ... disposes of it by way of gift ... or
> [iii] by way of distribution from a company in respect of shares in the company...

The transfer of an asset by a company in liquidation to its shareholders would normally be deemed to be for a consideration equal to the market value of the asset, under s.17(1)(a)[i] or [iii]. Thus a chargeable gain would normally accrue to the company on the disposal.

Section 257 TCGA provides (so far as relevant):

> (1) Subsection (2) below shall apply where a disposal of an asset is made otherwise than under a bargain at arm's length—
> (a) to a charity or a registered club...
> (2) [A] Sections 17(1) ... shall not apply;
> [B] but if the disposal is
> [i] by way of gift (including a gift in settlement) or
> [ii] for a consideration not exceeding the sums allowable as a deduction under section 38,
>
> then—
> (a) the disposal and acquisition shall be treated for the purposes of this Act as being made for such consideration as to secure that neither a gain nor a loss accrues on the disposal...

The transfer of an asset by a company in liquidation to its shareholders is not in principle a disposal made under a bargain at arm's length. So where the disposal is made to a charity, s.17 does not apply.[40]

If (exceptionally) there is an agreement between the charity and the company in liquidation under which the disposal is made for consideration, CGT is in principle charged by reference to the actual

40 See 23.3.3 (Position of donor).

consideration. This may happen for instance if the transfer is in satisfaction of a debt owed to the charity.

However the transfer is not in principle made for consideration. This accords with the SD and SDLT treatment of a distribution on liquidation: the transfer is not in principle subject to SD or SDLT which is payable on the consideration for the transfer.[41]

Section 122 TCGA does not apply to the company's disposal: that section applies only to the shareholder and not to the distributing company.

9.18.3 *Loss on disposal in liquidation?*

Section 257(2) [B] TCGA applies if the disposal is:

(1) by way of gift or
(2) for a consideration not exceeding the sums allowable as a deduction in computing the gain or loss of the person making the disposal...

The disposal by the company in liquidation is not "by way of gift". The disposal is also not normally "for a consideration". It might be argued that the words should be given their literal meaning, so s.257(2)[B] TCGA does not apply. On that view a loss would arise on the disposal.[42] But we think the better view is to construe the words purposively, understanding the words "for a consideration not exceeding..." to apply also to the case of a transfer for nil consideration. It is difficult to see why s.257(2)[B] should apply if there is a consideration of £1 but not if there is no consideration at all.

---

41 See Kessler, *Taxation of Non-Residents and Foreign Domiciliaries* (21st ed., 2022/23), App 4.2.6 (Transfer on liquidation).

42 But if there is a loss, it would not normally be of any use:
(1) If all the assets of the company are distributed to the charity, then the company will make no chargeable gains. The loss cannot be offset against prior chargeable gains of the company as a new accounting period will have started with the commencement of the winding up. Capital losses cannot be carried backwards and set against chargeable gains of prior accounting periods.
(2) If the charity controls the company then it will be connected with the company for CGT purposes, with the result that the loss will be deductible only from a chargeable gain accruing to the company on some other disposal of an asset to the charity: see s.18(3) TCGA. As already explained, however, there will normally be no such chargeable gain.
The loss (if there is one) may be important if the charity is a minority shareholder. If a main purpose of the arrangement is to obtain a tax advantage, s.16A TCGA would disallow the loss.

If (exceptionally) the charity-shareholder did give consideration for the asset, for example if the charity assumed liability for a mortgage, or released a debt due to the charity from the company, then:

(1) s.257(2)[B] TCGA would apply, creating a no gain/no loss disposal which effectively nullifies the loss, (if the consideration was less than the allowable expenditure); or

(2) the gain on the disposal would be computed by reference to the actual consideration (if the consideration exceeded the allowable expenditure).

9.19 Capital asset: No liquidation

For various reasons, liquidation of the company may not be acceptable. If the asset is transferred while the company is a going concern, the capital gains considerations are in principle the same. There are, however, two additional potential problems. First, if made for less than full consideration (as it normally will be, otherwise it will not be possible to avoid CT on the company in respect of the chargeable gain realised by it) the transfer must be justified as a matter of company law. Secondly, the transfer may also amount to a distribution of profits of the company for IT purposes: see 9.3.1 (Dividends).

9.19.1 *Dividend route*

One possibility is for the company to declare a dividend in specie. (Company law considerations would have to be borne in mind, in particular, whether the company had sufficient distributable profits.) Is there a CT liability in respect of the chargeable gain the company might realise in transferring the asset? For the same reason as transfer on liquidation of the company, no such gain will arise: see 9.18 (Liquidation). Instead, there may in principle be a loss.

9.19.2 *Sale at book value*

Another possibility is for the company to sell the asset at book value to the charity. (A sale at less than book value in principle constitutes a distribution.) The sale should not give rise to any charge to CT on the company provided, as will usually be the case, the book value is no higher than its allowable expenditure. As the charity would give some consideration, there would be no possibility of creating an allowable loss: see 9.18 (Liquidation).

The sale may or may not amount to a distribution. The amount of any distribution would be the difference between the consideration given by the charity and the market value of the asset sold. Prima facie, s.1020 CTA 2010 does deem there to be such a distribution. Section 1020 does not apply, however, where the company and the member receiving the benefit are both resident in the UK and either the former is a subsidiary of the latter or both are subsidiaries of a third company also so resident: s.1002 CTA 2010.

In the case of a charitable trust, s.1002 will not apply. In the case of a charitable company, however, a wholly-owned subsidiary is a subsidiary for the purposes of CTA 2010. This turns on whether the charity "beneficially" owns the shares in its subsidiary. It is considered that an incorporated charity does beneficially own its assets, just like any other body corporate, provided it does not hold them on charitable trusts.

It might be argued that, even if an incorporated charity were not the beneficial owner of its shares in the company, s.1002 CTA 2010 would prevent a distribution. Section 1002 prevents a transfer of assets other than cash between one company and another from being a distribution by virtue of s.1020 if both are resident in the UK and neither is a 51% subsidiary of a company not so resident (see s.1021 CTA 2010), provided that they were not under common control. In our opinion, s.1002 would not be in point for it applies only to a transfer to a company beneficially and not to a company as trustee of charitable trusts.

9.20 Distribution of trading stock

Where the company owns an asset as trading stock, CGT charity relief will not prevent the company realising a trading profit, either on the discontinuance of the trade (see Chapter 11 Part 3 CTA 2009) or if the asset is disposed of before the trade has been discontinued. Relief is, however, available for gifts of trading stock to charity: see 18.7.7 (Relief for gift of trading stock).

CHAPTER TEN

BUSINESS SPONSORSHIP AND ADVERTISING

Cross references

The following topics are considered elsewhere:
18.3 (Sponsorship: Position of sponsor)
Sponsorship also raises VAT issues, see:
35.12 (Sponsorship)
35.9.1 (Donation or sponsorship)

10.1 Introduction

This chapter considers the tax position of a charity or NPO benefiting from business sponsorship, or providing advertising for sponsors.

10.2 Is sponsorship a trade

Sponsorship activities may constitute a trade by a charity. Whether or not this is so depends on the circumstances. HMRC's view is set out in HMRC Guidance Note Annex iv:

> **22. Direct tax: is sponsorship income trading income?**
> The direct tax treatment of payments received by charities under sponsorship arrangements will depend on the nature of the arrangement. Just because a sponsor derives good publicity or public relations benefits from payments to charity, doesn't automatically mean that payments by the sponsor are trading income in the hands of the charity.
> If the charity doesn't provide goods or services in return for payment, sponsorship payments will normally have the character of charitable donations rather than trading income in the charity's hands.

The principle that a trade requires the provision of goods or services is so well established that one might doubt the need for the word "normally".[1]

> The fact that the business sponsor itself takes steps to publicise or exploit the affinity with the charity won't change the treatment of the payments in the hands of the charity, unless the charity also publicises the affinity itself.
>
> If, before payment is made by the business sponsor, a commercial participator agreement (required by the Charity Commission under Section 59 of the Charities Act 1992 or by the Office of the Scottish Charity Regulator under Section 81 Charities and Trustee Investment (Scotland) Act 2005) is in place, the tax treatment of the payment will be determined by the wording of the agreement. Otherwise, the tax treatment of the payments will be determined on the particular facts of the case.
>
> HMRC has agreed the Charity Commission guidance on whether university research paid for by a sponsor is charitable. Other charities may also find this guidance helpful.

This Charity Commission guidance, "Research by Higher Education Institutions"[2] relates to the charity law aspects but is not relevant to tax.

> **23. Direct tax: what if the charity provides goods or services to the sponsor?**
>
> If the charity provides some goods or services in return for the sponsorship payments they may be treated as trading income.
>
> Most commonly a charity will play a part in publicising the business sponsor's affinity with the charity by including references to the sponsor in publications, posters, etc. and at events organised by the charity. Provided that such references amount to no more than acknowledgements of the sponsor's contributions they will not cause the payments to be regarded as trading income.[3] However, references to a sponsor which amount to advertisements will mean the payments are trading income. HMRC Charities will regard a reference to a sponsor as an advertisement if it incorporates any of the following:
>
> - large and prominent displays of the sponsor's logo
> - large and prominent displays of the sponsor's corporate colours
> - a description of the sponsor's products or services
>
> For example, if a project organised by a charity is sponsored by a well

1 *Ransom v Higgs* [1974] 1 WLR 1594 at pp.1600, 1622.

2 *https://www.gov.uk/government/publications/research-by-higher-education-institutions*

3 On advertising as a benefit for Gift Aid, see 15.22 (Acknowledgement and advertising).

known company, and acknowledgement of the support of this company is in the form of its name and logo inserted in the corner of a project report, this wouldn't be considered to be advertising. However, if the name and logo was substantially and widely displayed throughout the report, this might constitute advertising in return for the sponsorship payment.

There are other services that a charity might provide in return for sponsorship payments that will be factors in determining whether the payments are trading income. Examples of such services are:

- use of the charity's mailing list
- use of the charity's logo
- endorsement of the sponsor's products or services
- links to the sponsor's sales website from the charity's own website
- exclusive rights to sell goods or services on the charity's premises

...

25. Direct tax: payments for use of a charity's logo

Where a charity allows its logo to be used in return for payment by a business as an endorsement for 1 or more of the business's products or services, and the charity likewise promotes the endorsement in its own literature, the payments are likely to be trading income of the charity.

Payments solely for the use of a charity's logo may not be trading income in the charity's hands.

The position for charitable companies, where the logo came into existence prior to 1 April 2002 and for charitable trusts whenever the logo came into existence is:

- A one-off payment (received without any deduction of tax). The income is charged to tax as miscellaneous income and no exemption is available apart from the small scale trading exemption.
- annual payments - the income is charged to tax as miscellaneous income - exemption is available under section 488(3)(b) Corporation Taxes Act (CTA) 2010 (for corporate charities) and section 536(3)(c) Income Tax Act (ITA) 2007 (for charitable trusts), if Income Tax is deducted by the payer then repayment of the tax can be claimed, provided the income is applied solely for charitable purposes - however, where the payer is a UK company, the payment can be made without the deduction of Income Tax provided the payer reasonably believes that the recipient is a charity (sections 930 and 936(2)(d) ITA 2007)

Whether payments for use of the logo are annual payments will depend on the precise terms of the agreement for the use of the logo. If they are annual payments then the payments must be made under a legal obligation, recur each year and be a pure donation in the hands of the

charity.

For charitable companies only, where the logo came into existence on or after 1 April 2002 the logo is an 'intangible fixed asset' within section 713 CTA 2009. Exemption from tax is available for related non-trading gains received by charitable companies from intangible fixed assets tax under section 488 CTA 2010.

A charity should in practice accept this rather than risk a dispute with HMRC.

The HMRC approach was however rejected in the Special Commissioner case *British Olympic Association v Winter* [1995] STC (SCD) 85. The objects of the British Olympic Association ("BOA") included the promotion of Olympic ideals and the organisation of the British entry to the Olympic Games. BOA was not a charity, but it was a non-profit organisation and there is no difference in this context between charities and other NPOs.

BOA raised funds by the following methods:

(1) granting commercial sponsors the right to exploit the BOA logo in return for the payment of a premium
(2) licensing fees from International Sports and Leisure, a Swiss organisation which exploits the Olympic connection internationally for the benefit of the various National Olympic Committees worldwide
(3) 'merchandising' which involves the receipt by BOA of fees for licensing the production of articles bearing the BOA logo
(4) donations from the public

The Special Commissioner held that BOA was not carrying on a trade.[4] He applied the test in *IRC v Livingstone* 11 TC 538 at p.542:

> I think the test, which must be used to determine whether a venture such as we are now considering is, or is not, "in the nature of trade," is whether the operations involved in it are of the same kind, and carried on in the same way, as those which are characteristic of ordinary trading in the line of business in which the venture was made.

Applying this test, the Special Commissioner said:

---

4 We do not understand why the trading issue mattered in the BOA case, since if the receipts were not trading income they would be royalty income on which BOA (not a charity) would be taxable. But that does not affect the relevance of the case on the trading issue.

> Some of BOA's activities appear to be commercial in that Mr Nicholson adopted a very commercial approach when dealing with prospective sponsors. On the other hand, it is common ground that many of BOA's activities and functions are non-commercial. The sending of the team to the Olympic games is partly financed by innumerable small gifts from the public. In addition, some sponsors are paying not only towards the sending of the team, but to be associated with them to support BOA's other activities. The donations alone are insufficient to finance the sending of a high quality team to the games. Without a high quality team being sent, sponsorship cannot be obtained.
>
> I have also been referred to *Religious Tract and Book Society of Scotland v Forbes* 3 TC 415 and *Grove v Young Men's Christian Association* 4 TC 613. In *Religious Tract Society* the book shops were held to be trading operations whilst the colportage was not. It was possible to separate the two operations which in my judgment is not possible in the instant appeals. Similarly in the YMCA case where the restaurant's profit was held to be taxable it was again possible to isolate the restaurant operation (which was carried on the usual commercial principles and was open to the public), from the other activities of the YMCA.
>
> Perhaps the closest analogy with the facts of the instant appeals is to be found in the case of *Noddy Subsidiary Rights Co Ltd v IRC* 43 TC 458 where the appellant company was formed to exploit Enid Blyton's creation of the fictitious character of Noddy in children's books. It was held that the company was carrying on the trade of exploiting intellectual property. In the instant case, however, BOA is not merely exploiting the logo. Its activities are far wider. Those activities are so intertwined as to form a melange.
>
> On the facts in my judgment BOA's activities as a whole are uncommercial and do not constitute a trade. I find that it is not possible to isolate the earning of the sponsorship income and I conclude that it was not earned simply by the grant of the right to use the logo.

On this basis charities earning sponsorship by exploitation of their logo will never be trading. This decision has been considered by the FTT in *Sir Keith Mills Team Origin LLP v HMRC* [2017] UKFTT 378 (TC). The FTT stated that following *BOA*, prima facie obtaining sponsorship income in return for the use of a logo can amount to a trade where done so in a commercial way as opposed to where contributions are made non-commercially (e.g. from the public).

10.3 Primary purpose sponsorship

HMRC Guidance Note iv para 24 provides:

Direct Tax: When is a sponsorship arrangement charitable trading?

Once it has been determined that sponsorship payments are trading income in the charity's hands the next step is to consider whether the sponsorship arrangement falls into the charitable or non-charitable parts of the charity's trade.

It is recognised that where a sponsor's funding is tied to a particular event or project, it may not be practical to confine the charity's response to a mere acknowledgement. However, HMRC may challenge any arrangement in which the charity's response is on such a scale that it appears to be a main purpose of the sponsor making the donation. In such a case, HMRC will want to consider the possibility of

[1] non-charitable trading by the charity and

[2] where the donor has claimed [corporate Gift Aid] tax relief on the payments, whether there has been a breach of the donor's benefits limits.

The "main purpose of the sponsor" is not the correct test. The correct question is whether the charity's activity is a trade, and whether it is a primary purpose trade. But in practice it probably comes to the same thing.

Examples

Example 1

A charitable theatre group's production is sponsored by a local business 'TaxCo'. TaxCo's logo is placed discreetly within the event programme. An executive of TaxCo appears on stage on the final night and is thanked. One sign of moderate size is positioned prominently in the hall stating that the event is sponsored by TaxCo.

In this case it could not reasonably be argued that a main purpose of the production is advertising TaxCo, and there would be no loss of direct tax reliefs for charity or donor.

Example 2

An arts organisation's broadcast national awards ceremony is sponsored by a nationally well-known brand 'CarCo'. The event is named 'The CarCo Awards', which brings CarCo's name up on television frequently in trailers and program breaks. CarCo's logo features prominently in the program. An executive of CarCo appears on stage and thus on television and is thanked. There are many prominent signs advertising CarCo in the venue.

In this case it could reasonably be argued that a main purpose of the donation is advertising CarCo, and there is the possibility of a loss of direct tax reliefs for charity and donor. (although the donor may be able to claim all or part of their payment as a business advertising expense).

We would not agree with the analysis in example 2. The question is whether the charity is trading, and its primary purpose. Example 1 correctly asks what is the main purpose of the charity's production, looking at the matter from the charity's point of view; not what is the main purpose of the donor's donation (looking at the matter from the donor's point of view).

CHAPTER ELEVEN

CHARITABLE COMPANIES

Cross references

The following topics are considered elsewhere:
24.39 (IHT on members of charitable co)

11.1 Charity company/trust: differences

For most purposes charitable companies and trusts are taxed in the same way. However there are differences. It is not possible to write a full list but they include the following:

(1) If tax is payable on income or gains:
    (a) A charitable trust pays income tax and CGT
    (b) A charitable company pays corporation tax[1]
(2) Charitable companies (but not trusts) have tax exemption for profits under various minor categories:
    (a) 4.18.2 (Swaps)
    (b) 4.14 (Life policies/annuities)
(3) Different double tax treaty reliefs may apply.

This chapter considers some other issues raised specifically by charitable companies.

---

1 See 4.5 (Rate of tax on income); 5.9 (Rate of tax on gains). Further consideration would be needed for non-resident charities.

11.2 Group relief

Section 1154 CTA 2010 provides:

> (1) Subsections (2) to (4) define, for the purposes of the Corporation Tax Acts, the circumstances in which a body corporate ("B") is a 51% subsidiary, a 75% subsidiary or a 90% subsidiary of another body corporate ("A").
> (2) B is a 51% subsidiary of A if more than 50% of B's ordinary share capital is owned directly or indirectly by A.
> (3) B is a 75% subsidiary of A if at least 75% of B's ordinary share capital is owned directly or indirectly by A.
> (4) B is a 90% subsidiary of A if at least 90% of B's ordinary share capital is owned directly by A.
> [(5), (6), not set out here, explain the concept of ownership in a commonsense way]

A non-charitable company held by a charitable company is a subsidiary of the parent company within s.1154. The companies form a group and qualify for group reliefs.[2]

By contrast, a non-charitable company held by a charitable *trust* is not a subsidiary of the trust, as defined, as the term only applies where a body corporate owns another body corporate.

A non-charitable company cannot hold a charitable company as a subsidiary so as to form a group. The charity will not normally have a share capital and so will not be a subsidiary. In exceptional cases a charitable company may have share capital, for instance, a charity which takes the form of a co-operative and community benefit society. However the charity cannot be an "effective 51% subsidiary" and so still cannot form part of a group.[3]

See too 35.24 (VAT groups).

11.3 Close company: definition

"Close company" is elaborately defined. The definition uses the terms "control" and "participator" which are themselves elaborately defined. For a full discussion, see Kessler, *Taxation of Non-Residents and Foreign Domiciliaries* (21st ed., 2022-23), Chapter 101 (Control, Connected,

---

2 This is self-evident, but if authority is needed, see *Noved v HMRC* [2006] STC (SCD) 120 at [56]-[60].

3 See s.171 TCGA.

Close and Related Expressions).[4]

The starting point is s.439 CTA 2010 which provides:

> (1) For the purposes of the Corporation Tax Acts, a "close company" is a company in relation to which condition A or B is met.
> (2) Condition A is that the company is under the control—
> (a) of 5 or fewer participators, or
> (b) of participators who are directors.

11.3.1 *Charitable close company*

Is a member of a charitable company a participator? Members do not fall within s.454(1) CTA 2010 (they have no share or interest in the capital or income of the company) and they do not fall within s.454(2)(b)-(e) (various financial rights). The question is whether a member falls within s.454(2)(a) on the ground that they possess "voting rights".

Members of a charitable company can in principle vote, but they are curtailed in that the vote must be used for the charitable purposes of the company. The expression "voting *rights*" should be read in the context of the definition which refers to rights held beneficially as against the company. A member of a charitable company does not possess voting rights within the meaning of the provision. There are only voting duties.[5] So it is suggested that a member of a charitable company is not a participator.

A charitable company is close if (in short) it is under the control of 5 or fewer participators, so it would follow that a charitable company is not close.

This view would reduce anomalies between charitable trusts and companies.

HMRC do not agree. The HMRC Guidance Note Annex III.8.1 provides:

> Many charitable companies are close companies for tax purposes (that's under the control of 5 or fewer participators).

If that were right, then a charitable company would also be close if the directors (regardless of their number) were a majority of the members (and so "control" the company in the relevant, ultra-wide sense).

---

4 online version *https://www.foreigndomiciliaries.co.uk*

5 Note the corresponding company law provision, and the definition of control in the ultra-wide sense, refer to voting *power*, not voting *rights*.

The issue is untested, and one should proceed on the cautious view that a member of a charitable company may be a participator, and a charitable company could be close.

11.3.2 *Subsidiary of charity*

A subsidiary of a charitable *company*:
(1) is close if the charity is close;
(2) is not usually close if the charity is not close.

A company held by a charitable *trust* will always be close. Section 1169 CTA 2010 provides:

> Chapter 2 of Part 9 of ITA 2007 (which relates to settlements and trustees) applies for the purposes of the Corporation Tax Acts as it applies for the purposes of the Income Tax Acts.

Section 474(1) ITA provides:

> For the purposes of the Income Tax Acts (except where the context otherwise requires), the trustees of a settlement are together treated as if they were a single person (distinct from the persons who are the trustees of the settlement from time to time).

Regardless how many trustees there are, the company is under control of that deemed person, so it is under the control of a single participator.

11.4 Significance of being close

It will not normally matter whether a charitable company is a close company, but there could be some issues:
(1) Tax charges on making/releasing loans to a participator or associate. HMRC Guidance Note Annex iii.8.1 says that HMRC will take the point:

> Many charitable companies are close companies for tax purposes ... Subsidiaries of such charities will also be close companies. In these cases liability under the provisions of Section 455 CTA 2010 can arise when the company lends or advances money to:
> • a participator in the company (for example one of the directors/governors/guarantors), or
> • an associate of a participator (spouse, civil partner etc.).

But this is likely to be caught as employment income in any event.
(2) Any benefit or facility provided by the company for a participator (or an "associate" of a participator) is prima facie a distribution, and gives

rise to a liability to income tax: s.1000 CTA 2010. However, the Company Taxation Manual para 60600 states that HMRC do not normally take this point:

> **CTM60600: Benefits to directors and employees** [June 2016]
>
> ...
>
> The extended meaning of distribution CTM60520[6] should also, normally, be regarded as not applying to expenses incurred in or in connection with the provision of benefits, etc, for a participator (or an associate of a participator) who is
>
> - a director or employee of a company which is a charity or
> - employed by a company which carries on business as a school (or other educational establishment), or
> - employed in lower paid employment
>
> unless exceptionally the benefits etc are excessive compared to those which might normally be provided for an individual holding a similar position with a company in which they were not a participator (or an associate of a participator).

Of course the ordinary employment income rules will normally tax such benefits.

11.5 Loan relationships

The corporation tax treatment of interest and other profits from loans is governed by a code known as the loan relationships provisions, contained in Part 5 CTA 2009. A full discussion requires a book to itself. This chapter focuses on matters closest to the themes of this work, but the subject can only be understood in the context of the provisions as a whole.

11.5.1 *"Loan relationship"*

In outline, s.302 CTA 2009 provides:

> (1) For the purposes of the Corporation Tax Acts a company has a loan relationship if—
>
> (a) the company stands in the position of a creditor or debtor as respects any money debt[7] (whether by reference to a security or

---

6 The reference should be CT6600.

7 The term 'money debt' is defined in s.303(1) CTA 2009:

For the purposes of this Part a money debt is a debt which—

(a) falls to be settled—

(i) by the payment of money,

(ii) by the transfer of a right to settlement under a debt which is itself a money

otherwise), and

(b) the debt arises from a transaction for the lending of money.

In short, a company has a "loan relationship" wherever the company stands in the position of a creditor or debtor as respects any money debt. Normally, the debt must be one arising from a transaction for the lending of money, unless an instrument has been issued for the purpose of representing security for the creditors.[8]

11.5.2 *Trading loan relationship*

Section 297 CTA 2009 provides:

> (1) This section applies so far as in any accounting period a company is a party to a loan relationship for the purposes of a trade it carries on.
> (2) The credits in respect of the relationship for the period are treated as receipts of the trade which are to be brought into account in calculating its profits for that period.
> (3) The debits in respect of the relationship for the period are treated as expenses of the trade which are deductible in calculating those profits.

In the trading case, the taxation of the profits of the loan relationship depends on whether the charity's trading profits qualify for exemption.

11.5.3 *Non-trading loan relationship*

Section 299(1) CTA 2009 imposes a charge on non-trading profits:

> The charge to corporation tax on income applies to any non-trading profits which a company has in respect of its loan relationships.

Section 301 CTA 2009 provides:

> (1) Whether a company has non-trading profits or a non-trading deficit from its loan relationships for an accounting period is determined as follows, using the non-trading credits and non-trading debits given by this Part for the accounting period.
> (2) In this Part—

---

debt, or

(iii) by the issue or transfer of any share in any company,

(b) has at any time fallen to be so settled, or

(c) may at the option of the debtor or the creditor fall to be so settled.

8 In the case of a money debt which does not arise from a loan relationship, the provisions apply but only as respects *interest* payable to or by a company.

> (a) "non-trading credits" means credits for any accounting period in respect of a company's loan relationships that are not brought into account under s.297(2), and
> (b) "non-trading debits" means debits for any accounting period in respect of a company's loan relationships that are not brought into account under s.297(3). ...
>
> (4) A company has non-trading profits for an accounting period from its loan relationships if the non-trading credits for the period exceed the non-trading debits for the period or there are no such debits.
> (5) The non-trading profits are equal to those credits, less any such debits.
> (6) A company has a non-trading deficit for an accounting period from its loan relationships if the non-trading debits for the period exceed the non-trading credits for the period or there are no such credits.
> (7) The non-trading deficit is equal to those debits, less any such credits.

In short, profits from a company's loan relationships (where it is the creditor) and deficits from a company's loan relationships (where it is the debtor) are to be computed for each accounting period. Normally, an accruals method can be used, although in some cases it is permissible to use a "mark to market" basis.

Trading credits and debts in respect of individual transactions are then aggregated. The net figure is added to (or, in the case of a deficit, deducted from) trading profits.

Non-trading credits and debits are aggregated separately. If a charity has balance of non-trading credits, this is taxable under s.299 CTA 2009 but qualifies in principle for a charity exemption: see 4.8 (Interest).

11.5.4 *Non-trading profits*

Where the profits consist of cash such as interest, the provisions do not give rise to any special difficulty. But what is the position where the profit which a charitable company is deemed to realise by the application of an accruals method of accounting is in fact an unrealised one? For example, a charity buys a zero coupon bond which in seven years will be redeemable at twice the issue price. Each year the charity is deemed to realise a part of the profit, yet in reality it realises nothing. How can it apply for charitable purposes a mere increase in value which it has not realised and therefore cannot spend? It is suggested that the answer is that merely retaining the bond on the terms of the charity is an application for charitable purposes. A similar issue arises for deemed gains for CGT, see 5.5 (Deemed gain).

11.5.5 *Non-trading deficits*

Section 457 CTA 2009 provides the basic rule for non-trading deficits:

> **456** (1) This Chapter applies if for any accounting period a company has a non-trading deficit from its loan relationships under s.301(6). ...
> **457** (1) The basic rule is that the deficit must be carried forward and set off against non-trading profits[9] of the company for accounting periods after the deficit period in accordance with subsection (3) and s.458. ...
> (3) So much of the amount carried forward from the deficit period as is not the subject of a claim under s.458(1) must be set off against the non-trading profits of the company for the next accounting period after the deficit period.
> (4) Those profits are reduced accordingly.

Section 458(1) CTA 2009 provides:

> The company may make a claim for so much of the amount carried forward from the deficit period as is specified in the claim to be excepted from being set off against non-trading profits of the first accounting period after the deficit period (the "first later period").

The company may claim for the deficit to be brought forward.
Section 459(1) CTA 2009 provides:

> The company may make a claim for the whole or part of the deficit—
> (a) to be set off against any profits of the company (of whatever description) for the deficit period, or
> (b) to be carried back to be set off against profits for earlier accounting periods. ...

In short, if a company has a deficit, eg because more interest is paid than received, the excess can be set off against various other profits of the company or other companies in the same group. However, s.459(3) CTA 2009 provides:

> Subsection (1) does not apply if the company is a charity.

This at first appears alarming in that it denies to charities a tax deduction allowed to any other taxpayer. Let us take as an example a charitable company whose function is to provide housing in the UK and which borrows to buy or improve properties and funds the interest out of the rents.

---

9 "Non-trading profits" is defined in s.457(5) CTA 2009.

If it were not a company, it would in principle be able to deduct the interest in computing its property income. For CT purposes, it cannot deduct interest otherwise than in accordance with the Loan relationship provisions: see s.464(1) CTA 2009:

> The amounts which are brought into account in accordance with this Part in respect of any matter are the only amounts which may be brought into account for corporation tax purposes in respect of it.

Section 459(3) prevents it from obtaining any deduction under the Loan relationship provisions. It would thus appear that a charitable company has an artificially high income as compared with a charitable trust or any other taxpayer, corporate or not.

There is normally no problem. The charitable company will in principle be exempt from tax on its property income. One of the conditions is that the income is "applied for charitable purposes only". Income will be so applied in so far as it is used in paying interest on a loan the proceeds of which were expended for its charitable purposes. Hence, the charity does in effect obtain tax relief in respect of the payment of the interest in that for every £1 of interest paid it will cease to be taxable on £1 of rent. The balance remaining after deducting the interest paid from the property income will qualify for the charitable exemption provided it is also applied for charitable purposes only. That is quite fair and exactly the position in which a charitable trust would find itself in similar circumstances. Section 459(3) CTA 2009 then makes sense as an attempt by the drafter to ensure that a deduction is not in effect obtained twice over.

11.6 Form of Charitable Companies

A charitable company usually takes the form of a company limited by guarantee. Members of a company limited by guarantee do not make any contribution to the company's capital for so long as the company remains a going concern, instead simply guaranteeing to contribute a certain amount (typically a nominal amount) in the event of insolvency. A company with shares is normally appropriate for a commercial enterprise as share capital prov ides the company's working capital and the shares allow for profit to be divided among the shareholders. A company limited by guarantee is appropriate for a charity which does not have these needs.

Whilst a charity must act only to further its charitable objectives, a company limited by shares is in general an entity that exists for the benefit of its shareholders, who have invested money, have a right to a share in the profits and capital on a winding up, and to change the company's articles as they see fit. So it is not entirely obvious that the powers of shareholders are compatible with the requirement that a charity have exclusively charitable objects.

It might be said that a company limited by guarantee is also afflicted by this conflict, in that it is also controlled by its members, and they have the power to change its articles such that they become entitled to call for profits or a share of capital in a winding up. This apparent difficultly is resolved by two observations: firstly, any such alteration would stop the company being a charity; secondly, section 197 and 198 of the Charities Act 2011 prevent abuse.[10]

The Charity Commission provides model company articles only for a company limited by guarantee.[11]

11.6.1 *Dual registered charities*

Whilst shares and shareholders are generally unnecessary for charitable companies, however, there is one situation in which they are desirable. This is where it is helpful for the company to be a registered charity in both the UK and the US. Dual registration is helpful, in particular, to enable individuals liable to tax in both the UK and the US to obtain reliefs for donations to the charity in each jurisdiction, as those reliefs are dependent on the charity being registered in the relevant jurisdiction. It is no use for the donor to get relief in one jurisdiction if all this does is reduce the double tax relief they get in the other.

Dual registration is available by making use of the "check the box" (disregarded entity) rules in the US. These rules (very broadly - US law is out of the scope of this book) allow a subsidiary company to be treated as part of its parent for tax purposes. So if a US charity owns a UK charity, and opts to treat the UK charity as a disregarded entity, a donation to the UK charity will secure UK tax relief whilst simultaneously being treated in the US as a donation to the parent and therefore qualifying for US charity reliefs.

However, for disregarded entity status to be achieved, the US parent charity must own all of the shares in the UK subsidiary charity. So the latter must be a company limited by shares.

---

10 See 3.27.2 (Temporary charitable company).

11 *https://www.gov.uk/government/publications/setting-up-a-charity-model-governin g-documents*

Despite the theoretical difficulties mentioned above, the Commission takes a practical approach, and will register a charitable company owned by shareholders. Sections 197 and 198 Charities Act provide sufficient protection from abuse. It is important when drafting articles for a company limited by shares to ensure that:

(1) the shareholders can receive no benefit from the company that is not in accordance with its charitable objects,

(2) the shareholders can receive a benefit from the company to the extent that that is in accordance with the objects (because often the parent will be a charity with similar objects, and the company will want to support it);

(3) that the articles themselves provide that the Charity Commission must be consulted if any changes are made to the objects or other substantive provisions (to ensure the company is charitable before it is registered and becomes subject to section 197 and 198).

The Charity Commission are familiar with this structure. It would be helpful, in order to ensure the application for registration finds them and so avoid unnecessary delays, to include in it an explanation for the choice of a company limited by shares, and a summary of the protections that have been incorporated.

The Charities Aid Foundation operate one such charity (the CAF American Donor Fund).

It may be possible to do the same in other jurisdictions.

Corporate donors to such charities will need to consider the hybrid mismatch rules in Part 6A TIOPA 2010.

CHAPTER TWELVE

EMPLOYEES & BENEFICIARIES OF CHARITIES

12.1 Charity employees

Employees[1] of charities are in principle taxed on their earnings, just as any other employees. There is in general no charitable tax relief, which is not surprising, because this concerns income arising to an individual, not to a charity.

However, charity employees enjoy some minor tax advantages:

(1) *Living accommodation*: the usual rule is that a company director who works part-time cannot escape the charge on the benefit in kind of living accommodation even though the accommodation may be:
   (a) necessary for the employee's duties, or
   (b) provided for the better performance of their duties.
   This restriction does not apply to the director of a charitable company: see s.99 ITEPA.
(2) *Ministers of religion*: these enjoy:
   (a) Reliefs relating to living accommodation under ss. 290, 290A and

---

1 The expression here includes directors of charitable companies.

290B ITEPA

(b) Certain expenses deductible under s.351 ITEPA. Employment Income Manual para 60040–48 lists clergymen's expenditure regarded by HMRC as deductible.

(c) Reliefs relating to benefits in kind, for ministers earning less than £8,500; see sections 290C - 290G ITEPA. We wonder how often that will apply.

(3) *Non-resident employees of missionary societies:* these enjoy personal allowances which are normally available only to EU residents: s.56(3) ITA.

It will be apparent that the first two of these reliefs are now only rarely of significance. The third and fourth are of limited application and are difficult to justify except on an historical basis. It is suggested that all four exemptions should be repealed in the interests of simplicity.

12.2 Taxation of charity trustees

The statutory residence test has rules which govern the question whether work done by unpaid directors of a charity affects their residence status.[2]

In *Children's Investment Fund Foundation v AG,* following the divorce of H and W:

(1) W resigned from being director of the Foundation.

(2) The Foundation proposed to transfer funds to a new charity (controlled by W).

This was held to be a benefit to W, within the meaning of a company article providing (in short) that a trustee must not receive a benefit from the charity except with the consent of the Charity Commission.[3] But HMRC accepted that no tax charge arose. The tax issue was whether the transfer would be taxed as a termination payment for W's loss of office under s.401 ITEPA, which provides:

> (1) This Chapter applies to payments and other benefits which are received directly or indirectly in consideration or in consequence of, or

---

2 This is not discussed here; see Kessler, *Taxation of Non-Residents and Foreign Domiciliaries* (21st ed., 2022-23), para 4.23.2 (Enquiry procedure) online version *https://www.foreigndomiciliaries.co.uk*

3 The article is not unusual: it is in the Charity Commission standard articles. The facts were in one respect unusual, in that W reduced her financial claim against H as a result of this transfer: it was something she was prepared to pay for.

> otherwise in connection with—
> (a) the termination of a person's employment...

The charge is on the amount of the benefit: s.403(1) ITEPA provides:

> The amount of a payment or benefit to which this Chapter applies counts as employment income of the employee or former employee for the relevant tax year if and to the extent that it exceeds the £30,000 threshold.

The Judge said:

> HMRC granted clearance that no such charge would arise. The clearance was, however, entirely dependent on the disclosure that had been made. One aspect of that disclosure was to the effect that the Grant, if made, would be approved by the court and not by the members of [the Foundation].
> ... [HMRC] would be highly unlikely ultimately to determine that the Grant would be taxable. This is because ... HMRC would not regard any intangible benefits that Ms Cooper might achieve by being the member or trustee of a charity with assets augmented by the Grant as being taxable benefits caught by [s.401 ITEPA]. There would be no value in [W's] membership of [the charity], which has exclusively charitable objects. ... I should, however, record that, in submitting that an increase in status is not taxed, [Counsel] asked that that statement should not be elevated into a general statement of principle.[4]

12.3 PAYE

Charities which are employers are treated like any other employer for PAYE. HMRC's PAYE audits include charity employers.

It seems to be the HMRC view that almost any person who receives regular sums from a charity for services is likely to be an employee. In one case in the authors' experience, HMRC took the view that those who taught at Sunday School religion classes for a nominal reward were employees of the charity concerned. A charity should consider PAYE carefully before making any payment to those who do any work for the charity. The Employment Procedures Manual at EP8545 formerly contained a special PAYE arrangement for "Local Religious Centres" but this does not seem to be in the current Manual.

---

4 [2017] EWHC 1379 (Ch) at [122], [124].

12.4 Volunteers

The main issue for volunteers is whether they are employees. Employment Income Manual 71100 [Aug 2016] provides:

Voluntary organisations: unpaid office holders

Voluntary workers

Before tax can be charged under the provisions relating to employment income there must be:

- either an office or an employment
- **and** earnings from that office or employment.

A person who does voluntary unpaid work for a voluntary organisation, for example, a charity or local society, will not normally be engaged under a contract of employment and will not normally be the holder of an office. If there is no office or employment, it follows that the reimbursement of any expenses incurred by voluntary workers in doing the work of the organisation will not give rise to liability to tax. Similarly, voluntary workers who are otherwise unpaid are **not** liable to tax on the reimbursement of the extra cost they might incur because they undertake such work, for example, the expenses of travel between home and the place where the work is done.

If expenses are paid that do more than reimburse the costs incurred, or are at scale rates (*see* EIM05200) that cannot reasonably be regarded as merely a reimbursement of what they spend, the voluntary workers may be receiving remuneration for their services. In that case, the payments will be taxable as employment income if it can be shown that they hold an office or employment. If they do not hold an office or employment, the payments may be Miscellaneous Income.

Unpaid office holders

The same principles apply in relation to:

- officials elected under the constitution of bodies such as sports clubs and social clubs and
- people who undertake unpaid work within normal commercial organisations, or within areas such as the health service, governing bodies of Further Education Colleges, or the courts.

Such people may well hold an office. But they will not have any taxable earnings unless it can be shown that the office holders are being remunerated for their services. If the sums involved are small, you should not spend time examining the amounts paid to such officials to compensate them for the extra expenses they incur as a result of holding office. These principles are intended to apply to small amounts of travelling and subsistence payments. However, if the expenses/reimbursements amount to £8,500 or more a year they will be treated as earnings by virtue of Section 72 ITEPA 2003.

If such an unpaid worker receives a financial loss allowance (*see* EIM01120) that allowance will not cause an otherwise non-taxable reimbursed expense to become taxable.

Employees of voluntary organisations

The above comments do not apply to ordinary employees of voluntary

> organisations who are engaged under contracts of employment. Payments to such employees will be chargeable to tax in accordance with normal principles (*see* EIM00510 onwards) and PAYE should be operated as necessary.

This is correct, though understandably it does not address the fraught issue of when is there a contract of employment. The passage is repeated in HMRC Guidance Note para 3.50.6 to 3.50.10 and in ESM2504 (Offices: officials of social clubs).

12.4.1 *Unpaid directors: Travel expenses*

Travel expenses of unpaid directors are exempted from income tax by section 241A ITEPA:

> (1) No liability to income tax arises in respect of a sum if or to the extent that it is paid wholly and exclusively for the purpose of paying or reimbursing travel expenses in respect of which conditions A to C are met.
> (2) Condition A is that—
> (a) the employee is obliged to incur the expenses as holder of the employment, and
> (b) the expenses are attributable to the employee's necessary attendance at any place in the performance of the duties of the employment.
> (3) Condition B is that the employment is employment as a director of a not-for-profit company.
> (4) Condition C is that the employment is one from which the employee receives no employment income other than sums to which Chapter 3 of Part 3 applies (expenses payments).
> (5) In this section—
> (a) "director" has the same meaning as in the benefits code (see section 67), and
> (b) "not-for-profit company" means a company that does not carry on activities for the purpose of making profits for distribution to its members or others.

12.5 Charity beneficiaries

Although all charities must be for the public benefit, an application of funds for charitable purposes will sometimes benefit certain individuals directly. For example, a student may be given a grant for the purposes of their education.[5] This section considers whether such individuals may be

5 This is self-evident, but if authority is needed, see *AG v Charity Commission* [2011] UKUT 42 at [37].

taxable in respect of benefits received from the charity. It is necessary to consider charitable trusts and companies separately.

12.5.1 *"Beneficiary" of charity*

The position of a person who receives a benefit from a charitable trust is different from that of a beneficiary of a non-charitable trust. Beneficiaries of non-charitable trusts may enforce the trust. Under English law, only the Attorney General or the Charity Commission can enforce a charitable trust. Individuals who benefit or might benefit have no *locus standi* and no interest in the trust assets. Such individuals are not "beneficiaries" in the strict trust law sense of that word.[6]

Nevertheless, in charity law, the term "beneficiary" is generally used in the wider sense, to include persons who receive benefits from charity.[7] Here the word is used in a loose non-chancery law sense, where it may of course apply in the context of charitable companies as well as charitable trusts. It is difficult to think of a more appropriate term. No harm need arise from that usage provided one bears in mind:

(1) A "beneficiary" of a charitable trust has a different status from a beneficiary of a non-charitable trust.
(2) In strict trust law terminology, the word "beneficiary" is not used in that wide sense.

---

6 "Individuals may benefit from the application of trust moneys but they are not, as individuals, the beneficiaries of the trust and may not enforce its terms." *Re Crown Forestry Rental Trust, Latimer v IRC* [2004] 4 All ER 588 at [29].
Likewise Law Commission, *Capital and Income in Trusts: Classification and Appointment* Consultation Paper No. 175 (2004) para 6.16
https://assets.publishing.service.gov.uk/government/uploads/system/uploads/attachment_data/file/248331/0426.pdf "The 'beneficiary' [of a charitable trust] is at all times the public (although the identity of the individuals who incidentally benefit from the carrying out of the charitable purpose may not remain constant)."
Likewise *AG v Cocke* [1988] Ch 414 at p.419: "... the nonsense of alleging that there is any beneficiary in any meaningful sense of that word under a public charitable trust of this nature. It seems probable to me that in almost all charitable trusts there are no individual beneficiaries."
For further discussion of the meaning of "beneficiary" see 32.6 (Is a charitable *trust* "a beneficiary").

7 For instance:
(1) s.525(1)(b) ITA; see 8.9 (Beneficiary worker trade).
(2) s.561 ITA; see 6.27 ("Approved charitable loan").
(3) s.117 Charities Act 2011.

In this section we use the term **"charity-beneficiary"** to describe someone who receives a benefit from a charity, in order to emphasise this distinction.

12.6 General rule: charity grant not taxable

12.6.1 *Payment from charitable trust*

In the case of a non-charitable trust, income payments to a beneficiary are taxable as income of the beneficiary. This is so even if the trust is a discretionary trust, ie the beneficiary is merely an object of the powers of the trustees. This was settled early in the history of income tax, in a case concerning an American will trust with power to apply income to maintain beneficiaries:

> The test is not, I think, whether there is an absolute interest in a foreign possession, but whether there is such an interest in a foreign possession that the party assessed derives income from it.[8]

Similarly, where trustees of a non-charitable trust apply income for the benefit of a beneficiary, for example by paying school fees, then that income becomes income of the beneficiary for tax purposes. even though they do not receive the cash in hand.

These principles do not apply to charitable trusts. In principle, a payment from a charity to a charity-beneficiary is not the income of the charity-beneficiary, since they have no interest in the trust or in the trust property.

It is of course true that the charity-beneficiary does benefit from the charity's application of its income for charitable purposes. However, just because there is a benefit does not mean there is taxable income.

It is well established that a simple gift, is in principle not income of the recipient for tax purposes; and a payment from a charitable trust could be described as a simple gift.

A payment from a charitable company to a charity-beneficiary is in principle not income of the recipient for tax purposes, and it would be strange if a charitable trust was treated differently.

Sections 493, 494 ITA provide:

> **493 Discretionary payments by trustees**
> (1) Sections 494 and 495 apply for income tax purposes if—
> (a) in a tax year the trustees of a settlement make an annual payment to a

8 *Drummond v Collins* 6 TC 525 at p.541.

person ("the beneficiary") in the exercise of a discretion (whether exercisable by the trustees or any other person),
(b) the trustees are UK resident for the tax year, and
(c) condition A or condition B is met.

(2) Condition A is that what is paid to the beneficiary is, only because of the payment, income of the beneficiary for income tax or corporation tax purposes. "Income" does not include employment income.

(3) [Condition B concerns payments to children of settlors and is not relevant here]

(4) The payment is referred to in ss.494 and 495 as "the discretionary payment".

...

494 Grossing up of discretionary payment and payment of income tax

(1) The discretionary payment is treated as if it were made after the deduction of a sum representing income tax at the trust rate on the grossed up amount of the discretionary payment.

(2) The grossed up amount of the discretionary payment is the actual amount of the discretionary payment grossed up by reference to the trust rate.

(3) The person mentioned in subsection (4) is treated as having paid income tax of an amount equal to the sum deducted as mentioned in subsection (1).

(4) That person is—
(a) if condition A in s.493 is met, the beneficiary ...

These sections only apply if the trustees of the trust make an "annual payment" to a beneficiary. A payment from a charitable trust to a charity-beneficiary is not normally an "annual payment" so the sections do not normally apply. As far as we are aware, HMRC accept this view.[9]

---

9 This is consistent with former Inspectors Manual para 1628:

"**Harkness Fellowship Payments** [Published: 9/95]
Payments received from the Commonwealth Fund of New York under the terms of the Harkness Fellowship Scheme are made at the discretion of the Harkness Fellowships. The payments are not chargeable to Income Tax under Schedule E (because a Fellowship does not constitute an office or employment) nor are they chargeable under Case V of Schedule D as income arising from a possession out of the UK (*because there is no enforceable right to the payments*)."

Likewise Insurance Policyholder Taxation Manual:

"**IPTM4600. Special types of annuity** [Jun 2016]
...The term 'annuity' when used to describe payments out of the London Stock Exchange benevolent fund refers to what is in fact a gift that should not be regarded as income in the hands of the recipient."

The Inspectors Manual was withdrawn in 2006 and there is no equivalent in the current Manuals, perhaps because such income should qualify for the scholarship exemption: s.776 ITTOIA.

However the provisions relating to inter-charity payments are drafted on the basis of the opposite view: see 4.3 (Inter-charity payment).

The position of a charity-beneficiary under a charitable trust governed by Scots law needs further analysis. Scots charity law (unlike the law of England and Northern Ireland) does permit a charity-beneficiary to enforce a charitable trust (though in practice it would be very rare for a charity-beneficiary to take action for a breach of a charitable trust). But no-one suggests that the taxation of charity-beneficiaries should depend on whether a charitable trust is governed by English law or Scots law. It is suggested that the rights of a charity-beneficiary under Scots law should not be regarded as sufficient that a payment of income from the charity to the beneficiary is taxable.

12.6.2 *Trust enforceable by beneficiary*

For completeness: It is in theory possible that a trust which confers enforceable rights on beneficiaries (in the strict sense), who do therefore have an interest in the trust, may qualify as a charitable trust. One example would be a trust whose beneficiaries were all charities.[10] It may perhaps also be possible where individuals are beneficiaries, so long as the trust was drafted in a manner which ensured that the beneficiaries could only benefit in a charitable manner.

If such trusts were created, it is arguable that a beneficiary is taxable on income distributions from the trust. However one might argue that the charity-beneficiary only received an indirect benefit. Indeed, one might say that a charity-beneficiary should not necessarily be regarded as receiving a "benefit", a wide word but one whose meaning depends on context.

In practice trusts of this kind are rarely if ever created. A possible exception is the Thalidomide Children's Trust, where HMRC apparently took the view that beneficiaries were taxable on charity distributions. HMRC said:

> Some payments from the trust to the children will rank as the children's income for tax purposes: others will not. Regular cash payments to the children would normally be taxable: but a payment by the fund, to meet e.g. the cost of house extensions or alterations, or for assistance with house purchase, would not be taxable.[11] Where a taxable payment is

---

10 Though the author of the SDLT relief had some doubt as to whether a trust whose beneficiaries were charities was itself charitable: see 39.4.5 ("Charitable trusts").

11 This view of the income/capital distinction is wrong, see *Stevenson v Wishart* 59 TC 740 but that does not affect the general issue of whether income payments from the charitable trust are taxable.

made, the trustees will deduct tax ...[12]

The TSE Manual provides:

> **TSEM5954: the Thalidomide Trust - payments to beneficiaries up to 4 August 2004** [3 Mar 2017]
> The Thalidomide Trust is a charitable trust. Charitable trusts are not taxed on their income, but payments to beneficiaries still fall within the normal rules.
> Up to 4 August 2004, income payments from the Thalidomide Trust to beneficiaries were discretionary. As such they were subject to the same rules that govern payments from all discretionary trusts (TSEM3755-3756).
> Income payments from the Trust counted towards the beneficiaries' taxable income and reduced their level of entitlement to tax credits.
> The beneficiaries were taxed on the payments at their marginal rate of tax with credit given at 34% (40% from 6 April 2004) under ICTA/S687(1) and (2).
> **TSEM5956: the Thalidomide Trust - payments to beneficiaries from 5 August 2004** [3 Mar 2017]
> During the tax year 2004-05 the Paymaster General approved a Treasury Order bringing the Thalidomide Trust within the 'structured settlements' legislation. The 'Thalidomide Children's Trust (Application of Section 329AA of the Income and Corporation Taxes Act 1988) Order 2004' came into effect on 5 August 2004.
> From 5 August 2004 income payments made by the Trust to beneficiaries are no longer subject to tax and no longer count as income for tax credits purposes. ...

The Explanatory Note to the Statutory Instrument provides:

> The Thalidomide Trust was set up in 1973 to support the Thalidomide victims as part of a compensation package agreed between Distillers (who manufactured the drug) and the victims whereby the victims received individual lump sums and a further entitlement to benefit from the trust fund.

If it was correct that income payments from the Thalidomide trust were taxable - we are not in a position to comment on this specific trust and the point is now academic - this could only be because this charitable trust did confer enforceable rights on beneficiaries in a way that a charitable trust normally does not. That would be most unusual, but the Thalidomide trust

12 Press release [1974] STI 448.

was set up in unusual circumstances.

12.6.3 *Payment from charitable company*

A voluntary payment by a charitable company is not in principle taxable in the hands of the recipient. This was accepted in *Stedeford v Beloe* 16 TC 505. (The actual point decided, that voluntary pensions were not taxable as employment income, has been reversed by statute. That does not alter the significance of the case in this context.)

If the recipient were a member of the company, the payment could be taxable as a distribution. Similarly, if the company were a "close company" and the recipient were a participator or an associate of a participator. This is a point HMRC will take; see 11.4 (Significance of being close).

12.7 Where charity grant is taxable

A grant from a charity to a charity-beneficiary could be taxable under the following heads (not a complete list):

- Employment income
- Trading income
- Miscellaneous income

In this context, similar principles apply to a charity grant as to a gift from a non-charity.

If a charity makes a payment to another charity, the sum is deemed to be income of the recipient charity and so might be taxable: see 4.3 (Inter-charity payment).

12.7.1 *Charity grant: Employment income*

A grant from a charity to a charity-beneficiary is taxable if the grant constitutes earnings of the beneficiary's employment or a pension.

The usual employment income principles must be applied here. Antique examples involving a charity include *Herbert v McQuade* 4 TC 484 (payment to augment curate's income held taxable); contrast *Turner v Cuxson* 2 TC 422 (payment in respect of faithful service as a clergyman, but not in respect of the particular curacy the clergyman holds, not taxable).

The EI Manual provides:

> **EIM74008: Payments exempted from or not charged to tax as pension income** [Aug 2016]
> ...The Church of England Pensions Board make payments out of two

charitable funds:

- The Clergy Pensions Augmentation Fund and
- The Clergy (Widows and Dependants) Augmentation Fund.

With the exception of certain payments to widows and dependants, to which the Board applies PAYE, payments made out of these funds are non-taxable gifts.

For HMRC views on scholarship income, see EIM06205.

12.7.2 *Charity grant: Trading receipt*

A grant from a charity to a charity-beneficiary is taxable if the grant is a receipt of the beneficiary's trade or profession (or vocation, though that is not likely to arise).

The BIM provides:

BIM50710: Authors and literary profits: awards and bursaries [Jan 2019]
There are many prizes and awards open to authors and other creative artists (one publication lists nearly 200 for authors alone) and entering competitions or seeking awards is a normal part of such professions.

Where an award, grant, bursary or prize is received, the determining factor in considering whether or not such an award etc is taxable is the quality of the award in the hands of the recipient. If it comes to the individual as an incident in the exercise of his or her profession or vocation (including a subsidiary or part-time activity the profits from which are charged to Income Tax as the profits of a profession), it should normally be treated as a professional receipt and included in the computation of the taxable profits. (See *Temperley v Smith* (1956) 37 TC 18, *Smart v Lincolnshire Sugar Co Ltd* (1937) 20 TC 643, *Duff v Williamson* (1973) 49 TC 1, *IRC v Falkirk Ice Rink Ltd* (1975) 51 TC 42, and *McGowan v Brown and Cousins* [1977] 52 TC 8). The facts relating to the award or prize should be considered for each case.

In some cases publishers enter works for competitions and entries direct from the author are not permitted although the permission of the author is usually a part of the entry conditions. To attract liability, it is not essential that the author should have applied for the award or prize personally. Nor does the author necessarily have to undertake to complete a particular piece of work during the currency of the award or to refund the award in the event of failure to complete a programme of work.

A prize or award is not a professional receipt in all cases.. The facts may show that the award is one of the following—

- Income from an office or employment (see EIM00510 onwards). Where an award is made to a person receiving full-time instruction at a university or other establishment and the award does not exceed certain financial limits, the exemption for scholarship income may be available (see EIM06205onwards). Such cases are likely to be rare, however, and, in particular, established academics or leading members of professions will be unlikely to qualify since they will not normally be receiving full-time education..

- A profit of a casual or occasional nature chargeable as miscellaneous income (see (a) of BIM100105).
- Exceptionally, chargeable as an annual payment not otherwise charged to Income Tax..

A literary etc prize which is unsolicited, and which is awarded as a mark of honour, distinction or public esteem in recognition of outstanding achievement in a particular field, including the field in which the recipient operates professionally, is not chargeable to tax. In 1979 the Special Commissioners found for the taxpayer in a case involving a literary award. The case attracted some press publicity as a reporter was admitted to the proceedings. The book was entered for the competition by the publisher without the author's consent. The decision turned very much upon its own facts and, in particular, a finding that the award was unsolicited and did not represent the proceeds of exploitation of the book by the author personally or by his publishers as agents on his behalf. The Inland Revenue and the Arts Council of Great Britain reviewed the tax treatment of awards, grants and bursaries then paid in 1978. The Arts Council published the agreement. If, exceptionally, you need to see a copy please contact CTISA (Technical).

Case of doubt or difficulty which cannot be resolved on the lines outlined above should be referred to Business Profits (Technical).

BIM65151: Research grants and fellowships: overview [Nov 2019]

Research grants and research fellowships paid to individuals which are not chargeable as employment income (see EIM06265 onwards) may give rise to liability to Income Tax in the following four situations;

- If the individual has an existing profession to which the award can be attached, the award is a receipt of that profession. The case of *Duff v Williamson* [1973] 49 TC 1 lends support to this view.
- The individual may have a vocation as a researcher, so that the award is a receipt of that vocation. The situation envisaged is that of a student who has a series of research awards spread over a number of years. Such cases will be rare.
- The award may be chargeable as an annual payment. It would be necessary to show that the payments were capable of being annually recurring, paid under a legal obligation and pure income profit in the hands of the recipient, before such liability could be attached. Where services are provided by the recipient in return for the award, even if these amount to no more than the production of a report at the end of the period of study, the award is unlikely to be chargeable as an annual payment but is more likely to be trading income or miscellaneous income. In cases of doubt or difficulty, further advice may be obtained from BAI (Business Profits)...

Any case in which one of the four situations appears to apply but the liability is disputed should be referred to CTISA (Technical) before a hearing before the Tribunal is considered.

BIM65155: Research grants and fellowships: British Academy [Jan 2017]

As a result of discussions with the British Academy, HMRC have agreed that in general, awards and grants it makes are not taxable. Where, however, such

> awards are received in the course of the beneficiary's profession or vocation, advice should be obtained from CTISA (Technical). As regards other awards, see EIM06205 onwards and BIM50710.

See Lane, "Wrong kind of gift?", Taxation Magazine, (26 April 2018, p.18).

The matter should now be decided in accordance with generally accepted accountancy practice, see s.25 ITTOIA, but I expect that comes to the same thing.

12.7.3 *Charity payment miscellaneous income*

A grant from a charity to a charity-beneficiary is taxable if the grant falls within s.687 ITTOIA (miscellaneous income), for instance, a payment for services falling short of trading.

The BIM provides:

> **BIM65151: Research grants and fellowships: overview** [Nov 2019]
> Research grants and research fellowships paid to individuals which are not chargeable as employment income (see EIM06265 onwards) may give rise to liability to Income Tax in the following four situations ...
>
> - There may be a liability under the sweep-up charge to Income Tax on miscellaneous income (see BIM100101 onwards), if the sums are paid under a contract and this is an enforceable contract for services but the activity does not constitute a profession or vocation (see *Brocklesby v Merricks* [1934] 18 TC 576). This is likely to be the situation where particular work is carried out for the paying body and it receives some service from the student such as a written report or articles for publication. However, if the paying body does not receive significant services there cannot be liability under the sweep-up charge even if there is a contract (see Lord Denning at page 321 in *Scott v Ricketts* [1967] 44 TC 303).

12.8 Apprenticeship Levy

FA 2016 introduced the apprenticeship levy. The levy is payable by employers, through PAYE, where employers have a pay bill over £3m.

12.8.1 *Pay bill*

Pay bill for these purposes is equal to the total amount of earnings in respect of which the employer incurs liabilities to pay secondary Class 1 contributions.[13]

12.8.2 *Rates and allowance*

The rate of the levy is 0.5% of the pay bill for the tax year, less the levy

---

13 s. 100(2) FA 2016

allowance, which is £15,000: s.99 FA 2016. So the levy is only payable by employers with a pay bill over £3m.

12.8.3 *Charities unit*

Section 102 FA 2016 provides:

> (1) Two or more charities form a "charities unit" for a tax year (and are the "members" of that unit) if—
> (a) they are connected with one another at the beginning of the tax year, and
> (b) each of them is entitled to a levy allowance for the tax year.

A charities unit is only entitled to one levy allowance. The unit may determine how that is shared between the charities concerned:

> (2) The members of a charities unit must determine what amount of levy allowance each of them is to be entitled to for the tax year (and the determination must comply with subsections (3) and (4)). But see subsections (6) and (11).
> (3) A member's levy allowance for a tax year may be zero (but not a negative amount).
> (4) The total amount of the levy allowances to which the members of a charities unit are entitled for a tax year must equal £15,000.
> (5) A determination made under subsection (2) (with respect to a tax year) cannot afterwards be altered by the members concerned (but this does not prevent the correction of a failure to comply with subsection (4)).

If the charities do not do that, HMRC will do it for them:

> (6) If subsection (8) applies—
> (a) HMRC must determine in accordance with subsection (7) what amount of levy allowance each of the relevant members (see subsection (8)(a)) of the unit concerned is to be entitled to for the tax year, and
> (b) accordingly subsection (2) is treated as never having applied in relation to that charities unit and that tax year.
> (7) The determination is to be made by multiplying the amount of levy allowance set out in each relevant return (see subsection (8)(a)) by—
> (15,000÷T)
> where T is the total of the amounts of levy allowance set out in the relevant returns.
> The result is, in each case, the amount of the levy allowance to which the relevant member in question is entitled for the tax year (but amounts may

be rounded up or down where appropriate provided that subsection (4) is complied with).

(8) This subsection applies if—

(a) HMRC is aware—

(i) that two or more members of a charities unit ("the relevant members") have made apprenticeship levy returns ("the relevant returns") on the basis mentioned in subsection (9), and

(ii) that those returns, together, imply that the total mentioned in subsection (4) is greater than £15,000,

(b) HMRC has notified the relevant members in writing that HMRC is considering taking action under subsection (6), and

(c) the remedial action specified in the notice has not been taken within the period specified in the notice.

(9) The basis in question is that the member making the return is entitled to a levy allowance (whether or not of zero) for the tax year concerned.

(10) If any member of the charities unit mentioned in subsection (8)(a) is not a relevant member, that member is entitled to a levy allowance of zero for the tax year.

(11) If subsection (13) applies—

(a) HMRC must determine in accordance with subsection (12) what amount of levy allowance each of the members of the unit concerned is to be entitled to for the tax year, and

(b) accordingly subsection (2) is treated as never having applied in relation to that charities unit and that tax year.

(12) Each member of the unit is to be entitled to a levy allowance for the tax year equal to—

(15,000÷N)

where N is the number of the members of the charities unit for the tax year. Amounts determined in accordance with the formula in this subsection may be rounded up or down where appropriate provided that subsection (4) is complied with.

(13) This subsection applies if—

(a) the total amount paid by the members of a charities unit in respect of apprenticeship levy for a tax year or any period in a tax year is less than the total of the amounts due and payable by them for the tax year or other period concerned,

(b) either the members of the unit have made no apprenticeship levy returns for any period in the tax year concerned or the returns that have been made do not contain sufficient information to enable HMRC to determine how the whole of the £15,000 mentioned in subsection (4) is to be used by the members of the

> unit for the tax year,
>
> (c) HMRC has notified all the members of the unit in writing that HMRC is considering taking action under subsection (11), and
>
> (d) the remedial action specified in the notice has not been taken within the period specified in the notice.
>
> (14) Subsection (4) is to be taken into account in calculating the total of the amounts due and payable as mentioned in subsection (13)(a).
>
> (15) The Commissioners may by regulations provide that in circumstances specified in the regulations the members of a charities unit may alter a determination made under subsection (2) (despite subsection (5)).
>
> (16) In this section "apprenticeship levy return" means a return under regulations under section 105(4).

12.8.4 *"Charity"*

These rules also apply to CASCs: s.102(17) FA 2016 provides:

> In this Part "charity" means—
>
> (a) a charity within the meaning of Part 1 of Schedule 6 to FA 2010;
>
> (b) the Trustees of the National Heritage Memorial Fund;
>
> (c) the Historic Buildings and Monuments Commission for England;
>
> (d) a registered club within the meaning of Chapter 9 of Part 13 of CTA 2010 (community amateur sports clubs).
>
> (18) Subsection (17) is subject to section 118(5).

12.8.5 *"Connected"*

Section 118(1) FA 2016 provides an elaborate definition:

> Two charities are connected with one another for the purposes of section 102(1) if—
>
> (a) they are connected with one another in accordance with section 993 of ITA 2007 (meaning of "connected persons"), and
>
> (b) their purposes and activities are the same or substantially similar.

Section 118(2) FA 2016 tweaks the usual definition of connected person:

> In the application of section 993 of ITA 2007 for the purposes of subsection (1)(a)—
>
> (a) a charity which is a trust is to be treated as if it were a company (and accordingly a person), including in this subsection;
>
> (b) a charity which is a trust has "control" of another person if the trustees (in their capacity as trustees of the charity) have, or any of them has, control of the person;
>
> (c) a person (other than a charity regulator) has "control" of a charity

which is a trust if—

(i) the person is a trustee of the charity and some or all of the powers of the trustees of the charity could be exercised by the person acting alone or by the person acting together with any other persons who are trustees of the charity and who are connected with the person,

(ii) the person, alone or together with other persons, has power to appoint or remove a trustee of the charity, or

(iii) the person, alone or together with other persons, has any power of approval or direction in relation to the carrying out by the trustees of any of their functions.

(3) For the purposes of section 102(1) a charity which is a trust is also connected with another charity which is a trust if at least half of the trustees of one of the charities are—

(a) trustees of the other charity,

(b) persons who are connected with persons who are trustees of the other charity, or

(c) a combination of both,

and the charities' purposes and activities are the same or substantially similar.

In a marginal case, the choice of trustees becomes very important.

(4) In determining if a person is connected with another person for the purposes of subsection (2)(c)(i) or (3)(b), apply section 993 of ITA 2007 with the omission of subsection (3) of that section (and without the modifications in subsection (2) above).

12.8.6 *Non-charitable subsidiary*

Section 118 FA 2016 provides:

(5) If a charity ("A") controls a company ("B") which, apart from this subsection, would not be a charity—

(a) B is to be treated as if it were a charity for the purposes of this Part, and

(b) A and B are connected with one another for the purposes of section 102(1).

(6) In subsection (5) "control" has the same meaning as in Part 10 of CTA 2010 (see sections 450 and 451 of that Act) (and a limited liability partnership is to be treated as a company for the purposes of that Part as applied by this subsection).

(7) For this purpose, where under section 450 of that Act "C" is a limited liability partnership, subsection (3) of that section has effect as if before

(a) there were inserted—

"(za) rights to a share of more than half the assets, or of more than half the income, of C,".

Section 119 FA 2016 provides:

(1) This section applies if—

(a) a charity ("A") is connected with another charity ("B") for the purposes of section 102(1), and

(b) B is connected with another charity ("C") for the purposes of section 102(1).

(2) A and C are also connected with one another for the purposes of section 102(1) (if that would not otherwise be the case).

(3) In subsection (1)—

(a) in paragraph (a) the reference to a charity being connected with another charity for the purposes of section 102(1) is to that charity being so connected by virtue of section 118 or this section, and

(b) in paragraph (b) the reference to a charity being connected with another charity for the purposes of section 102(1) is to that charity being so connected by virtue of section 118.

CHAPTER THIRTEEN

ACQUISITION OF COMPANIES

13.1 Acquisition of company

This chapter deals with questions which arise when a charity acquires an interest in a company by way of bargain at arm's length.

Shareholder-vendors are potentially exposed to taxation at two levels:

(1) *Tax at company level* If an asset is sold by the company, then the company will be taxable on chargeable gains (if the asset is a capital asset) or trading profits (if the asset is held as trading stock).

(2) *Tax at shareholder level* The shareholders will then normally be able to extract the profit from the company only at an additional cost,

whether in terms of IT on a dividend or other distribution, or CGT on a disposal of their shares on a liquidation of the company.

The shareholders could simply sell their shares in the company, thus being directly exposed to only one level of taxation. However, the purchase price would normally be discounted to allow for the fact that the asset held by the company could only be disposed of by the company at a further tax cost. A charity may be in a position to obtain the benefit of this discount and yet avoid the tax charge on the company.

13.2 Charitable expenditure rules

If there were a tax avoidance motive, expenditure by the charity in buying the shares would normally constitute non-charitable expenditure.[1]

13.3 Transactions in securities

The "lengthy and complicated"[2] provisions relating to transactions in securities (the "**TiS code**") requires a book to itself.

The rules are in:

(1) Chapter 1 part 13 ITA
(2) Part 15 CTA 2010

This chapter focuses on the points most relevant to charities.

Different rules apply to CT and IT so it is necessary to distinguish between **"CT TiS rules"** and **"IT TiS rules"**, though there are many points of overlap.

IRC v Universities Superannuation Scheme explains:

> Charities and other exempt bodies often participated in schemes for dividend stripping relying upon their exemption from tax ... [Counsel for the taxpayer] accepted that charities and other exempt bodies were within the scope of [the TiS rules].[3] ...

13.4 CT TiS rules: Introduction

Section 733(1) CTA 2010 provides:

> This section applies to a company in respect of a transaction in securities

---

1 See 6.22 (Other investments: Type 12).

2 *IRC v Laird Group* [2003] STC 1349 at [13].

3 70 TC 193 at p.212; *Greenberg v IRC* 47 TC 740 at p.257 assumes that a charity can fall within the TiS rules.

> or two or more such transactions if the company is in a position to obtain or has obtained a corporation tax advantage—
> (a) in circumstances where any of the provisions specified in subsection (2) applies in relation to the company, and
> (b) in consequence of—
> (i) the transaction, or
> (ii) the combined effect of the transactions.

Section 733(2) CTA 2010 sets out three sets of circumstances:

> The provisions are—
> section 736 (receipt of consideration representing company's assets, future receipts or trading stock (circumstance C)),
> section 737 (receipt of consideration in connection with relevant company distribution (circumstance D)), and
> section 738 (receipt of assets of relevant company (circumstance E)).

We refer to this as **"CT circumstances C to E"** to avoid confusion with the IT circumstances.

Section 733 CTA 2010 raises the following issues:

(1) Is there a transaction in securities?
(2) Does a company obtain an CT advantage?
(3) Does it obtain the tax advantage in consequence of the transaction in securities?
(4) Do CT circumstances C to E apply?

13.5 "Transaction in securities"

This expression is defined in s.751 CTA 2010:

> "transaction in securities" means transactions, of whatever description, relating to securities, and in particular—
> (a) the purchase, sale or exchange of securities,
> (b) issuing or securing the issue of new securities,
> (c) applying or subscribing for new securities, and
> (d) altering or securing the alteration of the rights attached to securities.

The IT equivalent is s.684(2) ITA but the definition is wider.
A sale of shares is of course a transaction in securities. A redemption of debentures is caught.[4]

---

4 This is self-evident but if authority is needed, see *IRC v Parker* 43 TC at p.434.

13.5.1 *"Securities"*

"Securities" is defined in s.751 CTA 2010/s.713 ITA:

> "securities"—
> (a) includes shares and stock, and
> (b) in relation to a company not limited by shares (whether or not it has a share capital) also includes a reference to the interest of a member of the company as such, whatever the form of that interest.

13.6 "CT advantage"

For corporation tax, the expression used is "corporation tax advantage" and for IT, "income tax advantage". We refer to these as **"CT advantage"** and **"IT advantage"**. The definitions are differently worded. CT advantage is defined in s.732(1) CTA 2010:

> In this Part "corporation tax advantage" means—
> (a) a relief from corporation tax or increased relief from corporation tax,
> (b) a repayment of corporation tax or increased repayment of corporation tax,
> (c) the avoidance or reduction of a charge to corporation tax or an assessment to corporation tax, or
> (d) the avoidance of a possible assessment to corporation tax.

We refer to **"limbs (a) to (d)"** of the definition. Section 732(2) CTA provides:

> For the purposes of subsection (1)(c) and (d) it does not matter whether the avoidance or reduction is effected—
> (a) by receipts accruing in such a way that the recipient does not pay or bear corporation tax on them, or
> (b) by a deduction in calculating profits or gains.

In *Sheppard v IRC (No. 2)*:[5]

(1) The shareholders in a company in effect gave 60% of their shares to a charitable trust.

(2) The shareholders (other than the charity) then waived their entitlement to a dividend in favour of the charity. Later on the same day the

5 65 TC 724.

charity was paid a dividend of £140,000 (net of the tax credit).[6]

The charity claimed repayment of the £60,000 tax credit. (This ceased to be possible in 1999 and tax credits have now been (more or less) abolished.) HMRC sought to prevent this under the TiS rules. The court held that the charity had not obtained a tax advantage. The court considered all four limbs of the definition. The case was considering the wording which is now found in the definition of CT advantage.

13.6.1 *"Repayment of tax": Limb (b)*

In order to understand *Sheppard* one must bear in mind that there was no tax advantage within limb (b) of the definition because the payment of the tax credit to the charity was not a "repayment" of tax. This point is now obsolete.

13.6.2 *"Avoidance or reduction of tax"*

What is "avoidance" of tax within limbs (c) and (d)? Lord Wilberforce said in *IRC v Parker*:

> The paragraph, as I understand it, presupposes a situation in which
> [1] an assessment to tax, or increased tax, either is made or may possibly be made,
> [2] that the taxpayer is in a position to resist the assessment by saying that *the way in which he received what it is sought to tax* prevents him from being taxed on it;
> [3] and that the Crown is in a position to reply that if he had received what it is sought to tax *in another way* he would have had to bear tax.
> In other words, there must be a contrast as regards the "receipts" between
> [a] the actual case where these accrue in a non-taxable way with
> [b] a possible accruer in a taxable way,
> and unless this contrast exists, the existence of the advantage is not established.[7]

In the following discussion:

(a) The actual case, where these accrue in a non-taxable way, is the **"actual receipt"**

---

6 If the same issue arose today, the shareholders would do best not to give the shares to charity but to receive the dividend themselves and make a Gift Aid donation to the charity.

7 43 TC 396 at 441 (emphasis added).

(b) The "possible accruer in a taxable way" is the **"comparator"**, (sometimes called the "hypothetical receipt").

The GAAR Guidance provides:

> The concept of a "tax advantage" is common in UK tax legislation. The language suggests that in ascertaining whether an advantage arises the actual tax position should be compared with another tax position. The appropriate comparator or alternative tax position will depend on the facts, but will usually derive from the arrangements that would have occurred absent the abusive tax purpose (which may include no arrangement at all). In situations where there is more than one alternative arrangement that might have been adopted if the taxpayer had not adopted an abusive arrangement then the appropriate comparator would be the transaction that the taxpayer would most likely have carried out.[8] This might not be the arrangement that would give rise to the greatest tax liability.[9]

The comparator need not be received as a result of the same kind of transaction as did the actual receipt. *IRC v Cleary*[10] concerned a share sale: the shareholder sold shares to a company for cash. The actual receipt of the proceeds of sale was not income-taxable. The comparator was a possible dividend from the company (which would have been income-taxable). So there was a "tax advantage" under limbs (c) or (d) of the definition.[11] A dividend and a sale are different types of transaction. The dividend would reduce the company's assets available for distribution (unlike the actual sale). That did not matter. So in short, the question under limbs (c) or (d) has been whether the company can pay a dividend to the shareholder equal to the amount which the shareholder received tax-free.

---

8 Footnote original: This follows the approach adopted by Lord Hoffmann in the Hong Kong case *IRC v Tai Hing Cotton Mill* (CACV 343/2005): "[The Commissioner] would not be entitled, as the more alarmist submissions of counsel for the taxpayer suggested, to make an assessment on the hypothesis that the taxpayer had entered into an alternative transaction which attracted the highest rate of tax. That would not be a reasonable exercise of power. But she may adopt the hypothesis which the evidence suggests was most likely to have been the transaction if the taxpayer had not been able to secure the tax benefit."

9 HMRC "GAAR Guidance" (2015) para C2.5 *https://www.gov.uk/government/publications/tax-avoidance-general-anti-abuse-rules*

10 44 TC 399 at 423.

11 At that time the definition applied in the same way to income tax and corporation tax.

The comparator must involve receipt of the same asset as the actual receipt. *Anysz v IRC* 53 TC 601 concerned a share for share exchange: the shareholder transferred shares in A Ltd to another company ("B Ltd") in exchange for an issue of shares in B Ltd. B Ltd could have declared a cash dividend, but cash was not a valid comparator to the actual receipt of B Ltd shares. However A Ltd could have:
(1) bought B Ltd shares, and
(2) distributed them to the shareholder by way of dividend in specie.

That was a valid comparator. Hence the shareholder obtained a "tax advantage".

However, a charity cannot usually obtain a CT advantage within limbs (c) or (d), applying the *Parker* test, because there is usually no possible taxable comparator.

In *Sheppard*, the *Parker* dictum was applied to limbs (a) and (b) of the definition (so a charity does not enjoy a tax advantage as defined even if the charity does benefit from a "relief"). At first sight this seems right. A charity (which is not subject to tax) does not obtain a tax advantage (in the normal sense of the term) simply by becoming entitled to income, even though the same income would be subject to tax in the hands of someone else. No matter how it took this profit, the charity could not have been taxable on it. Nevertheless, it was said in *IRC v Universities Superannuation Scheme* 70 TC 193 that the *Parker* test only applied to limbs (c)(d) of the definition of tax advantage. If that is right, a charitable company obtains a CT advantage within limb (a) whenever it receives any income, which is surprising. The basis of this view must be that we have here not a definition of "tax advantage" but an "artificial inclusion clause", under which the label "tax advantage" is used to include things that are not within the natural meaning of the words. In good drafting practice a defined term should not have a meaning far from its natural meaning. Nevertheless, this rule was breached elsewhere in the TiS provisions[12] (though the tax law rewrite slightly improved matters).

In what follows the expression is referred to as **"CT Advantage"** (initial capitals) to remind readers that it is used in a defined and artificial sense.

13.7 CT motive defence

Section 734 CTA 2010 provides:

---

12 See *IRC v Cleary* 44 TC 399 at p.428.

> (1) Section 733 does not apply to a company in respect of a transaction in securities or two or more such transactions if the company shows that the transaction or transactions meet conditions A and B.
> (2) Condition A is that the transaction or transactions are effected—
> (a) for genuine commercial reasons,[13] or
> (b) in the ordinary course of making or managing investments.
> (3) Condition B is that enabling corporation tax advantages to be obtained is not the main object or one of the main objects of the transaction or, as the case may be, any of the transactions.

We refer to this as the **"CT motive defence"**. Conditions A and B must both be satisfied.

13.7.1 *"Main object"*

IRC v Kleinwort Benson 45 TC 369 concerned a purchase by a dealer in securities of debenture stock with the right to unpaid arrears of interest. Cross J said:

> Here there was only a single indivisible transaction, and it was an ordinary commercial transaction, a simple purchase of debenture stock. As the purchaser was a dealer, he was entitled to keep the interest element out of his tax return and so was able to pay a higher price than an ordinary taxpayer would have been able to pay. Similarly, a charity, because it would have been able to reclaim the tax, would have been able to pay an equally large price and still make a profit. But it is to my mind an abuse of language to say that the object of a dealer or a charity in entering into such a transaction is to obtain a tax advantage.[14]

But subsequently the courts stepped back from this. In *IRC v Sema Group Pension Scheme Trustees* 74 TC 593, a pension scheme received the proceeds of a purchase of own shares, on which it could reclaim the tax credit. The Special Commissioners held that one of the main objects of the purchase was to obtain this credit. The issue was held to be one of fact, the traditional way for the court to express no view, so the decision of the Special Commissioners was upheld. Tax credits have now been abolished.

---

13 On the meaning of "genuine" see Kessler, *Taxation of Non-Residents and Foreign Domiciliaries* (21st ed., 2022-23), para 3.18.3 ("Genuine") online version *https://www.foreigndomiciliaries.co.uk*
Sheppard v IRC (No. 2) (discussed above) is an example of a case where transaction in securities was intended to benefit charity and so not "commercial".

14 45 TC 369 at p.382. The passage was approved in *Chilcott v IRC* 55 TC at p.474.

13.8 CT Circumstance C

Section 736(1) CTA 2010 provides:

> This section applies in relation to a company ("A") if subsections (2) to (4) apply.

13.8.1 *Receipt of distributable consideration*

Section 736(2) CTA 2010 provides:

> A receives consideration which—
> (a) is or represents the value of—
> (i) assets which are available for distribution by a company by way of dividend, or
> (ii) assets which would have been so available apart from anything done by the company,
> (b) is received in respect of future receipts of a company, or
> (c) is or represents the value of trading stock of a company.

Consideration is given an artificial definition in s.736(6) CTA 2010:

> In this section references to the receipt of consideration include references to the receipt of any money or money's worth.

It is convenient to have a label for this concept, which is here called **"Distributable Consideration"**.
Section 736(5) CTA 2010 restricts this concept:

> The assets mentioned in subsection (2) do not include assets which are shown to represent a return of sums paid by subscribers on the issue of securities, despite the fact that under the law of the country in which the company is incorporated assets of that description are available for distribution by way of dividend.

13.8.2 *Abnormal amount by way of dividend*

Section 736(3) CTA 2010 provides:

> The receipt is in consequence of a transaction whereby another person subsequently receives, or has received, an abnormal amount by way of dividend (see section 740).

Abnormal amount by way of dividend is not discussed here.

13.8.3 *Tax-free receipt*

Section 736(4) CTA 2010 provides:

> The receipt of the consideration is such that A does not pay or bear corporation tax on income in respect of it (apart from this Part).

Circumstance C could catch the vendor of the shares where the charity purchaser took an abnormal amount by way of dividend after the purchase. It could apply in situations, for example, where the company is a trading company and owns valuable trading stock on the disposal of which it would realise substantial profits. The purchasing charity could ensure that this profit were realised after the purchase of the shares. Circumstance C would then apply. But in these circumstances the motive defence may be available.

13.9 CT Circumstance D

Section 737(1) CTA 2010 provides:

> This section applies in relation to a company ("the section 733 company") if subsections (2) to (4) apply.

13.9.1 *Receipt by s.733 company*

Section 737(2) CTA 2010 provides:

> The section 733 company receives consideration in connection with—
> (a) the distribution, transfer or realisation of assets of a relevant company (see section 739), or
> (b) the application of such assets in discharge of liabilities.

13.9.2 *Distributable consideration*

Section 737 CTA 2010 provides:

> (3) The consideration—
> (a) is or represents the value of—
> (i) assets which are available for distribution by way of dividend by the relevant company, or
> (ii) assets which would have been so available apart from anything done by the relevant company,
> (b) is received in respect of future receipts of the relevant company, or
> (c) is or represents the value of trading stock of the relevant company.
>
> (5) The assets mentioned in subsection (3) do not include assets which are shown to represent a return of sums paid by subscribers on the issue of securities, despite the fact that under the law of the country in which the relevant company is incorporated assets of that description are available for distribution by way of dividend.

(6) In this section references to the receipt of consideration include references to the receipt of any money or money's worth.

This is comparable to the concept of distributable consideration found in circumstance C.

13.9.3 *Tax free receipt*

Section 737(4) CTA 2010 provides:

The section 733 company so receives the consideration that it does not pay or bear corporation tax on income in respect of it (apart from this Part).

13.9.4 *Relevant company*

"Relevant company" is defined in s.739 CTA 2010:

(1) A company is a relevant company for the purposes of sections 737 and 738 if it is—
- (a) a company under the control of not more than 5 persons (but see subsection (2)), or
- (b) any other company none of whose shares or stocks is—
  - (i) included in the official UK list, and
  - (ii) dealt in on a recognised stock exchange in the United Kingdom regularly or from time to time.

The restriction of this relief to UK quoted companies is not EU-law compliant.

(2) A company is not a relevant company for those purposes if it is under the control of one or more companies which are not relevant companies for those purposes.
(3) The reference in subsection (1)(b) to shares or stocks does not include debenture stock, preferred shares or preferred stock.
(4) Section 450 (meaning of "control" for the purposes of Part 10 (close companies)) applies for the purposes of this section.

The distributable consideration need not be received from the relevant company.[15]

Circumstance D is the widest. It applies in any case where there is a sale of shares in a relevant company and a "distribution of profits" (as defined) of that company. In such a case, a vendor would be caught unless they could rely on the motive defence.

---

15 This is self-evident but if authority is needed see *IRC v Wiggins* 53 TC 639.

13.10 CT Circumstance E

This involves, inter alia, a person receiving non-taxable consideration in the form of share capital or securities and would not therefore apply to a cash sale.

13.11 IT TiS rules: Introduction

The IT TiS rules were introduced in 2010 and amended in 2016.
Differences between the IT and the CT TiS include:
(1) The definition of IT advantage
(2) Replacing "relevant company" with "close company"
(3) Exemption for fundamental changes in ownership of shares

Section 684(1) ITA provides:

> (1) This section applies to a person ("the party") where—
> (a) the person is a party to a transaction in securities or two or more transactions in securities[16] ...
> (b) the circumstances are
> [i] covered by section 685 and
> [ii] not excluded by section 686,
> (c) the main purpose, or one of the main purposes, of the transaction in securities, or any of the transactions in securities, is to obtain an income tax advantage, and
> (d) the party or any other person obtains an income tax advantage in consequence of the transaction or the combined effect of the transactions.

Unlike the CT rules, the person must be a party to the transaction in securities.

13.12 IT TiS motive defence

Section 684(1)(c) ITA requires:

> the main purpose, or one of the main purposes, of the transaction in securities, or any of the transactions in securities, is to obtain an income tax advantage

13.12.1 *"IT Advantage"*

"Income tax advantage" is defined in s.687 ITA. It is not the standard definition of "tax advantage":

---

16 The words "or two or more transactions in securities" are otiose, but they do no harm.

(1) For the purposes of this Chapter [chapter 1 part 13] a person obtains an income tax advantage if—

(a) [i] the amount of any income tax which would be payable by the person in respect of the relevant consideration if it constituted a distribution[17] exceeds

[ii] the amount of any capital gains tax payable in respect of it, or

(b) [i] income tax would be payable by the person in respect of the relevant consideration[18] if it constituted a distribution and

[ii] no capital gains tax is payable in respect of it.

(2) So much of the relevant consideration as exceeds the maximum amount that could in any circumstances have been paid to the person or an associate of the person by way of a distribution at the time when Condition A or B in section 685 is met is to be left out of account for the purposes of subsection (1)....

In what follows the expression is referred to as Income Tax Advantage (initial capitals) to remind the reader that it is used in a defined and artificial sense.

This is differently worded from the CT motive defence. HMRC describe the IT expression as "narrower" than the CT expression.

HMRC say:

> The proposed legislation, through the definition of tax advantage would make it clear that the TiS legislation does not apply to TiS where an advantage in relation to tax on chargeable gains is obtained. This would be more relevant for corporation tax where the position is not clear from the existing [pre 2010] legislation.[19]

13.12.2 *Disregard for undistributable income*

Section 687(2) ITA provides:

> So much of the relevant consideration as exceeds the maximum amount that could in any circumstances have been paid to the person by way of

---

17 Subsection (4) provides: "In this section (a) "distribution" does not include a distribution which is a distribution for the purposes of the Corporation Tax Acts only because it falls within paragraph C or D in section 1000(1) of CTA 2010 (redeemable share capital or security issued as bonus in respect of shares in, or securities of, the company)".

18 Subsection (4) provides: "In this section ... (b) "relevant consideration" has the same meaning as in section 685."

19 See HMRC , "Simplifying Transactions in Securities Legislation" (2009) para 3.3 *https://www.taxation.co.uk/files/TransactionsSecuritiesLegislation.pdf*

> a qualifying distribution at the time when the relevant consideration is received is to be left out of account for the purposes of subsection (1).

13.12.3 *Amount of IT advantage*

The amount of IT Advantage has a commonsense definition in s.687(3) ITA:

> The amount of the income tax advantage is the amount of the excess or (if no capital gains tax is payable) the amount of the income tax which would be payable.

13.13 IT circumstances

Section 685(1) ITA provides:

> The circumstances covered by this section are circumstances where condition A or condition B is met.

We refer to **"IT circumstances A and B"**.

13.14 IT circumstance A

There are 3 types of circumstance A, which I call A(a), A(b) and A(c).

13.14.1 *Circumstance A(a)(b)*

Section 685(2) ITA provides:

> Condition A is that, as a result of the transaction in securities or any one or more of the transactions in securities, a relevant person receives relevant consideration in connection with—
> (a) the distribution, transfer or realisation of assets of a close company, [or]
> (b) the application of assets of a close company in discharge of liabilities...
>
> and the relevant person does not pay or bear income tax on the consideration (apart from this Chapter).

Examples are:

(1) The sale of a close company for cash, assuming that the sale is a "realisation of assets" of the company

(2) The repayment of a debt security, assuming the creditor receives relevant consideration

13.14.2 *Circumstance A(c)*

Section 685(2) ITA provides:

> Condition A is that, as a result of the transaction in securities or any one or more of the transactions in securities, a relevant person receives relevant consideration in connection with...
>
> (c) the direct or indirect transfer of assets of one close company to another close company,
>
> and the relevant person does not pay or bear income tax on the consideration (apart from this Chapter).

13.14.3 *"Relevant person"*

Section 685(3A) ITA provides:

> In subsections (2) and (3) "relevant person" means-
>
> (a) the party, or
>
> (b) any person other than the party in relation to whom the condition in section 684(1)(d) is met.

Unpacking the definition, this means:

(a) The parties to the transaction in securities and

(b) any person meeting the condition in s.684(1)(d), ie any person who obtains an Income Tax Advantage in consequence of the TiS.[20]

13.14.4 *"Relevant consideration"*

Section 685 ITA provides two definitions:

Subsection	**Definition for:**
(4)	Circumstance A(a)(b)
(5)	Circumstance A(c), B

> (4) In a case within subsection (2)(a) or (b) [in my terminology, Circumstance A(a)(b)] "relevant consideration" means consideration which—
>
> (a) is or represents the value of—
>
> (i) assets which are available for distribution by way of dividend by the company, or
>
> (ii) assets which would have been so available apart from anything done by the company,
>
> (b) is received in respect of future receipts of the company, or
>
> (c) is or represents the value of trading stock of the company.
>
> (5) In a case within subsection (2)(c) or (3) [in my terminology, Circumstance A(c) and Circumstance B] "relevant consideration" means consideration

20 That is, the phrase "in relation to whom the condition in section 684(1)(d) is met" governs the words "any person" not the words "the party".

[i] which consists of any share capital or any security issued by a close company and
[ii] which is or represents the value of assets which—
(a) are available for distribution by way of dividend by the company,
(b) would have been so available apart from anything done by the company, or
(c) are trading stock of the company.

13.15 IT circumstance B

Section 685(3) ITA provides:

> Condition B is that—
> (a) a relevant person receives relevant consideration in connection with the transaction in securities or any one or more of the transactions in securities,
> (b) two or more close companies are concerned in the transaction or transactions in securities concerned, and
> (c) the relevant person does not pay or bear income tax on the consideration (apart from this Chapter).

An example is the sale of shares in one close company to another close company in consideration of an issue of shares or loan notes.

13.16 Other definitions

13.16.1 *"Consideration"*

"Consideration" has an artificial definition. Section 685(8) ITA provides:

> References in this section to the receipt of consideration include references to the receipt of any money or money's worth.

"Sum" would be the more apt label.

13.16.2 *"Share capital"*

Section 685(7) ITA restricts the concept of share capital:

> [1] So far as subsection (2)(c) or (3) [circumstance A(c) and circumstance B] relates to share capital other than redeemable share capital, it applies only so far as the share capital is repaid (on a winding up or otherwise);
> [2] and for this purpose any distribution made in respect of any shares on a winding up or dissolution of the company is to be treated as a repayment of share capital.

13.16.3 *"Assets"*

Section 685 ITA deals with assets available for distribution:

> (7A) The references in subsection (4)(a)(i) and (ii) to assets do not include assets shown to represent return of sums paid by subscribers on the issue of securities merely because the law of the country in which the company is incorporated allows assets of that description to be available for distribution by way of dividend.
> (7B) The references in subsections (4)(a)(i) and (5)(a) to assets which are available for distribution by way of dividend by the company include assets which are available for distribution to the company by way of dividend by any other company it controls.

13.17 Fundamental change of ownership

Section 686(1) ITA provides:

> Circumstances are excluded by this section if—
> (a) immediately before the transaction in securities (or the first of the transactions in securities) the person (referred to in this section as "the party") holds shares or an interest in shares in the close company, and
> (b) there is a fundamental change of ownership of the close company.

Section 686 ITA goes on to define "fundamental change":

> (2) There is a fundamental change of ownership of the close company if—
> (a) as a result of the transaction or transactions in securities, conditions A, B and C are met, and
> (b) those conditions continue to be met for a period of 2 years.
> (3) Condition A is that at least 75% of the ordinary share capital of the close company is held beneficially by—
> (a) a person who is not connected with the party and has not been so connected within the period of 2 years ending with the day on which the transaction in securities (or the first of the transactions in securities) takes place, or
> (b) persons none of whom is so connected or has been so connected within that period.
> (4) Condition B is that shares in the close company held by that person or those persons carry an entitlement to at least 75% of the distributions which may be made by the company.

(5) Condition C is that shares so held carry at least 75% of the total voting rights in the close company.

13.18 Position if IT TiS rules apply

Subject to procedural requirements not discussed here, if the TiS provisions apply, HMRC may serve a counteraction notice. Section 698 ITA provides:

> (1) If—
> (a) a person on whom a notification is served under section 695 does not send a statutory declaration to an officer of Revenue and Customs under section 696 within 30 days of the issue of the notification, or
> (b) the tribunal to which such a declaration is sent under section 697 determines that there is a prima facie case for serving a notice on a person under this section,
>
> the income tax advantage in question is to be counteracted by adjustments.
>
> (2) The adjustments required to be made to counteract the income tax advantage and the basis on which they are to be made are to be specified in a notice served on the person by an officer of Revenue and Customs.
>
> (3) In this Chapter such a notice is referred to as a "counteraction notice".
>
> (4) Any of the following adjustments may be specified—
> (a) an assessment,
> (b) the nullifying of a right to repayment,
> (c) the requiring of the return of a repayment already made, or
> (d) the calculation or recalculation of profits or gains or liability to income tax.

13.19 Acquisition of all assets

The safest route will usually be for the charity to purchase and then liquidate the company and for the liquidator to distribute the asset in specie to the charity.[21] IT Circumstance A is satisfied. At first sight no IT Advantage has been obtained. There is a CGT saving, but that is not an *income* tax advantage. However, the vendor has an IT Advantage (as defined) because the vendor could have extracted the profits of the company by way of dividend. But the fundamental change of ownership defence will apply if the charity and the vendor are not connected persons.

---

21 See 9.18 (Liquidation).

13.20 Acquisition of part of assets

What if a charity wishes to purchase only part of the assets of a company? Suppose:

(1) a company ("X") owns Blackacre and Whiteacre the value of which exceeds its CGT base cost.

(2) A charity wishes to acquire only Blackacre and the present owners of X wish to retain Whiteacre.

The shareholders of X could sell an appropriate proportion of their shares to the charity and enter into a shareholders' agreement whereby X would be liquidated and the liquidator would distribute Blackacre in specie to the charity and Whiteacre to the other shareholders.

The loss realised by the company on the disposal of Blackacre to the charity may be allowable against the capital gain arising on the disposal of Whiteacre.[22] It is essential that the charity is not connected with X. If the charity has a majority of shares, then it will normally have "control" and thus be a connected person: s.286(6) and 288(1) TCGA and s.450 CTA 2010. Where the charity is not entitled to a majority of the share capital, care should still be taken to ensure that it does not have "control" by virtue of other provisions.

One major difficulty is s.286(6) and (7) TCGA. Section 286(6) provides that a company is connected with another person not only if that person has control of it but also if that person and persons connected with them together have control of it. When one bears in mind that any two or more persons "acting together to secure or exercise control of a company" are treated in relation to that company as connected with one another[23] (and with any person acting on the directions of any of them), care must be taken to ensure that the charity does not act together with the other shareholders to secure or exercise control of X. One solution might be for the shares in X to be redesignated A shares and B shares, carrying appropriate rights to distribution of assets in specie on liquidation, before any sale is negotiated. The articles would provide that the holders of either class of shares could procure a liquidation of the company. The A shares could then be sold to the charity which could, acting unilaterally, procure a liquidation of the company. It would not seek to exercise any other type of control over the company, either alone or in consort with the

---

22 See 9.18 (Liquidation).

23 See s.286(7) TCGA and *Steele v EVC* 69 TC 88.

B shareholders.

Where the shareholders in X wish to dispose of the company with all its assets but the charity does not wish to retain them, there is a potential problem. If the charity buys the shares simply with the intention of, in effect, buying the assets of the company at a discount and then selling them on at a profit, there must be a risk that this would amount to a trade or an adventure in the nature of a trade. It is possible that the proper accounting treatment would be to treat the shares in X as trading stock and similarly to treat the distribution in specie from X as trading stock, but acquired for no additional consideration. This would throw up a trading gain when the shares were disposed of. Where the assets of X consist of land, HMRC will also have the alternative argument that the charity is taxable under the transactions in land rules.[24]

Where a charity wishes to obtain part of the assets of X as an investment or for its own use and does not need the other part, it will be a question of fact and degree whether it is trading if it buys all the shares, liquidates the company and then sells on the assets it does not want. The greater the proportion of the assets of the company which the assets to be sold on represent, the greater the risk of trading. In such a case, it may be possible for the shareholders in X to effect a share reorganisation of the type mentioned above and to sell the A shares to the charity and the B shares to third parties desirous of obtaining the B assets. In this way, the charity could not be held to be trading or (unless the circumstances were unusual) be caught under the transactions in land rules. The B shareholders would, however, have the benefit of receiving the assets in specie subject to a much reduced, or possibly nil, charge to CT on capital gains on the company. This should enable the charity to negotiate a lower price for the A shares.

13.21 Dividend in specie

It might be asked whether the purchaser charity could extract an asset by a dividend in specie from the company; see 9.19.1 (Dividend).

The extraction by the charity of a dividend could bring the TiS rules into play. IT Circumstance A or CT Circumstance D apply. If the provisions did come into play, then the whole or part of the price paid to the vendor could constitute taxable income.

---

24 See 4.13.1 (Transactions in land).

13.22 Sale at book value

Another possibility is for the company to sell the asset at book value to the charity. See 9.19.2 (Sale at book value).

The sale of an asset at book value should not give rise to any charge to CT on the vendor as s.257 TCGA would normally prevent it realising any capital gain: see 9.18 (Liquidation). The base cost of the recipient charity would usually be equal to the allowable expenditure of the vendor company, so that if the charity sold the asset it would usually realise the inherent chargeable gain. Given the s.256(1) TCGA exemption for charities, that need not necessarily be a problem. The charity would, however, have to bear in mind the charitable expenditure rules: see 6.1 (Charitable expenditure rules).

Another possibility is for the gain to be extracted by means of Gift Aid. The vendor would need to consider whether they might be caught by the transaction in securities rules: see 13.3 (Transactions in securities).

13.23 Trading stock

Where the company owns an asset as trading stock, the best course of action will normally be for the asset to be sold to the charity at market value (even if on credit) *after* the charity has acquired the shares in the company: see 9.18 (Liquidation. Then consideration should be given to the company making Gift Aid payments to the charity.

A company cannot make a qualifying donation which is associated with the acquisition of property by the charity from the company.

CHAPTER FOURTEEN

DOUBLE TAXATION TREATIES AND CHARITIES

14.1 Introduction

A UK charity may wish to invest abroad. In the absence of treaty relief, the charity may well find that it is subject to foreign tax on its foreign investments, whereas it would not be subject to UK tax on its UK investment. The UK charity can only properly invest abroad if the net return, after foreign tax, would justify the investment.

The UK has a wide network of double taxation treaties, of which a UK charity can take the benefit. By contrast, a charity in a conventional tax haven does not benefit from such treaties. For a bona fide charity, the UK may therefore be better than a tax haven.

In this chapter we consider OECD Model Agreement (**"OECD Model"**) but refer from time to time to actual treaties. It will of course be necessary to review the actual treaty in any particular case.

The basic principle is that a UK charity, as a resident of the UK, is entitled to the same reliefs from foreign tax under a DTA as any other UK resident, even though it does not in general pay UK tax on its income or gains.

It is exceptional for a treaty to refer to charities expressly. The Ireland/UK treaty is the only UK treaty which provides mutual charity exemption (exemption for Irish source income of UK charities and UK source income of Irish charities).[1]

UK treaties do not override the UK domestic law rule that relief for donors is limited to gifts to UK and EU charities. (Contrast the US, where federal income tax charity relief applies only to gifts to US charities, but the relief is extended by DTAs with Mexico, Canada and Israel.)

For a general discussion of DTAs, see Kessler, *Taxation of Non-Residents and Foreign Domiciliaries*, (21st ed., 2022-23) Chapters 105-116.[2]

14.2 Charity resident of contracting state

Article 4.1 OECD Model provides:

> 1. For the purposes of this Convention, the term "resident of a Contracting State" means any person who, under the laws of that State, is liable to tax therein by reason of his domicile, residence, place of management or any other criteria of a similar nature ....

14.2.1 *"Person"*

Article 3.1(a) OECD Model provides:

> The term "person" includes an individual, a company and any other body of persons.

A charitable company is a "person".

An unincorporated association is a person for one or two reasons, either of which would be sufficient:

(1) it is a "body of persons"[3] and

(2) it may also be a "company" within OECD Model definition.[4]

At first sight it is not quite so obvious how to classify a trust (whether charitable or non-charitable). But although there is much that could be said on the topic, no-one seriously doubts the conclusion that trustees are a person for treaty purposes. We omit the discussion here because the

---

1 UK/Ireland Treaty Arts. 11, 14A, maintaining what would have been the position before the creation of the Irish Free State.

2 Online version *https://www.foreigndomiciliaries.co.uk*

3 See Avery Jones, "Bodies of Persons" [1991] BTR 453 and [2006] BTR at p.699. For completeness: the European Convention on the Recognition of the Legal Personality of International Non-governmental Organisations provides that the legal personality of certain international NGOs shall be recognised. But this does not affect the position of domestic NGOs.

4 See art 3(b).

matter is fully discussed elsewhere.[5]

14.2.2 *"Liable to tax"*

The generally held view is that a person may be "liable" to tax in a state (and so can be a resident of the state for DTA purposes) even if it enjoys exemption from tax in that state.[6]

HMRC agree. The International Manual provides:

> **INTM162040 whether the customer is a resident of the UK** [May 2019]
> The phrase 'liable to tax' means that they only have to be within the general scope to tax. Charities and pension funds can therefore be regarded as resident even if their income is exempt from tax.

OECD Commentary leaves the point open. It provides:

> 8.11 Paragraph 1 refers to persons who are "liable to tax" in a Contracting State under its laws by reason of various criteria. In many States, a person is considered liable to comprehensive taxation even if the Contracting State does not in fact impose tax. For example, charities and other organisations may be exempted from tax, but they are exempt only if they meet all of the requirements for exemption specified in the tax laws. They are, thus, subject to the tax laws of a Contracting State. Furthermore, if they do not meet the standards specified, they are also required to pay tax. Most States would view such entities as residents for purposes of the Convention ...
> 8.12 In some States, however, these entities are not considered liable to tax if they are exempt from tax under domestic tax laws. These States may not regard such entities as residents for purposes of a convention unless these entities are expressly covered by the convention. Contracting States taking this view are free to address the issue in their bilateral negotiations.

It seems reasonably clear that a UK charity "liable" to UK tax since

---

5 See Kessler, *Taxation of Non-Residents and Foreign Domiciliaries* (21st ed., 2022-23), para 9.21 (Treaty residence: Trusts)
online version *https://www.foreigndomiciliaries.co.uk*

6 This is assumed to be correct (without much consideration) in *General Electric Pension Trust v Director of Income-tax* 8 ITELR 1055 (Authority for Advance Rulings (Income-tax) New Delhi) and this view is adopted in *Assistant Director of IT v Green Emirate Shipping & Travels* 9 ITLR 1 (IT Appellate Tribunal).
For further discussion, if needed, see Ward, "The Use of OEEC-OECD Historical Documents in Interpreting Tax Treaties" in Baker & Bobbett (ed) *Tax Polymath* (2010) p.3.

charity exemptions (unlike, say, the exemption for Local Authorities) do not apply to all types of income, and are restricted by the charitable expenditure and other anti-avoidance rules.[7]

In particular, charitable common investment funds can qualify for the same treaty reliefs as similar non-charitable open ended investment companies or unit trusts.

14.2.3 *Non-OECD Model treaties*

Some treaties provide expressly that charities are residents of a contracting state. For instance, art 4(3) USA/UK DTA supplements a (roughly) standard OECD Model definition of "resident of a contacting state" with the following:

> The term "resident of a Contracting State" includes...
>
> c) an organization that is established exclusively for religious, charitable, scientific, artistic, cultural, or educational purposes and that is a resident of a Contracting State according to its laws, notwithstanding that all or part of its income or gains may be exempt from tax under the domestic law of that State.

This is not necessary, as a UK charity at least should be a resident under the basic OECD Model definition, but the position might be less clear in the USA. The USA Department of the Treasury Technical Explanation of the Convention provides:

> Paragraph 3 provides that certain tax-exempt entities such as pension funds and charitable organizations will be regarded as residents of a Contracting State regardless of whether they are generally liable for income tax in the State where they are established. The inclusion of this provision is intended to clarify the generally accepted practice of treating an entity that would be liable for tax as a resident under the internal law of a State but for a specific exemption from tax (either complete or partial) as a resident of that state for purposes of paragraph 1.
>
> ... Subparagraph (c) applies to an organization that is established exclusively for religious, charitable, scientific, artistic, cultural, or educational purposes and that is a resident of a Contracting State. Thus, an exempt section 501(c) organization (such as a U.S. charity) that is generally exempt from tax under U.S. law is a resident of the United States for all purposes of the Convention.[8]

---

7 Contrast the question whether charity income is "subject to tax": see 14.6 ("Subject to tax"); or "chargeable to tax": see 32.4 ("Capital payment").

8 *http://www.treasury.gov/resource-center/tax-policy/treaties/Documents/teus-uk.pdf*

So the omission of a clause of this kind in the vast majority of DTAs is not a matter of concern to charities.

Similarly, a protocol to the UK/Switzerland DTA dated 7 September 2009 supplements a (roughly) standard OECD Model definition of "resident of a contacting state" with wording very similar to the UK/US treaty. It is considered that this was not strictly necessary, at least for a UK charity; perhaps it was necessary for Swiss reasons.

14.3 Charity as beneficial owner

DT relief is often restricted to the "beneficial owner" of income (eg OECD Model Arts 10, 11 and 12, providing relief for dividends interest and royalties).

The expression "beneficial ownership" has (at least) three distinct meanings:

(1) The English property law/trust law meaning, where it may be contrasted with bare legal ownership and is (more or less) synonymous with equitable ownership.
(2) An international tax law meaning, in the context of DTAs.
(3) A meaning (or set of meanings) in the context of money laundering and CRS.[9]

These are all distinct and discussion of the meaning in one context has (more or less) no relevance in other contexts.

In English law, a charitable company is in principle the beneficial owner of its assets; charitable trustees are not the beneficial owners of their trust funds, they are the fiduciary, non-beneficial owners. However, even in domestic English legal usage the word "beneficial" may be used in a loose or non-technical sense under which:

(1) A charitable company may be regarded as not a beneficial owner;[10] or

---

9 See Kessler, *Taxation of Non-Residents and Foreign Domiciliaries* (21st ed., 2022-23), App 6.1 (Beneficial ownership: Meanings) online version *https://www.foreigndomiciliaries.co.uk*

10 *Von Ernst & Cie v IRC* [1980] STC 111 where the court had to consider whether charitable trusts and companies were persons:

> ... for whose benefit the settled property or income from it might be applied or who might become beneficially entitled to an interest in possession in it.

It was held that these words were not appropriate to a charitable trust or company. Buckley LJ said (at page 122):

> "In my judgment a corporation which is by its constitution debarred from using or acquiring assets for the purpose of making or obtaining any profit for itself or its

(2) A trust (charitable or non-charitable) may be regarded as a beneficial owner.[11]

In the context of DTAs "beneficial owner" has an international tax law meaning which is different from its meaning in English law. It excludes a mere nominee but does include someone, such as the trustees of a charitable trust, who are entitled to the trust property, in the sense that there is no third party who could claim a superior title to it than the trustees.[12] Thus it includes a charitable trust. HMRC agree. International Tax Manual formerly provided:

> **INTM162030: Certificates of Residence** [Jan 2013]
> ... *Where the only condition for exemption or relief is that the United Kingdom resident is the beneficial owner of the foreign income, the certificate [that treaty-relief applies] can be given whether or not he is subject to tax in the United Kingdom on that income. A certificate can therefore be given on claims by charities, registered pension schemes etc...*

We cannot find a similar statement in the current Manual, but there is no reason to think that HMRC practice has changed.

14.4 Treaty exemptions

14.4.1 *Business profits*

Article 7 OECD Model provides:

---

corporators, and which serves the purpose only of machinery for carrying on exclusively charitable activities, is not an object for whose *benefit* settled property or income from it can be applied or which might become *beneficially* entitled to an interest in possession in settled property within the meaning of para 3(2). For the purposes of applying para 3(2) one must look at the character of such a body to see whether it, rather than the purposes which it exists to serve, is capable of benefiting within the meaning of the paragraph and, in my judgment, it is not capable of doing so. It is a mere conduit pipe, just as in my view the trustees of an unincorporated charity are."

11 See 32.5 (Is a charitable *company* a "beneficiary"); 32.6 (Is a charitable *trust* "a beneficiary").

12 See para 12 of OECD Commentary to art 10:
"The term 'beneficial owner' is not used in a narrow technical sense, rather, it should be understood in its context and in light of the object and purposes of the Convention, including avoiding double taxation and the prevention of fiscal evasion and avoidance."
Contrast 32.5, 32.6 (Are charities beneficiaries within s.87 TCGA?).

> **Business Profits**
> 1. The profits of an enterprise of a Contracting State shall be taxable only in that State unless the enterprise carries on business in the other Contracting State through a permanent establishment situated therein. If the enterprise carries on business as aforesaid, the profits of the enterprise may be taxed in the other State but only so much of them as is attributable to that permanent establishment. ...

What is exempt from tax is the "business profits of an enterprise of a Contracting State". OECD Model provides:

> The term 'enterprise of a Contracting State' means an enterprise carried on by a resident of a Contracting State.

Hence, provided a charity carries on an "enterprise" it will be exempt from tax on the profits of the enterprise. See 9.16.1 (When is charity affected).

14.4.2 *Dividends*

Article 10 OECD Model provides:

> (1) Dividends paid by a company which is a resident of a Contracting State to a resident of the other Contracting State may be taxed in that other State.
> (2) However, such dividends may also be taxed in the Contracting State of which the company paying the dividends is a resident and according to the laws of that State, but if the beneficial owner of the dividends is a resident of the other Contracting State, the tax so charged shall not exceed:
> (a) 5 per cent of the gross amount of the dividends if the beneficial owner is a company (other than a partnership) which holds directly or indirectly 25 per cent of the capital of the company paying the dividends;
> (b) 15 per cent of the gross amount of the dividends in all other cases.

Note that a charitable company[13] obtains greater relief than a charitable trust. As charities can in principle make donations between themselves, without incurring any UK tax charge, there may be something to be said for a charitable trust to have a twin charitable company, so as to take the

---

13 "Company" is defined to mean:
"Any body corporate or any entity that is treated as a body corporate for tax purposes." (Art 3.1(b)).

maximum advantage of any particular provision in any given double tax treaty.

In some cases it might be appropriate to have an underlying company which is not a charity, as that entity may secure an exemption which would not be available to its parent.

14.4.3 *Interest and Royalties*

OECD Model provides for a ceiling on the liability of the resident of one Contracting State for tax imposed by the other Contracting State on interest (Art 11). Many actual treaties provide full exemption.

OECD Model provides that a resident of one Contracting State shall not in general be liable to tax in the other Contracting State in respect of royalties (Art 12).

14.4.4 *Capital gains*

Article 13(5) OECD Model provides:

> Gains from the alienation of any property, other than that referred to in paragraphs 1, 2, 3 and 4, shall be taxable only in the Contracting State of which the alienator is a resident.

14.4.5 *Cultural activities*

Article 17 OECD Model provides:

> 1. Notwithstanding the provisions of Articles 7 and 15, income derived by a resident of a Contracting State as an entertainer, such as a theatre, motion picture, radio or television artiste, or a musician, or as a sportsman, from his personal activities as such exercised in the other Contracting State, may be taxed in that other State.
> 2. Where income in respect of personal activities exercised by an entertainer or a sportsman in his capacity as such accrues not to the entertainer or sportsman himself but to another person, that income may, notwithstanding the provisions of Articles 7 [Business profits] and 15 (Income from Employment], be taxed in the Contracting State in which the activities of the entertainer or sportsman are exercised.[14]

This is sometimes qualified by a form of charity exemption. OECD Commentary provides:

---

14 For a discussion, see Kessler, *Taxation of Non-Residents and Foreign Domiciliaries* (21st ed., 2022-23), Chapter 23 (Performers) online version *https://www.foreigndomiciliaries.co.uk*

> 14. Some countries may consider it appropriate to exclude from the scope of the Article events supported from public funds. Such countries are free to include a provision to achieve this but the exemptions should be based on clearly definable and objective criteria to ensure that they are given only where intended...

The UK has about a dozen treaties of this kind. For instance, art 17(3) of the Austria/UK convention provides:

> Notwithstanding the provisions of paragraphs (1) and (2) of this Article, income derived from activities as defined in paragraph (1) performed under a cultural agreement or arrangement between the Contracting States or derived by a non-profit making organisation accepted as such on application to the competent authority of the Contracting State of which it is a resident under Article 27 of this Convention, or by an entertainer or athlete in respect of services provided to such an organisation shall be exempt from tax in the Contracting State in which those activities are exercised.

In such cases the incidence of UK tax would often be small or nil, because the expenses associated with the tour may exceed the receipts.

14.4.6 *Other income*

Article 21 OECD Model provides:

> 1. Items of income of a resident of a Contracting State, wherever arising, not dealt with in the foregoing Articles of this Convention shall be taxable only in that State.

14.5 Non-discrimination

Article 24 OECD Model provides:

> 1.[a] Nationals of a Contracting State shall not be subjected in the other Contracting State to any taxation or any requirement connected therewith, which is other or more burdensome than the taxation and connected requirements to which nationals of that other State in the same circumstances, in particular with respect to residence, are or may be subjected.
> [b] This provision shall, notwithstanding the provisions of Article 1, also apply to persons who are not residents of one or both of the Contracting States.

14.5.1 *"National"*

Article 3.1(g) defines "national":

the term "national", in relation to a Contracting State, means:

(i) any individual possessing the nationality or citizenship of that Contracting State; and

(ii) any legal person, partnership or association deriving its status as such from the laws in force in that Contracting State.

A charitable company incorporated under the laws of the UK is a UK national. The same should apply to a charitable trust incorporated under s.251 Charities Act 2011. It is not obvious that a charitable trust is a "national" of the UK though the better view is that this is the case where the trust is governed by a UK law.

14.5.2 *Application to charities*

OECD Commentary states that charities are in principle outside the scope of the non-discrimination article. Article 24(1) is not:

> ... to be construed as obliging a State which accords special taxation privileges to private institutions not for profit whose activities are performed for purposes of public benefit, which are specific to that State, to extend the same privileges to similar institutions whose activities are not for its benefit.
> ... if a State accords taxation privileges to certain private institutions not for profit, this is clearly justified by the very nature of these institutions' activities and by the benefit which that State and its nationals will derive from those activities.[15]

Thus in OECD view, a domestic NPO and a foreign NPO are not in the same circumstances, because the state and its nationals derive benefits from domestic NPOs but not from foreign NPOs. However this observation does not fit the UK, as a charity with foreign objects may be a UK charity even though no person in the UK could benefit.[16]

In *Pinacothèque d'Athènes*[17] the French Conseil d'État held that a foreign charity did benefit from the non-discrimination article. A Greek museum (a national of Greece) sold land in France. Under French domestic law the gain was taxable, though an equivalent French NPO would not have been taxable. The non-discrimination clause in the France/Greece DTA (1963)

15 Para 11-13. The same point is made in para 6-9 commentary to art 10 (non-discrimination) of OECD Model double taxation convention on estates and inheritances and on gifts (1982).

16 See 3.14 (Foreign charitable objects).

17 13 ITELR 375.

provided exemption. The article was not materially different from the current OECD Model:

Treaty	**OECD Model**
Les nationaux d'un État contractant ne sont soumis dans l'autre État contractant à aucune imposition ou obligation y rela tive, qui est autre ou plus lourde que les impositions et les obligations relatives auxquelles sont ou pourront être assujettis les nationaux de cet autre État se trouvant dans la même situation.	*Les nationaux d'un État contractant ne sont soumis dans l'autre État contractant à aucune imposition ou obligation y relative, qui est autre ou plus lourde que celles auxquelles sont ou pourront être assujettis les nationaux de cet autre État qui se trouvent dans la même situation, notamment au regard de la résidence....*

The omission of the words "in particular with respect to residence" does not matter as these were only inserted for the avoidance of doubt.

The court did not discuss OECD Commentary.

The museum also argued the EU-law point and would have won on that basis, but the court decided the case on the basis of the treaty.

If it were accepted in the UK that the non-discrimination article requires foreign charities to enjoy charity exemption, this would be far-reaching as there are many treaties with this clause with countries outside the EU who would benefit from treaty relief.

14.6 "Subject to tax"

Some treaties provide exemption for income which is "subject to tax". This is not in OECD Model, and only survives in a diminishing number of treaties; for instance art VI (Interest) of the Greece/UK treaty provides:

> Any interest or royalty derived from sources within one of the territories by a resident of the other territory, *who is subject to tax in that other territory in respect thereof* and does not carry on a trade or business in the first territory through a permanent establishment situated therein, shall be exempt from tax in that first territory.

It is considered that a UK charity is not "subject to tax" on income to which the charity exemption applies.[18] So far as the issue concerns foreign tax it would ultimately be decided by foreign tax authorities and

18 This is supported by *General Electric Pension Trust v Director of Income-tax* 8 ITELR 1055 (Authority for Advance Rulings (Income-tax) New Delhi).

courts, but the HMRC view may well represent an international consensus. So it is relevant to note that the HMRC Guidance Note Annex i.7 provides:

> **Foreign Tax**
>
> i.7.1. Occasionally charities seeking to claim exemption from foreign tax from an overseas tax authority may request confirmation that they're subject to UK tax. Certain Double Taxation Agreements provide that a resident of the UK will be entitled to exemption or relief from the foreign tax on certain types of income only if they're subject to tax on that income in the United Kingdom.
>
> i.7.2 Charities should be aware that a person isn't regarded as subject to tax in the UK if the income in question is statutorily exempt from tax.

The same point is made in International Tax Manual:

> **INTM332210: Double Taxation applications and claims - Subject to tax: Background** [Jun 2016]
>
> The expression "subject to tax" usually means that the person must actually pay tax on the income in their country of residence.
>
> However, a person is still regarded as "subject to tax" if, for example, he or she does not pay tax because their income is sufficiently small that it is covered by personal allowances that are available to set against liability to tax in the other country.
>
> A person is not regarded as "subject to tax" if the income in question is exempted from tax because the law of the other country provides for statutory exemption from tax. For example
>
> - the income is that of a charity
> - the income is that of an exempt approved superannuation scheme (pension fund).
>
> In such cases the "subject to tax" condition is not met and relief is not allowable.[19]

What if the income belongs beneficially to a non-charitable company owned by a charity to which it gives its profits to a charity under Gift Aid? It is considered that the income would be "subject to tax" in the UK, even

---

19 In *Weiser v HMRC* the tribunal agreed with this passage: [2012] UKFTT 501 (TC) at [38]. Similar points are made in INTM162090:

> "**'Subject to tax'** [Jan 2014]
>
> ...A person is not regarded as subject to tax in the UK if the income in question is exempted from UK tax by an extra-statutory concession or is statutorily exempt from tax, for example the income is that of a charity ..."

though the company did not pay tax on them, just as much as if the reason it did not pay tax on them was that it had trading losses which it set against them for UK tax purposes. Thus an underlying non-charitable company may secure an exemption which would not be available to its charitable parent.

14.7 Dual jurisdiction charity

It is possible to set up a structure that qualifies as a charity for UK and foreign (in particular, US) tax purposes. See 11.6.1 (Dual registered charities).

CHAPTER FIFTEEN

CASH GIFTS FROM INDIVIDUAL TO CHARITY (GIFT AID)

Cross references

The following topics are considered elsewhere:

7.21 (Tainted Gift Aid donation)
47.18 (Gift Aid audit)
For a discussion of corporate Gift Aid, see the next chapter.

15.1 Gift Aid: Introduction

The tax relief for cash gifts to charity is known as Gift Aid.[1]

---

1 A note on terminology. Statute originally used the formal and sober term "qualifying donations". But in keeping with the zeitgeist, the catchy and colloquial name slipped

In this book:

"Individual Gift Aid" means the income tax relief for cash gifts to charity by individuals.

"Corporate Gift Aid" means the corporation tax relief for cash gifts to charity by companies.

The rules for the two reliefs are similar but not identical. This chapter discusses individual Gift Aid and also corporate Gift Aid where the rules are the same or similar.

The rules matter: in 2014/15, £15m Gift Aid tax reclaims were denied to charities for technical breaches of Gift Aid rules.[2]

15.2 Gift Aid: History

Income tax relief was formerly available on a deed of covenant to charity. This was not in origin a specific charity tax relief but a fortuitous consequence of the rules governing annual payments. Deeds of covenant first became popular in the 1920s.

Churchill proposed abolition of the relief when Chancellor in 1927,[3] but that failed to pass. Relief was abolished for surtax in s.28 FA 1946. When surtax was replaced by higher rate tax in 1965 the rule continued that higher rate relief was not allowed.

Higher rate relief was then restored in 1980 but with a cap of £3,000; the cap was gradually raised until it was abolished in 1986, returning the position to what it was before 1946. However, attitudes had changed. Covenants to charity had formerly been considered by old Labour as a "racket". The relief was by 1986 an accepted part of the tax system, though many of its rules were eccentric.[4]

Gift Aid was introduced in 1990 and has been amended countless times since.

There was little point in having two overlapping tax reliefs, Gift Aid and covenants. The abolition of tax relief for covenants in 2000 was a sensible and logical consequence of the introduction of Gift Aid in 1990.

---

into statutory usage in 2000 and is now the standard term for the relief. It has now also been used as a verb. Text added to the HMRC guidance note in 2016 provides: "you can only Gift Aid your own donations". But "there is no noun that cannot be verbed".

2 HMRC correspondence.

3 Hansard 11 April 1927 col. 85-86 *http://hansard.millbanksystems.com/commons/1927/apr/11/tax-avoidance*

4 See Stopforth, "Charitable Covenants by Individuals – a History" [1986] BTR 101.

15.3 Requirements of Gift Aid

Section 414(1) ITA provides:

> An individual who makes a gift to a charity which is a qualifying donation is entitled to the relief set out in subsection (2).

There are three requirements here:
(1) a gift
(2) made to a charity
(3) which is a qualifying donation

15.4 "Gift"

Individual Gift Aid applies only if the payment is a gift. If a payment is made which is not a "gift", no relief is available.

The question of exactly what is a "gift" is conceptually interesting but of limited practical importance because of the benefit rule. A payment which confers a benefit in breach of the benefit rule does not qualify for relief, and it does not matter whether it is a gift. A payment which complies with the benefit rule is likely to be a gift.

Corporate Gift Aid does not have a "gift" requirement.[5]

15.4.1 *What is a gift?*

"Gift" is not defined. It is not a precise word: it has been defined or explained in different ways; it has a range of possible meanings which only context can resolve.[6]

Hyland states:

> The most adequate notion of the gift ... involves the transfer of an interest that occurs in conjunction with four additional elements.
> (1) The transfer is gratuitous, a characteristic that is often inferred either from the absence of a quid pro quo or from the fact that the donor acted without being obligated to do so.
> (2) Certain subjective factors are present, usually either donative intent or the parties' agreement about the gratuitous character of the transaction...[7]

---

5 See 17.3 Qualifying charitable donation).

6 See too 4.2.1 (Types of gift).

7 Hyland's last two elements are:
(3) The transaction takes place *inter vivos*, which distinguishes gifts from transfers made under a will.

In common law jurisdictions, the requirement of an absence of a *quid pro quo* is normally (though not invariably[8]) expressed as the absence of *consideration*.

In America, the Restatement (3d) of the Law of Property Wills and other Donative Transfers defines a gift as a transfer of an ownership interest to the donee without consideration and with donative intent.[9]

"Consideration" brings in contact law ideas. In *R v Brathwaite*:

> In our judgment the word "consideration" connotes the existence of something in the shape of a contract or a bargain between the parties. ... The word "gift" is the other side of the coin, that is to say it comes into play where there is no consideration and no bargain.[10]

This is long established in English law. Blackstone says:

> Gifts are always gratuitous, grants are upon some consideration or equivalent.[11]

The meaning of "grant" has shifted over the intervening 250 years, but "gift" has not changed.

The question is: how strictly does one insist on the absence of a *quid pro quo* for a transfer to qualify as a gift, or (to express the issue another way) what is meant by "consideration" or its antonym "gratuitous".

Hyland states:

> One of the features that most clearly distinguishes the modern gift transaction from most other transactions governed by the private law is

---

(4) The object of the transfer involves rights, particularly property rights, rather than services or other types of advantage.

In the context of Gift Aid, elements [3] and [4] are a given; it is the first two which matter here.

See Hyland, *Gifts: A Study in Comparative Law* (1st ed, 2009), p.10.

8 Duff, "The Tax Treatment of Charitable Contributions in Canada: Theory, Practice, and Reform", in *Not-for-Profit Law: Theoretical and Comparative Perspectives* (2014) (chapter 9, p.46): "In common law provinces, courts have defined a gift as "a voluntary transfer of property from one person to another gratuitously and not as a result of a contractual obligation without anticipation or expectation of material benefit". He cites *Woolner v The Queen* [2000] 1 CTC 35.

9 American Law Institute, *Restatement (3d) of the law of property wills and other donative transfers* (2011), para.6.1. Likewise Black's Law Dictionary 10th ed: "Gift: The voluntary transfer of property to another without compensation."

10 [1983] 1 WLR 385 at p.391. The Hong Kong Court of Appeal adopted this view in *Sanford Yung-tao Yung v CIR* [1979] 1 HKTC 1081.

11 Blackstone *Commentary on the Laws of England* (1766) Vol 2 chap 30.

its gratuitousness. Though the concept is intuitively simple - the donor gives something away and receives nothing in exchange - legal systems are rarely able to define the idea clearly. There are several reasons for the difficulty.

Hyland identifies two difficulties:

[1] To begin with, the consequences often weigh heavily on the definition. The characterization question is often raised for the first time post hoc, at the moment when a court is asked to invalidate a transaction that proceeded without the requisite formalities. In these circumstances, the validity of the transaction depends on whether it is characterized as gratuitous or whether, following civilian usage, it may be considered *onerous*. Fairness considerations thus influence the determination.

[2] Another reason for the difficulty is that, from a theoretical point of view, the notion of gratuitousness represents the boundary between market-orientated transactions and transactions designed to fulfill other sorts of needs and goals. Because, as Mauss taught, transactions frequently involve both types of motivation, the line proves difficult to draw. Due to the complexity of the problem, it is often resolved by reference to flexible concepts from the law of contracts, such as the consideration doctrine or the notion of natural obligation.[12]

It is difficult to identify examples of dispositions by individuals which are not made for consideration, but are not gratuitous (or have no donative intent), though it is possible for companies and trusts.[13]

A disposition may be a gift even though it is made as an inducement, or in the hope of some advantage. The position in relation to VAT is, however, less straightforward - see 35.9 (Grants and donations) for the applicable principles.

Accepting the absence of consideration as a general requirement of a gift, the question arises whether a "gift" should be regarded as:

(1) a payment made for no consideration whatsoever

(2) a payment even if made for nominal or small consideration[14]

---

12 Hyland, *Gifts: A Study in Comparative Law* (1st ed, 2009), p.135.

13 Examples are:

(1) Dividends paid by a company or distributions in the course of liquidation.

(2) A transfer from a trustee to a beneficiary under the terms of a trust.

14 Of course a range of views would be possible as to what constitutes "nominal or small".

(3) a payment, even if made for more than nominal consideration, as long made with donative intent and the value is significantly less than the value of the payment.[15]

Here the meaning of "gift" will vary according to context. The drafting of the QIDR rules assumes that a person may make a "gift" even though they receive benefits in consequence of making it.[16]

In the context of Gift Aid, the drafter clearly envisaged that something may be a "gift" even though:

(1) the donor receives a small benefit (ie one within the small benefit rules), or

(2) the payment is subject to a condition as to repayment.

So meaning (1) is ruled out. It is suggested that meaning (2) is the correct one in a Gift Aid context.[17] In principle it makes no difference here which of (2) or (3) is the correct nuance of "gift" since the Gift Aid benefit rule usually disqualifies gifts within (3).[18]

In *Hernandez v Commissioner* the US Supreme Court considered the American equivalent to Gift Aid, a relief for a "contribution or gift" to charity:

> The legislative history of the "contribution or gift" limitation, though

---

15 It is generally agreed that a sale for consideration less than market value is a "disposal by way of gift" in the IHT Gift with Reservation rule, ie "gift" there has meaning (3). Likewise "gift" in the IT settlement code includes any transaction with an element of bounty: *Jones v Garnett* 78 TC 597.
Contrast the meaning given to the word "donation" by the Neill Committee: see 5th Report of the Committee on Standards in Public Life (The Funding of Political Parties in the UK) Cm 4057-1, 1998, para 4.44.5 *http://www.public-standards.gov.uk* Here "donation" is understood to include: "cash gifts, gifts in kind, sponsorship and affiliation fees. ... The provision of paid employees' time and free use of equipment and facilities would all rank. So too would any goods or services supplied at below their true cost, the gift element being the difference between true cost and the charge actually made. Loans on other than arm's length open-market terms would be presumed to be in part donations, examples being interest-free loans, loans with uncommercial rates of return and loans which revert to gifts (at the time they revert)".

16 See 21.8.1 ("Relievable amount": Gift).

17 This is accepted by HMRC in the examples of permissible "small benefits": see below.

18 Unless the consideration is not received by a connected person. If the benefit is received by a person who is not connected but is a donor-linked person (which is a slightly wider concept) then the tainted donation rules may apply.

> sparse, reveals that Congress intended to differentiate between unrequited payments to qualified recipients [in short, charities] and payments made to such recipients in return for goods or services. Only the former were deemed deductible. The House and Senate Reports on the 1954 tax bill, for example, both define "gifts" as payments "made with no expectation of a financial return commensurate with the amount of the gift." Using payments to hospitals as an example, both Reports state that the gift characterization should not apply to
>
> > "a payment by an individual to a hospital *in consideration of* a binding obligation to provide medical treatment for the individual's employees. It would apply only if there were no expectation of any *quid pro quo* from the hospital."
>
> In ascertaining whether a given payment was made with "the expectation of any *quid pro quo*," the IRS has customarily examined the external features of the transaction in question. This practice has the advantage of obviating the need for the IRS to conduct imprecise inquiries into the motivations of individual taxpayers. The lower courts have generally embraced this structural analysis ... We likewise focused on external features in *United States v American Bar Endowment,* to resolve the taxpayers' claims that they were entitled to partial deductions for premiums paid to a charitable organization for insurance coverage; the taxpayers contended that they had paid unusually high premiums in an effort to make a contribution along with their purchase of insurance. We upheld the Commissioner's disallowance of the partial deductions because the taxpayers had failed to demonstrate, at a minimum, the existence of comparable insurance policies with prices lower than those of the policy they had each purchased. In so doing, we stressed that "*the sine qua non* of a charitable contribution is a transfer of money or property *without adequate consideration*."[19]

While the starting point is the objective test, the state of mind (donative intent) of the donor matters too, as the case goes on to say:

> The sole taxpayer in *American Bar Endowment* who had demonstrated the existence of a lower premium insurance program failed to show that he was aware of this less expensive option at the time he purchased his insurance.

HMRC Guidance Note provides at 3.4.5:

---

19 490 US 680 (1989) *http://supreme.justia.com/cases/federal/us/490/680/case.html#F8* Two members of the 7 judge court dissented, but not from this general statement. I have removed some references from the quote.

> Payments to a charity in return for services, rights or goods are not gifts to charity and so are not eligible for the Gift Aid Scheme. For example, the following cannot come within the Gift Aid Scheme:
> [a] payment of school fees for a specific person
> [b] payment to purchase books, jumble sale items, food

Points [a] and [b] are clearly correct (assuming price paid is market value). The HMRC Guidance Note continues:

> [c] payment for admission to events (jumble sales, concerts)

It is correct that the purchase of a concert ticket at market value is not a gift. We think that payment for entry to jumble sales or fetes (of a kind that are primarily fund-raising events) would be a "gift" if the ticket has no monetary value and the payment is made with gratuitous intent.

The HMRC Guidance Note continues:

> [d] payment for raffle or lottery tickets (including 100 clubs) - the payment to purchase a raffle ticket from a charity is not a gift but a payment for the right to enter the raffle - it does not matter that the chance or expectation of winning a prize is small or that the prize is of little value

We do not agree: the purchase of a lottery ticket is a "gift" if made with gratuitous intent and the value of the ticket is within the "small benefit" limit.

The HMRC Guidance Note also discusses this issue in the context of charitable events:

> **3.43 Charity events**
> 3.43.1 Charities often hold events (dinners, concerts, firework displays) to raise funds and this section explains whether all or part of the payment to attend the event can be gift aided.
> 3.43.2 To be eligible for the Gift Aid Scheme a payment must be a freewill gift of money to charity, that is, there must be no compulsion about making the payment. So the payment must be a wholly voluntary payment and not linked to attendance at the event.
> 3.43.3 A payment to purchase a ticket (or an admission charge) to attend a charity event is not a gift to charity but the purchase of a right to attend the event. Without buying a ticket a person cannot attend the event, so there's no freewill in making a payment - that is, a person must pay the ticket price to attend the event. Such payments are not eligible for Gift Aid.
> 3.43.4 In the same way, a payment described as a 'minimum donation'

> or a 'donation' to attend an event is not a freewill payment. Again, a person must make the payment to attend the event. The 'minimum donation' or 'specified donation' is, in fact, the admission charge.
>
> 3.43.5 The following payments to attend an event are not gifts to charity:
>
> - payment to purchase a ticket
> - payment to gain admission
> - a required minimum donation
> - a required specified donation
>
> All of the payments described must be paid in order to attend the event and so are not freewill gifts to charity. Such payments are not eligible for the Gift Aid Scheme.

For completeness we should mention *Osborne v HMRC,* a FTT decision in which the taxpayer was not represented by counsel. The taxpayer was a member of an unincorporated association (a masonic lodge). He paid a membership fee to the association, and the association made a payment (a fixed sum per member) to charity. The tribunal held that the membership fee was not a gift:

> If the contributions are mandatory (and hence not voluntarily made) they cannot qualify for Gift Aid. Section [414 ITA] requires there to be a "gift", which by its very definition requires a voluntary disposition.[20]

This is too broadly expressed, for it is clear that membership subscriptions may qualify for Gift Aid, and covenanted donations may constitute gifts, and neither of these are voluntary. The division between gifts and non-gifts is not quite so easily drawn.[21] In *Osborne* however the taxpayer did not make a gift because there was a single indivisible membership subscription and the subscription itself was a gift. One could not split the subscription into two parts.

The taxpayer should also have failed on the ground that the payment of the membership fee was not "to a charity". It was a payment to the association. The association would have qualified for corporate Gift Aid on its gift to charity (though it probably had no taxable income and so no need of the relief).

Gift Aid could have been available if the documentation had been appropriately drafted.

---

20 [2010] UKFTT 368 (TC).

21 See 15.31 (Membership subscription).

15.4.2 *Charity vouchers*

The HMRC Guidance Note provides at 3.4.5:

> Charities should also note that charity vouchers cannot be used to purchase services or goods from them.

This is correct because these services and goods would be improper use of the funds transferred by the charity pursuant to the charity vouchers.

15.5 Gift in tax avoidance context

HMRC have issued a statement on a tax avoidance scheme abusing Gift Aid:

> **Spotlight 9: Gift Aid with no real gift (March 2010)**
> An avoidance scheme exploiting the Gift Aid provisions has recently been disclosed to HMRC. The scheme seeks to exploit the rules which enable a charity to claim a repayment of tax at the basic rate on a qualifying donation by an individual. The individual may claim relief for the donation on the difference between the higher and basic rates of tax. The scheme depends upon a circular series of payments.
> [1] It starts with the charity purchasing, say, gilts of £100,000
> [2] which pass through a third party[22] to an individual taxpayer for perhaps £10.
> [3] The taxpayer is expected to make a sale for £100,000 and
> [4] [the taxpayer] passes the money to the charity.
> [5] There is an option that ensures the gilts will be returned to the charity if it does not receive a cash gift of £100,000 within one or two days.

The scheme only works if the payment at stage [4] is a gift. The HMRC analysis is as follows:

> In HMRC's view a gift has not been made to the charity as it is no better off than before entering the arrangements. Therefore Gift Aid is not due. HMRC will challenge the reliefs claimed in any instances where this scheme has been used and will litigate where appropriate.[23]

---

22 The role of the third party is not clear. Perhaps it is to procure the scheme vendor's fee.

23 *https://www.gov.uk/government/publications/spotlight-9-gift-aid-with-no-real-gift-29-march-2010/spotlight-9-gift-aid-with-no-real-gift-29-march-2010* See too 21.22 (QIDR "avoidance" schemes). An HMRC update in June 2013 adds:
"HMRC is now preparing to take legal action, but will first contact the remaining users of this scheme to invite them to reconsider their position and let HMRC know if they wish to withdraw their claims."

The scheme is only described in outline, and no doubt some variations are possible. As described, the scheme appears to face insuperable difficulties:

(1) The payment to the charity does not seem to be a gift (Possibly the position of the taxpayer might be strengthened if the individual paid more than the value of the gilts to the charity, and this does not apply to corporate donors).
(2) The individual seems to receive a benefit (release of the burden of the option) as a result of the gift.

The concepts of gift and causation seem sufficiently open ended to defeat avoidance schemes of this kind.

15.6 Gift "to a charity"

The gift must be made to a charity.

There are various ways that a gift may be made to a charity:

(1) As a simple gift: the charity holds beneficially (if a company) or on the terms of the charitable trust (if a trust). The charity can use the funds freely for any object within its charitable purposes.
(2) As a restricted fund
(3) As an agent/nominee/trustee of a separate charity

15.6.1 *Charity acting as agent/nominee*

Of course if a charity acts as agent, funds held as agent belong to the principal and not to the agent. Charities SORP (FRS 102) provides:

> 19.1. Charities may agree to administer the funds of another entity as its agent. As agent, a charity will act in line with the instructions of the entity that acts as the principal. For example, a charity may operate in an area of the world where the principal does not and so, by agreement with the principal, the charity administers the principal's funds in accordance with the instructions received. Within the charity sector, agency arrangements are sometimes referred to as conduit funding because the charity, in acting as agent, provides a conduit through which funds are passed in order to fund activities or assist the beneficiaries of the principal.
> 19.2. The agent is usually bound by an agency agreement and distributes

---

In practice the litigation did not take place. The persons who took part in the scheme wisely backed down.

> the funds it holds as agent to specified third parties in line with the instructions given by the principal. The funds transferred to the agent remain under the control of the principal and the principal remains responsible for the charitable application of those funds. A charity acting as agent should ensure that the terms of the agency agreement and the use of the funds are consistent with its own purposes.
> 19.7. Funds received by a charity as agent are not recognised as an asset in its accounts because the funds are not within its control. Consequently, the receipt of funds as agent is not recognised as income nor is its distribution recognised as the agent's expenditure.

15.6.2 *Restricted funds*

An individual may make a gift to a charity imposing a condition that the money be used for a specific charitable purpose which is narrower than the charitable objects of the charity. This is a gift to the charity. Charities SORP (FRS 102) explains the charity law background:

> 2.1 [A charity has] two primary classes of fund: those that are unrestricted in their use, which can be spent for any charitable purposes of a charity, and those that are restricted in use, which can only be lawfully used for a specific charitable purpose.

A gift to a restricted fund constitutes a gift to the charity:

> 5.14. Not all terms or conditions attaching to a grant or donation prevent its recognition as income. A term or condition that simply restricts the use of a grant or donation does not affect a charity's entitlement to the gift and recognition of income. However, a restriction does affect how the gift or grant is reported in the accounts.

> 19.4. A restricted donation is not an agency arrangement. A charity accounts for the receipt of a restricted fund as principal because the charity's trustees control how it is subsequently spent. For example, even if the purposes of the gift were narrowly defined by the donor, the trustees of a grant-making charity would still retain discretion as to the selection of grant recipients and the timing of the payment.

What if an individual makes a gift to a charity imposing a condition that the money be used for a non-charitable purpose? That may not be a gift "to the charity". If (contrary to our view) it were a gift to the charity, tax relief would be lost as charity funds would not be applied for charitable purposes. The issue is not likely to arise, as in practice it seems unlikely that a charity would or properly could accept a gift on such terms.

15.6.3 *Gift through fundraising charity*

It often happens that one person (the "fundraiser") raises money for a charity (the "ultimate charity"). The fundraiser is often (but not necessarily) itself a charity, in which case we call it the "fundraiser charity".

Questions which may arise include:

(1) Who may reclaim Gift Aid, the fundraiser (if a charity) or the ultimate charity? The question here is, to whom is the gift made?

(2) If the fundraiser charity reclaims Gift Aid, must it transfer that sum to the ultimate charity?

The arrangement may be carried out in various ways:

(1) The fundraiser charity may acquire the gifted money as nominee for the ultimate charity. In practice, if the fundraiser is a charity, that is less common.

(2) The fundraiser charity may acquire the gifted money beneficially, ie on its own account, but in due course, pursuant to a contractual obligation, or at its discretion, it may:
(a) transfer the money (or an equivalent sum) to the ultimate charity
(b) transfer its Gift Aid reclaim (or an equivalent sum, or the sum less costs) to the ultimate charity[24]

The position depends on the intention of the donor, which is in principle to be ascertained from the documentation relating to the donation. If the fundraising literature says, as one might expect, that

15.6.4 *Fundraiser charity is nominee*

HMRC Guidance Note considers the position where the fundraiser is itself a charity. It is consistent with the principles set out above:

> **3.36 Church collections**
> 3.36.1 Whether or not collections made for a particular charity by churches (which are themselves charities) can fall within the churches' Gift Aid Scheme will depend on the particular circumstances.
> 3.36.2 If the church has not exercised any discretion in collecting the donations and the donations are merely given to the church to simply pass on to a particular charity then the:
> - church has no entitlement to the donations (and they do not form part of the church's income)

---

24 See *Charity Commission v Framjee* [2015] 1 WLR 16.

- church is merely acting as a conduit and it's the charity that's the donee

More analytically, the church is acting as a nominee.

- charity must claim any Gift Aid tax relief (subject to the normal requirements, Gift Aid declaration and audit trail)

This is straightforward.

15.6.5 *Fundraiser charity is principal*

HMRC Guidance Note continues:

> 3.36.3 However, if the church exercises its discretion and decides to open a fund for donations to a particular charity, then the:
> - fund is a restricted fund of the church
> - church is the donee and the donations form part of the church's income
> - church is able to claim any Gift Aid tax relief (subject to the normal requirements)

The point is that this is a gift to the fundraiser charity (the church) and not a gift to the ultimate charity.

> 3.36.4 The church is legally obliged to pass the tax associated with a Gift Aid payment to the charity. The donor would have made their donation in expectation that both the Gift Aid donation and the associated Gift Aid tax would go to the charity for which the collection was made.

We agree that a general rule, in the absence of other indications, is that if the donation form says the gift will be paid on to the ultimate charity, that will include the Gift Aid repayment. That is also likely to correspond to what the donor would actually intend. But we would add that (i) it would be a matter of examining the documentation and facts of each case; (ii) a fundraising charity could if desired retain the Gift Aid reclaim, or some of it, by appropriate wording of the fundraising form, assuming the donor was content to give on such terms.[25]

15.6.6 *Payment of charity debt*

If an individual pays a debt of a charity, have they made a gift *to* the

---

25 See 15.49.4 (Ownership/use of tax reclaim).

charity? In the authors' view, the answer is, yes.[26] To avoid a possible dispute, the practical advice is to make the gift to the charity, and let the charity discharge the debt. This is not difficult unless the charity is insolvent.

Suppose an individual guaranteed a charity's debt. The making of the guarantee would not qualify for relief. If the guarantee was called upon, the donor would make a payment, which would arguably be a gift "to" the charity and qualify for relief if the documentation expressly provides that the individual has no right of subrogation against the charity. It may be appropriate to obtain an informal HMRC clearance; if that was not forthcoming, alternative arrangements could be devised which will qualify for the relief and satisfy the creditor's need for security.

15.7 Qualifying donation

"Qualifying donation" is a label which brings in a set of seven rules. The term is defined in s.416(1) ITA:

> A gift made to a charity by an individual is a qualifying donation for the purposes of this Chapter if
> (a) conditions A to F are met, and
> (b) the individual gives the charity a Gift Aid declaration relating to the gift (see s.428).

We refer to "**Gift Aid conditions A to F**".

15.8 Payment: Gift Aid condition A

Section 416(2) ITA provides:

---

26 This is supported by *Inglewood v IRC* [1983] STC 133 at p.139 ("The words 'to a beneficiary' cannot be construed literally. They must include, for example, payment of a minor's school fees or payment of his debts.") Likewise *IRC v Berrill* 55 TC 429 at p.455 ("Literally construed [s.493] ITA does not apply to the case where trustees of a conventional discretionary trust exercise their discretion in favour of a beneficiary by applying income for his benefit, for instance by paying rates on property which they occupy. The sum paid does not become the income 'of the person to whom it is paid' but becomes the income of the person for whose benefit it was paid. But [s.493] ITA must clearly have been intended to apply to such a case ... ." What is striking is that exactly the opposite conclusion was reached in the age of Lord Simonds: *Potts v IRC* (1950) 32 TC 211. Here the House of Lords held that the payment of tax owed by T was not a payment "to" T for the purposes of the IT settlement provisions. But that reflects the high tide of literal interpretation, an approach now long abandoned.

> Condition A is that the gift takes the form of a payment of a sum of money.

"Payment of a sum of money" is a composite phrase and not necessarily equal to the sum of its parts, but it is helpful for the purpose of analysis to consider "payment" and "sum of money" separately.

15.8.1 *"Payment"*

There are a variety of ways of making a "payment".[27] HMRC Guidance Note 3.4.1 provides:

> Donors must donate their own money. The donation can be made by cash, cheque, direct debit, credit card, debit card, postal order or standing order. 'Telegraphic transfer' is also acceptable.

These are all within the concept of "payment".

A payment to a person on trust to transfer the money to a charity is a "payment"; HMRC accept this, eg in relation to sponsored events.[28] A declaration by the donor that they hold money on trust for charitable purposes should likewise constitute a "payment".[29]

An entry in bankers books relating to a donor's bank account is a payment. Whether an entry in the books of the donor (not being a bank) amounts to a "payment" depends on the circumstances. The cases are discussed in *Minsham v Price* 63 TC 570. The issue will not often arise in relation to Gift Aid donations.

HMRC Guidance Note 3.4.3 provides:

> Donations by cheque are only valid pending clearance of the cheque. If the cheque is not honoured a donation has not been made.

This is correct. On releases of loans see 15.12 (Release of debt by charity).

15.8.2 *Payment by set-off*

If two pre-existing cross-demands for money immediately payable are set off against each other by agreement[30] without the formality of handing the

---

27 *Garforth v Newsmith Stainless Ltd* 52 TC 522. On "payment" generally, see Proctor, *Mann on the Legal Aspect of Money,* (7th ed, 2012) chap 7.

28 See 47.15.7 (Sponsored events).

29 I think this is clear without authority, but if authority is needed, one could find support in *Re Longman, Berry v IBS-STL* [2012] EWHC 666 (Ch) at [8].

30 It is different if there is no agreement: *Mellham v Burton* [2003] STC 441.

money over and handing it back again, the set-off constitutes a "payment".[31] HMRC accepted this in practice in relation to the former deposited covenant scheme. This would be relevant in a Gift Aid context if a person had promised by covenant to make a donation to a charity and the payment was satisfied by set-off. If there is a "payment" it is clearly a payment "of a sum of money"

15.9 "A sum of money"

The word "payment" alone normally implies the payment of money (rather than a non-cash asset), but statute states expressly that the payment must be "a sum of money". A gift of services or non-cash assets does not qualify for Gift Aid because the gift is:

(1) not a "payment"; and
(2) not a sum of money.[32]

If an individual contracts with a supplier, and pays money to the supplier for goods or services to be supplied to a charity, then the relief does not apply: the gift to the charity is a gift of goods or services rather than a sum of money. If the charity contracts for the goods or services, and the individual pays the debt, the position is different. The best course is to make a cash gift to the charity and allow the charity to use the money in the desired way. See too 15.40 (Retail Gift Aid).

If a debtor owes money to A, and A assigns the benefit of the debt to charity, Gift Aid does not apply as the assignment by A is not the payment of a sum of money. If the debtor subsequently pays the charity the sum due under the debt, there is a payment of a sum of money; however Gift Aid does not apply since it is not the case that *the gift* takes the form of the payment of a sum of money.[33] However if A directs the debtor to pay the sum due directly to charity, it is considered that that does constitute a payment of a sum of money.[34]

---

31 See *Coren v Keighley* 48 TC 370 at p.375. The same point is made in *Lowry v Consolidated African Selection Trust* 23 TC at p.288: "You need not pass cheques backwards and forwards across a table".

32 Qualifying investments have their own relief: see 21.1 (Gift of shares/land to charity). It may be possible to achieve income tax relief for gifts of services or other assets indirectly: see below.

33 This is self-evident but if authority is needed, see *Simpson v HMRC* [2009] STC (SCD) 226 at [34].

34 It appears that HMRC agree, since they conceded the point in *Simpson v HMRC* [2009] STC (SCD) 226 at [38].

15.9.1 *Foreign currency*

HMRC Guidance Note states at 3.4.1:

> Donations can be made in sterling or any foreign currency. When calculating claims the charity must convert foreign currency into sterling at the rate on the date when the donation was made.

This is correct, because "money" in its normal sense includes foreign currency.[35]

HMRC say:

> Bitcoins are not considered to be legal tender and therefore not recognised as money. Per S416(2) ITA 2007 therefore cannot be used to claim Gift aid donations.[36]

15.10 Gift by will

Gift Aid does not apply to a gift made by will even if the gift is a sum of money. The testator does not make a "payment", either when they make their will or on the occasion of death. The executors do not qualify for Gift Aid when they pay the legacy to the charity as they are not "individuals".

15.11 Loan to charity

A loan to a charity, even if it is interest-free or on beneficial terms, does not qualify for Gift Aid. A loan is disqualified on three grounds (any one of which would suffice):

(1) A loan is not a "gift".
(2) A loan is subject to a condition as to repayment.
(3) The donor may be said to receive a benefit, in the form of the right to repayment of the loan.[37]

15.12 Waiver of debt

15.12.1 *HMRC former view*

Waiver of a debt (or release, the terms are synonymous) qualifies for Gift

---

35 See Proctor, *Mann on the Legal Aspect of Money* (7th ed, 2012), para 1.86.

36 Charity Tax Forum Action Point Log *https://www.gov.uk/government/uploads/system/uploads/attachment_data/file/440570/Action_Point_Log_29_May_2015.pdf*
See Kessler, *Taxation of Non-residents and Foreign Domiciliaries*, (21st ed, 2022-23), para 99.36.1 (What cryptoassets are).

37 See 20.1 (Interest-free loans to charity).

Aid if it is a payment of a sum of money.

The word "payment" in its strict meaning is not apt to describe a voluntary waiver of a debt. On this basis the relief does not apply. However, the context may show that word should be given a wider meaning.[38] The context here, and a purposive view of the legislation, suggests that the waiver of a debt might be a payment.[39]

However, a debt (except a debt in the form of a bank account) is not a "sum of money". It would not be regarded as such by commercial business people. This can be seen clearly in the case of a charity unable or unwilling to repay its debt on demand; and the question whether or not a debt is a sum of money can hardly depend on the creditworthiness of the charity.

HMRC formerly took the view that the waiver of a debt did not amount to the payment of a sum of money, so it did not qualify for Gift Aid. HMRC Guidance Note 3.4.4 provided:

> *A donation must be a payment of a sum of money. A donation cannot be made... by loan waiver or by debt/loan conversion.*[40]

While perhaps unfair, this is considered to be strictly correct.

15.12.2 *HMRC current view*

In the course of the Covid pandemic, there were many instances where donors waived the right to repayment due for tickets which had to be cancelled. This highlighted the unfairness of the strict rule.

In May 2021 HMRC changed their view, and the Guidance Note now provides:

> 3.4.4 ... Donations made via the waiving of a refund or loan repayment can be considered a donation of a sum of money where there is a clear agreement to cancel a loan or not accept a refund...
>
> **3.45 Claiming Gift Aid on Waived Refunds and Loan Repayments**
>
> 3.45.1 HMRC will consider donations made from a waiver of a right to either a refund or loan repayment to be eligible for Gift Aid. This is provided there is a record of a formal waiver held by the charity and all other Gift Aid rules are met. The donation will be considered to have been made at the date of the waiver and not the date of the original

---

38 *National Grid plc v Mayes* [2001] 1 WLR 864 at [20].

39 See too 15.8.2 (Payment by set-off).

40 The context suggests the expression "debt/loan conversion" referred to the conversion of a debt or loan to a gift, ie it was a synonym of "waiver" of the debt or loan.

> payment. A Gift Aid declaration will need to be collected by the charity if one is not already held for the donor.
> 3.45.2 What HMRC considers to be a formal waiver depends on the amount being waived.

15.12.3 *Waiver of small amount*

The Guidance Note now continues:

> For a small amount, for example a couple of tickets to a fund-raising event, which has been cancelled. The charity should keep an auditable record of correspondence between the charity and the taxpayer, confirming that no refund is required and that this amount is to be treated as a donation. Examples of this correspondence could include:
> - an email exchange
> - a letter out to the taxpayer and their response
> - a recorded telephone call

This is concessionary, as a debt cannot be waived by these informal methods.[41]

15.12.4 *Waiver of larger amount*

> 3.45.3 Where the amount being waived is more than a nominal amount, such as a loan repayment, HMRC would expect there to be a legally enforceable document in place. Amongst other things, the document should include:
> - details of what is being waived (make it expressly clear that the lender is giving up all legal rights to any future repayment)
> - confirmation the amount waived is to be treated as a donation for Gift Aid
>
> The charity must keep a copy of this document for audit purposes and all other Gift Aid rules should be adhered to.

If English law applies, waiver must be by deed.[42] But even if the debt is validly waived, HMRC's view is still concessionary if, which we consider to be the better view, waiver of a debt is not payment of a sum of money.

The taxpayer might take the point if, exceptionally, it is discovered that gift aid treatment is not advantageous, eg if a donor finds they do not have sufficient income to cover the gift.

The statement binds HMRC. So for Gift Aid purposes, it is no longer

---

41 Different rules may apply in Scotland.

42 Likewise in Northern Ireland. Different rules may apply in Scotland.

necessary to find some other way to arrange the transaction, as was done previously.[43]

The new practice applies regardless of the time of the waiver, or purported waiver, so it applies to waivers before the date of change of practice.

As with all concessions, there is the difficulty that in the event of a dispute the taxpayer's remedy is by way of judicial review and not an appeal to the first-tier tribunal. But that is usually only theoretical.

Further thought may be needed in exceptional cases where:

(1) a fixed-term loan at less than commercial interest was repaid early; or

(2) a charity is insolvent and unable to repay the loan from its own resources.

15.12.5 *Waivers: Best practice*

The HMRC Guidance Note provides:

> 3.45.4 In all circumstances, HMRC expects the charity to explain clearly to the individual that they have a choice between obtaining a full refund or waiving the right to a refund and have this classed as a qualifying donation. There must be no pressure placed on the individual to waive their right to a refund. The individual must positively choose to waive their right.
> 3.45.5 The individual must ensure that they have paid sufficient tax to cover their donation, for the year in which the donation is deemed to be made.

In practice that should be complied with.

15.12.6 *A cautionary tale*

Battle Baptist Church v IRC[44] is a case of no legal importance. It may however be mentioned here as a cautionary tale.

Donors lent money to the charity and purported to waiver the loans. HMRC refused a Gift Aid refund on the grounds that the waiver of the loan was not a "payment of a sum of money". Just before this point came

---

43 Previously, either (1) the donor made a cash gift to the charity; and the charity used the funds to repay the donor; or (2) the charity repaid its debt to the donor; and the donor made a cash gift of the proceeds.
There is however an Inheritance Tax problem on the waiver of a substantial debt: see 24.8 (Charities/charitable purposes) so this practice might continue for IHT reasons.

44 [1995] STC (SCD) 176.

to the Commissioners, it was noticed that the loans were not effectively waived (waiver was not done by deed). So there was no question of Gift Aid. The appeal was withdrawn. This was, however, an effective victory for the charity, as its donors had the new opportunity to give cash, so as to allow the charity to repay the loans.

The charity survived to obtain its tax relief on another day. It did so only because it was unaware of both the general law *and* the tax law. If the charity had known the rules about waiver of loans and deeds, it might have executed a deed of waiver. Under the former HMRC practice, HMRC would not have allowed Gift Aid, and the charity would (probably) have lost its tax appeal. A little knowledge is a dangerous thing!

But if the same facts arose today, and provided a waiver was by deed, relief should have been allowed under the current HMRC practice.

15.13 Charity pays donor: Circularity

Suppose:

(1) (a) a donor gives a sum to charity and
(b) the charity repays the sum to the donor; or

(2) (a) the charity pays a sum to a donor and
(b) the donor gives the sum to the charity.

This may happen, for instance if:

(1) (a) The charity purchases services from the donor and
(b) the donor makes a cash gift of the fee back to the charity.

(2) (a) The charity discharges a liability owing to the donor and
(b) the donor makes a cash gift of the sum paid to them back to the charity.

(3) (a) The charity lends money to the donor as an investment and
(b) the donor makes a cash gift of the sum lent back to the charity.

Does the payment to the donor neutralise the donor's payment to the charity? In the authors' opinion it does not, provided that:

(1) the GAAR does not apply; and
(2) the transactions involved are not shams.

This is supported by much authority, in particular *Russell v IRC* 26 TC 242; *Nightingale v Price* [1996] STC (SCD) 116; *MacNiven v Westmoreland* 73 TC 1.[45] This was discussed in more detail in the 4th edition of this book but the text is now omitted because in most cases

45 For completeness, the same conclusion was also reached in *Simpson v HMRC* [2009] STC (SCD) 226 at [39] though the authorities were not fully discussed.

HMRC agree: see the next section. For circular payments to trading companies see 9.15 (Returning Gift Aid payment: Circularity).

15.14 Volunteer expenses

HMRC Guidance Note provides:[46]

> **3.41 Voluntary workers' expenses**
> 3.41.1 Voluntary workers sometimes incur expenditure when assisting charities to carry out their work (for example, travel costs, postal or photocopying charges, etc). Provided the expenses are reasonable and proper, a charity can reimburse a volunteer for the expenses incurred. Often a volunteer will forgo the expenses to which he/she is entitled. This section explains how the Gift Aid rules apply when volunteers agree to forgo their expenses.
> 3.41.2 One of the requirements of the Gift Aid Scheme is that the gift by a donor to a charity 'takes the form of a payment of a sum of money'. So a Gift Aid payment to a charity cannot be made by book entries following a waiver of expenses.
> 3.41.3 The charity must physically pay the expenses to the volunteer. The volunteer is then free to keep the money or pay part or all of it back to the charity as a Gift Aid payment. If they give all of the expenses paid back to the charity, they're not returning the expenses but making a payment of an equivalent amount.
> 3.41.4 The charity will need, as normal, a Gift Aid declaration and an audit trail to bring the payment into the Gift Aid Scheme. The payment will also need to meet the usual requirements of the Gift Aid Scheme (benefit rules etc).
> 3.41.5 For audit purposes, it is preferable that at least 1 of the payments by the charity or the volunteer is made by cheque.

Leonard Beighton, former deputy chairman of the Board of Inland Revenue, notes that "there are of course cultural issues here which would need to be weighed up in any particular case".[47]

15.15 "Social giving account"

In 2016 a section was added to the HMRC Guidance Note under the heading "Digital giving and social giving accounts".

The neologism "social giving", if it has an established meaning, appears to refer to peer-to-peer fundraising; with a nod to the term "social media".

---

46 For employment income and PAYE issues, see 12.4 (Volunteers).

47 *Tax Adviser*, December 2002, p.20.

The expression “social giving account” is not explained but appears to be a CAF account, or similar arrangement.

HMRC Guidance Note provides:

> **Chapter 3.44 Digital giving and social giving accounts**
> 3.44.1 We recognise that there are many new and innovative ways of giving to charity through digital platforms including social media and fundraising websites.
> 3.44.2 The general rule at 3.4.1 still applies, however, that donors must only claim Gift Aid when donating their own money when using social giving opportunities. The donor must also still give the charity a valid Gift Aid declaration, to declare that they have paid, or will pay, UK income tax or capital gains tax in support of a donation.[48]
> 3.44.3 So, you cannot Gift Aid
> [1] money collected from family, friends or work colleagues, or
> [2] money raised from fundraising activities such as jumble sales, raffles, tombola’s or ticket sales.

Who is the “you” to whom this is addressed? It must be referring to the donor or the person who procures a donation.

More analytically, the Gift Aid declaration must be given by the donor. So if A procures B to make a gift to charity, then B must make the Gift Aid declaration for B’s gift.

> 3.44.4 If
> [a] you have a social giving account with a charity fundraiser or
> [b] register a credit or debit card with a fundraising website
> then you can only Gift Aid your own donations made through your social giving account. You can use your account to transfer money given to you by others to pass on to charity, but you can only claim Gift Aid on your own donations that are charged to your account, and for which you do not receive a compensating payment from others.
> 3.44.5 If you donate to charity with a text message then you can use Gift Aid if you are donating your own money and you are the person who is legally responsible for paying the mobile phone bill.

It is therefore necessary to identify who is the donor. That should not be hard.

> 3.44.6 Some social giving accounts allow a donor to leave a supportive message for a fundraiser participating in a sponsored event, or a

48 Authors’ footnote: This is not an accurate description of a Gift Aid declaration, but that does not matter in the present context.

> dedication message in remembrance of a loved one. It is okay to extend such messages beyond the donor as long as the donation is still of the donors own money...

A series of six examples are then given. We set them all out, for completeness, though they are somewhat repetitious.

> 3.44.8 (Julia)
> J donates £50 of her own money to charity using her social giving account and completes a Gift Aid declaration. J includes a supporting note with her donation which says 'with best wishes – Julia Smith and family'. This donation would qualify for Gift Aid because the donation is solely from J, despite the inclusion of other names on the supporting message.
> 3.44.9 (Rahul and Peter)
> R is running a marathon. R's colleague P passes a collection around his office and raises £400.P uses his social giving account to donate this money to R's chosen charity and includes a supporting note which says 'good luck, Rahul – from all your colleagues'. This donation would not qualify for Gift Aid because the donation has not come solely from P.

The donations (the plural is more appropriate) would of course qualify for Gift Aid so far as the actual donors make Gift Aid declarations.

> 3.44.10 (Barry and Cindy)
> B is also running a marathon. His Mum, C, gives him £100 which B donates to his chosen charity using his own social giving account and includes the message 'From Mum and Dad'. This would not qualify for Gift Aid because B has not donated his own money.

The donation would qualify for Gift Aid if the mother made a Gift Aid declaration.

> 3.44.11 B runs a marathon again the following year. C now has her own social giving account and uses it to donate £100 to B's chosen charity and includes the message 'From Mum and Dad'. This donation would qualify for Gift Aid because the donation is solely from C, despite the inclusion of other names on the supporting message.

This is the same example as Julia.

> 3.44.12 (Kate)
> K organises a 'Fun Day and exhibition match' at her local rugby club in memory of her late father. Entry is by ticket only, and other funds are raised through a raffle, tombola, fairground rides and a bouncy castle.

> £1,000 is collected from all sources and K pays this to her chosen charity using her social giving account and includes the message 'In loving memory of my father, Frank'. This payment would not qualify for Gift Aid because it has been received in return for services, rights or goods provided to many people. No donations have been received, and the payment is not a donation from K.
>
> 3.44.13 (Daniel)
>
> D works as a barman and pledges to give his Friday tips from his shift to a fundraising telethon broadcast that night. D receives £30 in tips and uses his social giving account to donate this money to the telethon appeal. This donation would qualify for Gift Aid because the donation is solely from D. The tips were received from many people, but are part of D's income for tax purposes and he has decided to donate them to charity.
>
> 3.44.14 (Jenny)
>
> J organises a collection at The Red Lion to raise funds for a new lifeboat. She collects £240 from others and decides to top this up to £250 with £10 of her own money. J uses her social giving account to pay the £240 to a lifeboat charity and leaves a message 'from the regulars at The Red Lion'. J cannot claim Gift Aid on this payment because it is not a donation of her money. £240 has been charged to her debit card but she has been compensated by the £240 collected from the regulars who can now check online that their donation has been passed on to a lifeboat charity.

This is the same example as Rahul. The donations (the plural seems more appropriate) would qualify for Gift Aid so far as the actual donors make Gift Aid declarations.

> In a separate transaction, J donates £10 to the same lifeboat charity through her social giving account to top up to £250 and leaves a further message 'from J at The Red Lion'. This £10 donation would qualify for Gift Aid because the donation is solely from J.

Fundraising websites will typically charge a fee for processing donations and deduct this from the amount passed on to the charity. In this situation, the question arises as to whether the charity's Gift Aid claim should be based on the full amount taken from the donor's account or the amount net of the fee actually received by the charity. If the charity is liable for the fee then the analysis would be that the charity has received the full amount taken from the donor's account which it then uses to pay the fee (even though the mechanism for this is by deduction from the amount it receives) so that the full amount taken from the donor's account can be treated as a Gift Aided donation. Conversely, if the donor is contractually liable to pay the fee then the analysis would strictly be that the donor has paid the fee and donated the remaining amount to the charity so only this amount would qualify as a Gift Aided donation, though perhaps the contrary might be argued, and we wonder whether HMRC would take the point. Clearly the former approach is better, and it is noted that the major fund raising websites have tended to draft their contractual terms so as to achieve this result.

15.16 Repayment rule: Condition B

Section 416(3) ITA provides:

> Condition B is that the payment is not subject to any condition as to repayment.

We refer to this as the "**repayment rule**".

What if a payment is made subject to a condition as to repayment in part? It is suggested that repayment of part is not "repayment".[49] But if the gift is actually repaid in part, that constitutes a benefit which disqualifies the relief, and even the right to repayment may constitute a benefit.

15.16.1 *"Condition as to repayment"*

Under insolvency law, a gift may be set aside if the donor becomes bankrupt within a specified period.[50]

Under charity law, certain credit/debit card donations (gifts above £100 in response to broadcast appeals) can be revoked by the donor during a cooling-off period.[51]

A charity may in appropriate circumstances return a gift to a donor (eg in cases of hardship); or to an estate (eg if the testator intended to change their will but failed to do so).

Clearly, matters such as these[52] do not amount to a "condition as to

---

49 Contrast *Saunders v IRC* 37 TC 416 (power to revoke settlement in part not a "power of revocation").

50 Section 339 Insolvency Act 1986.

51 Section 61 Charities Act 1992.

52 Further examples can be given. Gifts to charity may be set aside on the death of the donor, if the validity of the gift is governed by a law which operates forced heirship clawback rules. Section 10 Inheritance (Provision for Family and Dependants) Act 1975 is a similar English law example (but that power to set aside is more limited).

repayment" or else Gift Aid would never apply. (If the gift is in fact set aside, for any of those reasons, the tax relief would be lost, because setting aside operates retrospectively to the date of the gift.[53])

It is suggested that rules of law unconnected with the terms of the gift do not constitute "conditions" as to repayment. In other words, the repayment rule only applies when the condition as to repayment is a term of the gift. To identify the terms of the gift requires an examination of the facts in the light of the law relating to gifts.

15.16.2 *Law relating to gifts*

A gift of money requires that:

(1) The donor transfers money to the donee.
(2) The donor intends the transfer to be a gift.

The intention of the donor is crucial. For instance, if a person transfers money but intends that the recipient should hold on trust for the transferor, the transfer does not take effect as a gift.

The intention of the donee is not relevant. A gift is valid at the time of the transfer even if the donee knows nothing at all about it. A gift is a *unilateral* transaction.[54]

A donor may make a gift subject to conditions. It is the *intention of the donor* which determines whether a gift is unconditional or subject to conditions (and if so, what the conditions are). The intention of the donee is irrelevant.[55]

The intention of the donor is ascertained objectively.[56] Chitty on

---

53 Alternatively it might be said that setting aside the gift constitutes a benefit, but it is not necessary to rely on that.

54 See *Standing v Bowring*, (1885) 30 Ch D 282 at p.288:

> "Now, I take the rule of law to be that where there is a transfer of property to a person, even although it carries with it some obligations which may be onerous, it vests in him at once before he knows of the transfer, subject to his right when informed of it to say, if he pleases, "I will not take it." When informed of it he may repudiate it, but it vests in him until he so repudiates."

See Hill, "The role of the donee's consent in the law of gift" [2001] LQR 127.

55 In *Dewar v Dewar* [1975] 2 All ER 728, A transferred £500 to B. A intended the payment to be a gift. B regarded it as a loan. The transfer was held to take effect as a gift. It was the intention of the donor which mattered.

A donee may seek to agree with the donor that a gift should be subject to conditions, but that would require the knowledge and agreement of the donor.

56 See *Day v Harris* [2014] Ch 211 at [69]: the intention of the donor is to be "objectively ascertained from his words and conduct".

Contracts says:

> The conditions [of a standard form contract] must be brought to the notice of the party to be bound before or at the time when the contract is made. If they are not communicated to him until after the contract is concluded, they will be of no effect.[57]

Thus if, for instance,
(1) a charity donee intended a gift to it to be revocable, but
(2) the donor did not have that intention, objectively determined,[58] eg they did not have reasonable notice of the charity's intention,
then the gift would not be revocable.

15.16.3 *Refund policy*

Charities may have refund policies. The Gift Aid position depends on
(1) the terms of the policy and
(2) whether the donor was reasonably aware of the policy.

There is no difficulty in a refund policy which states:
(1) The charity may refund gifts at its discretion.
(2) The charity will refund gifts made in error (the most common case is where a donor clicks on a website donate button more than once).

These are not conditions as to repayment. They simply restate the general law.[59]

15.16.4 *Cooling-off period*

A **"cooling-off"** refund policy is one which offers the donor an

57 (32nd ed., 2015), para 12-010 (Time of notice). A simple gift is not a contract, in English law (Scotland may be different). However similar principles apply as both the terms of both gifts and contracts are determined objectively.

58 In practice it seems unlikely that a donor would have the intention of making a revocable gift, in cases where:
(1) This is unfavourable as its effect is that Gift Aid does not apply. The charity loses its Gift Aid reclaim, which the donor wants the charity to have; and the donor would lose their own claim to higher rate tax relief.
(2) The donor completes a Gift Aid declaration.

59 That is self-evident, but if authority is needed, see: *Champions Fun Learning Centre v HMRC* [2018] UKFTT 516 (TC) at [195] - [196] " The appellant's website says that if a pupil is not able to attend a refund may be possible. ... We do not consider that the possibility of a refund of itself is [a condition as to repayment. If any particular monthly payments were refunded then we would agree that they were not gifts."

unconditional right to repayment if they change their mind within a relatively short specified period, typically 14 or 28 days.

Cooling-off periods ensure protection of donors, and it is good practice for a charity to allow a cooling-off period.[60] As such a cooling-off period is arguably not a condition as to repayment, (within the meaning of Gift Aid condition B read purposively).

If a cooling-off period were a condition as to repayment, it is alternatively arguable that there is a payment of a sum of money (to which Gift Aid applies) on the expiry of the cooling-off period.[61]

But HMRC do not agree, and in the absence of HMRC guidance on the point, charities should stick to the safe refund policy that refunds are made at its discretion and not as of right.

In practice, even where a charity formally adopts an unconditional cooling-off refund policy, it could not constitute a term of the gift unless the donor is reasonably aware of it. That depends on the facts, but is not generally the case. Donors do not read, and cannot be expected to read, legal small print of refund policies.

15.16.5 *Conditions as to use*

The repayment rule raises a problem when a charity is raising funds for purchasing an asset. Donors may give to the charity on terms that if sufficient funds are not raised, and the asset cannot be purchased, their contributions will be returned. A gift on those terms does not strictly qualify for Gift Aid. It may be that HMRC would not take the point in practice in a meritorious case. It would be essential to seek a binding advance clearance. Another solution is for donors to covenant to pay the amount they wish to give, conditional upon the charity raising sufficient funds to make the purchase. A payment under that covenant after the condition is satisfied would qualify for Gift Aid. This may also be desirable for IHT reasons.[62] But this solution raises practical administrative difficulties.

---

60 Note the statutory cooling-off period for credit card donations in response to broadcast appeals. Institute of Fundraising recommend that vulnerable donors, ie those that need additional care and support, should be allowed a cooling-off period: "Treating Donors Fairly" (2014) *http://www.institute-of-fundraising.org.uk/library/treatingdonorsfairly/*

61 See 15.8.1 (Payment).

62 See 24.15 (Conditional gift to charity).

15.16.6 *Donatio mortis causa*

The repayment rule disqualifies from relief a gift which qualifies as a *donatio mortis causa* (a gift made in anticipation of death). Such a gift may be revoked during the donor's lifetime. But in practice such gifts are rare and the point is theoretical.

15.16.7 *Purpose of repayment rule*

It is hard to see the purpose of the repayment rule. Presumably the drafter had in mind schemes where the donor obtained their relief and received their money back too. Perhaps they intended to stop interest-free loans to charity from qualifying. But these would have been caught by the Gift Aid benefit rule in any event.

15.17 Payroll giving: Condition C

Section 416(4) ITA provides:

> Condition C is that the payment is not a sum falling within s.713(3) of ITEPA 2003 (payroll deduction scheme).

Gifts within the payroll giving scheme are naturally excluded from Gift Aid. Such payments already qualify for tax relief.

15.18 Payment deductible for IT

Section 416(5) ITA provides:

> Condition D is that the payment is not deductible in calculating the individual's income from any source.

Of course if the payment is deductible the individual does not need Gift Aid. Unfortunately a charity cannot tell whether or not a payment is deductible, but if the donor gives a Gift Aid declaration, it should assume Gift Aid applies. See 18.2 (Charity gift: Deductible expense) .

HMRC say:

> **Professional organisation membership fees**
> Membership subscriptions paid to some professional organisations on HMRC's list of qualifying bodies can be treated as an expense deduction. Working members can claim tax relief on their subscription, but subscriptions can't be treated as Gift Aid payments.
> Retired or student members' subscription fees can be treated as a Gift Aid payment, but they must confirm that they don't have income from

which they can deduct professional membership subscriptions.[63]

15.19 Acquisition of property rule

It was desired to restrict Gift Aid to gifts of money, and to deny income tax relief for gifts of other assets. Without a specific anti-avoidance provision, donors could easily obtain that relief. They would give money to the charity, which the charity then used to purchase the asset from the donor.[64] In this way, what is effectively a gift of a non-cash asset could qualify for income tax relief.

Section 416(6) ITA therefore provides:

> Condition E is that the payment is not
> [a] conditional on,
> [b] associated with or
> [c] part of an arrangement involving,
> the acquisition of property by the charity from
> [i] the individual or
> [ii] a person connected with the individual.
> An acquisition by way of gift is ignored for the purposes of this condition.

We refer to this as the **"acquisition of property rule".**

The expression "conditional on, associated with or part of the arrangement involving" seems very wide, but HMRC do not necessarily understand it so strictly. See 15.33 (Multiple/single/split payment).

It may sometimes be possible to arrange a transfer of value to a charity without the acquisition of property. Examples are the surrender of a lease, and the variation of a company's articles. These are outside the scope of the acquisition of property rule.

Suppose there is an arrangement under which:

(1) a donor gives money to a charity; and

(2) the charity lends money to the donor.[65]

---

63 HMRC, "Gift Aid: what donations charities and CASCs can claim on" (Dec 2014) *https://www.gov.uk/gift-aid-what-donations-charities-and-cascs-can-claim-on*

64 The sale would not give rise to capital gains tax if the sale price did not exceed the donor's base cost. The sale price would not, of course, exceed the market value of the asset, or the charity would be acting in breach of trust.

65 Of course the loan would have to be on arm's length terms and raises other charity law issues. For the position where a gift is associated with a loan from the donor to the charity see 15.47 (Deposited donation: Carry-forward).

The charity has acquired property (the benefit of the debt). Has it acquired the property "from the donor"? It is suggested that the answer is, no. That is ordinary use of words and consistent with the purpose of the subsection.

Suppose there is an arrangement under which:

(1) a corporate donor gives money to a charity; and

(2) the charity subscribes for shares in that company.

The charity has acquired property (shares); has it done so "from the donor"? The company has not disposed of shares but is described as "issuing" shares. In this case, it is suggested that the acquisition is "from the company". The same applies to an issue of debentures.

The importance of the acquisition of property rule has been reduced by the introduction of QIDR. The best way to obtain IT relief for a gift of a non-cash asset which is outside QIDR is an arrangement under which:

(1) The donor makes a gift to the charity which qualifies for QIDR.

(2) The charity purchases the asset from the donor.[66]

There are other artificial ways around the acquisition of property rule.[67] IT relief can also be obtained for gift of assets by Will or by IOV: see 28.5 (Gift of non-cash asset to charity by Will).

For a discussion of the policy issues here, see 22.3 (IT relief for other assets: Critique).

15.19.1 *Connected person acquisition*

On the meaning of "connected person" see 15.32.1 (Connected person).

It is suggested that the question whether the person is connected is decided at the time of the acquisition, not at the time of the Gift Aid payment.

The corporate Gift Aid rule is slightly different: it applies to acquisitions from *associated* persons (whereas the IT rule applies to acquisitions from

---

66 See 21.20 (Gifts of non-qualifying assets via QIDR).

67 Suppose, for instance, that a donor wishes to give a picture to charity, but would like to qualify for income tax relief. The donor would sell the picture to the charity, and put the charity in funds in order to pay for the purchase in a manner which qualifies for tax relief. One method of doing this without infringing Condition E is to arrange for the purchase to be made by a charity other than the charity to whom the gift is made; in principle, an inter-charity loan or grant should achieve this. Alternatively the purchase might be made by a related non-charitable body. Watch the GAAR. The matter can also be dealt with by Will or by IOV: see 28.5 (Gift of non-cash asset to charity by will).

connected persons).[68]

15.20 Benefit rule: Condition F

Section 416(7) ITA provides:

> Condition F is that—
> (a) there are no benefits associated with the gift, or
> (b) there are benefits associated with the gift but the restrictions on those benefits are not breached.

This is here called the "**benefit rule**" or (when being compared to other areas) the "Gift Aid benefit rule". The term used in HMRC Guidance Note is "Donor Benefit Rule".

Section 417 ITA defines "associated":

> A benefit is associated with a gift for the purposes of this Chapter if it is received by the individual who makes the gift, or a person connected with the individual, in consequence of making the gift.

This is an exclusive definition, ie a benefit is associated if and only if it falls within s.417.

The benefit rule operates on an all-or-nothing basis. If there is a disqualifying benefit, tax relief for the gift is entirely forfeited. Small benefits (which are permitted) are discussed at 15.34 (Small benefits).

15.20.1 *Benefit rule: Cross references*

The following points are considered elsewhere:

Topic	**See para**
Is remuneration of charity worker a benefit	15.29
Is IHT relief a benefit	28.2.2

15.20.2 *Review of benefit rule*

In 2014 the Public Accounts Committee concluded:

> HMRC has not adequately simplified the tax rules for reliefs on donations. Recommendation: HMRC should examine ways in which the rules can be simplified to both reduce abuse and make the system easier and simpler for charities to claim the reliefs.[69]

---

68 See 17.4.4 (Acquisition of property rule).

69 Gift Aid and Other Tax Reliefs on Charitable Donations (Feb 2014)

The Government agreed with the recommendation.[70] But the response was understandably guarded: "The department will review all charity relief processes to ensure they are as easy to use as possible. However, in doing so this must be balanced against the need to ensure that the integrity of the reliefs is not compromised and systems and processes are not left open to the risk of fraud or abuse."

Budget 2014 provided:

> 2.96 The government will review benefits allowed to donors with a view to simplifying existing rules.

Autumn statement 2014 expanded on this:

> 2.82 The government will continue and extend the review of donor benefits launched at Budget 2014 to include consideration of the rules for claiming Gift Aid on membership and entrance fees. An update will be provided at Budget 2015. The government will also work with the sector on updating the guidance and making it easier to understand.

This is the background of the current review of the donor benefit rules and the 2017 rules for intermediaries

The matter is proceeded at a leisurely pace, which is in principle a good thing, though it might reflect a lack of enthusiasm on HMRC's part rather than an understanding that time is required to find the best solution. HMRC subsequently published a number of short and shallow papers:

- "Simplifying the Gift Aid Donor Benefit Rules: a call for evidence" (the **"donor benefit paper"**).[71]
- Simplifying the Gift Aid donor benefits rules: consultation"[72]
- "Simplifying the Gift Aid donor benefits rules: response to the consultation and further consultation"[73]

The matter is still ongoing.

---

70 Government responses on the Thirty Fifth to the Forty Fifth Reports from the Committee of Public Accounts: Session 2013-14. *https://www.gov.uk/government/uploads/system/uploads/attachment_data/file/302527/39796_Cm_8847_Print_Ready.pdf?j=689509&e=kessler@kessler.co.uk&l=346_HTML&u=15535401&mid=1062735&jb=0*

71 *https://www.gov.uk/government/uploads/system/uploads/attachment_data/file/446089/Donor_Benefits_call_for_evidence_web_v4.pdf* (July 2015)

72 *https://www.gov.uk/government/uploads/system/uploads/attachment_data/file/567994/Simplifying_the_gift_aid_donor_benefits_rule_consultation.pdf* (Feb 2016)

73 *https://www.gov.uk/government/consultations/simplifying-the-gift-aid-donor-benefits-rules-further-consultation* (Nov 2016)

15.21 "Benefit"

"Benefit" is undefined. It is often said to be a word of wide import. The word benefit is very common in tax statutes and in other areas of law.[74] So there is no shortage of material for discussion, though it is always necessary to consider the word in its context.

In the present context "benefit" means a financial benefit. (This is assumed in the small benefits exemption which refers to the "*value* of the benefits".)

In practice, giving is generally based on a combination of motives:

(1) Altruistic motives: to help others
(2) Private motives:
  (a) inward and personal: the "warm glow" of giving, or relief of guilt
  (b) public: to obtain recognition, honour or influence for the donor
  (c) sometimes, spite: to deprive heirs of an inheritance[75]

"No man giveth but with the intention of good to himself" thought Hobbes.[76] But even if motives for giving do include these private motives, the "benefit" obtained does not in principle amount to a benefit in the relevant sense of financial benefit.[77]

The benefit need not be received from the charity. Suppose A promises to make a payment to B if B makes a payment to charity. This is arguably a "gift" by B.[78] The payment to B is a benefit, however, so no relief is available.

Every higher rate taxpayer receives a benefit from their gift, in the form of higher rate tax relief. That, necessarily, does not disqualify a gift.

Allowing a donor to participate in religious worship does not constitute a benefit (in the relevant sense of financial benefit). The practice in US tax law is set out in *Hernandez v Commissioner*:

> The IRS ruled that
>
> > "pew rents, building fund assessments and periodic dues paid to a church ... are all methods of making contributions to the church,

---

74 For discussion see Kessler, *Taxation of Non-Residents and Foreign Domiciliaries* (21st ed., 2022-23), para 50.4 (Benefit) online version *https://www.foreigndomiciliaries.co.uk*

75 See Hyland, *Gifts: A Study in Comparative Law* (1st ed, 2009), p.50-53.

76 *Leviathan*, Part 1, Chapter 15. But the point is debatable: see Robinson's rewarding book *Definition* (1950), Ch IV s.4 and Ch VI s.5.

77 See 15.22 (Acknowledgement and advertising).

78 *Berry v Warnett* 55 TC 92.

> and such payments are deductible as charitable contributions."
> Similarly, notwithstanding the "form" of Mass stipends as fixed payments for specific religious services, the IRS has allowed charitable deductions of such payments.
> ... the IRS recently explained ...
>
> > "[i]n contrast to tuition payments, religious observances generally are not regarded as yielding private benefits to the donor, who is viewed as receiving only incidental benefits when attending the observances. The primary beneficiaries are viewed as being the general public and members of the faith. Thus, payments for saying masses, pew rents, tithes, and other payments involving fixed donations for similar religious services, are fully deductible contributions."
>
> ... In exchange for their payment of pew rents, Christians receive particular seats during worship services. Similarly, in some synagogues attendance at the worship services for Jewish High Holy Days is often predicated upon the purchase of a general admission ticket or a reserved seat ticket. Religious honors such as publicly reading from Scripture are purchased or auctioned periodically in some synagogues of Jews from Morocco and Syria. Mormons must tithe their income as a necessary but not sufficient condition to obtaining a "temple recommend," i.e., the right to be admitted into the temple.[79]

The same applies in the UK. Participation in religious worship does not constitute a benefit for Gift Aid purposes, and do not prevent the payment from constituting a gift, so that the payment in principle qualifies for Gift Aid.

15.22 Acknowledgement and advertising

HMRC Guidance Note provides:

> Some items do not count as benefits, for example:
> **Acknowledgements**
> 3.19.1 An acknowledgement of a donor's generosity, for example in a printed brochure or on a plaque. However this must be a simple acknowledgement and not an advertisement for the donor's business. So a small commemorative type plaque recording the name of the donor and that they provided a donation would be acceptable but a large sign which also promoted the donor's business would be an advert and so not

79 490 US 680 (1989). This passage is from a dissenting judgment, but it reflects the accepted practice.

allowed.

At first sight a distinction between acknowledgment and advertising seems meaningless. To most of us, the mere mention of a name of a trader or professional person is a form of advertising. But an acknowledgment/ advertising distinction may be helpful, as long as one bears in mind that it is only a way of approaching or clarifying the statutory question, which is whether there is a "benefit" within the meaning of the Gift Aid benefit rule. There are two reasons why a mere acknowledgment is not a benefit:

(1) Social norms of giving permit (and may expect or require) a donor to be acknowledged; such reputational benefit as follows from charitable giving should not be regarded as a "benefit" within the meaning of the section.
(2) The word "benefit" in tax law usually means a benefit which can be quantified in financial (money) terms, and a reputational benefit cannot be so quantified.

In fact a significant incentive for major donations is that they allow the donor to be recognised during their life, and memoralised after their death, by naming an institution, building, scholarship or academic chair. Gifts may be used to compete for places on a charitable board, and to establish social prestige.

The question is when one goes beyond mere acknowledgment or recognition. If a trading donor wants to receive more, the matter should be dealt with as a trading deduction.[80]

Whether VAT is payable should also be considered - see 35.9 (Grants and donations) for the applicable principles.

The HMRC Guidance Note provides:

> **Fund raising events in honour of a donor**
> 3.19.6 Charities that receive a large donation from a donor will often want to give some form of 'thank you' to the donor. For example they may hold a gala dinner to which they'll invite the donor as 'guest of honour', their family, friends, and other potential donors. If the purpose of the dinner is to both celebrate the donation and promote the charity to stimulate more donations from the others attending the event, this is a fund raising event and would not be treated as a benefit to the donor - the dinner is simply an opportunity to help raise more funds. However

---

80 See 18.2 (Charity gift: Deductible business expense) and 18.3 (Sponsorship: position of sponsor).

if the dinner is a private affair limited to the donor and a few guests and there's no significant element of additional fundraising involved then that's simply a private dinner for the donor and is a benefit. Trustees of charities considering holding fund-raising events of this kind can find further guidance in paragraph 3.43.

3.19.7 Where a fundraising event is held and the attendees are a mixture of previous donors and potential future donors there is still a benefit for the individual attending. The value of the benefit should be calculated using the normal rules. More information can be found at paragraph 3.43.

15.23 Naming rights

The HMRC Guidance Note originally provided:

> 3.19.7 Sometimes charities want to name a building or part of a building after a donor who's provided a substantial part of the funds to pay for the building. There's no monetary value attached to the naming of a building after an individual and therefore there's no benefit for Gift Aid purposes.

Now the paragraph reads:

> 3.19.8
> [1] Sometimes charities want to name a building or part of a building after a donor who's provided a substantial part of the funds to pay for the building. There's no monetary value attached to the naming of a building after an individual
> [2] but that does not necessarily mean there's no benefit for Gift Aid purposes. The naming of the building or part of the building needs to be unsolicited and not expected in return for the donation.

The words at [2] were added in 2019. Para [2] constitutes a reversal of HMRC practice. It is also inconsistent with point [1] because "benefit" in the Gift Aid rule specifically means a financial or monetary benefit. The point is important. We consider the original paragraph was correct.

15.24 Benefit "in consequence" of gift

Relief is not lost merely because a donor receives a benefit from the charity. The benefit must be "associated with" the gift, which means, received in consequence of the gift. This concept of causation can raise puzzling legal (and philosophical) questions, and has given rise to much discussion in many different areas of law.

There is no case law in a Gift Aid context, apart from a general comment in *Harris v HMRC*:

> [58] [Counsel for HMRC] sought to argue that a benefit would be in consequence of the making of a gift if it would not have arisen but for the gift. We do not accept this. The test is one of consequence which requires a different causal connection to a 'but for' test. It is not in our view sufficient that a benefit would not have been received but for the making of the gift. The making of the gift (including, as we have found, the underlying arrangements whereby the gift is made) must be the reason why the benefit is received; it must in short be the cause of the benefit. [Counsel for HMRC] sought to suggest further explanations of the meaning of 'in consequence of', including that the benefit must be 'integral to' the arrangements for the making of the gift, or by framing the question as: could the gift have been made other than with the benefit of the IHT saving? We do not consider that any further gloss is required to the plain meaning of 'in consequence of', which we regard as readily understandable on its own terms.[81]

In short, a "but for" test is a necessary but not a sufficient condition of causation. This is the usual legal concept of causation.[82]

In the following discussion:

the **"payment"** is the payment from the donor to the charity

the **"benefit"** is the benefit received by the donor.

15.25 Contract to provide benefit

If there is a contract under which the benefit is consideration for the payment (and the payment is consideration for the benefit) then the benefit

---

81 [2010] SFTD 1159 at [58].

82 A full discussion on causation needs a book to itself. In short, a causation test ought to be applied flexibly and in a manner sensitive to the context or purpose of the provisions.

It has been argued that the notion of causation in the law of negligence should be extended to include cases where a person contributed to a result, even though the but-for test is not satisfied. For instance, a director who voted for a resolution caused the result of the resolution even though the resolution would have been passed without that vote. See Stapleton, "Unnecessary Causes" [2013] LQR 39. It seems to us that a weakness of her argument is its exclusive focus on the tort of negligence, where an extension of the concept of causation does not matter as other rules will fill in the gap. Causation matters in many areas of the law. But that aside, this is not the normal view of causation. An individual who voted Conservative in 2015 did not cause the Conservative victory. It is also not the law even in the context of the tort of negligence.

is in consequence of the gift. It does not matter that the benefit is received before or after the time that the payment is made.[83] Since the donor is *entitled* to the benefit, it does not matter that the donor does not exercise their right to receive the benefit at all. For the right to receive the benefit is itself a benefit, received at the time of the gift. HMRC agree. The HMRC Guidance Note provides:

> 3.18.2 ... A right to receive a benefit, is also a benefit, whether or not the right is exercised.

The courts will exercise a degree of cynicism in cases where the parties have in substance agreed a fee for goods or services, there being no real doubt that the benefit will be conferred. In such a case the courts may find that there is a contractual entitlement, and dismiss any purported agreement to the contrary as a sham.

15.26 No contract to provide benefit

If there is no contract (ie no consideration), then the benefit may or may not be in consequence of the payment.

15.26.1 *Benefit before gift made*

Suppose
(1) a benefit is received by an individual from a charity, and
(2) subsequently, the individual makes a gift to the charity.
For instance, a charity may arrange a dinner for potential donors, who later make gifts. If the gifts are genuinely voluntary, this will not disqualify the gift, the benefit will not be a consequence of the gift. The gift may be a consequence of the benefit, or else independent of it.

Suppose A makes a gift to B on the understanding (not enforceable) that B will make a gift to charity. Subject to the GAAR, it is considered that Gift Aid applies.

15.26.2 *Benefits will be received*

Even in the absence of a contractual entitlement to a benefit, it is considered that Gift Aid will not apply if one can say at the time of the gift that the donor is certain to receive a benefit later. The delay alone does not prevent the benefit being "in consequence" of the gift.

---

83 Para 99 sch 2 ITA recognises that a benefit may be received before the date of the gift.

15.26.3 *Benefits may be received*

Suppose, however, that the donor is not contractually entitled to any benefit, receives no benefit at the time of the gift, and it is possible but not certain at the time of the gift, that they may receive a later benefit. Does the gift qualify for Gift Aid?

It is suggested that the condition applies if the donor receives a benefit in consequence of the gift at any time and, subject to time limits, any tax relief granted can be reclaimed by HMRC. But then the issue of whether the relief applies would never be determined (subject to time limit of assessments) because there is always a possibility of a subsequent benefit.

An alternative view is that the condition only applies if the donor receives the benefit in the same tax year as the gift. This approach is supported by the principle that income tax is an annual tax, so the question of tax relief should be determined in the year of payment. See *Vestey v IRC* 54 TC at 581 and s.4 ITA.

In practice this issue may not arise often, because a benefit which may possibly be received after the gift (but which may not be received at all) is less likely to be a benefit received in consequence of the gift.

15.27 Gift from parent to school

Payments to schools neatly raise the issue of causation. The position depends on the facts, which may need careful examination.

The payment of school fees does not qualify for Gift Aid for one and maybe two reasons:

(1) The payment is not a gift to charity: paying a fee is not a gift. (The payment involves a gift of education to the child, but Gift Aid requires a gift of a sum of money to a charity.)

(2) The benefit rule may apply: if the payor is a parent or grandparent, a connected person (the child) receives a benefit (education) in consequence of the gift. This does not arise if school fees are paid by a person who is not "connected" to the child (eg by an uncle or unrelated friend); but it does not matter as point (1) is sufficient.

Suppose parents are invited to make donations to the school. Suppose the payment is not obligatory, and all children receive the same treatment regardless of whether their parents contribute.[84] Yet as a result of the

84 In England this is required by law: s. 460 Education Act 1996.

donations as a whole, their children as a body receive some advantage. Is this a benefit "in consequence of" the gift?

The answer can be found this way. Suppose only one parent, A, gave a donation. A's child would benefit from the gift; but that benefit would clearly be *de minimis.* All the other schoolchildren benefit equally. Now suppose other parents also made donations. Those donations benefit A's child; but those benefits are not in consequence of A's gift. So A's donation still qualifies for relief under the Gift Aid rule.

It follows that gifts by parents to schools qualify for Gift Aid, provided that:

(1) All children are treated equally, regardless of parental contribution; and

(2) One parent's donation is not conditional on donations by others.

However, HMRC Guidance Note now states:

> **3.34 Educational trusts**
> 3.34.1 This section explains when educational trusts (Trusts)[85] can claim Gift Aid in respect of payments made to such Trusts by parents and persons connected to a pupil.
> 3.34.2 A Trust is established to provide education for children as an alternative to state education. Parents may pay for textbooks, exercise books, exam fees and consumable materials. However, they're often not required to pay any set fees to cover the costs of tuition and other overheads, but instead may make payments described as donations.
> 3.34.3 The payment of fees to a charity is not a gift to charity and so fees paid to a Trust are not eligible for the Gift Aid Scheme. Whether non-fee payments (donations) made by parents (and persons connected to them) to a Trust qualify as Gift Aid payments depends upon the surrounding circumstances and the situation for each Trust is judged on its own merits.
> 3.34.4 There's a cost in providing education for a child and if that cost is met in consequence of the Gift Aid payments being made to the Trust then that cost is a benefit for the purposes of the Gift Aid Scheme. This includes the cost of tuition, heating and lighting of premises and other administrative costs, which would be taken into account by a private school in setting fees.

More analytically, the benefit is the education provided to the child, not the cost. But that does not matter: the important point is that the child

85 Authors' footnote: It is assumed that the educational trust is a charity.

receives a benefit.

> Whether or not a benefit is received 'in consequence of' the Gift Aid payments is a question of fact to be determined in the light of the surrounding circumstances. In particular, it's important to consider whether the Trust would be able to meet the costs of providing the education in the absence of the donations.
> In considering whether the level of fees is sufficient to cover operating costs trusts can take account of reliable, ongoing income sources such as endowments, but not one-off or periodic donations or grants where no binding commitment exists.

Why not?

> 3.34.5 As far as alternative sources of funding are concerned, these are relevant only in as much as they form part of all the circumstances a court might look at in deciding whether the overall funding structure was genuinely able to maintain the activities of the charitable trust to the extent that additional contributions from individuals receiving a benefit were unnecessary.
> 3.34.6 Where the trust has a genuine fee structure in place HMRC will accept that the benefit of receiving education arises from payment of the fees. Consequently, the receipt of education would not be received as a consequence of making donations over and above the fees and so those donations could qualify for Gift Aid. A genuine fee structure is one where fees are charged in respect of all students and the fees are set at such a level that enables the Trust to operate without needing additional support.
> 3.34.7 Where there's no fee structure or only nominal fees are charged, insufficient to enable the trust to operate without additional donations the additional donations give rise to a benefit. Such consequential benefits will generally be in excess of the benefit limits for donations made by parents and persons connected to them and so the donations will usually fail as Gift Aid payments.
> 3.34.8 Where there's no fee structure or only nominal fees are charged, but sufficient alternative, unconnected, funding sources can be clearly identified, there will be no benefit arising as a consequence of donations from persons connected with the children receiving education. In situations where this is clearly the case, providing the other Gift Aid criteria are met, Gift Aid relief might (?) be available on those donations.

The fact (if it be a fact) that the school does not need a donation to operate is likely to be sufficient to show that the child of the donor does not receive a benefit in consequence of the donor's gift. On that basis HMRC say:

> Donations given for the following will usually qualify for Gift Aid:
> - building appeals
> - equipment appeals[86]

But the converse does not hold: it is not correct to say that where a school *does* need donations to operate, it follows that a child *does* receive a benefit from the parent's gift. HMRC have sometimes accepted this, notwithstanding the official policy set out in the Guidance Note.

15.28 *School trip*

School trips raise the same point, though the sums involved are much smaller. HMRC Guidance Note provides:

> 3.35.1 This section is intended for charitable schools and Parent Teacher Associations (PTAs)[87] who want to know if Gift Aid can be used in respect of voluntary contributions toward educational school trips.
> 3.35.2 In schools, other than independent fee paying schools, the education provided wholly or mainly during school hours is free. This means that head teachers may not impose a charge on parents for any visit that is undertaken as part of the National Curriculum and occurs during school hours. The head teacher may, however, ask for a voluntary contribution.
> Parents must be made aware that the contribution is not compulsory, and the children of parents who do not contribute must not be discriminated against. It's permissible for the school to ask parents to contribute more than the minimum amount in order to subsidise those pupils whose parents have not contributed. However, if there are not enough voluntary contributions and the shortfall cannot be made up, the visit may have to be cancelled.

We are not sure about the last sentence. In practice, we suspect that in many cases the school would use its funds to cover the shortfall. But perhaps that is what the author means by raising the possibility that the shortfall could be "made up".

---

86 HMRC, "Gift Aid donation claims for charities and CASCs" *https://www.gov.uk/guidance/gift-aid-what-donations-charities-and-cascs-can-claim-on#donations-to-schools-charities-involved-in-running-schools-and-educational-trusts*

87 Authors' footnote: It is assumed that the PTAs are charities.

> Such voluntary contributions to charitable schools or PTAs may be eligible for tax relief under the Gift Aid Scheme, provided the usual requirements of the scheme are satisfied and in particular:
>
> - parental contributions are made on the basis that they're not refundable (and are not in any event refunded) if the trip does not go ahead or if their child does not go on the trip
> - any benefit arising from the school trip does not exceed the maximum level of permissible benefit for the donation as explained below
>
> [The guidance summarises the small benefit limits, and continues:]
> Benefits include travel costs, trip insurance, cost of entry and associated educational material, cost of food and drink supplied and any other costs associated with the trip (costs averaged per pupil if appropriate).
> In general, however, it is likely that the benefits associated with a school trip contribution will exceed the maximum level of permissible benefits and so the donation will not come within the Gift Aid Scheme.
> **Example 1**
> The cost of an educational trip to a local museum amounts to £8 (transport £5 entry £2 and brochure £1). The school asks for a voluntary contribution of £10.
> The payment of £10 cannot be made under the Gift Aid Scheme as the benefit of £8 exceeds the 25% limit (80%).

We do not agree with example 1. It is correct that the child receives a benefit (the trip). But the benefit that the child receives is not a consequence of the *parent's* gift: it is a consequence of all the gifts made (as a whole) by unconnected persons. The case is clear if the facts are that the trip would go ahead whether or not a particular parent made their gift.

The HMRC Guidance Note concludes:

> However, where a payment is made in excess of the requested contribution the excess can be Gift Aided provided the requested contribution meets the cost of the trip (the benefit).
> **Example 2**
> The position is the same as in example 1 but a parent makes a voluntary contribution of £15 instead of the requested £10. The additional £5 can be made as a Gift Aid payment.

That is not contentious.

15.28.1 *Non-uniform day*

HMRC formerly said, in an attractively illustrated but technically lightweight publication:[88]

> ***Non-uniform days***
> *School charities often raise funds by organising non-uniform days. In return for the payment of a small fee[89] the child does not wear school uniform to school. The funds raised may be donated to an unconnected charity or may be donated to the school charity. Such payments only qualify as charitable donations if there is no link between who pays and the student who is allowed not to wear school uniform.*
> *In this example all pupils would need to be allowed not to wear school uniform, whether or not they have made a donation, in order for the payments received to be charitable donations.*
> *If the pupil has to pay to be allowed not to wear school uniform then this is not a charitable donation.*
> *As non-uniform days are normally organised so that pupils must make a donation to be allowed not to wear school uniform then payments made for such non-uniform days will not qualify for Gift Aid or Payroll Giving.*

HMRC did not say why Gift Aid is disallowed. One possible argument is that the payment is not a gift. Another is that the child receives a benefit - the privilege of not having to wear school uniform for a day. We think the payment may properly be described as a gift and the value of the benefit is nil. The privilege of not wearing school uniform is no more than a piece of fun and an acknowledgement of the gift, like a lapel sticker or poppy. Gift Aid does in principle apply on no-uniform days.

It appears that HMRC now accept this view. The publication was withdrawn in 2015.[90] HMRC now say:

> Donations given for the following will usually qualify for Gift Aid:
> - non-uniform days
> - sponsored events[91]

In practice this issue may not arise in a Gift Aid context as (1) the amount

---

88 "Gift Aid & Payroll Giving: A reference guide for school charities" (2011) *https://webarchive.nationalarchives.gov.uk/20120406073751/http://www.hmrc.gov.uk/charities/gift_aid/rules/school-charities-ezine.pdf*

89 Authors' footnote: The word "fee" is not apt to describe the nature of the payment.

90 Stated in the above URL, accessed 2 June 2015.

91 HMRC, "Gift Aid donation claims for charities and CASCs" *https://www.gov.uk/guidance/gift-aid-what-donations-charities-and-cascs-can-claim-on#donations-to-schools-charities-involved-in-running-schools-and-educational-trusts*

of each donation may be too small to justify a Gift Aid claim; and (2) the donor must be a taxpayer, and if the donor is the child (not the parent) they will not be a taxpayer. The point also matters for the Gift Aid Small Donation Scheme[92] but the amount involved will be small, because of the very low limit on GASDS claims.

15.29 Gift to support charity worker

The HMRC Guidance Note provides at 3.26:

> **Donations to support missionaries and other full-time[93] workers for a charitable cause**
> 3.26.1 Gift Aid only applies to unfettered gifts to a charity for its charitable purposes. Donors earmarking money for the support of relatives are, in principle, no different from those generally making payments to support other relatives, for whatever reason. These are not eligible for tax relief.

It is difficult to agree or disagree with this because of the imprecise terms "unfettered" and "earmark". In the context we take "fettered" and "earmarked" to mean a payment subject to a condition that the funds must be used (1) to provide a benefit for the individual and (2) not for charitable purposes. So read, this paragraph is correct. The payments are disqualified from Gift Aid for two reasons: they are not payments to charity and a connected person receives a benefit. The HMRC Guidance Note continues:

> Once a Gift Aid payment has been received it's for the charity to show that its income has been applied for charitable purposes only.

It would be pedantic to object that Gift Aid as such applies regardless of whether income is applied for charitable purposes.[94] HMRC's point is that if the charity does not apply the income for charitable purposes, one might well infer that the gift was made subject to a condition which prevents it from counting as a payment to charity. The HMRC Guidance Note continues:

> Gifts given on condition, rather than hope or expectation, that they'll be used to feed and clothe a relative are likely to breach the benefits rules

---

92 See 16.9.8 (GASDS benefit rule).

93 Although the heading refers to full-time workers, the same principles must govern part-time workers.

94 Though mis-application has other tax consequences.

> for Gift Aid.
> 3.26.2 HMRC takes the view that donations to cover the costs incurred by a charity such as a missionary society in supporting the relative of the donor, as a missionary, can qualify under the Gift Aid Scheme provided the missionary society is not merely channelling a donation to the donor's relative.

The HMRC Guidance Note goes on to explain what is meant by "merely channelling":

> [1] Where, for example, a missionary society says to its workers 'It costs us £10,000 a year to support you while you carry out your charitable work. We look to you to raise at least this amount of funds for the society through donations from family, etc' the donations may qualify under the Gift Aid Scheme.
> [2] Where, on the other hand, a missionary society says to its missionaries 'It is up to you to support yourself while you carry out your charitable work, with the help of your family, etc. If your family wishes to send you money they can do so via the Society' payments will not qualify under the Gift Aid Scheme.

Gift Aid does not apply in case [2] because there is no payment to charity; see 15.6 (Gift "to a charity"). What is more important is that HMRC accept Gift Aid does apply in case [1].

> 3.26.3 This situation equally applies where a church, for example, supports the charitable work of a Christian worker. The Christian worker is unlikely to be in the employment of the Church and so the onus in demonstrating that payments made to particular individuals are unfettered and only applied for charitable purposes falls to the trustees of the church.

Thus where T make a gift to a charity, and the money is used to pay T's salary, or the salary of an employee who is connected to T (or who is T himself) then HMRC accept Gift Aid applies. The reason is not clearly stated. It is considered that the payment of a fair salary is not a benefit.[95] It is also arguable that provided the charity is free to do what it likes with the money, the benefit (if any) is not in consequence of the gift. It is in consequence of the charity's independent decision to make the payment. This illustrates the importance of correct documentation.

---

95 See Kessler & John, *Drafting Trusts and Will Trusts* (14th ed, 2019), para 6.54 (Trustee remuneration clause: dispositive or administrative?).

15.30 Adventure fundraising events

This section concerns adventure fundraising events of the kind described in HMRC Guidance Note para 3.38.1:

> 3.38.1 Some charities organise adventure challenge events, frequently overseas treks and bike rides, (events) to raise funds. For example, cycling in Cuba, rafting the Grand Canyon or trekking in China. The same principles apply to similar events in the UK (for example, parachute jumps, helicopter flights).

We use the following terminology:
The **"participant"** is the person who takes part in the event.
The "**event cost**" is the payment made by the charity to the event organiser, the third party who organises the event on behalf of the charity (or if there is no event organiser, the costs directly incurred by the charity.)
The "**participation fee**" is the amount that the participant is required to pay towards the event cost.
The "**minimum sponsorship amount**" is the amount which the charity requires the participant to raise.

15.30.1 *Participator fee less than cost*

The HMRC Guidance Note first considers the position where the participation fee is less than the event cost:

> 3.38.2 Participants are asked to pay a non-refundable deposit/ registration fee (say, £200) and to raise sponsorship of a minimum set amount (say, £2,500) in return for going on the event.
> 3.38.3 The charity pays a third party to arrange the event (say, £1,200). The payment covers all a participant's costs, (travel, insurance, provision of specialist equipment (bike, raft etc), food, accommodation etc).
> **Gift Aid**
> 3.38.4 Sponsorship payments are eligible for the Gift Aid Scheme provided all the normal requirements of the scheme are satisfied, including the benefit rules. The relationship of the sponsor to the participant - whether they are 'connected' persons - generally decides whether sponsorship may be Gift Aided. [The guidance then outlines the definition of connected person].[96]

The HMRC Guidance Note continues:

---

96 See 15.32.1 ("Connected person").

> 3.38.5 In most instances a participant will receives a benefit equal to the cost of the event, less any payment they personally make towards the cost of the event (including any deposit/registration fee payable). Where the value of the benefit exceeds the permitted levels Gift Aid will not be available.

It is correct that the participant receives a benefit. (The words "in most instances" are presumably to allow for the exception where the participation fee equals the cost, which is discussed below.) It is not self-evident that the value of the benefit should be based on the cost of the event to the charity (less, of course, any participation fee) but that is a practical way of valuing the benefit, and should be taken as correct. This basis of valuation will normally favour the taxpayer (though often the precise value will not matter).

15.30.2 *Unconnected sponsor*

The HMRC Guidance Note provides:

> **Sponsors who are not connected persons**
> 3.38.7 Sponsorship payments made by persons not connected to the participant can be made under Gift Aid. So, if all the sponsorship raised by a participant is donated by persons not connected to the participant then all of those individual payments can be Gift Aided.

This is correct.

15.30.3 *Connected sponsor*

The HMRC Guidance Note provides:

> **Sponsors who are connected persons**
> 3.38.6 Sponsorship payments made by persons connected to the participant also, usually, fail the donor benefit rules (where the participant receives a benefit) and so will not qualify for Gift Aid but see para 3.38.9.

A gift is not disqualified merely because the donor receives a benefit. The donor (or connected person) must receive the benefit *in consequence of* the gift.

If the gifts made by the participant (and connected persons) are needed in order to reach the minimum sponsorship amount, then the benefit is in consequence of the gift.

The position is different if:

(1) The participant raises the minimum sponsorship amount (or more)

from non-connected persons. The participant then becomes entitled to attend the event whether or not they (and connected persons) make any further donations.

(2) The participant (and connected persons) subsequently make gifts.

The subsequent gifts are neither a necessary nor sufficient condition for receiving the benefit. In those circumstances the benefit should not be regarded as a "consequence" of those donations, and the donations qualify for Gift Aid.[97] Perhaps this is why the HMRC Guidance Note is qualified by the word "usually".

The best course, therefore, where the participant does not pay the full event fee is that:

(1) The participant fundraises from non-connected persons until they have raised the minimum sponsored amount.
(2) The participant then fundraises from connected persons.

15.30.4 *Payment from participator*

The HMRC Guidance Note states:

> **Participant**
> 3.38.8 Any deposit/registration fee paid by a participant will not be a donation to the charity and so cannot be a Gift Aid payment.

This is correct.

> Any donation made by the participant may also fail the benefit rules and cannot be Gift Aided.

The position is the same as for connected persons; this may explain why the guidance is qualified by the word "may".

15.30.5 *Participator fee exceeds cost*

The HMRC Guidance Note considers the case where the participation fee equals the event cost:

> **The participant pays the full cost of the event.**
> 3.38.9 If a participant personally pays the charity the full advertised cost of the event from his own resources, the value of the benefit of participating is reduced to nil. The benefit rules still apply but in this instance the value of the benefit will be nil. So, while the sum paid by

---

97 The benefit is (in philosophical terminology) *over determined*, that is, it has several causes, any one of which would have been enough to trigger the receipt on its own.

> the participant to meet the full cost of taking part in the event cannot be Gift Aided, the donations made by others (both connected and not connected persons) can be Gift Aided.
> 3.38.10 In the example above the benefit, which would arise is the full cost of the trip as advertised by the charity - £1,200 (that is, £200 deposit/registration fee plus £1,000 for the balance of the trip). If the participant pays the charity £1,200 they will reduce that benefit to nil. None of this payment will be a gift to the charity so none of the £1,200 can be a Gift Aid payment.
> 3.38.11 If the participant reduces the benefit to nil by paying the full cost of the trip then all sponsorship paid, whether by connected persons or otherwise, can be Gift Aided.

It is obviously correct that if the participation fee equals the value of the event, there is no benefit. The HMRC Guidance Note muddles or fudges the valuation issue by referring to the full *advertised* cost, but it assumes that the advertised cost is the sum the charity pays to the event organiser. Perhaps the point it seeks to make is that if the event costs the charity £1200 but the charity requires a participation fee of £1300, the value of the benefit should be regarded as the full £1300. In practice charities will no doubt set the participation fee equal to the event cost, or their best estimate of the cost, and that will suffice.

15.30.6 *Duty on charity*

The HMRC Guidance Note provides:

> 3.38.12 Charities should take all reasonable steps to ensure that Gift Aid payments are not received from persons connected to a participant. HMRC recognises that, in practice, a charity cannot be expected to check whether a participant and their sponsors are connected persons. However, a participating charity must include in the event literature and on the sponsorship form:
> - an explanation that sponsors connected to a participant cannot make their donations by Gift Aid unless exceptionally the participant pays the full advertised cost of the event
> - the definition of a 'connected person' (see paragraph 3.36).[98]

---

98 The full definition would take a page, and a full discussion of it needs a long chapter to itself. See 15.32.1 (Connected person). We suggest that the charity should in practice adopt the (incomplete) definition given in the HMRC Guidance Note para 3.38.4:

> "A 'connected person' is a person that is connected with a donor if that person is:
> - the wife, husband or civil partner

This passage is clearly not intended to apply where the participation fee equals the event cost[99].

We also do not think this would be appropriate in cases where the payments made by non-connected persons have exceeded the minimum set amount and have been received before receipt of the payments from the connected persons. But of course at the time the literature is prepared it may not be known whether this will be the case.

15.30.7 *Planning*

There are three ways to deal with adventure fundraising events:

(1) The participation fee may be less than the event cost. From a tax viewpoint, this is not the best course as it will lose Gift Aid on all (or at least a very substantial part) of the donations from the participator and connected persons.

(2) A better route is one under which the participator promises to pay the entire event cost[100] in return for going on the event. In this case Gift Aid will apply to all donations made apart from the participation payment.

(3) The best route for tax (but the most complex) is to provide that the donor must pay the event cost only so far as it exceeds donations received from unconnected persons, that is they must make a top-up payment. In this case, Gift Aid will apply to the gifts made by unconnected persons, and to gifts made by the participant and connected persons (except so far as the participant's top-up payment is made, if any is needed).

There are fundraising and cultural issues to consider apart from the tax: donors may not wish to sponsor a participant who is not "paying his way".

The documentation (which HMRC describe as event literature) needs to be drafted with the Gift Aid aspects in mind.

- a relative (brother, sister, ancestor (for example, mother) or lineal descendant (for example, grandson)
- the wife, husband or civil partner of a relative
- a company under the control of the donor, or under control of connected persons."

99 The passage was written before para 3.38.9 and 3.38.11 were added to the HMRC Guidance Note, but the author of those paragraphs failed to read to the end of the section and make the necessary consequential amendments.

100 Or any discount from the event cost falls within the permitted small benefit exemption.

15.31 Membership subscription

The terms member/membership cover a variety of distinct circumstances:

(1) Membership of company/unincorporated association:

  (a) Membership of company: this is a status, governed by company law, conferring on the member the rights and obligations set out in the company articles.

  (b) Membership of an unincorporated association (eg a club): this is a status, governed by contract law, conferring on the member the rights and obligations set out in the association constitution.

  We refer to this as **"formal membership"** and it will typically confer at least the right to vote and attend an AGM.

(2) An organisation may designate persons as "members" of the organisation, who are not (or need not be) members of the company or association in the formal sense (1). These members have rights and obligations set out in the contract. An example is members of a privately owned gym. The term "Friends" may also be used in this context. We refer to this as **"informal membership"**.

Membership generally requires some payment ("membership subscription"). The Gift Aid questions which arise are:

(1) Is the membership subscription a gift?

(2) If so, what is the value of benefits (if any) received as a result of the gift?

It is obviously impossible to answer that in the abstract. The nature of the subscription, and the benefits received as a result of that subscription, depend on the articles, constitution, or contract concerned. The subscription may or may not be a gift. Membership benefits (if any) may be valuable benefits, small benefits, or of no value at all.

The donor benefit consultation paper provides:

> 2.20 For the specific purpose of this review a 'member' is defined as someone who is given particular benefits or subscription rights for a fixed and specified period, e.g. one year, in return for a donation. Membership benefits therefore refer to the specific benefits that are provided in return for that donation.

The HMRC Guidance Note, we think, assumes this definition without expressly saying so, ie it assumes that the membership confers "particular benefits or subscription rights".

15.31.1 *"Membership subscription"*

HMRC Guidance Note provides:

> **3.37 Membership subscriptions**
> 3.37.1 There's a statutory requirement, under Gift Aid, for payments to be gifts. This means that payments that are made to acquire goods or services are not eligible for Gift Aid. However, there are rules within the Gift Aid legislation that allow charities to provide donors with token benefits, within specified limits, in recognition of their gifts.

This is basic and uncontroversial, and introductory to the main point:

> 3.37.2 [a] Most membership subscriptions are not gifts, they're made to gain access to the facilities and services provided by the charity.
> [b] However, membership subscriptions paid to charities that secure voting rights and the right to attend a charity's AGM are gifts provided they meet the conditions in the next paragraph. These payments will, of course, still have to satisfy the benefit rules referred to above.
> 3.37.3 The conditions referred to are that the:
> - payments do no more than secure membership of the charity
> - payments do not secure a right to personal use of any facilities or services provided by the charity

There are two propositions here.

The point at 3.37.2[b] and 3.37.3 is straightforward. Formal membership subscriptions to a charity, that confer only the right to vote and attend an AGM, qualify for Gift Aid, as
(1) They are gifts and
(2) The right to vote and attend an AGM is not a benefit, or is a benefit of nil value.

The point at 3.37.2[a] is that "most" membership subscriptions are "made to gain access to facilities[101] provided by the charity". This may be true, though it is not self-evident. However that may be, in at least some cases, charity membership subscriptions
(1) do not provide access to facilities or other benefits or
(2) provide access to facilities or benefits of small value and no-one pays

101 We refer to "facilities" as a shorthand for "facilities and services", the expression used in HMRC Guidance Note.

the subscription to gain access to them.

The second proposition is that payments that are "made to gain access to facilities" are not gifts, and so are not eligible for Gift Aid. This is only correct as a general proposition if one adds the words "wholly or mainly" after the word "made". If one makes a payment and receives goods or services of trivial value, the payment may be described as a gift.[102]

This is confirmed by s.430 ITA which provides:

> (1) In this Chapter "charity" includes ...
>
> (d) a club that is registered as a community amateur sports club for the purposes of Chapter 9 of part 13 of CTA 2010.
>
> (2) For the purposes of the application of s.414(1) *in relation to clubs that are charities as a result of subsection (1)(d) of this section*, membership fees are not gifts.
>
> (Emphasis added)

It is assumed that membership fees in relation to a charity (except a registered community amateur sports club) *can* be a gift.

However, this point does not much matter in practice because HMRC, having stated their position very broadly, go on to withdraw from it.

The HMRC Guidance Note draws a distinction[103] between:

(1) Mere membership.

(2) Provision of facilities.

It begins with examples of what HMRC regard as acceptable:

> 3.37.4 The provision to members of, for example,
>
> [1] periodic newsletters explaining the work of the charity, or
>
> [2] opportunities to visit and view the work of the charity would not breach these conditions.
>
> [3] So, a wildlife conservation charity that allowed members admission to its sites to view its conservation work would not be regarded as providing services or facilities for personal use.
>
> The payment of a subscription to a charity to simply receive a copy of its magazine is not a payment to become a member of the charity. Such a payment is the purchase of a magazine subscription and cannot be Gift Aided.
>
> 3.37.5 Similarly,

102 See 15.4 ("Gift").

103 The Note makes the same distinction at 3.46.7.

[4] opportunity to take part in activities by which the charity carried out its charitable objectives are acceptable as long as the activities do not amount to making personal use of its facilities.

[5] a youth organisation that provided various activities in furtherance of its broader educational objectives would not be regarded as providing services or facilities for personal use.

Then the HMRC Guidance Note turns to what HMRC regard as unacceptable:

> 3.37.6 Membership subscriptions that secure the right to personal use of facilities or services are not gifts. So, for example,
>
> [1] subscriptions that are made in order to obtain for an individual or individuals' tuition, coaching or other educational instruction are not gifts
>
> [2] Similarly, subscriptions to a sports charity or a charitable film society are not acceptable if they secured for members the free or discounted use of, say, a golf course or a swimming pool or the viewing of films that are not available on similar terms to non-members.

In the examples given in para 3.37.6 relief would in principle be lost under the benefit rule. If the value of the benefit fell within the "small benefit" rules (eg if a subscription allowed only one free swim per year) then Gift Aid would be applicable. But perhaps that will not often arise.

The distinction is similar to the elusive but important charity law distinction between public and private benefits.

HMRC accept that membership subscriptions to choral societies in principle fall on the right side of the line and do qualify for Gift Aid.[104]

---

104 *Taxation* 5 February 2009 p.126. See too the HMRC Guidance Note on membership subscriptions which offers this example:

"**Additional charges on top of a subscription**

If your charity provides a basic membership and charges separately for other activities and benefits, only the basic membership subscription will qualify for Gift Aid. The additional charges won't qualify.

Example

A musical society charges a basic membership subscription of £180 a year, with additional rehearsal or playing charges of £10 per hour. In the first month that Jane joins the society she pays £45, of which £15 is her monthly membership subscription and £30 is for three additional playing sessions. Only £15 of the total £45 paid can qualify for Gift Aid."

https://www.gov.uk/gift-aid-what-donations-charities-and-cascs-can-claim-on#professional-organisation-membership-fees

15.31.2 *Subscription: Split payments*

The HMRC Guidance Note continues with some tax planning advice:

> 3.37.7 Where a charity separates
> [1] that part of the membership subscription that simply gives the basic rights of membership and does no more than cover the basic administration costs of the charity from
> [2] any part that relates to the provision of services or facilities
> the membership element can be a gift.
> So, for example, a sports charity that charges a basic membership subscription, with additional, variable, training or playing charges depending on the member's standard, could regard the basic membership as a gift. The additional training or playing charges could not be treated as gifts.
> A charity that charges a standard membership fee that covers membership and participation could not treat any part of the subscription as a gift if participation in the activities involved personal use of services or facilities.

Documentation is, once again, very important. How does one apportion the total payment? See 15.33 (Multiple/single/split payments).

15.31.3 *Paying another's subscription*

The HMRC Guidance Note continues:

> **Family membership**
> 3.37.8 Many organisations offer family membership arrangements that give all the rights of individual membership, but at a reduced cost. Where a charity offers family membership the subscription is a gift to the charity provided the subscription:
> - secures membership for the donor
> - satisfies the conditions in 'Membership subscriptions'
>
> 3.37.9 The fact that the subscription gives members of the donor's family rights of membership too does not change this as the payment is, primarily, a gift from the donor to the charity. The donor must, however, be the person who has given a Gift Aid declaration to the charity.
> **Paying other people's subscriptions**
> 3.37.10 The payment to a charity to secure individual membership rights for a person other than the donor are not gifts to the charity. This includes an individual membership purchased for a family member (spouse, parent etc) that's not secured as part of a family membership scheme. This is because although the payment is made to the charity the gift is to the person whose membership subscription is being paid.

> However, this does not extend to payments made in respect of a donor's minor children (children under 18 years of age). So, a payment that satisfies the conditions to be treated as a gift if made in respect of the donor personally will be accepted as a gift if it's made for their minor child.[105]

Elsewhere HMRC say:

> [1] Gift Aid can't be claimed on a subscription payment paid on behalf of someone else. This is because it's considered a gift to the person whose membership is paid, not to the charity.
> [2] However, if the membership is paid for a child (under the age of 18), payment is accepted as a gift and is eligible.[106]

Point [1] is wrong because the fact that payment may be said to be a gift to the person whose membership is paid does not preclude it being a gift to the charity. The two are not inconsistent. If someone sponsors a friend running a marathon, they make a gift to charity, even though everyone knows it is also a favour to the friend. Point [2] is also not compatible with the argument at point [1].

15.31.4 *HMRC view*: *Critique*

The HMRC Guidance Note on membership is misguided or at least not well drafted. Whether a payment to charity is a "membership subscription" is an unhelpful way to approach the question. "Membership" is not a thing. It is simply a label for a set of rights or facilities whose content varies from one membership to another. A membership of a gym has nothing in common with membership of the Tiffany circle. This is the error of reification. The relevant questions are: does the donor receive a benefit in return for their gift and if so does the value of the benefit exceed the Gift Aid limits?

15.32 Benefit to connected/associated person

The benefit rule applies if a benefit is received by the donor or by a person

---

105 In the 2013 edition of this book, we noted that the HMRC Guidance Note inconsistently stated that HMRC did "not accept that payments made to a charity to secure individual membership rights for a person other than the donor ae gifts to the charity...", but this has now been deleted.

106 HMRC, "Gift Aid: what donations charities and CASCs can claim on"(8 Dec 2014) *https://www.gov.uk/gift-aid-what-donations-charities-and-cascs-can-claim-on*

connected with the donor.[107]

15.32.1 *"Connected person"*

"Connected person" is defined in s.993 ITA.[108] A full discussion of the definition needs a long chapter to itself, and is not considered here because James Kessler has dealt with it elsewhere.[109]

In outline, an individual ("A") is connected with another person ("B") if—

(a) A is B's spouse.[110]
(b) A is a relative of B; "relative" here means brother, sister, ancestor or lineal descendant.
(c) A is the spouse of a relative of B.
(d) A is a relative of B's spouse.
(e) A is the spouse of a relative of B's spouse.
(f) A is a partner of B.
(g) B is a company of which A has control.

The corporate Gift Aid rule is slightly different: it relates to benefits received by *associated* persons (whereas the IT rule relates to benefits received by *connected* persons).[111]

15.32.2 *Date of connection*

The benefit must be received by the donor or a person connected with them. Assuming that receipt of benefits after the gift may disqualify the relief, the question arises whether the person must be "connected":

(1) at the time of the gift; or
(2) at the time of the receipt of the benefit; or
(3) at either or both of these times.

This question would arise for instance if the benefit was provided after the death of the donor. It is considered that view (2) is the better reading of the statute; this view has not always been accepted by HMRC.

---

107 See 15.20 (Benefit rule: Condition F).

108 See s.1021(1) ITA.

109 See Kessler, *Taxation of Non-Residents and Foreign Domiciliaries* (21st ed., 2021-22), Chapter 101 (Control, Connected, Close and Related Expressions) online version *https://www.foreigndomiciliaries.co.uk*

110 In this section we use the word "spouse" to include a civil partner.

111 See 17.4.6 (Benefit rule: CGA condition F).

15.32.3 *Benefit to connected charity*

A donor is connected to the trustees of a settlement of which they are a settlor. A person is a settlor if they have provided any funds for the purpose of a settlement. That includes a charitable trust.

This raises a set of problems. Suppose:

(1) a donor makes a gift (the "Original Gift") to a charity ("charity A"), and a gift to another charity ("charity B, a charitable trust").
(2) Charity A shortly afterwards makes a gift to charity B.

It seems at first sight that Gift Aid on the Original Gift is lost because:
(1) The donor is connected with Charity B and
(2) Charity B receives a benefit in consequence of the Original Gift

This is part of a wider problem. Suppose:
(1) A donor makes a gift to a charitable trust and
(2) The donor then makes a second gift to the same trust.

It seems at first sight that Gift Aid relief on the second gift is lost, because:
(1) the donor is connected with the charity and
(2) the charity receives a benefit in consequence of the gift

Indeed even on the first gift the relief should be lost, as the donor becomes connected at the time of making the first gift.

One might think that this applies only to charitable trusts, and not charitable companies. A person is in general only "connected" with a company if they have control over it, or if persons connected with them have control of it.[112] Thus at least the charitable companies to which the donor has contributed funds are not "connected" with them and not within the scope of the connected person rule. But even this is not clear. A charitable company may be a "settlement" in the wide sense given to that word.[113] The company is also a "trustee" of this "settlement".[114] So the same problem arises.

No-one would seriously suggest that Gift Aid should be lost in these circumstances. The question is how to reach that conclusion.

One might simply say that the context shows that benefits to charity do

---

112 See s.993(6) ITA.
113 See s.620 ITTOIA.
114 See s.994(3) ITA.

not count. Or one might refer to *Von Ernst & Cie SA v IRC*.[115] In that case the issue was whether trust property was excluded property. The requirement was that:

> All known persons for whose *benefit* the settled property or income from it has been or might be applied ... are persons neither domiciled nor resident in the United Kingdom.[116]
> (Emphasis added)

In *Von Ernst* the beneficiaries consisted of:
(1) individuals who were not domiciled or resident in the UK; and
(2) two UK charities, a charitable trust and a charitable company

HMRC argued that the condition was not satisfied, since income might be applied for the benefit of the charities. It was stressed that a charitable company is the beneficial owner of its assets. But the Court of Appeal held that the condition was satisfied. The payment of money to the charitable trust, or even to the charitable company, was not "for the benefit" of the charities in the sense intended by the statute. It was for the "benefit" of the object of the charities. This would now be classified as a purposive construction. The Court of Appeal noted that there was no "possible ground of fiscal policy" which could justify the denial of the relevant tax relief. The same reasoning should be applied in the Gift Aid context.

15.33 Multiple/single/split payments

15.33.1 *Multiple v single payment*

There is a distinction between:
(1) *A multiple payment:* Eg, an individual makes:
    (a) a gift of (say) £50 combined with
    (b) a separate payment of £50 in return for a benefit.
(2) *A single payment:* An individual makes a payment of £100 in return for a benefit of £50.

In case (1) the £50 gift qualifies in principle for Gift Aid. In case (2) the £100 single payment does not in principle qualify for Gift Aid (but see below).

The distinction is a formal one in that it rests on the documentation: the

---

115 [1980] STC 111.
116 See s.48(4)(b) IHTA.

same economic result might be achieved either way.[117]

When are there two payments? One must look at all the circumstances and ask if a business person would regard the payment as one or two.[118] The clearest case of a multiple payment is if there are two separate payments, eg two cheques, but this is not strictly necessary. One cheque (or other money transfer) may constitute two distinct payments (a gift and a non-gift).

15.33.2 *Split payments*

HMRC Guidance Note provides:

> **3.25 Split Payments**
> 3.25.1 When a benefit given to a donor would exceed the benefit limits - so Gift Aid could not be claimed - it may be possible for the donor's payment to be split between an amount to cover the cost of the benefit and an amount that is treated as a gift. To do this the cost of the benefit is taken away from the total amount given to the charity and the remainder treated as the donation. Gift Aid can only be applied to the remainder if the:
> - benefit can be purchased separately by members of the public, who can choose not to make a donation
> - donor knows the value of the benefit they will receive, at the time the donation is made
>
> It's important that the donor is made aware by the charity of the 'split' between the amount that is to be treated as a qualifying donation and the amount that is used to purchase the benefit. This is to make sure the donor pays enough basic rate tax to cover the Gift Aid claim made by the charity and claim the correct amount of tax relief if they're a higher rate taxpayer.
> 3.25.2 The charity and donor should keep evidence of how the payment was to be split for example a copy of a dated letter accompanying the payment. Alternatively, separate payments could be made.

If separate payments are made, then the gift-payment qualifies for relief in the normal way. If a single payment is made, then relief is strictly concessionary, though the guidance note does not describe it as such. The HMRC Guidance Note gives two examples:

---

117 Compare *Spectros v Madden* 70 TC 349; see 23.4 ("Consideration"). A similar distinction is draw in the IHT gift with reservation rules.

118 We can take guidance from the approach of the courts to the CGT issue of whether there is one settlement or two.

Example 1
An arts charity has a patron scheme where, for a donation of £1,000, an individual can become a patron. In return the charity provides the benefit of ten free tickets (value £20 per ticket at the box office) for forthcoming events. In this case then the benefit received by the donor for the free tickets is £200.
The maximum benefit the donor can receive for a donation of £1,000 is £70. As the benefit received by the donor for the free tickets is £200 the Gift Aid benefit limit is exceeded and the whole of the donation does not qualify for Gift Aid.
However, the donor's aware that the cost of the benefit of the 10 free tickets is £200 and so elects to split the donation and treat £200 as payment for the tickets. The remaining balance of £800 is an eligible Gift Aid donation.
Example 2
The situation is as in Example 1:

- ten free tickets - total value £200 (£20 per ticket)

And the charity also offers the following benefits:

- dinner with the director - estimated value £30 but attending the dinner is not open to the general public
- an unlimited amount of tickets at a discount of 10%

The benefit is clearly in excess of the benefit limit of £70 as it amounts in excess of £230 - £200 for the tickets and an estimated £30 for the dinner. However, the benefit cannot be bought for the following reasons:

- all the benefits cannot be quantified at the outset - the benefit from the discounts is not known - nor is the actual value of the dinner
- the dinner is not available to the public and so can't be purchased separately

Therefore the split payment rule does not apply and no part of £1,000 donation is eligible for gift aid.
Items bought at a charity auction
For auction items, the option to split the payment only applies where the:

- item's commercially available
- donor is aware, at the time they make a successful bid that the item could be purchased separately and for what price

Your charity or CASC and the donor should keep evidence of this arrangement - for example an exchange of letters.

The donor benefit paper notes that the practice is concessionary:

1.14 Although not included in the current Donor Benefit Rules, HMRC currently permits a select number of Extra Statutory Concessions, which give charities certain prescribed flexibilities to provide benefits above and beyond the strict limits set out above. These are:

- The split payment rule: If a charity can accurately establish the cost of a benefit (through market value), and that product is sold separately and offered to the general public, the charity can separate that cost from the donation and claim Gift Aid on the rest of the money donated...[119]

15.33.3 *Charitable events*

The HMRC Guidance Note returns to this the topic of single/multiple payments in the context of charity events. It begins with a comment on charity law background:

> **Ticket price plus a suggested donation**
> 3.43.6 A charity can charge what it likes for a ticket to attend its event. However, it should not put the charity's funds at risk and, therefore, should set the ticket price at a level to at least recover its costs.

It is correct that the charity should not put its funds at risk. But it does not follow that it should therefore set ticket prices at a level to recover costs. Funds may be at risk if ticket prices are set at a level to recover costs (if ticket sales fall below expectation) and funds may be safe if ticket prices are below cost (because the charity is confident that donations will follow). This is accepted in example 6 below.

> 3.43.7 A charity can, therefore, charge a set ticket price (on which Gift Aid cannot be claimed) and, in addition, request a donation that can be gift aided. However, any suggested donation:
>
> - mustn't be compulsory such that it has to be paid, in addition to the set ticket price, to attend the event - that is, the payer must be able to pay only the ticket price to attend the event
> - the payer must be aware that the suggested donation is not compulsory and that they need only pay the set ticket price at the time they make the suggested donation (the ticket and/or event literature must make it clear)
> - the charity must not give any preferential treatment to those who do make a donation over those that choose not to - that is, the tickets must be allocated on a 'first come first served basis'

---

119 HMRC, "Simplifying the Gift Aid Donor Benefit Rules: a call for evidence (July 2015)
https://www.gov.uk/government/uploads/system/uploads/attachment_data/file/446089/Donor_Benefits_call_for_evidence_web_v4.pdf
The paper gives an example similar to example 1 in the HMRC Guidance Note.

> 3.43.8 A payment described as a 'minimum donation' or a 'specified donation' that has to be paid in addition to the set ticket price is not a freewill gift and cannot be gift aided. In these circumstances, the set ticket price plus the minimum donation or the specified donation is the actual ticket price and no part of the payment made (ticket price plus minimum/specified donation) can be gift aided.

The guidance gives six examples all based on the following facts:

> A charity organises a dinner dance and incurs the following costs:

Hire of venue	£1,000
Catering costs	£3,000
Orchestra/singer	£2,000
Total costs	£6,000

> The proposed number of attendees is 100 and the charity hopes to make (say) £4,000 on the event or £40 per attendee.
> The cost per attendee is £60 (£6,000/100) and so the charity is looking at a set ticket price at £100 (£60 + £40).

Example	**Facts**
1	£100 ticket charge
2	Ticket charge and minimum "donation"
3	Ticket charge and suggested donation
4	Donor pays dinner costs to charity
5	Suppliers waive their charges
6	No ticket charge and voluntary donation

> **Example 1** [£100 ticket charge]
> The charity charges £100 for each ticket.
> There's no gift to charity, all the proceeds (£10,000) are from ticket sales and none qualify as Gift Aid payments.
> Note: sometimes a charity seeks to claim Gift Aid on the £4,000 (£40 per person) on the basis that the amount over and above the costs is a donation. However, the £4,000 (proceeds £10,000 less costs £6,000) is a profit and not a donation.

More analytically, the £100 payment does not qualify for Gift Aid because
(1) the benefit exceeds the small benefit limit, and
(2) the split payment concession does not apply.

> **Example 2** [Ticket charge and minimum "donation"]
> The charity charges £65 per ticket and also asks for a minimum donation of £35.
> To attend the dinner an attendee must pay £100 (£65 + the minimum donation of £35). A person may not buy a ticket or attend by only paying

£65.
There's no gift, the whole of the £100 is a compulsory payment to attend the dinner and no part of it is eligible for the Gift Aid Scheme.

More analytically, the £35 is not properly described as a "donation" (the statutory terminology is "gift" but the terms may be regarded as synonymous) because it is compulsory and not voluntary.[120] The £100 payment does not qualify for Gift Aid because the benefit exceeds the small benefit limit, and the split payment concession does not apply.

Example 3 [Ticket charge and suggested donation]
The charity charges £80 per ticket and, in addition, asks for a suggested donation of £20. The charity makes it clear on the back of the ticket that the £20 is only a suggested donation and that attendance at the dinner can be obtained by only paying the set ticket price of £80.
The £80 paid for the ticket cannot be Gift Aided.
However, as the charity made it clear that a payment to attend the dinner was only £80 (the set cost of a ticket) then any payment made in excess of the £80 can be Gift Aided. So the suggested £20 donation or any other donation in excess of the £80 paid for a ticket can be Gift Aided.

Example 4 [Donor pays dinner costs to charity]
The charity charges £100 for each ticket.
However, a benefactor pays the full cost (£6,000) to the charity[121] so that it [the charity] can pay for the dinner.
For Gift Aid purposes, the situation is exactly the same as for example 1.
Who meets, or how the costs are met, is not important when determining whether a payment to attend the dinner is a gift. The charge to attend the event remains at £100 even though the charity's cost is met by the benefactor. So, none of the £100 payment can be Gift Aided.
Note: the benefactor has made a gift to the charity of £6,000 and so he can Gift Aid his £6,000 gift provided all the requirements of the Gift Aid Scheme are satisfied. Any free tickets (£100 each) given to the benefactor are benefits for the purposes of the Gift Aid benefit limit (which are £300 for a £6,000 donation) - so 1 free ticket valued at £100 is within the Gift Aid benefit limit.

Example 5 [Suppliers waive their charges]
The charity charges £100 for each ticket. However, the venue/ orchestra/caterer all waive their charges and so it costs the charity

120 See 15.4 ("Gift").
121 It would be different if donor paid the suppliers directly.

> nothing to put on the dinner dance.
> None of the £100 paid can be Gift Aided as it is a payment to purchase a ticket to attend the dinner.
> Unlike example 4, the venue/orchestra/caterer cannot Gift Aid their contributions because they have not made any payments to charity but simply waived their fees – that is, there's no payment of 'a sum of money'.

However the suppliers' taxable profits are reduced so they effectively obtain tax relief. There is also a *prima facie* VAT saving (where the charity cannot recover the VAT).

> **Example 6** [No ticket charge and voluntary donation]
> The charity decides that it will not make any charge to attend the event and will rely on expected donations from previous donors to more than cover costs.

HMRC attempt to discourage donation only events:

> Charity trustees are obliged to take proper care of charity funds and not expose them to undue risk. Any trustees considering this kind of approach would have to be able to demonstrate that they had made a properly informed and considered decision that a better return on funds laid out could be achieved by not charging for tickets. Failure to do this could result in the costs being treated as non-charitable expenditure and the trustees being personally liable for any loss of funds. Professional advice should be taken before embarking upon such a course....

However HMRC do accept that they could be effective for Gift Aid:

> ... Donations received in such circumstances could be eligible for Gift Aid [122]

The previous version of the guidance used the word "would" rather than "could" and so accepted that donation only events would qualify for relief. We think that was accurate.

15.33.4 *Single payment: small benefit*

The position is different where a donor receives a "small" benefit, that is, a benefit below the limits permitted by the benefit rule.[123] Again, there is a distinction between:

---

122 See too 35.9 (Grants and donations).
123 See 15.34 (Small benefits).

(1) A single payment of (say) £100, in return for which a donor receives a small benefit worth, say, £20.
(2) A multiple payment, say:
   (a) a gift of £80; and
   (b) a separate payment of £20 in return for the benefit of £20.

In this case the single payment allows Gift Aid on £100; in case (2) there is Gift Aid on £80.

Particular care is needed when donors to charity are offered a range of "subscriptions" with different benefits attached. The problem arises especially in relation to:
(1) charity literature, which can be a valuable benefit, because of HMRC concession on valuation: see 15.35.5 (Charity literature);
(2) membership subscriptions: see 15.31 (Membership subscription).

15.34 Small benefits

15.34.1 *Introduction*

The receipt of a benefit does not breach the benefit rule (Gift Aid condition F) where the value of the benefit falls within certain limits. We describe these as "**small benefits**".

Section 416(7) ITA provides:

> Condition F is that—
> (a) there are no benefits associated with the gift, or
> (b) there are benefits associated with the gift but the restriction on those benefits are not breached.

Section 418(1) ITA provides:

> For the purposes of s.416(7), the restrictions on benefits associated with a gift are breached if condition A or B is met.

We refer to this as **"small benefit conditions A and B"**.

15.34.2 *Condition A: Variable limit*

Section 418(2) ITA provides:

> Condition A is that the total value of the benefits associated with the gift exceeds the variable limit, which is—
> (a) in a case where the amount of the gift is £100 or less, 25% of that amount, and
> (b) in a case where the amount of the gift exceeds £100, the sum of £25 and 5% of the amount of the excess.

The test is that the total value of the benefits associated with the gift does not exceed a limit which (after the ITA) we call the "variable limit". The HMRC Guidance Note calls this the "relevant value test".

15.34.3 *Condition B: Absolute limit*

Section 418(3) ITA provides:

> Condition B is that the sum of-
> (a) the total value of the benefits associated with the gift, and
> (b) the total value of the benefits (if any) associated with each relevant prior gift,
>
> is more than £2,500.

Section 418(4) ITA defines "relevant prior gift":

> Relevant prior gift means a gift—
> (a) which has already been made by the individual to the charity in the tax year, and
> (b) which is a qualifying donation.

This has two consequences. Firstly, no benefit which exceeds £2,500 is permitted, even if it is less than 5% of the gift and so satisfies small benefit condition A. (This only affects donations exceeding £50,000.)

Secondly, one aggregates all gifts from the donor in the tax year up to the gift itself, and the maximum benefit allowed is £2,500 in value. This was not an easy administrative task for the charity when the figure was lower, but now that it is the substantial sum of £2,500, the problem will not often arise.

The HMRC Guidance Note refers to this as the "aggregate value test".

Example

Gift	**Amount of Gift**	**Benefit**
1	£100	£25
2	£49,600	£2,480

Gift 1 qualifies for relief. Gift 2 satisfies small benefit condition A but fails to meet small benefit condition B (if made in the same tax year as Gift 1).

Small benefit condition B might in theory be avoided by making gifts to separate charities, but small benefit condition A is so strict that this has little practical significance.

The HMRC Guidance Note summarises the law:

3.22 The aggregate value test

3.22.1 In addition to satisfying the relevant value test, the value of the benefits received in consequence of a donation must also satisfy the aggregate value test if the donation is to qualify as a Gift Aid donation. In other words:

- the value of the benefits received in consequence of making the donation
- plus the value of any benefits received in consequence of any Gift Aid donations by the same donor to the same charity earlier in the same tax year
- must not exceed £500 - for donations made between 6 April 2007 and 5 April 2011 or £2,500 for donations made on or after 6 April 2011

The value of benefits is not annualised for the purposes of the aggregate value test. It's the actual value, as opposed to an annual value, of the benefits that counts.

The HMRC Guidance Note then offers a more challenging example. This incorporates the facts of HMRC's example 1, which are as follows:

Example 1

Ms Smith makes 4 unconnected donations to a wildlife charity as follows:

Date	**Amount**	**Benefits**
6 May 2012	£30	nil
21 June 2012	£10	nil
18 August 2012	£25	nil
5 February 2013	£80	fashion book worth £30

As no benefits are received in consequence of making any of the first 3 donations, they all pass the relevant value test.

The book received in consequence of making the fourth donation does not fall into any of the categories above, so annualising does not apply. As the £30 value of the book exceeds the limit of £20 (25% of the £80 donation) the fourth donation fails the relevant value test and so does not qualify as a Gift Aid donation.

Using these facts as the basis for its example of the aggregate value test, the HMRC Guidance continues:

3.22.2 For example, suppose in example 1 (paragraph 3.21.6) Ms Smith makes 2 further donations to the charity in the tax year 2012 to 2013 as follows:

Date	**Amount**	**Benefits**
6 May 2012	£30	nil

21 June 2012	£10	nil
18 August 2012	£25	nil
5 February 2013	£80	fashion book value £30
11 March 2013	£9,600	weekend break worth £450
4 April 2013	£50,000	package of benefits valued at £2,500

As the value of the weekend break does not exceed the limit of £480 (ie 5% of the £9,600 donation) the fifth donation passes the relevant value test. Furthermore, it passes the aggregate value test (it's not aggregated with the benefit worth £30 received in consequence of the fourth donation, because that donation did not qualify as a Gift Aid donation). As the value of the package of benefits does not exceed the limit of £2,500 (ie 5% of the £50,000 donation) the sixth donation passes the relevant value test. However, it fails the aggregate value test, because the value of the package of benefits plus the value of the weekend break exceeds £2,500. (£450 + £2,500 = £2,950). Therefore, the sixth donation cannot qualify as a Gift Aid donation. The other 5 donations are unaffected.

15.34.4 *Fixed benefit cap: Critique*

McGregor calls for abolition of the fixed cap:

> **Remove the fixed cap ... on the benefits that a donor can receive from a charity. Rely entirely on the proportional cap (currently 5%). This allows the benefits provided by charities to be commensurate with the generosity of the gift, a much more suitable structure for eliciting high value gifts.** The benefits that a donor can receive from a charity (while remaining eligible for Gift Aid) are currently capped at £500. If a charity offers a donor a benefit valued at more than £500 the donation is no longer eligible for Gift Aid. Therefore the allowable benefits for a donation of £1m are no greater than those for a donation of £10,000. The most generous donors are not well served by this restriction. To encourage larger gifts it would help if the allowable benefits corresponded to the size of the donation. This could be achieved if the benefit cap was expressed as a percentage of the donation rather than a fixed amount. This would do much to promote philanthropy at no cost to HMRC.[124]

This reform would also be a simplification. Justine Greeing (then

124 Report on the Role Endowments Could Play in DCMS Funded Museums and Galleries (2010*)* *http://www.culture.gov.uk/images/publications/Endowments_paper_20101208.pdf.*

Economic Secretary to the Treasury) claimed that the increase in the Gift Aid limit from £500 to £2,500 "should ease the administrative burden on charities and donors who currently become involved in time-consuming paperwork to keep within the £500 limit."[125] The increased limit has in some cases eased the administrative burden but it has not removed it.

15.35 Valuation of benefit

Valuation of a benefit is important because it determines whether or not a benefit is large enough to breach the benefit rule.

There are several possible bases of valuation:

(1) The amount which someone would pay for the benefit.
(2) The cost to the charity providing it.
(3) The second-hand value.[126]

The normal meaning of valuation is market value, which is the amount someone would pay for the benefit on the open market, or (if there is no market) assuming there were an open market.[127] It is often the case that there are a range of reasonable values, though ultimately a tribunal would have to determine an actual value even if the choice is slightly arbitrary. In may cases the exact value does not need to be determined, since the question is not what is the value, but whether the value exceeds a relatively small limit.

HMRC Guidance Note provides:

> 3.23.1 The valuation of donor benefits can be difficult. However:
> [1] where an item or service is sold to the public, the benefit will be the sale price to the public - for example, for a ticket to attend a performance by an opera society that costs £20, the benefit will be £20
> [2] in other cases the charity will need to determine how much someone providing the benefit at arm's length would charge for it - evidence might be obtained from similar commercial transactions

Case [1] is easy, but valuation in case [2] may be difficult because benefits

---

125 Hansard 24 May 2011 *http://www.publications.parliament.uk/pa/cm201011/cmpublic/finance/110524/pm/110524s01.htm*

126 As in *Wilkins v Rogerson* 39 TC 344. This would produce a lower valuation.

127 Contrast *IRC v Botnar* [1998] STC p.81–85 where the valuation was on the basis of "what the benefit would have cost the individual taking into account the terms on which it was provided".

that charities provide often have no market: there are no comparable commercial transactions. But one just has to do the best one can.

> 3.23.2 Where the charity does not sell the benefit or there is no similar commercial transaction to base a valuation upon, HMRC will accept any method of valuation that it deems to be fair and reasonable.
> 3.23.3 The value of a benefit is always the value to the recipient, not the cost to your charity or CASC of providing the benefit. Even though your charity or CASC may get a discount on the cost of any benefits you give to donors, the benefit must be given its full value when working out whether a donation qualifies for Gift Aid.

HMRC give an example of the easy category of case:

> As an incentive, new members receive a teddy bear (on sale at £5 but cost £2 to the shop owner) in return for paying their membership subscription. The teddy bear is supplied direct to new members free of charge to the charity by a local shop owned by one of the charity's trustees on presenting a voucher given to new members by the charity. The benefit is £5 (cost to the public if they purchased a bear).

The HMRC Guidance Note provides:

> **Valuing goods and services**
> 3.23.3 For many benefits the value is simply the retail value of the item or service. For example if a donor receives a free theatre ticket, the value of the benefit is the face value of the ticket.
> 3.23.4 Where a retail value cannot be found, your charity or CASC must work out how much someone would be prepared to pay for the item or services - looking at similar commercial transactions will help.

15.35.1 *Private event*

The HMRC Guidance Note provides:

> 3.23.5 Where a benefit takes the form of attendance at an event that
> [1] is not open to the public (so that there's no ticket price) and which
> [2] is not a fund raising event ...
> the benefit should be valued by reference to the cost to the charity of staging the event and the number of people in attendance. Only direct costs associated with the one off event should be included in the calculation. The charity should not include apportioned everyday overheads within the calculation.

In the absence of a market, this basis (cost per attendee) seems a reasonable indicator of market value, in the absence of special features.

The donor benefit paper considers this topic:

> 1.14 Although not included in the current Donor Benefit Rules, HMRC currently permits a select number of Extra Statutory Concessions, which give charities certain prescribed flexibilities to provide benefits above and beyond the strict limits set out above. These are ...
>
> - The averaging method: A charity can average the cost of a benefit over a number of individual donors...
>
> **The averaging method**
>
> - Charity D hosts a fundraising dinner, at which David (a UK taxpayer) donates £100 and provides his consent for Gift Aid to be claimed on his donation.
> - Charity D does not know the exact cost[128] of the benefit David received at the fundraising dinner, in return for his donation, but it does know that there were 10 attendees and the total cost of hosting the dinner was £200.
> - Using the averaging method Charity D can calculate that the cost per attendee (of which David was one) was £20 (£200 divided by 10).
> - As a £20 benefit in return for a £100 donation is permissible under the current rules, i.e. it does not exceed 25% of the value of the donation, Charity D can claim Gift Aid on all of David's £100 donation.[129]

We do not regard this practice as a concession, for what other method of valuation might be better?

What is the position if a large number of persons are invited, but a small number attend? It is tentatively suggested that the non-attendees receive no benefit, and the attendees receive a benefit valued at cost per attendee. It is arguable that:

(1) the benefit is the right to attend, which is received by every member invited; and

(2) the value of the right to attend should be the cost (or anticipated cost) to the charity divided by the fraction of members invited.

---

128 More analytically, the question is not the cost of the benefit which the donor received, but the value of the benefit. One should not use the word "cost" as a synonym of value.

129 HMRC, "Simplifying the Gift Aid Donor Benefit Rules: a call for evidence (July 2015)
https://www.gov.uk/government/uploads/system/uploads/attachment_data/file/446089/Donor_Benefits_call_for_evidence_web_v4.pdf

15.35.2 *Life membership*

The HMRC Guidance Note provides:

> **Valuing benefits in return for life membership subscriptions**
> 3.23.6 Where the benefit is given in return for a donation is a life membership a value must be attributed to the lifetime membership. In cases where the charity sells lifetime membership, the value of the benefit would simply be the amount lifetime membership is being sold for. If the charity does not sell lifetime membership HMRC accepts that it would be reasonable to base the value of the benefit on the cost of a lifetime membership at an equivalent or similar organisation.
> In rare cases there will be no genuine equivalent or similar lifetime membership on which to base a valuation. In these situations the charity will need to value the benefit of a lifetime membership. When valuing the benefit of a lifetime membership a charity should only consider the benefits received in the first 10 years of membership. Any benefit received after 10 years does not need to be considered. However, when considering the value of benefits received in the first 10 years, the charity must take into account the diminishing value of the same benefit received, that is the value of entrance into an attraction in the tenth year will be lower than the value of the same right to entrance in the first year. How this is calculated is up to the charity but the method used should be fair and reasonable.

Strictly, the value of the benefit will depend on the life expectancy of the member but a valuation of a life benefit by 10 year's purchase is a pragmatic, rough and ready approximation. Benefits are to be valued at the time of the gift. If the benefit is to be provided later its value should be discounted to allow for the delay.

15.35.3 *Discount on goods/services*

Charities often offer a discount at a charity shop or café. The value of this benefit would be its commercial value. Research may show that the discount is not much used. The commercial value is then fairly low. HMRC accept this:

> **Valuing benefits which are discounts**
> 3.23.7 Where the benefit is a discount on goods or services, which an individual member may or may not take advantage of, the valuation of the benefit is based on the value of the benefit irrespective of whether or not the donor took up the option of the benefit. The average take-up of the benefit, by all the charity's members, can be used to calculate the

value of the benefit. This is called the averaging method. In order to establish the average benefit the charity must keep complete records of all the discounts received by its members. Where a charity agrees a discount with a third party organisation such as a café or retailer, this discount must also be valued as a benefit.

Example 1 - The Averaging Method

A charity has 500 members and offers a 10% discount on sales in its shop and has an agreement with a café to give members £10% discount. The charity and cafe keep complete records of discounts given to its members. The total discounts in the year are:

- £5,295 for the shop
- £3,410 for the café

The average benefit per member is £17.41 (£5,295 + £3,410 ÷ 500). This benefit must apply to all members whether they've received a discount or not. The other choice is to keep records to quantify the actual discount benefit received by each individual member.

Example 2 - The Averaging Method

A charity has 300 members and offers a 10% discount on sales in its shop. The charity fails to keep records of members' discounts.

The benefit is open-ended and so the membership subscriptions fail as Gift Aid donations as the charity cannot show that the maximum benefit available is not exceeded.

15.35.4 *Priority booking*

If a charity offers a priority booking facility, the value of the benefit depends on the circumstances. Priority booking for a popular event where tickets are not otherwise available (eg Wimbledon) would be a valuable benefit. Priority booking has no value at all if a person could otherwise obtain a ticket (even if it was necessary to act promptly).

15.35.5 *Charity literature*

HMRC Guidance Note provides:

3.24 Provision of literature

3.24.1 Where a charity sends literature to its donors, either in a physical or electronic format, the value of the literature is nil provided the:

- material is produced solely for the purpose of describing the work of the charity whether produced by the charity, or a third party
- material is relevant to and distributed exclusively in furtherance of the objects of the charity

This is an important statement which will often be helpful to charities.

As the donor benefit paper correctly notes,[130] this practice is strictly a concession, not law, since in some cases charity literature will have some value.[131]

The following text was added in 2019:

> For gifts made on or after 6 April 2019, a benefit associated with a gift is ignored if the benefit consists of promotional literature.
> Literature is promotional if it consists wholly or mainly of:
> - information about the activities or proposed activities of the charity to which the gift is made
> - material encouraging further gifts to that charity or otherwise promoting the objects of that charity
> - both of the above
>
> The fact that the literature has a cover price and is also on sale to members of the public is not relevant. This means that literature like newsletters, bulletins, annual reports, journals, magazines, members' handbooks and programmes of events will generally carry no value for the purposes of the donor benefit rules.
> **Example**
> A conservation charity provides its members with a free copy of the BBC's nature magazine. The magazine costs £4.50 but is supplied to the charity at a cost of £3 per copy.
> The value of the benefit is £4.50. The magazine may be connected to the purposes of the charity but it's neither about the specific work of the charity or produced by the charity.

15.36 Charity auction

In a normal commercial auction:
(1) the bidder does not make a gift, and
(2) the auction price is the best indicator of market value.

That is not the case for a charity auction, as the bidder may bid not with a view to obtaining the asset at the market price, but in order to support the charity. If that is the case:
(1) the bidder does make a gift; and

---

130 HMRC, "Simplifying the Gift Aid Donor Benefit Rules: a call for evidence (July 2015) *https://www.gov.uk/government/uploads/system/uploads/attachment_data/file/446089/Donor_Benefits_call_for_evidence_web_v4.pdf*

131 Whether the matter is one of concession or not does not matter in practice, except in the event of litigation or unless or until the concession is publically withdrawn.

(2) the auction price is not a reliable indicator of market value.

Of course, the bidder obtains a benefit (the auctioned asset) but the gift qualifies for Gift Aid if:
(1) the value of the benefit is below the small benefit limit; or
(2) if the split payment concession applies[132]

HMRC Guidance Note para 3.40 provides:

> 3.40.1 A payment for an item at a charity auction is not a gift to charity, it's a purchase.
> 3.40.2 However, when a person purchases a lot at a charity auction they may intentionally pay more than it is worth in order to support the charity. So, on that basis and depending upon the circumstances, part or all of a successful auction bid may qualify as a Gift Aid donation to the charity.
> 3.40.3 The payment will only qualify as a Gift Aid payment if the normal requirements of the Gift Aid Scheme are met, and that includes satisfying the Gift Aid benefit rules.

This accepts the analysis set out above.

> **Gift Aid benefit (valuation of an auction item)**
> 3.40.4 For an item that is commercially available, the benefit for Gift Aid purposes is the 'shop sale' price of the item. An item must have a clear and recognisable value (market value) and be available commercially for purchase separately by an individual otherwise than at the auction.

This is straightforward.

> 3.40.5 For a commercially available item that has had its value enhanced, for example because it has been owned by a celebrity, the market value (and hence the benefit for Gift Aid purposes) will not be the original price of the item but the amount it fetches in the auction.

It is in principle correct that the value of the asset would be higher the normal value of the item because of the celebrity association. However, it is incorrect to say that in such circumstances the auction price is the market value. At charity auctions many bidders deliberately overbid (as the HMRC Guidance Note recognises at 3.40.2). That may happen in the case of items which have celebrity association, or which are otherwise not

132 See 15.33.2 (Split payments).

commercially available. The only difficulty with such items is to ascertain what is the true market price. In most cases the true market price (whatever it is) is likely to exceed the modest Gift Aid limits, so the question of an exact valuation will not arise.

> 3.40.6 For an item not commercially available, its value is the auction price paid by the purchaser. So the benefit for Gift Aid purposes is the 'auction' price paid (effectively a benefit of 100% of the successful auction bid).

This is wrong for the same reason. In the case of an item not commercially available (say, a painting) the value is the value which may be far below the auction price.

Assuming the value of the benefit, correctly ascertained, exceeds the small benefit limit, the question is whether the split payment concession applies. The HMRC Guidance Note provides:

> **Buying the Gift Aid benefit (split payment)**
> 3.40.7 Where the value of the benefits exceeds the limits in the donor benefit rules (so that the whole of the donation fails as a Gift Aid donation) the donor may, as a concession, be able to treat part of his/her payment as buying the benefits (the value in monetary terms of the benefits) and Gift Aid the excess donation.
> The Gift Aid benefits can only be purchased if:
> - the benefits can be purchased separately
> - the donor is aware of the monetary value of the benefit at the time they make their donation
>
> 3.40.8 For auction items, this treatment only applies where:
> - the auction item can be purchased separately elsewhere
> - the donor is aware of the value of the benefit (the retail cost of the item) at the time they make their successful auction bid (donation)
>
> That is, the donor must know the monetary value of the item at the time they make their bid in order to 'buy the benefit' and so know that the excess is a donation.
> **Example 1**
> A charity auctions a football that is on sale in a well known store for £10.
> The football is commercially available for £10, so the Gift Aid benefit is £10. The benefit is £10 whether:
> - the charity buys the ball from the store
> - the store donates the ball to the charity
> - an individual purchases the ball from the store and donates it to the charity

This is in principle correct.

> **(a) An individual successfully bids £40 for the ball**
> The benefit is £10 and, as the benefit is 25% of the price paid of £40, the whole of the £40 is eligible as a Gift Aid payment.

This is correct.

> **(b) An individual successfully bids £30 for the ball but the charity did not tell bidders at the start of the auction that it could be bought locally for £10**
> The benefit is £10 and, as the benefit is 33% of the price paid of £30, the Gift Aid benefit limit is exceeded. So none of the £30 paid is eligible as a Gift Aid payment (the donor cannot buy the benefit).

This is correct because the small benefit limit is exceeded, and the conditions for the split payment concession are not satisfied.

> **(c) An individual successfully bids £30 for the ball and the charity told bidders at the start of the auction that it could be bought locally for £10**
> The benefit is £10 and, as the benefit is 33% of the price paid of £30, the Gift Aid benefit limit is exceeded. However, the donor can buy the benefit and so £20 is eligible as a Gift Aid payment (£30 paid less the bought benefit of £10).

This is correct: the conditions for the split payment concession are satisfied.

> **(d) The ball is signed by the local football team and sold for £100 (although the price paid is not relevant to the treatment described below)**
> The nature of the ball has changed by its being signed by the local football team. The signed ball is not the item on sale in the store and its value for Gift Aid benefit purposes is the auction price paid of £100. The benefit is 100% (£100 donation, £100 benefit) and so none of the £100 paid is eligible for the Gift Aid Scheme.

The valuation point is wrong. If the value correctly ascertained is less than £25, the payment qualifies for Gift Aid. If the value exceeds £25, there is no relief, as the conditions for the split payment concession are not met.

> **Example 2**
> An individual makes a wooden train that is similar to one on sale at a local store and it is bought at auction for £50

The train auctioned is not on sale in the store (and is not commercially available) and so its value for Gift Aid benefit purposes is the auction price paid of £50. The benefit is 100% (£50 donation, £50 benefit) and so none of the £50 paid is eligible for the Gift Aid Scheme.

This is the same as example 1(d) above.

Example 3
Often a charity (mainly churches) will hold an auction of ‘promises’. These are tasks that individuals have promised to carry out for successful bidders. For example:

- wash and polish a car
- cut the grass
- prepare and serve a meal
- make available a holiday cottage for the weekend
- baby sit for an evening

These are all items offered by the general public and are not usually (see exception below) on general sale. Similar items/services may be available commercially but not those offered as promises.
The value of a promise for Gift Aid benefit purposes is the auction price paid. The benefit will always be 100% of the donation and so none of the auction price paid to purchase a promise is eligible for the Gift Aid Scheme.

We think this is clearly wrong, as the correct value of these benefits can easily be ascertained.

Exception
Occasionally a promise offered is commercially available. For example:

- a cottage may be generally available for letting even though owned by a member of the public - if the promise is to make available the cottage for a weekend and the rent charged is usually £100 (and there is evidence available in support) then the Gift Aid benefit is £100 and the rules apply as in example 1
- a local garage may agree to supply a free ‘wash and polish’ for which they charge £10 - the Gift Aid benefit is £10 and the rules apply as in example 1

This is correct.

Example 4
Charities sometimes receive items owned or used by celebrities for auction. Such items have an enhanced value over and above their purchase price and bids to secure such items cannot be Gift Aided. For example:

A famous pop music star gives a pair of her shoes for a charity auction. These shoes normally retail for £150. Mr Webster purchases the shoes with a bid of £10,000.[133] Although the shoes retail for £150, because a celebrity has owned them, their value has been considerably enhanced and the £10,000 paid represents their market value. The benefit received is £10,000, 100% of the payment. Consequently the £10,000 cannot be paid under Gift Aid.

15.37 Benefit of uncertain value

There will sometimes be doubts as to the valuation of benefits. A charity should certainly not take any risk that the value of the benefit may exceed the permitted limit: too much tax is at stake. It may sometimes be possible to obtain an informal clearance from HMRC in doubtful cases. Can a donor undertake that, if the value of the benefit exceeds the limit, the donor will make an additional gift to the charity? That is not a solution. The undertaking is not a "payment of money", so it is not treated as part of the original gift. The donor can, however, undertake that if the value of the benefit exceeds the limits, they will make a payment to the charity in respect of the benefit. This undertaking will not increase the amount of the gift; but it will diminish the value of the benefit, and so in this way the tax problem can be avoided. Alternatively, use the relief for gifts of qualifying investments instead.

15.38 Annualisation

Annualisation is the term used in the HMRC Guidance Note for the rules in s.419 ITA.

Section 419 provides:

> (1) This section modifies the application of s.418(2) in relation to a gift if condition A, B, C or D is met.

We refer to the conditions as "**Annualisation Conditions A to D**".

> (2) Condition A is that a benefit associated with the gift relates to a period of less than 12 months.
> (3) Condition B is that a benefit associated with the gift consists of a right to receive benefits at intervals over a period of less than 12

---

133 Authors' footnote: That figure may seem implausibly high. But in 2020 a pair of Nikes worn by basketball player Michael Jordan sold at public auction for $615,000. In any case, all that matters is that the shoes have a value in excess of the Gift Aid limit (in this case, £500).

months.

(4) Condition C is that a benefit associated with the gift is one of a series of benefits which are—

(a) received at intervals, and

(b) associated with a series of gifts made at intervals of less than 12 months.

(5) Condition D is that—

(a) A benefit associated with the gift is not one of a series of benefits received at intervals, and

(b) the gift is one of a series of gifts made at intervals of less than 12 months.

The annualisation rules only apply for the purposes of s.418(2), ie small benefit condition A. It does not affect the application of small benefit condition B, the aggregate value test. This is clear under ITA but the same applies for corporation tax under CTA 2010. This is HMRC view. HMRC Guidance Note para 3.22 provides:

> The value of benefits is not annualised for the purposes of the aggregate value test. It's the actual value, as opposed to an annual value, of the benefits that counts.

15.38.1 *Benefits received over a period*

Section 419(6) ITA provides:

> If condition A, B or C is met, then for the purposes of s.418(2)-
>
> (a) the value of the benefit is taken to be the annual equivalent of its actual value, and
>
> (b) the amount of the gift is taken to be the annual equivalent of its actual amount.

The consequence is twofold:

(a) the value of the benefit is deemed to be the "annual equivalent" (not the true value).

(b) the amount of the gift is deemed to be the "annual equivalent" (not the true value).

The annual equivalent is defined in s.419(8) ITA.

> The annual equivalent of the value of a benefit, or of the amount of a gift, is calculated as follows.
>
> Step 1
>
> Multiply the value or amount by 365.
>
> Step 2
>
> If condition A or B is met in relation to the benefit (and neither

condition C nor condition D is met in relation to it), divide the result by the number of days in the period of less than 12 months referred to in subsection (2) or (as the case may be) subsection (3).

If condition C or D is met in relation to the benefit, divide the result by the average number of days in the intervals of less than 12 months referred to in subsection (4)(b) or (as the case may be) subsection (5)(b).

HMRC Guidance Note provides at 3.21.5:

> In practice, where the period or the intervals are measured in calendar months, annualising can be done by reference to calendar months, rather than days.

Example

Suppose:

(1) The gift is £100.

(2) The benefit consists of a season ticket for the period of one week and is worth £10.

Apart from the annualisation rules the gift would qualify for Gift Aid. But after annualisation, the value of the gift and benefit are deemed to be the annual equivalent and not the true value. The adjustment is to multiply them both by the amount (365 ÷ 7). Thus the amount of the gift is treated as £5,200 and the value of the benefit is treated as £520. A gift of £5,200 for a benefit of £520 does not qualify for Gift Aid, failing to meet small benefit condition A, so the gift actually made does not qualify.

HMRC Guidance Note at 3.21.6 gives examples:

> *Example 3*
>
> Mrs O'Connor makes a single payment of £120 to the same medical charity, in consequence of which she receives the right to receive 6 free monthly computer magazines worth £3 each. The benefit of the right to receive the magazines is therefore worth £18 (£3 × 6).
>
> The right to receive the magazines falls into the first category at paragraph 3.21.3 (a right to receive benefits at intervals over a period of less than 12 months) so annualising applies. The limits in the table at paragraph 3.21.1 therefore apply by reference to the annual amount of the donation £240 (£120 × 12 ÷ 6) and the annual value of the right to receive the magazines £36 (£18 × 12 ÷ 6). As the annual value of the right to receive the magazines exceeds the limit of £32 (annualised donation £240: 25% of £100 plus 5% of £140) the donation fails the relevant value test and so cannot qualify as a Gift Aid donation.
>
> *Example 4*
>
> Mr Green makes a single payment of £120 to a performing arts charity,

> in consequence of which he receives the right to a 5% discount on theatre tickets purchased in the next 6 months. The benefit of the right to the discount is worth, say, £18.
> The right to the discount falls into the second category above (a benefit relating to a period of less than 12 months) so annualising applies. The limits in the table at paragraph 3.21.1 therefore apply by reference to the annual amount of the donation £240 (£120 × 12 ÷ 6) and the annual value of the right to the discount £36 (£18 × 12 ÷ 6). As the annual value of the right to the discount exceeds the limit of £32 (annualised donation £240: 25% of £100 plus 5% of £140) the donation fails the relevant value test and so cannot qualify as a Gift Aid donation.

If the benefit relates to an entire year, it will not fall into this category of annualisation. HMRC Guidance Note 3.21.6 gives an example:

> *Example 2*
> Mr Patel makes a single payment of £240 to a medical charity, in consequence of which he receives the right to receive 12 free monthly computer magazines worth £3 each. The benefit of the right to receive the magazines is therefore worth £36 (£3 × 12).
> The right to receive the magazines does not [meet any of the Annualisation Conditions], so annualising does not apply. As the value of the right to receive the magazines (£36) exceeds the limit of £32 (donation £240: 25% of £100 plus 5% of £140) the donation fails the relevant value test and so cannot qualify as a Gift Aid donation.

This is correct, if the series of benefits extend over one entire year, not less than one year. But if Mr Patel makes a gift on 15 January, and immediately receives the *January* issue of the magazine, subsequently receiving the December issue on 1 December, then the annualisation rules would apply but it would probably not affect the result.

The general planning rule must be to avoid benefits for shorter periods than one year.

The same example continues:

> As the value of the right to receive the magazines (£30) exceeds the limit of £25 (ie the limit for donations of £100 - £1,000) the donation fails the relevant value test and so cannot qualify as a Gift Aid donation.

This is not strictly correct. The value of the right to receive the magazine is less than the face value because of the advance payment made. Magazines usually give substantial discounts to annual subscribers who pay in advance. But this valuation point does not affect the fundamental point of the example.

15.38.2 *Series of gifts, one benefit*

Section 419(7) ITA provides:

> If Condition D is met, the amount of the gift is taken for the purposes of s.418(2) to be the annual equivalent of its actual amount.

In this case there is no adjustment in the value of the benefit but the amount of the gift is deemed to be the annual equivalent instead of the actual value. The annual equivalent is explained in s.419(8) ITA, set out at 15.38.1 (Benefits received over a period).

Example

(1) A donor makes a series of four gifts over one month of £10 (ie £40 in total).
(2) The donor receives a single benefit worth £10 in consequence of the last gift.

Apart from the annualisation rules the last gift would not qualify for relief as it fails small benefit condition A, the relevant value test. But after annualisation the value of the gift is deemed to be the annual equivalent and not the true value. The adjustment is to multiply it by the amount (12 ÷ 1). So the last gift is treated as worth 12×10 = £120, so that the gift satisfies small benefit condition A.

HMRC Guidance Note 3.21.6 provides:

> *Example 1*
> Ms Smith makes four unconnected donations to a wildlife charity as follows:

Date	**Amount**	**Benefits**
6 May 2012	£30	nil
21 June 2012	£10	nil
18 August 2012	£25	nil
5 February 2013	£80	fashion book value £30

> As no benefits are received in consequence of making any of the first 3 donations, they all pass the relevant value test.
>
> The book received in consequence of making the fourth donation does not [meet any of the Annualisation Conditions], so annualising does not apply. As the value of the book (£30) exceeds the limit of £20 (i.e. 25% of the £80 donation) the fourth donation fails the relevant value test [Benefit Condition A] and so cannot qualify as a Gift Aid donation.

This is correct if the gifts are not a "series". It is possible, however, that even "unconnected" gifts (and *quaere* what "unconnected" is supposed to mean in this context) by the same person to the same charity form a "series".

HMRC Guidance Note formerly provided an example where the annualisation rules helps the taxpayer:

> *Example 6*
> Mr Wong makes monthly payments of £2 to a charity under an open-ended standing order. In consequence of starting the payments he receives a one-off benefit of a free pen worth £5.
> The pen falls into [Annualisation Condition D] (a one-off benefit received in consequence of making a donation which is 1 of a series of donations made at intervals of less than 12 months) so annualising applies to the donation, but not the benefit. The [Gift Aid limits] therefore apply by reference to the annual amount of the donation £24 (£2 × 12 ÷ 1) and the actual value of the pen £5. As the value of the pen does not exceed the limit of £6 (ie 25% of the £24 annual donation) the donation passes the relevant value test [small benefit condition A] and so can qualify as a Gift Aid donation.

But the example is deleted in the current guidance.

15.38.3 *Series of benefits and gifts*

This is Annualisation Condition C. HMRC Guidance Note formerly provided an example:

> *Example 5*
> Miss Tomkins makes monthly payments of £20 to a medical charity under an open-ended standing order, in consequence of which she receives a free monthly computer magazine worth £2.50.
> The right to receive the magazines falls into [Annualisation Condition C] (a benefit which is 1 of a series of benefits received in consequence of making a series of donations at intervals of less than 12 months) so annualising applies. The [Gift Aid limits] therefore apply by reference to the annual amount of the donation £240 (£20 × 12 ÷ 1) and the annual value of the right to receive the magazines £30 ([£2.50][134] × 12 ÷ 1). As the annual value of the right to receive the magazines exceeds the limit of £25 (ie the limit for donations of £100 - £1,000) the donation fails the relevant value test [small benefit condition A] and so cannot qualify as a Gift Aid donation.

134 The original erroneously reads: £2.20.

As the example shows, the series may extend over one year. But the example is deleted in the current guidance.

15.38.4 *Critique*

What is the purpose of the annualisation rules? HMRC Guidance Note 3.21.2 explains:

> Special rules apply to 'annualise' the amount of certain donations and the value of certain benefits for the purposes of applying the limits. Broadly, in the case of subscriptions under a membership scheme, the limits normally apply by reference to the amount of the annual membership subscription and the value of the annual membership benefits. This way:
> - a charity can tell whether the benefits in its membership scheme will exceed the limit simply by looking at the annual membership subscription and the annual membership benefits
> - the result will be the same whether the donor pays the subscription in a single payment, or half-yearly, quarterly, or monthly

Presumably the aim is to prevent avoidance of small benefit condition A by fragmentation of gifts. A person could not receive a benefit of £50 if they made one gift of £200. But they could make two gifts of £100 receiving two benefits of £25. But this (trivial) avoidance is only prevented at a considerable cost in complexity. The rules do not strike the right balance between simplicity and fairness. In practice it is unlikely that charities or HMRC pay any attention to the rules. It is certain that very few charities understand them, nor could they reasonably be expected to. They should be scrapped: the remedy is worse than the disease.[135]

15.39 Right of admission

15.39.1 *Admission relief*

This section considers the Gift Aid for rights of admission to view property.[136] We refer to this as **"admission relief"**.

Section 420(1) ITA provides:

---

135 The Tax Law Rewrite commented:

"A number of respondents expressed some exasperation about difficulties with the rules for annualisation of gifts and benefits. Many of the concerns raised go beyond the Project's remit and have been passed to appropriate colleagues."

Paper CC/SC (05) 27, (2005). But nothing happened.

136 For VAT aspects of rights of admission, see 35.21 (Admission charges).

> A benefit associated with a gift is ignored for the purposes of this Chapter if the benefit consists of a relevant right of admission.

Section 420(2) ITA defines "right of admission":

> "Right of admission" means a right which—
> (a) benefits the individual who makes the gift or that individual and one or more members of that individual's family (whether or not the right must be exercised by all of them at the same time),
> (b) authorises admission to premises or property to which the public are admitted on payment of an admission fee, and
> (c) authorises admission to those premises or that property without payment of the admission fee or on payment of a reduced fee.

Paragraphs (b) and (c) represent the normal meaning of "right of admission". Paragraph (a) restricts the normal meaning; it is discussed separately below.

"Relevant" right of admission is a label which brings in a number of rules. Section 420(3) ITA provides:

> A right of admission is a relevant right of admission if—
> (a) conditions A and B are met in relation to it, and
> (b) either Condition C or D is met in relation to it.

We refer to these as **"admission conditions A to D"**.

Admission conditions A & B are compulsory; conditions C & D are alternatives.

15.39.2 *Open to public: Condition A*

Section 420(4) ITA provides:

> Condition A is that the opportunity to make a gift and to receive the right of admission in consequence is available to the public.

The HMRC Guidance Note provides at 3.39.5:

> The opportunity to make a gift and to receive a right of admission in consequence must always be available to the public. This means that the right of admission to view charity property must not be made conditional upon the donor making a Gift Aid declaration.

And again:

> **Donors who do not make a Gift Aid declaration**
> 3.39.35 Some visitors will choose to make a donation to the charity but will be unable to make a Gift Aid declaration as they will not be UK

taxpayers, others may want to make a donation but prefer not to claim Gift Aid on their donation. These donors must receive exactly the same right of admission as donors who do make a Gift Aid declaration. This rule applies whether the charity operates the 'annual right of admission' option or the 'admission charge plus 10%' option.

3.39.36 Charities may decide to give annual right of admission to visitors who make a donation equal to, or less than, the standard daily admission charge. This is acceptable, but charities must be prepared to accept a donation and give the annual right of admission to any donor who chooses this option, whether or not he or she makes a Gift Aid declaration.

Example

A charity owns 3 properties and charges £10 for daily admission to any single property. The charity chooses to offer donors the annual right of free admission to all three properties in return for a minimum donation of just £25. The benefit of admission to all 3 qualifying properties in return for a donation can be disregarded for the purposes of Gift Aid, providing the 'discount' is offered to all donors, and not only to those making a Gift Aid declaration.

15.39.3 *Purpose*: *Condition B*

Section 420(5) ITA provides:

> Condition B is that the right of admission is a right granted by the charity for the purpose of viewing property preserved, maintained, kept or created by a charity for its charitable purposes.

We refer to property within s.420(5) as **"charity-purpose property"**.
Section 420(6) ITA provides an inclusive definition:

> The property mentioned in subsection (5) includes, in particular—
> (a) buildings,
> (b) grounds or other land,
> (c) plants,
> (d) animals,
> (e) works of art (but not performances),
> (f) artefacts, and
> (g) property of a scientific nature.

This list is inclusive and only illustrative.
The HMRC Guidance Note provides:

> **Property preserved, maintained, kept or created**
> 3.39.15 The property being viewed does not necessarily have to be

> preserved, maintained etc by the particular charity granting a right of admission but must be
> [1] preserved, kept etc. by a charity,
> [2] with similar objects to the charity making the admission charge.[137]

Point [2] is a slightly inaccurate paraphrase of the statutory requirement, but in practice it is not likely to matter.

The HMRC Guidance Note also provides:

> **Charities displaying loaned items or non-charity property**
> 3.39.20 Charities may also display property that does not belong to them, borrowing it from other charities or from private owners, public bodies etc.
> 3.39.21 A distinction has to be drawn between admission to view a charity's property, which may have been merely supplemented by items borrowed from others, including non-charities, and the display of other property - simply being displayed on a charity's premises.
> If the borrowed property and/or its preservation etc is within the defined objects of the charity it's being 'kept' by the charity and Gift Aid can apply, subject to all other conditions being met. If the borrowed property and its preservation would be outside the charity's objects and it's displayed by its owners rather than by the charity that is, the charity does not borrow the property for incorporation into its own displays, that property is not 'kept' by a charity.
> If the property - not regarded as 'kept' by the charity - constitutes a significant part of the attraction at a particular property, Gift Aid would probably not apply to the payment for admission as the value of viewing non-charity property would have to be accounted for as a non-charitable Gift Aid benefit.

HMRC published the clauses in draft on 21 January 2005 with a commentary which explained:

> The fact that the property must be preserved, maintained kept or created "in pursuance of its charitable purposes" means that commercial

---

137 The HMRC Guidance Note provides a straightforward example:

- A national child welfare charity – CWC – has a permanent exhibition at its headquarters, illustrating the value of toys and games as elements of a healthy childhood.
- The toys on display belong to a Museum of childhood (MOC), which is a charity with similar objects to CWC
- The charity (CWC) is therefore admitting visitors to view property kept, maintained etc by a charity – MOC

activities run solely to raise funds would not be eligible. For example, an amusement park in the grounds of a museum would not be eligible.

15.39.4 *Performances*

Section 420(6) ITA provides:

> The property mentioned in subsection (5) [charity-purpose property] includes, in particular ...
> (e) works of art (but not performances),

The HMRC Guidance Note provides:

> **Performances**
> 3.39.22 Performances are specifically excluded from the category of 'works of art' but Gift Aid may still be available on donations made for admission to view property where performances also take place.
> For example:
> - donations to admit visitors to a performance of a play at an historic theatre will not qualify
> - but the same theatre may be open at times when performances are not taking place, to allow visitors to view its architectural features
>
> 3.39.23 If a performance is merely incidental to the viewing of a charity's property or it can be regarded as integral to the viewing of that property it's not disqualified as a 'performance'.
> For example:
> - historic re-enactments illustrative of the property's former use
> - demonstrations of technical processes or crafts associated with the property
> - interactive experiments in a science museum
>
> 3.39.24 Rights of admission that include interactive experiments with an educational purpose and displays of military memorabilia will also qualify as being integral to the viewing of charity property.

HMRC does not regard showing a film as a performance.

15.39.5 *Annual admission: Condition C*

Section 420(7) ITA provides:

> Condition C is that the right of admission applies, during a period of at least 12 months, at all times at which the public can obtain admission.

Section 421 ITA dilutes the requirement that the right of admission must apply "at all times when the public can obtain admission":

> (2) Condition C is to be treated as met even if the right does not apply on

days which are specified by the charity as event days[138], provided that no more than 5 days are specified for that purpose in relation to the applicable period.

(3) The applicable period is—

(a) the period during which the right applies, in the case of a right which applies for a period of 12 months, or

(b) each calendar year during all or part of which the right applies, in the case of a right which applies for a period of more than 12 months.

The HMRC Guidance Note explains:

The annual right of admission option

3.39.6 This option applies where, in return for a donation, a charity grants a right of admission to view charity property for a period of at least 1 year, at all times that members of the public can gain admission. Charities can opt to:

(a) Accept a donation and allow free admission for all visits during the period covered (but the charity can specify up to five days when the right of free admission does not apply). However a visitor who chooses to make a donation but does not complete a Gift Aid declaration must also be able to gain free admission on the same terms. So in practice the '12 months entry' price must be available to all whether they chose to make a Gift Aid declaration or not.

(b) Accept a donation and grant a right of admission on payment of a reduced fee, which must apply for the first and all subsequent visits during the period covered. In this scenario only the initial donation will qualify for Gift Aid. The first and subsequent admission fees are not donations but are payments of a charge for admission to view the property. A visitor who chooses to make a donation but does not complete a Gift Aid declaration must also be able to gain the same reduced rate admission on the same terms for their first and all subsequent visits.

This is correct. The HMRC Guidance Note then becomes controversial:

3.39.7 A charity granting annual admission in return for a donation must apply 1 or the other of these scenarios rather than a mixture of the 2, that is, the same free or reduced rate admission must be applied for the first

---

138 Section 421(4) ITA provides a commonsense definition of "event day": "An 'event day' is a day on which an event is to take place on the premises to which the right relates."

and all subsequent visits.
A 12 month admission scheme where a donation, equal to the cost of a day admission, secures 1 free visit and repeat visits at reduced rates does not succeed because it mixes free and reduced price admission.

We cannot see the basis for this in the statute, but it would be wise to follow the guidance to avoid a dispute. The HMRC Guidance Note continues:

3.39.8 Charities are free to decide what minimum level of donation they'll accept before granting a right of admission for a year or more (so for example can choose to allow annual admission for a donation equal to the daily admission charge), but must always give an equivalent right of admission to all donors including those who do not make a Gift Aid declaration that is, the right of admission mustn't be made conditional upon the donor making a Gift Aid declaration. It must also be made clear to the donor before they're asked to complete a Gift Aid declaration that they can purchase the yearly right of admission without making the Gift Aid declaration for the same price as if they do make the declaration. For further guidance see paragraph 3.39.5.
3.39.9 Charities do not have to be open all year or every day to grant a right of admission for a period of a year or more. Gift Aid can apply as long as the right of admission is available to donors at all times when the property is open for viewing by members of the public. Charities may, however, specify up to 5 days per year when the donors' free or reduced rate right of admission will not apply. For further guidance see paragraph 3.39.25.
3.39.27 If a charity excludes donors from free or reduced rate admission to view the charity property when a special event is taking place, it may nonetheless admit donors for that day only, on payment of the public admission charge. The payment of the admission charge will not qualify for Gift Aid as it will be a payment to attend the event rather than to view the charity property.
Example 1
A charity allows donors the right of free annual admission to view its property but donors are excluded from free entry on 5 days per year because events with a separate admission charge are taking place, such as a Christmas fayre, Easter egg hunt, Fashion show, etc. On those days the charity charges donors the full public admission price, which does not qualify for Gift Aid. If there were 6 or more such events in the year none of the donations would qualify for Gift Aid.
Example 2
If donors with the annual right of free admission were charged a reduced

price for admission to a special event, the value of the discount would be taken into account as an additional benefit received in consequence of their donation. The payment of the reduced admission fee would not qualify for Gift Aid (see paragraph 3.39.30)
3.39.28 Special events that are held outside the times when the charity property is normally open to members of the public need not be taken into account when applying this restriction.

Example

A charity allows donors the right of free annual admission to view its property on weekdays only. It can exclude donors from free admission to special events, such as concerts, held on any Saturday or Sunday, but exclusion of donors from free admission on a weekday because a special event is taking place must be restricted to a maximum of 5 days in any 12 month period.

15.39.6 *Admission + 10%: Condition D*

Section 420(8) ITA provides:

Condition D is that—
(a) a member of the public could purchase the same right of admission and
(b) the amount of the gift is greater by at least 10% than the amount the member of the public would have to pay.

Section 421(5) ITA provides:

In condition D, "the same right of admission" means a right relating to the same property, classes of person and periods of time as the right received in consequence of the gift

The HMRC Guidance Note provides:

The 'admission charge plus 10%' option

3.39.10 This option applies where a member of the public could purchase a right of admission, but instead chooses to make a gift that is at least 10% more than the admission charge, and in return for that donation the charity grants the equivalent admission to view charity property. The whole amount received from a donor is treated as a donation for Gift Aid purposes, not just the additional 10%.
3.39.11 Any period of admission from 1 day to less than 12 months can be included within this option as long as members of the public could purchase an equivalent right of admission.

Example

A charity may sell a summer season ticket for a period of three months for £30. If the same right of admission is granted to an individual donating an additional 10% (that is, paying £33 in total), the whole £33 can qualify for Gift Aid.

3.39.12 For payments to qualify for Gift Aid, each visitor must be made aware at the time they're asked for payment that they can choose to pay the admission charge or make a voluntary donation of 10% more than the admission charge and receive the same right of admission. If the visitor is denied the right to choose to pay the standard admission charge, then payment of the extra 10% is not a freely given gift and cannot be a qualifying donation. Charities must clearly advertise their normal admission charges and make it absolutely clear to all visitors that they will be admitted upon payment of the lower admission charge if they choose not to make an additional 10% voluntary donation.

Classes of admission

3.39.37 A charity may make admission available at concessionary rates for different classes of visitor for example, pensioners, students, disabled visitors, the unwaged etc. When granting the right of entry in return for a donation of 10% more than the admission charge, the 10% extra is applied to the specific charge for each particular class of visitor.

Example

The standard adult admission charge to a charity property is £15, with a reduced admission charge of £10 available to pensioners.

Mr Green is a pensioner and makes an additional voluntary donation of £1.00 (10% of £10.00) - he can Gift Aid his whole donation of £11.00. His daughter Miss Green is not entitled to any concessions, so must make a voluntary donation of £1.50 (10% of £15.00) in order to Gift Aid her total donation of £16.50.

If Miss Green makes a donation to secure admission for both herself and her father, the total amount she must pay to qualify for Gift Aid is £27.50

15.39.7 *Joint admission*

The HMRC Guidance Note provides:

3.39.16 Gift Aid can apply to donations which give the donor a right of admission to the property of more than 1 charity. The visitor who chooses to make a donation must, however, know which charity or charities are sharing his donation, and in what proportions. There are 2 general scenarios possible:

(a) Where 1 charity manages the whole venue, and has a separate contractual arrangement with the other charities for providing that management service, any visitor choosing to make a donation will make it to the managing charity and the Gift Aid declaration need only specify that charity.

(b) Where each charity administers its own site but there are joint admission arrangements allowing for a split of the admission charge or donation between the charities then the visitor must be made aware, if he chooses to make a donation, of the amount of the donation 'per charity'. This must be clearly specified at the time of the donation. The Gift Aid declaration must also reflect this correctly.

Example 1

A joint admission ticket allows access to 3 different charity properties, specifying that the admission charge of £15.00 is allocated in equal proportions that is, £5.00 to each of the 3 charities offering admission to their property.

If a donor makes an additional voluntary contribution of £1.50 (10% of £15.00) each charity could claim Gift Aid on £5.50; HMRC will accept a joint declaration which specifies the names of each charity and shows that the donor is aware of the allocation when he makes his donation.

Example 2

2 charities together offer a qualifying right of annual admission to their properties in return for a donation of £100 to be allocated between them in the proportion 70:30.

The charities could claim Gift Aid on £70 and £30 respectively; The charities can use a joint declaration which specifies the names of each charity and shows that the donor is aware of the allocation when he makes his donation.

3.39.17 In these circumstances care must be taken regarding the format of the Gift Aid declaration, and charities considering this type of joint admission arrangement can contact HMRC Charities for assistance.

This is necessary since HMRC must know which charity is entitled to reclaim tax on the gift. The HMRC Guidance Note continues:

Mixed sites

3.39.18 Charities must also be very careful when they consider offering multiple admissions to a mixture of charity and non-charity properties. The right of entry to a non-charity property may have to be considered as a benefit received in consequence of the donation (unless it is clearly priced and paid for separately).

Charities in this position should contact HMRC Charities for guidance about specific scenarios or proposals.

Reciprocal arrangements with other charities

3.39.19 Gift Aid can apply to qualifying donations which grant a right of admission to the property of more than 1 charity as long as there's an equivalent right of admission granted to donors who opt not to make a Gift Aid declaration.

Example

2 zoos in different parts of the country may have a reciprocal arrangement to allow donors annual admission to the other's property. As long as each is a charity the benefit of admission to each site can be disregarded under this arrangement.

There's no additional benefit as donors receive a disregarded right of admission to each zoo.

15.39.8 *Benefit in addition to admission*

The HMRC Guidance Note provides:

> 3.39.29 Some charities give donors other benefits apart from the right of admission. Only the right of admission to view a charity property can be disregarded and any other benefits provided to a donor as a consequence of a donation must be valued separately and taken into account when considering whether the donation qualifies for Gift Aid. The value to be taken into account is the value to the donor not the cost to the charity. A charity may decide to provide visitors with benefits as a thank you for making an optional 10% donation; this is acceptable providing the benefits do not exceed the normal benefit rules.
>
> **Example:**
>
> - the admission charge to view a charity's property is £20.00
> - visitors making a donation (£22) of an extra 10% are granted free admission
> - the full amount donated, £22.00 qualifies for Gift Aid and the charity can therefore give other benefits with a value of
> - to £5.50 (being 25% of £22.00)
> - if the charity gives a soft toy worth £6 (the benefit to the donor is the retail value not the cost of the item to the (charity) no Gift Aid can be claimed on the donation as the benefit limit is exceeded
> - if the charity offers a voucher for £5.00 to spend in the restaurant, the donation will qualify for Gift Aid
>
> **Particular benefits - admission to special events**
>
> 3.39.30 If admission to a property also includes free or reduced rate entry into events that are held on the charity's premises, and for which a separate admission charge applies, then the value of free or reduced price entry into those special events must be taken into account as an additional benefit in consequence of a donation for Gift Aid purposes. Depending on the value of the event it may mean that the donation does not qualify for Gift Aid.

Example
A charity allows free annual admission to its estate in return for a donation. The charity holds an annual Easter egg hunt on the estate, for which there is a special public admission charge of £10. The charity allows free entry to the Easter egg hunt to donors. The additional benefit of £10 is not automatically disregarded for Gift Aid purposes but must be taken into account as an additional benefit in consequence of the donation.

Particular benefits - use of charity facilities
3.39.31 If the right of admission includes the use of charity facilities then the value of the use of those facilities must be taken into account as an additional benefit in consequence of a donation for Gift Aid purposes. Depending on the value of the use of those facilities it may mean that the donation does not qualify for Gift Aid.

Example
A charity charges visitors to view a historic building, visitors can pay an optional additional fee to use a swimming pool housed in the building. The charity allows free annual admission to the building and swimming pool in return for a donation. The right of admission to the building is disregarded for Gift Aid purposes, but the value of the right to use the swimming pool facilities must be taken into account as an additional benefit in consequence of the donation.
If you're in doubt about how to treat a particular item, site or event at a property covered by this legislation please contact HMRC Charities with full details.

15.39.9 *Refunded admission fee*

The HMRC Guidance Note formerly provided:

> 3.48.16 Some heritage[139] charities offer to refund visitors' admission fees if they agree to take out membership of the charity for, say, one year. For Gift Aid purposes the refunded admission fee is a benefit received in consequence of paying the membership fee. Refunding a previously paid admission fee is not equivalent to allowing a member free admission as, at the time they paid the admission fee, the visitor was not a member and not entitled to free admission. If the benefit exceeds the Gift Aid donor benefit limit the membership subscription will not qualify as a Gift Aid donation. However, if the charity has a special category of membership for paying visitors, that reduced membership subscription can qualify as a Gift Aid payment.

---

139 The relief for admission charges was formerly restricted to heritage charities.

Example 1
Admission charge paid to a "heritage" charity of £8.
Visitor pays membership subscription of £30 and receives refund of admission charge of £8 (only "other" benefit received for membership is right of free entry to view heritage property).
The benefit of £8 exceeds the donor benefit limit of 25% (£8 is 26.67% of £30) and so the £30 fails as a Gift Aid payment.
Example 2
The situation is the same as Example 1 but the charity offer a reduced membership fee of £22 to visitors that have paid an admission charge (no refund is given). The extra payment of £22 is eligible as a Gift Aid payment.

This is not now in the HMRC Guidance Note, but it is still correct: see 15.33 (Multiple/single/split payment).

15.39.10 *Restriction to family*

Section 420(2) ITA defines "right of admission":

> "Right of admission" means a right which—
> (a) [i] benefits the individual who makes the gift or
> [ii] that individual and one or more members of that individual's family (whether or not the right must be exercised by all of them at the same time)

The HMRC Guidance Note provides:

Family admission
3.39.38 The right of admission of the donor and 1 or more members of his/her family can be disregarded for Gift Aid purposes, whether or not that right of admission is exercised by all of the family members at the same time.
Example
Mr Smith makes a donation in return for which a charity grants the right of annual admission to Mr Smith, his wife and his two children. His donation will qualify for Gift Aid even if his wife and children visit the property without him, or if he visits the property alone.
3.39.39 What constitutes a 'family' for the purposes of a 'family ticket' depends on the circumstances. Typically a family ticket will be available to a couple and their minor children or to everyone living in the same home - which might include adult children and grandparents. Either is acceptable for Gift Aid purposes. It's each charity's responsibility to explain to visitors that in order for donations to qualify for Gift Aid, the right of admission must apply to family members only. HMRC

> recommends that charities draw attention to this requirement in literature and signage. There's no expectation that the charity will make detailed identity or relationship checks on individuals. However, it's in the charity's interests to monitor donations for 'family admissions', as HMRC may query claims for Gift Aid on unusual groups may be queried *if audited.*

These last two sentences are contradictory. However, the example which follows shows what is meant.

> If a charity wanted to introduce a different definition of 'family' to either of the two above and seek to claim Gift Aid on that ticket they should contact HMRC Charities explaining the definition of 'a family' they intend to use before submitting any Gift Aid claims for that ticket.
>
> *Example*
>
> If a visitor wishes to make a Gift Aid donation to admit a group of 8 adults (paying 8 times the single admission + 10% donation), he or she should be told that only donations giving the right of admission to the donor's own family members will qualify for Gift Aid. The visitor should be asked to confirm that 7 guests are indeed members of their own family. If audited, the charity is likely to be asked to demonstrate that its procedures included this confirmation. Whilst it's not a statutory obligation, charities might decide to include this confirmation on Gift Aid declarations/till receipts.
>
> 3.39.40 Many charities offer 'family tickets' at special prices. Each charity can decide its own policy for what they're prepared to accept in terms of family size and familial relationships when granting such a right of admission, but this is not directly relevant to the Gift Aid provisions.
>
> *Example*
>
> A charity may offer a 'family ticket' allowing annual admission for 2 adults and up to 3 children at a reduced rate.
>
> If Mr and Mrs Brown have 4 children, Mrs Brown may claim Gift Aid on her donation for a 'family ticket' obtaining a right of annual admission in accordance with the charity's rules for a family reduction. She can also make a Gift Aid donation for the additional child admission she obtains to take the whole family to view the property as she is merely making a second donation for 1 or more members of her family.
>
> **Group Admissions**
>
> 3.39.41 A donor cannot make a qualifying donation in respect of payment for a group of people who are not members of his/her family, for example a group arriving as a coach party.
>
> 3.39.42 An individual can, however, collect donations from members of a group and pass them on to the charity for administrative convenience.

> Each member of the group who makes a donation must individually fulfil the Gift Aid conditions (so the donation could be for his personal admission, or for himself and members of his family), and each donor must complete a personal Gift Aid declaration. Any cheques must be made payable to the charity rather than the group organiser.
> 3.39.43 The charity must take care only to claim Gift Aid in respect of those members of the group who make qualifying Gift Aid donations.

A membership option which contains the option to bring a guest (without specifying that the guest must be a family member) is not uncommon amongst charities. These charities are likely claiming Gift Aid on this membership option, but technically they should not be. Whilst it is difficult to see any purpose to this rule, which just adds to the paperwork (each family having to make its own donation), it is the current rule and therefore these charities may need to rethink this membership option or they may risk enquiry by HMRC.

15.39.11 *Admission relief : Critique*

The relief for rights of admission is responsible for slow moving queues at venues across the UK, as staff at entry booths labouriously enter in details for the Gift Aid declaration. As the reader stands in the queue, they may well ask: What is the policy behind admission relief? It is not the normal aim of charity tax relief, which is to encourage philanthropy.[140] The philanthropic element in the admission + 10% is minimal. It is reduced further by the practice of dealing with the donation by a notice saying *Price includes 10% donation,* which is overlooked by many if not most visitors, even though it gives the more observant and parsimonious an opportunity to refuse to make the donation.

Is there any reason why privileged admission-charities deserve special state subvention? Admission relief exists for historical reasons, and perhaps represents a powerful lobby.

A serious discussion of reform would require an estimate of the amounts of tax involved in this relief, and an estimate of the effect on admission-charities of withdrawal of the relief, which include culturally important charities such as the National Trust. We have not tried to do that. But the case for admission relief is, to say the least, far from self-evident. Those hostile to charity reliefs might do well to start here. Repeal of admission relief would be a simplification, too.15.40.1

140 See 1.4.2 (Tax reliefs of donor).

15.40 Retail Gift Aid

15.40.1 *No relief for gift of goods*

There is of course no Gift Aid for a gift of goods. The HMRC Guidance Note provides:

> **Selling donated goods**
> 3.42.1 Gift Aid applies only to gifts of money by an individual. So, if a person simply donates goods to a charity, Gift Aid does not apply. Charities cannot claim Gift Aid on donations of any physical items, such as clothes or books, only on donations of money.

On the other hand, there is relief if an individual sells the goods and gives the proceeds of sale.

> 3.42.2 However, in certain situations, Gift Aid can be claimed by charities or CASCs on the income from the sale of supporters' goods. The rules that apply are considered in the rest of this Chapter. References to charity or charities throughout should be taken to include CASCs unless otherwise stated.
> **Carrying out the sale of goods on behalf of the owner**
> 3.42.3 Charity shops may be run directly by the charity or by a subsidiary trading company. A charity or its trading company can offer to act as an agent for private individuals and sell goods on their behalf, so that at the point of sale the funds actually belong to the individual. The charity or its trading company can then ask the owner of the goods to donate the sale proceeds to the charity. If the owner agrees to donate the sales proceeds to the charity, Gift Aid can be claimed by the charity on the net sales proceeds subject to all other Gift Aid conditions being satisfied...

HMRC call this arrangement **"retail Gift Aid"**.

The lengthy section in the HMRC guidance note on this topic is a mix of legal requirements and HMRC's views of good practice, preferences or recommendations; the latter are not legally binding but are (wrongly) expressed in the guidance in imperative terms. In general it would be sensible to follow the guidance, but it is important to identify what is law (mandatory) and what is guidance (breach of which will not affect tax relief).

15.40.2 *Three methods*

> **Operating the Gift Aid process**
> 3.42.6 There are 3 ways charity shops can operate the Gift Aid process - the Standard Method, Method A and Method B.

> The first is the method that charities have been using up to 5 April 2013 and is called the 'Standard Method'. This is explained in paragraph 3.42.7 below. Please note the guidance on the standard method has changed and charities that continue to use this method should check that their process matches the changed guidance below....
> The other 2 methods, 'Method A' and 'Method B', can be used from 6 April 2013. The methods a charity can use will depend on how it operates its shops.
> If shops are operated by the charity directly, then the charity can use the Standard Method or Method A.
> If the shops are operated by a separate entity such as a trading subsidiary company then the Standard Method, Method A or Method B can be used.
> 3.42.10 If goods are given to a shop operated by the charity itself to sell those goods on behalf of the individual, the charity must use 'Method A' or the Standard Method to operate the Retail Gift Aid process. This is because the charity is both the donor's agent and recipient of any Gift Aid donations. However, if the goods are given to a shop operated by a trading subsidiary company of a charity that sells donated goods on behalf of an individual, it can use either 'Method A' or 'Method B' or the Standard Method.

This text twice states that trading subsidiaries may use either method A or B, but in fact it is envisaged that method A is only for charities; and method B is only for trading subsidiaries.

The three methods may be summarised as follows:

Method	Shop run by	In-year letter to donee	Date of gift
Standard	Charity or trading co	In all cases	21 days after letter
Method A	Charity	If gift above £100	21 days after sale (up to £100)
Method B	Trading co	If gift above £1,000	21 days after sale (up to £1k)

15.40.3 *Template letters*

All the methods involve the use of standard form letters sent to donors, which HMRC call template letters.[141] The HMRC Guidance Note provides:

> 3.42.6 ...[Charities] should check that the letters they issue to donors follow the wording of the model letters.
>
> 3.42.9 ... The charity must use the compulsory text in the standard method template letter below when writing to the individual. Charities are free to

141 For the text, see App 3.1 (Retail Gift Aid: Template Letters).

> add additional information to the letter or alter the opening and closing sections but the words in italics must be used...

The HMRC Guidance Note provides:

> 3.42.15 The charity must use the compulsory text in the templates when sending both in-year and end of tax year letters to the individual. Charities are free to add additional information to the letters or alter the opening and closing sections, but the words in italics must be used.

This is only guidance; of course it is not necessary to use the HMRC wording exactly.

> 'End of tax year letters' are compulsory for charities operating the retail Gift Aid process using Method A and Method B. In both cases the individual must always be sent a summary of the net proceeds raised from the sale of their goods for the tax year by 31 May each year. However, if the donor's total donations in a given year are less than £20, a letter only needs to be issued once every three years. Telling individuals of the net proceeds raised provides information which can help them check that they have paid sufficient tax to cover the Gift Aid that has been claimed. It also helps higher rate tax payers to claim in the additional tax relief on their donations.
>
> Any adjustments required as a result of the donor notifying the charity of a change in tax status or other details must be actioned by the charity within 2 months.
>
> HMRC recommend that all in-year and end-of-tax year Gift Aid letters are sent by post. Charities may use email, but if a charity is alerted to an email having been rejected by receiving an 'undeliverable' message, they must follow up and send the donor a letter by post too.

We think charities may prefer the email option, given the cost of post; but that is essentially a marketing/fundraising decision.

15.40.4 *Standard method*

The HMRC Guidance Note provides:

> 3.42.7 This method has been available since 2006. This guidance has been updated and charities that choose to use this method should ensure their process matches this guidance and in particular, that the letters they issue to donors include the compulsory wording of the model letters. See paragraph 3.42.9 onwards. Failure to follow this guidance could result in the subsequent Gift Aid claims being invalidated.
>
> 3.42.8 The way the Standard method works is that an individual takes goods to a charity shop and agrees that the shop will act as their agent in

> selling the goods (for which a commission plus related VAT will be deducted from the proceeds). A Gift Aid declaration is completed by the individual at this stage, if the charity does not already hold one. The charity marks the goods in some way so that the sales proceeds can be linked back directly to the donor.
> 3.42.9 After the goods are sold (but before the charity makes a gift aid claim) the charity shop writes (or sends an email) to the owner of the goods to advise them of the net sale proceeds. The letter / email explains that the charity intends to treat this amount as a gift to the charity unless the owner contacts the charity within 21 days (of the date of the letter / email) to say they want to keep the proceeds. The charity shop must then give the individual at least 21 days to respond to this letter / email before it treats the net sale proceeds as a donation to the charity.

The HMRC Guidance Note gives an example, but that does not add anything to the above.[142]

> **Alternative Methods 'A' and 'B'**
> 3.42.10 ... methods A and B allow the individual to specify when signing up to Gift Aid at the start of the process that they will donate net sales proceeds up to a certain amount in each tax year without the charity needing to ask them every time.

Methods A and B are easier to administer, and in practice we doubt if any well informed charity will choose to use the "standard method".

---

142 **Example 1**
Emma brings a bag of clothes to a shop run by a charity, and agrees that they can sell all the goods on her behalf.
She completes a Gift Aid declaration naming the charity operating the shop.
The shop assistant explains the process and tells Emma that she's under no obligation to donate the net sale proceeds.
When they sort and price Emma's goods, the shop links them to her using a unique donor number on each price tag or on a bar code on each label.
Every time the shop sells any of these goods, it records the amount received against her unique donor number. Before the charity can make a Gift Aid claim on the net proceeds from the sale of Emma's goods, it writes to her (using the template letter) to tell her the total net amount raised from selling her goods. The letter / email asks her to contact the charity within 21 days if she wants to keep any of the 'net sale proceeds 'from the charity.
Emma is happy to donate all the net sales proceeds mentioned in the letter / e-mail, so she doesn't reply. At the end of the 21 day period the charity can assume Emma is content to donate the net proceeds, and can treat them as a Gift Aid donation.

15.40.5 *Method A: Charity runs shop*

The HMRC Guidance Note provides:

> 3.42.11 Method A is for charities that directly operate their own shops. Under this method of operating the Retail Gift Aid process it is not necessary for a charity to send letters during the tax year to each individual when the net proceeds from selling their goods are less than £100 in that year. The charity must obtain the agreement of the individual when they bring the goods to the shop to sell. They must make it clear to the individual that, if the total net sale proceeds in a tax year are below £100, the individual will not be offered any money back before the charity treats the net proceeds as a donation and claims Gift Aid. This is on the basis that the individual has agreed to donate the money to the charity. If the net proceeds from the sale of goods are more than £100, the charity must contact donors to ask if they will also donate the proceeds over £100 to the charity.
>
> Once the limit of £100 has been exceeded in any given tax year, the company or charity can either:
>
> - send a letter or email to the individual and then write again each time further goods are sold
> - wait until the end of the tax year and send one letter or email detailing the total amount raised in the year
>
> and in either case the individual must be given at least 21 days to let the charity know whether they want to donate to the charity the amount raised in excess of £100.
>
> In either case, the charity will NOT be able to claim Gift Aid on the excess over £100 until the donor has been sent the notification by letter or email and 21 days have elapsed without a response.
>
> The individual should also be told that they will receive a letter or email at the end of the tax year informing them of the total amount raised from the sales of their goods. Individuals who can claim higher rate tax relief need this letter to enable them to claim their tax relief

There is no statutory basis for the £100 limit.

The HMRC Guidance Note continues:

> The charity must use the following template letters when writing to donors. Charities can add additional information to the letters or alter the opening and closing sections but the words in italics must be used.

This is only guidance; of course it is not necessary to use the HMRC wording exactly.

The HMRC Guidance Note then gives an example, though that does not add anything to the above.[143]

15.40.6 *Method B: Subsidiary runs shop*

The HMRC Guidance Note provides:

> 3.42.12 Method B is for charity shops where Retail Gift Aid is managed and operated by a subsidiary trading company of a charity. This method of operating the Retail Gift Aid process is similar to Method A but it can only be used where a trading company receives the goods, sells them on behalf of the donor, and then transfers the donated proceeds to the charity. For the purpose of this process it does not matter whether the company owns the lease to the shop or not.
> The trading company can:
> - be the operator of all the retail selling for the charity
> - just sell donated goods under Method B and operate that process for the charity
> - sell new goods, and the donated goods under Method B and operate that process for the charity

---

143 **Example 2**
Sam brings a bag of shoes to a shop run by a charity, and agrees that they can sell all the shoes on her behalf. The shop assistant explains the process and tells Sam that she's under no obligation to donate the sale proceeds.
Sam agrees to donate the net proceeds up to £100 and accepts that the charity will not contact her during the tax year if the sales proceeds do not exceed £100.
She completes a Gift Aid declaration naming the charity that operates the shop and signs an agreement for the charity to sell her donated goods.
The shop's staff link Sam's goods to her using a unique donor number or bar coded label on each price tag. When the shop sells any of her goods, it records the sale proceeds against her unique donor number.
The net proceeds raised from the sale of Sam's shoes is £83. As this is below £100, the shop does not need to ask her to confirm she wants to donate the proceeds to the charity.
If the charity had raised net sales proceeds of £120 from selling Sam's shoes, it would have to send her a letter or e-mail either during the year or at the end of the tax year telling her the amount of the sale proceeds and asking her to contact the charity if she has not paid sufficient tax or her details have changed. But they must also tell her to let the charity know within 21 days if she wants to keep any of the sale proceeds over £100.
Whatever amounts are raised from sales made under this method, at the end of the tax year the charity will send Sam a letter or e-mail informing her of the total net proceeds raised from the sale of her goods during the year. They should also ask her to contact the charity within 21 days, if she has not paid sufficient Income and / or Capital Gains Tax to cover the Gift Aid claimed back by the charity, or if her contact details have changed.

The company must monitor and record the total net sale proceeds raised from the goods sold on behalf of each individual during each tax year.
3.42.13 The procedure where an individual takes goods to a charity shop run by a subsidiary trading company is that they sign an agency agreement with the company to sell donated goods under Method B. The donor also makes a Gift Aid declaration to the charity operating the shop. The agreement confirms that the company will act as the individual's agent to sell the donated goods and that the net proceeds raised will be gifted to the charity automatically as long as they do not exceed £1,000 in any tax year. The agreement must state that the individual and the company are entering into an agency arrangement and that the company will sell goods on behalf of the individual in return for a commission (or may dispose of them if they cannot be sold). The company must make clear to the individual that, if the total net sale proceeds in a tax year are below £1,000, the individual will not be offered their money back before the charity claims Gift Aid, because the agreement committed the individual to donate the money to the charity.
£1,000 is the maximum net sale proceeds to which Method B can apply, with individuals committed to donate all the proceeds to the charity. Charities and their trading companies can offer a lower amount if individuals consider £1,000 to be too high for this purpose.
Once the limit of £1,000 has been exceeded in any given tax year, the company or charity can either:

- send a letter or email to the individual and then write again each time further goods are sold
- wait until the end of the tax year and send one letter or email detailing the total amount raised in the year and in either case give the individual at least 21 days to let the charity know if they do not want to donate to the charity the amount raised in excess of £1,000

In either case, the charity will NOT be able to claim Gift Aid on the excess over £1,000 until the donor has been sent the notification by letter or email and 21 days have elapsed without a response.

There is no statutory basis for the £1,000 limit.

The HMRC Guidance Note gives an example, though that does not add anything to the above.[144]

---

144 **Example 3**
Bill brings some paintings to a charity shop run by a trading company, and agrees that the shop sell them all on his behalf.
The shop assistant explains the process and tells Bill that he's under no obligation to donate the sale proceeds. Bill agrees that if the net sales proceeds from the paintings or subsequent donations are no more than £1,000 in the tax year, the

HMRC Guidance Note states:

> Method B isn't suitable for CASCs because subsidiary companies of a CASC can't donate profits to the CASC under corporate Gift Aid.

That is no longer correct as corporate Gift Aid does now apply to corporate gifts to CASCs.

15.40.7 *Change of method*

The HMRC Guidance Note provides:

> 3.42.14 If a charity uses the 'Standard Method' for claiming Gift Aid on donations raised from the sale of goods in its shops, it can switch to one of the simplified methods at any time. The appropriate limit of £100 or £1,000 will then apply during the remaining part of the tax year. Only goods sold after the simplified process is implemented fall within the new arrangements.
> The charity must consider how it will move its donors from the standard method to Method A or B. The easiest way is to move everyone at the start of a tax year, but there's no legal requirement to do this. A charity can choose to run 2 processes simultaneously if it so wishes.

---

charity will not contact him during the tax year to confirm he wishes to donate the proceeds to the charity.
Bill completes a Gift Aid declaration naming the charity represented by the shop, and also signs an agency agreement with the shop to sell his paintings.
When the shop's staff sort and price the goods, they link Bill's goods to him via a unique donor number on the price tag or a separate bar coded label.
When the shop sells any of these goods, it records the amount raised against Bill's unique donor number.
The shop keeps a record of the net sales proceeds from the sale of Bill's paintings and the total comes to £750.
The charity will need to write a letter or email to Bill at the end of the tax year informing him that during the tax year they raised a total of £750 from selling his paintings and asks him to contact the charity within 21 days, if he has not paid sufficient Income or Capital Gains Tax to cover the Gift Aid claimed back by the charity, or if his contact details have changed.
If there's a further sale in the year that raises net sales proceeds of £300, the total net sale proceeds will have exceeded the £1,000 limit and the charity must write to Bill each time the amount above £1,000 has been exceeded, or at the end of the tax year, to tell him the value of the net sale proceeds and ask him to contact the charity within 21 days if he wants to keep any of the net sale proceeds over £1,000. They must in any case write to him at the end of the tax year asking him to contact the charity if he has not paid sufficient tax during the year, or his details have changed.

When individuals have already signed an agreement with the charity to convert their donated goods into Gift Aid donations, a charity can either wait for them to visit their charity shop again and then ask them to sign a new agreement for the simplified method, or the charity can write to all existing donors and explain that its sale process has changed. The charity can tell people that it will assume they agree to the new process applying to the future sales of their donated goods unless they tell the charity otherwise within 21 days. The charity should remind the individual of the need to have paid sufficient Income Tax and / or Capital Gains Tax to cover amounts up to the new agreed limit, as well as amounts donated to other charities. It must also send the individual a letter at the end of the tax year confirming the net sales proceeds and requesting notification of any change in tax status or contact details.

15.40.8 *"Net sale proceeds"*

The HMRC Guidance Note provides:

> 3.42.16 When a charity offers an individual the proceeds from the sale of their goods, or claims Gift Aid on the proceeds if they're donated to the charity, the proceeds in question are the 'net sale proceeds'. This means the total proceeds raised after deduction of any sale commission and related VAT charged by a charity or its trading company subsidiary...

The HMRC Guidance Note then gives an example, though that does not add anything to the above.[145]

---

145 **Example 4**
John asks a charity shop run by a subsidiary trading company to sell a vase on his behalf and completes a Gift Aid declaration.
John is asked to sign an agency agreement under Method B and is told that there is a 5% commission for handling the sale.
The vase sells for £1,050.
Under the terms of his agency agreement John has told the shop that he does not want to receive net sale proceeds under £1,000.
The charity shop takes a sale commission of £52.50 plus £10.50 VAT out of the £1,050 and passes the balance to the charity.
The charity can claim Gift Aid on £987 but not the £63 commission fee (including VAT).
The charity or its trading subsidiary must account for VAT on commission fees that are a taxable supply of services. If the goods were sold by a shop operated directly by the charity (where the limit is £100 under Method A) and the charity was not registered or required to be registered for VAT, there would be no VAT to deduct.

15.40.9 *Agency agreement*

The HMRC Guidance Note provides:

> 3.42.17 Charities must ensure that the agency agreements they use make clear that they are legally binding contracts.
> The individual needs to be told that the charity or its trading subsidiary will be selling their goods on their behalf so that the net sale proceeds can be given to the charity as a Gift Aid donation. They need to be aware that they must pay enough Income Tax and/or Capital Gains Tax to cover the tax the charity will reclaim through Gift Aid on the donated sale proceeds.
> There needs to be a written agreement between the individual and the charity, and the charity needs to keep a record of each individual's agreement. The agreement can be a document signed by the donor, or a leaflet or information sheet given to the donor. The form of the agreement is for the charity to decide but it must cover the following points:
>
> - the individual must be made aware that the charity is acting as agent in selling their goods
> - the individual must be made aware that they're not donating the goods, but arranging for the charity to sell them on their behalf
> - the agreement must specify the rate of commission charged for selling the individual's goods on their behalf. Gift Aid can only be claimed on the balance donated after commission and related VAT has been deducted
> - the agreement should specify that if the cumulative net sales proceeds are less than £100 for Method A or £1,000 for Method B in a tax year, the charity will not have to notify the individual before it claims Gift Aid on the amount
> - if the net sales proceeds exceed £100 or £1,000, the agreement should specify that the charity will contact them, so that the individual has an opportunity to decide whether to donate the proceeds in excess of £100 or £1,000. The letter should give the individual 21 days to let the company know if they do not want to donate the additional amount to the charity
> - the agreement should specify that an end of tax year letter will be sent, whether or not the cumulative net sales proceeds are less than £100 or £1,000 in a tax year

It is important that the documentation is correct. It is (fortunately) not necessary for the donor to fully understand it.

15.40.10 *Gift Aid claim*

> **Tax implications for donors**
> 3.42.4 In order for the owner's donation of the proceeds of the sale of goods to qualify for Gift Aid, the following conditions must apply:
> - the private individual retains legal and beneficial ownership of the goods until they're sold

Strictly, all that matters is that the supporter retains beneficial ownership. Legal ownership is not relevant. But in practice the two are not likely to be split, so perhaps the criticism is pedantic.

> - it must be clear to potential customers that the shop is selling the goods on behalf of the owner and not the charity, and the owner of the goods and the charity must both understand that the charity (or its trading company) is acting as the individual's agent
> - the owner of the goods has the right to keep all of the net proceeds of the sale, but can choose to donate all or part of the proceeds if they wish
>
> Before the net proceeds of sale are donated to the charity, the owner of the goods must make a valid Gift Aid declaration to cover the proceeds they choose to donate to the charity.

The declaration could of course be made later, but the agency agreement should be made before the sale, and in practice all the documentation will be dealt with at the same time.

> The declaration will normally be made before the goods are sold, when they're taken into the shop. The donor must make a declaration confirming that in the tax year in which the donation is made they'll have paid UK Income and/or Capital Gains tax at least equal to the amount of Gift Aid tax relief that the charity, and any other charities they donate to, can claim on their donations.
> It's important that the owner of the goods understands the following:

The documentation must say the following, but fortunately it is not necessary for the owner of the goods to fully understand it, and we expect that few actually do.

> - the amount which qualifies for Gift Aid is the net sale proceeds - (after any sale commission and VAT are deducted) from the sale of the goods that they agree the charity may keep
> - the scheme is not available to non-taxpayers - the shop staff need to be aware that the individual must be a taxpayer and bear in mind that

children, the unemployed and many retired people are not likely to be taxpayers

- the goods must belong to the individual personally and not to any other person

15.40.11 *Commission on sale*

The HMRC Guidance Note provides:

> 3.42.18 Commissions charged by charities or their trading subsidiaries must be set at a reasonable rate to cover the costs of operating the scheme. Charities may be asked by HMRC to explain how they've set their commission rates.

Since the commission fee is taxable and VATable, one might think the better course would be for a charity not to charge a fee.

That is in principle a benefit to the donor, but it is not a benefit which arises by reason of the gift, so it does not breach the Gift Aid benefit rule. However, it is arguably a financial advantage which would make the gift a tainted donation.

15.40.12 *Disclosure to customers*

HMRC Guidance Note provides:

> 3.42.22 For Retail Gift Aid purposes the agent must be a disclosed agent. It is important that the charity makes their customers aware that they are selling goods on behalf of individuals. They can for example, put up a notice or poster to that effect in the shop window or by the till and ensure that items being sold under the Retail Gift Aid arrangements are clearly marked up using different coloured price tickets or labels.

There is no statutory requirement. In practice it may be wise to slap up a poster or notice, to avoid an argument. We doubt whether any customer will care whether the charity/trading company is selling on its own account or as undisclosed agent; only a practitioner with an interest in charity tax would understand all the implications.

15.40.13 *Record keeping*

The HMRC Guidance Note provides:

> **Tracking of sales of goods to individual**
> 3.42.27 All charities, whether using the Standard Method, Method A or Method B must be able to link the goods sold on behalf of each owner and keep a running total of the amounts raised from the sale of goods on

> their behalf in each tax year. Charity shops need to be able to identify when the total raised during a year from all goods sold on behalf of each individual has exceeded the agreed limit, and tell the donor the amount raised at the end of the tax year.
> Charity shops must allocate a unique identity code or number to each donor and use this on the price labels attached to their goods so that the proceeds from the sale of each item can be linked to the correct donor. Goods sold on behalf of individuals must be identifiable from other goods or stock that has been bought in by the shop. This is usually done using different price labels on the goods.

This must call for a significant investment of IT and of staff time.

> For audit purposes the charity should retain all documentation associated with claims for Gift Aid on the proceeds from the sale of goods on behalf of individuals.
> This includes the following items:
> - the donor's dated Gift Aid declaration
> - a copy of any written agreement with the individual under which the charity (or its trading subsidiary) is appointed as agent to sell goods on the person's behalf
> - records of any changes in process between the Standard Method, Method A or Method B and the movement of individuals from one process to another
> - records to show that the individual has been notified of the net sale proceeds where required
> - records to show that end of tax year letters have been sent to all donors by charities operating either Method A or B
> - records tracing Gift Aid claims back to the sales of donated goods to individual donors
> - if goods are sold by a trading subsidiary of a charity, records to show how the net sales proceeds are transferred to the charity
> - records of checks the charity has carried out on each of its shops to ensure that the Retail Gift Aid process is operated correctly

A charity should keep all of these, though (depending on circumstances) some gaps may not be fatal to tax reclaims.

> Charities should also keep records of staff/volunteer training and guidance, to demonstrate that all their staff and volunteers have a good understanding of the processes.

If the charity has the items in 3.42.17, the failure to produce these records would not matter, though in practice a well organised charity will no doubt keep this too.

3.42.28 ...[146]

If a Charity becomes aware that it has claimed Gift Aid on donations in error because the donor(s):

- has not completed a Gift Aid declaration
- informed the charity not to treat his/her donations as Gift Aid donations.
- payments to the charity were not gifts

Then the charity should make an appropriate adjustment to its next Gift Aid claim to repay the Gift Aid claimed to date.

If donors, whose goods have been converted into a Gift Aid donation, notify a charity, at any point, that they have become a non-taxpayer, then the charity is not responsible for paying back any Gift Aid claimed to date. The charity must ensure, however, that the donor's record is adjusted so that Gift Aid is not claimed on any further sales of the donor's goods or on any future donations.

15.40.14 *Compliance*

3.42.29 When a charity uses any of the 3 methods for operating Gift Aid on the sale of goods on behalf of individuals, it must ensure that the method chosen is operated correctly. In particular:

- all shop staff involved in the process must undergo training to understand the importance of following the correct procedures and to correctly explain the scheme to donors. Shop staff need to understand that goods cannot be sold on behalf of individuals who do not pay sufficient UK Income Tax and/or Capital Gains Tax. All staff operating the scheme should be aware that anyone who joins the charity's scheme and does not pay enough tax may have to pay back to HMRC the tax claimed by the charity
- operating incentive bonus schemes or other monetary rewards systems relating directly to operating a Retail Gift Aid Scheme is unacceptable. The take up of the Retail Gift Aid Scheme in individual shops within a charity may be monitored and reviewed, however, as an accepted part of the normal commercial and compliance management performance of the charity
- inappropriate schemes, specifically designed to increase Gift Aid income, including

  [a] targets for Gift Aid take up,

146 HMRC's comments the position where the donor has not paid sufficient tax are considered elsewhere, see 15.44 (Tax to cover Gift Aid).

> [b] publishing league tables of shops,
> [c] giving bonuses, incentives, or otherwise rewarding increased Gift Aid claims from individual shops
>
> might lead to some shop staff not following processes correctly. Charities with inappropriate schemes cannot claim Gift Aid on the proceeds from the sale goods sold on behalf of individuals. Where targets or other schemes are in place, they should only be used for monitoring performance and identifying training needs, rather than to directly reward shop staff

Of course this is wrong: it is a matter for charities to decide how to motivate staff. But shops which adopt these strategies may expect a more thorough HMRC audit.

> • charities must undertake regular audits on a periodic or sample basis, as appropriate, to ensure the processes are being followed correctly. Records of such audits must be kept.

This is not statutory, but it is sound advice.

15.41 Retail Gift Aid: Position of vendors

15.41.1 *VAT on commission*

The HMRC Guidance Note provides:

> 3.42.21 When a charity or its trading company is acting as an agent, it's providing a service of selling goods on behalf of an individual and if it's VAT registered, it will have to account for output VAT on its commission charges.

And again:

> 3.42.18 ... [1] Because the agency arrangement for selling goods on behalf of an individual is a business activity, commissions charged are a consideration for a taxable supply and VAT must be accounted for at the standard rate.
> [2] If the commissions charged do not reflect the real costs of acting as agent to sell goods on behalf of individuals, it will not constitute a business for VAT purposes. Under these circumstances any VAT incurred on costs associated with the agency arrangement will not be recoverable by the charity or subsidiary trading company.

Point [1] is correct, though point [2] on its face, is not an accurate statement of what is in reality a complex set of issues.

15.41.2 *VAT on sale of goods*

The HMRC Guidance Note provides:

> 3.42.19 A simple gift of goods to a charity by a private individual will have no VAT implications for the donor or the charity.

This is correct but irrelevant in the present context, as the retail Gift Aid scheme does not involve a gift of goods to the charity.

15.41.3 *Input VAT*

The HMRC Guidance Note provides:

> 3.42.20 The sale of donated goods by a charity (or by a trading company that donates its profits to the charity) is a zero-rated supply for VAT purposes. VAT incurred by a VAT-registered charity in relation to these supplies can therefore be reclaimed as input tax. No VAT reliefs are available to CASCs, so this paragraph applies only to charities.

This is again correct but irrelevant in the present context, as the retail Gift Aid scheme does not involve a sale of donated goods by a charity.

The HMRC Guidance Note provides:

> 3.42.23 When VAT is incurred on expenditure that directly relates to goods being sold through the agency arrangement, that VAT is not recoverable as input tax even if the charity or its trading company bears the cost. So if, for example, electrical goods need to be tested before they can be sold, any VAT charged on the costs of the testing can't be recovered as input tax. This is because the goods still belong to the individual for whom the charity or trading company is acting as agent...

It may be possible for the charity to recover the VAT, if the supply is made to the charity or the trading company, and the VAT is attributable to one of the services it provides in return for its sales commission.

15.41.4 *Third party sales agent*

The HMRC Guidance Note provides:

> 3.42.24 Charities can use commercial operators to sell certain goods on behalf of the individual, who then donates the proceeds to the charity. This usually happens when a charity shop puts some goods into a commercial auction or sells goods on a website. Commercial operators will charge their own sale commission, which is deducted from the sale proceeds. Commercial operators will almost certainly be VAT registered and so will charge VAT on the commission.

> The use of auctioneers or a website that charges commission is a complicating factor, but the charity or trading company could still act as agent for the individual in arranging the sale by auction. The auctioneer's commission and VAT would need to be deducted from the selling price before arriving at the amount that is due to the individual. The charity or trading company would then deduct its commission and VAT from this amount to arrive at the net sales proceeds.

The HMRC Guidance Note then discusses input VAT on the commercial operators commission:

> Under this arrangement the VAT charged on the auctioneer's commission is in effect borne directly by the individual, so the charity/trading company has no right to recover it as input tax.

The question, again, is who the supply is made to. It may be possible to arrange that the auctioneer's supply is made to the charity in which case the VAT should be recoverable as it would be attributable to the charity's own VATable supply.

The HMRC Guidance Note then gives an example, though that does not add anything to the above.[147]

15.41.5 *Income tax/CT on commission*

The HMRC Guidance Note provides:

> 3.42.25 Where charities sell donated goods that they own, the activity is not normally treated as trading and so any profits are not taxable.

---

147 **Example 5** (Fred)
F asks a charity shop to sell a table on his behalf and completes a Gift Aid declaration.
F is asked to sign an agency agreement and is told that there's a 5% commission for handling the sale.
The shop sends the table to an auction house for sale.
The table sells for £400.
The auction house deducts commission of £48 - 10% plus VAT - leaving £352.
The charity shop deducts its commission of £17.60 plus £3.52 VAT, leaving net sales proceeds of £330.88.
F, if notified by the charity under Standard Method or Method A, does not reclaim the sale proceeds.
The charity can claim Gift Aid on £330.88, but not the £17.60 commission fee, £3.52 VAT or the £48 paid to the auction house.
As long as the individual is under no obligation to give the proceeds to the charity, Gift Aid can be claimed on any amounts that are donated. Care should be taken to ensure that any Gift Aid declaration names that charity.

> However, if they provide a service in return for payment, in this case by selling goods on behalf of others in return for a commission, that service may amount to taxable trading activity. If no commission is charged, the charity will not be trading.

Although the text says "may", the sales commission is bound to constitute a trading receipt unless:

(1) the commission is a one-off event, in which case it may be taxed as a miscellaneous income, or
(2) the amount charged is so small that profits are impossible.

Elsewhere the HMRC Guidance Note says:

> Any commission received by the charity or its trading subsidiary company will be a trading receipt and potentially subject to Income Tax or Corporation Tax as well as VAT. For guidance about trading by charities read paragraph 3.42.22

15.41.6 *Non-charitable expenditure*

The HMRC Guidance Note provides:

> Regardless of whether a commission is charged, all direct and indirect costs incurred in selling goods on behalf of other people will be non-charitable expenditure, and may affect the charity's entitlement to tax exemption. This is different from the traditional method of charities simply selling only donated goods to raise money for the charity, which is not a trading activity and does not normally involve non-charitable expenditure. ...
> Charity trustees are required to show that the expected proceeds from selling goods on behalf of others are expected to exceed costs of running the scheme.

We do not agree. The costs of selling would be non-charitable expenditure if the charity does not reasonably expect to make a profit. In other cases the costs are charitable expenditure, like any other fundraising costs.[148] This was in fact what the HMRC Guidance Note previously stated (or at

---

148 The Charities SORP recognises that the costs of generating voluntary income are in principle proper expenses:
"Fundraising costs consist of three categories:
- costs of generating donations;
- fundraising trading costs, which are the costs of trading to raise funds and include the cost of goods sold and any other costs associated with a trading operation; and
- investment management costs."

least implied).[149]

If the charity is trading, a loss on the trade will count as non-charitable expenditure.[150] Though of course a loss-making activity is not so likely to constitute a trade.

In practice it may be better to use a subsidiary to avoid the issue.

> Charities may decide that using a subsidiary trading company is the best way of selling goods on behalf of others. The use of a trading company stops a charity incurring non-charitable expenditure or putting its charitable funds at risk. The trading company can then pass its profits to the charity under company Gift Aid, to minimise any corporation tax liability on the profits.

15.42 Retail Gift Aid: Donor's position

15.42.1 *CGT on sale*

The HMRC Guidance Note provides:

> 3.42.26 When an individual disposes of assets, a charge to Capital Gains Tax can arise, depending on the nature of the asset and its value. Where a personal possession worth more than £6,000 is sold, any gain made could be chargeable to Capital Gains Tax. ...

CGT is unlikely to arise, because of the CGT exemption for tangible movable property whose value does not exceed £6,000.[151]

> If a donor knows that a personal possession will be liable to a capital gains charge when it's sold on their behalf, they may want to consider whether it would be more beneficial to them to gift the asset directly to the charity instead. The donor would then be able to claim relief from Capital Gains Tax on the disposal of the item to the charity. The charity will not be able to claim Gift Aid on the net sale proceeds, but the charity will not be charged Capital Gains Tax when it sells the asset, if the proceeds are used for charitable purposes only.

This issue is discussed at 23.13 (Gift of assets v. sale & cash gift).

---

149 Before 1 August 2007 the HMRC Guidance Note provided:
"*[1] any expenditure incurred in selling the assets may fall to be treated as non-charitable expenditure, which may affect the charity's entitlement to tax exemption.*
[2] To be acceptable under charity law the trustees will need to be able to demonstrate that the likely proceeds are reasonably expected to exceed costs."

150 See 6.32 (Trading loss: Non-primary purpose trade),

151 Section 262 TCGA.

15.42.2 *Income tax if donor trading*

The HMRC Guidance Note provides:

- if [donors] sell significant quantities of goods, or are trading separately (as a sole trader) in those or similar goods, they might be deemed to be acting as a business and must therefore consider their own position in terms of potential liability to income tax and VAT on the proceeds, even if they donate them to the charity

The donor will not be trading in the goods which the charity sells as their agent, unless

(1) the donor is carrying on a separate trade and instructs the charity to sell stock in trade as an agent for the donor.

(2) the donor buys the goods for the purpose of selling though the agency of the charity; that seems unlikely.

In case (1) retail Gift Aid is not suitable. As the HMRC Guidance Note points out:

- any trader that asks a charity to sell trading goods on their behalf will need to include the full proceeds in their receipts and any commission charged as expenses in their accounts when calculating their taxable profits and when a charity is selling valuable goods on their behalf, [any Capital Gains Tax liability will remain the traders own responsibility][152]

In practice we do not expect that a trader would ever use the scheme for trading stock.

15.43 Mechanics of Gift Aid

15.43.1 *"Grossed Up amount"*

Statute uses the concept of the "grossed up amount" of a gift.
Section 415 ITA provides:

> In this Chapter [Chapter 2 Part 8 ITA] references to the grossed up amount of a gift are to the amount of the gift grossed up by reference to the basic rate for the tax year in which the gift is made.

For clarity, I write this with initial capitals.

---

152 The words in brackets are inapt as a sale by a trader would be subject to IT, not CGT.

The definition only applies for Chapter 2 Part 8 [individual Gift Aid], so it has to be repeated verbatim elsewhere: s.520(3), 521(3) ITA/s.471(3), 472(3) CTA 2010.

It may be easier to follow algebraically:

> N is the amount of the gift (**N**et gift)
> G is the Grossed Up amount of the gift
> B is the **B**asic rate (expressed as a fraction).

So: $N = G - BG$
or: $G = N \div (1 - B)$

Where the basic rate is 20%:

Net gift	**Grossed Up amount of gift**
£80	£100
£100	£125

In short:

- Add 25% to the Net gift to find the Grossed Up amount of the gift.
- Deduct 20% from the Grossed Up amount of the gift to find the Net gift

15.43.2 *IT higher rate relief*

Relief for income tax above the basic rate is given by the technique of increasing the basic rate and higher rate limits.

Section 414(2) ITA provides:

> The Income Tax Acts have effect in their application to the individual for the tax year in which the gift is made as if ...
> (b) [i] the basic rate limit and the higher rate limit (see section 10)
> [ii] and additionally, in the case of a Scottish taxpayer,
> [A] the upper limit for the Scottish basic rate and
> [B] the limits for any Scottish rates above the Scottish basic rate,
> were increased by an amount equal to the grossed up amount of the gift.

This links into s.10 ITA, under which (in short) an individual's total income is subject to income tax at the higher or additional rates to the extent that it exceeds the basic/higher rate limits:

> (2) Income tax on an individual's income up to the basic rate limit is charged at the basic rate ...

> (3) Income tax is charged at the higher rate on an individual's income above the basic rate limit and up to the higher rate limit.
> (3A) Income tax is charged at the additional rate on an individual's income above the higher rate limit.[153]

So the effect of the two provisions is that the individual enjoys higher rate relief on the Grossed Up amount of the gift.

The value of higher rate relief depends on the rate of tax paid on the top slice of income. The rate on the top slice of income may vary from 32.5% (the dividend upper rate) to 60% (the £100k - £125k band).[154]

Gift Aid does not apply for purposes of a computation under ss.535 to 537 ITTOIA (life policies top slicing relief): s.535(7) ITTOIA.

15.43.3 *CGT higher rate relief*

There are special rules for residential gains, carried interest gains, and Entrepreneurs and investors reliefs. Subject to that, s.1H TCGA provides:

> (3) Other chargeable gains accruing in a tax year to an individual are charged to capital gains tax at a rate of 10% or 20%.
> (4) The question as to which of the rates applies to the gains concerned is determined by section 1I (income taxed at higher rates or gains exceeding unused basic rate band).

So we turn to s.1I TCGA which provides:

> (1) If any of an individual's income for a tax year is chargeable to income tax at a higher income tax rate,[155] gains accruing to the individual in the tax year are charged—
> (a) at the rate of 28% (if they are residential property gains or carried interest gains), or
> (b) at the rate of 20% (if they are other kinds of gains).
> (2) If—
> (a) none of an individual's income for a tax year is chargeable to income tax at a higher income tax rate, but
> (b) the individual is chargeable to capital gains tax for the tax year on an amount that exceeds the unused part of the individual's

---

153 The equivalents for Scottish/Welsh taxpayers are s.11A/11B ITA.

154 See 15.43.7 (Personal allowance taper).

155 Section 1J(1) TCGA provides: "For the purposes of section 1I a "higher income tax rate" means—
(a) the higher rate or the default higher rate,
(b) the savings higher rate, or
(c) the dividend upper rate".

basic rate band,

the excess ("the higher rate excess") is charged at the rate of 28% (so far as comprising residential property gains or carried interest gains) or at the rate of 20% (so far as comprising other kinds of gains).

Thus in the absence of income, Gift Aid could in principle be used to reduce the rate of CGT from 20% to 10%, but in practice that may not be the best way to use the relief if as an alternative it could be set against income of future years.[156]

15.43.4 *Basic rate IT/lower rate CGT*

Gift Aid does not give relief as such against income tax at the basic rate, or CGT at the lower rate (10%). The benefit of Gift Aid is effectively enjoyed by the charity reclaiming basic rate tax: see 15.49 (Position of charity receiving gift from individual).

15.43.5 *No relief for NICs*

Gift Aid does not give relief against NICs. For individuals (and partnerships of individuals), which are subject to NICs, relief as a trading deduction is superior, if it is available.[157] Companies are not subject to NICs so it makes no difference for them.

15.43.6 *CGT interest surcharge (offshore trust)*

If a beneficiary receives income from an offshore trust, and gives the income (less tax paid) to a charity, the Gift Aid would broadly match the income tax charge. However, this does not work for CGT because of the interest surcharge.

Suppose a UK resident beneficiary receives a capital payment from an offshore trust. The payment is in principle chargeable under s.87 TCGA. Suppose, for instance, the capital receipt is £100 and the payment to charity £80. The charity reclaims £20 in the usual way. The individual has higher rate relief on the Grossed Up amount of £100. But they may also pay the interest surcharge up to 60% of the CGT charge. There is no Gift Aid relief for this.

Careful planning is therefore needed in this situation. One possibility is that the trust might make a capital payment to the charity, sufficient to

---

156 See 15.47 (Deposited donation: Carry-forward).

157 See 18.2 (Charity gift: deductible expense).

"wash" the trust gains.[158] A capital payment of the balance might be made to the beneficiary in order for the beneficiary to make further gifts to the charity.

15.43.7 *Personal allowance taper*

Section 35 ITA provides the normal personal allowance (2019/20 = £12,500). This allowance is withdrawn for higher income taxpayers.

Section 35(2) ITA provides:

> For an individual whose adjusted net income exceeds £100,000, the allowance under subsection (1) is reduced by one-half of the excess.

Thus (at 2019/20 rates) taxpayers with "net adjusted income" between £100k and £125,000 the marginal rate of income tax is 60%.

The rule has incurred some high level criticism from the IFS ("the absurd and arbitrary marginal income tax band").[159] But no-one has taken any notice.

The key term here is "net adjusted income". Section 58 ITA provides:

> (1) For the purposes of Chapters 2 and 3, an individual's adjusted net income for a tax year is calculated as follows.
> *Step 1* Take the amount of the individual's net income for the tax year.
> *Step 2* If in the tax year the individual makes, or is treated under section 426 as making, a gift that is a qualifying donation for the purposes of Chapter 2 of Part 8 (Gift Aid) deduct the grossed up amount of the gift.

Thus Gift Aid donations decrease the "net adjusted income".

The term is also used in the calculation of age-related personal allowances and the same points apply.

The same applies to qualifying investment donation relief,[160] though in that case the deduction comes in the definition of "net income". Section 23 ITA provides:

> To find the liability of a person ("the taxpayer") to income tax for a tax year, take the following steps.
> *Step 1*
> Identify the amounts of income on which the taxpayer is charged to income tax for the tax year.

---

158 See 32.1 (Payment to charity from non-resident trust). It is assumed that this is within the powers of the trustees.

159 IFS, *Tax By Design* (2011) para 4.3.1. (A Straightforward Income Tax Schedule).

160 See 21.14 (QIDR relief for individual).

> The sum of those amounts is "total income".
> Each of those amounts is a "component" of total income.
> *Step 2*
> Deduct from the components the amount of any relief under a provision listed in relation to the taxpayer in section 24 to which the taxpayer is entitled for the tax year.
> See section 25 for further provision about the deduction of those reliefs.
> The sum of the amounts of the components left after this step is "net income".

QIDR is one of the reliefs mentioned in s.24.

We coin the term **"marginal personal allowance taxpayers"** to refer to taxpayers in the (rather narrow) band whose net adjusted income exceeds £100k, before Gift Aid or QIDR, but who make charity donations bringing their net adjusted income below that limit.

For such taxpayers, a charitable gift brings the additional advantage of restoring their personal allowance and so their marginal cost of giving to charity is reduced. The amount involved is relatively small. For 2019/20, the personal allowance will be completely lost when a person's earnings exceed £125,000. However, as Gift Aid donations will be taken into account in determining his or her adjusted net income, a donation with a Grossed Up value of £25,000 to charity by Gift Aid would enable a donor with an income of £125,000 to receive the personal allowance in full, ie effectively the donor obtains relief at 60%. The rate of relief reduces as the income increases, eg with an income of £150k, the first £25k donation obtains effective relief at 45% and the next £25k donation obtains effective relief at 60%.

However payroll giving is missing from s.24 list so a marginal personal allowance taxpayer should not use the payroll giving scheme.

15.43.8 *Welsh/Scots taxpayers*

Section 414A ITA deals with the position if basic rate/devolved basic rates differ:

> (1) Subsections (3) and (4) apply if an individual makes a gift to a charity which is a qualifying donation, and for the tax year in which the gift is made—
> (a) the individual is a Scottish taxpayer or a Welsh taxpayer,
> (b) there is a difference between—
> (i) the applicable devolved basic rate, and
> (ii) the basic rate, and

(c) any of the individual's income is liable to the applicable devolved basic rate.

(2) In this section—

"the applicable devolved basic rate"—

- (a) is the Scottish basic rate if the individual is a Scottish taxpayer, and
- (b) is the Welsh basic rate if the individual is a Welsh taxpayer,

"the ADBR amount" is the amount of the individual's income liable to the applicable devolved basic rate, and

"the rate difference" means the difference between the basic rate and the applicable devolved basic rate.

(3) If, for the tax year in which the gift is made, the applicable devolved basic rate is above the basic rate—

- (a) the individual is entitled to a tax reduction for that tax year,
- (b) the tax reduction is given effect at Step 6 of the calculation in section 23,
- (c) where the ADBR amount is more than or equal to the grossed up amount of the gift, the amount of the tax reduction is equal to the grossed up amount of the gift multiplied by the rate difference, and
- (d) otherwise, the amount of the tax reduction is equal to the ADBR amount multiplied by the rate difference.

(4) If, for the tax year in which the gift is made, the applicable devolved basic rate is lower than the basic rate—

- (a) income tax is charged under this subsection for that tax year,
- (b) the individual is the person liable for the tax,
- (c) where the ADBR amount is more than or equal to the grossed up amount of the gift, the amount of the tax is equal to the grossed up amount of the gift multiplied by the rate difference, and
- (d) otherwise, the amount of the tax is the ADBR amount multiplied by the rate difference,

but see subsection (5).

(5) If, in the case of an individual (and ignoring this subsection), the total amount of tax charged under subsection (4) for a tax year is greater than the individual's section 414(2)(b) tax saving for that year, the total amount of that tax is limited so as to be equal to the individual's section 414(2)(b) tax saving for that year.

(6) For the purposes of subsection (5), the amount of an individual's "section 414(2)(b) tax saving" for a tax year is—

- (a) if the amount calculated at Step 5 of the calculation in section 23 in the individual's case for that year is less than it would be were section 414(2)(b) not to have effect, equal to the difference, and

(b) otherwise is nil.

EN Devolved Income Tax Rates (Consequential Amendments) Order 2019 provides:

> The background is that gift-aid donations received by charities will continue to treated as amounts received after deduction of tax at the main basic rate (even in the case of Scottish and Welsh taxpayers), with charities being able to reclaim tax at that rate from HMRC.
> New section 414A(3) ensures that where the Scottish basic rate or Welsh basic rate is higher than the main basic rate, the donor of a gift-aid donation is effectively taxed only at the main basic rate on so much of the grossed-up donation as would otherwise be more heavily taxed at the Scottish, or Welsh, basic rate. New section 414A(4) ensures that where the Scottish basic rate or Welsh basic rate is lower than the main basic rate, the donor of a gift-aid donation is effectively taxed at the main basic rate on so much of the grossed-up donation as would otherwise be more lightly taxed at the Scottish, or Welsh, basic rate. But new section 414A(5) ensures that new section 414A(4) does not make a donor worse off as a result of having made gift-aid donations.

The charities guidance note provides:

> **3.5.6 Scottish taxpayers**
> Following the introduction of the Scotland Act 2012 that gives the Scottish Parliament the power to set a Scottish rate of Income Tax to be administered by HMRC for Scottish taxpayers from April 2016, the Gift Aid scheme for charities and individuals will operate as follows:
> Charities - there is no change in the position for charities claiming Gift Aid on donations from Scottish taxpayers. Charities will continue to receive Gift Aid relief equal to the rest of the UK basic rate of tax.
> Individuals - there is no change in position for a Scottish taxpayer who pays the new starter or basic rate tax. Donors who pay tax at the intermediate, higher or top rate Scottish tax rates can claim the difference between the rate they pay and the Gift Aid claimed by the charity on the donations. The tax to cover rules in paragraph 3.5.1 will continue to apply to all these individuals.
> How to claim tax relief on your donations - the process for UK higher rate taxpayers to claim tax relief on donations made to charities is explained in tax relief when you donate to a charity. This process also applies to Scottish taxpayers paying tax above the Scottish basic rate.

HMRC say:

> 19. When a taxpayer makes a voluntary donation to a charity through Gift Aid, the donation is made net of income tax at the basic rate, and the charity is able to claim repayment of that tax from HMRC (section 520(2) of ITA). For example, with a basic rate of 20 per cent, a gift of £100 is treated as a gift of £125 on which £25 tax has already been deducted. The charity is therefore able to reclaim the £25.
> 20. If the Welsh basic rate of income tax were higher than the UK basic rate, charities would benefit as they could claim back more tax in relation to donations made by Welsh taxpayers. Likewise, if the Welsh basic rate of income tax were lower than the UK basic rate, charities would lose out as they could claim back less in relation to donations made by Welsh taxpayers.
> 21. The UK Government has had an ongoing dialogue with charity representative bodies about the impact of having to identify donors liable at devolved rates of income tax in order to make accurate claims. The UK Government took account of those views when implementing the Scottish income tax powers, agreeing that the additional burden placed on charities would be disproportionate. It therefore decided that Gift Aid for charities would continue to apply at the UK basic rate, regardless of the tax position of the donor. This will also be the case for donors liable at the Welsh rates for the same reasons.
> 22. The UK Government will keep this issue under review though so that, if the Welsh or Scottish and UK rates diverge considerably or it becomes possible to provide Gift Aid relief at the correct rate without the currently anticipated administrative burden, the position can be reconsidered.
> 23. Donors who are higher and additional rate taxpayers are also able to claim tax relief on their donations. This relief is the difference between the higher/additional rate of tax and the basic rate of tax on the total 'gross' value of their donation to the charity. For example, if a higher rate taxpayer makes a £100 donation to a charity, the charity can claim Gift Aid at the basic rate, making the total value of the donation £125. The taxpayer can claim the difference between the higher rate of tax at 40 per cent and the basic rate of tax at 20 per cent on the total value of their donation, so they can claim 20 per cent of £125, a total of £25. Total tax paid, at 40 per cent on the £125 donation is £50, of which the charity can claim £25 and the donor can claim £25.
> 24. Once the Welsh rates are introduced, Welsh taxpayers will be able to claim relief equal to the difference between the UK basic and the highest Welsh rate of tax that applies to them.

25. So, whatever the Welsh rates might be, the total value of a donation of £100 by a Welsh taxpayer would be treated as £125. And a taxpayer who pays tax at above the UK basic rate would be able to claim the difference between their marginal rate of tax and the UK basic rate. So, for example, if the Welsh higher rate were 11 per cent, the Welsh taxpayer would then claim the difference between their higher rate (41 per cent) and the UK basic rate (20 per cent) on the total valuation of the donation. This would be 21 per cent of £125, so a total of £26.25. Total tax paid, at 41 per cent on the £125 donation is £51.25, of which the charity can claim £25 and the donor can claim £26.25.[161]

15.43.9 *Claiming relief in tax return*

In practice an individual donor claims higher rate relief by entering the amounts in the relevant boxes, in form SA100 (2020/21) page TR4:[162]

Box	Rubric	Form SA150 Tax Return notes (2020/21)
5	Gift Aid payments made in the year to 5 April 2021	Put the total Gift Aid payments you made from 6 April 2020 to 5 April 2021 in this box. Do not include any payments under Payroll Giving.
6	Total of any "one-off" payments in box 5	To help us get your PAYE tax code right, if you have one, put any one-off payments you included in box 5 in box 6. These will be Gift Aid payments made from 6 April 2020 to 5 April 2021 that you do not intend to repeat in the year to 5 April 2022.
7	Gift Aid payments made in the year to 5 April 2021 but treated as if made in the year to 5 April 2020	Put in box 7 any Gift Aid payments that you made between 6 April 2020 and 5 April 2021, which you want us to treat as if you made them in the tax year 6 April 2019 to 5 April 2020.[163]
8	Gift Aid payments made after 5 April 2021 but treated as if made in the year to 5 April 2021	If you want us to treat Gift Aid payments you made between 6 April 2021 and the date you send us your tax return, as if you made them in the year to 5 April 2021, put the amount in box 8. For example, if you know you'll not be paying higher

161 HMRC, " Clarifying the Scope of the Welsh Rates of Income Tax: Technical Note" (2018) *https://assets.publishing.service.gov.uk/government/uploads/system/uploads/attachment_data/file/750621/Welsh_rates_of_Income_Tax_technical_note.pdf*

162 I set out the 2020/21 wording, but the wording has not changed materially from at least 2018/19.

163 See 15.45 (Carry-back relief).

		rate tax this year but you did in the year to 5 April 2021.[164]
12	Gift Aid payments to non-UK charities in box 5	You can claim relief for Gift Aid donations to certain non-UK charities. If any amounts included in box 5 are to charities outside the UK, put the amount in box 12 and give us details in 'Any other information' on page TR 7.

15.44 Tax to cover Gift Aid

15.44.1 *Tax deemed deducted from gift*

Section 414(2) ITA provides:

> The Income Tax Acts have effect in their application to the individual for the tax year in which the gift is made as if—
> (a) the gift had been made after deduction of income tax at the basic rate...

Tax is not actually deducted from the gift, but it is treated as deducted.

The tax treated as deducted from the gift will be **"amount A"** in the computation below.

15.44.2 *"IT which donor is charged"*

The legislation uses the expression the "total amount of income tax to which the donor is charged for a tax year". This will be **"amount B"** in the computation below. The expression is defined in s.425 ITA:

> (1) For the purposes of sections 423 and 424, the total amount of income tax to which an individual is charged for a tax year is the amount calculated as follows.
> (2) Calculate the individual's liability to income tax for the tax year in accordance with section 23, as modified by subsection (3).

There are so many adjustments that we prefer the expression **"creditable tax",** rather than the "total amount of income tax to which the donor is charged".

Section 425(3)(a) ITA makes a set of adjustments which increase the amount of creditable tax:

> In applying s.23—

164 See 15.45 (Carry-back relief).

> (a) at Step 6, ignore any tax reductions to which the individual is entitled[165] for the tax year under a provision listed in subsection (4)...

Section 425(4) ITA sets out three disregarded deductions:

> The tax reductions to be ignored are tax reductions under—
> (a) section 453 (qualifying maintenance payments),

At first sight it is hard to see the reason for s.425(4)(a). The reason may be that the maintenance payments are not income of the recipient. So if the deduction is not restored for the payor, then no relief would be available for payor or payee.

Section 425 continues:

> The tax reductions to be ignored are tax reductions under ...
> (b) sections 2 and 6 of TIOPA 2010 (double taxation arrangements: relief by agreement), or
> (c) section 18(1)(b) and (2) of TIOPA 2010 (relief for foreign tax where no double taxation arrangements).

It seems sensible to disregard DTA reliefs since in general the individual will have paid foreign tax.

Section 425(3)(b) ITA next makes a set of adjustments which decrease the amount of creditable tax:

> In applying s.23 ...
> (b) ignore Step 7.

So we turn to step 7 of s.23, which is:

> *Step 7* Add to the amount of tax left after Step 6 any amounts of tax for which the taxpayer is liable for the tax year under any provision listed in relation to the taxpayer in section 30.

So we turn to s.30 ITA:

> If the taxpayer is an individual, the provisions referred to at Step 7 of the calculation in section 23 are—

Section	**Topic**
s.424 ITA	Gift Aid: charge to tax
s. 809ZN ITA	Tainted Gift Aid donations: charge to tax

165 Section 425(6) ITA provides: "For the purposes of this section a person is treated as being entitled to a tax reduction under sections 2 and 6 of TIOPA 2010 if the person is entitled to credit against income tax under double taxation arrangements."

s. 809ZO ITA	Tainted charity donations by trustees: charge to tax
s. 205 FA 2004	Pension schemes: short service refund lump sum charge
s. 205A FA 2004	Pension schemes: serious ill-health lump sum charge
s. 206 FA 2004	Pension schemes: special lump sum death benefits charge
s. 208(2)(a) FA 2004	Pension schemes: unauthorised payments charge
s. 209(3)(a) FA 2004	Pension schemes: unauthorised payments surcharge
s. 214 FA 2004	Pension schemes: lifetime allowance charge
s. 227 FA 2004	Pension schemes: annual allowance charge
s. 7 F(No 2)A 2005	Social security pension lump sum
Chap 8 Pt 10 ITEPA	High income child benefit charge[166]

The list mostly relates to specialist pension charges which will not in practice arise.

The last set of adjustments decreases the amount of creditable tax. Section 425(5) ITA provides:

> From the amount calculated in accordance with subsections (2) to (4) deduct—
> (a) any tax treated as having been paid under—
> (i) s.399(2) of ITTOIA 2005 (distributions from UK resident companies etc on which there is no tax credit),
> (iv) s.530(1) of that Act (gains from contracts for life insurance), or
> (v) s.685A(3) of that Act (settlor-interested settlements), and
> (b) any tax treated as deducted from estate income under s.656(3) or 657(4) of ITTOIA 2005, so far as that income is treated under s.679 of that Act as paid from sums within s.680(4) of that Act.

For the interaction with the remittance basis claim charge, see Kessler, *Taxation of Non-Residents and Foreign Domiciliaries* (21st ed, 2022-23), para 108.23.1 (Interaction with Gift Aid).[167]

There is some scope for simplification here.

15.44.3 *Restriction on personal reliefs*

Section 423 ITA provides:

> (1) This section applies if—
> (a) an individual makes one or more gifts to charities in a tax year which are qualifying donations, and
> (b) amount A is greater than amount B.

---

166 For clarity I have set this out in tabular form rather than the layout of the statute.

167 Online version *https://www.foreigndomiciliaries.co.uk*

(2) In this section—

"amount A" means the total amount of the tax treated as deducted from the gifts under s.414, and

"amount B" means the total amount of income tax and capital gains tax to which the individual is charged for the tax year (before applying this section).

...

(4) The individual's entitlement to the reliefs mentioned in subsection (5) is extinguished, so far as is necessary to ensure that the total amount of income tax and capital gains tax to which the individual is charged for the tax year (after applying this section)—

(a) is equal to amount A, or

(b) if that is not possible, falls short of amount A by as little as possible.

(5) The reliefs are—

(a) an allowance under Chapter 2 of Part 3 of this Act (personal allowance and blind person's allowance),

(b) a tax reduction under Chapter 3 of Part 3 of this Act (tax reductions for married couples and civil partners), and

(c) relief under section 457 or 458 of this Act (payments to trade unions and police organisations).

15.44.4 *Gift Aid clawback charge*

If the loss of personal reliefs under s.423 is not enough to ensure that the donor pays tax equal to the tax treated as deducted from the gift, then s.424 ITA takes effect.[168]

Section 424 ITA provides:

(1) Income tax is charged under this section if—

(a) an individual makes one or more gifts to charity in a tax year which are qualifying donations, and

(b) amount A is greater than amount C.

(2) In this section—

"amount A" means the total amount of the tax treated as deducted from the gifts under s.414, and

"amount C" means the sum of—

(a) the amount of income tax to which the individual is charged for the tax year, and

168 HMRC Relief Instructions Manual previously contained useful worked examples. These may be found at para 15.38 of the sixth edition of this work. But there is no equivalent in the current manuals.

> (b) the amount of capital gains tax to which the individual would be chargeable for the tax year if the following were ignored—
>
> (i) any relief under sections 2 and 6 of TIOPA 2010 (double taxation arrangements: relief by agreement), and
>
> (ii) any relief under section 18(1)(b) and (2) of TIOPA 2010 (relief for foreign tax where no double taxation arrangements).
>
> (3) For the purposes of this section, the total amount of income tax to which the individual is charged for the tax year is the amount calculated in accordance with s.425, after taking into account any restriction of relief under s.423.
>
> (4) The amount of the tax charged under this section is equal to the difference between amount A and amount C.
>
> (5) Tax charged under this section is charged for the tax year in which the gift or gifts are made.
>
> (6) The person liable for any tax charged under this section is the individual.

We refer to this as the "**Gift Aid clawback charge**".

The HMRC Guidance Note summarises the position:

> **3.5 Tax to cover**
>
> 3.5.1 Donors must be charged an amount of Income Tax and/or Capital Gains Tax, whether at the basic rate or some other rate, for the tax year in which Gift Aid donations are made at least equal to the Income Tax treated as deducted from the total of all their Gift Aid donations made in the same tax year. Donors who have not been charged sufficient tax to cover the Income Tax deducted from their Gift Aid donations are responsible to pay any difference.
>
> *Example* (Mr Green)
>
> During the 2015 to 2016 tax year (basic rate of tax 20%), a donor (G) who only pays a small amount of Income Tax each tax year wins a tax free cash prize of £10,000 in a competition. He decides to share his good fortune and makes Gift Aid donations of £800 to charity A and £1,600 to charity B.
>
> Charity A claims Gift Aid tax relief of £200 and charity B £400 - the total Gift Aid tax claimed by the 2 charities on G's Gift Aid donations in the tax year is £600.
>
> However, G only paid Income Tax of £250 during the 2015 to 2016 tax year and so he owes the £350 difference in tax (£600 total Gift Aid tax claimed less £250 Income Tax paid by G) to HMRC.

Tax reliefs which reduce an individual's tax liability may therefore give rise to the Gift Aid clawback charge. the dividend allowance is one example:

> 3.5.2 The introduction of the Dividend Allowance on 6 April 2016, means that individuals will not pay tax on the first £5,000 of their income from dividends paid by companies that they own shares in. This means that only donors that have paid tax on dividend income over the £5,000 allowance will have some tax that can be used to cover their Gift Aid donations to charities and community amateur sports club (CASC's). Tax credits on dividends paid by UK companies, up to 5 April 2016 could be used by the donors to cover the tax reclaimed by the charity on their Gift Aid donations made before 6 April 2016.

The guidance is out of date; the reduction in the dividend allowance to £2,000 from 2018/19 reduces that problem. The savings allowance is another example:

> 3.5.3 The tax-free Personal Savings Allowance of £1,000 (£500 for higher rate taxpayers) for savings income or interest was introduced from 6 April 2016. This means that most people will no longer pay tax on savings interest because banks and building societies will stop deducting tax from interest they pay on savings accounts. Only donors who have savings income or interest of more than £1,000 (£500 for higher rate taxpayers) will have pay some tax that can be used to cover their Gift Aid donations to charities and CASCs.
> 3.5.4 Only Tax deducted from bank and building society interest, paid before 5 April 2016 and not repaid to the individual, can also be used to cover the tax reclaimed by a charity on Gift Aid donations received from a donor before 6 April 2016.

So the position needs to be reviewed each year:

> 3.5.5 The position of a taxpayer making Gift Aid donations can change from one tax year to the next. Charities should remind donors on a regular basis of the need for them to have paid sufficient Income and/or Capital Gains Tax on their donations. It need not be done in a separate letter to each donor, but could be included in any material sent to supporters, for example a newsletter.

This charge may arise even on a gift by a non-resident to a non-resident charity, if the donor has made a Gift Aid declaration. If a UK resident becomes non-resident, it would be wise to cancel Gift Aid declarations in favour of charities which the individual may continue to support, to avoid an accidental Gift Aid clawback charge.

15.44.5 *HMRC practice*

The practice is:

> Where HMRC finds that not enough tax has been paid to cover one or more donations to a charity it usually gives the charity the opportunity to make up the shortfall, without revealing the details about the donor. Many charities prefer to repay the Gift Aid themselves in these circumstances because they want to protect their relationship with their donor.[169]

HMRC also comment on this in the context of retail Gift Aid:

> 3.42.28 If during an audit or other review of a claim for repayment of tax on donations obtained from the sale of a donors' goods HMRC identifies individuals who have not paid enough Income Tax and/ or Capital Gains Tax to cover the tax claimed by a charity, the donor will be liable to repay the difference to HMRC. Under the 'Charge to tax' legislation (s.424 ITA 2007) the person liable for any tax charged under this section is the individual donor not the charity. HMRC will not tell a charity the name of any donors that are identified as not paying enough tax to cover the tax claimed following the conversion of their goods into Gift Aid payments.

As to whether the charity can properly pay the donor's tax, see 4.21.6 (Ex-gratia payments). Of course the charity may decline to pay, and the position becomes more difficult if the donor gives to two or more charities.

The authors have seen cases where HMRC refused to refund tax to charities in cases where donors had paid insufficient tax to cover donations; but that is wrong. That can only be done if the charity chose to accept that.

If an individual donor is assessed for tax, they should review whether they have made a valid Gift Aid declaration, (or if appropriate, received a valid Gift Aid statement). In practice declarations in the pre-2016 HMRC model form were valid only by concession;[170] but no assessment can be made on

---

169 HM Treasury "Gift Aid and digital giving" (2013) *http://www.gov.uk/government/uploads/system/uploads/attachment_data/file/210423/consult_gift_aid_and_digital_giving.pdf*
The same practice is referred to in Hansard, Standing Committee debate on the 2002 Finance Bill (13 Jun 2002): "In practice, where the Inland Revenue finds that a non-taxpayer's donation has been included in a Gift Aid claim from a charity, it invites the charity to make good the shortfall rather than pursuing the taxpayer."

170 See 15.51 (Gift Aid declarations).

a taxpayer under a concession.

15.44.6 *Tax to cover: Critique*

If these rules were enforced, there would be many difficulties. But the problem is not likely to arise for substantial gifts, where the donor is properly advised; and in relation to smaller gifts, it is not likely that HMRC seek to enforce the rules. In general, in comparison to the total amount of giving, the matter does not often arise. This is confirmed by the statistic that some £55m per annum is lost through Gift Aid declarations by non-taxpayers.[171] Although the NAO grumbled, it seems unlikely that much of that sum is sensibly collectable.

For a solution, see 15.50.1 (Gift Aid v deduction relief).

15.45 Carry-back relief

The donor's higher rate relief can be carried back one tax year. Section 426 ITA provides:

> (1) If—
> (a) an individual makes a gift to a charity that is a qualifying donation, and
> (b) the condition in subsection (2) is met,
> the individual may elect to be treated as if the gift had been made in the previous tax year ("year P"). ...
> (3) If an election is made, s.414 and 423 to 425 have effect in relation to the individual as if the gift were a qualifying donation made by the individual in year P.

Year P stands for the year **P**revious to the year of the gift.

We refer to this as **"carry-back relief"**.

In strictness, the relief is all or nothing: one must carry back the whole of a gift and not part. If an individual makes two or more distinct gifts they can elect to carry back some and not others. In practice HMRC have been known to say that a single gift may be apportioned between an amount carried back and an amount treated as made in the current year.[172] Under this practice it would not be necessary for an individual to make two or more distinct gifts in order to elect to carry back some and not others. That is sensible. However HMRC would not be bound by that practice, and the

---

171 National Audit Office, "Gift Aid and reliefs on donations" (2013) para 1.25 *http://www.nao.org.uk/wp-content/uploads/2013/11/10302-001-Gift-Aid-Book1.pdf*

172 Private correspondence.

taxpayer cannot rely on it, so for planning purposes, 2 distinct gifts would be the safer approach.

The relief does not apply for CGT.

The relief was introduced in 2003.

15.45.1 *Charge in previous year*

Section 426(2) ITA provides:

> The condition is that the individual's charged amount for year P (see s.427) is at least equal to the increased total of gifts.

Section 427 ITA defines "charged amount":

> (1) For the purposes of this Chapter, an individual's charged amount is the amount calculated as follows.
> (2) Calculate the amount of the individual's modified net income for year X (see section 1025).
> (3) Calculate the amount on which the individual is chargeable to capital gains tax for year X.
> (4) Add together the amounts calculated under subsections (2) and (3). The result is the individual's charged amount for year X.

This takes us to the elaborate rules in s.1025, but we leave the trail there.

Section 426 ITA defines "increased total of gifts":

> (4) The increased total of gifts is the sum of—
> (a) the grossed up amount of the gift, and of any gifts that are the subject of the same election or an election made at the same time,
> (b) the sum of the grossed up amounts of any gifts to charities made by the individual in year P which—
> (i) are qualifying donations, and
> (ii) are not themselves treated as made in the tax year before year P because of an election under this section, and
> (c) the sum of the grossed up amounts of any gifts which, as a result of an earlier election under this section, are treated as made in year P.
> (5) The grossed up amount of the gifts mentioned in paragraphs (a) and (c) of subsection (4) is to be determined as if the gifts were made in year P.

This would disapply the carry back election if the Grossed Up amount of the gift only slightly exceeded the income or gains of the individual in the earlier year.

15.45.2 *Election time limit*

The time limit for election is set out in s.426(6) ITA:

> An election must be made—
> (a) on or before the date on which the individual delivers a return for year P under s.8 of TMA 1970 (personal return), and
> (b) not later than the normal self-assessment filing date for year P.[173]

The election is made in the individual's tax return.[174] In short:
(1) The gift must be made by 31 January after the year of the gift (year P) in short, within 9 months; and
(2) The return for year P must go in after the gift is made.

After the return for year P has been submitted, it is too late to put in the election. In *Cameron v HMRC*:[175]
(1) The taxpayer submitted his 2005/06 return in September 2006
(2) He made a charitable donation in November 2006.
(3) He did not (and could not) make the election in his return, but tried to make it in an amended return in January 2007.

The election was invalid. HMRC effectively said: "if only Mr Cameron had not been so prompt and diligent in submitting his return, if only he had waited until 29 January 2007 before submitting his complete return, then all would have been well and he would have got his relief, but as it was his prompt compliance was his undoing." The judge thought this was "an odd stipulation and one for which no clear policy may be evident".[176] A possible reason is to save HMRC from the work of having to re-compute and (in some cases repay) higher rate tax. That may be regarded as sufficient reason to justify a rule which discourages prompt submission of tax returns, though views may differ. But by the time the return is ready to submit, the donor should normally have the data to decide whether or not he wishes to make a carry-back election.

Care must be taken to ensure that the carry-back election specifies the correct amount of the gift. In *Re Webster*[177] the taxpayer made a claim to carry back his donation in his tax return but accidentally inserted the wrong

173 Section 989 ITA provides: "normal self-assessment filing date", in relation to a tax year, means the 31 January following the tax year".
174 See 15.43.9 (Claiming relief in tax return).
175 [2010] UKFTT 104 (TC).
176 at [9] and [28].
177 [2020] EWHC 2275 (Ch).

figure. The election was invalid. Following *Cameron*, the mistake could not be corrected by amendment to the return. Instead, the taxpayer sought rectification of the return. No-one had ever thought of that before. A High Court master held that it had no jurisdiction to rectify a tax return, and while decisions of High Court masters are not binding precedents, that seems clearly right.

There is a small Covid-related extension for 2021:

> 5.1 ... the SA Filing deadline remained as 31 January 2021 for the 2019-20 tax returns. However, the £100 late filing penalty was not chargeable on any tax returns filed on or before 28 Feb 21...
> 5.4 Another query was around whether the gift aid deadline, based on the filing of the Tax Return, could also be extended to sync with no late filing penalties. We can confirm that claims for tax relief on donations included in the SA Return will be allowed if filed on or before 28 February 2021. For clarity, this is a claim for relief on donations made on or before 31 January – the donation still needs to have been made during the normal time period, but the claim for relief will be accepted if made via a return filed on or before 28 February 2021.[178]

15.45.3 *Position of charity*

The election does not affect the position of the charity: s.426(7) ITA provides:

> An election does not affect the position of the recipient of the gift (see s.520 (gifts to charitable trusts: income tax treated as paid) and sections 471 and 475 of CTA 2010 (charitable companies and eligible bodies: income tax treated as paid etc)).

15.45.4 *Carry-back relief: Merits*

Carry-back relief does a number of possible uses, as well as bringing forward the time that the taxpayer enjoys the benefit of Gift Aid relief.

The relief may allow for changes in circumstances. OTS give the example of a taxpayer who makes Gift Aid contributions in late April each year. In June he is made redundant. His 2020-21 income may be less than his personal allowance, so he may not pay tax in 2020-21. In the absence of carry-back relief, he would need to basic rate tax on the Gift Aid

---

178 Joint Expatriate Forum on Tax and NICs (April 2021) *https://www.gov.uk/government/groups/joint-forum-on-expatriate-tax-and-national-insurance-contributions*

payment. But a taxpayer may be better advised to make substantial donations in early April when their income is known; and if the facts of the example ever happened, the charity should in a deserving case offer to pay the tax directly.

The relief may be helpful if a person is a higher-rate taxpayer in one year and a basic rate taxpayer in the following year. If the donation had to be made in the year of a business sale, or if a bonus is paid towards the end of the tax year, it may be difficult to know by the end of the tax year what level of donation could be made.

In particular, the relief allows the taxpayer to mitigate the rule that phases out the personal allowance, under which (at 2021/22 rates) income in the band of £100k-125k pays tax at a marginal rate of 60% (61.5% in Scotland).[179] The rule gives the taxpayer an opportunity to make a Gift Aid payment to reduce their income down to £100k.

Is that sufficient to justify retention of the relief? Perhaps it depends on how much one values simplicity. If the "absurd and arbitrary"[180] 60% band were abolished, the authors would favour abolition of the relief. This simplification is not however one considered by the Office of Tax Simplification.

15.45.5 *OTS reform proposals*

If the relief is to be retained, the time limit for the election should be brought into line with normal practice. The OTS have made this point:[181]

> 3.101 When debating the measures though Parliament, one of the comments at that time was that the measure 'will act as a prompt and an incentive to higher rate taxpayers by making Gift Aid relief immediately available'. It was also noted that 'the link to the filing of the Self Assessment return for the previous year is a key part of the government's planned measure in offering the incentive of claiming relief early rather than waiting until completion of the return for the year in which the gift was made'...[182]

---

179 See s.35(2) ITA and Kessler, *Taxation of Non-Residents and Foreign Domiciliaries*, para 44.4 (IT allowances: high earners) (21st ed., 2022-23) online version *https://www.foreigndomiciliaries.co.uk*

180 The epithet from IFS, *Tax By Design* (2011) para 4.3.1 (A Straightforward Income Tax Schedule).

181 OTS Claims and elections review (2020) *https://assets.publishing.service.gov.uk/government/uploads/system/uploads/attachment_data/file/927023/Claims_and_elections_report_Oct_2020_-_web_copy.pdf*

182 Hansard Debate 4 July 2002.

> 3.105 ... the election (normally made on the individual's Self Assessment tax return) must be made on or before the date the individual files that tax return with HMRC and cannot be changed after that has been done.
> 3.106 Although this does give some certainty to HMRC (?), there is a difference between this and the general ability to be able to amend a tax return within one year of the normal filing deadline.
> 3.107 This seems odd, particularly as other entries in the tax return may need to be amended within normal timescales...
> 3.108 Another issue is that the election must relate to the whole of a specific Gift Aided donation, as there is no scope to carry back only part of the Gift Aided amount. This has the merit of simplicity, but can lead to unnecessary complication, perhaps because, when the donation is made, it is not always certain at that time how much can be carried back. Respondents said this could encourage taxpayers to delay filing their returns until very near the filing deadline...
> 3.110 The current measures apply to all levels of Gift Aid donations, so the legislation does cause some complexity particularly when smaller donations are in point. One concern is that advisors may feel they need to consider the carry back election for their clients, often where small amounts are involved, perhaps incurring additional costs for little overall benefit...
> 3.113 The OTS suggest that government consider restricting the ability to carry back gift aid donations to high value donations, perhaps those above £10,000, although this would need to be considered in more detail...[183]
> 3.114 For those that do make high value donations, the government should consider making changes to the process to make it easier for those who wish to make an election, by allowing part of a donation to be treated as carried back and allowing amendments within the normal timescales.

It remains to be seen if anyone will take any notice.

15.46 Minimum and maximum donation

There is no statutory minimum amount for a Gift Aid donation. Charities may decide for themselves that for small gifts it is not worth seeking Gift Aid declarations (or reclaiming tax if a declaration is made).

There is no statutory maximum amount, but there are two effective caps

---

183 Authors' footnote: the reader may think it inappropriate for OTS to make proposals which they do not consider in detail.

which impose a maximum:

(1) The donor's creditable tax should exceed the amount treated as deducted from the gift (to avoid a clawback change).

(2) A donor should if practical restrict giving to an amount which maximises higher rate tax relief (after allowing for carry-back relief).

15.47 Deposited donation: Carry-forward

There is no carry-forward of Gift Aid.

For this reason it is essential that an individual does not make a qualifying donation in excess of the tax due on their income and gains in any tax year. It must be borne in mind that the amount of an individual's income in any particular year may not be ascertained with certainty until some later time; and also that certain reliefs, if claimed, may retrospectively reduce the amount of an individual's income.

A donor may wish to make a gift to charity which exceeds taxable capacity in any one year.

The gift should then be spread over a number of years. In the meantime, the donor could lend the balance to charity.

Suppose an individual with an annual income of £100,000 wished to make a gift of £300,000 to charity. The gift could be spread over at least three years thus (computation assuming 20% basic rate):

Year	**Net Gift**	**Gross Gift**[184]	**Loan**	**Funds with Charity**
1	£80K	£100K	£200K	£300K
2	£80K	£200K	£100K	£300K
3	£80K	£300K	–	£300K

It may be advantageous to spread the relief in this way still further so that the relief is used only against income which is taxable at the higher rate, and not wasted on income taxed at the basic rate or which qualifies for personal allowances.

The arrangement would be particularly advantageous if tax rates rose. Conversely it would be disadvantageous if rates fell, or if Gift Aid relief were withdrawn. The arrangement is similar to the deposited covenant scheme which operated before the introduction of Gift Aid in 2000.

The arrangement appears at first sight to be simple and straightforward. However the association of the gift and loan may contravene Gift Aid Condition E.[185] For the loan involves the charity acquiring property,

184 Including tax reclaim.

185 See 15.19 (Acquisition of property rule (Gift Aid condition E)).

namely, the money loaned. There is an argument that an interest-free loan is an acquisition of property "by way of gift".[186] The arrangement is far from the target of s.416(6) and the better view is that condition E is satisfied, but the cautious might seek confirmation from HMRC. Alternatively, perhaps, the loan might be made to a charity other than the charity which receives the gift.

15.48 Donor on remittance basis

This section considers the position of an individual who is a remittance basis taxpayer. These are UK resident but non-UK domiciled individuals who claim the remittance basis. These individuals pay tax on their foreign income and gains so far as the income or gains are remitted in UK. These individuals, therefore, tend to retain their foreign income and gains outside the UK.

A remittance basis taxpayer ("T") making a gift to charity should give:
(1) money (including foreign currency), qualifying for Gift Aid relief or
(2) foreign assets, qualifying for qualifying investment donation relief.

The gift may be made out of foreign income/gains, or property derived from foreign income/gains. If the sum given is money the gift should be to a bank account in the name of the charity outside the UK.[187] The charity may bring the assets to the UK without a taxable remittance, provided the charity is not a relevant person in relation to T.

A charitable company would be a relevant person if it is a close company and T or some other relevant person is a participator.[188]

A charitable trust would be a relevant person if T or some other relevant person is a beneficiary. That should not be the case, so a charitable trust is not a relevant person. This is the case even if the individual is a trustee or owner and director of a corporate trustee of the charity. If limited

---

186 The argument is supported by s.620(5) ITTOIA which envisages that an interest-free loan is not made for consideration; see 20.2.1 (Loan by individual).

187 We understand that the CAF maintain an offshore account for this purpose (and no doubt some other charities do the same). This is not strictly necessary: see Kessler, *Taxation of Non-Residents and Foreign Domiciliaries* (21st ed., 2022-23), para 18.12.7 (Gift to non-relevant person)
online version *https://www.foreigndomiciliaries.co.uk* but HMRC may not agree with that view.

188 See s.809M ITA 2007 and see Kessler, *Taxation of Non-Residents and Foreign Domiciliaries* (21st ed., 2022-23), para 18.4 (Relevant person: Companies) online version *https://www.foreigndomiciliaries.co.uk*

liability is needed, the trust may have a corporate trustee.

What about a company wholly owned by a charitable trust ("a subsidiary company")? The charitable trustee is a participator, but it is not a relevant person so that is not a problem. For the same reason, s.809L(2)(h) ITA will not apply. So the subsidiary company is not a relevant person. I mention one exception for completeness: a loan creditor is a participator, so the subsidiary company is a relevant person if the individual (or any other relevant person) is a loan creditor of the subsidiary company. In practice funding for the subsidiary company will usually come from the charity, not from loans directly from the individual or other relevant persons, so this should not be a problem.

Outstanding loans from the individual to the charity would need further consideration.

15.48.1 *Non-dom giving: Reform*

A rule that a charity is not a relevant person would sensible and avoid the current illogical distinction between charitable trusts and charitable companies. HMRC say:

> 2.91 A number of responses from the arts and charity sectors suggested that the business investment relief[189] should be extended to allow non-domiciles to bring overseas income and gains to the UK tax-free for the purpose of making donations to, or investments (?) in, UK charities.

We suspect, though it is not completely clear, that the suggestion was that a gift directly to a UK bank account of a charity should not be regarded as a taxable remittance. That reform would make it unnecessary for charities to maintain a foreign bank account. That seems in principle sensible,[190] but

---

189 As far as I can see, the proposal has nothing to do with business investment relief; the proposal was framed that way because it was made in the context of a consultation on that relief.

190 There are two complications. (1) If one is going to change the rule, there is no good reason to limit the change to charities. The same rules should apply to a payment to the bank account of a non-charity, for instance, a gift to a non-relevant person should not have to be made via a foreign bank account. The point illustrates how well meaning reform proposed by those with special interests can complicate matters as they may fail to look at the broad picture. (2) The proposal assumes that at present a payment to a UK bank account is a remittance; that is the HMRC view, but it is not correct; see Kessler, *Taxation of Non-Residents and Foreign Domiciliaries* (21st ed., 2022-23), para 18.12.7 (Gift to non-relevant person) online version *https://www.foreigndomiciliaries.co.uk* so what is needed is a change of practice, not a change in the law.

HMRC rejected it:

> **Government response**
> 2.92 The Government is committed to encouraging philanthropy. However, there are already tax-efficient ways for non-domiciles to make donations to UK charities[191] and the Government has not seen any compelling evidence that extending the business investment relief in the way suggested would lead to a significant increase in the level of donations to UK charities by non-domiciles. It is also very likely that complicated legislation and anti-avoidance provisions would be required. The Government therefore does not intend to take any further action on this issue at the present time...[192]

Thus there is no current prospect of reform.

15.49 Position of charity

15.49.1 *Tax deemed deducted*

s.520 ITA	**s.471 CTA 2010**
(1) This section applies if [a] a gift is made to a charitable trust by an individual and [b] the gift is a qualifying donation for the purposes of Chapter 2 of Part 8 (Gift Aid).	(1) This section applies if [a] a gift is made to a charitable company by an individual and [b] the gift is a qualifying donation for the purposes of Chapter 2 of Part 8 of ITA 2007 (gift aid).
(2) The charitable trust is treated as receiving, under deduction of income tax at the basic rate for the tax year in which the gift is made, a	(2) The charitable company is treated as receiving, under deduction of income tax at the basic rate for the tax year in which the

---

Still, it could all be sorted out easily enough.

191 It does not say, but presumably this is a reference to planning by a gift to a foreign bank account.

192 The paragraph concluded "but [the Government] will consider how to increase awareness of ways for non-domiciles to make tax-efficient donations under the existing rules." Nothing was done. Perhaps that was not intended seriously. Or perhaps the Government realised that the current rules are so absurd that the less that is said about them, the better.
HMRC, *Reform of the taxation of non-domiciled individuals: summary of responses to consultation* (2011).
http://webarchive.nationalarchives.gov.uk/20130129110402/http://www.hm-treasury.gov.uk/d/condoc_responses_non_domicile_reform.pdf

gift of an amount equal to the grossed up amount of the gift.

[(3) defines the "grossed up amount of the gift"; see 15.43.1 (Grossed Up amount")]

(4) The income tax treated as deducted is treated as income tax paid by the trustees of the charitable trust.

gift is made, a gift of an amount equal to the grossed up amount of the gift.

[(3) defines the "grossed up amount of the gift"]

(4) The income tax treated as deducted is treated as income tax paid by the charitable company.

The charity is treated as receiving the Grossed Up amount of the gift. For instance, on the receipt of a £80 Gift Aid donation, the charity is deemed to have received £100 income and paid £20 tax. The £20 tax can be reclaimed from HMRC.

15.49.2 *Gift Aid charge & relief*

s.521 ITA

(1) This section applies if
[a] gifts are made to charitable trusts by individuals and
[b] the gifts are qualifying donations for the purposes of Chapter 2 of Part 8 (gift aid).

(2) Income tax is charged on the gifts under this section.
(3) It is charged on the grossed up amount of the gifts arising in the tax year.

(4) But a gift is not taken into account in calculating total income so far as it is applied to charitable purposes only.

[(5) defines the "grossed up amount of a gift"; see 15.43.1 (Grossed Up amount")

s.472 CTA 2010

(1) If
[a] a charitable company receives a gift from an individual and
[b] the gift is a qualifying donation for the purposes of Chapter 2 of Part 8 of ITA 2007 (gift aid),

the grossed up amount of the gift is treated as an amount in respect of which the company is chargeable to corporation tax, under the charge to corporation tax on income.

(2) But the grossed up amount of the gift is not taken into account in calculating total profits so far as that grossed up amount is applied to charitable purposes only.

[(3) defines the "grossed up amount of a gift"

(6) The trustees of the charitable trust are liable for any tax charged under this section.

(4) The exemption under subsection (2) requires a claim.

The charity will be taxable on its Gift Aid income if it fails to qualify for the exemption (eg if it does not apply the income for charitable purposes, or breaches the charitable expenditure rules).

At the time these rules were devised it was assumed that the charity would be UK resident. But it is considered that these rules apply on a Gift Aid donation to a non-resident charity.

15.49.3 *Tax reclaim*

The HMRC Guidance Note provides:

> 6.1.1 A charity or Community Amateur Sports Club (CASC) can claim repayment of UK basic rate tax that is treated as deducted from donations made to it by individuals under Gift Aid. There is no limit on the amount of a Gift Aid donation.
> 6.1.2 A charity cannot claim repayment of basic rate tax on donations made by companies, unincorporated businesses, trusts or other charities.
> 6.1.3 The basic rate tax which can be claimed on Gift Aid donations made by individuals in part or all of a tax year can be calculated by using the fraction:
>
> $$\frac{\text{Basic rate of tax for the year} \times \text{amount of Gift Aid donations received}}{(100 - \text{basic rate of tax for the year})}$$
>
> So, for example, where the basic rate in force for a tax year is 20%, the fraction will be 20/80 (20/ (100 – 20)).
> On a Gift Aid donation of £10, the tax reclaimable would be £2.50 (£10 × 20/80).

For the reclaim procedure, see 47.15 ("Charities online" repayment system).

15.49.4 *Ownership/use of tax reclaim*

Charities SORP FRS 102 deals with the terms of ownership and accountancy treatment of the amount reclaimed:

> 2.5...Similarly, any Gift Aid amount recovered on a donation forms part

of that gift and is an addition to the same fund as the initial donation unless the donor or the terms of the appeal have specified otherwise.

15.50 Gift Aid: Critique

15.50.1 *Gift Aid v deduction relief*

Charity income tax reliefs other than individual Gift Aid (payroll giving scheme, qualifying investments and corporate Gift Aid) all take the form of a deduction for the donor. We refer to this as the **"deduction system of relief."** Gift Aid relief is different. It consists of two components:

(1) *Transferred basic rate component:* Gift Aid gives (Grossed Up) basic rate relief to the donee charity.

(2) *Higher rate deduction component:* Gift Aid confers a deduction for higher rates of tax (for higher rate taxpayers).

The reason is historical: Gift Aid relief operates in the same manner as its predecessor, the relief for deeds of covenant.

At first sight, it seems preferable to treat Gift Aid in the same way as the other reliefs. The 1955 Royal Commission on the Taxation of Profits and Income preferred this in theory but rejected the change for two pragmatic reasons:

(1) The immediate result would be a reduction in the value of gifts to charities. It is not clear to what extent donors would increase their giving to allow for their tax relief.

(2) The administrative work giving a personal relief to each individual taxpayer would be greater than the present work of returning basic rate tax to charities, at least for basic rate taxpayers who are the great majority.[193]

These considerations still have some validity today, though perhaps less than in 1955 since:

(1) The changeover to the deduction system of relief was made for charitable companies in 2000, so there is a precedent.

(2) The administrative work could be mitigated by a minimum donation set at an administratively sensible level (say £100).

There is however a third and important consideration which favours the

---

193 Royal Commission on the Taxation of Profits and Income, final report Cmd. 9474, paras 182–185 *https://www.kessler.co.uk/wp-content/uploads/2012/05/Royal-Commission-on-the-Taxation-of-Profits-and-Income-1955-comments-on-what-is-a-trade.pdf*

deduction system of relief. This is the compliance risk: the prevention of fraudulent claims by charities or sham charities. The scope of such fraud increased significantly after the extension of charity tax reliefs to EU countries. Under the Gift Aid system, any fraudster can create a charity or sham charity which puts in a fraudulent repayment claim. These will often be difficult for HMRC to detect. There have been successful prosecutions, but it seems unlikely that will deter further attempts. Under the deduction system, the scope for significant fraud is limited to taxpayers with significant income, and it is easier for HMRC to supervise them.

A further disadvantage of the present system is that donors typically do not understand it. In particular donors often do not understand the Gift Aid declaration. Donor typically have little awareness of how much Income Tax they pay each year.[194]

Further disadvantages arise from the present system, which imposes a tax charge on donors who pay insufficient tax. Firstly that charge is more or less uncollectible. Secondly, it operates harshly on impecunious taxpayers. The Low Income Tax Reform Group is pressing HMRC not to pursue taxpayers for tax due on donations they make under Gift Aid, saying it is fairer that reimbursements should come from the charity.[195] This proposal seems sensible, until it is viewed in the context of the Gift Aid rules as a whole. Moving the onus on to the charity is not practical for various reasons. Charities could not properly budget for the tax. They would have to be given information confidential to donors. However a shift to a deduction system would solve these problems.

A possible compromise between the two systems would be one which allows the charity to reclaim tax on gifts up to an appropriate limit, say, £250 or £1,000 (gross) and larger gifts to be treated as deductions.

Ireland operates an interesting compromise between the two systems, with grossing up for PAYE only taxpayers (those whose tax is collected under PAYE). If the individual completes a self-assessment return, or does not pay tax under PAYE at all, there is no grossing up, and instead the

---

194 HMRC Research Report 334 "Gift Aid: Understanding donor behaviour" (2014) *https://www.gov.uk/government/uploads/system/uploads/attachment_data/file/372221/report344.pdf*
HMRC Research Report 366 "Charitable giving and Gift Aid behaviour amongst better-off individuals" (2015)
https://www.gov.uk/government/publications/charitable-giving-and-gift-aid-behaviour-amongst-better-off-individuals

195 *http://www.litrg.org.uk/latest-news/news/160324-press-release-check-your-tax-position-giving-under-gift-aid-because-imminent*

individual claims a deduction.[196]

15.50.2 *Redirection/composite rate*

Research by economists commissioned by HMRC considered two other theoretical methods of tax relief:

(1) *Redirection.* Under a redirection scheme, higher-rate and additional-rate taxpayers would no longer be entitled to higher-rate or additional rate relief; instead the donee charity would reclaim the relief, in short:
   (a) 45p[197] for every gross £1 donated out of net-of-tax income by additional-rate taxpayers,
   (b) 40p for higher rate taxpayers
   (c) 20p for basic-rate taxpayers
(2) *Composite rate.* Under a composite rate scheme, higher-rate[198] taxpayers would no longer be entitled to higher-rate relief; instead charities could reclaim at some rate (to be specified) that would apply equally to higher-rate and basic rate donors (and on a further variant, to non-taxpayer donors). This composite rate could be set anywhere. The research considered possible composite rates of 30% and 37%.[199]

Both methods eliminate the deduction component of Gift Aid; redirection transfers that relief from the higher-rate donors to charities receiving the gift; a composite rate increases the relief to charities receiving gifts from any taxpayer (or on another variant, from anyone at all).

This research only considered the effect on donors. It did not consider any other aspects of the proposed reform. In particular, it did not consider the impact of the redirection and composite rate options on compliance risks and operational costs. Nor did it address feasibility of implementation.[200]

Looking at the matter from a practitioners viewpoint, we think it is fairly

---

196 See booklet Chy "2" (Scheme of tax relief for donations to eligible charities and other approved bodies) *http://www.revenue.ie*

197 46p in Scotland.

198 To avoid undue repetition, where the context permits, references in this discussion to the "higher rate" include the top rate (which statute calls the additional rate); and we ignore the different rates of income tax which may be payable by Scottish/Welsh taxpayers.

199 Scharf & Smith, "Gift Aid donor research: Exploring options for reforming higher-rate relief" (2009) *https://webarchive.nationalarchives.gov.uk/20101006154205/http:/www.hmrc.gov.uk/research/report91.pdf*

200 At p.7.

clear that neither proposal is feasible.

Redirection is not feasible for practical reasons: Donors would have to tell charities whether they were higher-rate or additional-rate taxpayers in each year that a gift was made; they may not know until some time after the end of the year what their marginal rate of tax was; HMRC would have to police those declarations.[201]

Redirection is also unnecessary and illogical since under the present system a higher-rate donor could if they wanted achieve the end result of a redirection system by increasing their donation to allow for the relief; conversely under a redirection system a higher-rate taxpayer could (and no doubt many would) achieve the same result as the current system by reducing the donation to allow for the relief.

A report in 2019 also recommended redirection, but again without addressing the feasibility issues ("Research can determine how practical administrative obstacles – such as determining the unknown marginal tax rates of donors before the end of the tax year - could be overcome.")[202]

A composite rate is not feasible (or at least, raises severe difficulties).[203] for political reasons: the payment to charity would be treated in national accounts as public expenditure, not a tax relief (negative taxation).[204] Quite apart from that, there are major objections:

(1) It is unclear how the composite rate should be set. If it is adjustable the reform would add to uncertainty: charities need to be able to predict what their future income will be.

(2) The composite rate weakens the connection between the donor and the donee charity: as the message will in effect be "give to my charity and the government will give more to the sector - but not specifically to my charity"

(3) The proposal does not have universal support in the charity sector, as it has very significant losers as well as winners.

---

201 A variant system would make redirection optional at the decision of the donor. That would avoid the problems of compulsory redirection, but it would not offer any benefit as a donor who wanted to achieve that result could do so under the present system.

202 Charity Tax Commission, "Reforming charity taxation" (2019) p.26, 27 *https://www.ncvo.org.uk/images/documents/policy_and_research/funding/CharityCommissionReport__ForWeb_3.pdf*

203 Fanning agrees:"Gift Aid Forum - report to Economic Secretary to the Treasury" (2010) *http://www.cgap.org.uk/uploads/reports/gift_aid_forum_final_report.pdf*

204 See 1.5 (Matched funding incentives).

(4) The proposal would lead to more tax planning as donors sought ways to obtain relief for charitable support other than Gift Aid relief.

Nevertheless a (rather low) composite rate was proposed in the Liberal Democrat Manifesto 2010:

> Liberal Democrats will support the voluntary sector by ... reforming Gift Aid to operate at a single rate of 23% – giving more money to charity while closing down a loophole[205] for higher rate tax payers.

With a composite rate at 23% scarcely above the basic rate, this proposal was close to abolition of higher rate Gift Aid relief and a return to the system which applied between 1946 and 1980.[206]

15.50.3 *Minimum amount for relief*

Bill Dodwell has made two interesting policy proposals, minimum amounts for basic rate relief and for higher rate relief:

> If it's desired to cut administrative costs, then gift aid claims by charities for under £1,000 annually could be refused - which would cut out up to 40% of claims. No doubt some small claimants would redirect their donors to one of the intermediaries, such as the CAF, or Justgiving - which would achieve the sensible objective of passing claims to a body equipped to handle the administration.
> Higher-rate relief claims could be allowed only for total annual gifts over, say, £2,500. This would cut out about 80% of such claims and probably produce ... £100m .... At the same time, the incentive for major donors to support charities is continued.[207]

The rule to have no minimum amount for Gift Aid donations does seem strange. Perhaps it arose primarily for historical reasons, for there was never any minimum amount for deeds of covenant, and that rule was continued on the abolition of deeds of covenant by removing the former minimum amount for Gift Aid donations.

15.51 Gift Aid declaration

Section 416(1) ITA provides:

---

205 This use of the word "loophole" is a nice illustration of the tendency to use (a purist would say, misuse) that word to describe any tax rule that one wishes to change in favour of HMRC.

206 See 15.2 (IT reliefs for cash gifts to charity).

207 Tax, September 2010, p.6

> A gift made to a charity by an individual is a qualifying donation for the purposes of this Chapter if ...
>
> (b) the individual gives the charity a Gift Aid declaration relating to the gift (see s.428)

Section 428(1) ITA provides:

> In this Chapter "Gift Aid declaration" means a declaration which—
>
> (a) is given in the manner specified by regulations made by the Commissioners for HMRC, and
>
> (b) contains any information and any statements required by the regulations.

The requirements of the declaration for gifts made on or after 6 April 2017 are specified in:

- The Donations to Charity (Gift Aid Declarations) Regulations 2016 ("**DCGADR**")
- The Donations to Charity by Individuals (Appropriate Declarations) Regulations 2000 (the **"old regulations"**)

Regulation 1(2) of the old regulations provides:

> These Regulations shall have effect in relation to—
>
> (a) gifts made on or after 6th April 2000 and on or before 5th April 2017 which are not covenanted payments; and
>
> (b) covenanted payments falling to be made on or after 6th April 2000.

So the old regulations now apply only to covenanted payments. But covenanted payments by individuals (more or less) stopped after the introduction of Gift Aid in 2000, and there cannot be many pre-2000 covenants still in effect. So the old regulations are (more or less) defunct.[208] This chapter considers the rules for gifts made on or after 6 April 2017.

15.51.1 *Time limit for declaration*

Section 416(1) ITA requires that the "donor *gives* [present tense] the charity a Gift Aid declaration". But the donor is obviously not required to give the declaration simultaneously with the gift. There is no time limit at all; but relief is not available until the declaration is made. If the

---

208 For a discussion of the old regulations, see chapter 15 of the 10th (2015/16) edition of this work.

declaration is made after more than (in short) a four year delay, it will be too late for the charity or the individual to claim the relief. HMRC accept this. HMRC Guidance Note 3.6.4 provides:

> Donors are able to give the charity a declaration:
> - in advance of their donation, or
> - at the time of their donation, or
> - at any time after their donation subject to the normal time limit within which tax can be reclaimed.

15.51.2 *Donor/intermediary declaration*

Regulation 4(1) DCGADR provides:

> A gift aid declaration may be given—
> (a) by a donor to a charity, or
> (b) by a donor intermediary to a charity,[209]

Declaration by	**Declaration under**	**See para**
Donor	reg 4(1)(a)	15.52
Donor intermediary	reg 4(1)(b)	15.53

15.51.3 *Oral or in writing*

Regulation 4(2) DCGADR provides:

> A gift aid declaration may be given in writing or orally, including the use of written or oral methods of electronic communications.

HMRC Guidance Note provides at 3.6.3:

> Gift Aid declarations can be given in writing (including by email, fax, or text message) or orally (in person or by telephone).

15.52 Declaration by donor

15.52.1 *Declaration content: Summary*

Regulation 5(1) DCGADR provides:

> A gift aid declaration given by a donor under regulation 4(1)(a) must—
> (a) contain the name and home address of the donor,
> (b) name the charity (or be made in circumstances where the charity is identified),
> (c) identify the gift or gifts to which the gift aid declaration relates,

---

209 For completeness: the comma at the end of regulation 4(1) is a slip for a full stop.

and

(d) confirm that the identified gift or gifts are to be qualifying donations for the purposes of section 416 of ITA 2007 (meaning of qualifying donation).

This applies to oral and written Gift Aid declarations.

15.52.2 *Name and home address*

Regulation 5 DCGADR provides:

> (1) A gift aid declaration given by a donor under regulation 4(1)(a) must—
>
> (a) contain the name and home address of the donor,..

The HMRC Guidance Note provides:

> **3.9 Further Information on the contents of the Gift Aid Declaration**
>
> 3.9.1 The donor's name and home address
>
> The declaration should show:
>
> - the donor's full[210] name – as a minimum we will accept the donor's initial and surname.
> - the donor's full[211] home postal address – as a minimum we will accept the number (or name as appropriate) of their home and their full postcode.

The minimum then to satisfy HMRC is initial, surname, name/number of house and postcode. If the declaration does not have that, HMRC are entitled to say it does not meet the requirement of giving "name and home address" and so is invalid.

> If HMRC finds the details on a declaration are not enough to trace the donor, HMRC may ask the charity to get more check the claim. If the charity fails to obtain this information, it's likely that the declaration will be considered invalid. We would recommend that charities ask donors at regular intervals, possibly every 2 years, to check the personal details held. Any request like this would have to be GDPR compliant.

This is not strictly correct. The obligation is to provide "name and home address"; not details sufficient to enable HMRC to trace the donor (if that

---

210 The requirements to give a *full* name is not in the regulations but the words which follow indicate that HMRC regard that as best practice, not a requirement.

211 The requirement to give the *full* address is not in the regulations but the words which follow again indicate that HMRC regard that as best practice, not a requirement.

is different).

15.52.3 *Name of charity*

Regulation 5 DCGADR provides:

> (1) A gift aid declaration given by a donor under regulation 4(1)(a) must...
>
> (b) name the charity (or be made in circumstances where the charity is identified)

The HMRC Guidance Note provides:

> **3.9.2 A Gift Aid declaration must clearly identify the charity**
> A declaration should ideally show the charity's full name. The charity's working name or acronym is acceptable, provided it's sufficient to identify the charity beyond doubt.
> There are other ways in which a charity might be identified in a particular declaration, for example:
>
> - the use of a charity's logo on a pre-printed form
> - a reference to a particular appeal run by an individual charity
>
> This will usually be acceptable but care should be taken that the information is sufficiently clear to identify a particular charity beyond doubt.
> A telephone declaration might, for example, be made in response to a recorded message identifying the charity. An appropriate message will in itself be acceptable, there is no requirement for the donor personally to identify the charity.
> A declaration can include the name of more than one charity - for example, where a joint fund-raising event takes place. In such a situation the charities involved need to ensure that:
>
> - the donor is aware how his or her donation's to be split between the charities listed on the declaration.
> - they each keep records of how the donations have been divided between them - each charity will also need to be able to produce a copy of the declaration, if required.
>
> Where a charity changes its name (for example because of a merger) the charity will not need to obtain a new declaration from a donor so long as the charity can show beyond doubt that the name of the charity on the existing declaration is a name previously used by the charity.

A change of name does not matter. If the merger results in a different entity, then a new declaration would be needed.

15.52.4 *Identify the gift*

Regulation 5 DCGADR provides:

> (1) A gift aid declaration given by a donor under regulation 4(1)(a) must...
>
> (c) identify the gift or gifts to which the declaration relates

The HMRC Guidance Note provides:

> 3.9.3 Identify the gift or gifts to which the declaration relates
> Any appropriate description can be used in a declaration but it must be unambiguous. Donations considered to fall outside the description provided won't qualify for Gift Aid relief.
> Examples of some common descriptions include:
>
> - the donation of £x I made to you on dd/mm/yy;
> - the enclosed donation
> - all donations I make under the direct debit mandate below
> - all donations I make on or after the date of this declaration
> - all donations I make from this date until further notice
> - all donations I have made for the four years prior to this tax year

This list omits a formula offered in the HMRC Guidance Note before 1 November 2005 which seems the best of them all:

> - "all donations I have made since 6 April 2000 and all donations I make hereafter".

The HMRC Guidance Note continues:

> Whether the charity chooses from 1 or more of the above descriptions or devises its own, it's important to get the description right. The declaration won't cover any donations received that fall outside the description used. If a specific date isn't included in the description then it's essential that the Gift Aid declaration is dated so that the period it covers can be determined.
> Depending on the description used, a declaration may apply indefinitely to future donations to the named charity.
> If a donor wishes to alter the description of the gift or gifts shown on a declaration, they must cancel the declaration and make a fresh one.

15.52.5 *Confirm Gift Aid applies*

Regulation 5 DCGADR provides:

> (1) A gift aid declaration given by a donor under regulation 4(1)(a)

must...

(d) confirm that the identified gift or gifts are to be qualifying donations for the purposes of section 416 of ITA 2007 (Meaning of qualifying donation).

The HMRC Guidance Note provides:

> 3.9.4 Declaration that donations are to be treated as Gift Aid donations
> The declaration must confirm that the gifts described in it are to be Gift Aid donations and this is best done by a specific reference in the description of the donation(s) that are covered by the Gift Aid declaration - for example:-
> - 'Please treat the enclosed gift as a Gift Aid donation'
> - 'I want all my subsequent donations to be Gift Aid donations'

Before the text was amended in 2012, the HMRC Guidance Note offered another set of choices:

- "Please reclaim tax on my donations", or
- "I want the charity to reclaim tax on my donations", or
- "I want the charity to reclaim tax on my donations Yes/No (delete as appropriate)", or
- "Tick here if you want us to reclaim tax on your donations [ ]".

The authors have seen the form:

> All donations will be Gift Aided as your wish unless you tick here that you do not wish the charity to reclaim any tax you have paid on this and other future donations.

That opt out form may increase Gift Aid take-up. The requirement is that the words used "confirm that the gift is to be a qualifying donation". It is a question of construction whether any particular form of words meets this requirement. It is, in our view, clearly possible to draft an "opt-out" form which does so, but it would be desirable to clear the form used with HMRC.

15.52.6 *Date and signature*

HMRC Guidance Note provides:

> 3.6.8 ... Many charities believe a signature makes an individual more committed to their charity. However, there is no requirement for a declaration to contain a signature and so the 'signature requirement' can be removed if you wish.
> The declaration does not require a date but a date serves to identify the

> period covered by the Gift Aid declaration and where this is not otherwise clear from the terms of the declaration it is necessary to include a request for a date.

In practice, it is very unlikely to matter. But as a matter of good practice, it is desirable for a written Gift Aid declaration to be signed and dated.

15.52.7 *Declaration by joint donors*

The HMRC Guidance Note provides:

> **3.10.2 Joint declarations**
> It is possible for spouses, civil partners and other persons living together to make a 'joint' declaration on the same form (in effect, there are two Gift Aid declarations). The 'joint' declaration must include the full name and address of each person. Both parties will need to make clear to the charity involved how much of any donation relates to each of them. They will also need this information for their own tax affairs.[212] The charity will need to list each person separately on the schedule to the claim form ChR1 and show the donation received from each.

In practice joint declarations will rarely if ever be used. See too: 15.56 (Gift from joint account); 18.4.1 (Gift Aid from partnership).

15.52.8 *Duty to give tax explanation*

Regulation 5(2) DCGADR provides:

> An explanation of the effect of section 424 of ITA 2007 (charge to tax) must be given to the donor at the time the gift aid declaration in paragraph (1) [gift aid declaration by donor] is given in order for the gift aid declaration to have effect for the purposes of the Income Tax Acts (subject to paragraph (3) and regulations 10 and 11).

This is here called the **"tax explanation"**.
In outline, this explanation may be given in three ways:

(1) If the donor completes a written Gift Aid declaration, the explanation is in practice given in that form (though it could be made later).
(2) If the donor makes an oral Gift Aid declaration:
  (a) The charity may give the tax explanation orally, at the time the oral Gift Aid declaration is made by the donor. This is later

---

212 Authors' note: Donors only need this information if they are higher rate taxpayers and wish to claim higher rate relief on the gift.

recorded in a written statement.

(b) The charity may give the tax explanation by a written statement sent by the charity after the donor has made an oral Gift Aid declaration is made.

Failure to give the explanation results in an invalid Gift Aid declaration. Fortunately there is no requirement that the donor should read or understand the explanation!

The HMRC Guidance Note provides:

> 3.6.8 ... The charity must tell a donor of the tax implications of making a Gift Aid donation. The charity can choose to leave the tax explanation on their Gift Aid declaration or omit it. If it is omitted then the charity must ensure that they clearly explain the donor's tax requirement to their donors and are able to demonstrate to HMRC that they have done so.

What should this explanation say? The HMRC Guidance Note provides:

> A statement that 'I am a UK taxpayer' is not sufficient to meet the charity's requirement to advise a donor of the tax implications of making a Gift Aid donation.

That is correct, since that wording does not explain that the tax paid should equal the charity's tax reclaim.

> A full explanation is essential to protect the individual donor and the charity. If the donor has not paid enough tax to cover the tax deducted from their Gift Aid donation(s), HMRC may ask the donor to pay the difference in tax and donors must be made aware of this. If the explanation is insufficient the Gift Aid declaration will not be valid and the charity may need to repay tax to HMRC.

A fully accurate statement would be along the following lines:

> The effect of s.424 ITA will be as follows:
>
> (a) Your gift will be treated as made under deduction of income tax at the basic rate.
>
> (b) To the extent to which tax treated as so deducted exceeds the amount of income tax and capital gains tax with which you are charged for the year of assessment in which the gift is made, you are chargeable to income tax at the basic rate on so much of the gift as is necessary to recover an amount of tax equal to the excess.

However, it is safe to use a form of words approved by HMRC:

> I am a UK taxpayer and understand that if I pay less Income Tax and/or Capital Gains Tax in the current tax year than the amount of Gift Aid claimed on all my donations it is my responsibility to pay any difference.

15.52.9 *Charity declaration form*

HMRC Guidance Note provides:

> 3.6.6 A charity may want to add more information and notes of its own on a declaration form. For example, the inclusion of any General Data Protection Regulations (GDPR) that the charity feel is needed. HMRC has no objection to this or to the inclusion of a declaration in other documents, such as standing order mandates provided the statutory requirements for a Gift Aid declaration are met.
> [There is no para 3.6.7]
> 3.6.8 HMRC does not produce an official form for Gift Aid declarations, so a charity can design its own. But the HMRC website contains a model Gift Aid declaration and it is recommended that charities use the model adapted, as appropriate, to reflect the period of the intended Gift Aid donation(s).[213]
> The notes at the foot of the declaration are purely explanatory and can be omitted if you wish...
> 3.6.9 There's no need for a charity to get approval from HMRC for own-design declarations - but HMRC will review proposed designs on request.

15.52.10 *Reminder to donors*

The HMRC Guidance Note provides:

> 3.5.5 The position of a taxpayer making Gift Aid donations can change from one tax year to the next. Charities should remind donors on a regular basis of the need for them to have paid sufficient Income and/or Capital Gains Tax on their donations. It need not be done in a separate letter to each donor, but could be included in any material sent to supporters, example, a newsletter.

This is good practice but not compulsory, and we wonder how often it is done.

Before the guidance was rewritten in 2012, HMRC (correctly) noted that there was no obligation to do this:

213 See App 2.1 (Model Gift Aid declarations).

> *Where a donor provides a long term or open-ended Gift Aid declaration, it would be considerate of a charity to provide regular reminders of this requirement – perhaps in "thank you" correspondence or simply in a newsletter. There is, however, no obligation on a charity to do this.*

15.52.11 *Donor changes address*

Regulation 5(7) of the old regulations (the Donations to Charity by Individuals (Appropriate Declarations) Regulations 2000) provided:

> *Where a donor who has given an appropriate declaration to a charity notifies the charity of any change to his name or home address, the charity must keep a record of those changes with the declaration.*

HMRC Guidance Note provides at 3.9.1:

> If a donor subsequently changes their name or address, this won't invalidate the declaration. If the charity is notified of a change in the donor's name or address, it must keep a record of the updated information - this can be kept as an electronic copy such as a scanned document. The declaration itself does not need to be amended, but a record of the change should be kept on the charity's database.

This is not in the current DCGADR. But in practice good fundraising and administration would require this in any event.

15.52.12 *Right to cancel declaration*

Regulation 5(3) DCGADR provides:

> A donor is entitled to cancel the gift aid declaration referred to in paragraph (1) [a declaration given by the donor] by giving notice to the charity.

Regulation 5(4) DCGADR provides:

> The notification under paragraph (3) may be given in writing or orally, including the use of written or oral methods of electronic communications.

Regulation 11 DCGADR provides:

> Where a donor notifies a charity of the cancellation of a gift aid declaration, other than under regulation 9(7),[214] the gift aid declaration

214 See 15.53.4 (Cancellation of authorisation).

> ceases to have effect for the purposes of the Income Tax Acts from the date on which the charity receives that notification, or if the notice specifies a later date, from that date.

A donor may cancel a declaration at any time, but this cancellation only applies to gifts after the date of the cancellation, it does not affect gifts made before. In other words, this power of cancellation operates prospectively, not retrospectively.[215]

The HMRC Guidance Note provides:

> 3.8.2 A cancellation will normally have effect only in relation to donations received by the charity on or after:
> - the date on which the donor notifies the charity of the cancellation, or
> - such later date as the donor may specify in the cancellation.
>
> The charity mustn't reclaim tax in respect of such donations. Any donations received before the date of the donor's notification will still qualify as Gift Aid donations.

15.53 Declaration by intermediary

15.53.1 *Power of intermediary*

Section 416 ITA provides:

> (1) A gift made to a charity by an individual is a qualifying donation for the purposes of this Chapter if ...
>
> (b) the individual, or an intermediary representing the individual, gives the charity, or an intermediary representing the charity, a gift aid declaration relating to the gift (see section 428).

Section 416(1A) ITA provides the definition of "intermediary":

> For the purpose of subsection (1)(b) an intermediary is—
>
> (a) a person authorised by the individual to give a gift aid declaration on behalf of that individual to the charity,
>
> (b) a person authorised by a charity to receive a gift aid declaration on behalf of that charity, or
>
> (c) a person authorised to perform both of the roles described in paragraphs (a) and (b).

Regulation 2 DCGADR provides a commonsense definition of the term

---

215 For completeness, see 15.55.5 (Cancellation on receipt of statement) for a further cancellation right; though that does not often arise.

"donor intermediary":

> In these Regulations ... "donor intermediary" means a person who is or was authorised by a donor to give a gift aid declaration on behalf of that donor to a charity

Thus an intermediary representing the donor may give the declaration. Though we wonder how often this is actually done.

15.53.2 *Intermediary declaration: content*

The rules are almost the same as for declarations by donors.[216] It is helpful to read regulation 5(1) and 6(1) side by side:

reg 5(1): declaration by donor	**reg 6(1): declaration by intermediary**
A gift aid declaration given by a donor under regulation 4(1)(a) must—	A gift aid declaration given by a donor intermediary on behalf of a donor under regulation 4(1)(b) must—
(a) contain the name and home address of the donor,	[Identical]
(b) name the charity (or be made in circumstances where the charity is identified),	[Identical]
(c) identify the gift or gifts to which the gift aid declaration relates, and	(c) identify the gift to which the gift aid declaration relates, and
(d) confirm that the identified gift or gifts are to be qualifying donations for the purposes of section 416 of ITA 2007 (meaning of qualifying donation).	(d) confirm that the identified gift is to be a qualifying donation for the purposes of section 416 of ITA 2007.

The only difference is that gift or gifts (in reg 5) has become gift in the singular (in reg 6). But we consider that the singular in reg 6(1) includes the plural, so there is no difference in meaning.

15.53.3 *Authorisation and tax explanation*

Regulation 6 DCGADR provides:

> (2) Before giving a gift aid declaration a donor intermediary must have—

216 See 15.52 (Declaration by donor).

(a) been authorised by the donor to give a gift aid declaration on behalf of the donor, and

(b) given an explanation of the effect of section 424 of ITA 2007 to the donor,

in order for the gift aid declaration to have effect for the purposes of the Income Tax Acts (subject to paragraph (5) and regulation 10).

(3) A donor intermediary must obtain the authorisation referred to in paragraph (2)(a) and provide the explanation referred to in paragraph (2)(b) in every tax year in which it gives a gift aid declaration on behalf of the donor. This is subject to paragraph (4).

(4) Paragraph (3) does not apply in respect of a tax year if the donor intermediary obtained the authorisation referred to in paragraph (2)(a) and gave the explanation referred to in paragraph 2(b) on or after 1st March in the immediately preceding tax year.

15.53.4 *Cancellation of authorisation*

Regulation 6 DCGADR provides:

> (5) A donor is entitled to cancel the authorisation referred to in paragraph (2)(a) by giving notice to the donor intermediary.
>
> (6) The notification under paragraph (5) may be given in writing or orally, including the use of written or oral methods of electronic communications.
>
> (7) Where a donor notifies a donor intermediary under paragraph (5), the authorisation ceases to have effect from the date on which the donor intermediary receives that notification, or if the notice specifies a later date, from that date.

15.53.5 *Record keeping by intermediary*

Regulation 7 DCGADR provides:

> (1) For each authorisation given by a donor under regulation 6(2)(a), a donor intermediary must maintain a record of—
>
> (a) the name and address of the donor, and
>
> (b) the date on which the authorisation was received,
>
> in a form, and to a standard, which can be inspected and audited by HMRC.
>
> (2) The donor intermediary must preserve that record for six years from the end of the tax year, or where regulation 6(4) is relied upon from the end of the final tax year, to which the authorisation applies.
>
> (3) For each gift aid declaration given on behalf of a donor under regulation 6, a donor intermediary must maintain a record of the date on

which the explanation of the effect of section 424 of ITA 2007 was given to the donor in accordance with regulation 6(2)(b), in a form, and to a standard, which can be inspected and audited by HMRC.

(4) The donor intermediary must preserve that record for six years from the end of the tax year in which the gift aid declaration is given.

(5) For each notice of cancellation of authorisation received from a donor under regulation 6(5), a donor intermediary must maintain a record of—

(a) the name and home address of the donor, and

(b) the date on which notice of cancellation was received,

in a form, and to a standard, which can be inspected and audited by HMRC.

(6) The donor intermediary must preserve that record for six years from the end of the tax year in which the notice of cancellation is received.

(7) An officer of Revenue and Customs may by notice in writing require a donor intermediary to produce a record referred to in paragraph (1), (3) or (5) for inspection.

(8) Where a donor intermediary is required by a notice under paragraph (7) to produce a record for inspection, the donor intermediary must do so—

(a) within such period,

(b) at such time, by such means and in such form (if any), and

(c) at such place, other than a place used solely as a dwelling,

as is reasonably specified in the notice.

15.53.6 *Annual statements*

Regulation 8 DCGADR provides:

(1) By the 31st May immediately following the end of a tax year during which a donor intermediary has given a gift aid declaration on behalf of a donor under regulation 6, the donor intermediary must send the donor a statement in writing, or details as to how the donor can access a statement in writing stating-

(a) the aggregate value of donations made by the donor which have been subject to a gift aid declaration given by the donor intermediary during that tax year (the "gift aided donations"),

(b) the maximum amount of gift aid which charities may claim on the gift aided donations,

(c) that the statement does not include any gift aid declarations given by other donor intermediaries on behalf of the donor, or given by the donor directly to a charity, and

(d) that if the donor paid less income tax and capital gains tax in that tax year than the amount of gift aid claimed by charities on all the donor's donations in that tax year, it is the donor's responsibility to pay any difference.

This paragraph is subject to paragraph (2).

(2) Paragraph (1) does not apply to a tax year during which-

(a) the aggregate value of the gift aided donations is £20 or less, or

(b) only one gift aided donation is made.

(3) The donor intermediary must maintain a record of annual statements and details as to how to access annual statements sent under paragraph (1), in a form, and to a standard, which can be inspected and audited by HMRC.

(4) The donor intermediary must preserve that record for six years from the end of the tax year to which the annual statement relates.

15.53.7 *Penalties for intermediary*

Regulation 12 DCGADR provides:

(1) A donor intermediary is liable to a penalty of £50 in respect of each failure to—

(a) maintain a record of an authorisation, in accordance with regulation 7(1) and (2),

(b) maintain a record of the date on which the explanation of the effect of section 424 of ITA 2007 was given, in accordance with regulation 7(3) and (4),

(c) maintain a record of a notice of cancellation, in accordance with regulation 7(5) and (6),

(d) send an annual statement or details as to how to access an annual statement, in accordance with regulation 8(1), and

(e) maintain a record of an annual statement, in accordance with regulation 8(3) and (4).

Paragraph 12(4) DCGADR provides for an additional penalty:

(4) A donor intermediary who fails to comply with a notice under regulation 7(7) to produce a record for inspection is liable to a penalty of £300.

(5) If the failure mentioned in paragraph (4) continues after the date on which a penalty is imposed under that paragraph in respect of the failure, the donor intermediary is liable to a further penalty or penalties not exceeding £60 for each subsequent day on which the failure continues.

Regulations 13-17 DCGADR deal with the administration of the penalty regime and are not considered here.

15.54 Record keeping by charity

15.54.1 *Auditable records*

Regulation 9(1) DCGADR provides:

> A charity must either—
> (a) maintain an auditable record of the gift aid declarations received from a donor or a donor intermediary in respect of which it submits a claim for gift aid relief, or
> (b) comply with paragraphs (5) to (10) in relation to each such gift aid declaration.
> This is subject to paragraph (4).[217]

Para (a) (keeping auditable records) is the default requirement; para (b) (sending confirmation statements) applies where the conditions of para (a) are not met.

Regulation 9(2) DCGADR provides:

> The charity must preserve the auditable record for six years from the end of the tax year in which a gift aid declaration is given.

Regulation 9(3) DCGADR provides:

> An auditable record is a record of evidence—
> (a) of gift aid declarations and the giving of them, and
> (b) that (whether or not separate from the gift aid declarations) statements explaining the effect of section 424 of ITA 2007 were given to donors in accordance with regulation 5(2) or regulation 6(2)(b), as the case may be,
> in a form, and to a standard, which can be inspected and audited by HMRC.

Thus "auditable record" is a somewhat opaque technical term. Satisfactory (auditable) record might be clearer.

The HMRC Guidance Note provides:

> 3.7.2 ...Examples of what HMRC is likely to accept as evidence include:
> [1] a written declaration made by the donor or a ticked box confirmation by the donor that they wish Gift Aid to apply to the donation
> [2] an audio recording of the making of a declaration by the donor or an

217 See 15.54.2 (Power to require statements).

audio recording of the donor confirming a declaration where the declaration is pre-recorded by the charity

[3] a computer record of a declaration template filled in by the donor and containing a link to the donors banking details

[4] an emailed copy of a declaration

[5] a computer 'screen print' of the declaration sent to the charity

[6] a scanned image that's an exact replica of a declaration

[7] a copy of a mobile phone text message confirmation of a declaration

[8] Confirmation that a donor has been sent a written record confirming their oral declaration

Note: the transcribing of declarations given by donors into a database will not satisfy the requirements to have an auditable record as such a record does not demonstrate that the donor made the declaration.

3.7.3 A charity must also maintain records that provide an audit trail linking each donation to an identifiable donor who has given a valid Gift Aid declaration, and provide acceptable evidence that a donor has been advised that they are liable to tax if they have not paid an amount of Income Tax and/or Capital Gains Tax equal to the amount reclaimed by the charity.

Further guidance on audit procedures is available at Chapter 7 of these detailed guidance notes.

In the case of oral Gift Aid declarations, the only options are [2] and [8]. Telephone recording requires some specialist IT, if the recordings are to be kept available for six years and made available for HMRC audit. The requirement to give confirmation statements to the donor spoils the convenience of oral Gift Aid declarations, but it is still a convenient method for donors.

We would have thought it sufficient if a charity worker signs a statement saying they have received the Gift Aid declaration orally and given the tax explanation orally. But the HMRC Guidance Note does not say this. It would be necessary to check that HMRC would accept it.

The sanction for:

(1) failure to give a tax explanation; or

(2) a failure to keep satisfactory (auditable) records of:

  (a) Gift Aid declarations; and

  (b) Tax explanations

is that a charity fails to satisfy reg 9(1)(a). It must then satisfy reg 9(1)(b) (confirmation statements), or else the Gift Aid declarations are not valid.

HMRC may inspect and, if the record keeping of confirmation statements and cancellation notices is not to their satisfaction, they may cancel the appropriate Gift Aid declarations and reclaim the basic rate tax paid to the charity. They may also reclaim higher rate relief allowed to the donor, though the matter of record keeping is outside the donor's control. There is no right of appeal, though judicial review may be available.

15.54.2 *Power to require statements*

Regulation 9(4) DCGADR provides:

> If HMRC notify a charity that a record relating to a particular gift aid declaration or class of gift aid declarations, in respect of which it submitted a claim to HMRC, does not satisfy HMRC, the charity must comply with paragraphs (5) to (10) in relation to the Gift Aid declarations in question.

In short, HMRC may inspect and if the "auditable record" is not to their satisfaction, they may require the charity to satisfy record keeping condition (b). There is no right of appeal.

15.55 Lack of auditable records

This section considers the rules which apply if a charity fails to keep satisfactory auditable records.

15.55.1 *Reg 9(5) confirmation statements*

Regulation 9(5) DCGADR provides:

> In each case where paragraph (1)(b)[218] or (4)[219] applies, the charity must send the donor a written statement containing—
> (a) the information required by regulation 5(1)(a) to (d)[220] or 6(1)(a) to (d),[221] as the case may be,
> (b) an explanation of the effect of section 424 of ITA 2007,[222]
> (c) the date on which the charity sends the statement to the donor, and
> (d) a statement that the donor is entitled to cancel his declaration by giving notice in writing to the charity not later than 30 days following the date in sub-paragraph (c).

218 See 15.54.1 (Auditable records).
219 See 15.54.2 (Power to require statements).
220 See 15.52.1 (Declaration content: summary).
221 See 15.53.2 (Intermediary declaration: content).
222 See 15.52.1 Declaration content: Summary).

Do not confuse:

(1) The statement which the charity sends to the donor under regulation 9(5) (the **"reg 9(5) confirmation statement"**)

(2) The Gift Aid declaration which the donor (or intermediary) gives to the charity

These are distinct statements, though their contents largely overlap.
The HMRC Guidance Note contains an error at 3.8.1:

> 3.8.1 Invalid declarations
> ...If the written statement is marked 'returned to sender' or 'not known at this address' etc the charity should treat the declaration as if it has been cancelled. The charity must keep a record of the cancellation.

This statement (which was not in the former HMRC Guidance Note) is wrong. However it is *possible* in such a case that the reg 9(5) confirmation statement may have been sent to the wrong address. So a charity which receives a confirmation statement marked "not known at this address" should check the statement was correctly addressed. In practice we expect this problem will not often arise.

15.55.2 *Confirmation statement time limit*

Regulation 9(6) DCGADR provides:

> (6) The statement required by paragraph (5) must be sent-
> (a) within 30 days beginning with the day on which the charity receives-
> (i) the gift aid declaration, in a case falling within paragraph (1)(b), or
> (ii) the notification from HMRC, in a case falling within paragraph (4), or
> (b) by such other time as may be agreed between an officer of Revenue and Customs and the charity.

15.55.3 *Revocation after confirmation statement*

Regulation 9 DCGADR continues:

> (7) Where paragraph (5) applies, the donor is entitled to cancel the gift aid declaration by giving notice of cancellation ("cancellation notice") to the charity.
> (8) The cancellation notice may be given in writing or orally, including the use of written or oral methods of electronic communications.

This notice (which one might call a revocation rather than a cancellation) is unlike the prospective cancellation of a Gift Aid declaration[223] because:
(1) It must be exercised within 30 days; and
(2) It operates retrospectively.

We doubt if this right of cancellation is ever exercised.

15.55.4 *Confirmation statements: record keeping*

Regulation 9(9) DCGADR provides:

> The charity must maintain a record of-
> (a) statements sent under paragraph (5), and
> (b) cancellation notices received under paragraph (7),
> in a form, and to a standard, which can be inspected and audited by HMRC.

The HMRC Guidance Note provides at 3.8.1:

> HMRC will accept that a written confirmation has been issued where the charity can show it has issued a standard letter template in an acceptable format and provides a list of the donors to whom the letter was sent.

Regulation 9(10) DCGADR provides:

> The charity must preserve the record for six years from the end of the tax year in which the statement is sent or the cancellation notice is received, as the case may be.

15.55.5 *Cancellation on receipt of statement*

Regulation 10 DCGADR provides:

> A gift aid declaration shall be treated for the purposes of the Income Tax Acts as never having had effect where—
> (a) in a case where it is required to do so by regulation 9(5), the charity does not send a written statement in respect of the gift aid declaration to the donor by the date specified in regulation 9(6)(a), or the time agreed under regulation 9(6)(b), as the case may be,
> (b) the donor cancels the gift aid declaration by giving a cancellation notice under regulation 9(7), or

---

223 See 15.52.12 (Right to cancel declaration).

(c) in a case where the charity is required by regulation 9(9) and (10) to maintain and preserve a record of statements sent and notices of cancellation received in relation to a gift aid declaration, HMRC notify the charity that the record does not satisfy HMRC.

The sanction for failing to comply with record keeping condition (b), where applicable, is that Gift Aid is denied or retrospectively withdrawn.
The HMRC Guidance Note provides at 3.10.1:

> In the case of an oral [gift aid] declaration, the person taking the declaration on behalf of the charity might recite information already held by the charity to the donor and ask them to confirm it, rather than asking the donor to recite the information themselves.
> If a charity receives an oral declaration, and it does not keep an audible (and auditable) recording of the donor's oral declaration it must send the donor a written record of the declaration to include:
>
> - all the details provided by the donor in their oral [gift aid] declaration
> - an explanation that the donor must pay an amount of Income Tax and/or Capital Gains Tax equal to the tax deducted from their donations
> - an explanation of the donor's entitlement to cancel the declaration retrospectively within 30 days (see below)
> - the date on which the donor gave the charity the oral declaration
> - the date on which the charity sent the written record to the donor
>
> An oral [gift aid] declaration will not be effective unless and until the charity or its representative sends the donor the written record of the declaration. The charity cannot reclaim tax in respect of a donation covered by an oral declaration until it has sent the written record. Once the written record has been sent, the charity can reclaim tax in respect of any donations covered by the declaration, even if they were received before the written record was sent. If the oral declaration is cancelled within the 30 day period, however, any reclaimed tax will have to be repaid to HMRC.
> The written record of the declaration does not have to be recorded on paper. For example, the charity's representative might record the details on a computer, with an electronic copy being emailed to the donor, or a paper copy sent by post. If the charity uses an electronic means of recording the donor's information, it will need to be able to demonstrate at an audit that the electronic recording of the information generates a written record sent to the donor.

15.56 Gift from joint account

15.56.1 *Position of charity*

HMRC Guidance Note provides:

> **3.32 Donations from joint bank accounts**
> 3.32.1 If a charity receives a donation drawn on a joint bank account, and it's not been given a Gift Aid declaration by both account holders, it'll need to determine whether the donation is from the donor who has given a Gift Aid declaration. The charity may, however, assume that the donation is from the person who has made the Gift Aid declaration, even if it's authorised by the other account holder, unless it holds evidence to suggest that the donation is from that other account holder.
> 3.32.2 Similarly, if a credit card donation is received drawn on an account in respect of which there are joint authorised signatories, it can be assumed that the donation is from the authorised signatory who's made a Gift Aid declaration unless there's evidence to suggest that the donation's from the other authorised signatory.
> 3.32.3 If there's any doubt whether the donation's from the person who signs the cheque, etc or authorises the transaction, the charity should ask them to confirm whether the donation is from them.

The HMRC Guidance Note directs the charity to take a Gift Aid declaration at face value unless:

(1) "There's evidence to suggest that the donation's from the other authorised signatory"; or
(2) "There's any doubt whether the donation's from the person who signs the cheque, etc or authorises the transaction".

It seems clear from the HMRC Guidance Note that the mere fact that a cheque is signed by one person but the declaration is given by another is not "evidence", nor is it sufficient to constitute a "doubt". In practice a charity will rarely if ever have any other "evidence" or reason to "doubt" so that if it has the Gift Aid declaration it need do nothing more.

This is a sensible practice which avoids the necessity for a charity to make unproductive enquiries into difficult questions of the ownership of assets held in joint accounts.

15.56.2 *Position of donor*

However, those advising the donor may have to advise whether the gift is made by (and the Gift Aid declaration should be signed by) one or other or both account holders. The HMRC Guidance Note does not help here. In outline,[224] there is a distinction between:

(1) an account under which either signatory can draw a cheque; and

(2) an account on which both signatories must sign a cheque.

Where only one signatory is needed on a cheque, the gift would normally be made by that signatory alone.[225] Where the cheque is drawn on a joint account which requires both signatories on a cheque, the transaction will normally constitute a joint gift from the two account holders, and will be treated for Gift Aid purposes as if each account holder had made a separate gift of one half of the sum given.

On joint Gift Aid declarations, see 15.52.7 (Declaration by joint donors).

15.56.3 *Gifts by spouses: Reform*

The Government rightly rejected a proposal that Gift Aid should be transferrable between spouses, though the reason given is curious:

> This would sever the link between the individual donor and the tax which he or she has paid which is an important element to ensure that Gift Aid is classified as a tax relief, rather than expenditure.[226]

We find that surprising, but perhaps that is a more tactful way of declining than the right reason, which is that the benefit does not justify the complication.

15.57 Declarations for sponsored events

The HMRC Guidance Note provides:

> **3.10.4 Declarations linked to sponsored events**
> The money raised from a sponsored event does not belong to the individual who is being sponsored and it is not theirs to give as a Gift Aid donation. However, individual sponsors may Gift Aid their own personal donation.
> The sponsor needs to make a separate declaration to the charity on whose behalf the money is being raised. This is likely to be a one-off donation

---

224 For a discussion of the background law of joint accounts, see Kessler, *Taxation of Non-Residents and Foreign Domiciliaries* (21st ed., 2022-23), Chapter 92 (Joint accounts) online version *https://www.foreigndomiciliaries.co.uk*

225 *Re Figgis* [1969] 1 Ch 123.

226 Letter from Justine Greening (Economic Secretary to the Treasury) to CIOT December 2010
http://webarchive.nationalarchives.gov.uk/20130129110402/http://www.hm-treasury.gov.uk/d/gift_aid_forum_letter_to_peter_fanning_from_est_031210.pdf
See 15.50.2 (Redirection/composite rate).

and the declaration should reflect this.

Alternatively, it is possible for charities to design a sponsorship form that can also be used as a multiple declaration form. The suggested format is for the declaration to be placed at the head of each sheet, with each sponsor being able to opt to have his or her sponsorship money paid to the charity as a Gift Aid donation by, for example, ticking a box. The recommended method is to have the following boxes below the declaration for each sponsor to complete:

- Sponsor's full name
- Sponsor's full home postal address – as a minimum HMRC will accept the number (or name as appropriate) of their home and their full postcode
- Amount pledged
- Amount collected
- Date collected
- Tick box to have amount treated as a Gift Aid donation.

The date when the sums collected were handed over to the charity should also be entered on the Sponsorship and Gift Aid declaration form. A copy of a model Gift Aid sponsored event form can be found.[227]

Where a sponsor form is being passed around a workplace some donors may be reluctant to give their full home address. HMRC is prepared to accept that the home address has been provided if donors enter, as a minimum, the name and number of their home, and their full postcode.

Where the participant banks money collected in their own account before sending a cheque to the charity, they should ensure that the sum on the cheque matches the amount collected on the sponsorship forms so that the charity is provided with a clear audit trail.

For particularly large sponsorship events, a charity can use the modified procedure set out in section 6.6 of this guidance, Sponsored Events.

HMRC is happy to advise charities on how to operate Gift Aid for sponsorship events and to review draft sponsorship/declaration forms.

The HMRC Guidance Note also sets out a special procedure for tax reclaims on sponsorship donations at 6.6. However, as this pre-dates the introduction of the new Charities Online system, it is no longer up to date and we have not reproduced it here.

15.58 Gift Aid declaration database

This proposal was floated in a 2013 consultation:

227 See 2.4 (Gift Aid declaration: Sponsored gifts).

> 4.4 There have been various proposed models for operating a UGADD [Universal Gift Aid Declaration Database]. Common elements include:
>
> - Donors fill out a single Gift Aid declaration covering all their donations to all charities that are registered with the UGADD, and submit it to the UGADD administrator;
> - Donors' declarations are held on a single database;
> - Donors are given a unique identifier, which is provided to the charity along with their donation;
> - When charities receive a donation the unique donor identifier is used to check the database to see if the donor has a valid Gift Aid declaration; and
> - Gift Aid is claimed from HMRC using the declaration held in the UGADD.
>
> 4.5 In some variations the charity interrogates the UGADD to see if the donor has a valid declaration, and makes the Gift Aid claim to HMRC itself. In other variations the claim is made electronically from the UGADD to HMRC and the charity is paid any Gift Aid owing without needing to make a claim itself.[228]

The IT and administrative challenges are considerable, the cost significant, and the overall advantages seem marginal. The proposal was rejected in 2013, we think rightly.[229] In 2019 the Charity Tax Commission recommended that the proposal should be re-explored, on the basis that technology has advanced since the 2013 consultation,[230] but we doubt if anything will come of that.

15.59 Record keeping

The charity should have evidence to satisfy HMRC that the payment has been made and from whom. Difficulty cannot arise if payment is made by cheque or standing order. Payment made in cash should be receipted by the charity. Although a written receipt is desirable to avoid dispute, it is not

---

228 HM Treasury, "Gift Aid and digital giving" (2014) para 4.4. *https://assets.publishing.service.gov.uk/government/uploads/system/uploads/attachment_data/file/210423/consult_gift_aid_and_digital_giving.pdf*

229 HM Treasury, "Gift Aid and digital giving: consultation response" (2014) part 5. *https://assets.publishing.service.gov.uk/government/uploads/system/uploads/attachment_data/file/303094/PU1618_Gift_Aid_and_digital_giving_consultation_response.pdf*

230 Charity Tax Commission, "Reforming charity taxation" (2019) p.27, 28. *https://www.ncvo.org.uk/images/documents/policy_and_research/funding/CharityCommissionReport__ForWeb_3.pdf*

strictly essential: in the event of a dispute as to whether a payment has been made, the Commissioners would be entitled to accept oral evidence that a cash payment was made, even in the absence of any documentary record.

HMRC Guidance Note provides:

> **3.28 Records to be maintained**
>
> 3.28.1 The form of records to be kept is not prescribed in the legislation. In practice, it will depend on the size of the charity, the number of donors and the kind of systems used.
>
> 3.28.2 When HMRC audit a repayment claim, the auditor will normally review a sample of the donations on which a charity is claiming Gift Aid. For smaller charities all donations may be looked at. For each donation reviewed, the auditor will ask to see:
>
> - the relevant Gift Aid declaration
> - a copy of any written statement that the charity is required to send to the donor
> - all correspondence with the donor relating to the donation
> - notification by the donor of a change of name or address
> - notification by the donor of the cancellation of the Gift Aid declaration
>
> HMRC will accept that a written confirmation has been issued where the charity can show a standard letter template in an acceptable format and a list of the donors to whom the letter was sent.
>
> In the case of recorded oral declarations the auditor will ask to listen to the recording of the declaration.
>
> **3.29 Means of keeping records**
>
> 3.29.1 The charity does not have to keep records on paper. They may be held on the hard drive of a computer, floppy disc or CD-ROM, or stored on microfiche. If records are kept on computer, it's advisable to make regular back-ups and store these in a different location to the computer. Further details on the procedures to follow when transferring original records onto microfiche or an electronic medium can be found in paragraph 7.4 of Chapter 7.
>
> **3.30: How long records should be kept**
>
> 3.30.1 The time limits for keeping Gift Aid records depend on how the charity is treated for tax purposes. Most charities will be treated as companies for tax purposes. A charity will only be a trust for tax purposes if it was set up by a trust deed or a will.
>
> All charities will need to keep enduring Gift Aid declarations covering ongoing donations permanently. If the donations cease then the time limits below apply from the date of the last donation.
>
> A single Gift Aid declaration may apply to more than one donation, so a

charity will need to work out when the last gift specified on a particular declaration is received, and keep the declaration long enough to satisfy the rules set out below.

Most charities

3.30.2 A charity run as a charitable company, which most are, must keep tax records (including Gift Aid declarations and records) until 6 years after the end of the accounting period they relate to.

For example if a charitable company prepares its accounts to 31 December 2007 and makes a Gift Aid repayment claim for that period during 2008, it must keep the records until at least 31 December 2013.

If HMRC asks the charity questions about its tax return or repayment claim, the charity will need to keep the records until the enquiries are finished.

Charitable trusts

3.30.3 Charitable trusts should keep tax records (including Gift Aid declarations and records) until the later of:

- 6 years after the end of the tax year they relate to
- 12 months after the charity makes a Gift Aid repayment claim for that tax year

If the charity is asked to make a tax return there are different rules about how long records must be kept for.

Changes to time limits

3.30.4 If before January 2012 you followed previous guidance and destroyed records between 4 and 6 years old you will not be penalised. However, if you have kept your records from that period you must continue to keep them as you may be penalised if you destroy records which you're required to keep.

If HMRC asks the charity questions about its tax return or repayment claim, the charity will need to keep the records until the enquiries are finished.

15.60 Envelope for cash donation

HMRC Guidance Note provides:

3.31 Using envelopes to collect cash donations

3.31.1 Charities may choose to collect cash donations in envelopes, such as church stewardship envelopes, so that they can show an audit trail linking the donation to the donor. For one-off donations, charities may choose to pre-print the Gift Aid declaration on the envelope for completion by the donor. If the donor is a regular supporter, the charity may already hold his or her Gift Aid declaration, in which case the envelope need simply contain either:

- the donor's name
- some other unique identifier, such as a reference number which can be cross-referenced to a donor register.

3.31.2 Where a unique identifier is used, such as a reference number, ideally this should be unique to the donor. In practice, where envelopes containing the same unique identifier are used by the donor and his or her spouse and minor children, it can assumed that all the donations are from the donor, unless there is evidence to the contrary.

3.31.3 When the envelope is opened and the contents are counted, an official of the charity should record the sum that it contained both:

- on the envelope
- in a donor record.

3.31.4 Charities should retain for the period set out in Chapter 7

- all envelopes on which a Gift Aid declaration is printed
- a sample of other envelopes (normally for 1month of the year)
- the donor record.

15.61 VAT/Gift Aid interaction

HMRC Guidance Note formerly provided:

> *3.48.17 For purposes of the Gift Aid scheme the charity should make a claim in respect of the actual Gift Aid payment made by the donor. We mention this because HM Customs & Excise take the view that such donations fall within the scope of VAT as payments in lieu of admission and some charities have deducted the VAT element from the net Gift Aid donation in error.*

This is still correct. For further discussion see 35.21 (Admission charges).

15.62 Gift Aid and settlement provisions

For completeness, s.627(2) ITTOIA provides:

> The rule in section 624(1) does not apply to income which consists of—
> ... qualifying donations for the purposes of Chapter 2 of Part 8 of ITA 2007 (gift aid).

This is not necessary as it is impossible for s.624 ITTOIA to apply to a Gift Aid payment. Section 627(2) ought to be repealed. It survives for historical reasons: it was originally was needed for covenanted payments to charity (which were annual payments) and (arguably) for Gift Aid which was originally deemed to constitute annual payments, but that has not been the case since 2007.

15.63 Repealed Gift Aid reliefs

15.63.1 *SA donate: Gift in tax return*

It was formerly possible to claim Gift Aid on donations given through a self assessment tax return: s.429 ITA. This was sensibly abolished by s.50(1) FA 2012.[231]

15.64 The future

Spring statement 2022 provides:[232]

> 3.9 *Basic rate of income tax* – The government will reduce the basic rate of income tax to 19% from April 2024.

That falls conveniently close to the next general election in the UK, which is formally set for 2nd May 2024.

The amount which a charity can reclaim from HMRC is in principle the tax which is deemed to have been deducted from the gift at the basic rate. The lowering of the basic rate from 20% to 19% will leave charities in an worse position. The spring statement addresses this:

> A three-year transition period for Gift Aid relief will apply, to maintain the income tax basic rate relief at 20% until April 2027. The reduction in the basic rate for non-savings-non-dividend income will not apply for Scottish taxpayers because the power to set these rates is devolved to the Scottish Government.

There is a precedent: sch 19 FA 2008 provided a transitional relief for the charities called "Gift Aid supplement" for the years 2008/09 to 2010/11, following the reduction in the basic rate from 22% to 20% in 2008. For a discussion see the 7th edition of this work para 15.40.

---

231 In the 7th edition of this book, we argued that this was a gimmick which deserved to abolished.

232 *https://assets.publishing.service.gov.uk/government/uploads/system/uploads/attachment_data/file/1062708/Spring_Statement_2022_Print.pdf*

CHAPTER SIXTEEN

GIFT AID SMALL DONATIONS SCHEME

16.1 Introduction

This chapter discusses the Gift Aid Small Donations Scheme (**"GASDS"**).

The legislation is in the Small Charitable Donations Act 2012 (**"SCDA"**) and the Small Charitable Donations Regulations 2013 (**"SCDR"**).

The background can be found in:

- The GASDS consultative document (March 2012)
- Small Charitable Donations Bill House of Commons Research Paper 12/45 (14 August 2012)
- The explanatory note for the Small Charitable Donations Bill (**"EN SCDB"**);[1] there is also an explanatory note for the SCDA (**"EN SCDA"**), but this is shorter.
- The Small Charitable Donations and Childcare Payments Act 2017 made a number of amendments to the GASDS. These have effect for the tax years 2017-18 and onwards.

The HMRC Guidance Note has a section on GASDS, and HMRC has also published online guidance.[2]

The HMRC Guidance Note provides an introduction:

> **8.1 Eligibility conditions**
> If your charity or Community Amateur Sports Club (CASC) is eligible you may be able to claim a top-up payment on small cash or contactless donations under GASDS.
> If your charity or CASC is eligible for a top-up payment you'll need to work out how much you can claim.
> Factors that affect the amount you can claim include:
>
> - the basic rate of income tax (BRT)
> - the amount of eligible small donations collected
> - the cap on the amount of GASDS top-up you can claim
> - how much Gift Aid you have claimed in that tax year, sometimes called the 'matching rule'
> - whether your charity or CASC is connected to another charity or CASC
>
> ...
>
> Charities and CASCs can now make a claim for a top-up payment on eligible small donations without needing to:
>
> - have been registered as a CASC or established as a charity for tax purposes for at least the 2 previous complete tax years
> - have made a successful Gift Aid claim in at least 2 of the previous 4 tax years

---

1 *http://www.publications.parliament.uk/pa/bills/lbill/2012-2013/0058/en/13058en.htm*

2 *https://www.gov.uk/guidance/claiming-a-top-up-payment-on-small-charitable-donations*

16.2 "Charity"

Section 18(1) SCDA provides:

> In this Act "charity" means—
> (a) a charity within the meaning of Part 1 of Schedule 6 to the FA 2010;
> (b) the Trustees of the National Heritage Memorial Fund;
> (c) the Historic Buildings and Monuments Commission for England;
> (d) a registered club within the meaning of Chapter 9 of Part 13 of the Corporation Tax Act 2010 (community amateur sports clubs).

Thus GASDS applies to charities and to CASCs.

16.3 Entitlement to top-up payment

Section 1(1) SCDA provides:

> A charity is entitled to a payment from HMRC (a "top-up payment") if—
> (a) the charity is an eligible charity for a tax year,
> (b) the charity has made a successful gift aid exemption claim in respect of gifts made to it in the tax year,
> (c) small donations are made to the charity in the tax year, and
> (d) the charity makes a claim in respect of small donations made to it in the tax year.

The term "top-up payment" is not particularly apt, but it is best to adopt the statutory language.

Section 18(2) SCDA provides:

> "tax year" means a year beginning on 6 April and ending on the following 5 April;

That applies to charitable companies as well as to charitable trusts.

16.3.1 *"Successful"*

Section 18(3) SCDA provides a commonsense definition:

> For the purposes of this Act—
> (a) a gift aid exemption claim is "successful" if an amount falls to be exempt from income tax or corporation tax as a result of the claim;
> (b) a successful gift aid exemption claim is made in respect of a gift

to the extent that the gift, or the grossed up amount of the gift, falls to be exempt from income tax or corporation tax as a result of the claim;

(c) a successful top-up claim is made in respect of small donations if, and to the extent that, a top-up payment falls to be made because of the claim (and does not fall to be repaid under section 10);

(d) in determining whether a successful claim has been made in a tax year, it does not matter when the claim is determined.

16.4 Amount of top-up payment

Section 1(2) SCDA provides:

> The amount of the top-up payment is—
>
> $$SD \times \frac{R}{(100 - R)}$$
>
> where—
> SD is the amount of the small donations to which the claim relates, and
> R is the percentage rate of the basic rate of income tax for the tax year in question.

In short:

SD is **S**mall **D**onations
R is the basic **R**ate of tax
The top-up amount is the amount of Small Donations grossed up at the basic rate.

On 6 April 2017, R was 20%, so the top-up payment is 25% of the donation. So a small donation of £1 attracts a top-up payment of 25p.

16.4.1 *Rounding*

Section 11(9) SCDA provides:

> An amount calculated for the purposes of any provision of this Act is to be rounded to the nearest whole penny, taking 0.5p as nearest to the next whole penny.

16.5 Top-up claim limit

The GASDS consultation document refers to the "need to keep the cost of the GASDS within reasonable limits".

Section 1(3) SCDA provides:

A charity is not entitled to top-up payments in respect of small donations made to it in a tax year in excess of the maximum donations limit for the charity for the tax year.

16.5.1 *"Maximum donations limit"*

Although the term used is "maximum donations limit" the limit is in fact a limit on the top-up payment, not the donations.

Section 1 SCDA provides:

> (4) The "maximum donations limit" for a charity for a tax year is—
> (a) an amount equal to 10 times the gift aid donations amount for the charity for the tax year, or
> (b) if less, the specified amount for the charity for the tax year.
> (5) The "gift aid donations amount" for a charity for a tax year is the amount of the gifts made to the charity in the tax year and in respect of which it has made successful gift aid exemption claims.
> (6) The "specified amount" for a charity for a tax year is £8,000.

The maximum possible top-up payment for any charity is
8,000 × 25% = £2,000

That applies if the charity receives:
(1) Gift Aid donations of at least £800. Other types of gift (QIDR, payroll giving scheme) do not count.
(2) GASDS donations of at least £8,000.

In computing the Gift Aid donations for GASDS, one does not gross up the gift. For tax purposes, a charity is treated as receiving, under deduction of income tax at the basic rate for the tax year in which the gift is made, a gift of an amount equal to the grossed up amount of the gift,[3] but that does not apply as GASDS is not a tax provision.

HMRC refer to the limit in s.1(4)(a) as the matching rule. The HMRC Guidance Note provides:

> **How much Gift Aid you have claimed in that year - the 'matching rule'**
> The maximum amount of GASDS top up you can claim is 10 times the total amount of Gift Aid donations claimed on by the charity or CASC in that tax year.
> The maximum amount of GASDS top-up you can claim is 10 times the total amount of Gift Aid donations claimed on by the charity or CASC

3 See 15.49 (Position of charity).

in that tax year.
For example, to claim a top-up payment on £100 of small donations you need to successfully claim Gift Aid on at least £10 of eligible donations in the same tax year.
You can only match GASDS donations to Gift Aid donations made in the same tax year. It is the tax year the donation was actually made, not the year you claim Gift Aid which matters.
GASDS is always worked out on a tax year basis, so the Gift Aid donations to be taken into account must also be considered on a tax year basis, even if the charity or CASC has an accounting year that is different from the tax year.
You must consider what tax year the Gift Aid donation was actually made to the charity.
Example
A charity submits a claim in 2016/17 for the following donations which are all eligible for Gift Aid:

- £300 in tax year 2014 to 2015
- £50 in tax year 2015 2016
- £100 in tax year 2016 2017

This charity will only be able to claim GASDS top-ups on a maximum of £1000 in small donations in tax year 2016 to 2017. This is worked out by multiplying the £100 Gift Aid donation in tax year 2016 to 2017 by 10. The amounts on the Gift Aid claim which were collected in earlier tax years do not count.
...
If you're filling in the claim online, provide this information in the space on the declaration page.
If you're using a paper form, use the space in box 38.

The Charity Tax Commission recommend:

To improve accessibility further and reduce the administrative burden associated with the Gift Aid Small Donations Scheme, government should explore removing the matching requirement which stipulates that claims cannot be more than 10 times the Gift Aid claimed in the same tax year. Increasing the amount that can be claimed each year from £2,000 (on £8,000 worth of donations) would also encourage more organisations to engage with GASDS, while allowing text donations would reflect the increased use of smartphones and the growth in impulse donations.[4]

---

4 Charity Tax Commission, "Reforming charity taxation" (2019) p.30 *https://www.ncvo.org.uk/images/documents/policy_and_research/funding/Charity*

But we suspect that the matching rule is important in restricting fraud.

16.6 "Eligible charity"

This is a label for three requirements or sets of requirements:

(1) Requisite Gift Aid claims: the charity must have made a successful Gift Aid exemption claim in at least two of the previous four tax years, and there must not have been a period between claims of two or more consecutive tax years.
(2) Passing the start-up period: the charity must have been in existence for at least two complete tax years.
(3) Not incurring recent penalties.

The reason for these rules is to reduce the scope for fraud.[5] Fraud is an ever present risk when grants and tax refunds may be made.

16.7 Gift Aid claim history

Section 2(1) SCDA provides:

> A charity is an eligible charity for a tax year if it is not an excluded charifty for the tax year (see subsection (3)).

16.7.1 *Claims by collection agent*

The HMRC Guidance Note provides:

> If you only make Gift Aid claims through a collection agent you will need to tell HMRC:
> - who the agent was
> - how much the claims were for
> - when they were made

16.8 Recent penalties

Section 2 SCDA provides:

> (3) A charity on which a penalty has been imposed in connection with a gift aid exemption claim or top-up claim made by the charity is an excluded charity -
> (a) for the tax year in which the claim was made, and
> (b) for the next tax year,
> (even if the penalty was imposed after the tax year in which the claim

---

CommissionReport__ForWeb_3.pdf

5 GASDS consultative document para 1.7 and 3.7.

was made).

(4) For the purposes of this section ...

(b) "penalty" means a penalty under—

(i) Schedule 24 to the FA 2007, or

(ii) regulations under section 11;

(c) a penalty is not to be regarded as having been imposed if all of the penalty is suspended (or the decision that a penalty is payable is cancelled on appeal); but this does not apply to a suspended penalty that subsequently becomes payable.

The HMRC Guidance Note provides:

> You can't claim under the GASDS for 2 tax years if your charity or CASC receives a penalty relating to Gift Aid or a GASDS claim under Schedule 24 Finance Act 2007 or the Small Charitable Donations Regulations 2013.
> For example, a charity charged a penalty on the Gift Aid claim on donations collected in tax year 2017 to 2018 couldn't claim under GASDS until tax year 2019 to 2020.
> If a penalty has been suspended or overturned on appeal it won't count, and you can still claim under GASDS as long as the other conditions are met.
> Charities and CASCs are still able to make Gift Aid claims if they've been charged a penalty.

16.9 "Small donation"

Section 3(1) SCDA provides:

> In this Act "small donation" means a gift made to a charity by an individual in relation to which each of the conditions in the Schedule is met (but does not include a membership fee).

"Small donation" is a label for a large number of rules. The term is not wholly apt: the donation must be small, but there are many other requirements. However no short label could do justice to the concept. "Qualifying donation" might have been better but it was not available as that term has already been used in the context of Gift Aid.

16.9.1 *Membership fees*

"Membership fee" is undefined.

The rule that membership fees are not "small donations" seems an odd inconsistency with the Gift Aid rules where membership fees may qualify.[6] Perhaps the reason is that the formalities involved in a membership fee give the charity sufficient opportunity to complete a Gift Aid declaration. In any case, membership fees are perhaps not often collected in cash.

Schedule 1 sets out nine conditions, some of which are based on the Gift Aid conditions.

16.9.2 *£30 limit*

Para 1 sch 1 SCDA provides:

> (1) The gift must be £30[7] or less
> (1A) The gift must be made –
> (a) in cash, or
> (b) by contactless payment.
> (3) In this paragraph—
> "cash" means coins and notes in any currency;
> "contactless payment" means a payment made at a contactless payment terminal using the contactless payment facility of a card, mobile telephone or other device;

It is a welcome development that contactless payments are now included however, it seems rather strange that other credit card payments are not accepted. We guess that the reason is to encourage use of Gift Aid rather than GASDS where possible. The GASDS consultative document provides:

> 5.32 ... as a point of principle, organisations should continue to claim Gift Aid on donations wherever possible. The GASDS is not intended to be a substitute for Gift Aid. Instead it provides for Gift Aid type payments on donations where it is difficult, or too burdensome, to obtain Gift Aid declarations. Wherever possible donors should be encouraged to make use of Gift Aid but this is not always practical where the amounts collected are small or the donations are collected somewhere where obtaining a declaration is difficult – such as a street collection.

If a donor gives more than £30 (or makes a gift of money by cheque or card) the charity should seek a Gift Aid declaration.

Para 1 sch 1 SCDA provides:

---

6 See 15.31 (Membership subscription).
7 This was amended in 2019 to increase the small donation limit from £20 to £30.

> (2) Where a gift of cash is made to the charity and its managers do not know whether the gift is £30 or less, the condition in sub-paragraph (1) is to be treated as met if the managers[8] have taken reasonable steps to find out.

16.9.3 *Made in UK*

Para 2 sch 1 SCDA provides:

> The gift must be made in the United Kingdom.

Readers may reasonably ask if that rule is consistent with EU law.

16.9.4 *Deposit in UK bank account*

Para 3 sch 1 SCDA provides:

> (1) Where the gift is made in cash, the cash given to the charity must have been deposited in an account kept by or on behalf of the charity at a relevant institution and the deposit must have been made in the United Kingdom.
> (2) "Relevant institution" has the meaning given by section 109(3) of the Charities Act 2011.

Section 109(3) Charities Act 2011 provides:

> For the purposes of sections 107 and 108 and this section, a "relevant institution" means—
> (a) the Bank of England (acting otherwise than in its capacity as the Prudential Regulation Authority),
> (b) a person who has permission under Part 4A of the Financial Services and Markets Act 2000 to accept deposits,
> (c) an EEA firm of the kind mentioned in paragraph 5(b) of Schedule 3 to that Act which has permission under paragraph 15 of that Schedule (as a result of qualifying for authorisation under paragraph 12(1) of that Schedule) to accept deposits, or
> (d) such other person who may lawfully accept deposits in the United Kingdom as may be prescribed by the Secretary of State.

This is an anti-fraud measure.

---

8 Para 1(3) sch 1 SCDA provides: "In this paragraph—

...

"managers", in relation to a charity, means the persons having the general control and management of the administration of the charity."

16.9.5 *Eligible for other relief*

Obviously a gift which qualifies for some other tax relief should not also qualify under GASDS. There are three possible reliefs, so there are three rules to prevent this.

Para 4 sch 1 SCDA deals with Gift Aid:

> (1) The gift must be one in relation to which no gift aid declaration is given to the charity.
> (2) "Gift aid declaration" means a declaration which is a gift aid declaration for the purposes of Chapter 2 of Part 8 of the Income Tax Act 2007.

There is of course a practical difficulty here, but charities are just expected to do the best they can.

Para 5 sch 1 SCDA deals with the payroll giving scheme:[9]

> The gift must not be a sum falling within section 713(3) of the Income Tax (Earnings and Pensions) Act 2003 (payroll deduction scheme).

In practice it seems unlikely that a payment under the payroll giving scheme would meet the GASDS requirement of either contactless payment or payment in cash, but the exclusion does no harm.

Para 6 sch 1 SCDA deals with the possibility of a trading deduction:

> The gift must not be deductible in calculating the individual's income from any source for thc purposes of income tax.

See 15.18 (Payment deductible for IT).

16.9.6 *Repayment rule*

Para 7 sch 1 SCDA provides:

> The gift must not be subject to any condition as to repayment.

This is the Gift Aid rule: see 15.16 (Repayment rule: Condition B).

16.9.7 *Acquisition of property*

Para 8 sch 1 SCDA provides:

> (1) The gift must not be conditional on, associated with or part of an arrangement involving, the acquisition of property by the charity from

---

9 See 15.17 (Payroll giving: Condition C); 19.1 (Payroll giving scheme).

> the individual or a person connected[10] with the individual.
> (2) An acquisition by way of gift is to be ignored for the purposes of this condition.

This is the Gift Aid rule: see 15.19 (Acquisition of property rule).

16.9.8 *GASDS benefit rule*

Para 9 sch 1 SCDA provides:

> (1) There must be no benefits associated with the gift, or any benefits associated with the gift must be of negligible value (for example, a lapel sticker designed to acknowledge the making of a gift).

We would not have thought that a sticker was a benefit of negligible value: we would have thought it was not a benefit at all; but it does not matter.

> (2) For this purpose a benefit is associated with a gift if it is received by the individual who makes the gift, or a person connected[11] with the individual, in consequence of making the gift.

This is stricter than the Gift Aid benefit rule, which allows small benefits (which need not be of negligible value). See 15.20 (Benefit rule: Condition F).

16.10 Applied for charitable purposes

Section 3(2) SCDA provides:

> But if a small donation made to a charity is applied to purposes other than charitable purposes, or any part of the donation is applied to purposes other than charitable purposes, the donation or part is to be treated as if it were not a small donation.

This is the application for charitable purposes rule: see 4.21 (Application for charitable purposes).

---

10 Para 10 schedule 1 SCDA provides:
"For the purposes of this Schedule whether a person is connected with another person is to be determined in accordance with section 993 of the Income Tax Act 2007."

11 Para 10 schedule 1 SCDA provides:
"For the purposes of this Schedule whether a person is connected with another person is to be determined in accordance with section 993 of the Income Tax Act 2007."

Section 18 SCDA gives "charitable purpose" the necessary definition:

> (2) In this Act—
> "charitable purpose"—
> (a) in the case of a charity within subsection (1)(a) to (c), has the meaning given by section 2(1) of the Charities Act 2011 (reading the reference in section 2(1) to the law of England and Wales as including a reference to the law of Scotland and the law of Northern Ireland);
> (b) in the case of a charity within subsection (1)(d) [a CASC], means qualifying purpose within the meaning given by section 661(3) of the Corporation Tax Act 2010;

16.11 Connected charities rule

Section 4(1) SCDA[12] provides:

> This section applies if two or more charities—
> (a) are connected with one another in a tax year, and
> (b) are eligible charities for the tax year.

Sections 4(2) and (3) provide:

> (2) Section 1 applies to each of the charities in relation to the tax year as if references to small donations made to a charity included small donations made to any of the charities.
> (3) The specified amount for the purposes of section 1(4) for each of the charities for the tax year is an amount equal to—
> (a) £8,000, divided by
> (b) the number of the charities which make a top-up claim in respect of small donations made in the tax year.

We refer to this as the **"connected charities rule"** though there are strictly two rules, a pooling of the specified amount and a pooling of donations.

The HMRC Guidance Note deals with the pooling of the specified amount:

> **8.6 Connected charities and CASC**
> If a charity or CASC is connected to one or more other charities or CASCs this will affect the amount of GASDS top-up that you can claim. All references to charities in this chapter also apply to CASCs. Charities and CASCs are generally connected where one or more of the following

12 Flagged by s.1(7) SCDA.

applies:

- one charity controls another
- two or more charities are under common control
- control links a number of charities - for example, if Charity A controls Charity B and Charity B controls Charity C, then all 3 charities are connected

If 2 charities are connected but they have purposes and activities which are not substantially the same, then they will not be a connected charity under GASDS rules.

Example

- a primary school and a nursery both provide education for children and have purposes and activities which are substantially the same
- a school, a zoo and a museum all provide education for children but their activities are sufficiently different and would not be connected under CASC rules

16.12 "Connected"

There are two requirements to be connected: they may be described as:
(1) a constitutional connection and
(2) an activity connection.

16.12.1 *Constitutionally connected*

Section 5(3) SCDA provides:

> Section 993 of the Income Tax Act 2007 applies for determining whether a charity is connected with another charity at any time for the purposes of this section.

So we turn to s.993 ITA, which provides (so far as relevant) :

> (5) A company is connected with another company if—
> (a) the same person has control of both companies,
> (b) a person ("A") has control of one company and persons connected with A have control of the other company,
> (c) A has control of one company and A together with persons connected with A have control of the other company, or
> (d) a group of two or more persons has control of both companies and the groups either consist of the same persons or could be so regarded if (in one or more cases) a member of either group were replaced by a person with whom the member is connected.
> (6) A company is connected with another person ("A") if—
> (a) A has control of the company, or

(b) A together with persons connected with A have control of the company.

(7) In relation to a company, any two or more persons acting together to secure or exercise control of the company are connected with—

(a) one another, and

(b) any person acting on the directions of any of them to secure or exercise control of the company.

Section 994 ITA provides that "control" is to be read in accordance with sections 450 and 451 CTA 2010. A full discussion of this definition of control needs a long chapter to itself. We omit that here as we have dealt with it elsewhere.[13] In short, the definition of the word "control" is so wide that the word not apt to describe the concept ("some loose association" would be nearer the mark).

16.12.2 *Time of connection*

Section 5(1) SCDA provides:

> For the purposes of this Act a charity is connected with another charity in a tax year if it is connected with that other charity at any time in the tax year (as to which see subsections (3) to (7)).

16.12.3 *Chain of connected companies*

Section 5(2) SCDA provides:

> If—
>
> (a) a charity ("charity A") is connected with another charity ("charity B") (including by virtue of this subsection) in a tax year, and
>
> (b) charity B is connected with a further charity ("charity C") in the tax year,
>
> charity A and charity C are also connected with each other in the tax year for the purposes of this Act.

What if A is connected to B, B is connected to C and C is connected to D? It appears that A is connected to D. This is so wide we wonder if there are any charities which are not constructionally "connected".

---

13 See Kessler, *Taxation of Non-Residents and Foreign Domiciliaries* (21st ed., 2022-23), Chapter 101 (Control, Connected, Close and Related Expressions) online edition *https://www.foreigndomiciliaries.co.uk*

16.12.4 *Charitable trust*

Section 5 SCDA provides:

> (4) In the application of section 993 for the purposes of subsection (3)—
> (a) a charity that is a trust is to be treated as if it were a company (and accordingly a person), including in this subsection;
> (b) a charity that is a trust has "control" of another person if the trustees (in their capacity as trustees of the trust) have, or any of them has, control of the person;
> (c) a person (other than a charity regulator) has "control" of a charity that is a trust if—
> (i) the person is a trustee of the charity and some or all of the powers of the trustees of the charity could be exercised by the person acting alone or by the person acting together with any other persons who are trustees of the charity and who are connected with the person,
> (ii) the person, alone or together with other persons, has power to appoint or remove a trustee of the charity, or
> (iii) the person, alone or together with other persons, has any power of approval or direction in relation to the carrying out by the trustees of any of their functions.
>
> (5) A charity that is a trust is also to be regarded as connected with another charity that is a trust at a time for the purposes of this section if, at that time, at least half of the trustees of one of the charities are—
> (a) trustees of the other charity,
> (b) persons who are connected with persons who are trustees of the other charity, or
> (c) a combination of both.
>
> (6) In determining whether a person is connected with another person for the purposes of subsection (4)(c)(i) or (5)(b), apply section 993 of the Income Tax Act 2007, with the omission of subsection (3) of that section (and without the modifications in subsection (4) above).

The HMRC Guidance Note provides:

> **8.7: Controlling persons**
> There are different definitions of controlling persons of charities and CASCs, and of charitable trusts.
>
> **Controlling persons of charitable companies or CASCs**
> A person has control of a charitable company or CASC if they have control:
>
> - over the affairs of the company

- through voting power
- through share capital or through issued share capital
- over the income or assets of the company

Controlling persons of charitable trusts

A person has control of a charitable trust if:

- the person is a trustee of the charity and some or all of the powers of the trustees of the charity could be exercised by that person alone, or by that person acting together with any other persons who are trustees of the charity and who are connected with the person
- the person, alone or together with other persons, has power to appoint or remove a trustee of the charity
- the person, alone or together with other persons, has any power of approval or direction in relation to the carrying out by the trustees of any of their functions in administering a charity

If two or more charitable trusts have the same (or very similar) purpose, then they can be classed as connected if at least half of the trustees of each trust are:

- the same people
- persons connected to the trustees of the other charity
- a combination of the two.

16.12.5 *Similar activity*

Section 5(7) SCDA provides:

> But a charity is not to be regarded as connected with another charity at a time for the purposes of subsection (1) unless, at that time, the purposes and activities of the charities are the same or substantially similar.

Charities will not therefore necessarily be connected to one another merely because they are constitutionally "connected".

16.12.6 *Power to amend*

The drafter seems to have anticipated that this definition may not work. Accordingly, s.5(8) SCDA provides:

> The Treasury may by order amend this Act so as to change the circumstances in which a charity is connected with another charity in a tax year for the purposes of the Act.

16.13 Charities in community building

The HMRC Guidance Note provides:

8.4 Community buildings

A community building is a building (or part of a building) which a charity uses to run charitable activities.

These charitable activities must host 10 or more beneficiaries at least 6 times during the tax year.

To qualify as a community building a building (or part of a building) must meet the following conditions:

- your charity must carry out charitable activities in a community building for a group of at least 10 beneficiaries at the same time
- the beneficiaries do not need to be the same 10 people each time
- activities must be group activities - 10 beneficiaries being counselled on a one to one basis in 10 separate rooms would not be eligible
- beneficiaries must not be charged for access to the part of the community building where the charitable activity takes place
- the charitable activity must also be open to members of the general public (or a section of the public)
- activities must be run in the building on at least 6 occasions each tax year

For example, the building used by a charity running a school would be unlikely to qualify as a community building unless children who aren't pupils of the school can join in freely with the charitable activity.

In some cases employees and volunteers will count as beneficiaries of the charity for example, at a religious service.

However, in other cases they will not count as a beneficiary. For example, a social worker facilitating a self-help group would not be considered a beneficiary of the charity.

Section 6 SCDA[14] provides:

(1) This section determines the specified amount for the purposes of section 1(4) for a charity that runs charitable activities in one or more community buildings in a tax year (see sections 7 and 8 for the meaning of certain terms used in this section).

(2) The specified amount for the charity for the tax year is —

(a) £8,000, or

(b) if more, an amount equal to the sum of the amounts which, for each community building in which the charitable activities are run, is the community building amount.

---

14 Flagged by ss.1(7) and 5(4) SCDA.

16.13.1 *"Community building amount"*

Section 6(3) SCDA provides:

> (3) The "community building amount", in relation to a community building, means—
> (a) the sum of the small donations that are made to the charity in the community building in the tax year by group members while it is running charitable activities in the building, or
> (b) if less, £8,000.
> This is subject to subsections (3A) and (3B).
> (3A) A small donation may not be part of the community building amount for more than one of the community buildings in which the charity runs charitable activities in the tax year.
> (3B) Where a small donation would (but for subsection (3A)) be part of the community building amount for more than one community building—
> (a) if the small donation is made in one of those buildings, it is part of the community building amount for that building;
> (b) in any other case, it is part of the community building amount for whichever one of those buildings the charity determines.
> (3C) "Local authority area" means the area of—
> (a) in England, a district council, a county council for an area for which there is no district council, a London borough council, the Common Council of the City of London or the Council of the Isles of Scilly;
> (b) in Wales, a county council or a county borough council;
> (c) in Scotland, a council constituted under section 2 of the Local Government etc. (Scotland) Act 1994;
> (d) in Northern Ireland, a district council constituted under section 1 of the Local Government Act (Northern Ireland) 1972.
> (3D) For the purposes of the definition of "local authority area" in subsection (3C), the Inner Temple and the Middle Temple are to be taken as falling within the area of the Common Council of the City of London.

16.13.2 *HMRC examples*

The HMRC Guidance Note provides:

> **Claim limits for connected charities that run charitable events in community buildings**
> When one or more charities in the group have a community building then all of the connected charities should claim GASDS under the

community building rules.
Under the community building rules all eligible small donations must be collected in the same Local Authority area as the community building they are claimed under.
The only exception is if the group of connected charities agree to make an election to HMRC.
An election tells HMRC that they would like to share a single £8,000 limit for donations collected anywhere in the UK instead of claiming under the community building rules.
This may happen in rare cases when a group of connected charities work out that they are better off sharing a single £8,000 limit as it can be used on eligible donations collected anywhere in the UK.
This is only likely to happen if together the group of charities collect most of their small donations outside of the Local Authority area of any community buildings they have.
In most cases connected charities will not want to make this election because although one or a few charities may benefit, the organisation as a whole would not be able to claim as much.
Claim limits for connected charities that don't run charitable events in community buildings
When 2 or more CASCs are connected they must share a single £8,000 limit between them because they aren't eligible to claim under the community building rules.
When 2 or more eligible charities are connected in a tax year and none of these charities run charitable activities in a community building they must share a single limit of £8,000 a year.
The limit is divided by the number of connected charities or CASCs that make a claim under the scheme in respect of small donations received in the tax year.
This rule allows a group of connected charities or CASCs to decide which of them will claim under GASDS on the group's behalf for the small cash donations collected outside a community building.
Depending on the circumstances of each member in a particular group it may be possible to make a higher total claim if just one member claims on behalf of everyone than if each member makes its own claim.
If the connected charities or CASCs decide that only one of them is to make a claim, that charity or CASC is entitled to make a claim on up to the full £8,000 specified amount for small cash donations received by all of the connected charities or CASCs (provided the matching rule is satisfied).
The charity or CASC making the claim doesn't need to have received £8,000 of small donations itself since the small cash donations are

pooled to include the small cash donations received by connected charities or CASCs that aren't making a GASDS claim in the tax year. However for the purposes of matching Gift Aid donations with small cash donations, donations received under Gift Aid aren't pooled between the eligible charities or CASCs.

The charity or CASC that makes the GASDS claim must still match the pooled small cash donations to the actual Gift Aid donations that it has itself received.

Claim limits for CASCs

CASCs must share a single £8,000 limit between them because they are not eligible to claim under the community building rules.

16.14 Charitable activities in building

Section 7 SCDA provides:

> (1) For the purposes of this Act a charity "runs" charitable activities in a community building in a tax year if, on 6 or more occasions in the tax year—
>
> (a) it carries out a charitable activity with a group of people in the community building, at least 10 of whom are in the class of people for whose benefit the charitable activity is being carried out,
>
> (b) the activity is of a kind that the charity makes available to the public or a section of the public, and
>
> (c) none of the group is required to pay to access the building, or the part of the building, in which the activity is carried out.
>
> (2) For this purpose the people forming the group need not be the same on any two of the occasions.
>
> (3) The Treasury may by order amend the numbers for the time being specified in subsection (1).
>
> (4) In this Act "charitable activity" means an activity carried out for a charitable purpose, other than primarily for the purpose of fund-raising.

Careful record keeping may be required though we wonder if that will often be taken seriously.

16.14.1 *CASCs*

Section 7(5) SCDA provides:

> In this Act a reference to a "charity" that runs charitable activities does not include a registered club within the meaning of Chapter 9 of Part 13 of the Corporation Tax Act 2010 that runs such activities.

A CASC does not benefit from an increased entitlement on account of community buildings. Each CASC is entitled to a specified amount under clause 1 of £8,000 only. Why?

This may be another reason for a sports club to prefer charity status to CASC status.

16.15 "Community building"

Section 8(1) SCDA provides:

> In this Act "community building"—
> (a) means a building (such as a village hall, town hall or place of worship), or those parts of it, to which the public or a section of the public have access at some or all times, but
> (b) does not include any parts of a building excluded by subsection (2) or (3).

The HMRC Guidance Note provides:

> Examples of buildings that can be community buildings include:
> - village halls
> - mosques
> - churches
> - synagogues
> - cathedrals
> - scout huts
>
> ...
>
> Charities do not need to own a building for it to qualify as a community building.

16.15.1 *Exclusions*

Section 8(2) SCDA provides:

> Any parts of a building that are used wholly or mainly for residential purposes or the sale or supply of goods are excluded.

The HMRC Guidance Note provides:

> A building cannot be a community building if the building (or parts of it) is used wholly or mainly for residential purposes or the sale or supply of goods unless the charity is using part of that building exclusively to carry out a charitable activity.

Section 8(3) SCDA provides:

(3) Any parts of a building that are used wholly or mainly for other commercial purposes are excluded, but this is subject to subsection (3A).
(3A) The parts mentioned in subsection (3) are not excluded from being a community building in relation to a charity if—

(a) the charity carries out a charitable activity in those parts, and
(b) at all times while it does so, the parts are available for use exclusively by the charity in carrying out the activity.

The HMRC Guidance Note provides:

Example
The function room of a hotel could be a community building for a support group if the group met there at least 6 times each year to deliver charitable activities to 10 or more beneficiaries, provided the room was used exclusively by the group.
If the group meets in one part of a room and the rest of the room is used by other members of the public then the room won't qualify as a community building.
Examples of buildings which are not community buildings include:

- charity shops
- residential care homes

16.15.2 *Single building?*

Section 8(4) SCDA provides:

Where a person holds a freehold or leasehold interest[15] in land, any two or more buildings on the land, or on any adjoining land in which the person holds such an interest, are to be treated as a single building for the purposes of this Act.

The HMRC Guidance Note provides:

Two or more buildings on the same or adjacent land are treated as a single building where the same person or organisation holds a freehold or leasehold interest in the land.

16.15.3 *Power to amend definition*

Section 8 SCDA provides:

(5) The Treasury may by order—

---

15 Section 8(7) SCDA provides the equivalents in Scots law.

(a) provide for cases in which a building, or part of it, is or is not to be treated as a community building or as part of a community building for the purposes of this Act;

(b) provide for cases in which 2 or more buildings in the same vicinity are to be treated as a single building for the purposes of this Act.

(6) Provision under subsection (5) may be framed by reference to a description of building, the use to which it is put or any other circumstances; and the provision may be framed so as to apply at all times or at certain times only.

16.16 Connected charities in community building

There is a special version of the connected charity rule for community buildings. Section 9 SCDA[16] provides:

> (1) This section applies if—
>
> (a) two or more charities ("connected eligible charities") are connected with one another in a tax year and are eligible charities for the tax year, and
>
> (b) one or more of them runs charitable activities in a community building in the tax year,
>
> but see subsection (2).
>
> (2) This section does not apply if the condition in section 9A is met.
>
> (3) Where this section applies, the specified amount for the purposes of section 1(4) for a connected eligible charity for the tax year is determined as follows.
>
> (4) If the charity runs charitable activities in a community building in the tax year, the specified amount is an amount equal to the sum of the amounts which, for each community building in which the charitable activities are run, is the community building amount.
>
> (5) The "community building amount", in relation to a community building, is to be calculated in accordance with section 6(3) to (3B).
>
> (6) If the charity does not run charitable activities in a community building in the tax year, the specified amount is nil.

16.16.1 *"Election for s.9 not to apply"*

Section 9A SCDA provides:

> (1) The condition mentioned in section 9(2) is that HMRC have notice from each connected eligible charity that the charity does not want

16 Flagged by section 6(7) SCDA.

section 9 to apply to the connected eligible charities for the tax year.
(2) "Connected eligible charity"has the same meaning as in section 9.
(3) A notice under subsection (1) may be withdrawn before the condition in that subsection is met, but may not be withdrawn after the condition in that subsection has been met.
(4) Regulations under section 11 may in particular make provision—
- (a) imposing a time limit for giving a notice under subsection (1);
- (b) about the form and contents of the notice (including provision for them to be determined by HMRC);
- (c) requiring the notice to be accompanied by information specified in the regulations or determined by HMRC.

16.17 Overpayment

Section 10 SCDA provides:

If—
- (a) an amount is paid to a charity under section 1, and
- (b) the charity was not, or has ceased to be, entitled to it (because of section 2(3), 3(2), 4 or 9, or otherwise),

the amount must be repaid to HMRC.

The SCDR provides:

Overpayments: time limit for assessment
8.—(1) Subject to paragraphs (2) and (3), an assessment of an overpayment may be made at any time not more than 4 years after the end of the tax year to which it relates.
(2) An assessment involving an overpayment brought about carelessly by a charity, or by a person acting on its behalf, may be made at any time not more than 6 years after the end of the tax year to which it relates.
(3) An assessment involving an overpayment brought about deliberately by a charity, or by a person acting on its behalf, may be made at any time not more than 20 years after the end of the tax year to which it relates.
(4) An assessment of an overpayment shall not be out of time if it is made before the relevant date.
(5) The relevant date for the purposes of paragraph (4) is the later of—
- (a) the last day of the tax year following that in which an officer of Revenue and Customs discovered the overpayment; or
- (b) where a top-up claim made by a charity is enquired into by an officer of Revenue and Customs, the day on which, by virtue of paragraph 7(1) of Schedule 1A to TMA 1970 as applied by

regulation 3, the enquiry is completed.

(6) An objection to the making of an assessment of an overpayment on the ground that it is out of time shall only be made on an appeal against the assessment.

Overpayments: altering an assessment and payment of amount assessed

9.—(1) After the notice of an assessment of an overpayment has been served on a charity, the assessment shall not be altered except in accordance with the provisions of TMA 1970 applied to it by regulation 11(1).

(2) Subject to section 55 of TMA 1970 as applied by regulation 11(2), an amount assessed as an overpayment must be paid to HMRC within 30 days of the date of service on the charity of the notice of assessment.

Overpayments: appeal against assessment

10.—(1) An appeal may be brought against an assessment of an overpayment.

(2) Notice of an appeal under paragraph (1) must—

- (a) specify the grounds of appeal, and
- (b) be given—
  - (i) in writing to the officer of Revenue and Customs by whom the notice of assessment was given;
  - (ii) within 30 days of the date of service on the charity of the notice of assessment.

Overpayments: application of TMA 1970 to appeals against assessments

11.—(1) The following provisions of TMA 1970 apply to an appeal against an assessment of an overpayment as they apply to an appeal against an assessment to tax—

- (a) section 49 (late notice of appeal);
- (b) sections 49A to 49I (appeal: HMRC review or determination by tribunal);
- (c) section 50(6), (7), (10) and (11)(a) and (b) (procedure);
- (d) section 54 (settling of appeals by agreement).

(2) Subject to the modification in paragraph (4), section 55 (recovery of tax not postponed) of TMA 1970 applies to an appeal against an assessment of an overpayment as it applies to an appeal to the tribunal against an assessment to tax other than a self-assessment.

(3) Subject to the modification in paragraph (4), section 56 (payment of tax where there is a further appeal) of TMA 1970 applies for the purposes of payment of an amount determined as an overpayment as it applies to an amount of tax determined as payable or repayable.

(4) The modification is that a reference to tax is to be treated as a

reference to an overpayment.

Collection and recovery

12. Part 6 of TMA 1970 (collection and recovery) applies to overpayments, interest and penalties which have become due and payable under these Regulations as it applies to income tax, interest charged and penalties imposed under that Act.

Persons chargeable in a representative capacity

13. Sections 71 (bodies of persons) and 75 (receivers appointed by a court) of TMA 1970 apply to overpayments as they apply to income tax chargeable to any person.

16.18 Administration

Section 11(1) SCDA provides:

> Matters relating to top-up payments are to be under the management of HMRC.

The details are left to regulations. Section 11 SCDA provides:

> (2) HMRC may by regulations make provision—
> (a) about the administration of top-up payments;
> (b) otherwise for the purposes of fully implementing this Act.
> (3) Regulations under subsection (2) may in particular—
> (a) make provision in relation to top-up claims applying or incorporating, with or without modifications, any enactment that applies in relation to gift aid exemption claims;
> (b) make provision in relation to top-up payments applying or incorporating, with or without modifications, any enactment that applies in relation to repayments of income tax treated as having been paid;
> (c) make provision in relation to overpayments applying or incorporating, with or without modifications, any enactment that applies in relation to amounts of income tax or corporation tax which are due and payable;
> (d) make other provision applying or incorporating, with or without modifications, any enactment relating to the collection or management of income tax or corporation tax;
> (e) make provision postponing the determination of a top-up claim in prescribed circumstances.
> (4) The enactments mentioned in subsection (3) include, in particular, enactments—
> (a) providing for the payment of interest;
> (b) requiring the provision of information;

(c) conferring a power of entry onto land;
(d) providing for the imposition of a civil penalty;
(e) creating a criminal offence (including, in particular, offences relating to the provision of false or misleading information or failure to provide information);
(f) providing for enforcement of sums owed (whether by action on a debt, by distraint against goods or in any other way);
(g) providing for appeals.

(5) A power conferred by subsection (3) to apply or incorporate a provision creating an offence does not include power to increase the level of any punishment for which a person may be liable on conviction for the offence.

(6) A power conferred by subsection (3) to apply or incorporate a provision imposing a civil penalty does not include power to increase the maximum amount of the penalty.

(7) In subsection (3) "enactment" includes—

(a) a provision of an Act passed after the day on which this Act is passed, and
(b) a provision made, or that may be made, under an enactment.

(8) In subsection (3)(c) "overpayment" means an amount to which section 10 applies.

Section 19 SCDA provides:

There is to be paid out of money provided by Parliament any increase attributable to this Act in the sums payable under any other Act out of money so provided.

Why is this needed?

16.18.1 *How to claim*

Regulation 3 SCDR provides:

3.—(1) Subject to the modifications in paragraph (2), and to paragraph (3), Schedule 1A to TMA 1970(3) (claims etc not included in returns) applies in relation to—

(a) making and amending top-up claims and giving effect to top-up claims and amendments;
(b) enquiring into top-up claims and completing an enquiry by issue of a closure notice;
(c) amending a top-up claim in a closure notice and appealing against any such amendment,

as it applies to a claim or election under the Tax Acts(4) made otherwise than in a return.

(2) The modifications are—

- (a) a reference to an amount of tax to be discharged or repaid is to be treated as a reference to an amount of top-up payment to be made;
- (b) a reference to the discharge or repayment of tax is to be treated as a reference to the making of a top-up payment;
- (c) a reference to a year of assessment or accounting period is to be treated as a reference to a tax year;
- (d) in paragraph 4(1), for "Subject to sub-paragraphs (1A), (3) to (5)" substitute "Subject to sub-paragraph (3)".

(3) In applying Schedule 1A to TMA 1970 for the purposes of this regulation, omit—

- (a) paragraph 2(2);
- (b) in paragraph 2A—
  - (i) sub-paragraph (2A);
  - (ii) in sub-paragraph (3), "sub-paragraph (3A) and";
  - (iii) sub-paragraph (3A);
  - (iv) in sub-paragraph (4), "Subject to sub-paragraph (5) below,";
  - (v) sub-paragraphs (5) and (7);
- (c) in paragraph 4—
  - (i) sub-paragraphs (1A) and (2);
  - (ii) in sub-paragraph (3), "or (2)";
  - (iii) sub-paragraphs (4) and (5);
- (d) in paragraph 5—
  - (i) in sub-paragraph (1), "or, in the case of a partnership claim, any successor of that person";
  - (ii) in sub-paragraph (3), paragraph (b) and the "or" immediately preceding it;
- (e) paragraph 7(3) and (8);
- (f) in paragraph 8—
  - (i) in sub-paragraph (1), the words from "whether—" to the end;
  - (ii) sub-paragraphs (2) and (3);
- (g) in paragraph 9—
  - (i) in sub-paragraph (1), paragraph (b) and the "or" immediately preceding it;
  - (ii) sub-paragraphs (2) and (5).

The HMRC Guidance Note provides:

The rules for making and administering claims under GASDS are set out in the Small Charitable Donations Regulations 2013 (as amended in 2017).

The rules for claims, amendments to claims, overpayments, enquiries and information powers are the same as apply to Gift Aid claims except:

- all claims for GASDS must be made on a tax year basis, not the accounting period of the charity or CASC
- charities or CASCs must make a claim for top-up payments within two years of the end of the tax year in which the donation is received

Claims must be made online using the Charities Online process that is also used for claiming Gift Aid.[17]

16.18.2 *Time limit for claim*

Regulation 3(4) SCDR provides:

> No top-up claim may be made more than 2 years after the end of the tax year to which the claim relates.

This is different from the Gift Aid rule. The GASDS consultative document explains the reason for the difference:

> Gift Aid claims may be made within four years of the tax year or accounting period in which the donations are received; this enables charities and CASCs to deal with late claims by donors who may make a claim to Gift Aid within four years after the end of the tax year in which the donation is made. There is no reason for an extended claim period for the GASDS because there is no interaction with donors' tax affairs, and charities and CASCs should follow best practice in relation to cash handling and make timely claims. A short claim period also reduces administrative costs for HMRC and assists government accounting for the costs of the scheme, which will be paid for through public spending.

16.18.3 *Record keeping*

The HMRC Guidance Note provides:

> **Record keeping**
> If you want to claim GASDs top up payments you need to keep sufficient records to support your claims.
> What records you need to keep is a matter for you, but you should be able to show that:
>
> - your charity or CASC collected the small donations in the UK and

17 See 47.15 ("Charities online" repayment system).

kept records to confirm this
- your charity or CASC banked any cash donations in a UK branch of a bank or other relevant institution, for example a building society
- cash was banked in an account held in the name of or on behalf of the charity or CASC
- contactless donations were credited into a UK bank account held in the name of or on behalf of the charity
- you kept any records of contactless donations produced by the contactless terminal so that you can monitor for any 'multiple donations' from the same person
- you can identify how much was collected on each contactless terminal so that you can work out how much was collected in a particular Local Authority area
- you've kept a record of the denomination of all notes received (£5, £10, £20) and have removed any £50 notes which are above the £20 [now £30] limit

It is important that small cash donations are banked if your charity or CASC wants to claim a GASDS top-up.

If your charity or CASC uses small cash donations to pay for expenses without banking the donations first you won't be able to claim a top-up payment.

It's also a good idea to provide fundraisers with bank giro credit forms so that they can pay any amounts collected directly into the charity account. The counterfoil receipt which notes the breakdown of the coins and notes collected should then be given to the charity for audit purposes.

If your charity wants to claim GASDs top up payments based on amounts collected in a Local Authority Area near a community building, you must also keep a record of:
- the address of the community building
- a record to show that the building qualified as a community building
- the date(s) that the money was collected
- the location(s) that the money was collected - this should include full address and postcode
- which community building the donations will be allocated to for the purposes of the GASDS claim

16.19 Power to amend SCDA

Section 14 SCDA provides:

(1) The Treasury may by order amend—

(a) section 1(6) (the specified amount),

> (b) section 4(3)(a),
> (c) section 6(2)(a) and (3)(b),
> by substituting a different sum for the sum for the time being specified in each of those provisions.
>
> (2) The Treasury may by order amend this Act for the purpose of—
> (a) amending the gift aid matching rule;
> (b) abolishing that rule;
> (c) reinstating that rule (if previously abolished), with or without amendment.
>
> (3) In subsection (2) "the gift aid matching rule" means the rule that limits the amount of top-up payments to which a charity is entitled by reference to the amount of gifts made to the charity in respect of which it has made successful gift aid exemption claims.
>
> (4) The Treasury may by order amend section 2 (meaning of "eligible charity").
>
> ...
>
> (6) The Treasury may by order amend paragraph 1(1) and (2) of the Schedule (limit on value of individual donations) by substituting a different sum for the sum for the time being specified in each of those provisions.

Practical charity administrators and their advisers may regard this as unimportant; though it does raise important constitutional questions on the appropriate roles of parliament and the Government in determining the rules which govern taxation and similar legislation. The power in subsection (6) was exercised in February 2019 in The Small Charitable Donations Act (Amendment) Order 2019, which raised the cap from £20 to £30.

16.20 Nature of top-up payment

The GASDS consultative document provides:

> 1.5 Dropping the link between the donor and the top-up payment on the donation means that payments made under the GASDS will not be repayments of tax. The GASDS, unlike Gift Aid, will not be a tax relief but will instead be funded through public expenditure. This means the scheme cannot be legislated through the tax code already in place, but must be legislated for separately, outside the annual Finance Bill process.

Section 15 SCDA provides:

> A top-up payment is not to be treated as income for any purpose of the

Tax Acts.

The Gift Aid rule is the opposite: see 15.49 (Position of charity).

16.21 Scotland & Northern Ireland

Section 20 SCDA provides:

> This Act extends to—
> (a) England and Wales,
> (b) Scotland, and
> (c) Northern Ireland.

Legislation for the whole of the UK is much more fraught than it was before the Blair government's steps towards devolution.

Taxation is reserved for Westminster; but the SCDA is not a tax measure.

Section 16 SCDA provides:

> In Schedule 2 to the Northern Ireland Act 1998 (excepted matters), before paragraph 10 insert—
> "9C The operation of the Small Charitable Donations Act 2012."

This takes SCD administration outside the scope of the Northern Ireland Assembly, and reserves it for Westminster.

As regards Scotland and Wales, EN SCBA simply states:

> 113.Section 20 provides that the Act extends to England and Wales, Scotland and Northern Ireland.

The more detailed EN SCBA provides:

> 13.The Small Charitable Donations Bill extends to the whole of the UK.
> 14.At introduction, the Bill's provisions relate to matters which are within the legislative competence of the Northern Ireland Assembly. The Bill includes a provision to make the scheme an excepted matter for the purposes of the Northern Ireland devolution settlement. A legislative consent motion was approved by the Northern Ireland Assembly on the 20th November 2012 providing consent for the UK Parliament to proceed with the Bill and also to amend Schedule 2 to the Northern Ireland Act 1998 to make the scheme an excepted matter.
> 15.This Bill does not contain any provisions falling within the terms of the Sewel Convention. Because the Sewel Convention provides that Westminster will not normally legislate with regard to devolved matters in Scotland without the consent of the Scottish Parliament, if there are

amendments relating to such matters which trigger the Convention, the consent of the Scottish Parliament will be sought for them.

16.In relation to Wales, the Bill does not relate to devolved matters or confer functions on the Welsh Ministers.

16.22 Human rights

EN SCDB has an interesting discussion:

> **Article 1 Protocol 1 ("A1P1")**
>
> 129. A1P1 protects the right to peaceful enjoyment of possessions. The top-up payments are akin to a tax relief but are not a repayment of tax. It is a grant and perhaps similarities as to what amounts to a possession may be looked for in the non-contributory benefit cases.[18] Even if A1P1 is engaged, States have what is described by the Court as a 'wide margin of appreciation' when framing and implementing policies when it comes to general measures of economic or social strategy.[19] This means that the Court will leave a wide discretion to the State in how they design their taxation, social or economic systems, and only interfere where an individual's rights are clearly breached. In ascertaining whether there has been such a breach, the Court will look at the aim of the measure, and then consider whether the measure is a proportionate way to achieve that aim. In doing so the Court will seek to discover whether a fair balance

---

18 Footnote original: In *R oao Carson & Reynolds v Secretary of State for Work and Pensions* [2005] 4 All ER 545 at [12]-[13] and [74]-[75] the House of Lords concluded that jobseeker's and income support were not "possessions" for the purpose of A1P1, in contrast to contributory benefits, which are "possessions" . [See too decision of the Court of Appeal [2003] 3 All ER 577 at [47]]. This was followed in *Campbell v South Northamptonshire DC* [2004] 3 All ER 387, paras 31-39 and 61. This appears to conflict with the Grand Chamber in *Stec v United Kingdom* (2005) 41 EHRR SE18 para 54 in that it held that non-contributory benefits were possessions. However, *Stec* was considered in *R oao RJM v Secretary of State for Work and Pension* [2008] 3 WLR 1023, para 28-34 where the HL held that a disability premium was a possession for the purposes of A1P1.

19 Footnote original: See for example *James v United Kingdom,* judgment of 21 February 1986, Series A no. 98, § 46; *National and Provincial Building Society v United Kingdom*, judgment of 23 October 1997, Reports 1997-VII, § 80; as referred to in paragraph 52 of the merits decision in *Stec v United Kingdom* (Applications nos. 65731/01 and 65900/01), dated 12 April 2006. This is because of their direct knowledge of their society and its needs, the national authorities are in principle better placed than the international judge to appreciate what is in the public interest on social or economic grounds, and the court will generally respect the legislature's policy choice unless it is "manifestly without reasonable foundation"' *Runkee and White v UK* Applications nos. 42949/98 and 53134/99.

has been struck between interests of the community and protection of individual rights, and whether the measure imposes an excessive or individual burden.[20] This Convention right is relevant to the following clauses:

130.Clause 2(3) provides that a charity or CASC is not an eligible charity or CASC where a penalty is incurred in respect of a Gift Aid exemption claim or a top-up claim. It is the Government's view that A1P1 is not engaged as the non-compliant charity or CASC cannot have a legitimate expectation of acquiring an effective enjoyment of a property right. If a charity or CASC receives a penalty for non-compliance with Gift Aid formalities it is difficult to see how it can then argue that it had a legitimate expectation of benefiting from a scheme that waives these formalities. If a charity or CASC does not comply with the correct requirements of Gift Aid then it cannot expect to partake in a scheme which removes those safeguards. In addition, a right under A1P1 only arises where the conditions to entitlement for a payment under the scheme are met. If a charity or CASC no longer fulfils the conditions of entitlement they do not have a right to that payment. Even if A1P1 is engaged, any interference is justified as this provision is the most proportionate way to achieve the desired result which is a waiver of Gift Aid formalities for compliant charities and CASCs thereby allowing for a Gift Aid style payment to be given in respect of small cash donations received by them. It is right for the State to determine eligibility criteria for the scheme so as to ensure the scheme is operated properly and is not open to abuse. This does not affect a charity's or CASC's entitlement to claim for Gift Aid instead provided the formalities are complied with. The non-eligibility is also for a limited time (2 tax years) provided the charity or CASC is compliant for those years.

131.Clause 4 and the connected charity rule - the Government's view is that the provisions of clause 4 do not engage A1P1 of the Convention as charities or CASCs cannot have a legitimate expectation of being able to fragment into smaller charities or CASCs in order to gain extra entitlement. Even if there is a possession falling within A1P1 so that A1P1 is engaged, any interference is justified. There is only a finite amount of money available under this Scheme and the State enjoys a wide margin of appreciation when framing and implementing policies when it comes to general measures of economic or social strategy. This is a proportionate response to counteract abuse and to level the playing

20 Footnote original: For a summary of the court's position see paragraphs 62 and 63 of *Bulges AD v Bulgaria* Application no 3991/03.

fields between those charities and CASCs able to organise themselves into smaller charities or CASCs and those who do not have that resource.

132.Clause 6 - it is the Government's view that increasing support for charities that operate through local branches or undertake regular meetings in the local community does not engage A1P1 rights as there is no possession here to interfere with. Even if A1P1 is engaged then any interference can be justified and falls within the wide margin of appreciation enjoyed by the state in matters of economic and social strategy.

133.Clause 9 - connected charities and community buildings. The Government's view is that the provisions of clause 9 do not engage A1P1 of the Convention as there is no possession here to interfere with. A charity or CASC cannot have a legitimate expectation of remaining eligible for the £8,000 entitlement if it becomes connected with another charity or CASC. The charity will still be entitled to the £8,000 limit if it runs charitable activities in a community building, but the standard allocation is to be shared between the connected charities or CASCs that submit a claim in relation to non-community building donations. Even if there is a possession falling within A1P1 so that A1P1 is engaged, any interference is justified. There is only a finite amount of money available under this Scheme and the State enjoys a wide margin of appreciation when framing and implementing policies when it comes to general measures of economic or social strategy. This is a proportionate response to counteract abuse otherwise there would be an incentive for charities or CASCs to fragment to increase their entitlement. Restricting entitlement in this way also ensures a level of consistency between charities or CASCs that are structured in different ways.

Article 14 taken with Article 1 Protocol 1

134.Consideration was also given as to whether A1P1 was engaged when taken with article 14 - whether any charity or CASC has been denied a benefit which has been extended to others on discriminatory grounds. In particular, different treatment was considered between charities or CASCs with a good compliance record and those subject to a penalty, charities or CASCs who are connected with each other and those who are not, and charities with community buildings and those with no community buildings. These characteristics are not specifically listed in Article 14. The Government does not consider that the courts would accept that "other status" includes any of these characteristics while noting that it has been accepted in a number of cases that "other status" should be widely construed[21]. It is the Government's view that

---

21 Footnote original: *Michalak* [2003] 1 WLR 617, para 34.

A1P1 taken with article 14 only prohibits differences in treatment based on personal characteristics and that such characteristics must be independent of the treatment complained of.[22]

135.Even if "status" does include such differential treatment the argument would then move to objective justification and the Government's view is that the aims of the Scheme can be objectively justified and are proportionate[23] for the reasons already given in relation to A1P1. Provided that a coherent and legitimate policy rationale is offered for the difference in treatment in relation to the enjoyment of an ECHR right, the courts are less likely to find discrimination on the basis of a status that is not based on one of the suspect categories specially referred to in Article 14 than it is in relation to a status within one of those suspect categories: States have a broader margin of appreciation in relation to the former than the latter.

Article 6

136.Clause 11 - Article 6 of the ECHR (right to a fair trial) only applies in the determination of civil or criminal rights and obligations and not public law obligations. Direct tax involves the relationship of state and citizen to which Article 6 does not apply (*Ferrazzini v Italy* [2002] 34 EHRR 1068). Whether the provision of a grant in circumstances akin to Gift Aid relief is still invoking public law obligations need not be debated as it is likely the penalty provisions will be classed as criminal in nature for Convention purposes and there is also a power to create a criminal offence. In so far as Article 6 is in issue there is provision in the Bill for an appeals process which will be Article 6 compliant. The clause also provides safeguards so that the regulation making power does not include a power to increase the maximum amount of penalty or level of punishment from that found in the corresponding provision of the relevant enactment which is being applied to top-up claims.

16.23 Planning

It may be helpful to summarise the basic planning points for a charity to maximise GASDS income:

---

22 Footnote original: *Clift v UK* (Application No. 7205/07). Also in *R oao Clift v Secretary of State for the Home Department* [2007] 1 AC 484 the House of Lords confined the scope of article 14 to discriminatory treatment having as its legal basis or reason a personal characteristic by which persons or groups of persons are distinguishable from each other, rejecting a challenge of differential treatment on the basis of length of sentence.

23 Footnote original: Lord Nicholls in *R oao Carson v Secretary of State for Work and Pensions* [2006] AC 173, para 3.

(1) Ensure that the charity receives some gift aid donation each year (with no more than one year's gap). The amount does not matter so £4 (reclaiming £1) or even 4p (reclaiming 1p) will suffice, until HMRC introduce a minimum gift aid requirement. See 16.7 (Gift aid claim history).

(2) Ensure that the charity receives sufficient gift aid donations in each year:

- (a) In a year with small donations, gift aid donations must be 10% of the small donations; see 16.5 (Top-up claim limit).
- (b) in a year where there are no small donations, a nominal gift aid donation may be needed to qualify in a future year: see 16.7 (Gift Aid claim history).

(3) Take care about appointing trustees if that may make two charities "connected": see 16.12 ("Connected").

(4) Careful choice of where to collect may affect the GASDS limits: see 16.13 (Charities in community buildings).

(5) Claim Gift Aid relief (rather than GASDS) where possible if necessary to avoid small donations above the £5k limit (which do not qualify for any relief); see 16.5 (Top-up claim limit).

16.24 GASDS: Critique

16.24.1 *Cost to taxpayer*

EN SCDB provides:

> 120.Costs for the scheme were published at Budget 2011 and Budget 2012 and have been certified by the Office for Budget Responsibility.

	2013/14	**2014/15**	**2015/16**	**2016/17**
Exchequer Impact	-£50m	-£85m	-£105m	-£115m

The estimates were reviewed in the 2012 Autumn Statement[24], which increased them by the following amounts:

2013-14	*2014-15*	*2015-16*	*2016-17*	*2017-18*
10	15	10	20	30

The actual figures when published in a few years time will be interesting but like all raw data will need careful evaluation. Some of the GASDS figures will reflect amounts which would (in the absence of GASDS) have been claimed anyway under Gift Aid.

---

24 *https://www.gov.uk/government/news/autumn-statement-2012-policy-decisions*

16.24.2 *Cost to charity*

EN SCDB provides:

> 124.... The costs to charities and CASCs of using the scheme are expected to be negligible, as any administration and record-keeping to support claims under GASDS fall within current best practice. The cost savings to charities and CASCs will also be negligible, as there may be some substitution from Gift Aid exemption claims to GASDS, where the administration requirements are less.

The claim that the administrative costs of GASDS for charities will be negligible seems implausible. Mastering the rules would require a significant investment of resources, but HMRC do not seriously expect charities to do that. GASDS consultative document provides:

> 2.1 In practice many smaller organisations will not be aware of the technical differences between Gift Aid and the GASDS.

The fact that the scheme is too complex for charities can be seen in the response to the GASDS consultative document by The Office of Tax Simplification. The evidence they compiled showed that "a small number said they found aspects of the rules confusing" and "six respondents felt the scheme was too complicated to administer, particularly for volunteers, and three respondents suggested that HMRC's guidance was unclear".[25] Likewise the Charity Tax Commission reported:

> Some charities are unaware or unable to navigate the rules, with research indicating that over a third of small charities (£10,000-100,000 income) report it difficult or very difficult to find out about the scheme.[26] Many small charities consider it not worth the effort to engage with a scheme that seems difficult to use and disproportionate in its reporting requirements.[27]

---

25 Gift Aid Small Donations Scheme - Consultation response by the Office of Tax Simplification *https://www.gov.uk/government/uploads/system/uploads/attachment_data/file/535498/Response_GASDS_consultation_290616.pdf*

26 Footnote original: *https://blogs.ncvo.org.uk/wp-content/uploads/andrew-o-brien/CFG-IoF-NCVO-GASDS-Briefing.pdf*

27 Charity Tax Commission, "Reforming charity taxation" (2019) *https://www.ncvo.org.uk/images/documents/policy_and_research/funding/CharityCommissionReport__ForWeb_3.pdf*

16.24.3 *Tax complication*

As tends to happen in tax, the idea is simple but the implementation was not. The anomalies - and need for planning - are obvious.

16.24.4 *GASDS: Evaluation*

The GASDS consultative document states that the object of GASDS is to encourage charitable giving. It is therefore relevant to ask:
(1) whether the scheme will actually increase charitable giving; and
(2) if so by how much: will the additional donations exceed the costs of the scheme - is the scheme value for money?

There has been no research or evidence to suggest that it will: that has been assumed as self-evident.

The view that GASDS will have a very significant effect on charitable giving seems to us implausible:
(1) The sums involved for an individual donor are trivial: while there is a notional £30 cap, we expect typical cash donations are much smaller. If someone is giving £1, or £5, no-one would regard the top-up payment of 25p or £1.25 as an incentive.[28]
(2) There is no incentive effect on giving to charities which receive more than the £8,000 limit. Indeed if donors were to take the relief seriously (which we doubt) they would need to ask themselves whether the charity (including connected charities) has (or will in the tax year) reach the £8,000 limit. The idea that donors will ask themselves this question, and increase or target their donations accordingly, seems fanciful.

GASDS is primarily a subvention to charities which raise small donations by passing round a collecting box. It is (to say the least) not clear why that method of fundraising should be given particular support. If there really were a case for GASDS, it should be uncapped, or at least subject to a very much greater cap than £8,000.

It is possible that GASDS actually may reduce charities income, if the result is that donors do not bother to fill in Gift Aid declarations in favour of charities which cannot collect the full top-up as they collect substantially more than £8,000.

---

28 This is self-evident, but evidence is also available: Smith,"Increasing Charitable Giving: What Can We Learn from Economics?" (2012), Fiscal Studies, 33: 449–466.

16.24.5 *The future*

If studies are carried out in a few years time it will be interesting to see the results. We would be surprised if they find that GASDS has increased charitable giving. It may not be practical politics to scrap GASDS: it was politics rather than policy which caused its introduction. Whilst the top-limit for the scheme has increased from £5,000 to £8,000 this has still not done enough to ensure the relevance of the scheme. The scheme could become (even) more irrelevant if this new £8,000 top-up limit is frozen allowing inflation to whittle it away. That seems a likely outcome. But the most satisfactory solution is repeal of the entire scheme.

This view is not universally held. John Hemming, Chairman of the Charity Tax Group, stated:

> In respect of the Gift Aid Small Donations Scheme the relaxation of the eligibility requirements, clarification of the community buildings rules and extension to contactless payments are all welcome and we hope that these changes will help to widen accessibility to the Scheme, particularly among smaller charities. However, we encourage the Government to continue to review the effectiveness of these changes, and consider further reforms, if there is no significant additional take-up. The charity sector will work hard to ensure that it maximises the value of this important relief and CTG will work with others in the sector and Government to promote the Scheme as much as possible.[29]

29 *https://www.charitytaxgroup.org.uk/press-release/ctg-welcomes-gasds-changes-highlights-cumulative-tax-burden/*

CHAPTER SEVENTEEN

CORPORATE GIFT AID

Cross references

The following topic is considered elsewhere:
9.7 (Donation exceeds distributable profit)

17.1 Corporate Gift Aid: Introduction

In this chapter I use the following terminology:
Corporate Gift Aid: CT relief for cash gifts to charity by companies
Individual Gift Aid: IT relief for cash gifts by individuals

Most of the rules of corporate Gift Aid are the same or very similar to individual Gift Aid, as to which see 15.1 (Gift Aid: Introduction). One could simplify the law by aligning the two sets of rules more closely; but the differences hardly matter, and it seems more trouble than it is worth.

17.2 Corporate Gift Aid

Section 189 CTA 2010 provides:

> (1) Qualifying charitable donations made by a company are allowed as deductions from the company's total profits in calculating the corporation tax chargeable for an accounting period.
> (2) They are deducted from the company's total profits for the period

> after any other relief from corporation tax other than group relief.
> (3) The amount of the deduction is limited to the amount that reduces the company's taxable total profits for the period to nil.
> (4) Except as otherwise provided, a deduction is allowed only in respect of qualifying charitable donations made by the company in the accounting period concerned.

We call this **"corporate Gift Aid"**.

17.2.1 *History of corporate Gift Aid*

CTA 2010 sensibly replaced the opaque term "charge on income" with the more transparent term "qualifying charitable donation". EN CTA 2010 comments on the old terminology:

> 749. For corporation tax purposes charges on income are now reduced to charitable donations only ... A more accurate description has therefore been substituted for "charges on income". The term "charges on income" was dispensed with for income tax purposes by ITA and this Act now follows that path.
> 750. It is not considered that by relabelling "charges on income" as "qualifying charitable donations" there is any danger of either depriving a company of a relief which is due or allowing relief that is not due for a payment.

The relief for charges on income formerly applied not only to gifts to charities but also to various other types of payment. Some old provisions relating to charges on income have survived (rewritten to refer to qualifying charitable donations) though they are not now needed, and exist for historical reasons only.

17.3 Qualifying charitable donation

"Qualifying charitable donations" is defined in s.190(1) CTA 2010:

> The following are qualifying charitable donations for corporation tax purposes—
> (a) payments which are qualifying payments for the purposes of Chapter 2 (certain payments to charity), and
> (b) amounts treated as qualifying charitable donations under Chapter 3 (certain disposals of investments to charity).

The category which interests us here is qualifying payments. For disposals of investments, see 21.1 (Gift of shares/land to charity).

17.3.1 *"Donation"*

Individual Gift Aid relief applies only if the payment is a "gift". [1] Corporate Gift Aid does not have this requirement. The CTA 2010 does use the expression "qualifying charitable donation", and "donation" may be regarded as a synonym of "gift", but the expression is just a label and its definition does not state that the payment must actually be a gift or a donation (whatever that would mean). The Gift Aid benefit rule covers (more or less) the same ground, and with rather greater clarity, so it makes no difference.

This difference between corporate/individual Gift Aid may be a fortuitous accident of drafting. Or it may have been deliberate; the drafter may have felt some unease with the idea that a company could make a gift; though of course that depends on what one means by the imprecise word gift. But it is not necessary to pursue that here.

17.4 Qualifying payment

Section 191(1) CTA 2010 provides:

> A payment made to a charity by a company is a qualifying payment for the purposes of this Chapter if each of conditions A to F is met.

We refer to **"corporate Gift Aid conditions A to F"**.

17.4.1 *Payment of sum of money*

Section 191(2) CTA 2010 provides:

> Condition A is that the payment is a payment of a sum of money.

This is the same as individual Gift Aid: see 15.8 (Payment: Gift Aid condition A)).

17.4.2 *Repayment rule: CGA condition B*

Section 191(3) CTA 2010 provides:

> Condition B is that the payment is not subject to a condition as to repayment (but see section 192).

This is the same as individual Gift Aid: see 15.16 (Repayment rule: Condition B). For the exception in s.192, see 9.5.5 (Estimation relief).

---

1 See 15.4 ("Gift").

17.4.3 *Non-charitable company donor*

Section 191(4) CTA 2010 provides:

> Condition C is that the company making the payment is not itself a charity.

A charity whose manager is not a "fit and proper" may be in a better position than other charities, since it is not a charity for tax purposes and so will qualify for corporate Gift Aid! Thus one can envisage circumstances where a charity argues that a manager is not fit and proper and HMRC argue that they are.

17.4.4 *Acquisition of property rule*

Section 191(5) CTA 2010 provides:

> Condition D is that the payment is not disqualified under section 193 (associated acquisition etc by the charity).

This takes us to s.193 CTA 2010 which provides:

> (1) A payment is disqualified under this section if—
> (a) it is conditional on an acquisition of property by the charity from the company or a person associated with the company,
> (b) it is associated with such an acquisition, or
> (c) it is part of an arrangement involving such an acquisition.
> (2) An acquisition by way of gift is to be ignored for the purposes of this section.

This is broadly the same as individual Gift Aid (though the rule there is called condition E): for a discussion, see 15.19 (Acquisition of property rule).

One difference is that the acquisition of property rule for individual Gift Aid applies to acquisitions by connected persons. The corporate rule applies to acquisitions by *associated* persons.

17.4.5 *Associated persons*

The definition of associated persons matters for:
(1) The acquisition of property rule: corporate Gift Aid condition D
(2) The benefit rule: corporate Gift Aid condition F

Section 201 CTA 2010 provides:

> For the purposes of this Chapter a person is associated with a company

> if the person is connected with—
> (a) the company, or
> (b) a person connected with the company.

The definition uses the concept of connected person, but is wider.

"Connected person" is defined in s.1122(1) CTA 2010; see s.1176(1) CTA 2010, which is the equivalent of the IT provisions discussed above.[2]

17.4.6 *Benefit rule: CGA condition F*

Section 191(7) CTA 2010 provides:

> Condition F is that the payment is not disqualified under section 195 (associated benefits).

This takes us to s.195(1) CTA 2010 which provides:

> A payment is disqualified under this section if—
> (a) benefits are associated with the payment, and
> (b) the restrictions on benefits associated with a payment are breached.

Section 196 CTA 2010 defines associated benefits:

> For the purposes of this Chapter a benefit is associated with a payment if—
> (a) it is received by the company which made the payment or by a person associated with the company, and
> (b) it is received in consequence of making the payment.

We refer to this as the **"benefit rule"**.

The rule is similar to that for individual Gift Aid.[3] One difference is that the individual Gift Aid rule applies to benefits received by connected persons. The corporate rule applies to benefits received by *associated* persons. That term is more widely defined.[4] We wonder if that difference rests on a conscious decision and if so what is its reason.

Another difference is that individual Gift Aid requires there to be a "gift". That does not apply to corporate Gift Aid. But that makes no difference in practice as the benefit rule covers the same ground. It is probably just a accidental quirk of the drafting.

Sections 197 and 198 CTA 2010 set out de minimis (small benefit) rules

---

2 See 15.32 (Benefit of connected/associated person).

3 See 15.20 (Benefit rule: Condition F).

4 See 17.4.5 (Associated persons).

and annualisation rules, which are the same as for individual Gift Aid.

The HMRC Guidance Note para 3.13.2 provides this example:

> On 1 June 2015 ABC Retailing Ltd donates £1,250 to a museum which is a charity.
> As a consequence of the donation its 4 directors receive free entry to an event at the museum, worth £20 each. The benefit to connected persons[5] of the company is £80 (4 × £20).
> The value of the benefit received by the 4 directors is greater than the relevant value allowed, which is in this case 5% of the donation, £62.50.
> The whole of the donation of £1,250 fails to be a 'qualifying charitable donation' for Gift Aid purposes.

This assumes that the directors are associated with the company (which may, but need not, be the case).

17.4.7 *Payment otherwise deductible*

Section 190(2) CTA 2010 provides:

> However, no payment that is otherwise deductible from total profits, or in calculating any component of total profits, is a qualifying charitable donation.

This is the same as individual Gift Aid: see 15.18 (Payment deductible for IT).

It would have been neater drafting to place this rule with the other conditions in s.191, but it does not matter.

Section 1301B CTA 2009 provides:

> In calculating a company's income from any source for corporation tax purposes, no deduction is allowed in respect of qualifying charitable donations.

It is not clear to us why s.1301B was thought necessary. We suspect it is otiose and exists for accidental historical reasons only.[6]

17.4.8 *Sale of leasing company*

For completeness: corporate Gift Aid is restricted in cases where there has been a sale of a leasing company and an election under s.398A CTA 2010: see s.398D(1) CTA 2010. This very specialist area is not discussed here.

---

5 The correct term is associated persons.

6 See 17.2.1 (History of corporate Gift Aid).

17.5 Distribution rule: Condition E

Section 191(6) CTA 2010 provides:

> Condition E is that the payment is not disqualified under section 194 (certain distributions).

This takes us to s.194(1) CTA 2010:

> A payment is disqualified under this section if it is to be regarded as a distribution by reason of any provision of the Taxes Acts (within the meaning of TMA 1970) except section 1020 (transfers of assets or liabilities treated as distributions).

We refer to this as the **"distribution rule."**

We therefore need to ask whether the payment is a "distribution". This term is elaborately defined. The starting point is s.1000(1) CTA 2010 which provides:

> In the Corporation Tax Acts "distribution", in relation to any company, means anything falling within any of the following paragraphs.

Only the first two paragraphs are relevant here:

> A. Any dividend paid by the company, including a capital dividend.
> B. Any other distribution out of assets of the company in respect of shares in the company...

In the following discussion a **"s.1000 distribution"**, is a distribution within s.1000 CTA 2010. In practice the focus is on para B.

We need to consider whether a payment which otherwise qualifies for corporate Gift Aid could be a s.1000 distribution. One could identify three requirements:

(1) A distribution
(2) Out of the assets of the company
(3) In respect of shares

Note that "distribution" in the company law sense does not have exactly the same meaning as the s.1000 definition.[7]

A gift is plainly "out of the assets of the company". Section 1117(3) CTA 2010 provides:

7 A gift is capable of being a distribution in a company law sense; see 9.7 (Donation exceeds distributable profit).

> For the purposes of this Part a distribution is treated as made out of assets of a company if the cost falls on the company.

The important issue is whether the gift is "in respect of shares". This expression is explained (after a fashion) in s.1113 CTA 2010:

> (3) For the purposes of this Part a thing is regarded as done in respect of a share if it is done to a person—
> (a) as the holder of the share, or
> (b) as the person who held the share at a particular time.
> (4) For the purposes of this Part a thing is also regarded as done in respect of a share if it is done in pursuance of a right granted, or an offer made, in respect of a share.

In *Noved Investment v HMRC* [2006] STC (SCD) 120 the Special Commissioners correctly held that this definition is inclusive, not exhaustive,[8] but the circumstances in which this matters will be rare.

In *Noved* the charity held A shares in a company. The A shares conferred the right to require the company to make charitable gifts out of the company's "A fund". Gifts made pursuant to that right were clearly gifts "in respect of shares" both in the normal sense and within s.1113(3).

However, the Special Commissioners realised that this might upset the apple cart for the common case of a non-charitable subsidiary making a

8 "41... If, as in the Articles in this case, the right in the share permits the shareholder to direct that another person should benefit from a distribution, and in pursuance of that right the company distributes assets to that person, is that a payment within 209(2)(b)? It is clearly not done to the third party as being the holder of a share, neither, if it is a gift to that third party, is its receipt in pursuance of any right other than the right of the shareholder in the Articles. If this is correct such Articles would permit distributions (other than dividends – because they are covered by section 209(2)(a)) to be paid to, for example, a shareholder's husband or wife in a form which was not a distribution which, had they been directly distributed to the shareholder, would be a distribution. ...
42. This difficulty, however, is capable of resolution if the words of section 254(12) are treated as imposing sufficient but not necessary conditions for something to be treated as done in respect of shares. Subsection (12) merely says that something is done in respect of shares "if" conditions are satisfied. It does not say "only if", or "if and only if". ... If subsection (12) imposes only a sufficient but not necessary condition then a wider enquiry is permissible as to whether, on the ordinary meaning of the words, something has been done in respect of shares. It seems to us clear that the exercise by a shareholder of a right to require a payment to a third party, and the subsequent payment out of the assets of the company to the third party would be a payment in respect of a share even though it is not made to the holder."

gift to its parent charity[9] and they went some way to deal with this at [55]:

> We should add that we do not think that this conclusion means that a gift by a trading company to a charity by which the company is owned is always a distribution within section 209(2)(b) [now s.1000 CTA 2010]. It would only be such if it was made in respect of shares, and it seems to us that it will be possible for such gifts to be made otherwise than pursuant to a collateral right, or to the charity in its capacity as shareholder, and otherwise than in such a way that the distribution generally is in respect of the shareholding.

In short, *Noved* was a special case:

> In the case of [*Noved*] the gifts were compelled by an agreement which related to shares and the rights and interests of the A shareholder; a voluntary gift need not be in respect of a shareholding even though it may be to a member.

17.5.1 *HMRC view*

HMRC Guidance Note para 3.16.2 formerly provided:

> *Whether a payment made by a company to a charity is a distribution in respect of shares is a question of fact. It should also be noted that a 'distribution in respect of shares' has a wider meaning than 'dividend'. Broadly, any payment made by a company to a charity in its capacity as a shareholder is regarded as a distribution in respect of shares in the company, and as such will not qualify as a Gift Aid donation ....*

How do we decide whether a payment is made to the charity in its capacity as a shareholder?

> *Factors that HMRC would take into account in deciding whether a payment is a distribution, made to a charity in respect of its shareholding, would include evidence from underlying documents (e.g. the company's minutes of meetings; correspondence between the company and its shareholders; whether payments were made to the non-charity shareholders – and if so when and in what amounts).*
> ***Example***
> *A company, A to Z Trading Ltd is jointly owned by a two companies: A Ltd, which owns 60% of the issued share capital and is a trading company, and Z Ltd, which owns 40% of the issued share capital and is a charity.*

9 *Noved* was decided before the enactment of the relief discussed at 17.5.3 (Company wholly owned by charity).

Diagrammatically:[10]

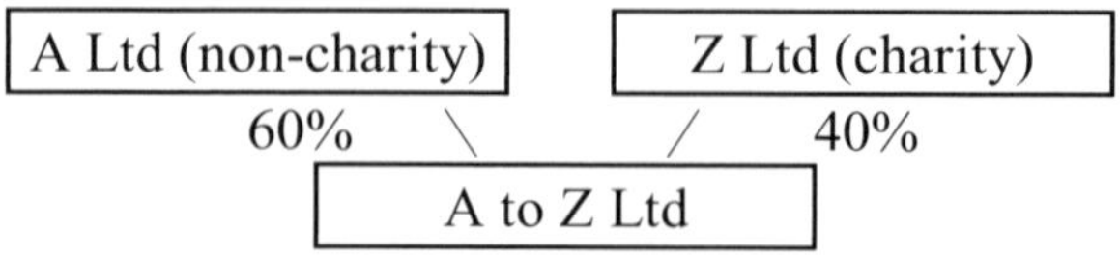

> *The company made a profit of £75,000 in its accounting period ended 31 March 2007.*
> *On 1 October 2007 the company made payments of £30,000 to A Ltd and £20,000 to Z Ltd.*
> *The minutes of a directors' meeting on 30 September 2007 recorded that the directors resolved to distribute current reserves to the shareholders, and the payments made were in direct proportion to the shareholdings.*

On these facts, the Guidance Note said:

> *These payments are distributions of profit, so the £20,000 paid to Z Ltd would not qualify as a Gift Aid donation.*

More analytically, the £20k payment to Z Ltd was a s.1000 distribution, so corporate Gift Aid condition E is not satisfied.

The result would be different if A Ltd was a charity.[11]

The guidance lastly gave a case where a charitable gift is not a distribution:

> *On 1 November 2007 the company made a payment of £15,000 to Z Ltd, in response to a public appeal by that charity.*
> *This payment would be accepted as a qualifying charitable donation.*

That is correct.

In May 2015 this passage was deleted, but there is no reason to think that the HMRC view has changed.

17.5.2 *Charity/non-charity joint venture*

Noved may be seen as an (unsuccessful) attempt to avoid the distribution rule. A solution for joint ventures between a charity and a non-charity is to insert a trading subsidiary into the structure, so the joint venture is run between that subsidiary and the non-charity:[12]

---

10 I have added the diagram for ease of exposition.

11 See 17.5.3 (Company wholly owned by charity).

12 I take this idea from Lloyd and Walker, *Charities, Trading and the Law* (2nd ed, 2009) para 7.249.

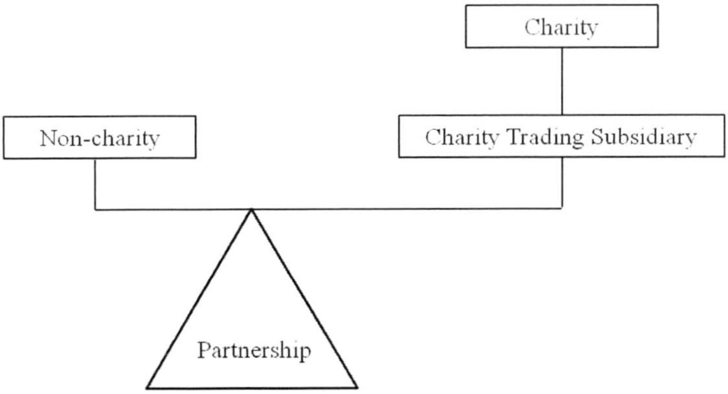

The partnership is not subject to tax. For tax purposes, its profits are in principle regarded as accruing to the partners. So far as its profits accrue to the charity trading subsidiary, they may be given to the charity and qualify for Gift Aid relief. The partnership rules introduced by the FA 2014 would need to be considered in the light of the circumstances of the particular case. Alternatively a joint venture company may be used instead of a partnership.

17.5.3 *Company wholly owned by charity*

The distribution rule makes sense for companies which are owned partly by charities and partly by non-charities. In the absence of that rule, a distribution would qualify for corporate Gift Aid relief so far as it went to the charity shareholder; the relief should in principle apply only to gifts which are borne by all the shareholders as a body.

The distribution rule is not appropriate for companies which are wholly owned by a charity. Section 194(3) CTA 2010 provides relief for this situation:

> A payment (other than a dividend) made by a company which is wholly owned by a charity is not to be regarded as a distribution for the purposes of subsection (1).

This provision is not required for a non-charitable company wholly owned by a single charity, as a gift to the parent is not regarded as a distribution. However it is needed where one non-charitable company is held by several charities. EN FB 2006 explains:

> 11. Some charities conduct activities through subsidiary companies.

> This organisational structure enables those charities to carry on activities that may be outside their primary purpose. For a company wholly owned by a single charity, company gift aid can be used to pass up the profits of the subsidiary company to the parent charity. Those profits then do not incur corporation tax.
> 12. Where a subsidiary is owned by more than one charity and that subsidiary makes payments to the parent charities in proportion to their shareholdings, the payments will be distributions of profit. Such distributions are not allowable as gift aid payments, and so are not deductible in computing profits for tax purposes. This results in a tax charge on the subsidiary and reduces the income flow to the charities from the subsidiary.
> 13. This clause allows companies jointly owned by charities to donate their profits to parent charities using gift aid.

If the company pays a *dividend*, as opposed to any other type of distribution, then corporate Gift Aid relief does not apply. That is not altogether sensible, but it does no harm in practice as profits can be, and always are, extracted by way of gift, without giving rise to a dividend.

17.6 Carry-back/forward of relief

HMRC Guidance Note provides at 3.12.2:

> Charitable donations can't be used to create or add to a company's trading losses, nor can excess charitable donations be carried forward or back although they may be surrendered as group relief.

This is broadly correct, under s.189(3)(4) CTA 2010. A companies must therefore take care not to make gifts in excess of its profits in any accounting period. If necessary, they could make loans followed by gifts in later years which can be set against later profits.

In a few exceptional cases, carry-back or carry-forward of charitable donations is permitted:

(1) Companies wholly owned by charities may carry back donations.[13]
(2) Gifts for the purpose of a company's investment business may be carried forward.
(3) Gifts which are deductible business expenditure may augment trading losses and so be carried forward.

---

13 See 9.4 (Carry-back relief).

17.7 Non-resident company donor

A non-resident company within the charge to corporation tax[14] qualifies for corporate Gift Aid relief.

A non-resident company outside the scope of corporation tax, but paying income tax, does not qualify for any relief; but now that companies pay CT on UK property income this is less likely to happen.

HMRC agree: HMRC Guidance Note 3.12.4 provides:

> Non resident companies within the UK Corporation Tax regime can also make Gift Aid donations; this will generally apply to companies trading in the UK through a branch or agency. Non-resident companies that are only chargeable to UK Income Tax in respect of income arising in the UK can't get Gift Aid relief on donations to charities or CASCs because corporate Gift Aid donations are only deductible against Corporation Tax profits.

This discrimination against foreign companies may be in breach of EU law, if the company is established in an EU member state. The discrimination is also irrational. The object of the relief is to encourage gifts to charity, and it does not make sense to encourage gifts from UK companies but not from non-UK companies. But after 2020 the point is not likely to arise.

Non-discrimination articles in double taxation treaties are narrowly construed, and it appears that HMRC would reject an argument that such an article could override this rule.[15]

---

14 ie a company carrying on a trade in the UK through a permanent establishment, or disposing of UK land.

15 When there was formerly a rule that non-resident companies did not qualify for the relief, the non-discrimination article was only accepted as overriding the rule for companies carrying on a trade in the UK through a branch or agency. Double Taxation Relief Manual (in a passage now very out of date) provides:

DT1959: Non-residents: UK income: Gift Aid payments [February 2006]

... ICTA88/S339(2) provides that [Gift Aid] relief shall not be due unless the company making the payment is resident in the United Kingdom. Section 25(2)(i) FA 1990 similarly confines relief to individuals resident in the United Kingdom.

Where a Gift Aid payment is made by a company or an individual resident in a state with which the United Kingdom has an agreement which includes a non-discrimination Article, relief may be given provided that the non-resident company or the non-resident individual is carrying on business in the United Kingdom through a permanent establishment and the payment is made by that permanent establishment. In the case of individuals, this excludes people who perform

17.8 Claims and record keeping

No claim is required for corporate Gift Aid and no declaration or certificate is required. The relief is compulsory.

HMRC Guidance Note para 3.11.3 provides:

> Charities and CASCs receiving Gift Aid donations from companies should keep accurate accounting records of company donations received, so that they can identify these in their accounts and include them on their tax return.

HMRC Guidance Note para 3.12.3 provides:

> 3.12.3 The donor company should keep
> [a] normal accounting records to support entries on its CTSA return along with
> [b] any other relevant documentation for example, correspondence with the charity or CASC in relation to the donation such as a 'thank you' letter.

Point [b] may be best practice, but the failure to retain a thank-you letter will not prejudice tax relief on the company's gift; there should always be sufficient evidence in the form of banking records that the gift was made. But now communication is by email, rather than paper, the point is not likely to arise.

17.9 Position of charity receiving gift

17.9.1 *Deemed income*

Under general principles, a gift from a company to a charity would not in principle be income of the charity.[16] However, s.522 ITA provides:

> (1) This section applies if gifts of sums of money are made to charitable trusts by companies.
> (2) But this section does not apply to a gift of a sum of money made by a company that is itself a charity (see section 523).
> (3) Income tax is charged on the gifts under this section.
> (4) It is charged on the full amount of the gifts arising in the tax year.
> (5) But a gift is not taken into account in calculating total income so far

professional services through a fixed base.

In addition, the non-resident company or individual must comply with whatever requirements are imposed by the legislation on United Kingdom resident payers. ...

16 See 4.2 (Are gifts"income").

> as it is applied to charitable purposes only.
> (6) The trustees of the charitable trust are liable for any tax charged under this section.

Similarly, s.473 CTA 2010 provides:

> (1) If a charitable company receives a gift of a sum of money from a company which is not a charity, the gift is treated as an amount in respect of which the charitable company is chargeable to corporation tax, under the charge to corporation tax on income.
> (2) But the gift is not taken into account in calculating total profits so far as it is applied to charitable purposes only...

This applies to all corporate gifts of money; a gift is still deemed to be income of the charity even if corporate Gift Aid does not apply, eg if:

(1) The conditions of the relief are not met (eg the donor receives a benefit)
(2) The donor has no profits
(3) The donor is a non-resident company outside the scope of corporation tax

This is odd, but it does not normally matter, because the charity will normally qualify for tax relief on the deemed income.

17.9.2 *No tax reclaim*

The charity does not reclaim tax on a gift from a company, and the company does not deduct tax from the gift. HMRC Guidance Note correctly states at 3.11.2:

> Gift Aid donations made to charities and CASCs by companies are paid gross and so, unlike the individual Gift Aid Scheme, no tax is repayable to charities or CASCs. For a charity or CASC the donation is treated as potentially taxable income, but is exempt from tax provided the donation is applied for charitable purposes by a charity or qualifying purposes by a CASC.

CHAPTER EIGHTEEN

GIVING BY BUSINESSES TO CHARITY

18.1 Introduction

This chapter considers the special opportunities for giving to charities and NPOs which are open to persons carrying on a business. This applies to persons carrying on a trade, profession or property business, alone or in partnership. It also applies to a company carrying on an investment business.

18.2 Charity gift: Deductible expense

18.2.1 *Relief from statutory disallowance*

For IT, s.45(1) ITTOIA normally disallows a deduction for gifts:

> The general rule is that no deduction is allowed in calculating the profits of a trade for expenses incurred in providing entertainment or gifts in

connection with the trade.

However there is an exception for gifts to charity: s.47 ITTOIA provides:

> (1) The prohibition in section 45 on deducting expenses incurred in providing gifts does not apply in any of cases A, B, C and D.
>
> ...
>
> (5) Case D is where the gift is given to—
> (a) a charity...[1]

The corporation tax equivalents are ss.1298 and 1300 CTA 2009.

18.2.2 *Wholly and exclusively*

A gift is only deductible if it satisfies the usual rules for business expenditure.

In the case of a trade, profession or property business, the gift must be incurred wholly and exclusively for the purposes of the business; see s.54 CTA 2009/s.34 ITTOIA.

A gift to charity may be made not for the purposes of the business, but out of charitable feelings, or because the donor feels some moral duty. No deduction is allowable if a gift is made with mixed motives, ie partly for some business advantage and partly out of charitable motives. The donor must make the donation entirely out of self-interest.

In several cases, the Commissioners decided that gifts to charity were not deductible for this reason In *Bourne and Hollingsworth v Ogden*[2] a draper made a gift to a hospital which gave some priority to the taxpayer's employees; in *Hutchinson v Turner*[3] there was a gift by a publisher to a charity for the benefit of individuals in the publishing trade. In each case the High Court held that the Commissioners were entitled to reach their decision that the gifts were not *purely* motivated by self-interest. The decisions now seem harsh; but they need to be understood in the context of the time: there was then no general Gift Aid relief for gifts to charity: the courts wished to prevent traders obtaining charity relief by dressing up charitable gifts as business expenditure, and a strict application of the wholly and exclusively rule was the way this was achieved.

Although these old cases do not encourage the would-be business donor,

---

1 The relief is extended to the Historic Buildings and Monuments Commission for England. See App 5.3 ("Eligible bodies").

2 14 TC 349.

3 31 TC 495.

they turn on their facts, and it is still possible for a charitable gift to be deductible. In the "well known judgment"[4] of *Bentleys Stokes & Lowless v Beeson*, the Court of Appeal regarded it as self-evident that charitable donations could be deductible:[5]

> The sole question is whether the expenditure in question was "exclusively" laid out for business purposes, that is: What was the motive or object in the mind of the two individuals responsible for the activities in question? It is well established that the question is one of fact: and again, therefore, the problem seems simple enough. The difficulty however arises, as we think, from the nature of the activity in question. ... Giving to charity ... involves inevitably the object of benefaction. ... But the question ... is: Was ... the charitable subscription, ... undertaken solely for the purposes of business, that is, solely with the object of promoting the business or its profit earning capacity?
>
> It is, as we have said, a question of fact. And it is quite clear that the purpose must be the sole purpose. The paragraph says so in clear terms. If the activity be undertaken with the object both of promoting business and also with some other purpose, for example, with the object of ... supporting a charitable or benevolent object, then the paragraph is not satisfied though in the mind of the actor the business motive may predominate. For the statute so prescribes. Per contra, if in truth the sole object is business promotion, the expenditure is not disqualified because the nature of the activity necessarily involves some other result, or the attainment or furtherance of some other objective, since the latter result or objective is necessarily inherent in the act.

There has been significant change in business practice and attitudes since these cases were decided. It is generally accepted that it is a duty of business as business to support the community, and to do so is enlightened self-interest.[6]

The costs of setting up a charitable foundation were allowed as a deduction in *Northern Rock v Thorpe*.[7] Here the reason for the charitable expenditure was as follows:

> The Board also considered that making a contribution to the community was important for the following reasons: It can improve the wellbeing of the community and in turn make it a better place to do business;

---

4 *Robinson v Scott Bader* 54 TC 757 at p.764.

5 33 TC 491 at p.503.

6 See eg *https://en.wikipedia.org/wiki/Corporate_social_responsibility*

7 [2000] STC (SCD) 317.

> Developing a closer affinity with a particular community increases the goodwill of the people in that community who may, other factors being equal, be more loyal to and therefore more likely to do business with, Northern Rock plc; and it can improve the morale and motivation of employees.

Normally set-up costs will be capital rather than income, but they were held to be income on the unusual facts of the case.

Gifts to a CASC were disallowed as trading expenses in *Interfish v HMRC* [2015] STC 55, where sponsorship of a professional rugby club was undertaken partly to promote a business and partly to support the club. But now CASC Gift Aid has been extended to companies, this is not likely to arise.

18.2.3 *Expense of management*

Similarly a donation by an investment company may be deductible an expense of management under s.1219 CTA 2009.

Section 1223 CTA 2009 provides for a carry-forward of unused relief:

> (1) This section applies if, in an accounting period of a company with investment business, any amount falling within subsection (2) cannot be deducted in full because—
> (a) the profits from which the amount is deductible are insufficient, or
> (b) in the case of an amount falling within subsection (2)(c)—
> (i) a claim relating to the whole of the amount has not been made under subsection (3B), or
> (ii) section 269ZD of CTA 2010 (restrictions on deductions from total profits) has effect for the accounting period, or
> (iii) section 269CC of CTA 2010 (restriction on deductions for management expenses) has effect for the accounting period.
> (2) The amounts are—
> (a) expenses of management deductible under section 1219,
> (b) qualifying charitable donations made in the accounting period, so far as they are made for the purposes of the company's investment business, and
> (c) amounts brought forward to the period under this section.
> (3) The excess is treated for the purposes of section 1219 as expenses of management deductible for the next accounting period.
> (3A) But subsection (3) does not apply in relation to so much of the excess as is surrendered as group relief under Part 5 of CTA 2010 or as group relief for carried-forward losses under Part 5A of that Act.

> (3B) A deduction in respect of the excess may be made under section 1219 for the next accounting period only on the making by the company of a claim.
> (3C) A claim may relate to the whole of the excess or to part of it only.
> (3D) A claim must be made—
> (a) within the period of two years after the end of the next accounting period, or
> (b) within such further period as an officer of Revenue and Customs may allow.
> (3E) Subsection (1A) of section 1219 does not apply in relation to a deduction in respect of the excess made for the next accounting period.

It is not clear to us why s.1223(2)(b) was thought necessary but we suspect it exists for historical reasons only.[8]

18.2.4 *HMRC practice*

The Business Income Manual provides:

> **BIM47405: Subscriptions: charitable and political subscriptions** [Dec 2016]
> S34(1) Income Tax (Trading and Other Income) Act 2005, S54(1) Corporation Tax Act 2009
> Subscriptions for general charitable purposes, and those to, for example, political parties are almost always made wholly or partly for non-trade purposes and should not be allowed as deductions in calculating the profits of a trade.
> Where the trader has a direct trade connection with a charity or its objects, the allowance of a relatively small annual subscription may be allowed, provided that the subscription can reasonably be claimed as an expense incurred in earning profits.
> Subscriptions to churches, chapels etc are normally inadmissible deductions, but may, in exceptional circumstances, be treated as admissible welfare expenditure.
> For certain charitable non-cash donations, see BIM45150 onwards. Gift Aid may also be relevant in some specific instances (see RE1830 to RE1841 for individuals and CTM09060 for companies).
> **BIM47410: subscriptions: annual subscriptions to charities by employers** [December 2016]
> S34(1) Income Tax (Trading and Other Income) Act 2005, S54(1) Corporation Tax Act 2009

8 See 17.2.1 (History of corporate Gift Aid).

An ordinary annual subscription by an employer to a charity, claimed as made for the benefit of his employees, may be allowed as a trade expense where:

- the availability of the charity to his employees or their immediate dependants can reasonably be regarded as a direct and valuable advantage to the employer's business, and
- the subscription is not of such magnitude that it can only be regarded as arising from munificence (see *Bourne & Hollingsworth Ltd v Ogden* [1929] 14 TC 349 and BIM37510).

Reasonable annual subscriptions made by an employer to, for example, a general hospital in the locality of his place of business, or to a trade charity maintained primarily for the benefit of employees in the employer's type of trade, are within this category. It can also cover subscriptions made to charities of benefit to a specific section of the employees.

Charity Special Appeal

A claim to deduct a special contribution made to a charity in response to a special appeal may be allowed if an annual subscription would be allowed as above, provided that:

- the employer has been or has become an annual subscriber
- the proceeds of the appeal are to be used to meet revenue as opposed to capital expenditure, (to be decided by the office handling the charity's tax affairs), and
- the amount is reasonable.

Chartered Accountants Benevolent Association

Contributions to The Chartered Accountants' Benevolent Association (CABA) by accountancy firms who employ members of the Institute of Chartered Accountants of England and Wales or Institute students may normally be allowed in computing profits for tax purposes. The contributions in any year should not exceed an amount equivalent to the annual subscription of a voting member of the Association, for each Institute member or student so employed.

See too 43.5 (Gift to political party: IT relief).

18.2.5 *Interaction with Gift Aid*

A gift which fails the requirements to be deductible as a business expense on the grounds that it has a philanthropic motive may still qualify for Gift Aid relief. For a company it usually makes no difference whether the deduction is a trading deduction or a corporate Gift Aid donation. For an individual it does make a difference but the combined effect of higher rate relief on the grossed up donation, and the repayment of basic rate to the taxpayer, means that (for a higher rate taxpayer) HMRC is worse off overall if Gift Aid applies.

If HMRC seek to disallow a deduction in trading accounts, they should be referred to the HMRC litigation strategy:

> 8. HMRC seeks to secure the best practicable return for the Exchequer…
> 15. ... HMRC will not usually persist with a tax dispute unless the revenue flows potentially involved justify doing so.[9]

18.2.6 *Deduction/Gift Aid compared*

A person carrying on a business who wishes to make a cash gift to charity may be able to do so in two ways:
(1) A simple gift, treated as an allowable business expense
(2) A gift qualifying for Gift Aid relief

One advantage of claiming a business deduction (as against Gift Aid) is that the onerous rules relating to Gift Aid need not be satisfied. A gift may be made for a benefit. Indeed, when cash gifts are made for a benefit, or not to a charity, the only possibility for relief is in the form of a business deduction. Another advantage (for individuals within the scope of NIC) is that the gift is deductible for NIC purposes. Also there is the possibility of carrying the deduction forward in the form of the relief for trading losses. Of course for individuals the mechanics of relief operate differently: a simple gift is deductible in computing business profits and the charity does not reclaim tax at the basic rate.

From the point of view of the charity, a simple gift may be preferable as the gift (if from an individual, not a company) is not income of the charity for tax purposes. In practice that will not normally be a material consideration.

A payment deductible in computing profits does not qualify for Gift Aid relief.[10]

18.3 Sponsorship: position of sponsor

This section considers the position of the sponsor. For the position of the charity, see 10.1 (Business sponsorship and advertising).

The Business Income Manual provides:

---

9 *https://www.gov.uk/government/publications/litigation-and-settlement-strategy-lss*
10 See 15.18 (Payment deductible for IT).

BIM42555: Advertising expenses: sponsorship [10 June 2016]
Sponsorship is a way for businesses to obtain the commercial benefit of bringing their name, products or services to public attention.
Sponsorship is often a form of advertising. A business tries to obtain benefits for its products, goodwill or reputation and public image by association with a popular or successful event or person.
Although often associated with sporting or cultural events, business sponsorship is not confined to those areas. For example, there is growing expenditure on 'product placement' - paying to ensure that a particular product or service features prominently in a successful television series or film.
Sports clubs and cultural venues offer a range of options for potential sponsors. These include:

- corporate sponsorship packages, often advertised on the club or venue website,
- sponsoring individual productions, players or races,
- long term deals such as sponsoring a football club.

These packages may include both advertising (for example in the event's programme, on clothing, at the venue, through to the name of the event) and hospitality. The hospitality may simply be a certain number of tickets or it may include meals or access to hospitality boxes.
Sponsorship costs are allowable in arriving at the profits of a trade or profession except where they are:

- capital expenditure,
- expenditure not made wholly and exclusively for business purposes, or
- expenditure which is specifically disallowed (such as any entertaining expenditure - see BIM45000 onwards).

18.3.1 *Capital expenditure*

The Business Income Manual provides:

BIM42555. Sponsorship [10 June 2016]
...*Capital expenditure*
Sponsorship costs may be disallowable as capital expenditure (see BIM BIM35000) if, for example:

- a contribution to a permanent exhibition provides an enduring benefit, or
- the sponsor buys capital assets such as racehorses or cars.

Where enduring benefit takes the form of an intangible asset and the sponsor is incorporated, relief may be available under the intangible assets regime. See BIM35501. Such relief is not, however, available under the regime where the intangible asset is linked to a right over land or over a tangible, moveable property. See CIRD25030 for further guidance on this point.

Where the sponsor acquires capital assets such as horses or cars they may be able to claim capital allowances. Guidance on the type of asset that qualifies for relief can be found in the Capital Allowances Manual. Guidance on animals as plant is at CA21220.

18.3.2 *Wholly and exclusively*

The Business Income Manual provides:

BIM42555. Sponsorship [10 June 2016]

...*Wholly & exclusively*

Sponsorship costs are subject to the 'wholly and exclusively' test as with any other expenditure. This means that if there is a non-business purpose to the sponsorship (even if there is also a business purpose) no allowance is due. See BIM38210 for guidance on purpose.

The purpose or purposes of expenditure is a question of fact to be determined by the Tribunal, in cases of dispute. Further guidance on the type of evidence to look for is at BIM42565.

For an example of where the Special Commissioners found that payments of sponsorship were not paid wholly & exclusively for the purposes of the trade, see the discussion of *Executive Network v O'Connor* [1996] SpC56 at BIM42565.

BIM42565. Sponsorship: purpose [10 June 2016]

To be an allowable expense the cost of sponsorship must be incurred wholly and exclusively for the purposes of the trade. Commercial sponsorship is rarely limited to paying over funds to the sponsored activity. The sponsorship will be part of a targeted marketing scheme. When significant sums are involved, the payer will look to maximum exploitation of the sponsorship vehicle.

[The Manual makes some general points on the wholly and exclusively test and continues:]

Typically (but not exclusively) there may be a non-business purpose where:

- the sponsored person is a relative or close friend of the business proprietor or controlling director, or
- the business proprietor or controlling director has a personal involvement in the sponsored activity (such involvement often pre-existing the sponsorship).

The purpose or purposes of expenditure is ultimately a question of fact to be determined by the Tribunal. It is important to obtain and review the contemporary factual evidence.

The type of evidence to look for includes (but is not limited to):

- details of negotiations, including correspondence and contracts;
- how did they become aware of that particular event/person?
- why was it decided to sponsor that particular event/person?
- what alternatives were considered and why were they rejected?
- a copy of the business plan that is usually prepared in commercial sponsorship cases;
- copies of any material prepared by the person/entity seeking sponsorship;
- details of how the sponsorship was intended to bring the name of the business or its products before the intended target audience (including how prominent are any adverts);
- how the sponsorship is exploited in terms of point of sale publicity, the local media, or other available avenues?
- the arrangements to assess and refine the effect of the sponsorship.

The Internet is a useful additional source of information:

- What is said about the sponsorship on the web-site of the business?
- Is there any information on general sites about that sort of activity?
- Is there evidence of previous involvement in the sport or activity?
- What does the person/entity sponsored have to say about their sponsors?

A demonstrable lack of commerciality in the transaction may indicate a non-trade purpose. However, this requires more than simply poor commercial judgment. A sponsor may make a poor choice of vehicle for sponsorship, but that decision may still have been taken purely for business purposes. A bad decision made with purely commercial motives, is still a decision made for the purposes of the trade. Lord Reid made the point in *Ransom v Higgs* [1974] (50 TC 1 at page 82) that:

> "If a trader is actuated by none but commercial motives the Revenue cannot merely say that he has paid too much. He may have been foolish or he may have had what could be fairly regarded as a good commercial reason for paying too much."

The type of evidence that may show a demonstrable lack of commerciality includes:

- sponsoring a relative or close friend,
- paying as much as the sponsored party wants without negotiation of consideration,
- not appearing to have regard to the commercial effect of the activity sponsored, for example, a small local business operating solely in the Newcastle-upon-Tyne area sponsoring an event in Plymouth,
- not considering any other option.

In particular where the parties are connected you should pay close attention to commerciality of the sponsorship.

The case of *Executive Network (Consultants) Ltd v O'Connor*, [1996]

SpC56 (see BIM37970), is an example of where the Special Commissioner found that sponsorship payments were not made wholly & exclusively for the purposes of the trade. The Special Commissioner found that the fact that the amount paid was determined by the amount that the sponsored party needed. This showed that the purpose of the payment was at least partly that of the sponsored party.

As the test is the purpose of the expenditure, the success (or otherwise) of the sponsorship (either in terms of generating commensurately more income or the success of the sponsored person/entity in their chosen field of endeavour) is not by itself a relevant factor. Where the sponsorship fails to generate commensurately more sales it is reasonable to expect, in a purely commercial arrangement, that steps will be taken to improve matters. Failure to identify and take the necessary measure may indicate that the arrangement is uncommercial.

Further evidence that may show a lack of commerciality includes:

- no review of the effect on the trade of the sponsorship,
- the review only considers the success of the sponsored party, not the effect on the trade.

Novices

The fact that a trader chooses to sponsor a novice does not, of itself, mean that they have not acted from a commercial motive. Novice sports persons do seek commercial sponsorship.

The trader may be able to demonstrate that they wanted their name and brand to be associated with a rising star and obtain publicity as a result. If this is their only purpose then the sponsorship is allowable. If the novice sports person is a relative or associate of the proprietor/ director(s), then there may also be a non-business purpose to the sponsorship as in *Executive Network (Consultants) Ltd v O'Connor*. If so, the whole of the expenditure is disallowable.

For example, a trader may decide, for purely commercial reasons, to sponsor a novice athlete who had appealed for sponsorship in the local media after reaching the finals of a major tournament at an unusually early age. There is an agreement between the parties setting out how much the trader will be paying and what services the sports person will perform in return; including a requirement that their equipment will be prominently marked with the sponsor's name. In addition they will appear at certain corporate events. The cost of the sponsorship is allowable (apart from any sums disallowable as capital or entertaining - see BIM42555).

18.3.3 *Entertaining and benefits in kind*

The Business Income Manual provides:

BIM42560: Sponsorship: entertaining and benefits in kind [10 June 2016]

In addition to the advertising, the sponsor may receive other benefits such as tickets to the event or access to hospitality boxes.

For example, a trader may enter a corporate sponsorship package with a theatre. The package includes advertising in the programme and in the foyer. In addition the package includes tickets and meals.

Although the theatre may emphasise the opportunities for business entertaining in its advertisements for sponsorship, the trader may have no use for these tickets or may use the tickets to entertain staff or guests. It is therefore important to establish the facts of the particular case before deciding whether a deduction for the expenditure is allowable.

The type of evidence to look for would include any business plan relating to the sponsorship, minutes of directors meetings and evidence as to how the facilities were actually used.

Entertaining

Where the sponsorship costs include an element of hospitality, this is disallowable under the rules at BIM45055.

Where a single sum is paid for a package that includes both advertising and hospitality, then the sum should be apportioned (see BIM37007).

You should look to see if the sponsored party also offers elements of the package separately as this will provide evidence as to the value of the different parts of the package.

Employment-related benefits in kind

Sponsorship may result in a taxable benefit for employees, including directors.

For example, the controlling director of a company has an existing personal interest in motor racing and is a member of a racing team. The director decides that the company will sponsor that team. The company pays bills for maintaining the team's cars. You should consider whether the expenditure gives rise to benefits taxable on the director as part of their remuneration. See EIM20001 for further guidance on employment-related benefits.

Where corporate hospitality is provided to an employee or director by reason of their employment it may represent an employment-related benefit (EIM21729). If expenditure is incurred as part of the remuneration package then it should be considered as part of the cost of employing the person concerned and a deduction allowed accordingly.

18.4 Gift from partnership

In many cases partnerships should obtain a trading deduction for their giving[11] or sponsorship. However it may happen that a partnership charitable gift is not deductible, in which case the partners will want Gift Aid relief or QIDR. That is in principle possible, as partnerships are transparent for IT.

18.4.1 *Gift Aid from partnership*

The HMRC Guidance Note provides:

> **3.10.3 Donations from all form of partnerships**
> ... when a business[12] partnership makes a donation to a charity or CASC it will be necessary for each individual partner to make their own Gift Aid declaration in order to reflect the correct legal position. Each partner's Gift Aid declaration must contain their name and full home address and be given to the charity or CASC. The amount of each partner's share of the whole donation also needs to be specified in their declaration or in any supporting correspondence given to a charity or CASC...
> The name and address of each partner that makes a Gift Aid donation to a charity or CASC must be recorded and shown separately on the Gift Aid schedule when it makes its claim for repayment of tax to HMRC.[13]

18.4.2 *Company is partner*

Section 1262(2) CTA 2009 provides:

> If a firm makes qualifying charitable donations,[14] a partner's share of the donations is determined for corporation tax purposes in accordance with the firm's profit-sharing arrangements during the accounting period of the firm in which the donations are made.

There is no IT equivalent, and we think this provision exists only for historical reasons.

18.4.3 *Partnership Gift Aid: Reform*

The Office of Tax Simplification recommend a new relief:

---

11 See 18.2 (Charity gift: Deductible expense).

12 There is no such thing as a non-business partnership. But the point may be that we are considering a partnership in the legal sense, not partners in the family or social sense of cohabitees.

13 The position before 2016 is considered in the 2019/20 edition of this work, but the material is now omitted as it is of historical interest only.

14 See 17.3 (Qualifying charitable donation).

> The firm may simply take a deduction for the donation in its computation of trading profits. In this case it would be treated as a gross donation with no eligibility for the charity to reclaim basic rate tax, in parallel to the gift aid system for companies.

That would essentially be a relaxation of the current wholly and exclusively rule. It would be anomalous if the relief applied to partnerships and not to individuals. It would not be a simplification. The OTS do not consider the NIC aspects of the proposal.

One could turn Gift Aid into a deduction relief, which would be a simplification[15] but that is another matter altogether.

The OTS had not thought the matter through. HMRC responded quite correctly:

> The Gift Aid rules for companies operate in a very different way from those for individuals, and the proposal would create inconsistencies with the tax treatment for unincorporated businesses when compared to partnerships, and would involve a major change in primary legislation. Allowing Gift Aid on donations by partnerships would require significant legislation around the Gift Aid declaration and attributing the donations and tax to individual partners. This would likely introduce complexities for the partnership and the individual partners.
> The alternative might be to treat the partnership as though it were a company and provide a new tax relief against profits. This means that all the relief would go to the business and the charity wouldn't be able to claim the BR tax relief. This is very likely to reduce charity income (experience is that donors do not usually increase their donations to take account of their tax relief). It would, however, be a brand new tax relief and would very likely open up obvious questions as to why sole proprietor businesses shouldn't also get the relief. All of this means additional complexity through changes in processes, less income for charities and risks for the Exchequer.[16]

It seems safe to predict that nothing will change.

18.5 Gift of services to charity

Expenditure incurred in the provision of free services to a charity may be disallowed as a business expense on the grounds that it is not incurred for

---

15 See 15.50 (Gift Aid: Critique).

16 OTS, "Review of partnerships: final report" (2015) Annex D, p.53. *https://www.gov.uk/government/uploads/system/uploads/attachment_data/file/396668/ots_partnerships_report_final.pdf*

the purposes of the business; see 18.2 (Charity gift: Deductible expense). However, it will often be the case that services are provided to the charity without incurring any such expenditure. Special provisions apply to seconded employees.

18.6 Secondment of employees

The expenditure of paying the salary of an employee seconded to charity might have been disallowed, as it may not be incurred for the purposes of the trade. Section 70 CTA 2009 provides relief:

> (1) This section applies if a company carrying on a trade ("the employer") makes the services of a person employed for the purposes of the trade available to -
> (a) a charity, or
> (b) an educational establishment[17]
> on a basis that is stated and intended to be temporary.
> (2) In calculating the profits of the trade, a deduction is allowed for expenses of the employer that are attributable to the employee's employment during the period of the secondment...

For income tax the legislation is in s.70 ITTOIA.

"Temporary" is not defined; it is suggested that any period less than one year would qualify as "temporary"; a secondment of a period of less than one year, which was later extended for a further period, would also be "temporary" so long as the decision to extend the secondment was made bona fide and was not preordained. Before seconding an employee to a charity the employer should write to the charity concerned setting out the basis and the proposed duration of the secondment.

No relief is available if the person provides the services of persons who are not their employees (eg services of independent contractors).

It may sometimes be better for the trader to make gifts of cash so that the charity itself would be able to engage independent contractors. It would be necessary to consider whether irrecoverable VAT paid by the charity to the independent contractors would exceed National Insurance contributions on earnings.

There is no objection if the charity pays the employer something for the secondment, or bears some of the expenses of the secondment. The payment may be taxable in the hands of the employer and subject to VAT.

---

17 Section 71 CTA 2009 lists the bodies to be treated as "educational establishments" under s.70(3) CTA.

With regard to VAT: secondments normally give rise to supplies of staff which are subject to VAT at the standard rate. However, there is a concession in VAT Notice 700/34 (Supply of staff and staff bureaux) [31 December 2020]:

> **6.1 Meaning of secondment by an employer**
> An employer (other than an employment business within the meaning of the Employment Agencies Act 1973) may second a member of its staff (the employee) to another business which:
> (a) exercises exclusive control over the allocation and performance of the employee's duties during the period of secondment
> (b) is responsible for paying the employee's remuneration directly to the employee
> (c) discharges the employer's obligations to pay to any third party PAYE, National Insurance Contributions, pension contributions and similar payments relating to the employee
>
> Any payments as are mentioned in paragraphs (b) and (c) above that form the consideration, or part of the consideration for the secondment of the employee to the other business, shall be disregarded in determining the value of seconding the employee...
>
> **6.2 Exceptions**
> An employer shall not be treated as seconding an employee to another business, if the placing of the employee with that other business is done with a view to the employer's (or any other person associated with them) deriving any financial gain from either:
> (a) the placing of the employee with the other business
> (b) any other arrangements or understandings (whether or not contractually binding and whether or not for any consideration) between the employer (or any other person associated with him) and the other business (or any person associated with it) with which the employee is placed

HMRC operates another concession specific to charities - see VAT Notice 701/1 (How VAT affects charities) [31 December 2020]:

> **5.17 Supplies of staff between charities**
> Income received for the supply of staff is a business activity and is normally taxable at the standard rate. But if staff are jointly employed there is no supply of staff for VAT purposes. Staff are regarded as jointly employed if their contracts of employment or letters of appointment make it clear that they have more than one employer and who the employers are. See Companies that supply staff and staff bureaux (VAT Notice 700/34) for more information.
>
> In some circumstances the income from the hire or loan of staff from one

charity or voluntary organisation to another can be treated as non-business and outside the scope of VAT. This is subject to the following conditions, the:

- employee has been engaged only in the non-business activities of the lending charity or organisation and is being seconded to assist in the non-business activities of the borrowing charity or organisation
- payment for the supply of the employee's services does not exceed the employee's normal remuneration

A 'voluntary organisation' is a body who operates other than for profit, but does not include any public or local authority. 'Normal remuneration' means the total costs incurred by the lending charity or organisation in employing the member of staff including National Insurance and pension scheme contributions.

Although not mentioned specifically in paragraph 5.17 of VAT Notice 701/1, the word "business" in a VAT context does not always share the same meaning as in an everyday or even direct tax context, so care is advised when construing the term "non-business" in the above - see 35.14 (Business).

18.7 Gift of trading stock, plant/machinery

18.7.1 *Cost of trading stock allowable*

The HMRC view was formerly set out in Tax Bulletin 23 (RI 151 Donations of trading stock to charities):

> Provided that the trading stock was originally manufactured and/or purchased for sale in the ordinary course of trade, its later donation [to charity] will not cause its cost to be disallowed for tax purposes.

Strictly, the question is whether the expenditure was incurred wholly and exclusively for the purposes of the trade. RI 151 is now classified as obsolete but there is no reason to think that HMRC the view has changed.

18.7.2 *Deemed trading receipt*

The relevant legislation is found in Chapter 10 Part 3 CTA 2009 and, for income tax, Chapter 11A Part 2 ITTOIA 2005. This puts into statute the former case law rule that when a trader takes stock from their business, or they transfer stock to their business stock the transfer should be treated for tax purposes as if it were a sale or purchase at market value.[18]

---

18 *Sharkey v Wernher* 36 TC 275.

For completeness: Transfer pricing rules take precedence over this rule but that topic is not discussed here.

18.7.3 *"Trading stock"*

Section 156 CTA 2009 provides:

> (1) In this Chapter "trading stock", in relation to a trade, means anything (whether land or other property)--
> (a) which is sold in the ordinary course of the trade, or
> (b) which would be so sold if it were mature or its manufacture, preparation or construction were complete.
> (2) It does not include--
> (a) materials used in the manufacture, preparation or construction of any such thing,
> (b) any services performed in the ordinary course of the trade, or
> (c) any article produced, or any material used, in the performance of any such services.

The trading stock rules discussed here apply only to trading stock in the strict sense. They do not apply to professions, and they do not apply to a person who donates their services to charity. In such cases one does not substitute market value. Thus if an artist makes a gift of their painting to charity, one does not substitute market value and there is no need of relief under s.105 CTA 2009. This continues the position as it was before the enactment of the rules discussed below.[19]

18.7.4 *Appropriation from trading stock*

Section 157 CTA 2009 provides:

> (1) This section applies if trading stock of a company's trade is appropriated by the company for any other purpose.
> (2) In calculating the profits of the trade--
> (a) the amount which the stock appropriated would have realised if sold in the open market at the time of the appropriation is brought into account as a receipt, and
> (b) the value of anything in fact received for it is left out of account.
> (3) The receipt is treated as arising on the date of the appropriation.

18.7.5 *Disposal not in the course of trade*

Section 159 CTA 2009 provides:

---

19 *Mason v Innes* 44 TC 26.

(1) This section applies if--
(a) trading stock of a trade is disposed of otherwise than in the course of the trade, and
(b) section 157 does not apply.
(2) In calculating the profits of the trade--
(a) the amount which the stock disposed of would have realised if sold in the open market at the time of the disposal is brought into account as a receipt, and
(b) any consideration obtained for it is left out of account.
(3) The receipt is treated as arising on the date of the disposal.

18.7.6 *Acquisition not in course of trade*

Section 160 CTA 2009 provides:

(1) This section applies if--
(a) trading stock of a trade has been acquired otherwise than in the course of the trade, and
(b) section 158 does not apply.
(2) In calculating the profits of the trade--
(a) the cost of the stock is taken to be the amount which it would have realised if sold in the open market at the time of the acquisition, and
(b) the value of anything in fact given for it is left out of account.
(3) The cost is treated as being incurred on the date of the acquisition.

18.7.7 *Stock gift to charity*

Section 105 CTA 2009 provides:

(1) This section applies if a company carrying on a trade ("the donor") gives an article for the purposes of--
(a) a charity, a registered club[20] or a body listed in subsection (4)[21], or
(b) a designated educational establishment (see section 106),
and the article is one manufactured, or of a class or description sold, by the donor in the course of the trade.
(2) In calculating the profits of the trade, no amount is required to be brought into account as a receipt in consequence of the disposal of the article.

---

20 ie a CASC: see 41.2 (Types of club and terminology).

21 Subsection (4) provides: "The bodies referred to in subsection (1)(a) are--
(a) the Trustees of the National Heritage Memorial Fund, and
(b) the Historic Buildings and Monuments Commission for England"

Section 105(6) signposts two exceptions:

> This section is subject to
> [a] section 203 of CTA 2010 (certain disposals of investments to charity)[22] and
> [b] section 939F of that Act (removal of corporation tax relief in respect of tainted charity donations etc).[23]

Section 107 CTA 2009 provides an overlapping relief for (in short) a gift by a company of trading stock of medical supplies or medical equipment. There is no requirement that the gift be made to a charity, it must instead by made "for humanitarian purposes" (s.107(1)(b)) and the supply of equipment is for human use (s.107(1)(c)). This means the gift may be made directly to a foreign body (which need not be a charity in the tax sense). Section 107 is an example of the sort of micro-detailed provision which transgresses the traditional objects of fiscal policy: equity and simplicity. No doubt it reflected effective lobbying and the Chancellor's need for a good headline. Charity tax is particularly vulnerable to this tinkering.[24]

18.7.8 *Gift of plant/machinery*

Section 63 Capital Allowances Act 2001 provides relief from the balancing charge which might otherwise apply:

> (2) If a person carrying on a relevant qualifying activity makes a gift of plant or machinery used in the course of the activity—
> (a) to a charitable trust,
> (aa) to a charitable company,
> (ab) to a registered club within the meaning of Chapter 9 of Part 13 of CTA 2010 (community amateur sports clubs),
> (b) to a body listed in section 468 of CTA 2010 (various heritage bodies and museums)[25], or
> (c) for the purposes of a designated educational establishment within the meaning of section 110 of ITTOIA 2005 or section 106 of CTA 2009 (gifts to educational establishments),
>
> the disposal value of the plant or machinery is nil.
> (3) In subsection (2) "relevant qualifying activity" means a qualifying

---

22 In short: QIDR has priority: See 21.14 (QIDR relief: Position of donor).
23 For income tax the legislation is in s.108 ITTOIA.
24 For another example, see 25.1 (IHT 10% incentive relief).
25 See App 5.3 (National/eligible bodies).

activity consisting of—
- (a) a trade,
- (b) an ordinary property business,
- (c) a furnished holiday lettings business,
- (d) an overseas property business, or
- (e) a profession or vocation.

(4) Subsection (2)
- (a) needs to be read with section 109 of ITTOIA 2005 and section 108 of CTA 2009 (which provide for a charge to tax if subsection (2) applies in circumstances in which the donor or a connected person receives a benefit attributable to the gift) and
- (b) is subject to section 809ZM of ITA 2007 and section 939F of CTA 2010 (removal of tax relief in respect of tainted charity donations etc).

18.7.9 *Clawback of relief*

Section 108 CTA 2009 provides a clawback charge on benefits:

> (1) This section applies if a company carrying on a trade makes a gift in relation to which relief is given under -
> - (a) section 105 [gifts of trading stock to charities]
> - (b) section 107(2) [gift of medical supplies or equipment], or
> - (c) section 63(2) of CAA 2001(gifts to charities etc of plant or machinery used in the trade)
>
> and the company, or a person connected with company, receives a benefit which is in any way attributable to the making of the gift.
>
> (2) This section also applies if -
> - (a) relief is given under section 107(3) for costs of transportation, delivery or distribution incurred by a company carrying on a trade, and
> - (b) the company, or a person connected with the company, receives a benefit which is in any way attributable to the company's incurring of those costs.
>
> (3) An amount equal to the value of the benefit -
> - (a) is brought into account in calculating the profits of the trade, as a receipt of the trade arising in the accounting period in which the benefit is received, or
> - (b) if the company has permanently ceased to carry on the trade before the benefit is received, is treated as a post-cessation receipt (see Chapter 15).

The IT equivalent is s.109 ITTOIA.

18.8 Lease to charity at undervalue

Property Income Manual provides a sensible concession here:

> **PIM2220: Properties not let at a commercial rent** [14 Oct 2016]
> ... If a property is let at less than the full commercial rent, any expenditure relating to that property will normally have been incurred partly for a benevolent or philanthropic purpose and will consequently fail the 'wholly and exclusively' test in ICTA88/S74(1)(a) and ITTOIA05/S272. Although, in strictness, no expenditure on such properties is admissible as an expense of the rental business, expenses can be deducted up to the amount of rent derived from that property.

18.9 Gift of goods and services: VAT

18.9.1 *Disposal of goods to charity*

The disposal of business goods for no consideration is treated for VAT purposes as a supply of goods: para 5(1) sch 4 VATA 1994 provides, subject to immaterial exceptions:

> 5(1) ... where goods forming part of the assets of a business are transferred or disposed of by or under the directions of the person carrying on the business so as no longer to form part of those assets, whether or not for a consideration, that is a supply by him of goods.
>
> ...
>
> (5) ... sub-paragraph (1) ... above shall [not] require anything which a person carrying on a business does otherwise than for a consideration in relation to any goods to be treated as a supply except in a case where that person or any of his predecessors is a person who (disregarding this paragraph) has or will become entitled—
>
> (a) under sections 25 and 26, to credit for the whole or any part of the VAT on the supply or importation of those goods or of anything comprised in them; or
>
> (b) under a scheme embodied in regulations made under section 39, to a repayment of VAT on the supply or importation of those goods or of anything comprised in them.
>
> ...
>
> (6) Anything which is a supply of goods or services by virtue of sub-paragraph (1) ... above is to be treated as made in the course or furtherance of the business (if it would not otherwise be so treated); and in the case of a business carried on by an individual—
>
> (a) sub-paragraph (1) above applies to any transfer or disposition of goods in favour of himself personally ...

(This is an exception to the usual rule that anything done for no consideration is not a supply.) The value of the supply, when the supply is for *no* consideration, is generally deemed to be (in effect) market value: see para 6 Part 2 sch 6 VATA 1994:

> 6(1) Where there is a supply of goods by virtue of—
>
> ...
>
> (b) paragraph 5(1) or 6 of Schedule 4 but otherwise than for a consideration) ...
>
> ...
>
> then, except where the person making the supply opts under paragraph A1(3) above for valuation on the flat-rate basis or paragraph 10 below applies, the value of the supply shall be determined as follows.
> (2) The value of the supply shall be taken to be—
> (a) such consideration in money as would be payable by the person making the supply if he were, at the time of the supply, to purchase goods identical in every respect (including age and condition) to the goods concerned; or
> (b) where the value cannot be ascertained in accordance with paragraph (a) above, such consideration in money as would be payable by that person if he were, at that time, to purchase goods similar to, and of the same age and condition as, the goods concerned; or
> (c) where the value can be ascertained in accordance with neither paragraph (a) nor paragraph (b) above, the cost of producing the goods concerned if they were produced at that time.
> (3) For the purposes of sub-paragraph (2) above the amount of consideration in money that would be payable by any person if he were to purchase any goods shall be taken to be the amount that would be so payable after the deduction of any amount included in the purchase price in respect of VAT on the supply of the goods to that person.

It should be noted that the "open market value" concept set out in s19(5) VATA 1994 is deliberately not used:

> (5) For the purposes of this Act the open market value of a supply of goods or services shall be taken to be the amount that would fall to be taken as its value under [s19(2) VATA 1994] if the supply were for such consideration in money as would be payable by a person standing in no such relationship with any person as would affect that consideration.

If, therefore, the business making the gift of goods to a charity were in such relationship with the producer of those goods as to be able to purchase those goods at a less-than-market price, that would be a relevant consideration for the purposes of para 6 Part 2 sch 6 VATA 1994.

Because of the provisions of para 6 Part 2 sch 6 VATA 1994, the gift of business goods to a charity may give rise to a VAT charge. If the charity undertakes to pay the VAT, any payment it makes would be consideration for VAT purposes. This would take the transaction outside the rules on "gifts".

There is a relief for the donation of goods for sale or export or letting by a charity or "profits-to-charity person": this is a zero-rated supply; see Item 2 Group 15 sch 8 VATA 1994.

The alternative is for the trader to sell the goods to the charity at a nominal consideration. The VAT charge is then calculated by reference to the actual (nominal) consideration. The rule in para 6 Part 2 Sch 6 only applies if the supply is "otherwise than for a consideration".

18.9.2 *Loan of goods to charity*

Similar problems arise if a trader wishes to allow a charity to have the use of business assets (for any purpose other than a purpose of the trader's own business). For VAT purposes this amounts to a supply of services, even if the goods are made available for no consideration: para 5(4) sch 4 VATA 1994. If goods are made available for *no* consideration, the value of the supply is normally deemed to be the full cost of providing the services: para 7 Part 2 sch 6 VATA 1994.

Similar rules apply to gifts of land or allowing the free use of land: para 9 sch 4 VATA 1994.

It will often be better to charge the charity a nominal sum. Then the value of the supply is the actual (nominal) amount charged, and VAT is charged accordingly. Sales or loans of assets at an undervalue can therefore lead to considerable VAT savings for the donor (the transaction would only be for no consideration for VAT purposes if the charity is making no payment to the donor, including VAT).

18.9.3 *Provision of services to charity*

The provision of services for no consideration is not usually a supply for VAT purposes, and does not give rise to a VAT charge.

18.9.4 *Goods/services from connected person*

Paragraph 1 Part 2 sch 6 VATA 1994 is intended to counteract VAT avoidance. That paragraph applies when a person makes a supply for a consideration in money at an undervalue to a connected person who is not entitled to recover all its input tax. The Commissioners may then direct that the supply should be taken to be at open market value (as defined - see s19(5) VATA 1994) for VAT purposes. A direction may be made up to three years after the supply, so that if supplies are made on a regular basis a direction may lead to a substantial VAT liability.

However, no problem arises unless the trader and the charity are "connected" as defined by s.1122 CTA 2010. A trader is connected with the trustees of a charitable trust if they are the settlor or "connected" with the settlor. The provision of goods at an undervalue to a charitable trust may constitute the trader a "settlor" having regard to the wide definition of "settlor" which applies (see s.1122 CTA 2010). Charitable trustees are also connected with a close company (or quasi-close company) in which they are participators, and any company controlled by such a company. However, an individual trader is not connected with a charitable company unless they (alone or with others) have "control"[26] of the company. No problem can thus arise whenever a trader is dealing with a charitable company of which they have no control.

18.10 Payroll giving scheme

Employers can also assist charities by encouraging employees to give, in particular by providing a payroll giving scheme. The payroll giving scheme is only open to employees whose employer chooses to operate the scheme. See 19.2 (Payroll giving: Operation).

26 For the definition of control, see s.450 CTA 2010.

CHAPTER NINETEEN

PAYROLL GIVING

19.1 Payroll giving scheme

This chapter considers the payroll giving scheme, also called the payroll deduction scheme. ITEPA uses both expressions but "payroll giving" is more common, perhaps as it sounds more attractive to the donor.

19.1.1 *Payroll giving: History*

The scheme was introduced in 1986.

In 1997 the Review of Charity Taxation Consultative Document called it a "disappointment". It records that in 1997/98, 370,000 employees gave £27 million. Since then the Government have run a series of schemes to encourage payroll giving. An uncharitable commentator would dismiss them as gimmicks. The first was a 10% supplement funded by "money provided by parliament". That applied from 2001 to 2004. The supplement broadly equalled the NIC deduction on the salary (for which there is no relief). Next, in 2004 the Government announced a £8.3m programme for small and medium enterprises. This ended in 2007.[1]

By 2006, 600,000 employees gave a total of £87m and in 2009/10,

1 See Institute of Fundraising, "A Review of the Payroll Giving SME Grants Programme" (April 2008) *http://www.payrollgivingcentre.com/attachments/SME_Grants_Programme_Report_20508.pdf*

724,000 donors gave £106m, so the scheme now perhaps seems worthwhile, though only marginally, since:

(1) the figures are tiny compared to Gift Aid; and
(2) All the money given under the payroll giving scheme could be given under Gift Aid, and most of it probably would.

A further round of consultation in 2013 did not immediately come up with any ideas beyond tinkering details.[2]

On 24 March 2015, a Memorandum of Understanding ("MOU") was signed by representatives of the Treasury, Payroll Giving Agencies and some charities in response to the consultation. This explains:

> This voluntary agreement has been drawn up following extensive contacts between Government, Payroll Giving Agencies and representatives from the charity sector. Whilst not a legally binding document its authority is derived from its endorsement by the participants. Payroll Giving Agencies, the Government and charities agree to work together constructively in our complementary roles.[3]

The MOU sets out standard information to be included in Payroll Giving Agencies' disbursement reports and details of an online portal for reporting figures for giving through the various Agencies.

19.1.2 *Welsh/Scots taxpayers*

HMRC say:

> 26. Tax relief for donations made to charity under the payroll giving scheme is given at source before an employee's PAYE tax is calculated, and is given at their marginal rate. Where the employee's marginal rate is derived from the Welsh rates of income tax then the relief will apply at that marginal rate.[4]

19.2 Payroll giving: Operation

Section 713(1) ITEPA provides:

---

2 HM Government "Payroll Giving: summary of responses" (September 2013) *https://www.gov.uk/government/uploads/system/uploads/attachment_data/file/239476/payroll_giving_summary_of_responses.pdf*

3 *http://www.institute-of-fundraising.org.uk/library/payroll-giving-mou/*

4 HMRC, " Clarifying the Scope of the Welsh Rates of Income Tax: Technical Note" (2018) *https://assets.publishing.service.gov.uk/government/uploads/system/uploads/attachment_data/file/750621/Welsh_rates_of_Income_Tax_technical_note.pdf*

This section applies if—

(a) an individual is entitled to receive payments of, or on account of, PAYE income[5] in respect of which PAYE regulations require deductions or repayments of income tax in accordance with those regulations, and

(b) at the request of the individual, the person making the payments (the "payer") withholds sums from them as donations.

The scheme only applies to a donor who is an individual. This excludes companies and trustees; but such persons will not usually be in receipt of PAYE income.

Section 713 ITEPA then sets out the relief:

(2) In determining whether there is such a requirement under PAYE regulations for the purposes of subsection (1)(a), any requirement under the regulations which requires the deduction of an amount in calculating the payments of, or on account of, PAYE income is to be disregarded.

(3) The amount of the donations is allowed as a deduction in calculating the amount of the individual's income which is charged to tax in accordance with subsection (4).

(4) In the case of a payment of, or on account of—

(a) taxable earnings from an employment, the deduction is allowed from the taxable earnings from the employment in calculating the net taxable earnings from the employment for the relevant tax year for the purposes of Part 2 (see section 11(1));

(b) taxable specific income from an employment, the deduction is allowed from that taxable specific income in calculating the net taxable specific income from the employment for the relevant tax year for the purposes of Part 2 (see section 12(1));

(c) taxable pension income for a pension, annuity or other item of pension income, the deduction is allowed from that taxable pension income in calculating the net taxable pension income for that income for the relevant tax year for the purposes of Part 9 (see section 567(3));

(d) taxable social security income for a taxable benefit, the deduction is allowed from that taxable social security income in calculating the net taxable social security income for that benefit for the relevant tax year for the purposes of Part 10 (see section 658(3)).

(5) For the purposes of subsection (4) "relevant tax year" means—

(a) in the case of paragraphs (a) and (b), the tax year in which the

5 "PAYE Income" is defined in s.683 ITEPA.

> donation is withheld, and
>
> (b) in the case of paragraphs (c) and (d), the tax year for which the income referred to in subsection (1)(a) is taxable pension income or taxable social security income, as the case may be.

The main features of the scheme are as follows:

(1) It is up to the individual to decide:
  - (a) Whether to join the scheme.
  - (b) How much to donate, up to the amount of their PAYE income. There is no maximum limit on donations. However, the amount of relief cannot exceed the PAYE income of the year.
  - (c) To which charity the money is to be paid.

(2) The person paying the PAYE income deducts the appropriate sum from the PAYE income and pays it to an agent.

(3) The agent pays the sum (less its expenses) to the charity; or it may give the employee a voucher to pass on to the charity of their choice by way of gift.

The donation is not deductible for the purposes of National Insurance contributions.

Regulation 3 Income Tax (PAYE) Regulations 2003 provides that the donation is deducted in computing "Net PAYE income":

> (1) "Net PAYE income" means PAYE income less any—
>
> (a) allowable pension contributions, and
>
> (b) allowable donations to charity.
>
> (2) In paragraph (1) ...
>
> "allowable donations to charity" means any donation which is withheld from the payment of PAYE income and for which a deduction must be allowed under section 713 of ITEPA (donations to charity: payroll deduction scheme).

This takes the payment out of the scope of PAYE: see regulation 4. 21.

See too 15.43.7 (Personal allowance taper).

19.2.1 *Tainted donation rules*

Section 713(6) ITEPA provides:

> This section is subject to section 809ZM of ITA 2007 (removal of income tax relief in respect of tainted charity donations etc).

See 7.22 (Tainted payroll giving).

19.3 Approved scheme/agency

19.3.1 *Approved scheme*

Section 714(2) ITEPA provides:

> In this section—
> "approved scheme" means a scheme which is approved (or is of a kind approved) by an officer of Revenue and Customs and under which—
> (a) the payer is required to pay sums withheld to a body which is an approved agent at the time of the withholding, and
> (b) the approved agent is required—
> (i) to pay sums withheld to the specified charity or charities, or
> (ii) in a case where the agent is itself a specified charity, to retain any sum due to itself;

19.3.2 *Approved agent*

Section 714(3) ITEPA provides:

> For the purposes of this section a body is an "approved agent" if it is approved by an officer of Revenue and Customs for the purpose of paying donations to one or more charities.

A list of agencies approved to operate payroll giving schemes is available on the HMRC website.[6] The three largest agencies are:

Charities Aid Foundation (which has the trade name: Give as You Earn)
Charities Trust
Charitable Giving, previously South West Charitable Giving

A few agencies are set up by a single employer, eg Saatchi Charitable Trust, Minet Employees Charitable Trust. A few are affiliated to a particular charity, eg Motor & Allied Trades Benevolent Fund.

19.3.3 *Regulations*

Section 715 ITEPA provides:

> (1) The Treasury may by regulations prescribe the circumstances in which an officer of Revenue and Customs may grant or withdraw approval of any—
> (a) scheme,

6 *https://www.gov.uk/government/publications/payroll-giving-approved-agencies/list-of-approved-payroll-giving-agencies*

(b) kind of scheme, or
(c) agent.

(2) The circumstances, whether relating to the terms of schemes or the qualifications of agents or otherwise, are to be such as the Treasury think fit.

(3) The Treasury may by regulations make provision—

(a) requiring a payer or agent who participates (or has at any time participated) in an approved scheme under this Part—
  (i) to comply, within a prescribed period, with any notice which an officer of Revenue and Customs give to the payer or agent to make available for their inspection documents or records of a prescribed kind,
  (ii) in prescribed circumstances, to furnish to an officer of Revenue and Customs prescribed information;

(b) for, and in relation to, appeals against a refusal by an officer of Revenue and Customs to approve, or the officer's withdrawal of approval from, any—
  (i) scheme,
  (ii) kind of scheme, or
  (iii) agent;

(c) generally for giving effect to sections 713 and 714.

In this subsection "prescribed" means prescribed by the regulations.

The regulations are the Charitable Deductions (Approved Schemes) Regulations 1986. These were amended by the Charitable Deductions (Approved Schemes) (Amendment) Regulations 2014, which reduced the amount of time that the approved agency has to distribute the funds to the designated charity from 60 days to 35 days.

19.4 Conditions for relief

It is essential that the individual's employer operates the scheme. If an employer does not choose to operate the scheme then their employees cannot participate in it.

Charities may prefer to raise funds by informal payroll giving, obtaining tax relief through Gift Aid. Indeed that may be better for the charities as they obtain the basic rate tax (rather than the donor receiving the relief),

19.5 "Donations"

The word "donation" is used as a label which brings in a number of rules. Section 714(1) ITEPA provides:

For the purposes of this Part "donations" means sums which—

(a) are withheld by the payer under a scheme which is an approved scheme at the time of the withholding,
(b) constitute gifts by the individual to one or more specified charities under the scheme, and
(c) satisfy the conditions (if any) set out in the scheme.

19.5.1 *"Gift"*

The donation must be a "gift" to the charity. On the meaning of "gift", see 15.4 ("Gift"). A charity may offer certain rights of admission, in return for Gift Aid payments; but this does not apply to payroll gifts. A charity may offer "small" benefits in return for a Gift Aid donation. There is no equivalent provision for payroll giving, but if the benefits are only nominal, or non-contractual, the payment may still be a "gift".

HMRC Guidance Note provides at 4.4.9:

> **Charity giving benefits to an employee in return for donations**
> If a charity provides benefits (for example, free admission to properties or free or discounted tickets to events) in return for donations, the employee's donations will not qualify for relief under Payroll Giving. However, items of low value, for example newsletters, stickers or badges, would still allow an employee's donation to qualify for relief under the scheme.

19.5.2 *"Specified charity"*

Section 714(2) ITEPA provides:

> In this section—
> "charity" includes each of the bodies mentioned in section 468 of CTA 2010;[7]
> "specified charity" means a charity specified by the individual.

The individual must be free to select any charity they wish to receive their donation.

The agent operating the scheme, who will receive the sums deducted from the individual's PAYE income, must be prepared to pay those sums on to the charity of the individual's choice. However, charities associated with particular industries or areas need not be deterred from acting as collecting agent for companies associated with their particular area or concern. To satisfy the tax requirement, all that is necessary is to draw

---

7 See App 5.3 (National/eligible bodies).

fairly to the employee's attention the fact that they have an option to donate either to the agent charity or to others. Nothing in the legislation restricts the agent's role to "impartial canvassing"; publicity or propaganda for the particular charity involved does not involve any conflict of interest.

19.6 Position of charity receiving donation

Section 521A ITA provides:

> (1) This section applies if gifts are made to charitable trusts by individuals and the gifts are donations for the purposes of Part 12 of ITEPA 2003 (payroll giving).
> (2) Income tax is charged on the gifts under this section.
> (3) It is charged on the full amount of the gifts arising in the tax year.
> (4) But a gift is not taken into account in calculating total income so far as it is applied to charitable purposes only.
> (5) The trustees of the charitable trust are liable for any tax charged under this section.

For charitable companies, the corporation tax equivalent is s.472A CTA 2010.

19.7 Donation not qualifying for relief

It may happen that HMRC argues that a donation which was thought to fall under the payroll giving scheme does not qualify for tax relief. By the time the dispute arises, the PAYE deduction will already have been made. HMRC then have three remedies:

(1) They may collect the tax due from the employee by issuing a new PAYE Code under Regs 13, 14, and 14A Income Tax (Pay As you Earn) Regulations 2003 (the "PAYE Regulations"). They collect the unpaid tax by increasing the level of deductions made by the employer in the future.

(2) HMRC may collect tax directly from the employee if (in short) the employer has been operating PAYE in good faith: reg. 72 PAYE Regulations.

In either case, the employee has a right of appeal.

(3) HMRC may collect tax from the employer, as it is tax on PAYE income which should have been deducted by the employer and was not: reg 80 PAYE Regulations. This does not apply to tax which has already been subject to a direction under reg 72 PAYE Regulations.

In this case, the employer has a right of appeal.

In practice it is rare that a payment made under Payroll Giving will not qualify for relief. One of the roles of the Payroll Giving approved agencies is to carry out due diligence into the recipient charities. HMRC's Guidance Note makes clear that it is HMRC's view that the responsibility of the Agency to ensure the charity qualifies:

> 4.2.3 The Agency is responsible for ensuring that the donations that it receives are only distributed to organisations that are charities. If the Agency cannot be certain that a nominated organisation is a charity it can ask HMRC Charities for confirmation.

19.8 Employer's expenses

HMRC accept that the employer's expenses of operating the payroll giving scheme will normally be deductible as incurred wholly and exclusively for the employer's business. HMRC Guidance Note states:

> **Employer's costs**
> 4.3.6 There may be some additional cost for the employer in running the scheme but these are likely to be absorbed in the existing payroll costs. Any additional costs are allowable as an expenses deduction when calculating the employer's profits for tax purposes.

If the employer makes payments to the agent to cover the agent's expenses, the payments are deductible for trading purposes, or may be treated as expenses of management of an investment company. See ss.72 and 1236 CTA 2009 and s.72 ITTOIA. HMRC's Guidance Note states:

> **Other costs**
> 4.3.7 Most Agencies make a small charge to cover their administration expenses. Their charge is usually deducted from the employees' donations before they're passed on to charities. An Agency's charges should be included in the contract with an employer. If the employer decides to pay the Agency's cost then this is also allowable as a deductible expense against the employers profit.
> Some Agencies don't charge for administration because they're funded by fundraising organisations that help employers to promote payroll giving in the workplace. They may charge the charities that they recruit new donors for instead.

The employer is not required to pay the agent's expenses (the agent might fund itself out of the employees' donations) but the scheme would obviously be more attractive to employees if their donations reach the charity of their choice without deduction for administrative expenses.

19.9 Gift Aid interaction/comparison

Gifts within the payroll deduction scheme are excluded from Gift Aid relief. See 15.17 (Payroll giving: Condition C)).

It may be helpful to summarise briefly the differences between the payroll giving scheme and Gift Aid:

(1) The payroll giving scheme is only open to individuals whose employers operate the scheme: Gift Aid is available to all.
(2) The individual need not make a Gift Aid declaration.
(3) The payment is made gross: the charity does not recover tax on the payment. Instead the donor enjoys the benefit of tax relief on the amount given. (But this is more a difference of procedure than substance. A donor could give more to allow for the benefit of tax relief.)
(4) The "benefit rules" are different.
(5) The gift is deductible from PAYE income only.

19.10 Salary sacrifice scheme

CIOT say:

> There is a way in which an employee can get relief from all taxes on donations to charity. An employer can nominate one or more charities and invite employees to accept a reduced salary or bonus in return for the employer itself making a donation to the charity under Gift Aid. An individual who then donates £100 to charity not only gets full income tax relief for the donation but also gets relief for employee NIC purposes (and the employer also saves at 13.8% (currently) in terms of employer NIC). The employer may then (and often does) contribute the saved employer NIC to the charity.
>
> 2.6 We understand that HMRC accept that such salary or bonus sacrifice arrangements are effective where it is the employer that nominates the charity or charities concerned and we are aware of examples where this happens in practice. Consequently, this option is currently more attractive for individuals than either Payroll Giving or Gift Aid if the employer nominates a charity the individual wants to donate to. In our view the NIC saving is a significant point and one that detracts from the attraction of using Payroll Giving.
>
> 2.7 For reasons which are not entirely clear, HMRC seem to accept the arrangement described above (at 2.5 and 2.6) where the employer nominates one or more charities but not where the employee nominates

> the charity (eg under a letter of wishes) to which he (or she) would like their employer to contribute. The suggestion is that the employee is simply re-directing income to which they would be entitled to a charity, but we believe that where a proper salary waiver or letter of wishes is effected this should not be a problem that cannot be overcome.
>
> 2.8 Furthermore, this appears to differ from HMRC's position concerning for example, reductions in bonus in return for employer contributions into registered pension schemes (eg see *http://www.hmrc.gov.uk/manuals/eimanual/EIM42785.htm*). It is unclear why HMRC take a different approach for pension contributions compared to charitable donations and we think that charitable giving would be significantly increased if this were not the case.
>
> 2.9 We can understand that allowing relief for employee NICs on Payroll Giving may lead to an imbalance with Gift Aid, and may dis-incentivise some individuals from making one-off Gift Aid donations if regular Payroll Giving donations are more tax efficient, but if the Government wants to encourage employers to offer Payroll Giving arrangements, and the case is by no means made that Payroll Giving should be encouraged over other forms of giving such as Gift Aid, allowing a deduction for employer NICs would encourage this.[8]

19.11 Payroll giving: Critique

In December 2010 Justine Greening said in a public letter to CIOT:

> I do not propose to bring Payroll Giving within Gift Aid. Payroll Giving is a quite separate scheme which gives all tax relief to the donor and which many employers operate extremely successfully. I would like to maintain the variety in giving mechanisms. However, I would like to examine Payroll Giving to see if there are ways to improve its operation and encourage take up.[9]

We suggest that everything that could be done to encourage take up has now been done.[10]

It is suggested that the payroll giving scheme should be repealed.

It made some sense when introduced in 1986, as an alternative to the cumbersome relief for charity deeds of covenant. There has been no need

---

8 *http://www.tax.org.uk/Resources/CIOT/Documents/2013/04/130419%20Payroll%20Giving%20Consultation%20-%20CIOT%20comments.pdf*

9 *http://webarchive.nationalarchives.gov.uk/20130129110402/http://www.hm-treasury.gov.uk/d/gift_aid_forum_letter_to_peter_fanning_from_est_031210.pdf*

10 See 19.1 (Payroll giving scheme).

for it since the introduction of Gift Aid in 2000. Employers can still arrange payroll giving, and income tax relief can be obtained under Gift Aid as easily as it can under the Payroll Giving scheme.

That would be a worthwhile simplification. In principle there should be at no cost to charity or to the Revenue. In fact, charities may slightly benefit overall, since they would obtain the benefit basic rate relief. Abolition will also avoid anomaly that relief under the payroll giving scheme will be at the (future) Scottish rate of income tax, and relief under deeds of covenant will be at the basic rate of income tax.[11]

The justification for the relief is that it has the beneficial effect of a public statement encouraging payroll giving. Quite apart from the fact that it has not been particularly successful, it is questionable whether tax legislation is the place to make such statements.

11 See 15.63 (Repealed Gift Aid reliefs).

CHAPTER TWENTY

INTEREST-FREE LOANS TO CHARITIES

Cross references

The following topic is considered elsewhere:
9.9 (Loan from subsidiary co to charity)

20.1 Interest-free loan to charity

A person may be prepared to make an interest-free loan to a charity, thereby in effect giving the income and gains which the money lent would otherwise have generated. At first sight, this looks like a relatively painless and convenient way of giving. As the lender ceases to have any income from the money lent, they in effect obtain tax relief at all rates on the income and gains forgone. Moreover, if the loan is repayable on demand, or at short notice, their commitment to the charity may be terminated at any time.

Interest free loans normally raise no tax problems, but there are several provisions which need consideration.

20.2 IT settlement provisions

20.2.1 *Loan by individual*

Section 624(1) ITTOIA provides:

> Income which arises under a settlement is treated for income tax purposes as the income of the settlor and of the settlor alone if it

arises—

(a) during the life of the settlor, and

(b) from property in which the settlor has an interest.

A loan on beneficial terms is in principle a "settlement"[1] and one in which the lender (settlor) has an interest.[2]

However, s.620(1) ITTOIA provides that "settlement" does not include a charitable loan arrangement. This term is defined in s.620(5):

> "charitable loan arrangement" means any arrangement so far as it consists of a loan of money made by an individual to a charity either—
>
> (a) for no consideration, or
>
> (b) for a consideration which consists only of interest ...

A loan is by definition made for consideration, the promise of the borrower to repay. That obviously does not count.

It is considered that a loan of "money" includes a loan made in a foreign currency.

So the income tax settlement provisions could only apply in the case of a loan by an individual which is:

(1) issued at a discount or for a premium; or

(2) made to a non-charity (eg to a non-charitable subsidiary of a charity)

In these cases one would need to consider whether any income arises under the settlement. It is considered that this would only be the case if there is some special feature of the loan, eg if the terms of the loan required the borrower to invest in a particular income producing asset.[3]

20.2.2 *Loan by company*

Section 624 ITTOIA does not apply to a lender which is a company. Section 627(4) ITTOIA provides:

> The rule in section 624(1) does not apply in relation to income which—
>
> (a) arises under a settlement, and

1 *IRC v Levy* 56 TC 68.

2 *Wachtel v IRC* 46 TC 543; see Kessler, *Taxation of Non-Residents and Foreign Domiciliaries* (21st ed., 2022-23), para 47.6.4 (Beneficial loan or guarantee) online version *https://www.foreigndomiciliaries.co.uk*

3 See *Jones v Garnett* [2007] UKHL 35 at [29]; Kessler, *Taxation of Non-Residents and Foreign Domiciliaries* (21st ed., 2022-23), App 2.2.4 (Identifying the arrangement) online version *https://www.foreigndomiciliaries.co.uk*

(b) originates from any settlor who was not an individual.[4]

Corporate lenders must however consider the loan relationship rules.[5]

20.3 Loan or credit transactions

Section 809CZC ITA provides:[6]

> (1) This section applies if—
> (a) under a loan or credit transaction a person transfers income arising from property,
> (b) the person is not, as a result of Chapter 5B (finance arrangements), chargeable to income tax on the income transferred, and
> (c) the person is within the charge to income tax.
> (2) In such a case—
> (a) income tax is charged under this section,
> (b) the tax is charged on an amount equal to the full amount of the income transferred,
> (c) the tax is charged for the tax year in which the transfer takes place, and
> (d) the person who transfers the income is liable for the tax.
> (3) This section does not prejudice the liability of any other person to tax.

There is no exemption for charities.

So far this has no effect on an interest-free loan. However s.809CZC(4) provides:

> For the purposes of this section a person transfers income if the person surrenders, waives or forgoes it.

This does not apply to an interest-free loan. One does not "forgo" income by making such a loan. Income is only foregone if it is income to which one is otherwise entitled.[7]

---

4 For the background to this provision, see Kessler, *Taxation of Non-Residents and Foreign Domiciliaries* (21st ed., 2022-23), para 47.16 (Corporate settlor) online version *https://www.foreigndomiciliaries.co.uk*

5 See 11.5 (Loan relationships).

6 The CT equivalent is s.779 CTA 2010.

7 For full discussion of this provision see Kessler, *Taxation of Non-Residents and Foreign Domiciliaries* (21st ed., 2022-23), para 26.25 (Loan or credit transaction) online version *https://www.foreigndomiciliaries.co.uk*

20.4 CGT position of lender

A loan of sterling which is repaid without any premium cannot give rise to any capital gains tax charge on the lender. A loan in a foreign currency would normally qualify for the relief for debts in s.251 TCGA. There could be a charge if:

(1) the loan amounted to a "debt on a security"; or
(2) if the right to the debt had been assigned.

20.5 IHT position of lender

20.5.1 *Loan repayable on demand*

The IHT Manual correctly states:

> **IHTM14317: Gifts with reservation (GWRs): the gift: interest free loans** [Jun 2016]
> The grant of an interest free loan repayable on demand ... is not a transfer of value (because the value of the loan is equal to the amount of it).

If a loan is made interest free (or on favourable terms as to interest) but is repayable on demand, then in principle the lender does not make a transfer of value as there is no diminution in the value of their estate. Before the loan is made they own the money and after the loan is made they own the right to be repaid the money. The value of the right to repayment would be less than its face value where there was any doubt as to whether the borrower would be good for repayment, and it might be argued that the value of the right to repayment would always be slightly less than face value. However, these objections are overcome by s.166 IHTA which provides:

> In determining the value of a right to receive a sum due under any obligation it shall be assumed that the obligation will be duly discharged, except if or to the extent that recovery of the sum is impossible or not reasonably practicable and has not become so by any act or omission of the person to whom the sum is due.

20.5.2 *Debt becomes statute barred*

What if the lender allowed the debt to become statute-barred? Section 3(3) IHTA provides:

> Where the value of a person's estate is diminished, and the value—

> (a) of another person's estate, or
> (b) of any settled property, other than settled property treated by s.49(1) below as property to which a person is beneficially entitled,
>
> is increased by the first-mentioned person's omission to exercise a right, he shall be treated for the purposes of this section as having made a disposition at the time (or latest time) when he could have exercised the right, unless it is shown that the omission was not deliberate.

It appears that a deliberate decision to allow the debt to become statute barred will be a chargeable transfer (the IHT charity exemption will not apply) and if it is a matter of oversight (more common) there is no transfer of value. However, it is likely that s.166 applies in both cases so
(1) there is no transfer of value in any case, but
(2) the benefit of the debt continues to form part of the estate.
In practice take care the debt does not become statute barred.

20.5.3 *IHT on term loan*

Making a loan will normally involve a transfer of value where the loan is interest free (or at a favourable rate of interest) and is not repayable on demand. If the loan is made to a charity, will the transfer of value qualify for the IHT charity exemption? Section 23(1) IHTA provides that transfers of value are exempt "to the extent that the values transferred by them are attributable to property which is given to charities". Section 23(6) provides that property is "given to charities" if it becomes the property of charities or is held on trust for charitable purposes only. This exemption does cover a loan of money (or other fungibles). The money which is lent to the charity is "given" to the charity. There is no obligation on the charity to return the same money to the lender. The transfer of value is attributable to the property "given". The transfer of the cash represents a gross diminution in the lender's estate. The partial consideration which the lender receives in return, namely the right to be repaid a like sum in the future, simply diminishes the value transferred.

Section 23(2) prevents the IHT charity exemption being available if the disposition by which the property is given is defeasible, but a loan is not defeasible.

Section 23(4) prevents (subject to certain exceptions) the s.23(1) exemption being available as respects property (which is not land or a building) which is given subject to an interest reserved or created by the donor. A term loan is not a transfer of money subject to an interest.

Section 23(5) prevents the IHT charity exemption being available in relation to property if it or any part of it may become applicable for purposes other than charitable purposes. Now it is possible that the borrower-charity may use the cash originally transferred or cash into which it is traceable to repay the loan. Nevertheless, the repayment of the loan would be an application for charitable purposes in that the debt of the charity would be thereby discharged.

The same result can be reached by the application of s.29 IHTA. Section 29 provides:

> **Loans—modifications of exemptions**
> (1) If or to the extent that a transfer of value is a disposition whereby the use of money or other property is allowed by one person to another ("the borrower"), the preceding provisions of this Chapter shall apply to it with the following modifications.
>
> ...
>
> (5) For the purposes of sections 23 to 25—
> (a) the value transferred shall be treated as attributable to the property of which the borrower is allowed the use, and
> (b) that property shall be treated as given to, or as becoming the property of, the borrower unless the use allowed includes use for purposes other than charitable purposes or those of a body mentioned in section 24 or 25 or, where it is land, of a body mentioned in section 24A;
>
> sections 23(2) to (6), 24 (3) and (4), 24A(3), and 25(2) shall not apply

Section 29 disapplies the anti-avoidance rules of s.23(2) to (6). The section is clearly applicable to (and useful in) the case of the loan of an asset which is to be returned *in specie*, for example land or a chattel. It is not strictly needed in the case of a loan of money where the borrower is under no obligation to return *in specie* the money lent.

20.5.4 *Reservation of benefit*

Since the making of the loan repayable on demand is not a transfer of value, the IHT charity exemption does not apply (because it only applies to a transfer of value). The GWR provisions would not then be disapplied by s.102(5)(d) FA 1986.

The IHT Manual provides:

> **IHTM14317 - Gifts with reservation (GWRs): the gift: interest free loans** [Jun 2016]
> The grant of an interest free loan repayable on demand ... is a gift

> because there is a clear intention to confer bounty: the property disposed of is the interest forgone.
> But the grant of such a loan is not, in itself, a GWR...

We agree that an interest free loan is not in principle a gift with reservation of benefit. It would be absurd if it was a GWR, because the benefit of the loan is an asset in the lender's estate. There is no need for GWR here. The only question is: *why* is an interest free loan outside GWR? The HMRC view that the property disposed of was the "interest forgone" is implausible because one cannot dispose of property that does not exist. In our view, the correct analysis is that an interest free loan repayable on demand is not a disposal "by way of gift" so that s.102 FA 1986 is not in point.

The making of a favourable term loan *is* a transfer of value to which the IHT charity exemption applies, so that qualifies for the GWR relief in s.102(5)(d) FA 1986.

20.6 Position of charity

20.6.1 *Income used to repay loan*

The charity will in due course have to repay the loan. If the money lent has been applied in discharging the income expenses of the charity then, if the repayment is made out of capital, the charity will in effect have expended capital for an income purpose. That might or might not be justified under the constitution of the charity.

It will be important for the charity to show that the funds used to repay the loan have been applied for charitable purposes only. In our opinion this condition is met provided the proceeds of the loan have been applied for charitable purposes.

20.6.2 *Charitable expenditure rules*

Neither the borrowing nor the repaying of money borrowed should bring the charitable expenditure rules into play. See 6.1 (Charitable expenditure rules).

20.6.3 *Capital gains*

A gain could arise from the repayment of a loan (normally in the case of a foreign currency loan). Such a gain arises from a liability and not an asset, and is therefore outside the scope of CGT.

CHAPTER TWENTY ONE

GIFT OF SHARES/LAND TO CHARITY

Cross references

The following topics are considered elsewhere:

15.48 (Donor on remittance basis)
28.3 (QIDR)

21.1 Gift of shares/land to charity

This chapter discusses the relief for gifts of shares, securities and land to charities. We refer to the relief as "**Qualifying Investment Donation Relief**" or "**QIDR**".

The relief is set out in Chapter 3 Part 8 ITA/Chapter 3 Part 6 CTA 2010

Non-tax practitioners sometimes refer to this relief as Gift Aid, but the parliamentary drafter never does that; and to avoid confusion "Gift Aid" should only be used for the relief for cash gifts, which is a distinct relief.

21.2 Conditions for relief

21.2.1 *Individual/corporate donor*

s.431(1) ITA	**s.203 CTA 2010**
An individual who disposes of the whole of the beneficial interest in a qualifying investment (see section 432) to a charity is entitled to relief if—	(1) This section applies if— (a) a company disposes of the whole of the beneficial interest in a qualifying investment to a charity,
(a) the disposal is otherwise than by way of a bargain made at arm's length, and	(b) the disposal is otherwise than by way of a bargain made at arm's length,
	(c) the company is not itself a charity, and
(b) the individual makes a claim	(d) the company makes a claim.

The relief applies to individuals and companies, but not to trustees. The relief applies to non-resident individuals, and non-resident companies within the scope of corporation tax. This is consistent with Gift Aid.

For CT, the rules are the same except for the additional requirement that the donor company must not be a charity. That is consistent with corporate Gift Aid.

In the case of a disposal by a company, relief applies even if the disposal is a distribution; contrast corporate Gift Aid (which does not apply to a distribution).

If a company disposes of an asset to a corporate charity which is a member of the same group[1] the interaction with group relief will need to

1 See 11.2 (Group relief).

be considered.

21.2.2 *Disposal to charity*

The disposal must be:
(1) to a charity[2] and
(2) otherwise than by way of a bargain made at arm's length.

In the tax avoidance scheme of *Ferguson v HMRC*[3] these conditions were held not to be satisfied, on the basis of a *Ramsay* approach, "looking at the overall effect of a composite transaction, rather than considering each step individually." This case does not shed any light on the meaning of these conditions outside the context of a tax avoidance scheme, and fact patterns of this kind are not likely to occur after the enactment of the GAAR.
HMRC Guidance Note provides:

> **5.5 Making a gift of shares or securities**
> 5.5.1 You should first contact the charity you have selected to ensure that it can accept the proposed gift. If it agrees, you then need to sign a transfer form ...

It is not strictly necessary to contact the charity first, though in most cases that will no doubt happen.

21.2.3 *Date of disposal*

HMRC Guidance Note provides:

> **5.12 The date to use as the date of gift for the purposes of establishing the market value of the qualifying investments**
> 5.12.1 The date on which the qualifying investments are transferred to the charity. In the case of shares and securities, this is likely to be the date that you sign and hand over the stock transfer document. For gifts of land you should take the date on which you disposed of your beneficial interest in the land. Normally this will be the date on which you conveyed the property to the charity. However, if the disposal was made under a contract, perhaps a sale at below market value, you should take the date on which the contract was made. If the contract was conditional take the date on which the conditions were all satisfied. If the

---

2 This requirement is the same as for Gift Aid; for a discussion see 15.6 (Gift "to a charity").

3 [2014] SFTD 934. For a summary of the scheme, see 2.6.2 (Gift of gilt subject to option).

gift was made by a declaration of trust you should take that date. If you have granted a lease to a charity you should take the date you granted the lease.

21.2.4 *Claims*

HMRC Guidance Note provides:

> **5.10 Claiming the relief**
> 5.10.1 You can claim relief by completing the appropriate section of your Self Assessment return, or requesting that your PAYE code is amended for the current tax year, or requesting that your Self Assessment Payments on Account are reduced.
> 5.10.2 If you are not sent a tax return at the end of the tax year, or if you want to claim relief before the end of the current tax year, you should write to your Tax Office, giving full details of the gift, in order to claim the relief.
> 5.10.3 Companies should include the amount of relief they are claiming in the 'Charges Paid' box on their Corporation Tax Self Assessment return.

In practice an individual donor makes the claim by entering the amount of the relief in the relevant boxes, in tax return form SA100 (2020/21) page TR4:

Box	**Title**	**Form SA150 Tax Return notes (2020/21)**
9	Value of qualifying shares or securities gifted to charity	Put in box 9 the net benefit of the shares or securities, minus any amounts or benefits received from the charity. Add any incidental costs for the transfer, such as brokers' fees or legal fees.
10	Value of qualifying land and buildings gifted to charity	Put in box 10 the net benefit of the land, minus any amounts or benefits received from the charity. Add any costs of the gift or sale, such as legal or valuer's fees.
11	Value of qualifying investments gifted to non-UK charities in boxes 9 & 10	You can claim relief for gifts of qualifying shares, securities, land or buildings to certain non-UK charities. If any amounts included in box 9 or box 10 are to charities outside the UK, put the amount in box 11 and give us details in 'Any other information' on page TR 7.

21.3 Whole beneficial interest rule

The donor must dispose of the "whole of the beneficial interest in a qualifying investment".[4] The relief will not apply if:
(1) the donor retains any beneficial interest; or
(2) if the donor does not possess the entire beneficial interest, even though they may give away all that they have.

We refer to that as the **"whole-interest rule"**.

The purpose of the rule is presumably that the charity should not be lumbered with:
(1) shares of assets, which may have little value or be difficult to value; or
(2) assets subject to rights, such as options, which may allow the donor to recover the assets.

Lord Radcliffe observed that:

> the terminology of our legal system has not produced a sufficient variety of words to represent the various meanings which can be conveyed by the word "interest"[5]

There are broadly two ways in which this requirement might be interpreted.

The "whole of the beneficial interest" might be construed in the same way as "beneficial ownership" in a group relief context. In that case:
(1) A person owns the whole beneficial interest in an investment which is subject to an option[6] and a gift of such an investment qualifies for QIDR.
(2) A person does not own the whole beneficial interest in an asset which is subject to a contract of sale, even if the contract is conditional,[7] and a gift of such an asset would not qualify for QIDR. Instead the purchaser under the contract holds the whole beneficial interest.

---

4 See 21.2 (Conditions for relief).
5 *Comr of Stamp Duties v Livingston* [1965] AC 694 at p.712.
6 *Sainsbury v O'Connor* 64 TC 208. However this case is problematic: see Kessler, *Taxation of Non-Residents and Foreign Domiciliaries* (21st ed., 2022-23), App 6.2 (English-law beneficial ownership)
online version *https://www.foreigndomiciliaries.co.uk*
The issue is discussed but not decided in *Ferguson v HMRC* [2014] SFTD 934 at [22] to [28]; perhaps some conclusions will emerge in the forthcoming appeal.
7 *Wood Preservation v Prior* 45 TC 112.

An alternative and, one might have thought, preferable view would be that a person only owns the "whole of the beneficial interest" if there is no other person who has any beneficial interest in the asset. In that case an asset subject to an option would not qualify for QIDR if given to charities subject to the option. The same would apply if shares were given subject to a right to receive dividends, or restrictions over the votes attached to shares. Indeed, one might have thought that the Whole-interest rule was designed to prevent just this. However, the drafter of s.433(5) ITA clearly assumed that the holder of an agreement to purchase land had the whole interest, or else s.433(5) ITA would not be necessary.[8] So the first view is the better one.

A gift of an asset subject to a right of pre-emption would be a gift of the "whole of the beneficial interest" if the right of pre-emption were not regarded as an interest in the asset. This is a controversial issue of property law, but there is authority that a right of pre-emption over land is not an interest in land.

Where an individual holds an asset subject to a lock-in agreement, they hold the whole of the beneficial interest in the asset. The party who holds the benefit of a lock-in agreement does not have any beneficial interest in the asset if all they can do is prevent a sale.

For the application of the whole-interest rule in relation to land, see 21.5.5 (Whole beneficial interest).

21.4 "Qualifying investment"

Section 432(1) ITA/s. 204(1) CTA 2010 provides:

> In this Chapter
> (a) shares or securities which are
> [i] listed on a recognised stock exchange or
> [ii] dealt in on any designated market in the UK
> (b) units in an authorised unit trust,
> (c) shares in an open-ended investment company,
> (d) an interest in an offshore fund, and
> (e) a qualifying interest in land.

Qualifying investments are, in short, listed securities and mutual funds.

21.4.1 *"Recognised stock exchange"*

This term is defined in s.1005 ITA 2007. HMRC say:

8 See 21.5.4 (Contract to acquire land).

Recognised stock exchanges

1. The term 'recognised stock exchange' occurs throughout the Taxes Acts and in various tax regulations. For example it is used in the definition of investments which may be held in Individual Savings Accounts (ISAs) and in the qualifying criteria for the quoted Eurobond exemption. Recognised stock exchange legislation is found under section 1005 Income Tax Act 2007 (ITA).
2. HMRC will consider the designation of a stock exchange as a recognised stock exchange under section 1005 ITA on receipt of a request made by a stock exchange. The fact that a particular exchange is not recognised may simply mean that recognition has not been requested.
3. Recognition under section 1005 ITA is for tax purposes only and confers no other status on the exchange concerned. It does not constitute any form of recognition or approval for regulatory or other purposes nor does it provide any form of approval or recommendation of any of the investments which are listed or traded on that exchange.
4. The definition of a recognised stock exchange is given in section 1005(1) ITA. It includes any market of a recognised investment exchange designated as a recognised stock exchange by an order made by the Commissioner for HMRC and any market outside the UK designated in such an order, these stock exchanges are listed in Table 1. In the case of the jurisdictions in Table 2 the stock exchanges which meet recognised stock exchange status are those which are stock exchanges within the law relating to stock exchanges of that jurisdiction.
5. All recognised stock exchanges prior to 19 July 2007 were designated under section 841(1)(b) Income and Corporation Tax Act 1988 (ICTA). Any stock exchanges designated under section 841(1)(b) ICTA are treated as designated for the purposes of section 1005 ITA going forward.

21.4.2 *"Listed"*

Sections1005(3) ITA/1137CTA 2010 provide:

> References in the Income Tax Acts/Corporation Tax Acts to securities which are listed on a recognised stock exchange are to securities—
> (a) which are admitted to trading on that exchange, and
> (b) which are included in the official UK list[9] or are officially listed

9 Defined in subsection (5): "References in the Income Tax Acts to securities which are included in the official UK list are to securities which are included in the official list (within the meaning of Part 6 of FISMA 2000) in accordance with the provisions of that Part."

in a qualifying country outside the UK[10] in accordance with provisions corresponding to those generally applicable in EEA states.

The HMRC statement continues:

> 6. The term is often used in the phrase 'listed on a recognised stock exchange' or in similar or related expressions. The tables below therefore include the markets which meet the HMRC definition of 'listed' as set out in paragraph 7 below. While we try to maintain an up to date list this is not always possible because markets frequently rename, re-structure or merge. It is possible that you may identify stock exchanges within the law of a named jurisdiction (Table 2) which we have not yet identified, but which would meet recognised stock exchange status. Equally you may identify a market of a recognised stock exchange where we have not given an opinion as to whether it meets the HMRC definition of listed. If you meet either of these situations please contact HMRC using the contact points below.
> 7. The phrase 'listed on a recognised stock exchange' in respect of shares and securities is now defined at section 1005(3) ITA. This means shares and securities which:
> a) are admitted to trading on that exchange and
> b) included in the official UK list maintained by the Financial Services Authority (in its capacity as the UK Listing Authority) or are officially listed in a qualifying country outside the UK in accordance with provisions corresponding to those generally applicable in EEA states.
> 8. HMRC recognise that in certain cases markets use terms such as 'listed', 'admitted to trading', or 'quoted'. Both Table 1 and Table 2 identify the markets which we consider would meet the HMRC definition of 'listed'...[11]

21.4.3 *Designated market*

s. 432(2) ITA	**s.204(3) CTA 2010**
In this section— "designated" means designated by an order made by the Commissioners for HMRC for	In paragraph (a) of subsection (1) "designated" means designated by an order made by the Commissioners for Her Majesty's Revenue and Customs

10 Defined in subsection (4): "For this purpose "qualifying country outside the UK" means any country outside the UK in which there is a recognised stock exchange."

11 *https://www.gov.uk/recognised-stock-exchanges*

the purposes of subsection (1)(a).[12]	for the purposes of that paragraph.

The alternative investment market ("AIM") is part of the London Stock Exchange. AIM shares are not regarded as "listed" because they are not included in the Official List.[13] However, in 2009 AIM became a

---

12 The CT equivalent is s.204(3)(4) CTA 2010. For completeness, s.432(3) ITA provides:

> "An order under subsection (2) may—
> (a) designate a market by name or by reference to any class or description of market, and
> (b) vary or revoke a previous order under that subsection."

13 CG Manual provides:

> "**CG50255 London stock exchange: History: The Alternative Investment Market** [Jun 2016]
> The Stock Exchange introduced a new, less regulated, market in June 1995. This is the Alternative Investment Market (AIM). It is designed primarily to enable trading in new, small and growing companies. A Press Release dated 20 February 1995 confirmed that shares and securities on AIM do not fall to be treated as quoted or listed for tax purposes."

The position is not affected by the reformation of the definition of RSE in 2007. See the note published 29 March 2007 (recognised stock exchange–Budget 2007):

> **"(a) AIM**
> AIM is a market platform of the London Stock Exchange and the London Stock Exchange is a recognised stock exchange (RSE). So AIM shares are already traded on a RSE. What differentiates them from the main market for most tax treatments is that they are not included in the official UK List maintained by the Financial Services Authority as the UK listing authority.
> **Capital Gains Tax Business Asset Taper Relief**
> This example uses business asset taper relief as representative of a tax treatment that is dependent upon shares not being "listed on a RSE". Similar reasoning will apply to other instances where a particular tax treatment is dependent on whether the shares are "listed on a RSE".
> In certain circumstances one of the conditions that must be met for business asset taper relief to apply to a capital gain arising on a disposal of company shares or securities is that the shares (etc) in question are not listed on a RSE. "Listed" here means included in the official UK List maintained by the Financial Services Authority as the UK listing authority.
> Shares solely admitted to trading on AIM are not included in the official UK List maintained by the Financial Services Authority (FSA), as the UK listing authority. Therefore the shares in a company which are traded solely on AIM are not "listed on a RSE".
> If a company's shares currently meet the business asset taper relief condition of being unlisted it will continue to meet the condition under the proposed new rules.

designated market, along with the PLUS-quoted Market. HMRC said:[14]

> **Designation of the Alternative Investment Market (AIM) of the London Stock Exchange and the PLUS-quoted Market of the PLUS Markets Group for the purposes of Tax Relief for Gifts of Qualifying Investments to Charities ...**
> With effect from 20 May 2009 HMRC have made Orders to designate the AIM and PLUS-quoted market as designated markets in the UK for the purposes of the definition of qualifying investments in Sections 432(1)(a) Income Tax Act 2007 (ITA) and [now s.205(5) CTA 2010] (Gifts of qualifying investments to charity) ...
> Until 18 July 2007, AIM shares and securities were qualifying investments for the purposes of S432 ITA, [now s.203 CTA 2010]... because they met the requirements of those sections by being 'shares or securities dealt in on a recognised stock exchange' (see note 1). From 19 July 2007 the legislation provided that qualifying shares and securities included those dealt in on markets specifically designated for the purpose of that legislation. It was intended to make a designation order in respect of AIM to maintain the status of AIM shares and securities. It was also intended to make a designation order in respect of the PLUS-quoted market following the designation of PLUS Markets as a recognised investment exchange by the Financial Services Authority on 19 July 2007.
> The Orders are now being put in place as of 20 May 2009. However, since 19 July 2007 until the date of these orders, shares and securities traded on AIM have been treated as qualifying investments for the purposes of sections 432 (1) (a) ITA , 421L (6) (b) ITEPA and [now s.204(1) CTA 2010] as if the Orders were in place.
> In the case of PLUS-quoted shares if anyone has failed to claim charitable gift relief or been denied this relief in the period following 19 July 2007, please contact HMRC. The HMRC Charities team will consider on a case by case basis any donor who had given PLUS-quoted shares to charity on or after 19 July 2007 if they had failed to claim gift relief because PLUS-quoted had not been designated for the purposes of sections 432 (1)(a) ITA and [now s.204 CTA 2010] ...
> The signing of the Orders does not signify any change in practice for AIM shares but puts in place the necessary designation Orders to ensure

---

The shares would however cease to meet the condition if they were to be included in the official UK List maintained by the FSA or listed on a recognised stock exchange outside the UK – where the listing met the HMRC definition for official listing."

14 This is no longer available online.

the continuing treatment of AIM shares/securities as qualifying investments for the purposes of sections 432 (1)(a) ITA and [now s.204 CTA 2010] ... It also allows Plus-Quoted shares to benefit from these particular tax treatments.

...

Notes

1. The term 'recognised stock exchange' occurs throughout the Tax Acts and in various tax regulations ... For example it is used in the definition of investments which may be held in ISAs. The term is often used in the phrase 'listed on a recognised stock exchange' or 'dealt in on a recognised stock exchange'.

The definition of a recognised stock exchange is given in section 1005 Income Tax Act 2007 (ITA). It includes the London Stock Exchange and PLUS-listed market and any such stock exchange outside the UK as is designated in an Order of the Commissioners of HMRC.

2. In the case of sections 432 (1)(a)ITA , 421L (6)(b) ITEPA 2003 and [now s.204 CTA 2010], the power to designate markets as 'dealt in on a designated UK market' lies within that legislation and is not covered by the section 1005 ITA recognised stock exchange legislation.

It was therefore necessary to put in place Orders to designate AIM under those sections to ensure the continuing tax treatment of AIM shares and securities for Tax Relief on Gifts of Shares to Charities ... and to allow PLUS-quoted shares to benefit from these particular tax treatments.

21.4.4 *Offshore fund*

s. 432(2) ITA	**s. 204(2) CTA 2010**
In this section ... "offshore fund" has the same meaning as in Chapter 5 of Part 17 of ICTA (see sections 756A to 756C of that Act).	In this section— "offshore fund" has the meaning given by section 355 of TIOPA 2010.

The definition of offshore fund in s.756A to 756C ICTA was introduced in 2004, amended in 2007 (unfortunately the amendment was botched) repealed in 2009, and replaced by s.80A to 80F FA 2008, which was in turn rewritten by TIOPA 2009. Amidst all this frenetic activity, the need to update this reference in ITA was overlooked, so the reference is very out of date. But it should take effect as a reference to the current legislation. This is consistent with the CT equivalent, where the legislation is correctly drafted.

For a discussion of the TIOPA definition, see Kessler, *Taxation of Non-*

Residents and Foreign Domiciliaries.[15]

21.4.5 *Open-ended investment co*

Section 432(2) ITA/s.204(2) CTA 2010 provides:

> In this section ...
> "open-ended investment company" is to be read in accordance with sections 613 and 615 of CTA 2010.

21.5 Gift of land

21.5.1 *"Qualifying interest in land"*

Section 433(1) ITA/s. 205 CTA 2010 provides:

> In this Chapter "qualifying interest in land" means—
> (a) a freehold interest in land in the UK, or
> (b) a leasehold interest in land in the UK which is a term of years absolute.[16]
>
> This is subject to subsections (2) to (5).

The restriction to UK land is not compatible with EU law, though the significance of that would need to be reconsidered post-brexit.

Comparable definitions apply in Scotland, framed for Scots property law.

21.5.2 *Easement*

s. 433(2) ITA	**s. 205(2) CTA 2010**
Subsection (3) applies if an individual with a beneficial interest in a freehold or leasehold interest mentioned in subsection (1)(a) or (b) makes a disposal to a charity of—	Subsection (3) applies if a company with a beneficial interest in a freehold or leasehold interest mentioned in subsection (1)(a) or (b) makes a disposal to a charity of—
(a) the whole of the beneficial	[identical]

15 (21st ed., 2022-23), Appendix 7 (Offshore Funds CIS/OEIC) online version *https://www.foreigndomiciliaries.co.uk*

16 "Term of years absolute" is not defined but the context suggests that the definition in s.205(1)(xxvii) Law of Property Act 1925 should apply. If that were wrong some erudite questions of land law could arise because a lease which is a "term of years absolute" for the purposes of the Law of Property Act might not be a "term of years" or "absolute" in the normal sense of those words (whatever that might be); but in practice this is likely to be academic.

interest, and
(b) an easement, servitude, right or privilege so far as benefiting the land in question.

In the absence of express provision:

(a) The gift of the freehold or leasehold would be a gift of a qualifying interest in land which would in principle qualify for QIDR.
(b) The gift of the easement would not be a gift of a qualifying interest in land (as an easement is not a freehold or a leasehold) and so would not qualify for QIDR.

Accordingly,

s.433(3) ITA

The disposal mentioned in subsection (2)(b) is regarded for the purposes of this Chapter as a disposal by the individual of the whole of the individual's beneficial interest in a qualifying interest in land separate from the disposal mentioned in subsection (2)(a).

s. 205(3) CTA 2010

The disposal mentioned in subsection (2)(b) is regarded for the purposes of this Chapter as a disposal by the company of the whole of its beneficial interest in a qualifying interest in land separate from the disposal mentioned in subsection (2)(a).

21.5.3 *Grant of lease to charity*

s. 433(4) ITA

If an individual who has a freehold or leasehold interest in land in the UK grants a lease for a term of years absolute to a charity of the whole or part of that land, the grant of the lease is regarded for the purposes of this Chapter as a disposal by the individual of the whole of the beneficial interest in the leasehold interest so granted.

s. 205(4) CTA 2010

If a company which has a freehold or leasehold interest in land in the United Kingdom grants a lease for a term of years absolute to a charity of the whole or part of the land, the grant of the lease is regarded for the purposes of this Chapter as a disposal by the company of the whole of the beneficial interest in the leasehold interest so granted.

Why is this needed? Presumably in the absence of this provision, it might be said that a person who grants a lease does not dispose of the whole of the interest in a qualifying interest in land:

(1) The grantor does not *dispose* of the lease: the grantor *creates* the lease.
(2) The grantor does make a part-disposal of the freehold, at least in the CGT sense of disposal, but that part-disposal is not the disposal of the whole of the beneficial interest in the freehold.

If the individual holds a lease, and transfers it to a charity, that is the disposal of the whole of the beneficial interest in a qualifying investment.

21.5.4 *Contract to acquire land*

Section 433(5) ITA/s. 205(5) CTA 2010 provides:

> Neither an agreement to acquire a freehold interest nor an agreement for a lease is a qualifying interest in land.

21.5.5 *Whole-interest rule*

The donor must dispose of the "whole of the beneficial interest" in the qualifying interest in land.[17] This rule was framed when qualifying investments were restricted to shares and securities and it makes less sense when applied to land.

In English land law, two legal estates (freehold and leasehold), each regarded as separate items of property, can subsist simultaneously in respect of the same land. If an individual owns a lease and a reversion, it is considered that a gift of the reversion to charity meets the whole beneficial interest requirement, as the qualifying interest in land is the freehold, and a lease is not an interest in the freehold. If that were wrong, no-one could ever give a freehold investment to charity, where the investment property was let to a third party, which would be surprising as an investment property which is let on arm's length terms is likely to be more valuable than one with vacant possession.

Is an easement an interest in a freehold or leasehold estate? If so, QIDR does not apply to a gift of land subject to an easement. That seems surprising. In the case of newly created easements, it may be possible to avoid this problem by careful conveyancing: instead of giving land to a charity subject to an easement retained by the donor, the donor may give the easement to the charity (along with other land) and retain the land.

In an appropriate case, it may be desirable to obtain HMRC clearance before making the gift.

---

17 See 21.3 (Whole beneficial interest).

21.5.6 *Certificate of gift of land*

s. 441 ITA	**s. 213 CTA 2010**
(1) This section applies if the qualifying investment is a qualifying interest in land.	[identical]
(2) No individual may make a claim for relief under this Chapter unless the individual has received a certificate given by or on behalf of the charity.	(2) A company may not make a claim under section 203 unless the company has received a certificate given by or on behalf of the charity.
(3) The certificate must— (a) describe the qualifying interest in land, (b) specify the date of the disposal, and (c) state that the charity has acquired the qualifying interest in land.	[identical]

HMRC Guidance Note states at 5.6.3:

> There's no prescribed certificate for this purpose and the charity can determine the form its certificate takes.

A letter is appropriate, but an email would suffice.

Presumably the intention is to make fraudulent claims easier to identify. It is not obvious that this is needed (or if it is needed, why it should apply to gifts of land and not gifts of shares). In practice it is just one more item of paperwork, and no problem should arise.

21.6 "Disqualifying events"

Section 444(2) ITA and s.216(2) CTA provide a claw-back of relief if there is a "disqualifying event" in the "provisional period":

s. 444(2) ITA	**s. 216(2) CTA 2010**
If a disqualifying event occurs at any time in the provisional period, the following are treated as never having been entitled to relief under this Chapter in respect of the	[identical]

disposal of the qualifying interest in land—	
(a) in a case to which section 442 does not apply,[18] the individual who made the disposal, or	(a) in a case where sections 214 and 215 do not apply, the company which made the disposal, and
(b) in a case to which section 442 applies, each individual who is an owner.	(b) in a case where those sections apply, each qualifying company which is an owner.

21.6.1 *"Provisional period"*

s. 444(7) ITA	**s. 216(7) CTA 2010**
"The provisional period" is the period beginning with the date of the disposal of the qualifying interest in land and ending with the fifth anniversary of the normal self-assessment filing date for the tax year in which the disposal was made.	"The provisional period" is the period beginning with the date of the disposal of the qualifying interest in land and ending with the sixth anniversary of the end of the accounting period in which the disposal was made.

21.6.2 *"Disqualifying event"*

The key term is "disqualifying event". This is defined in:

s.444 ITA	**s. 216 CTA 2010**
(4) A disqualifying event occurs if a person mentioned in subsection (5) becomes, otherwise than for full consideration in money or money's worth–	(4) A disqualifying event occurs if a person mentioned in subsection (5) becomes (otherwise than for full consideration in money or money's worth) —
(a) entitled to an interest or right in relation to all or part of the land to which the disposal relates, or	Identical
(b) party to an arrangement under which the person enjoys some right in relation to all or part of that land.	(b) party to an arrangement under which he enjoys some right in relation to all or part of that land.

18 Section 442 applies to land in joint ownership, see 21.7 (Joint ownership).

(5) The persons are—	(5) The persons are—
(a) in a case to which section 442 does not apply[19]—	(a) in a case where sections 214 and 215 do not apply
(i) the individual who made the disposal, or	[i] the company which made the disposal, or
(ii) a person connected with that individual, and	[ii] a person connected with that company, and
(b) in a case to which section 442 applies—	(b) in a case where those sections apply,
(i) a person who is an owner, or (ii) a person connected with such a person.	Identical

Thus there are two types of disqualifying event: in short, type (a) involves becoming entitled to a right; type (b) involves enjoying a right.

This is obscure but the courts will have to make it work.[20]

Suppose:

(1) a donor gives land to a charity; and
(2) the donor (or a connected person) continues to live there (without paying a market rent).

The charity which provides property at an undervalue to a donor (or connected person) would prima facie commit a breach of trust. The donor would not have the right of occupation (or any right in relation to the land)[21] and at first sight there is no disqualifying event. However, the donor as occupier would have the right to exclude anyone other than the charity from the land, and that would be sufficient to constitute a disqualifying event.

If the charity was acting lawfully, the donor would have a valid licence or lease and there would be a disqualifying event.

If a full rent is paid, there is no disqualifying event.

Suppose the donor carries out an *Ingram* scheme, that is:

---

19 Section 442 applies to land in joint ownership, see 21.7 (Joint ownership).

20 The drafting is loosely based on s.102A FA 1986 (gifts with reservation: interests in land) but that section is itself notoriously obscure.

21 In the case of land in England, s.117 Charities Act 2011 may also render the lease void.

(1) the donor grants themselves a lease (not at a market rent); and
(2) the donor subsequently gives the land to the charity subject to the lease.

There is a disqualifying event under (a) when the lease is granted: the donor becomes entitled to an interest in the land. However, that disqualifying event does not take place in the relevant period, so the anti-avoidance provision does not apply. When the reversion is given to the charity, there is probably a disqualifying event under (b): the gift is an arrangement under which the donor enjoys the right of occupation. So there is a disqualifying event unless the occupation is for full consideration. (Some like to argue that the payment of the purchase price when the donor originally purchased the property is full consideration, but while literally correct, that would defeat the obvious intention of the anti-avoidance provision, and the courts are likely to prefer a purposive construction.)

Suppose a donor grants a short lease of land to a charity. In principle the grant of the lease qualifies for relief. On the expiry of the lease, the donor becomes entitled to possession of the land again. This is not a disqualifying event. The donor does not "become" entitled to any interest or right. The reversionary interest simply falls into possession. It is suggested that there is no "arrangement" under head (b).

Section 444(6) ITA/s. 216(6) CTA 2010 provides:

> A disqualifying event does not occur if a person becomes entitled to an interest or right as mentioned in subsection (4)(a) as a result of a disposition of property on death (whether the disposition is effected by will, under the law relating to intestacy or otherwise).

This would cover the situation where:
(1) A grants a lease to charity, qualifying for relief.
(2) A dies and B (a connected person) acquires A's reversion under A's Will.

By contrast, if A had given the freehold reversion to B by a lifetime gift, then the gift would have been a disqualifying event. When enacted, back in the year 2000, anomalies of this kind were still a cause of surprise, and earlier editions of this book raised a quiet protest:

> What is the purpose of this? Do not look to Hansard for elucidation, for the point was fairly raised by the Opposition (briefed by the Law Society) but dismissed with bluster by the Government: the provision

> was "clear" and since it was "there to prevent avoidance" no further justification needed to be given.

But since 2000 sloppy anti-avoidance legislation and disregard of professional opinion no longer to excite surprise or special comment.

21.7 Joint ownership

s. 442 ITA	**s. 214 CTA 2010**
(1) This section applies if the qualifying investment is a qualifying interest in land.	[identical]
(2) It applies if two or more persons ("the owners")— (a) are jointly beneficially entitled to the qualifying interest in land, or (b) are, taken together, beneficially entitled in common to the qualifying interest in land.	[identical]
(3) Relief under this Chapter is available if—	[identical]
(a) at least one of the owners is an individual, and	(a) at least one of the owners is a qualifying company, and
(b) all the owners dispose of the whole of their beneficial interest in the qualifying interest in land to the charity.	[identical]
(4) Relief under this Chapter is available to each of the owners who is an individual.	(4) Relief as a result of this Chapter is available to each of the owners which is a qualifying company (and section 215 applies).

This extends the relief. In the absence of this provision, co-owners would not qualify for relief because neither disposes of the whole of the beneficial interest.

Section 442 ITA then deals with the quantum of relief for the joint owners:

> (5) The amount of relief under this Chapter to be given to an individual is such share of the relievable amount as is allocated to the individual by an agreement made between those owners who are—

(a) individuals, or
(b) qualifying companies.[22]

The "relievable" amount is the amount of relief given.[23] This is, broadly, the value of the entire interest in the property. This prevents lost relief due to the fact that a (say) one half share in property is worth less than one half of the value of the whole property.

It appears that joint owners can agree to share the relief on the gift of property in proportions which are different from their ownership of property. For instance, if the property is shared equally, the joint owners may nevertheless agree that one of them should obtain 90% of the relief for the gift to charity, and the other only 10%.

The corporation tax equivalent is s.214 CTA 2010.

21.8 Amount of relief

The amount of relief is the "relievable amount".[24] There are different definitions depending on whether the qualifying investment is given to the charity, or sold at an undervalue.

21.8.1 *"Relievable amount": Gift*

Section 434(1) ITA/s. 206(1) CTA 2010 provide:

> If the disposal is a gift, the relievable amount is given by the formula—
> V + IC - B

In short, V stands for **V**alue of the asset, IC stands for **I**ncidental **C**osts and B stands for **B**enefits received by the individual (if any).

In full detail, s.434(1) ITA/s. 206(1) CTA 2010 provides:

> V is the value of the net benefit to the charity at, or immediately after, the time when the disposal is made, whichever is less,
> IC is the amount of the incidental costs of making the disposal to the individual making it, and
> B is the total value of any benefits received in consequence of making the disposal by the individual making the disposal or a person connected with the individual.

---

22 Section 442(6) defines qualifying company: "A company is a qualifying company if ... it is not itself a charity".

23 See 21.8 (Amount of relief).

24 See 21.14 (QIDR relief: Position of donor).

The following issue has its equivalent in respect of cash gifts.[25] Here, we run into a theoretical problem where the charity is a charitable trust and the donor its founder. The problem is that the charity is connected with the donor if it is a charitable trust and the donor is a settlor in relation to it. If one has to include the benefit received by the charity this will reduce the relievable amount to nil . It is difficult to avoid this conclusion on a strict reading of the legislation but for the reasons set out in the discussion on Gift Aid, a purposive construction ought to apply.

A charity may be connected with the donor, but the context shows that benefits received such a charity do not count for the purpose of ascertaining item B.[26]

21.8.2 *Sale at undervalue*

Section 434(2) ITA/s. 206(2) CTA 2010 provide:

> If the disposal is at an undervalue, the relievable amount is given by the formula—
> E + C - B

In short, E stands for **E**xcess (the undervalue), C stands for allowable incidental **C**osts, and B for **B**enefits. In full detail:

> E is the amount (if any) by which V (as defined in subsection (1)) exceeds the amount or value of the consideration for the disposal,
> C is given by subsection (4), and
> B is as defined in subsection (1).

There is a complex formula for ascertaining what proportion of the incidental costs are allowable:

> (4) C is found by taking the following steps.
> *Step 1*
> Calculate the consideration for which the disposal is treated as made for the purposes of TCGA 1992 as a result of section 257(2)(a) of that Act (in case of disposal to charity etc, consideration to be such that no gain or loss accrues).
> *Step 2*
> Find the excess (if any) of the amount calculated at Step 1 over the amount or value of the consideration for the disposal.
> If there is such an excess, C is the amount of that excess or, if less, the

---

25 See 15.32.3 (Benefit to connected charity).
26 See 15.32.3 (Benefit to connected charity).

amount of the incidental costs of making the disposal to the individual making it.
If there is no such excess, C is nil.

So, where the sale is for consideration, the incidental costs of disposal are only added to the relievable amount to the extent that:
(1) the [actual] consideration for the disposal is less than
(2) the consideration for which a disposal is treated as made by virtue of s.257(2)(a) TCGA (that is, such consideration as secures that neither a gain nor a loss accrues on the disposal, ie consideration equivalent to the allowable expenditure).[27]

Since incidental costs are usually nominal, it would have been easier just to allow them or disallow them, but there it is.

21.8.3 *Benefit exceeds gift*

Section 434(3) ITA/s. 206(3) CTA 2010 provides:

> But if the amount given by the formula in subsection (1) or (2) is a negative amount, the relievable amount is nil.

That is self-evident.

21.8.4 *Gift Aid benefit rule compared*

The Gift Aid rule (in short) is that benefits from the disposal are deducted in computing the relief. The discussion in 15.20 (The Benefit rule: Gift Aid condition F) applies here except:
(1) QIDR does not have an equivalent to the Gift Aid exemptions for small benefits and rights of admission.
(2) Benefits restrict the relief, but do not nullify it altogether.

21.8.5 *Welsh/Scottish taxpayers*

HMRC say:

> 27. Individuals who donate certain shares or land to a charity qualify for income tax relief (at the basic, higher and additional rates). All the tax relief has to be claimed through the Self Assessment return. The approach here will follow that taken for other donations to charities where relief is claimed through Self Assessment – therefore if an individual is a Welsh taxpayer they would receive relief at the Welsh

---

27 See 23.3.3 (Position of donor).

rates.[28]

21.9 Incidental costs of disposal

s. 435 ITA	**s. 207 CTA 2010**
References in section 434 to the incidental costs of making the disposal to the individual making it are to—	References in section 206 to the incidental costs of making the disposal to the company making it are to—
(a) fees, commission or remuneration paid for the professional services of a surveyor, valuer, auctioneer, accountant, agent or legal adviser which are wholly and exclusively incurred by the individual for the purposes of the disposal,	(a) fees, commission or remuneration paid for the professional services of a surveyor, valuer, auctioneer, accountant, agent or legal adviser which are wholly and exclusively incurred by the company for the purposes of the disposal,
(b) costs of transfer or conveyance wholly and exclusively incurred by the individual for the purposes of the disposal,	(b) costs of transfer or conveyance wholly and exclusively incurred by the company for the purposes of the disposal,
(c) costs of advertising to find a buyer, and	[identical]
(d) costs reasonably incurred in making any valuation or apportionment required for the purposes of this Chapter.	[identical]

It was surprising that in 2000 the section went to the trouble of dealing with incidental costs of disposing of qualifying investments (then, shares and securities) because the incidental costs of transferring shares and securities to charity would normally be trivial.[29] But the provision could

28 HMRC, " Clarifying the Scope of the Welsh Rates of Income Tax: Technical Note" (2018) *https://assets.publishing.service.gov.uk/government/uploads/system/uploads/attachment_data/file/750621/Welsh_rates_of_Income_Tax_technical_note.pdf*

29 The explanation may be found in the former IR178 (Giving shares and securities to charity, 2006) which stated that the "relevant amount" includes:

> "any incidental costs incurred in transferring the investments (such as broker's fees *or stamp duty*)".

be useful after the extensions of the relief to land in 2002, because the cost of transferring land to charity may not be trivial. In the case of a lease to charity, for instance, this would include the legal costs of drafting the lease.

HMRC Guidance Note provides:

> 5.13.3 For gifts of real property, you need to determine the market value of the property on the date you wish to gift the property to charity. Generally you'll need to obtain professional advice as to the market value. The incidental costs of this advice may be added to the market value if they relate to the valuation of the property for that particular gift.[30]

It is suggested that the law should be simplified without significant cost or unfairness by ignoring incidental costs in computing the relief.

21.10 Net benefit to charity

The expression the "value of the net benefit to the charity" is used as a label to bring in rules relating to:

(1) recently acquired property and

(2) disposal-related liabilities.

Section 437(1) ITA/s. 209(1) CTA 2010 provides:

> For the purposes of this Chapter the value of the net benefit to a charity is—
>
> (a) the relevant value of the qualifying investment, or
>
> (b) if the charity is, or becomes, subject to a disposal-related obligation, the relevant value of the qualifying investment reduced by the total amount of the disposal-related liabilities of the charity.

21.11 Recently acquired property

"Relevant value" is a label which is used to bring in rules relating to recently acquired property. The rules are intended to prevent an avoidance arrangement under which:

In fact there is no stamp duty on a gift or sale to charity, and if there were, it would not be payable by the transferor but by the charity. The passage suggests that those responsible for the legislation overlooked this. Perhaps under the erroneous impression that a QIDR donation may give rise to substantial stamp duty, they allowed QIDR relief for incidental costs generally.

30 See CG Manual 15250 [Jun 2016] for further discussion of incidental costs.

(1) A person acquired a qualifying investment (relatively) cheaply.
(2) The person gave the asset to charity, claimed a deduction for the then value of the asset, and argued, due to some valuation quirk or other, that the value at the time of the gift greatly exceeded the acquisition cost.

s. 437 ITA	**s. 209 CTA 2010**
(1A) In subsection (1) "relevant value" means—	[identical]
(a) where subsection (1B) applies, the lower of the market value and the acquisition value, and	[identical]
(b) otherwise, the market value.	[identical]
(1B) This subsection applies where—	[identical]
(a) the qualifying investment, or anything from which it derives or which it represents (whether in whole or in part and whether directly or indirectly), was acquired by the individual making the disposal within the period of 4 years ending with the day on which the disposal is made,	(a) the qualifying investment, or anything from which it derives or which it represents (whether in whole or in part and whether directly or indirectly), was acquired by the company making the disposal within the period of 4 years ending with the day on which the disposal is made,
(b) the acquisition was made as part of a scheme, and	[identical]
(c) the main purpose, or one of the main purposes, of the individual in entering into the scheme was to obtain relief, or an increased amount of relief, under this Chapter.	(c) the main purpose, or one of the main purposes, of the company in entering into the scheme was to obtain relief, or an increased amount of relief, as a result of this Chapter.
(1C) In subsection (1B) "scheme" includes any scheme, arrangement or understanding of any kind, whether or not legally enforceable, involving a single transaction or two	[identical]

or more transactions.

Section 438A ITA/s. 210A CTA 2010 define acquisition value:

s. 438A ITA	**s. 210A CTA 2010**
(1) For the purposes of this Chapter the acquisition value of a qualifying investment disposed of by an individual is—	(1) For the purposes of this Chapter the acquisition value of a qualifying investment disposed of by a company is—
(a) where the qualifying investment was acquired by the individual within the period of 4 years ending with the day on which the disposal is made, the cost to the individual of acquiring it, or	(a) where the qualifying investment was acquired by the company within the period of 4 years ending with the day on which the disposal is made, the cost to the company of acquiring it, or
(b) where something from which the qualifying investment derives or which it represents was so acquired, such proportion of the cost to the individual of acquiring that thing as is just and reasonable to attribute to the qualifying investment.	(b) where something from which the qualifying investment derives or which it represents was so acquired, such proportion of the cost to the company of acquiring that thing as is just and reasonable to attribute to the qualifying investment.
(2) A reference in subsection (1) to the cost to the individual of an acquisition is to—	(2) A reference in subsection (1) to the cost to the company of an acquisition is to—
(a) the consideration given by the individual for the acquisition, less	(a) the consideration given by the company for the acquisition, less
(b) any amount that is received in connection with the acquisition, by the individual or a person connected with the individual, as part of the scheme in question.	(b) any amount that is received in connection with the acquisition, by the company or a person connected with it, as part of the scheme in question.

HMRC Guidance Note para 5.9.7 gives this example:

> Example 5 (Mr Jones)
> J enters into an agreement with company X, which sells tax avoidance schemes, to buy £200,000 of shares in a FTSE 100 company from company X for £30,000. The shares come with an option attached for

company X to buy them back after three years for £1.
2 days after purchasing the shares J donates them to charity B and makes a claim for relief of £200,000. He claims that the fact that the option to buy back the shares exists isn't taken into account in valuing the shares because the option is a contingent liability which is ignored.
Because the shares were acquired as part of a scheme or arrangement less than 4 years before they were gifted to charity B and the reason J purchased them was so that he could donate them to charity and claim the relief, his relief is restricted to the lower of market value or acquisition cost. Therefore, J is only entitled to relief of £30,000.

21.12 Disposal-related liabilities

21.12.1 *Purpose of rule*

This section discusses anti-avoidance provisions aimed at tax avoidance schemes where the market value of the asset given to the charity is greater than the economic value received by the charity. HMRC explain:

> 3. For example, two trusts might each buy for a token amount options to purchase from a charity any gilts that may be donated to that charity during a specified period, if a certain condition is met. The conditions for the exercise of the two options are near-mirror images of each other–e.g., Trust A having the option to purchase if X does happen and Trust B having the option to purchase if X does not happen. Each option to purchase will be at a tiny fraction of the market value of the gilts (e.g., £5,000 for £1 million gilts). The options may be dressed up so that, for example, the charity has to sell the gilts at market value and then hand over the cash realised (so that strictly the value of the gilts is not affected). Various arrangements can be put in place to secure the transfer of benefit back to the donor from the trust.
> 4. The effect of the avoidance scheme is to eliminate most of the value of the gift in the hands of the charity, while potentially returning virtually the whole value of the gift to the control of the donor. In short, the donor gets substantial tax relief while potentially getting his donation back.[31]

21.12.2 *Disposal-related obligation*

The first step is to decide whether there is a "disposal-related obligation". Section 439(1) ITA/s. 211 CTA 2010 provide:

31 Press Release, 2 July 2004.

> In this Chapter an obligation[32] is a "disposal-related obligation" in relation to a qualifying investment, if condition A or condition B is met in relation to it.

We refer to "**disposal-related obligation conditions A and B**".

s. 439(2) ITA	**s. 211(2) CTA 2010**
The obligation may be to any person (whether or not the individual making the disposal or a person connected with the individual).	The obligation may be to any person (whether or not the company making the disposal or a person connected with it).

21.12.3 *Condition A*

Section 439(3) ITA/s. 211(2) CTA 2010 provides:

> Condition A is that it is reasonable to suppose that the disposal of the qualifying investment to the charity would not have been made in the absence of the obligation. ...

This is too widely expressed. Taken literally it could apply whenever a charity with an overdraft raises funds in order to pay off its debts. But clearly there is intended to be a much closer link between the disposal and the obligation.

s.439(5) ITA	**s. 211(5) CTA 2010**
In applying condition A, all the circumstances must be taken into account (including, in particular, the difference in the value of the net benefit to the charity calculated under section 437(1)(a) and that value calculated under section 437(1)(b)).	In applying condition A all the circumstances must be taken into account (including in particular the difference in the value of the net benefit to the charity calculated under section 209(1)(a) and that value calculated under section 209(1)(b) on the assumption that the obligation under consideration is a disposal- elated obligation).

---

32 "Obligation" is defined. Section 439(7) ITA provides:

> "In this Chapter "obligation" includes a reference to each of the following—
> (a) a scheme, arrangement or understanding of any kind, whether or not legally enforceable, and
> (b) a series of obligations (whether or not between the same parties)."

At first sight the oxymoron "unenforceable obligation" is difficult to understand. But an obligation may be enforceable in honour and with a sanction, eg that no further gifts will be made to a non-complying charity. We cannot see the point of subsection (7)(b) in this definition.

That hardly seems worth saying, though it does no harm.

21.12.4 *Condition B*

Section 439 ITA/s. 211 CTA 2010 provide:

> (4) Condition B is that the obligation (whether in whole or in part) relates to, is framed by reference to, or is conditional on the charity receiving, the qualifying investment or a disposal-related investment.
>
> ...
>
> (6) In subsection (4) "disposal-related investment" means any of the following—
>
> (a) an asset of the same class or description as the qualifying investment (irrespective of size, quantity or amount),
>
> (b) an asset derived from, or representing, the qualifying investment, whether in whole or in part and whether directly or indirectly, and
>
> (c) an asset from which the qualifying investment is derived, or which the qualifying investment represents, whether in whole or in part and whether directly or indirectly.

21.12.5 *"Disposal-related liability"*

Having determined whether or not there is a "disposal-related obligation", one is in a position to consider whether there is a "disposal-related liability". Section 440(1) ITA/s. 212(1) CTA 2010 provides the definition:

> In this Chapter a liability is a "disposal-related liability" in the case of a qualifying investment if it is a liability of the charity under a disposal-related obligation in relation to the qualifying investment.

21.12.6 *Valuation of liabilities*

We then need to ascertain the amount of the liabilities. Section 440(2) ITA provides:

s. 440(2) ITA	**s. 212(2) CTA 2010**
If the disposal-related obligation is contingent, the amount to be brought into account for the purposes of section 437 at any time in respect of the disposal-related liability, so far as contingent, is—	If the disposal-related obligation is contingent, the amount to be brought into account for the purposes of section 209 at any time in respect of the disposal related liability, so far as contingent, is—

(a) if the contingency occurs, the amount or value of the liability actually incurred in consequence of the occurrence of the contingency, or	[identical]
(b) if the contingency does not occur, nil.	

There is no time limit for any contingency.

This only addresses some of the problems of valuation. Valuation of (say) a lock-in agreement may be hard to ascertain.

21.12.7 *HMRC example*

HMRC Guidance Note para 5.9.7 gives this example:

> Example 4 (Roger)
> R owns and gifts gilts with a market value of £10,000 to a charity and receives in return a free ticket to a concert worth £30. The charity is under an obligation, for which it received a payment of £750, to sell any gilts it receives to a third party (not connected to R) at 10 per cent of their market value. The charity sells the gilts to the third party for £1,000, so the net benefit to the charity from the receipt of the qualifying investment is £1,000.

Deductions/additions	Amount £
The deduction R can make is the market value of the gilt	£10,000
Less the market value of the charity's liability under the obligation to sell the gilts at 10 per cent of their market value (market value £10,000 less proceeds £1,000)	- £9,000
(the net benefit to the charity)	£1,000
Less the value of the benefit received	£30
Total	£970

21.13 "Market value"

"Market value" is defined. Section 438 ITA/210 CTA 2010 provides:

> (1) The market value of a qualifying investment for the purposes of this Chapter is determined in accordance with sections 272 to 274 of TCGA 1992 (subject to Part 1 of Schedule 11 to that Act).
> (2) But, in the case of an interest in an offshore fund for which separate buying and selling prices are published regularly by the managers of the fund, the market value for the purposes of this Chapter is equal to the buying price (that is the lower price) published on—

(a) the day of the disposal, or
(b) if none were published on that day, on the latest day on which the prices were published before that day.

Some of these rules are designed to give a high valuation, which usually favours HMRC in the context of CGT, but favours the taxpayer here. Perhaps this is an unintended consequence of incorporating the CGT rules by reference. Perhaps it was a deliberate decision to encourage gifts to charities.

HMRC Guidance Note provides:

> **5.14 Obtaining confirmation of the value of a gift before claiming relief**
> 5.14.1 If you've made a gift of land to charity you may want to obtain confirmation from HMRC that they agree the value of your gift before you claim relief in your Self Assessment or CTSA Return. As long as you have a valuation of the land at the time you made the gift HMRC can check that valuation for you.
> 5.14.2 This service is only available for checking your valuation. They are not able to provide valuations of your property. HMRC can only check your valuation after you have made a gift, not before.

Share valuation is a large subject, on which many books have been written. For QIDR examples, see *Green v HMRC*[33], *Netley v HMRC*[34] and *Nice v HMRC*.[35] However the approach to share valuation in a QIDR context is no different from share valuation generally, and the topic is not discussed here as it falls too far from the themes of this book.

21.14 QIDR relief: Position of donor

The method of relief is different from Gift Aid. There is no grossing up of the donation and no tax reclaim by the charity. Instead relief is given by a deduction from total income.

s. 431(2) ITA:	**s. 203(2) CTA 2010**
The relief is given by deducting the relievable amount in calculating the individual's net income for the tax year in which the disposal is made	The relievable amount is treated for corporation tax purposes as a qualifying charitable donation made by the company in the accounting

33 [2014] UKFTT 396 (TC).
34 [2017] UKFTT 442 (TC).
35 [2021] UKFTT 285 (TC).

(see Step 2 of the calculation in section 23). period in which the disposal is made.

The relief is ignored for the purposes of calculating top slicing relief: s.535(7) ITTOIA.

Gift Aid may be more valuable than QIDR for a taxpayer who has dividend income, because of the quirky dividend rates.

See too 15.43.7 (Personal allowance taper).

There is no relief against CGT on chargeable gains accruing to the donor. So the donor should limit a donation to their total taxable income or (to maximise the tax advantage) total income subject to tax at the top rates.

For completeness, s.445(1) ITA provides:

> If a claim is made for relief under this Chapter in respect of a disposal—
> (a) section 108 of ITTOIA 2005 (gifts of trading stock to charities etc) does not apply in relation to the disposal, and
> (b) no relief in respect of the disposal is allowable under any other provision of the Income Tax Acts.

The corporation tax equivalent is s.445(1)(a) is s.203(3) CTA 2010.

The exclusion of s.108 ITTOIA (s.105 CTA 2010) prevents a double deduction for dealers in shares or land.[36] It is not clear what "other provision" of the IT Acts is in point and it does not matter that this has no corporation tax equivalent.

The method of giving relief to a company is the same as corporate Gift Aid.

A qualifying charitable donation is deductable against profits,[37] so the relief can be set against chargeable gains of a company as well as its income.

21.15 CGT relief for donor

Perhaps generously, the QIDR disposal also qualifies for CGT charity relief on disposals to charity.

21.16 Position of charity

21.16.1 *CGT position of charity*

Section 257 TCGA provides:

---

36 See 18.7.7 (Relief for gift of trading stock).

37 See 17.2 (Corporate Gift Aid).

(2A) Subsection (2B) applies if relief is available under
[a] Chapter 3 of Part 8 of ITA 2007 or
[b] as a result of Chapter 3 of Part 6 of CTA 2010
(gifts of shares, securities and real property to charities) in relation to the disposal of a qualifying investment to a charity (whether or not a claim for relief is actually made).

(2B) The consideration for which the charity's acquisition of the qualifying investment is treated by virtue of subsection (2) above as having been made—
(a) is reduced by the relievable amount within the meaning of Chapter 3 of Part 8 of ITA 2007 if relief in relation to the disposal is available only under that Chapter,
(b) is reduced by the relievable amount within the meaning of Chapter 3 of Part 6 of CTA 2010 if relief in relation to the disposal is available only as a result of that Chapter,
(c) is reduced by the relievable amount within the meaning of Chapter 3 of Part 8 of ITA 2007 if relief in relation to the disposal is available both under that Chapter and as a result of Chapter 3 of Part 6 of CTA 2010 because of section 442 of ITA 2007 and section 214 of CTA 2010 [joint ownership], or
(d) is reduced to nil if that consideration is less than the amount referred to in paragraph (a), (b) or (c) (as the case may be).

(2C) In subsection (2A) and (2B)—
"qualifying investment" has the same meaning as in Chapter 3 of Part 8 of ITA 2007 (see section 432 of that Act).

In short, the donor's QID relief is deducted from the charity's base cost for CGT. This will not normally concern the charity, because it will qualify for CGT charity relief on a gain accruing on a subsequent disposal of the asset.

This rule applies on a gift even though no claim is made for QIDR. That is daft, but consistent with the corporate Gift Aid rule.[38] It does not matter in practice, because a claim should almost always be made, and because a charity is not normally concerned with CGT base cost.

21.16.2 *Income tax position of charity*

The gifted investment is not treated as income of the charity for tax purposes; contrast the Gift Aid position. But the tainted donation rules may apply.

38 See 17.9 (Position of charity receiving gift).

21.17 Share/cash gifts compared

Cash gift: gift aid	**Share gift: Qualifying investment relief**
Individual donor	
Basic rate reclaim/higher rate relief	Simple deduction for donor
Right of admission relief	No right of admission relief
Gift aid declaration needed	Claim needed
Company donor	
Deduction for donor	*Same*
Distribution rule	No express restriction
Carry-back relief	No carry-back relief
No claim needed	Claim needed
All donors	
Chargeable gain n/r	Relief for gain on disposal
Small benefit relief	No small benefit relief
Benefits reduce relief	No-benefit rule disqualifies relief
Repayment rule	No express equivalent; may not matter?
Payment deductible for IT/CT	No express equivalent; may not matter?
Acquisition of property rule	No equivalent rule

A sale of shares[39] and gift of the proceeds of sale will be better when a loss accrues on the disposal.

In the following discussion it is assumed that a chargeable gain would accrue on the disposal (greater than the CGT annual exemption), and the donor has sufficient income to utilise the IT relief.

If shares are given to charity, there is:

(1) income tax relief on the value of the shares
(2) no capital gains tax on the donor

That is better than an arm's length sale and gift of the proceeds, which gives Gift Aid relief on the proceeds, but CGT on the sale.

For individuals, there is an important difference between a cash gift and a gift of shares[40]:

(1) In a cash gift, the basic rate tax is reclaimed by the charity and only the higher rate relief is enjoyed directly by the donor.
(2) In a gift of shares, the whole of the tax relief (which may equal the

---

39 For convenience we refer to shares, but the same applies to gifts of other types of qualifying investment.

40 For convenience we refer to shares, but the same applies to gifts of other types of qualifying investment.

total of the CGT and the IT marginal rates)[41] is enjoyed by the donor.

So the practical consequences of a gift of cash is different from the consequences of a gift of shares worth the same amount. (It would however be possible to reduce the size of the cash gift to confer the same position as the gift of shares).

This distinction does not apply to company donors: they enjoy the same tax relief under both Gift Aid and QIDR.

HMRC Guidance Note provides:

> **5.17 Donating the qualifying investments or selling them and giving the proceeds to charity using Gift Aid**
> 5.17.1 For companies, relief for cash gifts is given in the same way as relief for gifts of qualifying investments and in most cases the relief will be the same whichever method of donating you choose.
> 5.17.2 If you're an individual, it depends on your circumstances and whether you wish the charity or yourself to gain the greater benefit from the tax relief. A charity can claim Gift Aid on a qualifying gift of money but can't make any claims in respect of the gift of an asset.
> 5.17.3 Generally, giving the shares to charity will be simpler, both in terms of the paperwork on the disposal and in completing your tax return, than selling the shares yourself and giving the cash to the charity.

HMRC Guidance Note formerly gave a worked example. That was subsequently deleted. Perhaps it was too much trouble to redo it with constantly changing tax rates, or perhaps HMRC did not want to dwell on the topic. The example is as follows (based on 2007/08 tax rates):

> **Example 4** (Paula)
> P is a higher rate taxpayer and has shares worth £100,000. If she sells them, she would make a net gain of £25,000 after all reliefs and allowances, and liable to capital gains tax.
> **Option A** P sells the shares and gives the proceeds to charity under Gift Aid

Gross proceeds of sale of shares	£100,000
less capital gains charge (£25,000 @ 40%)	£10,000
Net proceeds after tax	£90,000

> Under Gift Aid, the charity can recover from us the amount of the gift multiplied by

$$\frac{\text{the basic rate of income tax (22\%)}}{\text{100 minus the basic rate (i.e.78)}}$$

> So, if P gives the £90,000 to a charity under Gift Aid, the charity can reclaim

41 If the qualifying investments are offshore funds, the saving could be up to twice the income tax marginal rate.

£90,000×22/78 = **£25,384**
When this is added to the gift, the charity receives in total
£90,000 + £25,384 = **£115,384**
P claims tax relief at the difference between the basic rate (22%) and the higher rate (40%) on
£115,384 (18%×£115,384) = **£20,769**
So, the gift has cost her
£100,000 – £20,769 = **£79,231**

Option B P gives the shares to charity

The charity receives shares to sell or retain as investments	£100,000
P gets tax relief on £100,000 at the higher rate of tax (40%)	£40,000
So, the gift has cost P £100,000 – £40,000 =	£60,000

Example 5 (Norman)
N is a basic rate taxpayer and has shares worth £780, which came free as part of a demutualisation. He has not made any other capital gain in the year.
Option A N sells the shares and gives the proceeds to the charity under Gift Aid

Gross proceeds of sale of shares	**£780**
Capital gains charge (within annual exempt amount)	nil
Net proceeds	£780

If N gives the £780 to a charity under Gift Aid, the charity can claim basic rate income tax of
£780×22/78 = **£220**
When this is added to the gift, the charity receives in total
£780 + £220 = **£1,000**
N has nothing further to claim and the gift has cost him **£780**
Option B N gives the shares to charity
The charity receives shares to sell or retain as investment **£780**
N gets tax relief on £780 @ 22% = £171.60
So, the gift has cost N £780 – £171.60 = **£608.40**

5.17.3 Generally, giving the shares to charity will also be simpler, both in terms of the paperwork on the disposal and in completing your tax return, than selling the shares yourself and giving the cash to the charity.

In theory, a charity should try to impress on an individual donor the true (post tax) size of the gift they are making, in terms of:
(1) the real cost to them; and
(2) the real benefit conferred on the charity.

But in reality that may not be practical, except in the case of substantial gifts by well-advised donors.

21.18 Sale to charity at undervalue

An optimum saving is achieved if the donor:
(1) sells to the charity for such a price as will involve realising no gain

and no loss for capital gains tax purposes; and
(2) gifts to the charity an amount equal to the proceeds of sale.

Total relief will be at the donor/vendor's marginal IT rate + the CGT rate. There will be no stamp duty or stamp duty reserve tax on the sale to the charity.

21.18.1 *Position of charity purchaser*

The charity will have to consider whether it is proper to buy the assets at the suggested price. It is just possible that exotic qualifying investments:
(1) may be outside the scope of a charity's power of investment (unlikely after the Trustee Act 2000); or
(2) may not be "qualifying investments" for the purposes of the charitable expenditure rules. In that case a claim must be made that the investment was made for the benefit of the charity and not for the avoidance of tax.[42] Otherwise the charity's tax reliefs may be reduced.

HMRC Guidance Note correctly states at 5.24.3:

> Any gift of investments to a charity is not an investment by the charity. So the charity won't be treated as having made an investment that is not a "qualifying investment" for the purposes of Sections 558 and 559 Income Tax Act 2007 or Sections 511 and 512 Corporation Tax Act 2010 where the cost of non-qualifying investments is treated as "non-charitable expenditure" and can give rise to a tax charge. A sale of investments to a charity at undervalue does, strictly, involve the charity in making an investment. Where those investments are not "qualifying investments" for the purposes of Sections 558/559 ITA or Sections 511/512 CTA HMRC would be unlikely to treat their cost as "non-qualifying expenditure" if they were acquired for significantly less than they were worth and no tax avoidance was involved.

21.18.2 *Procedure and documentation*

If a donor wishes to give shares to a charity which wishes to receive cash, the following procedure may be convenient:
(1) to give the investments to the charity by declaration of trust;
(2) sell as nominee for the charity; and
(3) transfer the sale proceeds to the charity.

---

42 See 6.9 ("Approved charitable investment").

HMRC rightly accept that the investment can be sold immediately by the charity without affecting the relief on the gift. HMRC Guidance Note provides:

> 5.15.1 If you contact the charity about making a gift of shares and securities and the charity asks you to sell them on its behalf, you can do so. However, you'll need satisfactory evidence (such as an exchange of letters) to show that you've made the gift of the investment to the charity and that the charity asked you to dispose of the investments on its behalf. Otherwise, you may be treated as having made a disposal on your own account and the cash you give to the charity may be treated as a Gift Aid donation. This may also incur a Capital Gains Tax charge.
> 5.15.2 Once the company registrar has received the stock transfer form and ownership has been transferred, you can no longer dispose of the shares for the charity.

The same applies in the case of a sale at an undervalue, which may leave title of the shares with the vendor, who sells as nominee for the charity.

It is essential that the documentation is correct, or else QIDR will be lost, and the transaction may be treated as a cash gift to charity.

The CAF offer a scheme where it accepts gifts of shares, or sale at an undervalue, sells the shares, and transmits the proceeds of sale of the shares to any charity.[43] It provides standard form documentation for this purpose.

21.19 Gift of small shareholdings

ShareGift offers a useful service here. Its website provides:

> ShareGift (Registered Charity no. 1052686) provides a charitable solution to the business problem of small shareholdings. Often unwanted because they are too small to sell, these shares can be transferred to ShareGift at no cost to the shareholder, aggregated and sold to benefit different registered charities. The result is a significant funding stream for the charitable sector which would not otherwise exist, along with substantial savings for companies in administrative costs.

21.20 Gift of non-qualifying asset

It was decided in 1990 to restrict Gift Aid relief to gifts of cash, and to deny income tax relief for gifts of other assets. Without a specific anti-

---

43 *https://www.cafonline.org/my-personal-giving/long-term-giving/share-giving/sell-shares*

avoidance provision, a donor could easily obtain that relief in two steps:
(1) Give money to the charity under Gift Aid.
(2) The charity then purchases the asset from the donor for full value or at CGT base cost.

In this way, what is effectively a gift of an asset could qualify for income tax relief. Statute therefore provides that Gift Aid relief does not apply to a gift from an individual (or a company) which is (in short) part of an arrangement involving the acquisition of property by the charity from the individual or a connected person.[44]

QIDR has no comparable restriction. So in this type of situation it should be possible for an individual or a company to obtain tax relief for what is effectively a gift of assets which are not qualifying investments:
(1) Give qualifying investments to the charity under QIDR;
(2) The charity then purchases the asset from the donor for full value.

It is debatable whether this is tax avoidance, but consider the GAAR.

21.21 Record keeping

HMRC Guidance Note provides:

> 5.11.1 You'll need some evidence of the transfer of ownership of the qualifying investments. In the case of a gift of property, you'll need to obtain from the charity the sort of certificate mentioned above.[45] For a gift of shares, evidence will take the form of a dated copy of the transfer form or some other dated document irrevocably giving the qualifying investments to the charity.
> 5.11.2 This is important because the shares will come out of your name on the company's register at a later date, by which time the value of the shares may have changed. You may also continue to receive communications, including dividends, from the company until the transfer has been registered.

21.22 QIDR "avoidance" schemes

HMRC Guidance Note provides:

> 5.23.2 Since this relief was introduced it has been the subject of a number of marketed tax avoidance schemes. These schemes focus on obtaining increased relief for the donor and there's rarely any

44 See 15.19 (Acquisition of property rule (Gift Aid condition E)).
45 See 21.5.6 (Certificate of gift of land).

> substantial value passed to the charity. If your charity receives a gift of shares or securities where there is a discrepancy between the apparent value and the amount that the charity is able to realise we would like you to tell HMRC so that action can be taken to protect this relief for genuine donors.
> 5.23.3 Sometimes a scheme provider may approach a single charity to act as the recipient for all the 'gifts' in their tax avoidance scheme. The charity may receive a fee for this but won't benefit from the full value of the investments which usually just pass through the charity. The amount of the fee may be very tempting but if an offer looks too good to be true then it probably is.
> Acting as a conduit in this way may also amount to non primary purpose trading and any profits would be taxable.
> If you're asked to take part in such a scheme we would like you to tell us.

HMRC have issued a statement on a more sinister scheme involving Gift Aid as well as QIDR:

> **Spotlight 7: Avoidance using Gift Aid (5 August 2010)**
> HMRC are aware of schemes that seek to generate Gift Aid and Gift of Shares tax relief claims. A cash donation to a nominated charity is required and in return shares are received from an unnamed non UK 'philanthropist'. These shares are claimed to be worth up to eight times the amount of the cash donation and are in companies listed on a stock exchange that is not recognised by HMRC, for example The Open Market of The Frankfurt Stock Exchange. The scheme anticipates that the shares will be donated to the nominated charity.
> There is also strong evidence that these schemes have links to share scams such as 'boiler rooms'. They usually involve a high level of upfront 'fee', paid to the scheme promoters, which is concealed within the original cash 'donation' given to the charity.
> HMRC's view is that no Gift Aid is due on the cash donation because the donor receives a benefit (the shares) that is in excess of the donation. HMRC also consider that no Gift of Shares relief is due because the requirement that the shares are listed on a stock exchange recognised by HMRC is not met.[46]

This arrangement involves two gifts:
(1) A gift of cash. The Gift Aid benefit rule in principle disqualifies the

---

46 *https://www.gov.uk/government/publications/spotlight-7-avoidance-using-gift-aid-6-january-2010/spotlight-7-avoidance-using-gift-aid-6-january-2010* See too 15.5 ("Gift" in tax avoidance context).

relief, but the donors (the word should perhaps be victims) might be able to argue that the cash gift to charity qualifies for Gift Aid relief on the grounds that the value of the shares they receive is in fact nil. A full investigation of the facts would be needed which is not possible on the basis of the brief HMRC description.

(2) A gift of shares. As the scheme is described, the relief on the gift is likely to be nil, either because QIDR conditions are not met, or because the shares have no value.

As described, this is not a tax avoidance scheme: it is a fraudulent scheme under which the promoters in principle commit criminal offences: obtaining money from the victims by deception, as well as tax evasion.

21.23 Planning by grant of lease

It is common for a person to own land and to allow a charity to use it rent-free. Now the owner of the land should grant a lease of the land to the charity for an appropriate period, so as to obtain income tax relief on the value of the lease.

Index

This is mainly an index to chapter numbers. The start of each chapter has a full list of headings and cross references.

You may search the text online: *https://www.taxationofcharities.co.uk*
Vol 1 Chap 1 - 21 Vol 2 Chap 22 - App. 9